Los Angeles,
San Diego &
Southern California

Santa Barbara
County
p345

Los Angeles
p66

Palm Springs
& the Deserts
p291

Disneyland &
Orange County
p234

San Diego
p386

Andrea Schulte-Peevers, Andrew Bender, Cristian Bonetto,
Jade Bremner, Benedict Walker, Clifton Wilkinson

SANTA BARBARA WINE COUNTRY P365

NTI ST CLAIR /GETTY IMAGES ©

ALAN CROSTHWAITE / 500PX ©

LA JOLLA P432

Contents

SURVIVAL GUIDE

SPECIAL FEATURES

Welcome to Southern California

Southern California (SoCal to the locals) inhabits a dreamlike otherworld – a place where breathtaking natural beauty merges with modern mythology.

Pop Culture

SoCal is Valhalla for pop-culture fiends. Where else can you sip martinis in Jack Nicholson's favorite booth, hike your way to Batman's cave and gaze up at the stars just like Jimmy Dean in *Rebel Without a Cause*? Not that LA gets all the glory: wine and dine at Cary Grant's former party pad in Palm Springs, a desert resort laden with Rat Pack anecdotes; or hit Orange County for TV-famous beaches and stars of the cartoon realm at Disneyland, the world's best-loved theme park.

Natural Beauty

Iconic beaches, snowcapped crags, sculpted deserts: in case you hadn't noticed, Mother Nature plays favorites with SoCal. Whether you're a punk surfer, aspiring pro-volleyball nut or new-school bohemian, there's an idiosyncratic SoCal beach and adjacent beach town just for you. Offshore, the Channel Islands are a jewel-like archipelago and part of what is one of the planet's richest marine ecosystems. Back on the mainland, escape to Big Bear Lake's cooler alpine climes or turn up the heat in Death Valley, Joshua Tree or Anza-Borrego, where dusty 4WD roads and hiking trails lead to hidden canyons and mirage-like oases.

Epicurean Highs

Think of SoCal as one huge, heavily laden table, passionately prepared by forward-thinking chefs and artisan purveyors. At one end are San Diego's incomparable fish tacos, at the other Santa Barbara and its luscious bottles of red. In between is a cornucopia of flavors, textures and thrills: decadent red-wine burgers in a pocket-sized Hollywood bistro, freshly steamed crab by the South Bay surf, fragrant *pho* in a loud, proud OC throwback. Whether you're hankering for freshly made tamales at a proper *panadería* or cognoscenti pastas in a slinky downtown warehouse, SoCal delivers. Dig in!

Arts & Architecture

Home to many of the world's leading actors, writers, musicians, artists and designers, SoCal explodes with creative energy. Heart of the action is LA, home to many of America's richest, riskiest and most innovative art collections, influential live-music venues, and a slew of neighborhoods jammed with grassroots galleries, artisan studios and street art. Not enough inspiration for you? Turn your attention to SoCal's architecture. Everything from Spanish-flavored missions and art-deco theaters to modernist prototypes and cutting-edge concert halls, it's an unmatched eclectic mash-up.

Why I Love Southern California

By Cristian Bonetto, Writer

The list is long and varied: warm winter sun and coastal drives, modernist homes and Hollywood lore, martinis and wildflowers in the desert. Despite the plastic clichés, LA is one of the world's great cultural cities, home to exceptional art collections, world-shaking architecture and a kaleidoscope of cultures. And when I tire of it all (rarely), lush mountain retreats and arid landscapes, Santa Barbara wineries and San Diego's cult-status fish tacos are all within driving distance. As a child I longed to be a part of this place. As an adult, I get to live the dream.

For more about our writers, see p512

Above: Channel Islands National Park (p383)

Los Angeles, San Diego & Southern

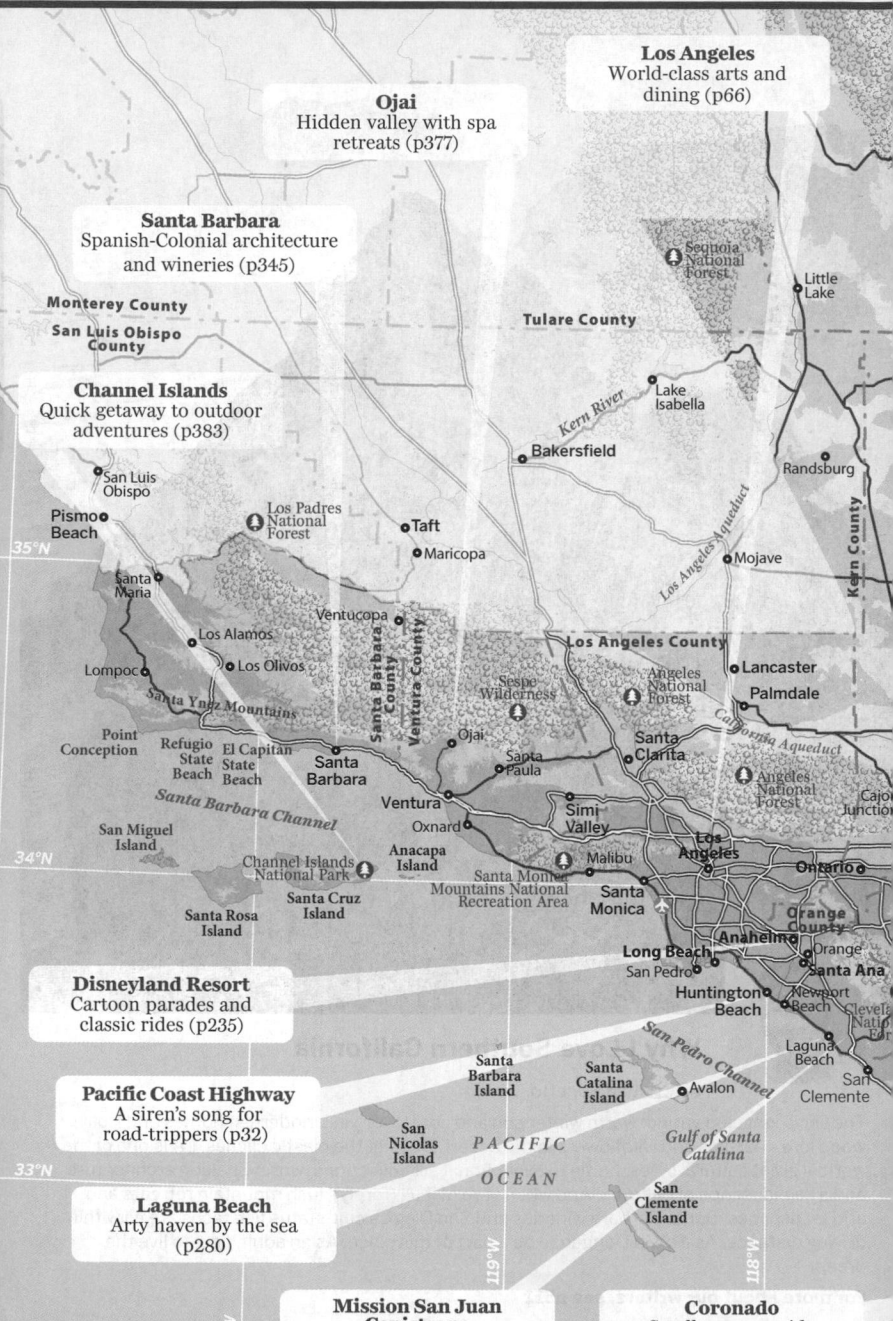

California

0 — 100 km
0 — 50 miles

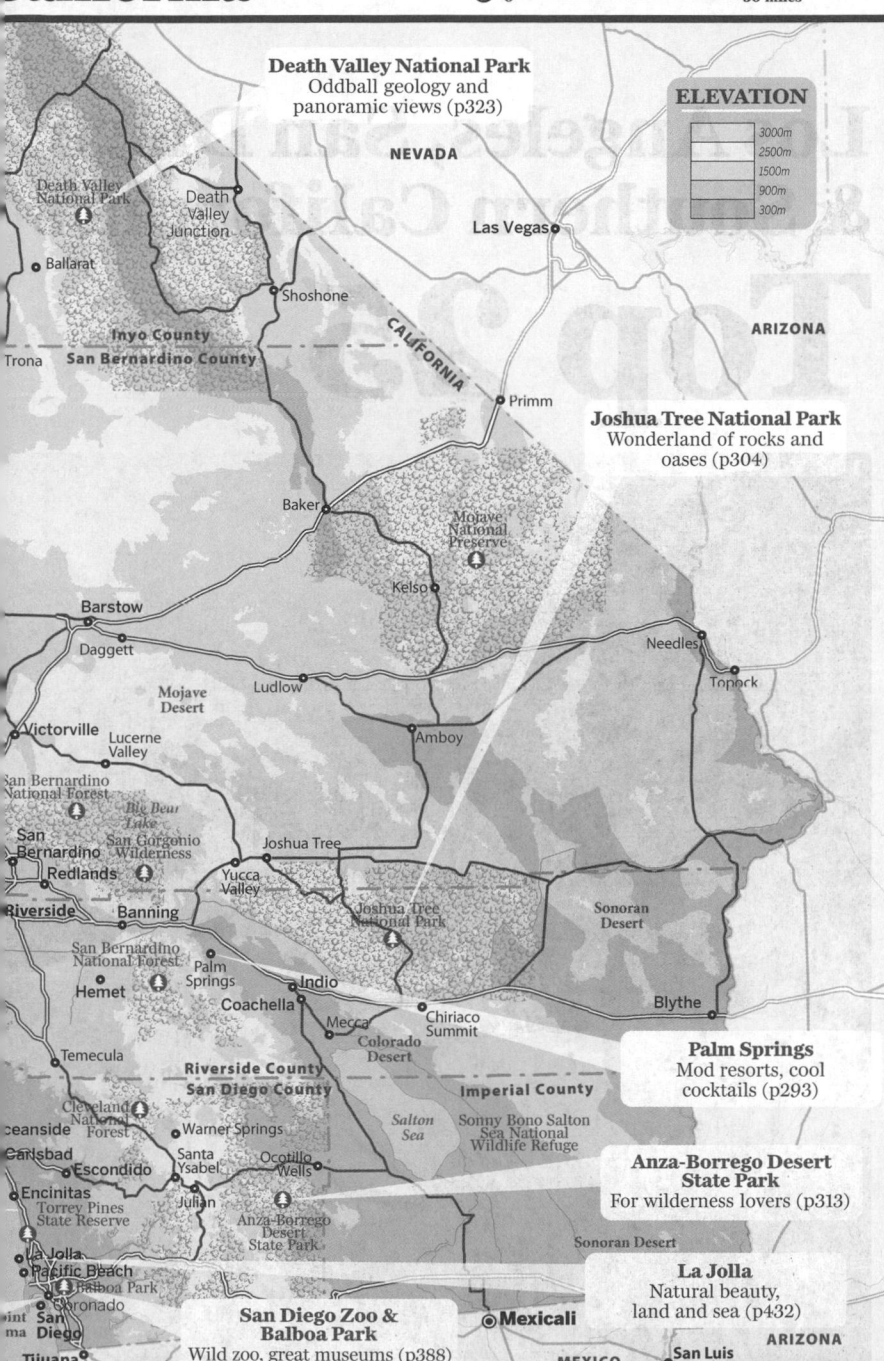

Death Valley National Park
Oddball geology and panoramic views (p323)

ELEVATION

3000m
2500m
1500m
900m
300m

NEVADA

Death Valley National Park
Death Valley Junction
Ballarat
Shoshone

Las Vegas

CALIFORNIA

ARIZONA

Inyo County
San Bernardino County
Trona

Primm

Joshua Tree National Park
Wonderland of rocks and oases (p304)

Baker

Mojave National Preserve

Kelso

Barstow
Daggett

Needles
Topock

Mojave Desert
Ludlow

Victorville
Lucerne Valley

Amboy

San Bernardino National Forest
Big Bear Lake
San Gorgonio Wilderness
San Bernardino
Redlands

Joshua Tree
Yucca Valley

Sonoran Desert

Riverside
Banning

Joshua Tree National Park

San Bernardino National Forest
Palm Springs
Hemet
Indio
Coachella
Mecca
Colorado Desert
Chiriaco Summit

Blythe

Temecula

Riverside County
San Diego County

Imperial County

Salton Sea

Sonny Bono Salton Sea National Wildlife Refuge

Palm Springs
Mod resorts, cool cocktails (p293)

Cleveland National Forest
Oceanside
Carlsbad
Escondido
Encinitas
Torrey Pines State Reserve
La Jolla
Pacific Beach
Balboa Park
Coronado
San Diego
Tijuana

Warner Springs
Santa Ysabel
Ocotillo Wells
Julian
Anza-Borrego Desert State Park

Sonoran Desert

Anza-Borrego Desert State Park
For wilderness lovers (p313)

La Jolla
Natural beauty, land and sea (p432)

Mexicali

San Diego Zoo & Balboa Park
Wild zoo, great museums (p388)

MEXICO

San Luis

ARIZONA

Los Angeles, San Diego & Southern California's
Top 25

Pacific Coast Highway

1 Make your escape from SoCal's tangled, traffic-jammed freeways and cruise the coast's spirit-lifting slow lanes. Legendary Hwy 1 snakes past dramatic sea cliffs and sun-soaked beach towns, each with its own idiosyncratic personality, from nostalgic Carpinteria to rich-and-fabulous Montecito (p3765). In between, you'll uncover hidden beaches and coves, the locals' favorite surf breaks and rustic seafood shacks dishing up the day's freshest catch. And once the day wraps up, nostalgic wooden piers await with yet another flawless sunset over endless Pacific horizons.

Los Angeles

2 If you think LA (p66) is little more than New York's soulless, surgically enhanced nemesis, think again. Beyond the tired clichés of celebrity culture, gridlocked traffic and Botoxed babes is one of the world's most complex urban conglomerations, made up of dozens of independent cities and no less than 185 languages. Sure, you can star-spot in Beverly Hills and envy chiselled abs in Santa Monica and Venice, but you can also lose yourself in superlative art collections, maverick architecture and spectacular hiking trails high above the city you *thought* you knew. Below right: Los Angeles Theater (p91).

SUPREECHA S:MANSUKUMAL / SHUTTERSTOCK ©

A KATZ / SHUTTERSTOCK ©

2

LOS ANGELES

LOS ANGELES

Disneyland Resort

3 Where orange groves and walnut trees once grew, there Walt Disney built his dream, throwing open the doors to the Magic Kingdom in 1955. Today, Disneyland (p235) is SoCal's most-visited tourist attraction, a childlike universe of giant spinning tea cups, selfie-snapping mice and glittery fireworks over a storybook castle. Despite the crowds and prices, it's hard not to feel a quiet pang for childhood. The good times roll on next door at Disney California Adventure, a Golden State–themed amusement park with (more) thrill rides, parades and after-dark spectaculars.

Death Valley National Park

4 Just uttering the name brings up visions of the scattered skeletons of ill-fated pioneers. And yet, the most surprising thing about Death Valley (p323) is just how full of life it is. Spring wildflower blooms explode with a painter's palette of hues across camel-colored hillsides, while its resident critters include coyotes, kit foxes and desert bighorn sheep. Feeling adventurous? Twist your way up narrow canyons sheltering geological oddities, stand atop volcanic craters formed by violent prehistoric explosions or explore Wild West mining ghost towns where fortunes were made and lost.

Santa Barbara

5 California's 'Queen of the Missions', Santa Barbara (p347) is a rare beauty, graced with red-roofed, whitewashed adobe buildings that will make you want to order lunch in Spanish. Downtown was rebuilt in Spanish Colonial style after a devastating earthquake in 1925, resulting in distinctly harmonious streetscapes. Add to this sinuous palms, powdery beaches and fishing boats in the harbor, and the city's self-proclaimed title as the 'American Riviera' seems totally justified. Come escape LA for the day or, better still, stay for a wine-soaked weekend in the country.

Palm Springs

6 A star-studded oasis in the Mojave ever since the heyday of old Blue Eyes and his Rat Pack, Palm Springs (p293) draws LA urbanites in need of a little retro-chic R&R. Follow the lead of A-list stars and hipsters: lounge by the pool at your mid-century-modern hotel, hit the galleries and vintage stores, then refresh with post-sunset cocktails. Too passive? Then break a sweat on hiking trails that wind through desert canyons across Native American tribal lands, or scramble to a summit in the San Jacinto Mountains, accessed via aerial tramway.

Laguna Beach

7 Orange County's Huntington Beach may draw the hang-loose surfer crowd, while Newport Beach's marina is the darling of Gold-Amex yachties, but further south, Laguna Beach (p280) tempts with a more sophisticated blend of salubrity, culture and natural beauty. Startling seascapes led an early-20th-century artists' colony to put down roots here, and Laguna's bohemian past shows in downtown art galleries, arts-and-crafts bungalows tucked among multimillion-dollar mansions and an annual Festival of Arts and Pageant of the Masters, famed for turning famous paintings into living, 3D artworks.

Joshua Tree National Park

8 Not named after a U2 album, Joshua trees reach up toward heaven like a biblical prophet. You'll find no shortage in their namesake national park (p304), where a network of hiking trails promise to lead you to even more natural wonders. Escape to native fan-palm oases that look airlifted straight out of Africa and soak up vistas that include the otherworldly Salton Sea and snow-dusted peaks of the San Bernardino Mountains. If you have kids in tow, boulder-hop in the park's Wonderland of Rocks, an outdoor playground for rock jocks.

COREY JENKINS / GETTY IMAGES ©

EMYU / GETTY IMAGES ©

San Diego Zoo & Balboa Park

9 A vast green patch in the center of the city, beautiful Balboa Park is where San Diegans let their hair down when they're not at the beach. Yet San Diego's communal backyard offers more than sunning sessions along El Prado promenade. The 1200-acre space is home to more than a dozen art, cultural and science museums, a faithful reconstruction of Shakespeare's Old Globe theater, not to mention elegant Spanish Colonial Revival architecture. It's most famous resident, however, is the San Diego Zoo (p389), widely considered one of the finest in the world.
Above left: Leopard, San Diego Zoo

La Jolla

10 On what some argue is the most beautiful stretch of San Diego's coastline, La Jolla (p431) is no average SoCal beach town. Atop rocky bluffs just a whisper's breath from the sea, its salubrious downtown is crowded with some of the city's finest boutiques, cafes and restaurants. But what's right on the shoreline is even more precious. It's here that you'll stumble across the nature-sculpted fish bowl of La Jolla Cove and, further along the coast, the windswept Torrey Pines State Natural Reserve, where migratory whales swim and leap by.

Route 66

11 The SoCal section of this poetically lonely, world-famous heritage highway (p318) appears for a stretch in the Mojave Desert before being gobbled up by the interstate. You'll know you've succeeded in finding America's Mother Road once again when you start cruising by neon-lit diners, drive-ins, retro motels and kitschy roadside attractions tailor-made for your Instagram feed. Speed west through atmospheric ghost towns and sleep inside a 1940s faux wigwam before getting your final kicks on the bustling, carnival-like pier at oceanside Santa Monica.

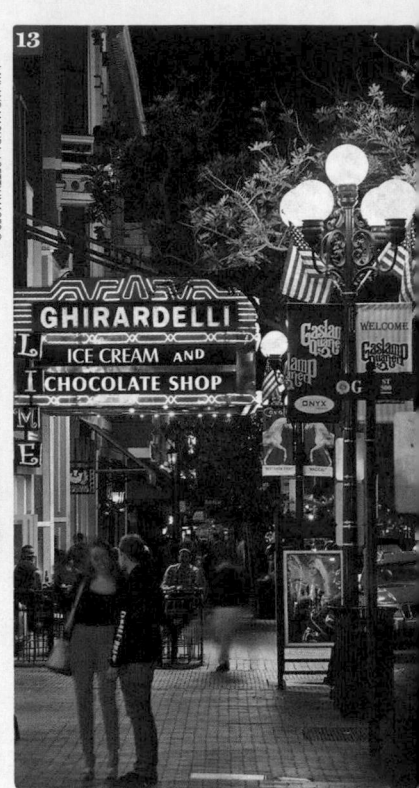

LAYLAND MASUDA / GETTY IMAGES ©

Venice Boardwalk

12 Strap on those Rollerblades, hop on a pastel-pink beach cruiser or simply slip into your trunks or bikini and shake what yo' mama gave you. Captured in countless movies and music videos, Venice's oceanfront walk (p184) is where SoCal's wilder side lets it all hang out. It's like one long, skunk-scented runway of eccentricity, flanked by soaring palms, tattoo parlors and street art, and packed with new-age bohemians, hippie tribal-drummers, street artists, bulging Schwarzenegger wannabes, inked skaters and proud, loud freaks after a cameo in that screenplay you're writing.

Gaslamp Quarter

13 If you can tear yourself away from San Diego's bodacious beaches after dark, hit the restaurants, bars and clubs of this cobblestone-clad downtown district. Just don't be fooled by those gracious gas lamps. This rollickin' neighborhood's true historical legacy is a heady jumble of long-gone gambling dens, saloons and bordellos. Nowadays the party scene spills out onto the sidewalk nightly, while cocktails and DJs lure the hordes indoors at hot spots like Bang Bang (p421). Best of all, the quarter takes all comers, so you won't be fighting those pesky velvet-rope bouncers.

Studio Tours

14 LA is the world's movie-making capital, and snooping around its famous studios is one of the city's most idiosyncratic experiences. Top billing goes to Warner Bros (p210), home to the biggest set construction project in studio history, as well as a booty of Batmobiles. Filmmaking and theme-park thrills join forces at Universal Studios, while Hollywood itself is home to Paramount Pictures, America's second-oldest studio and the very site on which classics including *Breakfast at Tiffany's*, *Grease* and TV series *Happy Days* were shot. Are you ready for your close up? Top Right: Universal Studios Hollywood (p205)

14

15

Foxen Canyon Wine Trail

15 Napa what? Forget Northern California's chichi wine country. SoCal beckons with the fog-kissed Santa Ynez and Santa Maria Valleys, aka *Sideways* wine country. Less than an hour's drive from Santa Barbara, you can tread through fields of grapes, tipple Pinot Noir, Syrah or Malvasia, and graze on regional edibles. Start in the dandified village of Los Olivos, overflowing with wine-tasting rooms and cafes. Then follow the rural Foxen Canyon Wine Trail (p366) along winding country roads where big-name vineyards rub shoulders with risk-taking boutique winemakers.

YASKOCREATIVE / GETTY IMAGES ©

RON THOMAS / GETTY IMAGES ©

Anza-Borrego Desert State Park

16 When you start feeling crushed by SoCal's almost 20 million residents, head inland from San Diego until you can breathe easy again in the wide-open desert. California's largest state park (p313) is an incredible place to get lost. Follow 4WD roads or hiking trails to find hidden canyons, wind caves, cactus gardens and even herds of endangered bighorn sheep. In the middle of the park is pocket-sized Borrego Springs, the first Californian town officially dedicated to protecting the night sky from light pollution. (Don't forget to look up!)

Channel Islands

17 Tossed like so many lost pearls off the coast, the Channel Islands (p383) are SoCal's last outpost of civilization. They've been that way for thousands of years, ever since seafaring Chumash tribespeople established villages on these remote rocks. The islands support an abundance of marine life, from coral reefs to giant elephant seals. Get back to nature in rustic Channel Islands National Park, a wildlife haven beckoning with fantastic sea kayaking and snorkeling, or go glam with a mod-con getaway to Med-style Catalina Island. Top right: Sea anenome, Anacapa Island (p384)

Tacos

18 Tacos are a staple of the SoCal lifestyle, whether you're a beach-bum surfer or an actor rushing between auditions, or both. You'll find them served all over SoCal, from curbside food trucks to trendy urban eateries. San Diego is especially famous for its Baja-style fish taco, a corn tortilla wrapped around fried or grilled fish on a bed of cabbage slathered with pico de gallo salsa and drizzled with a piquant white sauce. Savor the flavor at standout eateries such as Pacific Beach Fish Shop (p421). We bet you'll like it.

Coronado

19 Who says you can't turn back time? Speed over the 2-mile bay bridge or board the ferry from San Diego to seaside Coronado, a civilized reminder of a more genteel era. Revel in the late-19th-century socialite atmosphere at the palatial Hotel Del Coronado (p402) where royalty and presidents have bedded down and Marilyn Monroe cavorted in the 1950s screwball comedy *Some Like It Hot*. Then pedal past impossibly white beaches all the way down the peninsula's Silver Strand, stopping for ice cream and cotton candy.

Temecula

20 Make a weekend getaway from San Diego to this Old West town (p450), the jumping-off point for a wine-tasting tour through gently rolling vineyards. Luiseño tribespeople, present when Spanish missionaries first traipsed through in 1797, called it *temecunga* (place of the sun). It became a ranching outpost for Mission San Luis Rey, and later a stop on the Butterfield stagecoach line and a railroad. These days, its nourishing sunshine, ocean breezes and nighttime fog provide the alchemy needed to turn Mediterranean varietals into some of California's most arresting wines.

19

20

Santa Monica

21 With more than 250 miles of Pacific coastline, SoCal has an overwhelming number of beaches to choose from. Yet few offer the buzz, pop-culture references and diversions of Santa Monica (p174), an easy metro ride from downtown LA. Sure, you can learn to surf, but you can also ride a solar-powered Ferris wheel on a Hollywood-famous pier, pump iron at Muscle Beach, or simply dip your toes in the ocean and catch another heart-melting SoCal sunset. You won't be the first to never want to leave.

Surfing

22 Even if you never set foot on a board – and we, like, totally recommend that you do, dude – there's no denying the influence of surfing on all aspects of SoCal life, from fashion to the way everyday people talk. With gnarly local waves, you won't need to jet over to Hawaii to experience the adrenaline rush for yourself. Pros ride world-class breaks off Huntington Beach (p262), aka 'Surf City USA', Malibu, San Diego and Santa Barbara, while newbies get schooled at 'surfari' camps along SoCal's sun-kissed coastline.

SAN JUAN CAPISTRANO / GETTY IMAGES ©

AIJOHN784 / GETTY IMAGES ©

Ojai

23 The scenery is so surreal that Frank Capra set the 1937 movie *Lost Horizon* about a mythical Shangri-La in this mountain valley, flush with orange orchards. Ojai (p377) has delighted generations of artists, bohemians and new-age mystics. Doing nothing much is the goal for most visitors, especially those on retreat at one of Ojai's spas, but you can happily spend an afternoon ambling around downtown's quaint shops or dropping by the bountiful Sunday farmers market. Then, at around sunset, catch a legendary 'pink moment,' when the mountains emanate a rosy glow. Above: Post office tower, Ojai

Mission San Juan Capistrano

24 When you visit SoCal, you can't help but follow in at least a few of the footsteps of early Spanish conquistadors and Catholic priests. Mission San Juan Capistrano (p286), nicknamed the 'Jewel of the Missions,' was founded by peripatetic priest Junípero Serra in 1776. Authentically restored, the mission today deserves its nickname, with gorgeous gardens, stone arcades and fountains, and a chapel adorned with spiritual frescoes. In mid-March the whole town celebrates the swallows' famous return from South America to nest in the mission's walls.

Julian

25 Winding through pine-covered mountains and tree-shaded valleys east of San Diego, you'll finally arrive at the one-horse town of Julian (p317). Settled by ex-Confederate soldiers after the US Civil War, flecks of gold were found in a creek here in 1869, sparking a short-lived burst of speculation. Today you can tour an underground 19th-century mine, then dig into homemade apple pie waiting in the windows of false-fronted shops on Main St. If it's fall, show up for apple picking in the orchards. Bottom right: Panning for gold, Julian

Need to Know

For more information, see Survival Guide (p487)

Currency
US dollar ($)

Language
English

Visas
Generally not required for stays of 90 days or less for citizens of Visa Waiver Program (VWP) countries with ESTA approval (apply online at least 72 hours in advance).

Money
ATMs are widely available. Credit cards are usually required for reservations at hotels and some restaurants. Travelers checks (US dollars) and non-local checks rarely accepted. Tipping is customary, not optional.

Cell Phones
Cell-phone coverage is spotty in deserts. The only foreign phones that will work in the USA are GSM multiband models. Buy prepaid SIM cards or disposable cell phones locally.

Time
Pacific Standard Time (UTC -8).

When to Go

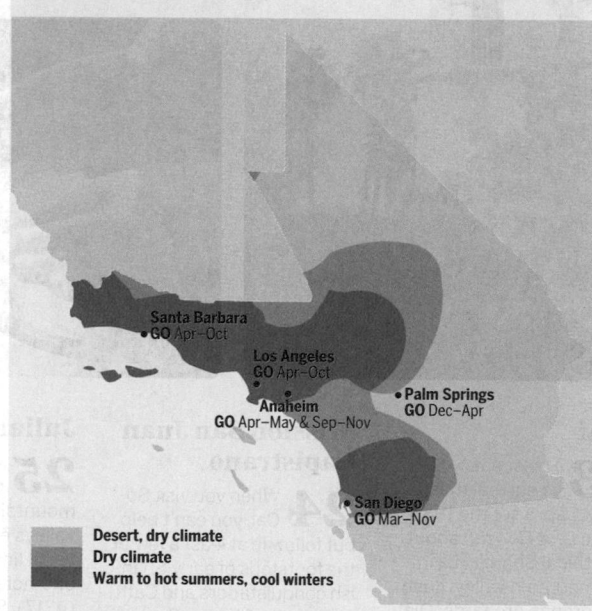

Santa Barbara
• GO Apr–Oct

Los Angeles
GO Apr–Oct

Anaheim
GO Apr–May & Sep–Nov

• Palm Springs
GO Dec–Apr

• San Diego
GO Mar–Nov

Desert, dry climate
Dry climate
Warm to hot summers, cool winters

High Season
(Jun–Aug)

➡ Accommodation prices up 50–100%.

➡ Major holidays are even busier and more expensive.

➡ Thick clouds may blanket the coast during 'June gloom.'

➡ Coincides with low season in the desert.

Shoulder
(Apr–May & Sep–Nov)

➡ Crowds and prices drop off, especially along the coast.

➡ Temperatures remain mild, with sunny, cloudless days in early autumn.

➡ Weather typically wetter in spring, drier in autumn.

Low Season
(Dec–Mar)

➡ Accommodations rates drop near the coast, but not always in cities.

➡ Chillier temperatures, more frequent rainstorms and mountain snow.

➡ Coincides with peak season in the desert regions.

Useful Websites

Lonely Planet (www.lonelyplanet.com/california) Destination information, hotel bookings, traveler forum and more.

California Tourism (www.visitcalifornia.com) Trip-planning guides, themed inspiration and other tips.

Caltrans (www.dot.ca.gov) Current highway conditions and construction updates.

LA Times Travel (www.latimes.com/travel) Daily news, SoCal travel deals and travel blogs.

Theme Park Insider (www.themeparkinsider.com) Reviews, tips and discussion boards.

Important Numbers

All phone numbers have a three-digit area code followed by a seven-digit local number. For long-distance and toll-free calls, dial 1 plus all 10 digits.

Country code	☏1
International dialing code	☏011
Operator	☏0
Emergency (ambulance, fire & police)	☏911
Directory assistance (local)	☏411

Exchange Rates

Australia	A$1	$0.76
Canada	C$1	$0.78
Euro zone	€1	$1.18
China	Y10	$1.51
Japan	¥100	$0.88
Mexico	MXN10	$0.52
New Zealand	NZ$1	$0.68
UK	£1	$1.32

For current exchange rates see www.xe.com.

Daily Costs

Budget: Less than $75

➡ Dorm bed: $25–40

➡ Takeout meal: $6–10

➡ Beach parking: Free–$15

Midrange: $75–200

➡ Two-star inland motel or hotel double room: $75–150

➡ Rental car per day, excluding insurance and gas: $30–75

Top End: More than $200

➡ Three-star beach hotel or resort double room: $150–275

➡ Three-course meal (excluding drinks) in top restaurant: $75–100

Opening Hours

Standard opening hours are as follows. Individual opening hours vary widely.

Banks 9am–5pm Monday to Thursday, to 6pm Friday, some 9am–1:30pm Saturday

Bars 5pm–2am

Business hours (general) 9am–5pm Monday to Friday

Post offices 9am–5pm Monday to Friday, some 9am–noon Saturday

Restaurants 7:30–10:30am, 11:30am–2:30pm and 5:30–10pm

Shops 10am–6pm Monday to Saturday, noon–5pm Sunday (malls open later)

Supermarkets 8am–9pm

Arriving in Southern California

Los Angeles International Airport (LAX) (p496) Taxis around town ($30 to $50) take 30 minutes to one hour. Door-to-door shuttles ($16 to $27) operate 24 hours. The FlyAway bus ($8) runs to downtown LA, Hollywood, Westwood (West LA) and the San Fernando Valley. Free shuttles will get you to LAX City Bus Center & Metro Rail station. For ride hailing services (Uber, Lyft), pick up and drop off are on the upper (departure) level only.

San Diego International Airport (SAN) (p497) Taxis to downtown ($10 to $25) take 15 to 30 minutes. Door-to-door shuttles ($8 to $20) operate 24 hours. Bus No 992 ('the Flyer'; $2.25) runs to downtown San Diego every 15 to 30 minutes from 5am to 11pm. Ride hailing services are also available.

Getting Around

SoCal is famously car country, but plenty of alternatives exist. Cars are still SoCal's go-to, traffic notwithstanding, but LA has an expanding light-rail and subway network, and regional trains connect some coastal and inland destinations. In San Diego, trolleys are a popular alternative despite limited routes. Metropolitan bus travel is typically the cheapest, slowest option, but with the most extensive route network. If traveling by taxi, you must generally call for a cab, unless there is a taxi stand (don't try to hail one). Popular smartphone apps such as Uber and Lyft generally beat taxis on fares and convenience, although they are subject to 'surge pricing' at peak times.

For much more on **getting around**, see p498

If You Like...

Theme Parks

If visiting Disney's 'happiest place on earth,' getting a thrill from Hollywood's movie magic or riding heart-in-throat roller-coasters is on your itinerary, you've definitely come to the right place.

Disneyland Topping almost every family's must-do fun list is Walt Disney's 'imagineered' theme park, with Disney California Adventure next door. (p235)

Universal Studios Hollywood Cinematic theme park with a studio backlot tram tour, tame rides and live-action, special-effects shows. (p205)

Six Flags Magic Mountain Hair-raising roller-coasters to scare the bejeezus out of speed-crazed teens. (p231)

Knott's Berry Farm Adrenaline-pumping roller-coasters set against a wholesome, all-American backdrop. (p253)

Legoland Low-key theme park made of those beloved building blocks for tots. (p446)

Quaffing Wine

Northern California's Napa and Sonoma Valleys may be more famous, but So-Cal's wine countries hold their own. Just crack open a bottle from these sun-kissed vineyards and you'll become a believer.

Foxen Canyon Wine Trail Pastoral country roads wind past some of Santa Barbara's most famous vintners. (p366)

Los Olivos The poshest village in Santa Barbara's wine country, where quaint streets are graced with wine-tasting rooms. (p371)

Santa Rita Hills Independent innovators artfully crush grapes in the Santa Rita Hills, west of Hwy 101. (p367)

Temecula Stroll past Old West–style storefronts, then head out into San Diego's hot wine country. (p450)

Urban Wine Trail Amble on foot between wine bars and tasting rooms in Santa Barbara's 'Funk Zone'. (p362)

Ethnic Food

Especially around LA, celebrity restaurateurs have conquered many neighborhoods. But dollar for dollar, SoCal's flavorful cornucopia of mom-and-pop ethnic eateries is what will really satisfy your belly and soul.

Little Tokyo Slurp on ramen or snap at sashimi in Downtown LA's mini version of Nippon. (p88)

Koreatown Juicy barbecue and fiery kimchi in LA's heavyweight Korean enclave. (p1312)

Thai Town Tangy flavors worthy of a Bangkok night market just east of Hollywood. (p120)

San Gabriel Valley Dim-sum carts, seafood feasts and fluffy bean-stuffed buns in the suburbs of LA. (p216)

San Diego Just north of the border, Mexican taquerias – and the city's famous fish tacos – are serious business. (p415)

Fairfax District Jewish delis old and new rub shoulders in this traditionally Orthodox LA neighborhood. (p143)

Glendale LA's Armenian American community cheers on belly dancers over hummus and kabobs. (p207)

Freebies

Who says you need to max the credit card to have a good time in SoCal? Many of the most beautiful beaches are free, and that's just for starters.

Broad Schmooze with Warhol, Rauschenberg, Haring and Sherman at LA's hottest new art museum. (p90)

Getty Center Arrive by public transportation, and stroll a multimillion-dollar art collection with priceless LA vistas. (p1152)

Griffith Observatory Ponder the mysteries of the universe while gazing at the stars in LA's Griffith Park. (p124)

Frederick R Weisman Art Foundation Book a guided tour of an LA mansion dressed head to toe in blockbuster modern art. (p153)

Getty Villa Malibu's trove of ancient Greco-Roman art is a can't-miss freebie (but you'll have to pay for parking). (p168)

El Pueblo Historical Monument Get a feel for LA's earliest days along lively, adobe building–lined Olvera St.

Hollywood Forever Cemetery DIY tours of the verdant final resting place of bygone entertainment legends. (p109)

Old Town San Diego Step back in time at a 19th-century Mexican and American pueblo. (p400)

Anza-Borrego Desert State Park Hike to hidden canyons, soak up jaw-dropping viewpoints and even pitch your tent for *nada*. (p313)

Scenic Drives

SoCal's coastal highways are the stuff of legend, while inland detours beckon adventure-seeking road trippers. So drop the convertible top, cue up the Red Hot Chili Peppers and step on it!

Pacific Coast Hwy SoCal's most famous scenic drive delivers beautiful ocean vistas as it hopscotches between beach towns. (p32)

Hwy 190 Deep inside Death Valley, horizons look boundless and roadside geology makes for otherworldly scenery. (p323)

Rim of the World Scenic Byway Hairpin turns to make you gasp on your way to rugged Big Bear Lake. (p232)

Palms to Pines Scenic Byway Carved into the San Jacinto Mountains above Palm Springs, a road that leads to Idyllwild. (p293)

Mulholland Dr So famous David Lynch named a movie after it; a twisting mix of LA views and movie-star mansions. (p114)

Top: Pacific Coast Highway (p9)
Bottom: *Back to the Future* film set, Universal Studios (p201)

Retail Therapy

SoCal covers all retail bases, from resale shops selling fashion straight off movie sets, to deeply discounted outlet malls and quirky boutiques peddling local designs. Ready, set, spend!

Melrose Ave Everyone from the Olsen twins to the Kardashians have their boutiques just east of La Cienega in LA. (p151)

Robertson Blvd Coveted strip of hip, higher-end boutiques popular with celebs and the paparazzi in LA. (p150)

It's a Wrap! Racks of castoffs from real TV shows and movies for sale in the San Fernando Valley. (p210)

Abbot Kinney Blvd An eclectic, artful mix of unique and indie boutiques by the beach in Venice. (p191)

Costa Mesa Shop luxe at South Coast Plaza or hit Camp and The Lab for an offbeat 'anti-mall' experience. (p276)

Palm Springs Especially good for mid-century design, thrift shops and outlet malls. (p303)

Retro Row Where *Mad Men* costume designers go to find mid-century treasures in LA. (p198)

Rose Bowl Flea Market The granddaddy of all flea markets awaits in Pasadena. (p219)

Museums & Galleries

Who says SoCal's only obsessions are pop culture and fame? You could spend your trip immersed in world-famous art galleries, moving museums and interactive high-tech exhibits.

Balboa Park One San Diego park with a string of engaging museums, taking in everything from top-notch art to history and science. (p388)

Getty Center Art museum as fascinating as the architecture and setting in West LA. (p152)

LA County Museum of Art More than 150,000 works of art span the ages and cross all borders. (p135)

Broad A cutting-edge temple to pop art and other modern movements in Downtown LA. (p90)

Museum of Tolerance A moving multimedia center in West LA exploring the Holocaust and the importance of compassion. (p157)

Noah Purifoy Desert Art Museum Ponder installations by a world-famous artist at a desert studio north of Joshua Tree. (p309)

Wende Museum An out-of-the-box collection in LA exploring East German life before the wall came down. (p165)

California Science Center An interactive, multi-level wonderland, complete with a real-deal space shuttle in LA. (p224)

History

Native American tribes, Spanish Colonial presidios (forts), Catholic missions, Mexican pueblos (villages) and mining ghost towns have all left traces here.

Julian Pan for real gold in this historic mining town in the hills east of San Diego. (p317)

Old Town San Diego Turn back time on the site of California's first civilian Spanish Colonial pueblo. (p400)

Mission Santa Barbara The 'queen of the missions' was the only one to survive secularization under Mexican rule. (p349)

La Brea Tar Pits Where prehistoric mammoths, sloths and saber-toothed cats once roamed in what is now LA. (p136)

Mission San Juan Capistrano A painstakingly restored treasure along 'El Camino Real,' California's mission trail. (p286)

Los Angeles City Hall Head to level four for black-and-white photographs of SoCal's fledgling megalopolis. (p83)

Celebrity Spotting

While no one can guarantee you'll run into Ryan Gosling or Emma Stone on their way for coffee, it's more likely to happen in SoCal than anywhere else on the planet.

Malibu Millionaire movie stars love their privacy, but you can often glimpse them in Malibu's shopping plazas. (p167)

Runyon Canyon Don't let those baseball caps and shades fool you. Even the stars love hiking the hills. (p110)

Hotel Bel-Air A well-known celebrity hideaway in LA; discreetly scan the back tables at its Wolfgang Puck restaurant. (p158)

Melrose Ave & Robertson Blvd Hipper stars head to these LA strips to buy their skinny jeans, heels and candles. (p119)

Chateau Marmont On the restaurant patio or in the lounge, expect to spot the odd celeb at this fabled LA hotel. (p141)

Grove Everyone from Justin Bieber to Demi Lovato and Kylie Jenner shop this alfresco LA mall. (p150)

TV-show taping Fawn over famous faces at a sitcom or talk-show taping in LA. (p112)

Brentwood Country Mart No shortage of actors and models graze and browse at this cute little LA hub. (p162)

Month by Month

January

One of the two wettest month in SoCal, January is a slow time for coastal travel. Mountain ski resorts are busy, as are desert destinations. Post-rain days see LA at its clearest.

☆ Rose Bowl Parade

Held before the Tournament of Roses college football game, this New Year's Day parade of flower-festooned floats, marching bands and the crowning of the Rose Queen and her court draws around one million spectators to Pasadena, outside LA.

February

✨ Chinese New Year

Firecrackers, parades, lion dances and street food celebrate the lunar new year. SoCal's biggest celebrations take place in LA, where a Golden Dragon Parade snakes its way through Chinatown.

👁 Modernism Week

Join other mid-century-modern aficionados in Palm Springs mid-February for a blockbuster celebration of mid-20th-century design and style. Expect more than 250 events, from architectural tours and lectures, to art shows, film screenings and parties. (p298)

☆ Academy Awards

The biggest Sunday of the year in LA, Oscar night sees Hollywood's heavyweights grace the red carpet at the Dolby Theatre. Usually held in late February or early March, this is the best time for celebrity-spotting in town. (p67)

March

The rain eases, so travelers head back to the SoCal coast, especially during spring break (varies, depending on school schedules and the Easter holiday). High season in the deserts. Ski season ends.

🏃 LA Marathon

On a Sunday in mid-March, more than 25,000 athletes race along a 26.2-mile course from Dodger Stadium to Santa Monica Pier. Even if you're not running, come cheer and enjoy the live entertainment on stages through the city. (p67)

April

Peak wildflower season in the high desert. Shoulder season in the mountains and on the coast means lower prices, except during spring break. Music royalty hits the Coachella Valley.

☆ Coachella Music & Arts Festval

Indie no-name bands, cult DJs and superstar rock bands and rappers descend on Indio, outside Palm Springs, for a musical extravaganza held over two weekends in mid-April. (p297)

May

Last month before vacationing school kids swarm attractions. Despite the warmer weather, some coastal areas are blanketed by fog ('May gray'). The Memorial Day holiday weekend is one of the year's busiest travel times.

✨ Cinco de Mayo

¡Viva México! Margaritas, music, piñatas and Latino-flavored merriment commemorate the victory of Mexican forces against the French at the Battle of Puebla on May 5. LA and San Diego do it up in style.

June

Once school's out for the summer, nearly everywhere in SoCal gets busier, from beaches to theme parks to mountain resorts. In the deserts, it's just too hot. Some coastal fog lingers ('June gloom').

 LA Pride

Pulling crowds of around 400,000, SoCal's biggest LGBT celebration takes place in West Hollywood over a long weekend in June, with live music, entertainment and a Sunday pride march. (p70)

July

Beach season gets into full swing on the coast. Theme parks are mobbed by vacationing families, as are mountain resorts, but the deserts are deserted. The July 4 holiday is summer's peak travel weekend.

◉ Festival of Arts

Running throughout July and August, Laguna Beach's Festival of Arts includes exhibitions, workshops and live music. One if its best-loved events is the Pageant of the Masters, which sees world-famous paintings recreated using costumed folk. (p285)

August

Warm weather and water temperatures keep beaches busy. School summer vacations come to an end, but everywhere (except the hot deserts) stays packed. Travel slows slightly before Labor Day weekend.

✕ Los Angeles Food & Wine Festival

A four-day, multi-location celebration of LA's booming food scene, with culinary demonstrations, food and drink tastings, special lunches and no shortage of celebrated chefs talking shop and sharing tips. (p70)

September

Summer's last hurrah is the Labor Day holiday weekend, which is extremely busy everywhere (except the deserts). After kids go back to school, the beaches and cities get fewer visitors.

◉ Miramar Air Show

The USA's largest air show (http://miramarairshow.com) wows the crowds at the Marine Corps Air Station Miramar, just north of San Diego, in late September. Expect death-defying aerial shows and military marching-band tunes.

October

Shoulder season means things quieten down just about everywhere in SoCal, despite the sunny weather. Travel deals abound along the coast, in cities and in the desert, where temperatures cool off.

◉ Fleet Week

San Diego's military muscle is on proud display during Fleet Week, with sea and air parades, ship-board tours and live music. (p410)

✵ West Hollywood Halloween Carnival

On October 31 WeHo serves up LA's wildest Halloween street party (www.visit-westhollywood.com/halloween-carnaval). Around 500,000 revelers squeeze onto Santa Monica Blvd in a mass of risque costumes, polished flesh, live music and DJ sets.

November

Temperatures drop, with scattered winter rains starting. Beach areas, cities, theme parks and even the deserts are less busy, except around the Thanksgiving holiday. Ski season just barely begins.

◉ Dia de los Muertos

Mexican communities, including those in LA and San Diego, honor their deceased relatives on November 2 with costumed parades, sugar skulls, graveyard picnics, candlelight processions and elaborate altars.

December

Winter rains usually begin in coastal areas. Travel to typically sunny, drier desert regions picks up. Christmas and New Year's Eve are extremely crowded travel times, though there's usually a short-lived lull between them.

◉ Christmas Boat Parade

Festooned with spectacular lights and Yuletide decorations, up to 150 boats float through Newport Beach's harbor the week before Christmas in what is one of the city's oldest and best-loved traditions. (p270)

Itineraries

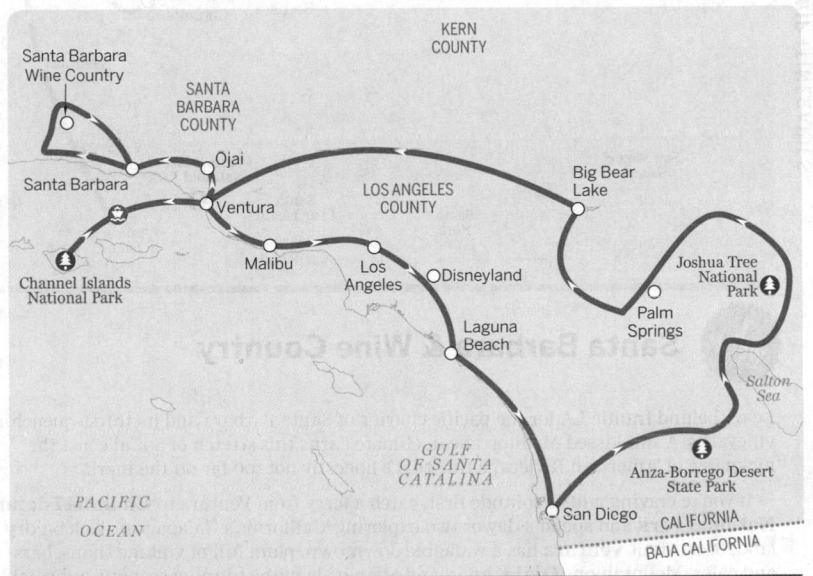

2 WEEKS SoCal Classics

From the high-gloss drawcards of LA to SoCal's answer to the Galapagos Islands, this two-week jaunt offers a satisfying mix of big-hitters and lesser-known treasures.

Kick things off in **Los Angeles**, an extraordinary force of world-class art, architecture, food and nature. Next, hang with Mickey at Disneyland or allow a day of sybaritic downtime in **Laguna Beach** before hitting **San Diego** for fish tacos, surf and the cultural draws of Balboa Park. Leaving civilization behind, shoot northeast to starkly beautiful **Anza-Borrego Desert State Park**. Cruise around eerie **Salton Sea** and into **Joshua Tree National Park**, beckoning with its 'Wonderland of Rocks.' Squeeze in a day of poolside margaritas in mid-century-mecca **Palm Springs** before escaping to **Big Bear Lake** for hiking, biking, fishing and skiing. Wind west via the Rim of the World Scenic Byway to **Ventura** for a boat trip to the unique flora and fauna of the **Channel Islands National Park**, then head inland to arty **Ojai** to catch a 'pink moment' at sunset. Take a breather in seaside **Santa Barbara**, with its gorgeous Spanish-Mediterranean downtown, then stock up on Pinot Noir in **Santa Barbara Wine Country** before heading back to LA via star-studded **Malibu**.

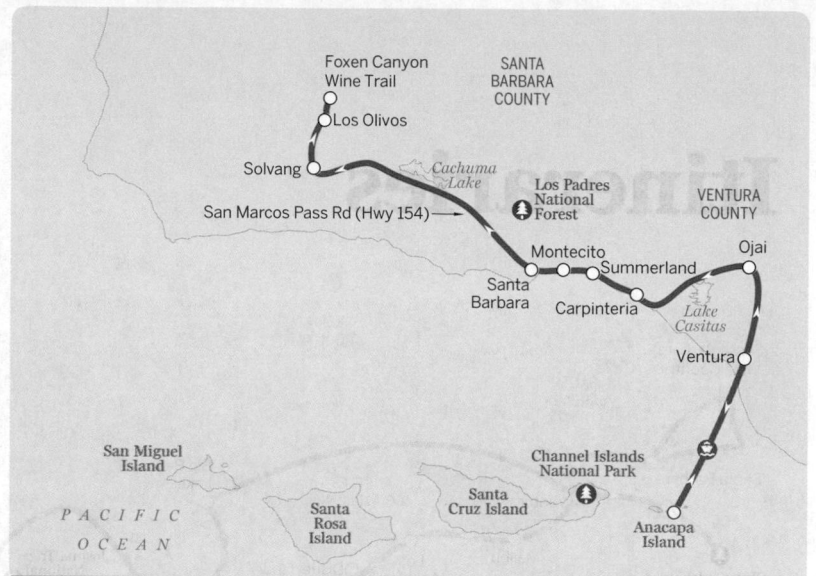

1 WEEK Santa Barbara & Wine Country

Leave behind frantic LA for the pacific charms of Santa Barbara and its thirst-quenching vineyards. A sun-kissed Mediterranean climate earns this stretch of SoCal coast the nickname of 'American Riviera', a title that's honestly not too far off the mark.

If you're craving a little solitude first, catch a ferry from Ventura to **Channel Islands National Park** and spend a day or two exploring 'California's Galapagos.' Back on dry land, oceanfront **Ventura** has a walkable downtown, plum full of vintage shops, bars and cafes. Mountainous **Ojai** is an inland Shangri-la with stunning scenery, unbeatable spa experiences and vibes both spiritual and artistic.

It's less than an hour's drive from Ojai to Santa Barbara, but why rush? Once you hit the coast, drop by **Carpinteria** for a lazy afternoon chilling on the beach, browsing surf shacks and shops on its vintage main street, and chowing down tacos or a darn good burger paired with fries and a hand-mixed milkshake. Just up Hwy 101 lie **Summerland** and **Montecito**, more affluent Santa Barbara suburbs for antiques and boutique shoppers.

Ah, **Santa Barbara**. Strut down State St, with its sea of red-tile roofs, then climb to the top of the courthouse for bird's-eye vistas. Down at Stearns Wharf, dig into a bowl of chowder on the pier. Refueled, join a pickup game of volleyball on East Beach or take your sweetheart to shamelessly romantic Butterfly Beach. Awaiting inland is Santa Barbara's 'Queen of the Missions,' as are several petite museums, exploring everything from art to maritime and Spanish Colonial history. After dark, hit the buzzing restaurants, bars and wine-tasting rooms of Santa Barbara's Funk Zone, down by the railroad tracks.

Take a scenic drive on San Marcos Pass Rd (Hwy 154) past **Los Padres National Forest** and **Cachuma Lake Recreation Area** up to Santa Barbara's friendly, rolling wine country. Drive west to kitschy Danish **Solvang**, with its faux windmills and historical mission, then north to chichi **Los Olivos**, a Napa-style town punctuated with bistros, boutiques and wine-tasting rooms. Just out of town is the beginning of the gorgeous **Foxen Canyon Wine Trail**, which lazily winds along rural roads past wineries where you can swill and savor the region's celebrated Pinot Noir, Syrah, Chardonnay and more.

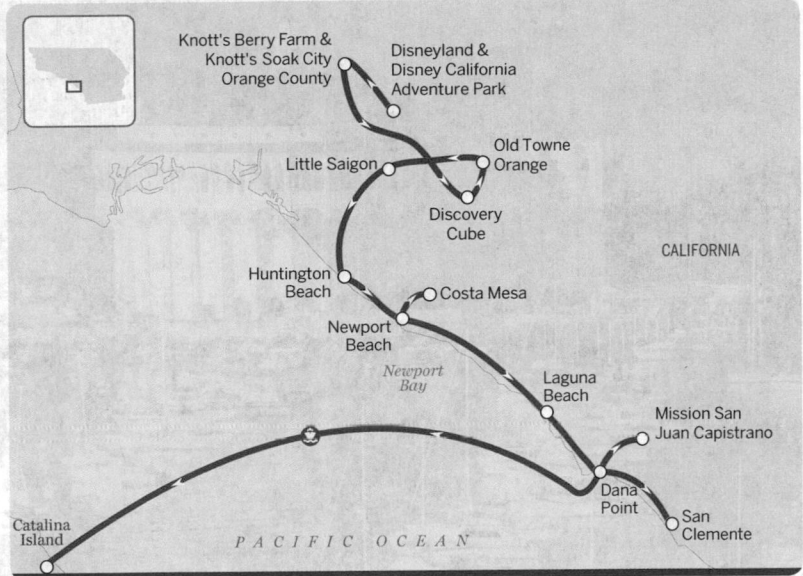

 Disneyland & Orange County

It's no secret: many of SoCal's most popular attractions are in Orange County, famed for its prime-time beaches, sunny skies and theme parks. But there's more to discover here, too, from high-tech museums to historic Spanish missions.

It will leave the kids thrilled and you exhausted, but there's no question that a trip to Disneyland is a quintessential SoCal experience. Skip down Main Street, USA or dive into **Disney California Adventure Park** next door. Then head to nearby **Knott's Berry Farm**, America's oldest theme park, which pairs Old Western cowboy themes with futuristic roller-coasters. If it's too darn hot, slip into your swimsuit and cool off at **Knott's Soak City Orange County** water park.

Just so you don't think SoCal is all about theme-park thrills, drop by the interactive **Discovery Cube** in Santa Ana, where the whole family can virtually experience the shake, rattle 'n' roll of a 6.4-magnitude earthquake. Also near Anaheim, **Old Towne Orange** offers another break from Disney jingles, with its antique and vintage shops and eclectic restaurants. A little further southwest in Westminster, **Little Saigon** trades theme-park hot dogs for fragrant bowls of authentic *pho* (noodle soup).

Continue south toward the OC's unbeatable beaches, the perfect place to chill, dude. Take a day off in **Huntington Beach**, aka 'Surf City USA'. Rent a board, slam a volleyball on the sand, then build a bonfire around sunset. When the sun rises, roll south to **Newport Beach** and people-watch by the piers. Make a quick stop for power shopping or eclectic eats in **Costa Mesa**, then continue south to soulful **Laguna Beach**, a former artists' colony with more than two dozen public beaches, a worthy art museum and chic downtown shopping and dining scenes.

From **Dana Point** you could catch a ferry to Med-style **Catalina Island**. Otherwise slingshot back toward the I-5, stopping off at **Mission San Juan Capistrano** for a sun-baked sampling of Spanish Colonial and Mexican rancho heritage. Alternatively, continue with the beach-bum attitude by slacking south to nostalgic surf enclave **San Clemente**, near Trestles, a year-round surf break. Just prepare to never want to leave.

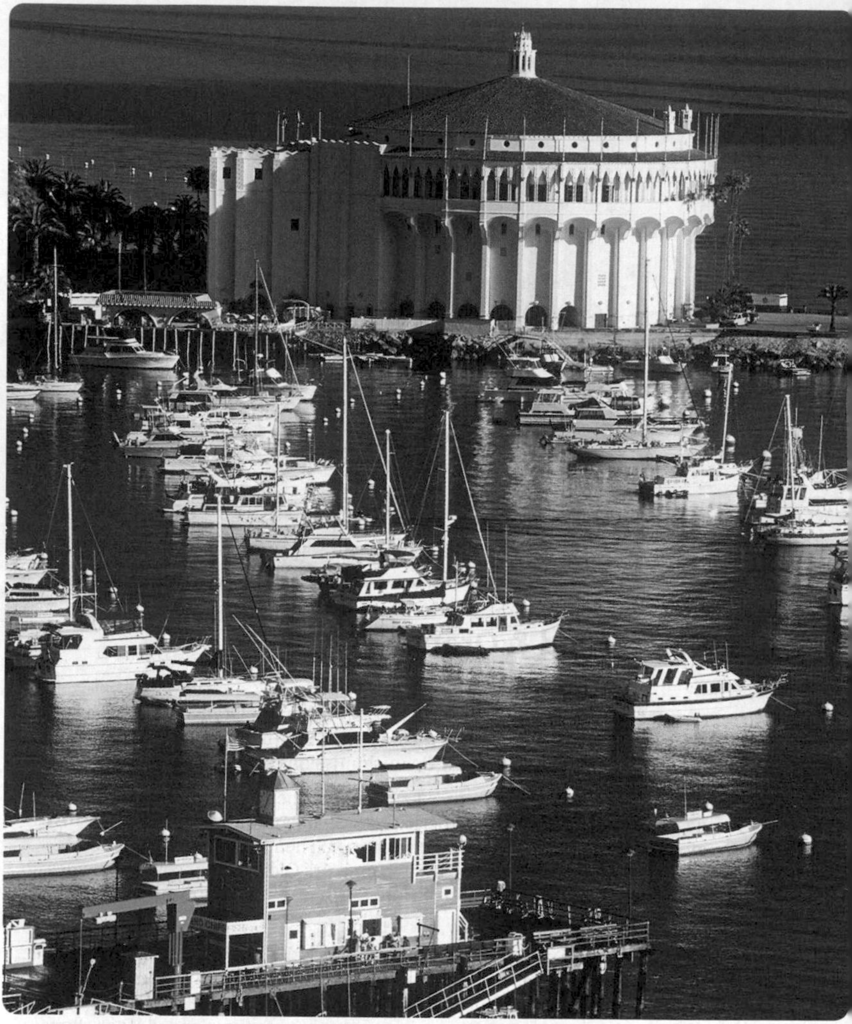

KIRK WESTER / SHUTTERSTOCK ©

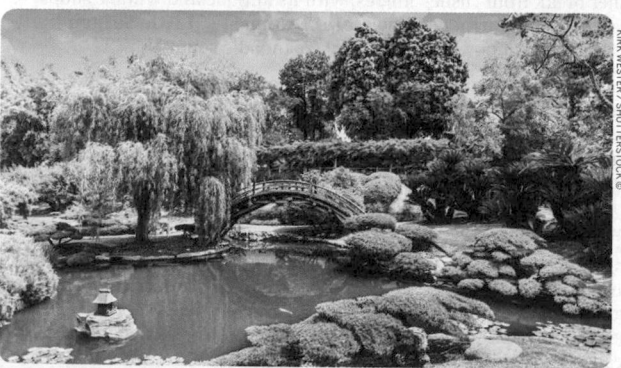

Top: Avalon Harbor, Catalina Island (p228)

Bottom: Huntington Botanical Gardens (p211)

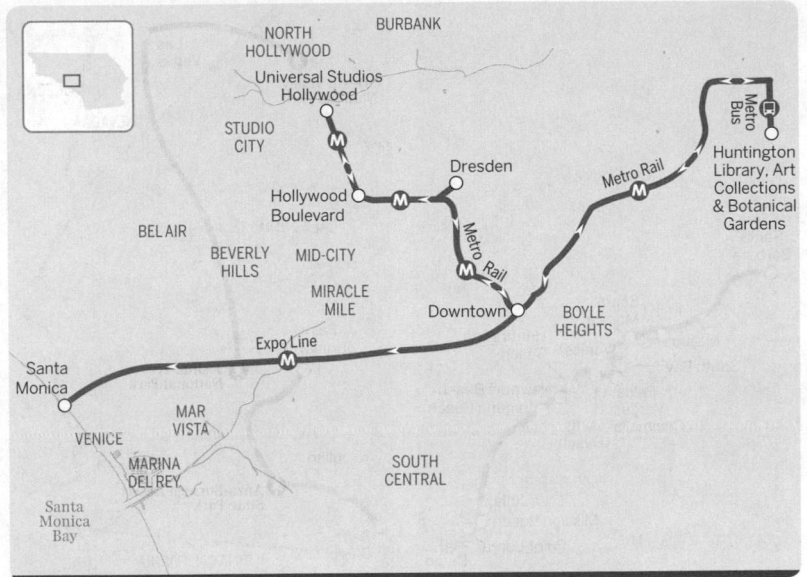

Los Angeles: No Car Required

Hollywood Walk of Fame. Walt Disney Concert Hall. Melrose Ave. Beverly Hills. The beaches. Yup, it can all be done in LA without a car, we promise. You'll just need patience, a good sense of direction and a Metro Tap Card. Get an early start and double-check bus and subway route maps and timetables with **Metro** before heading out.

Downtown makes a handy base of operation and puts you within walking distance – or a short bus ride – of the Broad and MOCA Grand Ave art museums, the Walt Disney Concert Hall, City Hall, Little Tokyo, and the colonial buildings of the El Pueblo Historical Monument. It also means easy access to the Arts District and its so-hot-right-now galleries, restaurants, bars and shopping. Spend your first day exploring the local area.

On the morning of day two, catch the Metro Red Line north up to **Hollywood Boulevard**. Explore its famous star-studded walk and Chinese Theatre and get up close and personal with Hollywood props, costumes and sets at the time-warped Hollywood Museum. Done, get back on the Red Line and continue north to **Universal Studios** for a backlot tour and some theme-park downtime. Come evening, hop back on the Red Line and alight at Vermont/Sunset station, from where the iconic **Dresden** lounge is a short walk north on Vermont Ave. The last train back to Downtown departs at 1:16am (2:36am on Friday and Saturday nights).

On day three, pack a swimsuit because you're headed to the beach. But first, catch the Metro Gold Line to Allen Station and transfer to southbound Metro bus 10, alighting at the corner of Allen Ave and Del Mar Blvd. From here, the extraordinary **Huntington Library, Art Collections and Botanical Gardens** is a half-mile walk further south on Allen. Spend a few hours then head back on the Gold Line, transferring to a Red or Purple Line train at beautiful Union Station and to an Expo Line train at 7th St/Metro Center. The Expo Line's final stop is **Santa Monica**. Spend the rest of the day checking out its world-famous pier, strolling the sand and squeezing in some shopping along Third Street Promenade. Lungs filled with ocean air, ride the Expo Line back to Downtown, the last service leaving at 12:56am (1:36am on Friday and Saturday nights).

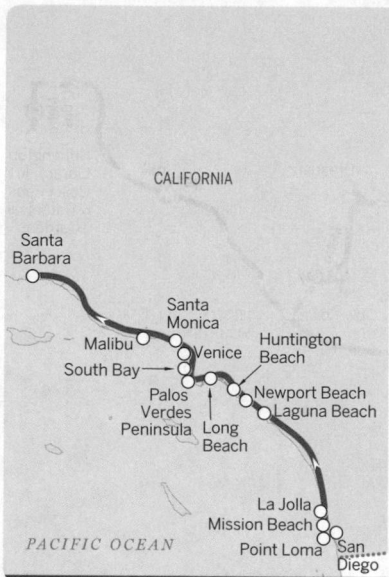

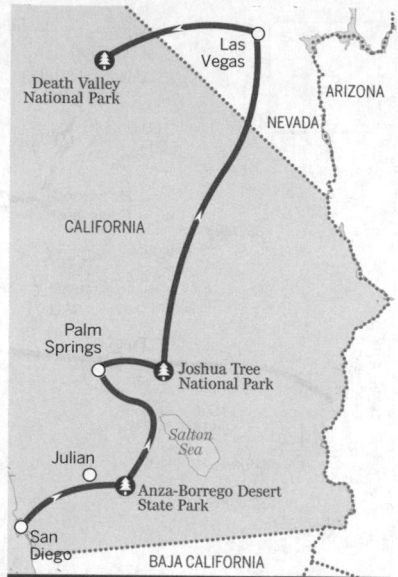

 Pacific Coast Highway

1 WEEK

Drop the convertible top, cue up 'California Girls' and step on it. This famous route starts in San Diego and hugs the Pacific throughout most of SoCal.

Before heading north soak up 360-degree views from **Point Loma**, buff surfers in **Mission Beach** and the underwater treasures of **La Jolla**. Our vote for prettiest Orange County town is cultured **Laguna Beach**, whose secluded coves and cliffs enchant. For yachts and glitz, plow on to **Newport Beach**. Just up the road is **Huntington Beach**, 'Surf City USA'.

Across the LA County line is **Long Beach**, home to an impressive aquarium and museum of Latin American art. Continue around beautiful **Palos Verdes Peninsula** before plunging into LA's **South Bay** beach towns. North of boho-chic **Venice**, **Santa Monica** beckons with its carnival pier, shopping and vibrant street life.

The busy coast highway has more surprises in store further north, with surreal ocean vistas en route to celebrity hideaway **Malibu**. Wrap up your trip in **Santa Barbara**, a seductive mélange of red-tile roofs, lauded wineries and soul-lifting beaches.

 Desert Escapes

1 WEEK

SoCal's desertscapes range from the poetically beautiful to the downright surreal. This route takes you through striking arid corners, with a splash of urban glitz thrown in for refreshment.

Start your trip in surfside **San Diego** and head northeast for **Julian**, an Old West mining town where you can pan for gold and gorge on apple pie. Drop into **Anza-Borrego Desert State Park**, where dirt roads and trails lead to hidden canyon oases, Native American petroglyphs and 19th-century stagecoach stops.

Watch for endangered bird species at the strange and salty **Salton Sea** before heading north to retro-chic **Palm Springs**, the once-again hip resort hangout of Elvis and the Rat Pack. Refreshed, continue to mystical **Joshua Tree National Park**, whose namesake trees have inspired artists and poets.

Next stop: **Las Vegas**, where you can climb the Eiffel Tower, make out in a gondola and catch an exploding volcano, all in the same day. Partied out, drive back west into California to **Death Valley National Park**, a mesmerizing jigsaw puzzle of sand dunes, sun-baked salt flats, volcanic cinder cones and ghost towns.

Plan Your Trip
Southern California's Beaches

With miles and miles of wide, sandy beaches, you'll find it hard to resist getting wet in Southern California. Beach life and surf culture are part of the free-wheeling SoCal lifestyle, so play hooky any day of the week and go hit the waves like locals so often do.

Beaches & Swimming

Ocean temperatures for swimming become tolerable in SoCal by about May, peaking in July and August. During the hottest dog days of summer, another way to keep kids' temperatures cool is at water parks such as Six Flags Hurricane Harbor (p231) north of LA, Legoland (p446) north of San Diego, the recently revamped Knott's Soak City (p255) in Buena Park (Orange County) and Wet 'n' Wild Palm Springs (p296).

Top Swimming Beaches

Coronado (p403), San Diego

Mission Beach (p405), San Diego

Balboa Peninsula (p268), Newport Beach

Pacific Beach (p405), San Diego

Main Beach (p280), Laguna Beach

Doheny State Beach (p287), Dana Point

San Buenaventura State Beach (p381), Ventura

El Capitán State Beach (p352), near Santa Barbara

Venice (p184), Los Angeles

SoCal's Best Beaches

Los Angeles County

Santa Monica (p174) & **Venice** (p184) Giant-sized sunsets and a cycling path.

Malibu (p167) Hidden strands of paradisiacal sand.

South Bay (p192) Surfing, beach volleyball and beautiful people.

Orange County

Huntington Beach (p262) Officially, 'Surf City USA'.

Newport Beach (p268) Eclectic social scenes between two piers.

Crystal Cove State Park (p279) Wild, rugged coastline pocked with tide pools.

San Diego County

Coronado (p403) Miles of coveted white sand along the Silver Strand.

Mission & Pacific Beaches (p405) Surfing, amusement-park rides and beach bums.

La Jolla (p432) Epic surf and windblown rambles.

Santa Barbara County

Leadbetter Beach (p352) Where local families picnic and splash about.

East Beach (p352) Lazy sunbathing near a historic wharf.

Carpinteria State Beach (p352) Palm trees, sand dunes and carefree swimming.

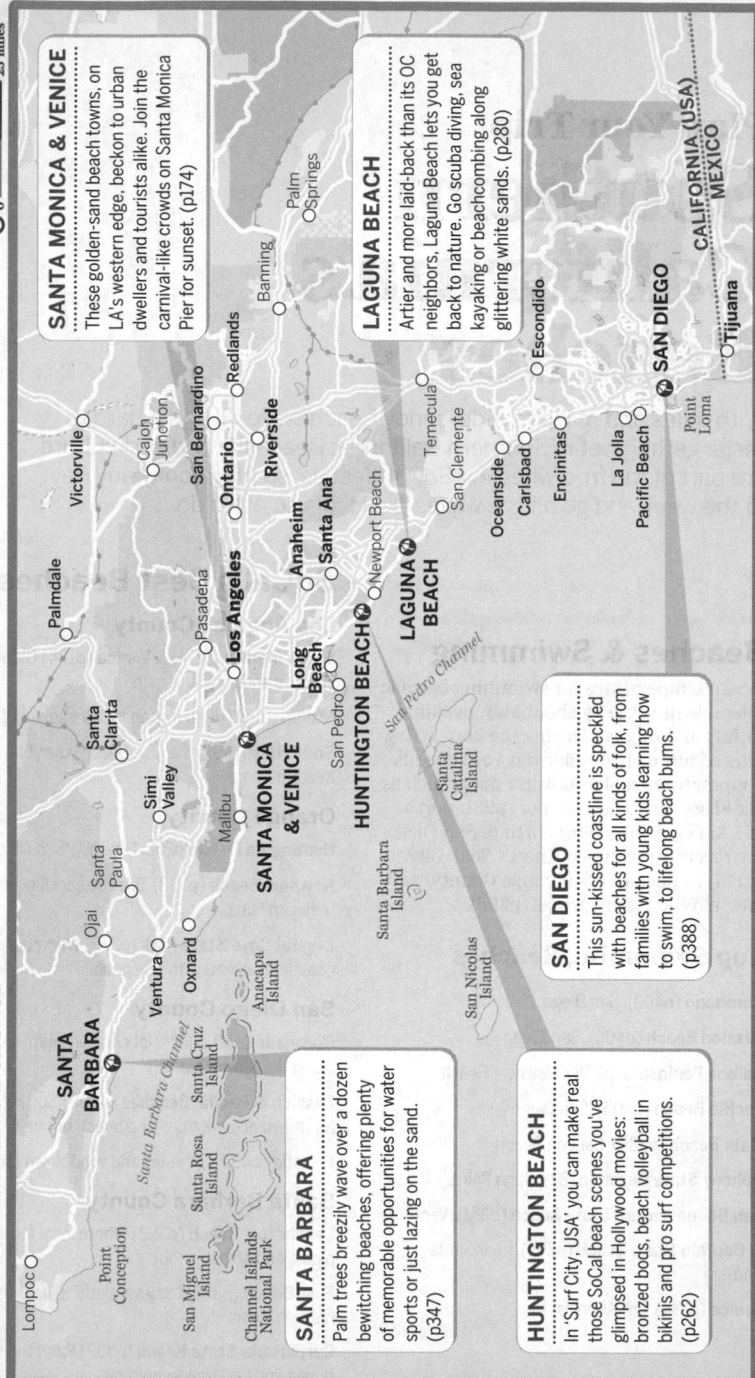

Southern California's Beaches

SANTA MONICA & VENICE

These golden-sand beach towns, on LA's western edge, beckon to urban dwellers and tourists alike. Join the carnival-like crowds on Santa Monica Pier for sunset. (p174)

LAGUNA BEACH

Artier and more laid-back than its OC neighbors, Laguna Beach lets you get back to nature. Go scuba diving, sea kayaking or beachcombing along glittering white sands. (p280)

SAN DIEGO

This sun-kissed coastline is speckled with beaches for all kinds of folk, from families with young kids learning how to swim, to lifelong beach bums. (p388)

SANTA BARBARA

Palm trees breezily wave over a dozen bewitching beaches, offering plenty of memorable opportunities for water sports or just lazing on the sand. (p347)

HUNTINGTON BEACH

In 'Surf City, USA' you can make real those SoCal beach scenes you've glimpsed in Hollywood movies: bronzed bods, beach volleyball in bikinis and pro surf competitions. (p262)

Best Family-Friendly Beaches

Silver Strand State Beach (p403), Coronado

Leo Carrillo State Park (p167), Malibu

Balboa Peninsula (p268), Newport Beach

Carpinteria State Beach (p352), Santa Barbara County

Arroyo Burro Beach County Park (Hendry's) (p352), Santa Barbara

Best Beaches for Beach Volleyball

Manhattan Beach (p192), LA's South Bay

Hermosa Beach (p193), LA's South Bay

Huntington Beach (p262), Orange County

Ocean Beach (p405), San Diego

East Beach (p352), Santa Barbara

Beach Safety Tips

➡ Most beaches have flags to distinguish between surfer-only sections and sections for swimmers. Flags also alert beachgoers to dangerous water conditions.

➡ Popular beaches have lifeguards, but can still be dangerous places to swim. Obey all posted warning signs and ask about local conditions before venturing out.

➡ Stay out of the ocean for at least three days after a major rainstorm because of dangerously high levels of pollutants flushed out through storm drains.

➡ Water quality varies from beach to beach, and day to day. For current water-safety conditions and beach closures, check the Beach Report Card (http://brc.healthebay.org) issued by the nonprofit organization Heal the Bay (https://healthebay.org).

Books & Maps

The outstanding *California Coastal Access Guide* (University of California Press; www.ucpress.edu) has comprehensive maps of every public beach, reef, harbor, cover, overlook and coastal campground, with valuable information about parking, hiking trails, facilities and wheelchair access. It's especially helpful for finding secret pockets of uncrowded sand.

Surfing

Surf's up! Are you down? Even if you have never set foot on a board, there's no denying the influence of surfing on every aspect of SoCal beach life, from clothing to lingo. It's an obsession up and down the coast, particularly in San Diego and Orange County.

The most powerful swells arrive in late fall and winter, while May and June are generally the flattest months, although they do bring warmer water. Speaking of temperature, don't believe all those images of hot blonds surfing in skimpy swimsuits – without a wet suit, you'll likely freeze your butt off except at the height of summer.

Crowds can be a problem at many surf spots, as can overly territorial surfers. Befriend a local surfer for an introduction before hitting SoCal's most famous waves, such as Windansea or Trestles. Sharks do inhabit California waters but attacks are rare.

Top Surf Spots for Pros

California comes fully loaded with easily accessible world-class surf spots, the lion's share of which are in SoCal – lucky you!

➡ Near San Clemente in Orange County, Trestles (p289) is a premier summer spot with big but forgiving waves, a fast ride, and both right and left breaks.

➡ Huntington Beach (p262) in Orange County may have the West Coast's most consistent waves, with miles of breaks centered on the pier.

➡ San Diego's Windansea Beach (p435) is a powerful reef break, while nearby Big Rock (p435) churns out gnarly tubes.

➡ Malibu's Surfrider Beach (p167) has a clean right break that just gets better with bigger winter waves.

➡ Santa Barbara County's Rincon Point in Carpinteria (p352) is a legendary right point break that peels forever.

Best Surf Breaks for Beginners

The best spots to learn to surf are at beach breaks at long, shallow bays where the waves are small and rolling. Popular places for beginners in SoCal, where many surf schools offer lessons, include:

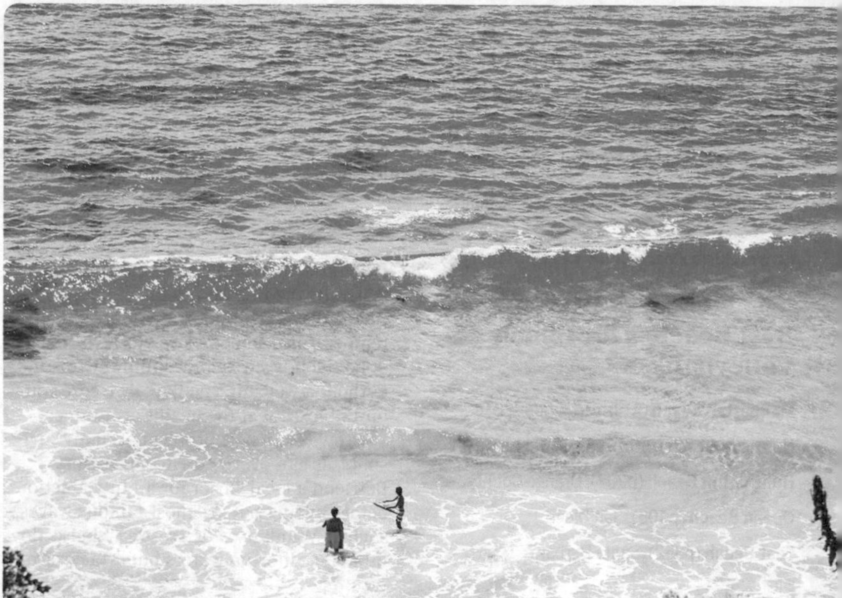

DOBINO / SHUTTERSTOCK ©

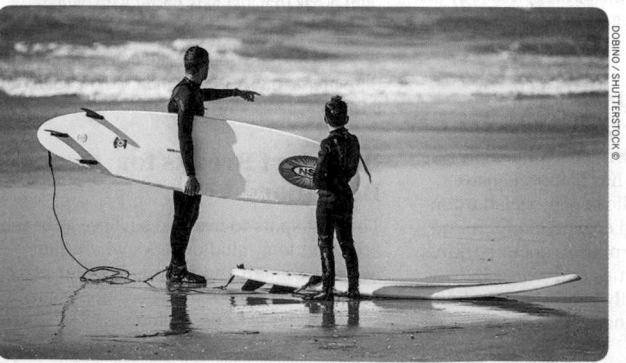

Top: Crystal Cove State Park (p279)

Bottom: Surfers, La Jolla Shores (p433)

La Jolla (p432)

San Diego Mission Beach, Pacific Beach, La Jolla and Oceanside

Orange County Seal Beach, Huntington Beach, Newport Beach and Laguna Beach

Los Angeles Santa Monica and Malibu

Santa Barbara Leadbetter Beach and Carpinteria

Rentals & Lessons

You'll find board rentals on just about every patch of sand where surfing is possible. Expect to pay from around $10 to $15 per hour (or around $40 per day) for a board, with wet-suit rental around another $10 to $15 for half a day (or around $20 per day).

Two-hour group lessons for beginners start at around $100 per person, while private, two-hour instruction costs over $125. If you're ready to jump in the deep end, many surf schools offer weekend surf clinics and weeklong 'surfari' camps.

Stand-up paddleboarding (SUP) is easier than learning how to board surf, and it's skyrocketing in popularity. You'll find similarly priced SUP rentals and lessons popping up all along the coast, from San Diego to Santa Barbara.

Books & Maps

➡ Water-resistant *Surfer Magazine's Guide to Southern California Surf Spots* (2006) is jam-packed with expert reviews, information, maps and photos.

➡ *Surfing California: A Guide To The Best Breaks And SUP-Friendly Spots On the California Coast* (2013) sheds light on more than 200 surf spots along the Californian coast, with information on best tide height, swell direction, wave size and more.

Online Resources

➡ Surfer (www.surfer.com) Orange County–based magazine's website has travel reports, gear reviews, newsy blogs, forums, videos and swell reports for the entire SoCal coast.

➡ Riptionary (www.riptionary.com) If you're a kook, bone up on your surf-speak so the locals don't go aggro and give you the stink eye.

Plan Your Trip

The Great Outdoors

Weather forecasters in Southern California have one of the easiest gigs in the world. 'Plenty of sun today. More sun tomorrow. And a high chance of sun later in the week.' Blessed with Mediterranean-style warmth and superlative natural diversity, SoCal is practically one giant playground made for alfresco thrills.

Best ...

Time to Go

Swimming and beach volleyball July and August

Surfing and windsurfing September to November

Kayaking, snorkeling and diving June to October

Whale-watching January to March

Hiking April to May and September to October

Skiing and snowboarding December to March

Outdoor Experiences

Surfing Malibu, Huntington Beach, Trestles or Rincon Point (Carpinteria)

Sea kayaking and whale-watching The Channel Islands

Snorkeling or scuba diving La Jolla

Beach volleyball LA's Manhattan Beach

Cycling LA's South Bay or Santa Barbara

Rock climbing or hiking Joshua Tree National Park

Snorkeling & Scuba Diving

Not surprisingly, Southern California has some excellent snorkeling and diving spots – from rock reefs to shipwrecks to kelp forests – suited for all skill and experience levels. Just don't expect crystal-clear waters like those in Hawaii or the Caribbean, as local dive spots can be murky. Ocean waters are warmest between July and September. That said, wet suits are recommended year-round.

Top Diving & Snorkeling Spots

➡ Outstanding spots, especially for first-time divers, are San Diego–La Jolla Underwater Park Ecological Reserve (p432) and Casino Point (Avalon Underwater Park) on Catalina Island (p228). Accessible right from shore, both have fertile kelp beds teeming with critters close to the surface.

➡ More experienced divers might want to steer toward Orange County's Crystal Cove State Park (p279) and Divers Cove (p281) around Laguna Beach, as well as Wreck Alley, near San Diego's Mission Bay (p388), where you can explore sunken military aircraft and ships.

➡ Many popular dive spots are also good for snorkeling, for example, Channel Islands

Kayaker, Catalina Island (p228)

National Park (p383). Guided dive boats and combo kayaking-and-snorkeling trips to the park's islands leave from Ventura and Oxnard, between Santa Barbara and LA.

Rentals, Lessons & Tours

Local dive shops are your best resources for equipment, guides, instructors and dive-boat trips. To explore California's deep waters, you must have an Open Water certificate from the Professional Association of Dive Instructors (PADI) or another recognized organization. If you already have your certification, you can book boat dives for about $65 to $150 (reserve trips at least a day in advance).

If you just want to dabble in diving, look for outfitters offering beginner courses that include basic instruction, followed by a shallow beach or boat dive, for around $150. If you're serious about learning and have the time and money, sign up for a multi-day Open Water certificate course, which costs from $250 to $600.

Snorkelers can rent a mask, snorkel, fins and even a wet suit for about $20 to $45 per day from concessionaires at some beaches and in towns near snorkeling

sites. If you're going to take the plunge more than once or twice, it's probably worth buying your own high-quality mask and fins. Remember not to touch anything while you're out snorkeling and don't snorkel alone.

Books, Magazines & Online Resources

➡ Lonely Planet's *Diving & Snorkeling Southern California & the Channel Islands* by David Krival is a hands-on guide to happy encounters with garibaldi, sheephead, calico bass and other offshore creatures in SoCal's waters.

➡ Scuba Diving (www.scubadiving.com) and Sport Diver (www.sportdiver.com) have comprehensive websites dedicated to underwater adventures.

Kayaking

Few water-based sports are as accessible and fun for the whole gang as kayaking, and most people manage to get paddling along quickly with minimal instruction.

AVOIDING SEASICKNESS

Choppy seas can be nauseating for some landlubbers. To avoid seasickness, sit outside on the boat's second level – not too close to the diesel fumes in back. Over-the-counter motion-sickness pills such as Dramamine are effective, though always ensure you choose a non-drowsy formula. Staring at the horizon works for some people, as does chewing ginger or wearing acupressure wristbands.

Whether you're looking for adventure and exploring sea caves or just serenely paddling along coastal bluffs, opportunities abound along SoCal's coast.

Best Places to Kayak

➡ Sea kayaking is fabulous in Channel Islands National Park (p383), offshore from Ventura, and at Catalina Island (p228), closer to LA. Both are ideal overnight getaways for experienced paddlers.

➡ Day trips are equally rewarding, especially for beginners who launch their kayaks in the calm, protected waters of San Diego's Mission Bay and Dana Point or Huntington Harbor in Orange County.

➡ You can explore sea caves while floating above the kelp forests and reefs of San Diego–La Jolla Underwater Park Ecological Reserve (p432).

➡ You'll find even more coastal kayaking in Malibu, Orange County's Laguna Beach and among the sea caves of Gaviota, west of Santa Barbara.

Rentals & Tours

Most kayaking outfitters offer a choice between sit-upon (open) kayaks and sit-in (closed-hull) ones; the latter usually require some training before you head out. Kayak rentals average $30 to $50 for a half-day, and you'll usually have a choice between single and tandem kayaks. A reputable outfitter will make sure you're aware of the variable tide schedule and wind conditions for your proposed route.

Many kayaking outfitters lead half-day ($50 to $90) or full-day (starting at $100) coastal trips. Some offer kayak–hike

combos or thrilling sunset or after-dark paddles. There's nothing quite like seeing the reflection of the moon and stars glittering on the water and hearing the gentle splash of water on your kayak's hull. Small group tours led by local guides with natural history knowledge are best.

Whether you're taking a guided tour or renting kayaks, try to make reservations at least a day beforehand.

Online Resources

Kayak Online (www.kayakonline.com) Dozens of links to local kayaking outfitters, schools and organizations, plus handy advice for beginners to experts.

California Kayak Friends (www.ckfkayak.club) Hosts discussion forums about anything from popular paddling destinations and put-ins to recent trip reports and upcoming events.

Whale-Watching

Every summer an estimated 20,000 gray whales feed in the Arctic waters between Alaska and Siberia, and every fall they start moving south down the west coast of Canada and the USA to sheltered lagoons in the Gulf of California off Baja California. In spring these whales turn around and head back to the Arctic. During their 12,000-mile round-trip, the whales pass just off the California coast, typically between late December and early April.

And it's not only gray whales that make appearances in SoCal. Blue, humpback, sperm and killer whales, as well as schools of dolphins and porpoises, can be seen swimming offshore throughout the summer and fall, but spotting these marine mammals is not quite as predictable.

On Land vs at Sea

You can try your luck whale-watching while staying ashore (eg at lighthouses) – it's free, but you're less likely to see whales and you'll be at a distance from all the action. Point Vicente (p193) on the Palos Verdes Peninsula in LA and San Diego's Point Loma (p403) are two well-known whale-watching spots, but you could get just as lucky somewhere else.

For bigger thrills, just about every SoCal port town worth its salt offers

Top: Rock climber, Joshua Tree National Park (p307)

Bottom: Humpback whale, Channel Islands (p383)

VIKKI HUNT / SHUTTERSTOCK ©

SOCAL'S DESTINATION SPA RESORTS & DAY SPAS

If the road has left you feeling frazzled and achy, an hour or more at a day spa may be just what the doctor ordered. There are literally hundreds of spas throughout So-Cal, from simple storefronts in strip malls to luxurious oases in rich-and-famous zip codes such as Palm Springs.

Every spa has its own 'treatment menu,' usually including a variety of massages such as Thai, shiatsu, deep-tissue, Swedish, tandem (two therapists equals four hands) and hot-stone. Beauty treatments range from classic facials and botanical wraps to exotic elixir baths and body cocktail scrubs.

For a treat, detour to Glen Ivy Hot Springs (www.glenivy.com), aka 'Club Mud,' located in inland Orange County. Famous for its red-clay mud bath, Glen Ivy also offers clear mineral-water tubs and a large swimming pool. In the mountains north of Ventura, closer to LA, Ojai Valley Inn & Spa (p378) is another renowned retreat. In LA itself, Koreatown is well known for its 24-hour Eastern-style spas. One of the best is Wi Spa (p132).

Wherever you go, massage sessions typically cost at least $80 for 50 minutes, while a facial will set you back $60 or more. By the time you've added a 20% tip, the final tab may be high enough to warrant another stress-relieving treatment.

whale-watching boat tours, especially during winter. Don't forget your binoculars! Half-day whale-watching boat trips (from around $30 to $90 per adult, usually discounted for children) last from two to four hours, and sometimes include snacks and drinks. Tours are sometimes cheaper on weekdays than weekends. Make reservations at least a day or two in advance.

Look for whale-watching boat tours that limit the number of people and have a trained naturalist or marine biologist onboard. Some tour-boat companies will let you go again for free if you don't spot any whales on your first cruise.

Windsurfing & Kiteboarding

Experienced windsurfers tear up the waves along the coast, while newbies and those who want a mellower ride skim along calm bays and protected beaches. There's almost always a breeze, but the best winds blow from September through November. Wet suits are a good idea year-round.

Best Places to Windsurf & Kiteboard

Basically, any place that has good windsurfing also has good kiteboarding. Look for the people doing aerial acrobatics as

their parachute-like kites yank them from the water. In wide open spaces devoid of obstacles such as piers and power lines, you won't have to worry about unexpected flights that could slam you into concrete.

➡ In San Diego, beginners should check out Santa Clara Point in Mission Bay.

➡ Santa Barbara's Leadbetter Beach (p352) is another good place for beginners to learn.

➡ In LA, you'll see lots of action off **Belmont Shore** (Map p200; Long Beach; ▣ Red Passport) near Long Beach and Point Fermin (p199) near San Pedro.

Rentals & Lessons

The learning curve in windsurfing is steeper than other board sports – imagine balancing on a fast-moving plank through choppy waters while trying to read the wind and angle the sail just so. At most windsurfing hot spots, you'll spend about $100 to $150 for an introductory lesson.

Although it's harder to get started kiteboarding, experts say it's easier to advance quickly once the basics are down. Beginner kiteboarding lessons start at over $200, usually taking place over a few days. The first lesson is spent learning kite control on the beach and the second lesson gets you into the water.

Windsurfing-gear rentals cost about $50 to $75 per half-day for a beginner's board and harness. Most windsurfing shops at

SOCAL'S TOP 10 NATIONAL & STATE PARKLANDS

PARK	FEATURES	ACTIVITIES	BEST TIME TO VISIT
Anza-Borrego Desert State Park	badlands, canyons, fan-palm oases, hot springs, caves; bighorn sheep, birds	4WD, stargazing, hiking, horseback riding, birding	Nov-Mar
Channel Islands National Park	rocky islands with steep cliffs; elephant seals, sea lions, otters, foxes	snorkeling, diving, kayaking, hiking, birding	Apr-Oct
Crystal Cove State Park	beach, woodland, marine park, tide pools, historic cottages, wildflowers; bobcats	swimming, diving, kayaking, hiking, mountain biking	year-round
Death Valley National Park	unique geology, sand dunes, canyons, volcanic craters, wildflowers; desert tortoise, bighorn sheep, bats	hiking, 4WD, horseback riding, mountain biking, birding	Oct-Apr
Joshua Tree National Park	rocky desert, fan-palm oases, Joshua trees, cacti, wildflowers; desert tortoise, bighorn sheep, coyotes, snakes	rock climbing, hiking, 4WD, mountain biking, birding	Sep-May
Los Padres National Forest	canyons, chaparral-covered foothills, mountains, forests, waterfalls, hot springs; California condors, mule deer, coyotes, black bears	hiking, birding, wildlife-watching, mountain biking, swimming	Apr-Oct
Mt San Jacinto State Park	alpine mountains, forests, meadows, aerial tramway, wildflowers; deer, mountain lions, foxes	hiking, cross-country skiing, snowshoeing, birding	year-round
Upper Newport Bay Nature Preserve	estuary, beach, salt marsh, mud flats, sand dunes, coastal scrub grasslands; birds	birding, kayaking, cycling, horseback riding, hiking	Oct-Apr
Santa Monica Mountains National Recreation Area	tree- and chaparral-covered coastal range, wildflowers; lizards, mountain lions, bobcats, snakes, raptors	hiking, mountain biking, birding	year-round
Torrey Pines State Natural Reserve	coastal lagoon, beaches, salt marsh, pine trees, coastal sage; seals, sea lions, foxes, birds	hiking, birding, tide pooling	year-round

least dabble in kiteboarding, but usually won't rent kiteboarding gear to people who aren't taking lessons from them.

Online Resources

iWindsurf (www.iwindsurf.com) Wind reports, weather forecasts, live wind-cams and active discussion forums.

iKitesurf (www.ikitesurf.com) Prime locations for both the experienced and the aspiring, wind reports and more.

Hiking

Got wanderlust? With awesome scenery, Southern California is perfect for exploring on foot. That's true no matter whether you've got your heart set on peak-bagging 10,000-footers, trekking to palm-tree oases, hiking among fragrant pines or simply going for a wander on the beach beside the booming surf. During spring and early summer, a painter's palette's worth of wildflowers bloom on shaggy hillsides, in mountain meadows, on damp forest floors and most famously, in desert sands.

Best Places to Hike

No matter where you find yourself in Southern California, you're never far from a trail, even in the metropolitan areas. The best trails are often amid the jaw-dropping scenery of national and state parks, national forests, recreation areas and other public lands. You'll find the gamut of routes, from paved trails negotiable by wheelchairs and baby strollers to multiday backpacking routes through rugged wilderness.

➡ In Los Angeles you can hike for miles in **Griffith Park** (Map p120; ☑323-644-2050; www.laparks.org; 4730 Crystal Springs Dr; ◷5am-10pm, trails sunrise-sunset; P) FREE, one of America's largest urban parks.

➡ Outside LA, the Santa Monica Mountains (p166) and Big Bear Lake are both cooler escapes during summer.

➡ East of San Diego, Cleveland National Forest is another cool summer hiking place.

➡ The Santa Ynez Mountains and Los Padres National Forest beckon around Santa Barbara, especially during the more temperate spring and fall seasons.

➡ Offshore, more rugged trails crisscross Channel Islands National Park (p383) and Catalina Island.

➡ Palm Springs delivers fantastic hiking in summer atop its aerial tramway inside Mt San Jacinto State Park (p296), and in winter at Indian Canyons (p296) and Tahquitz Canyon (p296).

➡ For spectacular spring wildflower displays, head deeper into the desert to Anza-Borrego Desert State Park (p313), Death Valley National Park (p323), the Mojave National Preserve (p322) and Joshua Tree National Park (p304).

➡ In San Diego and Orange Counties, you can hike along coastal bluffs, including at Torrey Pines State Natural Reserve (p433) and Crystal Cove State Park (p279), or in the canyons above Laguna Beach.

Safety Tips

➡ Pay attention on the trail and be aware of potential dangers. Even a minor injury such as a twisted ankle can be life-threatening, especially if you're alone or in inclement weather.

➡ Always let someone know where you're going and how long you plan to be gone. When available, use sign-in boards at trailheads or ranger stations.

➡ Always carry extra water, snack food and extra layers of clothing.

WARNING: POISON OAK

Watch out for western poison oak in forests throughout California, especially in areas below 5000ft in elevation. Poison oak is a shrub most easily identified by its shiny reddish-green tripartite leaves, which turn crimson in the fall, and its white berries. In the winter months, when the plant has no leaves, it looks brown and twiggy, but can still cause a serious allergic reaction. If you brush against poison oak, remove any affected clothing and scrub the exposed area immediately with soap and cool water or an over-the-counter remedy such as Tecnu, a soap specially formulated to remove the plant's itchy urushiol oils.

➡ Don't rely on your cell phone: service is spotty or nonexistent in many areas, especially in the forest, mountains, deserts and canyons.

➡ Weather can be unpredictable. Afternoon summer thunderstorms, for instance, are quite common in the deserts. Double-check the forecast before heading out.

➡ Encounters with mountain lions and black bears are extremely rare but possible. Rattlesnakes and spiders also present potential dangers. Watch your step!

➡ Be aware of the warning signs and symptoms of heat exhaustion, heatstroke and hypothermia.

Fees

➡ Most California state parks charge a daily parking fee of $4 to $15. Don't park on the road's shoulder outside a state park just to avoid paying the fee.

➡ National park entrance averages $15 to $25 per vehicle ($5 per bicycle or hiker), and is usually good for seven consecutive days. There's no fee to enter Channel Islands National Park (p383).

➡ For unlimited admission to national parks, national forests and other federal recreation lands, buy the 'America the Beautiful' annual pass ($80). They're sold at national park visitor centers and entry stations, as well as at most USFS ranger stations. Lifetime 'America the Beautiful' passes are free for US citizens (and permanent residents) with disabilities, and $10 for those aged 62 and over.

➡ If you don't have an 'America the Beautiful' pass, you'll need a National Forest Adventure Pass (per day $5, annual pass $30) to park in some recreational areas of the San Bernardino, Cleveland, Angeles or Los Padres National Forests. Buy passes from USFS ranger stations or local vendors (check the website for a current list), or order them online in advance.

Maps & Information

There are bulletin boards showing basic trail maps and other information at most major trailheads, some of which also have free trail brochure dispensers. Most national parks and forests, and some state parks, have a visitors center or ranger station with clued-in staff happy to offer trail tips and suggestions.

For short, well-established hikes in national or state parks, the free trail maps handed out at ranger stations and visitors centers are usually sufficient. Occasionally a more detailed topographical map may be necessary, depending on the length, difficulty and remoteness of your hike.

Books

➡ Former *Los Angeles Times* columnist John McKinney's excellent hiking guides include the *Day Hiker's Guide to California State Parks*, *Hike the Santa Monica Mountains* and *Coast Walks Santa Barbara*. For more titles, see www.thetrailmaster.com.

➡ The late Jerry Schad's *101 Hikes in Southern California* and *Top Trails: Los Angeles* detail many locals' favorite trails with insider tips. The latest edition of his *Afoot & Afield: San Diego County* was co-authored by Scott Turner.

Online Resources

Modern Hiker (http://modernhiker.com) SoCal hiking guru Casey Schreiner's site is a virtual encyclopedia of hiking trails, especially in national forests and recreation areas around LA. Also includes newsy blog entries and hiking-gear reviews.

Tralls.com (www.tralls.com) Search for descriptions of myriad trails that explore SoCal's mountains, deserts and more; trail summary overviews are free.

Leave No Trace Center for Outdoor Ethics (http://lnt.org) Learn how to minimize your impact on the environment while hiking and camping in the wilderness.

Cycling & Mountain Biking

Strap on your helmet: Southern California is outstanding cycling territory, no matter whether you're off for a leisurely spin along the beach, an adrenaline-fueled mountain-bike ride or a multiday road-cycling tour along the coast. Avoid the mountains in winter (too much rain and snow at higher elevations) and the deserts in summer (too dang hot). Know your own skill and fitness levels, and plan accordingly.

Best Bike-Friendly Cities & Parks

For the inside scoop on SoCal's cycling and mountain-biking scenes, ask the knowledgeable staff at local bicycle shops.

BUT WAIT, THERE'S MORE!

ACTIVITY	LOCATION	DESCRIPTION
fishing	Big Bear Lake	Catch trout in the mountains northeast of LA.
	Dana Point	Popular departure point for sportfishing boats.
	Malibu	Fish right from the pier, or take a sportfishing tour.
	Marina Del Rey	Offers lots of sportfishing trips, including to Catalina Island.
	San Diego	Dangle a rod from public piers, or take a sportfishing trip.
hang-gliding & paragliding	Torrey Pines	Glide at SoCal's gliding capital, near La Jolla.
	Santa Barbara	Soar by the coast from this spot.
hot-air ballooning	Del Mar	SoCal's ballooning capital, in northern San Diego County.
horseback riding	Santa Monica Mountains	Canter where film stars once shot Hollywood Westerns on location.
rock climbing	Joshua Tree	Offers world-class, mostly short technical rock climbs, plus bouldering.
skiing & snowboarding	Big Bear Lake	This family-friendly sports resort is the closest powder to LA.
yoga	Los Angeles	Indoor studios abound, from traditional Hatha and heated Bikram to power and martial-arts styles.

➜ SoCal's cities are not terribly bike-friendly, but shining exceptions include Palm Springs, Santa Barbara and Santa Monica, as well as several smaller beach towns.

➜ For photo-worthy scenery, paved oceanfront cycling routes include LA's South Bay Trail (p172); between Huntington State Beach and Bolsa Chica State Beach in Orange County; between San Buenaventura State Beach and Emma Wood State Beach in Ventura; along the harborfront in Santa Barbara; and between El Capitán State Beach and Refugio State Beach, west of Santa Barbara.

➜ Mountain bikers can follow tracks in the Santa Monica Mountains outside LA; in Orange County at Crystal Cove State Park (p279) and Aliso & Wood Canyons Park, both near Laguna Beach; and at Anza-Borrego Desert State Park (p313), east of San Diego.

➜ Fat-tire speed freaks also sing the praises of Snow Summit park at Big Bear Lake, in the San Bernardino Mountains outside LA.

Road Rules

➜ In national parks, bikes are usually limited to paved and dirt roads and are not allowed on trails or in designated wilderness areas.

➜ Most national forests and BLM lands are open to mountain bikers. Stay on established tracks (don't create any new ones) and always yield to hikers and horseback riders.

➜ At California state parks, trails are off-limits to bikes unless otherwise posted, while paved and dirt roads are usually open to both cyclists and mountain bikers.

Maps & Online Resources

Local tourist offices can usually supply you with cycling route ideas, maps and advice.

Adventure Cycling Association (www.adventure cycling.org) Sells long-distance cycling route guides and touring maps and apps, including for the entire Pacific Coast.

Biking in LA (http://bikinginla.com) Lists bike retailers and rental outlets, bike co-ops and other cycling resources in the LA area.

California Association of Bicycling Organizations (www.cabobike.org) Provides freeway access info for cyclists, printable e-guides and cycling maps, and links to partner organizations statewide.

Los Angeles Bicycle Coalition (http://la-bike.org) Organizes occasional group rides in the LA area, including the annual Los Angeles River Ride fundraiser.

MTBR.com (www.mtbr.com) and **SoCal Trail Riders** (www.socaltrailriders.org) Host online forums and user reviews of mountain-biking trails all over SoCal.

Santa Barbara Bicycle Coalition (www.bike-santabarbara.org) Offers downloadable do-it-yourself cycling tours, including of Santa Barbara's Wine Country, and links to bicycle rental shops, tour companies and bike-friendly accommodations.

Golf

The Palm Springs and Coachella Valley resort area is SoCal's undisputed golfing center, offering more than 100 courses. San Diego, LA and Orange Counties have many more places to get in a round, and even Catalina Island has a notably historic course to play.

Most cities and bigger towns in Southern California have public golf courses

with reasonable greens fees, although many of the top-ranked courses are at private golf clubs, where you may have to be invited by a member or get a referral from the pro at your home club. Semiprivate clubs are open to nonmembers, except at peak times such as weekend mornings.

Fees

Green fees vary hugely, from around $15 to $250 or more for 18 holes, depending on the course, season and day of the week, and that usually doesn't include cart or club rental. Golfers can save money – sometimes as much as 50% – by booking twilight play, when desert courses also happen to be cooler. Book tee times well in advance.

Online Resources

For a searchable directory of golf courses throughout Southern California, as well as tee-time bookings, visit www.scga.org.

Handy regional golfing websites:

City of Los Angeles Golf (http://golf.lacity.org)

Los Angeles County Golf Courses (http://parks.lacounty.gov)

Orange County: California's Golf Coast (www.occgolf.com)

Palm Springs Golf (http://palmspringsgolf.com)

Golf San Diego (www.golfsd.com)

Santa Barbara Golfing (www.santabarbara.com/activities/golf)

Plan Your Trip
Disneyland Trip Planner

The Best...

Times to Visit

Mid-April–mid-May Miss both spring-break and summer-vacation crowds, but still have a good chance of sunny weather.

Mid- to late September Summer vacationers depart after Labor Day and temperatures cool down, but it's still sunny.

Late November–early December As visitation dips between Thanksgiving and Christmas, holiday decorations spruce up the parks.

Weekdays Year-round, they're less busy than weekends.

Adventure Rides

Indiana Jones Adventure (p238), Adventureland

Hyperspace Mountain (p237), Tomorrowland

Splash Mountain (p238), Critter Country

California Screamin' (p239), Paradise Pier, Disney California Adventure (DCA)

Soarin' Around the World (p239), Grizzly Peak, DCA

Big Thunder Mountain Railroad (p238), Frontierland

Grizzly River Run (p239), Grizzly Peak, DCA

Matterhorn Bobsleds (p237), Fantasyland

Radiator Springs Racers (p239), Cars Land, DCA

Mickey's Fun Wheel (p240), Paradise Pier, DCA

Timing Your Visit

➡ Both Disneyland and Disney California Adventure (DCA) are open 365 days a year; hours vary. Check the current schedule (www.disneyland.com) in advance.

➡ During peak summer season (roughly mid-June to early September), Disneyland's hours are usually 8am to midnight; the rest of the year, it's open from 10am to 8pm or 10pm. DCA closes at 10pm or 11pm in summer, earlier in the off-season.

➡ Opening hours may be extended during spring break (March/April) and the winter holidays, from a week before Christmas through New Year's Day.

➡ Off-season, some attractions and shows may not be running, including fireworks. Check the website in advance to avoid disappointment.

➡ Don't worry about getting stuck waiting for a ride or attraction at closing time. Parks stay open until the last guest in line has had their fun.

Busiest Times to Go

Mar–Apr Unless you love crowds and the chance of rain showers, don't visit when schools take their spring-break vacation, especially the weeks before and after Easter.

Jul–Aug The hottest dog days of summer are the busiest time in the parks, with families taking summer vacations.

Oct Although the weather is balmy and summer crowds have vanished, Halloween celebrations make this a busy time, too.

Mid–late Nov The week leading up to the Thanksgiving long weekend is crowded. Plus, there's a chance of rainfall, and not all of the holiday decorations are up yet.

Special events High schoolers take over the parks on 'Grad Nites' in late May and June. Unofficial, queer-friendly 'Gay Days' in early October are also popular.

Weekends Year-round, the parks are busiest on Saturdays and Sundays.

Beating the Crowds

➡ Arrive when parking lots and ticket booths open, an hour before the theme parks' official opening times.

➡ The parks are busiest between 11am and 4pm, making that a great time to go back to your hotel for a midday swim (and a nap!). Then return after dinner.

➡ Downtown Disney's restaurants and shops get crowded after 5pm. Visit around lunchtime for smaller crowds and cheaper menu prices.

➡ Disneyland and Disney California Adventure's FASTPASS system (p251) can cut wait times significantly for some rides and attractions.

➡ Look for shorter, single-rider lines.

➡ Smartphone apps may also help you avoid long queues in the parks.

Buying Tickets

➡ Tickets never sell out, but buying them in advance will save you time waiting in ticket lines and probably some money.

➡ Ticket prices rise annually. Children's tickets apply to kids aged three to nine. Single day ticket prices vary daily but on low traffic days (typically Monday to Wednesday in the off or shoulder season) start at adult/child $97/91 for either Disneyland or Disney California Adventure (DCA).

➡ Two-day passes for the same park cost adult/child $199/187, up to $305/290 for five days.

➡ 'Park Hopper' tickets (single day per adult/child $157/151) let you visit both parks in one day.

➡ Multiday 'Park Hopper' tickets cost from $244/232 for two days to $350/335 for five days.

➡ Some 'Park Hopper' tickets include one 'Magic Morning' early-bird admission to select attractions on certain days (arrive 75 minutes before the theme park opens to the general public).

➡ A Deluxe Annual Passport for unlimited theme-park entry on 315 pre-selected days of the year costs $619 per person, regardless of age; a Premium Annual Passport with no blackout dates costs $1049, including parking (which otherwise costs $20 per day).

DISNEYLAND TO-DO LIST

While you *could* do Disney on the fly, a little planning can save you time, money and aggravation once you get there.

A Month or More in Advance

☐ Make area hotel reservations or book a Disneyland vacation package.

☐ Sign up for online resources including blogs, e-newsletters and resort updates, such as Disney Fans Insider.

A Week or Two Ahead

☐ Check the parks' opening hours, live show and entertainment schedules online.

☐ Make dining reservations for sit-down restaurants or special meals with Disney characters.

☐ Buy print-at-home tickets and passes online.

The Day or Night Before

☐ Recheck the next day's opening hours and Anaheim Resort Transportation or hotel shuttle schedules.

☐ Pack a small day pack with sunscreen, hat, sunglasses, swimwear, change of clothes, jacket or hoodie, lightweight plastic rain poncho, and extra batteries and memory cards for digital and video cameras.

☐ Fully charge your electronic devices, including cameras and phones.

☐ Download the Disneyland app to your smartphone.

Discounts & Deals

➡ Look for specials online such as the five-day 'Park Hopper' tickets for the regular three-day price.

➡ Southern California residents (defined by zip code, extending as far north as San Luis Obispo County) may be eligible for discounted theme-park admission tickets and passports.

➡ Anyone can buy a **Southern California CityPass** (adult/child from $328/284), covering three-day 'Park Hopper' admission to Disneyland and Disney California Adventure, plus one-day admission to SeaWorld San Diego (p405) and Universal Studios Hollywood (p205). The CityPass price is at least $100 off of the combined regular ticket prices.

Bringing the Kids

You're never too young or too old for Disneyland. You'll see huge, multi-generational families all enjoying the parks together – mothers with newborn babes in arms, young honeymooners and elderly great-grandparents.

Infants & Toddlers

➡ Stroller rentals are available but can only be used in the theme parks, not Downtown Disney.

➡ Your own stroller will save time, money and a headache if the parks' rentals are all taken, especially during peak season or later in the day.

GET SMART

If you've got a smartphone, make sure you bring it with you to Disneyland fully charged (with an extra battery and a plastic bag to keep it dry on water rides). Probably the most useful app you can get is Disney's own, but there's a fierce market for competitors offering all the details you need – restaurant menus, insider 'Hidden Mickey' tips, live webcams, park opening hours and show schedules and, most importantly, current wait times at rides and attractions. Some of the best apps are free, so check out app user reviews before spending any money.

➡ Strollers are not allowed on escalators or the parking-lot tram. Fold up strollers before bringing them on the monorail.

➡ Stroller parking areas are available outside most park rides and attractions.

➡ Baby centers, including diaper-changing and nursing facilities with comfy rocking chairs, are available at Disneyland (Main Street, U.S.A.) and Disney California Adventure (Pacific Wharf).

➡ Day lockers are available.

➡ The 'rider swap' system lets two parents with babies or small children each ride without standing in line twice. Ask a staff member at any ride for a pass (both adults must be present). The first adult waits in line and rides, while the other stays with the kids, then they swap.

Kids & Tweens

➡ Tell kids that if they get lost, contact the nearest Disney staff, who will escort them to a 'lost children' center (on Disneyland's Main Street, U.S.A. or at Disney California Adventure's Pacific Wharf).

➡ Study online the minimum-height charts for rides and attractions in advance, to avoid whining and disappointment when you get to the park.

➡ If you've booked a Disneyland Resort vacation package, schedule a complimentary pre-trip phone call for your kids from Mickey, Minnie or Goofy.

➡ Every restaurant has a kids' menu.

➡ If you're here for a birthday, inquire about decorate-your-own-cake parties and personal-size cakes (at least 48 hours in advance), and stop by Disneyland's City Hall for a free 'It's My Birthday!' badge.

➡ Kids aged nine years and under may wear costumes inside the park (but no masks, toy weapons or other sharp objects). During Halloween time, preteens may also wear costumes.

➡ For sensitive children, many kids' rides – including Roger Rabbit's Car Toon Spin and Mr. Toad's Wild Ride – can be surprisingly scary.

Teens

➡ Tell your teens that if their cell phones don't work, they can leave a message for 'Lost Parents' at City Hall, just inside Disneyland's entrance.

DISNEYLAND DO'S & DON'TS

Dos

➡ Buy tickets in advance.

➡ Designate a meeting place in case someone in your group gets lost.

➡ Leave pets at home, or board them for the day at Disneyland's **kennels** (☑714-781-7662; https://disneyland.disney.go.com/guest-services/kennel; Disneyland; per animal per day $20; ⊘30min before park opening to 30min after park closing).

➡ Allow time for a security check before entering Disneyland Resort.

➡ Drink plenty of fluids to avoid dehydration.

➡ Arrive early at the parks, then take a midday break back at your hotel.

➡ Use FASTPASS and/or the Disney app to skip long lines at select rides and attractions.

➡ Keep your ticket and get a hand stamp if you leave and want to return later.

Don'ts

➡ Don't try to cram both theme parks into one day – allow two days minimum.

➡ Don't arrive at 11am – it's almost always the busiest time to buy tickets and enter the parks.

➡ Don't bring the following into the park: selfie sticks, soft-sided coolers bigger than a six-pack, any kind of wheels (eg rolling luggage, bikes, skateboards, even shoes with wheels!), any kind of seating.

➡ Don't show up without restaurant reservations if you want a sit-down meal.

➡ Don't walk up *and* down Downtown Disney – use the monorail as a one-way shortcut to/from Disneyland.

➡ Don't light up in the parks, except at specially designated smoking areas.

➡ Clothing or tattoos with language, graphics or designs deemed offensive are prohibited, as is displaying what Disneyland deems an 'excessive' amount of bare skin (eg bikini tops). Same goes for grownups, by the way!

Visitors with Special Needs

Disneyland Resort may be the most accessible place in all of Southern California for anyone with mobility issues or other disabilities. If you need something, just ask.

Mobility Support

➡ Rental wheelchairs ($12 per day manual) and electric conveyance vehicles (ECVs, $50 per day) are available, but it's best to bring your own because rentals are only for use in the parks (not Downtown Disney). They may also run out.

➡ Most rides are either fully accessible to those in wheelchairs or scooters or allow guests to board via a 'transfer access vehicle.'

➡ Companion restrooms are available at Disneyland and Disney California Adventure; consult park maps.

Other Services

➡ Service animals (eg guide dogs) may accompany guests into the parks but must remain on a leash or harness at all times and are not allowed on some rides and attractions.

➡ Braille guides, digital audio tours, supplemental audio descriptions, assisted listening systems, captioning and sign-language interpretation services are all available free of charge but may require a same-day refundable deposit or advance notice.

Grand Central Market, Los Angeles (p90

Plan Your Trip
Eat & Drink
Like a Local

While Los Angeles is known for its celeb chefs and hot spot restaurants, you don't have to drop a Benjamin to eat well here. Southern California's culinary scene is diverse, cutting edge and caters to all budgets. Many culinary trends have started in its coastal kitchens, and the region's cuisine keeps redefining and refining itself – and along with it, the way the rest of America eats.

A Year of SoCal Feasting

dineLA (p67) Take advantage of wallet-friendly multicourse menus from some of LA's hottest chefs for two weeks in January and July.

San Diego Restaurant Week (www.sandiegorestaurantweek.com) Special deals on prix-fixe menus at nearly 200 restaurants for one week in mid-January and late September.

National Date Festival (www.datefest.org) Save the date (get it?) for Indio's February celebration of its prime local product. Bonus: camel races!

Spring Weekend (p370) Wine tastings, talks and vineyard dinners are the focus of this four-day Wine Country event in April.

California Strawberry Festival (http://castrawberryfestival.org) Oxnard's family-fun festival features recipe cook-offs and chefs' demos in mid- to late May.

Los Angeles Food & Wine Festival (p70) Four days of food, wine and beer tastings, special lunches, cooking demonstrations and other culinary events across LA. In August.

Latino Food Fest (https://latinfoodfest.com) San Diego celebrates pan-Latin flavors with food tastings, cooking demos and celebrity chefs over four days in August.

Little Italy Festa (p410) More than 120,000 hungry folks turn out for San Diego's Italian food and cultural celebration in early October.

California Avocado Festival (p377) Curious to see the world's largest vat of guacamole? Come to Carpinteria, just south of Santa Barbara, in early October.

Celebration of Harvest Weekend (p370) SoCal's premier wine country celebrates the annual grape harvest with a four-day bash in early October.

San Diego Beer Week (p410) Taste stellar craft brews from all around SD, SoCal and the country, plus local restaurant and food-truck fare, in early November.

San Diego Bay Wine & Food Festival (p410) Food, wine and beer tastings, plus dinners and top-chef classes and competitions in mid-November.

Indio International Tamale Festival (www.tamalefestival.net) The Coachella Valley celebrates one of Latin America's best-loved street foods over two days in early December.

California Cuisine

While California cuisine is widely celebrated, it is also inherently ambiguous. How do you actually define it? While chefs, critics and diners argue the finer points over their salads of pickled vegetables, avocado and daikon sprouts, the state's trademark style does have some inherent characteristics. First and foremost is a loyalty to fresh and seasonal ingredients. Locally grown, organic and sustainable produce is favored, not to mention food that is minimally processed and prepared. After all, all those gorgeous natural flavors should speak for themselves. Dishes are driven by the chef rather than by specific cuisines or genres, with influences from various corners of the world common on the one plate. Cooking methods often celebrate old traditions with modern twists, and menus prefer 'small plate' dining, the latter concept encouraging the ordering and sharing of numerous dishes at the table, similar to Spanish tapas or family feasting. Perhaps no one has done as much to popularize California's salubrious, fusion-style cuisine nationwide as much as peripatetic Austrian-born chef Wolfgang Puck, who began his career as a celebrity restaurateur in Beverly Hills.

It's All & Nuts, Honey

Make all the jokes you want about this being the land of fruits, nuts and flakes. It's true, and locals couldn't be prouder. You name it, Southern California grows it. Avocado, citrus, dates, berries and all manner of vegetables are just a sampling of the crops that flourish between Santa Barbara County and the Mexican border.

In salads, forget iceberg lettuce (although that's grown here too): a SoCal salad is likely to include endive, radicchio, arugula and other greens that may not pass your smartphone's spell-checker. Other classics: the Cobb salad (invented on LA's Wilshire Blvd), the Caesar salad (invented in Tijuana, Mexico) and the Chinese chicken salad (popularized in LA during the health-conscious 1970s) made with sliced Napa cabbage, slivered carrot, green onion, grilled chicken, toasted sesame seeds and a tangy soy-based dressing.

An Omnivore's Feast

You may associate SoCal with vegetarianism, but locals ardently love meat too. Trendy new steakhouses open all the time, many proudly printing on the menu the names of local ranches supplying grass-fed, free-range and hormone-free beef, pork, lamb, chicken, duck and even heritage-breed turkeys. When it comes to comfort-food classics, downtown LA's Phillipe the Original claims to have invented the French-dip roast beef sandwich way back in 1908.

With hundreds of miles of coastline, fishing is not only a huge industry in SoCal, but also a popular sport. As you travel between Santa Barbara and San Diego, you'll often see halibut, rockfish, sablefish (black cod) and sand dabs on restaurant menus, much of it locally caught. Another popular surf treat is Dungeness crab, usually found as far south as Point Conception, just west of Santa Barbara.

A rare and pricey treat is farm-raised abalone, which has a delicate flavor and texture similar to squid.

Tacos

Small World, Big Tastes

No less than Ruth Reichl, the one-time California chef, food writer and former *New York Times* restaurant critic, has said that LA's real culinary treasure is its ethnic restaurants. With more than 180 nationalities in LA County alone, you will only be scratching the surface with the next great Korean barbecue truck, Japanese ramen shop or Persian ice-cream parlor.

You'll find Mexican restaurants all over SoCal. Japanese eateries are concentrated in LA neighborhoods such as Downtown's Little Tokyo and Torrance inland from the South Bay. Downtown LA's Chinatown and communities in the San Gabriel Valley are the epicenter of Chinese cooking. LA's Koreatown and Orange County's Little Saigon are each the largest respective ethnic expat communities outside their home countries, while Anaheim's Little Arabia is best for Middle Eastern fare. San Diego has a thriving Little Italy too.

If you want to taste all of SoCal in just one place, downtown LA's Grand Central Market (p90) is the place to head. It's crammed with energetic vendors dishing up street food from around the globe, from Latin American *pupusas* (filled corn tortillas) and fresh-squeezed fruit *jugos* (juices) to freshly made pasta, tangy Thai barbecue and juicy falafel rolls.

Tamale

Mexican

Mexican food is iconic here, and not exclusively among people of Latino heritage. Until you've sampled *carnitas* (braised pork), *al pastor* (marinated and grilled pork) or San Diego–style fish tacos washed down with a cold beer or a margarita, you haven't experienced SoCal culture.

Virtually any Cal-Mex meal starts with tortillas (flatbread made of wheat or corn flour). Small ones are wrapped around meat, cheeses and vegetables and called tacos; larger, rolled versions are enchiladas (traditionally pan-fried and covered in sauce then baked), while burritos are huge tortillas, stuffed with the same, well, stuff, plus rice and beans. Rather than slushy supermarket brands, locally made salsa is a finely diced mix of fresh tomatoes, onions, cilantro and jalapeño peppers. Another commonly found Mexican classic is the tamale, which generally consists of *masa* (cornmeal dough) rolled with seasoned ground meat or beans, wrapped in a corn husk or banana leaf and steamed.

Given LA's size and status as the world's second-largest 'Mexican' city, it makes sense that the city offers the greatest variation of regional Mexican cuisines in SoCal, from world-renowned Oaxacan dishes to rarer bites from western states such as Nayarit, Sinaloa, Jalisco and Colima.

Japanese

Angelenos were happily chowing down sushi and sashimi when most of America still considered it foreign fare not to be trusted. Yet SoCal's Japanese food scene goes far beyond raw piscine treats. Many a good meal starts with *edamame* (boiled soybeans in the pod) and continues with *yakitori* (grilled skewers of chicken or vegetables), tempura (lightly battered and fried vegetables or fish) and an endless variety of artful hot and cold appetizers, most often shared by groups of friends at an *izakaya* (gastropub). Some restaurants offer *omakase* (Japanese version of a tasting menu), with dishes selected for diners by the chef.

Other Japanese eateries might specialize in just one dish, such as ramen (noodle soup), *sukiyaki* and *shabu-shabu* (cook-it-yourself hot pots), or *okonomiyaki* (vegetable, seafood and pork-filled pancakes topped with a savory, barbecue-like sauce, Japanese mayonnaise and crispy seaweed flakes).

THESABRINA / GETTY IMAGES ©

LA Cocktail

tarts. Other regional cuisines also abound, including fiery Szechuan and Hunan.

Then, of course, there's Chinese American food, Chinese-based dishes tweaked over the generations for local palates. One of its best-loved classics is General Tso's chicken, crispy, deep-fried chicken served in a sweet, vinegary sauce. LA is home to the largest and most diverse choice of Chinese eateries, with many of the best located in the San Gabriel Valley.

Korean

LA's expansive Koreatown is home to America's largest (and best) selection of Korean eateries. The quintessential culinary experience is chowing down at a Korean BBQ joint, where beef, pork and other meats of your choice are grilled fresh at your table. Among the favorite meats to grill is *kalbi* (beef ribs), marinated in soy, sesame oil, green onion and garlic. The meats are usually served with bottomless Korean sides, from *musaengchae* (spicy radish salad) to *kimchi* (spicy pickled cabbage). Another Korean culinary must is *bibimbap,* a large bowl of mixed Korean vegetables, sliced meat (usually beef) and a fried egg topped with hot chili sauce over a mini mountain of rice.

Chinese

California serves up the country's best Chinese food; hardly surprising given its huge and historical Chinese population, not to mention its perch on the Asia Pacific rim. Don't miss a Cantonese dim-sum brunch; channeling Hong Kong, it usually sees a small army of servers strolling around cavernous dining rooms, pushing carts loaded with *char siu bao* (steamed pork buns), dumplings like *har gao* (shrimp) and *shu mai* (pork), veggie dishes like Chinese broccoli with oyster sauce and creamy egg

Vietnamese

Vietnam's national dish is *pho*: white rice noodles in clear beef broth, topped with sliced meat (usually beef) and served with a plate of bean sprouts and Thai basil, which you add into the soup along with sliced chilies and maybe hoisin sauce or freshly squeezed lime juice. You'll find the best (and most authentic) Vietnamese grub in the Orange County city of Westminster, home to the country's largest Vietnamese community.

FISH TACOS, SAN DIEGO–STYLE

San Diego may not have an official food, but the city obsesses over where to get the best fish tacos. The fish used can vary, but a firm fish like mahimahi works well. It's cut into bite-sized pieces, then seasoned and grilled, or – for 'Baja-style' tacos – battered and deep-fried. The cooked fish is placed inside a tortilla (purists say it must be made of corn) and drizzled in a creamy white sauce of sour cream and mayonnaise seasoned with jalapeño peppers, capers, cayenne pepper and other spices. On top of that goes shredded cabbage and fresh *pico de gallo* (chopped tomato, onion and chili) salsa. Squeeze a little lime, take a bite, and say Hola to the culinary addiction you never knew you had. Top spots to savor the flavor include Pacific Beach Fish Shop (p421), South Beach Bar & Grille (p420) and Puesto La Jolla (p437).

Santa Barbara Wine Country (p365)

Wine, Beer & Beyond
Made in SoCal: Wine & Beer

California is America's vineyard heavyweight, producing around 85% of the country's wine. Indeed, the Golden State bottles more than 600 million gallons of vino annually, making it the world's fourth-largest producer after France, Italy and Spain. Excellent drops are produced up and down the length of the state, with more than 117 varietals grown in its soils. The state's most widely planted varietal is Chardonnay, followed by Cabernet Sauvignon and Merlot.

One of the largest growing regions in Southern California is Santa Barbara County, known for Pinot Noir, Chardonnay and Rhône varietals such as Syrah and Viognier. The other prominent region in SoCal is upstart Temecula, a Wild West frontier town on the edge of the desert outside San Diego. Aside from producing notable Chardonnay, Merlot and Sauvignon Blanc, the region is also known for its Mediterranean varietals, among them Viognier, Syrah and Pinot Gris.

Many SoCal winemakers are implementing their passion for the vine in earth-conscious ways, using organic practices and biodynamic farming techniques, of which they'll enthusiastically share their knowledge in winery tasting rooms and on guided vineyard tours.

Those more excited by head than legs will appreciate SoCal's ever-expanding booty of award-winning microbreweries. Innovation, seasonality and experimentation are common themes running through the taps, whether it's a barrel-aged red ale, an apricot-infused sour or a Yuletide choc-peppermint stout. This is also the home of the West Coast IPA, very generally defined by its strong 'hoppy' aromas, invigorating bitterness and higher alcohol content.

While San Diego remains SoCal's craft-beer epicenter, you'll find standout microbreweries across the region, from the Coachella Valley to Santa Barbara. Los Angeles itself is now home to a booming craft-beer scene, with a number of notable microbreweries spread across the city. It's a trend not lost on outsiders either, with globally influential Copenhagen microbrewery Mikkeller (p100) opening its fourth Californian branch in downtown LA.

SoCal Cocktails, Old & New

The margarita (traditionally made with tequila, triple sec and lemon or lime juice, either frozen and blended or served straight up 'on the rocks' with ice) is the drink of choice with Mexican cuisine. The finest are made using 100% agave tequilas. These higher-grade tequilas are also reputedly better for avoiding hangovers.

Quality underscores a growing number of SoCal cocktail bars, where bartenders are judged not by flashy tricks, but by their knowledge of the boutique liquors from California's burgeoning micro-distilleries. Knowledge of a drink's history is another source of kudos, as is the ability to competently reinterpret classics in clever ways. The penchant for local, seasonal and organic ingredients on modern Californian menus also drives many of the region's best bars, where herbal and fruit infusions are often made in-house. The barkeeps at LA's Library Bar (p115) go one further, ditching the drinks list altogether and basing their libations on whatever fresh market produce is at their disposal.

And while neither LA nor San Diego can claim a world-famous namesake cocktail (New York, stop gloating...), SoCal is not without its own homegrown curiosities. Take LA-born Chareau, a delicate liqueur made by distilling Californian grapes into an eau-de-vie (clear brandy), infusing it with locally sourced cucumber, spearmint, muskmelon and lemon peel and finally adding fresh-pressed aloe vera juice. Savor it in a Milano Swizzle, a refreshing combination of Chareau, citrus, Italian vermouth and strawberry-cucumber shrub.

Coffee Evolution

While coffee snobs from coffee-literate countries like Australia and New Zealand may grimace at SoCal's abundance of coffee chains and jumbo-sized coffee 'drinks,' change is in the air. The specialty coffee scene continues to expand, with a growing number of local roasters and specialty coffee bars taking a more artisanal approach to their Joe. Here, the emphasis is on single-origin and seasonal beans, lightly roasted in small batches and brewed using any number of methods, from classic espresso to Hario V60, Aeropress, drip brew and others. The aim is to showcase the nuances of each coffee varietal. Some places even run regular (and often free) cupping sessions, allowing customers to hone their coffee-tasting skills. Among these is **Brū** (Map p128; 323-664-7500; www.brucoffeebar.com; 1866 N Vermont Ave, Los Feliz; 7am-8pm;), one of an expanding legion of superlative coffee peddlers in LA that also includes Eightfold Coffee (p122), **Intelligentsia** (Map p128; 323-663-6173; www.intelligentsiacoffee.com; 3922 W Sunset Blvd; 6am-8pm Sun-Wed, to 10pm Thu-Sat;), Cognoscenti Coffee (p165) and Australian-influenced Paramount Coffee Project (p147).

Vegetarians, Vegans & Locavores

California cuisine is all about being local, organic and seasonal, so eating green like a slow food–loving 'locavore' isn't a tall order. Certified farmers markets abound, as do natural and organic food stores. Many top chefs make a point of using organic

Farmers market produce

produce whenever possible and only order fish, seafood or meat that's from local, sustainable sources. In fact, Southern California is so vegetarian-friendly that it's a cliché. While strictly vegetarian, vegan or raw-food restaurants are rare outside bigger cities, almost every restaurant offers at least a handful of vegetarian choices. And bottled water shipped over from Fiji or France? No thank you, filtered tap will be fine (and cheaper).

To Market, to Market

Picture it: crates bursting with heirloom tomatoes, berries and apriums, stalls lined with crusty sourdough loaves and piquant cheeses, jars filled with raw wildflower honey: Southland's farmers markets are cornucopias of prime Californian produce.

Held weekly in cities and towns across SoCal, these markets allow farmers and artisanal food producers to sell their wares direct to the public; keep an eye out for specialty items that are only available seasonally. Prices are higher than at supermarkets, but quality is excellent and much of what's on offer is organic. Best of all, most vendors offer free samples too. Most farmers markets also offer specialty coffee, cheap eats and even live entertainment, rendering them veritable pop-up versions of Europe's old market squares. One of the country's very best is the Santa Monica Wednesday Farmers Market (www. santamonica.com), a well-known shopping destination for many of LA's top chefs. For a handy map of farmers markets across Southern California, see http://projects. latimes.com/farmers-markets.

Plan Your Trip

Travel with Children

Southern California is unquestionably one of the most child-friendly vacation spots on the planet. The kids will be begging to go to theme parks and teens to celebrity hot spots. Get those over with (you might enjoy them too), then introduce them to many other worlds, big and small.

Best Regions for Kids

Orange County

Disneyland is a natural with kids, and Knott's Berry Farm is a more old-time, Americana attraction with a summer water park. Speaking of water, there are any number of gorgeous beaches to choose from.

Los Angeles

See stars in Hollywood and get behind the movie magic at Universal Studios, then hit the beaches and Griffith Park for SoCal fun in the sun. What, it's raining? Dive into the city's many kid-friendly museums instead.

San Diego

From pandas to koalas, flamingos to elephants, San Diego Zoo is paws-down the best zoo in Southern California. Also make time for the zoo's safari park in Escondido, as well as the other family-oriented attractions in Balboa Park, maritime sites along downtown's Embarcadero and colorful Legoland in Carlsbad.

Southern California for Kids

SoCal's sunny skies and warm temperatures lend themselves to outdoor activities of all kinds. Here's a small sampling: swimming, surfing, snorkeling, cycling, kayaking, hiking and horseback riding. Many outdoor outfitters and tour operators have dedicated kids' activities. On those rare cold, rainy days – or if you need a break from all that sun – you'll find top-notch museums and indoor entertainment galore.

Sometimes no organized activity is even needed. We've seen young kids thrill at catching their first glimpse of a palm tree, and teens with sophisticated palates bliss out over their first taste of heirloom tomatoes at a farmers market or shrimp dumplings at a dim-sum palace. The bottom line: if the kids are having a good time, you will be too.

Eating Out

Most restaurants in Southern California – not just fast-food places – are easygoing places to bring kids. A good measure is the noise level: the louder, the more kid-friendly. Casual eateries in well-trafficked neighborhoods typically have high chairs and children's menus available, and some break out the paper place mats and crayons for drawing. Even restaurants without special kids' menus can usually whip up something your children will eat. Generally, dining earlier (say, before 6pm) is better for families with young ones.

Theme parks have dozens of ways to get the kids hopped-up on sugar and salt at expensive prices, and many don't permit picnics or food to be brought in. One way to get around this is to carry a cooler in the car and have a picnic in the parking lot (although be sure to get everyone's hand stamped for park re-entry before you do).

One place kids are generally *unwelcome* is at high-end restaurants. Unless your children are exceptionally well behaved, properly dressed and old enough to appreciate the meal, neither the staff nor the other diners are likely to be charmed.

If all else fails, supermarket chains such as Trader Joe's, Whole Foods and Gelson's have healthy takeout food. Baby food, infant formula, disposable diapers (nappies) and other necessities are also widely sold at supermarkets and pharmacies.

Children's Highlights
Theme Parks

Disneyland (p235) & Disney California Adventure (p239), Anaheim (Orange County)

Legoland (p445), Carlsbad, San Diego

Universal Studios Hollywood (p205), San Fernando Valley, Los Angeles

Six Flags Magic Mountain (p231), north of LA

Knott's Berry Farm (p253) & Soak City (p255), Buena Park (Orange County)

Aquariums & Zoos

San Diego Zoo (p389), Balboa Park (San Diego)

San Diego Zoo Safari Park (p446), Escondido (San Diego)

Aquarium of the Pacific (p198), Long Beach (LA)

Los Angeles Zoo (p125), Griffith Park (LA)

Living Desert Zoo & Gardens (p296), Palm Springs

Birch Aquarium (p433), La Jolla (San Diego)

Museums

Reuben H Fleet Science Center (p389) & San Diego Natural History Museum (p391), Balboa Park (San Diego)

California Science Center (p224) & Natural History Museum of Los Angeles (p223), Exposition Park (LA)

La Brea Tar Pits (p136), Los Angeles

USS Midway Museum (p401), San Diego

New Children's Museum (p397), San Diego

Discovery Cube (p256), Santa Ana (OC)

Planning

A word of advice: Don't pack your schedule too tightly. Traveling with kids always takes longer than expected, especially when navigating metro areas such as LA, where you'll want to allow extra time for traffic jams and getting lost.

Children's discounts are available for everything from museum admission and movie tickets to bus fares. The definition of a 'child' varies from 'under 18' to age six. A limited number of venues offer student discounts for older children and university students.

At amusement parks, some rides may have minimum-height requirements, so let younger kids know about this in advance, to avoid disappointment – and tears.

Many public toilets have a baby-changing table. Bigger, private 'family' bathrooms may be available at airports, museums etc.

For all-round information and advice, check out Lonely Planet's *Travel with Children*.

What to Pack

Sunscreen. Lots of sunscreen.

And bringing sunscreen should remind you to bring hats, swimsuits, goggles and flip-flops. If you like beach umbrellas and sand chairs, pails and shovels, you'll probably want to bring your own or buy them at local supermarkets and pharmacies. At many beaches, you can rent bicycles and water-sports gear (eg snorkel sets) for kids.

For mountain outings, bring broken-in hiking shoes, plenty of food and water, and your own camping equipment. Outdoor gear can be purchased or sometimes rented from local outdoor outfitters and sporting-goods shops. But remember that the best time to test out gear is before you take your trip. Murphy's Law dictates that wearing brand-new hiking shoes results in big blisters, and setting up a new tent in the dark ain't easy.

SOCAL'S TOP FIVE PIERS FOR FAMILIES

Santa Monica Pier (p174) – LA's coastal gem, built in 1908, has its own amusement park on top, an aquarium underneath and summer twilight concerts.

Balboa Island (p274), Newport Beach – It's not one but two piers, plus a peanut-sized amusement park made famous on TV's *The OC*.

Stearns Wharf (p351), Santa Barbara – The West Coast's oldest continuously operating pier hosts the engaging Ty Warner Sea Center.

Crystal Pier (p414), Pacific Beach – If you're lucky enough to book the Crystal Pier Hotel, the surf lapping beneath your cottage on the pier is a natural lullaby.

Paradise Pier (p239), Disney California Adventure – Granted, it's not technically a pier (it's nowhere *near* the ocean), but who cares when the rides are so good?

Accommodations

Rule one: if you're traveling with kids, always mention it when making reservations. At a few places, notably B&Bs, you may have a hard time if you show up with little ones unannounced. When booking, be sure to request the specific room type you want, although this is not often guaranteed.

Motels and hotels often have rooms with two beds or an extra sofa bed. They may also have rollaway beds or cots available (request these when making reservations), typically for a surcharge. Some offer 'kids stay free' promotions, although this may apply only if no extra bedding is required; ask when booking. Some hotels provide free breakfast for the whole family too.

Bigger hotels and resorts may offer daytime activity programs for kids, especially during summer. Fees can be cheaper than babysitting and everyone may enjoy the change of pace. At some hotels, the front-desk staff or concierge can help you make babysitting arrangements. Ask whether babysitters are licensed and bonded, what they charge per hour per child, whether there's a minimum fee and if they charge extra for transportation and meals.

Transportation

Airlines usually allow infants (up to age two) to fly for free as a 'lap child' – bring proof of age – while older children require a seat of their own and don't usually qualify for reduced fares. Children do receive substantial discounts on Amtrak trains and Greyhound buses.

California law requires all passengers in private cars to wear seat belts. Any child under age six or weighing less than 60lb must be buckled up in the car's back seat in a child or infant safety seat. Most car-rental agencies rent these for about $10 per day, but you must book them in advance.

For better or for worse, being on the road is an essential part of the SoCal experience. So is traffic, especially in LA. From LA to all but the most remote destinations in the Southland, travel time is theoretically two hours or less, but can easily multiply in traffic, especially on weekends and holidays.

Plan some in-car distractions in case the kids get fidgety. On the road, rest stops on freeways are few and far between, and gas stations and fast-food bathrooms are frequently not very clean. However, you're usually never far from a shopping mall, which generally have well-kept restrooms.

Useful Websites

Baby's Away (https://babysaway.com) and **Traveling Baby Company** (www.travelingbaby.com) Rent cribs, Pack 'n Plays (portacots), strollers, car seats, high chairs, beach gear and more. Rates vary according to equipment, rental duration and delivery charges.

Lonelyplanet.com (www.lonelyplanet.com) Ask questions and get advice from other travelers in the Thorn Tree's 'Kids to Go' and 'USA' forums.

Travel for Kids (www.travelforkids.com) Has no-nonsense listings of kid-friendly sights, activities, hotels and recommended children's books for LA, San Diego and Orange Counties.

Visit California (www.visitcalifornia.com) The state's official tourism website lists family-friendly attractions, activities and more – just search for 'Family Fun' and 'Events'.

Regions at a Glance

Southern California may span a small section of the state, but its natural diversity and cultural riches could outshine entire nations. Sprawling Los Angeles claims much of SoCal's best art, dining, entertainment and shopping. To the southeast, LA bleeds into Orange County, known for its beaches, theme parks and conservative voters. Straddling the US–Mexico border is surf-loving, easy-living San Diego, while east of LA and Orange County lies the mid-century-modern chic of Palm Springs. South, east and north of Palm Springs lie extraordinary desert landscapes, while northwest of LA sits Santa Barbara county, a salubrious blend of Med-style architecture and prized vineyards.

Los Angeles

Culture
Architecture & Museums
Food

Many Worlds in One

LA is a sprawling tapestry of tribes and cultures: should you brunch with celebs in Brentwood, catch breaks with surfer dudes in Hermosa Beach, chow tacos with Mexican workers in Boyle Heights, or chat post-punk with indie artists in Highland Park?

Architecture & Museums

Storybook mansions, modernist studios, space-age concert halls: LA architecture is eclectic and extraordinary. Add to this a mind-expanding collection of museums exploring everything from neon art and cinema to Cold War Germany and you'll be re-evaluating those vapid LA clichés.

A Feast of Flavor

Culinary angels are smiling down on La La Land, with hot-spot eateries opening by the week. Whet the appetite at Grand Central Market then dive into a multiculti scene of real-deal tamales and breakfast tacos, French–Mexican fusion and farm-to-table Californian.

p66

Disneyland & Orange County

Family Fun
Beaches
Surfing

Theme Parks

No other SoCal county will make you and your kids scream and grin quite like the OC. This is theme-park heartland, home to Knott's Berry Farm, Disney California Adventure Park and the original fantasy wonderland, Disneyland.

'The OC'

You've lusted after Orange County's beautiful beaches in countless movies and TV shows. Now soak it up in all its 3D glory along this achingly gorgeous stretch of coastline between LA and San Diego.

Surf City USA

You'll find SoCal's surf culture personified at Huntington Beach, though the OC's legendary breaks don't stop there. Earn your wave-riding chops with a learn-to-surf class or step it up with a wild weekend 'surfari' camp.

p234

Palm Springs & the Deserts

Design
Outdoors
Nightlife

Retro Modern

Hang-out of Elvis, the Rat Pack and Hollywood celebs, PS is a hip-again hub of mid-century modern. Tour architectural gems, fill your shopping bags with vintage treasures or simply soak up the sun by your Hockney-style pool.

Desert Thrills

It's not just PS's spas that will rejuvenate you. From Joshua Tree's fan-palm oases and Anza-Borrego's hidden canyons, to Death Valley's sand dunes and salt flats, SoCal's deserts are unique and beckoning with adventure.

Dirty Weekends

When it comes to nightlife down in the deserts, nothing beats the neon-lit Las Vegas Strip, blinking away just across the California–Nevada state line. There aren't many reasons to ever leave SoCal, but 'Sin City' is one.

p291

Santa Barbara County

Wine
Beaches
History

Premium Vineyards

Even before *Sideways*, Santa Barbara's wine country was cherished for its pinot noir. Taste award-winning vintages with polished Angelenos, or search out unpretentious tasting rooms on country back roads.

American Riviera

That touristy tagline only stretches the point a bit. With white sands and swaying palms, Santa Barbara's sun-kissed coast easily competes with SoCal's best, whether you're a surfer or a creature of luxury.

State Street

Rebuilt in Spanish Colonial Revival style, Santa Barbara is awash in red-tiled roofs and white-stucco walls. Climb the county courthouse bell tower for cinematic vistas, then tour a gorgeous 18th-century Spanish mission.

p345

San Diego

Beaches
Food
Museums

Coastal Living

Almost always a perfect 68°F, San Diego's climate is the country's best. Take your pick of more than a dozen beach towns, each with its own eclectic personality, then count your blessings with bronzed bods on golden sands.

Fish Tacos

Home to more taco shops per capita than LA, San Diego dishes up outstanding south-of-the-border grub. The fish tacos here are the stuff of legend, and leaving without having devoured a few is a serious culinary crime.

Cultural Assets

Dumb-blond surfer jokes are lame, dude. San Diego city has a surprising wealth of cultural attractions, from dedicated museums of contemporary art, photography, maritime history and more, to one of the world's most impressive zoos.

p386

On the Road

Santa Barbara County
p345

Los Angeles
p66

Palm Springs & the Deserts
p291

Disneyland & Orange County
p234

San Diego
p386

Los Angeles

Best Places to Eat

➜ Cassia (p182)

➜ Bestia (p99)

➜ Otium (p98)

➜ Gjelina (p191)

➜ Joss Cuisine (p160)

Best Places to Sleep

➜ Palihouse (p179)

➜ Chateau Marmont (p141)

➜ Hotel Indigo (p95)

➜ Terranea (p194)

➜ Petit Ermitage (p141)

Why Go?

LA runs deeper than her blonde beaches, rolling hills and beemers-for-days would have you believe. She's a myth. A beacon for countless small-town dreamers, rockers and risk-takers, an open-minded angel who encourages her people to live and let live without judgement or shame. She has given us Quentin Tarantino, Jim Morrison and Serena and Venus Williams; spawned skateboarding and gangsta rap; popularized implants, electrolysis and Spandex; and has nurtured not just great writers, performers and directors, but also the ground-breaking yogis who first brought Eastern wisdom to the Western world. LA is best defined by simple life-affirming moments: a cracked-ice, jazz-age cocktail on Beverly Blvd, a hike high into the Hollywood Hills sagebrush, a swirling pod of dolphins off Point Dume, a pink-washed sunset over a thundering Venice Beach drum circle, the perfect taco. And her night music. There is always night music.

When to Go
Los Angeles

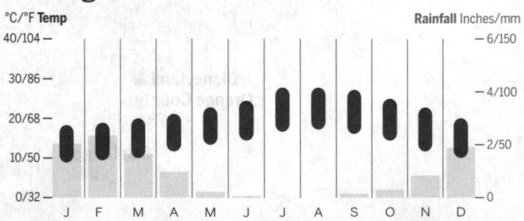

Dec–Feb
The wettest time of the year, though there's still plenty of sunshine.

Mar–May
Ideal time to visit. Rainfall drops, and the summer heat and crowds are still at bay.

Sept–Nov
Summer crowds have thinned, though temperatures remain warm.

History

LA's human history begins with the Gabrielino and Chumash, who roamed the chaparral and oak-dotted savannah as early as 6000 BCE. Their hunter-gatherer existence ended in the late 18th century with the arrival of Spanish missionaries and Mexican settlers who founded the El Pueblo de la Reina de Los Angeles. This settlement became a thriving farming community, but remained a far-flung outpost for decades.

During the Mexican–American War (1846–48), American soldiers encountered some resistance from General Andrés Pico and other Mexican commanders, but eventually LA came under US rule along with the rest of California. The city was incorporated on April 4, 1850.

A series of seminal events caused LA's population to swell to two million by 1930: the collapse of the Northern California gold rush in the 1850s, the arrival of the railroad in the 1870s, the birth of the citrus industry in the late 1800s, the discovery of oil in 1892, the launch of San Pedro harbor in 1907, and the opening of the LA aqueduct in 1913.

During WWI the Lockheed brothers and Donald Douglas established aircraft manufacturing plants in LA. Two decades later, aviation – helped along by billions of federal dollars for military contracts – was among the industries that contributed to a real-estate boom and sparked suburban sprawl. Another, of course, was the film biz, which took root in 1908.

Over the years, LA has had its share of nefarious water barons (William Mulholland), socialist politicians (Gaylord Wilshire) and philanthropic magnates (Colonel Griffith J Griffith). There was a certain filmmaker turned aviation renegade turned agoraphobe (Howard Hughes), a groundbreaking ballplayer (Jackie Robinson), an actress turned studio magnate (Mary Pickford), a newspaper editor turned civil-rights activist (Charlotta Spears Bass), a professional raconteur and polyamorous publishing legend who eventually saved the Hollywood sign (The Hef) and more than a few celebrity murders, deadly overdoses, divorces and scandals, all of which left their mark on the city. But arguably the biggest impact was made by Detroit's big three automakers who bought then dismantled the famed LA trolley system after WWII and built freeways – lots of them.

✪ Festivals & Events

From the Rose Parade to the Hollywood Christmas Parade, from the Oscars to the LA Times Festival of Books, from the Fiesta Hermosa street fair to the candy colored mayhem of Halloween in WeHo, LA has its share of annual parades, festivals, carnivals and live-music throwdowns.

Rose Parade   PARADE
(www.tournamentofroses.com) This cavalcade of flower-festooned floats snakes through Pasadena on New Year's Day. Get close-ups during post-parade viewing at Victory Park. Avoid traffic and take the Metro Rail Gold Line to Memorial Park.

DineLA   FOOD & DRINK
(www.discoverlosangeles.com) The winter edition of DineLA runs over two weeks, with both high-end and more casual restaurants offering prix-fixe menus showcasing their best dishes. A summer version takes place in July.

Chinese New Year   CULTURAL
(www.lachinesechamber.org) SoCal's biggest celebration of the lunar new year, with Chinese bites, lantern processions, fashion shows and other special events. The main draw is the cacophonous Golden Dragon Parade, which snakes its way through Chinatown.

Pan African Film Festival   FILM
(www.paff.org; Baldwin Hills Crenshaw Plaza) This festival, which celebrated its 25th anniversary in 2017, has been recognized as one of America's best, featuring screenings, talks, galas and more. Most screenings are at Baldwin Hills Crenshaw Plaza (p227).

Academy Awards   FILM
(www.oscars.org) Ogle your favorite film stars from the Dolby Theatre's red-carpet-adjacent bleachers. Apply in November or December for one of around 700 lucky spots.

LA Marathon   SPORTS
(www.lamarathon.com) This marathon is a 26.2-mile party through the city from Dodger Stadium to the Santa Monica Pier. Rally the 25,000 runners and wheelchair racers then wander among performance stages and finish-line festivities.

Blessing of the Animals   CULTURAL
On the Saturday before Easter, pets, farm animals and their human companions descend on Olvera St for the Blessing of the Animals. The event sees the Archbishop of Los Angeles lead the procession of paws, hooves and feet along Downtown's oldest street.

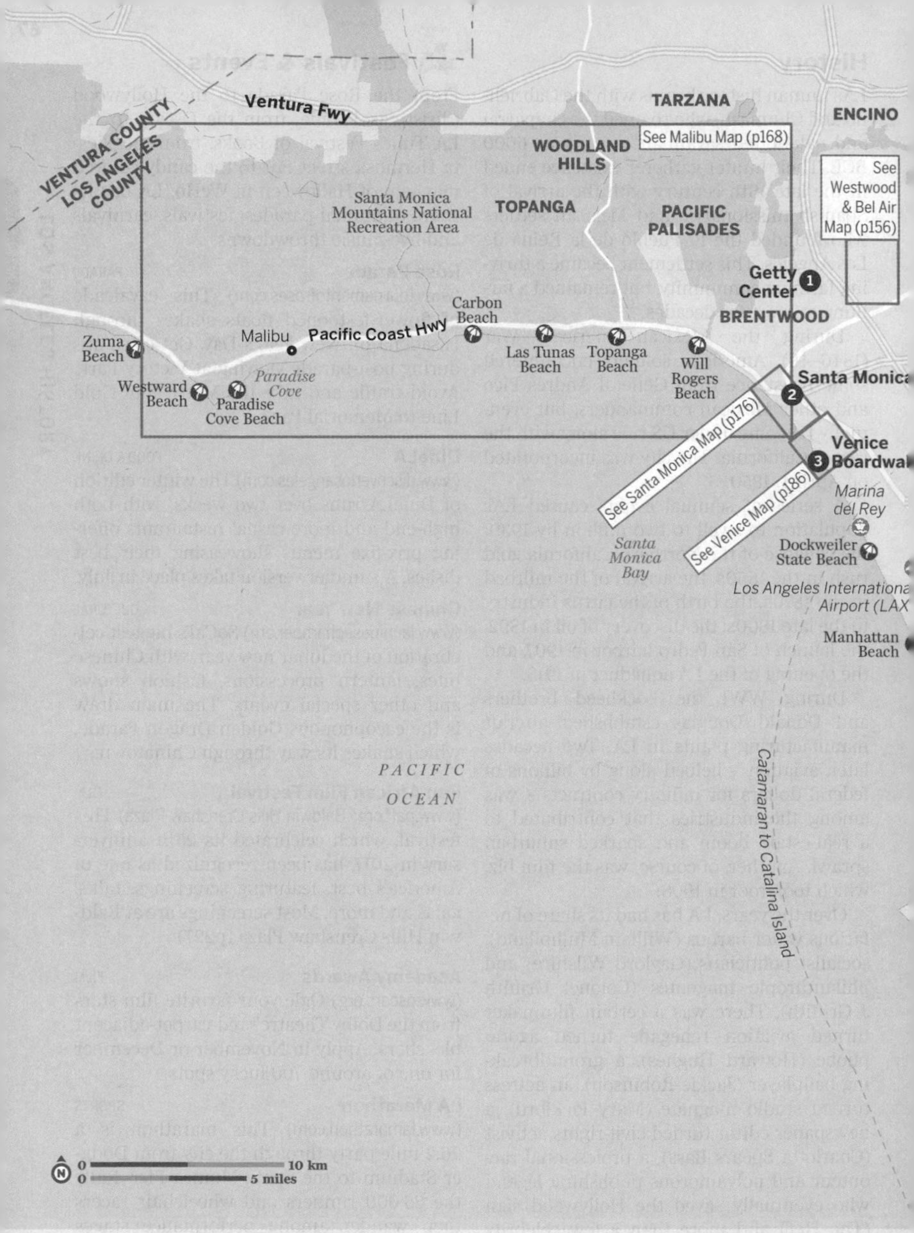

Map labels:

TARZANA

ENCINO

Ventura Fwy

VENTURA COUNTY / LOS ANGELES COUNTY

WOODLAND HILLS

See Malibu Map (p168)

See Westwood & Bel Air Map (p156)

Santa Monica Mountains National Recreation Area

TOPANGA

PACIFIC PALISADES

Getty Center **1**

BRENTWOOD

Carbon Beach

Zuma Beach

Malibu

Pacific Coast Hwy

Las Tunas Beach

Topanga Beach

Will Rogers Beach (p176)

Santa Monica **2**

Westward Beach

Paradise Cove

Paradise Cove Beach

Venice Boardwalk **3**

See Santa Monica Map (p176)

Marina del Rey

Santa Monica Bay

See Venice Map (p186)

Dockweiler State Beach

Los Angeles International Airport (LAX)

Manhattan Beach

PACIFIC OCEAN

Catamaran to Catalina Island

N
0 — 10 km
0 — 5 miles

Los Angeles Highlights

1 Getty Center (p152)
Feeling your spirits soar in this glorious hilltop alchemy of art, architecture and gardens.

2 Santa Monica (p174)
Catching the SoCal vibe in this sassy beach town imbued with irresistible boho-glamour.

3 Venice Boardwalk (p184)
Getting your freak on milling with snake charmers and tarot readers on this glorious beachside strip.

4 Hollywood (p105)
Hitting the bars and clubs of Tinseltown for a night of tabloid-worthy decadence.

5 Runyon Canyon (p110)
Joining the buff, the famous and their canine companions

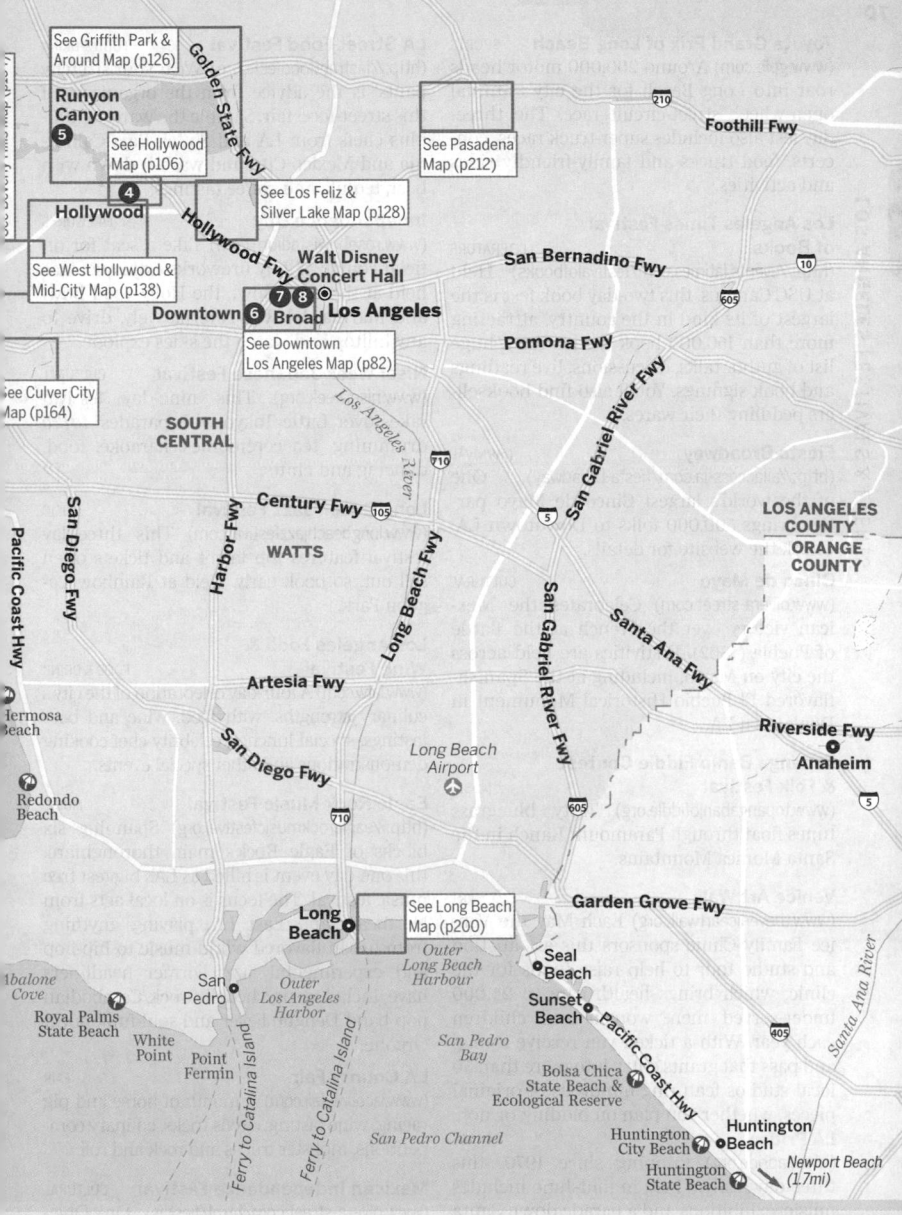

See Griffith Park & Around Map (p126)

Runyon Canyon ⑤

See Hollywood Map (p106)

④

Hollywood

See West Hollywood & Mid-City Map (p138)

See Los Feliz & Silver Lake Map (p128)

See Culver City Map (p164)

See Pasadena Map (p212)

Foothill Fwy

Golden State Fwy

Hollywood Fwy

Walt Disney Concert Hall

Downtown ⑥ ⑦ ⑧ **Broad** **Los Angeles**

See Downtown Los Angeles Map (p82)

San Bernadino Fwy

Pomona Fwy

Los Angeles River

SOUTH CENTRAL

San Gabriel River Fwy

San Gabriel River Fwy

Santa Ana Fwy

LOS ANGELES COUNTY

ORANGE COUNTY

Century Fwy

WATTS

Harbor Fwy

Long Beach Fwy

Pacific Coast Hwy

San Diego Fwy

Artesia Fwy

San Diego Fwy

Hermosa Beach

Redondo Beach

Long Beach Airport

Riverside Fwy

Anaheim

Santa Ana Fwy

Garden Grove Fwy

Long Beach

See Long Beach Map (p200)

Outer Long Beach Harbour

Seal Beach

Sunset Beach

Pacific Coast Hwy

Santa Ana River

Abalone Cove

Royal Palms State Beach

San Pedro

White Point

Point Fermin

Ferry to Catalina Island

Ferry to Catalina Island

Outer Los Angeles Harbor

San Pedro Bay

San Pedro Channel

Bolsa Chica State Beach & Ecological Reserve

Huntington City Beach

Huntington Beach

Huntington State Beach

Newport Beach (1.7mi)

---

on a hike through this Hollywood Hills park.

⑥ **Downtown** (p77) Rubbing shoulders with fashionistas, sipping cocktails in rooftop lounges and sampling world-

class cuisine in LA's historic center.

⑦ **Broad** (p90) Feasting your eyes on this Aladdin's cave of modern art-masters from Warhol to Murakami.

⑧ **Walt Disney Concert Hall** (p85) Giving a standing ovation to this Frank Gehry-designed answer to Sydney's Opera House and London's Royal Albert Hall.

Toyota Grand Prix of Long Beach   SPORTS
(www.gplb.com) Around 200,000 motor heads roar into Long Beach for the city's annual open-wheel, street-circuit race. The three-day fest also includes super-truck races, concerts, food trucks and family-friendly rides and activities.

Los Angeles Times Festival of Books   LITERATURE
(http://events.latimes.com/festivalofbooks) Held at USC Campus, this two-day book fest is the largest of its kind in the country, attracting more than 150,000 book worms for a huge list of author talks, discussions, live readings and book signings. You'll also find booksellers peddling their wares.

Fiesta Broadway   CARNIVAL
(http://allaccess-la.com/fiesta-broadway) One of the world's largest Cinco de Mayo parties brings 500,000 folks to Downtown LA. Check the website for details.

Cinco de Mayo   CULTURAL
(www.olvera-street.com) Celebrates the Mexican victory over the French at the Battle of Puebla (1862). Festivities are held across the city on May 5, including at the Spanish-flavored El Pueblo Historical Monument in Downtown LA.

Topanga Banjo Fiddle Contest & Folk Festival   MUSIC
(www.topangabanjofiddle.org) Tasty bluegrass tunes float through Paramount Ranch in the Santa Monica Mountains.

Venice Art Walk   ART
(www.theveniceartwalk.org) Each May the Venice Family Clinic sponsors this art auction and studio tour to help raise funds for the clinic, which brings health care to 24,000 under-served men, women and children each year. With a ticket, you receive a map and pass that grants entry into more than 50 local studios featuring hundreds of original pieces, whether you plan on bidding or not.

LA Pride   PARADE
(www.lapride.org) Running since 1970, this three-day festival held in mid-June includes music, exhibitions and a parade down Santa Monica Blvd.

Long Beach Bayou   MUSIC
(http://longbeachbayou.com) A weekend of sultry cajun, zydeco and blues music against the backdrop of the *Queen Mary*.

LA Street Food Festival   FOOD & DRINK
(http://lastreetfoodfest.com) 'Wear your stretchy pants' is the advice from the organizers of this street-food fair. Sample the wares of 100-plus chefs from LA and SoCal, Baja California and Mexico City, and wash it down with beer, tequila and coffee tastings.

Independence Day   FIREWORKS
(www.rosebowlstadium.com) Take a seat for official Fourth of July fireworks extravaganzas held at the Rose Bowl, the Hollywood Bowl and Marina del Rey. Alternatively, drive to any hilltop and watch the skies explode.

Nisei Week Japanese Festival   CULTURAL
(www.niseiweek.org) This nine-day festival takes over Little Tokyo with parades, *taiko* drumming, tea ceremonies, karaoke, food, dancing and crafts.

Long Beach Jazz Festival   MUSIC
(www.longbeachjazzfestival.com) This three-day festival features top talent and tickets often sell out, so book early. Held at Rainbow Lagoon Park.

Los Angeles Food & Wine Festival   FOOD & DRINK
(www.lafw.com) A four-day celebration of the city's culinary strengths, with food, wine and beer tastings, special lunches, celebrity-chef cooking demonstrations and other special events.

Eagle Rock Music Festival   MUSIC
(http://eaglerockmusicfestival.org) Spanning six blocks of Eagle Rock's main thoroughfare, this one-day event is billed as LA's biggest free music festival. The focus is on local acts from Northeast and East LA, playing anything from urban-flavored world music to hip-hop and experimental jazz. Former headliners have included psychedelic rock/Cambodian pop band Dengue Fever and soul-funk outfit Orgone.

LA County Fair   FAIR
(www.lacountyfair.com) A month of horse and pig racing, wine tasting, circus tricks, culinary competitions, monster trucks and rock and roll.

Mexican Independence Festival   CULTURAL
(www.olvera-street.com/html/fiestas) On Olvera St, a free mid-September celebration of Mexico's independence from Spain, with live performers and delicious food.

Abbot Kinney Festival   STREET CARNIVAL
(www.abbotkinney.org) Soak up the groovy Venice vibe at this annual celebration of local

arts, crafts, music, food and eccentrics, held in late September. It's been going since 1975.

Watts Towers Day of the Drum & Jazz Festival   ART, MUSIC
(http://wattstowers.org) Multicultural beats on Saturday followed by a day of jazz, gospel and blues. Late September.

West Hollywood Halloween Carnaval   CARNIVAL
(www.visitwesthollywood.com/halloween-carnaval) This rambunctious street fair brings 500,000 revelers – many in over-the-top and/or X-rated costumes – out for a day of dancing, dishing and flirting on Halloween.

Día de los Muertos   CULTURAL
(Day of the Dead) LA's Mexican community honors its deceased relatives on November 2 with costumed parades, sugar skulls, grave-yard picnics, candlelight processions and fabulous altars. Events are held across the city, including on Olvera St and at the Holly-wood Forever Cemetery.

Hollywood Christmas Parade   PARADE
(www.thehollywoodchristmasparade.com) On the Sunday after Thanksgiving, Hollywood and Sunset Blvds turn into a glittering Yuletide river of Christmas floats, marching bands and waving celebrities. Attracting around a million spectators, the parade inspired Gene Autry's dangerously catchy 'Here Comes Santa Claus'.

Marina del Rey Holiday Boat Parade PARADE
(www.mdrboatparade.org) Boats decked out in twinkling holiday cheer promenade for priz-es in the marina. Check it out from Burton Chace Park.

Las Posadas   CULTURAL
(www.olvera-street.com;) Free candlelight pro-cessions that re-enact Mary and Joseph's journey to Bethlehem, followed by piña-ta-breaking and general merriment on Olve-ra St. Run over nine days in the lead up to Christmas.

❶ Information

DISCOUNT CARDS
The Go Los Angeles Card (www.smartdestinations.com) offers discounted admission to over 30 attractions and tours, including major theme parks (Disneyland excepted). One-day and multi-day passes are available, with one-day passes costing $85 ($69 for children aged three to 12). Purchase passes online, at the Los Angeles Visitor Information Center, or see the website for other vendors.

MEDIA
KCRW 89.9 FM (www.kcrw.com) LA's cultural pulse, the best radio station in the city beams National Public Radio (NPR), eclectic and indie music, intelligent talk and hosts shows and events throughout Southern California.

KPFK 90.7 FM (www.kpfk.org) Part of the Pacifica radio network; news and progressive talk.

La Opinión (www.laopinion.com) Spanish-language daily newspaper.

LA Weekly (www.laweekly.com) Free alter-native news, live music and entertainment listings.

Los Angeles Downtown News (www.downtownnews.com) The finger on the cultural, political and economic pulse of the booming Downtown district.

Los Angeles Magazine (www.losangelesmagazine.com) Monthly lifestyle magazine with a useful restaurant guide and some tremendous feature stories.

Los Angeles Sentinel (www.losangelessentinel.com) African-American weekly.

Los Angeles Times (www.latimes.com) Major, center-left daily newspaper.

MEDICAL SERVICES
Cedars-Sinai Medical Center (☑ 310-423-3277; http://cedars-sinai.edu; 8700 Beverly Blvd, West Hollywood; ⊘24hr) 24-hour emer-gency room skirting West Hollywood.

Keck Medicine of USC (☑ 323-226-2622; www.keckmedicine.org; 1500 San Pablo St, Downtown; ⊘24hr emergency room) 24-hour emergency department just east of Downtown.

Ronald Reagan UCLA Medical Center (☑ 310-825-9111; www.uclahealth.org; 757 Westwood Plaza, Westwood; ⊘24hr emergency room) 24-hour emergency room on the UCLA campus.

TOURIST INFORMATION
Beverly Hills Visitors Center (Map p154; ☑ 310-248-1015; www.lovebeverlyhills.com; 9400 S Santa Monica Blvd, Beverly Hills; ⊘9am-5pm Mon-Fri, from 10am Sat & Sun; ☎) Sightseeing, activities, dining and accom-modations information focused on the Beverly Hills area.

Downtown LA Visitor Center (Map p82; www.discoverlosangeles.com; Union Station, 800 N Alameda St; ⊘9am-5pm; Ⓜ Red/Purple/Gold Lines to Union Station) Maps and general tour-ist information in the lobby of Union Station.

Long Beach Area Convention & Tourism Bu-reau (☑ 562-628-8850; www.visitlongbeach.com; 3rd fl, One World Trade Center, 301 E Ocean Blvd, Long Beach; ⊘11am-7pm Sun-Thu, 11:30am-7:30pm Fri & Sat Jun-Sep, 10am-4pm Fri-Sun Oct-May) Tourist office located in downtown Long Beach.

Greater Los Angeles

N 0 ___ 10 km
0 ___ 5 miles

WINNETKA
LAKE BALBOA
Van Nuys
VALLEY GLEN
Vanowen St
Burbank Hollywood Airport
Victory Pl
Wildwood Canyon Park
LA CAÑADA FLINTRIDGE
17
Altadena
Angeles National Forest

Los Angeles River
SAN FERNANDO VALLEY
Burbank Junction
North Glendale
40 Pasadena
Arcadia
Santa Anita
27

Encino Reservoir
TARZANA
See Malibu Map (p168)
44
ENCINO
State Canyon Reservoir
Laurel Canyon Blvd
See Griffith Park & Around Map (p126)
Hollywood Reservoir
West Glendale
31
Adams Square
5
134
Eagle Rock
28
Pasadena Map (p212)
3
San Marino
Huntington Library, Art Collections & Botanical Gardens
Temple City

Topanga State Park
405
Atwater
20
See Los Feliz & Silver Lake Map (p128)
43
Elephant Alhambra
Hill
San Gabriel
Stoneman
41
Rosemead

Brentwood Heights
See Westwood & Bel Air Map (p156)
21
West Hollywood
Santa Monica Blvd
Silver Lake Reservoir
33
Aurant
San Bernardino Fwy
10

Westgate
Bel Air
10
HOLLYWOOD
23
46 Elysian Park
Ascot Hills Park
Monterey Park
South San Gabriel

Brentwood
See Beverly Hills Map (p154)
West Los Angeles
See West Hollywood & Mid-City Map (p138)
4
Museum of Tolerance
15
29
19 18
16
Belvedere
South El Monte
Legg Lake

Sawtelle
9
Culver Junction
52
12
See Downtown Los Angeles Map (p82)
Boyle Heights
Los Angeles River
Bandini

See Santa Monica Map (p176)
Santa Monica
Ocean Park
See Venice Map (p186)
Mar Vista
49
Culver City
See Culver City Map (p164)
Sentous
Rodeo Blvd
W Adams Blvd
W Jefferson Blvd
25
47
Exposition Park
32
14
S Central Ave
Greyhound Bus Terminal
110
Montebello
Bartolo
Hellman Wilderness Park
Whittier Junction
Whittier

Marina del Rey
Alsace
Alla
N Jefferson Blvd
Slauson Ave
W Vernon Ave
Wildasin
SOUTH LOS ANGELES
Slauson Ave
Bell
Bell Gardens
5
Bandini
Pico Rivera

7
Westchester
Morningside Park
Florence
Cudahy
Los Nietos

Greater Los Angeles

Los Angeles Visitor Information Center (Map p106; ☑ 323-467-6412; www.discover losangeles.com; Hollywood & Highland, 6801 Hollywood Blvd; ☺ 8am-10pm Mon-Sat, 9am-7pm Sun; Ⓜ Red Line to Hollywood/Highland) The main tourist office for Los Angeles, located in Hollywood. Maps, brochures and lodging information, plus tickets to theme parks and attractions.

Marina del Rey (☑ 310-305-9545; www.visit marinadelrey.com; 4701 Admiralty Way, Marina del Rey; ☺ 9am-5pm Mon-Fri, 10am-4pm Sat & Sun) Maps and information on sights, activities, events and accommodations in the Marina del Rey area.

Santa Monica Visitor Information Center (Map p176; ☑ 800-544-5319; www.santa monica.com; 2427 Main St) The main tourist information center in Santa Monica, with free guides, maps and helpful staff.

Visit Pasadena (Map p212; ☑ 626-795-9311; www.visitpasadena.com; 300 E Green St, Pasadena; ☺ 8am-5pm Mon-Fri, 10am-4pm Sat) Visitor information with a focus on Pasadena attractions and events.

Visit West Hollywood (Map p138; www. visitwesthollywood.com; Pacific Design Center Blue Bldg, 8687 Melrose Ave, Suite M60, West Hollywood; ☺ 9am-5pm Mon-Fri; 🛜) Information on attractions, accommodations, tours and more in the West Hollywood area.

WEBSITES

Lonely Planet (www.lonelyplanet.com/usa/ los-angeles) Destination information, hotel bookings, traveler forum and more.

Discover Los Angeles (www.discoverlosange les.com) Official Convention and Visitors' Bureau website.

LA Curbed (www.la.curbed.com) Delicious bites of history, neighborhood esoterica and celebrity real-estate gossip.

Eater LA (http://la.eater.com) Up-to-the-minute news and reviews covering the city's ever-evolving food scene.

LA Times (www.latimes.com) Excellent coverage of local news, arts and culture.

Los Angeles Magazine (www.lamag.com) Up-to-date news and articles covering LA dining, arts, fashion, civic issues and more. Also offers handy 'Things to Do' lists.

❶ Getting There & Away

AIR

The main LA gateway is Los Angeles International Airport (p496). Its nine terminals are linked by the free LAX Shuttle A, leaving from the lower (arrival) level of each terminal. Cabs and hotel and car-rental shuttles stop here as well. A free minibus for travelers with disabilities can be ordered by calling ☑ 310-646-6402. Ticketing and check-in are on the upper (departure) level.

The hub for most international airlines is the Tom Bradley International Terminal.

Some domestic flights operated by Alaska, American Eagle, Delta Connection, JetBlue, Southwest and United also arrive at Burbank Hollywood Airport (p497), which is handy if you're headed for Hollywood, Downtown or Pasadena.

To the south, on the border with Orange County, the small Long Beach Airport (p497) is convenient for Disneyland and is served by Alaska, JetBlue and Southwest.

BUS

The main bus terminal for **Greyhound** (☑ 213-629-8401; www.greyhound.com; 1716 E 7th St) is in an industrial part of Downtown, so try not to arrive after dark. Take bus 18, 60, 62 or 760 to the 7th St/Metro Center metro station, from where metro trains head to Hollywood (Red Line), Koreatown (Purple Line), Culver City and Santa Monica (Expo Line) and Long Beach (Blue Line). Both the Red and Purple Lines reach Union Station, from where you can catch the Metro Gold Line (for Highland Park and Pasadena).

Some Greyhound buses go directly to the terminal in **North Hollywood** (11239 Magnolia Blvd) and a few also pass through **Long Beach** (1498 Long Beach Blvd).

CAR & MOTORCYCLE

If you're driving into LA, there are several routes by which you might enter the metropolitan area.

From San Francisco and Northern California, the fastest route to LA is on I-5 through the San Joaquin Valley. Hwy 101 is slower but more pic-turesque, while the most scenic – and slowest – route is via Hwy 1 (Pacific Coast Hwy, or PCH).

From San Diego and other points south, I-5 is the obvious route. Near Irvine, I-405 branches off I-5 and takes a westerly route to Long Beach and Santa Monica, bypassing Downtown LA entirely and rejoining I-5 near San Fernando.

From Las Vegas or the Grand Canyon, take I-15 south to I-10 then head west into LA. I-10 is the main east–west artery through LA and continues on to Santa Monica.

TRAIN

Amtrak (www.amtrak.com) trains roll into Downtown's historic **Union Station** (☑ 800-872-7245; www.amtrak.com; 800 N Alameda St). Interstate trains stopping in LA are the daily *Coast Starlight* to Seattle, the daily *Southwest Chief* to Chicago and the thrice-weekly *Sunset Limited* to New Orleans. The *Pacific Surfliner* travels numerous times daily between San Diego, Santa Barbara and San Luis Obispo via LA.

❶ Getting Around

BICYCLE

Most buses have bike racks, and bikes ride for free, although you must securely load and unload them yourself. Remember to remove all loose items not attached to your bike – including helmets, bags and lights – and take them on the bus with you. When disembarking, always advise the driver that you need to unload your bike and exit through the front door. Folding bikes with wheels no larger than 20 inches can be taken on board, folded. Bicycles are also allowed on Metro Rail trains at all times.

LA has a number of bike-sharing programs. The following are especially useful for visitors:

Metro Bike Share (https://bikeshare.metro.net) Has more than 60 self-serve bike kiosks in the Downtown area, including Chinatown, Little Tokyo and the Arts District. Pay using your debit or credit card ($3.50 per 30 minutes). You can also pay using your TAP card, though you will first need to register it on the Metro Bike Share website. Download the Metro Bike Share smartphone app, which offers real-time bike and rack availability.

Breeze Bike Share (p178) Runs self-serve kiosks all over Santa Monica, Venice and Marina del Rey. Sign up online, download the Social Bicycles app, or pay on the spot, and you can borrow bikes and return to the nearest kiosk. You can rent hourly ($7 per hour), or long-term memberships include up to 90 minutes' daily ride time. The monthly student rate ($7) is the best deal in town.

CAR & MOTORCYCLE

Unless time is no factor – or money is extremely tight – you're going to want to spend some time behind the wheel, although this means contending with some of the worst traffic in the country. Avoid rush hour (7am to 9am and 3:30pm to 6pm).

Parking at motels and cheaper hotels is usually free, while fancier ones charge anywhere from $8 to around $45 for the privilege. Valet parking at nicer restaurants and hotels is commonplace, with rates ranging from $3.50 to $10.

The usual international car-rental agencies have branches at LAX and throughout LA, and there are also a couple of companies renting hybrid vehicles. If you don't have a vehicle already booked, use the courtesy phones in the arrival areas at LAX. Offices and lots are outside the airport, but each company has free shuttles leaving from the lower level.

For Harley rentals, go to Route 66 (p500). Rates start from $149 per six hours, or $185 for one day. Discounts are available for longer rentals.

PUBLIC TRANSPORTATION

Most public transportation is handled by **Metro** (☑ 323-466-3876; www.metro.net), which offers maps, schedules and trip-planning help through its website.

To ride Metro trains and buses, buy a reusable TAP card. Available from TAP vending machines at Metro stations with a $1 surcharge, the cards allow you to add a preset cash value or day passes. The regular base fare is $1.75 per boarding, or $7 for a day pass with unlimited rides. Both single-trip tickets and TAP cards loaded with a day pass are available on Metro buses (ensure you have the exact change). When using a TAP card, tap the card against the sensor at station entrances and aboard buses.

TAP cards are accepted on DASH and municipal bus services and can be reloaded at vending machines or online on the TAP website (www.taptogo.net).

Metro Buses

Metro operates about 200 bus lines across the city and offers three types of bus services:

➡ Metro Local buses (painted orange) make frequent stops along major thoroughfares throughout the city.

➡ Metro Rapid buses (painted red) stop less frequently and have special sensors that keep traffic lights green when a bus approaches.

➡ Commuter-oriented Metro Express buses (painted blue) connect communities with Downtown LA and other business districts and usually travel via the city's freeways.

Metro Rail

The Metro Rail network consists of two subway lines, four light-rail lines and two express bus lines. Six lines converge in Downtown.

Red Line The most useful for visitors. A subway linking Downtown's Union Station to North Hollywood (San Fernando Valley) via central Hollywood and Universal City; connects with the Blue and Expo Lines at the 7th St/Metro Center station in Downtown and the Metro Orange Line express bus at North Hollywood.

Purple Line Subway line between Downtown LA, Westlake and Koreatown; shares six stations with the Red Line.

Expo Line Light-rail line linking USC and Exposition Park with Culver City and Santa Monica to the west and Downtown LA to the northeast, where it connects with the Red Line at 7th St/Metro Center station.

Blue Line Light-rail line running from Downtown to Long Beach; connects with the Red and Expo Lines at 7th St/Metro Center station and the Green Line at Willowbrook/Rosa Parks station.

Gold Line Light-rail line running from East LA to Little Tokyo/Arts District, Chinatown and Pasadena via Union Station, Mt Washington and Highland Park; connects with the Red Line at Union Station.

Green Line Light-rail service between Norwalk and Redondo Beach; connects with the Blue Line at Willowbrook/Rosa Parks.

Orange Line Express bus linking the west San Fernando Valley to North Hollywood, from where the Red Line subway shoots south to Hollywood and Downtown LA.

Silver Line Express bus linking the El Monte regional bus station to the Harbor Gateway Transit Center in Gardena via Downtown LA. Some services continue to San Pedro.

Most lines run from around 4:30am to 1am Sunday to Thursday, and until around 2:30am on Friday and Saturday nights. Frequency ranges from up to every five minutes in rush hour to every 10 to 20 minutes at other times. Schedules for all lines are available at www.metro.net.

Municipal Buses

Santa Monica–based **Big Blue Bus** (☑ 310-451-5444; www.bigbluebus.com) serves much of western LA, including Santa Monica, Venice, Westwood and LAX ($1.25). Its express bus 10 runs from Santa Monica to Downtown ($2.50, one hour).

The **Culver City Bus** (www.culvercity.org/enjoy/culver-city-bus) runs services throughout Culver City and the Westside. This includes a service to Aviation/LAX station on the metro Green Line ($1), from where a free shuttle connects to LAX.

Long Beach Transit (www.lbtransit.com; $1.25 per ride) serves Long Beach and surrounding communities.

All three municipal bus companies accept payment by TAP card.

DASH Buses

These small, clean-fuel shuttle buses, run by the LA Department of Transportation (www.

ladottransit.com), operate along 33 routes serving local communities (50¢ per boarding, 0.25¢ for seniors and passengers with disabilities), but only until around 6:30pm to 7pm and with limited services on weekends. Many lines connect with other DASH routes; see the website for details. Here are some of the most useful lines:

Beachwood Canyon Route (Monday to Saturday) Useful for close-ups of the Hollywood Sign; runs from Hollywood Blvd and Vine St up Beachwood Dr.

Downtown Routes (daily) Five separate routes hit all the hot spots. Route A runs from Little Tokyo to City West, Route B connects Chinatown to the Financial District, Route D travels between Union Station and South Park, Route E connects City West to the Fashion District, and Route F connects the Financial District to Exposition Park and USC. Routes A, B and D do not run on weekends.

Fairfax Route (Monday to Saturday) Makes a handy loop past the Beverly Center mall, the Pacific Design Center, western Melrose Ave, the Farmers Market/Grove and Museum Row.

Hollywood Route (daily) Covers Hollywood east of Highland Ave and links with the short Los Feliz Route (daily) at Franklin Ave and Vermont Ave.

TAXI

→ Because of LA's size and its traffic, getting around by cab will cost you.

→ Cabs are best organized over the phone, though some prowl the streets late at night, and they are always lined up at airports, train stations, bus stations and major hotels.

→ Fares are metered and vary by the company. The **Uber**, **UberX** and **Lyft** smartphone apps are extremely popular for cheaper rides in LA.

→ In the city of LA, taxi rates are $2.85 at flagfall plus about $2.70 per mile. Cabs leaving from LAX charge a $4 airport fee. For details, check www.taxicabsla.org.

Taxi companies include the following:

Beverly Hills Cab (☑ 800-273-6611; www. beverlyhillscabco.com) A solid, dependable company, with good rates to the airport and a wide service area.

Checker (☑ 800-300-5007; http://ineedtaxi. com) Services both the airport and a large swathe of the LA metro area.

Taxi Taxi (☑ 310-444-4444; www.santamonica taxi.com) Easily the best and most professional fleet available. It'll drive you anywhere, but can only pick up in Santa Monica.

Downtown Los Angeles

Though still sketchy in patches, Downtown (DTLA) continues its upward swing. New condos and hotels are sprouting like mushrooms, joined by buzz-inducing eateries, bars, boutiques and galleries. It's here that you'll find the space-age Broad museum and Walt Disney Concert Hall, which povide dramatic counterpoints to the crumbling opulence of Broadway theaters, the Spanish curves of historic Olvera St and the hulking warehouses of the booming Arts District. Across the concrete Los Angeles River lies East LA, the oldest and largest Mexican community outside of Mexico and home to earthy, vibrant Boyle Heights.

◉ Sights

Downtown is divided into numerous areas. Bunker Hill is home to major modern-art museums and the Walt Disney Concert Hall. To the east is City Hall and, further east still, Little Tokyo. Southeast of Little Tokyo lies the trendy Arts District. Broadway is flanked by glorious heritage buildings, while the city's oldest colonial buildings line Olvera St, north of City Hall and the 101 freeway. Further north still is Chinatown.

◉ El Pueblo de Los Angeles

Compact, colorful and car-free, El Pueblo is a vibrant historic district near the spot where LA's first colonists settled in 1781. It preserves the city's oldest buildings, some dating back to its days as a dusty, lawless outpost. More than anything, though, El Pueblo is a microcosm of LA's multi-ethnic heritage and the contributions made by immigrants from Mexico, France, Italy and China.

LA Plaza MUSEUM
(La Plaza de Cultura y Artes; Map p82; ☑ 213-542-6200; www.lapca.org; 501 N Main St; ☺ noon-5pm Mon, Wed & Thu, to 6pm Fri-Sun; ⊕) **FREE** This museum offers snapshots of the Mexican–American experience in Los Angeles, from Spanish colonization in the late 18th century and the Mexican–American War (when the border crossed the original pueblo), to the Zoot Suit Riots, activist César Chávez and the Chicana movement. Exhibitions include a re-creation of 1920s Main St as well as

Los Angeles Neighborhoods

Los Angeles, the nation's second-biggest metro area, is a quilt of self-contained neighborhoods. These are our favorites.

1. Downtown (p77)
A gleaming nightlife beacon with an arty, funky population of dreamers.

2. Hollywood (p105)
Not just about the glitterati – we love Hollywood for LA's beloved Thai Town and its nocturnal hot spots.

(Hollywood ™ and Hollywood Walk of Fame™ & Design © 2014 HCC. All Rights Reserved . Used with permission of the Hollywood Chamber of Commerce).

3. Los Feliz & Griffith Park (p124)
Laid-back, hip and tasteful, with cafes, landmark architecture and LA's signature green space.

4. Silver Lake & Echo Park (p119)
Silver Lake's kitchens and shops are tip top. Echo Park and its fountain lake are for the young, freaky and funky.

5. West Hollywood & Mid-City (p135)
The set-piece Sunset Strip, terrific shopping, the hub of Gay LA and some of the city's best museums and galleries are all here.

6. Culver City & Mar Vista (p162)
Art galleries, cutting-edge architecture, stucco subdivisions, East German–inspired museums and more hipster communities (Westside edition) all converge just inland from Venice Beach. *(Sony Pictures, Culver City)*

7. Bel Air, Brentwood & Westwood (p152)
Celebrity mansions in Bel Air, the Getty Center in Brentwood, and the wonderful Hammer Museum in Westwood.
Getty Center, designed by Richard Meier

8. Malibu & Pacific Palisades (p167)
Stop by the Getty Villa on your way to epic beaches and an underrated coastal mountain range laced with trails.

9. Santa Monica (p174)
LA's most beloved beach city, for countless reasons.

10. Venice & Marina del Rey (p184)
Venice retains its status as LA's bohemian dream incarnate, despite now being flush with high-tech cash. Marina del Rey is awash with pricey sailboats.

11. South Bay Beaches (p192)
Looking for the archetypal golden-sun small-town beach dream in a big city? Come here.

12. Burbank, Universal City & San Fernando Valley (p205)
Tour Universal Studios Hollywood, and dine on Sushi Row.

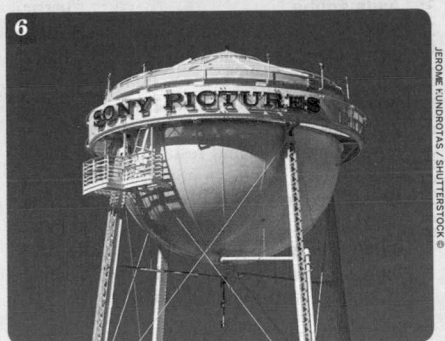

rotating showcases of modern and contemporary art by LA-based Latino artists.

Olvera Street
LANDMARK

(Map p82; www.calleolvera.com; 🚇) It may be a festive Mexican marketplace with gaudy decorations and souvenir stalls that scream 'tourist trap', but you can still find authentic experiences here. Shop for Chicano art, slurp thick, Mexican-style hot chocolate, or pick up handmade candles and candy. At lunchtime, construction workers and cubicle drones swarm the little eateries for tacos, *tortas* (sandwiches) and burritos.

Avila Adobe
MUSEUM

(Map p82; ☎213-628-1274; www.elpueblo.lacity. org; 10 Olvera St; ⊙9am-4pm) FREE The oldest surviving house in LA was built in 1818 by wealthy ranchero and one-time LA mayor Francisco José Avila. After subsequent lives as a boarding house and restaurant, the abode was restored to offer a glimpse into domestic LA life circa 1840. Rooms are filled with period furniture and furnishings, including a handful of items that belonged to the Avila family. Among these is the sewing machine. The house is open for self-guided tours.

Italian American Museum of Los Angeles
MUSEUM

(IAMLA; Map p82; ☎213-485-8432; www.iamla. org; 644 N Main St; ⊙10am-3pm Tue-Sun) FREE Aptly located inside Italian Hall – built in 1908 as a social hub for the area's Italian community – this small, interactive museum sheds light on the oft-overlooked history of Southern California's Italian diaspora. Panels, touch screens and a handful of historical artifacts explore numerous themes, including early Italian pioneers, discrimination and Italian-American success stories (look out for Frank Zappa's 1987 Grammy Award trophy). The museum also hosts rotating exhibitions of Italian-American art.

Listed on the National Register of Historic Places, Italian Hall itself is the site of *América Tropical,* a celebrated mural by 20th-century Mexican artist David Alfaro Siqueiros. To view it, head to the América Tropical Interpretive Center a few doors down from the museum.

América Tropical Interpretive Center
MUSEUM

(Map p82; ☎213-485-6855; www.elpueblo.lacity. org; 125 Paseo De La Plaza; ⊙10am-3pm Tue-Sun) FREE Everyone from Hollywood stars to LA intellectuals attended the 1932 unveiling of *América Tropical,* a rooftop mural by David Alfaro Siqueiros, one of Mexico's great early 20th-century muralists. Depicting a crucified Native American in front of a Mayan pyramid, the artwork proved too provocative for some and it was subsequently whitewashed. Multimedia exhibits explore the artist, politics and artistry behind the mural, as well as its rehabilitation by the Getty Conservation Institute. Upstairs, a viewing platform grants a close-up view of the faded work. The viewing platform is usually closed on rainy days.

Old Plaza
LANDMARK

(Map p82; Olvera St) El Pueblo's central, magnolia-shaded square is crowned by a pretty wrought-iron gazebo. Sleepy and a little sketchy during the week, it often turns into a full-blown fiesta zone on Saturdays and Sundays, drawing mariachis, costumed dancers, kissing couples and strolling families.

The best time to be here is for one of the many Mexican festivals, such as Cinco de Mayo or Día de los Muertos. Dotted around the plaza are statues of such key historical figures as Felipe de Neve, who led the first group of settlers, and King Carlos III of Spain, who financed the venture. The colonists' names are engraved on a nearby bronze plaque.

Pico House
LANDMARK

(Map p82; 430 N Main St) South of Old Plaza are a number of historic buildings, including the 1870 home of Pío Pico, California's last Mexican governor. It was the city's first three-story building, and later a glamourous hotel with 21 parlors and two interior courtyards. At the time of writing the building is closed to the public while it undergoes a seismic retrofit.

Plaza Firehouse
MUSEUM

(Map p82; 134 Paseo de la Plaza; ⊙10am-3pm Tue-Sun) FREE The city's oldest fire station (1884) is now a one-room museum filled with dusty old fire-fighting equipment and photographs.

La Placita
CHURCH

(Map p82; www.laplacita.org; 535 N Main St; ⊙6am-8:30pm) Founded as La Iglesia de Nuestra Señora la Reina de Los Ángeles (Our Lady the Queen of the Angels Church) in 1781, and now affectionately known as

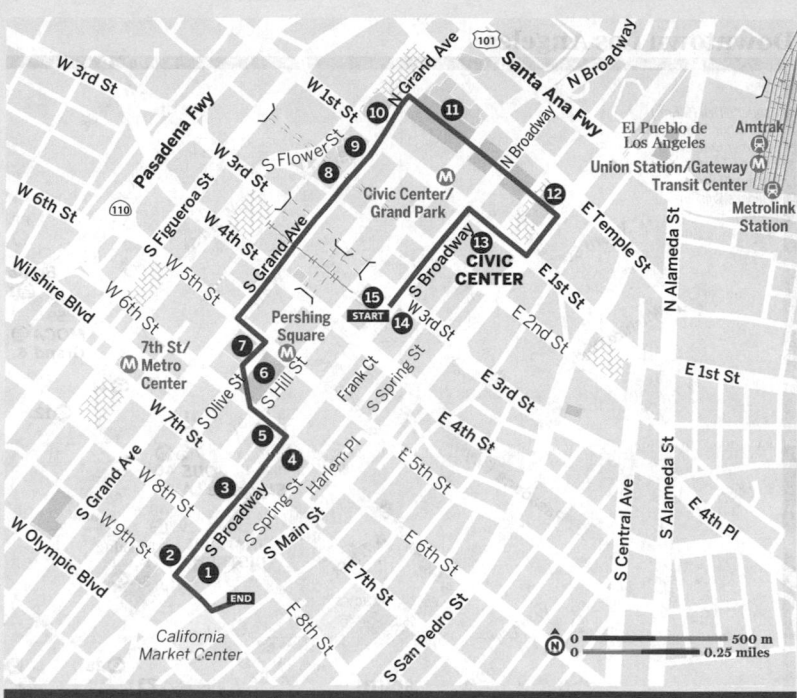

City Walk
Downtown: Art, History & Architecture

START VERVE
END GRAND CENTRAL MARKET
LENGTH 2.5 MILES; 2½ TO 3 HOURS

Grab a coffee at **1** **Verve** (p100) then head one block northwest along 9th St to Broadway. Dominating the intersection is the turquoise-and-gold **2** **Eastern Columbia Building** (p91), an art-deco beauty with a spectacular entrance. Head north on Broadway through the old theater district. Its heady soup of beaux-arts architecture, retro theater marquees, discount jewelers and trendy new enterprises sums up the Downtown rennaisance in just a few short blocks. Take note of the **3** **State Theatre** (p91), **4** **Palace Theatre** (p91) and **5** **Los Angeles Theatre** (p91). The Palace made a cameo in Michael Jackson's *Thriller* music video.

Turn left at 6th St and continue for two blocks, passing **6** **Pershing Square** (p89) en route to the historic **7** **Millennium Biltmore Hotel** (p96); cameos include *Ghostbusters*, *Fight Club* and *Mad Men*. Step inside for a look at its opulent interiors and find the Historical

Corridor to scan the fascinating photograph of the 1937 Academy Awards.

Head right into Grand Ave, which leads to the extraordinary contemporary building: modern-art museum **8** **Broad** (p90). The courtyard – planted with century-old olive trees – is home to restaurant Otium, whose exterior features a mural by British artist Damian Hirst. On the other side of Broad is Frank Gehry's showstopping **9** **Walt Disney Concert Hall** (p85), home to the LA Philharmonic. Beside it is the Phil's former home, '60s throwback **10** **Dorothy Chandler Pavilion** (p78). Across the street is **11** **Grand Park** (p78), a good spot to rest and post those pics using the free wi-fi.

At the end of the park is **12** **City Hall** (p83). Head up its tower for stunning (free) views and take in the breathtaking rotunda on level three. Then head south along Main St, turning right into 1st St and passing the art-deco headquarters of the **13** **Los Angeles Times** (p94). Turn left onto Broadway, eyeing up the beautiful atrium inside the **14** **Bradbury Building** (p91) before a well-earned lunch at the **15** **Grand Central Market** (p90).

Downtown Los Angeles

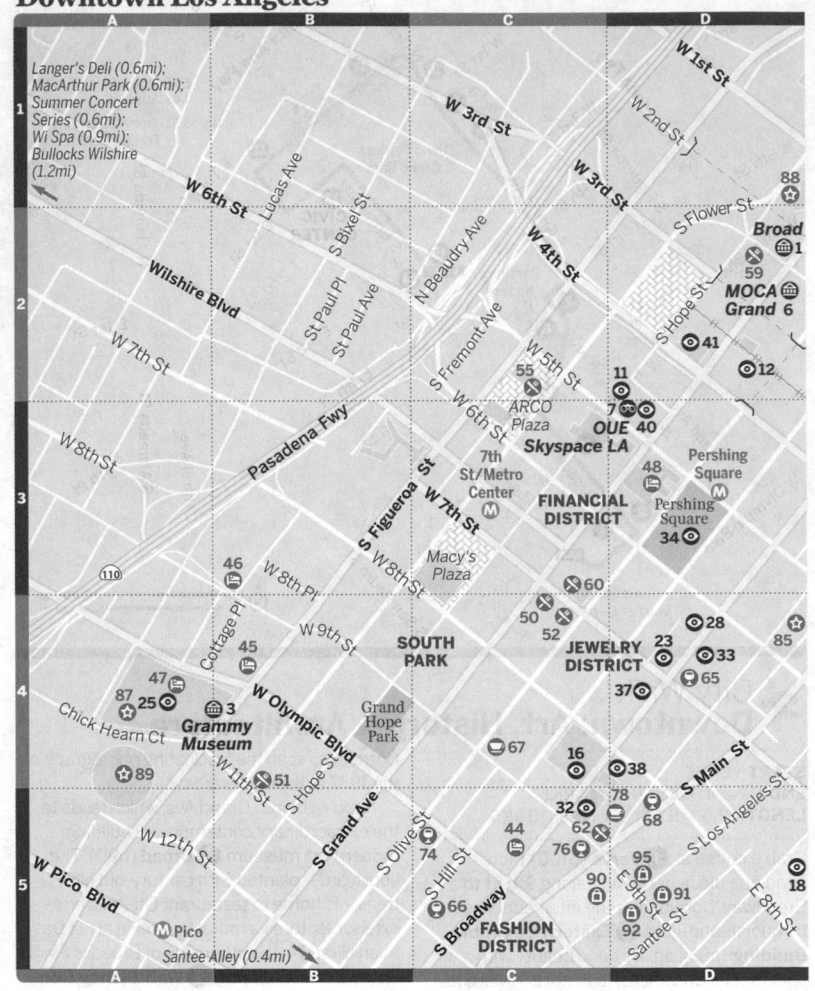

Langer's Deli (0.6mi);
MacArthur Park (0.6mi);
Summer Concert
Series (0.6mi);
Wi Spa (0.9mi);
Bullocks Wilshire
(1.2mi)

'Little Plaza.' Head inside for a peek at the gilded altar and painted ceiling.

Chinese American Museum
MUSEUM
(Map p82; ☎213-485-8567; www.camla.org; Garnier Bldg, 425 N Los Angeles St; adult/child $3/2; ◉10am-3pm Tue-Sun) Follow the red lanterns to the small 1890 Garnier Building, once the unofficial Chinatown 'city hall'. Changing exhibits highlight various historical, cultural and artistic aspects of the Chinese–American experience.

Union Station
NOTABLE BUILDING
(Map p82; www.amtrak.com; 800 N Alameda St; Ⓟ) Built on the site of LA's original Chinatown, Union Station opened in 1939 as America's last grand rail station. It's a glamourous exercise in Mission Revival style with art-deco and American Indian accents. The marble-floored main hall, with cathedral ceilings, original leather chairs and 3000-pound chandeliers, is breathtaking. The station's Traxx Bar was once the telephone room, complete with operator to place customers' calls. The LA Conservancy

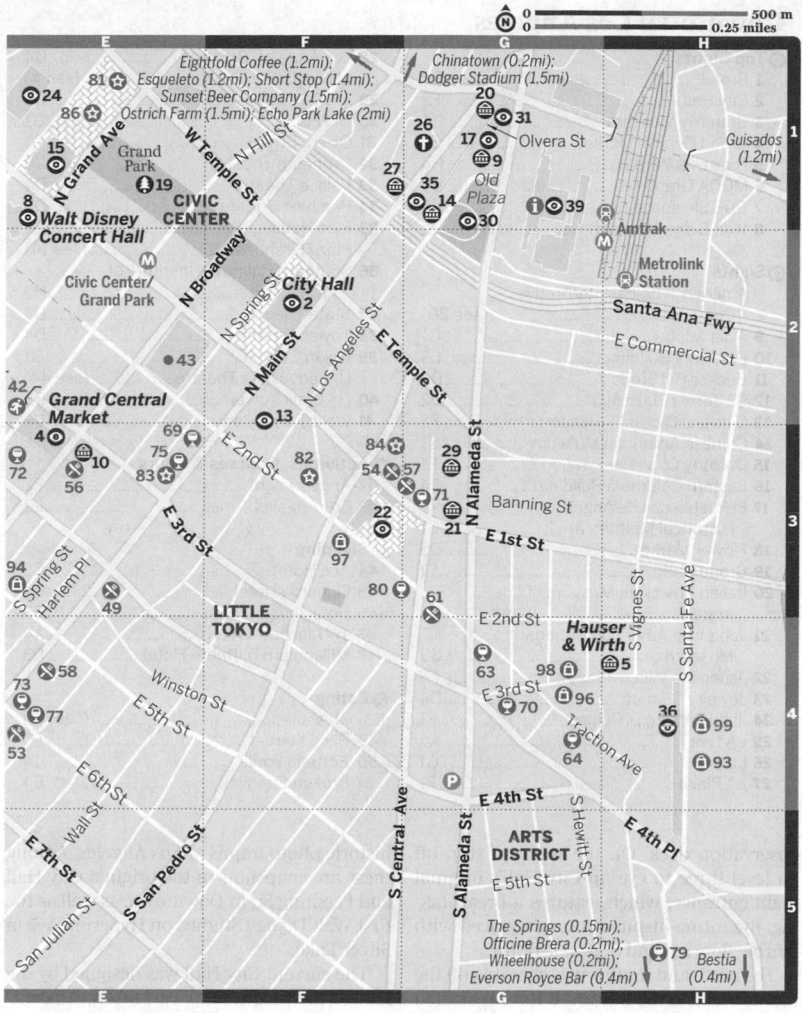

runs 2½-hour walking tours of the station on Saturdays at 10am (book online).

The tiled twin domes north of the station belong to the Terminal Annex, once LA's central post office before it was closed and later reopened as an active postal branch. This is where Charles Bukowski worked, inspiring his 1971 novel *Post Office*.

◉ Bunker Hill & City Hall

South of the 101 freeway stands City Hall, worth a visit for its breathtaking interiors and (free) tower viewpoint. Lining up along

Grand Ave to the west are the blockbuster art museums and cultural institutions of Bunker Hill, among them the Broad, MOCA Grand and Walt Disney Concert Hall.

★ City Hall
LANDMARK

(Map p82; ☑213-485-2121; www.lacity.org; 200 N Spring St; ⊙9am-5pm Mon-Fri) **FREE** Until 1966 no LA building stood taller than the 1928 City Hall, which appeared in the *Superman* TV series and 1953 sci-fi thriller *War of the Worlds*. On clear days you'll have views of the city, the mountains and several decades of Downtown growth from the

Downtown Los Angeles

observation deck. On the way up, stop off on level three to eye up City Hall's original main entrance, which features a breathtaking, Byzantine-inspired rotunda graced with marble flooring and a mosaic dome.

The north and south wings shooting off the rotunda lead to the Edward R Roybal Session Room and the John Ferraro Council Chambers respectively. Both are worth a peek for their elegant interiors. The Edward R Roybal Session Room is usually open between 10am and around noon on Monday, Wednesday and Friday, while the John Ferraro Council Chambers is usually open Tuesday, Wednesday and Friday during the same hours. Close to the John Ferraro Council Chambers is the Clerk Office (open 8am to 4pm weekdays), home to a fascinating old map documenting Los Angeles' gradual annexation of surrounding cities and settlements.

One floor up, level four offers impressive views of the rotunda's geometric floor and dome mosaics. It's also home to a series of historic photographs of Los Angeles. Among these are snapshots of the original City Hall and Pershing Sq in Downtown, as well as the first Walt Disney Studios on Hyperion Ave in Silver Lake.

The current City Hall was designed by the lauded architects John Parkinson, Albert C Martin and John C Austin, whose inspiration for the building's iconic terracotta tower was the Mausoleum at Halicarnassus, one of the world's seven ancient wonders.

The public entrance is on Main St.

Grand Park PARK
(Map p82; www.grandparkla.org; 227 N Spring St; Ⓜ Red/Purple Lines to Civic Center) Everything from free lunchtime yoga to music concerts and long days of lounging and people-watching takes place at this preened Downtown park, cascading from the Music Center down to City Hall. You'll find manicured lawns and plenty of benches on each tier, as well as free wi-fi.

Dorothy Chandler Pavilion NOTABLE BUILDING
(Map p82; ☎213-972-7211; www.musiccenter.
org; 135 N Grand Ave; Ⓜ Red/Purple Lines to Civic
Center/Grand Park) Downtown's '60s-era concert hall was home to the LA Philharmonic
until it moved to the acoustically superior
Walt Disney Concert Hall. These days, the
3200-capacity venue is mostly used by the
LA Opera and touring companies. Try to reserve seats on the upper floors, which offer
the best sound.

John Ferraro Building NOTABLE BUILDING
(Map p82; 111 N Hope St) Home to the Los Angeles Department of Water and Power, this
16-story Ferraro-designed classic dates back
to 1964. While it isn't LA's biggest, tallest or
edgiest building, it is an architectural standout, defined by sharp horizontal lines and
framed by a reflection pond that seemingly
hovers over the underground parking lot.
Interestingly, the pond feeds the building's
cooling towers while the parking lot's shade

structure is a solar farm. Head in at twilight,
when the skyline twinkles in the water.

★ **Walt Disney Concert Hall** NOTABLE BUILDING
(Map p82; ☎323-850-2000; www.laphil.org; 111 S
Grand Ave; ⊙ guided tours usually noon & 1:15pm
Thu-Sat, 10am & 11am Sun; Ⓟ; Ⓜ Red/Purple Lines
to Civic Center/Grand Park) FREE A molten blend
of steel, music and psychedelic architecture,
this iconic concert venue is the home base of
the Los Angeles Philharmonic, but has also
hosted contemporary bands such as Phoe-
nix and classic jazz musicians such as Sonny
Rollins. Frank Gehry pulled out all the stops:
the building is a gravity-defying sculpture of
heaving and billowing stainless steel.

In contrast, the auditorium feels like the
inside of a finely crafted cello, clad in walls
of smooth Douglas fir with terraced 'vineyard' seating wrapped around a central
stage. Even seats below the giant pipe organ
offer excellent sight lines. Free, self-guided
audio tours are available most days, and

NITO / SHUTTERSTOCK © USED WITH PERMISSION OF THE HOLLYWOOD CHAMBER OF COMMERCE

1. Hollywood Sign (p108) 2. Hollywood Boulevard (p105)
3. Walt Disney Concert Hall (2003), designed by Frank Gehry
(p85) 4. Eastside bar scene, Silver Lake (p122)

SEAN PAVONE / SHUTTERSTOCK ©

Los Angeles Highlights

Griffith Observatory & Hollywood Sign

The crown atop LA's most beloved urban green space, the landmark 1935 observatory, has had star turns in feature films and offers a nice vantage point for the iconic Hollywood Sign.

LACMA

From stunning permanent collections, to special exhibitions and live Friday night jazz in the summertime, there's a reason this is one of LA's favorite cultural oases.

Walt Disney Concert Hall & the Broad

An abstract, melting mass of brushed steel, Frank Gehry's downtown masterpiece, the Walt Disney Concert Hall, harmonizes beautifully with its new neighbor, the Broad, a jewel box of contemporary art that opened in September 2015.

Explore the Eastside

Los Angeles culture and nightlife once revolved around the Sunset Strip and points west, but no longer. These days the hippest hoods – with prime dining, shopping, drinking and dancing – are in Los Feliz, Silver Lake, Echo Park and Highland Park.

Westward Beach

A wide swath of golden sand on the open ocean side of Point Dume, with good surf, *beaucoup* bikinis, and crystal-clear waters that teem with wildlife.

Downtown

Rapidly evolving, Downtown is LA's most intriguing neighborhood, a bustling beehive where cutting-edge art and architecture meet mariachi tunes, old movie palaces and many of the city's hottest restaurants, bars, galleries and boutiques.

CHINATOWN

Walk north from El Pueblo and you'll breach the dragon gates of **Chinatown** (www.chinatownla.com). After being forced to make room for Union Station, Chinese immigrants resettled a few blocks north along Hill St and Broadway. Chinatown is still the community's traditional hub, even though many Chinese Americans now live in the San Gabriel Valley. There are no essential sights here, but the area (a stop on Metro Gold Line) is fun for an aimless wander. Restaurants beckon with dim sum and crispy duck, while shops overflow with curios, ancient herbal remedies and lucky bamboo.

there are one-hour guided tours available too, but they won't let you see the auditorium. The best way to experience the hall is to see a show. Tour times are subject to change, so always check the website for exact times.

★**MOCA Grand** MUSEUM
(Museum of Contemporary Art; Map p82; ☑213-626-6222; www.moca.org; 250 S Grand Ave; adult/child $15/free, 5-8pm Thu free; ☺11am-6pm Mon, Wed & Fri, to 8pm Thu, to 5pm Sat & Sun) MOCA's superlative art collection focuses mainly on works created from the 1940s to the present. There's no shortage of luminaries, among them Mark Rothko, Dan Flavin, Willem de Kooning, Joseph Cornell and David Hockney. Their creations are housed in a postmodern building by award-winning Japanese architect Arata Isozaki. Galleries are below ground, yet sky-lit bright.

Tickets are also good for same-day admission at MOCA Geffen (p89) in Little Tokyo, a quick DASH bus ride away – catch it at the corner of Grand Ave and 1st St. Visitors with a Tap card enjoy two-for-one general admission.

California Plaza LANDMARK
(Map p82; www.grandperformances.org; 350 S Grand Ave; Ⓜ Red/Purple Lines to Pershing Sq) MOCA Grand is dwarfed by the soaring California Plaza office towers. The outdoor water-court amphitheater is host to **Grand Performances** (Map p82; ☑213-687-2190; www.grandperformances.org; California Plaza, 300 & 350 S Grand Ave; ☺Jun-Sep; Ⓜ Red/Purple Lines to Pershing Sq) **FREE**, which is one of the best free summer performance series in the city.

Wells Fargo Center NOTABLE BUILDING
(Map p82; 333 S Grand Ave; ☺ Wells Fargo History Museum 9am-5pm Mon-Fri) Featuring two granite polygonal skyscrapers connected by a three-story atrium, this 1983 office complex is the work of renowned Chicago architecture firm Skidmore, Owings & Merrill (SOM). The center houses a number of sculptures, including works by Jean Dubuffet, Robert Graham and Joan Miró, as well as a small museum documenting the history of the Wells Fargo bank in Southern California.

◉ Little Tokyo & Arts District

Little Tokyo swirls with outdoor shopping malls, Buddhist temples, public art, traditional gardens and some of the most authentic sushi bars, izakayas and shabu-shabu parlors in town. The community can trace its roots back to the 1880s, but only a few historic buildings survive along E 1st St.

Caltrans District 7 Headquarters LANDMARK
(Map p82; www.dot.ca.gov; 100 S Main St) **FREE** OK, maybe Caltrans didn't earn its $150-million digs based on performance, but that doesn't change the fact that this floating steel-mesh-and-glass-skinned behemoth is worthy of praise. Completed in 2004, the building won its designer – LA-based architect Thom Mayne – the prestigious Pritzker Architecture Prize a year later. The hulking structure is true to Mayne's futuristic style, with dramatic geometric forms, space-grey hues and perforated metal screens. Its Main St steps have become a vortex for Downtown's skate punks.

Japanese Village Plaza LANDMARK
(Map p82; btwn 1st & 2nd Sts; Ⓜ Gold Line to Little Tokyo/Arts District) The unusual-looking tower is a *yagura*, a traditional fire-lookout tower typically found in rural Japan. It's the gateway to this kitschy outdoor mall, flanked by Japanese grocery stores, stalls and boutiques selling Hello Kitty kitsch and Japangeles T-shirts, with a couple noteworthy eateries. A good spot for people watching.

Japanese American National Museum MUSEUM
(Map p82; ☑213-625-0414; www.janm.org; 100 N Central Ave; adult/child $10/6, 5-8pm Thu & all day 3rd Thu of month free; ☺11am-5pm Tue, Wed & Fri-Sun, noon-8pm Thu; ♿; Ⓜ Gold Line to Little Tokyo/Arts District) A great first stop in Little Tokyo, this is the country's first museum dedicated to the Japanese immigrant experience. The

2nd floor is home to the permanent 'Common Ground' exhibition, which explores the evolution of Japanese-American culture since the late 19th century and offers moving insight into the painful chapter of America's WWII internment camps. Afterwards relax in the tranquil garden and browse the well-stocked gift shop.

MOCA Geffen
GALLERY

(Map p82; 213-625-4390; www.moca.org; 152 N Central Ave; adult/student/child under 12yr $15/8/free, 5-8pm Thu free; 11am-6pm Mon, Wed & Fri, to 8pm Thu, to 5pm Sat & Sun; Gold Line to Little Tokyo/Arts District) MOCA showcases its big names and blockbuster exhibits at its main building on Grand Ave, freeing its original site in Little Tokyo to focus on more experimental, cutting-edge and conceptual works. The gallery itself was converted from a police car warehouse by LA-based starchitect Frank Gehry.

★ Hauser & Wirth
GALLERY

(Map p82; 213-943-1620; www.hauserwirthlosangeles.com; 901 E 3rd St; 11am-6pm Wed & Fri-Sun, to 8pm Thu) FREE The LA outpost of internationally acclaimed gallery Hauser & Wirth has art fiends in a flurry with its museum-standard exhibits of modern and contemporary art. It's a huge space, occupying 116,000 sq ft of a converted flour mill complex in the Arts District. Past exhibits have showcased the work of luminaries such as Louise Bourgeois, Eva Hesse and Jason Rhoades. The complex is also home to a superlative art bookshop.

Southern California Institute of Architecture
NOTABLE BUILDING

(Sci-Arc; Map p82; www.sciarc.edu; 960 E 3rd St; gallery admission free; gallery 10am-6pm) The surrounding area got a nod of respectability when this institute moved into the former Santa Fe Freight Yard in 2001. It's a progressive laboratory with faculty and students who continually push the envelope in architectural design. You can see some of the results in one of the two galleries or attend a lecture or film screening; see the website for upcoming events.

◉ Financial District & Jewelry District

LA's traditional business and financial district sits south and west of Bunker Hill and got its skyscraper-studded skyline during an aggressive building boom in the 1970s and '80s. A few steps away is Pershing Sq, LA's oldest park, with the Jewelry District just beyond.

US Bank Tower
LANDMARK

(Map p82; 633 W 5th St, Downtown; Red/Purple Lines to Pershing Sq) Although the spire-topped 73-story Wilshire Grand Tower is technically LA's tallest building by architectural height, the 1018ft US Bank Tower remains the city's tallest building to roof height. Destroyed by aliens in *Independence Day* and by a mega-quake in *San Andreas,* the skyscraper is home to the OUE Skyspace LA a multilevel observation deck offering a spectacular 360-degree view of the city, hills, ocean and (in winter) snowcapped mountains.

★ OUE Skyspace LA
VIEWPOINT

(Map p82; 213 894 9000; https://oue-skyspace.com; US Bank Tower, 633 W 5th St, Downtown; adult/senior/child $25/22/19; 10am-9pm Sun-Thu, to 10pm Fri & Sat;) Perched atop the city's tallest building to roof level, this is LA's loftiest observation deck, offering knockout views of LA, its hills, ocean and distant mountains. The experience begins with interactive displays on the 54th floor before a second set of elevators whisks you up to the indoor and outdoor decks straddling levels 69 and 70. For an extra $8, visitors can experience the Skyslide, a see-through outdoor slide connecting the two observation-deck floors – a short, somewhat underwhelming 'thrill'.

Weekends can get especially busy, so consider buying timed tickets online to avoid any lengthy queues. Needless to say, the best times to head up are on a clear day and just before sunset, allowing you to see the city slip on its glittering evening coat.

Bunker Hill Steps
LANDMARK

(Map p82) The US Bank Tower abuts the Bunker Hill Steps, a cheesy set-piece staircase (there's an escalator, too) that links 5th St with the Wells Fargo Center (p88) and other hilltop office complexes. At the top is a small fountain featuring a female nude by Robert Graham.

Pershing Square
LANDMARK

(Map p82; www.laparks.org; 532 S Olive St;) LA's first public park in 1866, Pershing Sq is now a postmodern concrete patch enlivened by public art, summer concerts and a holiday-season ice rink. Criticism of its heavily built-up appearance led to a 2015 competition seeking proposals for its future redevelopment. The winner was French landscape

A BROAD COLLECTION

From the instant it opened in September 2015, the **Broad** (Map p82; ☎ 213-232-6200; www.thebroad.org; 221 S Grand Ave; ⊙ 11am-5pm Tue & Wed, to 8pm Thu & Fri, 10am-8pm Sat, to 6pm Sun; Ⓟ 👪; Ⓜ Red/Purple Lines to Civic Center/Grand Park) – rhymes with 'road' – became a must-visit for contemporary-art fans. It houses the world-class collection of local philanthropist and billionaire real-estate honcho Eli Broad and his wife Edythe, with more than 2000 postwar pieces by dozens of heavy hitters, including Cindy Sherman, Jeff Koons, Andy Warhol, Roy Lichtenstein, Robert Rauschenberg, Keith Haring and Kara Walker.

The striking building is an attraction in itself. Designed by New York–based firm Diller Scofidio + Renfro (designers of Manhattan's iconic High Line) in collaboration with SF-based firm Gensler, it's shrouded in a white lattice-like shell that lifts at the corners, allowing visitors to access the cavernous, undulating lobby. It's in here that you can (and should) register to experience Yayoi Kusama's super-popular *Infinity Mirrored Room*. Once it's your turn to view the installation, you will receive a text message from the museum (note: waiting times are sometimes shorter than the estimation given, so check your phone regularly).

Once you've eyed up the temporary exhibitions on the lobby floor, an escalator whisks you up through a narrow tunnel to the 35,000-sq-ft 3rd-floor gallery, where Jeff Koons charms visitors with his giant bunch of stainless-steel tulips. The flowers are framed by equally bold, poptastic artworks by Japanese artist Takashi Murakami. The surrounding galleries rotate works from the Broad's permanent collection, considered one of the world's most prominent holdings of postwar and contemporary artworks.

And while we generally don't have much of an opinion on museum docents, the Broad's are surprisingly knowledgeable and helpful. Plus, an excellent smartphone app gives further descriptions of the art and artists.

Admission is free (except during special exhibitions), but you'll want to reserve a timed ticket online, as the line for same-day walk-ups can be long (arrive 45 minutes before opening for best results).

architecture firm Agence Ter, whose design envisioned a flatter, greener, more open space. Flanking the western side of the square is the hulking 1923 Millennium Biltmore Hotel (p96).

Jewelry District AREA
(Map p82) South of Pershing Sq is one of the country's largest jewelry districts. Centered on Broadway and Hill St (between 6th and 7th Sts), the main currency here is gold and diamonds. Sadly many of the working-class Latinos who frequented these businesses have moved on in recent years and the combination of rapid gentrification and soaring rents in the area has forced a growing number of long-standing traders to shut shop.

⊙ Broadway & Around

South of Bunker Hill and City Hall lies Downtown's Historic Core, bordered by E 3rd, Olympic Blvd, Hill St and Los Angeles St. The district's star is raffish Broadway, home to a cachet of beautiful historic buildings as well as the vibrant Grand Central Market. Until eclipsed by Hollywood in the mid-1920s, Broadway was LA's entertainment hub with no fewer than a dozen theaters built in a riot of styles, from beaux arts to east Indian to Spanish Gothic. East of Los Angeles St, south of 3rd St, west of Alameda St and north of 7th Ave is the notorious Skid Row, a squalid area best avoided.

★ **Grand Central Market** MARKET
(Map p82; www.grandcentralmarket.com; 317 S Broadway; ⊙ 8am-10pm; Ⓜ Red/Purple Lines to Pershing Sq) LA's Grand Central Market has been satisfying appetites in this beaux-arts building since 1917. Originally leased to the Ville de Paris department store, this was the city's first fireproof, steel-reinforced commercial building, designed by prolific architect John Parkinson and once home to an office occupied by Frank Lloyd Wright. Lose yourself in its bustle of neon signs, stalls and counters, peddling everything from fresh produce and nuts, to sizzling Thai street food, hipster egg rolls, artisanal pasta and specialty coffee.

Bradbury Building HISTORIC BUILDING
(Map p82; www.laconservancy.org; 304 S Broadway; ☻ lobby usually 9am-5pm; Ⓜ Red/Purple Lines to Pershing Sq) Debuting in 1893, the Bradbury is one of the city's undisputed architectural jewels. Behind its robust Romanesque facade lies a whimsical galleried atrium that wouldn't look out of place in New Orleans. Inky filigree grillwork, rickety birdcage elevators and yellow-brick walls glisten golden in the afternoon light, which filters through the peaked glass roof. Such striking beauty hasn't been lost on Hollywood – the building's star turn came in the cult sci-fi flick *Blade Runner*.

Million Dollar Theatre THEATER
(Map p82; ☏ 213-617-3600; www.milliondollar.la; 307 S Broadway) The first theater built by Sid Grauman of Chinese Theatre and Egyptian Theatre fame. While the top floors were designed by Albert Carey Martin Sr (co-designer of City Hall), the theater facade – decorated with bison heads and longhorn cattle skulls – is the work of William Lee Woollett. Big bands played here in the '40s and, a decade later, it became the first Broadway venue to cater to Spanish speakers. Briefly a church, it's now rented out for film shoots.

Los Angeles Theatre THEATER
(Map p82; ☏ 213-488-2009; www.losangelestheatre. com; 615 S Broadway) Designed by celebrated theater designer S Charles Lee, this 1931 jewel was the last major movie palace to be built in Downtown. A breathtaking swansong, it's the most lavish theater on the strip, with a soaring lobby inspired by Louis XIV's Hall of Mirrors at Versailles. Here, Corinthian columns, crystal chandeliers and a grand central staircase lead to an auditorium where Albert Einstein and other luminaries enjoyed the premiere of Charlie Chaplin's *City Lights*. Restored, it presents special events and screenings.

Palace Theatre THEATER
(Map p82; ☏ 213-488-2009; www.palacedowntown.com; 630 S Broadway) Dating back to 1911, the Palace is one of the city's oldest theaters. The facade is a curious fusion of early Renaissance Florentine architecture and pure theatrical whimsy, with colorful terracotta swags, masks, fairies and flora. The four panels depicting song, dance, music and drama (the four muses of vaudeville) are the work of celebrated Spanish sculptor Domingo Mora. Inside, the theater is pure French baroque fantasy, laced with pastoral-themed murals and garland-draped columns.

These days the venue is hired out for special events and film shoots.

State Theatre THEATER
(Map p82; 703 S Broadway) This beaux-arts creation is Broadway's biggest entertainment complex, seating close to 2500 people. The theater debuted in 1921 with a vaudeville show and the silver-screen premiere of *A Trip to Paradise*. The facade features terracotta ornamentation while the building's lobby and auditorium find their inspiration in a Spanish castle. These days the theater functions as a Spanish-language church.

Tower Theatre THEATER
(Map p82; 802 S Broadway) The world's first talkie, *The Jazz Singer*, starring Al Jolson, premiered here in 1927. The first theater designed by celebrated architect S Charles Lee, it's a suitably lavish affair, melding French baroque, Romanesque, Spanish and Moorish influences. These days the interior is often used for location shoots.

Orpheum Theatre THEATER
(Map p82; ☏ 877-677-4386; www.laorpheum.com; 842 S Broadway) This 1926 theater was built for vaudeville and has hosted such entertainers as Judy Garland, George Burns and Nat King Cole. A truly sumptuous place, its French baroque style is accented with silk tapestries, a gilded, coffered ceiling, an old brass box office and a still-functioning Wurlitzer organ that can replicate over 1400 orchestral sounds. Fully restored, the venue runs an eclectic entertainment calendar. See a show here if you can.

Eastern Columbia Building NOTABLE BUILDING
(Map p82; www.easterncolumbiahoa.com; 849 S Broadway) Architect Claud Beelman's extraordinary 1929 Eastern Columbia Building is a masterpiece of art moderne architecture. Clad in turquoise-and-gold terracotta tiles, the 13-storey tower originally housed two clothing companies belonging to industrious Polish immigrant Adolph Sieroty. Now home to luxury lofts, the building features a striking gilded sunburst entrance that's especially impressive when lit after dark. One-bedroom lofts rent for upwards of $3000 a month – Johnny Depp allegedly bought the penthouse for a cool $2.1 million. One can dream.

Southern California's Best Beaches

Hundreds of miles of Pacific beaches edge SoCal's golden coast – which makes choosing just one to visit almost impossible. Take your pick depending on what you prefer doing: launching your surfboard onto a world-famous break; snapping on a snorkel mask and peeking at colorful marine life; or just lazing on the sand.

1. Santa Monica (p174)
A carnival pier with a solar-powered Ferris wheel and a tiny aquarium for the kiddos sits atop this idyllic 3-mile long strand where LA comes to play.

2. Malibu (p167)
Celebrity residents aren't keen to share their paradisaical pocket beaches, but with persistence and some insider tips, you too can indulge in these million-dollar views.

3. Huntington Beach (p262)
Officially 'Surf City, USA,' Huntington Beach is everything you imagined SoCal beach life to be, from surfing by the pier to sunset bonfires on the sand.

4. Mission Beach (p405)
A day trip to San Diego's most fun-crazed beach should begin with a ride on the Giant Dipper wooden roller coaster and end with sunset along Ocean Front Walk.

5. Crystal Cove State Park (p279)
Tired of manicured beaches filled with bikini babes? Escape instead to this wilder, undeveloped Orange County gem for beachcombing and scuba diving.

6. Coronado (p402)
Pedal a beach cruiser along the Silver Strand, or frolic like Marilyn Monroe did on the golden sand fronting San Diego's landmark Hotel del Coronado.

7. East Beach (p352)
Next to historic Stearns Wharf (pictured), where Santa Barbara meets the sea, this easy-access beach fills in summer with swimmers, volleyball players and even sea kayakers.

8. Carpinteria State Beach (p376)
Even tots can get their feet wet or poke around the tide pools at this Santa Barbara County classic, where palm trees wave above soft sands.

2

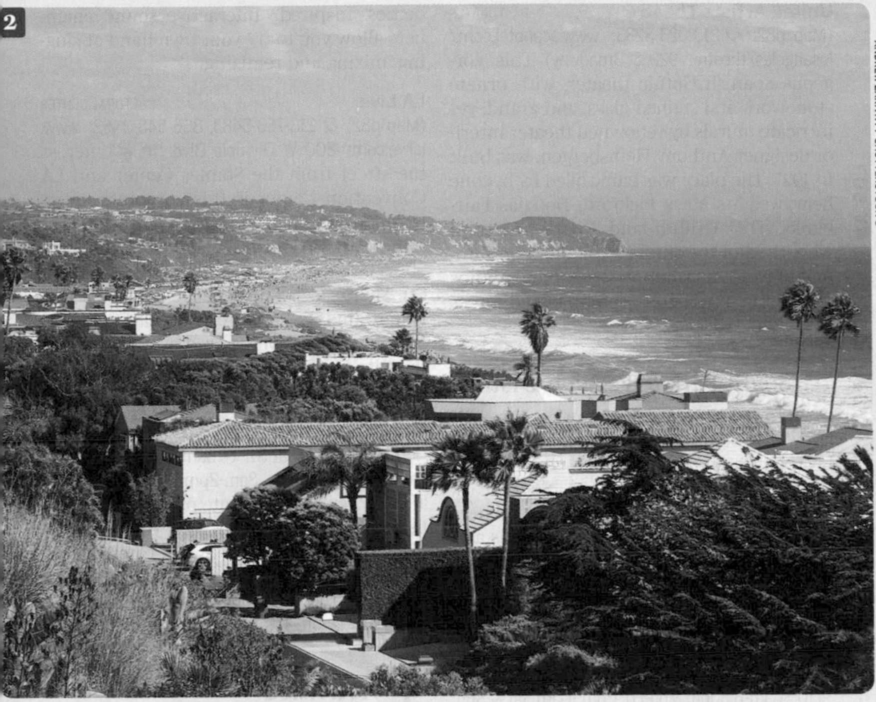

ANDREW ZARIVNY / SHUTTERSTOCK ©

5

TRACEROUDA / GETTY IMAGES ©

6

CHARLES DAVIES / 500PX ©

7

GIMAS / SHUTTERSTOCK ©

8

ASHLEYWILEY / GETTY IMAGES ©

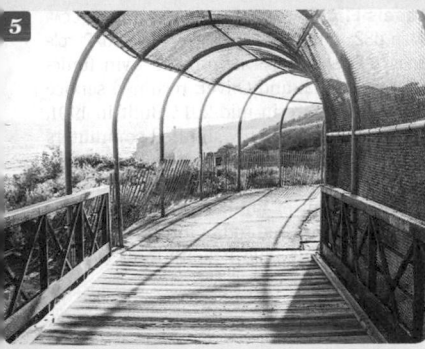

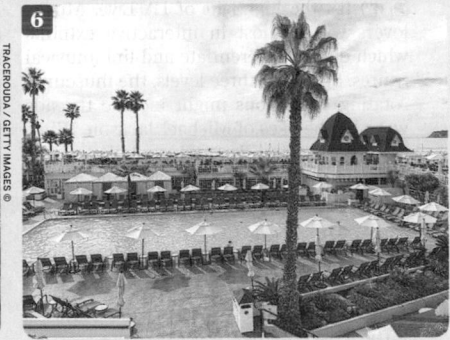

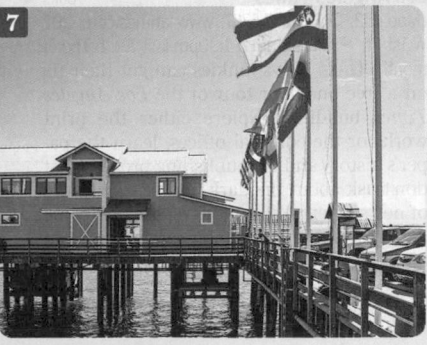

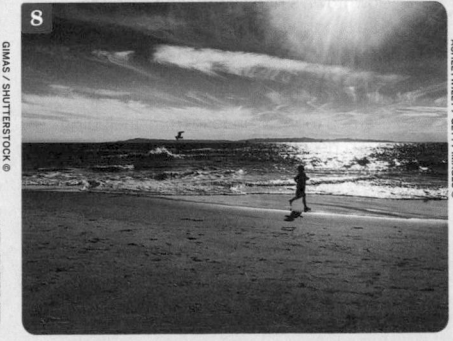

United Artists Theatre
THEATER

(Map p82; ☑ 213-623-3233; www.acehotel.com/losangeles/theatre; 929 S Broadway) This gorgeous Spanish Gothic theater, with ornate stonework and stained glass, and grand, yet intricate murals by renowned theater interior designer Anthony Heinsbergen, was built in 1927. The place was bankrolled by bygone heavyweights Mary Pickford, Douglas Fairbanks, DW Griffith and Charlie Chaplin who, tired of the studio stronghold on filmmaking and distribution (back then studios owned the movie houses, too), joined forces as United Artists.

◎ South Park & Fashion District

Downtown's revamped southwest corner – known as South Park – is home to the LA Live entertainment complex, the Staples Center and Grammy Museum. South Park segues into the Fashion District, where fashionistas flaunting the latest threads and accessories wander among crack heads and drunks in neck tattoos and a perma-haze.

★ Grammy Museum
MUSEUM

(Map p82; ☑ 213-765-6800; www.grammymuseum.org; 800 W Olympic Blvd; adult/child $13/11; ◷ 10:30am-6:30pm Mon-Fri, from 10am Sat & Sun; ℗⛨) It's the highlight of LA Live. Music-lovers will get lost in interactive exhibits which define, differentiate and link musical genres. Spanning three levels, the museum's rotating exhibitions might include threads worn by the likes of Michael Jackson, Whitney Houston and Beyoncé, scribbled words from the hands of Count Basie and Taylor Swift and instruments once used by rock

---

ⓘ HISTORIC WALKING TOURS

The most rewarding way to explore Downtown's rich history and architecture is on a weekend walking tour run by the **Los Angeles Conservancy** (☑ 213-623-2489; www.laconservancy.org; adult/child $15/10). There are several themed tours to choose from, including an art deco tour, an exploration of Union Station and a tour of Broadway's historic theaters (this tour does not guarantee entry into the theaters themselves). Most tours run around 2½ hours. See the conservancy's website for tour schedules and to book tickets.

---

deities. Inspired? Interactive sound chambers allow you to try your own hand at singing, mixing and remixing.

LA Live
CULTURAL CENTER

(Map p82; ☑ 213-763-5483, 866-548-3452; www.lalive.com; 800 W Olympic Blvd; ℗⛨) Across the street from the Staples Center and LA Convention Center is this corporate entertainment hub, which includes the 7100-seat **Microsoft Theater** (Map p82; ☑ 213-763-6020; www.microsofttheater.com; 777 Chick Hearn Ct). There's also a megaplex cinema, a dozen restaurants, ESPN's LA headquarters and a 54-story hotel tower shared by Marriott and the Ritz-Carlton. Parking costs $10 to $30.

Flower Market
MARKET

(Map p82; www.laflowerdistrict.com; Wall St; admission Mon-Fri $2, Sat $1; ◷ 8am-noon Mon & Wed, 6am-noon Tue & Thu, 8am-2pm Fri, 6am-2pm Sat; ℗) Cut flowers at cut-rate prices are the lure here, where a few dollars gets you armloads of Hawaiian ginger or sweet roses, a potted plant or elegant orchid. The market is busiest in the wee hours when florists stock up. Bring cash. It's located between 7th and 8th Sts.

🏃 Activities

Angels Flight
CABLE CAR

(Map p82; https://angelsflight.org; Ⓜ Red/Purple Lines to Pershing Sq) Downtown's twin funicular cars, Sinai and Olivet, resumed service to much fanfare in mid-2017. Built in 1901, the funicular originally shuttled commuters between Downtown and the long-gone Victorian abodes that graced Bunker Hill. The redevelopment of Bunker Hill into the corporate hub you see today forced the funicular's move half a block south to its current location in 1969.

↰ Tours

Los Angeles Times
TOURS

(Map p82; ☑ 213-237-5757; www.latimes.com; 202 W 1st St; ◷ tours 11am & 1:30pm last Tue & Thu of month) FREE News junkies can get their fix on a free one-hour tour of the Los Angeles Times building. Explore either the print works or the editorial offices, learn the paper's history and the publishing process; just don't ask about the dark and murky future of newspapers. Kids under eight can't come and reservations must be made weeks in advance.

GUIDED TOURS

Whatever your pleasure – dark or light, tragic or profane, sweet or salty – LA has a guided tour for you.

Los Angeles Conservancy (p94) Non-profit walking tours of architectural pearls in Downtown LA and beyond.

Architecture Tours LA (☏323-464-7868; www.architecturetoursla.com; tours from $75; ⊙tours 9:30am & 1:30pm) Neighborhood- and architect-themed bus tours for fans of bold, beautiful and unusual buildings.

Esotouric (☏213-915-8687; www.esotouric.com; tours $58) Bus tours that explore the city's hypnotic underbelly, from real-life crime stories to the seedy LA of Chandler and Bukowski.

TMZ Celebrity Tour (Map p106; ☏844-869-8687; www.tmz.com/tour; 6925 Hollywood Blvd; adult/child $54/44; ⊙tours departing Hard Rock Cafe Hollywood 12:15pm, 3pm & 5:30pm Thu-Tue, 12:15pm & 3pm Wed; Ⓜ Red Line to Hollywood/Highland) Irreverent celeb-culture bus tours of Hollywood, WeHo and Beverly Hills.

Dearly Departed (☏855-600-3323; www.dearlydepartedtours.com; tours $50-85) A bus tour of scandal and blood, because life and Hollywood can be dark and tragic.

Out & About Tours (p148) Closeted heart-throbs, underground bars and brave radicals are all celebrated on these straight-friendly walking tours of LGBT+ Hollywood, WeHo and Downtown.

Melting Pot Food Tours (☏424-247-9666; www.meltingpottours.com; adult/child from $59/45) Appetite-piquing walking tours of LA's Original Farmers Market, old Pasadena town and Latino-flavored East LA.

Perry's Legends Beach Bike Tour (☏310-939-0000; www.perryscafe.com; adult/senior & student/child under 13 $59/50/35; ⊙May-Sep) Hit the pedal for the lowdown on Muscle Beach mysteries, Jim Morrison's house and Skateboard Mamma on this easy coastal bike ride.

Metro Art Moves (www.metro.net/about/art/art-tours; ⊙10am 1st Sat & Sun of month) **FREE** Free guided tours of the art-gracing Union Station and Red Line metro stops.

🛏 Sleeping

Downtown's renaissance extends to its hotel stock, with a number of properties recently opened or under construction. Options range from hip, boutique-style chains to more generic business hotels.

★**Hotel Indigo** HOTEL $$$
(Map p82; ☏877-270-1392; www.ihg.com; 899 Francisco St, Downtown; d from $229; Ⓟ❄🛜🏊; Ⓜ Red/Purple Lines to 7th St/Metro Center) This freshly minted, 350-room property celebrates Downtown's colorful backstory: wagon-shaped lobby lights pay tribute to the Fiesta de Las Flores, blown-up paparazzi shots around the elevators nod to vaudeville and early movie days, while the restaurant's tunnel-like booths allude to speakeasies. Rooms are plush and svelte, with city-themed splashbacks and deco-inspired bathrooms that pay tribute to early film star Anna May Wong.

Ace Hotel HOTEL $$$
(Map p82; ☏213-623-3233; www.acehotel.com/losangeles; 929 S Broadway; lofts from $400; Ⓟ❄🛜🏊) The ever-hip, buzzy, 182-room Ace is big on quirky details: Haas Brothers murals in the lobby and restaurant, whimsically themed cocktails at the rooftop bar and retro-inspired rooms with boxer-style robes, blank music sheets and, in many cases, record players or guitars. Small rooms can feel tight, so consider opting for a medium. Valet parking is $36 a night.

The safari-themed rooftop bar comes with knockout city views and a small pool (transformed into a steamy Jacuzzi in the cooler months), while the small lobby store stocks many of the rooms' designer details, including those coveted Pendleton blankets.

JW Marriott LA Live HOTEL $$$
(Map p82; ☏213-765-8600; www.marriott.com; 900 W Olympic Blvd, Downtown; r from $279; Ⓟ❄🛜🏊) This 878-room behemoth flanks

the massive LA Live entertainment complex. Chef Ben Ford (son of Harrison) heads the Californian restaurant in the lofty, light-filled lobby, while the 4th floor is home to a spacious, alfresco pool deck. Rooms are fresh, plush and contemporary, with abstract art prints, modernist lounge chairs and crisp, white comforters on blissful beds. Generously sized showers. Parking is $45 per night.

Millennium Biltmore Hotel
HOTEL $$$

(Map p82; ☑ 213-624-1011; www.thebiltmore.com; 506 S Grand Ave; r from $269; P @ 🛜 🛋) Graced with chandeliers, Renaissance-inspired ceilings and legend (the Academy Awards were founded in the Crystal Ballroom in 1927), this grand dame will leave you feeling like Julia Roberts in *Pretty Woman*. The indoor pool is an art deco beauty, though the modestly sized, dated rooms are less inspiring. That said, the beds are wonderful and we love the framed stills of movies shot on site. Parking is $45 per night.

Figueroa Hotel
BOUTIQUE HOTEL $$$

(Map p82; ☑ 877-724-1973, 213-627-8971; http://hotelfigueroa.com; 939 S Figueroa St; r from $309; P ✳ 🛜 🛋; Ⓜ Red/Purple Lines to 7th St/Metro Center) What was originally a 1920s hostel for women is now one of Downtown's coolest slumber pads, recently revamped and adorned with specially commissioned artworks from LA-based artists such as Sarah Awad. Rooms offer sharp, idiosyncratic style, with hard-wood floorboards, bespoke wallpaper, Spanish-style decorative tiles and vintage-inspired bathrooms. Sip craft cocktails by the foliage-fringed mosaic pool.

There are Basque-inspired dishes at the on-site restaurant. Parking costs $45 per night.

✖ Eating

The DTLA dining scene is booming and diverse, with an ever-expanding cache of on-trend restaurants and cafes, plus no-fuss cheapies. Hubs include Grand Central Market for fresh, multiculti bites, Little Tokyo for quality ramen and sashimi, Chinatown for Chinese and both the Arts District and the Downtown core for hot-spot bistros and produce-driven menus. Across the LA River, humble Boyle Heights is a top choice for authentic, low-frills Mexican street food.

★ Mariscos 4 Vientos
MEXICAN $

(☑ 323-266-4045; www.facebook.com/Mariscos4Vientos; 3000 E Olympic Blvd; dishes $2.25-14; ⊙ 9am-5:30pm Mon-Thu, to 6pm Fri-Sun) You'll find the greatest shrimp taco of your life at no-frills Mariscos 4 Vientos. Order from the truck (if you're in a hurry) or grab a table inside the bustling dining room. Either way, surrender to corn tortillas folded and stuffed with fresh shrimp, then fried and smothered in *pico de gallo* (fresh salsa).

★ Guisados
TACOS $

(☑ 323-264-7201; www.guisados.co; 2100 E Cesar Chavez Ave, Boyle Heights; tacos from $2.75; ⊙ 10:30am-8pm Mon-Thu, to 9pm Fri, 9am-9pm Sat, 9am-5pm Sun; Ⓜ Gold Line to Mariachi Plaza) Guisados' citywide fame is founded on its *tacos de guisados;* warm, thick, nixtamal tortillas made to order and topped with sultry, smoky, slow-cooked stews. Do yourself a favor and order the sampler plate ($7.25), a democratic mix of six mini tacos. The *chiles torreados* (blistered, charred chili) taco is a must for serious spice-lovers.

The Springs
VEGAN $

(☑ 213-223-6226; www.thespringsla.com; 608 Mateo St; lunch $11-15; ⊙ 7am-8pm Mon-Fri, 9am-6pm Sat & Sun; P 🛜 ⏩) Plant-based fare gets sexy at The Springs, an airy warehouse cafe and lounge splashed with bar seating, common tables and design-literate lounges. Standouts on the short, artful, market-driven menu include a moreish Phil wrap (wholewheat tortilla packed with yuba, roasted shiitake, caramelized onion and cashew fondue). Nutrient-packed drinks include cold-pressed juices, probiotic sangria and health shots (try the spicy turmeric Wellness Shot).

Lemonade
CALIFORNIAN $

(Map p82; ☑ 213-488-0299; www.lemonadela.com; 505 S Flower St; meals $8-13; ⊙ 11am-3pm Mon-Fri; 🛜 ⏩; Ⓜ Red/Purple Line to 7th St/Metro Center) In the basement food hall of City National Plaza, trendy Lemonade offers the Cafeteria 2.0 experience – counter slop ditched for super-fresh gourmet grub. There are six food stations – Market Place, Leafy Greens, Land and Sea, Sandwiches, Hot Dishes and Dessert – serving up the likes of watermelon radish and seared ahi tuna salad, and Thai-inspired pineapple chicken with crisp beans and toasted coconut.

Knead & Co Pasta Bar + Market
ITALIAN $

(Map p82; ☑ 213-223-7592; http://kneadpasta.com; Grand Central Market, 317 S Broadway, Downtown; mains $9-16; ⊙ 11am-8pm Mon-Wed, to 9pm Thu & Fri, 9am-9pm Sat, 9am-8pm Sun; Ⓜ Red/Purple Lines to Pershing Sq) Knead is one of our favorite stalls at Grand Central

Market, its just-made pasta singing in dishes such as sultry butternut squash ravioli with chili, sage and amaretti cookies, or garlicky *malfadine* (ribbon-shaped pasta) with olive oil and sharp Grana Padano cheese. Italo-American comfort options include chicken and meatball parm sandwiches and a fontina-pimped mac-n-cheese.

BS Taqueria
MEXICAN $

(Map p82; ☑ 213-622-3744; http://bstaqueria.com; 514 W 7th St, Downtown; lunch mains $12-15, dinner mains $12-24; ☺ 11:30am-2:30pm & 5:30-11pm Mon-Fri, 5:30-11pm Sat & Sun; Ⓜ Red/Purple Lines to 7th St/Metro Center) Mexican street food goes freestyle at this colorful, counter-service eatery. Here, *al pastor* tacos might ditch pork for cauliflower and *ceviche tostadas* might pair lime curd basa with pomegranate. Chef Ray Garcia's creative flair shines brightest in the dinner menu, with cult-status dishes such as a phenomenal clams and lardo taco and a *tres leches* cake worth every calorie.

Madcapra
MIDDLE EASTERN $

(Map p82; ☑ 213-357-2412; www.madcapra.com; Grand Central Market, 317 S Broadway, Downtown; salads & sandwiches $11-13; ☺ 11am-5pm Sun-Wed, to 9pm Thu-Sat; Ⓜ Red/Purple Lines to Pershing Sq) This hectic stall peddles flawless falafel sandwiches. The flatbread is rolled and grilled fresh, then filled with pillowy falafel with just the right amount of crunch. Choose from four color-coded sandwiches (the 'red' is the most popular), all of which can also be made as a salad. Pair with an iced cardamon coffee or *shandria* (ginger lemonade, beer and fruit).

Eggslut
DINER $

(Map p82; www.eggslut.com; Grand Central Market, 317 S Broadway; dishes $6-9; ☺ 8am-4pm) A classic breakfast counter has been brought back to life by local foodie punks who, among other things, stuff house-made turkey sausage, eggs and mustard aioli in brioche, and make a dish known only as 'the slut': a coddled egg nestled on top of potato puree poached in a glass jar and served with sliced baguette. To avoid the queues, head in around 9am Monday to Wednesday.

Marugame Monzo
JAPANESE $

(Map p82; www.facebook.com/marugamemonzo; 329 E 1st St; mains $7-16; ☺ 11:30am-2:30pm & 5-10pm Mon-Fri, 11:30am-10pm Sat & Sun) If you care to step up from ramen to udon, slip into this special udon emporium, where the

TEN STANDOUT LA BITES

→ The decadent Bic Mec double cheeseburger at **Petit Trois** (p113).

→ Crisp, golden, off-the-menu *farinata* (Italian chickpea pancake) at **Officine Brera** (p98).

→ Flawless deep-fried shrimp tacos at **Mariscos 4 Vientos** (p96).

→ Vietnamese *pot au feu* with short ribs, veggies and bone marrow at **Cassia** (p181).

→ Soul-coaxing brisket sandwich at **HomeState** (p129).

→ Squid-ink tagliatelle with piquillo pepper, tomato ragu, Thai basil and breadcrumbs at **MB Post** (p196).

→ Soft, warm, made-from-scratch red falafel sandwich at **Madcapra**.

→ Vegan artichoke 'oysters' at **Crossroads** (p143).

→ Almond brittle with salted ganache ice cream at **Salt & Straw** (p188).

→ Burnt brioche with house-made ricotta and jam at **Sqirl** (p120).

noodles are made fresh in the open kitchen. Appetizers include tempura-fried chicken skin and raw, sliced scallops dolloped with flying-fish roe, but the perfectly chewy udon is what draws the raves.

Cole's
SANDWICHES $

(Map p82; ☑ 213-622-4090; http://213hospitality. com/project/coles; 118 E 6th St; sandwiches $10-13.50; ☺ 11am-midnight Sun-Wed, to 2am Thu-Sat; ☏) An atmospheric old basement tavern with vintage vinyl booths, original glass lighting and historic photos, Cole's is known for originating the French Dip sandwich way back in 1908, when those things cost a nickel. You know the drill – French bread piled with sliced lamb, beef, turkey, pork or pastrami, dipped once or twice in *au jus*.

Daikokuya
JAPANESE $

(Map p82; ☑ 213-626-1680; www.daikoku-ten.com/ locations/littletokyo/; 327 E 1st St; dishes $8.50-22; ☺ 11am-midnight Mon-Thu, to 1am Fri & Sat, to 11pm Sun) If you're partial to Japanese noodles, follow your nose to this funky Little Tokyo diner. You can smell the scallions and bubbling broth from the sidewalk, where many line up to grab a tan vinyl booth or red bar stool (write your name on the clipboard list and wait to be called). The place also serves rice bowls, but ramen is king. Cash only.

★ Manuela
MODERN AMERICAN $$

(Map p82; ☎323-849-0480; www.manuela-la.com; 907 E 3rd St; ☺5:30-10pm Sun-Thu, to 11pm Fri & Sat, also 11:30am-3:30pm Wed-Fri & 10am-4pm Sat & Sun; ☜) Young Texan chef Wes Whitsell heads this deserving it-kid inside the Hauser & Wirth arts complex. The woody warmth of the loft-like space is echoed in the oft-tweaked menu, a beautiful fusion of local ingredients and smokey southern accents. Pique the appetite with a house-pickled appetizer then lose yourself in deceptively simple soul-stirrers like sultry pork ragù over flawless polenta.

★ Maccheroni Republic
ITALIAN $$

(Map p82; ☎213-346-9725; www.maccheronirepublic.com; 332 S Broadway; mains $11-18; ☺11:30am-2:30pm & 5:30-10pm Mon-Thu, 11:30am-2:30pm & 5:30-10:30pm Fri, 11:30am-10:30pm Sat, 11:30am-9pm Sun) Tucked away on a still-ungentrified corner is this gem with a leafy heated patio and tremendous Italian slow-cooked food. Don't miss the *polpettine di gamberi* (flattened ground shrimp cakes fried in olive oil), and its range of delicious housemade pastas. Perfectly al dente, the pasta is made using organic semolina flour and served with gorgeous crusty bread to mop up the sauce.

Bottega Louie
ITALIAN $$

(Map p82; ☎213-802-1470; www.bottegalouie.com; 700 S Grand Ave, Downtown; pizzas $22, dishes $12-36; ☺6:30am-11pm Mon-Thu, to midnight Fri, 8am-midnight Sat, 8am-11pm Sun; ☜; Ⓜ Red/Purple Lines to 7th St/Metro Center) Divided into a patisserie, bar and dining room, this sprawling, loft-like space recalls the grand cafes of northern Italy: dapper barkeeps pour Aperol spritzers, waiters carry trays high and confidently, and a democratic mix of couples, suits and tourists tuck into decent bistro fare (go for the giant, Neapolitan-style pizzas). The macarons here are famous, though, frankly, we've had better elsewhere.

Woodspoon
BRAZILIAN $$

(Map p82; ☎213-629-1765; www.woodspoonla.com; 107 W 9th St; mains $15-29; ☺11am-3pm & 5-10pm Tue-Sat; ☜) We love it all: the handpicked china, the cracked terrazzo floor, and the fact that the affable Brazilian owner-operator is still chefing it up. Her pork ribs fall off the bone in a bath of grits and gravy, while her takes on steak frites, chicken pot pie and *moqueca* (seafood stew) have a way of melting away the day's troubles.

Bäco Mercat
FUSION $$

(Map p82; ☎213-687-8808; www.bacomercat.com; 408 S Main St; lunch $13-17, dinner mains $16-38; ☺11:30am-2:30pm & 5:30-11pm Mon-Thu, 11:30am-3pm & 5:30pm-midnight Fri & Sat, 11:30am-3pm & 5-10pm Sun) A low-key, industrial hangout with chipped steel bench, butcher's paper place mats and old-school classroom chairs, Bäco Mercat is known for its warm flatbread sandwiches, filled with combos such as panko-crumbed shrimp, house-made Sriracha sauce and coleslaw. The fusion-focused dinner menu might see yellowtail collar coupled with yuzu kosho or hand-torn pasta channel the Middle Eastern with kale, soujouk, tomato, pine nuts and raisins.

Nickel Diner
DINER $$

(Map p82; ☎213-623-8301; www.nickeldiner.com; 524 S Main St; mains $8-15; ☺8am-3:30pm Tue-Sun, 6-10pm Tue-Sat) Named for the intersection of 5th and Main, termed 'the Nickel' by nearby Skid Row residents who used to come to this corner for their daily meds, this kitschy red-vinyl joint re-imagines American diner fare. Avocados are stuffed with quinoa salad, burgers are piled with poblano chilies, and don't sleep on the maple-glazed bacon donut.

★ Officine Brera
ITALIAN $$$

(☎213-553-8006; http://officinebrera.com; 1331 E 6th St; lunch mains $24-34, dinner mains $26-54; ☺11:30am-2:30pm & 5:30-10pm Mon-Thu, 11:30am-2:30pm & 5:30-11pm Fri, 5-11pm Sat, 4:30-9:30pm Sun; Ⓟ) Hidden down a seemingly barren street is this stylish northern Italian restaurant, an expansive industrial space with rustic wooden accents. Stacked logs fuel beautiful wood-fired dishes such as chestnut-egg pasta with wood-braised goose sugo and pecorino cheese, or roasted pork shank with aromatic herbs, polenta and kale. The risottos are heavenly as is the must-try, off-the-menu specialty: *farinata*, a flawless Genoese crepe.

The restaurant's obsession with fresh produce is evident in the menu, tweaked twice daily according to what's available that day.

★ Otium
MODERN AMERICAN $$$

(Map p82; ☎213-935-8500; http://otiumla.com; 222 S Hope St, Downtown; dishes $15-45; ☺11:30am-2:30pm & 5:30-10pm Tue-Thu, 11:30am-2:30pm & 5:30-11pm Fri, 11am-2:30pm & 5:30-11pm Sat, 11am-2:30pm & 5:30-10pm Sun; ☜) In a modernist pavilion beside the Broad is this fun, of-the-moment hot spot helmed by chef Timothy Hollingsworth. Prime ingredients conspire in unexpected ways, from the crunch of wild rice and amaranth in an eye-candy salad of avocado, beets and pomegranate, to a twist of lime and sake in flawlessly al dente whole-wheat bucatini with Dungeness crab.

★ **Broken Spanish** MEXICAN $$$
(Map p82; ☑ 213-749-1460; http://brokenspanish. com; 1050 S Flower St; mains $22-49; ☉ 5:30-10pm Sun-Thu, to 11pm Fri & Sat; ☎) Despite retro design nods such as concrete blocks, macrame plant hangers and terracotta lampshades, Ray Garcia's sleek Downtown eatery is all about confident, contemporary Mexican cooking. From the *chochoyoes* (masa dumplings with green garlic and pasilla pepper) to a rich, intense dish of mushrooms with black garlic, flavors are clean and intriguing, and the presentation polished. Beautiful wines, cocktails and over 100 mezcals seal the deal.

★ **Q Sushi** SUSHI $$$
(Map p82; ☑ 213-225-6285; www.qsushila. com; 521 W 7th St; per person lunch/dinner from $75/165; ☉ noon-1:30pm Tue-Fri, 6-9pm Tue-Sat; ☑) Sushi and sashimi hit dizzying highs at this *omakase* heavyweight, where bite-sized bliss comes from the likes of tender octopus braised in sake and brown sugar, or blow-torched toro made with rice fermented for a month. Dinner consists of 20 courses (lunch about half that), all created by Japanese sushi savant Hiro Naruke, who lost his business in the post-tsunami aftermath. Reserve ahead.

★ **Bestia** ITALIAN $$$
(☑ 213-514-5724; www.bestiala.com; 2121 7th Pl; pizzas $16-19, pasta $19-29, mains $28-120; ☉ 5-11pm Sun-Thu, to midnight Fri & Sat; ☑) Years on, this loud, buzzing, industrial dining space remains the most sought-after reservation in town (book at least a week ahead). The draw remains its clever, produce-driven take on Italian flavors, from charred pizzas topped with housemade '*nduja* (a spicy Calabrian paste), to a sultry stinging-nettle raviolo with egg, mixed mushrooms, hazelnut and ricotta. The wine list celebrates the boutique and obscure.

★ **Sushi Gen** JAPANESE $$$
(Map p82; ☑ 213-617-0552; www.sushigen.org; 422 E 2nd St; sushi $11-23; ☉ 11:15am-2pm & 5:30-9:45pm Tue-Fri, 5-9:45pm Sat; ☑; ⓜ Gold Line to Little Tokyo/Arts District) Come early to grab a table at this classic sushi spot, where bantering Japanese chefs carve thick slabs of melt-in-your-mouth salmon, buttery *toro* (tuna belly), Japanese snapper and more. At lunch, perch yourself at the sushi counter for à la carte options, or queue for a table in the dining room, where the sashimi lunch special ($17) is a steal. You'll find it in Honda Plaza.

71 Above MODERN AMERICAN $$$
(Map p82; ☑ 213-712-2683; www.71above.com; 633 W 5th St; 2-course set lunch $35, 3-course set dinner $70; ☉ 11:30am-11pm Mon-Thu, to midnight Fri, 5pm-midnight Sat, 5-10pm Sun; ☑; ⓜ Red/Purple Lines to Pershing Sq) Reserve ahead for a window table at fine-dining 71 Above, perched 950ft above Downtown streets. While it's difficult to upstage the views, chef Vartan Abgaryan offers strong competition with his creative, globally influenced flavors. Scan the skyline over dishes such as beets with chocolate wheat berries and blood orange, or lobster with Vadouvan curry, coconut, almond and barrel-aged fish sauce.

☕ Drinking & Nightlife

Whether you're craving G&Ts in a steampunk basement, mai tais in a secret tiki lounge or dirt-cheap beers in a gay Latino dive, this corner of town has your back. Bars are scattered across the Downtown area, with many serving up live music at least a few nights a week.

★ **Everson Royce Bar** COCKTAIL BAR
(☑ 213-335-6166; www.erbla.com; 1936 E 7th St; ☉ 5pm-2am) Don't be fooled by the unceremonious grey exterior. Behind that wall lies a hopping Arts District hangout, with a buzzy, bulb-strung outdoor patio. The barkeeps here are some of the city's best, using craft liquor to concoct drinks such as the prickly-pear Mateo Street Margarita. Bar bites are equally scrumptious, including the roasted pork-belly steamed buns.

★ **Edison** COCKTAIL BAR
(Map p82; ☑ 213-613-0000; www.edisondowntown. com; 108 W 2nd St; ☉ 5pm-2am Wed-Fri, from 7pm Sat; ⓜ Red/Purple Lines to Civic Center/Grand Park) Accessed through easy-to-miss Harlem Pl alleyway, this extraordinary basement lounge sits in a century-old power plant. It's like a dimly lit, steampunk wonderland, punctuated with vintage generators, handsome leather lounges and secret nooks. Look

for celebrity signatures in the original coal furnace and stick around for the live tunes (anything from jazz to folk), burlesque or aerialist performances.

★ Mikkeller DTLA
BEER HALL

(Map p82; ☑213-596-9005; www.mikkellerbar. com/la; 330 W Olympic Blvd, Downtown; ☺bar 5pm-midnight Sun-Wed, to 2am Thu-Sat, cafe 8am-5pm daily) This cool, influential Copenhagen import puts a contemporary spin on the old beer hall. Fitted out with booths, communal bar tables and cartoon artwork by Philly-based artist Keith Shore, the industrial loft peddles craft beers from some of the world's most interesting microbreweries. Look for LA brewers such as Eagle Rock and Mumford, as well as Mikkeller's own renowned suds.

★ EightyTwo
BAR

(Map p82; ☑213-626-8200; http://eightytwo. la; 707 E 4th Pl; ☺6pm-2am Tue-Thu, from 5pm Fri, from 2pm Sat & Sun) Cocktails, pinball machines and arcade games makes for oh-so-retro good times at this graffiti-soaked warehouse bar. Named for 1982 (the height of the 'Arcade Age'), its 40-plus consoles include classics Donkey Kong, Space Invaders and Ms Pac-Man (with drink coasters for grown-up '80s kids). Nightly DJs and rotating food trucks fuel the crowds. Head in before 9pm to avoid long waits, especially later in the week. The venue also hosts regular tournaments; check the website for upcoming events.

★ Upstairs at the Ace Hotel
BAR

(Map p82; www.acehotel.com/losangeles; 929 S Broadway, Downtown; ☺11am-2am) What's not to love about a rooftop bar with knockout Downtown views, powerful cocktails and a luxe, safari-inspired fit out? Perched on the 14th floor of the Ace Hotel, this chilled, sophisticated space has on-point DJs and specially commissioned artworks that include an installation made using Skid Row blankets.

★ Varnish
BAR

(Map p82; ☑213-817-5321; http://213hospitality.com/the-varnish; 118 E 6th St; ☺7pm-2am; Ⓜ Red/Purple Lines to Pershing Sq) Tucked into the back of Cole's (p97) is this cubby-hole-sized speakeasy, where good live jazz burns Sunday through Tuesday.

★ Villains Tavern
BAR

(Map p82; ☑213-613-0766; www.villainstavern.com; 1356 Palmetto St; ☺5:30pm-2am Tue-Sat) Behind Villains Tavern is restaurateur and interior designer Dana Hollister, who turned a run-down Arts District deli into this dark-wood and iron den of bluesy cool. There's a salvaged bar top, church-pew seating, high ceilings dangling with vintage chandeliers and a 1600-sq-ft open-air patio where live folk, bluegrass and outlaw country rocks the stage.

Angel City Brewery
MICROBREWERY

(Map p82; ☑213-622-1261; www.angelcitybrewery. com; 216 S Alameda St; ☺4pm-1am Mon-Thu, to 2am Fri, noon-2am Sat, noon-1am Sun) Where suspension cables were once manufactured, craft brews are now made and poured. Located on the edge of the Arts District, it's a popular spot to knock back an India pale ale or chai-spiced Imperial stout, listen to some tunes and chow down some food-truck tacos.

Cognoscenti Coffee
COFFEE

(Map p82; ☑213-263-3349; www.popupcoffee. com; 868 S Olive St, Downtown; ☺7am-7pm; 🛜) Soaked in natural light, this airy mix of glass, marble and concrete brews fantastic coffee, including espresso, drip and cold brew. Beans are seasonal and from a rotating cast of microroasteries. You'll find decent baked goods, as well as attitude-free baristas, free wi-fi and an easy, laid-back vibe.

Arts District Brewing Co
MICROBREWERY

(Map p82; ☑213-519-5887; http://213hospitality. com/project/artsdistrictbrewing; 828 Traction Ave; ☺3pm-midnight Mon-Thu, to 2am Fri, noon-2am Sat, noon-midnight Sun; 🛜) A loud, cavernous, industrial Arts District hot spot, with huge brewing vats behind the bar, vintage Skee-Ball tables and a Charles Bukowski quote glowing in blue neon. Slurp on ales, porters, IPAs, stouts and sours, brewed on-site or from guest brewers such as LA's Eagle Rock and Colorado's Avery. Sud-soaking grub includes a lip-smacking turkey burger.

Verve
CAFE

(Map p82; ☑213-455-5991; www.vervecoffee.com; 833 S Spring St, Downtown; ☺7am-7pm Mon-Fri, to 8pm Sat & Sun; 🛜) Santa Cruz microroastery Verve turns ethically sourced beans into beautiful cups of coffee at its loft-like DTLA branch, an industrial combo of concrete walls and columns, sculptural lighting and timber tabletops. Power sockets, reliable wi-fi and sweet staff make it a popular workspace for local media, fashion and artistic types. There's an impressive range of excellent (albeit pricey) cold-pressed juices.

Wolf & Crane
BAR

(Map p82; 213-935-8249; www.wolfandcranebar.com; 366 E 2nd St; ⊙5pm-2am Mon-Fri, from 4pm Sat & Sun; ; Gold Line to Little Tokyo/Arts District) A fun Little Tokyo bar with waxed concrete floors, a blonde-wood slab bar, common tables and built-in bench seating. Expect ball games on the flat screens, Japanese art and a clued-up mix of Californian craft beers, small-batch spirits and Japanese whiskeys. Our personal favorite is the house special, Wolf & Crane: a shot of Johnnie Red and a Sapporo.

Crane's Bar
BAR

(Map p82; 213-239-0047; www.facebook.com/Cranes-Bar-Downtown-412971755514506; 810 S Spring St; ⊙5pm-2am Mon-Thu, from 4pm Fri, from 2pm Sat & Sun) In a former bank vault, Crane's is one of our favorite Downtown dives, complete with jukebox, butcher-block bar (carved from a 130-year-old Douglas fir) and red vinyl booths.

Far Bar
BAR

(Map p82; 213-617-9990; www.farbarla.com; 347 E 1st St; ⊙11am-2am Mon-Fri, from 10am Sat & Sun; Gold Line to Little Tokyo/Arts District) A vintage bar with old-school funk, groovy tunes on the stereo, sports on strobing flat screens and taps pouring suds from Cali craft brewers such as Cismontane, Port Brewing and 21st Amendment. Fusion bites reflect the bar's Little Tokyo address, from garlic-spiked wasabi fries to sushi and sake-braised pork tacos.

Pattern Bar
BAR

(Map p82; 213-627-7774; www.patternbar.com; 100 W 9th St; ⊙noon-10pm Sun-Wed, to midnight Thu, to 2am Fri & Sat;) A retro-spirited watering hole with twirling ceiling fans, parlor floors and cocktails celebrating its Fashion District address. Chat hemlines and fabrics over tequila-fueled Chanels or gin-pimped McQueens, or butch it up with craft brews from as far afield as Iceland. Bites include ceviche, cheese, charcuterie, panini and gourmet salads.

La Cita
CLUB

(Map p82; 213-687-7111; www.lacitabar.com; 336 S Hill St; ⊙11am-2am Mon-Fri, from 10am Sat & Sun; Red/Purple Lines to Pershing Sq) Pulling everyone from hipsters to urban *vaqueros* and nostalgic Latino aunties, this red-vinyl Mexican dive bar just keeps on kicking, despite Downtown's ongoing gentrification. DJs whip the crowd into a frenzy with hip-hop, reggae, ska and post-punk, while Sundays feature veteran band Doble Poder, who keep the floor heaving with old-school Latin dance tunes between 2pm and 9pm.

Club Mayan
CLUB

(Map p82; www.clubmayan.com; 1038 S Hill St, Downtown; cover $10-25; ⊙9pm-2:30am Fri & Sat, varies Sun-Thu) Kick up your heels during Saturday's Tropical Nights when a salsa band turns the heat up against the faux Mayan-temple backdrop. Don't know how? Come early for lessons, but there is a dress code. On Fridays it's mainly house and hip-hop, and the club also hosts its share of wrestling events, indie bands and DJs with a following.

Association
BAR

(Map p82; 866-687-4499; www.theassociation-la.com; 110 E 6th St; ⊙9pm-2am Tue-Sun; Red/Purple Lines to Pershing Sq) This dark basement lounge flashes old-school glamour with leather bar stools and lounges tucked into intimate coves. But the bar is the thing, armed with dozens of whiskeys, ryes, rums and tequilas, poured straight or mingling in potent drinks such as the sexy Empire (dark rum, sweet vermouth, spiced bitters and orange zest).

Las Perlas
BAR

(Map p82; http://213hospitality.com/lasperlas; 107 E 6th St; ⊙5pm-2am Mon-Fri, from 1pm Sat & Sun; Red/Purple Lines to Pershing Sq) With an old Mexico whimsy, more than 400 agave spirits and friendly barkeeps who mix ingredients such as egg whites, blackberries and port syrup into new-school takes on the classic margarita, there's a reason hipsters flock to Downtown's finest mezcal bar. True connoisseurs select a highland variety and sip it neat.

☆ Entertainment

Downtown is home to some of LA's major entertainment venues, serving up world-class music, theater and sports. You'll also find independent theater stages and cinema.

★ Blue Whale
JAZZ

(Map p82; 213-620-0908; www.bluewhalemusic.com; 123 Onizuka St, Suite 301; cover $5-20; ⊙8pm-2am, closed 1st Sun of month; Gold Line to Little Tokyo/Arts District) An intimate, concrete-floored space on the top floor of Weller Court in Little Tokyo, Blue Whale serves top-notch jazz nightly from 9pm. The crowd is eclectic, the beers craft and the bar bites decent. Acts span emerging and edgy to established, and the acoustics are excellent. Note: bring cash for the cover charge.

★ Mark Taper Forum
THEATER

(Map p82; ☑ 213-628-2772; www.centertheatre group.org; 135 N Grand Ave) Part of the Music Center, the Mark Taper is one of the three venues used by the Center Theatre Group, SoCal's leading resident ensemble and producer of Tony-, Pulitzer- and Emmy-winning plays. It's an intimate space with only 15 rows of seats arranged around a thrust stage, so you can see every sweat pearl on the actors' faces.

★ Los Angeles Philharmonic
CLASSICAL MUSIC

(Map p82; ☑ 323-850-2000; www.laphil.org; 111 S Grand Ave) The world-class LA Phil performs classics and cutting-edge works at the Walt Disney Concert Hall (p85), under the baton of Venezuelan phenom Gustavo Dudamel.

Ahmanson Theatre
THEATER

(Map p82; ☑ 213-628-2772; www.centertheatre group.org; 135 N Grand Ave) This grand space is a Center Theatre Group venue in the Music Center, used primarily for big-time musicals on their way to or from Broadway.

CLIFTON'S MAGICAL MYSTERY LAIR

Opened in 1935 and back after a $10-million renovation, multilevel, mixed-crowd **Clifton's Republic** (Map p82; ☑ 213-627-1673; www.cliftonsla.com; 648 S Broadway; ⊙ 11am-midnight Tue-Thu, to 2am Fri, 10am-2:30am Sat, 10am-midnight Sun; 🗲; Ⓜ Red/Purple Lines to Pershing Sq) defies description. You can chow retro-cafeteria classics (meals around $15) by a forest waterfall, order drinks from a Gothic church altar, watch burlesque performers shimmy in the shadow of a 40ft faux redwood, or slip through a glass-paneled door to a luxe tiki paradise where DJs spin in a repurposed speedboat.

Located on the 4th floor, the tiki bar is our favorite of Clifton's booty of bars, its look a Polynesia-Manhattan mash-up and its smashing tropical libations including an addictive Painkiller (concocted with house-made coconut cream). Head up by 9:30pm to avoid the queues, especially on weekends.

Staples Center
STADIUM

(Map p82; ☑ 213-742-7100; www.staplescenter. com; 1111 S Figueroa St) South Park got its first jolt in 1999 with the opening of this saucer-shaped sports and entertainment arena. It's home court for the Los Angeles Lakers, Clippers and Sparks basketball teams, and home ice for the LA Kings. The stadium also hosts pop and rock concerts. Parking costs $10 to $30, depending on the event.

Downtown Independent
CINEMA

(Map p82; www.downtownindependent.com; 251 S Main St; Ⓜ Red/Purple Lines to Pershing Sq) Cinephiles head here for independent films, movie-related Q&As and film festivals showcasing anything from Asian-Pacific cinema to arty dirty shorts. Craft beers and wines available on site.

United Artists Theatre
LIVE MUSIC, DANCE

(Map p82; ☑ 213-623-3233; www.acehotel.com/ losangeles/theatre; 929 S Broadway, Downtown) A historic gem of a theater restored by the Ace Hotel, which curates the calendar. Offerings are eclectic, ranging from music performances to dance acts and film screenings. Recent events include the West Coast premiere of Tyler Hubby's documentary film *Tony Conrad: Completely in the Present,* with a post-screening conversation moderated by Henry Rollins. Check the website for what's on.

Orpheum Theatre
LIVE PERFORMANCE

(Map p82; ☑ 877-677-4386; www.laorpheum.com; 842 S Broadway) Currently the most active of Broadway's historic theaters, the Orpheum hosts everything from touring musicals and rock bands to comedy shows and galas. Check the website for upcoming events.

Redcat
THEATER

(Map p82; ☑ 213-237-2800; www.redcat.org; 631 W 2nd St) Downtown's most avant-garde performance laboratory where theater, dance, music, poetry and film merge into impressive exhibitions presented in its own theater and gallery within the Walt Disney Concert Hall (p85) complex. The curious name is an acronym for Roy and Edna Disney/Cal Arts Theater. Admission to the gallery (noon to 6pm Tuesday to Sunday) is free. Theater ticket prices vary.

East West Players
THEATER

(Map p82; ☑ 213-625-7000; www.eastwestplayers. org; 120 N Judge John Aiso St) Founded in 1965, this pioneering Asian-American ensemble seeks to build a bridge between Eastern and

FREE SOUNDS OF SUMMER

Summer in LA means free concert series across the city, most of which take place weekly. Toast to long days and soul-lifting tunes at the following standouts.

Twilight Concert Series (Map p176; www.santamonicapier.org/twilight; ⊘ 7-10pm Thu Jul-early Sep) FREE Some of the biggest crowds rock up to Santa Monica Pier for a mix of indie pop, rock, reggae, Latin, soul, classical and more, every Thursday from early July to early September.

Saturdays Off the 405 (p153) From May to September, the Getty Center courtyard fills with evening crowds for a delicious collision of art, brilliant live acts and beat-pumping DJ sets.

KCRW Summer Nights (http://summernights.kcrw.com; ⊘ Jun-Aug) A popular, weekly concert series popping up at different locations across the city from June to August. DJs, live bands, food trucks, craft beer and art workshops.

Jazz at LACMA (Map p138; www.lacma.org; 5905 Wilshire Blvd, Mid-City; ⊘ 6pm Fri) FREE A hugely popular Friday-night series at one of LA's finest art museums, with top-tier jazz acts and open galleries. Runs from April to November.

Grand Performances (p88) Serves up local and international music acts on Downtown's California Plaza on Friday and Saturday nights from June to September. Expect everything from world music and hip-hop to theater and other cultural events.

Pershing Square (p89) This Downtown square hosts a busy program of cultural events from early July to mid-August. This includes its Saturday-night concert series, featuring anything from Brit dance acts to '80s rock icons.

Western theatrical styles. Its repertoire of Broadway to modern classics takes a backseat to acclaimed premieres by local playwrights. Alumni have gone on to win Tony, Emmy and Academy awards.

Los Angeles Theatre Center THEATER
(Map p82; ☎ 213-489-0994; www.thelatc.org; 514 S Spring St; Ⓜ Red/Purple Lines to Pershing Sq) Built in 1915, the Old Pacific Stock Exchange building is home to the commendable Latino Theater Company. Expect excellent stage shows exploring culturally diverse material and often showcasing emerging playwrights.

LA Lakers BASKETBALL
(Map p82; ☎ 888-929-7849; www.nba.com/lakers; tickets from $30) One of two NBA basketball teams in Los Angeles beside, based at Downtown's Staples Center.

LA Clippers BASKETBALL
(Map p82; ☎ 213-204-2900; www.nba.com/clippers; tickets from $20) The other NBA basketball team in Los Angeles beside the Lakers, the Clippersalso play their home games at the Staples Center.

🔒 Shopping

For cool boutiques selling fashion and design, hit the Arts District. Little Tokyo also offers a scattering of idiosyncratic stores. In the Downtown core, you'll find a handful of fashionable, higher-end boutiques around 9th and Broadway, and one of LA's best bookstores at 5th and Spring. Both the Broad (p90) and Japanese American National Museum (p88) have great gift shops, while the Fashion District lures with its monthly sample sales.

★ Raggedy Threads VINTAGE
(Map p82; ☎ 213-620-1188; www.raggedythreads. com; 330 E 2nd St; ⊘ noon-8pm Mon-Sat, to 6pm Sun; Ⓜ Gold Line to Little Tokyo/Arts District) A tremendous vintage Americana store just off the main Little Tokyo strip. There's plenty of beautifully ragged denim, with a notable collection of pre-1950s workwear from the US, Japan and France. You'll also find a good number of Victorian dresses, soft T-shirts and a wonderful turquoise collection at decent prices.

★ Last Bookstore in Los Angeles BOOKS
(Map p82; ☎ 213-488-0599; www.lastbookstorela. com; 453 S Spring St; ⊘ 10am-10pm Mon-Thu, to 11pm Fri & Sat, to 9pm Sun) What started as a one-man operation out of a Main St storefront is now California's largest new-and-used bookstore, spanning two levels of an old bank building. Eye up the cabinets of

LOCAL KNOWLEDGE

LA FASHION DISTRICT DEMYSTIFIED

Bargain hunters love the frantic, 100-block warren of fashion in southwestern Downtown that is the Fashion District. Deals can be amazing, but first-timers are often bewildered by the district's size and immense selection. For orientation, check out www.fashiondistrict.org.

Basically, the area is subdivided into several distinct retail areas, with womens wear and accessories constituting the bulk of the offerings:

Women Santee St between 9th St and Pico Blvd; Pico Blvd between Main and Santee Sts; Wall and Maple Sts between Olympic Blvd and 12th St

Children 12th St and Pico Blvd between Maple Ave and San Julian St

Men Main, Los Angeles and Santee Sts, between Pico Blvd and 16th St, plus Los Angeles St between 7th and 9th Sts

Textiles The blocks bordered by 8th St, Olympic Blvd, Maple Ave and San Julian St

Jewelry and accessories Santee Alley, Olympic Blvd between Main St and Wall St, plus Main and Santee Sts between Olympic and Pico Blvds

Shops are generally open from 10am to 5pm daily, with Saturday being the busiest day because that's when many wholesalers open up to the public. Around a third of the shops are closed on Sunday. Cash is king and haggling may get you 10% or 20% off, especially when buying multiple items. Refunds or exchanges are a no-no, so choose carefully and make sure items are in good condition. Most stores don't have dressing rooms. Sample sales are usually held on the last Friday of every month, with popular showrooms including the **California Market Center** (Map p82; ☑213-630-3600; www.california marketcenter.com; 110 E 9th St), **Cooper Design Space** (Map p82; ☑213-627-3754; www. cooperdesignspace.com; 860 S Los Angeles St), **New Mart** (Map p82; ☑213-627-0671; www. newmart.net; 127 E 9th St) and the **Gerry Building** (Map p82; www.gerrybuilding.com; 910 S Los Angeles St). Upcoming sales are posted on the LA Fashion District Facebook page (www.facebook.com/LAFashionDist).

rare books before heading upstairs, home to a horror-and-crime book den, a book tunnel and a few art galleries to boot. The store also houses a terrific vinyl collection.

Hennessey + Ingalls   BOOKS
(Map p82; ☑213-437-2130; www.hennesseyingalls. com; 300 S Santa Fe Ave; ☺10am-8pm) Directly opposite the Southern California Institute of Architecture, this spacious new-and-used bookstore focuses primarily on design in its various forms, from architecture, interiors and landscaping, to graphics, fashion and photography. There's a dedicated section for out-of-print titles, as well a good selection of niche magazines and journals. Check out the cool, vintage, LA-themed cards.

Wittmore   FASHION & ACCESSORIES
(Map p82; ☑213-626-0780; https://shopwittmore. com; The Yards at One Santa Fe, 300 S Santa Fe Ave; ☺11am-7pm) Wittmore stocks sharp edits of men's threads and accessories best described as high-end Californian cool...think layers, muted colors and pieces that can be dressed up or down. Scan the space for stylish lei-

surewear from Vancouver's Raining Champ, roll-neck wool sweaters from California's Mollusk, and Wittmore's own LA-made tees. Beautiful accessories include cult-status sunglasses, artisan jewelry, leathergoods, ceramics and LA-themed photography.

Shinola   GIFTS & SOUVENIRS
(Map p82; ☑213-613-1355; www.shinola.com; 825 E 3rd St; ☺10am-8pm Mon-Sat, to 6pm Sun) Detroit design company Shinola is well known for its wristwatches, as well as its beautiful, handcrafted leathergoods, from stylish wallets, iPhone covers, toiletry bags and backpacks, to classic duffle, messenger and laptop bags. Adding to the sharply curated mix is anything from designer journals and power cords to Detroit photography tomes. There's another branch in Silver Lake.

Poketo   BOUTIQUE
(Map p82; ☑213-537-0751; www.poketo.com; 820 E 3rd St; ☺noon-7pm Mon, from 11am Tue-Sun) Located in the Arts District, this is Poketo's flagship store. Shop the shelves for a thoughtful mix of mainly US-designed lifestyle products,

from hand-poured scented candles and beauty products, to hand-painted ceramics, jewelry, bags and super-cool textiles.

Wheelhouse
SPORTS & OUTDOORS

(☎213-628-3117; www.thewheelhouse.bike; 1375 E 6th St; ☺cafe 7am-6pm, bike store from 10am) Love led to marriage and the opening of this one-stop bike store, service center and cafe for Chase and Tami Spenst. Driven by a philosophy that bikes should be every-day props, the couple sells vintage-inspired two-wheelers suitable for both urban com-mutes and country rides. Everything from the saddle to the wheels can be customized and the store stocks design-savvy accesso-ries like leather wine-bottle carriers.

The space is also worth a peek for Tami's ghostly wall installation, which sees a bri-gade of bicycles seemingly emerge from a solid concrete wall.

Santee Alley
CLOTHING

(www.thesanteealley.com; cnr Santee & 12th Sts; ☺9:30am-6pm) Yes, it's an actual alley, open every day and packed with solid bargains spanning everything from on-trend threads and kitschy gowns, to kicks, bling, eyewear, perfumes and more.

RIF.LA
SHOES

(Map p82; ☎213-617-0252; www.riflosangeles. com; 334 E 2nd St; ☺noon-5pm Mon, to 7pm Tue-Sat, to 6pm Sun) Your one-stop shop for new and used limited-edition, imported and old-school sneakers. T-shirts and hats are avail-able in its annex two doors down.

Jewelry District
JEWELRY

(Map p82) For bargain bling head to this shrinking Downtown district. Centered on Broadway and Hill St (between 6th and 7th Sts), you can snap up watches, gold, silver and gemstones at up to 70% off retail prices. The mostly traditional designs are unlikely to be seen on the red carpet, but the selection is un-questionably huge. Quality, however, varies.

Hollywood

No other corner of LA is steeped in as much mythology as Hollywood. It's here that you'll find the Hollywood Walk of Fame, the Cap-itol Records Tower and Grauman's Chinese Theatre, where the hand- and footprints of entertainment deities are immortalized in concrete. Look beyond the tourist-swamped landmarks of Hollywood Blvd and you'll discover a nuanced, multifaceted neighbor-hood where industrial streets are punctuat-ed by edgy galleries and boutiques, where strip malls hide swinging French bistros, and where steep, sleepy streets harbor the homes of long-gone silver-screen stars.

◎ Sights

Many of Hollywood's tourist attractions gravitate around the intersection of Holly-wood Blvd and Highland Ave. While many are gimmicky (wax-model Angelina Jolie, anyone?), there are some notable attractions here, namely the Grauman's Chinese Thea-tre, Dolby Theatre (home of the Oscars) and the engrossing Hollywood Museum. Further south on (and off) Highland Ave is a clus-ter of top-notch commercial art galleries, including Regen Projects. The southern end of Hollywood is home to a pair of worthy pit stops: the Hollywood Forever Cemetery and, right behind it, the Paramount Studios.

★ Grauman's Chinese Theatre
LANDMARK

(TCL Chinese Theatres; Map p106; ☎323-461-3331; www.tclchinesetheatres.com; 6925 Hollywood Blvd; guided tour adult/senior/child $16/13.50/8; ⍟; Ⓜ Red Line to Hollywood/Highland) Ever won-dered what it's like to be in George Clooney's shoes? Just find his footprints in the fore-court of this world-famous movie palace. The exotic pagoda theater – complete with temple bells and stone heaven dogs from China – has shown movies since 1927 when Cecil B. DeMille's *The King of Kings* first flickered across the screen.

To see the inside, buy a movie ticket or join a half-hour guided tour offered throughout the day (check in at the kiosk by the cinema entrance). Of course, most Tinseltown tour-ists are content to find out how big Arnold's feet really are, or to search for Betty Grable's legs or Whoopi Goldberg's braids.

Hollywood Walk of Fame
LANDMARK

(Map p106; www.walkoffame.com; Hollywood Blvd; Ⓜ Red Line to Hollywood/Highland) Big Bird, Bob Hope, Marilyn Monroe and Aretha Frank-lin are among the stars being sought out, worshipped, photographed and stepped on along the Hollywood Walk of Fame. Since 1960 more than 2600 performers – from legends to bit-part players – have been hon-ored with a pink-marble sidewalk star.

Dolby Theatre
THEATER

(Map p106; ☎323-308-6300; www.dolbytheatre. com; 6801 Hollywood Blvd; tours adult/child, senior & student $23/18; ☺10:30am-4pm; Ⓟ; Ⓜ Red

LOS ANGELES HOLLYWOOD

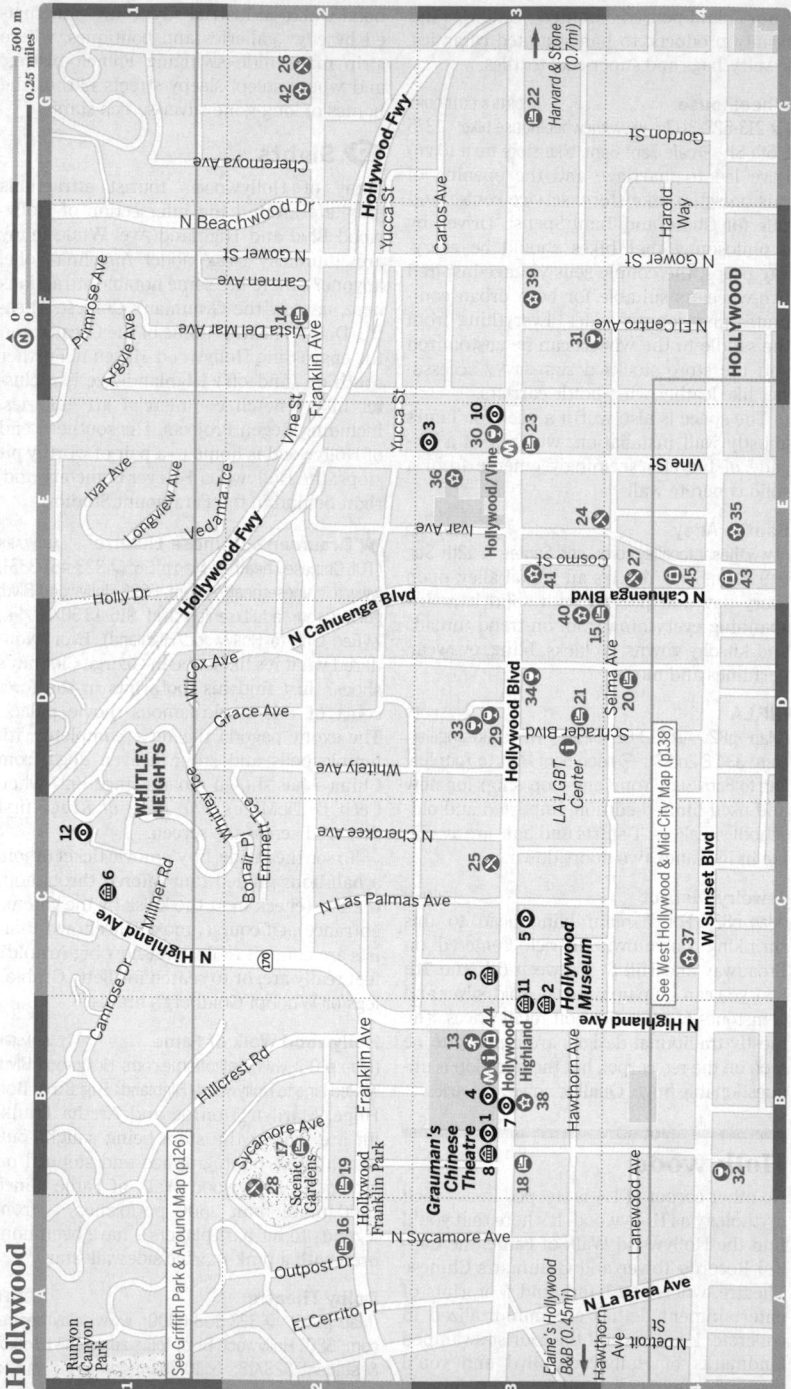

Hollywood

Line to Hollywood/Highland) The Academy Awards are handed out at the Dolby Theatre, which has also hosted the *American Idol* finale, the Excellence in Sports Performance Yearly (ESPY) Awards and the Daytime Emmy Awards. The venue is home to the annual PaleyFest, the country's premier TV festival, held in March. Guided tours of the theater will have you sniffing around the auditorium, admiring a VIP room and nosing up to an Oscar statuette.

Madame Tussaud's   MUSEUM
(Map p106; ☏ 323-798-1670; www.madametussauds.com; 6933 Hollywood Blvd; adult/child $31/26; ◷ 10am-6pm Mon, to 7pm Tue-Fri, to 8pm Sat & Sun; 🅿; Ⓜ Red Line to Hollywood/Highland) The better of Hollywood's two wax museums, this is the place to take selfies with motionless movie stars (Salma Hayek, Tom Hanks and Patrick Swayze), old-school icons (Charlie Chaplin, Marilyn Monroe, Clark Gable), movie characters such as Hugh's Wolverine from *X-Men*, chart-topping pop stars

and all-time-great directors. To save money, book online and opt for the 'Late Night Saver' option (adult/child $14.95/11.45), which grants entry after 4pm.

El Capitan Theatre   LANDMARK
(Map p106; ☏ 800-347-6396; https://elcapitantheatre.com; 6838 Hollywood Blvd) Spanish Colonial meets East Indian at the flamboyant El Capitan movie palace, built for live performances in 1926 and now run by Disney. The first flick to show here was *Citizen Kane* in 1941 and it's still an evocative place to catch a film, often accompanied by a live show.

Ripley's Believe It or Not!   MUSEUM
(Map p106; www.ripleys.com/hollywood; 6780 Hollywood Blvd; adult/child $20/10; ◷ 10am-midnight; Ⓜ Red Line to Hollywood/Highland) Life's pretty strange and it'll feel stranger still after you've visited Ripley's, where exhibits range from the gross to the grotesque. If shrunken heads, a sculpture of Marilyn Monroe made

HOLLYWOOD SIGN

LA's most famous landmark, the **Hollywood Sign** (Map p126), first appeared in the hills in 1923 as an advertising gimmick for a real-estate development called 'Hollywoodland'. Each letter is 50ft tall and made of sheet metal. Once aglow with 4000 light bulbs, the sign even had its own caretaker who lived behind the 'L' until 1939.

In 1932 a struggling young actress named Peggy Entwistle leapt her way into local lore from the letter 'H'. The last four letters were lopped off in the '40s as the sign started to crumble. In the late '70s Alice Cooper and Hugh Hefner joined forces with fans to save the famous symbol, and Hef was back at it again in 2010 when the hills behind the sign became slated for a housing development. The venerable Playboy donated the last $900,000 of the necessary $12.5 million it took to buy and preserve the land. The sign made the news once again on New Year's Day in 2017 when artist Zachary Cole Fernandez sneakily turned the last two 'O's into 'E's to form 'Hollyweed'.

Technically it's illegal to hike up to the sign, but viewing spots are plentiful, including **Hollywood & Highland** (p119), the top of Beachwood Dr and the **Griffith Observatory** (p124).

from shredded $1 bills and a human-hair bikini capture your imagination, this place is calling your name.

Starbucks   ARCHITECTURE
(Map p138; ☏ 323-493-1868; 859 N Highland Ave) Quite possibly the most novel coffee shop in town, this drive-thru branch of the famous Seattle chain occupies a lovingly restored, art-deco gas station. Dating back to 1935, the building's fetching form has led to numerous Hollywood cameos, including in *LA Story* and *48 Hrs*. There's a small outdoor patio for those wanting to linger.

Hollywood Heritage Museum   MUSEUM
(Map p106; ☏ 323-874-2276; www.hollywood heritage.org; 2100 N Highland Ave; adult/child under 12 $7/free; ☉noon-4pm Sat & Sun) Hollywood's first feature-length film, Cecil B. DeMille's *The Squaw Man,* was shot in this building in 1913–14, originally set at the corner of Selma and Vine Sts. DeMille went on to co-found Paramount and had the barn moved to the lot in the '20s. The building is now a quaint museum, mainly showcasing projectors and cameras from the early days of filmmaking as well as a re-creation of DeMille's office.

Hollywood Bowl Museum   MUSEUM
(Map p126; ☏ 323-850-2058; www.hollywood bowl.com/visit/hollywood-bowl-museum; ☉10am-showtime Tue-Sat & 4pm-showtime Sun late Jun-late Sep, 10am-5pm Tue-Fri rest of year) **FREE** The Bowl (as it's affectionately known around town) enjoys a glamorous history, and this is where you can literally listen to it, and watch it. Classic Bowl moments are

yours thanks to audio and video footage of musical deities such as the Beatles, the Stones and Mr James Hendrix.

★**Hollywood Museum**   MUSEUM
(Map p106; ☏ 323-464-7776; www.thehollywood museum.com; 1660 N Highland Ave; adult/child $15/5; ☉10am-5pm Wed-Sun; Ⓜ Red Line to Hollywood/Highland) For a taste of Old Hollywood, do not miss this musty temple to the stars, its four floors crammed with movie and TV costumes and props. The museum is housed inside the Max Factor Building, built in 1914 and relaunched as a glamourous beauty salon in 1935. At the helm was Polish-Jewish businessman Max Factor, Hollywood's leading authority on cosmetics. And it was right here that he worked his magic on Hollywood's most famous screen queens.

The makeup rooms, complete with custom hues and lighting to complement the ladies' varying complexions and hair colors, are still located on the ground floor, along with personal items from the likes of Joan Crawford, Judy Garland and Marilyn Monroe. Also on the floor is the 1965 Silver Cloud Rolls-Royce once owned by Cary Grant. Lurking downstairs is Hannibal Lecter's cell from *The Silence of the Lambs*.

Museum of Broken Relationships   MUSEUM
(Map p106; ☏ 323-892-1200; http://brokenships.la; 6751 Hollywood Blvd; adult/student & senior $18/15; ☉11am-6pm Mon-Wed, to 7pm Thu & Sun, noon-8pm Fri & Sat; Ⓜ Red Line to Hollywood/Highland) The everyday-looking items in this museum – clothing, perfume bottles, stuffed animals, silicone breast implants – take on entirely new meanings when you read the descriptions by

their donors – emotion-filled stories of relationships that are no more. Some are wistful, others poignant, others make you want to wince. About 100 pieces – and 100 stories – are on display at any one time, and there's a confessional booth should you want to tell your own. Admission isn't cheap, but maybe emotions shouldn't be either.

Egyptian Theatre
LANDMARK

(Map p106; 📞 323-461-2020; www.egyptiantheatre.com; 6712 Hollywood Blvd; M Red Line to Hollywood/Highland) The Egyptian, the first of the grand movie palaces on Hollywood Blvd, premiered *Robin Hood* in 1922. The theater's lavish getup – complete with hieroglyphs and sphinx heads – dovetailed nicely with the craze for all things Egyptian sparked by the discoveries of archaeologist Howard Carter. These days it's a shrine to serious cinema thanks to the nonprofit American Cinematheque.

Pantages Theatre
NOTABLE BUILDING

(Map p106; http://hollywoodpantages.com; 6233 Hollywood Blvd; M Red Line to Hollywood/Vine) Scottish architect Benjamin Marcus Priteca designed this 1930 survivor, the last theater commissioned by Greek-born theater magnate Alexander Pantages. Adorned with art-deco chevrons, ziggurats, zigzags and octagons, the theater hosted the Academy Awards between 1949 and 1959, when Howard Hughes owned the place. The building itself has made numerous screen cameos, including in Michael Jackson's music video for *You Are Not Alone*. Next door,

the Frolic Room (p115) bar appeared in *LA Confidential*.

Capitol Records Tower
LANDMARK

(Map p106; 1750 Vine St) **FREE** You'll have no trouble recognizing this iconic 1956 tower, one of LA's great mid-century buildings. Designed by Welton Becket, it resembles a stack of records topped by a stylus blinking out 'Hollywood' in Morse code. Some of music's biggest stars have recorded hits in the building's basement studios, among them Nat King Cole, Frank Sinatra and Capitol's current heavyweight, Katy Perry. Outside on the sidewalk, Garth Brooks and John Lennon have their stars.

Hollywood Forever Cemetery
CEMETERY

(📞 323-469-1181; www.hollywoodforever.com; 6000 Santa Monica Blvd; ⊙ usually 8:30am-5pm, flower shop 9am-5pm Mon-Fri, to 4pm Sat & Sun; P) Paradisiacal landscaping, vainglorious tombstones and epic mausoleums set an appropriate resting place for some of Hollywood's most iconic dearly departed. Residents include Cecil B. DeMille, Mickey Rooney, Jayne Mansfield, punk rockers Johnny and Dee Dee Ramone and *Golden Girls* star Estelle Getty. Valentino lies in the Cathedral Mausoleum (open from 10am to 2pm), while Judy Garland rests in the Abbey of the Psalms. For a full list of residents, purchase a map ($5) at the flower shop.

Despite being an eternal resting place, these hallowed grounds are anything but dead. Summer brings outdoor screenings of classic movies (p111), while in late October or early November the gates open for Día de

---

OLD HOLLYWOOD'S GLAMOUR HOOD

For a taste of Old Hollywood, wander the narrow, winding streets of **Whitley Heights** (Map p106), a residential preservation zone bordered by Franklin Ave to the south, Highland Ave to the west, and split in two by the 101 freeway to the north and east. Peppered with beautiful Moorish, Renaissance and Italianate-style villas, this was the city's first 'Beverly Hills,' a salubrious estate designed by architect AS Barnes in the early 1900s and inspired by Mediterranean villages.

The neighborhood's proximity to silent-era movie studios made it popular with the day's stars. Among its silver-screen residents was heartthrob Valentino, whose home on Wedgewood Pl was demolished to make way for the 101 freeway. Acclaimed actor Marie Dressler lived at 6809 Iris Circle, while Jean Harlow reputedly called 2015 Whitley Ave home. Watsonia Tce is an especially beautiful street in the neighborhood, framed by lush gardens and houses that wouldn't look out of place in Italy. Of particular note is Villa Vallombrosa at number 2074, a Venetian-inspired mansion designed by architect Nathan Coleman and home (at different stages) to screenwriter Ben Hecht, Hollywood fashion designer Gilbert Adrian and composer Leonard Bernstein. Close by, number 2058 was Gloria Swanson's base while filming *Sunset Boulevard*.

los Muertos (p71), complete with costumes, dancing and exhibitions.

Regen Projects   GALLERY
(Map p138; ☑ 310-276-5424; www.regenprojects. com; 6750 Santa Monica Blvd; ☺ 10am-6pm Tue-Sat) FREE A standout private gallery, known for propelling the careers of some of LA's most successful and innovative artists, among them Matthew Barney, Glenn Ligon and Catherine Opie. Its stable also includes a number of international big guns, from Anish Kapoor to Wolfgang Tillmans. Expect bold, edgy shows showcasing everything from photography, painting and video art, to ambitious installations.

Kohn Gallery   GALLERY
(Map p138; ☑ 323-461-3311; www.kohngallery.com; 1227 N Highland Ave; ☺ 10am-6pm Tue-Fri, from 11am Sat; P) One of the city's top private gallery spaces, with museum-standard exhibitions of modern and contemporary art. Recent shows have included a retrospective of American conceptual artist Joe Goode and painter John Altoon, as well as the premiere of a digitally restored version of Bruce Conner's seminal experimental short film, *A Movie*.

🏃 Activities

★ Runyon Canyon   HIKING
(Map p126; www.runyoncanyonhike.com; 2000 N Fuller Ave; ☺ dawn-dusk) A chaparral-draped cut in the Hollywood Hills, this 130-acre public park is as famous for its buff runners and exercising celebrities as it is for the panoramic views from the upper ridge. Follow the wide, partially paved fire road up then take the smaller track down to the canyon, where you'll pass the remains of the Runyon estate.

Free morning yoga sessions (bring your own mat) are run daily in the park; click the link on the website for details.

Lucky Strike   BOWLING
(Map p106; ☑ 323-467-7776; www.bowlluckystrike. com/locations/hollywood; 6801 Hollywood Blvd; ☺ noon-1am Mon-Wed, to 2am Thu & Fri, 11am-2am Sat, 11am-1am Sun; M Red Line to Hollywood/Highland) These 12 lanes are as stylish as bowling gets. There's a DJ booth, projection screens, bottle service and leather seating.

☞ Tours

Red Line Tours   WALKING
(Map p106; ☑ 323-402-1074; www.redlinetours. com; 6708 Hollywood Blvd; adult/child from $25/15; ☺ 75min Hollywood Behind-the-Scenes Tour 10am, noon, 2pm & 4pm; M Red Line to Hollywood/Highland) Learn the secrets of Hollywood on Red Line's 'edutaining' Hollywood Behind-the-Scenes Tour, a 75-minute walking tour that comes with nifty headsets to cut out traffic noise. Guides use a mix of anecdotes, fun facts, trivia and historical and architectural data to keep their charges entertained.

🛏 Sleeping

Elaine's Hollywood B&B   B&B $
(☑ 323-850-0766; www.elaineshollywoodbed andbreakfast.com; 1616 N Sierra Bonita Ave, Hollywood; r $120-140; P ❖ ✿ @ 🛜 🐾; M Red Line to Hollywood & Highland) This B&B offers four rooms in a lovingly restored 1910 bungalow on a quiet street. Your outgoing hosts speak several languages, serve a generous continental breakfast and will happily help you plan your day. Cash only.

USA Hostels Hollywood   HOSTEL $
(Map p106; ☑ 800-524-6783, 323-462-3777; www. usahostels.com; 1624 Schrader Blvd; dm $38-49, r with bath from $120; ❖ @ 🛜; M Red Line to Hollywood/Vine) This sociable hostel puts you within steps of the Hollywood party circuit. Private rooms are a bit cramped, but making new friends is easy during staff-organized barbecues, comedy nights and various walking tours. Freebies include wi-fi and a cook-your-own-pancake breakfast. It has cushy lounge seating on the front porch and free beach shuttles, too.

Vibe Hotel   HOTEL $
(Map p106; ☑ 323-469-8600; www.vibehotel.com; 5922 Hollywood Blvd; r $84-110; P ❖ @ 🛜; M Red Line to Hollywood/Vine) Especially popular with young international travelers, this blue-hued motel-hotel comes with an outdoor tiki lounge area and the choice of basic or premium rooms. While both are pretty simple, the latter come with their own full kitchen. Budget rooms have a fridge and microwave and all rooms have flat-screen TVs, free wi-fi and private bathroom. Free, limited parking on site, too.

★ Mama Shelter   BOUTIQUE HOTEL $$
(Map p106; ☑ 323-785-6666; www.mamashelter. com; 6500 Selma Ave; r from $179; ❖ @ 🛜; M Red Line to Hollywood/Vine) Hip, affordable Mama Shelter keeps things playful with its lobby gumball machines, foosball table and live streaming of guests' selfies and videos. Standard rooms are small but cool, with quality beds and linen and subway-tiled bathrooms

with decent-sized showers. Quirky in-room touches include movie scripts, masks and Apple TVs with free Netflix. The rooftop bar (p115) is one of LA's best.

Magic Castle Hotel — HOTEL $$

(Map p106; ☑ 323-851-0800; www.magiccastle hotel.com; 7025 Franklin Ave; r from $204; P ✱ @ 🛜 ☒) Walls at this perennial pleaser are a bit thin, but otherwise it's a charming base of operation with large, modern rooms, exceptional staff and a petite courtyard pool where days start with fresh pastries and gourmet coffee. Inquire about access to the Magic Castle, a fabled members-only magic club in an adjacent Victorian mansion. Parking costs $13.

Highland Gardens Hotel — HOTEL $$

(Map p106; ☑ 323-850-0536; www.highland gardenshotel.com; 7047 Franklin Ave; r from $169; P ✱ @ 🛜 ☒; Ⓜ Red Line to Hollywood/Highland) The lobby at this residential-style motel is more glamourous than the '70s-time-warped rooms. Brad Pitt stayed here when he first arrived in Hollywood and wore a chicken suit for nearby El Pollo Loco. Janis Joplin overdosed in room 105. Rooms facing Franklin St tend to be noisy. More positively, parking and wi-fi is free and Hollywood Blvd attractions and the metro are a walk away.

Best Western Plus Hollywood Hills Hotel — HOTEL $$

(Map p106; ☑ 323-464-5181; www.bestwestern california.com; 6141 Franklin Ave; r from $167; P ✱ @ 🛜 ☒; Ⓜ Red Line to Hollywood/Vine) Not all rooms are created equal at this family-run hotel with colorful retro touches. For more space and quiet, get one in back facing the sparkling pool. Self-caterers will welcome the refrigerator and microwave, although the on-site coffee shop serves some pretty good comfort food and is open late. Parking is $20.

★ Dream — BOUTIQUE HOTEL $$$

(Map p106; ☑ 323-844-6417; www.dreamhotels. com; 6417 Selma Ave; r from $382; P ✱ 🛜 ☒; Ⓜ Red Line to Hollywood/Vine) This 179-room complex is inspired by mid-century style and designed by the acclaimed Rockwell Group. It's a hip, sceney spot, with a massive rooftop pool area and a branch of legendary New York bar Beauty & Essex. Entry-level rooms aren't especially strong on space, though all offer floor-to-ceiling windows and pared-back elegance in neutral, hangover-friendly hues.

★ Hollywood Roosevelt Hotel — HISTORIC HOTEL $$$

(Map p106; ☑ 323-856-1970; www.thehollywood roosevelt.com; 7000 Hollywood Blvd; d from $282; P ✱ @ 🛜 ☒; Ⓜ Red Line to Hollywood/Highland) Roosevelt heaves with Hollywood lore: Shirley

---

MOVIES UNDER THE STARS

Angelenos love their movies and their fine weather, so it's only logical that they combine the two. Screenings under the stars are a popular annual tradition. Come early to stake out a good spot and bring pillows, blankets and snacks.

From mid-May to September, **Cinespia** (☑ 323-221-3343; www.cinespia.org; tickets $14; ⊙ Sat May-Oct) has a to-die-for location at **Hollywood Forever Cemetery** (p109), the place of perpetual slumber for a galaxy of old-time movie stars. Classics by Milos Forman, Robert Altman and Alfred Hitchcock are projected onto a mausoleum wall around 8:30pm, but the hipster crowd starts lining up long before gates open at 6:45pm for picnics and drinks (wine and beer are allowed, spirits are not!) while a DJ spins smooth soundtracks.

If that's too morbid for you, catch the Pacific sea breeze while camping out on the Santa Monica Pier where the **Front Porch Cinema at the Pier** (Map p176; www.santa monicapier.org/frontporchcinema; Santa Monica Pier) presents populist faves every Friday night from late September through October. Music usually starts playing at 6:30pm, with films screening at 7:30pm. Tickets are free.

Early fall is also the time for Sunday-evening flicks at **Barnsdall Art Park** (Map p128; www.barnsdallartpark.com; 4800 Hollywood Blvd; Ⓜ Red Line to Vermont/Sunset). Here, classic and cult-status films are screened on the west lawn of Frank Lloyd Wright's first Californian project, Hollyhock House. The season usually runs from early September to early October.

YOUR 15 MINUTES OF FAME

Be in a Studio Audience

Sitcoms and game shows usually tape between August and March before live audiences. To nab free tickets, check with TV Tickets (www.tvtix.com) or **Audiences Unlimited** (p118. Tickets to *Jimmy Kimmel Live,* which conveniently tapes at its namesake theater beside Hollywood's El Capitan Theatre, are available through http://1iota.com. If you don't have tickets, try your luck getting standby tickets at the theater 90 minutes before the 4pm showtime. For assistance, ask the ushers outside the theater. The website is also the go-to for tickets to *The Late, Late Show with James Corden,* filmed at **CBS Television City** (Map p138; ☑ 323-575-2345; www.cbs.com; 7800 Beverly Blvd; ⊙ 9am-5pm Mon-Fri). Most shows have a minimum age of 18; always bring a valid driver's license or passport as ID.

Become an Extra

If you'd like to see yourself on screen, check with Be In a Movie (www.beinamovie.com) on how to become an extra in a big crowd scene at major film shoots. There's no money in it, but the behind-the-scenes experience and chance of seeing a big star live and in person should make you a hit back at the office water cooler.

Become a Game Show Contestant

Jeopardy and *Wheel of Fortune* are among the game shows that tape in LA, but the chances of actually becoming a contestant are greatest on *The Price is Right,* taped at CBS Television City. Check www.on-camera-audiences.com/shows/The_Price_is_Right for details.

Temple learned to tap dance on the stairs off the lobby, Marilyn Monroe shot her first print ad by the pool (later decorated by David Hockney) and the ghost of actor Montgomery Clift can still be heard playing the bugle. Poolside rooms channel a modernist, Palm Springs vibe, while those in the main building mix contemporary and 1920s accents.

W Hollywood HOTEL $$$
(Map p106; ☑ 888-625-4955, 323-798-1300; www. whollywoodhotel.com; 6250 Hollywood Blvd; r from $360; P❄@🐾🏊; Ⓜ Red Line to Hollywood/Vine) The W's soaring, sparkly atrium makes quite an impression, as does the sceney, palm-fringed rooftop pool deck. In shades of grey, silver and white, rooms are minimalist and modern, with white leather headboards, down comforters and a pillow menu for fussy sleepers. Many of the Wonderful, Spectacular or Fabulous category rooms are small. Corner Fantastic Suites are the best bet.

Hollywood Hills Hotel HOTEL $$$
(Map p106; ☑ 323-850-1909, 800-741-4915; www. hollywoodhillshotel.com; 7025 Franklin Ave; r from $450; P❄🏊) Breathtaking city views, a curvaceous pool guarded by a 17th-century pagoda, and roomy digs with balcony and kitchen are among the assets at this older

but well-kept hillside hotel. A partial refurbishment has seen rates skyrocket, making the place less value these days. That said, we love the tranquility and proximity to central Hollywood. Check in at the adjacent Magic Castle Hotel (p111). No children allowed.

🍴 Eating

Hyperactive Hollywood Blvd is home to a plethora of casual eateries, most of them touristy and mediocre. Clued-in locals tend to gravitate to Highland Ave, where you'll find a handful of great midrange eateries, including Salt's Cure and La Carmencita at the intersection of Lexington Ave, and Petit Trois and Osteria Mozza at the intersection of Melrose Ave. Melrose Ave itself is home to LA's highly acclaimed fine-dining superstar, Providence.

Stout Burgers & Beers BURGERS $
(Map p106; ☑ 323-469-3801; www.stoutburgers andbeers.com; 1544 N Cahuenga Blvd; burgers $11-13, salads $8-12; ⊙ 11:30am-4am; P🐾🏊; Ⓜ Red Line to Hollywood/Vine) Cool, casual Stout flips gourmet burgers and pours great craft brews. The beef is ground in-house, the chicken is organic and the veggie patties are made fresh daily. One of our favorites here is the Six Weeker, a beef-patty burger jammed

with brie, fig jam, arugula and caramelized onions.

Square One
CAFE $

(Map p128; ☑ 323-661-1109; www.squareonedining.com; 4854 Fountain Ave; mains $11-15; ⊗ 8:30am-3pm) In the shadow of the looming Scientology campus is this homely breakfast and lunch spot, complete with quirky egg-carton ceiling. Indeed, eggs feature prominently on the all-day-breakfast menu, from braised mustard and collard greens served with baked eggs and grits, to tacos filled with scrambled eggs and jalapeños. Check the board for specials such as lemon ricotta pancakes and creative salads.

Oaks Gourmet
DELI $

(Map p106; ☑ 323-871-8894; www.theoaksgourmet.com; 1915 N Bronson Ave; mains $9-13; ⊗ 7am-midnight; P🐾) A hipster deli and wine shop with a devoted following, where you can browse Californian wines, specialty bottled cocktails, artisanal cheeses and other gourmet treats while waiting for your crowd-pleasing BLT (heirloom tomato, creamy Camembert cheese, avocado and black-forest bacon on toasted sourdough). The breakfast burrito is special.

Hollywood Farmers Market
MARKET $

(Map p106; http://hfm.la; cnr Ivar & Selma Aves; ⊗ 8am-1pm Sun; 🐾; Ⓜ Red Line to Hollywood/Vine) On the shortlist for the city's best farmers market, this Sunday-morning sprawl offers organic and specialty produce from well over 100 local farmers, producers and artisans. Some of the city's top chefs shop here and the market also peddles decent ready-to-eat bites for the peckish.

Yamashiro Farmers Market
MARKET $

(Map p106; http://yamashirohollywood.com/farmers-market; 1999 N Sycamore Ave; ⊗ 5-9pm Thu mid-May–early Sep; P) The best farmers market views in LA are yours from Yamashiro's spectacular perch. In addition to organic produce, expect tasty prepared food and live music. There's also a wine-tasting bar.

★ Petit Trois
FRENCH $$

(Map p138; ☑ 323-468-8916; http://petittrois.com; mains $14-36; ⊗ noon-10pm Sun-Thu, to 11pm Fri & Sat; P) Good things come in small packages...like tiny, no-reservations Petit Trois! Owned by acclaimed TV chef Ludovic Lefebvre, its two long counters (the place is too small for tables) are where food-lovers squeeze in for smashing, honest,

Gallic-inspired grub, from a ridiculously light Boursin-stuffed omelette to a show-stopping double cheeseburger served with a standout foie gras–infused red-wine bordelaise.

Given its size, popularity and no-reservations policy, waits can be long. Your best bet is to head in between 3pm and 6pm or after 9pm. If you do have to wait, affable staff and top-notch cocktails ease the pain. Credit-card payment only.

★ Salt's Cure
MODERN AMERICAN $$

(Map p138; ☑ 323-465-7258; http://saltscure.com; 1155 N Highland Ave; mains $17-34; ⊗ 11am-11pm Mon-Thu, to midnight Fri, 10am-midnight Sat, 10am-11pm Sun) Wood-paneled, concrete-floored Salt's Cure is an out, proud locavore. From the in-season vegetables to the house-butchered and cured meats, the menu celebrates all things Californian. Expect sophisticated takes on rustic comfort grub, whether it's capicollo with chili paste or tender duck breast paired with impressively light oatmeal griddle cakes and blackberry compote.

The weekend brunch is a longstanding hit, as are the well-crafted cocktails.

★ Musso & Frank Grill
STEAK $$

(Map p106; ☑ 323-467-7788; www.mussoandfrank.com; 6667 Hollywood Blvd; mains $15-52; ⊗ 11am-11pm Tue-Sat, 4-9pm Sun; P; Ⓜ Red Line to Hollywood/Highland) Hollywood history hangs in the thick air at Musso & Frank Grill, Tinseltown's oldest eatery (since 1919). Charlie Chaplin used to knock back vodka gimlets, Raymond Chandler penned scripts in the high-backed booths, and movie deals were made on the old phone at the back (the booth closest to the phone is favored by Jack Nicholson and Johnny Depp).

La Carmencita
MEXICAN $$

(Map p138; ☑ 323-701-2063; www.lacarmencita.com; 1156 N Highland Ave; tacos $4.50-6, dishes $8-16; ⊗ 11am-11pm Mon-Sat; 🐾) Colorful, affable La Carmencita peddles delicious, made-from-scratch Baja Californian grub. Go easy on the house-made blue-corn tortilla chips as you'll need space for the vibrant ceviche and hearty shrimp *cazuela*, a creamy, peppery, stew-like dish topped with a cheesy baked crust. Best of the tacos are the rich, succulent lamb and generous battered fish.

The Edmon
NEW AMERICAN $$

(☑ 323-645-5225; http://theedmon.com; 5168 Melrose Ave; mains $19-32; ⊗ 6pm-midnight Tue-Thu,

MULHOLLAND DRIVING TOUR

What To See

If you found David Lynch's 2001 movie *Mulholland Drive* a tad bizarre, perhaps a drive along the road itself will clear things up. The legendary road winds and dips for 24 miles through the Santa Monica Mountains, skirting the mansions of the rich and famous (Jack Nicholson's is at No 12850, Warren Beatty's at No 13671) and delivering iconic views of Downtown, Hollywood and the San Fernando Valley at each bend. Named for its creator, California aqueduct engineer William Mulholland, it's especially pretty just before sunset (go west to east, though, to avoid driving into the setting sun) and on clear winter days when the panorama opens up from the snowcapped San Gabriel Mountains to the shimmering Pacific Ocean.

At the very least, drive up to the Hollywood Bowl Overlook for classic views of the Hollywood sign and the beehive-shaped bowl below. Other pullouts offer hiking-trail access, for instance to Runyon Canyon and Fryman Canyon. Note that pulling over after sunset is verboten and may result in a traffic ticket.

Time & Route

Driving the entire route takes about an hour, but even a shorter spin is worthwhile. Mulholland Dr runs from the US-101 Fwy (Hollywood Fwy; take the Cahuenga exit, then follow signs) to about 2 miles west of the I-405 (San Diego Fwy). About 8 miles of dirt road, closed to vehicles but not to hikers and cyclists, links it with Mulholland Hwy. If you are driving, turn right at Calneva Dr (which becomes Hayvenhusrt Ave) and then left onto Ventura Blvd. Continue west along Ventura Blvd, turning left onto Topanga Canyon Blvd, right onto Mulholland Dr and then left onto Mulholland Hwy. From here, Mulholland Hwy continues a serpentine route through the mountains for another 31 miles as far as Leo Carrillo State Beach.

to 2am Fri & Sat; ⓟ🛜) Old Hollywood glamour is back in vogue at this sultry newcomer, where the wallpaper is deco, the bar hand-carved and the waitstaff bow-tied. Part of the 1927 Hollywood Historic Hotel, its menu pulls retro dishes into the present, whether it's brûléed avocado with roasted root vegetables and preserved grapefruit, or potato and black garlic-filled pierogi paired with fried quail egg.

★**Providence**   MODERN AMERICAN **$$$**
(Map p138; 📞323-460-4170; www.providencela. com; 5955 Melrose Ave; lunch mains $40-45, tasting menus $120-250; ⊗noon-2pm & 6-10pm Mon-Fri, 5:30-10pm Sat, 5:30-9pm Sun; ⓟ) The top restaurant pick by preeminent LA food critic Jonathan Gold for four years running, this two-starred Michelin darling turns superlative seafood into arresting, nuanced dishes that might see abalone paired with eggplant, turnip and nori, or spiny lobster conspire decadently with macadamia nut and earthy black truffle. À la carte options are available at lunch only.

★**Osteria & Pizzeria Mozza**   ITALIAN **$$$**
(Map p138; 📞osteria 323-297-0100, pizzeria 323-297-0101; http://la.osteriamozza.com; 6602 Melrose Ave; pizzas $11-25, osteria mains $29-38; ⊗pizzeria noon-midnight, osteria 5:30-11pm Mon-Fri, Sat, 5-10pm Sun; ⓟ) Osteria Mozza crafts fine cuisine from market-fresh, seasonal ingredients, but being a Mario Batali joint, you can expect adventure – think squid-ink *chitarra freddi* with Dungeness crab, sea urchin and jalapeño – and consistent excellence. Reservations are recommended. Next door, Pizzeria Mozza is more laid-back and cheaper, its gorgeous thin-crust pies topped with combos such as squash blossoms, tomato and creamy *burrata*.

🍷 Drinking & Nightlife

Hollywood's bar scene is diverse and delicious, with a large number of venues on or just off Hollywood Blvd. You'll find everything from historic dive and cocktail bars once frequented by Hollywood legends, to velvet-rope hot spots, buzzing rooftop hotel bars, and even a rum-and-cigar hideaway. Some of the more fashionable spots have dress codes or reservations-only policies, so always check ahead.

★Sassafras Saloon BAR

(Map p138; ☑ 323-467-2800; www.sassafrasholly wood.com; 1233 N Vine St; ⊙ 5pm-2am) You'll be pining for the bayou at the hospitable Sassafras Saloon, where hanging moss and life-size facades evoke sultry Savannah. Cocktails include a barrel-aged Sazerac, while themed nights include live jazz on Sunday and Monday, brass bands and acrobatics on Tuesday, burlesque and blues on Wednesday, karaoke on Thursday, and DJ-spun tunes on Friday and Saturday.

★Rooftop Bar at Mama Shelter BAR

(Map p106; ☑ 323-785-6600; www.mamashelter. com/en/los-angeles/restaurants/rooftop; 6500 Selma Ave; ⊙ 11am-midnight; Ⓜ Red Line to Hollywood/Vine) Less a hotel rooftop bar than a lush, tropical-like oasis with killer views of the Hollywood sign and LA skyline, multi-colored day beds and tongue-in-cheek bar bites like a 'Trump' turkey burger. Pulling everyone from hotel guests to locals from the nearby Buzzfeed and Lulu offices, it's a winning spot for languid cocktail sessions, landmark spotting and a game of Jenga Giant.

★Library Bar COCKTAIL BAR

(Map p106; ☑ 323-769-8888; www.thehollywood roosevelt.com/about/food-drink/library-bar; Roosevelt Hotel, 7000 Hollywood Blvd; ⊙ 6pm-1am; ⊛; Ⓜ Red Line to Hollywood/Highland) Evoking an old hunting lodge with its timber panels, Chesterfield sofas and mounted antlers, this handsome hideaway sits off the Roosevelt Hotel's fountain-studded lobby. You won't find a cocktail menu here; simply tell the barkeeps what you're in the mood for and let them work their magic.

★Sayers Club CLUB

(Map p106; ☑ 323-871-8233; www.facebook.com/ TheSayersClub; 1645 Wilcox Ave; cover varies; ⊙ 9pm-2am Tue & Thu-Sat; Ⓜ Red Line to Hollywood/Vine) When established stars such as the Black Keys, and even movie stars such as Joseph Gordon-Levitt, decide to play secret shows in intimate environs, they come to the back room at this brick-house Hollywood nightspot, where the booths are leather, the lighting moody and the music always satisfying.

★No Vacancy BAR

(Map p106; ☑ 323-465-1902; www.novacancyla. com; 1727 N Hudson Ave; ⊙ 8pm-2am; Ⓜ Red Line to

Hollywood/Vine) If you prefer your cocktail sessions with plenty of wow factor, make a reservation online, style up (no sportswear, shorts or logos) and head to this old shingled Victorian. A vintage scene of dark timber panels and elegant banquettes, it has bars in nearly every corner, tended by clever barkeeps while burlesque dancers and a tightrope walker entertain the droves of party people.

★Dirty Laundry BAR

(Map p106; ☑ 323-462-6531; http://dirtylaundry barla.com; 1725 N Hudson Ave; ⊙ 10pm-2am Tue-Sat; Ⓜ Red Line to Hollywood/Vine) Under a cotton-candy-pink apartment block of no particular import is this funky den of musty odor, low ceilings, exposed pipes and good times. There's fine whiskey, funkalicious tunes on the turntables and plenty of eye-candy peeps with low inhibitions. Alas, there are also velvet-rope politics at work, so reserve a table to make sure you slip through.

★Harvard & Stone BAR

(☑ 323-466-6063; http://harvardandstone.com; 5221 Hollywood Blvd; ⊙ 8pm-2am; Ⓜ Red Line to Hollywood/Western) With daily rotating craft whiskey, bourbon and cocktail specials, Harvard & Stone lures peeps with its live bands, solid DJs and burlesque troops working their saucy magic on Fridays and Saturdays. Think Colorado ski lodge meets steampunk industrial, with a blues and rockabilly soul. Note the dress code, which discourages shorts, shiny shirts, baggy clothes, sports gear and flip-flops.

★La Descarga LOUNGE

(☑ 323-466-1324; www.ladescargala.com; 1159 N Western Ave; ⊙ 8pm-2am Tue-Sat) This tastefully frayed, reservations-only rum and cigar lounge is a revelation. Behind the marble bar sit more than 100 types of rum from Haiti, Guyana, Guatemala and Venezuela. The bartenders mix specialty cocktails, but you'd do well to order something aged, and sip it neat as you enjoy the Mambo and Son sounds and the burlesque ballerina on the catwalk. Guys, wear smart shoes and shirts. No jeans. Ladies wear heels and a dress or dark pants.

Frolic Room BAR

(Map p106; ☑ 323-462-5890; 6245 Hollywood Blvd; ⊙ 11am-2am; Ⓜ Red Line to Hollywood/ Vine) The neon sign is worth a trip alone, but Frolic Room offers more than colored lights. This is one of Hollywood's true dives, a vinyl-lined relic where the drinks are stiff and the regulars quirky. It has served them

LOS ANGELES FOR CHILDREN

Los Angeles is sometimes touted as not especially child friendly, and looking around Rodeo Dr or the Sunset Strip, you might think that young Angelenos have been banished to a gingerbread cottage in the woods. In reality, LA offers a plethora of child-friendly attractions, from theme parks to interactive museums.

Museums

Griffith Observatory Watch eyes widen inside the world's top planetarium (p124) then scan the skies through a telescope.

La Brea Tar Pits Get up close and personal with curious prehistoric beasts, right beside an ancient death pit (p136).

California Science Center Hands-on, high-tech exhibits (p224) exploring nature and technology, plus a real-deal NASA space shuttle and seven-story IMAX screen.

Natural History Museum of Los Angeles You'll find one of the world's most impressive dinosaur exhibits at LA's Natural History Museum (p223), as well as creepy bugs and a dedicated Nature Lab.

Zimmer Children's Museum Play instruments, fly planes and drive ambulances at this community-minded museum (p136), specially designed for children aged eight and under.

Museum of Tolerance Explore the life of Anne Frank and the importance of compassion and cultural understanding at this interactive educational center (p157).

Kidspace Children's Museum Get wet and a just a little muddy at Pasadena's nature-driven museum (p213), complete with educational gardens and water features.

Coastal Fun

Santa Monica Fun-fair attractions, wide sweeps of golden sand and wade-friendly shallows beckon families at Santa Monica (p174).

---

all, from Judy Garland to Charles Bukowski, and it's here that Kevin Spacey downs a drink in the film *LA Confidential*.

Good Times At Davey Wayne's BAR
(Map p106; ☑ 323-962-3804; www.goodtimesatdaveywaynes.com; 1611 N El Centro Ave; ⊙5pm-2am Mon-Fri, from 2pm Sat & Sun; Ⓜ Red Line to Hollywood/Vine) Enter the faux garage, walk through the refrigerator door and emerge in a dim, rocking ode to 1970s Californication, complete with pine paneling, 'groovy' wallpaper and enough interior-design kitsch to make your sideburns explode. The draught beers are craftsman and there's a second bar (housed in a camper) and barbecue on the back deck. Attracts mainly 20- to 30-something hipsters.

☆ Entertainment

Hollywood serves up a plethora of entertainment options, from mainstream and art-house films, to Broadway musicals and indie bands. The neighborhood is home to the famous Hollywood Bowl, as well as the Upright Citizens Brigade Theatre, one of LA's best live-comedy venues. Hollywood's Theatre Row – a stretch of Santa Monica Blvd roughly bordered by McCadden Pl and El Centro Ave – is dotted with small, independent theater companies.

★**Hollywood Bowl** CONCERT VENUE
(Map p126; ☑ 323-850-2000; www.hollywoodbowl.com; 2301 N Highland Ave; rehearsals free, performance costs vary; ⊙ Jun-Sep) Summers in LA just wouldn't be the same without alfresco melodies under the stars at the Bowl, a huge natural amphitheater in the Hollywood Hills. Its annual season – which usually runs from June to September – includes symphonies, jazz bands and iconic acts such as Blondie, Bryan Ferry and Angélique Kidjo. Bring a sweater or blanket as it gets cool at night.

Thankfully, big projection screens ensure that even folks in the 'nosebleed' sections (from around $18) enjoy close-ups of the performers. Come early to claim a table in the park-like grounds for a preshow picnic

Aquarium of the Pacific Eye up strange creatures from the shallows and the deep at Long Beach's knockout aquarium (p198), which also runs harbor cruises and seasonal whale-watching trips.

Manhattan Beach Long shallows and an aquarium (☎ 310-379-8117; www.roundhouseaquarium.org; Manhattan Beach Pier, Manhattan Beach; suggested donation $2-5; ☻ 2-5pm Mon-Fri & 10am-sunset Sat & Sun early Sep-late May, until 8pm daily late May-early Sep; ⊕) **FREE** with touch pool at the end of the pier.

Cabrillo Beach Tide pools, the choice of calmer waters and the nearby Cabrillo Marine Aquarium (p200) make this stretch of sand perfect for younger kids.

Thrills

Six Flags Magic Mountain Hair-raising, adrenaline-searing roller coasters are the main drawcard at this massive Valley theme park (p231).

Hurricane Harbor Magic Mountain's adjacent water park (p231) cools kids (and kids at heart) with its wave pool, 1300ft river and soaring, fully enclosed speed waterslides.

Universal Studios Hollywood Studio tours, live shows and theme-park rides keep the families coming to Universal Studios Hollywood (p205).

Sunset Ranch Hollywood Explore LA's wilder side with a horseback tour (p127) through rugged Griffith Park.

Budding Artists

Getty Center A blockbuster art museum (p152) with child-friendly interactive displays, a kids' gift shop, entertainment and play-friendly gardens.

LACMA Giant sculptures and a hands-on children's gallery will keep little art fiends buzzing at must-see LACMA (p135).

(some picnic areas open up to four hours before show time and alcohol is permitted). There are numerous food stands on site if you don't want to lug your own grub.

The bowl is the summer home of the LA Philharmonic and the Hollywood Bowl Orchestra. Open rehearsals are held on some Tuesdays and Thursdays during the season (always call ahead to confirm).

Parking is free during the day, but expensive and limited on performance nights. Save yourself the headache and take a shuttle, such as the one running from Hollywood & Highland (p119), which costs $6 per person round trip.

★ **Upright Citizens Brigade Theatre**   COMEDY
(Map p106; ☎ 323-908-8702; http://franklin.ucb theatre.com; 5919 Franklin Ave; tickets $5-12) Founded in New York by *Saturday Night Live* alums Amy Poehler and Ian Roberts along with Matt Besser and Matt Walsh, this sketch-comedy group cloned itself in Hollywood in 2005. With numerous nightly shows spanning anything from stand-up comedy to improv and sketch, it's arguably the best comedy hub in town. Valet parking costs $7.

Pantages Theatre   THEATER
(Map p106; ☎ 323-468-1770; http://hollywood pantages.com; 6233 Hollywood Blvd; Ⓜ Red Line to Hollywood/Vine) The splendidly restored Pantages Theater is an art deco survivor from the Golden Age and a fabulous place to catch a hot-ticket Broadway musical. Recent shows include *An American in Paris, The Book of Mormon* and *Hamilton*. Tidbit: the theater hosted the Academy Awards ceremony between 1949 and 1959.

ArcLight Cinemas   CINEMA
(Map p106; ☎ 323-464-1478; www.arclight cinemas.com; 6360 W Sunset Blvd; Ⓜ Red Line to Hollywood/Vine) Assigned seats, exceptional celeb-sighting potential and a varied program that covers mainstream and art-house movies make this 14-screen multiplex the best around. If your taste dovetails with its schedule, the awesome 1963 geodesic Cinerama Dome is a must. Bonuses: age-21-plus screenings where you can booze it up, and

Q&As with directors, writers and actors. Parking is $3 for four hours.

Bardot
CLUB

(Map p106; ☑323-462-8900; www.avalonholly wood.com; 1735 N Vine St; ☺7:30pm-1am Mon, 9pm-2am Tue, 10pm-2am Thu & Sat, 9:30pm-2am Fri; Ⓜ Red Line to Hollywood/Vine) On Monday nights, KCRW's Chris Douridas brings **School Night** (www.itsaschoolnight.com), a free live-music club featuring buzz-worthy talent to the atmospheric top floor of the old Avalon theater. There is no exclusivity here, but you do have to RSVP and show up early enough to get in prior to max capacity.

iO West Theater
COMEDY

(Map p106; ☑323-962-7560; http://ioimprov.com/ west; 6366 Hollywood Blvd; admission free-$10; Ⓜ Red Line to Hollywood/Vine) This long-running, multispace theater serves up at least four comedy shows a night, starting on the hour. Saturday night's The Armando Show ($5) is hosted by a celebrity guest and hinges on suggestions from the audience. Sunday-night staple Top Story! Weekly ($5), written by some of the industry's top comedy scriptwriters, takes an irreverent look at the week's news headlines.

Fonda Theatre
CONCERT VENUE

(Map p106; ☑323-464-6269; www.fondatheatre. com; 6126 Hollywood Blvd; Ⓜ Red Line to Hollywood/ Vine) Dating back to the Roaring Twenties, the since-restored Henry Fonda Theatre remains one of Hollywood's best venues for live tunes. It's an intimate, (mostly) general-admission space with an open dance floor and balcony seating. Expect progressive bands such as The Radio Dept and Pussy Riot, groove masters like Clean Bandit and next-gen rappers like Kanye protégé Desiigner.

ⓘ PARKING IN HOLLYWOOD

Many of Hollywood's main tourist sights are easily accessible by metro (Red Line). If you are driving, however, parking at the Hollywood & Highland mall is especially convenient. Parking costs $2 for two hours (with validation from participating mall shops and eateries, among them Starbucks), or $2 for four hours with validation from Grauman's Chinese Theatre. Enter the parking garage from either Highland Ave or Orange Dr.

El Floridita
DANCE

(Map p138; ☑323-871-8612; www.elfloridita.com; 1253 N Vine St; cover $10-15, with dinner free; ☺11:30am-1:45am Mon, Fri & Sat, to 9pm Tue-Thu & Sun; ☎; Ⓜ Red Line to Hollywood/Vine) The place for grown-up salseros. Order a mojito and watch the beautiful dancers do their thing (or join in if you feel you've got the moves). Live shows run on Monday, Friday and Saturday only; Monday's long-running salsa night (from 8pm) is especially popular, so make reservations at least a week in advance.

Audiences Unlimited
BOOKING SERVICE

(☑818-260-0041; www.tvtickets.com) Booking service for a variety of free TV-show tapings, including Big Bang Theory and 2 Broke Girls. Tickets for most shows are released 30 days prior to the show date. See the website for schedules.

El Capitan Theatre
CINEMA

(Map p106; ☑800-347-6396; www.elcapitantheatre. com; 6838 Hollywood Blvd; ♿; Ⓜ Red Line to Hollywood/Highland) Disney rolls out family-friendly blockbusters at this movie palace, sometimes with costumed characters putting on the Ritz in live preshow routines. The best seats are on the balcony in the middle of the front row. VIP tickets ($28) allow you to reserve a seat and include popcorn and a beverage.

Hotel Cafe
LIVE MUSIC

(Map p106; ☑323-461-2040; www.hotelcafe.com; 1623 N Cahuenga Blvd; Ⓜ Red Line to Hollywood/ Vine) An anomaly on glittery Cahuenga Corridor, this intimate venue is the place for handmade music by message-minded singer-songwriters. It's mainly a stepping stone for newbie balladeers (a fresh-faced Adele wowed the crowd here back in 2008). Get there early and enter from the alley. Doors usually open at 6:30pm (check the website).

Catalina Bar & Grill
JAZZ

(Map p106; ☑323-466-2210; www.catalinajazzclub. com; 6725 W Sunset Blvd; cover $15-40 plus dinner or 2 drinks) It might be tucked in a ho-hum office building (enter through the garage), but once you're inside this sultry, premier jazz club all is forgiven. Expect a mix of top touring talent and emerging local acts – performers have included Roy Hargrove, Monty Alexander, Barbara Morrison, Kenny Burrell and Chick Corea. One or two shows nightly, best reserved ahead.

Ford Theatres
CONCERT VENUE

(Map p126; ☑ 323-461-3673; www.fordtheatres.org; 2580 Cahuenga Blvd E; tickets $25-125; ☺ Jun-Oct) Every seat is within 100ft of the stage at this up-close-and-personal outdoor amphitheater. Recently renovated and with the Hollywood Hills as a backdrop, it's an atmospheric spot to catch indie bands, foreign movies and dance troupes from June to October. Picnics welcome.

🛍 Shopping

Hollywood Blvd is the epicenter of tacky souvenirs, while Highland and Melrose Aves are well known for their sharply curated galleries and showrooms selling expensive furniture and design pieces, including mid-century design pieces.

Amoeba Music
MUSIC

(Map p106; ☑ 323-245-6400; www.amoeba.com; 6400 W Sunset Blvd; ☺ 10:30am-11pm Mon-Sat, 11am-10pm Sun) When a record store not only survives but thrives in this techno age, you know it's doing something right. Flip through 500,000 new and used CDs, DVDs, videos and vinyl at this granddaddy of music stores, which also stocks band-themed T-shirts, music memorabilia, books and comics. Handy listening stations and the store's outstanding *Music We Like* booklet keep you from buying lemons.

Check the website for free in-store live performances by touring bands.

Just One Eye
FASHION & ACCESSORIES

(Map p138; ☑ 888-563-6858; http://justoneeye.com; 700 Romaine St; ☺ 10:30am-7pm Mon-Sat) Coveted fashion and art collide at Just One Eye. A dramatic concept store hidden inside Howard Hughes' former headquarters, its racks are hang with bold, creative, expensive threads from big-guns such as Gucci, Stella McCartney and Bruno Cucinelli and cognoscenti labels like Beau Souchi. Intriguing jewelry, eye-catching kicks and a smattering of collectable furniture, sculpture and other artworks (Warhol, anyone?) complete the picture.

To find it, head through the door to the right of the main gated entrance (itself an art-deco treat) and turn right into the hallway.

Counterpoint
MUSIC, BOOKS

(Map p106; ☑ 323-957-7965; www.counterpointrecordsandbooks.com; 5911 Franklin Ave; ☺ 11am-11pm) Woodblock stacks are packed high with used fiction, while crude plywood bins are stuffed with vinyl soul, classical and jazz. The real gems (the rare first editions and vintage rock posters) are in the collectible wing next door.

Hollywood & Highland
MALL

(Map p106; www.hollywoodandhighland.com; 6801 Hollywood Blvd; ☺ 10am-10pm Mon-Sat, to 7pm Sun; 🚻; Ⓜ Red Line to Hollywood/Highland) It's appropriate that a Disney-fied shopping mall should be the spark for Hollywood Blvd's rebirth. A marriage of kitsch and commerce, the main showpiece is a triumphal arch, inspired by DW Griffith's 1916 movie *Intolerance* and framing the Hollywood sign. The limited retail mix is mainly midrange and mainstream; souvenir hunters may want to check out the Dodgers Clubhouse store on level three.

Space 15 Twenty
MALL

(Map p106; www.space1520.com; 1520 N Cahuenga Blvd; ☺ Pharmacy Boardshop 11am-8pm Mon-Thu, to 9pm Fri, 10am-9pm Sat, 11am-7pm Sun, Free People 11am-7pm Mon-Sat, to 6pm Sun) The hippest mini-mall in Hollywood, this designer construct of brick, wood, concrete and glass is home to streetwear-cum-skateboard store Pharmacy Boardshop and women's boho-chic boutique Free People. The venue is also home to a branch of Umani Burger, plus a salon and regular pop-ups and other special events; see the website for details.

Silver Lake & Echo Park

Pimped with stencil art, inked skin and skinny jeans, Silver Lake and Echo Park are the epicenter of LA hipsterdom. Silver Lake is the more upwardly mobile of the pair, home to revitalized modernist homes, sharing-plate menus and obscure fashion labels on boutique racks. To the southeast lies grittier Echo Park, one of LA's oldest neighborhoods. Despite its own ongoing gentrification, it continues to offer a contrasting jumble of rickety homes, Mexican *panderias* (bakeries), indie rock bars, vintage stores, design-literate coffee shops and the serenity of its namesake lake, featured in Polanski's *Chinatown*.

◉ Sights

Echo Park claims a pair of LA icons: its eponymous lake and hilltop Dodgers Stadium. More niche in nature is the Tom of Finland House, a small house museum dedicated to world-famous homoerotic artist Touko Laaksonen. Silver Lake's own home-turned-museum is the Neutra VDL House, former abode and office of acclaimed architect Richard Neutra. Alas, Silver Lake's usually picturesque reservoir is expected to remain empty until 2018.

Dodger Stadium
STADIUM

(☏866-363-4377; http://m.mlb.com/dodgers/tickets/tours; 1000 Elysian Park Ave; tours adult/child & senior from $20/15; ⊙tours 10am, 11:30am & 1pm; ℗) Built in 1962, and one of Major League Baseball's classic ballparks, Dodger Stadium offers behind-the-scenes tours. Your 1½ hours will cover the press box (base camp of the legendary Vin Scully), the Dodger dugout, the Dugout Club, the field and the Tommy Lasorda Training Center. Reservations are strongly advised.

During the season (April to October), tours are held almost daily – except on game days. In the off-season they are less frequent. Of course, the best way to experience the stadium is to go to the ol' ball game with MLB's most dedicated fan base. LA does love its Dodgers.

Neutra VDL House
ARCHITECTURE

(www.neutra-vdl.org; 2300 Silver Lake Blvd, Silver Lake; adult/senior/child $15/10/free; ⊙guided tours 11am-3pm Sat, last tour commences 2:30pm) Built in 1932, burnt to a crisp in 1963 then subsequently rebuilt, the light-washed former home and laboratory of modernist architect Richard Neutra is a leading example of mid-century Californian design. Indeed, the site was declared a National Historic Landmark in 2017. Thirty-minute guided tours of the property run most Saturdays, shedding light on the Austrian-born architect's theories and stylistic evolution. Reservations not required.

Always check the website as tours are not run some weeks.

Echo Park Lake
PARK

(www.laparks.org; 751 Echo Park Ave, Echo Park; ℗) Surrounded by shingled craftsmen homes that rise with the steep streets and looming hills to the north, and blessed with keyhole Downtown views to the south, this fountain lake park is patronized by cool rockers, laid-back *vatos* (dudes), flocks of ducks and crows, and is home to wild, wind-rustled palms.

Tom of Finland House
MUSEUM

(☏213-250-1685; http://tomoffinlandfoundation.org; 1421 Laveta Tce, Echo Park; ⊙by appointment) This craftsman cottage was once home to artist Touko Laaksonen (aka Tom of Finland), internationally renowned for his illustrations of well-endowed, leather-clad beefcakes in all sorts of erotic scenarios. Today the property is home to the Tom of Finland Foundation, dedicated to cataloging Laaksonen's work and supporting erotic artists. Tours of the collection are available on request and the venue also runs life-drawing sessions, usually on the second Sunday of the month (check the website).

🛏 Sleeping

Sunset Blvd is speckled with dated, uninspiring motels. The most popular option for travelers in these two neighborhoods is the private rental of local homes or bedrooms.

🍴 Eating

Silver Lake and Echo Park offer vibrant dining scenes, spanning everything from fashionable neighborhood bistros serving seasonal sharing plates, to low-fuss joints pumping out everything from vegan fare and pho, to ramen, Thai and Mexican street food, and out-of-the-box breakfasts. Sunset Blvd is the area's dining spine. In Silver Lake you'll also find good options on Silver Lake Blvd (near Effie St), Rowena Ave and Hyperion Ave.

★ Sqirl
CAFE $

(Map p128; ☏323-284-8147; http://sqirlla.com; 720 N Virgil Ave; dishes $5-15; ⊙6:30am-4pm Mon-Fri, from 8am Sat & Sun; ☏🅿; Ⓜ Red Line to Vermont/Santa Monica) Despite its somewhat-obscure location, this tiny, subway-tiled cafe is forever pumping thanks to its top-notch, out-of-the-box breakfast and lunch offerings. Join the queue to order made-from-scratch wonders such as long-cooked chicken and rice porridge served with dried lime, ginger, turmeric, cardamon ghee and tomato, or the cult-status ricotta toast, a symphony of velvety housemade ricotta, thick-cut 'burnt' brioche and Sqirl's artisanal jams.

★ Night + Market Song
THAI $

(Map p128; ☏323-665-5899; www.nightmarketla.com; 3322 Sunset Blvd; dishes $7-15; ⊙noon-3pm Mon-Fri, 5-11pm Mon-Sat; 🍴) After cultivating a cult following in WeHo, this gleefully garish temple to real-deal Thai and Cambodian street food is killing it in the hipster heartlands. Invigorate the taste buds with spicy larb (minced-meat salad), proper pad Thai and harder-to-find specialties such as Isaan-style fermented pork sausage.

Mohawk Bend PUB FOOD $

(📞213-483-2337; http://mohawk.la; 2141 Sunset Blvd, Echo Park; pizzas $13-15, dinner mains $12-15; ⏰11:30am-11:30pm Mon-Thu, to 1am Fri, 9:30am-1am Sat, 9:30am-11:30pm Sun; 🛜🍴) This former vaudeville theater is now a casual, industrial-style bar and eatery packed with skinny jeans and beards. Local produce dominates the vegan-friendly menu, its standouts including buffalo cauliflower and an almond-ricotta and kale pizza. Seventy-two taps pour Californian craft beers, wines, ciders, kombucha and cold brew.

Silver Lake Ramen RAMEN $

(Map p128; 📞323-660-8100; www.silverlakeramen.com; 2927 Sunset Blvd; ramen $9.75-12.50; ⏰11:30am-11pm Sun-Thu, to 1:45am Fri & Sat; 🅿) In a retro strip mall on Sunset is this toasty, super-popular ramen spot. You'll probably have to wait for a table or a seat at the counter, but the wait is worth it. Once seated, order the classic *tonkotsu* ramen with pork belly. The meat is beautifully charred and the broth is full bodied and creamy.

Sage VEGAN $

(📞213-989-1718; www.sageveganbistro.com; 1700 W Sunset Blvd, Echo Park; dishes $9-15; ⏰11am-10pm Mon-Wed, to 11pm Thu & Fri, 9am-4pm & 5-11pm Sat, to 10pm Sun; 🛜🍴🚼) Popular, loft-like Sage dishes out organic vegan fare, from a spicy buffalo-cauliflower salad and tempeh-loaded burger, to tacos stuffed with jackfruit 'carnitas' or walnut cranberry 'meat.' If you're undecided, go for the butternut-squash ravioli. Servings are generous and delicious, and the team friendly. For a sweet, guilt-free epilogue, try the organic, vegan KindKreme ice cream (the caramel topping is the bomb).

★**Ostrich Farm** MODERN AMERICAN $$

(📞213-537-0657; http://ostrichfarmla.com; 1525 Sunset Blvd; dinner mains $19-29; ⏰10am-2pm Tue-Fri, to 3pm Sat & Sun, also 5:30-10pm Mon-Thu, 5:30-11pm Fri & Sat) Flickering tea lights and charming, competent barkeeps crank up the charm at this intimate, convivial space, owned and run by a husband-and-wife team. You won't find ostrich on the menu (the name refers to a former railway that reached Griffith Park), just beautiful, honest takes on American classics, many of them cooked over the kitchen's wood-fired grill.

Whatever you choose, conclude with the salty dark-chocolate tart.

★**Kettle Black** ITALIAN $$

(Map p128; 📞323-641-3705; www.kettleblackla.com; 3705 W Sunset Blvd, Silver Lake; pizzas $13-18, mains $23-26; ⏰5-10:45pm Sun-Wed, to 1:15am Thu-Sat) Kettle Black belongs to the new Silver Lake guard, a dark, stylish cocktail bar-restaurant with fashionable diners, communal bar tables and a dizzying back bar lined with clued-in craft spirits. The wood-fired oven delivers gorgeous, dense pizzas and the house-made pastas are superb. The enlightened wine list is an all-Italian affair, though we suggest an invigorating G&T made with local Mulholland Distilling gin.

★**Elf Cafe** VEGETARIAN $$

(📞213-484-6829; www.clfcafe.com; 2135 Sunset Blvd, Echo Park; mains $16-23; ⏰6-11pm Mon-Sat; 🍴) This intimate Echo Park mainstay is one of the best – if not the very best – vegetarian restaurants in LA. The menu has distinct Mediterranean and Middle Eastern leanings, evident in thoughtful dishes such as baked feta wrapped in grape leaves and a gorgeous mushroom kofta with preserved lemon purée and herbed saffron yogurt.

Fat Dragon CHINESE $$

(Map p128; 📞323-667-9193; www.fatdragonla.com; 3500 W Sunset Blvd, Silver Lake; mains $15-18; ⏰5-10pm Tue-Fri, from 11:30am Sat & Sun; 🅿) Lo-fi, counter-service Fat Dragon pumps out tweaked takes on old-school American Chinese to the sound of hip-hop and woks. Chow down hearty, flavor-packed dishes such as sweet-and-tangy eggplant with spicy garlic sauce, chili-spiked pork-and-shrimp wontons or stir-fry pork jowl with tofu, bell peppers and Chinese celery. Unlike many old-school Chinese dives, the focus here is on fresh, quality ingredients.

Black Cat NEW AMERICAN $$

(Map p128; 📞323-661-6369; www.theblackcatla.com; 3909 W Sunset Blvd, Silver Lake; mains $15-38; ⏰4pm-midnight Mon-Fri, from 11am Sat & Sun) In 1966, two years before New York's Stonewall Riots, LGBT protesters bravely stood up to police harassment at this very site. These days, the Black Cat is a slinky, inclusive neighborhood restaurant and bar, with produce-driven comfort bites – think gorgeous kale and roasted garlic salads, bluecheese burgers, and yams with smoked fig, balsamic and chili.

Alimento ITALIAN $$

(Map p128; ☑323-928-2888; www.alimentola.com; 1710 Silver Lake Blvd, Silver Lake; dishes $8-19; ☉5:30-10pm Tue-Thu & Sun, to 11pm Fri & Sat) In a small, simple, modern space packed with convivial locals, chef Zach Pollack delivers contemporary takes on regional Italian cooking. The pasta – made in-house using locally milled flour – includes a subversive take on *tortellini in brodo* (tortellini in broth), with the liquid sealed inside the pasta. If you're partial to seafood, try the flawlessly charred octopus with black barley. Reservations recommended.

★Wolfdown MODERN AMERICAN $$$

(Map p128; ☑323-522-6381; www.wolfdownla.com; 2764 Rowena Ave, Silver Lake; dishes $8-45; ☉5:30-10pm Tue-Thu, to 11pm Fri & Sat; 🍽) Young Korean-American chef Jason Kim has created a buzz with his latest venture, a snug, discreet restaurant with a 'deconstructed farmhouse' design, adorable outdoor patio and convivial pine-clad bar (the best seat in the house). Kim personally picks his market produce, creating seductive dishes like coconut black rice with oil-cured vegetables and a crunchy, sweet Korean fried chicken (opt for the chili version).

🍷 Drinking & Nightlife

You won't go thirsty in these parts, with a diverse and eclectic choice of drinking holes that range from hipster coffee shops and dive bars, to hidden cocktail lounges, fun and dirty gay bars and an old-school German beer joint. The greatest concentration of venues in both neighborhoods is on (or just off) Sunset Blvd.

★Eightfold Coffee CAFE

(☑213-947-3500; www.facebook.com/eightfoldcoffee; 1294 Sunset Blvd, Echo Park; ☉7am-5pm; 🍽) Eastside stylists, bloggers and musicians flock to this cool, whitewashed coffee shop to talk gigs, browse niche journals and sip superlative, Portland-roasted coffee. There's a small selection of decent pastries, artisan bagels and (on weekdays) breakfast burritos, plus a couple of power sockets at the back if your laptop needs juice.

★Virgil BAR

(Map p128; ☑323-660-4540; www.thevirgil.com; 4519 Santa Monica Blvd, Silver Lake; ☉7pm-2am) An atmospheric, vintage-styled neighborhood

hangout serving quality cocktails to local hipsters and arty types. A stocked calendar of entertainment includes top-notch live-comedy nights, with hilarious, subversive erotic fan-fiction improv on the third Sunday of the month. Other rotating events include booze-fueled spelling bees, storytelling events, bands and themed club nights, including '80s-themed Funkmosphere on Thursdays. Did we mention the jukebox?

Red Lion Tavern BEER HALL

(☑323-662-5337; http://redliontavern.net; 2366 Glendale Blvd, Silver Lake; ☉11am-2am, beer garden to 11pm Sun-Thu & 1am Fri & Sat; 🍽) Chipped, worn and armed with retro cigarette vending machine, this old-school beer dive has been pouring German suds since 1959. The snug, woody downstairs bar feels like a Teutonic version of *Cheers,* while upstairs is an even cozier bar and a super-popular beer garden. Beer flights are $10 and edibles include fantastic pretzels and a sausage platter large enough for two.

Sunset Beer Company BAR

(☑213-481-2337; http://sunsetbeerco.com; 1498 Sunset Blvd, Echo Park; ☉bar 4-11pm Mon-Thu, 2pm-midnight Fri & Sat, 1-10pm Sun) What's better than a beer store? One with a bar. That's what you get here, where clued-up, attitude-free staffers are happy to help you decide between that Imperial India Pale Ale from Coronado, or the Eagle Rock Solidarity on Nitro. It's a snug, low-key spot and always a good bet before a Dodgers game.

Short Stop CLUB

(☑213-482-4942; 1455 W Sunset Blvd, Echo Park; ☉5pm-2am Mon-Fri, from 2pm Sat & Sun) Echo Park's beloved and deceptively sprawling dive has a dance floor in one room, a bar strobing ballgames on flat-screens in another, and a pool table and pinball machines in yet another section. Longtime Echo Park locals and new-breed hipsters bump shoulders and more here...especially on Motown Mondays, when vintage jams fill the room with joy.

Thirsty Crow BAR

(Map p128; ☑323-661-6007; www.thirstycrowbar.com; 2939 W Sunset Blvd; ☉5pm-2am Mon-Fri, from 2pm Sat & Sun) A divey, hipster-pulling whiskey bar on Sunset where (small-batch) bourbon is the preferred poison. The $5 happy-hour drinks, offered 5pm to 8pm on weekdays and 2pm to 8pm on weekends, are a steal.

☆ Entertainment

★ Echo
LIVE MUSIC

(www.attheecho.com; 1822 W Sunset Blvd, Echo Park; cover varies) Eastsiders hungry for an eclectic alchemy of sounds pack this super-packed dive, basically a sweaty bar with a stage and a back patio. On the music front, expect anything from indie and electronica, to dub reggae and dream and power pop. Monday nights are dedicated to up-and-coming local bands, with regular club nights including Saturday's always-a-blast Funky Sole party.

★ Dodger Stadium
BASEBALL

(☎ 866-363-4377; www.dodgers.com; 1000 Vin Scully Ave) Few clubs can match the Dodgers when it comes to history (Jackie Robinson, Sandy Koufax, Kirk Gibson and Vin Scully), success and fan loyalty. The club's newest owners bought the organization for roughly $2 billion, an American team-sports record.

Satellite
LIVE MUSIC

(Map p128; ☎ 323-661-4380; www.thesatellitela.com; 1717 Silver Lake Blvd, Silver Lake) On the radar since 1995, divey Satellite remains immensely popular thanks to its kicking lineup of indie bands. Rock on downstairs or escape to the upstairs bar. Monday nights showcase up-and-coming bands on one-month Satellite residences, with indie-pop club night Dance Yourself Clean (www.danceyourself-clean.com) on Saturdays. Young crowds and cheap valet parking ($5).

🔒 Shopping

Silver Lake offers painfully cool fashion and concept stores selling niche threads, fragrances and accessories, to specialist stores stocking records, handmade leather goods and collectable bar props. Most line Sunset Blvd, though you'll also find a handful of interesting retailers on Silver Lake Blvd and Rowena Ave. Further southeast on Sunset Blvd, Echo Park's eclectic retail mix includes local art, fabulous vintage fashion and accessories and sculptural, handmade jewelry.

★ Mohawk
General Store
FASHION & ACCESSORIES

(Map p128; ☎ 323-669-1602; www.mohawkgeneral-store.com; 4017 W Sunset Blvd, Silver Lake; ⊙ 11am-7pm Mon-Sat, to 6pm Sun) Stylish individualists hit Mohawk for edgy, progressive men's fashion and accessories, including hard-to-find fragrances from the likes of Byredo and jewelry by local designer Matthew Ready. Fashion-forward labels include Belgium's Jan Van Essche and Mohawk's own Smock. The mezzanine level is dedicated to Dries Van Noten and, unexpectedly, a small collection of vintage hi-fi equipment. The women's store lies a few doors down.

★ Esqueleto
JEWELRY

(☎ 213-947-3508; http://shopesqueleto.com; 1298 Sunset Blvd, Echo Park; ⊙ 11am-7pm Mon-Thu, to 6pm Fri-Sun) Esqueleto showcases highly imaginative, affordable collections of fine jewelry from mostly West Coast and New York–based designers. Among them is the work of the store's Oakland-based owner, Lauren Wolf, inspired by vintage design and oceanic textures. Silver jewelry starts at around $30, with gold pieces starting from about $200. Tapestry weavings, ceramics and art are also in the mix.

★ Luxe De Ville
VINTAGE

(☎ 213-353-0135; http://luxedeville.com; 2157 Sunset Blvd, Echo Park; ⊙ 12:30-7pm Mon, from noon Tue-Sat, noon-5pm Sun) Mention Oskar de la Cruz to LA stylists and chances are they know (and love) Oskar and his Echo Park boutique. His sharp eye for rare, uber-stylish and impeccably maintained vintage threads and accessories is legendary, whether it's a deco-tasseled Lillie Rubin frock, a vintage ostrich coat or a 1960s mod-style hat.

Clare V
FASHION & ACCESSORIES

(Map p128; ☎ 323-665-2476; www.clarev.com; 3339 W Sunset Blvd, Silver Lake; ⊙ 11am-7pm Mon-Sat, to 6pm Sun) The eponymous store of French transplant Claire Vivier, who sells her cool, idiosyncratic bags and leather goods (we love the iPad Notebook sleeves) alongside bold local jewelry, French scented candles, vegan sneakers, chic luggage tags and cute office accessories. Vivier also collaborates with other designers, producing anything from playful graphic tees to '50s-inspired eyewear.

Lemon Frog
VINTAGE

(☎ 213-413-2143; http://lemonfrogshop.com; 1202 N Alvarado St, Echo Park; ⊙ 10:30am-5:30pm Mon-Wed & Sat, to 6:30pm Thu, 11:30am-7:30pm Fri, noon-5pm Sun) Bold, vibrant patterns and colors dominate at this jam-packed treasure trove of vintage fashion. Owner Micki Curtis displays cheaper items at the front, with the pricier goods deeper in the store. It's a mostly '60s and '70s affair, with a little '90s thrown in for on-trend millennials and a small, precious booty of '20s frocks and accessories on the wall.

Nico & Bullitt
GIFTS & SOUVENIRS

(☎213-674-7755; www.nicoandbullitt.com; 2205 Sunset Blvd, Echo Park; ☉11am-7pm Tue-Sun) Cassette-themed paintings, leather satchels, felt coasters, retro-themed mugs, kitsch tomes, hand-printed LA-themed cards: Nico & Bullitt is all about good vibes and quirky objects from local and independent designers. Buy a kitschy pin from the vending machine or scan the racks for retro-inspired threads for girls and guys, from '70s-style tees to denim overalls and summery, LA-designed frocks.

Foxhole LA
VINTAGE

(Map p128; ☎213-290-7175; www.foxholela.com; 3318 W Sunset Blvd, Silver Lake; ☉noon-5pm Mon-Sat) Lovebirds Jeff and Fox stock their shop with a solid selection of lovingly worn and reworked denim, from classic 501s to funky bell-bottoms, jackets and shirts. Match with retro tees, which include Foxhole's own coveted numbers. Best of all, the guys also provide expert tailoring, guaranteed to make that butt look good in your new denim favorites.

The Odells
FASHION & ACCESSORIES

(Map p128; ☎323-515-7385; https://theodellsshop.com; 3906 W Sunset Blvd, Silver Lake; ☉11am-7pm Mon-Sat, to 6pm Sun) Not only do owners Laura Stang and Jason O'Dell sell their own Cali-cool label here – think women's oversized smocks, spaghetti jumpsuits, cropped culottes and boldly patterned frocks for little fashionistas – they also stock some of their favorite fashion labels for both women and men. Goods for guys include retro-inspired tees, button-down shirts, hoodies, cardigans, Swedish denim and hipster essentials like bow ties and boots.

Mush
GIFTS & SOUVENIRS

(Map p128; ☎323-664-6874; www.m-u-s-h.com; 1617 Silver Lake Blvd, Silver Lake; ☉11am-6pm Tue-Sun) An inspiring gift, antique and home-decor boutique filled with color, style and sheer originality. Stop by for stalactite rings and sterling-silver Navajo cuff bracelets, collectable lamps and eclectic armchairs, original paintings, Japanese incense, loose-leaf teas and everything in between. There seems to be an anecdote behind almost every object, happily recounted by the owner.

Clover
GIFTS & SOUVENIRS

(Map p128; ☎323-661-4142; www.facebook.com/Cloversilverlake; 2756 Rowena Ave, Silver Lake; ☉10am-7pm Mon-Sat, noon-6pm Sun) Free-spirited Clover stocks an eclectic mix of fashion, accessories and gifts. Head in for outstanding, locally designed jewelry, boho-chic threads, designer denim, wallets, clutches, even LA-neighborhood-themed coffee mugs.

Los Feliz & Griffith Park

Easy-living Los Feliz – (mis)pronounced *Fee-liz* – is home to screenwriters, low-key celebrities and some legendary bars. It's here that you'll find Jeff Goldblum tickling the ivories at the Rockwell, and Marty and Elayne jazzing it up at the Dresden lounge. Walt Disney opened his first studio on Hyperion Ave and the neighborhood's lush hillside mansions have housed greats such as Cecil B. DeMille and Norma Talmadge. North of Los Feliz lie the deep canyons and hiking trails of Griffith Park, whose own fabled icons include the mighty Griffith Observatory.

◎ Sights

Five times the size of New York's Central Park, Griffith Park is home to the world-famous Griffith Observatory, the oft-overlooked Autry Museum of the American West and the take-it-or-leave-it city zoo. Rising above the southern edge of Los Feliz, Barnsdall Art Park is crowned by architect Frank Lloyd Wright's Californian debut, Hollyhock House.

★ Griffith Observatory
MUSEUM

(Map p126; ☎213-473-0890; www.griffithobservatory.org; 2800 E Observatory Rd; admission free, planetarium shows adult/child $7/3; ☉noon-10pm Tue-Fri, from 10am Sat & Sun; P⊞; ☐DASH Observatory) FREE LA's landmark 1935 observatory opens a window onto the universe from its perch on the southern slopes of Mt Hollywood. Its planetarium claims the world's most advanced star projector, while its astronomical touch displays explore some mind-bending topics, from the evolution of the telescope and the ultraviolet Xrays used to map our solar system to the cosmos itself. Then, of course, there are the views, which (on clear days) take in the entire LA Basin, surrounding mountains and Pacific Ocean.

The public is welcome to peer into the Zeiss Telescope on the east side of the roof where sweeping views of the Hollywood Hills and the gleaming city below are especially spectacular at sunset. After dark, staff wheel additional telescopes out to the front lawn for star gazing.

Inside the building, you'll definitely want to grab a seat in the Planetarium – the aluminum-domed ceiling becomes a massive screen where lasers are projected to offer a tour of the cosmos, while another laser-projection show allows you to search for water, and life, beyond Earth. Downstairs, the Leonard Nimoy Event Horizon Theater screens a fascinating 24-minute documentary about the observatory's history, which includes an extraordinary engineering feat that saw the entire building lifted from its foundations during its expansion in the early 2000s.

The observatory itself has starred in numerous movies, most famously *Rebel Without a Cause* with James Dean. Outside, have your picture snapped beside the actor's bust with the Hollywood Sign caught neatly in the background.

Those relying on public transit can reach the observatory by hopping on the DASH Observatory shuttle bus, which runs between Vermont/Sunset metro station on the Red Line and the observatory. Buses run every 20 minutes from noon to 10pm on weekdays and from 10am to 10pm on weekends.

★ **Autry Museum**
of the American West   MUSEUM
(Map p126; ☑ 323-667-2000; www.autrynational center.org; 4700 Western Heritage Way, Griffith Park; adult/senior & student/child $14/10/6, 2nd Tue each month free; ☺ 10am-4pm Tue-Fri, to 5pm Sat & Sun; P 🖪) Established by singing cowboy Gene Autry, this expansive, underrated museum offers contemporary perspectives on the history and people of the American West, as well as their links to the region's contemporary culture. Permanent exhibitions explore everything from Native American traditions to the cattle drives of the 19th century and daily frontier life; look for the beautifully carved vintage saloon bar. You'll also find costumes and artifacts from famous Hollywood westerns such as *Annie Get Your Gun*, as well as rotating art exhibitions.

Hollyhock House   ARCHITECTURE
(Map p128; ☑ 323-913-4031; www.barnsdall.org/hollyhock-house/about; Barnsdall Art Park, 4800 Hollywood Blvd, Los Feliz; adult/student/child $7/3/free; ☺ tours 11am-4pm Thu-Sun; P; Ⓜ Red Line to Vermont/Sunset) Oil heiress Aline Barnsdall commissioned Frank Lloyd Wright to design this hilltop arts complex and residence

in 1919. With its central courtyard, porches and pergolas, the residence is seen as a transitory moment in the architect's style, which evolved into a more open-plan, indoor-outdoor style that would help define modern Southern Californian living. The building's aesthetic evokes Mayan temple architecture – popular at the time – while its abstract imagery of the hollyhock is a nod to Aline's preferred flower.

Los Angeles Zoo & Botanical Gardens   ZOO
(Map p126; ☑ 323-644-4200; www.lazoo.org; 5333 Zoo Dr, Griffith Park; adult/senior/child $20/17/15; ☺ 10am-5pm, closed Christmas Day; P 🖪) Home to 1100 finned, feathered and furry friends from more than 250 species, the LA Zoo rarely fails to enthrall the little ones. Adults who have been to zoos in Hawaii, San Diego or Singapore, however, may find the place a little average. To save time, purchase tickets online. To save money, bring your own food and drinks as the offerings at the zoo are expectantly overpriced.

Griffith Park
Merry-Go-Round   MERRY-GO-ROUND
(Map p126; www.laparks.org; Griffith Park; rides $2; ☺ 11am-5pm daily early Jun-Aug, Sat & Sun Sep-early Jun; P 🖪) This richly festooned 1926 merry-go-round was brought to its current home in 1937, where Walt Disney would bring his young daughters and find inspiration for his future Anaheim theme park (look for the salvaged park bench Walt would perch on). The real horsehair tails on the carved horses were added and subsequently donated by actor Hugh Laurie, who featured the location in his TV series *House*.

Travel Town   MUSEUM
(Map p126; ☑ 323-662-5874; www.traveltown.org; 5200 W Zoo Dr, Griffith Park; ☺ 10am-4pm Mon-Fri,

Griffith Park & Around

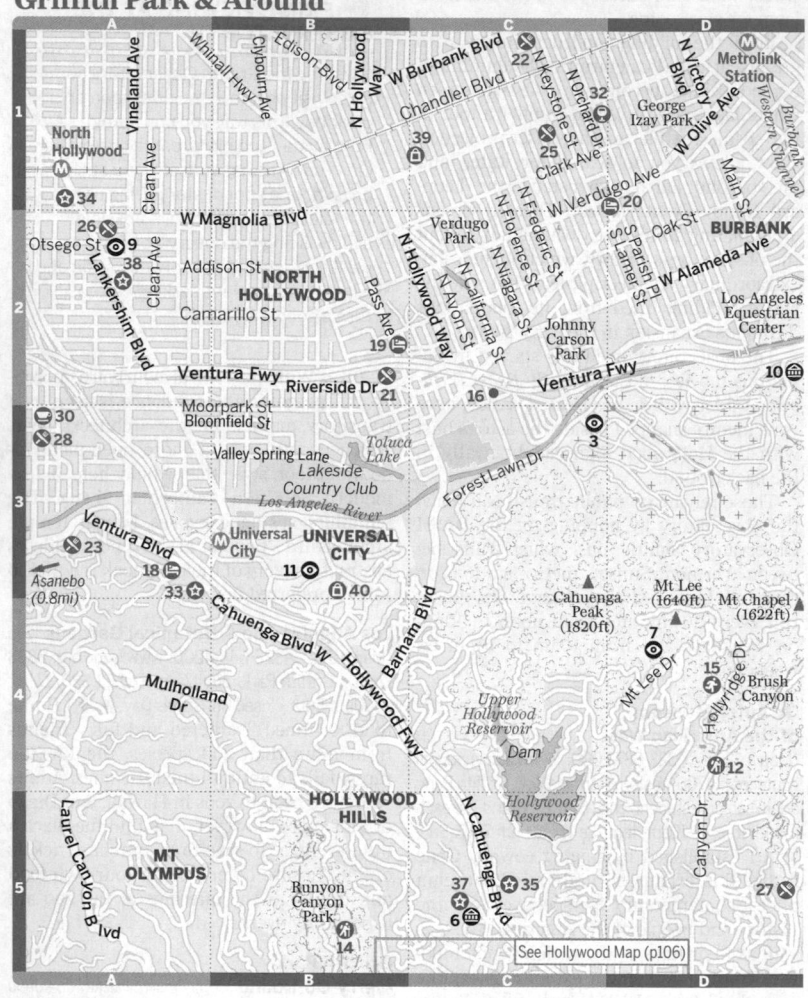

See Hollywood Map (p106)

to 5pm Sat & Sun; **P** **♿**) **FREE** This delightful rail yard displays dozens of vintage railcars and locomotives, the oldest from 1864. Kids are all smiles imagining themselves as engineers, clambering around the iron horses, and there's a 1-mile toy-train loop that costs $2.75 ($2.25 for seniors).

🏃 Activities

Griffith Park is the city's sprawling playground, with more than 50 miles of hiking trails, as well as golf courses, playgrounds and a historic merry-go-round that inspired Walt Disney's Disneyland. If you'd rather ride than hike, the park is home to a bike-rental concession as well as Sunset Ranch Hollywood, which offers horseback adventures through the hills.

Bronson Canyon   HIKING
(Map p126; ☎ 818-243-1145; www.laparks.org; 3200 Canyon Dr; ⊙ 5am-10:30pm) Although most of the pretty people prefer to do their running, walking and hiking in Runyon Canyon, we always prefer Bronson. A wide fire road rises to a lookout point and links to the Hollywood sign, Griffith Park and the famed **Bronson Caves** – where scenes from

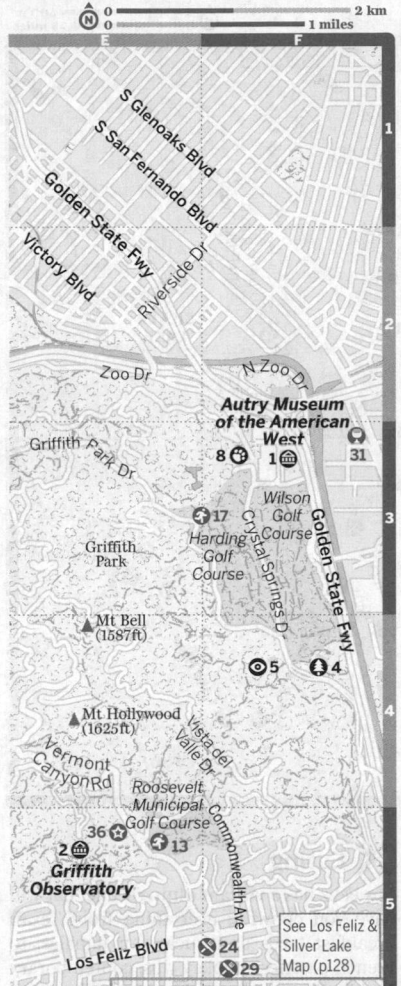

Griffith Park & Around

◎ Top Sights

the old *Batman* and *The Lone Ranger* series were shot.

Head north on Canyon Dr and park in the last lot before the locked gate at Hollywoodland Camp. Walk back south then turn left and head past a gate and up the fire road. For the Bronson Caves, turn left when the trail forks and the caves will be right there. The trail continues on the other side of the caves.

Sunset Ranch Hollywood　　　HORSE RIDING
(Map p126; ☎ 323-469-5450; www.sunsetranch
hollywood.com; 3400 Beachwood Dr; 1hr/2hr rides
$50/75; ☻) Escape the rat race on horseback

Los Feliz & Silver Lake

with a gallop through Griffith Park. Daytime one- and two-hour rides aside, the outfit runs famous two-hour sunset rides ($95), and 7-mile lunch and dinner rides (from $100) to a Mexican restaurant in Burbank. Advanced reservations are highly recommended (and obligatory for sunset, lunch and dinner tours). Private Saturday lessons (Western or English riding) start at $85 per hour.

Wilson Harding Golf Course   GOLF
(Map p126; ☑ 323-663-2555; http://golf.lacity.org/cdp_harding.htm; 4730 Crystal Springs Dr; green fees 18 holes $35-45; ☺ dawn-dusk) The tranquil, bucolic Wilson Harding golf complex is actually two 18-hole courses with electric golf carts ($28) available for rent. Alternatively, play a short round at the nine-hole **Roosevelt Municipal Golf Course** (Map p126; ☑ 323-665-2011; http://golf.lacity.org/cdp_roosevelt.htm; greens fees $16-20.50; ☺ dawn-dusk), which slopes down the mountain on the other side of the park. Golf clubs are available for rent.

✗ Eating

Los Feliz has a vibrant dining scene that will have you chowing everything from Texan breakfast tacos and Yucatecan tamales, to French pastries, smokey ribs, contemporary Middle Eastern share plates and cult-status, seasonally inspired ice cream. The scene is focused on Vermont and Highland Aves, with a burgeoning scene now luring diners on Hollywood Blvd between the two. In Griffith Park, outdoor Trails is a popular lunch spot for hikers.

★ HomeState   TEX-MEX $
(Map p128; ☑ 323-906-1122; www.myhomestate.com; 4624 Hollywood Blvd, Los Feliz; tacos $3.50, dishes $7-10; ☺ 8am-3pm; Ⓜ Red Line to Vermont/Sunset) Texan expat Briana Valdez is behind this rustic ode to the Lone Star State. Locals queue patiently for authentic breakfast tacos such as the Trinity, a handmade flour tortilla topped with egg, bacon, potato

Los Feliz & Silver Lake

and cheddar. Then there's the *queso* (melted cheese) and our lunchtime favorite, the brisket sandwich, a coaxing combo of tender meat, cabbage slaw, guacamole and pickled jalapeños in pillow-soft white bread.

★ **Jeni's Splendid Ice Creams**   ICE CREAM $
(Map p128; ☑ 323-928-2668; https://jenis. com; 1954 Hillhurst Ave, Los Feliz; 2/3/4 flavors $5.50/6.50/7.50; ⊙ 11am-11pm) Rarely short of a queue, this Ohio import scoops some of the city's creamiest, most inventive ice cream. Forget plain vanilla. Here, signature flavors include brown butter almond brittle and a riesling poached-pear sorbet. Then there are the limited-edition offerings, which might leave you tossing up between a juniper and lemon-curd combo, or a spicy Queen City Cayenne. Tough gig.

Trails   CAFE $
(Map p126; ☑ 323-871-2102; 2333 Fern Dell Dr, Los Feliz; pastries $3-4, meals $5-9; ⊙ 8am-5pm; 🛜🚼) Hungry hikers gravitate to this adorable walk-up cafe, a few blocks north of Los Feliz Blvd. Almost everything from its tiny timber-cabin kitchen is made from scratch, from the blissful egg-salad sandwich to the quiche and apple pie. Order at the counter then devour at one of its picnic benches, under the shade of sycamores, Chinese elms and carob trees.

Yuca's   MEXICAN $
(Map p126; ☑ 323-662-1214; www.yucasla.com; 2056 Hillhurst Ave, Los Feliz; items $4-10; ⊙ 11am-6pm Mon-Sat) Location, location, location... is definitely not what lures people to this former shoeshine booth turned parking-lot snack shack. It's the tacos! And the tortas, burritos, Yucatecan tamales and other Mexican faves that earned the Herrera family the coveted James Beard Award in 2005. Make sure to send matriarch 'Mama' Socorro Herrera our love.

★ **Mess Hall**   PUB FOOD $$
(Map p126; ☑ 323-660-6377; www.messhallkitchen.com; 4500 Los Feliz Blvd, Los Feliz; mains $16-35; ⊙ 9am-10pm Sun-Thu, to 11pm Fri & Sat; 🅿🛜) What was formerly The Brown Derby, a swing dance spot made famous by the film *Swingers,* is now a handsome, cabin-style hangout with snug booths, TV sports and a comfy, neighborly vibe. The feel-good factor extends to the menu, with standouts that include comforting mac-n-cheese and smoky baby-back ribs with slaw and house fries.

Figaro Bistrot   FRENCH $$
(Map p128; ☑ 323-662-1587; www.figarobistrot. com; 1802 N Vermont Ave, Los Feliz; cakes $6.20, brunch $10-14, dinner mains $23-35; ⊙ 8:30am-10:30pm Sun-Thu, to 11pm Fri & Sat) A culinary ménage à trois involving a boulangerie,

bistro and lounge, Figaro channels fin-de-siècle Paris with its heavy framed mirrors, sidewalk tables and Gallic-inspired fare. Grab a goat-cheese tart to go, or settle in for the popular brunch, where dishes such as eggs with crab cakes are best washed down with a refreshing carafe of mimosa.

 ## Drinking & Nightlife

★ Dresden
COCKTAIL BAR
(Map p128; ☑ 323-665-4294; www.thedresden.com; 1760 N Vermont Ave, Los Feliz; ⊙ 4:30pm-2am Mon-Sat, to midnight Sun; Ⓜ Red Line to Vermont/Sunset) Marty and Elayne have been a Los Feliz fixture since 1982 when they first brought their quirky Sinatra style to the Dresden's mid-century lounge. He rumbles on the drums and the upright bass; she tickles the ivories and plays the flute. Both sing. Their fame peaked when they made a brief appearance in the film *Swingers.*

Tiki-Ti
BAR
(Map p128; ☑ 323-669-9381; www.tiki-ti.com; 4427 W Sunset Blvd; ⊙ 4pm-2am Wed-Sat) Channeling Waikiki since 1961, this tiny tropical tavern packs in everyone from Gen-Y hipsters to grizzled old-timers in 'non-ironic' Hawaiian shirts. Drinks are strong and smooth; order the tequila-fueled Blood and Sand and expect a ritual that involves raucous cheers and a charging bull. The brown-paper tags are notes written by regulars, some of them dating back to the '60s.

Maru Coffee
COFFEE
(Map p128; ☑ 323-741-8483; http://marucoffee.com; 1936 Hillhurst Ave, Los Feliz; ⊙ 7am-7pm Mon-Sat, 8am-6pm Sun) Mellow, minimalist Maru brews superb specialty coffee, poured into handmade Portland ceramics and elegantly presented on little timber trays. Espresso and pour-over aside, liquids include beautiful teas and matcha lattes. The team's Korean side is evident in the selection of fresh pastries, which includes a curiously delicious Spam and kimchi croissant.

Good Luck Bar
BAR
(Map p128; ☑ 323-666-3524; www.goodluckbarla.com; 1514 Hillhurst Ave, Los Feliz; ⊙ 7pm-2am Mon-Fri, from 8pm Sat & Sun; Ⓜ Red Line to Vermont/Sunset) Is it a Chinese restaurant? A '70s massage parlor? Actually, it's one of Los Feliz's older hipster dive bars. Step through the velvet curtains and into a bordello-red hideaway of Chinese lanterns, skinny jeans and strong, tropical cocktails with endear-ingly lame names such as All Wong and Fist of Fury. Never short of a crowd and plenty of bar seating.

☆ Entertainment

★ Greek Theatre
LIVE MUSIC
(Map p126; ☑ 844-524-7335; www.lagreektheatre.com; 2700 N Vermont Ave; ⊙ Apr-Oct) The 'Greek' in the 2010 film *Get Him to the Greek* is this 5900-capacity outdoor amphitheater, tucked into a woodsy Griffith Park hillside. A more intimate version of the Hollywood Bowl, it's much loved for its vibe and variety – recent acts include PJ Harvey, John Legend and Pepe Aguilar. Parking (cash only) is stacked, so plan on a postshow wait.

Rockwell
LIVE MUSIC
(Map p128; ☑ 323-669-1550; http://rockwell-la.com; 1714 N Vermont Ave, Los Feliz; Ⓜ Red Line to Vermont/Sunset) If you like to be enter-tained while you chew, come to this table and stage. Make a reservation for Wednes-day night, when Jeff Goldblum and his Mil-dred Snitzer Orchestra usually take to the stage. The Hollywood veteran knows how to charm his crowd, encouraging selfies with the star.

Vista Theatre
CINEMA
(Map p128; ☑ 323-660-6639; www.vintagecinemas.com/vista; 4473 W Sunset Blvd, Los Feliz; Ⓜ Red Line to Vermont/Sunset) Dating back to 1923, the single-screen Vista has played some colorful roles, nominally vaudeville theat-er and gay-porn cinema. It's now back to screening mainstream new releases in its wonderfully kitsch 'ancient Egyptian' interior. At the front is a humbler, more indie-orientated version of Hollywood's Chi-nese Theatre forecourt, with the concrete imprints of names such as Spike Jonze.

🔒 Shopping

You'll find a booty of interesting shops on N Vermont Ave between Hollywood Blvd and Franklin St, stocking everything from vin-tage threads and furniture, to street wear, quirky homewares and books. On Hillhurst Ave, hunt for vintage, jewelry and gifts as well as cut-price designer fashion between Franklin and Finley Ave. For offbeat art, party supplies and fabulously weird novelty items, hit Hollywood Blvd between N Ver-mont and Hillhurst Aves.

★ **Steven Alan Outpost** FASHION & ACCESSORIES
(Map p128; ☑ 323-667-9500; www.stevenalan.
com; 1937 Hillhurst Ave, Los Feliz; ⊘11am-7pm
Mon-Sat, to 6pm Sun) The fashion cognoscenti love New York designer Steven Alan for
his super-cute men's and women's threads,
which fuse preppy style with unique detailing and effortless casual cool. And it's here,
at his Los Feliz outpost, that you can bag his
shirts, tees, trousers, dresses, skirts and bags
at heavily discounted prices.

★ **Skylight Books** BOOKS
(Map p128; ☑ 323-660-1175; www.skylightbooks.
com; 1818 N Vermont Ave, Los Feliz; ⊘10am-10pm)
Occupying two adjoining shopfronts, this
much-loved Los Feliz institution carries
everything from art, architecture and fashion tomes, to LA history titles, vegan cookbooks, queer literature and critical theory.
There's a solid selection of niche magazines
and local zines, some great lit-themed tees
and regular, engaging in-store readings and
talks (with the podcasts uploaded onto the
store's website).

SquaresVille VINTAGE
(Map p128; ☑ 323-669-8464; www.squaresville
vintage.com; 1800 N Vermont Ave, Los Feliz;
⊘noon-7pm Mon & Sun, 11am-8pm Tue-Thu,
11am-9pm Fri & Sat) One of our favorite unisex consignment stores in LA, SquaresVille
is never short of fun, unique and just plain
outrageous wearables. Dive in and expect
to find anything from pink-leather pants,
denim jumpsuits and Landlubber jeans, to
vintage designer frocks, TV-sitcom-print
tees and groovy '70s sweaters. And did we
mention the shoes, bags and jewelry? New
stock added daily.

Spitfire Girl GIFTS & SOUVENIRS
(Map p128; ☑ 323-912-1977; www.spitfiregirl.com;
1939 Hillhurst Ave, Los Feliz; ⊘11am-7pm Mon-Fri
& Sun, to 7:30pm Sat) This is one of the city's
coolest, quirkiest gift boutiques, where fine
jewelry, art tomes, papier-mâché mounts
and aromatic candles mingle with stuffed
gnomes and the odd taxidermy item. We
especially love the store's unisex fragrances and handmade pillows, the latter's
graphic prints ranging from 19th-century
photographs to pop-art comics and quotes
straight out of a drag queen's mouth.

Wacko COLLECTIBLES
(Map p128; ☑ 323-663-0122; www.soapplant.
com; 4633 Hollywood Blvd, Los Feliz; ⊘11am-7pm
Mon-Wed, to 9pm Thu, to 10pm Fri & Sat, noon-6pm

Sun; Ⓜ Red Line to Vermont/Sunset) Billy Shire's
giftorium of camp and kitsch has been a
fun browse for over three decades. Pick up
a *Star Wars* tote, some Gauguin socks or a
Hillary Clinton paper doll. You'll find a great
selection of comics and books by LA authors
such as Ray Bradbury and Philip K. Dick.

Out back is La Luz de Jesus, one of LA's
top lowbrow-movement art galleries. The
gallery's opening parties (on the first Friday of the month) are the stuff of local
legend.

Westlake & Koreatown

Once a glamourous enclave for silent-film
stars and tycoons, Westlake is now Downtown's raffish western neighbor, tempered by
lake-studded MacArthur Park, the very one
that 'melts in the dark' in the eponymous
Jimmy Webb song made famous by Donna
Summer. Despite the faint whiff of gentrification, the neighborhood remains a gritty bastion of working-class Latino *vida*. Further
west, Westlake spills seamlessly into vast
and vibrant Koreatown, a platter of sizzling
BBQ joints, 24-hour spas and karaoke bars,
all splashed with a dash of glorious art-deco
architecture from the area's gilded past.

◉ Sights

Westlake's one main attraction is MacArthur
Park, located in the heart of the neighborhood and safest during daylight hours. The
park is dissected by Wilshire Blvd, which
shoots west to Koreatown. The thoroughfare
is where you'll find many of the area's most
impressive historic buildings.

MacArthur Park PARK
(cnr Wilshire Blvd & Alvarado St; Ⓜ Red/Purple
Lines to Westlake/MacArthur Park) The centerpiece of MacArthur Park is its 14ft-deep
lake. Originally a swamp, the lake reached
6th St before the extension of Wilshire Blvd
sliced right through it in the 1930s, leading
to the draining of its northern half. Today
its glassy waters ripple with tales of suicide,
drownings and showbiz lore: a bound Harry Houdini once plunged into (and escaped
from) the lake, while Charlie Chaplin shot
numerous films here, including his 1914
comedy, *Twenty Minutes of Love*.

In the summer, the park's historic band
shell hosts free **concerts** (www.levittla.org;
MacArthur Park, 2230 W 6th St; Ⓜ Red/Purple Lines

to Westlake/MacArthur Park), ranging from world music to child-friendly marionette shows.

Bullocks Wilshire
ARCHITECTURE

(www.swlaw.edu/campus/building; 3050 Wilshire Blvd; M Red/Purple Lines to Wilshire/Vermont) Clad in terracotta tiles and adorned with copper decorative motifs, this 1929 art-deco diva was the country's first department store designed for shoppers arriving by car. Its main entrance was placed at the rear of the building, where shoppers were welcomed by valets at the porte cochere. The 241ft metal tower originally housed a searchlight, shining boldly to lure shoppers. Sadly, the luxury store closed in 1992 and is now a law school rarely open to the public.

Wilshire Boulevard Temple
SYNAGOGUE

(213-835-2195; www.wbtla.org; 3663 Wilshire Blvd; ⊙ guided tour by appointment; M Purple Line to Wilshire/Western) The construction of this Byzantine-revival behemoth was overseen by Edgar Magnin, dubbed 'Rabbi of the Stars' due to his numerous Hollywood pals. Movie theaters inspired the synagogue's design, while the impressive murals, depicting 3000 years of Jewish history, were commissioned by Hollywood Warner Brothers moguls. Guided tours of the building are available by emailing or calling in advance.

Chapman Plaza
ARCHITECTURE

(3465 W 6th St) It might look like an extravagant Spanish baroque villa, but this complex began life as one of the first drive-in markets in the western US. Opened in 1929, its design allowed motorists to access grocery stores in the inner courtyard lined with a flouncy Spanish Revival archway. Today the courtyard is packed with valet-parked cars and flanked by a handful of popular Korean restaurants, coffee shops, boutiques and a karaoke bar.

Across Alexandria St is Chapman Plaza's imposing sibling, **Chapman Park Studio**. Both buildings were designed by Los Angeles architecture firm Morgan, Walls and Clements – its other LA landmarks include the Mayan Theater in Downtown.

🏃 Activities

★ Wi Spa
SPA

(213-487-2700; www.wispausa.com; 2700 Wilshire Blvd; spa access $25-35, 1hr massage from $60; ⊙ 24hr) Sprawling Wi is the king of 24-hour Korean spas, complete with salt and clay saunas (yes, the clay is imported

from Korea), a Jade Room with sodium and minerals embedded in the walls, and an ice sauna. There's also a Korean restaurant, gym, sleeping rooms and plenty of spa treatments, including massage, body scrubs, manicures and pedicures. Reserve treatments in advance.

🛏 Sleeping

★ Line Hotel
HOTEL $$

(213-381-7411; www.thelinehotel.com; 3515 Wilshire Blvd; r from $170; P ❄ @ 🛜 ➷; M Purple Line to Wilshire/Normandie) Behind the Line is Roy Choi, the man who sparked the LA food-truck revolution and became a celebrity chef. Interiors are sleek and industrial: think (slightly chipped) concrete walls, quirky artworks and floor-to-ceiling windows overlooking the city. Bathrooms are spotless and in-room tech allows smartphones and music players to be plugged into the flat-screen TV and sound system.

There's a smart rooftop pool, a gym, free Saturday yoga for guests and bikes for guest use. Both the lobby bar and Choi's restaurant, Pot, are sterling. Valet parking is $35.

🍴 Eating

Koreatown has the largest number of Korean eateries Stateside, with food that leans towards the authentic and traditional. You'll find eateries on 6th St, S Vermont Ave (between Beverly and W Olympic Blvds), 8th St (between S Vermont and S Western Aves) and Wilshire Blvd. Westlake is most famous for its retro Jewish deli Langer's, home to the city's best pastrami sandwiches.

Slurpin' Ramen
RAMEN $

(213-388-8607; www.slurpinramenbar.com; 3500 W 8th St; ramen from $8; ⊙ 11:30am-1am; P 🛜) The communal bar tables and window counters at this casual joint are rarely short of K-Town locals and USC students, slurping on superlative ramen. The broth has a satisfying, Korean-influenced kick, though there's a non-spicy option for heat-o-phobes. Spicy or not, the ramen is fragrant and full-bodied, dressed with dried seaweed and black-garlic oil and best paired with lean *chashu* (pork).

Somi Somi
ICE CREAM $

(213-568-3284; 621 S Western Ave; ice cream $5.95; ⊙ noon-10pm Mon-Thu, 12:30-10:30pm Fri-Sun; M Purple Line to Wilshire/Western) Tucked away on the 2nd floor of Madang Mall, pocket-sized Somi Somi serves super-cute,

THE WONDERS OF WILSHIRE WALK

Start Bullocks Wilshire

End Wiltern Theatre

Length 1.4 miles; two hours

Begin your walk at the striking **Bullocks Wilshire**, the former luxury department store where Marlene Dietrich would buy her men's trousers. Head west along Wilshire Blvd to the corner of S Catalina St, home to the **Robert F Kennedy Community Schools**. This sprawling property once housed the Ambassador Hotel, host of two Academy Awards ceremonies and the very place where Palestinian man Sirhan Bishara Sirhan fatally shot Robert Kennedy on June 5, 1968. The hotel was demolished in 2005. Across the street are the **Gaylord Apartments**, completed in 1924 and once described by the *Los Angeles Times* as the largest and most pretentious apartment houses in the nation. Former residents included thespian John Barrymore, while current ones include hipster drinking spot HMS Bounty, pouring since 1962. Next door, **Brown Derby Plaza** is named for the long-gone Brown Derby, the iconic, hat-shaped LA restaurant that invented the Cobb salad. Take a quick detour north along S Alexandria Ave to view striking **Chapman Plaza**, one of the first automobile-centric markets designed in the US. The market was developed by the Chapman brothers, who donated the land to build the **Wilshire Christian Church** (Oasis Church) on the corner of Wilshire Blvd and Normandie Ave. The current Romanesque Revival church replaced the original in 1927. Soaring two blocks further west on Wilshire Blvd is the concrete **St Basil Catholic Church**, completed in 1969 and sliced by dramatic, 3-D stained-glass windows. Its $3-million price tag drew outrage in the Chicano community, which argued that the money would have been better spent on helping the archdiocese's poor. Upstaging it on the next block west is the octagonal **Wilshire Boulevard Temple**, capped with a Byzantine-like dome and adorned with extraordinary murals by Hugo Ballin. Byzantine makes way for Italian on the next block, where Edward Durell Stone's 1970 masterpiece, the Wilshire Colonnade, recalls 1930s Rome with its muscular arches, travertine skin and Carrara-marble paving. Across the street is your final stop, the still-thriving **Wiltern Theatre** (p134), considered one of America's finest art deco creations.

---

soft-serve ice cream worthy of its Instagram fame. The heavenly scented, fish-shaped, waffle-like cones are freshly made on site, then squirted with your choice of filling (custard, Nutella or red bean) and your preferred ice-cream flavor (the green tea is justifiably popular). Hashtags and selfies optional.

Ma Dang Gook Soo NOODLES $
(☑ 213-487-6008; 869 S Western Ave; dishes $6-9; ⊙ 9am-10pm; Ⓜ Purple Line to Wilshire/Western) A humble little noodle spot known for its house-made, knife-cut noodles and wonderful house-made chili sauce. Portions are huge.

★**Langer's Deli** JEWISH $$
(☑ 213-483-8050; www.langersdeli.com; 704 S Alvarado St; pastrami sandwiches from $15, mains $13-28; ⊙ 8am-4pm Mon-Sat; Ⓜ Red/Purple Lines to Westlake/MacArthur Park) The best pastrami sandwiches aren't in New York. They're at this retro deli, where the recipe and hand-carving of the meat hasn't changed since 1947. Sandwich 19 is the ultimate prize

(peppery pastrami, Swiss cheese and coleslaw on double-baked rye). If you feel like mixing it up, opt for 'Soup and Half Sandwich' and swoon over both the sandwich and some matzo-ball soup.

Oo-Kook KOREAN $$
(☑ 213-385-5665; www.oo-kook.com; 3385 W 8th St; lunch/dinner $24/29; ⊙ 11am-midnight; Ⓟ) Unlike many of its competitors, this good-value, all-you-can-eat Korean BBQ joint takes reservations (the upstairs can get frustratingly loud so request a table on the ground floor). Grills are built into the tables and the meats are hand-cut, fresh and good quality; top choices include the US Kobe marinated thin-slice beef, marinated chicken and corn cheese. The bottomless condiments are also delicious.

Chosun Galbee KOREAN $$
(☑ 323-734-3330; www.chosungalbee.com; 3330 W Olympic Blvd; dishes $10-45; ⊙ 11am-11pm) An ideal K-Town BBQ habitat that has both

class and charm, thanks to superb heated patio seating. Grills are built into the tables of course, and aside from the paper-thin rib eye, which you'll cook yourself, it does a nice bibimbap, and black cod stew. Says one local in the know, 'the fish is like butter.'

Buil Sam Gye Tang   KOREAN $$
(📞 213-739-0001; 4204 W 3rd St; mains $13-21; ⊗ 11am-9:30pm Mon-Sat; 🅿) Who doesn't love a chicken in a pot? Of course, you can opt for deer antler or abalone instead, but we (alongside other Korean food geeks) are partial to the *samgyetang*, a soul-soothing concoction of chicken in a bubbling pot filled with ginseng broth, teeming with herbs and swirling with rice. It may need salt, but it's healing.

Jun Won   KOREAN $$
(📞 323-731-0509; 414 S Western Ave; dishes $11-26; ⊗ 11am-2:45pm & 5:30-8:45pm Mon-Sat; 🅿🛜; Ⓜ Purple Line to Wilshire/Western) It steams pollock and cod, but we love the pan-fried mackerel: crispy skin, tender morsels of fish flesh and an array of sides that will occupy nearly your entire table, including greens drizzled in rice vinegar, fried tofu topped with chili, and spicy pickled cabbage. You may need to wait but it's worth it.

★ Ahgassi Gopchang   KOREAN $$$
(📞 213-249-9678; www.facebook.com/Ahgassi Gopchang; 3744 W 6th St; beef/pork combo for 2 persons $56/50; ⊗ 11am-2pm; 🅿🛜; Ⓜ Purple Line to Wilshire/Normandie) Especially popular with young, trendy Koreans, Ahgassi Gopchang (or 'young lady's…small intestines') doesn't translate well into English, but the fatty satisfaction of grilled small intestine (made from beef and pork, not young ladies) are perfect with an ice-cold beer. If you don't like small intestines, opt for the melt-in-your-mouth prime rib eye. Arrive by 7pm to avoid the mobs.

★ Taylor's   STEAK $$$
(📞 213-382-8449; www.taylorssteakhouse.com; 3361 8th St; lunch $14-29, dinner mains $15-39; ⊗ 11:30am-9:30pm Mon-Thu, to 10:30pm Fri, 4-10:30pm Sat, 4-9:30pm Sun; 🅿🛜) Fifties throwback Taylor's is all old-school LA, from the dark-leatherette booths and wood-paneled walls, to the vest-clad old-school waiters. Some consider it an LA institution for its decent, affordable meats (go for the char-broiled options), paired with bistro classics such as bacon-wrapped scallops and a fabulously cheesy French onion soup.

Whatever you order, pair with one (or two) of Taylor's well-regarded martinis.

🍷 Drinking & Nightlife

Koreatown's nightlife is eclectic, ranging from hip hotel bars to retro speakeasies and craft-beer dens.

★ Prince   BAR
(3198 W 7th St; ⊗ 4pm-2am; Ⓜ Red/Purple Lines to Wilshire/Vermont) In the movie *Chinatown*, Faye Dunaway meets with Jack Nicholson at this snug, retro warren of semicircular booths, quirky lamps and, these days, Gen-Y hipsters. Also featured in hits such as *Mad Men* and *New Girl*, it's an atmospheric spot for '80s-inspired cocktails, a dose of soju and perhaps a serve of its rather fine Korean fried chicken.

Beer Belly   PUB
(📞 213-387-2337; www.beerbellyla.com; 532 S Western Ave; ⊗ 11:30am-11pm Sun-Tue, to midnight Wed & Thu, to 1am Fri & Sat; 🛜; Ⓜ Purple Line to Wilshire/Western) Tucked off the western strip is this wood-paneled barrel of craft beer and creative pub grub, written in colorful script on the chalkboard behind the bar. Quench your thirst with a coffee stout or *kölsch* from Inglewood, a sour ale from Pasadena, and far darker, funkier concoctions where the alcohol content hits the double digits.

R Bar   LOUNGE
(📞 213-387-7227; www.facebook.com/rbarktown; 3331 W 8th St; ⊗ 7pm-2am Mon & Tue, from 5pm Wed-Fri, from 11am Sat & Sun; 🛜; Ⓜ Purple Line to Wilshire/Normandie) The jukebox is stocked with classics and neo-classics, and you have to know the password to get past the gatekeeper. Seriously. Call or log on to its Facebook page for the password, as it's always changing. Patrons hit the mic for karaoke on Wednesdays, Thursdays and Sundays, with other rotating events including live music, trivia nights and more.

☆ Entertainment

★ Wiltern Theatre   THEATER
(📞 213-388-1400; www.wiltern.com; 3790 Wilshire Blvd; Ⓜ Purple Line to Wilshire/Western) Soaring confidently at the intersection of Wilshire and Western Blvds (get it?), this extraordinary, turquoise-hued deco landmark started life as a movie theater (*West Side Story* premiered here). These days it's an epic venue for live music, comedy and occasional screenings

of cult-status movies: recent live acts included Passenger, David Crosby and comic Adam Devine of *Modern Family* fame.

West Hollywood & Mid-City

Welcome to West Hollywood (WeHo), an independent city with way more personality (some might say frivolity) than its 1.9-sq-mile frame might suggest. Upscale and low-rent (but rising), gay fabulous and Russian-ghetto chic, this is a bastion of LA's fashionista best and home to some of the trashiest shops you'll ever see.

Mid-City, to the south and east, encompasses the Miracle Mile (home to some of the best museums in the west), the Orthodox-Jewish-meets-hipster Fairfax district and the legendary rock, punk and vintage shopping strip of Melrose Ave.

◉ Sights

Top of the list for any visit to LA is Museum Row, as Wilshire Blvd is known between about Fairfax and La Brea Aves. If nothing else, be sure to take in at least a portion of the huge Los Angeles County Museum of Art and the newly refurbished and very striking Petersen Automotive Museum.

★ Los Angeles County Museum of Art   MUSEUM

(LACMA; Map p138; ☑ 323-857-6000; www.lacma. org; 5905 Wilshire Blvd, Mid-City; adult/child $15/ free, 2nd Tue each month free; ⊙ 11am-5pm Mon, Tue & Thu, to 8pm Fri, 10am-7pm Sat & Sun; ℗; 🚇 Metro lines 20, 217, 720, 780 to Wilshire & Fairfax) The depth and wealth of the collection at the largest museum in the western US is stunning. LACMA holds all the major players – Rembrandt, Cézanne, Magritte, Mary Cassatt, Ansel Adams – plus millennia's worth of Chinese, Japanese, pre-Columbian and ancient Greek, Roman and Egyptian sculpture. Recent acquisitions include massive outdoor installations such as Chris Burden's *Urban Light* (a surreal selfie backdrop of hundreds of vintage LA streetlamps) and Michael Heizer's *Levitated Mass,* a surprisingly inspirational 340-ton boulder perched over a walkway.

Between 2008 and 2010, architect Renzo Piano designed two of the newer gallery buildings on the western side of the campus (the **Broad Contemporary Art Museum** (BCAM) and the **Resnick Pavilion**, which hosts temporary exhibits).

The rest of the campus is now about to see a major makeover, courtesy of Swiss architect Peter Zumthor. Renovation plans call for most of the current mid-century pavilions (so in need of work as to be untenable) to be razed and airy, cantilevered galleries to replace them, straddling Wilshire Blvd. The redesign is scheduled for completion in 2023. Until then, some of the galleries will remain open (thankfully the jewel-box Pavilion for Japanese Art is staying put) and parts of the collection will be exhibited elsewhere around LA.

Check the website for construction schedules and to learn which galleries will remain open during the renovation.

Currently under construction adjacent to and behind LACMA is the **Academy Museum** (Map p138; www.oscars.org/museum; cnr Wilshire Blvd & Fairfax Ave, Mid-City), operated by the Academy of Motion Picture Arts and Sciences (the Oscars people). It's scheduled to open in 2019.

★ Petersen Automotive Museum   MUSEUM

(Map p138; ☑ 323-930-2277; www.petersen.org; 6060 Wilshire Blvd, Mid-City; adult/senior & student/child $15/12/7; ⊙ 10am-6pm; ℗ 🚼; 🚇 Metro lines 20, 217, 720, 780 to Wilshire & Fairfax) A four-story ode to the auto, the Petersen Automotive Museum is a treat even for those who can't tell a piston from a carburetor. A headlights-to-brake-lights futuristic make over (by Kohn Pederson Fox) in late 2015 left it fairly gleaming from the outside; the exterior is undulating bands of stainless steel on a hot-rod-red background. The once-dowdy inside is now equally gripping, with floors themed for the history, industry and artistry of motorized transportation.

Start by on the history floor (3rd floor) brimming with a regularly changing selection of classic and concept cars. In the Cars of Film and Television gallery you might see the DeLorean from *Back to the Future,* the convertible from *Thelma & Louise* and a Batmobile. The 2nd (industry) floor shows how it's done, including in a kids' section inspired by the movie *Cars;* there's a custom-built Lightning McQueen. The ground floor focuses on the art of the automobile, mostly in special exhibits.

What's the 4th floor? The basement vault of 100-plus rare and special cars, which can be visited by tour ($20 surcharge, age 10 and over only). On our visit, we saw a Model T

Ford, Pope John Paul II's Popemobile, limos for US presidents and Saddam Hussein, and Fred Astaire's Rolls-Royce, complete with Louis Vuitton luggage.

The museum's design won the prestigious American Architecture Award for significant new buildings. Parking is $12.

La Brea Tar Pits & Museum   MUSEUM
(Map p138; www.tarpits.org; 5801 Wilshire Blvd, Mid-City; adult/student & senior/child $12/9/5, 1st Tue of month Sep-Jun free; ⊙9:30am-5pm; 🅿️👤) Mammoths, saber-toothed cats and dire wolves used to roam LA's savannah in prehistoric times. We know this because of an archaeological trove of skulls and bones unearthed here at the La Brea Tar Pits, one of the world's most fecund and famous fossil sites. A museum has been built here, where generations of young dino hunters have come to seek out fossils and learn about paleontology from docents and demonstrations in on-site labs.

Thousands of Ice Age critters met their maker between 40,000 and 10,000 years ago in gooey crude oil bubbling up from deep below Wilshire Blvd. Animals wading into the sticky muck became trapped and were condemned to a slow death by starvation or suffocation. A life-size drama of a mammoth family outside the museum dramatizes such a cruel fate. Also outside the museum, visitors can observe the pits where fossils are still being discovered.

The tar pits were recently taken over by the Natural History Museum of Los Angeles (p223). Inside the museum's 3-D cinema the 25-minute film *Titans of the Ice Age* screens 10am to 4pm daily (extra charge adult/child $4/3).

Fun fact: *la* is Spanish for the and *brea* is Spanish for tar, so you're really saying 'the the Tar Tar Pits'.

Wall Project   PUBLIC ART
(Map p138; www.wendemuseum.org/collections/berlin-wall-segments; 5900 Wilshire Blvd) FREE Ten slabs of the old Berlin Wall, augmented by well known street artists, are on display on the lawn of a Wilshire high-rise across the street from LACMA as part of the global Wall Project, curated by the fabulous Wende Museum in Culver City. It's the largest stretch of the wall outside of Germany – LA and Berlin are sister cities.

Craft & Folk Art Museum   MUSEUM
(Map p138; 📞323-937-4230; www.cafam.org; 5814 Wilshire Blvd, Mid-City; adult/student & senior/under 12yr $7/5/free, 1st Thu of month free 6:30-9:30pm;

⊙11am-5pm Tue-Fri, to 6pm Sat & Sun; 👤; 🚌MTA line 20 to Wilshire & Curson) This well-respected, intimate, three-story museum features an eclectic mix of world-renowned and local, up-and-coming artists in the folk and craft art worlds. Exhibits change a few times per year, but the museum's goal is to straddle the lines between the contemporary-art, socio-political movements and craft media you don't always see: fiber arts, metal working, book-binding and more. Exhibits change every few months, so check for closing dates and for family-oriented hands-on workshops, usually held on Sundays.

The gift store is one of the best in town, with hand-crafted gifts, including many by local makers, with an emphasis on jewelry, housewares, textiles and games.

Zimmer Children's Museum   MUSEUM
(Map p138; 📞323-761-8984; www.zimmermuseum.org; 6505 Wilshire Blvd, Mid-City, Suite 100; admission $7.50; ⊙10am-5pm Mon-Thu, to 4pm Fri, 12:30-4:30pm Sun; 🅿️👤; 🚌Metro line 20 to Wilshire & La Jolla) In the Jewish Federation Center, this charming museum brims with interactive exhibits that gently teach kids about tolerance, generosity and community spirit. Kids 'fly' to exotic lands, become ambulance drivers, work the newsroom and take other fun journeys. Check the calendar for a roster of singalongs and workshops.

★ Original Farmers Market   MARKET
(Map p138; 📞323-933-9211; www.farmersmarketla.com; 6333 W 3rd St, Fairfax District; ⊙9am-9pm Mon-Fri, to 8pm Sat, 10am-7pm Sun; 🅿️👤) Long before the city was flooded with farmers markets, there was *the* farmers market. Fresh produce, roasted nuts, doughnuts, cheeses, blini – you'll find them all at this 1934 landmark. Casual and kid friendly, it's a fun place for a browse, snack or for people-watching.

From late May to mid-September it holds the Summer Music Series (7pm to 9pm). On Thursday nights it's all jazz, and on Fridays the bands can range from zydeco to pop.

Parking is free for the first 1½ hours with validation.

CBS Television City   STUDIO
(Map p138; www.cbs.com; 7800 Beverly Blvd) North of the Farmers Market is CBS (p134), where game shows, talk shows, soap operas and other programs are taped, often before a live audience, including the *Late Late Show with James Corden, Real Time with Bill*

Maher and the perennially popular *Price is Right* game show. Check online for tickets.

Grove
MALL

(Map p138; www.thegrovela.com; 189 The Grove Dr; P; MTA lines 16, 17, 780 to Wilshire & Fairfax) Next door to the farmers market is a faux-European and rather corporate, yet attractive, shopping mall built around a central plaza with a musical fountain (nicest after dark, almost magical at Christmas time). Little-known secret: the views of the city and Hollywood Hills from the top floor of the parking structure are stunning, especially at sunset.

Sunset Strip
STREET

(Map p138; Sunset Blvd) A visual cacophony of billboards, giant ad banners and neon signs, the sinuous stretch of Sunset Blvd running between Laurel Canyon and Doheny Dr has been nightlife central since the 1920s.

Mobster Bugsy Siegel and his posse hung out at clubs such as Ciro's (now the Comedy Store; p147); Marilyn Monroe had her first date with Joe DiMaggio at the Rainbow Bar and Grill, which later became the preferred late-night hub of Guns N' Roses. The **Whisky-a-Go-Go** (Map p138; 310-652-4202; www.whiskyagogo.com; 8901 W Sunset Blvd, West Hollywood) gave birth to both the Doors and go-go dancing, and Led Zeppelin raced motorcycles in the Andaz (p142) hotel, formerly the Hyatt House, and henceforth known as the 'Riot House.' In the late '90s, the strip recaptured the limelight with the House of Blues (HOB), the ultraposh Sky Bar at the Mondrian (p141) hotel and the sexy Standard Hollywood (p142).

These days, though, it seems to be coasting on its fabled legacy. The young, hip and fickle have moved west to Abbot Kinney in Venice and east to Downtown, leaving the Strip to the buttoned-down, cashed-up suburbanites, though midweek and during awards season, the celebs still appear.

Schindler House
ARCHITECTURE

(Map p138; 323-651-1510; www.makcenter.org; 835 N Kings Rd, West Hollywood; adult/senior & student/under 12 $10/7/free, 4-6pm Fri free; 11am-6pm Wed-Sun; MTA line 4) The former home and studio of Vienna-born architect Rudolph Schindler (1887–1953) offers a fine primer on the modernist elements that so greatly influenced mid-century California architecture. The open floor plan, flat roof and glass sliding doors, while considered avant-garde back in the 1920s, all became design staples after WWII.

Today Schindler's old pad houses the **MAK Center for Art and Architecture**, which runs a roster of other exhibitions and activities.

Pacific Design Center
LANDMARK

(PDC; Map p138; www.pacificdesigncenter.com; 8687 Melrose Ave, West Hollywood; 9am-5pm Mon-Fri) Interior design is big in WeHo, with more than 120 trade-only showrooms at the Pacific Design Center and dozens more in the surrounding **Avenues of Art & Design** (Beverly Blvd, Robertson Blvd and Melrose Ave). PDC showrooms generally sell only to design pros, but often you can get items at a mark-up through the Buying Program.

The PDC itself is an architectural landmark designed by Cesar Pelli of Petronas Twin Towers (Kuala Lumpur) fame. Best viewed from a Runyon Canyon trail or a hotel rooftop, the three glass buildings, one each in race-car red, forest green and cobalt blue, bear a rather striking footprint.

MOCA Pacific Design Center
GALLERY

(Map p138; 310-289-5223; www.moca.org; 8687 Melrose Ave, West Hollywood; 11am-5pm Tue-Fri, to 6pm Sat & Sun; P) FREE Standing a bit forlorn amid the glassy behemoths is the small satellite branch of Downtown's Museum of Contemporary Art (p88). Exhibits usually have an architectural or design theme. Entrance is off San Vicente Blvd.

Check the website before setting out, as it may be closed between exhibitions. Parking is free for the first 20 minutes, and $1.50 per 20 minutes thereafter.

🏃 Activities

Duff's Cake Mix
COOKING

(Map p138; 323-650-5555; www.duffscakemix.com; 8302 Melrose Ave, Mid-City; decorating 6 cupcakes/1 cake $28/34 plus $12 per person; 12:30pm-7:30pm Mon-Thu, to 8pm Fri, 10am-8pm Sat, to 6:30pm Sun) Cake lovers, rejoice! Your sweet tooth will lead to artistic breakthroughs (or not) at this glass-box bakery by celebrity baker Duff Goldman of the Food Network's *Ace of Cakes*. Choose your cake, fillings, frosting and decorations. It also sells cakes ($34 to $91) and cupcakes ($3.50) from Duff's Charm City Cakes West.

West Hollywood & Mid-City

WEST HOLLYWOOD

Norton Ave

Santa Monica Blvd

Romaine St

Willoughby St

Waring Ave

Melrose Ave

BEVERLY CENTER DISTRICT

Clinton St

Rosewood Ave

Oakwood Ave

FAIRFAX DISTRICT

Beverly Blvd

W 1st St

Farmers'

W Sunset Blvd

Sunset Strip

WEST HOLLYWOOD

Holloway Dr

WEST HOLLYWOOD DESIGN DISTRICT

Alden Dr

See Beverly Hills Map (p154)

Melrose Ave

Santa Monica Blvd

W 3rd St

Burton Way

Colgate Ave

Clifton Way

Wilshire Blvd

Charleville Blvd

Dayton Way

Colgate Ave

Original Farmers Market

MID-CITY

Los Angeles County Museum of Art

Hancock Park

Petersen Automotive Museum

S Almont Dr

W Olympic Blvd

La Cienega Park

S Roxbury Dr

W Pico Blvd

Packard St

Stearns Dr

N Doheny Dr

N Palm Ave

N San Vicente Blvd

Huntley Dr

West Knoll Dr

N La Cienega Blvd

N Orlando Ave

N Kings Rd

N Sweetzer Ave

N Crescent Heights Blvd

N Edinburgh Ave

N Laurel Ave

N Hayworth Ave

N Fairfax Ave

N Orange Grove Ave

N Ogden Dr

N Ogden Dr

N Robertson Blvd

N Arnaz Dr

S Robertson Blvd

S Wooster St

S Shenandoah St

S Sherbourne Dr

S Corning St

S Orlando Ave

S Sweetzer Ave

S La Jolla Ave

S San Vicente Blvd

S Crescent Heights Blvd

S Ogden Dr

S Spaulding Ave

S Fairfax Ave

Market Pl

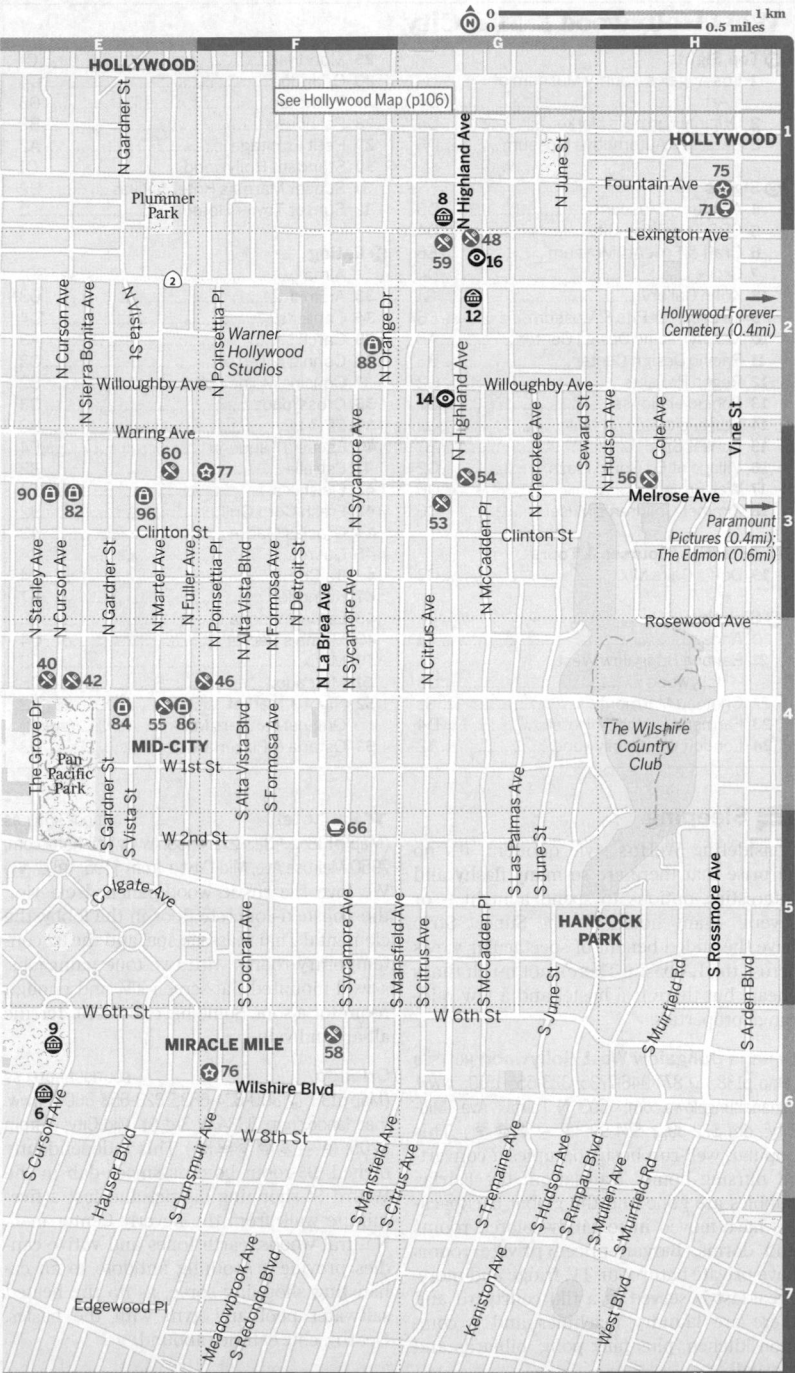

0 — 1 km
0 — 0.5 miles

HOLLYWOOD

See Hollywood Map (p106)

HOLLYWOOD

N Gardner St

Plummer Park

N Highland Ave

N June St

Fountain Ave   75
71

Lexington Ave

8
59   **48**
16

12

N Curson Ave
N Sierra Bonita Ave
N Vista St

N Poinsettia Pl

Warner Hollywood Studios

N Orange Dr
88

N Highland Ave

Hollywood Forever
Cemetery (0.4mi)

Willoughby Ave   Willoughby Ave

Waring Ave   **14**

N Cherokee Ave

Seward St

N Hudson Ave

Cole Ave

Vine St

60
77

54

56

Melrose Ave

90   82
96

Clinton St

53

Clinton St

Paramount
Pictures (0.4mi);
The Edmon (0.6mi)

N Stanley Ave
N Curson Ave
N Gardner St
N Martel Ave
N Fuller Ave
N Poinsettia Pl
N Alta Vista Blvd
N Formosa Ave
N Detroit St

N La Brea Ave

N Sycamore Ave

N Citrus Ave

N McCadden Pl

Rosewood Ave

40   **42**

46

84   55   86

MID-CITY

W 1st St

S Gardner St
S Vista St
S Alta Vista Blvd
S Formosa Ave

S Sycamore Ave
S Mansfield Ave
S Citrus Ave
S McCadden Pl

S Las Palmas Ave
S June St

*The Wilshire
Country
Club*

The Grove Dr

Pan
Pacific
Park

Colgate Ave

W 2nd St

66

S Cochran Ave

**HANCOCK
PARK**

S Muirfield Rd

S Rossmore Ave

S Arden Blvd

W 6th St

W 6th St

9

MIRACLE MILE

58

6

76

Wilshire Blvd

S Curson Ave

Hauser Blvd

S Dunsmuir Ave

W 8th St

S Mansfield Ave
S Citrus Ave

S Tremaine Ave
S Hudson Ave
S Rimpau Blvd
S Mullen Ave
S Muirfield Rd

Edgewood Pl

Meadowbrook Ave
S Redondo Blvd

Keniston Ave

West Blvd

West Hollywood & Mid-City

🛏 Sleeping

Considering WeHo's style quotient, it's no surprise that there are so many flashy and interesting options to spend a night – or several. Many hotels on the Sunset Strip have the added benefit of spectacular views across the LA basin. There's not much that's cheap, but there is a hostel and a few mid-range properties.

Banana Bungalow West Hollywood HOSTEL $
(Map p138; ☎877-946-7735, 323-655-1510; www.bananabungalows.com; 603 N Fairfax Ave, Mid-City; dm $22-39, r $74-99; 🅿❂❄@❖) This popular, well-run hostel occupies a converted nursing home. Translation: the Fairfax bubbies are gone and the global backpackers have moved in to candy-colored rooms and dorms. Bargain-priced private rooms have private bathroom, TV, fridge and more. Breakfast is served in a tiki courtyard and there are laundry machines and a common kitchen, plus ping pong, billiards and foosball.

★Palihotel BOUTIQUE HOTEL $$
(Map p138; ☎323-272-4588; www.pali-hotel.com; 7950 Melrose Ave, Mid-City; r from $195; 🅿@❖) We love the rustic wood-panelled exterior, the polished-concrete floor in the lobby, the elemental Thai massage spa, and the 32 contemporary rooms with two-tone paint jobs, a wall-mounted flat-screen TV, and enough room for a sofa. Some have terraces. Terrific all-around value.

Orlando BOUTIQUE HOTEL $$
(Map p138; ☎800-624-6835, 323-658-6600; www.theorlando.com; 8384 W 3rd St, Mid-City; r from $205; 🅿❂❄@❖❄❖) This independently owned, 95-room hotel is smack-dab in the W 3rd St shopping district and just a five-minute walk from the Beverly Center mall. Natural woods, earth tones and votive candles provide a soothing antidote to an exhausting shopping spree, as do the heated saltwater pool and gym with the basics. Nearby, chic eateries abound.

★**Petit Ermitage**　　　　BOUTIQUE HOTEL **$$$**
(Map p138; ☑310-854-1114; www.petitermitage.com; 8822 Cynthia St, West Hollywood; ste from $315; P✳@🖢🐾) Bohemian-chic environs with Turkish rugs, old-world antiques, rooftop bars and fine booze set apart this intimate, one-of-a-kind hotel. No two of its 79 suites are the same, but all feature Venetian-style plaster walls, fireplaces, fun minibar snacks, and some have wet bar and kitchenette. Guests have exclusive access to an impressive art collection lining the halls, lots of chill spaces, and the rooftop bar/butterfly sanctuary.

★**Mondrian**　　　　HOTEL **$$$**
(Map p138; ☑323-650-8999, reservations 800-606-6090; www.mondrianhotel.com; 8440 Sunset Blvd, West Hollywood; r/ste from $329/369; P@🖢🐾) This chic, sleek tower has been an LA showplace since the 1990s. Giant doors facing the Sunset Strip frame the entrance, opening to a lobby of minimalist elegance: white walls, blond woods, billowy curtains

and model-good-looking staff. Upstairs, mood-lit hallways with tiny light boxes (by famed light artist James Turrell) lead to rooms with chandeliers, rain showers and down duvets.

★**Chateau Marmont**　　　　HOTEL **$$$**
(Map p138; ☑323-656-1010; www.chateaumarmont.com; 8221 W Sunset Blvd, Hollywood; r $450, ste from $820; P⊖✳🖢🐾) The French-flavored indulgence may look dated, but this faux castle has long lured A-listers with its hilltop perch, five-star mystique and legendary discretion. Howard Hughes used to spy on bikini beauties from the same balcony suite that became the favorite of U2's Bono. If nothing else, it's worth stopping by for a cocktail at Bar Marmont (p146).

The garden cottages are the most romantic, but the superstitious might want to steer clear of No 2, where John Belushi set his final speedball in 1982.

Palihouse
BOUTIQUE HOTEL $$$

(Map p138; 323-656-4100; www.palihousewest hollywood.com; 8465 Holloway Dr, West Hollywood; r from $315; P❄️🛜) Between Santa Monica Blvd and the Sunset Strip, this cool spot offers 36 suites starting at a super-spacious 600 sq ft, well equipped with galley kitchens, washer/dryers and 'urban lodge' decor: dark woods, raw-bulb lighting, marble counters, arty furniture and tall windows. The lobby has nooks and crannies to chill, sip coffee or cocktails, or play foosball. No pool, though.

Andaz
HOTEL $$$

(Map p138; 323-656-1234; www.westhollywood. andaz.hyatt.com; 8401 W Sunset Blvd, West Hollywood; r from $285; P@🛜🏊) Built in 1958 in the heart of the Sunset Strip, the Andaz boasts a mod, urban aesthetic while paying tribute to the building's heritage as the Hollywood Hyatt House (aka Riot House). Rooms have marble bathrooms, complimentary snacks and nonalcoholic drinks, and it's got LA's tallest rooftop pool for awesome city and Hollywood Hills views.

Sunset Marquis Hotel & Villas
HOTEL $$$

(Map p138; 310-657-1333; www.sunsetmarquis hotel.com; 1200 N Alta Loma Rd, West Hollywood; r from $325; P❄️@🛜🏊) 'Rock-and-roll retreat' may sound like an oxymoron, but not at this quiet, secluded, tropical-garden hideaway that often hosts visiting music royalty, including Mick Jagger and Eric Clapton. There's even a recording studio on site and an inspiring gallery of rock photography.

FUN FACT

The previous incarnation of the Andaz Hotel earned its 'Riot House' moniker from the rock stars – Led Zeppelin, the Who and Santana among them – who stayed here and partied like, well, rock stars. Keith Richards mooned the crowd on Sunset Blvd below, Slash passed out in the elevator, and numerous TVs were tossed from room balconies (maybe that's why they're now windowed off like sunrooms). The infamous John Bonham party tore up the 6th floor. A presumably more sedate tenant, Little Richard, lived here for 20 years. These days, look for a changing selection of rock 'n' roll art on the 2nd floor above the lobby.

Sunset Tower Hotel
HISTORIC HOTEL $$$

(Map p138; 323-654-7100; www.sunsettower hotel.com; 8358 W Sunset Blvd, West Hollywood; r from $345; P@🛜🏊) This 1929 art-deco marvel evokes the romance of Hollywood's Golden Age, when Errol Flynn, Truman Capote and Marilyn Monroe resided here. Recently renovated, the 81-unit tower offers soothing rooms, nightly piano and bass in the flirty bar (in Bugsy Siegel's former apartment), a clubby restaurant, city-view pool deck and a top-notch spa with Turkish hammam (steam bath).

London West Hollywood
LUXURY HOTEL $$$

(Map p138; 866-282-4560; www.thelondon westhollywood.com; 1020 N San Vicente Blvd, West Hollywood; ste incl breakfast from $379; P❄️🛜🏊🐾) A grand all-suite property, favored by the entertainment industry, hides in plain sight just off the Sunset Strip. Fresh from a $30-million renovation, the decor features pearl-toned mosaic motifs in the lobby and guestrooms, where there's Berber carpeting, generous marble desks, silver washbasins, selfie-worthy bathroom lighting, gorgeous inlaid wood paneling and complimentary phone calls to London.

Standard Hollywood
HOTEL $$$

(Map p138; 323-650-9090; www.standardhotel. com; 8300 Sunset Blvd, West Hollywood; r/ste from $235/335; P❄️@🛜🏊) The first hotel in the Standard chain brings fun, cool and hipster sass to the Sunset Strip. Behind its undulating, mid-century facade, a shagadelic lobby leads to sizable rooms with balconies, minimalist furniture and pops of color such as Warhol poppy-print curtains. On summer weekends, the pool rocks amid a cobalt-blue Astroturf deck and views across the LA basin.

Farmer's Daughter Hotel
MOTEL $$$

(Map p138; 800-334-1658, 323-937-3930; www. farmersdaughterhotel.com; 115 S Fairfax Ave, Mid-City; r from $240; P🐾❄️@🛜🏊) Gingham bedspreads, country-style throw pillows and down-home art lend this flirty motel a farmhouse vibe, mixed with big-city sophistication such as floor-to-ceiling mirrors, wall-of-glass bathrooms and a chill pool deck. Adventurous lovers should ask about the secluded No Tell Room, which has a full wet bar and a mirror on the ceiling.

Long ago, a young Charlize Theron stayed here with her mom when they were hunting for a Hollywood career.

SO MANY MEN, SO LITTLE PARKING

That's a slogan we saw on an actual t-shirt in WeHo, and it's true. Street parking enforcement in West Hollywood can be described as fascist (read signs carefully), but you'll find two hours of free parking at some municipal lots, and the library and many businesses offer validated parking. The parking situation is a big reason so many locals have taken to ride-hailing apps like Uber and Lyft – they can be cheaper than paid parking, and certainly cheaper than a ticket.

Mid-City neighborhoods usually have plenty of street parking (hint: free parking is usually a block or two off main streets). DASH buses serve the area on the Fairfax Route and the Hollywood/West Hollywood Route. And the Metro Purple line subway is under construction through Mid-City along Wilshire Blvd (hooray!) though it's not scheduled to begin operating until 2023 (awwww!).

And if you want to 'come on down' and be a contestant on the TV game show *The Price is Right* at CBS Television City (p136) across the street, the hotel runs a clinic for guests looking to better their chances.

✖ Eating

★ Night + Market
THAI $

(Map p138; ☑ 310-275-9724; www.nightmarketla. com; 9043 W Sunset Blvd, West Hollywood; dishes $8-15; ⏰ 11:30am-2:30pm Tue-Thu, 5-10:30pm Tue-Sun) Set behind Talésai, a long-running Thai joint, this related kitchen pumps out outstanding Thai street food and Thai-inspired hybrids such as catfish tamales. Pique the appetite with *larb lanna* (chopped pork salad), push the envelope with rich *pork toro* (grilled pork collar) then move onto winners like *chien-grei* herb sausage and a pad Thai that makes standard LA versions seem overly sweet.

Just leave room for the not-to-be-missed coconut ice cream.

Fleishik's
DELI $

(Map p138; ☑ 323-746-5750; www.fleishiks.com; 7563 Beverly Blvd, Mid-City; sandwiches $10-14; ⏰ 11am-3pm Sun-Fri, 1hr past sundown-midnight Sat) Chef Eric Greenspan pushes boundaries (his Grilled Cheese truck set off an LA and then nationwide trend), but his new restaurant (opened 2017) brings him back to his Jewish roots – sort of. Everything here is kosher, meaning no pork, shellfish or dairy served with meat. That said, if you're looking for an everyday corned beef on rye, go elsewhere.

Original Farmers Market
MARKET $

(Map p138; ☑ 323-933-9211; www.farmersmarket-la.com; 6333 W 3rd St; mains $6-12; ⏰ 9am-9pm Mon-Fri, to 8pm Sat, 10am-7pm Sun; P ⏹) The Farmers Market is a great spot for a casual meal any time of day, especially if the rug rats are tagging along. There are lots of options here, from gumbo and diner food to Singapore-style noodles and tacos, sit-down or takeout. Before or afterwards, go check out the Grove (p137), next door.

Komodo
FUSION $

(Map p138; ☑ 310-246-5153; www.komodofood. com; 8809 Pico Blvd; tacos, burritos & bowls $3-11, mains $11-15; ⏰ 11am-9pm Mon-Thu, to 10pm Fri & Sat; ❄) If 'Latin-Asian fusion' and 'counter service' don't necessarily go together in your mind, Komodo may be a realignment. Choose a taco, burrito or rice bowl and fill it with an eclectic selection from Asian-marinated or banh mi chicken, Java pork, Hawaiian-style *loco moco*, or the MP3 steak with sunny-side egg, tater tots, garlic aioli and cilantro.

Fresh Corn Grill
AMERICAN $

(Map p138; ☑ 310-855-9592; www.freshcorngrill. com; 8714 Santa Monica Blvd, West Hollywood; mains $10-15; ⏰ 11am-10pm Mon-Sat, to 9pm Sun; P ☎) A fantastic, fresh, all-natural counter-service joint with affordable grilled-veggie salads, pastas, semi-authentic tacos, pizzas (the grilled chicken is a big hit), home-baked desserts and good coffee. It's a perfect choice for quick healthy eats, and the side of grilled corn is fantastic. Service is friendly and upbeat, and you can sit in the up-to-date indoors or streetside.

★ Gracias Madre
VEGAN, MEXICAN $$

(Map p138; ☑ 323-978-2170; www.gracias madreweho.com; 8905 Melrose Ave, West Hollywood; mains lunch $10-13, dinner $12-18; ⏰ 11am-11pm Mon-Fri, from 10am Sat & Sun; ☝) Gracias Madre shows just how tasty – and chichi – organic, plant-based Mexican cooking can be. Sit on the gracious patio or in the cozy interior and feel good as you eat healthily: sweet-potato flautas, coconut 'bacon,' plantain 'quesadillas,' plus salads and bowls.

We're consistently surprised at innovations like cashew 'cheese,' mushroom 'chorizo' and heart-of-palm 'crab cakes.'

★ Crossroads VEGAN $$

(Map p138; ☑ 323-782-9245; www.crossroadskitchen.com; 8284 Melrose Ave, Mid-City; brunch mains $7-14, dinner mains $12-22; ⊙10am-2pm daily, 5-10pm Sun-Thu, to midnight Fri & Sat; ✍) Tal Ronnen didn't get to be a celebrity chef (Oprah, Ellen) by serving ordinary vegan fare. Instead, seasonal creations include 'crab cakes' made from hearts of palm, artichoke 'oysters,' and porcini-crusted eggplant, alongside pizzas and pastas incorporating innovative 'cheeses' made from nuts. Leave the Birkenstocks at home; this place is sophisticated, with full bar and cool cocktails.

Canter's DELI $$

(Map p138; ☑ 323-651-2030; www.cantersdeli.com; 419 N Fairfax Ave, Mid-City; ⊙24hr; ℗) As old-school delis go, Canter's is hard to beat. A fixture in the traditionally Jewish Fairfax district since 1931, it serves up the requisite pastrami, corned beef and matzo-ball soup with a side of sass by seen-it-all waitresses, in a rangy room with deli and bakery counters up front.

The adjacent Kibitz Room is part-restaurant, part-dive-bar, and has been visited over the decades by rockers from Frank Zappa to Joni Mitchell, Guns N' Roses and Jakob Dylan. There are still performances most nights. Who knows? You might catch tomorrow's big star.

EP & LP SOUTHEAST ASIAN $$

(Map p138; ☑ 310-855-9955; http://eplosangeles.com; 603 N La Cienega Blvd, West Hollywood; small plates $10-18, large plates $20-34; ⊙5pm-2am Mon-Fri, from noon Sat & Sun) Louis Tikaram, Australia's Chef of the Year in 2014, has brought the creative, bold flavors of his Fijian-Chinese heritage – *kakoda* (Fijian-style ceviche), Chiang Mai larb (spiced salmon stands in for meat), and crispy chicken with black vinegar, chili and lemon – to some of LA's most enviable real estate, at the corner of Melrose and La Cienega.

Estrella CALIFORNIAN $$

(Map p138; ☑ 310-652-6613; www.estrellasunset.com; 8800 Sunset Blvd, West Hollywood; lunch mains $11-26, dinner mains $18-38; ⊙8-11am & 11:30am-3pm Mon-Fri, 10am-3pm Sat & Sun, 5:30-10pm Sun-Thu, 5:30-11pm Fri & Sat) In its prime Sunset Blvd location, Estrella looks almost too polished for inventive cooking, but looks can deceive. Executive chef Dakota Weiss' menu boasts veggie-forward lunch dishes such as grilled cauliflower and roasted-grape lettuce wraps, light and lovely *michelada* Caesar salad (with pickled clams), or maple-syrup-grilled squash sandwich. We especially like the terrace inspired by 1960s-era Laurel Canyon bungalows.

Cousins Maine Lobster SEAFOOD $$

(Map p138; ☑ 424-204-9923; www.cousinsmainelobster.com; 8593 Santa Monica Blvd, West Hollywood; mains $10-17; ⊙11am-10pm Tue-Sun, to 9pm Mon; ℗; 🚈MTA line 4, 704) It's a classic LA success story: cousins Jim and Sabin moved to LA with a dream of a business drawing on their New England heritage. They started with a food truck and – here's the LA part – found their way onto TV's *Shark Tank*. Now they've gone brick-and-mortar, selling lobster rolls, lobster BLTs, lobster salads and tater tots.

Alma AMERICAN $$

(Map p138; ☑ 323-822-3131; www.standardhotel.com; Standard Hotel, 8300 Sunset Blvd, West Hollywood; dishes daytime $14-28, dinner mains $15-36; ⊙24h; ℗) Like its home, the Standard Hotel (p142), Alma's a hub of millennial cool. Menus feature hipster standards during the day – think avocado toast, chicken club or marinated-mushroom sandwich – and avant-garde dinner items such as frozen foie gras with seaweed and tofu beignet, and charred octopus with black garlic. Enjoy yours in the retro mid-century dining room, or poolside.

Petty Cash Taqueria MEXICAN $$

(Map p138; ☑ 323-933-5300; www.pettycashtaqueria.com; 7360 Beverly Blvd, Mid-City; tacos $5-6.50, other dishes $6-21; ⊙5-10pm Mon, to 10:30pm Tue-Thu, noon-11pm Fri & Sat, noon-10pm Sun) A big, funky, reimagined taco joint with raw-light-bulb chandeliers, a pounded-metal bar, bright-pink-paper menu and handmade, fresh-grilled tortillas. *Conchinita pibil* (marinated pulled pork shoulder) tacos come folded with pickled onion and black-bean purée. The grilled octopus taco is garnished with *chile de arbol,* peanuts, jack cheese and avocado.

Escuela Taqueria MEXICAN $$

(Map p138; ☑ 323-932-6178; www.escuelataqueria.com; 7615 Beverly Blvd, Mid-City; tacos & burritos $4-12; ⊙11am-11pm) An upscale, new-school taqueria. Vegetarians may opt for the roasted poblano and jack cheese tacos; fish heads will dig the branzino, shrimp or lobster (hell yes!).

It also serves carnitas, and the crispy beef and pickle is its answer to a burger in taco clothing. It doesn't serve alcohol, but you can bring your own for $4 per person.

Mama's Secret
TURKISH $$

(Map p138; ☎323-424-3482; www.mamassecret bakery.com; 8314 W 3rd St, Mid-City; mezzes $8-13, mains $11-18; ☺8am-6pm Mon-Wed, to 8pm Thu-Sun) A delightful Turkish cafe where tables spill from a whitewashed interior (with colorful handprints on the walls) onto the sidewalk. Gyros are wrapped in freshly baked lavash, burgers are made with Mediterranean meatball patties, and *gozleme* (flatbreads) are filled with your choice of spinach and feta, potato, spicy *soujouk* sausage, haloumi cheese or ground beef.

Mercado
MEXICAN $$

(Map p138; ☎323-944-0947; www.mercado restaurant.com; 7910 W 3rd St, Los Angeles; dishes $9-26; ☺5-10pm Mon-Wed, to 11pm Thu & Fri, 11am-3pm & 4-11pm Sat, 11am-3pm & 4-10pm Sun; ⓟ) Terrific *nuevo* Mexican food served in whitewashed brick environs, with dangling bird-cage chandeliers and a terrific marble tequila bar. The slow-cooked carnitas melt in your mouth. It also spit-roasts beef, grills sweet corn and folds tasty tacos and enchiladas. Its *hora feliz* (happy hour) is among the best in the city.

Ita Cho
JAPANESE $$

(Map p138; ☎323-938-9009; www.facebook.com/itachorestaurant; 7311 Beverly Blvd, Mid-City; dishes $4-20; ☺11:30am-11:30pm, to midnight Fri & Sat; ⓟ) Simply put, this is some of the best Japanese food available in Los Angeles, served izakaya style with fusion sushi. Order any of its small plates, but don't miss the *nasu miso* (eggplant coated in sweet miso sauce), the buttery enoki, the broiled *unagi* and anything sashimi, served in a post-modern, industrial-style room. Celeb sightings happen here.

Terroni
ITALIAN $$

(Map p138; ☎323-954-0300; www.terroni.ca; 7605 Beverly Blvd, Mid-City; mains $12-21; ☺11:30am-10:30pm Mon-Thu, to 11:30pm Fri, 10am-11:30pm Sat, 10am-10:30pm Sun) Traditional southern Italian cuisine, by way of, um...Toronto? Facts is facts, and you will love the *carpaccio di tonno*, the thin-crust *pizze* and exquisite *pasta al limone*. Just don't expect pizza cutters or substitutions. Terroni doesn't change nuthin' for nobody! But do demand the awesome, vinegary, fiery red chilies.

Village Idiot
PUB FOOD $$

(Map p138; ☎323-655-3331; www.villageidiotla.com; 7383 Melrose Ave, Mid-City; mains $14-29; ☺11:30am-2am Mon-Fri, from 10am Sat & Sun; ⓟ) Fantastic pub fare with recommended fish and chips, American and English breakfasts and other comfort food in a habitat that lures a smart, but plenty-boisterous crowd. The kitchen stays open until midnight. Drinks flow until 2am, and when it's game time, high-mounted mirrors slide to reveal TVs.

★Catch LA
FUSION $$$

(Map p138; ☎323-347-6060; http://catchrestau rants.com/catchla; 8715 Melrose Ave, West Hollywood; shared dishes $11-31, dinner mains $28-41; ☺11am-3pm Sat & Sun, 5pm-2am daily; ⓟ) An LA-scene extraordinaire. You may well find sidewalk paparazzi stalking celebrity guests and a doorman to check your reservation, but all that's forgotten once you're up in this 3rd-floor rooftop restaurant/bar above WeHo. The Pacific Rim–inspired menu features super-creative cocktails and shared dishes such as truffle sashimi, black-cod lettuce wraps, and scallop and cauliflower with tamarind brown butter.

★Connie & Ted's
SEAFOOD $$$

(Map p138; ☎323-848-2722; www.connieandteds.com; 8171 Santa Monica Blvd, West Hollywood; mains $13-44; ☺4-10pm Mon & Tue, 11:30am-10pm Wed & Thu, 11:30am-11pm Fri, 10am-11pm Sat, 10am-10pm Sun; ⓟ) At this modernized version of a New England seafood shack by acclaimed chef Michael Cimarusti, there are always up to a dozen oyster varieties at the raw bar, classics such as fried clams, grilled fish (wild and sustainably raised), lobsters and steamers, lobster rolls served cold with mayo or hot with drawn butter, and shellfish marinara is a sacred thing.

★Republique
BISTRO $$$

(Map p138; ☎310-362-6115; www.republiquela.com; 624 S La Brea Ave, Mid-City; mains lunch $11-19, dinner $14-56; ☺8am-4pm daily, 5:30-10pm Sun-Thu, to 11pm Fri & Sat; ⓟ🚻; 🚍MTA line 20, 720) A design gem with the gourmet ambition to match. The old interior of LA's dearly departed Campanile is still an atrium restaurant with stone arches, a brightly lit front end scattered with butcher-block tables, and a marble bar peering into an open kitchen. There are tables in the darker, oakier backroom too.

★Ray's
MODERN AMERICAN $$$

(Map p138; ☎323-857-6180; www.raysandstark bar.com; 5905 Wilshire Blvd, Los Angeles County

Museum of Art; mains $17-36; ⊙11:30am-8pm Mon-Tue & Thu, to 10pm Fri, 10am-8pm Sat & Sun; ℗; 🚇MTA 20) Seldom does a restaurant blessed with as golden a location as this one – on the plaza of LACMA (p135) – live up to the address. Ray's does. Menus change seasonally and often daily with farm-to-table fresh ingredients – some grown in the restaurant's own garden. You can expect some form of burrata, kale salad and pizzas to be on the menu.

It's attached to Stark Bar, known for cocktails and its own water sommelier. Yup.

Pump
ITALIAN $$$

(Map p138; ☎310-657-7867; www.pumprestaurant. com; 8948 Santa Monica Blvd, West Hollywood; appetizers $14-18, salads $14-26, dinner mains $18-38, brunch mains $14-24; ⊙5pm-2am Mon-Fri, from 11:30am Sat & Sun; ℗) It's a veritable scene at the crossroads of WeHo, where reality TV's *Vanderpump Rules* star Lisa Vanderpump has opened this showplace. There's always a buzz around the gorgeous, twinkly-lit bar and plush, garden-style dining room where model-good-looking staff serve dishes such as tuna tartare with pomegranate seeds, chicken Milanese and pistachio-crusted salmon. And cocktails. Lots of cocktails.

Animal
GRILL $$$

(Map p138; ☎323-782-9225; www.animalrestaurant. com; 435 N Fairfax Ave, Mid-City; dishes $6-39; ⊙6-10pm Mon-Thu, to 11pm Fri, 10:30am-2:30pm & 6-11pm Sat, 10:30am-2:30pm & 6-10pm Sun) Carnivorous foodies pray at the altar of Animal, the restaurant that put food bros Jon Shook and Vinny Dotolo on the map. Begin with chicken-liver toast or spicy beef tendons (with charred-onion pho dip) then get the smoked turkey leg with celery root, apple and white barbecue sauce, or foie gras loco moco. Simultaneously serious and playful.

The Ivy
CALIFORNIAN $$$

(Map p154; ☎310-274-8303; www.theivyrestaurants. com; 113 N Robertson Blvd, West Hollywood; mains $22-97; ⊙8am-11pm; ℗) Amid the modeling agencies and couture boutiques, and with a long history of celebrity power lunches, this flower-festooned and cushioned cottage is where Southern comfort food (such as fried chicken and crab cakes) has been elevated to haute cuisine. Service is refined and impeccable, and paparazzi etiquette (among one another and their prey) is a fluid, dynamic beast.

Gusto
ITALIAN $$$

(Map p138; ☎323-782-1778; www.gusto-la.com; 8432 W 3rd St, Mid-City; mains $17-32; ⊙6-10pm Sun-Thu, to 11pm Fri & Sat) This neighborhood Italian joint feels like it's belonged here since forever, though it opened in 2012. That's when it was named one of *Esquire*'s best new restaurants. We suggest you start with the octopus with heirloom cannellini beans then move onto black spaghetti with anchovy and chili or bucatini carbonara.

Son of a Gun
SEAFOOD $$$

(Map p138; ☎323-782-9033; www.sonofagunrestaurant.com; 8370 W 3rd St, Mid-City; dishes $8-32; ⊙noon-3pm daily, 6-10pm Sun-Thu, to 11pm Fri & Sat; 🚇MTA line 16) The guys behind Animal also operate this creative fish and seafood kitchen festooned with beach-shack decor. The menu changes daily, but you might find chefs glazing and grilling kampachi collars, searing octopus with chili or fixing a classic trout amandine. They also make a mean lobster roll, terrific linguine and clams and plate their burrata with uni.

🍸 Drinking & Nightlife

WeHo is party central, especially on Sunset and Santa Monica Blvds. For SoCal's LGBT community, Santa Monica Blvd between about Robertson and La Cienega Blvds is also known as Boys Town, complete with rainbow-painted crosswalks – it's super fun and flirty, especially on weekend nights. Off this strip are some of America's best comedy clubs, classic cocktail and tequila bars, and even a new cat cafe.

★ Bar Marmont
BAR

(Map p138; ☎323-650-0575; www.chateaumarmont.com; 8171 Sunset Blvd, Hollywood; ⊙6pm-2am) Elegant, but not stuck up; been around, yet still cherished. With high ceilings, molded walls and terrific martinis, the famous and the wish-they-weres still flock here. If you time it right you might see celebs – the Marmont doesn't share who (or else they'd stop coming – get it?). Come midweek. Weekends are for amateurs.

Stark Bar
BAR

(Map p138; Los Angeles County Museum of Art, 5905 Wilshire Blvd, Los Angeles) The closest you can get to LACMA's *Urban Light* with a drink in your hand, this bar on the museum's plaza specializes in draft cocktails and frozen ones like the Hemingway daiquiri, and uses spirits from small-batch distillers. The water sommelier can match bottled water to the bites you get from Ray's next door.

Crumbs & Whiskers
CAT CAFE

(Map p138; ☑ 323-879-9389; www.crumbsandwhiskers.com; 7924 Melrose Ave, Mid-City; 75min visit weekdays/weekends $22/25; ⊙ 11am-7:45pm Thu-Tue; ☐) Humans commune with kitties at LA's first cat cafe. The spare, stylish black-box storefront is kitted out with fluffy futons and climbing shelves, and humans can observe and gently touch felines while drinking coffee and tea. Resident cats were rescued from high-kill shelters and are up for adoption, but here you're in their environment, not the other way around.

Graffiti Sublime Coffee
CAFE

(Map p138; 180 S La Brea Ave, Los Angeles; ⊙ 9am-8pm; ☎) The organic coffees and limited menu of well-chosen soups, pastries and such here are complemented by the serene, artfully hip black-and-white decor, Eames-style chairs and minimalist, bright-white tables. The warehouse-style room never feels crowded even when it's full. Great for people-watching without looking like you're people-watching (and it's great people-watching). No one under 18 allowed (see 'serene').

El Carmen
BAR

(Map p138; ☑ 323-852-1552; www.elcarmenla.com; 8138 W 3rd St, Mid-City; ⊙ 5pm-2am) A pair of mounted bull heads and *lucha libre* (Mexican wrestling) masks create an over-the-top, 'Tijuana North' look and pull in an industry-heavy crowd at LA's ultimate tequila tavern (over 300 to choose from). If you don't know an *añejo* from a *reposado*, do a tasting and find out (from $25), or just get a perfect tequila cocktail.

Beverly Hills Juice Club
JUICE BAR

(Map p138; ☑ 323-655-8300; www.beverlyhillsjuice.com; 8382 Beverly Blvd, Mid-City; ⊙ 7am-6pm Mon-Fri, from 9am Sat) This 1975 hippie classic – the first on the LA health-food, raw-power bandwagon – started out on Sunset when Tom Waits and Rickie Lee Jones used to stumble in between shows. It still attracts an in-the-know crowd craving wheatgrass shots and banana-manna shakes. Get yours with a shot of algae. No, seriously.

Paramount Coffee Project
CAFE

(Map p138; ☑ 323-746-5480; www.pcpfx.com; 456 N Fairfax Ave, Mid-City; ⊙ 7am-5pm Mon-Sat, from 8am Sun) Aussie-run PCP gets its coffee from Sydney's famed Reuben Hills coffee roaster, and it makes its own almond milk and macadamia milk. Food includes breakfast and all-day sandwiches, avocado toast, noodles and salads. Sit in the long, narrow, modernist room or order to-go from the window.

Roger Room
COCKTAIL BAR

(Map p138; ☑ 310-854-1300; www.therogerroom.com; 370 N La Cienega Blvd, West Hollywood; ⊙ 6pm-2am Mon-Fri, from 7pm Sat, from 8pm Sun) Cramped but cool; too cool even to have a sign out front. When handcrafted, throwback cocktails first migrated west and south from New York and San Fran, they landed here, amid velvet booths and well-dressed, mustachioed bartenders.

☆ Entertainment

Comedy Store
COMEDY

(Map p138; ☑ 323-650-6268; www.thecomedystore.com; 8433 W Sunset Blvd, West Hollywood) There's no comedy club in the city with more street cred than Sammy and Mitzi Shore's Comedy Store on the strip. Sammy launched the club, but Mitzi was the one who brought in hot young comics such as Richard Pryor, George Carlin, Eddie Murphy, Robin Williams and David Letterman. There are three stages, meaning something's on just about every night.

Improv
COMEDY

(Map p138; www.improv.com; 8162 Melrose Ave, Mid-City; prices vary; ⊙ show times vary) Launch pad for countless stand-up comics from Richard Pryor to Jerry Seinfeld, Ellen DeGeneres and Dave Chapelle, the Improv still gets headliners (Maz Jobrani, Nikki Glazer, Jay Mohr and, um, more), but it's mostly up-and-comers these days. Tuesday evenings at 5:45pm anyone can grab the mic.

Largo at the Coronet
LIVE MUSIC, PERFORMING ARTS

(Map p138; ☑ 310-855-0530; www.largo-la.com; 366 N La Cienega Blvd, Mid-City) Ever since its early days on Fairfax Ave, Largo has been progenitor of high-minded pop culture (it nurtured Zach Galifianakis to stardom). Now part of the Coronet Theatre complex, it features edgy comedy, such as Sarah Silverman and Nick Offerman, and nourishing night music such as the Preservation Hall Jazz Band.

LA'S LGBT COMMUNITY

LA is one of the country's gayest cities and has made many contributions to gay culture. Your gaydar may well be pinging throughout the county, but the rainbow flag flies especially proudly in Boystown, along Santa Monica Blvd in West Hollywood, which is flanked by dozens of high-energy bars, cafes, restaurants, gyms and clubs. Most cater to gay men, although there's plenty for lesbians and mixed audiences. Thursday through Sunday nights are prime time.

Beauty reigns supreme among the buff, bronzed and styled of Boystown. Elsewhere the scene is considerably more laid back and less body conscious. The crowd in Silver Lake is more mixed age and runs from cute hipsters to leather-and-Levi's, while Downtown's burgeoning scene is an equally eclectic mix of hipsters, East LA Latinos, general counterculture types and business folk. Venice and Long Beach have the most relaxed, neighborly scenes.

If nightlife isn't your scene, there are plenty of other ways to meet, greet and engage. Outdoor options include the **Frontrunners** (www.lafrontrunners.com) running club and the **Great Outdoors** (www.greatoutdoorsla.org) hiking club. The latter runs day and night hikes, as well as neighborhood walks. For insight into LA's fascinating queer history, book a walking tour with **Out & About Tours** (www.thelavendereffect.org/tours; tours from $30).

There's gay theater all over town, but the **Celebration Theatre** (Map p138; ☑323-957-1884; www.celebrationtheatre.com; 6760 Lexington Ave, Hollywood) ranks among the nation's leading stages for LGBT plays. The **Cavern Club Theater** (Map p128; www.cavernclubtheater.com; 1920 Hyperion Ave, Silver Lake) pushes the envelope, particularly with uproarious drag performers; it's downstairs from Casita del Campo restaurant. If you're lucky enough to be in town when the **Gay Men's Chorus of Los Angeles** (www.gmcla.org) is performing, don't miss out: this amazing group has been doing it since 1979.

The **LA LGBT Center** (Map p106; ☑323-993-7400; www.lalgbtcenter.org; 1625 Schrader Blvd; ◷9am-9pm Mon-Fri, to 1pm Sat) is a one-stop service and health agency, and its affiliated **Village at Ed Gould Plaza** (Map p138; ☑323-993-7400; https://lalgbtcenter.org; 1125 N McCadden Pl, Hollywood; ◷6-10pm Mon-Fri, 9am-5pm Sat; ℗) offers art exhibits, theater and film screenings throughout the year.

The festival season kicks off in mid- to late May with the **Long Beach Pride Celebration** (☑562-987-9191; www.longbeachpride.com; 450 E Shoreline Dr, Long Beach; parade free, festival admission adult/child & senior $25/free; ◷mid-May) and continues with the three-day **LA Pride** (p70) in mid-June with a parade down Santa Monica Blvd. On Halloween (October 31), the same street brings out 500,000 outrageously costumed revelers of all persuasions.

WeHo

Abbey (Map p138; ☑310-289-8410; www.theabbeyweho.com; 692 N Robertson Blvd, West Hollywood; ◷11am-2am Mon-Thu, from 10am Fri, from 9am Sat & Sun) It's been called the best gay bar in the world, and who are we to argue? Once a humble coffee house, the Abbey has expanded into WeHo's bar/club/restaurant of record. It has so many different-flavored martinis and mojitos that you'd think they were invented here, plus a full menu of upscale pub food (mains $14 to $21).

Fiesta Cantina (Map p138; ☑310-652-8865; www.fiestacantina.net; 8865 Santa Monica Blvd, West Hollywood; ◷noon-2am) The essence of cheap and cheerful, Fiesta packs in a vibrant crowd of 20-something twinks and other assorted revelers, thanks to extra-long happy hours, reasonably priced nachos, downright cheap Taco Tuesdays, a busy sidewalk patio, beach-shack vibe and a roof deck. Nothing fancy, but always busy.

Micky's (Map p138; www.mickys.com; 8857 Santa Monica Blvd, West Hollywood; ◷5pm-2am Mon-Thu, to 4am Fri, 3pm-4am Sat, 2pm-2am Sun) A two-story, quintessential WeHo dance club, with go-go boys, expensive drinks, attitude and plenty of eye candy. There's a marble circle bar, exposed steel girders and doors that open all the way to the street. Check online for special events. Valet parking available.

Rage (Map p138; ☑310-652-7055; www.ragenightclub.com; 8911 Santa Monica Blvd, West Hollywood) Two-story Rage does theme nights – Asian Fridays, Latin Saturdays etc – with thumping music and lotsa bars and boys. We admit to having a soft spot for the more intimate Musical Mondays, when a ragtag troupe of amateurs with makeshift props acts out Broadway and Hollywood videos projected on big screens, and performers from local stage productions guest star.

Trunks (Map p138; ☑310-652-1015; www.trunksbar.com; 8809 Santa Monica Blvd, West Hollywood; ⊙1pm-2am) With pool tables and sports on the flat-screen TVs, this brick-house, low-lit dive is a long-running boulevard staple that is less fabulous and more down to earth than most in WeHo. And that can be a very good thing.

Marix (Map p138; ☑323-656-8800; www.marixtexmex.com; 1108 N Flores St, West Hollywood; mains $13-22; ⊙11:30am-11pm Mon-Fri, 11am-11pm Sat, 11am-10pm Sun; ℗) Marix is barely more than a glassed-in patio with a retractable roof, but it's been a party place for a generation of LGBT Angelenos and those who love them. Strong margaritas are dispensed by the pitcher (splurge on the good tequila; you're welcome), chips and salsa are plentiful and the kitchen seems to dish out sizzling fajitas approximately every minute.

Chi Chi Larue's (Map p138; ☑800-997-9072; www.chichilarues.com; 8932 Santa Monica Blvd, West Hollywood; ⊙10am-midnight Sun-Wed, to 2am Thu-Sat) If other erotica stores are too tame or hetero-friendly for you, make your way to this (not just) gay-oriented store owned by a legendary drag queen. You can size up in the manhood department, pick up aromas, oils and films to spark the mood, grab some assless chaps, and otherwise combine your love of retail with the joy of sex.

Beyond WeHo

Akbar (Map p128; ☑323-665-6810; www.akbarsilverlake.com; 4356 W Sunset Blvd, Silver Lake; ⊙4pm-2am) Fun-loving, Casbah-style Akbar is a hit with queer Eastsiders of all ages – skinny-denim hipsters, greying daddies, skyscraping drag queens. There's no shortage of theme nights, from lip-sync comps and karaoke, to weekend dance sessions with gyrating go-go boys. Drinks are rightfully potent.

Eagle LA (Map p128; ☑323-669-9472; www.eaglela.com; 4219 Santa Monica Blvd, Silver Lake; ⊙4pm-2am Mon-Fri, from 2pm Sat & Sun; 🛜) A dark, sexy demi-monde where the walls are black, the lights red and the videos hardcore, the Eagle is as close as LA gets to a proper gay leather bar, especially on themed nights (see the website). It's a friendly neighborhood hangout, with pool table, the odd topless barkeep and a crowd of mixed body types and ethnicities. Cash only.

New Jalisco Bar (Map p82; ☑213-613-1802; 245 S Main St, Downtown; ⊙noon-2am Mon-Fri, from 2pm Sat & Sun) The ultimate gay dive bar, with all the thrilling prerequisites: no cover charge, regular drag shows, a heaving dance floor and wallet-friendly drinks (including $2 local beers from 1pm to 7pm Monday to Thursday). The crowd is a fun, democratic mix of Latino locals, Downtown hipsters and other queer revelers yearning for something less plastic than the WeHo scene. Cash only.

Redline (Map p82; ☑213-935-8391; www.redlinedtla.com; 131 E 6th St, Downtown; ⊙5pm-2am Tue-Sat, 11am-midnight Sun) Part of Downtown's booming gay scene, Redline's metal-pressed bar draws everyone from laid-back old timers to twinks and punks. Head in for $5 happy-hour drinks and bites from 5pm to 8pm Tuesday to Friday, and book ahead for Wednesday's Dragalicious, where drag shows collide with $6 martinis. See the website for regular themed events, which include DJs and butt-shaking dancers.

Faultline (Map p128; ☑323-660-0889; www.faultlinebar.com; 4216 Melrose Ave; ⊙5pm-2am Wed-Fri, from 2pm Sat & Sun) One of LA's naughtier gay bars, with no shortage of beards and brawn. Take off your shirt and join the Sunday-afternoon beer bust (it's an institution), but get there early or expect a long wait.

Groundlings

COMEDY

(Map p138; ☎ 323-934-4747; www.groundlings. com; 7307 Melrose Ave, Mid-City; tickets $10-20) This improv school and company launched Lisa Kudrow, Will Ferrell, Maya Rudolph and other top talent. Its sketch comedy and improv can be belly-achingly funny, especially on Thursdays when the main company, alumni and surprise guests get to riff together in 'Cookin' with Gas'.

Mint

CONCERT VENUE

(Map p138; www.themintla.com; 6010 W Pico Blvd; cover $5-25) Built in 1937, Mint is an intimate, historic venue. Legends such as Ray Charles and Stevie Wonder played here on the way up, and axe-man Ben Harper got his start here, too. Expect a packed slate of terrific jazz, blues and rock shows, sensational sound, and you'll never be more than 30ft from the performance stage.

El Rey

LIVE MUSIC

(Map p138; www.theelrey.com; 5515 Wilshire Blvd, Mid-City; cover varies) A 1931 art-deco dance hall decked out in red velvet and chandeliers and flaunting an awesome sound system and excellent sightlines. Although it can hold nearly 800 people, it feels more intimate. It brings in everything from cover bands to pretty big names, so check the calendar.

Laugh Factory

COMEDY

(Map p138; ☎ 323-656-1336; www.laughfactory. com; 8001 W Sunset Blvd, Hollywood) The Marx Brothers used to keep offices at this long-standing club. It still gets some big names (such as Kevin Nealon and Dave Chappelle) as well as up-and-comers.

🛍 Shopping

WeHo and Mid-City are by far the best and most diverse shopping territory in a city that often feels like it's built by and for shopaholics. Melrose Ave, between La Brea and Fairfax Aves, gets most of the buzz, thanks to the boutiques stuck together like block-long hedgerows. Most of their gear is rather lowbrow and low-end, with some unique gems and fab vintage stores. If you want the high-end stuff, make your way west of Fairfax on Melrose or 3rd St. Both Beverly Blvd and La Brea Ave are stocked with gorgeous interiors showrooms and galleries, with the occasional fashion boutique mixed in. Fairfax Ave, between Beverly and Melrose, is where hip-hop and skate culture collide.

Then there are the megamalls: the Beverly Center and its smaller sister, Beverly Connection, across the street, and the Grove, each with dozens of high-to-middle-end shops and department stores, and often big hangout spots in their own right.

★ Reformation

FASHION & ACCESSORIES

(Map p138; www.thereformation.com; 8253 Melrose Ave, Mid-City; ⊗11am-7pm Mon-Sat, to 6pm Sun) 🖉 Here's classic, retro-inspired, fashionable women's wear that's eco-conscious without the granola. It does it by using pre-existing materials, which means no additional dyeing of fabrics and half the water use of other fashion brands, and with an eye toward minimizing waste from sourcing to production, sales and even recycling. Everything is made locally.

★ Mystery Pier Books

BOOKS

(Map p138; www.mysterypierbooks.com; 8826 W Sunset Blvd, West Hollywood; ⊗11am-7pm Mon-Sat, noon-5pm Sun) An intimate, hidden-away courtyard shop that specializes in selling signed shooting scripts from past blockbusters, and 1st editions from Shakespeare ($2500 to $4000), Salinger ($21,000) and JK Rowling ($30,000 and up).

★ Fred Segal

FASHION & ACCESSORIES

(Map p138; ☎ 323-651-4129; www.fredsegal.com; 8100 Melrose Ave, Mid-City; ⊗10am-7pm Mon-Sat, noon-6pm Sun) Celebs and beautiful people circle for the very latest from Babakul, Aviator Nation and Robbi & Nikki at this warren of high-end boutiques under one impossibly chic but slightly snooty roof. The only time you'll see bargains (sort of) is during the two-week blowout sale in September.

★ Wasteland

VINTAGE

(Map p138; www.shopwasteland.com; 7428 Melrose Ave, Mid-City; ⊗11am-8pm Mon-Sat, from noon Sun) Large, popular and rather-polished vintage boutique with racks packed with skirts and tops, fur-collared jackets and Pendleton wool shirts.

Grove

MALL

(Map p138; ☎ 323-900-8080; www.thegrovela. com; 189 The Grove Dr; ⊗10am-9pm Mon-Thu, to 10pm Fri & Sat, to 8pm Sun; 🚌 MTA line 16) This faux Italian palazzo is one of LA's most popular shopping destinations, with 40 name-brand stores, a fountain and a trolley rolling down the middle.

Melrose Avenue
FASHION & ACCESSORIES

(Map p138) A popular shopping strip as famous for its epic people-watching as it is for its consumer fruits. You'll see hair (and people) of all shades and styles, and everything from Gothic jewels to custom sneakers to medical marijuana to stuffed porcupines available for a price. The strip is located between Fairfax and La Brea Aves.

Book Soup
BOOKS

(Map p138; ☑ 310-659-3110; www.booksoup.com; 8818 W Sunset Blvd, West Hollywood; ☺9am-10pm Mon-Sat, to 7pm Sun) A bibliophile's indie gem, sprawling and packed with entertainment, travel, feminist and queer studies, eclectic and LA-based fiction, with appearances by big-name authors.

Shopaholic
CLOTHING

(Map p138; ☑ 323-930-9909; www.shopaholicsamplesales.com; 8032 W 3rd St, Mid-City; ☺11am-6pm) While everyone else pays retail at the Beverly Center and the Grove down the street, Shopaholic specializes in sample sales – basically, ways for designers to get rid of excess inventory. The stock at this shop is always changing, but if you find what you want it could be 50% to 80% off the retail price.

ASH
FASHION & ACCESSORIES

(A Sexy Habit; Map p138; ☑ 323-944-0529; 7614½ Melrose Ave, Mid-City; ☺noon-8pm) This thumping shop sells street wear and designer wear mostly for men, with brands such as Tokyo's Iro-ichi (band jackets of embroidered denim) and Black Pyramid (singer Chris Brown's clothing line). But we love LA designer Rik Villa's amazing repurposing of old duffel bags, deconstructed jeans and more to create cool, one-of-a-kind jackets.

Beverly Center
MALL

(Map p138; ☑ 310-854-0070; www.beverlycenter. com; 8500 Beverly Blvd, Los Angeles; ☺10am-9pm Mon-Fri, to 8pm Sat, to 6pm Sun) Mall shoppers will want to head to this eight-story monolith anchored by Bloomingdale's and Macy's department stores and home to some 100 other national and international brands. It's undergoing a $500-million facelift and interior redesign, scheduled for completion by late 2018 – shops remain open for the duration.

Curve
FASHION & ACCESSORIES

(Map p154; ☑ 310-360-8008; www.shopcurve.com; 154 N Robertson Blvd, West Hollywood; ☺11am-7pm Mon-Sat, noon-6pm Sun) A funky fashion boutique that isn't as stiff as some of the other players on Robertson. It offers Acne denim, Rona Pfeiffer jewelry and a range of funky trenches, spiked heels, sexy minis, leather vests, baby-doll dresses and some wonderful leather high tops from Maison Martin Margiela.

Madison
FASHION & ACCESSORIES

(Map p154; ☑ 310-275-1930; www.madisonlos angeles.com; 8745 W 3rd St, Mid-City; ☺11am-7pm Mon-Sat, noon-5pm Sun) An essential shopping destination for LA women who move seamlessly from casual days to glitzy nights. It stocks denim from Current/Elliott and Rag and Bone, dresses by ALC and Alexander Wang, and handbags and heels by Valentino.

Nudie Jeans
DENIM

(Map p138; ☑ 323-951-0677; www.nudiejeans.com; 710 N Edinburgh Ave, Mid-City; ☺11am-7pm Mon-Sat, noon-6pm Sun) This is the West Coast's only branded shop from the Swedish-owned Nudie denim line. Jeans come in a variety of colors, and prices include free hemming and repair. The shop itself is a converted house outfitted with blackboard walls, one of which offers suggestions on when to wash your new denim. Short answer: every five to six months. Seriously.

Gibson
HOMEWARES

(Map p138; ☑ 323-934-4248; www.garygibson. com; 7350 Beverly Blvd, Mid-City; ☺9am-6pm Mon-Fri, noon-5pm Sat) If you love vintage interiors, step into this gem of a gallery, where (almost) everything from vintage baseball bats to armchairs and desks to the art on the walls was birthed in another era (or reproduced to look that way). It's owned and operated by noted designer Gary Gibson, who operates his interior-design studio out back.

Supreme
FASHION & ACCESSORIES

(Map p138; ☑ 323-655-6205; www.supremenew york.com; 439 N Fairfax Ave, Mid-City) Fans are fanatical about the skate and street wear from this New York–based fashion house: colorful, patterned, padded, faux fur, patches and more. Cool. Fans have been known to line up for half a block to get a taste of the new line. It also has a half-pipe in the store. Also cool.

Kayo
FASHION & ACCESSORIES

(Map p138; ☑ 323-677-2104; www.thekayostore. com; 464 N Fairfax Ave, Mid-City; ☺11am-7pm Mon-Sat, from noon Sun) This hip-hop skater retailer on Fairfax is set in a converted bank building and it has the vault to prove it. It deals in labels such as Organika and has some of the best and most interesting T-shirt designs on the block. It also hocks decks, trucks and wheels if you need a ride.

Espionage VINTAGE
(Map p138; ✆323-272-4942; www.espionagela. com; 7456 Beverly Blvd, Mid-City; ⊙11am-6pm Tue-Sat, to 5pm Sun) A fabulous boutique blessed with a tasteful melange of new and vintage goods. Its jewelry is fantastic, as are the chunky vintage perfume bottles and ashtrays. The leather chairs work perfectly with the brass-and-glass end tables, and it offers a collection of vintage couture clothing sold on consignment.

Le Labo PERFUME
(Map p138; ✆323-782-0411; www.lelabofragrances. com; 8385 W 3rd St; ⊙11am-7pm Mon-Sat, to 5pm Sun) The West Hollywood branch of this noted fragrance lab based in New York offers 15 fragrances, including one you can only purchase here. All are alchemized with hundreds of natural oils such as patchouli, vetiver, iris and ylang ylang. It'll make a bottle fresh for you. It also has addictive shower gel, body lotion, massage oil and balm.

Record Collector MUSIC
(Map p138; ✆323-655-6653; 7809 Melrose Ave, Mid-City; ⊙10am-5pm daily) If you dig vinyl – specifically jazz and classical on vinyl – you must check out this record trader. It's stuffed floor to ceiling and staffed with a shopkeeper who would love to help you hunt down the gems, but it's best to have something particular in mind – then they can really help you. They've been doing it since 1974.

Great Frog JEWELRY
(Map p138; ✆323-879-9100; www.thegreatfrog london.com; 7955 Melrose Ave, Mid-City; ⊙11am-7pm Mon-Sat, noon-6pm Sun) A sterling-silver jewelry company known for its skulls, Great Frog started in London, has a shop in NYC and this is its latest offering. It casts in gold as well, and sells leather jackets. We loved the vintage motorcycle engines in the jewelry case and the stunning 1941 Indian in the window.

American Girl Place DOLLS
(Map p138; www.americangirl.com; 189 The Grove Dr, Grove Mall, Mid-City; ⊙10am-7pm Mon-Thu, to 9pm Fri & Sat, to 6pm Sun; ♠) Little girls go gaga for this make-believe toy land where

they can take their plastic friends to lunch or afternoon tea at the cafe or a revue-style show, get photographed for a mock *American Girls* magazine cover at the photo studio, or give them a makeover in the doll hair salon.

Beverly Hills, Bel Air, Brentwood & Westwood

A triptych of megamansions, luxury wheels and tweaked cheekbones, Beverly Hills, Bel Air and Brentwood encapsulate the LA of international fantasies. Beverly Hills lures with its high-end boutiques and swanky bistros, the latter of which are popular with power-lunching movie execs. Hollywood deities hide away in luxurious homes in discreet Bel Air and Brentwood, which is home to hilltop cultural heavyweight, the Getty Center. West of Beverly Hills, past the mini-downtown of Century City, lies cerebral Westwood, home to University of California, Los Angeles (UCLA) and its neo-Romanesque buildings, and a little cemetery that houses Hollywood greats.

⊙ Sights

The major cultural sight here is the Getty Center, located in the hills of Brentwood. Westwood is home to the well-tended UCLA campus, the contemporary-art-focused Hammer Museum and the star-studded Westwood Village Memorial Park Cemetery, all three of which are within walking distance of each other. Beverly Hills claims Rodeo Dr, a prime people-watching spot. Guided tours of celebrity homes depart from Hollywood.

★ **Getty Center** MUSEUM
(✆310-440-7300; www.getty.edu; 1200 Getty Center Dr, off I-405 Fwy; ⊙10am-5:30pm Tue-Fri & Sun, to 9pm Sat; P ♠; ☐734, 234) FREE In its billion-dollar, in-the-clouds perch, high above the city grit and grime, the Getty Center presents triple delights: a stellar art collection (everything from medieval triptychs to baroque sculpture and impressionist brushstrokes), Richard Meier's cutting-edge architecture, and the visual splendor of seasonally changing gardens. Admission is free, but parking is $15 ($10 after 3pm).

On clear days, you can add breathtaking views of the city and ocean to the list. A great time to visit is in the late afternoon after the crowds have thinned. Sunsets create a remarkable alchemy of light and shadow and are especially magical in winter.

Even getting up to the 110-acre 'campus' aboard a driverless tram is fun. From the sprawling arrival plaza a natural flow of walkways, stairs, fountains and courtyards encourages a leisurely wander between galleries, gardens and outdoor cafes. Five pavilions hold collections of manuscripts, drawings, photographs, furniture, decorative arts and a strong assortment of pre-20th-century European paintings. Must-sees include Van Gogh's *Irises*, Monet's *Wheatstacks*, Rembrandt's *The Abduction of Europa* and Titian's *Venus and Adonis*. Don't miss the lovely Cactus Garden on the remote South Promontory for breathtaking city views.

Tours, lectures and interactive technology (including valuable audio guides) help make the art accessible to all. Children can take a Family Tour, visit the interactive Family Room, borrow a kid-oriented audio guide, or browse the special kid bookstore. It even hosts garden concerts for kids.

Concerts, lectures, films and other cultural events for grown-ups keep the space buzzing with locals. Most are free, but some require reservations (or try standby). In summer, the free weekly concert series **Saturdays Off the 405** (☉6-9pm Sat May-Sep) serves up some tremendous progressive pop and world-music acts in the Getty courtyard.

Skirball Cultural Center MUSEUM
(☎310-440-4500; www.skirball.org; 2701 N Sepulveda Blvd; adult/student & senior/under 13yr $12/9/7, Thu free; ☉noon-5pm Tue-Fri, 10am-5pm Sat & Sun; P🚼) Although it is, technically speaking, the country's largest Jewish museum and cultural center, the Skirball has something for all. The preschool set can board a gigantic wooden **Noah's Ark**, while grown-ups gravitate to the permanent exhibit, an engagingly presented romp through 4000 years of history, traditions, trials and triumphs of the Jewish people.

★**Frederick R Weisman Art Foundation** MUSEUM
(☎310-277-5321; www.weismanfoundation. org; 265 N Carolwood Dr; ☉90min guided tours 10:30am & 2pm Mon-Fri, by appointment only)

FREE The late entrepreneur and philanthropist Frederick R Weisman had an insatiable passion for art, a fact confirmed when touring his former Holmby Hills home. From floor to ceiling, the mansion (and its manicured grounds) bursts with extraordinary works from visionaries such as Picasso, Kandinsky, Miró, Magritte, Rothko, Warhol, Rauschenberg and Ruscha. There's even a motorcycle painted by Keith Haring. Tours should be reserved at least a few days ahead.

University of California, Los Angeles
UNIVERSITY
(UCLA; www.ucla.edu; P) Founded in 1919, the alma mater of Jim Morrison, Kareem Abdul Jabbar and Jackie Robinson ranks among the nation's top universities. The campus is vast: walking briskly from one end to the other takes at least 30 minutes. You could easily spend a couple of hours exploring its manicured, sycamore-shaded lawns, profuse gardens, Romanesque Revival architecture and cultural assets.

Among these assets is the Fowler Museum at UCLA (p154), which presents intriguing multimedia ethno-exhibits. Close by, the **Powell Library** (☎310-825-1938; www.library. ucla.edu/powell; ☉vary) houses the **UCLA Film and TV Archive** (☎310-206-5388; www. cinema.ucla.edu; ☉office hours 8:30am-5:30pm Mon-Fri) **FREE**, the country's second-largest after the Library of Congress, with more than 350,000 movies and 160,000 TV shows. It's only open to researchers, but regular screenings take place at the state-of-the-art Billy Wilder Theater in the Hammer Museum, located just south of the campus in Westwood Village.

Northeast of historic Royce Quad is the **Franklin D. Murphy Sculpture Garden**, considered one of the country's most comprehensive. Set amid jacaranda, redwood and coral trees, its 70-plus sculptures include works by American and European greats such as Henry Moore, Auguste Rodin, Hans Arp, Alexander Calder and Jacques Lipchitz. We're partial to the giant, torqued ellipse by Richard Serra in the adjoining plaza of the **Broad Art Center** (☎310-825-0557; www.art.ucla.edu; ☉gallery 9am-4:30pm Mon-Fri; P). Designed by Richard Meier, the Broad houses the UCLA visual-arts programs and an MFA student gallery.

In the campus' southeastern corner, the tranquil **Mildred E Mathias Botanical Garden** (☎310-825-1260; www.botgard.ucla.edu/

Beverly Hills

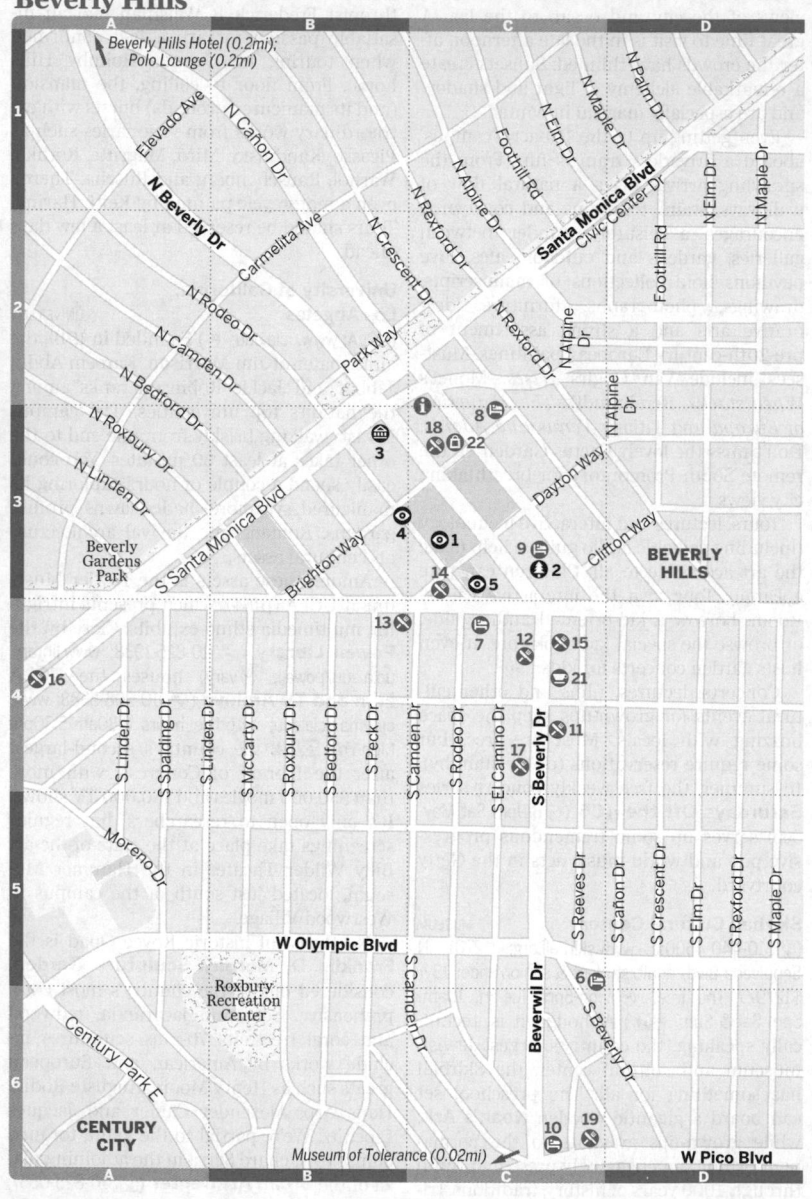

bg-home.htm; ⊗8am-5pm Mon-Fri, to 4pm Sat; Ⓟ) **FREE** is home to more than 3000 native and exotic plants and flowers. Guided tours of the garden run on the first Saturday of the month at 1pm and depart from the Nest. Enter on Tiverton Ave.

Fowler Museum at UCLA   MUSEUM
(☏310-825-4361;   www.fowler.ucla.edu;   308 Charles E Young Dr N; ⊗noon-8pm Wed, to 5pm Thu-Sun; Ⓟ) **FREE** Near the Film and Television Archive in UCLA, this museum presents oft-intriguing ethno-exhibits. Previous

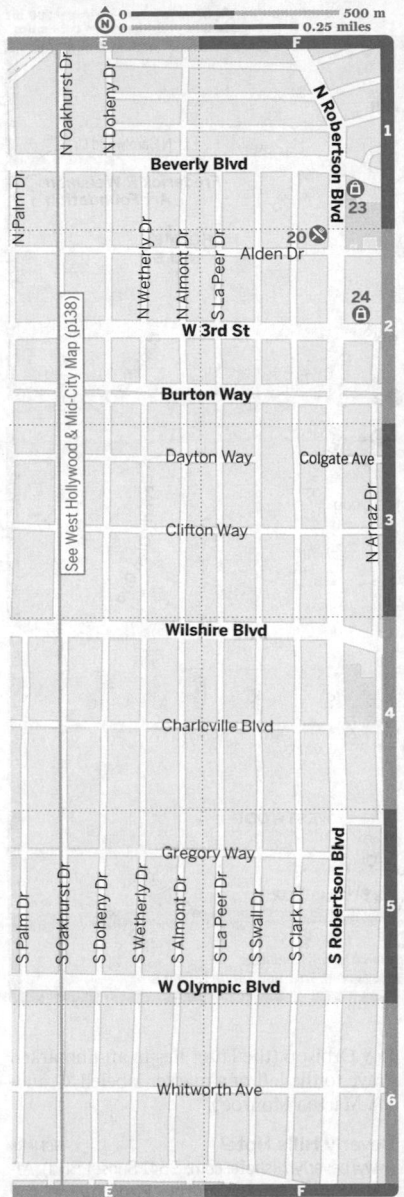

permanent silver collection includes a chalice reputedly gifted to Rasputin by his lover, the Empress of Russia, as well as an impressive set of 16th-century English plates, engraved with scenes depicting the adventures of Hercules.

Hammer Museum MUSEUM
(📞310-443-7000; www.hammer.ucla.edu; 10899 Wilshire Blvd, Westwood; ⏰11am-8pm Tue-Fri, to 5pm Sat & Sun; 🅿) FREE Once a vanity project of the late oil tycoon Armand Hammer, this eponymous museum has become a widely respected art space. Selections from Hammer's personal collection include relatively minor works by Monet, Van Gogh and Mary Cassat, but the museum really shines when it comes to cutting-edge contemporary exhibits featuring local, under-represented and controversial artists. Best of all, it's free.

multimedia shows have explored everything from the dance and fashion subcultures of Johannesburg to the extraordinary jewelry of India's Thar Desert. The museum's

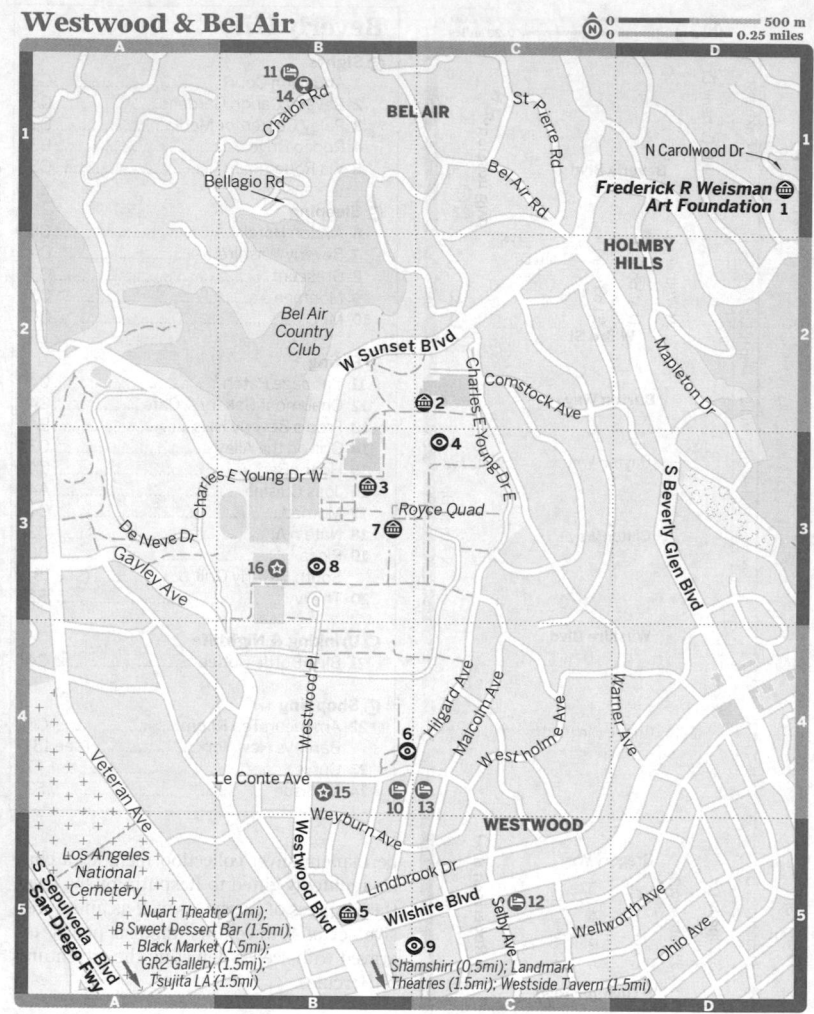

Westwood Village Memorial Park Cemetery
CEMETERY

(☎310-474-1579; 1218 Glendon Ave, Westwood; ◷8am-6pm; P) You'll be spending quiet time with entertainment heavyweights at this compact cemetery, hidden behind Wilshire Blvd's wall of high-rise towers. The northeast mausoleum houses Marilyn Monroe's simple crypt, while just south of it, the Sanctuary of Love harbors Dean Martin's crypt. Beneath the central lawn lie a number of iconic names, including actress Natalie Wood, pin-up Bettie Page and crooner Roy Orbison (the latter lies in an unmarked grave to the left of a marker labeled 'Grandma Martha Monroe').

Beverly Hills Hotel
LANDMARK

(www.beverlyhillshotel.com; 9641 Sunset Blvd) Affectionately known as the 'Pink Palace,' the Beverly Hills Hotel has served as unofficial hobnobbing headquarters for the industry elite since 1912. In the 1930s its Polo Lounge was a notorious hangout of Darryl F Zanuck, Spencer Tracy, Will Rogers and other lords of the polo crowd.

Westwood & Bel Air

◎ **Top Sights**

◎ **Sights**

🛏 **Sleeping**

🍷 **Drinking & Nightlife**

🎭 **Entertainment**

Greystone Mansion & Park NOTABLE BUILDING
(☑ 310-286-0119; www.greystonemansion.org; 905 Loma Vista Dr, Beverly Hills; ⊙ 10am-6pm mid-Mar–Oct, to 5pm Nov-early Mar; ℗) Known for inducing bouts of real-estate envy, this Tudor Revival mansion dates back to 1927. Hoover Dam architect Gordon Bernie Kaufmann designed the estate, which was a generous gift from oil tycoon Edward L. Doheny to his son Ned and his family. In 1929 the oil heir was found with a bullet in his head along with his male secretary in an alleged murder-suicide – a mystery that remains unsolved to this day.

Rodeo Drive STREET
(Map p154) It might be pricey and unapologetically pretentious, but no trip to LA would be complete without a saunter along Rodeo Dr, the famous three-block ribbon of style where sample-size fembots browse for Gucci and Dior. Fashion retailer Fred Hayman opened the strip's first luxury boutique

– Giorgio Beverly Hills – at number 273 back in 1961. Famed for its striped white-and-yellow awning, the store allowed its well-heeled clients to sip cocktails while shopping and have their purchases home delivered in a Rolls-Royce.

These days, most visitors to Rodeo Dr gravitate to Euro-flavored Via Rodeo, a compact cobbled lane lined with pastiche European facades, a smattering of cafe tables and no shortage of star-struck Japanese and Chinese tourists photographing its string of luxury boutiques.

The street is also home to Frank Lloyd Wright's 1953 commercial-residential complex **Anderton Court** (Map p154; 322 N Rodeo Dr), which features an angular ramp that leads up and around a hexagonal light well.

Via Rodeo STREET
(Map p154; cnr Rodeo Dr & Wilshire Blvd) One of the most popular corners of Rodeo Dr is this kitschy, cobbled outdoor mall, lined with mock-European facades and home to a small but exclusive cache of European fashion boutiques and galleries. There's a popular cafe at the southern end, though you'll be seeing more selfie-obsessed tourists than actual stars.

Paley Center for Media MUSEUM
(Map p154; ☑ 310-786-1091; www.paleycenter.org; 465 N Beverly Dr, Beverly Hills; suggested donation adult/child $10/5; ⊙ noon-5pm Wed-Sun; ℗) The main lure of the Paley Center, located in a crisp white building by Getty Center architect Richard Meier, is its mind-boggling archive of TV and radio broadcasts dating back to 1918. The Beatles' US debut on the *Ed Sullivan Show*? The moon landing? The *All in the Family* pilot? All here and yours to view without the need to book ahead. The center also hosts regular discussions with the casts of hit TV shows.

★ **Museum of Tolerance** MUSEUM
(☑ reservations 310-772-2505; www.museumoftolerance.com; 9786 W Pico Blvd; adult/senior/student $15.50/12.50/11.50, Anne Frank Exhibit adult/senior/student $15.50/13.50/12.50; ⊙ 10am-5pm Sun-Wed & Fri, to 9:30pm Thu, to 3:30pm Fri Nov-Mar; ℗) Run by the Simon Wiesenthal Center, this powerful, deeply moving museum uses interactive technology to engage visitors in discussion and contemplation around racism and bigotry. Particular focus

MEETING ANNE FRANK

One of the most engrossing drawcards at the Museum of Tolerance is the $2.5-million **Anne Frank Exhibit**. A multimedia journey, it documents the life of the Holocaust's young victim, who dreamed of Hollywood stardom. Her father, Otto, was an officer in the German army during WWI. When he landed a job in Amsterdam just ahead of the Holocaust, Otto chose to resettle the family there because it was as neutral as Switzerland and was considered a safe haven for Jews. Then the Nazis steamrolled into the Netherlands and the Franks went into hiding.

Throughout the exhibit, its halls lined with recovered concentration-camp prison robes, you will see Anne's words, and hear them through the sound system. They come from her diaries and from her original letters to an Iowa pen pal, also on display. The exhibit also captures her shifting perspective, from dreamy and naive, to insightful, profound and inspiring. And you'll spend time in a mock-up attic, like the one that sheltered her family for years.

The Franks were discovered on August 4, 1944, and divided. Anne and her big sister, Margot, died of typhus together in Bergen-Belsen just weeks before that camp was liberated. Otto was the only survivor, and it was he who published Anne's diary, which has since been translated into almost 70 languages and is among the most widely read books of all time.

is given to the Holocaust, with a major basement exhibition that examines the social, political and economic conditions that led to the Holocaust as well as the experience of the millions persecuted. On the museum's 2nd floor, another major exhibition offers an intimate look into the life and effect of Anne Frank.

🛏 Sleeping

Hilgard House Hotel　　　　　HOTEL $$
(☎ 800-826-3934, 310-208-3945; www.hilgard house.com; 927 Hilgard Ave, Westwood; r from $188; P❄️🔔) This 55-room, Euro-style hotel near UCLA is an unflashy, unpretentious abode. Rooms are smallish, but the high ceilings make them feel airy, and the marble entryways and antiques add an elegant touch. Wi-fi is free and it's always a good idea to ask about special room rates when making a reservation. On-site parking is $10.

★ Montage　　　　　　　　HOTEL $$$
(Map p154; ☎ 888-860-0788; www.montage beverlyhills.com; 225 N Canon Dr, Beverly Hills; r/ste from $695/1175; P@🔔🏊) Drawing on-point eye candy and serious wealth, the 201-room Montage balances elegance with warmth and affability. Models and moguls lunch by the gorgeous rooftop pool, while the property's sprawling five-star spa is a Moroccan-inspired marvel, with both single-sex and unisex plunge pools. Rooms are classically styled, with custom Sealy mattresses,

dual marble basins, spacious showers and deep-soaking tubs.

Beverly Hills Hotel　　　LUXURY HOTEL $$$
(☎ 310-276-2251; www.beverlyhillshotel.com; 9641 Sunset Blvd, Beverly Hills; r/bungalows from $525/715; P❄️@🔔🏊🐾) The revered 'Pink Palace' packs more Hollywood lore than any other hotel in town. Slumber in one of 208 elegantly appointed hotel rooms or – if money isn't an issue – live like the stars in one of 23 discreet, self-contained bungalows. Interiors in the latter are inspired by the stars who've stayed there, from Liz Taylor in number 5 to Frank Sinatra in 22.

Hotel Bel-Air　　　　　　　HOTEL $$$
(☎ 310-472-1211; www.hotelbelair.com; 701 Stone Canyon Rd, Bel Air; r from $525; P❄️🔔🏊) This tranquil, 12-acre Spanish Colonial estate is a popular hideaway for royalty – Hollywood or otherwise. Leafy and low-key (we love the outdoor fireplaces), it exudes intimacy and restrained luxury, from the plush, living-room-style lobby with central fireplace to the dark, slinky bar and discreet alcoves of Wolfgang Puck's outstanding Californian restaurant. The pink-stucco rooms come with private entrances and French furnishings.

W Los Angeles - West Beverly Hills　　　　　　　HOTEL $$$
(☎ 310-208-8765; www.wlosangeles.com; 930 Hilgard Ave, Westwood; r from $299; P❄️@🔔🏊) Despite a $25-million renovation, wear and tear is evident in the W's lobby, an aquatically

themed space with wave-shaped wooden panels, digital art and modernist-inspired furniture. The wonderfully spacious rooms are more impressive, graced with silvery palm-themed wallpaper, watery photography by Amber Grey and large showers. There's a gym with mostly cardio equipment, a spa and a verdant pool area with DJs on Sundays.

Crescent HOTEL $$$
(Map p154; ☑ 310-247-0505; www.crescentbh. com; 403 N Crescent Dr, Beverly Hills; r from $395; P@🐾🛜📶) What was once an apartment complex for stars of the silent-movie era is now the Crescent, its eclectic fireside lounge splashed with turquoise accents, chandeliers and Old Hollywood photographs. Single rooms are a tight squeeze, with queen rooms offering more space and better value.

Beverly Wilshire HOTEL $$$
(Map p154; ☑ 310-275-5200; www.fourseasons. com/beverlywilshire; 9500 Wilshire Blvd, Beverly Hills; r from $595, ste $780-1330; P🏊@🛜📶) Now part of Four Seasons, the Beverly Wilshire has corked Rodeo Dr since 1928. Home to 395 elegantly appointed rooms and suites, it exudes a formal elegance more akin to Manhattan than LA, especially in the original Wilshire wing. Guests have access to Ferragamo amenities and 12 concierges, the highest number in California. The Tuscan-style outdoor pool is on the smaller side.

Avalon Hotel HOTEL $$$
(Map p154; ☑ 844-328-2566, 310-277-5221; www. avalon-hotel.com/beverly-hills; 9400 W Olympic Blvd, Beverly Hills; r from $289; P🏊@🛜📶🐾) Mid-century modern gets a 21st-century spin at this fashion-crowd fave, which was Marilyn Monroe's old pad in its days as an apartment building. Funky retro rooms are all unique, but most have arched walls, marble slab desks and night stands, as well as playful art and sculpture. Perks include a sexy hourglass-shaped pool. Call it affordable glamour.

Kimpton Hotel Palomar HOTEL $$$
(☑ 310-475-8711; www.hotelpalomar-lawestwood. com; 10740 Wilshire Blvd, Westwood; r from $310; P🏊@🛜📶) 🐾 Recently renovated, the Palomar mixes elegance and playfulness in the lounge, where handsome wooden panels, modernist-style furniture and sculptural lighting meet pool table and Skee-Ball. Rooms are comfortable and stylish, with

leather-studded lounges, superb bedding and 42in plasma TVs. South-facing nests have views of the Mormon Temple and beyond. Facilities include a gym and smallish outdoor pool. Pets are welcome.

Mr C HOTEL $$$
(Map p154; ☑ 877-334-5623; www.mrchotels.com; 1224 Beverwil Dr; r/ste from $350/850; P🏊🛜📶) This long-standing tower hotel was redesigned by the Cipriani brothers, who included a replica of Harry's Bar in Venice (expect a Bellini on arrival). Alfresco lounges at the front of the 137-room property faintly echo an Italian Riviera feel, while the jazz-loving lobby lounge includes Venetian chandeliers and a rare glass-topped pool table.

🍴 Eating

Beverly Hills is known for high-end bistros, steakhouses and Italian restaurants, though you will find a scattering of moderately priced eateries. There's a plethora of dining options either side of Rodeo Dr and some solid options on S Beverly Dr. If you're taking out, head for Beverly Canon Gardens. Westwood Village serves its large student population with plenty of affordable cafes and bistros, pizza parlors and burger joints.

Chaumont Bakery & Cafe CAFE $
(Map p154; ☑ 310-550-5510; 143 S Beverly Dr, Beverly Hills; pastries from $3; ⊙ 6:30am-6:30pm Mon-Fri, to 5pm Sat, 7:30am-2pm Sun) Owned by a true-*bleu* French couple, this pretty patisserie serves fabulous croissants (opt for the almond version), *pain au chocolat* and other too-cute-to-eat treats, from fruit-topped tarts to eclairs. For something a little more substantial, opt for the flawless Gruyère and mushroom omelette, the French toast or the smoked-salmon and poached-egg croissant. *Très bon!*

B Sweet Dessert Bar DESSERTS $
(☑ 310-963-9769; www.mybsweet.com; 2005 Sawtelle Blvd; desserts from $5; ⊙ noon-11pm Wed-Sat, to 8pm Sun) Dessert fans flock to this hip, adorable storefront in Sawtelle Japantown for its weekly-changing selection of bread pudding from over 40 flavors: maple bacon, chocolate donut, salted caramel etc. Then there's the halo, an ice-cream sandwich pressed like hot panini inside a glazed donut...mercy! Get yours with coffee and teas on tap, or brownies from 'fudgiest' to 'sluttiest'.

Cabbage Patch
CAFE $

(Map p154; ☑ 310-550-8655; www.cabbagepatchla.com; 214 S Beverly Dr; mains $8-13; ⊙11am-9pm Mon-Fri, to 4pm Sat; 🐾) This busy, fast-food-style place won't be winning awards for atmosphere anytime soon, but you're here for fresh, tasty, wallet-friendly salads, sandwiches and sides. Favorites include the roasted beet salad with avocado, mint and goat's cheese, with larger plates including falafel and a chicken kebab made using free-range poultry from respected purveyor Mary's.

★ Joss Cuisine
CHINESE $$

(Map p154; ☑ 310-277-3888; www.josscuisine.com; 9919 S Santa Monica Blvd, Beverly Hills; dishes $15-30; ⊙noon-3pm Mon-Fri, 5:30-10pm daily) With fans including Barbra Streisand, Gwenyth Paltrow and Jackie Chan, this warm, intimate nosh spot serves up superlative, MSG-free Chinese cuisine at noncelebrity prices. Premium produce drives a menu of exceptional dishes, from flawless dim sum and ginger fish broth, to crispy mustard prawns and one of the finest Peking ducks you'll encounter this side of East Asia. Reservations recommended.

Honor Bar
MODERN AMERICAN $$

(Map p154; ☑ 310-550-0292; http://honorbar.com/locations/beverlyhills; 122 S Beverly Dr, Beverly Hills; sandwiches & burgers $14-16, sushi $15-19; ⊙11am-11pm Sun-Thu, to midnight Fri & Sat) Sharing the same owners as its bigger neighbor, South Beverly Grill, this smart, handsome bar serves smashing cocktails, sandwiches, burgers and sushi to a mix of film execs, earthy workers and the odd celebrity (hello, Taylor Swift). Don't go past the Ding's crispy chicken sandwich, a succulent, neatly sliced burger crammed with gloriously golden chicken, tomato, cheddar and kale.

Fred's Beverly Hills
INTERNATIONAL $$

(Map p154; ☑ 310-777-5877; www.barneys.com/store/R-store-902; 9570 Wilshire Blvd, Beverly Hills; mains $22-32; ⊙11am-7pm Mon-Sat, 11:30am-6:30pm Sun; 🅿🐾) Perched on the top floor of Barneys department store, mid-century-inspired Fred's is a hit with on-point lunching girlfriends and power suits. Call ahead to reserve a table on the balcony, where views of the Hollywood Hills call for one of Fred's superlative mimosas. Quality produce underscores the modern, bistro-style dishes, from crunchy Asian chicken salad to a gorgeous rigatoni with brisket ragù.

South Beverly Grill
MODERN AMERICAN $$

(Map p154; ☑ 310-550-0242; http://southbeverlygrill.com; 122 S Beverly Dr, Beverly Hills; salads $14-26, mains $18-48; ⊙11am-10pm Sun-Thu, to 11pm Fri & Sat; 🅿) With its handsome bar and red leather booths peppered with movie execs talking shop, this dim, buzzing restaurant offers a genuine slice of Beverly Hills life. Eavesdrop over classics such as fried oysters with creamed spinach and artichoke, tuna Niçoise salad or a succulent cheeseburger. If you're here Thursday to Saturday, try the celebrated Dover sole meunière.

Tsujita LA
NOODLES $$

(☑ 310-231-7373; http://tsujita-la.com; 2057 Sawtelle Blvd; ramen $10-15; ⊙11am-1:30am, annex 11am-11:30pm) This super-popular noodle joint is famed for its barbecued pork ramen, the broth of which is simmered for 60 hours to produce a heavier, more robust version than most in town. Indeed, the demand for the ramen became so great, the place was compelled to build an annex caddy corner.

Momed
MEDITERRANEAN $$

(Map p154; ☑ 310-270-4444; www.atmomed.com; 233 S Beverly Dr, Beverly Hills; lunch $9.50-24.50, dinner mains $15.50-28.50; ⊙11am-9:30pm Mon-Thu, to 10pm Fri, 9am-10pm Sat, to 9:30pm Sun) Yes, it has traditional Mediterranean dishes covered, but Momed (short for Modern Mediterranean) also melts avocado into its hummus, crafts shawarma from duck breast, oven-dried tomatoes and fig confit, and loads wood-fired flatbread with akawi cheese, spicy beef *soujuk* (spicy dry sausage) and red onions. While it probably won't knock your socks off, the food is generally consistent and tasty.

Westside Tavern
GASTROPUB $$

(☑ 310-470-1539; www.westsidetavernla.com; 10850 W Pico Blvd, Westwood; mains $14-25; ⊙11am-10pm Sun-Thu, to 11pm Fri & Sat; 🅿🐾) Modern, woody, warm – this gastropub is a good standby if you're catching a film at the adjoining **Landmark Theatres** (☑ 310-470-0492; www.landmarktheatres.com; 10850 W Pico Blvd, Westwood; adult/child & senior $14/11). The menu's focus is quality comfort grub, with standouts including the cheeseburger and the roasted lamb dip with caramelized onions, horseradish cream and thyme jus. Decent cocktails to boot. Find it on the ground floor of the Westside Pavilion shopping mall.

Shamshiri IRANIAN $$

(☑ 310-474-1410; www.shamshiri.com; 1712 Westwood Blvd, Westwood; mains $11-25; ☺ 11:30am-10pm Mon-Thu, to 11pm Fri, noon-11pm Sat, noon-10pm Sun; P ♿) One of a string of Persian kitchens, these guys bake their own pita, which they use to wrap chicken, beef and lamb shwarma, kebabs and falafel served with a green, *shirazi* or tabouli salad. They also do broiled lamb and seafood platters, and vegan stews. Come for one of their good-value weekday lunch specials ($9 to $12).

Nate 'n Al DELI $$

(Map p154; ☑ 310-274-0101; www.natenal.com; 414 N Beverly Dr; dishes $7-22; ☺ 7am-9pm; ♿) Dapper seniors, chatty girlfriends, busy execs and even Larry King have kept this New York–style nosh spot busy since 1945. The huge menu brims with corned beef, lox, matzo-ball soup and other old-school favorites, but we're partial to the pastrami, made fresh on-site.

Grill on the Alley STEAK $$$

(Map p154; ☑ 310-276-0615; www.thegrill.com; 9560 Dayton Way, Beverly Hills; mains $16-47; ☺ 11:30am-9pm Mon, to 10pm Tue-Thu, to 10:30pm Fri & Sat, 5-9pm Sun) A back-alley marble, oak and leather steak house where Hollywood heavyweights – who flock here from nearby agencies – slug it out over lunch. While it's rightfully known for steaks, other menu standouts include the chicken pot pie, crab cakes with *beurre blanc* sauce, and the pan-fried John Dory. Pair with a Red Velvet martini (lemon-infused vodka, pomegranate juice and Chambord).

Picca SOUTH AMERICAN $$$

(Map p154; ☑ 310-277-0133; www.piccaperu.com; 9575 W Pico Blvd; dishes $8-24; ☺ 5:30-9:30pm Sun-Thu, to 10pm Fri & Sat) Years on, Peruvian flavors, Japanese influences and Cali ingredients continue to make a solid team at still-hip Picca. Standouts include the ceviche *crocante* (halibut and crispy calamari), the scallops and the black-cod *anticucho* with miso and crispy sweet potatoes. Whatever you order, make sure to wash it down with a piquant pisco sour.

🍷 **Drinking & Nightlife**

This part of town is all about cocktails in plush hotel bars. The Polo Lounge at the Beverly Hills Hotel heaves with Hollywood lore, while nightly jazz sessions make the Hotel Bel-Air and Vibrato Grill Bar seductive options. Cocktails at these venues average around $20, though the atmosphere and history make it worth the expense. Collegiate Westwood is a more laid-back affair, with numerous sports bars and laptop-friendly cafes.

★ **Bar & Lounge at Hotel Bel-Air** COCKTAIL BAR

(☑ 310-909-1644; www.dorchestercollection.com/en/los-angeles/hotel-bel-air; Hotel Bel-Air, 701 Stone Canyon Rd, Bel Air; ☺ 2:30pm-midnight Mon-Thu, to 2am Fri & Sat, 11am-midnight Sun) You'll be clinking crystal at the Hotel Bel-Air's dark, intimate hideaway, a deco-inspired bar-lounge graced with white-marble fireplace and blown-up photography by Norman Seeff. The grand piano is tickled nightly with silky jazz; try catching the fabulous Maria de la Vega Trio on Wednesday nights. Flawless cocktails aside, the bar offers an exceptional food menu by celebrity chef Wolfgang Puck. Style up.

★ **Polo Lounge** COCKTAIL BAR

(☑ 310-887-2777; www.dorchestercollection.com/en/los-angeles/the-beverly-hills-hotel; Beverly Hills Hotel, 9641 Sunset Blvd, Beverly Hills; ☺ 7am-1:30am) For a classic LA experience, dress up and swill martinis in the Beverly Hills Hotel's legendary bar. Charlie Chaplin had a standing lunch reservation at booth 1 and it was here that HR Haldeman and John Ehrlichman learned of the Watergate break-in in 1972. There's a popular Sunday jazz brunch (adult/child $75/35).

Blue Bottle Coffee COFFEE

(Map p154; ☑ 510-653-3394; https://bluebottle coffee.com; 132 S Beverly Dr, Beverly Hills; ☺ 7am-7pm) Coffee snobs in Beverly Hills can now gravitate to this celebrated San Francisco import, known for its meticulous baristas and rotating selection of single origins and limited-edition blends. A minimalist, light-filled, split-level space, its caffeinated offerings include rich, thick espresso and refreshing cold brew. While the focus is coffee, a small selection of edibles include pastries, oatmeal and avocado toast.

☆ **Entertainment**

★ **Geffen Playhouse** THEATER

(☑ 310-208-5454; www.geffenplayhouse.com; 10886 Le Conte Ave, Westwood) American magnate and producer David Geffen forked over $17 million to get his Mediterranean-style playhouse back into shape. The center's season includes both American classics and freshly minted works, and it's not unusual to see well-known film and TV actors treading the boards.

UCLA Basketball
SPECTATOR SPORT

(www.uclabruins.com; Pauley Pavilion, UCLA; ☺Nov-Feb) In all American sports, it would be hard to find a more dominant team than the UCLA squads under the late, great John Wooden, who led his teams to 10 national titles in 12 years (including seven straight). The Bruins remain a competitive bunch, feeding studs such as Minnesota's Kevin Love into the NBA.

Nuart Theatre
CINEMA

(☏310-473-8530; www.landmarktheaters.com; 11272 Santa Monica Blvd, Westwood; adult/senior & child $11/9) This dank, but still hip, art and revival house presents the best in offbeat and cult flicks, including a highly interactive screening of *The Rocky Horror Picture Show* ($12) supported by an outrageous live cast at midnight on Saturdays. Bring glow sticks and toilet paper.

🔒 Shopping

Downtown Beverly Hills is the area's retail heartland, heaving with both well-known and more obscure luxury fashion and jewelry brands from mainly Europe and the US. The most famous (and most expensive) strip is Rodeo Dr (p157), with boutiques also on the surrounding streets. Among these is N Beverly Dr, dotted with higher-end midrange fashion and lifestyle brands. To the south, Wilshire Blvd offers high-end department stores, including fashion-forward Barneys.

Barneys New York
DEPARTMENT STORE

(Map p154; ☏310-276-4400; www.barneys.com; 9570 Wilshire Blvd; ☺10am-7pm Mon-Wed, Fri & Sat, to 8pm Thu, 11am-6pm Sun; ☎) The Beverly Hills branch of New York's most fashion-forward department store delivers four floors of sharply curated collections for women and men. Expect interesting pieces from luxe Euro brands such as Givenchy and Gucci, as well as unique pieces from home-grown labels like 3.1 Philip Lim and Warm.

GR2 Gallery
ART

(☏424-246-7626; www.giantrobot.com; 2062 Sawtelle Blvd; ☺noon-6pm Wed & Thu, to 8pm Fri & Sat, to 7pm Sun) Anime fans can browse and bag original artworks and prints from prolific and emerging artists at this gallery space. Expect work from the likes of LA artist and

graphic novelist David Choe and Japanese master Katsuya Terada.

Brentwood Country Mart
SHOPPING CENTER

(Map p168; www.brentwoodcountrymart.com; 225 26th St; ☺individual shops vary) A long-running, barn-red complex filled with high-end boutiques such as skincare emporium Space NK, unisex LA fashion brand James Perse and independent bookstore Diesel. Keep your eyes (discreetly) peeled for the odd celebrity sighting.

Black Market
FASHION & ACCESSORIES

(www.blackmarketla.com; 2023 Sawtelle Blvd; ☺10:30am-9pm Sun-Fri, to 10pm Sat) Black Market stocks an eclectic selection of cool, casual threads, from Pendleton knits, Obey sweat tops and Nudie jeans, to an especially kicking selection of tees. Accessorize with quirky socks, awesome sneakers and Herschel backpacks.

American Tea Room
DRINKS

(Map p154; ☏310-271-7922; www.americantearoom.com; 401 N Canon Dr; ☺10am-6pm Mon-Sat, 11am-5pm Sun; ☎) If you consider fine tea one of life's great pleasures, you'll find kindred spirits at this savvy tea purveyor. Spanning Africa to northern China and Japan, its 80-plus varieties of quality leaves include an especially popular Earl Grey Shanghai. Tastings are welcome and the in-store cafe includes single-estate teas as well as pastries from cult-status LA bakery Cake Monkey.

Culver City & Mar Vista

Hollywood's less-famous sibling, Culver City has been calling 'Lights, Camera, Action' since the 1920s. It was right here that Dorothy tapped her ruby slippers and that Gene Kelly crooned in the rain. While films and TV shows are still shot here, the place has broken free of its studio-town roots, evolving into a vibrant hub of contemporary-art galleries, design stores and buzzing restaurants. Wedged between it and Santa Monica is Mar Vista, a down-to-earth real-estate hot spot dotted with mid-century abodes and a handful of coffee shops, quirky boutiques and tattoo parlors.

👁 Sights

Downtown Culver City is home to the offbeat Museum of Jurassic Technology. To the northeast of downtown are the commercial art galleries of the Culver City Arts District, while to the southwest are the Sony Pictures Studios. Much further south is the intriguing Cold War–focused Wende Museum. West of Culver City, Mar Vista is predominantly residential, though fans of mid-century architecture may find interest walking through the suburban streets of the Mar Vista Tract, the first post-war modern historic district in the City of Los Angeles.

Culver City Arts District   AREA

(Map p164; https://culvercityartsdistrict.com; La Cienega Blvd, Culver City) The Helms complex marks the beginning of Culver City's vital Arts District, which runs east along Washington Ave to La Cienega Blvd and up one block to Venice Blvd. Most of the galleries on Washington are clustered at the La Cienega end, with the best on La Cienega itself.

Museum of Jurassic Technology   MUSEUM

(MJT; Map p164; 310-836-6131; www.mjt.org; 9341 Venice Blvd; suggested donation adult/student & senior/under 13yr $8/5/free; 2-8pm Thu, noon-6pm Fri-Sun; Expo Line to Culver City) Nope, this kooky museum has nothing to do with dinosaurs and even less to do with technology. Instead you'll find madness nibbling at your synapses as you try to read meaning into displays about Cameroonian stink ants, a tribute to trailer parks and a sculpture of the Pope squished into the eye of a needle.

It may all be a mind-bending spoof, an elaborate hoax or a complete exercise in ironic near-hysteria by founder David Wilson. Maybe. For an entertaining read about the place, pick up *Mr Wilson's Cabinet of Wonder* by ex–*New Yorker* staff writer Lawrence Weschler.

🛏 Sleeping

Accommodation options are limited in this part of town, with a small scattering of generic midrange chains. The one notable exception is the historic, higher-end Culver Hotel in the heart of Culver City.

Culver Hotel   HOTEL $$$

(Map p164; 310-558-9400; www.culverhotel. com; 9400 Culver Blvd; r from $290; P ❄ @ 🖤; Expo Line to Culver City) The Munchkins bunked in this 1924 heritage hotel in downtown Culver City while filming *The Wizard of Oz*. A mahogany-paneled lobby gives way to rooms with the odd antique furnishing and marble bathrooms but surprisingly few amenities. Parking is $26.

🍴 Eating

You'll find a good number of eateries on (and off) Culver Blvd in downtown Culver City, serving everything from Italian to Mexican and modern Californian. A little further north on Washington Blvd, both the Platform development and the Helms Bakery District are home to a handful of quality, trendy eateries. Mar Vista's options are more limited and mostly located on (or just off) Venice Blvd between Inglewood Blvd and Beethoven St.

Sunny Blue   JAPANESE $

(310-751-6306; www.sunnyblueinc.com; 12608 Washington Blvd; rice balls from $3.15; 11am-9pm Mon-Sat, to 8pm Sun) In Japan *omusubi* (rice balls, aka *onigiri*) are an everyday staple, and this counter-service shop aims to make them popular Stateside. Before your eyes, the cheerful staff stuff fluffy rice with dozens of fillings such as miso beef, spicy salmon and chicken curry – and veggie-friendly options such as miso mushroom and *hijiki* seaweed – then wrap it in a crunchy *nori* seaweed wrapper.

Humble Potato   BURGERS $

(310-881-9498; www.humblepotato.com; 12608 W Washington Blvd; burgers from $11; 11:30am-10pm Mon-Fri, noon-10pm Sat & Sun) A quality, Japanese-inspired burger-and-sandwich joint. If you're undecided, order the Battle Royale, jammed with applewood bacon, garlic jam, caramelized onion, avocado, romaine, tomato, spicy sauce and fried egg. Pair with the shichimi garlic parmesan fries.

Samosa House   INDIAN $

(Map p164; 310-559-6350; www.samosahouse. com; 10700 Washington Blvd; samosas $1.50, dishes $3.50, meals $9; 11am-10pm; P 🖤) This family-owned vegetarian steam table serves chunky, cheap samosas, as well as more substantial dishes such as charcoal-smoked cauliflower daal, *aloo* curry and *pakara* curry. It's a basic, unadorned place and better for a quick bite than a lingering lunch or dinner.

Father's Office   PUB FOOD $$

(Map p164; 310-736-2224; www.fathersoffice. com; 3229 Helms Ave; mains $10.50-19; 5-11pm Mon-Thu, noon-midnight Fri & Sat, noon-10pm Sun; Expo Line to Culver City) Modern, timber-lined Father's Office spills onto an outdoor patio, where you can sip any of 36

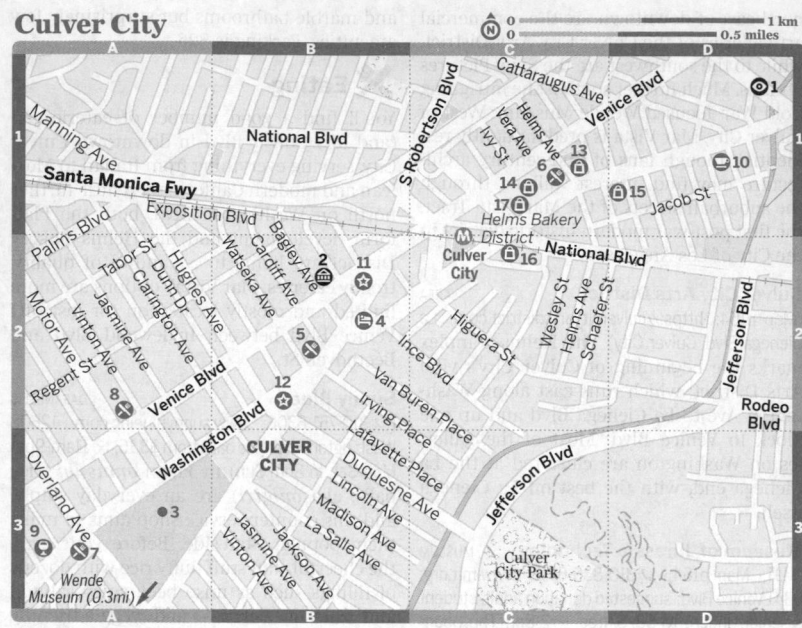

Culver City

Culver City

◎ Sights
1 Culver City Arts District D1
2 Museum of Jurassic Technology B2

✈ Activities, Courses & Tours
3 Sony Pictures Studios A3

⌂ Sleeping
4 Culver Hotel B2

✖ Eating
5 Akasha B2
6 Father's Office C1
   Lukshon .... (see 6)
7 Samosa House A3
8 Versailles A2

☕ Drinking & Nightlife
9 Blind Barber A3
10 Cognoscenti Coffee D1

★ Entertainment
11 Actors' Gang Theater B2
12 Kirk Douglas Theatre B2

🛍 Shopping
13 Arcana C1
14 Helms Bakery District C1
15 Midland D1
16 Platform C2
   Room & Board .... (see 6)
17 Surfas C1

craft beers, munch on smoked eel, spread roasted bone marrow on toast and devour the beloved Office burger, topped with Gruyère and Maytag blue cheese and enjoyed by the likes of Leonardo DiCaprio and Jake Gyllenhaal. Order at the bar and don't ask for any menu substitutions.

Akasha   MODERN AMERICAN **$$**
(Map p164; ☎310-845-1700; www.akasharestaurant. com; 9543 Culver Blvd; dinner mains $15-30, cafe dishes $4-13.50; ⏱restaurant 11:30am-2:30pm & 5:30-9:30pm Mon-Thu, to 10:30pm Fri, 10:30am-

2:30pm & 5:30-10:30pm Sat, 10:30am-2:30pm & 5-9pm Sun, cafe 8am-5pm Mon-Fri, 9am-5pm Sat, 9am-9pm Sun; Ⓟ⛊; Ⓜ Expo Line to Culver City) Once Michael Jackson's chef, Akasha Richmond helms her eponymous eatery, a lofty, timber-meets-concrete space where seasonal, sustainable produce meets global flavors. Options span creative salads and burgers, to tandoori-spiced wings with tamarind-date chutney and knockout, melt-in-your-mouth star-anise short ribs. The cocktails are notable and the place includes a cheaper cafe

THE OPEN SOURCE MUSEUM

Newly housed in the former National Guard Armory, the under-the-radar **Wende Museum** (🖉310-216-1600; www.wendemuseum.org; 10808 Culver Blvd, Culver City; ⊘10am-9pm Fri, to 5pm Sat & Sun; P) stands out for its vast, yet niche collection. German for 'turning point', Wende collects anything and everything made, bought, sold and created in Soviet Bloc countries from the end of WWII to the fall of the Berlin Wall. It's the brainchild of Oxford grad Justin Jampol, who has produced two documentary films on the Cold War, as well as urban art programs, including The Wall Project.

Saving countless films, photographs and artifacts from incinerators and garbage dumps, his collection reveals how typical Germans lived behind the wall. If that sounds dry to you, don't worry, it's anything but. He's revealed the strange world of the Soviet hippie, now owns an extensive East German film archive, and has over 100,000 pieces all told, including a wonderful Lenin bust painted pink and turquoise by a 1980s street artist.

Guided tours of the museum are available; see the website for details.

peddling fresh pastries, breakfast grub and lunchtime sandwiches and salads.

Versailles CUBAN $$
(Map p164; 🖉310-558-3168; www.versaillescuban. com; 10319 Venice Blvd; mains $14-20; ⊘11am-10pm Sun-Thu, to 11pm Fri & Sat; P 🖼) A comforting, old-school combo of TV sports, vested waiters and mission-brown panels and chairs, Versailles draws everyone from college kids to grizzled grips with its Cuban-style roast-garlic chicken (tip: the half chicken is more flavorful than the leaner breast). Other standouts include the empanadas, oxtail soup and pork dishes. Most mains are served with sweet fried plantains, beans and rice.

★ Lukshon ASIAN $$$
(Map p164; 🖉310-202-6808; www.lukshon.com; 3239 Helms Ave; dishes $10-34; ⊘11:30am-2:30pm & 5:30-10pm Tue-Thu, to 10:30pm Fri & Sat; Ⓜ Expo Line to Culver City) This upscale, teak-clad restaurant is one of LA's underrated highs. Chef and owner Sang Yoon steers a sharp, well-rounded menu of sharing dishes inspired by East and Southeast Asia. Special shout-outs go to the tangy Sichuan-style pork dumplings and the Vietnamese-style lobster roll jammed with poached lobster tail, pig-ear terrine and spicy green papaya slaw.

🍷 Drinking & Nightlife

★ Blind Barber BAR
(Map p164; 🖉310-841-6679; www.blindbarber.com; 10797 Washington Blvd, Culver City; ⊘6pm-2am Mon-Sat) Clippers and cocktails conspire at this winning speakeasy. The front section is an actual barbershop, complete with vintage

barber chairs and inked staffers. Behind that back-wall door, however, is a dimly lit hideaway, decked out in checkered floors, studded booths and eye-candy barkeeps crafting on-point cocktails. Decent tunes and killer grilled-cheese sandwiches seal the deal.

Cognoscenti Coffee CAFE
(Map p164; 🖉310-363-7325; www.popupcoffee. com; 6114 Washington Blvd; ⊘8am-5pm Mon-Sat, 9am-3pm Sun; 🛜) Coffee geeks flock to Cognoscenti, a clean, bright, contemporary cafe showcasing a rotating cast of specialty micro-roasters such as San Francisco's Ritual and Portland's Heart. Brewing methods span espresso, filter and V60 pour over, and you'll also find cold-pressed juices and decent pastries. Seating is limited to a communal table, a handful of window-counter seats and a small outdoor area.

☆ Entertainment

Kirk Douglas Theatre THEATER
(Map p164; 🖉213-628-2772; www.centertheatre group.org; 9820 Washington Blvd, Culver City) What was originally an art-deco movie house is now a 317-seat theater used by the Center Theatre Group to stage oft-terrific new plays by fresh, up-and-coming local talent. Recent productions include world premieres by award-winning Californian playwrights Ngozi Anyanwu and Lauren Yee.

Actors' Gang Theater THEATER
(Map p164; 🖉310-838-4264; www.theactorsgang. com; 9070 Venice Blvd, Culver City; Ⓜ Expo Line to Culver City) The 'Gang' was founded in 1981 by Tim Robbins and other renegade UCLA acting-school grads. Robbins remains the

artistic director and the company's daring, topical works and offbeat reinterpretations of classics have a loyal following.

🔒 Shopping

Washington Blvd is home to a booty of hip retailers peddling unique homewares, interesting fashion and designer furniture. The main hubs are the Helms Bakery District – great for furniture, furnishings and art tomes – and the Platform development, home to hip homewares and gifts and a small mix of casual and higher-end threads. Mar Vista is home to one of LA's best-loved farmers markets.

Helms Bakery District   FURNITURE
(Map p164; www.helmsbakerydistrict.com; 8800 Venice Blvd, Culver City; M Expo Line to Culver City) From points north, this distinguished 1932 moderne-style former bakery complex is the gateway to Culver City. The warehouses and studios house one of the most stylish collections of furniture galleries in the city. Among these is **Room & Board** (Map p164; ☑ 310-736-9100; www.roomandboard.com), whose primary focus is artisan American furnishings and accessories. The district is also home to popular eateries and superlative art-focused bookstore **Arcana** (Map p164; ☑ 310-458-1499; www.arcanabooks.com; ☺ 11am-7pm Tue-Sun).

Platform   SHOPPING CENTER
(Map p164; www.platformla.com; 8840-8850 Washington Blvd, Culver City; M Expo Line to Culver City) Contemporary architecture, fashion and design collide at this mixed-use development. Eye up the street art and shop-hop its small, sharply curated booty of retailers. Drop into

Magasin for avant-garde men's threads, Poketo for quirky gifts and design, Aesop for botanical skincare, and Tom Dixon for edgy (albeit expensive) design objects and women's fashion.

Surfas   FOOD & DRINKS
(Map p164; www.surfasonline.com; 8777 W Washington Blvd, Culver City; ☺ 9am-6pm Mon-Sat, 11am-5pm Sun; M Expo Line to Culver City) More than 75 years old, Surfas stocks professional cooking gadgets and tools, as well as gourmet deli goods for serious epicureans.

Midland   DESIGN
(Map p164; ☑ 424-298-8333; http://shop-midland.com; 8634 Washington Blvd; ☺ 11am-6pm Mon-Sat, to 5pm Sun; M Expo Line to Culver City) Channeling a cool Southwest vibe, this gorgeous lifestyle store showcases a mix of local, American and international designers. Shop local with Saint Rita Parlor vintage-inspired eyewear, Lucy Michel ceramics, Rachel Craven linen kaftans and Venice-roasted Canyon Coffee. You'll find small-batch colognes, stylish leather goods (including naturally dyed booties for bubs), vintage turquoise jewelry and a modest selection of clothing for guys.

Mar Vista Farmers Market   MARKET
(www.marvistafarmersmarket.org; Grand View Blvd at Venice Blvd; ☺ 9am-2pm Sun) Mar Vista's weekly Sunday farmers market is one of LA's finest. Fill your bags with quality local fruit and vegetables, artisan breads, pasta, raw honey and chocolates, and keep an eye out for locally made crafts, from jewelry to ceramics. If you're feeling peckish, you won't go hungry, with some great ready-to-eat

---

HIKING IN LA

If hiking doesn't feel like an indigenous LA activity to you, you need to reassess. This town is hemmed in and defined by two mountain ranges and countless canyons. In the **San Gabriel Mountains**, trails wind from Mt Wilson into granite peak wilderness, once the domain of the Gabrielino people and the setting for California's last grizzly-bear sighting. The Chumash roamed the **Santa Monica Mountains** (www.nps.gov/samo/index.htm), which are smaller, but still offer spectacular views of chaparral-draped peaks with stark drops into the Pacific. The **Backbone Trail** spans the range, but our favorite hike is to Sandstone Peak. Day hikes in **Topanga Canyon State Park** (p170), **Malibu Canyon** (p171), Point Mugu and **Leo Carrillo** (p167) state parks are also recommended. If you only have an hour or two, check out **Runyon** (p110) or **Bronson** (p126) canyons in Hollywood. For more advice about trails in and around Southern California check out www.trails.com, or buy any of *Afoot and Afield: Los Angeles County: A Comprehensive Hiking Guide* (Wilderness Press; 2009), *Secret Walks: A Walking Guide to the Hidden Trails of Los Angeles* (Santa Monica Press; 2015) or *60 Hikes Within 60 Miles* (Menasha Ridge Press; 2009).

options spanning anything from crepes to lobster rolls.

Malibu & Pacific Palisades

Malibu enjoys near-mythical status thanks to its large celebrity population (it's been celebrity central since the 1930s) and the incredible beauty of its 27 miles of coastal mountains, pristine coves, wide sweeps of golden sand and epic waves.

Despite its wealth and star quotient, the best way to appreciate Malibu is through its natural assets, so grab your sunscreen and a towel and head to the beach.

◉ Sights

The beach is king, of course, and whether you find a sliver of sand among the sandstone rock towers and topless sunbathers at El Matador or enjoy the wide loamy blonde beaches of Zuma and Westward, you'll have a special afternoon.

Culture more your bag? The Getty Villa, a replica of a 1st-century Roman villa stocked with Greek and Roman antiquities, is a showstopper.

For hikers, Topanga Canyon State Park (p170) offers 36 miles of trails, while Will Rogers State Historic Park (p169) and Temescal Canyon State Park are closer to Santa Monica, more easily managed and very popular among locals.

Leo Carrillo State Park　　BEACH, PARK
(☑ 310-457-8143; www.parks.ca.gov; 35000 W Pacific Coast Hwy, Malibu; per car $12; ⊗ 8am-10pm; ℗ ⛟) Families love this summer-camp-style beach with enough stimulating tide pools, cliff caves, nature trails and great swimming and surfing to tire out even the most hyperactive kids.

★ El Matador State Beach　　BEACH
(☑ 818-880-0363; 32215 Pacific Coast Hwy, Malibu; ℗) Arguably Malibu's most stunning beach, where you park on the bluffs and stroll down a trail to sandstone rock towers that rise from emerald coves. Topless sunbathers stroll through the tides, and dolphins breech the surface beyond the waves. It's been impacted by coastal erosion, but you can still find a sliver of dry sand tucked against the bluffs.

Zuma Beach　　BEACH
(Map p168; 30000 Pacific Coast Hwy, Malibu; ℗; ▣ MTA 534) Zuma is easy to find, and thanks to the wide sweep of blonde sand that has

MALIBU BEACHES FOR ALL

Malibu's locals, famous for their love of privacy, don't want you to know this, but you're actually free to be on any beach as long as you stay below the high-tide line. That means you can walk, swim and beachcomb on Carbon Beach, Broad Beach, Little Dume and wherever the famous like to frolic. You may get nasty looks from security guards, but there's nothing they can legally do to stop you from being there. Driving along Pacific Coast Hwy, keep an eye out for the brown 'Coastal Access' signs. Locals have been known to take them down and put up 'Private Beach' or 'No Trespassing' signs; don't be deterred. For the full scoop and 'secret' access points, download the handy map and guide at www.laurbanrangers.org/site/malibu, or get the free **Our Malibu Beaches** app for your smartphone, developed by a local environmental writer and beachcombing populist, Jenny Price.

been attracting valley kids to the shore since the 1970s, it gets busy on weekends and summer afternoons. Pass around Point Dume to **Westward Beach** (Map p168; 6800 Westward Rd, Malibu; ℗; ▣ MTA 534).

Point Dume State Beach begins once you pass through the parking gate south of the Sunset restaurant. Keep walking down the beach and navigate a short trail to semiprivate Pirate's Cove.

Malibu Pier　　LANDMARK
(Map p168; www.malibupier.com; 23000 Pacific Coast Hwy, Malibu; ⊗ 6:30am-sunset) The pier marks the beginning of Malibu's commercial heart. It's open for strolling and license-free fishing (note the brackets for your rod and reel) and delivers fine views of surfers riding waves off Surfrider Beach. The restaurant at the end caters to tourists. You can rent a rod and reel ($14 for two hours), and buy bait ($5) here, too. Although the Pier management stops at sunset, some businesses stay open later.

Adamson House　　LANDMARK
(Map p168; ☑ 310-456-8432; www.adamsonhouse. org; 23200 Pacific Coast Hwy, Malibu; adult/child $7/2; ⊗ 11am-3pm Thu-Sat; ℗) Up on a bluff overlooking Surfrider Beach is this gorgeous Spanish-style villa, which used to belong to

Malibu

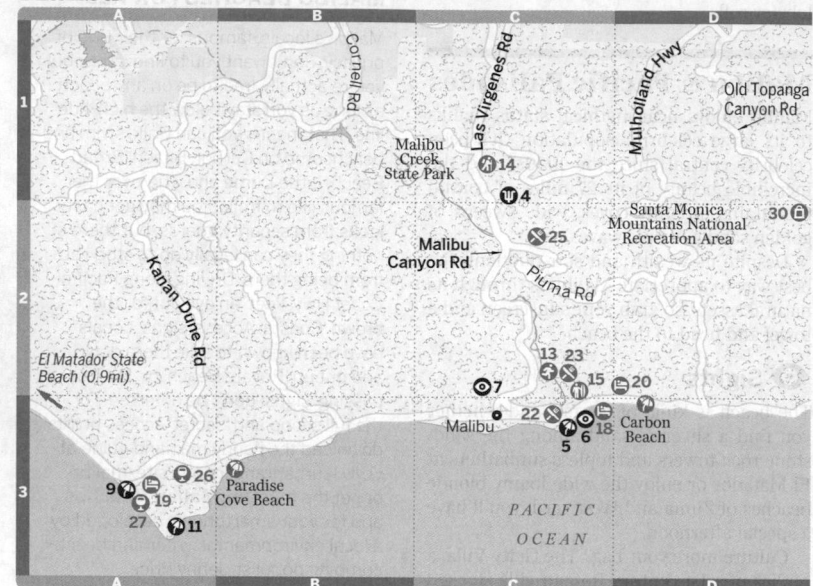

LOS ANGELES MALIBU & PACIFIC PALISADES

the Rindge family and is awash in locally made, hand-painted tiles. Check out the 'Persian rug' in the entryway and the tiled dog bath outside. The last tour leaves at 2pm.

To learn more about Malibu's arc of history – Chumash to glamour town – pop into the adjacent **Malibu Lagoon Museum**.

From here it's a pleasant stroll through the marsh to Surfrider Beach.

Pepperdine University UNIVERSITY
(Map p168; www.pepperdine.edu; 24255 Pacific Coast Hwy, Malibu; P) Self-assuredly holding court on 830 acres atop a grassy slope down to the ocean where deer graze at sundown, this private, Christian institution has views of the Pacific and the mountains and is consistently ranked one of America's most beautiful campuses.

Notable faculty over the years have included Ben Stein (former law professor who played the teacher in *Ferris Bueller's Day Off*, and current political gadfly) and former law-school dean Kenneth Starr, who previously was the independent investigator who revealed to the world where Bill Clinton put his cigars.

Art fans should check out the latest show at the university's Frederick R Weisman Museum of Art (p169), which rotates edgy works created by contemporary American artists.

★**Getty Villa** MUSEUM
(Map p168; 310-430-7300; www.getty.edu; 17985 Pacific Coast Hwy, Pacific Palisades; 10am-5pm Wed-Mon; P; line 534 to Coastline Dr) FREE
Stunningly perched on an ocean-view hillside, this museum in a replica 1st-century Roman villa is an exquisite, 64-acre showcase for Greek, Roman and Etruscan antiquities. Dating back 7000 years, they were amassed by oil tycoon J Paul Getty. Galleries, peristiles, courtyards and lushly landscaped gardens ensconce all manner of friezes, busts and mosaics, millennia-old cut, blown and colored glass and brain-bending geometric configurations in the Hall of Colored Marbles. Other highlights include the Pompeii fountain and Temple of Herakles.

**Self-Realization Fellowship
Lake Shrine** GARDENS
(Map p168; 310-454-4114; www.lakeshrine. org; 17190 Sunset Blvd, Pacific Palisades; 9am-4:30pm Tue-Sat, noon-4:30pm Sun; P) FREE No matter your religious persuasion, any negative vibes seem to disappear while strolling through these uplifting meditation gardens. Paths meander around a spring-fed, artificial lake and past clumps of flowers and swaying palms to the **Windmill Chapel**, where George Harrison's memorial was

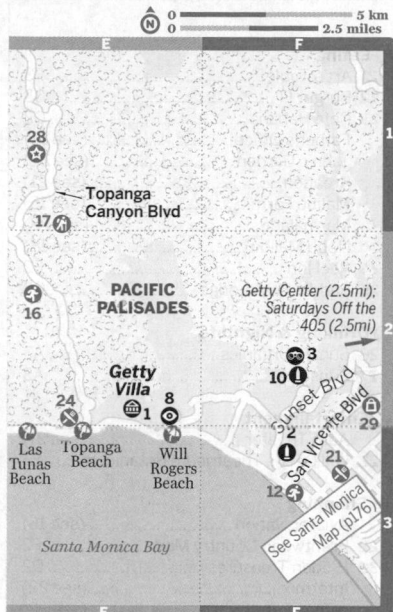

10am-4pm Sat & Sun) and lived here until his tragic 1935 death in a plane crash.

Free guided tours allow you to nose around the Western art and Native American rugs and baskets, and marvel at the porch swing right in the living room.

The park's chaparral-cloaked hills, where Rogers used to ride his horses, are laced with trails and offer an easy escape from the LA hubbub. The best time for a ramble is late in the day when the setting sun delivers golden views of the mountains, city and ocean from **Inspiration Point** (Map p168; Will Rogers State Historic Park, Pacific Palisades). They're yours after an easy-to-moderate 1.5-mile trek. Trails continue along the Backbone Trail into Topanga State Park.

A big polo fan, Will Rogers built his own field to battle such famous buddies as Spencer Tracy, Gary Cooper and Walt Disney. The **Will Rogers Polo Club** (Map p168; www. willrogerspolo.org; 1501 Will Rogers State Park Rd, Pacific Palisades; ⏰2-5pm Sat, 10am-1pm Sun late Apr-early Oct) **FREE** still plays in the park on what is the city's only remaining polo field.

Frederick R Weisman Museum of Art
GALLERY

(Map p168; ☑310-506-4851; www.pepperdine.edu/arts/museum; 24255 Pacific Coast Hwy, Malibu, Pepperdine University; ⏰11am-5pm Tue-Sun; P) **FREE** This art museum on the Pepperdine University (p168) campus hosts temporary exhibits of mostly 20th-century art (Claes Oldenburg, Dale Chihuly, Roy Liechtenstein and more), with a focus on Californian art. Check the website for current offerings.

Malibu Hindu Temple
HINDU TEMPLE

(Map p168; www.malibuhindutemple.org; 1600 Las Virgenes Canyon Rd, Topanga; ⏰9am-12:30pm & 5-8pm Mon-Fri Apr-Oct, to 7pm Nov-Mar, 8am-7pm Sat & Sun; P) **FREE** This house (or, more precisely, these houses) of Hindu gods sneaks up on you as you drive up Malibu Canyon, but you won't miss the ivory towers located 6.5 miles north of Pepperdine. Temple grounds are shaped and dappled like a big blissful sandcastle and include a series of shrines to various deities.

Visitors are welcome any day, but it's best to visit on a Hindu holiday, when colorfully robed flocks descend with fruit, flowers and smoldering incense in hand. Kick your shoes off before stepping up to the marble platform.

held, and back to a shrine containing some of the ashes of Mahatma Gandhi.

Sprinkled throughout are quotes from Hindu and Christian saints. The gold-lotus-peaked sanctuary situated on the hillside is where meditation services and lectures are held by resident monks on Thursday evenings at 8pm and Sunday mornings at 9am and 11am, and are open to the public. The fellowship was founded in 1925 by charismatic Paramahansa Yogananda, one of the first yogis to come to the West from India. His teachings blend traditions and stories from the five major religions.

Will Rogers State Historic Park
MONUMENT, PARK

(Map p168; ☑310-454-8212; www.parks.ca.gov; 1501 Will Rogers State Park Rd, Pacific Palisades; parking $12; ⏰8am-sunset, ranch house tours hourly 11am-3pm Thu & Fri, 10am-4pm Sat & Sun; P; ☐MTA lines 2 & 302) This park sprawls across ranch land once owned by Will Rogers (1875–1935), an Oklahoma-born cowboy turned humorist, radio-show host and movie star (in the early 1930s he was the highest-paid actor in Hollywood). In the late '20s, he traded his Beverly Hills manse for a 31-room **ranch house** (Map p168; ☑tours 310-454-8212; ⏰tours hourly 11am-3pm Thu & Fri,

Malibu

🏃 Activities

★ Mishe Mokwa Trail & Sandstone Peak
HIKING

(www.nps.gov/samo; 12896 Yerba Buena Rd, Malibu) On warm spring mornings, when the snowy blue *ceonothus* perfumes the air with honeysuckle, there's no better place to be than this 6-mile loop trail that winds through a red-rock canyon dotted with climbers, into the oak oasis at **Split Rock** and up to Mt Allen (aka Sandstone Peak), the tallest peak in the Santa Monica Mountains.

The mountain is a spectacular perch overlooking the sea and the West San Fernando Valley, with golden eagles and red-tail hawks riding the thermals – this is what silence sounds like.

Take the Pacific Coastal Hwy past Trancas to Yerba Buena Rd (look for Neptune's Net; p172). Make a right on Yerba Buena and follow it to the ranger station at Circle X Ranch. Maps and trail conditions are available at the ranger station, but it's usually only staffed on weekends. You can also download a map online. The trailhead is 1 mile past the station, on the left. Hike for 0.5 miles up the fire road (spoiler alert – this steep yet wide trail leads directly to the peak in 1.5 miles) before verging onto the Mishe Mokwa connector trail, a spur that will lead you to the gorgeous Mishe Mokwa trail. Picnic beneath the oaks then keep humping up to the peak – you won't be able to miss it. After enjoying the view, don't double back on Mishe Mokwa; keep hiking down the fire road all the way to the parking lot. It gets crowded on weekends.

Topanga Canyon State Park
HIKING

(Map p168; ☎ 310-455-2465; www.parks.ca.gov; 20828 Entrada Rd, Topanga; per vehicle $10; ☺ 8am-dusk) America's largest state park located entirely with city limits (Los Angeles), this scenic, 11,529-acre park boasts 36 miles of trails winding through grass savannah and aromatic chaparral, ducking beneath shady oaks, climbing to peaks and skirting cliffs with inspirational ocean views.

Most trails link with the Santa Monica Mountains' contiguous **Backbone Trail**, which means you can hike north and south from here to other canyons and parks. A quick day hike from park headquarters leads 2.2 miles south to a seasonal waterfall along the **Santa Ynez Trail**. The **Eagle Rock Trail** (2 miles) leads to a picnic area surrounded by contoured ridges.

Topanga Canyon SCENIC DRIVE
(Map p168; Topanga Canyon Rd) Take this sinuous road from the sea and climb into a primordial canyon cut deep in the Santa Monica Mountains. The drive lays bare naked boulders and reveals jagged chaparral-covered peaks from every hairpin turn. The road is shadowed by lazy oaks and glimmering sycamores, and the whole thing smells of wind-blown black sage and 'cowboy cologne' (artemisia).

About halfway to the pass, the cute country town of Topanga sprouts on both sides of the road.

Malibu Canyon SCENIC DRIVE
(Map p168; Malibu Canyon Rd, Malibu) One of the most beautiful drives through the Santa Monica Mountains starts right next to Pepperdine on Malibu Canyon Rd, which cuts through Malibu Creek State Park. Expect tight curves and canyon vistas. Malibu Canyon Rd eventually bisects Mulholland Hwy (beyond which it's called Las Virgenes Rd) and joins with the 101 (Ventura Fwy) near Agoura Hills.

Malibu Creek State Park HIKING, SWIMMING
(Map p168; ☑ 818-880-0367; www.malibucreek statepark.org; 1925 Las Virgenes Rd, Cornell; parking $12; ⊙ dawn-dusk) A beautiful spot in the Santa Monica Mountains, *M*A*S*H* and *Planet of the Apes* were shot here. Laced by a creek with swimming holes in the spring, this park has excellent hiking, with trails leading past craggy oaks and stately sycamores. The park is about 5 miles north of Pacific Coastal Hwy via Malibu Canyon Rd.

Malibu Surf Shack SURFING
(Map p168; ☑ 310-456-8508; www.malibusurf shack.com; 22935 Pacific Coast Hwy, Malibu; kayaks per day $35, surfboards per day $25-35, SUP per 2hr/ overnight $45/75, wetsuits per day $10-15, surf/SUP lessons per person $125/100; ⊙ 10am-6pm) This barefoot surf shop rents (and sells) kayaks, SUP kits and surfboards. Surf and SUP lessons take place on Surfrider beach, last 1½ hours and include a full day's rental of the board and wetsuit. The paddling between here and Point Dume is excellent, with frequent dolphin and sea-lion sightings.

Malibu Long Boards SURFING
(☑ 310-467-6898; www.malibulongboards.com; per person surf or SUP lessons 1/2hr from $75/120) Private lessons in Malibu given by college-level surf and SUP instructors.

🛏 Sleeping

The M Malibu MOTEL $$
(Map p168; ☑ 310-456-6169; www.themmalibu. com; 22541 Pacific Coast Hwy, Malibu; r $189-389; P ⊖ ❋ 🙅 🖭 🐾) This recently modernized, 18-room motel offers a minimalist cool vibe with comfy beds draped in crisp linen, slate floors in the bathrooms, plus coffee makers, bottled water and simple breakfast snacks. Second- and 3rd-floor rooms have ocean views. Light sleepers should gear up with earplugs (provided) to combat Pacific Coast Hwy traffic noise.

Malibu Country Inn INN $$
(Map p168; ☑ 310-457-9622; www.malibucountry inn.com; 6506 Westward Beach Rd, Malibu; r $190-400; P ⊖ 🙅 🖭 🐾) Perched above the highway and overlooking Westward Beach is this humble shingled inn with 16 fairly large rooms that are clean and white with subdued colors, fridges, coffee makers, working faux fireplaces, sun patios and some have massive sea views.

★ Malibu Beach Inn INN $$$
(Map p168; ☑ 310-651-7777; www.malibubeachinn. com; 22878 Pacific Coast Hwy, Malibu; r from $595; P ❋ 🙅) This intimate, adult-oriented hacienda was recently given a four-star upgrade by Waldo Hernandez, celebrity designer who has done work for the likes of the former Brangelina. The look is ocean-friendly grays and blues, and you might just find yourself face-to-face with well-curated art pieces by the likes of Jasper Johns, Robert Indiana and Andy Warhol.

🍴 Eating

To eat where the locals do, head for the Malibu Country Mart and Lumberyard, but there are some other lovely, rather chic spots up and down the coast, some with a sky-high celebrity quotient and prices to match. Some of LA's most beloved restaurants are inland, up Malibu and Topanga Canyons.

John's Garden
DELI **$**

(Map p168; ☏ 310-456-8377; www.johnsgardenmalibu.com; 3835 Cross Creek Rd, Malibu Country Mart; salads & sandwiches $7-12; ☺ 9am-5pm Mon-Wed, to 6pm Thu & Fri, to 7pm Sat & Sun; ℗) At Malibu's favorite lunch counter you can order fresh daily soups such as curry tomato lentil and Louisiana gumbo, salads that echo Greece, Italy, Cape Cod and Korea, Italian sandwiches and classics such as the Woody (corned beef and Swiss on rye), the Surfer Princess (turkey and avocado) and the Malibu Club, a tuna and veg triple-decker.

Burger Fi
BURGERS **$**

(Map p168; ☏ 310-317-0200; www.burgerfi.com; 3939 Cross Creek Rd, 2nd fl, Malibu Lumber Yard; hot dogs & burgers $4-10; ☺ 11am-late (closing times vary); ℗ ♿; ◻ MTA line 534) This new burger joint stacks them double, and the burgers top out at $10 – a nice surprise for Malibu. The CEO burger blends Wagyu and brisket burgers with bacon tomato jam, truffle aioli and Swiss cheese, while the Conflicted has both Angus and veggie patties. Eat inside or on the terrace with sweeping views of the Malibu Hills.

Malibu Farm
CALIFORNIAN **$$**

(Map p168; ☏ 310-456-1112; www.malibu-farm.com; 23000 Pacific Coast Hwy, Malibu Pier, Malibu; mains breakfast $11-16, lunch & dinner $13-32; ☺ 7am-9pm, until 10pm Sat; ◻ MTA line 534) A lovely antidote to the seafood and burger shacks that dominate piers up and down California's coast, this suite of whitewashed dining rooms is beachy keen and a perfect place to munch on farm-to-table brunches, pizzas (try the ones with cauliflower crust) and skirt-steak sandwiches.

Marmalade
AMERICAN **$$**

(Map p168; ☏ 310-317-4242; www.marmaladecafe.com; Malibu Country Mart, 3894 Cross Creek Rd, Malibu; mains lunch $12-20, dinner $14-23; ℗; ◻ Metro line 532) All-American comfort food has kept locals coming to this cafe-restaurant with French-country-style decor. Look for a classic grilled cheese and tomato bisque, pasta dishes such as blackened chicken penne, the cafe burger and 'breakfast for lunch,' while dinnertime brings heartier fare such as free-range chicken pot pie and beef pot roast. A cafe counter adds tasty muffins and cookies.

Reel Inn
SEAFOOD **$$**

(Map p168; ☏ 310-456-8221; www.reelinnmalibu.com/; 18661 Pacific Coast Hwy, Malibu; mains $12-21; ☺ 11am-9pm; ℗ ♿; ◻ 534 to Topanga Canyon Blvd) Since the '80s, this rambling shanty has been reeling them in for fresh fish and seafood. Order at the counter (simply grilled, blackened, fried etc) with sides such as fries, slaw and Cajun rice then grab a picnic table on the deck, or a booth by the window, for views across PCH to the ocean.

Café Habana
MEXICAN, CUBAN **$$**

(Map p168; ☏ 310-317-0300; www.habana-malibu.com; 3939 Cross Creek Rd, Malibu Lumber Yard; sandwiches & tacos $14-18, mains $15-26; ☺ 11am-11pm Sun-Tue, to 1am Wed-Sat; ℗ ♿; ◻ MTA line 534) This Mexican joint with a Cuban name serves terrific margaritas in sumptuous booths on the heated patio, salsa on the sound system and two dishes that prevail above all else: the shrimp and the *carne asada* tacos. Both come piled with either chili and lime sautéed rock shrimp, or cubes of ancho-rubbed and grilled steak. Ask for one of each.

Neptune's Net
SEAFOOD **$$**

(☏ 310-457-3095; www.neptunesnet.com; 42505 Pacific Coast Hwy; mains $7-21; ☺ 10:30am-8pm Mon-Thu, to 9pm Fri, 10am-8pm Sat & Sun, closes 1hr earlier Oct-Apr; ♿ 🐾) Not far past the Malibu line in Ventura County, Neptune's Net catches Range Rovers, road bikes and rad choppers with fried-shrimp-and-beer hospitality on inviting wooden porches.

★ Saddle Peak Lodge
AMERICAN **$$$**

(Map p168; ☏ 818-222-3888; www.saddlepeaklodge.com; 419 Cold Canyon Rd, Calabasas; appetizers $14-23, mains $34-62; ☺ 5-9pm Mon-Fri, to 10pm Sat, 10:30am-2pm & 7-9pm Sun; ℗) Rustic as a Colorado mountain lodge, and tucked into the Santa Monica Mountains with a creek running beneath, Saddle Peak Lodge serves up elk, venison, buffalo and other game in a setting watched over by mounted versions of the same. Though the furnishings are rustic timber, this is fine dining, so don't come here after a day on the trail.

★ Nobu Malibu
JAPANESE **$$$**

(Map p168; ☏ 310-317-9140; www.noburestaurants.com; 22706 Pacific Coast Hwy, Malibu; dishes $8-46; ☺ noon-10pm Mon-Thu, 9am-11pm Fri & Sat, to 10pm Sun; ℗) Chef Nobu Matsuhisa's empire of luxe Japanese restaurants began in LA, and the Malibu outpost is consistently one of LA's hot spots. East of the pier, it's a cavernous, modern wood chalet with long sushi bar and a dining room that spills onto a patio overlooking the swirling sea. Remember, it's the cooked food that built the brand.

Drinking & Nightlife

While there isn't much of a bar culture in Malibu – and especially not in the Palisades – many restaurants and hotels offer great wines and cocktails, and snacks to go with them.

Sunlife Organics   JUICE BAR
(Map p168; www.sunlifeorganicsmalibu.com; 29169 Heathercliff Rd, Malibu; ⊙ 7am-7pm Mon-Sat, 8am-7pm Sun) The place to come for everything from wild honey, organic chocolate, supplements galore to its raison d'être – a fabulous juice bar where ingredients such as almond butter, banana, bee pollen, cacao, coconut, dates, maca, royal jelly and almond milk are blended into creative smoothies that cultivate a regular following (that recipe is their most popular concoction, the Wolverine).

Sunset   BAR
(Map p168; ☑ 310-589-1007; www.thesunsetrestaurant.com; 6800 Westward Beach Rd, Malibu; ⊙ noon-9pm Mon-Thu, to 10pm Fri, 11am-10pm Sat, to 9pm Sun; ⊛) Right across from the ocean is this low-slung, converted whitewashed beach house with tasty flatbreads and a popular weekend brunch. But we consider it to be the perfectly strange oasis after a day at the beach, mostly because the happy-hour crowd gets weird – rich, celebrity, plastic-surgery, comb-over weird. We do love us some Malibu.

☆ Entertainment

Will Geer's Theatricum Botanicum THEATER
(Map p168; ☑ box office 310-455-3723, main office 310-455-2322; www.theatricum.com; 1419 N Topanga Canyon Blvd, Topanga; adult/child tickets from $25/10; ⊛) Actor Will Geer (TV's Grandpa Walton) founded this beloved open-air theater as a refuge for blacklisted actors like himself during the McCarthy years. The woodsy setting is a perfect backdrop for such classic crowd pleasers as Shakespeare's *A Midsummer Night's Dream* and Bram Stoker's *Dracula,* and modern works such as Jon Robin Baitz's *Other Desert Cities.*

The season runs from June to early October. To get there, head north on Pacific Coast Hwy, turn inland on Topanga Canyon Blvd and proceed for 6 miles; the theater will be on your left.

Bring extra layers for nighttime performances. Topanga nights can get chilly, even in summer.

Shopping

The twin shopping centers of the Malibu Country Mart and Malibu Lumberyard are the area's big-ticket shopping items, featuring low-key yet high-quality fashion boutiques from local and international designers. Meanwhile, lovers of funky fashion and vintage ware won't want to miss Topanga Village.

★ Hidden Treasures   VINTAGE
(Map p168; ☑ 310-455-2998; www.hiddentreasurestopanga.com; 154 S Topanga Canyon Blvd, Topanga; ⊙ 10:30am-6:30pm Apr-Oct, shorter hours Nov-Mar) This one-of-a-kind store pops from the Topanga Canyon roadside, thanks to skeletons and mannequins dressed like Egyptian eunuchs and Viking warriors, standing sentry among the old wagons and totem poles out front. Inside it's a sprawling vintage boutique of (mostly well-curated) sweaters and coats, sweatshirts, ponchos and wool flannels, denim jackets and leather bombers – all the retro-hippie essentials.

Aviator Nation   CLOTHING
(Map p168; ☑ 310-456-1532; www.aviatornation.com; 22967 Pacific Coast Hwy, Malibu) If you find yourself getting chilly at Malibu Pier, cross PCH to this chill shop for coastal-chic hoodies, T-shirts and more, made in LA and emblazoned with signature stripes of yellow, orange and red. You can get accessories such as guitar picks with the same pattern, plus Pendleton blankets with the same sort of cool.

Malibu Lumberyard   MALL
(Map p168; www.themalibulumberyard.com; 3939 Cross Creek Rd, Malibu; 🛜; 🚌 Metro bus 534) Steps from the **Malibu Country Mart** (Map p168; ☑ 310-456-7300; www.malibucountrymart.com; 3835 Cross Creek Rd, Malibu; ⊙ 10am-midnight Mon-Sat, to 10pm Sun; 🛜; 🚌 MTA line 534) is this newer 'lifestyle mall' done up in teak and (elegantly) rusted metal. It's got upscale casual clothing stores such as **James Perse** (Map p168; ☑ 310-469-6030; www.jamesperse.com; 3939 Cross Creek Rd, Malibu Lumber Yard; ⊙ 10am-6pm; 🚌 Metro line 534) and **Intermix** (Map p168; www.intermixonline.com; 3939 Cross Creek Rd, Malibu, Mailbu Lumberyard; ⊙ 10am-7pm Mon-Sat, from 11am Sun), rock and crystal shops and some decent restaurants, and we love the signs reading 'paparazzi-free zone.'

Santa Monica

Santa Monica is LA's cute, alluring, hippie-chic little sister, its karmic counterbalance and, to many, its salvation. Surrounded by LA on three sides and the Pacific on the fourth, SaMo is a place where real-life Lebowskis sip White Russians next to martini-swilling Hollywood producers, celebrity chefs dine at family-owned taquerias, and soccer moms and career bachelors shop at abundant farmers markets. All the while, kids, out-of-towners and those who love them flock to wide beaches and the pier, where the landmark Ferris wheel and roller coaster welcome one and all.

◎ Sights

Sightseers should head to the Pier, of course, where Pacific Park amusement park beckons you out over the water to glimpse the open Pacific – then turn around and see the beauty of the city on your walk back. The beach straddles either side. Even if you're not a shopper, it's fun to hang out on Third Street Promenade, catch some street performers and observe everyday folk going about their days.

★**Santa Monica Pier**   LANDMARK
(Map p176; ☑310-458-8901; www.santamonicapier.org; ☒) Once the very end of the mythical Route 66 and still the object of a tourist love affair, the Santa Monica Pier dates back to 1908 and is the city's most compel-

---

ANNENBERG COMMUNITY BEACH HOUSE
....

Like a fancy beach club for the rest of us, this sleek and attractive **Annenberg Community Beach House** (Map p168; ☑310-458-4904; www.annenbergbeachhouse.com; 415 Pacific Coast Hwy; per hour/day Nov-Mar $3/8, Apr-Oct $3/12, pool admission adult/senior/child $10/5/4), built on actress Marion Davies' estate (she had a thing with William Randolph Hearst), opens to the public on a first-come-first-served basis. It has a lap pool, lounge chairs, yoga classes, beach volleyball, fitness room and art gallery.

There's a cafe nearby, and it's set on a sweet stretch of Santa Monica Beach. Opening hours are seasonal; see the website for details.

---

ling landmark. There are arcades, carnival games, a vintage carousel, a Ferris wheel, a roller coaster and an aquarium, and the pier comes alive with free concerts (Twilight Dance Series) and outdoor movies in the summertime.

There are also a number of bars and restaurants, but the thing here is the view: the pier extends almost a quarter-mile over the Pacific, so you can stroll to the edge, hang out among the motley anglers and lose yourself in the rolling, blue-green sea.

Kids get their kicks at **Pacific Park** (Map p176; ☑310-260-8744; www.pacpark.com; 380 Santa Monica Pier; per ride $5-10, all-day pass adult/child under 8yr $32/18; ☺daily, seasonal hours vary; ☒), a small amusement park with a solar-powered Ferris wheel, kiddy rides, midway games and food stands. Check the website for discount coupons.

Near the pier entrance, nostalgic souls and their offspring can giddy up the beautifully hand-painted horses of the 1922 **carousel** (Map p176; ☑310-394-8042; ☺hours vary; ☒), also featured in the movie *The Sting*.

Peer under the pier – just below the carousel – for Heal the Bay's **Santa Monica Pier Aquarium** (Map p176; ☑310-393-6149; www.healthebay.org; 1600 Ocean Front Walk; adult/child $5/free; ☺2-6pm Tue-Fri, 12:30-6pm Sat & Sun; ☒) ✆. Sea stars, crabs, sea urchins and other critters and crustaceans scooped from the bay stand by to be petted – ever so gently – in their adopted touch-tank homes.

South of the pier is the **Original Muscle Beach** (Map p176; www.musclebeach.net; 1800 Ocean Front Walk; ☺sunrise-sunset), where the Southern California exercise craze began in the mid-20th century. New equipment now draws a fresh generation of fitness fanatics. Close by, the search for the next Bobby Fischer is on at the International Chess Park. Anyone can join in. Following the South Bay Bicycle Trail (p178), a paved bike and walking path, south for about 1.5 miles takes you straight to Venice Beach. Bike or in-line skates are available to rent on the pier and at beachside kiosks.

Santa Monica State Beach   BEACH
(Map p176; ☑310-458-8411; www.smgov.net/portals/beach; ☒Big Blue Bus 1) There are endless ways to enjoy this 3.5-mile stretch of sand, running from Venice Beach in the south to Will Rogers State Beach in the north. Sunbathing and swimming are obvi-

TOP 10 LA BEACHES

Long before the Beach Boys sang the praises of Californi-a and its girls, Southern California was an American dream destination for one reason: the beach. With miles of wide, sandy beaches hemmed in by ragged, towering bluffs, and gentle, rolling surf that serves beginners but can get big enough to charge up even old sea dogs, LA remains an epic coastal mecca.

The following beaches are listed north to south.

Leo Carrillo (p167) Families love this summer-camp-style beach with enough stimulating tide pools, cliff caves, nature trails and great swimming and surfing to tire out even the most hyperactive kids.

El Matador (p167) An intimate, remote hideaway with sandstone spires that rise from the swirling azure sea. A popular filming location thanks to battered rock cliffs and giant boulders, the surf is wild and clothing is optional.

Westward Beach (p167) Around the bend from Point Dume and just south of Zuma, Malibu locals favor this wide, blonde beach for crystal water, resident dolphin pods and sea lion colonies. The shallows aren't made for kiddies, though.

Zuma (p167) Two miles of pearly sand. Mellow swells make for perfect bodysurfing. Come early on weekends to snag parking.

Paradise Cove The site of a kitschy beach restaurant, Paradise Cove is close enough to Point Dume to get set-piece rock formations and mellow waves. Eating at the restaurant cuts the $35 parking fee ($50 on weekends and holidays) down to $6 ($8 on weekends and holidays).

Santa Monica (p174) Wide slab of sand where beach-umbrella-toting families descend like butterfly swarms on weekends to escape the inland heat. Water quality is poor right by the pier but OK a few hundred yards south.

Venice Beach (p184) Get your freak on at the Venice Boardwalk. During Sunday's drum circle, there's a crescendo of bongos, and dancers turn to silhouettes as the sun dips into the ocean. The wide beaches south of the Venice Pier are an oft-ignored gem with excellent bodysurfing.

Manhattan Beach (p192) A brassy SoCal beach with a high flirt factor and hard-core surfers hanging by the pier.

Hermosa Beach (p192) LA's libidinous, seemingly never-ending beach party with hormone-crazed hard bodies getting their game on over beach volleyball and in the raucous pubs along Pier Ave. If you're free on July 4, come here.

Malaga Cove This crescent-shaped, cliff-backed shoreline is the only sandy Palos Verdes beach easily accessible by the hoi polloi. It blends into rocky tide pools and serves up decent rolling waves for surfers (at Haggerty's), but no lifeguards.

---

ous options, but you can also reserve time on a beach volleyball court or, for more cerebral pursuits, settle in at a first-come first-served chess table at **International Chess Park** (Map p176; ☑310-458-8450; www.smgov.net; Ocean Front Walk at Seaside Tce; ☉sunrise-sunset), just south of the Santa Monica Pier.

Palisades Park PARK
(Map p176; ☑800-544-5319; Ocean Ave btwn Colorado Ave & San Vicente Blvd; ☉5am-midnight) **FREE** Perhaps it's appropriate that Route 66, America's most romanticized byway, formerly ended at this gorgeous cliffside park

perched dramatically on the edge of the continent. Stretching 1.5 miles north from the pier, this palm-dotted greenway sees a mix of resident homeless people, joggers and tourists taking in the ocean and pier views. Sunsets are priceless.

Tongva Park PARK
(Map p176; 1615 Ocean Ave; ☉6am-11pm; Ⓜ Expo Line to Downtown Santa Monica) This meticulously designed green space connects Ocean Ave to the Santa Monica Civic Center area. Well-lit and maintained, there are palms and agave groves, kinetic sculptures, cas-

Santa Monica

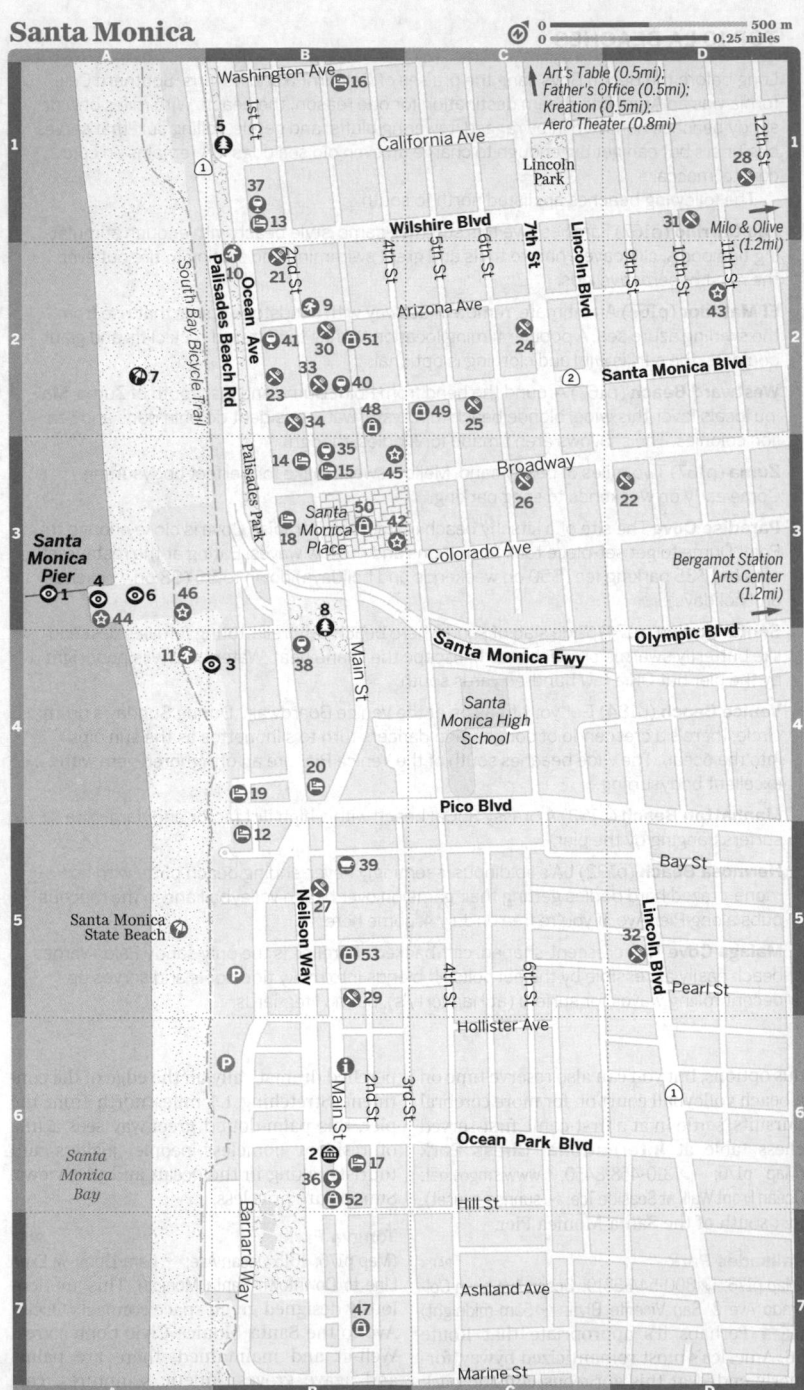

0 — 500 m
0 — 0.25 miles

Washington Ave

16

1st Ct

California Ave

5

Art's Table (0.5mi);
Father's Office (0.5mi);
Kreation (0.5mi);
Aero Theater (0.8mi)

Lincoln
Park

12th St

28

37

13

Wilshire Blvd

6th St

7th St

Lincoln Blvd

31

Milo & Olive
(1.2mi)

9th St

10th St

11th St

43

Ocean Ave

Palisades Beach Rd

10

2nd St

21

4th St

5th St

Arizona Ave

9

41

30

51

24

South Bay Bicycle Trail

7

33

23

40

Santa Monica Blvd

48

34

49

25

Palisades Park

14

35

15

45

Broadway

26

22

**Santa
Monica
Place**

18

50

42

Colorado Ave

Bergamot Station
Arts Center
(1.2mi)

**Santa
Monica Pier**

1

4

6

46

44

8

38

Main St

Santa Monica Fwy

Olympic Blvd

11

3

*Santa
Monica High
School*

Nelson Way

20

19

Pico Blvd

12

Bay St

39

*Santa Monica
State Beach*

7

27

53

32

Lincoln Blvd

Pearl St

29

4th St

6th St

Hollister Ave

*Santa
Monica
Bay*

2nd St

Main St

3rd St

1

Ocean Park Blvd

2

17

36

52

Hill St

Barnard Way

Ashland Ave

47

Marine St

Santa Monica

cading fountains, amphitheater seating, trim lawns and an adorable, ergonomic playground for tots. Designer James Corner Field Operations also worked on, among other projects, the High Line in New York City.

California Heritage Museum MUSEUM
(Map p176; ☑ 310-392-8537; www.californiaheritage museum.org; 2612 Main St; adult/student & senior/under 12yr $5/3/free; ☺ 11am-4pm Wed-Sun; P; 🚍 Big Blue Bus line 8, Metro line 733) For a trip back in time, check out the latest exhibit at this museum housed in one of Santa Monica's few surviving grand Victorian mansions – this one built in 1894. Curators do a wonderful job presenting pottery, colorful tiles, craftsman furniture, folk art, vintage surfboards and other fine collectibles in as dynamic a fashion as possible.

Eames House & Studio MONUMENT
(Map p168; ☑ 310-459-9663; www.eamesfoun dation.org; 203 Chautauqua Blvd, Pacific Palisades; adult/child $10/free; ☺ 10am-4pm Mon, Tue & Thu-Sat; P) In Santa Monica Canyon, the striking Eames House and Studio, built in 1949 by design deities Charles and Ray Eames, resembles a Mondrian painting in 3-D. It's still used by the Eames family, but with at least 48-hour advance reservation you can study the exterior, walk around the garden (which was a natural meadow preserved by the Eames) and peek through the window into the kitchen and living room.

Bergamot Station Arts Center ARTS CENTER
(www.bergamotstation.com; 2525 Michigan Ave; ☺ 10am-6pm Tue-Fri, 11am-5:30pm Sat; P; 🚍 Expo Line to 17th St/Bergamot Station) This former rail yard has been converted to one of LA's

best centers for art galleries, mostly for con-temporary art. A couple dozen of them keep varying hours, so check the website before setting out.

That's the good news. The bad news is that Bergamot Station has been imperiled since 2016 as galleries have been threatened with, in some cases, a tripling of their rent. Several key galleries and other tenants had closed up shop as we went to press.

🏃 Activities

What's the number-one activity destination in Santa Monica? That would be that loamy, quarter-mile-deep, 5-mile stretch of golden sand lapped by the Pacific. Water temperatures become tolerable by late spring and are highest – about 67°F (20°C) – in September. Water quality varies; for updated conditions check the **Beach Report Card** (www.healthebay.org).

The waves in Santa Monica are gentle and well shaped for beginner surfers, as well as bodyboarders and bodysurfers. The best swimming beaches are Will Rogers State Beach on the border of Pacific Palisades, and the beach south of the pier.

ⓘ SHARE A BIKE

Breeze Bike Share (www.santamonica bikeshare.com; per hour $7, monthly/annually $25/99) Bike sharing finally came to the beach in 2016. These sturdy green bikes, with baskets emblazoned with the Hulu logo, can be found at self-serve kiosks all over Santa Monica, Venice and Marina del Rey and are perfect for getting you to and from the new Expo Line stations, around town and along the South Bay Bicycle Trail.

Sign up online, download the Social Bicycles app, or pay on the spot, and you can borrow bikes and return to the nearest kiosk. You can rent hourly (pro-rated), or long-term memberships include up to 90 minutes' daily ride time. The monthly student rate ($7) is the best deal in town.

Other bike rental facilities around town, such as **Perry's** (Map p176; ☑ 310-939-0000; www.perryscafe.com; Ocean Front Walk; bikes per hour/day from $10/30, boogie boards $7/20; ⓒ 9am-7:30pm Mon-Fri, from 8:30am Sat & Sun), provide a wider assortment of recreational equipment.

South Bay Bicycle Trail   CYCLING
(Map p176; ⓒ sunrise-sunset; 🚲) The South Bay Bicycle Trail parallels the sand for most of the 22 miles between Will Rogers State Beach on the north end of Santa Monica and Torrance County Beach in the south.

On weekday mornings you may have the trail mostly to yourself, while weekends can get jammed with riders and skaters and you may have to swerve to avoid pedestrians, lollygaggers, surfers and stray volleyballs in the 'bike only' lanes.

Soul Cycle   GYM
(Map p176; ☑ 310-622-7685; www.soul-cycle.com; 120 Wilshire Blvd; 1st class $20, thereafter $30; ⓒ classes 6am-8:30pm; 🚌 MTA 20, 720) A spin class mashed up with aerobics and turned up to hyper-speed has made addicts out of (mostly) women, young and old. At this, the first LA location of a New York transplant, there are lockers, showers, drinking water and the special shoes. When you aren't heaving and trying not to die, it's fun.

Trapeze School New York   TRAPEZE
(Map p176; ☑ 310-394-5800; www.trapezeschool. com; 370 Santa Monica Pier; 2hr classes $35-65; ⓒ class schedule varies) Ever wanted to learn how to fly on the trapeze? In a cordoned-off and netted area on the Santa Monica Pier, you'll get your chance. So chalk up and leave your fear of heights and inhibitions at the door. The public is watching.

Bhakti Yoga Shala   YOGA
(Map p176; www.bhaktiyogashala.com; 207 Arizona Ave; suggested donation $10-20) Donation-based yoga and meditation classes offered in a simple space near the promenade. You won't feel like om-ing cattle here. There are two to seven classes daily.

🛌 Sleeping

Let's face it. Santa Monica is not the place to come for a cheap sleep or a party hotel, but if you want the genuine high-end beachfront experience, it's hard to do better. And, in fact, there are some bargains to be had. At the lowest end, the youth hostel is one of the best we've seen.

HI Los Angeles – Santa Monica   HOSTEL $
(Map p176; ☑ 310-393-9913; www.hilosangeles. org; 1436 2nd St; dm low season $27-45, May-Oct $40-55, r with shared bath $109-140, with private bath $160-230; ⓒ ❄ @ 🛜; 🚇 Expo Line to Downtown Santa Monica) Near the beach and Promenade, this hostel has an enviable location

and recently modernized facilities that rival properties charging many times more. Its approximately 275 beds in single-sex dorms are clean and safe, private rooms are decorated with hipster chic and public spaces (courtyard, library, TV room, dining room, communal kitchen) let you lounge and surf.

Rates include breakfast, and the hostel programs activities such as tours, pub crawls and comedy nights. That said, if you're looking to party, you're better off in Venice or Hollywood.

Hotel Carmel
BOUTIQUE HOTEL **$$**

(Map p176; ☑800-445-8695, 310-451-2469; www. hotelcarmel.com; 201 Broadway; r from $189; P ⊖ ✳ ⊛; M Expo Line to Downtown Santa Monica) Behind the charming historic facade, this older boutique hotel around the corner from the Promenade has just redone its rooms with craftsman-style furniture and updated bathrooms. Rooms are smallish but fairly bright and have ceiling fans; some on the upper floors have ocean views. There's only one elevator, but management is fastidious, in a good way.

Sea Shore Motel
MOTEL **$$**

(Map p176; ☑310-392-2787; www.seashoremotel. com; 2637 Main St; r $125-175, ste $200-300; P ✳ ⊛) The friendly, family-run lodgings at this comfy 25-unit motel put you just a Frisbee toss from the beach on happening Main St (quadruple-pane windows help cut street noise). The tiled, rattan-decorated rooms are basic, but 2nd-floor rooms have high ceilings and families can stretch out in the suites (basically full apartments) with kitchen and balcony a few doors down.

★ Shutters on the Beach
HOTEL **$$$**

(Map p176; ☑310-458-0030; www.shuttersonthe beach.com; 1 Pico Blvd; r $525; P @ ⊛) Bringing classic Cape Cod charm to the Pacific coast, the 198 rooms here have a beach-cottage feel with marble baths, wood floors, spectacular ocean views and tiny balconies with white-washed shutters. The in-house beach cafe is charming and tasty, and the chichi One Pico restaurant draws rave reviews. This is as upscale as Santa Monica nests get.

Slink into a lounge chair on the ocean-view deck around the pool, or treat yourself to a spa treatment. Parking is $45.

★ Palihouse
BOUTIQUE HOTEL **$$$**

(Map p176; ☑310-394-1279; www.palihousesanta monica.com; 1001 3rd St; r/studios from $315/350; P ✳ @ ⊛ ⊛) LA's grooviest hotel brand (not named Ace) occupies the 38 rooms, studios and one-bedroom apartments of the 1927 Spanish Colonial Embassy Hotel, with antique-meets-hipster-chic style. Each comfy room is slightly different, but look for picnic-table-style desks and wallpaper with intricate sketches of animals. Most rooms have full kitchens (and we love the coffee mugs with lifelike drawings of fish).

The lobby is fitted out with terracotta floors, beamed ceilings, leaded-glass windows and coffee bar, plus booths, leather sofas and an intimate back garden, and there's a vintage elevator leading upstairs. Continental breakfast is included on Saturdays and Sundays, and it has a fleet of local Linus bikes for rent for the day.

Service could not be better, which is probably why some guests stay for months. Discounts for longer stays. Overnight parking is $39.

Casa del Mar
HOTEL **$$$**

(Map p176; ☑310-581-5533; www.hotelcasadelmar. com; 1910 Ocean Way; r from $525; P ⊖ ✳ @ ⊛ ⊛ ⊛) This mid-1920s beachfront building has alluring Spanish-Mediterranean style and 129 rooms and suites in whites and pale blues designed by Michael Smith, who did the Obama family's private residence. Room rates basically correlate with best views. 'Casa' is most definitely not a thumping pool-party scene, but there is a beach concierge for bikes, blades and umbrellas.

It's across the street from Shutters (p179), its sister hotel. Parking is $45.

Fairmont Miramar
HOTEL **$$$**

(Map p176; ☑310-576-7777; www.fairmont.com/ santa-monica; 101 Wilshire Blvd; r from $342; P ⊖ ✳ @ ⊛ ⊛; ⬜ MTA line 704, M Expo Line to Downtown Santa Monica) Santa Monica's original grand dame, Fairmont Miramar is a block from the bluffs and the Promenade, shaded by gorgeous palm and fig trees, and home to the fabulous Fig (Map p176; ☑310-319-3111; www.figsantamonica.com; 101 Wilshire Blvd, Fairmont Miramar Hotel; mains lunch $13-24, dinner $18-34; ⊙7am-2pm & 5-10pm Mon-Fri, 7am-2:30pm & 5-10pm Sat & Sun) restaurant and The Bungalow (p182), one of Santa Monica's best night spots. Rooms are four-star comfortable – most have some sort of ocean view – and the modern, indoor-outdoor gym is stunning.

A $25 resort covers wi-fi, car transport within 3 miles, and more. Parking is $46.

Viceroy
BOUTIQUE HOTEL $$$

(Map p176; ☎800-622-8711, 310-260-7500; www.viceroysantamonica.com; 1819 Ocean Ave; r from $399; P🅟❄@🛜🏊🐕) Starving for some LA glam by the sea? With porcelain hounds guarding the elevators, frosted glass, framed mirrors and white-vinyl lounge chairs in the lobby, and shag carpet in the library, the Hollywood Regency decor by *Top Design*'s Kelly Wearstler works, and the pool deck is hemmed by tall hedges and palms. It gets plenty of 'industry' and tech guests.

Ambient electronic music infuses public spaces, there's a flashy bar scene and it's a block from the beach.

Upstairs, rooms are so slick even the marble bathroom is hip. A $26 guest fee takes care of morning coffee, e-readers and bike rentals. Parking is $38.

Shore Hotel
HOTEL $$$

(Map p176; ☎310-458-1515; www.shorehotel.com; 1515 Ocean Ave; r from $379; P🅟❄🛜🏊🐕; 🚌Big Blue Bus line 8, Ⓜ Expo Line to Downtown Santa Monica) 🌿 Modern with clean lines, lots of woods, whites with pops of orange and aqua, this is Santa Monica's only gold LEED-certified (low carbon footprint) hotel. Case in point: the lovely back garden is seeded with drought-tolerant plants. The 164 rooms have ocean, city or garden views and private terraces, and the pool deck faces Ocean Ave and the Pacific.

✗ Eating

There's good food scattered all around SaMo, particularly on Main St and around Third Street Promenade. You'll also find a sort of gourmet glut around 10th St and Wilshire Blvd.

★ Santa Monica Farmers Markets
MARKET $

(Map p176; www.smgov.net/portals/farmers market; Arizona Ave, btwn 2nd & 3rd Sts; ⊙Arizona Ave 8:30am-1:30pm Wed, 8am-1pm Sat, Main St 8:30am-1:30pm Sun; 🚼) 🌿 You haven't really experienced Santa Monica until you've explored one of its outdoor farmers markets stocked with organic fruits, vegetables, flowers, baked goods and freshly shucked oysters. The mack daddy is the Wednesday market, around the intersection of 3rd and Arizona – it's the biggest and arguably the best for fresh produce, and often patrolled by local chefs.

Satdha
THAI, VEGAN $

(Map p176; ☎310-450-6999; www.satdhakitchen.com; 2218 Lincoln Blvd; mains $11-13; ⊙11am-3pm & 5-9:30pm Tue-Sun; 🍴) This vegan Thai restaurant draws fans from all over town to an unassuming stretch of Lincoln Blvd for vibrant dishes such as endive cups filled with cashew 'tuna', coconut, ginger, lemongrass, peanuts and more; green papaya or snap pea salads; beet-dyed noodles; and eggplant served catfish-style in curry paste. The vibe is comfy, contemporary and friendly.

Bay Cities
DELI, ITALIAN $

(Map p176; www.baycitiesitaliandeli.com; 1517 Lincoln Blvd; sandwiches $5-9; ⊙9am-6pm Tue-Sun; 🅟) The best Italian deli in LA, period. The signature sandwich is the sloppy, spicy Godmother (piled with salami, mortadella, coppacola, ham, prosciutto, provolone and pepper salad). It also has house-roasted tri-tip, eggplant parmigiana, tangy salads, imported meats, cheeses, breads and oils to salivate over. The outdoor seating is just OK, so we take ours to the beach or Hollywood Bowl.

Father's Office
GASTROPUB $

(Map p168; ☎310-736-2224; www.fathersoffice.com; 1018 Montana Ave; dishes $5-15; ⊙5pm-1am Mon-Thu, 4pm-2am Fri, noon-2am Sat, noon-midnight Sun) Chef Sang Yoon's elbow-to-elbow, counter-service gastropub is famous for its Office Burger, a dry-aged-beef number dressed in smoky bacon, sweet caramelized onion and an ingenious combo of Gruyère and blue cheese. Pair it with fries served in a mini shopping cart and a mug of handcrafted brew chosen from the three dozen on tap. No substitutions tolerated.

Samosa House
INDIAN $

(Map p176; ☎310-314-0821; www.samosahouse.com; 2301 Main St; combo plates $6-10; ⊙11am-10pm; 🍴) A Bollywood and Indian hip-hop playlist animates this corner shop, with cheap, generous combo plates of South Indian vegetarian and vegan cuisine. The changing menu, served cafeteria-style with rice and your choice of bread baked before your eyes, might include charcoal-smoked cauliflower, jackfruit curry and veggie chicken, alongside pakoras, the namesake samosas and Indian ice-cream sticks.

★ Erven
VEGAN $$

(Map p176; ☎310-260-2255; www.ervenrestaurant.com; 514 Santa Monica Blvd; sandwiches $7-15, snacks $5, dinner mains $15-21; 🛜; Ⓜ Expo Line to Downtown Santa Monica) 🥢 In this city that teems with vegetarian and vegan dining, chef Nick Erven's restaurant ticks it up a few notches in this airy, modern space. Lunch and dinner are different experiences – counter service versus refined sit-down, with different menus – and there's a marketplace counter that's open even when the kitchen is closed.

★ **Milo & Olive** ITALIAN $$
(☎310-453-6776; www.miloandolive.com; 2723 Wilshire Blvd; dishes $7-20; ⊙7am-11pm) We love this place for its small-batch wines, incredible pizzas, terrific breakfasts (creamy polenta and poached eggs anyone?), breads and pastries, all of which you may enjoy at the marble bar or shoulder to shoulder with new friends at one of two common tables. It's a cozy neighborhood joint so it doesn't take reservations.

Santa Monica Seafood SEAFOOD $$
(Map p176; ☎310-393-5244; www.santamonicaseafood.com; 1000 Wilshire Blvd; appetizers $7-15, mains $14-30; ⊙9am-9pm Mon-Sat, to 8pm Sun; P🖶) The best seafood market in Southern California offers a tasty oyster bar and market cafe, where you can sample delicious chowder, salmon burgers, albacore melts, oysters on the half shell and pan-roasted cod.

Art's Table AMERICAN $$
(Map p168; www.artstablesm.com; 1002 Montana Ave; mains lunch $13-24, dinner $17-29; ⊙11am-10:30pm Mon-Fri, from 9:30am Sat & Sun) Creative New American cooking takes center stage at this multi-windowed cafe with lots of sidewalk seating on Montana Ave. The Greek corn salad is lovely, and the Belly of the Beast Cuban sandwich packs a punch, especially with its Gruyère fondue dipping sauce. Fun fact: the restaurant was actually founded by five guys named Art.

Ye Olde King's Head BRITISH $$
(Map p176; ☎310-451-1402; www.yeoldekingshead.com; 116 Santa Monica Blvd; breakfast dishes $6-14, sandwiches & salads $10-15, mains $14-23; ⊙9am-10pm Mon-Wed, to 11pm Thu & Fri, 8am-11pm Sat, 8am-10pm Sun) Fancy LA's best fish and chips? Or some bangers and mash, shepherd's pie or curry? This been-there-forever pub is a slice of 'jolly old' on the left coast. Breakfasts span beans on toast to the 'king size English breakfast' (eggs, bacon, sausage etc – basically the full monty).

Inotheke MEDITERRANEAN $$
(Map p176; ☎310-458-3366; www.inotheke.com; 606 Broadway Ave; dishes $6-17; ⊙noon-2:30pm Mon-Fri, 5-9:30pm Sun-Thu, to 10pm Fri & Sat; ❉; 🚌Big Blue Bus lines 1, 2, Metro line 720, Ⓜ Expo Line Downtown Santa Monica) Greek cooking gets a 21st-century update, courtesy of a Cypriot chef who trained with Alain Ducasse. Greek salad comes with generous serves of sheep's milk, zucchini for *mousakas* is grilled not fried, eggplant-tahini salad perfectly balances acid and sweetness, and shrimp *saganaki* is flamed with ouzo and has overtones of cinnamon. All this just steps from Third St Promenade.

800 Degrees PIZZA $$
(Map p176; ☎310-566-0801; www.800degreespizza.com; 120 Wilshire Blvd; salads $6-10, pizzas $8-14; ⊙11am-1:30am Sun-Wed, to 2am Thu-Sat; 🖶) The name refers to the temperature of this restaurant's wood-fired pizza oven. Your job: follow the line into the big, splashy, marble-floored environs and create your own Neapolitan-style pizza.

Kreation CAFE $$
(Map p168; ☎310-458-4880; www.kreationkafe.net; 1023 Montana Ave; ⊙7am-10pm; 🅿) 🥢 This combination juicery-cafe is the original in a growing local chain. The juice bar blends coconut milk and blueberries, blood orange with carrots and turmeric, and all the greens. The cafe has a rustic Persian twist. It offers fresh poached salmon, tasty frittatas and organic chicken and beef kebabs.

Sugarfish SUSHI $$
(Map p176; www.sugarfishsushi.com; 1345 2nd St; 'Trust me' meals lunch $19-37, dinner $$22-42; ⊙11:30am-10pm Mon-Sat, noon-9pm Sun) The Santa Monica shingle of a popular sushi chain imagined by LA's reformed Sushi Nazi, Chef Nozawa. You can order à la carte or one of the three set 'Trust Me' *omakase* menus, which are reasonably priced, fulfilling and delicious. The special rice recipe offers just a hint of sweetness, and don't miss out on the blue crab roll. Phenomenal.

Blue Plate Oysterette SEAFOOD $$
(Map p176; ☎310-576-3474; www.blueplatesantamonica.com; 1355 Ocean Ave; dishes $11-26; ⊙11:30am-10pm Sun-Thu, to 11pm Fri & Sat) At this New England–style seafood shack across from the ocean, there's only one reason to ignore a raw bar that includes a ceviche of the day, delectable oysters, prawns and clams – you've ordered the lobster roll or the

lobster mac-n-cheese. Fried fish or seared ahi tacos add a West Coast flavor.

★ M Street Kitchen
CALIFORNIAN $$

(Map p176; ☑310-396-9145; www.mstreetkitchen. com; 2000 Main St; mains $7-21; ⊘8am-10pm Sun-Thu, to 11pm Fri & Sat; Ⓟ⚑) This wildly popular breakfast and lunch choice, with abundant sunshine patio seating, conjures farmers market produce and all-natural ingredients into comfortable creations such as pulled chicken nachos, terrific fried-egg sandwiches at breakfast, house-made veggie burgers at lunch and soft-taco platters that have their own cult following. There's a huge bakery section if you just want takeout.

★ Cassia
SOUTHEAST ASIAN $$$

(Map p176; ☑310-393-6699; 1314 7th St; appetizers $12-24, mains $18-77; ⊘5-10pm Sun-Thu, to 11pm Fri & Sat; Ⓟ) Ever since it opened in 2015, open, airy Cassia has made about every local and national 'best' list of LA restaurants. Chef Bryant Ng draws on his Chinese-Singaporean heritage in dishes such as *kaya* toast (with coconut jam, butter and a slow-cooked egg), 'sunbathing' prawns, and the encompassing Vietnamese pot-au-feu: short-rib stew, veggies, bone marrow and delectable accompaniments.

Even the building is cool – the 1937 art-deco Santa Monica Telephone Building.

Rustic Canyon
CALIFORNIAN $$$

(Map p176; ☑310-393-7050; www.rusticcanyon winebar.com; 1119 Wilshire Blvd; dishes $13-40; ⊘5:30-10:30pm Sun-Thu, to 11pm Fri & Sat) At this 'wine bar and seasonal kitchen', almost all the ingredients for the daily-updated menus come from local organic producers (credited on the menu, no less!). You can expect handmade pasta dishes and an assortment of stunning small plates such as *pozole verde* (mussels, hominy, poblano chilies and tortilla) and 'beets & berries' served with avocado, quinoa, fennel and pistachio 'soil'.

🍸 Drinking & Nightlife

Santa Monica has luxe lounges, its share of dive bars and a couple stunning clubs by which others are measured.

★ Dogtown Coffee
CAFE

(Map p176; www.dogtowncoffee.com; 2003 Main St; ⊘5:30am-5pm Mon-Fri, from 6:30am Sat & Sun) Set in the old Zephyr surf shop headquarters, where skateboarding was invented during a 1970s drought that emptied pools across LA, it brews great coffee and makes a mean breakfast burrito, the preferred nutritional supplement of surfers the world over. And it's open for dawn patrol.

★ Bungalow
LOUNGE

(Map p176; www.thebungalowsm.com; 101 Wilshire Blvd, Fairmont Miramar Hotel; ⊘5pm-2am Mon-Fri, noon-2am Sat, noon-10pm Sun) A Brent Bolthouse nightspot, the indoor-outdoor lounge at the Fairmont Miramar was one of the hottest nights out in LA when it burst onto the scene a couple of years ago. It's since settled down, and like most Westside spots can be too dude-centric late in the evening, but the setting is elegant, and there's still beautiful mischief to be found here.

★ Basement Tavern
BAR

(Map p176; www.basementtavern.com; 2640 Main St; ⊘5pm-2am) A creative speakeasy, housed in the basement of the Victorian, and our favorite well in Santa Monica. We love it for its craftsman cocktails, cozy booths, island bar and nightly live-music calendar that features blues, jazz, bluegrass and rock bands. It gets way too busy on weekends for our taste, but weeknights can be special.

Onyx
ROOFTOP BAR

(Map p176; www.shangrila-hotel.com; 1301 Ocean Ave, Hotel Shangri-La; ⊘4pm-midnight Mon-Wed, to 2am Thu, 3pm-2am Fri & Sat, 3pm-midnight Sun) Santa Monica's only indoor-outdoor roof bar has a swinging-'70s, Studio 54 vibe – brass-plated fireplace, hexagonal ceiling tiles – a bar made of a giant onyx slab (get it?) and cocktails such as the TamieTini (Ketel One, basil, passion fruit and cava) and the Shangri-La Mojito. But we most love surveying the view from the Pier to Malibu from seven stories up. There's also a small-plates menu. After sunset the dress code is urban chic, so leave the flip-flops and shorts behind.

Copa d'Oro
BAR

(Map p176; www.copadoro.com; 217 Broadway; ⊘5:30pm-midnight Mon-Wed, to 2am Thu-Sat) The cocktail menu was created by the talented Vincenzo Marianella – a man who knows his spirits, and has trained his team to concoct addictive cocktails from a well of top-end spirits and a produce bin of fresh herbs, fruits, juices and a few veggies. The rock tunes and the smooth, dark ambience don't hurt.

Misfit
LOUNGE

(Map p176; ☏ 310-656-9800; www.themisfitbar. com; 225 Santa Monica Blvd; ☺ noon-late Mon-Fri, from 11am Sat, from 10:30am Sun) This darkly lit emporium of food, drink and fun is notable for the decent menu and phenomenal cocktails made from craftsman spirits. Set in a historic building decked out with a retro interior, it's busy from brunch to last call.

Chez Jay
BAR

(Map p176; www.chezjays.com; 1657 Ocean Ave; ☺ 11:45am-2pm & 5:30-9:30pm Mon-Fri, 9am-1:45pm & 5:30-9:30pm Sat & Sun) Rocking since 1959, this nautical-themed dive has seen its share of Hollywood intrigue from the Rat Pack to the Brat Pack. To this day it's dark and dank and all the more glorious for it. The classic steak and seafood menu's not bad, either.

Bar Chloe
LOUNGE

(Map p176; www.barchloe.com; 1449 2nd St; ☺ 6pm-midnight Mon-Wed, to 1am Thu, 5pm-2am Fri, 7pm-2am Sat, 5-11pm Sun) Cozy, dark and elegant with dangling chandeliers, twinkling candles, intimate booths, crisp white tablecloths and a chamomile mai tai that has earned rave reviews. We wouldn't know; we ordered a whiskey neat. The tapas and sliders are decent, too.

☆ Entertainment

★ Harvelle's
BLUES

(Map p176; ☏ 310-395-1676; www.harvelles.com; 1432 4th St; cover $5-15) This dark blues grotto has been packing 'em in since 1931, but somehow still manages to feel like a well-kept secret. There are no big-name acts here, but the quality is usually high. Sunday's Toledo Show mixes soul, jazz and cabaret, and Wednesday night brings the always-funky House of Vibe All-Stars.

Arclight Cinemas
CINEMA

(Map p176; ☏ 310-566-2810; www.arclightcinemas. com; 395 Santa Monica Pl 330; adult $13.75; Ⓜ Expo Line to Downtown Santa Monica) New Santa Monica outpost of LA's most admired cinema chain. Sitting atop Santa Monica Pl, the cinema offers assigned seating in plush seats, ultra-clean theaters, cocktails in the snack bar, hosts who make sure the projection is just so and – our favorite part – no commercials. Sure, it's pricey, but what price perfection? Discounted weekday matinee tickets are available.

Aero Theater
CINEMA

(Map p168; www.americancinematheque.com; 1328 Montana Ave) Santa Monica's original movie theater (c 1940) is now operated by American Cinematheque (p101), where it screens old and neo classics, and offers Q&A sessions with bigwigs from time to time. Check its online calendar for upcoming shows.

Broad Stage
THEATER

(Map p176; ☏ 310-434-3200; www.thebroadstage. com; 1310 11th St) A 499-seat, state-of-the-art theater anchors Santa Monica College's striking, modernist performing-arts complex, which is a satellite campus on its own. Touring shows bring everything from new interpretations of classic Shakespeare to one-man productions, edgy plays and classical and world-music performances.

McCabe's Guitar Shop
LIVE MUSIC

(☏ 310-828-4497; www.mccabes.com; 3101 Pico Blvd; tickets $15-30) Sure, this mecca of musicianship sells guitars and other instruments, but you want to come for the concerts in the back room. Since 1969 everyone from indie rockers to the the likes of Beck, Jackson Browne, Charlie Hunter and Liz Phair have performed here.

🛍 Shopping

For big chains such as Anthropologie, and the flagship Apple, Guess and Converse (where you can build your own shoes), make your way to the Third Street Promenade. Santa Monica Place offers more upscale, corporate consumption. For more indie-minded boutiques, head to Montana Ave and Main St.

Santa Monica Place
MALL

(Map p176; www.santamonicaplace.com; 395 Santa Monica Pl; ☺ 10am-9pm Mon-Sat, 11am-8pm Sun) The mall at the south end of the Promenade offers posher shops than those on the comparatively dated Promenade. Think All Saints, Juicy Couture, Bloomingdales and Nordstrom, Michael Kors, Swarovski, Tiffany, Uniqlo and there's a Nike flagship too, along with epic views from the dining deck.

Third Street Promenade
MALL

(Map p176; 3rd St between Broadway & Wilshire Blvd) Stretching for three long blocks sprawled between Broadway and Wilshire Blvd, 'the Promenade' is a case study in how to morph a dilapidated, dying main street into a dynamic and happening strip. It offers carefree and car-free strolling accompanied by the sound of flamenco guitar or hip-hop acrobatics courtesy of street performers.

Puzzle Zoo
GAMES

(Map p176; ☑ 310-393-9201; www.puzzlezoo.com; 1411 Third St Promenade; ⊙10am-10pm Sun-Thu, to 11pm Fri & Sat; 🛉) Those searching galaxy-wide for the caped Lando Calrissian action figure, look no more. Puzzle Zoo stocks every imaginable *Star Wars* or anime figurine this side of Endor. There's also an encyclopedic selection of puzzles, board games and toys. Kids adore it.

Church of Type
ART

(☑ 310-310-3951; www.churchoftype.com; 3215 Pico Blvd; ⊙10am-8pm Mon-Fri, 11am-7pm Sat, noon-6pm Sun; 🚌 Big Blue Bus line 7) Retro printing seems oh-so-hipster cool, but this workmanlike storefront workshop gets both fun and serious, lined with drawer after drawer of moveable type that goes back to the 1700s and still works. It sell prints, posters, printed fabric pillows and more ($10 to *how much?*) and offers occasional workshops; check website for times.

Vital Hemp
FASHION & ACCESSORIES

(Map p176; ☑ 310-450-2260; www.vitalhemp.com; 2305 Main St; ⊙10am-6pm) 🌿 A boutique stocked with designer, ecofriendly hemp goods made in Downtown LA. It has fitted tees, chinos, hoodies and more, perfectly suited to the coastal casual look.

REI
SPORTS & OUTDOORS

(Map p176; www.rei.com; 402 Santa Monica Blvd; ⊙10am-9pm Mon-Sat, 11am-7pm Sun) This 'cathedral to outdoor gear' makes it easy to stock up on everything from wool socks to speed-dry underwear, rolling backpacks to Everest-capable sleeping bags. The staff are friendly and knowledgeable. It also rents camping equipment.

Undefeated
SHOES

(Map p176; www.undefeated.com; 2654 Main St; ⊙10am-7pm Mon-Sat, to 5pm Sun) Get your kicks at this slammin' sneaker store specializing in vintage and limited editions, hand selected from the manufacturer by the manager. When new shipments arrive, expect sidewalk campouts.

Free People
FASHION & ACCESSORIES

(Map p176; www.freepeople.com; 2925 Main St; ⊙11am-7pm Mon-Sat, to 6pm Sun) Hippie-chic women's gear with a dash of retro cool. Santa Monica's pretty, pouty, upscale flower children get dressed here.

Venice, Marina Del Rey & Playa del Rey

If you were born too late, and have always been a little jealous of the hippie heyday, come down to the Boardwalk and inhale a (not just) incense-scented whiff of Venice, a boho beach town and longtime haven for artists, new agers, road-weary tramps, freaks and free spirits. This is where Jim Morrison and the Doors lit their fire, where Arnold Schwarzenegger pumped himself to stardom, and the place the late Dennis Hopper once called home. These days, even as tech titans move in, the Old Venice spirit endures.

◎ Sights

Be it beach, canal or wetlands, you're never far from water in these oceanside communities. Prepare for sensory overload on Venice's Boardwalk, a one-of-a-kind experience. Buff bodybuilders brush elbows with street performers and sellers of sunglasses, string bikinis, Mexican ponchos and medical marijuana, all while cyclists and rollerbladers whiz by on the bike path and skateboarders and graffiti artists get their own domains. A few blocks away, the Venice Canals offer a genteel escape among funky to modernist homes around the waterways that lent the neighborhood its name. For a quieter beach scene, head down the Marina Del Rey peninsula (one of America's largest pleasure-boat harbors is just inland), or head around the Ballona Wetlands to the wide open beaches of Playa del Rey.

★ Venice Boardwalk
WATERFRONT

(Ocean Front Walk; Map p186; Venice Pier to Rose Ave) Life in Venice moves to a different rhythm and nowhere more so than on the famous Venice Boardwalk, officially known as Ocean Front Walk. It's a freak show, a human zoo and a wacky carnival alive with Hula-Hoop magicians, old-timey jazz combos, solo distorted garage rockers and artists (good and bad) – as far as LA experiences go, it's a must.

The Sunday-afternoon drum circle draws hundreds of revelers for tribal jamming and spontaneous dancing on the grassy mounds (sometimes beats migrate to the sand, as well). If the noise doesn't guide you there, just follow your nose towards skunky cigarettes, which are sold over the counter at several MMJ (medical marijuana) dispensaries.

Don't miss the tagged-up towers and the free-standing concrete wall, forever open to aerosol Picassos.

★ Abbot Kinney Boulevard   AREA

(Map p186; 🚌 Big Blue Bus line 18) Abbot Kinney, who founded Venice in the early 1900s, would probably be delighted to find that one of Venice's best-loved streets bears his name. Sort of a seaside Melrose with a Venetian flavor, the mile-long stretch of Abbot Kinney Blvd between Venice Blvd and Main St is full of upscale boutiques, galleries, lofts and sensational restaurants. A few years back, GQ named it America's coolest street, and that cachet has only grown since.

In late September, the Abbot Kinney Festival draws thousands of revelers, as does the First Friday (www.abbotkinneyfirstfridays.com; ⏱ 5-11pm 1st Fri each month) street fair, when galleries and shops stay open late and you'll roam all night with the tramps, hippies, weirdos, fashionistas, yuppies and squares.

★ Venice Canals   AREA

(Map p186) Even many Angelenos have no idea that just a couple of blocks from the Boardwalk madness is an idyllic neighborhood that preserves 3 miles of Abbot Kinney's canals. The Venice Canal Walk threads past eclectic homes, over bridges and along waterways where ducks preen and locals lollygag in little rowboats. It's best accessed from either Venice or Washington Blvds.

Ballona Wetlands   NATURE RESERVE

(www.ballonafriends.org; cnr Lincoln & Jefferson Blvds, Playa del Rey) FREE These last remaining wetlands in LA County are home to at least 200 migrating and resident bird species, including the great blue heron. Their habitat, however, has shrunk significantly since Playa Vista, a much-debated custom-planned luxury community for about 11,000 residents, took root across Lincoln. Still, the developers get points for restoring and expanding the healthiest intact marsh, which has seen increasing bird activity.

🏃 Activities

Beaching is the main activity in Venice and the Marina down to Dockweiler State Beach around Playa del Rey. The South Bay Bicycle Trail (p178) also cuts along the beach before darting inland at Washington Blvd to circle around the Marina and Fisherman's Village,

LOS ANGELES VENICE, MARINA DEL REY & PLAYA DEL REY

VENICE ART WALK

Who needs galleries when you've got great outdoor art? Venice has plenty of both, so keep your eyes open as you stroll around town (and let us know your favorite finds!). This leisurely tour starts at the corner of Rose Ave and Main St, where Jonathan Borofsky's 30ft-high, tutu-clad **Ballerina Clown** (Map p186; cnr Rose Ave & Main St, Venice; 🚌 Big Blue Bus lines 1, 8, 18, Metro line 733), 1989, offers up a surreal presence. One block south, Frank Gehry's **Binoculars Building** (Map p186; 340 Main St, Venice) (now – sign of the times – a Google outpost) is fronted by massive binoculars by Claes Oldenburg and Coosje van Bruggen.

But Venice's real strength is its murals. Fine specimens along the Venice Boardwalk include Chagall Returns to Venice Beach by Christina Schlesinger, and **Venice Reconstituted** (Map p186; 25 Windward Ave, Venice) by Rip Cronk. The latter is a parody of Botticelli's Renaissance work *Birth of Venus*, containing a cacophony of figures, many of them real Venetians. As you walk around, you'll find many more Cronk murals. His **Homage to a Starry Night** (Map p186; Ocean Front Walk, at Wavecrest Ave) was inspired by the Van Gogh original. The same artist also created the epic 30ft-high portraits of one-time Venice resident **Jim Morrison** (Morning Shot; Map p186; 1881 Speedway, Venice) and city founder **Abbot Kinney** (Map p186; cnr N Venice Blvd & Pacific Ave, Venice).

With such a strong mural tradition, it only makes sense that the nonprofit **Social and Public Art Resource Center**, which promotes, preserves and produces public murals throughout LA, is based in Venice. It has a gallery here, too.

Each May the Venice Family Clinic sponsors an art auction and studio tour also known as the Venice Art Walk (p70) to help raise funds for the clinic, which brings health care to 24,000 under-served men, women and children each year. With a ticket, you receive a map and pass that grants entry into more than 50 local studios featuring hundreds of original pieces, whether you plan on bidding or not.

Venice

connecting along the Ballona Canal to the ocean again at Playa del Rey.

★ **Venice Skatepark** SKATEBOARDING
(Map p186; www.veniceskatepark.com; 1500 Ocean Front Walk, Venice; ☉dawn-dusk) Long the destination of local skate punks, the concrete at this skate park has now been molded and steel-fringed into 17,000 sq ft of vert, tranny and street terrain with unbroken ocean views. The old-school-style skate run and the world-class pool are most popular for high flyers and gawking spectators. Great photo opps, especially as the sun sets.

★ **Muscle Beach** GYM
(Map p186; ☎310-399-2775; www.musclebeach. net; 1800 Ocean Front Walk, Venice; per day $10; ☉8am-7pm Mon-Sat, 10am-4pm Sun Apr-Sep, shorter hours rest of year) Gym rats with an exhibitionist streak can get a tan and a workout at this famous outdoor gym right on the Venice Boardwalk, where Arnold Schwarzenegger and Franco Columbo once bulked up.

Venice Bike & Skate CYCLING, SKATING
(Map p186; ☎310-301-4011; http://venicebike andskates.com; 21 Washington Blvd, Venice; per hour/ day cruisers $8/24, rollerblades & skates $8/24; ☉9:30am-5pm Mon-Fri, 8:30am-6pm Sat & Sun) Get outfitted for a day on the bike path here.

🛌 Sleeping

The most Venice way to stay is on the beach. Several properties of different budgets are on or right off the Boardwalk, offering great views and an only-in-Venice feel (though note that 'only-in-Venice' can sometimes include homeless folks and late-night carousers).

Samesun HOSTEL $
(Map p186; ☎310-399-7649, reservations 888-718-8287; www.samesun.com; 25 Windward Ave, Venice; dm $39-60, r with shared/private bath from $110/150; ☻❄️🛜) This hostel in a refurbished

Venice

1904 building has spectacular rooftop views of Venice Beach, bright, beachy swatches of color and four- to eight-person dorms, as well as some private rooms with either en suite or shared bathrooms. Breakfast is included and it's steps from the beach, restaurants and nightlife. All guests must present a passport. Other amenities include laundry machines, activities and free wi-fi. Towel rental costs $2.

Rose Hotel   INN $$
(Map p186; ☑310-450-3474; www.therosehotel venice.com; 15 Rose Ave, Venice; r from $185, ste $450-485; ❀❋☏) This intimate, low-slung, pension-style inn was built in 1908 and recently refurbished with beach-cottage cool. It's on a quiet street just off the beach and offers small (150-sq-ft) rooms with bathrooms down the hall, coffee and croissants for breakfast, surfboards for loan and bikes for rent. Larger, family-friendly suites have private baths, kitchens and living rooms.

Inn at Venice Beach   MOTEL $$
(Map p186; ☑310-821-2557; www.innatvenice beach.com; 327 Washington Blvd, Venice; r from

$199; Ⓟ❀❋@☏) Close to the beach, the Venice canals, bars and restaurants, this mid-century-themed, 43-room motel sports brightly hued rooms with a good range of amenities. All wrap around a central courtyard perfect for munching your free breakfast in the morning.

Venice Beach Suites & Hotel   HISTORIC HOTEL $$
(Map p186; ☑310-396-4559; www.venice beachsuites.com; 1305 Ocean Front Walk, Venice; r from $209; @☏) Old Venice funky and old-sandal comfy, this place right on the Boardwalk scores big for bend-over-backwards staff. Take Betsy, the creaky 1913 elevator, upstairs to access the new roof deck. Below, rooms have exposed-brick walls, wrought-iron bed frames, kitchenettes, wood floors, rattan furniture, built-in closets and rates that vary with the view. It's ideal for long stays.

★ Hotel Erwin   BOUTIQUE HOTEL $$$
(Map p186; ☑310-452-1111; www.hotelerwin.com; 1697 Pacific Ave, Venice; r from $280; Ⓟ❀@☏) This old motor inn has been dressed up,

colored and otherwise funkified in retro style. Think eye-popping oranges, yellows and greens, framed photos of graffiti art and ergo sofas in the spacious rooms. Book online for the best deals. Whether or not you stay here, the High (p191) rooftop lounge is a wonderful place for a sundowner.

Venice Suites INN $$$
(Map p186; ☑ 310-566-5224; www.venicesuites. com; 417 Ocean Front Walk, Venice; studios from $175, 1-bedroom ste from $270; ⓟ➌☎) This former apartment building offers tasty one-bedroom suites and studios right on the Boardwalk with a beachy, modern-minimalist aesthetic, hardwood floors, pillow-top mattresses, kitchens, pops of color and marble trim in the bathrooms. There are coin-op laundry machines, a special rooftop deck with a barbecue and views from the ocean to the mountains. Good for extended stays.

Venice Breeze Suites BOUTIQUE HOTEL $$$
(Map p186; ☑ 310-566-2222; www.venice-breezesuites.com; 2 Breeze Ave, Venice; r from $175; ➌✳@☎) This 31-room beachfront property feels like home away from home. A cool wooden elevator takes you up to stylish studios and suites boasting wood floors, exposed-brick walls, full kitchens, floating beds and rain showers in modernist bathrooms. There's a guest-use laundry and communal barbecue area with wraparound sofas on the rooftop. It'll even provide a beach bag.

Su Casa BOUTIQUE HOTEL $$$
(Map p186; ☑ 310-452-9700; www.sucasavenice. com; 431 Ocean Front Walk, Venice; r/1-bedroom ste from $169/239; ⓟ➌✳☎✿) Set in a string of boho studio and apartment hotels overlooking the Boardwalk, rooms here are fairly large with new wood floors, wall-mounted flat-screen TVs, kitchenettes to full kitchens and framed black-and-white photos of old-school surfers, around a deeply grained wooden staircase. The reception desk is off Paloma Ave.

✖ Eating

Venice has some of LA's best dining, and Abbot Kinney Blvd is the main restaurant row, with everything from juice bars and falafel stands to high-flying gourmet dinners. That said, there are interesting eats all over Venice and the Marina, down to Playa.

Eggslut BREAKFAST $
(Map p186; ☑ 424-438-7818; www.eggslut.com; 1611 Pacific Ave, Venice; mains $7-9; ☺8am-4pm)

Westside outpost of the DTLA hipster foodie favorite. This cozy, post-industrial storefront's best seller is the Fairfax sandwich (a lovably gooey mess of scrambled eggs, caramelized onion and sriracha mayo) served in adorable mini paper bags. The namesake 'eggslut' is a coddled egg nestled on top of potato purée in a glass jar and served with toasted crostini.

Salt & Straw ICE CREAM $
(Map p186; ☑ 310-310-8429; www.saltandstraw. com; 1537 Abbot Kinney Blvd, Venice; ice cream from $4; ☺10am-11pm) There always seems to be a line out the door at this branch of the hipster-cool Portland-based ice-cream fantasy land. Maybe it's because there's always something new to try: adventurous, seasonal flavors that change monthly – think farmers-market veggies to late-summer harvest. Check the website for current offerings.

Wurstkuche GERMAN $
(Map p186; ☑ 213-687-4444, ext 2; www.wurstkuche.com; 625 Lincoln Blvd, Venice; dishes $4-8.50; ☺11am-midnight; ✳; ☒Big Blue Bus line 3 or R3) Set in a hipster-chic brick-house loft, but sealed off from the on-rushing madness of Lincoln Blvd, this German sausage and beer *haus* specializes in three things: classic, gourmet and exotic grilled sausages (bratwurst to rattlesnake and rabbit, plus vegetarian options); fine Belgian, German and North American beers; and Belgian fries with ample dipping sauces.

Komodo FUSION $
(Map p186; ☑ 310-255-6742; www.komodofood. com; 235 Main St, Venice; dishes $3-11, meals $10-15; ☺11am-9pm Sun & Mon, to 10pm Tue-Sat; ☒Big Blue Bus lines 1, 8, 18, Metro line 733) *What the...?* Asian-Latin-Mediterranean fusion combos are the thing at this airy, counter-service spot. Tacos, burritos or rice bowls are filled with selections such as banh mi chicken, Alaskan cod with grapes, roasted almonds and sour-cream salad; or the Komodo 2.0 (steak, jalapeño aioli and Southwestern corn salad) and more. Plate meals include Hawaiian-style chicken and *nasi goreng*.

Humble Potato BURGERS $
(☑ 323-989-2242; www.humblepotato.com; 8321 Lincoln Blvd, Playa del Rey; burgers from $8.50; ☺11:30am-10pm Mon-Fri, noon-10pm Sat & Sun) A super-fun anime aesthetic animates this Japanese-inspired, not-quite-fast-food burger-and-sandwich joint between Marina del Rey and LAX. Order a burger (our favorite:

LA'S MOBILE KITCHEN CRAZE

Any LA foodie will tell you that some of the best bites in town come on four wheels. Food trucks are no less popular here than in any other cool, food-loving metropolis, with their mobile kitchens serving up a global feast of old- and new-school flavors. You can track food trucks at Roaming Hunger (www.roaminghunger.com), or check the websites, Twitter or Instagram feeds of the following LA favorites.

Free Range (www.freerangela.com) Famed for its signature tempura-fried chicken with Fresno-chili slaw and honey mustard sauce, jammed into a toasted Portuguese bun. Don't eat meat? Go for the sourdough toast topped with avocado mash, egg over easy, spicy Sriracha and pickled onions. Credit cards accepted.

Yeasty Boys (http://yeastieboysbagels.com) Fluffy-centered, hand-rolled bagels available in plain, poppy, sesame cheddar and everything. Top billing goes to the Game Over, a spot-hitting combo of soft scrambled eggs, peppered bacon, beer cheese, tomato and jalapeño spread in a cheddar bagel. Takes credit cards.

Kogi BBQ (http://kogibbq.com) Chef Roy Choi is a founding dude of the LA food-truck scene and his four trucks (Roja, Verde, Naranja and Rosita) peddle standout Korean-Mexican fusion fare. Sink your teeth into the signature short-rib taco, an expert balancing act of double-caramelized Korean BBQ, salsa roja and chili-soy slaw on griddled corn tortillas. Tofu available and cards accepted.

Plant Food for People (http://pffp.org) Smashing plant-based street food good enough for herbivores *and* omnivores. Crowd favorite is the Super Crazy Taco, which sees organic yellow corn tortillas laden with marinated jackfruit 'carnitas', slow-cooked pinto beans, cabbage slaw, pico de gallo, chipotle mayo and tomatillo salsa. Supporting options include nachos and tortas. Cards accepted.

Guerrilla Tacos (www.guerrillatacos.com) Chef Wes Avila brings his fine-dining background to his blue-hued truck, which offers an oft-tweaked, seasonal Mexican menu using quality, sustainable produce from local farms and artisanal purveyors. Expect fresh, inspired tacos topped with combos such as roasted sweet potato, almond chile, fried corn nuts, feta and scallions. Takes cards.

Ta Bom Truck (www.tabomtruck.com) Take one mom from Sao Paolo, add two daughters and a shared passion for Brazilian food and, presto, you get Ta Bom. Kill the hunger pangs with ground-beef pastel (a *brasiliano* take on the empanada) and don't skimp on the the the garlic fries, pimped with grilled minced garlic, homemade garlic-herb mayo, grated Parmesan cheese and parsley. Accepts cards.

the supremely gooey Battle Royale, loaded with applewood bacon, garlic jam, caramelized onion, avocado, romaine, tomato, spicy sauce and fried egg) and fries with *shichimi* powder, garlic and nori, and wait for the fun to unfold.

Lemonade CALIFORNIAN $
(Map p186; ☑ 310-452-6200; www.lemonadela.com; 1661 Abbot Kinney Blvd, Venice; meals $8-13; ☺ 11am-9pm; 🚌 Big Blue Bus line 18 to Venice Blvd, 🚌 Metro line 733 to Abbot Kinney Blvd) This imaginative, local-market, cafeteria-style shop serves a lineup of tasty salads (watermelon radish and chili or tamarind pork and spicy carrots), and stockpots bubbling with lamb and stewed figs or miso-braised short ribs. It has six kinds of lemonade augmented with

blueberries and mint or watermelon and rosemary. Yummy sweets, too.

⭐ **Butcher's Daughter** VEGETARIAN, CAFE $$
(Map p186; ☑ 310-981-3004; www.thebutchersdaughter.com; 1205 Abbot Kinney Blvd, Venice; dishes $10-22; ☺ 8am-10pm) Find yourself a seat around the central counter or facing busy Abbot Kinney to tuck in to stone-oven pizzas, handmade pastas and veggie faves such as whole roasted cauliflower and butternut-squash risotto. It's Aussie-owned, meaning great coffee. Light, airy and fun. Welcome to California!

⭐ **Gjusta** CALIFORNIAN $$
(Map p186; ☑ 310-314-0320; www.gjusta.com; 320 Sunset Ave, Venice; mains $7.50-20; ☺ 7am-9pm; 🚌 Big Blue Bus lines 1, 18) The folks behind the

standard-setting Gjelina (p190) have opened this very casual, very gourmet, *very* Venice bakery, cafe and deli behind a nondescript storefront on a hidden side street. The menu changes regularly, but if we say lunches of chicken, cabbage and dumpling soup, house-cured charcuterie and fish (such as gravlax, smoked Wagyu brisket and leg of lamb), does that help?

★ Rose Café
CALIFORNIAN $$

(Map p186; ☎ 310-399-0711; www.rosecafevenice. com; 220 Rose Ave, Venice; breakfast $10-17, lunch mains $10-28, dinner mains $20-32; ☺ 7am-10pm Tue-Thu, to 11pm Fri, 8am-11pm Sat, 8am-10pm Sun; P ✦) This sprawling Venice institution (established 1979) was recently given a major, very welcome makeover. If the new version is less funky (though you'll still find laptop-toting writers, tech geeks and beefcakes from nearby Gold's Gym), it's also more fun and more sophisticated. Display cases show off lovely salads, prepared dishes and pastries, which you can take to a hedge-framed patio.

Plant Food + Wine
VEGAN $$

(Map p186; ☎ 310-450-1009; www.matthewkenneycuisine.com/hospitality/plant-food-and-wine; 1009 Abbot Kinney Blvd, Venice; mains lunch $14-22, dinner $17-24; ☺ noon-4pm Mon-Fri, 11am-4pm Sat & Sun, 5-11pm daily; ✎; ▣ Big Blue Bus lines 1, 18, Metro line 33) Not only do noted vegan chef/author/activist Matthew Kenney and chef Scot Winegard work miracles with raw vegetables, grains, nuts and seeds here, they do it in one of LA's most beautiful dining spaces. Look for standards such as Caesar salad with sea beans and sunflower-nori dust, zucchini lasagna with spicy marinara, basil pesto and ricotta made from macadamia nuts.

Superba Food & Bread
CALIFORNIAN $$

(Map p186; ☎ 310-907-5075; www.superbafoodandbread.com; 1900 Lincoln Blvd, Venice; breakfast $8-16, lunch mains $12-22, dinner mains $12-27; ☺ 7am-10pm Sun-Thu, to 11pm Fri & Sat; P ✳; ▣ Big Blue Bus line 3, Metro lines 33, 733) This industrial-sleek, indoor-outdoor space on an up-and-coming stretch of Lincoln Blvd has fab breads and pastries, excellent coffees and flawless (if trendoid) California cooking. For breakfast try avocado toast, chia-seed pudding or the Hangtown Fry (scrambled eggs with crispy oysters). Lunch brings salads and sandwiches, and dinner adds bigger plates. Vegetarians are well served (cauliflower alla Romana – *muah!*).

Café Gratitude
VEGAN $$

(Map p186; ☎ 424-231-8000; http://cafegratitude venice.com; 512 Rose Ave, Venice; mains $10-16; ☺ 8am-10pm; ✎) An anchor of Venice's vegan corridor, Café Gratitude's all-organic menu items are named for affirmations such as 'I am Magical' (that's a house-made veggie burger), 'I am Gracious' (seasonal grain salad), 'I am Pure' (Asian kale salad) and 'I am Whole'"(macrobiotic bowl of sea vegetables, braised yams, adzuki beans, sautéed greens and kimchi).

Cerveteca
MEXICAN $$

(Map p186; ☎ 310-310-8937; www.cervetecala.com; 523 Rose Ave, Venice; mains $12-21; ☺ 11:30am-11pm Mon-Fri, 10:30am-3pm & 4-11pm Sat & Sun) A gourmet Mexican kitchen with fusion digressions (such as the chorizo burger and the mac-n-cheese with bacon). The patio is inviting, but so is the stylish interior, with a wide marble bar, craftsman drafts (this is a *cerveteca*, or beer bar, after all), and global tunes on the sound system.

La Cabaña
MEXICAN $$

(Map p186; ☎ 310-392-7973; www.lacabanavenice. com; 738 Rose Ave, Venice; combination plates $11-18.50; ☺ 11am-3am; ✦) They make the tortillas before your eyes at this rangy, atmospheric warren of a cantina in business since the early '60s. A small troop of black-jacketed, red-bow-tied waiters serves tableside guacamole, authentic *chile rellenos* (stuffed peppers), *carne asada* (marinated, grilled beef), 'super burritos' such as El Verde with green salsa and melted cheese, and 10 kinds of quesadillas.

Propagator
PUB FOOD $$

(☎ 310-439-8264; www.firestonebeer.com; 3205 Washington Blvd, Marina del Rey; dishes $9-18, large plates $15-23, beer brunch mains $11-13; ☺ 11am-11pm Mon-Thu, to midnight Fri, 10am-11pm Sat & Sun; P; ▣ Big Blue Bus route 3 to Washington Blvd) There's always fresh brew on tap at this postmodern barn of a beer hall, owned by Firestone Walker Brewery, and the comforting pub grub is way better than it needs to be: pizzas and pretzels from a wood-burning oven, pork belly carnitas lettuce cups, tacos such as drunken cauliflower, and a knock-your-socks-off brisket sandwich with mushrooms, Gruyère and horseradish aioli.

Figtree's Beach Cafe & Grill
CALIFORNIAN $$

(Map p186; ☎ 310-392-4937; www.figtreescafe. com; 429 Ocean Front Walk, Venice; appetizers $8-13, mains $11-16; ☺ 8am-9pm; ✎) The best eats on the boardwalk. Here you can munch shiitake omelets made with organic eggs, ginger noodles, or a pesto-brushed, arugula-dressed salmon sandwich. The veg-heads will appreciate the spinach nut burger. Meals come with complimentary sea views.

★ **Gjelina** AMERICAN $$$

(Map p186; ✆310-450-1429; www.gjelina.com; 1429 Abbot Kinney Blvd, Venice; veggies, salads & pizzas $10-18, large plates $15-45; ⊙8am-midnight; 🖼; 🚌Big Blue Bus line 18) If one restaurant defines the new Venice, it's this. Carve out a slip on the communal table between the hipsters and yuppies, or get your own slab of wood on the elegant stone terrace, and dine on imaginative small plates (raw yellowtail spiced with chili and mint and drenched in olive oil and blood orange) and sensational thin-crust, wood-fired pizza.

Tasting Kitchen ITALIAN $$$

(Map p186; ✆310-392-6644; www.thetastingkitchen.com; 1633 Abbot Kinney Blvd, Venice; mains $16-40; ⊙10:30am-2:30pm Sat & Sun, 5:30pm-midnight daily) From the salt-roasted branzino, to the porcini-crusted hangar steak, to the burger and the quail, it's all very good here. The pastas are especially good (that bucatini is a gift from the gods), as are the cocktails. Which is why it's almost always packed. Book ahead.

Scopa ITALIAN $$$

(Map p186; ✆310-821-1100; www.scopaitalianroots.com; 2905 Washington Blvd, Venice; dishes $6-49; ⊙5pm-midnight Mon-Fri, to 1am Sat & Sun, 11am-2:30pm Sat & Sun) Venice cool has leaked into the Marina Del Rey border regions with wonderful results. This place is big and open with polished concrete floors and an expansive marble L-shaped bar. The crudo bar serves scallops and steak tartare, four varieties of oysters, uni and mussels, while mains include a whole roasted branzino and a 24oz T-bone.

🍷 Drinking & Nightlife

★ **High** ROOFTOP BAR

(Map p186; ✆424-214-1062; www.highvenice.com; 1697 Pacific Ave, Hotel Erwin, Venice; ⊙3-10pm Mon-Thu, to midnight Fri, noon-midnight Sat, noon-10pm Sun) Venice's only rooftop bar is quite an experience, with 360-degree views from the shore to the Santa Monica Mountains – if you can take your eyes off the beautiful people. High serves creative seasonal cocktails (blood-orange julep, lemon apple

hot toddy, Mexican hot chocolate with tequila) and dishes like beef or lamb sliders, meze plates and crab dip. Reservations recommended.

Intelligentsia Coffeebar CAFE

(Map p186; ✆310-399-1233; www.intelligentsiacoffee.com; 1331 Abbot Kinney Blvd, Venice; ⊙6am-8pm Mon-Thu, to 10pm Fri, 7am-10pm Sat, 7am-8pm Sun; 🛜; 🚌Big Blue Bus line 18) In this hip, industrial, minimalist monument to the coffee gods, perfectionist baristas – who roam the central bar and command more steaming machines than seems reasonable – never short you on foam or caffeine, and the Cake Monkey scones and muffins are addictive. The tunnel-like front vestibule is an oh-so-SoCal chill space.

Venice Ale House PUB

(Map p186; www.venicealehouse.com; 2 Rose Ave, Venice; ⊙10am-midnight Mon-Thu, to 2am Fri, 9am-2am Sat, 9am-midnight Sun) A fun pub right on the Boardwalk on Venice's north end, blessed with ample patio seating for sunset people-watching, long boards suspended from the rafters, rock on the sound system, and plenty of local brews on tap. Beer flights are served in a drilled-out skate deck, and the pub grub works.

Townhouse & Delmonte Speakeasy BAR

(Map p186; www.townhousevenice.com; 52 Windward Ave, Venice; ⊙5pm-2am Mon-Fri, from noon Sat & Sun) Upstairs is a cool, dark and perfectly dingy bar with pool tables, booths and good booze. Downstairs is the speakeasy, where DJs spin pop, funk and electronic music, comics take the mic, and jazz players set up and jam. It's a reliably good time almost any night.

Brig BAR

(Map p186; www.thebrig.com; 1515 Abbot Kinney Blvd, Venice; ⊙4pm-2am Mon-Wed, from 2pm Thu & Fri, from noon Sat & Sun) Old-timers remember this place as a divey pool hall owned by ex-boxer Babe Brandelli (that's him and his wife on the outside mural). Now it's a bit sleeker and attracts a trendy mix of grown-up beach bums, arty professionals and professional artists. On First Fridays, the parking lot attracts a fleet of LA's famed food trucks.

🛍 Shopping

Abbot Kinney Blvd has become one of LA's top shopping destinations. Bargains are few and far between here, but there's a lot of tantalizing stuff – clothing, gifts, accessories and more. As rents have risen here, there has been spillover to surrounding streets.

Along the Venice Boardwalk, shops and stalls sell everything from cheap sunglasses and microbikinis to incense and the inevitable tacky T-shirts.

General Admission
CLOTHING, ACCESSORIES

(Map p186; ☑310-399-1051; www.general admission.us; 52 Brooks Ave, Venice; ☺11am-7pm) A block from the Abbot Kinney strip, this shop sells coastal-cool clothing and accessories, from sage-green Converse sneakers to surfboards, sunglasses and a line of watches and ineffably chic towels with art prints. As if it needed more hipster cred, it also operates a coffee bar across the street in an old Airstream trailer.

Salt
GIFTS & SOUVENIRS, ART

(Map p186; ☑310-452-1154; www.saltvenice.com; 1114 Abbot Kinney Blvd, Venice; ☺11am-6pm Tue-Sat, noon-5pm Sun & Mon; ☐Big Blue Bus line 18) Art, gifts and gifts that are art are the jam here. Artist-designed, one-of-a-kind trophies, snow globes with the F-word inside, handmade boxes that look like hardback books and ingenious children's books that even adults will enjoy. Whimsical, practical, fun and occasionally naughty.

Mystic Journey
SPIRITUALITY

(Map p186; ☑310-399-7070; www.mysticjourney bookstore.com; 1624 Abbot Kinney Blvd, Venice; ☺10am-8pm Sun-Thu, until 11pm Fri & Sat) This spot serves all manner of spirituality, from Hindu to Wiccan, magic to no religion at all, with books, ritual objects, sound bells and bowls, crystals, self-improvement slogans and teas that support your chakras. A backroom hosts lectures and events. As Abbot Kinney gentrifies, it's great to know that this Old Venice institution continues to flourish.

Aviator Nation
CLOTHING

(Map p186; ☑310-396-9100; www.aviatornation. com; 1224 Abbot Kinney Blvd, Venice; ☺10am-8pm) Coastal-chic hoodies, tees and blankets, even guitar picks come emblazoned with the signature stripes of yellow, orange and red. Behind the store is an awesome chill space with a DJ station, ping-pong table and plenty of couches to chill and listen to the bands it sometimes brings in.

Will
FASHION & ACCESSORIES

(Map p186; www.willleathergoods.com; 1360 Abbot Kinney Blvd, Venice; ☺10am-8pm Mon-Sat, 11am-7pm Sun; ☐Big Blue Bus line 18) A terrific leather-goods store out of Eugene, Oregon, and one of just eight nationwide. It sells fine leather bags, briefcases, backpacks, belts, wallets and sandals for men and women – and custom-embosses initials or messages. Our favorite is the bike messenger bag inlaid with colorful remnant Oaxacan wool.

Burro
GIFTS & SOUVENIRS

(Map p186; www.burrogoods.com; 1409 Abbot Kinney Blvd, Venice; ☺10am-7pm; ☐Big Blue Bus line 18) One of our favorite shops on Abbot Kinney deals in quality aromatherapy candles, art books, a smattering of boho-chic attire for ladies, fair-trade beach bags from India and beaded jewelry. It serves tots at the kid's store two doors down.

South Bay Beaches

When you've had all the Hollywood ambition, artsy pretension, velvet ropes and mind-numbing traffic you can take, head south of the airport, where this string of beach towns along Santa Monica Bay will soothe that mess from your psyche in one sunset. Buff volleyballers brush elbows with well-to-do University of Southern California (USC) alumni and an increasingly interesting restaurant scene.

◉ Sights

No matter what you do in the South Bay, you're never far from the water. Whether it's biking the strand in Manhattan or Hermosa Beaches, playing the arcade by Redondo Beach Pier, or driving with inspirational ocean views in Palos Verdes, the vast Pacific is always there.

Manhattan Beach
AREA

(www.citymb.info; ☐MTA 126, 439) If Manhattan Beach had its own magazine, it would surely be called *Gorgeous Living*. Classy beachside cottages, bougainvillea-lined walk streets, bustling sidewalk patios, friendly boutiques, surfers silhouetted against the setting sun over the ocean, and babies who never seem to cry – all within half a mile of a portrait-worthy pier. It's that impossibly perfect.

Its downtown area along Manhattan Beach Blvd has seen an explosion of trendy restaurants, boutiques and hotels, yet it remains a serene seaside enclave with prime surf on either side of the pier.

Hermosa Beach   AREA

Strolling down Hermosa Beach's Pier Ave on a summer weekend, you're immediately struck by two things: everybody's wearing flip-flops, tiny tees and a tan, and they all seem to be having way too much fun. The short, car-free strip is party central in a small town (within a big town) that's always lived the easy life.

Once home to long-haired hippies and underground punk bands such as Black Flag, it's now solidly ruled by USC frat boys and sorority girls, financially challenged, hormone-crazed surfers and the beautiful people who love them all. Rents are lower here than in Manhattan Beach, and the scene trashier, but that's part of the charm.

Hermosa's beach is indeed *muy hermosa* (Spanish for 'beautiful') – long, flat and dotted with permanent volleyball nets. Go to 16th St to see local pros bump, set and spike in preparation for the AVP Hermosa Open in August. And if you prefer a cool, casual distance from the Pier Ave fracas, just belly up to one of the town's epic dives.

Redondo & Torrance Beaches   AREA

Redondo Beach is a working-class beach town, the largest in the South Bay and the most ethnically diverse. As it wanders inland it bleeds into neighboring Torrance, where there's a huge Japanese influence, especially from car manufacturers' US headquarters. Redondo's heart is at King Harbor, where the dated **pier** (www.redondopier.com; 100 W Torrance Blvd, Redondo Beach; P) is still an excursion-worthy detour on your way south to an absurdly beautiful coastline. Around Redondo's southern end, framed by the Palos Verdes Peninsula, is the Riviera neighborhood.

★ Abalone Cove Shoreline Park   BEACH

(www.rpvca.gov/Facilities/Facility/Details/Abalone-Cove-Shoreline-Park-1; Palos Verdes Dr, Palos Verdes; parking first 30min/2hr/daily max free/$6/12; ◎9am-dusk, parking lot 9am-4pm; P ⚑) The best place to hunt for starfish, anemones and other tide-pool critters is in and around this rock-strewn eco-preserve. The walk down to the beach gets pretty steep in some sections, so watch your footing. Note: as we went to press parts of the cove were shut due to erosion. Check website for latest.

★ Wayfarers Chapel   CHURCH

(☑310-377-1650; www.wayfarerschapel.org; 5755 Palos Verdes Dr S, Palos Verdes; ◎10am-5pm, grounds open at 9am; P) The most stunning non-natural attraction on Palos Verdes was built by Lloyd Wright (son of Frank) in 1951, and no matter where you stand among the great saints, this place will touch your soul. It's a glass church cradled by soaring redwood trees. Not surprisingly, it's a popular spot to tie the knot, so avoid coming on weekends.

South Coast Botanic Garden   GARDENS

(☑310-544-1948; www.southcoastbotanicgarden. org; 26300 Crenshaw Blvd, Palos Verdes; adult/student/child 5-12yr $9/6/4; ◎9am-5pm; P) It's hard to believe that this 87-acre, flowering and fruiting, sprouting and sprawling blast of life (we're talking around 2000 species) was reclaimed from former landfill. Plant shows and sales take place year-round. Themed gardens include Mediterranean, rose, drought-friendly (always an issue in California), herb, Japanese and more.

Point Vicente Interpretive Center   VIEWPOINT

(☑310-377-5370; www.rpvca.gov/Facilities/Facility/Details/Point-Vicente-Interpretive-Center-13; 31501 Palos Verdes Dr W, Rancho Palos Verdes; donations appreciated; ◎10am-5pm; P ⚑) FREE Binocular-toting whale watchers gather north of the adjacent **lighthouse** (www.palosverdes. com/pvlight; 31550 Palos Verdes Dr W, Rancho Palos Verdes; ◎lighthouse museum 10am-3pm 2nd Sat each month; P) FREE between December and April when Pacific gray whales embark on their fascinating and arduous migration from Alaska to Mexico. Inside are fun exhibits for boning up on the specifics. You'll also glimpse giant mako shark fossils and Tongva ceramics and arrowheads. Picnic beneath palm trees and stroll along the bluff-top trail.

🏃 Activities

Palos Verdes Peninsula   SCENIC DRIVE

(Palos Verdes Dr, Palos Verdes; ⚑) For awesome eyefuls of stunning shoreline, take this scenic drive. From Redondo Beach, take Palos Verdes Blvd and turn right at Palos Verdes Dr W. Follow it as steep cliffs tumble to rocky shores and secluded coves as the roadway ribbons past rambling multi-million-dollar mansions (the street becomes Palos Verdes Dr S).

The route ends at Point Fermin Park (p199) in San Pedro, where Catalina Island looms across the sparkling Pacific, and near the White Point Nature Preserve (p199) and **Royal Palms Beach** (http://beaches.lacounty.gov/white-point-royal-palms-beach; 1799 Paseo del Mar, San Pedro; P 🚻).

Nikau Kai WATER SPORTS
(Manhattan Beach; 🗐 310-545-7007; www.nikaukai.com; 1300 N Highland Ave; lessons private $90-95, semi-private $70-75, group lessons $55-60, surfboard rentals per hour/day $15/40, SUP rentals per hour/day $35/65, wetsuit rentals $15; ⊙10am-6pm Mon-Fri, 9am-7pm Sat & Sun) Just across the street from Uncle Bill's (p195) you'll find this terrific surf shop with board shorts and tees, flip-flops and boards. It runs SUP and surf rentals and lessons, which are an hour long. Book them a day in advance.

Hermosa Cyclery CYCLING
(🗐 310-374-7816; www.hermosacyclery.com; 20 13th St, Hermosa Beach; bike rental per hour/day from $8/24; ⊙9am-7pm; 🚻) Get your cruisers, six-speeds, boogie boards and beach chairs by the hour or day. Rates are competitive and the quality is high.

🛏 Sleeping

From dignified oceanside resorts to hostels for party people, the South Bay offers a good variety of lodging for most budgets, including some beachside bargains.

Surf City Hostel HOSTEL $
(🗐 310-798-2323; www.surfcityhostel.com; 26 Pier Ave, Hermosa Beach; dm/r Oct–mid-Jun from $27/70, mid-Jun–Sep from $45/92; ⊛@🛜; 🖵) Steps from the sand, the halls of this convivial hostel with a newly renovated kitchen offer mostly co-ed four- and six-person dorms. Even the private rooms have shared baths. If you're looking to spend your days beaching and your nights partying, this is your place.

Redondo Inn & Suites MOTEL $
(🗐 310-540-1888; www.redondoinn.com; 711 S Pacific Coast Hwy, Redondo Beach; r from $89; P🛜) Rooms aren't huge at this simple motor hotel, but it's fresh and clean, the bathroom tiles sparkle, there's a mini-fridge and microwave in rooms, staff are helpful and it's just two blocks from the beach.

Miyako Hybrid Hotel BOUTIQUE HOTEL $$
(🗐 310-212-5111; www.miyakohybridhotel.com; 21381 S Western Ave, Torrance; r from $119; P⊛@🛜) 🍃 This friendly, sophisticated, Japanese-owned hotel is slice of Tokyo in downtown Torrance. The inland location (near Honda's US headquarters) isn't close to much tourist stuff and attracts suits midweek, but it has a commendable sustainable ethos (recycled wallpaper, recyclable carpeting and solar power), plus only-in-Japan touches such as deep-soaking tubs, robo-toilets and spa with hot-stone sauna.

Portofino Hotel & Yacht Club HOTEL $$
(🗐 310-379-8481; www.hotelportofino.com; 260 Portofino Way, Redondo Beach; r $189-259; P@⊛🛜☀) This '60s property on its own peninsula north of the Redondo Pier blends urban sophistication with nautical light-heartedness. Get an ocean-side room with a balcony for watching the sunset and an adorable sea-lion colony. Marina-facing views overlook not only boats, but also a power plant, partially hidden behind a Wyland whale mural.

Belamar Hotel HOTEL $$
(🗐 310-750-0300; www.thebelamar.com; 3501 Sepulveda Blvd, Manhattan Beach; r from $187; P⊝❄🛜☀) A mile from Manhattan Beach and 10 minutes' drive from the airport, the 127-room Belamar is a bit off the beaten track on busy Sepulveda Blvd, so it's often overlooked. Still, decent rates buy stylish rooms with sea-blue accents and aromatherapy bath products, plus easy access to a nature trail to the beach for jogging off your jet lag.

Sea View Inn MOTEL $$
(🗐 310-545-1504; www.seaview-inn.com; 3400 N Highland Ave, Manhattan Beach; r $175-275, apt & ste $200-375; P❄🛜☀) This one-time motel turned boutique spans all four corners of Highland Ave and 34th St with luxurious, ocean-facing rooms on the west side, and nicely appointed rooms on the east side. All of them are just uphill from the beach, and it offers free bikes, beach chairs and boogie-board rentals.

Sea Sprite Motel MOTEL $$
(🗐 310-376-6933; www.seaspritemotel.com; 1016 The Strand, Hermosa Beach; r $149-199, ste from $199, higher prices mid-May–mid-Sep; P⊝🛜☀) The rooms here are pretty simple, but they come with full kitchen, or kitchenette and wood furnishings, and the location – right on the beach, overlooking the bustling Strand – could not be better, especially at this price.

★ Terranea RESORT $$$
(🗐 866-547-3066; www.terranea.com; 100 Terranea Way, Palos Verdes; r from $395; P⊝❄@🛜☀☀) Nature trails wrap this 120-acre property, skirt the wild coast and are open

to the public at LA's best five-star beach resort. Rooms are flooded with natural light and have been designed in classic California style, and even the smallest are spacious at 450 sq ft – 92% of them have ocean views.

Free activities for guests include nature walks and a meet-and-greet with the resort's own falconer. Paid activities include SUP, cycling excursions and painting classes.

Even if you don't stay here, it's worth stopping to stroll the grounds and enjoy a meal or drink at one of the eight restaurants and bars (chic and costly **mar'sel** is our favorite for Sunday brunch). Or come for a treatment at the spa – the Terranea Seaside Renewal uses salt scrub from the local shores. Or you might want to shoot a round on the nine-hole golf course.

Overnight guest parking is $38.

Fun fact: Terranea was once the domain of trick sea mammals, on the site of the old Marineland water park.

★ **Shade Hotel**   BOUTIQUE HOTEL **$$$**
(☑ 310-546-4995; www.shadehotel.com; 1221 N Valley Dr, Manhattan Beach; r from $350; P ☺ ✿ @ ☎ ☎ ☎) Look for cool, subdued craftsman-inspired design with splashes of color. All rooms have outdoor space and marble bathrooms with spa tubs big enough for two; sliding frosted-glass doors give you privacy (or not, as you wish!). Downstairs rooms have daybeds; top-floor rooms have fireplaces. The beach is just three blocks away and the Zinc Lounge bar is buzzy.

★ **Beach House at**
Hermosa Beach   BOUTIQUE HOTEL **$$$**
(☑ 310-374-3001, 888-895-4559; www.beach-house.com; 1300 The Strand, Hermosa Beach; r from $299; P ☺ ✿ ☎; ☐ MTA 130, 439) ✈ This upscale beachfront inn epitomizes California's laid-back lifestyle. Open the balcony door of your lofty ocean-view suite to let in the ocean breezes, soak in a deep, warm tub, or fall asleep to the light of a gas fireplace. There's a fitness center and a Jacuzzi with a **Bo Bridges** (☑ 310-937-3764; www.bobridgesgallery.com; 1108 Manhattan Ave, Manhattan Beach; ☺ 11am-7pm, extended hours in summer) mural.

✗ **Eating**

There are some serious gems to be had in the South Bay dining scene. In Manhattan Beach, the area around Manhattan Ave and Manhattan Beach Blvd is a particularly

happy hunting ground for upscale restaurant browsers, while the Riviera Village neighborhood on the south side of Redondo Beach is a little more midrange. Don't overlook the Japanese eateries and markets in Torrance, which are there largely to serve employees of the Japanese auto manufacturers headquartered nearby.

Local Place   HAWAIIAN **$**
(☑ 310-523-3233; www.thelocalplace.com; 18605 S Western Ave, Torrance; mains $6.75-10.50; ☺ 7am-9pm Sun-Thu, to 10pm Fri & Sat; P ☎) King's Hawaiian Bakery is beloved in these parts for its sweet bread rolls and day-glo cakes, and its sister, counter-service restaurant sells sandwiches and lunches to match. *Loco moco* is a lovable mess of burgers, eggs, brown gravy and rice, *lau lau* are like Hawaiian pork or salmon tamales stuffed, and the *kalua* pork sandwich is so wrong it's right.

Standing Room   BURGERS, KOREAN **$**
(☑ 310-374-7575; www.thestandingroomrestaurant.com; 144 N Catalina Ave, Redondo Beach; burgers & sandwiches $8-18.50, plates $16-20; ☺ 11am-9:30pm Mon-Sat, noon-8pm Sun) South Bay heads who know descend on this tiny Korean-American fusion takeout grill, built into the back of a liquor store with a few outdoor tables. It specializes in burgers and re-imagines other greasy-spoon delights. The massive Napoleon comes topped with bacon, three cheeses, greens, fried egg, braised short rib, Korean aioli *and* truffle parmesan fries – whew!

Green Temple   VEGETARIAN **$**
(www.greentemple.net; 1700 S Catalina Ave, Redondo Beach; appetizers $5-12, mains $10-16; ☺ 11am-4pm & 5-9pm Tue-Thu, to 10pm Fri & Sat, 9am-4pm & 5-9pm Sun; ☑) ✈ Sit in the flowery courtyard, or amid the Asian-inspired atmosphere, at this sanctuary where meat is a no-no and organic, local produce is plentiful. Salads, including the tasty Sproutada, come with a slice of homemade walnut bread. Folks come back for the organic tofu sauce, served on dishes such as white lasagna and tostaditas.

Uncle Bill's Pancake House   DINER **$**
(☑ 310-545-5177; www.unclebills.net; 1305 N Highland Ave, Manhattan Beach; dishes $8-15; ☺ 6am-3pm Mon-Fri, from 7am Sat & Sun; ☎) Grab a stool, a booth or, better yet, an ocean-view table at this tiny, greet-the-day, intimate South Bay

institution. Sexy surfers, tottering toddlers and gabbing girlfriends – everybody's here for the famous pancakes and big fat omelets (try the 'Istanbul' made with turkey). Put your name on the list – the wait's worth it.

Martha's 22nd St Grill
DINER $

(☑ 310-376-7786; 25 22nd St, Hermosa Beach; dishes $6-13; ⊙ 7am-3pm; 🖩) Locals swear by the eggs at this unassuming beachside patio joint. It does sandwiches such as the Monte Cristo and salads too, but the eight varieties of Benedict eggs and omelettes, stuffed with veggies, havarti, avocado, bacon, cheddar, hummus, sun-dried tomatoes and goat cheese are the draw.

★ Fishing with Dynamite
SEAFOOD $$

(☑ 310-893-6299; www.eatfwd.com; 1148 Manhattan Ave, Manhattan Beach; oysters from $3, dishes $9-26; ⊙ 11:30am-10pm Mon-Wed, to 10:30pm Thu & Fri, 10am-10:30pm Sat, 10am-10pm Sun) You'll love this tiny, modernist place for its oysters, raw bar and menu mixing 'old school' (chowder, crab cakes) and 'new school' (miso black cod, serrano scallops seared and garnished with uni). The menu is constantly shifting, but trust us, if you like binge eating on fine seafood, starve yourself for a day, then come here. It has cocktails that rock, and the bar stays open late.

★ Abigaile
PUB FOOD $$

(☑ 310-798-8227; www.abigailerestaurant.com; 1301 Manhattan Ave, Hermosa Beach; dishes $10-30; ⊙ 5pm-late Mon-Fri, from 11am Sat & Sun) Hermosa's gastropub deluxe, in a space that used to be a church and, later, punk rock band Black Flag's rehearsal space. History continues with a graffiti wall and equally anarchic daily-changing menu divided into 'swimmers', 'carnage', 'ruffage' and, um, 'plats principaux': dishes such as PIG pop tarts (smoked pork confit, bacon and Gruyère in puff pastry), escargot poppers and pho-poached chicken salad.

Dia De Campo
MEXICAN $$

(☑ 310-379-1829; www.diadecampohb.com; 1238 Hermosa Ave, Hermosa Beach; lunch mains $12-14, dinner mains $18-25, large plates $35-40; ⊙ 11:30am-10pm Mon-Thu, to 1am Fri-Sun, brunch from 11am Sat & Sun) The most refined joint in Hermosa, this upscale Mexican kitchen does mole scallops, braised lamb nachos and chorizo-stuffed dates, and has a full raw bar, including eight varieties of ceviche. Lunchtime features bowls such as grilled ahi or albacore, and 'sandos' like *carne asada*. The

interior is classy with red leather bar stools and mod picnic-table booths.

Locale 90
PIZZA $$

(☑ 310-540-9190; www.locale90.com; 1718 S Catalina Ave, Redondo Beach; pizzas & salads $10-16; ⊙ 11:30am-3pm & 5-9pm Mon-Thu, 11:30am-10pm Fri & Sat, to 9pm Sun; 🖩) Families gather in this brick and dark-wood spot in the Hollywood Riviera for pizzas served *rossa* (with red sauce) or *bianca* (white), such as the classic margherita, caprese with pesto and pine nuts, or the deceptively simple cotto, with cream, tomato and basil. It's family-run, and the chef is from Sicily.

Fishbar
SEAFOOD $$

(☑ 310-796-0200; www.fishbarmb.com; 3801 Highland Ave, Manhattan Beach; mains $13-30; ⊙ 11am-11pm Mon-Thu, to 1am Fri, 9am-1am Sat, 9am-11pm Sun; 🖩) Aficionados of old-school fish houses will enjoy this divey joint near Manhattan Beach's north end, decked out with rattan furnishings, aquariums and flat-screen TVs. The menu includes seared tuna and lobster tacos (cheap on Taco Tuesday, one of several daily-changing specials), 10 varieties of mesquite grilled fish and a high-flying surf and turf. It's popular for weekend brunch.

Petros
GREEK $$

(☑ 310-545-4100; www.petrosrestaurant.com; 451 Manhattan Beach Blvd, Manhattan Beach; mains lunch $10-20, dinner $19-39; ⊙ 11am-11pm Mon-Thu, to midnight Fri, 10am-midnight Sat, to 11pm Sun; 🅿) Finally a Greek restaurant for the 21st century, on a comfortably modern courtyard. There's a feta-encrusted rack of lamb, a smoky eggplant and walnut dip, and people cross town for its *avgolemono* soup (lemon chicken and rice). Grab a seat on the people-watching patio, or lose the baseball cap for a dress-code-worthy experience indoors.

★ MB Post
FUSION $$$

(☑ 310-545-5405; www.eatmbpost.com; 1142 Manhattan Ave, Manhattan Beach; small plates $9-13, mains $11-39; ⊙ 5-10pm Mon-Thu, 11:30am-10:30pm Fri, 10am-10:30pm Sat, 10am-10pm Sun; 🖩) There's a lot to love here, from the reclaimed wood-paneled exterior to the exposed rafters and wood-block common tables where you'll munch pomegranate couscous with lavender feta, house-cured charcuterie, oak-grilled squid, pomegranate couscous, charcuterie and cheeses such as house-made ricotta, and the Elvis dessert (chocolate pudding, peanut butter mousse and bacon). The bacon cheddar buttermilk biscuits have their own Facebook page.

Strand House
FUSION $$$

(☏ 310-545-7470; www.thestrandhousemb.com; 117 Manhattan Beach Blvd, Manhattan Beach; mains $24-44; ☺5pm-late Mon, 11:30am-3pm & 5pm-late Tue-Fri, 10am-late Sat & Sun) A splashy place perched a block from the sand with three floors dedicated to dining and drinking, and floor-to-ceiling windows revealing the Pacific. Start with a Korean pork belly with kimchi, and finish with branzino in black truffle risotto or a New York strip and creamed broccolini. It's ambitious and packed on weekends.

★ Standing Room
BURGERS, KOREAN

(☏ 310-318-1272; www.thestandingroomrestaurant.com; 1320 Hermosa Ave, Hermosa Beach; mains $8-20; ☺11am-10pm Mon-Thu, until 1am Fri, 8am-1am Sat, 8am-10pm Sun; ▣) New brick-and-mortar incarnation of the gourmet fave, Korean-fusion burger stand (p195) that started in Redondo Beach. It's a hipster-cool spot for the Cash burger (shishito pepper, bacon, American and cheddar cheeses, crispy onion strings, Korean aioli, hoisin barbecue), the gooey, massive Napoleon and adventurous plate meals. On Saturdays and Sundays, it does a Hawaiian-inflected brunch – *kalua* pork omelet, anyone?

🍷 Drinking & Nightlife

The South Bay offers amusements from dive bars and ocean-view extravaganzas to one of LA's best comedy clubs.

Old Tony's
BAR

(Tony's On The Pier; ☏ 310-374-1442; www.oldtonys.com; 210 Fishermans Wharf, Redondo Beach; ☺11:30am-10pm Sun-Thu, to 11pm Fri & Sat) This holdover from 1952 is as cool as the Redondo Pier gets, with its classic neon sign, 360-degree views from the glass octagonal lounge upstairs and waves crashing below the long, terracotta bar downstairs. Both have gas fireplaces roaring and local barflies buzzing. The food (seafood, Italian) is whatever. Have a beverage.

Smog City Brewing Co.
BREWERY

(☏ 310-320-7664; www.smogcitybrewing.com; 1901 Del Amo Blvd, Torrance; ☺tap room & tours 3-10pm Tue-Thu, noon-10pm Fri & Sat, noon-8pm Sun) Despite its nondescript Torrance office-park location, this family-run craft brewery is making waves in the LA culinary scene. It has a tap room where you can taste experimental and unreleased brews alongside regular offerings such as the Little Bo Pils, Hoptonic IPA, Sabre-tooth Squirrel and Coffee Porter.

Barnacle's
BAR

(☏ 310-798-9064; www.barnaclesbarandgrill.com; 837 Hermosa Ave, Hermosa Beach; ☺11:30am-2am Mon-Thu, from 11am Fri, from 8:30am Sat & Sun) Nestled thankfully off the Pier Ave crush, this decidedly grungy neighborhood joint has friendly (not bubbly) blondes behind the bar, boards (snow, skate, surf) in the rafters, Creedence on the stereo and ball games on the TVs, but you may as well wander outside to the sun patio to gaze at the big blue sea.

Simmzy's Pub
PUB

(www.simmzys.com; 229 Manhattan Beach Blvd; mains $10-14; ☺11am-11pm Mon-Thu, to midnight Fri, 10am-midnight Sat, 10am-11pm Sun) A terrific gastropub with 24 beers on tap. The bacon and blue burger is popular (with blue cheese and carmelized bacon), as are the spice-and-vinegar pulled pork and the Sammy – wood-fired grilled salmon, avocado and buttermilk sauce on a brioche bun.

Ercoles 1101
BAR

(☏ 310-372-1997; http://m.mainstreethub.com/ercoles1101#; 1101 Manhattan Ave, Manhattan Beach; ☺10am-2am) A nice counterpoint to the design-heavy sports bars on Manhattan Beach Blvd. This locals-heavy hole is dark, neon-lit and cozy, the tiles are chipped and faded, there are burgers to munch on, and the barn door has been open to everyone from salty barflies to yuppie pub crawlers to volleyball stars and wobbly co-eds since 1927.

☆ Entertainment

★ Comedy & Magic Club
LOUNGE

(www.comedyandmagicclub.com; 1018 Hermosa Ave; ☺Tue-Sun) Live music and comedy right on the Hermosa strip. It has something going almost every night, including some big names: David Spade, Arsenio Hall, Alonzo Bodden, Jon Lovitz, and 10 – count 'em, 10! – comedians most Fridays and Saturdays. Sunday means Jay Leno live and up close; he's the place's big draw.

Saint Rocke
CONCERT VENUE

(☏ 310-372-0035; www.saintrocke.com; 142 Pacific Coast Hwy, Hermosa Beach; ☺6pm-late

Tue-Sun) The South Bay's best live-music venue lies within a dated brick house with nightly live bands ranging from the up-and-coming to the past-their-prime and still doing it well.

🛍 Shopping

★ **Stars Antique Market**　ANTIQUES
(www.starsantiquemarket.com; 526 Pier Ave, Hermosa Beach; ⊙11am-6pm Mon-Sat, to 5pm Sun) If you dig old stuff, weird stuff and weird old stuff, stop by this old barn crammed with Brunswick record players and Hammond typewriters. There are vintage watches, china, glassware, signage, furniture, lanterns and chandeliers. It's a terrific browse.

Daiso Japan　GIFTS & SOUVENIRS
(☎424-558-3646; www.daisojapan.com; 21557 S Western Ave, Torrance; ⊙10am-9pm Mon-Sat, to 8pm Sun) In Japan, 100 yen stores are the counterpart to dollar stores, except filled with ingenious stuff. In this Japanese part of Torrance, this shop sells most items for $1.50, from the everyday to the irrepressibly cute: animal-shaped hats, notebooks, minimalist white dishes, Japanese folk toys and sushi key rings, snacks from Japan and thousands more items.

Long Beach & San Pedro

Long Beach and San Pedro straddle the LA River and together form the ports of Los Angeles and Long Beach, America's first and second busiest respectively, but they're about a lot more than shipping.

Long Beach has come a long way since its working-class, port, oil rig and navy days. California's seventh-largest city in population (SoCal's third-largest), its star attractions are the Aquarium of the Pacific and retired ocean liner Queen Mary, while the Museum of Latin American Art stages consistently high-quality shows. Elsewhere, **Retro Row** (www.4thstreetlongbeach.com; 4th St btwn Junipero St & Cherry Ave, Long Beach) and the East Village Arts District (p201) provide a more local, chill city vibe. Long Beach is also home to America's largest Cambodian community.

On any given (not just) Saturday night, the restaurants, clubs and bars along lower Pine Ave and the upscale loft district the Promenade are abuzz with everyone from buttoned-down conventioneers to hipsters, the testosterone-fueled frat pack and diners in big-chain eateries in waterside **Shoreline Village**, the departure point for boat cruises.

Across the LA River, just northwest of Long Beach, the neighborhood of San Pedro (San *Pee*-dro) has retained its working-class harbor-town feel. The area around San Pedro Bay is gradually being redeveloped as the **LA Waterfront**, trying to appeal to both locals and passengers from the numerous cruise ships docking here, with attractions such as the Battleship Iowa.

A couple miles west, the area around Point Fermin Park and the historic Fort MacArthur provide inspirational views of the ocean, Catalina Island and southeast all the way to Orange Country.

◉ Sights

★ **Aquarium of the Pacific**　AQUARIUM
(Map p200; ☎tickets 562-590-3100; www.aquariumofpacific.org; 100 Aquarium Way, Long Beach; adult/senior/child $30/27/19; ⊙9am-6pm; 🅿️♿) Long Beach's most mesmerizing experience, the Aquarium of the Pacific is a vast, high-tech indoor ocean where sharks dart, jellyfish dance and sea lions frolic. More than 11,000 creatures inhabit four re-created habitats: the bays and lagoons of Baja California, the frigid northern Pacific, tropical coral reefs and local kelp forests.

In the Shark Lagoon, you can pet young sharks in a touch pool and go nose-to-nose – through a window – with their adult-sized cousins patrolling a larger tank.

There's also a popular penguin habitat.

Elsewhere, you'll be entertained by the antics of sea otters, spooked by football-sized crabs with spiny 3ft-long arms, and charmed by Seussian-looking sea dragons. The Ocean Science Center shows films and live video feeds of environmental phenomena.

It's a wondrous world that'll easily keep you enthralled for a few hours.

The best time to be here is during the daily feeding sessions (check the schedule online or in the lobby). On weekdays, avoid the field-trip frenzy by arriving around 2pm; on weekends beat the crowd by getting here as early as possible.

For an extra fee, the aquarium offers behind-the-scenes tours and ocean-boat trips. Or, for $299 per person, divers with open water certification can enter the tropical reef tank (reservation required); all equipment is provided including the underwater camera.

Parking is $8 with validation. Look for discounted combination tickets with other attractions such as the Los Angeles Zoo and Battleship Iowa.

★ Battleship Iowa   MUSEUM, MEMORIAL

(☑877-446-9261; www.pacificbattleship.com; Berth 87, 250 S Harbor Blvd, San Pedro; adult/senior/child $20/17/12; ⏱10am-5pm, last entry 4pm; P ♿ ; ⏚Metro Silver Line) This WWII to Cold War–era battleship is now permanently moored in San Pedro Bay and open to visitors as a museum. It's massive – 887ft long (that's 5ft longer than *Titanic*) and about as tall as an 18-story building. Step onto the gangway and download the app to take a self-guided audio tour of everything from the stateroom where FDR stayed to missile turrets and the enlisted men's galley, which churned out 8000 hot meals a day during WWII.

Queen Mary   SHIP

(Map p200; ☑877-342-0738; www.queenmary.com; 1126 Queens Hwy, Long Beach; tours adult/child from $27/17.50; ⏱tours 10am-6pm or later; P ♿ ; ⏚Passport, ⏚AquaBus, AquaLink) Long Beach's 'flagship' attraction is this grand – and supposedly haunted! – British luxury liner. Larger and more luxurious than even the *Titanic*, she transported royals, dignitaries, immigrants, WWII troops and vacationers between 1936 and 1966 and has been moored here since 1967. Sure it's a tourist trap, but spend time with the memorabilia and you may envision dapper gents escorting ladies in gowns to the art-deco lounge for cocktails, or to the sumptuous Sir Winston's for dinner.

Basic admission, aka the Queen Mary Passport, includes a 4-D theater screening and either the Glory Days Historical Tour or the hokey Haunted Encounters special-effects tour, which features strange apparitions in the 1st-class swimming pool and the boiler room.

Various other tours and packages are also available. Combination tickets with the Aquarium of the Pacific cost $45/29 per adult/child, or $39/23 for combos with the Battleship Iowa. Parking costs $18 ($8 with restaurant validation), and opening hours can vary seasonally; check the website for times before you visit.

For the full treatment, consider staying for the night in one of its staterooms (p202). At least pop in for a drink at the art-deco Observation Bar (p203).

The Cold War–era Soviet submarine Scorpion (p201) is moored next door.

★ Museum of Latin American Art   MUSEUM

(Map p200; ☑562-437-1689; www.molaa.org; 628 Alamitos Ave, Long Beach; adult/senior & student/child $10/7/free, Sun free; ⏱11am-5pm Wed, Thu, Sat & Sun, to 9pm Fri; P) This gem of a museum is the only one in the US to present art created since 1945 in Latin America and in Latino communities in the US, in important temporary and traveling exhibits. Blockbuster shows have recently included Caribbean art and the works of LA's own Frank Romero.

Point Fermin Park & Around   PARK

(San Pedro) Locals come to this grassy community park on the bluffs to jog, picnic, watch wind- and kitesurfers, cool off in the shade of spreading magnolias, gaze at the silhouette of Catalina Island, wonder at never-ending waves pounding a rugged crescent coastline and enjoy live jazz on balmy summer Sundays.

In the park is the Point Fermin Lighthouse, and nearby are Fort MacArthur Military Museum, Korean Friendship Bell and the aging biker bar, Walker's Cafe (p204).

Fort MacArthur Military Museum   MUSEUM

(☑310-548-2631; www.ftmac.org; 3601 S Gaffey St, Angels Gate Park, San Pedro; suggested donation adult/child $5/3; ⏱noon-5pm Tue, Thu, Sat & Sun; P ♿) Just north of Point Fermin and west

WHITE POINT NATURE PRESERVE & BEACH

A former Nike missile site has gone back to nature in the White Point Nature Preserve (☑310-541-7613; www.pvplc.org; 1600 W Paseo del Mar, San Pedro; ⏱dawn-dusk, nature center 10am-4pm Wed, Sat & Sun; P ♿), which protects 102-acres of coastal sage-scrub habitat. Hiking trails run from from 0.8 miles to a 7-mile loop, and there are monthly children's programs, guided naturalist hikes, bird walks and plant sales, all from the preserve's nature education center.

Across the street, the county-run White Point-Royal Palms Beach has 1.5 miles of rocky shoreline and 30 acres of parkland. You can scramble among tide pools to see sea anemones and other wildlife, although it's not a good swimming beach due to the rocky shore.

Long Beach

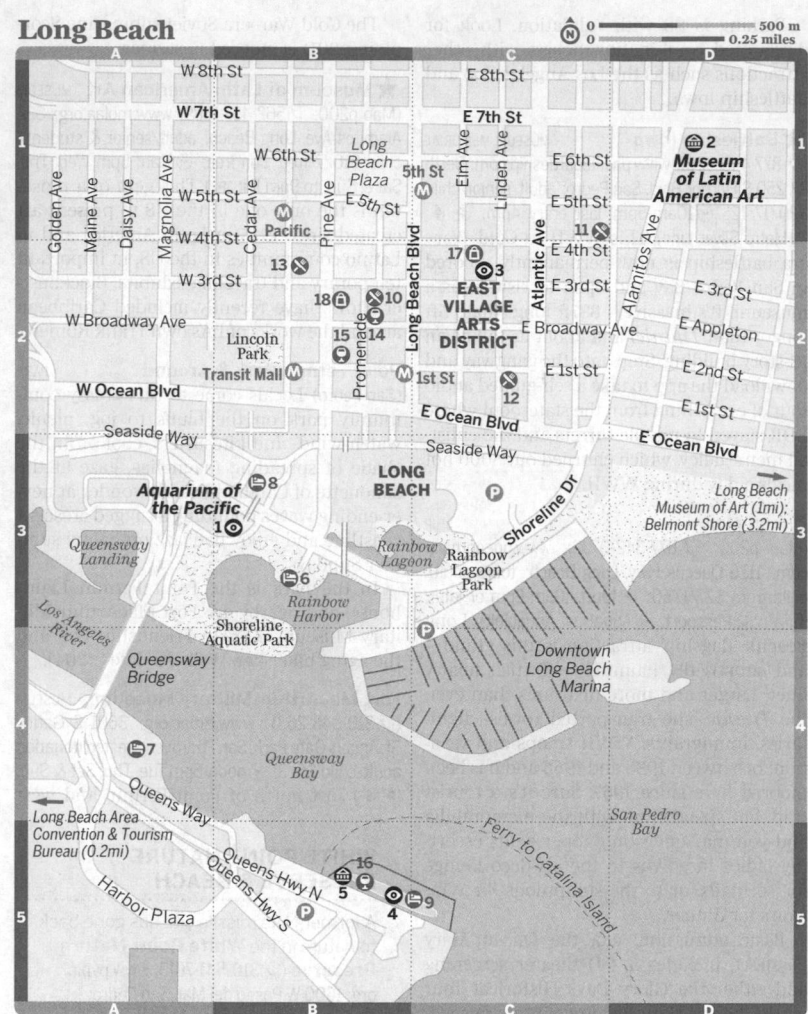

of the Korean Friendship Bell, this rambling, 20-acre facility was an LA harbor defensive post until 1945, as well as LA air-defense headquarters until 1975. Indoor galleries showcase this history, but we find it even more interesting to enter gun batteries and search for secret tunnels on the sprawling hillside with impressive views of the ocean.

Korean Friendship Bell
LANDMARK

(www.kccla.org; 3601 S Gaffey St, San Pedro; ◎10am-6pm; P🚇) A gift from South Korea for the US bicentennial in 1976, this nearly 12ft-tall, 18.75 ton bronze chime dominates the hillside and

makes for a fantastic lookout point. The bell is suspended inside a pagoda-style pavilion intricately painted in the traditional Korean, multicolored *dancheong* style.

It's adjacent to Fort MacArthur Museum and just uphill from Point Fermin Park.

Cabrillo Marine Aquarium
AQUARIUM

(☎310-548-7562; www.cabrillomarineaquarium. org; 3720 Stephen M White Dr, San Pedro; suggested donation adult/child & senior $5/1; ◎noon-5pm Tue-Fri, from 10am Sat & Sun; P🚇) This city-owned aquarium is the smaller, older, low-tech cousin of Long Beach's Aquarium of the

Long Beach

Pacific. It's also a lot lighter on your wallet and less overwhelming for small children. Spiky urchins, slippery sea cucumbers, magical jellyfish and other local denizens will bring smiles to even the most iPad-jaded youngster.

East Village Arts District　　　　AREA
(Map p200; www.eastvillagelongbeach.com; btwn Ocean Blvd, 7th St, Long Beach Blvd & Alamitos Ave, Long Beach) Don't get overly excited just because the words 'East Village' and 'Arts' happen to appear in the same sentence. Still, this rather small corner of downtown Long Beach does have a funky feel, with some groovy cafes, restaurants and boutiques to explore.

The East Village tends to be most lively during the **2nd Saturday Art Walk** (www.artwalklb.com; East Village, Long Beach; ⊙4-10pm 2nd Sat each month).

Scorpion　　　　MUSEUM
(Map p200; adult/child $14/12) This Cold War–era Soviet submarine is moored alongside the Queen Mary (p199). As you scramble around, imagine how 78 crew shared 27 bunks and two bathrooms, often for months at a time...definitely not for the claustrophobic.

Point Fermin Lighthouse　　　　LIGHTHOUSE
(☑310-241-0684; www.pointferminlighthouse.org; Point Fermin Park, 807 W Paseo Del Mar, San Pedro; ⊙1-4pm Tue-Sun; 🅿) **FREE** Ostensibly the main visitor attraction in Point Fermin Park (p199) is this restored 1874 lighthouse, which looks like a Victorian home and is one of the oldest lighthouses in the West. The first keepers of the light were trailblazing sisters Mary and Ellen Smith.

It's accessible by guided tour at 1pm, 2pm and 3pm. Admission is free, but visitors are requested to make a donation.

Los Angeles Maritime Museum　　　　MUSEUM
(☑310-548-7618; www.lamaritimemuseum.org; Berth 84, San Pedro; adult/senior/child $5/3/free; ⊙10am-5pm Tue-Sun; 🅿🚹) Galleries in LA's historic ferry building (on the National Register of Historic Places) tell the story of the city's relationship with the sea and display enough ship models, deep-sea-diving dioramas, figureheads and navigational equipment to keep your imagination afloat for an hour or so.

Long Beach Museum of Art　　　　MUSEUM
(☑562-439-2119; www.lbma.org; 2300 E Ocean Blvd, Long Beach; adult/seniors & students/child $7/6/free, Fri free; ⊙11am-8pm Thu, to 5pm Fri-Sun; 🅿) The beachfront location is breathtaking; permanent collections boast pop art, mid-20th-century furniture and sculpture and some contemporary work; and the restaurant, in a nicely detailed 1912 arts-and-crafts mansion, serves tasty lunches with a ceramics exhibit on the side. You may want to check about special exhibits before heading over.

🛏 Sleeping

Some of the best accommodations in Long Beach are on and around the harbor. Access is a bit easier to shopping, restaurants and nightlife if you're staying on the harbor's north side.

★Hotel Maya　　　　BOUTIQUE HOTEL $$
(Map p200; ☑562-435-7676; www.hotelmayalongbeach.com; 700 Queensway Dr, Long Beach; r from $179; 🅿🅰@🛜🏊🐕) West of the *Queen Mary*, this boutique property hits you with hip immediately upon entering the rusted-steel, glass and magenta-paneled lobby. The feel continues in the 199 rooms (coral tile, river-rock headboards, Mayan-icon accents), set in four 1970s-era hexagons with views of downtown Long Beach that are worth the upcharge.

Queen Mary Hotel
SHIP $$

(Map p200; ☑877-342-0738; www.queenmary.
com; 1126 Queens Hwy, Long Beach; r from $99;
P❋@☎; ☒Passport) There's an irresistible
romance to ocean liners, and this nostal-
gic retreat time warps you to a long-gone,
slower-paced era. Yes, the rooms are small,
but hallways are lined with bird's-eye maple
veneer, period artwork and display cases of
memorabilia from the Cunard days. First-
class staterooms are atmospherically refur-
bished with original art-deco details.

Dockside Boat & Bed
B&B $$

(Map p200; ☑562-436-3111, 800-436-2574; www.
boatandbed.com; Dock 5, Rainbow Harbor, 330 S Pine
Ave, Long Beach; r from $175; ☻☎) Get rocked
to sleep by the waves aboard your choice of
five yachts sleeping three to five people. Each
yacht is different, but all have galley kitchens
and entertainment centers. Boats are moored
right along the waterfront promenade, with
some big restaurants nearby. Continental
breakfast is delivered to your vessel.

Hyatt Centric at the Pike
HOTEL $$$

(Map p200; ☑562-432-1234; www.thepike-
longbeach.centric.hyatt.com; 285 Bay St, Long
Beach; r from $239; P❋@☎☒) This sleek,
splashy hotel is in the Pike Center complex,
a short walk from the aquarium and outlet
shopping. Spacious rooms have modern,
hardwood furniture, ultra comfy beds, bath-
rooms outfitted with streaky marble and
even small sitting areas. We love the rooftop
pool deck with 360-degree views across the
city and harbor.

✖ Eating

Pine Ave, the main drag in downtown Long
Beach, is happy hunting ground for res-
taurants: Italian, Spanish, Greek, seafood,
bagels, burgers and more. A couple blocks
east of Pine Ave, the Promenade is a restau-
rant-lined pedestrian street, while along the
waterfront south of Pine Ave are (mostly
chain) restaurants around Rainbow Harbor.
Hipsters and those who love them will enjoy
the fun, quirky and often-gourmet one-off
eateries of the East Village Arts District and
Retro Row, while 2nd Ave in Belmont Shore
caters to a more upscale crowd of young
families and professionals.

★ Steelcraft
FOOD HALL $

(www.steelcraftlb.com; 3768 Long Beach Blvd, Long
Beach; prices vary by shop; ☉7am-10pm, individual
shop hours vary; P) Shipping containers have

been repurposed with mini-kitchens churn-
ing out burgers (at Pig Pen Delicacy), pizzas
(DeSano), ramen (Tajima), waffles (Waffle
Love), Coffee (Steel Head), craft beer (Smog
City Brewing Co) and more. Order at the
counters, grab a communal-table seat in the
Astroturfed courtyard – your choice of cov-
ered or not – and get grazing.

Phnom Penh Noodle Shack
CAMBODIAN $

(☑310-433-0032; www.thenoodleshack.com;
1644 Cherry Ave, Cambodia Town, Long Beach;
noodles $4.50-8; ☉7am-3pm Tue-Sun; ☒line 22)
First-timers and old Cambodia hands love
this friendly, neat-as-a-pin breakfast and
lunch place on the corner. Choose your noo-
dle type (rice, egg, etc) and it arrives in soup
or stir-fried with your choice of beef, pork,
chicken or seafood. Soups are heady with
cilantro, green onion and garlic.

Omelette Inn
DINER $

(Map p200; ☑562-437-5625; www.omeletteinn
lbc.com; 318 Pine Ave, Long Beach; dishes $7-
14; ☉7am-3pm; ✚) From clerks to cops to
city-council members, *everybody's* got a
soft spot for this unassuming joint where
breakfasts and sandwiches are served in
belt-loosening portions. Build your own
omelettes from more than 40 ingredients,
or pick from tried-and-true menu favorites
such as the Sicilian or Grecian Formula.

★ Fourth & Olive
ALSATIAN $$

(Map p200; ☑562-269-0731; www.4thandolive.
com; 743 E 4th St, East Village, Long Beach; mains
$15-29; ☉4:30-10pm Mon & Tue, 11am-10pm Wed,
Thu & Sun, 11am-11pm Fri & Sat) There's much
to love about this new Cal-French bistro:
farmers-market produce, small-farm-raised
beef and pork, housemade sausages, classic
dishes such as *steak frites* and *choucroute
garnie*, and low-key service, all under a
high-raftered roof with generous windows
to watch the world go by. *And* many of its
staff are disabled veterans, so you're doing
good while eating well.

San Pedro Fish Market & Restaurant
SEAFOOD $$

(☑310-832-4251; www.sanpedrofish.com; 1190
Nagoya Way, San Pedro; meals $9-18; ☉8am-8pm;
P✚) Seafood feasts don't get more decadent
and divey than at this family-run, harbor-view
institution. Buy fresh fish or seafood at the
counter and the price includes cooking. You'll
see entire families gathered around plastic
trays piled high with meaty crabs, plump
shrimp, slimy oysters, melty yellowtail and

tender halibut, spiced and cooked to order with potatoes, tomatoes and peppers.

Lug your tray to a picnic table, fold up your sleeves and dig right in. Don't forget to order some buttery garlic bread and a pile of extra napkins. It's so sprawling, confusingly laid out and often crowded that it can be overwhelming, but it's been in business since the 1950s, and the formula works.

You can save a buck or two next door at **Crusty Crab**, doing the same exact work.

Number Nine   VIETNAMESE $$
(☑562-434-2009; www.numberninenoodles.com; 2118 E 4th St, Retro Row, Long Beach; ⊙11am-9:30pm Sun-Thu, to 10pm Fri & Sat; ⊕; ⊒22) On Retro Row, Vietnamese noodles, banh mi sandwiches and craft beers are served in a spare, minimalist spot (concrete floors, white Formica tables) that looks like it could be an art gallery in other circumstances. Ingredients are free-range, sustainable, grass-fed etc. There's also outdoor seating in a simple pocket park out front.

James Republic   MODERN AMERICAN $$
(Map p200; ☑562-901-0235; www.jamesrepublic. com; 500 E 1st St, East Village, Long Beach; $11-26; ⊙6:30-10:30am Mon-Fri, 10:30am-3pm Sat & Sun, 4-10pm Mon-Sat, 4-9pm Sun) James Republic does farm-to-table New American cooking, though some dishes have an Asian twist. It serves cheese and charcuterie boards, grill cauliflower and steaks, spoon kimchi farro fried rice and foie gras parfait, and makes grass-fed burgers, pastrami sandwiches with Gruyère and beer mustard, and wonderful roast chicken.

Simmzy's   GASTROPUB $$
(☑562-439-5590; www.simmzys.com; 5271 E 2nd St, Belmont Shore, Long Beach; mains $10-16; ⊙11am-11pm Mon-Thu, to midnight Fri, 10am-midnight Sat, 10am-11pm Sun; ⊕) The Belmont Shore branch of this Manhattan Beach favorite (p197). It serves tasty burgers, a terrific salmon sandwich, wood-fired pizzas and a huge craft-beer selection. The design here is special, too. The doors roll up completely to the street for great people-watching and there are butcher-block common tables and a marble bar.

Beachwood BBQ   BARBECUE $$
(Map p200; ☑562-436-4020; www.beachwoodb-bq.com; 210 E 3rd St, East Village, Long Beach; mains $10-24; ⊙11:30am-midnight) This friendly, open spot fronting the Promenade serves up dry-rubbed barbecue brisket, pulled pork, smoked chicken and ribs (try one of the house sauces) and has 22 beers on tap, including award-winning house brews such as the Belgian-style sour. Grab a seat at the bar or on the sunny patio.

🍷 Drinking & Nightlife

Downtown Long Beach, especially along lower Pine Ave and the pedestrianized Promenade, is chockablock with bars, cafes and music joints. Around Retro Row you'll find establishments from coffee houses to live music bars, juice bars and the historic Art Theatre art-house cinema.

★Pike   BAR
(☑562-437-4453; www.pikelongbeach.com; 1836 E 4th St, Long Beach; ⊙11am-2am Mon-Fri, from 9am Sat & Sun; ⊒line 22) Adjacent to Retro Row, this nautical-themed dive bar, owned by Chris Reece of the band Social Distortion, brings in the cool kids for live music acts every night – with no cover, thank you – and serves beer by the pitcher or bottle and cocktails such as the Mezcarita and Greenchelada (a *michelada* with cucumber, jalapeño and lime).

Observation Bar   BAR
(Map p200; ☑562-499-1740; www.queenmary. com/dining-bars/dining-bars/observation-bar; Queen Mary, 1126 Queens Hwy, Long Beach; ⊙4pm-midnight Sun-Thu, 11:30am-2am Fri & Sat) If you like your cocktails with a sidecar of history, the main bar on the *Queen Mary* is the place to be. The ocean liner's one-time 1st-class lounge still has art-deco furniture, art and finishings. Slink into a Singapore sling or a dark and stormy, or a curated selection of beers, wines and classic bar snacks.

★Federal Bar   BAR
(Map p200; ☑562-435-2000; www.lb.thefederal bar.com; 102 Pine Ave, Long Beach; ⊙11:30am-late Mon-Fri, from 10:30am Sat & Sun) This converted, historic bank with its weighty granite bar, crystal chandeliers and burly wooden columns offers a good selection of craft beers and booze. In the downstairs former vault, it hosts DJ nights (soul, funk, hip-hop and more), local bands and the occasional nationally known standouts.

Congregation Ale House   PUB
(Map p200; ☑562-432-2337; www.congregation alehouse.com; 201 E Broadway Ave, Long Beach; ⊙11:30am-1am Mon-Thu, to 2am Fri & Sat, to midnight Sun) A popular pub on the Promenade on the ground floor of a historic building, Congregation Ale House has nearly 30 craft

beers on tap and a nice patio out front. It has decent pub grub, too.

Brouwerij West
BREWERY

(☎ 310-833-9330; www.brouwerijwest.com; 110 E 22nd St, San Pedro; ⏱ 4-9pm Wed & Thu, 3-10pm Fri, noon-10pm Sat, noon-8pm Sun) In San Pedro's old warehouse district, this brewery opens to the public five days a week for tastings from beers such as the Popfuji unfiltered pilsner, Starfish IPA and blueberry-flavored Dog Ate My Homework. Enjoy yours in the cavernous warehouse or on the loading dock, or get selected brews to go by the can, bottle or growler.

Portfolio Coffeehouse
CAFE

(☎ 562-434-2486; www.portfoliocoffeehouse.com; 2300 E 4th St, Retro Row, Long Beach; ⏱ 5:30am-9pm Mon-Fri, 6:30am-9pm Sat & Sun) Portfolio has been supporting the arts, and nurturing Retro Row, since 1990, with poetry readings, art exhibit space and live jazz performances on Fridays and indie bands on Saturdays. Lounge around on mid-century furniture (what else?). The coffee and vittles are pretty great, too: cold brew on tap comes out with a head like Guinness.

Riley's
SPORTS BAR

(☎ 562-856-1612; www.rileyson2nd.com; 5331 E 2nd St, Belmont Shore; ⏱ 11am-midnight Sun-Thu, to 2am Fri & Sat) Local sports freaks and sun worshippers collide at Riley's during big games. Ice-cold beer is poured into massive goblets, the pub grub is decent and the outdoor patio is usually populated.

Salud
JUICE BAR

(☎ 562-528-8444; www.saludjuice.com; 1944 E 4th St, Retro Row, Long Beach; ⏱ 7am-8pm Mon-Fri, from 8am Sat & Sun) There seems to be a juice bar on every LA block, but only this one is owned by the gregarious Angela, who will pound a (spicy ginger) shot with you to cure what ails ya. Other fave juice concoctions include the energy-boosting, lung-clearing Shroot Farm and the immune-boosting Indian Summer.

Walker's Cafe
DINER

(☎ 310-833-3623; 700 Paseo del Mar, San Pedro; ⏱ 9:30am-8pm Tue-Fri, 8:30am-8pm Sat & Sun, opens later Mon) Bessie Walker started selling sandwiches at this classic Americana divey biker bar in 1943, and the place has hardly changed a lick since: sloping linoleum floor, retro jukebox, greasy burgers and cold beers

sold cheap. Sandwiches run $3 to $7.50. *And* it was featured in *Chinatown.*

☆ Entertainment

Art Theatre
CINEMA

(☎ 562-438-5435; www.arttheatrelongbeach.org; 2025 E 4th St, Retro Row, Long Beach; 🚆 Line 22) An anchor of Retro Row, this lovingly restored 1924 art-deco gem is Long Beach's only single-screen cinema, showing a compelling mix of classic and art house cinema, plus *Rocky Horror* Saturdays at midnight. Bonus: you can buy a bottle of wine at the shop next door and take it inside.

🛍 Shopping

Retro Row is one of our favorite shopping strips in all of LA County, where lovers of the *Mad Men* era go to shop in cool specialty shops with goods for the body and the home. Elsewhere, downtown Long Beach, near the convention center, has an evolving retail scene, including the Pike Outlets, where you'll find large national and international retailers such as H&M and Nike.

★ Retro Row
VINTAGE

(www.4thstreetlongbeach.com; 4th St btwn Cherry Ave & Junipero St, Long Beach) Everyone from today's hipsters to Hollywood costumers comes to shop at Retro Row's dozens of vintage stores, cafes, hair salons and happening restaurants.

Made by Millworks
ARTS & CRAFTS, CLOTHING

(Map p200; ☎ 562-584-6233; www.madebymillworks.com; 240 Pine Ave, Long Beach; ⏱ 10am-6pm Sun & Tue-Thu, to 9pm Fri & Sat; Ⓜ Blue Line) This large storefront is laid out like a museum gift shop with the works of some 150 artisans who make or source their wares locally: apparel, soaps, even handmade foods, many with a 21st-century hipster sensibility.

Meow
VINTAGE

(☎ 562-438-8990; www.meowvintage.com; 2210 E 4th St, Retro Row, Long Beach; ⏱ noon-7pm Mon-Fri, 11am-7pm Sat, noon-6pm Sun) If you have time for only one shop on Retro Row, make it this one. The owner has quite an eye, making it hard not to find something you didn't know you needed amid the neatly jumbled aisles of vintage and dead-stock (stuff that never sold first time around) clothing, accessories and home decor.

Meow is also like a museum of vintage signage, and – holy Napoleon Dynamite! – it even makes its own line of tube socks.

In Retrospect
VINTAGE
(📱562-433-6600; www.inretrospect.co; 2122 E 4th St, Retro Row, Long Beach; ⊙noon-7pm Mon-Thu, 11am-8pm Fri & Sat, 11am-6pm Sun; 🚇line 22) At 4000 square feet, In Retrospect feels like a vintage department store: clothing, vinyl, furniture, tableware, even Pez dispensers, most from the 1950s to '70s. If the large collection of silkscreen prints by David Weidman looks familiar, it could be because they were featured on *Mad Men*.

Fingerprints
MUSIC
(Map p200; 📱562-433-4996; www.fingerprints music.com; 420 E 4th St, East Village Arts District, Long Beach; ⊙10am-9pm Sun-Thu, until 10pm Fri & Sat; 🚇Passport Blue Line) An anchor of the East Village Arts District, this beloved record store sells vintage to modern vinyl and CDs and has live in-store performances – book early when big names such as Ryan Adams come through town. Or just chill at the Berlin Bistro coffee shop on site.

Long Beach Outdoor Antique & Collectible Market
MARKET
(www.longbeachantiquemarket.com; Veteran's Memorial Stadium, 4901 E Conant St, Long Beach; admission $6; ⊙6:30am-2pm 3rd Sun of month) Bargains abound at this sprawling market with more than 800 stalls hawking everything from vintage postcards to pottery, and fur to furniture near the Long Beach Airport.

San Fernando Valley

Angelenos think of two things first when it comes to the Valley: major studios and urban sprawl. One, they think, is worth visiting. The other, not so much.

It's true that the Valley does sprawl; car culture was basically invented here, along with the mini-mall, the drive-in movie theater, drive-in bank and drive-in restaurant. But look closer, and you'll see there's a lot more there. This is where the real folk live, making it more laid-back and down to earth than other areas in the city.

⊙ Sights

The Valley's big-ticket items are its studios. Universal Studios (p205) and Warner Bros (p206) open to the public, although in very different ways. Universal is more a theme park, while Warner Bros admits visitors by small-group guided tours. Other highlights are scattered across the Valley, from the

Museum of Neon Art (p206) in Glendale to the **Ronald Reagan Presidential Library** (📱ticketing 805-577-4066; www.reaganfoundation. org; 40 Presidential Dr, Simi Valley; adult/senior/ teen $16/9/13; ⊙10am-5pm; 🅿) in Simi Valley, while to the north, technically in the Santa Clarita Valley, are the hair-raising roller coasters of Six Flags Magic Mountain (p231).

Universal Studios Hollywood
AMUSEMENT PARK
(Map p126; 📱800-864-8377; www.universalstudios hollywood.com; 100 Universal City Plaza, Universal City; admission from $99, child under 3yr free; ⊙daily, hours vary; 🅿🚻; 🚇Red Line to Universal City) Although Universal is one of the world's oldest continuously operating movie studios, the chances of seeing any filming action here, let alone a star, are slim to none. But never mind. This theme park on the studio's back lot presents an entertaining mix of thrill rides, live-action shows and a tram tour.

First-timers should head straight for the 45-minute narrated **Studio Tour** aboard a multi-car tram that drives around the sound stages in the front lot then heads to the back lot past the crash site from *War of the Worlds,* vehicles from *Jurassic Park* and the spooky Bates Motel from *Psycho.* Also prepare to brave a flash flood, survive a shark attack, a spitting dino and an 8.3-magnitude earthquake, before facing down King Kong in a new 3-D exhibit created by Peter Jackson. It's a bit hokey, but fun.

Newly opened, the phenomenally popular **Wizarding World of Harry Potter** is the park's biggest attraction. Climb aboard the **Flight of the Hippogriff** roller coaster and the 3-D ride **Harry Potter and the Forbidden Journey**. Buy wizarding equipment and 'every-flavour' beans in the fantasy-themed shops then dig into a feast platter with frosty mugs of 'butterbeer' at Three Broomsticks restaurant.

Elsewhere in the park, the **Jurassic Park** ride is a gentle float through a prehistoric jungle with a rather 'raptor-ous' ending. **Revenge of the Mummy** is a short, but thrilling, indoor roller-coaster romp through 'Imhotep's Tomb' that at one point has you going backwards and hits speeds of up to 45mph. A ride based on **The Simpsons** sends guests rocketing along with the Simpson family to experience a side of Springfield previously unexplored. You can also get a flight-simulated thrill on the new **Transformers** 3-D ride. Another 3-D ride certain to get the kids smiling is the delightful **Despicable Me Minion Mayhem**.

Try to budget a full day, especially in summer. To beat the crowds, get there before the gates open or invest in the Front of Line Pass (from $199) or the deluxe guided VIP Experience (from $359). Some rides have minimum height requirements. Buying online tickets usually yields discounts and coupons.

Snack food and drinks, including beer and margaritas, are available throughout the park, although you'll have more choices at the adjacent Universal CityWalk, a promenade of restaurants, shops, bars and entertainment venues. Be sure to get your hand stamped for re-entry. General parking costs $10 to $18. Opening hours vary by season.

Museum of Neon Art   MUSEUM
(☑ 818-696-2149; www.neonmona.org; 216 S Brand Blvd, Glendale; adult/student $10/8; ⊙ noon-7pm Thu-Sat, to 5pm Sun) Neon signage is a defining element of LA's cityscape, and the collection at this museum in the heart of Glendale's commercial district includes signage from some of the region's best-known establishments, from the legendary (departed) Brown Derby to the Pep Boys auto-repair shops. In addition to both permanent and temporary exhibits of signage and other light art, MONA also holds twice-monthly Neon Cruises on open-topped double-decker buses, to see works around town up close.

Mission San Fernando Rey de España   CHURCH
(☑ 818-361-0186; www.missiontour.org; 15151 San Fernando Mission Blvd, Mission Hills; adult/senior/child 7-15yr $5/4/3; ⊙ 9am-4:30pm; P) One of the original chain of Spanish missions, Mission San Fernando dates from 1797, and the rambling grounds include the original 1822 *convento,* with its 4ft-thick adobe walls and Roman arches showing construction of the time (and enclosing the only known remaining mission wine cellar). There's also a historical museum, replicated church and many gardens.

NoHo Arts District   NEIGHBORHOOD
(Map p126; www.nohoartsdistrict.com) North Hollywood (NoHo) was a down-on-its-heels neighborhood of artists, but thanks to redevelopment it now boasts some 20 stage theaters in 1 sq mile and a burgeoning community of galleries, restaurants and vintage-clothing stores around them.

It's situated at the end of both the Metro Red Line to Downtown LA and the Orange Line busway across the Valley.

Forest Lawn Memorial Park – Glendale   CEMETERY
(☑ 323-254-3131; www.forestlawn.com; 1712 S Glendale Ave, Glendale; ⊙ 8am-5pm, until 6pm late Mar-early Nov; P) The final home of such Golden Age superstars as Clara Bow, Humphrey Bogart and Jimmy Stewart. Alas, many of their graves are in mausoleums and are off-limits to the public. It doesn't help that cemetery staff strongly discourage star seekers.

You can download maps from the internet (for example, www.seeing-stars.com), but be discreet or risk having them confiscated.

Forest Lawn Memorial Park – Hollywood Hills   CEMETERY
(Map p126; www.forestlawn.com; 6300 Forest Lawn Dr; ⊙ 8am-5pm; P) Pathos, art and patriotism rule at this humongous cemetery next to Griffith Park. A fine catalog of old-time celebrities, including Lucille Ball, Bette Davis and Stan Laurel, rests within the manicured grounds strewn with paeans to early North American history.

🛏 Sleeping

The fact that the Valley has no real center, being instead a selection of small neighborhoods, makes choosing where to stay a bit of a challenge. You'll find the usual international assortment of chain hotels across the Valley, but there are some one-off properties with unusual stories and charm.

Sportsmen's Lodge   HOTEL $$
(☑ 818-769-4700; www.sportsmenslodge.com; 12825 Ventura Blvd, Studio City; r from $149; P ❂ ✿ @ 🛜 ⌷) This valley classic (Clark Gable, Katharine Hepburn and other Hollywood stars once stayed here) had fallen on hard times but is back and swinging after a renovation. Okay, it's still a glorified motel, but much more inviting. Spacious rooms have orange and lime-green disco sheets, wall-mounted flat-screen TVs and two-tone walls. There's a sexy pool area, too.

BLVD Hotel   HOTEL $$
(Map p126; ☑ 818-623-9100; www.blvdstudiocity.com; 10730 Ventura Blvd, Studio City; r from $179; P ❂ ✿ ⌷) A fun, great-value boutique property and walkable to Universal Studios in about .5 miles, the BLVD has 69 spacious, IKEA-chic rooms with pillow-top beds, wood floors, rain showers, high ceilings and

plush linens. Amenities include a heated indoor pool, massage services (extra charge) and a lobby bar.

Safari Inn
MOTEL **$$**

(Map p126; ☑818-845-8586; www.safariburbank.com; 1911 W Olive Ave, Burbank; r $139-169; P ⊝ ✲ @ ☎ ✇) This 1950s motel boasts a vintage neon sign, beds are draped in animal-print bedspreads, and framed poster art adds charm to rooms that are otherwise on the smallish side; a renovation was planned as we went to press. The pool is nice, the staff professional, and it's close to the studios – for free shuttle service, reserve in advance.

Hotel Amarano
BOUTIQUE HOTEL **$$**

(Map p126; ☑818-842-8887; www.hotelamarano.com, 322 N Pass Ave, Burbank; r weekend/midweek from $179/235; P ⊝ ✲ @ ☎ ✇) Close to Warner Bros, the 100 rooms at this boutique business hotel are inspired by Hollywood movie sets, from doors like those on actors' dressing rooms to movie-reel artwork and the script from *Casablanca* discreetly printed on headboards. Even the basic superior rooms are large and sunny, and bedding is soft and welcoming.

Embassy Suites
HOTEL **$$**

(☑818-550-0828; www.embassysuites.com; 800 N Central Ave, Glendale; r from $189; P ✲ @ ☎ ✇) Ignore the oh-so-corporate moniker. This tower hotel with a frosted-glass facade has class and value around a soaring atrium lobby. All rooms are suites, there's a lap pool on the 2nd-floor ledge, a full fitness center and full breakfast included. It's in downtown Glendale, within walking distance of busy Brand Blvd and the Americana (p210) mall.

✗ Eating

Some of the most interesting dining options across the Valley are ethnic ones: Armenian/Lebanese, Cuban, Filipino, Japanese, Israeli and Mexican. For restaurant browsing, the area around Brand Blvd in downtown Glendale is a good place for a roam, especially the high-end restaurants at the Americana at Brand, while Universal CityWalk is a good for a break from Universal Studios, with quick-service options.

Porto's
CUBAN, BAKERY **$**

(☑818-956-5996; www.portosbakery.com; 315 N Brand Blvd, Glendale; ⊙6:30am-8pm Mon-Sat, 7am-6pm Sun; ☝) Locals obsess over Porto's. There always seems to be a queue somewhere in this sprawling bakery-cafe, where

different stations dispense hearty sandwiches, luscious cakes and obsession-worthy *pasteles* (small pastries). Deep-fried potato balls filled with meat or cheese and jalapeño define comfort food, as do flaky guava-cheese pastries and meaty sandwiches such as *medianoche* and Cuban. There's simple cafeteria-style seating. Olé, y'all!

Republic of Pie
PIES **$**

(Map p126; ☑818-308-7990; www.republicofpie.com; 11118 Magnolia Blvd, North Hollywood; slice of pie from $5.95; ⊙8am-10pm Mon-Thu, to 11pm Fri & Sat, to 9pm Sun; ☝; Ⓜ Red Line to North Hollywood) Pies from fruit to meat star at this reclaimed-wood-built shop in the NoHo Arts District. It's got all the standard comfort-food pies and quiches and pushes the envelope with creations such espresso chocolate cream and Earl Grey cream pies and the Triple Threat – three pies stacked and baked together inside a cake (don't try this at home, kids).

Chili John's
AMERICAN **$**

(Map p126; ☑818-846-3611; 2018 W Burbank Blvd, Burbank; mains $6.90-13.30; ⊙11am-7pm Mon-Fri, to 4pm Sat; P ☝; ☒ line 145 to Keystone & Burbank Blvd) A neighborhood institution dishing out chili around a U-shaped counter since 1946. It's most popular served over spaghetti, but it'll do chili dogs, sandwiches such as the Sloppy John (think Sloppy Joe with chili) and the open-faced Messy Mary. Chili comes in beef, chicken and vegetarian versions, spiced from mild to hot.

Quenelle
ICE CREAM **$**

(Map p126; ☑818-843-1035; www.quenelleicecream.com; 2214 W Magnolia Blvd, Burbank; ⊙11am-9pm Tue-Thu, to 10pm Fri & Sat; ☝) This ice-cream shop often pops up on lists of America's best. That's due in part to the hundreds of flavors it's created, some quite outlandish: yuzu mojito, root beer float, PB&J, raspberry merlot and blackberry lychee, and popsicles made with Red Bull and Tang, not to mention funnel cake ice-cream sandwiches.

Bob's Big Boy
DINER **$**

(Map p126; ☑818-843-9334; www.bigboy.com; 4211 W Riverside Dr, Burbank; burgers, sandwiches & salads $9-11.50, mains $9.50-14.50; ⊙24hr; P ☝; ☒ line 155 to Riverside Dr & Rose St) Bob, that cheeky, pompadoured kid in red-checkered pants, hasn't aged a lick since serving his first double-decker more than half a century ago. This Wayne McAllister–designed,

Googie-style 1949 coffee shop is the oldest remaining Bob's Big Boy in America, serving a down-home menu centered around burgers, fries and chicken.

This location takes great pride in its history and architecture. The cantilevered roof seems to float above the restaurant and recall the work of Frank Lloyd Wright, and even its 70ft-tall sign is a local landmark.

On Fridays from about 4pm to 10pm, classic hot rods roar into the parking lot, while the weekend car-hop service (5pm to 10pm Saturday and Sunday) brings in families and love doves.

★ **Daichan**   JAPANESE $$
(Map p126; ☏ 818-980-8450; 11288 Ventura Blvd, Studio City; mains $8-20; ⏰ 11:30am-3pm & 5:30-9pm Mon-Fri, noon-3pm & 5-9pm Sat; 🅿) Tucked away in an unassuming mini-mall, and stuffed with knickknacks, pasted with posters and staffed by a sunny, sweet owner-operator, this offbeat, home-style Japanese diner offers some of the best (and tastiest) deals on Sushi Row. Fried seaweed tofu gyōza are divine and so are the bowls – especially the *negitoro* bowl, which puts fatty tuna over rice, lettuce and seaweed.

★ **Carousel**   MIDDLE EASTERN $$
(☏ 818-246-7775; www.carouselrestaurant.com; 304 N Brand Blvd, Glendale; mezes $6.75-11, mains lunch $12-18.50, dinner $15.50-28; ⏰ 11am-9:30pm Tue-Thu, to 10:30pm Fri & Sat, to 8:30pm Sun; 🅿) Carousel may call itself a Lebanese restaurant, but this huge place has a commensurately huge following among Glendale's Armenian community. We can see why: succulent shawarma and kebabs, mounds of *mezzas* (small plates, hummus to steak tartare) and desserts made with *ashta* (condensed milk) and honey are knockouts.

Barrel & Ashes   BARBECUE $$
(☏ 818-623-8883; www.barrelandashes.com; 11801 Ventura Blvd, Studio City; mains $11-19; ⏰ 11am-3pm Mon-Fri, 5-10pm Sun-Thu, until 11pm Fri & Sat, 10:30am-3pm Sat & Sun; 🅿) Barbecue with a pedigree: there's a concept. This stylish shop was founded by alumni of the Napa Valley's famed French Laundry and smokes meats such as beef brisket and pork spare ribs over California red oak. The 1940s building shows off original tile around contemporary communal tables, a sidewalk patio and a cool bar.

Vitello's   ITALIAN $$
(Map p126; ☏ 818-769-0905; www.vitellosrestaurant. com; 4349 Tujunga Ave, Studio City; mains lunch $12-24, dinner $17-32; ⏰ 11am-10pm Mon-Thu, to 11pm Fri, 10am-11pm Sat, 10am-10pm Sun; 🅿) This sophisticated spot with brick and black-mottled walls has been in business since 1964 thanks to dishes such as chicken penne, branzino filet, plenty of pastas and hearty dinners like double-bone pork chops and American Wagyu flat iron steaks. Upstairs, the E-Spot supper club gigs in jazz, pop, rock and comedy (cover varies). There's even a new speakeasy.

Max's   FILIPINO $$
(☏ 818-637-7751; www.maxschicken.com; 313 W Broadway, Glendale; mains $10-16.50; ⏰ 10:30am-10pm Mon-Thu, until 1am Fri, 9:30am-11pm Sat, 8:30am-10pm Sun; 🅿♿) There always seems to be a (manageable) line of hungry Filipino families waiting to get into this friendly, Manila-style temple to fried chicken – it deep fries the whole bird and serves it with French fries and sweet-potato fries. There are other dishes such as sizzling beef *kaldereta* (beef stew) or Pinatuyong pork *adobo* (marinated pork), but chicken is king.

Itzik Hagadol   ISRAELI $$
(☏ 818-784-4080; www.itzikhagadol.com; 17201 Ventura Blvd, Encino; mains $12-33; ⏰ 11am-11pm; 🅿✏; 🖥) The informal, modern, spotless LA branch of this Tel Aviv restaurant is known for kebabs, steaks, chicken and lamb, but we're satisfied – stuffed, rather – with the assortment of 20 salads spread across the table – cucumber, baba ghanoush, beans, Moroccan-spiced carrots, vegetarian chopped liver and seasonal selections – refillable and served with falafel and chewy, fresh-baked bread.

Commonwealth   CALIFORNIAN $$
(☏ 818-845-2225; www.restaurantcw.com; 222 S Glenoaks Blvd, Burbank; dishes $8-16; ⏰ 6-10pm Mon-Thu, to 10:30pm Fri & Sat) This dinner-only, small-plates restaurant is a foodie favorite and a local restaurant that draws people from all over. Chefs get inventive with dishes such as bacon and burrata with onion compote, grapefruit and crispy leeks; hangar steak with sauteed onions and mushrooms and horseradish cream; and the CW sundae (vanilla ice cream, bacon, maple syrup and blue-cheese mascarpone mousse).

Reservations strongly suggested. Note that it takes only two seatings: 6pm or 6:30pm, and 8pm or 8:30pm.

★ **Asanebo**   SUSHI $$$
(☏ 818-760-3348; www.asanebo-restaurant. com; 11941 Ventura Blvd, Studio City; dishes $3-21;

⊗ noon-2pm & 6-10:30pm Tue-Fri, 6-10:30pm Sat, to 10pm Sun; P; MTA lines 150, 240) Although it's in a strip mall (welcome to the Valley), Asanebo is a Sushi Row standout thanks to dishes such as halibut sashimi with fresh truffle, and *kanpachi* with miso and serrano chilies. Chef Tetsuya Nakao was one of the chefs who helped launch the Nobu Japanese restaurant empire at Matsuhisa in Beverly Hills.

 Drinking & Nightlife

Ventura Blvd in Studio City has everything from cocktail bars to one of LA's longest-running gay clubs, Oil Can Harry's. Craft-beer lovers will want to beeline for the brew pub at Golden Road Brewing, and Aroma Coffee & Tea is as close to a destination as a coffee house gets.

Aroma Coffee & Tea   CAFE
(Map p126; ☑818-508-7377; www.aromacoffeeand tea.com; 4360 Tujunga Ave, Studio City; ⊗6am-11pm Mon-Sat, from 6:30am Sun) This popular cafe is in a converted, artsy, multi-room (yet somehow still cozy) house; outside, tables crowd leafy, heated patios and the line runs out the door. Coffees are great, and the humongous menu (mains $11 to $15) includes goat-cheese-and-walnut salads, popular turkey burgers and breakfasts such as *chilaquiles* and breakfast enchiladas, to veggie Reuben and lobster club sandwiches.

Pub at Golden Road Brewing   MICROBREWERY
(Map p126; ☑213-373-4677; www.goldenroad.la; 5410 W San Fernando Rd; ⊗11am-midnight Mon-Thu, to 2am Fri, 10am-2am Sat, 10am-midnight Sun; Metro line 94 to Doran St) In an industrial area between Glendale and Burbank, this brewery takes up most of a city block, but the pub on the old loading dock is warm and welcoming under strings of white lights. Beers such as 329 Days of Sun lager and Wolf Among Weeds IPA pair with sandwiches like the Latin-spiced Chickano and the Drop the Funky Beet burger.

Tony's Darts Away   CRAFT BEER
(Map p126; ☑818-253-1710; www.tonysda.com; 1710 W Magnolia Blvd, Burbank; ⊗noon-2am Mon-Thu, 11am-2am Fri, 10am-2am Sat, 11am-1am Sun; MTA line 183) ⊘ This old-shoe-comfy neighborhood bar is renowned for its extraordinary beer selection – a changing choice of 38 craft beers on tap, plus wines and ciders. The food menu features a wide range of sausages ($7 to $9), including vegan versions.

There is a dart board (and pool table), but it's really about the beer.

Black Market Liquor Bar   BAR
(☑818-446-2533; www.blackmarketliquorbar.com; 11915 Ventura Blvd, Studio City; ⊗5pm-1am daily, 11am-3pm Sat & Sun) Under a vaulted brick ceiling, this upscale neighborhood tavern had us at its list of Bloodys (Mary with vodka, Maria with tequila, hell with gin, etc), make-your-own mimosas, unusual cocktails and offbeat beers flavored with watermelon, grapefruit and coffee. They go great with plates such as fried cauliflower with lemon aioli and meatballs with garlic crisps.

Laurel Tavern   PUB
(www.laureltavern.com; 11938 Ventura Blvd, Studio City; ⊗noon-1am; MTA lines 150, 240) This new, tastefully modern pub with wood floors, wood-slab bar and brick walls has an extensive craftsman beer and wine list on the chalkboard. It has sports on the TV, enticing pub grub and a full bar, and there's a covered sidewalk terrace to enjoy the weather.

Firefly   LOUNGE
(☑818-762-1833; www.fireflystudiocity.com; 11720 Ventura Blvd, Studio City; ⊗5pm-2am Mon-Sat, 11am-3pm & 5pm-1am Sun; MTA lines 150, 240) The bar at this restaurant has the sexiest library this side of an Anne Rice novel – bordello-red lighting, low-slung couches and flickering candles, all surrounded by shelves of somber-looking tomes. Not that anyone's opened one – the members of this upwardly mobile crowd are too busy reading each other.

☆ **Entertainment**

The NoHo, aka North Hollywood, arts district is sprinkled with theaters and venues offering plays and stand-up comedy. The El Portal is one of the biggest, and ACME Comedy Theatre, an improv troupe, has a branch here, too.

El Portal   THEATER
(Map p126; ☑818-508-4200; www.elportaltheatre. com; 5269 Lankershim Blvd, North Hollywood; M Red Line to North Hollywood) The stage of this one-time vaudeville house from 1926 has been graced by headliners from Debbie Reynolds to Smokey Robinson, Carol Channing to James Corden. Restored to its former glory after the 1994 Northridge earthquake, it's now a mainstay of the NoHo Arts District. Shows run on three stages (42 to 360 seats).

Zombie Joe's Underground Theatre THEATER
(Map p126; ☑818-202-4120; www.zombiejoes.
com; 4850 Lankershim Blvd, North Hollywood;
shows $15) Oh, the horror! Part theater, part
haunted house, Zombie Joe's presents for
your entertainment shows that are at turns
creepy, campy, Goth, killer-thriller, deranged,
downright jump-out-of-your-pants scary and
(paradoxically?) well respected. There's an
annual series called *Urban Death* – get the
idea? Shows are short – under an hour.

Baked Potato JAZZ, BLUES
(Map p126; www.thebakedpotato.com; 3787 Cahuenga Blvd, Studio City; cover $10-25, plus 2
drinks; ⏰7pm-2am) Near Universal Studios,
a dancing spud beckons you to come inside
this diminutive jazz-and-blues hall where
the schedule mixes no-names with big-tim-
ers. Drinks are stiff, and actual baked potatoes ($6.50 to $15) are optional.

 Shopping

Americana at Brand MALL
(www.americanaatbrand.com; 889 Americana Way,
Glendale; 🚼) If you dig the Grove (p137) in
Mid-City then you'll enjoy this set-piece
shopping mall, developed by the same folks,
that feels like an extended walking street.
There's an 18-screen multiplex, some 30 res-

taurants and food stalls and some very good,
albeit very corporate, shopping.

It's a Wrap! CLOTHING
(Map p126; ☑818-567-7366; www.itsawrapholly
wood.com; 3315 W Magnolia Blvd, Burbank; ⏰11am-
7pm Mon-Fri, to 6pm Sat, noon-6pm Sun) Here are
fashionable, post-production wares worn
by TV and film stars. What that means to
you is great prices on mainstream designer
labels, including racks of casual and formal
gear worn on such shows as *Nurse Jackie*
and *Scandal*. The suits are a steal, and so is
the denim. New arrivals are racked by show
affiliation.

Universal CityWalk MALL
(Map p126; ☑818-622-4455; www.citywalkholly
wood.com; 100 Universal City Dr, Universal City;
⏰11am-9pm Mon-Thu, to 11pm Fri-Sun; 🚼; Ⓜ Universal City) Flashing video screens, oversized
facades and garish color combos (think
Blade Runner meets Willy Wonka) animate
the outdoor shopping concourse adjacent to
Universal Studios. CityWalk's 65 shops, restaurants and entertainment venues offer a
mix of mid- and lowbrow attractions, with
low leading by a nose.

BEHIND THE CURTAIN: MOVIE MAGIC UNMASKED

Did you know it takes a week to shoot a half-hour sitcom? Or that you rarely see ceilings on shows because the space is filled with lights and lamps? You'll learn these and other nuggets of information about the make-believe world of film and TV while touring a work-ing studio. Star-sighting potential is better than average, except during 'hiatus' (May to August) when studios are deserted. Reservations are required and so is photo ID.

Paramount (☑323-956-1777; www.paramountstudiotour.com; 5555 Melrose Ave; tours from $55; ⏰tours 9:30am-5pm, last tour 3pm) *Star Trek, Indiana Jones* and *Shrek* are among the blockbusters that originated at Paramount, the longest-operating movie studio and the only one still in Hollywood proper. Two-hour tours through the back lots and sound stages are available daily year-round and are led by passionate, knowledgeable guides.

Sony (Map p164; ☑310-244-8687; www.sonypicturesstudiostours.com; 10202 W Washington Blvd; tour $45; ⏰tours usually 9:30am, 10:30am, 1:30pm & 2:30pm Mon-Fri) Running on week-days only, this two-hour tour includes visits to the sound stages where *Men in Black, Spider-Man,* and *Charlie's Angels* were filmed. Munchkins hopped along the Yellow Brick Road in *The Wizard of Oz,* filmed when this was still the venerable MGM studio.

Warner Bros (Map p126; ☑877-492-8687, 818-972-8687; www.wbstudiotour.com; 3400 W Riverside Dr, Burbank; tours adult/child 8-12yr from $62/52; ⏰8:30am-3:30pm, extended hours Jun-Aug; 🚌155, 222, 501 stop about 400yd from tour center) This tour offers the most fun and authentic look behind the scenes of a major movie studio. Consisting of a two-hour guided tour and a self-guided tour of Studio 48, the adventure kicks off with a review of WB's greatest film hits – among them *Rebel Without a Cause* and *La La Land* – before a tram whisks you to sound stages, back-lot sets and technical departments, including props, costumes and the paint shop. Tours run daily, usually every half-hour.

Pasadena & the San Gabriel Valley

One could argue that there's more blue-blood, meat-eating, robust Americana in Pasadena than in all other LA neighborhoods combined. Here you'll find a community with a preppy old soul, a historical perspective, an appreciation for art and jazz and a progressive undercurrent. The Rose Parade and Rose Bowl football game may have given Pasadena its long-lasting fame, but it's the spirit of this genteel city and its location beneath the lofty San Gabriel Mountains that make it a charming and attractive place to visit year-round.

⊙ Sights

Pasadena is home to some world-renowned gems of high culture, chief among them the Huntington Library, Norton Simon Museum and Gamble House. Or you can just stroll the area around Old Pasadena and the 1920s Pasadena's Civic Center, which is a reflection of the great wealth and local pride that have governed the city since its early days, especially the Spanish Renaissance–style City Hall.

If fresh air is more your deal, try strolling the manicured expanses of Descanso Gardens, northwest of Pasadena, or the LA County Arboretum, or head north to lose yourself (not literally, please) hiking in the expanse of the Angeles National Forest.

★ **Huntington Library, Art Collections & Botanical Gardens**   MUSEUM, GARDEN
(🖂 626-405-2100; www.huntington.org; 1151 Oxford Rd, San Marino; adult weekday/weekend & holidays $23/25, child $10, 1st Thu each month free; ☉ 10am-5pm Wed-Mon; 🅿) One of the most delightful, inspirational spots in LA, the Huntington is rightly a highlight of any trip to California thanks to a world-class mix of art, literary history and over 120 acres of themed gardens (any one of which would be worth a visit on its own), all set amid stately grounds. There's so much to see and do that it's hard to know where to begin; allow three to four hours for even a basic visit.

You might start with the library. Only a fraction of its six million rare books and related items can possibly go on display to the public, but they're pretty darned impressive: a Gutenberg Bible, a manuscript of *the Canterbury Tales* by Geoffrey Chaucer, books by Marco Polo and Christopher Columbus and numerous items relating to the US Civil War, westward expansion, women's suffrage and early California.

Nearby, in the galleries of European and American art, you can lose yourself in the brushstrokes of Thomas Gainsborough's the *Blue Boy* and Thomas Lawrence's *Pinkie*, or take in American classics by the likes of Mary Cassatt, Edward Hopper, Andy Warhol and Frank Stella. There's also decorative arts from intricately patterned furniture to porcelain and gleaming silver service.

Then there are the gardens – about a dozen – meticulously curated like museums. Among our favorites is the Chinese Garden, where the Jade Ribbon Bridge straddles a pond surrounded by rockeries and a cafe. In the Japanese Gardens, hills, valleys and waterways are lined with precision-pruned pine trees around a 1904 Japanese house, and paths lead to a Zen garden and courtyards of bonsai. The landscapes of the Desert Garden are surprisingly full of life, and in the Rose Garden guests can enjoy high tea in the tea room (p218; reservations strongly suggested any day and well in advance on weekends).

The Huntington was established in 1919 as the genteel country estate of railroad, utility and real-estate tycoon Henry Huntington and his wife, Arabella.

Advance tickets are required for free-day admission.

★ **Gamble House**   ARCHITECTURE
(Map p212; ☑ info 626-793-3334, tickets 844-325-0712; www.gamblehouse.org; 4 Westmoreland Pl, Pasadena; tours adult/child $15/free; ☉ tours 11:30am-3pm Thu & Fri, noon-3pm Sat & Sun Sep-May, 11am-3pm Thu-Sat, noon-3pm Sun Jun-Aug, bookstore 11am-2pm Tue, 10am-5pm Thu-Sun; 🅿) This mansion in northwest central Pasadena has been called one of the 10 most architecturally significant homes in America, a 1908 masterpiece of California arts-and-crafts architecture built by Charles and Henry Greene for Procter & Gamble heir David Gamble. Incorporating 17 woods, art glass and subdued light, the entire home is a work of art, with its foundation, furniture and fixtures all united by a common design and theme inspired by its Southern California environs and Japanese and Chinese architecture.

Note the sleeping porches, iridescent stained glass and subtle appearances of the Gamble family's rose and crane crest.

Other Greene and Greene homes, including **Charles Greene's former private residence** (Map p212; 368 Arroyo Tce, Pasadena), line

Pasadena

0 — 500 m
0 — 0.25 miles

Rose Bowl Flea Market (0.7mi); Rose Bowl Stadium (0.7mi)

Brookside Park

Lincoln Ave

N Arroyo Blvd

Linda Vista Ave

5

Foothill Fwy

Lake

210

Gamble House **1**

Arroyo Tce

N Orange Grove Blvd

Grand Ave

3

Ventura Fwy

Memorial Park

E Walnut St

E Foothill Blvd

N Lake Ave

PASADENA PLAYHOUSE DISTRICT

OLD PASADENA

19 20

11

E Union St

6

W Colorado Blvd

Memorial Park

21

7

Paseo Colorado

25

22

E Colorado Blvd

134

Glendale (6mi)

24

14

W Green St

17 **12**

23

13

E Green St

Pasadena City College Flea Market (0.1mi); Saga Motor Hotel (0.3mi)

4

Ventura Fwy

W Colorado Blvd

8

S Pasadena Ave

S De Lacey Ave

Central Park

15

S Oakland Ave

S Madison Ave

S El Molino Ave

S Oak Knoll Ave

S Hudson Ave

Cordova St

Lower Arroyo Park

16

Del Mar

E Del Mar Blvd

Arroyo Seco

Arbor St

Waverly Dr

W Del Mar Blvd

9

S Grand Ave

S Orange Grove Blvd

18

S Fair Oaks Ave

S Raymond Ave

S Arroyo Pkwy

S Marengo Ave

S Euclid Ave

S Los Robles Ave

S Lake Ave

Shoppers Lane

N Mentor Ave

N Catalina Ave

N Wilson Ave

SOUTH LAKE DISTRICT

2

Palmetto Dr

10

La Loma Rd

La Loma Rd

Bradford St

W California Blvd

Fair Oaks Pharmacy (1.1mi); Gus's BBQ (1.1mi); Crossings (1.5mi); Mike & Anne's (1.5mi)

Fillmore

Magnolia Ave

E California Blvd

Langham (1mi)

Huntington Library, Art Collections & Botanical Gardens (1mi); Rose Garden Tea Room (1mi)

Downtown Los Angeles (8mi)

Pasadena

nearby Arroyo Tce and Grand Ave. Pick up a self-guided walking-tour pamphlet at the Gamble House bookstore ($1.50).

Los Angeles County Arboretum & Botanic Garden
GARDENS
(www.arboretum.org; 301 N Baldwin Ave, Arcadia; adult/student & senior/child 5 12yr $9/6/4, 3rd Tue of month free; ⊙9am-4:30pm) It's easy to spend hours amid the global vegetation, waterfalls, spring-fed lake and historic buildings of this fantastic, rambling, 127-acre park. Originally the private estate of real-estate tycoon Elias 'Lucky' Baldwin, it's so huge there's even a tram to haul those who are foot-weary.

Kidspace Children's Museum
MUSEUM
(Map p212; ☎626-449-9144; www.kidspacemuseum.org; 480 N Arroyo Blvd, Pasadena; admission $13; ⊙9:30am-5pm Tue-Fri, from 10am Sat & Sun, plus 9:30am-5pm Mon mid-Mar–early Sep; 🅿️👶) Kidspace is one of the best children's museums we've seen, with hands-on exhibits, outdoor learning areas and gardens luring the single-digit set. It makes great use of the SoCal sunshine with trails rambling uphill in the Arroyo Adventure, an indoor nature exchange, plenty of water features and ways to learn through play in the Galvin Physics Forest. For a quieter experience, come after 1:30pm, when the field-trip crowd has left.

Norton Simon Museum
MUSEUM
(Map p212; www.nortonsimon.org; 411 W Colorado Blvd, Pasadena; adult/child $12/free; ⊙noon-5pm

Mon, Wed & Thu, 11am-8pm Fri & Sat, 11am-5pm Sun; 🅿️) Rodin's *The Burghers of Calais* standing guard by the entrance is only a mind-teasing overture to the full symphony of art in store at this exquisite museum. Norton Simon (1907–93) was an entrepreneur with a Midas touch and a passion for art who parlayed his millions into an admirable collection of Western art and Asian sculpture. Meaty captions really help tell each piece's story.

The accessible, user-friendly galleries teem with choice works by Renaissance and impressionist artists, including Rembrandt (eg *Self-Portrait*), Renoir (*Young Woman in Black*), Canaletto (*Piazzetta in Venice Looking North*) and Van Gogh portraits, as well as an outstanding array of paintings and sculpture by Degas. Twentieth-century masterpieces span Picasso and LA's own Sam Francis.

Asian sculpture – principally Buddhist and Hindu imagery in stone, bronze and copper – is in the basement, while Western sculpture graces the gorgeous garden inspired by Monet's garden at Giverny, France.

California Institute of Technology
UNIVERSITY
(Caltech; Map p212; ☎tours 626-395-6341; www.caltech.edu; 551 S Hill Ave, Pasadena; ⊙tours 11:15am year-round, 2:15pm Mar, Apr, Jul & Aug) **FREE** With 34 Nobel laureates among its faculty and alumni (not to mention that it's the fictional setting of TV's *The Big Bang Theory*), it's no surprise that Caltech is regarded

MOUNTAIN ESCAPE

The first national forest in California, Angeles National Forest was established in 1908 and today rubs up against the vast metropolitan sprawl of Los Angeles. With your own wheels, it offers a quick and easy respite from the urban hubbub and the summer heat.

Angeles Crest Scenic Byway (https://scenicbyways.info/byway/10245.html; Hwy 2) The two-lane Angeles Crest Scenic Byway treats you to fabulous views of big-shouldered mountains, the Mojave Desert and deep valleys on its 55-mile meander from La Cañada to the resort town of Wrightwood. The road skirts LA County's tallest mountain, officially called **Mt San Antonio** (10,064ft), but better known as Old Baldy for its treeless top.

You'll pass ranger stations along the way, but the main **Chilao Visitors Center** (📞626-796-5541; www.fs.fed.us; Angeles National Forest; ⊘8am-4pm Sat & Sun mid-Apr–mid-Oct) has natural exhibits and trails and is about 27 miles from the turnoff.

Mt Wilson Observatory (📞626-440-9016; www.mtwilson.edu; Red Box Rd, Mt Wilson; tours adult/child & senior $15/12; ⊘10am-5pm) As you drive into the Angeles National Forest take the Red Box Rd turn-off, which, 5 miles later, dead ends atop 5715ft Mt Wilson. Operating since 1904, this was the world's top astronomical research facility in the early 20th century and is still in use today.

You can walk around the grounds (download a handy self-guided tour from the website) and visit the museum. Free guided tours run at 1pm on Saturdays and Sundays April to November. The website also has details on how to schedule a viewing session using the 1908 60-inch telescope (half-/full night $1000/1700 for groups of up to 25 people). It's closed in bad weather.

Kenyon Devore Trail (www.fs.fed.us; Mt Wilson Observatory, Red Box Rd, Mt Wilson) Named after a longtime San Gabriel Mountain man, this trail begins 0.25 miles from the Mt Wilson summit on Red Box Rd and drops down the mountain for 3000ft through stunning oak and pine habitat, meandering on both sides of the year-round Strayns Canyon Creek.

It's stunning countryside, especially in the spring – when wildflowers pop – and the fall when valley and black oaks turn gold and drop their spinning leaves. Follow the trail for about 4 miles to West Fork Campground before turning back. It's a strenuous 9-mile round trip. You can also cross Strayns Canyon Creek and make a right at the Gabrielino Trail, which leads back up the mountain in a 10.5-mile loop. Whatever your game plan, be sure to pick up a good map and carry plenty of water.

with awe in academic circles. Earthquake studies were essentially pioneered here in the 1920s with the inventions of the seismograph and the Richter scale, and to this day Caltech scientists are usually the first experts to be consulted whenever a shaker strikes.

Descanso Gardens   GARDENS
(📞818-949-4200; www.descansogardens.org; 1418 Descanso Dr, La Cañada Flintridge; adult/student & senior/child 5-12yr $9/6/4; ⊘9am-5pm; 🅿) The 160-acre Descanso Gardens put on a dazzling show all year, but especially in January and February when some 34,000 camellias, some as tall as 20ft, brighten the LA winter. In spring lilacs perfume the air, followed by roses in summer. It's easy to spend a whole day amid the greenery, waterways and bird sanctuary.

San Gabriel Mission   LANDMARK
(📞626-457-3035; www.sangabrielmission.org; 428 S Mission Dr, San Gabriel; adult/child 6-17yr $6/3; ⊘9am-4:30pm Mon-Sat, 10am-4pm Sun; 🅿♿) In 1781, settlers departed from this mission to found El Pueblo de Los Angeles in today's Downtown area. Set about 3 miles southeast of Pasadena in the city of San Gabriel, it's the fourth in the chain of 21 missions in California and is one of the prettiest.

Its church boasts Spanish Moorish flourishes, a copper baptismal font, carved statues of saints and a 1790 altar made in Mexico City. The mission surroundings are also well worth a quick stroll. Following Mission Dr takes you past the 1927 Civic Auditorium, the Civic Center, a historical museum and galleries.

Pasadena Museum of California Art
MUSEUM

(Map p212; ☑ 626-568-3665; www.pmcaonline.org; 490 E Union St, Pasadena; adult/student & senior/child $7/5/free, 1st Fri & 3rd Thu of month free; ⊗ noon-5pm Wed-Sun, to 8pm 3rd Thu each month; P) This progressive gallery is dedicated to art, architecture and design created by California artists since 1850; there's always a mix of contemporary and historic art. Shows change every few months and have included masterpieces by Maynard Dixon, collages by beatnik artist Jess and vinyl toys by Gary Basemen. Also swing by the **Kosmic Kavern**, which is what this former garage has become thanks to spray-mural pop artist Kenny Scharf.

Colorado St Bridge
BRIDGE

(Map p212) Spanning some 150ft above and nearly 1500ft across the Arroyo Seco, this stunning bridge was the world's tallest concrete bridge when it was completed in 1913. The bridge balances on soaring arches. The bridge had a star turn in *La La Land* when Mia and Sebastian crossed it on a date at sunset.

Tournament House & Wrigley Gardens
LANDMARK

(Map p212; ☑ 626-449-4100; www.tournamentof roses.com; 391 S Orange Grove Blvd, Pasadena; ⊗ 2pm & 3pm Thu Feb-Aug) FREE Chewing-gum magnate William Wrigley spent his winters in the elegant Italian Renaissance–style mansion where the Tournament of Roses Association now masterminds the annual Rose Parade. When they're not busy, you can tour the rich interior and inspect Rose Queen crowns and related memorabilia. Feel free to nose around the rose garden any time.

Rose Bowl Stadium
STADIUM

(☑ 626-577-3100; www.rosebowlstadium.com; 1001 Rose Bowl Dr, Pasadena) One of LA's most venerable landmarks, the 1922 Rose Bowl Stadium can seat up to 93,000 spectators and has its moment in the sun every New Year's Day when it hosts the famous Rose Bowl post-season college football game. At other times the UCLA Bruins play their home games here, and the occasional concert or special event also brings in the masses, as does a monthly flea market.

The Rose Bowl is surrounded by **Brookside Park**, which is a nice spot for hiking, cycling and picnicking. Families should check out the excellent Kidspace Children's Museum (p213), and architecture nuts should look for the nearby, palatial 1903 **Richard**

H Chambers Courthouse
(former Vista del Arroyo Hotel; Map p212; ☑ 626-229-7251; www.gsa. gov/portal/ext/html/site/hb/category/25431/ac tionParameter/exploreByBuilding/buildingId/825; 125 S Grand Ave, Pasadena; ⊗ 9am-5pm Mon-Fri except when court is in session; P) FREE, once a grand hotel.

🛏 Sleeping

Pasadena has a variety of lodgings from historic motels to a luxury resort that would easily cost much more if it were elsewhere.

Green Tree Pasadena Inn
MOTEL $

(Map p212; ☑ 626-795-8401; www.greentreepasa denainn.com; 400 S Arroyo Pkwy, Pasadena; r from $109; P@ 🗟 ≋) On busy Arroyo Pkwy, and situated around a parking lot, this older but recently renovated property offers shut-eye at a modest tariff. In the morning drag your coffee and Danish out to the pool area. The adjacent Thai restaurant makes a decent curry if you don't feel like hoofing it to Old Pasadena, a 15-minute walk away.

★ Bissell House B&B
B&B $$

(☑ 626 441 3535; www.bissellhouse.com; 201 S Orange Grove Ave, South Pasadena; r from $159; P 🗟 ≋) Antiques, hardwood floors and a crackling fireplace make this secluded Victorian (1887) B&B on 'Millionaire's Row' a bastion of warmth and romance. The hedge-framed garden feels like a sanctuary, and there's a pool for cooling off on hot summer days. The Prince Albert room has gorgeous wallpaper and a claw-foot tub. All seven rooms have private baths.

Saga Motor Hotel
MOTEL $$

(☑ 800-793-7242, 626-795-0431; www.thesaga motorhotel.com; 1633 E Colorado Blvd, Pasadena; r from $105; P ❋ @ 🗟 ≋) This peach-tinted, palm-shaded, 70-room motel isn't fancy or as cool as its vintage 1950s sign makes it look. But even if some of the decor could use a refresh, rates include simple continental breakfast (toast, muffins) and rooms are clean and have fridges, tubs, showers and some homey touches such as shutters on the window and books on the shelves.

★ Langham
RESORT $$$

(☑ 626-568-3900; www.pasadena.langhamhotels. com; 1401 S Oak Knoll Ave, Pasadena; r from $289; P ❋ @ 🗟 ≋) Opened as the Huntington Hotel in 1906, this place spent several decades as the Ritz-Carlton before recently donning the robes of Langham. But some things don't change, and this incredible 23-acre, palm-dappled, beaux-arts country estate – complete with rambling gardens, giant swimming pool and covered picture bridge – has still got it. Rooms would cost hundreds more elsewhere in town.

Westin
HOTEL $$$

(Map p212; ☑ 626-792-2727; www.westin.com; 191 N Los Robles Ave, Pasadena; r from $249; P@⑨⑨⑨) Downtown Pasadena's slickest sleep is a 350-room, modern, Spanish-style complex with comfortable, newly renovated rooms, large, well-equipped gym with steam and sauna and a pool deck with bang-on views of the city hall dome. It gets a lot of business travelers on weekdays, and groups on weekends. A nice, four-star choice. Parking is $15 per night.

✗ Eating

There's a huge variety of eating options in Pasadena and in the San Gabriel Valley. Pasadena and South Pasadena are the place to go for smart, all-American lunches and dinners with a little bit of hipster thrown in, while in the SGV it's all about Chinese food – some of the best in the country.

★ Din Tai Fung
CHINESE $

(☑ 626-574-7068; www.dintaifungusa.com; 1108 S Baldwin Ave, Arcadia; dumplings $10-14, dishes $4.50-11.50; ☺ 11am-9:30pm Mon-Fri, 10am-9:30pm Sat, 10am-9pm Sun; P) It's a testament to the SGV's ethnic Chinese community that Taiwan's most esteemed dumpling house opened its first US outpost here. The menu of dumplings, greens, noodles, desserts, teas and smoothies is as long as the phone directory at a medium-size corporation, but everyone orders pork *xiaolongbao* – steamed dumplings juicy with rich broth. Expect long waits – it's worth it.

NBC Seafood
DIM SUM $

(☑ 626-282-2323; www.nbcrestaurant.com; 404-A Atlantic Blvd, Monterey Park; dim sum $3-7, mains $10-17; ☺ 8am-10pm, dim sum until 3pm; P) Behind the rotunda facade, this SGV dim-sum institution seats 388 at a time. At peak hours (roughly 10am to 1pm on weekends) all seats are full, with a line out the door. Shrimp *har gao,* pan-fried leek dumplings and addictive shrimp on sugarcane are worth the wait, as are dozens of other small plates wheeled around on carts.

85°C Bakery & Cafe
BAKERY $

(Map p212; ☑ 626-792-8585; www.85cbakerycafe. com; 61 S Fair Oaks Ave, Pasadena; breads & pastries from $1.20; ☺ 7am-10pm Mon-Thu, to midnight Fri & Sat, 8am-10pm Sun; P ; Ⓜ Gold Line to Del Mar) If Pasadena is the San Gabriel Valley's East-meets-West melting pot, then this outpost of a Taiwanese bakery chain may be the oven that heats it. It churns out western-style brioche, breads and filled buns, plus dozens of Asian-inflected mashups, including matcha rolls, calamari bread, coconut raisin tarts and tuna Danish (hey, don't knock it 'til you try it!).

Indiana Colony
FOOD HALL $

(Map p212; www.indianacolonymarket.com; 59 E Colorado Blvd, Pasadena; ☺ 7am-10pm daily; Ⓜ Gold Line to Memorial Park) Cool your jets in the heart of Old Pasadena with some of LA's hippest purveyors of sweets and treats assembled under one roof. Amid the space's downtown-cool vibe, try Coolhaus for ice-cream sandwiches, mile-high pies from the Pie Hole and drinks from Legacy Tea and Intelligentsia Coffee, to name a few.

★ Union
ITALIAN $$

(Map p212; ☑ 626-795-5841; www.unionpasadena.com; 37 E Union St, Pasadena; dishes $14-38; ☺ 5-11pm Mon-Fri, from 4pm Sat & Sun) A cheerful, sophisticated energy animates James Beard–nominated chef Bruce Kalman's restaurant, offering California interpretations of northern Italian cuisine. The menu changes daily, but standards include pork meatballs, squid-ink pasta, fish caught from the waters of nearby Santa Barbara and a subtle and delicious olive-oil cake for dessert. Everything's made in-house, from breads to pastas to cheeses.

Gus's BBQ
BARBECUE $$

(☑ 888-799-3251; www.gussbbq.com; 808 Fair Oaks Ave, South Pasadena; mains $12-22; ☺ 11am-10pm Mon-Thu, to 11pm Fri, 8:30am-11pm Sat, 8:30am-10pm Sun; Ⓜ Gold Line to South Pasadena) In business since 1946 and under a neon sign, Gus's smokes its baby back ribs, chicken, brisket and more in pecan wood and serves them Memphis or St Louis style, alongside fried chicken and corn bread served in a skillet. Enjoy them all at the vintage lunch counter or red leatherette booths, or in the more contemporary back dining room.

La Grande Orange
CALIFORNIAN $$

(Map p212; ☑ 626-356-4444; www.lgostationcafe. com; 260 S Raymond Ave, Pasadena; mains lunch $15-23, dinner $15-34, pizzas $13-16; ☺ 11am-10pm Mon-Thu, to 11pm Fri, 10am-11pm Sat, 9am-9pm Sun; P ; Ⓜ Gold Line to Del Mar) Pasadena's original train station (circa 1911) has been handsomely renovated into this cheery, popular dining room beneath lovingly aged wooden beams. The kitchen in the former ticket booth serves a menu of New American cooking: burgers, salads and build-your-own taco platters such as short rib or grilled ahi. Watch today's Gold Line trains go by from the generous bar.

From 5pm Monday to Friday (from noon Saturday and Sunday), the former luggage room turns into the, uh, Luggage Room, a stylish bar and pizzeria.

Little Flower   CAFE $$

(Map p212; ☑ 626-304-4800; www.littleflowercandyco.com; 1424 W Colorado Blvd, Pasadena; mains $9-16; ⊘ 7am-7pm Mon-Sat, 9am-4pm Sun) An adorable, locally loved cafe set just a mile over the Colorado Bridge from Old Pasadena. There's a diverse menu, from the Goddess Salad, to banh mi sandwiches with chicken, roast beef or tempeh, and bowls stuffed with such things as dahl, raita, curried eggplant and steamed spinach. And you can't miss the case of delectable cakes.

Mike & Anne's   MODERN AMERICAN $$

(☑ 626-799-7199; www.mikeandannes.com; 1040 Mission St, South Pasadena; mains $10-25; ⊘ 8am-2:30pm & 5-9pm Tue-Thu, to 10pm Fri & Sat, 8am-3pm & 5-9pm Sun; P; M Gold Line to South Pasadena) Right on the Mission St drag in South Pasadena, Mike & Anne's is popular for its inviting patio (or minimalist wood and concrete dining room), lemon and ricotta pancakes with caramelized blueberry compote at breakfast, lunchtime salads and sandwiches (pulled pork to grilled eggplant or meatloaf and cheese) and dinners such as mushroom risotto, chicken pot pie and flatiron steak.

Saladang Garden   THAI $$

(Map p212; ☑ 626-793-5200; www.saladang-thai.com; 383 S Fair Oaks Ave, Pasadena; dishes $10-20; ⊘ 11am-9:30pm Sun-Thu, to 10pm Fri & Sat; P) Traditional Thai is served in contemporary environs at this pseudo-industrial outpost hemmed in by artfully rendered concrete walls and lovely tapestries. It serves simple curries, barbecue chicken with curry powder and herbs, and vermicelli with fish balls steamed in green curry.

Sea Harbour   CHINESE $$

(☑ 626-288-3939; 3939 Rosemead Blvd, Rosemead; dim sum $3.50-8.50, dishes $12-32; ⊘ 10:30am-2:30pm & 5-8pm Mon-Fri, 10am-2:30pm & 5-10pm Sat & Sun; P) Dim sum classics here are served off a menu instead of carts, not that it matters much. When we see pork *shu mai* dumplings, golden-fried sesame balls, shredded pork wrapped in sticky rice and a lotus leaf, or shrimp folded into thick flat noodles and soaked in sweet soy, all we do is eat. It's just off Valley Blvd, the SGV's main drag.

Ración   SPANISH $$$

(Map p212; ☑ 626-396-3090; www.racionrestaurant.com; 119 W Green St, Pasadena; small plates $4-14, mains $20-58; ⊘ 6-10pm Mon-Thu, 11:30am-3pm & 6-10:30pm Fri, 11:30am-3pm & 5:30-10:30pm Sat, 5:30-10pm Sun; M Gold Line to Memorial Park or Del Mar) A foodie favorite, this minimalist, Basque-inspired spot offers tapas such as *conservas* (pâté), chicken croquettes and seared prawns in salsa verde. It house cures yellowfin tuna in anchovy vinaigrette, and offers larger plates *(raciones)* ranging from a wild market fish with heirloom beans to duck breast with date jam and slow-braised lamb belly.

Crossings   MODERN AMERICAN $$$

(☑ 626-799-7001; www.crossings-restaurant.com; 1010 Mission St, South Pasadena; mains $18-50; ⊘ 5:30-9:30pm Sun-Thu, to 10pm Fri & Sat, 10am-1:30pm Sun; M Gold Line to South Pasadena) In a handsomely renovated brick building near South Pasadena station (hence the name), there's an open kitchen downstairs and a cozy bar upstairs – a striking backdrop for specialties such as fresh oysters, black cod with Spanish chorizo, dry-aged New York steak with foie gras butter, swordfish with charred sweet onion risotto, and wild-boar mac-n-cheese. Brunch served Sundays.

Bistro 45   AMERICAN $$$

(Map p212; ☑ 626-795-2478; www.bistro45.com; 45 S Mentor Ave, Pasadena; mains $23-45; ⊘ 5-9:30pm Tue-Sat, to 8:30pm Sun; P) Touted as the best fine-dining in the 'dena, this pink-and-green, art-deco dining room is elegant, yet not stiff, and the ingredients are organic wherever possible. It's the kind of place top Central Californian winemakers choose if they're hosting a dinner for potential buyers. The pizzas, seafood, steaks and chops are all seriously good.

Westfield Santa Anita FOOD HALL
(www.westfield.com/santaanita; 400 S Baldwin Ave, Arcadia; ☺10am-9pm Mon-Sat, 11am-7pm Sun; Ⓟ) Upstairs in this megamall is a spiffy new East Asian food hall. Among the selections are **Side Chick** (Hainan chicken and rice with habit-forming ginger-garlic sauce) by the folks behind trendy Eggslut (p97), **EMC** (raw bar and hotpot), **Monkey Bar** (Japanese whiskey and Chinese-inflected American comfort food), **Uncle Tetsu** (ramen) and a branch of famed dumpling house Din Tai Fung (p216).

Many of the restaurants are counter service, with seating at tables and stools styled after early California orange crates.

Enter the mall near Chinese superstore **Wing Hop Fung** (📞626-508-8888; www.winghopfung.com; Westfield Santa Anita, 400 S Baldwin Ave, Arcadia; ☺11am-8pm Sun-Thu, to 9pm Fri & Sat), lest you find yourself confronted with – heaven forbid – a conventional mall food court.

🍸 Drinking & Nightlife

While there's a decent selection of bars in Old Pasadena, it's in its tea rooms that it really excels. Also look at some of the Asian restaurants and cafes, such as 85°C (p216), for an interesting selection of Asian-inspired drinks.

★Rose Garden Tea Room TEAHOUSE
(📞626-405-2236; www.huntington.org/dining; Huntington Library, 1108 Oxford Rd, San Marino; ☺noon-5pm Mon & Wed-Fri, 10:30am-5pm Sat & Sun) High tea ($35) at the Rose Garden has been a grand tradition inside the Huntington (p211) for generations. Try your choice of herbal and fair-trade teas (including jasmine, tropical fruit, vanilla and signature bergamot blend) with crumpets, scones, finger sandwiches, seasonal fruit and mini-desserts. Allow about 1½ hours for the full experience. Reservations are recommended; book well in advance for weekends.

Note: Huntington admission is required for access, sold separately.

Chado Tea Room TEAHOUSE
(Map p212; 📞626-431-2832; www.chadotea.com; 79 N Raymond Ave, Pasadena; ☺11:30am-7pm; Ⓜ Gold Line to Memorial Park) Sensible ladies descend to this Indian-owned emporium for affordable afternoon-tea service (full tea service $18): tea, scones, half-sandwiches and desserts. Chado serves teas from all over the globe – about 400 in all – from milky oolong to white teas, green Darjeeling and the

best-selling Mauritius, heady with vanilla aromas. If the spirit moves you, it also sells loose teas and accessories.

Vertical Wine Bistro WINE BAR
(Map p212; www.verticalwinebistro.com; 70 N Raymond Ave, Pasadena; ☺5pm-late Tue-Sun) Although this is a sophisticated wine bar dressed in cocoa and candlelight, don't worry if you can't tell your pinot noir from your pinot grigio. Tapas come with a wine recommendation and you can sample 2oz tastes from most of the 400-plus bottles in the cellar.

☆ Entertainment

Ice House COMEDY
(Map p212; 📞626-577-1894; www.icehousecomedy.com; 38 N Mentor Ave, Pasadena) Since it opened in 1960, this legendary comedy club has helped launch the careers of dozens of comics, including household names such as David Letterman, Ellen DeGeneres, George Lopez, Lily Tomlin, Jerry Seinfeld and Jay Leno. Who knows? Maybe America's next great comic will be here during your visit.

Santa Anita Park HORSE RACING
(📞tickets 626-574-6366, tour info 626-574-6677; www.santaanita.com; 285 W Huntington Dr, Arcadia; adult/child from $5/free; ☺racing season Christmas–mid-Apr, late Sep-early Nov, tram tours 8:30am & 9:45am Sat & Sun during racing season; 📶♿) Home of the legendary Seabiscuit, this stunning, art deco thoroughbred racetrack is the oldest and one of the most prestigious in Southern California. Free **tram tours** take you to Seabiscuit's barn, the jockey's room and other sights during racing season.

The track opened in 1934 and pioneered the use of the automated starting gate, photo finish and electrical timer. Stars who kept and raced their horses here have ranged from Bing Crosby and Errol Flynn to Mark McGrath (of the band Sugar Ray), Alex Trebek and Burt Bacharach.

There's also an altogether shameful part of its history. During WWII it served as internment camp for Japanese-Americans, whose only crime was their ancestry.

Pasadena Playhouse THEATER
(Map p212; 📞626-356-7529; www.pasadenaplayhouse.org; 39 S El Molino Ave, Pasadena) This attractive, adobe-style complex was founded in 1917 and by 1937 had developed such a reputation that it was named State Theater of California. It's since premiered hundreds

---

LOCAL KNOWLEDGE

FLEA MARKET STANDOUTS

Flea markets are like urban archaeology: you'll need plenty of patience and luck when sifting through other people's trash and detritus, but oh, the thrill when you finally unearth a treasure! Arrive early, bring small bills, wear walking shoes and get ready to haggle. These are the best of the best.

Rose Bowl Flea Market (www.rgcshows.com; 1001 Rose Bowl Dr, Pasadena; admission from $9; ⊙9am-4:30pm 2nd Sun each month, last entry 3pm, early admission from 5am) Pasadena's massive monthly Sunday market draws hunters and collectors from across the US.

Melrose Trading Post (Map p138; www.melrosetradingpost.org; Fairfax High School, 7850 Melrose Ave, Mid-City; admission $3; ⊙9am-5pm Sun; ▣MTA lines 217, 218 and 10) Held at Fairfax High School, this is one of LA's trendiest secondhand hot spots, with vintage furniture, decorative objects, fashion, accessories and more.

Pasadena City College Flea Market (www.pasadena.edu; 1570 E Colorado Blvd, Pasadena; ⊙8am-3pm 1st Sun of each month) The Rose Bowl's free, less-hyped sibling, with fashion, accessories, crafts and an especially notable selection of vinyl.

---

of works and hosted leading actors of their generations. It still books the occasional big names, recently including Al Pacino, Lawrence Fishburne and Taraji P Henson.

🔒 Shopping

From giant malls such as Westfield (p218) Santa Anita and El Paseo in Old Pasadena to LA's top flea market and some surprisingly edgy fashion and accessories, there's something for about every taste in Pasadena and the San Gabriel Valley.

★**Gold Bug**   ART
(Map p212; ☑626-744-9963; www.goldbugpasadena.com; 22 E Union St, Pasadena; ⊙10am-5pm Mon, to 6pm Tue-Sat, noon-5pm Sun) An amazing boutique with a steampunk vibe, Gold Bug shows work and collections created (or curated) by 100 area artists. We saw a robotic, metallic Cheshire cat, exquisite vintage jewelry and lamps, raw crystals and selenite, and a terrific art-book collection.

Lather   BODY CARE
(Map p212; ☑626-396-1973; www.lather.com; 17 E Colorado Blvd, Pasadena; ⊙11am-9pm Mon-Thu, to 10pm Fri & Sat, until 7pm Sun; Ⓜ Gold Line to Del Mar or Memorial Park) This Pasadena-based company supplies natural hand creams, exfoliants and other treatments, and at its flagship store you can try them. The bamboo lemongrass body scrub left our hands feeling all smooth and silky. Products are made with natural ingredients such as cranberry, kelp and chamomile.

Vroman's Bookstore   BOOKS
(Map p212; ☑626-449-5320; www.vromansbookstore.com; 695 E Colorado Blvd, Pasadena; ⊙9am-9pm Mon-Thu, to 10pm Fri & Sat, 10am-8pm Sun; 🖶) In business since 1894, Vroman's is a Pasadena institution and claims to be the largest and oldest bookstore in all of SoCal. It's practically a required stop for authors on book tours, making for events virtually daily, from book signings to story time for the kids (10am Wednesday and Saturday) – check website for details.

Highland Park & Eagle Rock

Highland Park is hot. Once plagued by gang activity, its low-key, low-rise streets have been transformed into an in-the-know hub of gentrified Craftsman homes, blog-worthy coffee shops, restaurants, bars, galleries, shops and offbeat museums, all of which live side by side with throwback taquerias, barbers and Mexican grocery stores. Further north, Dodger-loving, Laker-rootin' Eagle Rock revels in its small-town air. Short on sights, it's still worth a detour for its nostalgic mix of mid-century signage, retro delis and pizza parlors...not to mention its discreet infiltration of attitude-free new-school cafes and eateries.

To make the most of Highland Park's offerings, consider hitting the neighborhood in the early afternoon. This way an exploration of the boutiques, vintage stores and coffee shops on N Figueroa St and York Blvd can be seamlessly followed by dinner and drinks on either strip. On the second Saturday of the month, many of the neighborhood's art galleries and businesses stay open late for the area's monthly gallery night.

◉ Sights

Los Angeles Police Museum MUSEUM
(☎323-344-9445; http://laphs.org; 6045 York Blvd, Highland Park; adult/senior/under 13yr $9/8/free; ☺10am-4pm Tue-Fri, also 9am-3pm 3rd Sun of month; ℗) Crime fighting goes under the spotlight at Police Station No 11, now better known as the Los Angeles Police Museum. Exhibits trace the history of the LAPD, from its humble beginnings in 1869 to the modern force of today. There's fascinating background on some of the city's most infamous crimes, plus a collection of historic police vehicles. Built in 1926, the handsome station itself isn't short of anecdotes, with former captives including notorious Mexican mafioso Joe 'Pegleg' Morgan.

Self Realization Fellowship NOTABLE BUILDING
(☎323-225-2471; www.yogananda-srf.org; 3880 San Rafael Ave, Mt Washington; ☺9am-5pm; ℗⛪) When Parmanhansa Yogananda first came to LA from India in the 1920s to spread his yoga love, he set up shop at this beautiful estate, which remains a working monastery that offers stunning views of the Downtown skyline from its garden. The house doors are also open. Peek into the library where you'll find a number of books by 'yogiji' (as he's affectionately called), as well as his letter opener, robes and locks of his hair.

🏃 Activities

★Highland Park Bowl BOWLING
(☎323-257-2695; http://highlandparkbowl.com; 5621 N Figueroa St, Highland Park; bowling per lane per hr $50-70; ☺5pm-2am Mon-Fri, from 11am Sat & Sun; Ⓜ Gold Line to Highland Park) It's a bowling alley, Jim. But not as we know it. You'll be hard-pressed to find a bowling alley as stunningly original as this one, its steampunk fit out including upcycled pinsetters turned chandeliers, leather Chesterfield sofas and twin bars serving rotating craft cocktails and beers. Bites include decent wood-fired Neapolitan-style pizzas: place is best earlier in the week when the crowds are thinner.

Second Saturday Gallery Night WALKING
(www.nelaart.org) On the second Saturday of the month, dozens of art galleries and businesses in Highland Park and Eagle Rock keep their doors open till late to encourage locals and visitors alike to explore the area's creative side. Behind it all is the Northeast Los Angeles Arts Organization, established to support local creatives. See the website for event details and map.

🍴 Eating

Highland Park's dining scene is diverse, exciting and ever-evolving. Focused on N Figueroa St and York Blvd, you'll find everything from vibrant vegetarian grub and fashionable sharing plates, to ramen, old-school Mexican and gourmet doughnuts. Although options in Eagle Rock are a little more limited, its main thoroughfare (Colorado Blvd) serves up some decent options, including a long-loved pizza joint.

★Kitchen Mouse VEGETARIAN $
(☎323-259-9555; http://kitchenmousela.com; 5904 N Figueroa St, Highland Park; dishes $8.50-12.50; ☺8am-4pm Mon-Fri, from 7am Sat & Sun; 🛜🅿🐾; Ⓜ Gold Line to Highland Park) A super-cute cafe with tied-back curtains, freshly picked flowers and sidewalk tables, Kitchen Mouse is Highland Park's favorite herbivore. Everyone from alt-fashion bloggers to mature middle-class couples flock here for generous, mood-lifting vegan and vegetarian dishes such as the avocado TLT, a moreish combo of avocado, cherry tomatoes and tempeh spiked with hot Dijon mustard and crunchy sunflower brittle. Good coffee, too.

Donut Friend DESSERTS $
(☎213-995-6191; http://donutfriend.com; 5107 York Blvd, Highland Park; donuts from $2.50; ☺7am-10pm Sun-Thu, to midnight Fri & Sat) 'Donuts. Done differently' is its slogan, and it's not kidding. Here, holed treats are sprinkled with coconut bacon, stuffed with vegan cream cheese and fresh basil, or drizzled in glazes such as matcha tea and maple. Picky gluttons can even customize their own donut from a range of fillings and glazes. The biggest hit is the Strawberrylab, jammed with fresh strawberries and whipped cream.

Mr Holmes Bakehouse BAKERY $
(☎323-739-0473; http://mrholmesbakehouse.com; 111 S Ave 59, Highland Park; pastries from $3.50; ☺8am-3pm; Ⓜ Gold Line to Highland Park) The (neon) writing is on the (brick) wall: I Got Baked in Los Angeles. Mr Holmes promises highs of the sugary type at this airy, buzz-inducing bakery. Scan the designer

counter for just-made matcha and chocolate croissants, pillowy doughnuts packed with velvety almond cream, and the signature cruffin (love child of the croissant and muffin). Expect queues, especially on weekends.

Casa Bianca
PIZZA $

(📞323-256-9617; www.casabiancapizza.com; 1650 Colorado Blvd, Eagle Rock; pizzas $6-21; ⏱4pm-midnight Tue-Thu, to 1am Fri & Sat; 🖅) This 'White House' has been peddling moreish thin-crust pizzas since 1955. Jonathan Gold, LA's erstwhile, Pulitzer Prize–winning restaurant critic, swears by the square-cut pizza here; he suggests ordering yours topped with fried eggplant and sweet-and-spicy homemade sausage. Pizzas aside, the place also pumps out decent lasagna and antipasto salad. Cash only.

Eagle Rock Italian Bakery
DELI $

(📞323-255-8224; 1726 Colorado Blvd, Eagle Rock; sandwiches from $4.50; ⏱8am-6pm Mon-Sat, 9:30am-1pm Sun) The Carfachia family has been running this old-school Italian deli for over 40 years, and everyone from local matriarchs to laborers and hipsters hit the place for its hulking lunchtime sandwiches. Mamma of them all is the Italian Combo, a fleshy fantasy of salami, ham, mortadella and capocollo (pork cold cut) encased in the bakery's oven-fresh bread.

Ramen of York
RAMEN $

(📞323-999-7988; www.ramenofyork.com; 5051 York Blvd, Highland Park; ⏱11:30am-10:45pm Sun-Thu, to 11:45pm Fri & Sat) It's just not a hipster hood without a decent ramen joint, and this skinny, black-walled bolthole is it for Highland Park. The hero dish is the *tonkotsu,* best ordered with the pork belly (vegetarian options available) and a side of black garlic oil for added flavor. Another favorite is the *tsukemen,* which has you dipping dry noodles into a separate bowl of broth.

Scoops
ICE CREAM $

(📞323-906-2649; 5105 York St, Highland Park; scoops $4, pints $8; ⏱2-9pm Mon-Sat) Locals (rightly) drool like fools at the mere mention of Scoops, which has several branches across the city. It's famed for its artisan ice cream and out-of-the-box flavors such as lavender, rosemary and lychee yuzu. Crowd favorites include the brown butter, though it's pretty hard to go wrong. The place also peddles vegan flavors that actually taste like ice cream.

★ Cafe Birdie
MODERN AMERICAN $$

(📞323-739-6928; http://cafebirdiela.com; 5631 N Figueroa St, Highland Park; dinner mains $11-27; ⏱5:30-10pm Mon-Thu, to 11pm Fri, 10am-2:30pm & 5-11pm Sat, 10am-2:30pm & 5-10pm Sun; M Gold Line to Highland Park) Market-fresh ingredients drive elevated comfort dishes at this slinky Highland Park hot spot, complete with prerequisite marble-topped bar, designer lighting and a dark, buzzing vibe. Cleanse the palate with one of the delicate, seasonal salads before sinking teeth into the stand-out Moroccan fried chicken. Birdie's pasta dishes are equally gorgeous, especially the pappardelle with pork-cheek ragù.

Check paid, retreat to Birdie's rear speakeasy, Good Housekeeping.

Little Beast
MODERN AMERICAN $$

(📞323-341-5899; www.littlebeastrestaurant.com; 1496 Colorado Blvd, Eagle Rock; small plates $8-15, mains $18-30; ⏱5-10pm Sun-Thu, to 11pm Fri & Sat; P 🖥) Less beastly than adorable, this friendly restaurant offers a string of snug nooks inside an old Craftsman cottage, as well as a larger, less atmospheric outdoor patio. The menu is a seasonal, modern American affair, spanning everything from creative salads to comfort grub. Not all the dishes quite hit the mark, though solid options include the duck liver mousse and risotto.

🍸 Drinking & Nightlife

Highland Park's bar scene is seriously kicking, with both N Figueroa St and York Blvd drawing a cool, indie crowd. Should you slurp cocktails in a bowling alley or in an intimate speakeasy? Or perhaps beers while rocking out to live local bands? Coffee snobs will find decent specialty joe in both Highland Park and Eagle Rock.

★ ETA
COCKTAIL BAR

(www.facebook.com/ETAHLP; 5630 N Figueroa St, Highland Park; ⏱6pm-1am Sun-Thu, 5pm-2am Fri & Sat; M Gold Line to Highland Park) One of the city's top cocktail dens, intimate ETA serves innovative, complex libations such as its famous Penultimate Word, an out-of-the-box mix of gin, mezcal, green chartreuse, cucumber puree and lime. The mural you're looking at is by local artist Johnny Tarajosu and, while the venue offers limited snacks, the team doesn't mind if you bring in something from outside.

★ **Good Housekeeping** COCKTAIL BAR
(☑ 323-739-6928; 5635 N Figueroa St, Highland Park; ⊘ 6pm-midnight Sun-Thu, to 2am Fri & Sat) Step out the back door of restaurant Cafe Birdie (p221) and you'll find this red-brick speakeasy. A neighborly oasis of tealights, leather booths and competent barkeeps, its on-point cocktails are fond of Californian spirits and ingredients. The cognoscenti tell the barkeeps they're here to see about a 'science kit,' code for a secret cocktail of Japanese whiskey, vermouth and smoked applewood.

Civil Coffee COFFEE
(http://civilcoffee.com; 5629 N Figueroa St, Highland Park; ⊘ 7am-5pm) A lofty, minimalist coffee shop with photogenic floor-tiles, Civil peddles a rotating cast of single-origin espresso, cold brew and drip coffees to Highland Park's hip brigade. The handful of quality edibles (available until 2pm) include avocado toast topped with shiitake 'bacon', and baguette-style gourmet sandwiches. If you're in retail mode, bag some grounded beans or a stylish, branded tote.

Sonny's Hideaway COCKTAIL BAR
(☑ 323-255-2000; www.sonnyshideaway.com; 5137 York Blvd, Highland Park; ⊘ 5pm-late Tue-Sun) Mission brown is back in vogue at this retro-inspired cocktail bar and eatery, decked out in brown dining booths and drawing a mixed, low-key crowd spanning hipsters to kooky couples. While the food menu is a competent, comfort affair, we prefer perching at the long, chatty bar for the smashing cocktails, shaken or stirred by congenial, attention-driven barkeeps.

Budget-conscious imbibers will appreciate the $6 cocktail specials, available 5pm to 7pm Tuesday to Saturday (from 4pm Sunday) and also from 11pm to 1am Tuesday to Thursday.

Villa Sombrero BAR
(☑ 323-256-9014; 6101 York Blvd, Highland Park) This '70s throwback is technically a Mexican restaurant, but the real reason to stop here is for the killer margaritas. Considered by many to be the best in town, they're huge, strong and not sickly sweet.

Feel the power while pondering the framed depiction of Aztec warrior Popocatépetl grieving his sweetheart Iztaccihuatl, who died brokenhearted after mistakenly believing that Popocatépetl had been slain in battle.

Found Coffee COFFEE
(☑ 323-206-5154; www.foundcoffeela.com; 1355 Colorado Blvd, Eagle Rock; ⊘ 7am-6pm Mon-Sat, 8am-5pm Sun; 🐾) Neighborly, light-soaked Found showcases a rotating cast of mostly Californian specialty coffee roasters, including LA's Demitasse and Peri Coffee, Ventura's Prospect Coffee Roasters and San Jose's Chromatic Coffee. Whatever the roaster, expect full-bodied, quality brews. Food options are limited to baked goods and packaged snacks. Common tables, free wi-fi and a few power sockets make the place popular with keyboard-tapping creatives.

Low End Theory CLUB
(www.lowendtheoryclub.com; 2419 N Broadway Ave, Lincoln Heights; 18 & over cover $10; ⊘ 9:30pm-2am Wed) On Wednesdays, gritty dive bar Airliner hosts Low End Theory, one of the city's top electronica nights, with loud, body-shaking beats spanning dubstep and glitch to IDM. The club was founded by resident DJs Daddy Kev and Gaslamp Killer and gained notoriety for launching the great Flying Lotus into the international limelight.

Special guests such as Q-Tip from Tribe Called Quest have been known to roll through and spin.

🛍 **Shopping**

Highland Park retail focuses on the eclectic and the artisanal. You'll find everything from warehouses crammed with mid-century lamps and armchairs, to quirky little shops selling everything from obscure vinyl and vintage tees, to one-of-a-kind frocks, jewelry, art, ceramics and hand-printed stationery, much of it designed and made locally. Most offerings are on York Blvd and on (or just off) N Figueroa St between Aves 56 and 60.

★ **Sunbeam Vintage** VINTAGE
(☑ 323-908-9743; www.sunbeamvintage.com; 106 S Ave 58, Highland Park; ⊘ 10am-6pm; Ⓜ Gold Line to Highland Park) Nirvana for fans of mid-century-modern design, Sunbeam Vintage stocks an utterly fabulous collection of retro furniture and homewares. Dive in for pineapple-shaped brass lamps, bar carts, elegant velvet armchairs, timber side tables, metallic art, even giant metal letters from old marquees. There's a second, smaller branch around the corner on Figueroa St.

Matters of Space
DESIGN

(☎ 323-743-3267; www.mattersofspace.com; 5005 York Blvd, Highland Park; ☉10am-6pm Mon-Sat, 11am-5pm Sun) Both an interior-design firm and store, Matters of Space sells its own mid-century-inspired furniture and a sharply curated collection of homewares and accessories from independent American and international designers. Look for photo collages by Hamish Robertson, glazed pottery by Highland Park's own Lily King and funky polymer-clay necklaces from Athens, Greece. We especially love the handmade, geometric-motif rugs from Brooklyn's Aelfie.

Mindfulnest
GIFTS & SOUVENIRS

(☎ 323-999-7969; www.mindfulnest.com/highland-park; 5050 York Blvd, Highland Park; ☉11am-6pm) A quirky concept store dedicated to Stateside designers, artists and artisans. Stock up on contemporary photography and digital art, playful buttons, canvas flasks, reworked vintage threads, even botanical teas. There's no shortage of LA and Californian items, include edgy handmade jewelry from Highland Park. You'll find other branches in Burbank and Santa Monica; see the website for details.

Galco's Old World Grocery
FOOD & DRINKS

(☎ 323-255-7115; www.galcos.com; 5702 York Blvd, Highland Park; ☉9am-6:30pm Mon-Sat, to 4pm Sun) You'll find around 700 small-batch and heritage sodas at this family-run grocery store, from botanically brewed British cola to American almond cream soda. You can even make your own soda from flavors such as toasted marshmallow and cotton candy. Heighten the sugar rush with some old-school candy, guaranteed to induce playground flashbacks in anyone with a star-spangled childhood.

Permanent Records
MUSIC

(☎ 323-739-6141; www.facebook.com/permanent recordsla; 5116 York Blvd, Highland Park; ☉noon-8pm) Permanent's black crates are jammed with new and used vinyl. The Chicago import pays decent money for vinyl, which translates into a strong offering of collectable and limited-edition discs. Fortes include garage, psych and hard rock, as well as some deliciously obscure treasures (we scored Mistress Mary's album *Housewife* on our last visit). The bargain bin usually harbors a gem or two.

Avalon Vintage
VINTAGE

(☎ 323-309-7717; www.facebook.com/avalon records; 106 N Ave 56, Highland Park; ☉1-8pm Tue-Sun; Ⓜ Gold Line to Highland Park) One the best-loved consignment stores in LA, known for stocking more unusual retro frocks and outfits. It's hardly surprising since store owner Carmen Hawk was Milla Jovovich's former design partner at Jovovich-Hawk. You'll also find an eclectic collection of old vinyl records spanning artists as varied as Janis Joplin, Kool & the Gang, Madonna and The Mars Volta.

Exposition Park & South LA

The world's oldest beings (dinosaur skeletons) and space-age technology (the Space Shuttle Endeavour) come together under one roof at the California Science Center, one of a trio of great museums in 'Expo Park,' a quick train ride from Downtown LA and a straight shot on the same train to Santa Monica. Several miles away, you may be equally inspired by Watts Towers, a masterpiece of folk art 33 years in the making, and by the spirit of Leimert Park, the heart of LA's African-American community.

◉ Sights

Exposition Park is home to three quality museums (the Natural History Museum, California Science Center and California African American Museum), a robust and rambling Rose Garden and the 1923 Los Angeles Memorial Coliseum. Eventually the **Lucas Museum of Narrative Art** is due to open here, scheduled for 2021.

Otherwise, one sight not to miss is the fabulous Watts Towers, a 30-year-plus labor of love by Simon Rodia.

Natural History Museum of Los Angeles
MUSEUM

(☎ 213-763-3466; www.nhm.org; 900 Exposition Blvd, Exposition Park; adult/student & senior/child $12/9/5; ☉9:30am-5pm; Ⓟ♿; Ⓜ Expo Line to Expo/Vermont) Dinos to diamonds, bears to beetles, hissing roaches to African elephants – this museum will take you around the world and back, through millions of years in time. It's all housed in a beautiful 1913 Spanish Renaissance–style building that stood in for Columbia University in the first Toby McGuire *Spider-Man* movie – yup, this was where Peter

Parker was bitten by the radioactive arachnid. There's enough to see here to fill several hours.

Special exhibits usually draw the biggest crowds, but don't miss out on a spin around the permanent halls to see such trophy displays as the **Dinosaur Hall**, featuring the world's first T. rex growth series (baby, juvenile and adult). There are the requisite **dioramas of animals** from North America and Africa, as well as the **bird hall** and a gallery of **Aztec and Latin American artifacts**. If diamonds are your best friend, head to the **Gem and Mineral Hall** with its walk-through gem vault and a Fort Knox–worthy gold collection, including the world's second-largest-known gold nugget.

Kids will have plenty of ooh-and-aah moments in the spruced-up **Discovery Center**, where they can assemble a T. rex puzzle, handle bones, antlers and minerals and get close to tarantulas, scorpions and other creepy-crawlies. Other interactive programs include the **Nature Lab**, which encourages local kids to survey their neighborhoods for biodiversity, and a bug-sorting lab.

One of the newest permanent exhibits, **Becoming Los Angeles**, takes a serious look at the region from the native Gabrieleño-Tongva peoples through the missions, Mexican independence, joining the US, movies, aviation and innovations such as the catalytic converter and solar panels.

Outside are 3.5 acres of **nature gardens**, including native plants, and a seasonal pavilion showcasing butterflies or spiders (not at the same time!).

For grown-ups, the museum turns up the volume during its **First Fridays** event series, which combines brainy lectures, live music and KCRW DJs in the African Mammal Hall, bars and late-night access to the exhibits, which are all bathed in nocturnal light. Check the website for upcoming dates. The $18 charge includes museum admission.

California Science Center   MUSEUM

(⌨ film schedule 213-744-2019, info 323-724-3623; www.californiasciencecenter.org; 700 Exposition Park Dr, Exposition Park; IMAX movie adult/child $8.50/5.25; ⊙10am-5pm; 🚼) **FREE** Top billing at the Science Center goes to the Space Shuttle Endeavour, one of only four space shuttles nationwide, but there's plenty else to see at this large, multistory, multimedia museum filled with buttons to push, lights to switch on and knobs to pull. A simulated earthquake, baby chicks hatching and a giant techno-doll

named Tess bring out the kid in everyone. Admission is free, but special exhibits, experiences and IMAX movies cost extra.

Behind its stately facade facing Expo Park, the Science Center is quite modern inside, the enormous space divided into themed areas. Upstairs on the left, **World of Life** focuses mostly on the human body. You can hop on a red blood cell for a computer fly-through of the circulatory system, visit the Digestion Diner to ask Gertie the waitress how long your insides really are, watch open-heart surgery, and learn about homeostasis from Tess, a giant, talking animatronic body billed as '50ft of brains, beauty and biology.' Tots may have trouble understanding the science, but they will remember Tess.

Creative World is all about the ingenious ways humans have devised to transport things and build structures. Meet a family of crash-test dummies, fly a virtual hovercraft and get all shook up during a fake earthquake. **Ecosystems** takes visitors through a variety of habitats: desert, river, island, urban and forest.

Aircraft and space travel take center stage in the **Sketch Foundation Gallery**, in an adjacent Frank Gehry building (yes, he's everywhere). Spirits will soar at the sight of a pioneering 1902 Wright glider; the original Gemini XI capsule flown by US astronauts in 1996; and a replica Soviet Sputnik, the first human-made object to orbit the earth in 1957.

But these days, the **Space Shuttle Endeavour** is the Science Center's star attraction (get it?). Exhibits leading up to it show it in one of the Mission Control centers (which operated here in LA County, no less!) and shuttles' inner workings from food prep to toilets. A remarkable time-lapse video shows Endeavour's much ballyhooed final voyage in 2012 – a meandering flyover of the city on the back of a Boeing 747, then its tow through city streets that lasted a couple days in the ultimate slow-speed chase (and this was with no traffic!).

When you finally get to see Endeavour, it dominates its pavilion, looking as it was after its 25th and last space flight, damaged heat-shield tiles and all. It will be kept in this temporary pavilion until its permanent home in the **Samuel Oschin Air and Space Center** is built (the Science Center is in the midst of a fundraising campaign). Just outside is one of the external fuel tanks used for liftoff, which is even longer than the shuttle itself. The gift shop sells space goods and super-cute plush toys such as the space chimp. During peak periods and holidays, visiting Endeavour requires a timed-ticket reservation (fee $2). To avoid crowds of schoolkids, arrive at the Science Center after 2pm on school days.

Rose Garden
GARDENS

(☎ 213-763-0114; www.laparks.org/expo/garden; 701 State Dr, Exposition Park; ⊘ 8:30am-sunset Mar 16–Dec 31; P; M Expo Line to Exposition Park/USC) FREE This stately garden in front of the California Science Center opened to the public in 1928 and today displays 145 varieties of plants.

California African American Museum
MUSEUM

(☎ 213-744-7432; www.caamuseum.org; 600 State Dr, Exposition Park; ⊘ 10am-5pm Tue-Sat, 11am Sun; P ⊕) FREE CAAM does an excellent job of showcasing African-American artists and the African-American experience, with a special focus on California and LA. Exhibits change a few times each year in galleries around a sunlit atrium.

Los Angeles Memorial Coliseum
STADIUM

(☎ 213-741-0410; www.lacoliseum.com; 3911 S Figueroa St, Exposition Park; guided/self-guided tours $25/10; ⊘ self-guided tours 10am-4pm Wed-Sun, guided tours 10:30am & 1:30pm Wed-Sun; M Expo Line to Exposition Park/USC) Built in 1923, this grand stadium hosted the 1932 and 1984 Summer Olympic Games, the 1959 baseball World Series and two Super Bowls, is the temporary home stadium for the Los Angeles Rams (p227) and permanent home of University of Southern California Trojans (American) football teams. Informative guided tours dish the history and take you inside locker rooms, press box, the field and more (blackout dates apply).

Self-guided tours are also available, but don't let you inside the bowl.

The adjacent indoor Los Angeles Memorial Sports Arena dates from 1959 and is still used for the rare rock concert.

University of Southern California
UNIVERSITY

(USC; ☎ 213-740-6605; www.usc.edu; cnr Exposition Blvd & Figueroa St, University of Southern California; M Expo Line to Expo Park/USC) FREE George Lucas, John Wayne and Neil Armstrong are among the famous alumni of this well-respected private university, founded in 1880, just north of Exposition Park. Free 50-minute, student-led tours depart from the admissions center Monday to Friday, and touch on campus history, architecture and student life. Reservations are strongly recommended. You can also pick up a self-guided tour at the admissions center or online.

To see changing art exhibits of noted artists and student shows, visit the USC Fisher Museum of Art.

USC Fisher Museum of Art
GALLERY

(☎ 213-740-4561; http://fisher.usc.edu; 823 W Exposition Blvd, Harris Hall, University of Southern California; ⊘ noon-5pm Tue-Fri, to 4pm Sat) FREE The university's art museum presents changing selections from its ever-expanding collection of American landscapes, British portraits, French Barbizon School paintings and modern Mexican masters such as Salomón Huerta and Gronk (Glugio Nicandro). It offers an annual student exhibition timed to commencement ceremonies each May.

★ Watts Towers
LANDMARK

(☎ 213-847-4646; www.wattstowers.us; 1761-1765 E 107th St, Watts; adult/child 13-17yr & senior/child under 13yr $7/3/free; ⊘ tours 11am-3pm Thu & Fri, 10:30am-3pm Sat, noon-3pm Sun; P; M Blue Line to 103rd St) The three Gothic spires of the fabulous Watts Towers rank among the world's greatest monuments of folk art. In 1921 Italian immigrant Simon Rodia set out 'to make something big' and then spent 33 years cobbling together this whimsical free-form sculpture from concrete, steel and a motley assortment of found objects: green 7Up bottles, sea shells, tiles, rocks and pottery.

The towers reach up to 99.5ft in height, just below the city's legal limit of 100ft. You can admire Watts Towers from beyond the fencing any time, but to get inside you must take the tour. A 12-minute black-and-white documentary from the 1950s tells the story through rare archival footage.

Admission is by cash or check only.

The adjacent Watts Towers Art Center sponsors workshops, performances and classes for the community, hosts art exhibits and organizes the acclaimed Watts Towers Day of the Drum and Jazz Festival in late September or early October.

Watts Labor Community Action Committee
CULTURAL CENTER

(WLCAC; ☎ 323-563-5639; www.wlcac.org; 10950 S Central Ave, Watts; tours adult/child $5/free; ⊘ 8:30am-5pm Mon-Fri; P ⊕; ◻ MTA line 53, M Blue Line to Willowbrook) Watts was around the epicenter of two sets of LA riots – first in 1965 and then in 1992 – when this vibrant community and cultural center was burned to the ground. The neighborhood is still teeming with large numbers of kids growing up poor and angry, but there are pockets of improvements, thanks in part to such groups as this.

Founded by Ted Watkins and run by his son, Timothy, the headquarters doubles as a cultural theme park. A huge bronze sculpture of a black woman called *Mother of Humanity* dominates the campus, and the **Cecil Ferguson Gallery** rotates exhibits of LA's best African-American artists, such as Willie Middlebrook and Michael Massenburg.

The most powerful exhibit, though, is the **Civil Rights Museum**, which is only accessible on guided tours that must be booked at least a day in advance. Guides take you through the hull of the *Amistad* (the actual facade used in the Spielberg film), a body-filled slave ship, and along the Mississippi Delta Rd to displays about Martin Luther King, the Black Panther Party and the 1960s Civil Rights movement.

There's also a wonderful new skate park (open 8am to dusk) where South LA's growing crew of skaters freelance and grind with incredible skill.

Central Avenue
HISTORIC SITE
(South LA) From the 1920s to the 1950s, Central Ave was the lifeblood of LA's African-American community, not by choice but because segregation laws kept black people out of other neighborhoods. It was also a hotbed of jazz and R&B, a legacy commemorated every July with the **Central Avenue Jazz Festival** held outside the 1928 **Dunbar Hotel** (4225 S Central Ave, South LA).

Duke Ellington once maintained a suite at the Dunbar, which was LA's only 1st-class hotel for African Americans. It's now a low-income seniors center, but has been renovated and the facade faithfully restored. It's worth a peek.

Leimert Park
AREA
The soft lilt of a saxophone purrs from a storefront. Excited chatter streams from a coffee house. The savory aroma of barbecue wafts into the steamy noontime air. Welcome to Leimert (*luh-MERT*) Park, the cultural hub of LA's African-American community.

About 2.5 miles west of Exposition Park, the mostly residential neighborhood was designed by the Olmsted brothers of New York Central Park fame, and was nicknamed 'the black Greenwich Village' by filmmaker and local resident John Singleton (*Boyz n the Hood*). Here, bongo freaks gather in the park for Sunday-afternoon drum circles. Nearby, the World Stage is a destination for jazz aficionados. Check out the **Sankofa Passage** (Leimert Park's walk of fame), paying homage to local figures such as LA jazz legends Horace Tapscott, Dexter Gordon and Buddy Collette.

Art + Practice
GALLERY
(☏323-337-6887; www.artandpractice.org; 3401 W 43rd Pl, Leimert Park; ⊙noon-6pm Mon-Sat) **FREE** Founded in 2014 by artist Mark Bradford, art collector and philanthropist Eileen Harris Norton and community activist Allan DiCastro, Art + Practice stages free exhibitions of world-class art in Leimert Park, with a special focus on artists living or working in LA. Its community outreach programs target youth in foster care. Exhibits change a few times a year, so check the calendar before setting out to make sure the gallery is open.

✖ Eating

★ Mercado La Paloma
FOOD HALL $
(www.mercadolapaloma.com; 3655 S Grand Ave; ⊙shop hours vary; P; MExpo Line to Jefferson/USC) If you're near Expo Park or USC, it's totally worth the five-minute walk under the freeway to this fabulous food hall. About a dozen restaurant stalls sell everything from Yucatan to Ethiopian cuisine, ceviche to coffee, while other stalls sell Mexican souvenirs, sports merchandise and more.

Everytable
AMERICAN $
(☏213-973-5095; www.everytable.com; 3650 W Martin Luther King Blvd, Baldwin Hills Crenshaw Plaza; mains $4-5.50; ⊙10:30am-9pm Mon-Sat, 11am-7pm Sun; P; MTA lines 210, 710 or 740 Crenshaw & MLK, MExpo Line to Crenshaw Blvd) A micro-chain with a social conscience: fresh, healthy grab-and-go meals in a bowl, priced lower in under-served communities and higher in more affluent ones. There's a simple but diverse and satisfying menu (think chicken tamales, Jamaican jerk chicken, kale Caesar salad and Cajun blackened fish), plus a kids' menu and cheerful staff.

It's in the food court of Baldwin Hill's Crenshaw Plaza. Free parking. There's another location (1101 W 23rd St) a short walk north of USC.

Locol
BURGERS $
(www.welocol.com; 1950 E 103rd St, Watts; burgers & bowls $5-7, snacks & sides from $2; ⊙11am-8pm) Clean lines, loud hip-hop and a gourmet pedigree animate this fast-food concept

from Roy Choi, the chef credited with starting LA's food-truck revolution. Locol does bargain-priced yet quality burgers, fried chicken burgers and chicken 'nugs', plus less expected fast food such as tasty shrimp and grits, waffles with chicken wings and hearty 'foldies', which are like modified quesadillas.

You can even get green juice or indulge in soft-serve ice cream or shakes, and it's all served on plant-based biodegradable disposable plates and utensils.

The best part, though, is its mission: to bring quality food to the one-time 'food desert' of Watts and employ local people to get a leg up. In part for this, Locol was named *Los Angeles Magazine*'s restaurant of the year in 2017.

Ackee Bamboo
JAMAICAN **$$**

(☎ 323-295-7275; www.ackeebamboojacuisine.com; 4305 Degnan Blvd, Leimert Park; meals $10-20; ⊙ 11am-8pm Tue-Thu, to 9pm Fri & Sat, 11:30am-6pm Sun) Does all the authentic Jamaican favorites: saltfish and ackee at breakfast; curry goat, jerk chicken and oxtails at lunch. The brown stew chicken is popular, as is the fish soup, which it serves on Friday and Saturday only.

☆ Entertainment

Los Angeles Rams
SPECTATOR SPORT

(www.therams.com; 3911 S Figueroa St, Los Angeles Memorial Coliseum; Ⓜ Expo Line to Exposition Park) Professional football returns to LA after a 22-year hiatus. The Rams were the first NFL team in Southern California, starting in 1946, but unbelievably the nation's second-largest market was without pro football once the Rams (and the now Oakland Raiders) left in 1994. High hopes and high spirits abound. Catch the Rams live at the Coliseum (p225), if you're lucky enough to snag a ticket.

Barbara Morrison
Performing Arts Center
JAZZ

(☎ 310-462-1439; www.barbaramorrisonpac.com; 4305 Degnan Blvd, Leimert Park) Grammy-nominated jazz singer and educator Barbara Morrison has sung with the likes of Ray Charles and Dizzy Gillespie and at jazz festivals worldwide, but her passion is teaching and programming performances here in Leimert Park. Jazz and blues concerts happen weekly. During April, for International Jazz Day, there are performances almost every day.

World Stage
JAZZ

(☎ 323-293-2451; www.theworldstage.org; 4321 Degnan Blvd, Leimert Park; suggested donation for most shows $5) Founded by the late hard-bop drummer Billy Higgins, this place doesn't serve food or drink, just good music from some of the best emerging talents in jazz. There are jam sessions to drum circles, vocal and writing workshops and open-mic events. On Sundays the open Sisters of Jazz (women-only performers) jam hums till midnight.

🛍 Shopping

The vibrant Leimert Park district is full of antique and art galleries, particularly focused on the African-American experience. Nearby, the Baldwin Hills Crenshaw Plaza offers a fun South LA shopping scene every day and night. It has movie theaters, too.

★ Sika
ART

(☎ 323-295-2502; 4330 Degnan Blvd, Leimert Park; ⊙ noon-6pm) It would be hard to find a better collection of antiques, masks, clothes and jewelry outside of West Africa than those found in this owner-operated treasure chest, a pillar of Leimert Park. It's also known for nose piercings. It co-sponsors a three-day **Labor Day Music, Food & Art Festival** in the lot next door.

Eso Won Books
BOOKS

(☎ 323-290-1048; www.esowonbookstore.com; 4327 Degnan Blvd, Leimert Park; ⊙ 10am-7pm Mon-Sat, noon-5pm Sun) Nearly 30 years in business and still going strong in an Amazon world, this store focuses on African-American literature, fiction and nonfiction. Luminaries such as Maya Angelou, BB King, Kareem Abdul-Jabbar and Ta-Nehisi Coates have held book signings here, and Presidents Bill Clinton and Barack Obama have both stopped by.

Gallery Plus
ART

(☎ 323-296-2398; 4333 Degnan Blvd, Leimert Park; ⊙ 11am-6pm) Since the early '90s this store has been dealing in African textiles – kente, mudcloth, kuba, indigo and more – as well as posters, dolls, bowls and baskets that tell both the African and African-American experience.

Baldwin Hills Crenshaw Plaza
MALL

(☎ 323-290-6636; www.baldwinhillscrenshawplaza.com; 3650 W Martin Luther King Jr Blvd, South LA; ⊙ 10am-9pm Mon-Sat, 11am-7pm Sun) This giant mall between Leimert Park and the Expo Line station looks ready to revitalize the neighborhood. It's anchored by Macy's department store, with dozens of other stores from fashion to fast food.

AROUND LOS ANGELES

Make like Jack Kerouac, ditch the congestion, crowds and smog, and use LA as a hub to all the natural glory of California. Get an early start to beat the commuter traffic (or catch a ferry, Greyhound bus or Amtrak train) and point the compass across the ocean, up into the mountains or into the vast and imposing desert.

Catalina Island

Mediterranean-flavored Santa Catalina Island is a popular getaway for harried Angelenos drawn by fresh air, seemingly endless sunshine, seaside fun and excellent hiking in a unique microclimate.

Originally the home of Tongva Nation, Catalina has gone through stints as a hangout for Spanish explorers, Franciscan friars, sea-otter poachers, smugglers and Union soldiers. In 1919 it was snapped up by chewing-gum magnate William Wrigley Jr (1861–1932), who had buildings constructed in the Spanish Mission style and for years sent his Chicago Cubs baseball team here for spring training. Apart from its human population (about 4100), Catalina's highest-profile residents are a herd of bison, brought here for a 1924 movie shoot and who ended up breeding.

Today most of the island is owned by the Catalina Island Conservancy (☑ 310-510-2595; www.catalinaconservancy.org; 125 Clarissa Ave, Avalon; biking/hiking permits $35/free), and 88% of the island's 75 square miles is a nature preserve requiring (easily available) permits for access to hiking and cycling.

Even if Catalina sinks under the weight of day-trippers in summer and whenever cruise ships anchor offshore, if you stay overnight you may well feel the ambience go from frantic to, as the song says, 'romance, romance, romance, romance.'

Commercial activity is concentrated in the town of Avalon (population about 3775), which is small enough to be explored in an hour or two, so there's plenty of time for hiking, swimming and touring.

The only other settlement is Two Harbors (population about 300) on the remote west coast, which has a general store, a dive and kayak center, a snack bar and a lodge.

⊙ Sights

Casino LANDMARK
(1 Casino Way, Avalon; tours adult/child 40 min $14/13, 70 min $29/26) It's a nice stroll along the waterfront to the cylindrical, 1929 art deco casino, Avalon's biggest landmark. It's not a gambling casino but an entertainment hall where big bands once played, and it's still used for events, celebrations and nightly movie screenings. Otherwise, it's accessible only by tour, showing off the gorgeous murals, a massive pipe organ, twinkling ceiling in the movie theater and a fabulous ballroom.

Catalina Island Museum MUSEUM
(☑ 310-510-2414; www.catalinamuseum.org; 217 Metropole Ave, Avalon; adult/student & senior/child $12/9/free; ⊙10am-5pm) Opened in a spiffy new building in 2016, this museum has a permanent collection showcasing Catalina's history from the province of the indigenous people to playground of Hollywood's elite – everyone from Errol Flynn and Charlie Chaplin through to John Wayne, Marilyn Monroe and George Harrison visited. A 12-minute newsreel-style video tells the story. Other sections are dedicated to the Wrigley family, local legends and characters, Catalina's clay-tile industry and artifacts such as the telephone switchboard used until 1978.

**Wrigley Memorial
& Botanic Gardens** GARDENS
(☑ 310-510-2595; www.catalinaconservancy.org/index.php?s=visit&p=wrigley_memorial_and_botanic_garden; 1400 Avalon Canyon Rd, Avalon; adult/senior/child $7/5/free; ⊙8am-5pm) About 1.5 miles inland from central Avalon, this nearly-38-acre park emphasizes indigenous California plants: agave, aloe, Catalina cherry, cedar, island scrub oak, silver dollar plant, yucca and more. It slopes uphill to the 1934 memorial to William Wrigley Jr, 180ft tall and made of concrete mixed with crushed local stone for an almost terrazzo effect, with accents of local tile. Here you'll get inspirational views down the canyon to the harbor and mainland on a clear day.

🏃 Activities

There are plenty of activities right in Avalon and on the harbor, as well as hiking, mountain biking and ziplining inland with the chance to spot eagles and bison. If you're going into the backcountry, there's very little shade, so take a hat, sunscreen and plenty of water.

In Avalon you can hang out on the privately owned **Descanso Beach** (☑310-510-7410; www.visitcatalinaisland.com/activities-adventures/descanso-beach-club; 1 St Catherine Way, Avalon). There's good snorkeling at **Lovers' Cove** and at **Casino Point (Avalon Underwater Park)**, a marine reserve that's also the best shore dive. Another way to escape the throngs is by kayaking to the quiet coves along Catalina's rocky coastline. **Catalina Island Expeditions** (Descanso Beach Ocean Sports; ☑310-510-1226; www.kayakcatalinaisland.com; Descanso Beach Club; single/double kayak rental per hour $22/30, per day $52/72, SUP per hour/day from $24/60, 2hr tours per person $48) rents snorkeling gear, SUP kits and kayaks, and also runs guided kayaking tours and kayak camping trips.

To get into the protected backcountry, hop on the **Safari Bus** (☑310-510-4205; www.visitcatalinaisland.com/activities-adventures/two-harbors/safari-bus; ☺mid-Jun—early Sep), which goes all the way to Two Harbors. You must book in advance and get a permit (and maps) from the Catalina Island Conservancy if you're going to be hiking or mountain biking.

Alternatively, you could just hop on an air-conditioned tour bus and let someone else show you around. Both **Catalina Adventure Tours** (☑877-510-2888; www.catalinaadventuretours.com; Green Pier, Avalon; tours adult/child & senior from $45/42) and **Discovery Tour Plaza** (☑800-626-1496; www.visitcatalinaisland.com/island-info/tour-plaza; 10 Island Plaza, Avalon; tours $19-124) operate historical Avalon itineraries and jaunts further out with memorable views of the rugged coast, deep canyons and sandy coves, and possible encounters with eagles and a herd of bison.

Snorkelers and certified scuba divers can rent equipment at Descanso Beach to glimpse local shipwrecks and kelp forests. **Two Harbors Dive and Recreation Center** (☑310-510-4272; www.visitcatalinaisland.com/activities-adventures/two-harbors/dive-recreation-center; 1 Banning House Rd, Two Harbors; guided trips from $99; ☺9am-5pm) accesses pristine dive sites off the island's less developed coast.

Silver Canyon Pottery　　　　　CRAFT
(☑310-499-8799; www.silvercanyonpottery.com; address provided upon reservation; tour & tile-making $60) When the Wrigleys were developing Catalina, tile-making was a thriving local industry. Tile-maker and native islander Robin Cassidy has restored many of the tiles

around Avalon and is a congenial guide to the history and process. Her 90-minute studio visit includes your chance to press three tiles based on traditional designs, which are custom glazed, fired and shipped to you.

Zip-Line Eco Tour　　　ADVENTURE SPORTS
(☑800-626-1496; www.visitcatalinaisland.com/activities-adventures/land/zip-line-eco-tour; Descanso Beach; from $119; ☺9am-5pm) Get airborne with this two-hour, five-line zip course as you descend about 600 vertical feet from Catalina's inland mountains to the shore, at speeds up to 30mph. Experienced guides outfit you with all the gear and coach you on the technique, and plaques along the way describe Catalina's unique flora and fauna.

Tours meet behind Descanso Beach Club.

🛏 Sleeping

Avalon lodging has long been pretty dowdy, but recent renovations are upgrading rooms while preserving the island's traditional charm. Rates soar on weekends and between May and September; they're about 30% to 60% lower at other times. For camping information, see www.visitcatalinaisland.com/avalon/camping.php.

Hotel Atwater　　　　　HOTEL $
(☑877-778-8322; www.visitcatalinaisland.com/hotels-packages/avalon/hotel-atwater; 120 Sumner Ave, Avalon; r from $98) At this historic hotel a block inland from the beach, the 91 rooms were getting a chic, modern makeover as we went to press: dark wood furniture, silvery wallpaper, marble vanities and showers and tile accents. Rooms have varying degrees of natural light, and you'll pay more for good views.

★ Pavilion Hotel　　　　　HOTEL $$
(☑877-778-8322; www.visitcatalinaisland.com/hotels-packages/avalon/pavilion-hotel; 513 Crescent Ave, Avalon; r from $185; ☺🏵🌐) This low-slung, sweet but not swanky resort feels much more intimate than its 71 units would suggest. Rooms have attractive rattan furnishings, comfy beds and pillows and private lanai overlooking the water or the manicured courtyard. Rates include full breakfast buffet, afternoon wine and cheese service and classes at the **Island Spa** (☑310-510-7300; www.islandspacatalina.com; 163 Crescent Ave, Avalon; massage from $95, body therapy from $105, day pass from $75 for 4hr; ☺9am-6pm Nov-Apr, to 8pm May-Oct).

Staff will pick up your luggage at the dock. Even if room rates can easily double in peak season, it's a nice choice.

★ **Banning House Lodge**   B&B $$
(☑ 877-778-8322; www.visitcatalinaisland.com/ho-tels-packages/two-harbors/banning-house-lodge; 1 Banning House Rd, Two Harbors; r from $129; 🛜) Built in 1910 by the Banning brothers, who owned the island at the time, this classic craftsman has been converted into an inviting B&B. All 12 rooms are uniquely decorated and have private baths. Sip wine by the fire in the living room and enjoy breakfast on a lanai with spectacular mountain and sea views.

Hotel Metropole   BOUTIQUE HOTEL $$$
(☑ 800-541-8528, 310-510-1884; www.hotel-metro-pole.com; 205 Crescent Ave, Avalon; r from $189 incl breakfast; ⊜@🛜) Around a leafy courtyard lined with shops and cafes, the Metropole has spotless rooms with dark wood floors, crisp white bedding, fireplaces, soaker tubs and spectacular sea views from upper floors. The design is more classic California than edgy – it works perfectly on this island – and there's a roof deck with tiny hot tub.

🍴 Eating & Drinking

Lloyd's of Avalon   DESSERTS $
(☑ 310-510-7266; www.catalinacandy.com; 315 Crescent Ave, Avalon; saltwater taffy $12 per 1lb; ⊗ 7am-6pm) Like at any good seaside candy shop, Lloyd's makes saltwater taffy before your eyes and sells penny candy by the pound, but – whoa! – how about those offbeat flavors of fudge such as mint chocolate swirl and the ridonkulous caramel apples (Heath bar, anyone?)? It's been at it since 1941.

The Sandtrap   SNACK BAR $
(☑ 310-510-2505; www.catalinasandtrap.com; 501 Avalon Canyon Rd, Avalon; mains $3-13; ⊗ 8am-3pm) Across from Avalon's golf course and en route to the botanic gardens (p228), this snack bar is nothing fancy (omelets, burgers and such served outdoors), but the authentic Mexican food at lunch is better than expected – especially the tacos. Bonus: full bar.

Maggie's Blue Rose   MEXICAN $$
(☑ 310-510-3300; www.maggiesbluerose.com; 417 Crescent St, Avalon; mains $11-30; ⊗ lunch from 11am, breakfast from 9am (seasonally); closing time varies) This new, central spot does Mexican standards and cooking with an island twist such as ancho-chile spiced shrimp served with avocado, greens, cucumber and pickled onion presented inside a (wait for it) hollowed-out half-watermelon. That's alongside award-winning mole-braised duck taquitos and pork adobo with grilled pineapple salsa.

Bluewater Grill   SEAFOOD $$$
(☑ 310-510-3474; www.bluewatergrill.com; 306 Crescent Ave, Avalon; mains lunch $14-34, dinner $19-34; ⊗ 11am-10pm) With an unbeatable location right over the water, Bluewater Grill is the most popular restaurant on the island thanks to dishes such as miso-glazed cod, cedar-plank salmon, lemon-pepper-seasoned mahi mahi, chicken under a brick and steamed lobster and crab.

Catalina Island Brew House   MICROBREWERY
(417 Crescent Ave, Avalon; ⊗ 6am-6pm, later in summer) This storefront across from the water does triple duty: cafe, bakery and possibly California's micro-est brewery. Tiny tanks in the corner dispense brews such as the Island Hop IPA and Gariblondie blond ale. It also does flatbread and sandwiches ($8.50 to $13.45) and its in-house bakery churns out treats such as pretzel rolls served free with your beer.

ℹ️ Information

Tourist Office (☑ 310-510-1520; www.catalin-achamber.com; Green Pier, Avalon) One-stop shopping for all island information.

ℹ️ Getting There & Away

A few companies operate ferries to Avalon and Two Harbors. Reservations are recommended at any time and especially during summer. The use of cars on Catalina is restricted, so there are no vehicle ferry services.

Catalina Express (☑ 800-613-1212; www.catalinaexpress.com) Ferries to Avalon from San Pedro, Long Beach and Dana Point in Orange County, and to Two Harbors from San Pedro. It takes one to 1½ hours, with up to three ferries daily. You'll ride free on your birthday...true story.

Catalina Flyer (☑ 800-830-7744; www.catalinaferries.com) Catamaran to Avalon and Two Harbors from Balboa Harbor in Newport Beach (one to 1½ hours).

ℹ️ Getting Around

Avalon and Two Harbors are small enough to get around on foot, and passenger cars are not permitted on the island. Should you need wheeled transportation, bike/4-person golf-cart rentals start at $5/45 per hour at shops around town. For public transportation, the city-operated **Garibaldi** (☑ 310-510-0081; www.cityofavalon.com/transit) bus loops around Avalon. Access to the inner portions of the island is by Safari Bus (p228).

Six Flags Magic Mountain & Hurricane Harbor

Velocity is king at **Six Flags Magic Mountain** (📞661-255-4111; www.sixflags.com/parks/magicmountain; 26101 Magic Mountain Pkwy, Valencia; adult/child under 4ft $80/55; ☉open daily late Mar-late Aug, check online calendar for rest of year; 🖟), the ultimate roller-coaster park, where you can go up, down and inside-out in ways only Space-X can outdo. The park's world-record 19 roller coasters include the aptly named Scream, which goes through seven loops, including a zero-gravity roll and a dive loop, with you sitting in a floorless chair.

If you've got a stomach of steel, X2 lets you ride in cars that spin 360 degrees while hurtling forward and plummeting all at once. Other favorites include the classic 4990ft-long, wooden Twisted Colossus (recently reinforced with steel on those twists for extra oomph), and the new-school Batman, where your seats dangle backwards from a track above. The world's tallest loop coaster, Full Throttle, takes you first inside the loop and then over the top. When the Superman: Escape from Krypton ride blasts off, it sounds like a fighter jet.

Note that many rides have minimum-height restrictions, ranging from 36in to 58in. However, there are plenty of tamer rides for the elementary-school set in the park's Bugs Bunny World, plus shows, parades and concerts to keep everyone entertained, as well as the Six Flags Hurricane Harbor water park next door.

Discounts and package deals, available on the website, can help you save buckage, and pay-in-advance parking passes can save you time. If you're looking to minimize your wait time for rides (some are 45 minutes or more), the Flash Pass system costs extra but can help a lot. Plans run $30 to $95 per person; purchase Flash Pass across from the main entrance.

Next to Magic Mountain, **Six Flags Hurricane Harbor** (www.sixflags.com/parks/hurricaneharborla; 26101 Magic Mountain Pkwy, Valencia; adult/child under 4ft $43/35; ☉late May-late Sep; 🖟) is a jungle-themed, 22-acre water park where you can chill in a tropical lagoon, brave churning wave pools and plunge

down wicked high-speed slides with names like Banzai Pipeline and Taboo Tower.

The Six Flags parks are in the Santa Clarita Valley, north of the San Fernando Valley, about 22 miles north of the US-101–I-405 Fwy interchange or about 32 miles from Santa Monica (via I-405 and I-5); about 26 miles from Universal Studios (via the CA-170 and I-5 freeways), and 36 miles north of Downtown LA (via I-5). Parking is $23. Some hotels and/or hostels in LA offer Magic Mountain shuttles.

Big Bear Lake

Big Bear Lake is a low-key, family-friendly mountain resort (elevation 6750ft) about 110 miles northeast of LA. Snowy winters lure scores of ski bunnies and boarders to its two mountains, while summer brings hikers, mountain bikers and watersports enthusiasts wishing to escape the stifling heat down in the basin. Even getting here via the spectacular, curvy, panorama-filled **Rim of the World Scenic Byway** (Hwy 18) is a treat.

The purchase of Big Bear's two mountains – Snow Summit and Bear Mountain – by the owners of Mammoth Mountain ski resort in the Eastern Sierra has injected the town not only with money but also with new energy. The vibe has especially picked up in downtown area, the Village, where upscale bars, restaurants and shops have opened.

🏃 Activities

★**Big Bear Mountain Resort**   SKIING
(📞844-462-2327; www.bigbearmountainresorts.com; 2-park lift ticket adult/child $56/46; ☉usually Dec-Apr; 🖟) SoCal's premier ski area is built around two mountains. The higher of the two, **Bear Mountain** (8805ft), is nirvana for freestyle freaks with over 150 jumps, 80 jibs and four pipes, including a 580ft in-ground superpipe. **Snow Summit** (8200ft) is more family-focused and has traditional downhill trails for everyone. Recent improvements include a ski school and mountaintop restaurant.

Scenic Sky Chair   CABLE CAR
(www.bigbearmountainresort.com; 1-way $12, day pass $25; ☉May–start of ski season) This mile-long chairlift ride has hikers, mountain bikers and sightseers swinging above the

RIM OF THE WORLD

While most folks are in a hurry to get to the mountains, which means picking up Hwy 330 in San Bernardino, consider taking the slow road, blessed with hair-raising cliff drop-offs and postcard canyon views. The Rim of the World Drive is one of America's Scenic Byways and with good reason. Pick up Hwy 138 at the Cajon Pass off the I-5 and head east past Silverwood Lake and Lake Gregory. Next climb Hwy 18 into quaint Blue Jay and Lake Arrowhead. Here the vistas get serious and the hairpins exciting. Lake Arrowhead's fashionable mall and ski resort makes a nice respite from the road. Once back on the highway, the most photogenic stretch of road takes you into Big Bear Lake.

San Bernardino forest en route to the Snow Summit mountaintop at 8200ft.

Bear Valley Bikes   MOUNTAIN BIKING
(☑909-866-8000; www.bvbikes.com; 40298 Big Bear Blvd; bikes per half/full day incl helmet $30/40; ⏱10am-5pm Sun & Tue-Fri, 9am-6pm Sat) This all-around bike shop has maps, tickets and bike rentals, and can also fix your wheels. Rates for full suspension and fat bikes are higher.

Big Bear Off-Road Adventures   DRIVING
(☑909-585-1036; www.offroadadventure.com) If you don't have your own 4WD but want to discover the area's off-track beauty spots, sign up for a driving tour with this outfit. Guides have the inside scoop on flora, fauna and local history and are highly trained drivers to boot.

🛏 Sleeping

On snowy winter weekends, demand often exceeds Big Bear's capacity, so plan ahead. The two hostels offer the cheapest digs, private villas the priciest and in between you'll find plenty of aging motels along the main highway and 2000 private cabins tucked into the woods.

ITH Mountain Adventure Lodge   HOSTEL $
(☑909-866-2532; www.ithhostels.com; 657 Modoc Dr; dm $27-33, d $51-87; P🐾) Over a century old, this rustic mountain lodge is as welcoming as a friend's hug. Choose from dorms or doubles with or without bath and meet fellow guests around the fireside lounge, over hot breakfast and dinner or during one of the daily activities such as yoga, hiking or pub crawls. Great for solo travelers.

Big Bear Hostel   HOSTEL $
(☑909-866-8900; www.bigbearhostel.com; 527 Knickerbocker Rd; dm $20-40, d $45-68; P@🐾) This clean and friendly hostel on the edge of the village is run by people happy to provide advice about the best trails, runs and all things extreme. Linen is provided, but BYO towel.

★Knickerbocker Mansion   B&B $$
(☑877-423-1180, 909-878-9190; www.knickerbockermansion.com; 869 Knickerbocker Rd; r $125-186; P@🐾) Characterful and ornate, this B&B in a hand-built 1920s log home is secluded from the tourist fray and has a dozen elegantly rustic rooms spaced over three buildings. The restaurant serves a popular Creole brunch from 10am to 2pm Thursday to Sunday. Two-night minimum stay on weekends.

Marina Resort   HOTEL $$
(☑toll free 800-600-6000; https://marinaresort.com; 40770 Big Bear Blvd; d $130-230; P🐾🏊) You can't get any closer to the lake when staying at this central resort where every room has water-facing balconies or patios. Updated rooms have knotted-pine beds and soothing natural tones, and there's free coffee and tea in the lobby with its soaring ceiling.

🍴 Eating & Drinking

Big Bear's dining scene has vastly improved in recent years and now covers the entire spectrum from greasy-spoon diners to fine lakeside dining. Restaurants cluster in the Village but there are plenty of others worth a drive.

Amangela's Sandwich & Bagel House   DELI $
(☑909-878-0015; www.amangelas.com; 40729 Village Dr; sandwiches $8-10; ⏱8am-5pm Mon-Thu, to 6pm Fri & Sat; 🐾) Mash up Angela and Amanda and you get Amangela, a sister-owned cafe with humble looks but stellar freshly made sandwiches – turkey pesto to French dip – alongside nicely chewy bagels slathered with four varieties of homemade hummus. Save room for a peppermint patty.

★Big Bear Brewing Co   GASTROPUB $$
(☑909-878-0283; www.bblbc.com; 40827 Stone Rd; mains $13-30; ⏱11am-10pm Sun-Thu, to 2am Fri & Sat; P🐾) Try a Barely Legal Honey Blonde or a Whispering Pine IPA at this

local brewpub with view of the steel vats from the woodsy drinking and dining area. The food is upscale pub fare with wagyu-beef burgers and beer-battered fish 'n' chips the standout picks.

Peppercorn Grille   AMERICAN $$
(☎909-866-5405; www.peppercorngrille.com; 553 Pine Knot Ave; mains lunch $9-30, dinner $12-55; ⊗11am-9pm Sun-Thu, to 10pm Fri & Sat; ℗🖧) Upscale by Big Bear standards, with table-cloths at dinner, this cozy burrow gets a thumbs up for quality steaks but also man-ages to satisfy noncarnivores with a broad selection of pizzas, pastas and salads.

Murray's Saloon & Eatery   BAR
(☎909-866-1444; www.facebook.com/murrays saloon; 672 Cottage Lane; ⊗10am-2am Mon Fri, 8am-2am Sat & Sun) The self-proclaimed 'best five-star hole-in-the-wall' has cheap beers, nightly karaoke and opening hours that might just keep you off the slopes or trail the following day. Skip the food.

❶ Information

Big Bear Visitors Center (☎909-866-7000; www.bigbear.com; 630 Bartlett Rd; ⊗9am-5pm; 🖧) Has lots of free flyers, maps and wi-fi, and sells trail maps and the National Forest Adventure Pass.

Big Bear Discovery Center (☎909-382-2790; http://mountainsfoundation.org; 40971 N

Shore Dr/Hwy 38, Fawnskin; ⊗8am-4:30pm, closed Wed & Thu mid-Sep–mid-May) Nonprofit visitor center dispenses information and maps on all outdoor-related activities around Big Bear, including camping. Also sells the National Forest Adventure Pass.

❶ Getting There & Away

Big Bear is on Hwy 18, an offshoot of Hwy 30 in San Bernardino. A quicker approach is via Hwy 330, which starts in Highland and intersects with Hwy 18 in Running Springs. If you don't like serpentine mountain roads, pick up Hwy 38 near Redlands, which is longer, but easier on the queasy. It has less traffic too, handy on peak weekends.

Mountain Transit (☎909-878-5200; http://mountaintransit.org) buses connect Big Bear with the Greyhound and Metrolink stations in San Bernardino at least twice daily ($10, 1¼ hours).

❶ Getting Around

There's free parking in the Village and on the streets. Public buses operated by **Mountain Transit** serve Big Bear on two routes (per ride $1.50).

Weekend Trolley (☎909-878-5200; http://mountaintransit.org; pass $5; ⊗7:30am-8pm Fri & Sat, 10:30am-3:30pm Sun) On weekends, a trolley links the Village with the Alpine Slide, Moonridge Zoo/Bear Mountain and various hotels and restaurants.

Disneyland & Orange County

Best Places to Eat

➜ Walt's Wharf (p260)

➜ Napa Rose (p246)

➜ Driftwood Kitchen (p284)

➜ Garlic & Chives (p261)

➜ Ramos House Café (p287)

Best Places to Sleep

➜ Paséa (p264)

➜ Disney's Grand Californian Hotel & Spa (p242)

➜ Montage (p283)

➜ Crystal Cove Beach Cottages (p279)

➜ Casa Tropicana (p290)

Why Go?

LA and Orange County are the closest of neighbors, but in some ways they couldn't be more different. If LA is about stars, the OC is about surfers. LA: ever more urban, OC: proudly *sub*urban, built around cars, freeways and shopping malls. If LA is SoCal's seat of liberal thinking, the OC's heritage is of megachurches and ultraconservative firebrands. If LA is Hollywood glam, the OC is *Real Housewives*.

Tourism is dominated by Disneyland in Anaheim in northern OC, and beach communities promising endless summer – and very different lifestyles as you progress down the coast from Seal Beach to Huntington Beach, Newport Beach to Laguna Beach.

While there's some truth to those stereotypes of life behind the 'Orange Curtain,' this diverse county's 789 sq miles, 34 cities and 3.15 million people create deep pockets of individuality and beauty, while cool, urbanesque spots keep the OC 'real,' no matter one's reality.

When to Go
Anaheim

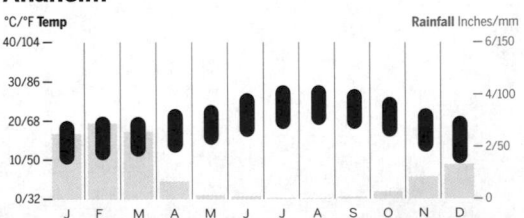

May Visitation dips from spring break to Memorial Day. Mostly sunny, balmy temperatures.

Jul & Aug Summer vacation and beach season peak. Surfing and art festivals by the coast.

Sep Blue skies, cooler temperatures inland, fewer crowds. Tall Ships Festival at Dana Point.

DISNEYLAND & ANAHEIM

Mickey is one lucky guy. Created by animator Walt Disney in 1928, this irrepressible mouse caught a ride on a multimedia juggernaut (film, TV, publishing, music, merchandising and theme parks) that rocketed him into a global stratosphere of recognition, money and influence. Plus, he lives in Disneyland, the 'Happiest Place on Earth,' an 'imagineered' hyper-reality where the streets are always clean, employees – called 'cast members' – are always upbeat and there are parades every day.

Sure, every ride seems to end in a gift store, prices are sky-high and there are grumblings that management could do more about affordable housing and health insurance for employees – but even determined grouches should find reason to grin. For the more than 14 million kids, grandparents, honeymooners and international tourists who visit every year, Disneyland Resort remains a magical experience.

History

When Walt Disney opened Disneyland on July 17, 1955, he declared it the 'Happiest Place on Earth.' Over six decades later, it's hard to argue.

Carved out of orange and walnut groves in Anaheim, the construction of the 'theme park' (another Disney term) took just one year. Disneyland's opening day was a disaster, however. Temperatures over 100°F melted asphalt underfoot, leaving women's high heels stuck in the tar. There were plumbing problems: all of the drinking fountains quit working. Hollywood stars didn't show up on time, and more than twice the number of expected guests – some 28,000 by day's end – crowded through the gates, some holding counterfeit tickets. But none of this kept eager Disney fans away for long, as more than 50 million tourists visited in its first decade alone.

During the 1990s, Anaheim undertook a staggering $4.2 billion revamp and expansion, cleaning up rundown stretches and establishing the first tourist police force in the US. In 2001 a second theme park, Disney California Adventure (DCA), was added, designed to salute the state's most famous natural landmarks and cultural history. More recently added was **Downtown Disney**, an outdoor pedestrian mall. The ensemble is called Disneyland Resort.

WHEN YOU WISH UPON A STAR

It's hard to deny the change in atmosphere as you're whisked by tram from the parking lot into the heart of the resort. Wide-eyed children lean forward with anticipation while stressed-out parents sit back, finally relaxing. Uncle Walt's in charge, and he's taken care of every possible detail.

Walk through the Disneyland gates and along the red-brick path and a floral Mickey Mouse blooms before you. A sign above the nearby archway reads 'Here you leave today and enter the world of yesterday, tomorrow and fantasy.' It's an apt if slightly skewed greeting that's indicative of the upbeat, slightly skewed 'reality' of the park itself – and the undeniable delight of millions who visit every year.

Meanwhile, Anaheim continues to fill in with malls like Anaheim GardenWalk (p249) (2008) and shopping and entertainment areas like the Packing District (p248) and **Center Street** (www.centerstreetanaheim.com), plus improved roads and transit.

◉ Sights

Disneyland is open 365 days a year; hours vary seasonally and sometimes daily, but generally you can count on at least 10am to 8pm. Check the current schedule (www.disneyland.com) in advance when timing your visit (p48). Don't worry about getting stuck waiting for a ride or attraction at closing time. Parks stay open until the last guest in line has had their fun.

There is a multitude of ticket options (p49). Single-day ticket prices vary daily but on low-traffic days (typically Monday to Wednesday in the off or shoulder season) one-day tickets start at adult/child $97/91 for either Disneyland or Disney California Adventure, and a variety of multiday and 'park-hopper' passes are available. Children's tickets apply to kids aged three to nine.

◉ Disneyland Park

Spotless, wholesome Disneyland is still laid out according to Walt's original plans. It's here you'll find plenty of rides and some of the attractions most associated with the Disney name – Main Street, U.S.A., Sleeping Beauty Castle and Tomorrowland.

Main Street, U.S.A., gateway to the park, is a pretty thoroughfare lined with old-fashioned Americana ice-cream parlors and shops. Though kids will make a beeline for the rides, adults may enjoy lingering on Main Street for the antique photos and history exhibit just inside the main park entrance at Great Moments with Mr Lincoln (p237).

At the far end of the street is Sleeping Beauty Castle (p237), an obligatory photo op and a central landmark worth noting – its towering blue turrets are visible from many areas of the park. The different sections of Disneyland radiate from here like spokes on a wheel.

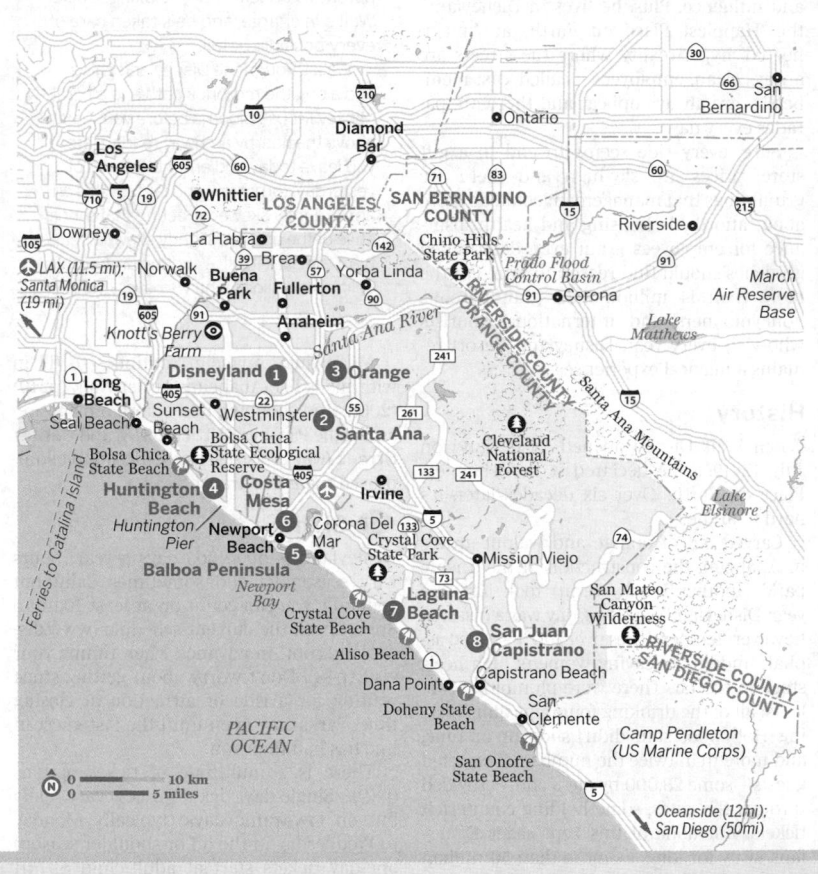

Disneyland & Orange County Highlights

1 Disneyland Resort (p235) Meeting Mickey, screaming your head off on Space Mountain, then fireworks.

2 Discovery Cube (p256) Stand inside the eye of a hurricane in Santa Ana.

3 Old Towne Orange (p257) Shopping for vintage and slurping milkshakes.

4 Huntington Beach (p262) Building a beach bonfire after a day of surfing killer waves.

5 Balboa Peninsula (p268) Cycling past the as-seen-on-TV sands of Newport Beach.

6 Costa Mesa (p276) Discovering Orange County's alternative side (yes, there is

one) at the Lab and the Camp 'antimalls.'

7 Laguna Beach (p280) Watching the sun dip below the horizon from the art-filled bluff-tops.

8 Mission San Juan Capistrano (p286) Being awed by Spanish colonial history and beauty.

Main Street, U.S.A. AREA

Fashioned after Walt's hometown of Marceline, Missouri, bustling Main Street, U.S.A. resembles the classic turn-of-the-20th-century, all-American town. It's an idyllic, relentlessly upbeat representation, complete with barbershop quartet, penny arcades, ice-cream shops and a steam train. The music playing in the background is from American musicals, and there's a flag-retreat ceremony every afternoon.

Great Moments with Mr. Lincoln (Map p240; https://disneyland.disney.go.com/attractions/disneyland/disneyland-story; Main Street USA; ▣), a 15-minute Audio-Animatronics presentation on Honest Abe, sits inside the fascinating **Disneyland Story** exhibit. Nearby, kids love seeing old-school Disney cartoons like *Steamboat Willie* inside **Main Street Cinema**.

Main Street ends in the **Central Plaza** (Main Street USA; ▣). Lording over the plaza is **Sleeping Beauty Castle** (https://disneyland.disney.go.com/attractions/disneyland/sleeping-beauty-castle-walkthrough; ▣), the castle featured on the Disney logo. Inside the iconic structure (fashioned after a real 19th-century Bavarian castle), dolls and big books tell the story of Sleeping Beauty. As if you didn't know it already.

Tomorrowland AREA

How did 1950s imagineers envision the future? As a galaxy-minded community filled with monorails, rockets and Googie-style architecture, apparently. In 1998 this 'land' was revamped to honor three timeless futurists: Jules Verne, HG Wells and Leonardo da Vinci. These days, though, the *Star Wars* franchise gets top billing. **Hyperspace Mountain** (Map p240; https://disneyland.disney.go.com/attractions/disneyland/hyperspace-mountain; ▣), Tomorrowland's signature attraction and one of the USA's best roller coasters, hurtles you into complete darkness at frightening speed, and **Star Wars Launch Bay** (Map p240; https://disneyland.disney.go.com/attractions/disneyland/star-wars-launch-bay; ▣) shows movie props and memorabilia.

Meanwhile, **Star Tours** (Map p240; https://disneyland.disney.go.com/attractions/disneyland/star-tours; ▣) clamps you into a Starspeeder shuttle for a wild and bumpy 3D ride through the desert canyons of Tatooine on a space mission.

If it's retro high-tech you're after, the **monorail** glides to a stop in Tomorrowland, its rubber tires traveling a 13-minute, 2.5-mile round-trip route to Downtown Disney. Just

IS IT A SMALL WORLD AFTER ALL?

Pay attention to the cool optical illusion along **Main Street, U.S.A.** (p237). As you look from the entrance up the street toward **Sleeping Beauty Castle** (p237), everything seems far away and bigger-than-life. When you're at the castle looking back, everything seems closer and smaller – a technique known as forced perspective, a trick used on Hollywood sets where buildings are constructed at a decreasing scale to create an illusion of height or depth. Welcome to Disneyland.

outside Tomorrowland station, kiddies will want to shoot laser beams on **Buzz Lightyear Astro Blasters** (Map p240; https://disneyland.disney.go.com/attractions/disneyland/buzz-lightyear-astro-blasters; ▣) and drive their own miniature cars in the classic **Autopia** (https://disneyland.disney.go.com/attractions/disneyland/autopia; Tomorrowland; ▣) ride. Then jump aboard the **Finding Nemo Submarine Voyage** (Map p240; ▣) to look for the world's most famous clownfish from within a refurbished submarine and rumble through an underwater volcanic eruption.

Fantasyland AREA

Fantasyland is filled with the characters of classic children's stories. If you only see one attraction here, visit **it's a small world**, a boat ride past hundreds of Audio-Animatronics children from different cultures all singing an earworm of a theme song.

Another classic, the **Matterhorn Bobsleds** (Map p240; https://disneyland.disney.go.com/attractions/disneyland/matterhorn-bobsleds) is a steel-frame roller coaster that mimics a bobsled ride down a mountain. Fans of old-school attractions will also get a kick out of *The Wind in the Willows*–inspired **Mr. Toad's Wild Ride** (Map p240; ▣), a loopy jaunt in an open-air jalopy through London.

Younger kids love whirling around the **Mad Tea Party** (Map p240; ▣) teacup ride and **King Arthur Carrousel** (Map p240; https://disneyland.disney.go.com/attractions/disneyland/king-arthur-carrousel ▣), then cavorting with characters in nearby **Mickey's Toontown** (Map p240; ▣), a topsy-turvy minimetropolis where kiddos can traipse through Mickey and Minnie's houses and dozens of storefronts.

ℹ️ FLYING SOLO

If you're on your own, ask the staff at the entrance to park rides if a single-rider line is available, where you wait in a separate, shorter line. Availability may depend on the size of the crowd – and also on how that particular cast member is feeling that day, so be nice! Disneyland's single-rider attractions include the ever-popular **Indiana Jones Adventure** (p238) and **Splash Mountain** (p238). At Disney California Adventure, look for single-rider lines at **Soarin' Around the World** (p239), **California Screamin'** (p239), **Goofy's Sky School** (p242), **Grizzly River Run** (p239) and **Radiator Springs Racers** (p239).

Frontierland   AREA

This Disney 'land' is a salute to old Americana: the Mississippi-style paddle-wheel **Mark Twain Riverboat** (Map p240; https://disneyland. disney.go.com/attractions/disneyland/mark-twain-riverboat; 👪), the 18th-century replica **Sailing Ship Columbia** (Map p240; https://disneyland.disney.go.com/attractions/disneyland/sailing-ship-columbia; 👪), a rip-roarin' Old West town with a shooting gallery and the **Big Thunder Mountain Railroad** (Map p240; https://disneyland.disney.go.com/attractions/disneyland/big-thunder-mountain-railroad; 👪), a mining-themed roller coaster. The former Tom Sawyer Island – the only attraction in the park personally designed by Uncle Walt – has been reimagined in the wake of the *Pirates of the Caribbean* movies and renamed the **Pirate's Lair on Tom Sawyer Island** (Map p240; https://disneyland.disney.go.com/attractions/disneyland/pirates-lair-on-tom-sawyer-island; Frontierland; 👪).

Adventureland   AREA

(👪) Loosely deriving its jungle theme from Southeast Asia and Africa, Adventureland has

TOP FIVE THEME PARK AREAS FOR YOUNG KIDS

Fantasyland (p237)

Mickey's Toontown (p237)

Critter Country (p238)

Paradise Pier (p239)

Cars Land (p239)

a number of attractions, but the hands-down highlight is the safari-style **Indiana Jones Adventure** (Map p240; https://disneyland.disney.go.com/attractions/disneyland/indiana-jones-adventure; Adventureland; 👪). Nearby, little ones love climbing the stairways of **Tarzan's Treehouse** (Map p240; https://disneyland.disney.go.com/attractions/disneyland/tarzans-treehouse; 👪). Cool down on the **Jungle Cruise** (Map p240; https://disneyland.disney.go.com/attractions/disneyland/jungle-cruise; 👪), viewing exotic Audio-Animatronics animals from rivers of South America, India, Africa and Southeast Asia. And the classic **Enchanted Tiki Room** (Map p240; https://disneyland.disney.go.com/attractions/disneyland/enchanted-tiki-room; 👪) features carvings of Hawaiian gods and goddesses and a show of singing, dancing Audio-Animatronics birds and flowers.

New Orleans Square   AREA

(👪) New Orleans Square has all the charm of the eponymous city's French Quarter but none of the marauding drunks. New Orleans was the favorite city of Walt and his wife Lillian, and he paid tribute to it by building this stunning square lined with restaurants and attractions.

Pirates of the Caribbean (Map p240; https://disneyland.disney.go.com/attractions/disneyland/pirates-of-the-caribbean; 👪) is the longest ride in Disneyland (17 minutes) and provided 'inspiration' for the popular movies. You'll float through the subterranean haunts of tawdry pirates, where dead buccaneers perch atop their mounds of booty and Captain Jack Sparrow pops up occasionally. Over at the **Haunted Mansion** (Map p240; https://disneyland.disney.go.com/attractions/disneyland/haunted-mansion; 👪), 999 'happy haunts' – spirits, goblins, shades and ghosts – appear and evanesce while you ride in a cocoon-like 'Doom Buggy' through web-covered graveyards of dancing skeletons.

Critter Country   AREA

(👪) Critter Country's main attraction is **Splash Mountain** (Map p240; https://disneyland.disney.go.com/attractions/disneyland/splash-mountain; 👪), a flume ride through the story of Brer Rabbit and Brer Bear, based on the controversial 1946 film *Song of the South*. Just past Splash Mountain, hop in a mobile beehive on **The Many Adventures of Winnie the Pooh** (Map p240; https://disneyland.disney.go.com/attractions/disneyland/many-adventures-of-winnie-the-pooh; 👪). Nearby on the Rivers of America, you can paddle **Davy Crockett's Explorer Canoes** (Map p240; https://disneyland.disney.go.com/attractions/disneyland/davy-crocketts-explorer-canoes; 🚶) on summer weekends.

👁 Disney California Adventure

Across the plaza from Disneyland's monument to fantasy and make-believe is **Disney California Adventure** (Map p240; DCA; ☎714-781-4565; https://disneyland.disney.go.com; 1313 Harbor Blvd, Anaheim; single day ticket prices vary daily, 2-day pass adult/child from $199/187; ℗ 🚶), an ode to California's geography, history and culture – or at least a sanitized G-rated version. DCA, which opened in 2001, covers more acres than Disneyland and feels less crowded, and it has more modern rides and attractions inspired by coastal amusement parks, the inland mountains and redwood forests, the magic of Hollywood, and car culture by way of the movie *Cars*.

DCA's entrance was designed to look like an old-fashioned painted-collage postcard. After passing under the Golden Gate Bridge, you'll arrive at a homage to a 1920s Los Angeles streetscape, complete with a red trolley running down the street.

Cars Land　　　　　　　　　　　AREA
(🚶) This land gets kudos for its incredibly detailed design based on the popular Disney Pixar *Cars* movies. Top billing goes to the wacky **Radiator Springs Racers** (Map p240; https://disneyland.disney.go.com/attractions/disney-california-adventure/radiator-springs-racers), a race-car ride that bumps and jumps around a track painstakingly decked out like the Great American West.

Tractor-towed trailers swing their way around the 'dance floor' at **Mater's Junkyard Jamboree** (Map p240; https://disneyland.disney.go.com/attractions/disney-california-adventure/maters-junkyard-jamboree; 🚶), ride inside cars choreographed to classic retro tunes at **Luigi's Rollickin' Roadsters** (Map p240; https://disneyland.disney.go.com/attractions/disney-california-adventure/luigis-rollickin-roadsters; 🚶) or ride along with Route 66–themed gift shops and diners like the tipi-style **Cozy Cone Motel** will take on that special glow of nostalgia underneath neon lights in the evening.

Grizzly Peak　　　　　　　　　　AREA
(🚶) Grizzly Peak is broken into sections highlighting California's natural and human achievements. Its main attraction, **Soarin' Around the World** (Map p240; https://disney-

TOP RIDES FOR TEENS

For the adventure seekers in your brood, try the following:

Indiana Jones Adventure (p238), Adventureland

Hyperspace Mountain (p237), Tomorrowland

Splash Mountain (p238), Critter Country

California Screamin' (p239), Paradise Pier, Disney California Adventure (DCA)

Soarin' Around the World (p239), Grizzly Peak, DCA

Big Thunder Mountain Railroad (p238), Frontierland

Grizzly River Run (p239), Grizzly Peak, DCA

Matterhorn Bobsleds (p237), Fantasyland

Radiator Springs Racers (p239), Cars Land, DCA

Mickey's Fun Wheel (p240), Paradise Pier, DCA

land.disney.go.com/attractions/disney-california-adventure/soarin; 🚶), is a virtual hang-gliding ride using Omnimax technology that 'flies' you over famous landmarks. Enjoy the light breeze as you soar, keeping your nostrils open for aromas blowing in the wind.

Grizzly River Run (Map p240; 🚶) takes you 'rafting' down a faux Sierra Nevada river – you will get wet, so come when it's warm. While fake flat-hatted park rangers look on, kids can tackle the **Redwood Creek Challenge Trail**, with its 'Big Sir' redwoods, wooden towers and lookouts, and rock slide and climbing traverses.

Paradise Pier　　　　　　　　　AREA
(🚶) If you like carnival rides, you'll love Paradise Pier, designed to look like a combination of all the beachside amusement piers in California. The state-of-the-art **California Screamin'** (Map p240; https://disneyland.disney.go.com/attractions/disney-california-adventure/california-screamin; 🚶) roller coaster resembles an old wooden coaster, but it's got a smooth-as-silk steel track: it feels like you're being shot out of a cannon. Just as popular is **Toy Story Midway Mania!** (Map p240; https://disneyland.

Disneyland Resort

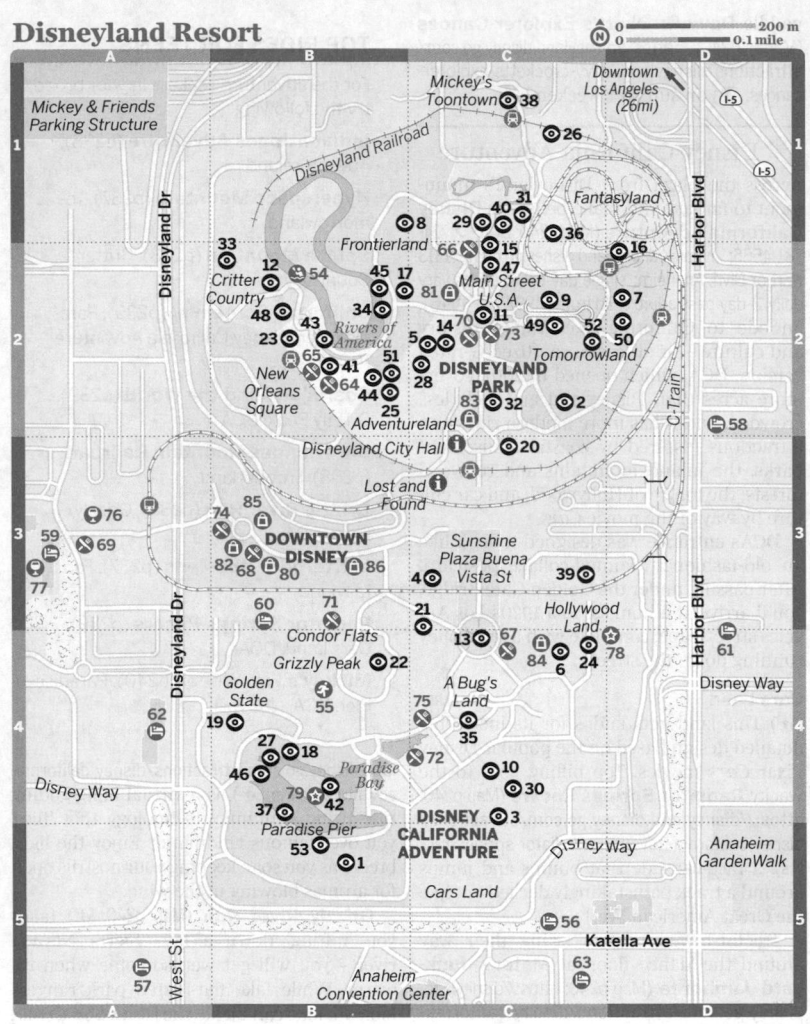

disney.go.com/attractions/disney-california-adventure/toy-story-mania) – a 4-D ride where you earn points by shooting at targets while your carnival car swivels and careens through an oversize, old-fashioned game arcade.

Want a bird's-eye view of the park? Head to **Mickey's Fun Wheel** (Map p240; https://disneyland.disney.go.com/attractions/disney-california-adventure/mickeys-fun-wheel;), a 15-story Ferris wheel where gondolas pitch and yaw in little loops as well as the big one (unless you've requested one of the stationary ones).

About half of Paradise Pier is dedicated to kid-friendly rides. Nearby, **Silly Sym-phony Swings** is a hybrid carousel with tornado-like chair swings, the pre-school set can ride a more sedate version on the **Golden Zephyr** (Map p240; https://disneyland.disney.go.com/attractions/disney-california-adventure/golden-zephyr;) and bounce along on the **Jumpin' Jellyfish** (Map p240; https://disneyland.disney.go.com/attractions/disney-california-adventure/jumpin-jellyfish; Paradise Pier;). **Goofy's Sky School** (Map p240;) is a cute and relatively tame cartoon-themed coaster ride. Cool your jets or get a pick-me up at the **Boudin Bakery** or

Disneyland Resort

DISNEYLAND IN...

One Day

Get to **Disneyland Park** early. Stroll **Main Street, U.S.A.** (p237) toward Sleeping Beauty Castle. Enter **Tomorrowland** (p237) to ride **Hyperspace Mountain** (p237). In **Fantasyland** (p237) don't miss the classic **'it's a small world'** (p237) ride or race down the **Matterhorn Bobsleds** (p237). Grab a FastPass for the **Indiana Jones Adventure** (p238) or the **Pirates of the Caribbean** (p238) before lunching in **New Orleans Square** (p238). Plummet down **Splash Mountain** (p238), then visit the **Haunted Mansion** (p238) before the **fireworks** begin.

Two Days

On the second day, at Disney California Adventure (p239), take a virtual hang-gliding ride on **Soarin' Around the World** (p239) and let kids tackle the **Redwood Creek Challenge Trail** (p239) before having fun at **Paradise Pier** (p239) with its roller coaster, Ferris wheel and carnival games. Watch the **Pixar Play Parade**, then ride the **Radiator Springs Racers** (p239) in **Cars Land** (p239) or cool off – fast! – on the **Grizzly River Run** (p239). After dark, drop by **World of Color** (p249) show.

the **Ghirardelli Soda Fountain and Chocolate Shop**.

Hollywood Land   AREA
(🎦) California's biggest factory of dreams is presented here in miniature, with soundstages, movable props, and – of course – a studio store. A *Guardians of the Galaxy*–themed ride was in the works as we went to press, but for now one of the top attractions is a one-hour live stage version of *Frozen*, at the Hyperion Theater (p249).

Learn how to draw like Disney in the **Animation Academy** or simply be amazed by the interactive **Sorcerer's Workshop**, both housed inside the **Animation Building** (https://disneyland.disney.go.com/attractions/disney-california-adventure/animation-academy; 🎦).

Children can navigate a taxicab through 'Monstropolis' on the **Monsters, Inc: Mike & Sulley to the Rescue!** (Map p240; https://disneyland.disney.go.com/attractions/disney-california-adventure/monsters-inc; Hollywood Land; 🎦) ride heading back toward the street's beginning.

If you arrive early in the day, you'll get an unobstructed look at the forced-perspective **mural** at the end of the street, a sky-and-land backdrop that looks, at least in photographs, like the street keeps going.

🛏 Sleeping

🛏 Disneyland Resort

For the full-on Disney experience, there are three different hotels within Disneyland Resort, though there are less-expensive options just beyond the Disney gates in Anaheim. If

you want a theme-park hotel for less money, try Knott's Berry Farm (p255).

Each of the resort's **hotels** (Map p240; ☎ 800-225-2024, reservations 714-956-6425; www.disneyland.com) has a swimming pool with a waterslide, kids' activity programs, fitness center, restaurants and bars, business center, and valet or complimentary self-parking for registered guests. Every standard room can accommodate up to five guests and has a minirefrigerator and a coffeemaker. Staying at one of Disney's resort hotels may also get you early admission to the parks. Lodging and admission-ticket packages can save money.

★ Disney's Grand Californian
Hotel & Spa   RESORT $$$
(Map p240; ☎ info 714-635-2300, reservations 714-956-6425; https://disneyland.disney.go.com/grand-californian-hotel; 1600 S Disneyland Dr; d from $360; P ❋ @ 🛜 ≋) Soaring timber beams rise above the cathedral-like lobby of the six-story Grand Californian, Disney's homage to the arts-and-crafts architectural movement. Cushy rooms have triple-sheeted beds, down pillows, bathrobes and all-custom furnishings. Outside there's a faux-redwood waterslide into the pool. At night, kids wind down with bedtime stories by the lobby's giant stone hearth.

Disneyland Hotel   HOTEL $$$
(Map p240; ☎ 714-778-6600; www.disneyland.com; 1150 Magic Way, Anaheim; r $210-395; P @ 🛜 ≋) Built in 1955, the year Disneyland opened, the park's original hotel has been rejuvenated with a dash of bibbidi-bobbidi-boo. There

are three towers with themed lobbies (adventure, fantasy and frontier), and the 972 good-sized rooms now boast Mickey-hand wall sconces in bathrooms and headboards lit like the fireworks over Sleeping Beauty Castle (p237).

Disney's Paradise Pier Hotel   HOTEL $$$

(Map p240; ☎info 714-999-0990, reservations 714-956-6425; http://disneyland.disney.go.com/paradise-pier-hotel; 1717 S Disneyland Dr, Anaheim; d from $240; P✳@🖵🏊) Sunbursts, surfboards and a giant superslide are all on deck at the Paradise Pier Hotel, the smallest (472 rooms), cheapest and maybe the most fun of the Disney hotel trio. Kids will love the beachy decor and game arcade, not to mention the pool and the tiny-tot video room filled with mini Adirondack chairs.

🛏 Anaheim

While the Disney resorts have their own hotels, there are a number of worthwhile hotels just off-site or a few miles away, and every stripe of chain hotel you can imagine. Generally Anaheim's hotels are good value relative to those in the OC beach towns.

Many Anaheim area motels and hotels offer packages combining lodging with theme-park tickets; most have family rooms or suites that sleep four to six people. Some local accommodations operate complimentary guest shuttles to Disneyland. Otherwise, consider staying within walking distance of the parks or along the public shuttle routes operated by Anaheim Resort Transportation (p252).

Ayres Hotel Anaheim   HOTEL $$

(Map p240; ☎714-634-2106; www.ayreshotels.com/anaheim; 2550 E Katella Ave; r incl breakfast $139-219; P⊖✳@🖵🏊) This well-run mini chain of business hotels delivers solid-gold value. The 133 recently renovated rooms

have microwaves, minifridges, safes, wet bar, pillow-top mattresses and design inspired by the Californian arts-and-crafts movement. Fourth-floor rooms have extra-high ceilings. Rates include a full breakfast and evening social hours Monday to Thursday with beer, wine and snacks.

Best Western Plus Stovall's Inn   MOTEL $$

(Map p240; ☎714-778-1880, ext 3 800-854-8175; www.bestwestern.com; 1110 W Katella Ave; r $99-175; P⊖✳@🖵🏊) Generations of guests have been coming to this 289-room motel about 15 minutes' walk to Disneyland. Around the side are two pools, two Jacuzzis, fitness center, kiddie pool and a garden of topiaries (for real). The remodeled sleek and modern-design rooms sparkle; all have air-con, a microwave and minifridge. Rates include a hot breakfast and there's a guest laundry.Go on the right night, and you might even catch a movie and s'mores by the pool.

Residence Inn Anaheim Resort/Convention Center   HOTEL $$

(Map p240; ☎714-782-7500; www.marriott.com; 640 W Katella Ave; r from $179; P⊖✳@🖵🏊) This new hotel near the convention center, yet only about 10 minutes on foot to Disneyland, shines with sleek linens, marble tables and glass walls within in-room kitchens, big windows and a sweet rooftop pool deck with Jacuzzi and a splash zone for kids. Rates include full breakfast, and there's also a gym and laundry machines.

Hotel Indigo Anaheim   BOUTIQUE HOTEL $$

(☎714-772-7755; www.ihg.com; 435 W Katella Ave; r from $170; P⊖@🖵🏊) This friendly, professional 104-room hotel has a clean, mid-century modernist look with hardwood floor and pops of color, fitness center, pool and guest laundry. Mosaic murals are modeled after the walnut trees that once

---

DCA SHOWS & PARADES

DCA's premier show is **World of Color** (p249), a dazzling nighttime display of lasers, lights and animation projected over Paradise Bay. It's so popular, you'll need a FastPass ticket (p251). Otherwise, reserved seating (714-781-4400, per person $15) includes a picnic meal; make reservations up to 30 days in advance.

During the day, don't miss the **Pixar Play Parade**, led by hot-rodder Lightning McQueen from *Cars* and featuring energetic, even acrobatic appearances by characters from other popular animated movies like *Monsters, Inc, The Incredibles, Ratatouille, Finding Nemo* and *Toy Story*. Be prepared to get squirted by aliens wielding water hoses.

DCA's other live entertainment includes mini musical extravaganzas like *Frozen*, based on the movies. Check out what's playing at the **Hyperion Theater** (p249) in Hollywood Land. Arrive 30 to 60 minutes early to get good seats.

THE WHAMMY

Have you gotten the Disneyland whammy yet? Don't worry, it's not a hex that cast members put on you for cutting in line. It's what fanatics call riding all three of Disneyland's 'mountain' rides – **Splash Mountain** (p238), **Hyperspace Mountain** (p237) and the **Big Thunder Mountain Railroad** (p238) – in one day. Overachievers can jump on the **Matterhorn Bobsleds** (p237) for extra credit.

bloomed here. It's about 15 minutes' walk or a quick drive to Disneyland and steps from shops and restaurants at Anaheim Garden-Walk (p249).

Grand Legacy at the Park HOTEL
(Map p240; ☎714-772-0440, 800-854-6097; www. grandlegacyhotel.com; 1650 S Harbor Blvd; r from $139; P❄❉@☎☒) About five minutes on foot to Disneyland, the large, four-story motel is recently renovated (though won't win any awards for chic design) around a large pool deck and parking lot. Rates include a snack bag with bottled water, fruit and kid-friendly snacks. Our fave spot is **The Fifth**, the rooftop bar with views of the Disneyland fireworks (Tue-Sun).

Anaheim Majestic Garden Hotel HOTEL $$
(☎714-778-1700, 844-227-8535; www.majestic gardenhotel.com; 900 S Disneyland Dr; r from $99; P❄❉@☎☒☒) Though the Majestic's a bit off on its own north of Disneyland (get there by free hotel shuttle), it's good value for the spacious rooms and gracious gardens around a Tudor-style building. If you're traveling with kids, there's a pool and game arcade, some rooms have castle-themed bunk beds, and the hotel even has its own princess, Corinne.

Alpine Inn MOTEL $
(Map p240; ☎714-535-2186, 800-772-4422; www. alpineinnanaheim.com; 715 W Katella Ave; r $99-149; P❉@☎☒) Connoisseurs of kitsch will hug their Hummels over this 42-room, snow-covered chalet facade on an A-frame exterior and icicle-covered roofs – framed by palm trees, of course. Right on the border of Disney California Adventure, the inn also has Ferris-wheel views. It's circa 1958, and

air-con rooms are well kept. Simple grab 'n' go breakfast served in the lobby.

Camelot Inn & Suites MOTEL $$
(Map p240; ☎714-635-7275, 800-828-4898; www. camelotinn-anaheim.com; 1520 S Harbor Blvd; r from $159; P@☎☒) This five-story, 200-room motel with accents of English Tudor style has minifridges and microwaves in every room, plus on-site laundry, a pool and hot tub. It's across the street from Disneyland, about five minutes on foot. The pool deck and some top-floor rooms have fireworks views.

✖ Eating

From stroll-and-eat Mickey-shaped pretzels ($4) and jumbo turkey legs ($10) to deluxe, gourmet dinners (sky's the limit), there's no shortage of eating options, though mostly pretty expensive and targeted to mainstream tastes. Phone **Disney Dining** (☎714-781-3463; http://disneyland.disney.go.com/dining) to make reservations up to 60 days in advance. Restaurant hours vary seasonally, sometimes daily. Check the Disneyland app or Disney Dining website for same-day hours.

✖ Disneyland Park

From snack stands to cafes and expensive sit-down meals, there are numerous dining options throughout Disneyland, with something for pretty much any taste. The selections here are some of the best. At most establishments, the formula is pretty simple: a few key dishes or plate meals for adults and some kind of kids menu. Individual eateries' hours vary with the park's opening hours; check the website or app for details. And if you're looking to dine at one of the fancier restaurants, reserve well in advance through Disney Dining (p244).

Jolly Holiday Bakery Cafe RESTAURANT, BAKERY $
(Map p240; https://disneyland.disney.go.com/ dining/disneyland/jolly-holiday-bakery-cafe; Main Street USA; mains $8.50-11; ⊗breakfast, lunch & dinner; ⊕) At this Mary Poppins–themed restaurant, the Jolly Holiday combo (grilled cheese and tomato basil soup for $9) is a decent deal and very satisfying. The cafe does other sandwiches on the sophisticated side, like the mozzarella caprese or turkey on ciabatta. Great people-watching.

Café Orleans
CAJUN, CREOLE $$

(Map p240; https://disneyland.disney.go.com/din ing/disneyland/cafe-orleans; New Orleans Square; mains $16-22; ⊙hours vary; ☖) This Southern-flavored restaurant is famous for its three-cheese Monte Cristo sandwiches at lunch. Breakfast served seasonally.

Plaza Inn
AMERICAN $$

(Map p240; https://disneyland.disney.go.com/din ing/disneyland/plaza-inn; Main Street USA; mains $12-17, breakfast buffet adult/child 3-9yr $27/13; ⊙breakfast, lunch & dinner; ☖) Finger-lickin' good fried chicken platter and pot roast come with mashed potatoes, buttermilk biscuits and veggies at this 1950s original. There's a fun breakfast buffet with Disney characters. The rest of the day, if you can snag an outdoor table you'll also enjoy great people-watching here, at the crossroads of Main Street, U.S.A.

Carnation Cafe
AMERICAN $$

(Map p240; https://disneyland.disney.go.com/ dining/disneyland/carnation-cafe; Main Street USA; mains $13-19; ⊙breakfast, lunch & dinner; ☖) Near the Disneyland entrance, this old-timey, wood-built spot serves baked potato soup, sourdough bacon cheese melt, meatloaf and gravy, fried chicken and Mickey-shaped breakfast waffles.

Next door, the **Gibson Girl** ice-cream parlor and candy store serves a dizzying selection of desserty decadence.

Blue Bayou
SOUTHERN US $$$

(Map p240; ☎714-781-3463; https://disneyland. disney.go.com/dining/disneyland/blue-bayou-restaurant; New Orleans Sq; mains lunch $28-41, dinner $30-48; ⊙lunch & dinner; ☖) Surrounded by the 'bayou' inside the Pirates of the Caribbean (p238) attraction, this is the top choice for sit-down dining in Disneyland Park and is famous for its Creole and Cajun specialties at dinner. Order fresh-baked pecan pie topped by a piratey souvenir for dessert.

Disney California Adventure

Like Disneyland, DCA has a number of eating options: counters for casual snacks and meals around Pacific Wharf and Paradise Pier (p239), all the way up to some of the resorts' best dining at Carthay Circle.

Pacific Wharf Cafe
FOOD HALL $

(Map p240; https://disneyland.disney.go.com/din ing/disney-california-adventure/pacific-wharf-cafe; mains $10-11.50; ⊙breakfast, lunch & dinner; ☖) This counter-service collection of restaurants shows off some of California's ethnic cuisines (Chinese, Mexican etc) as well as hearty soups in sourdough-bread bowls, farmers-market salads and deli sandwiches. We like to eat at umbrella-covered tables by the water.

Wine Country Trattoria
ITALIAN $$

(Map p240; https://disneyland.disney.go.com/ dining/disney-california-adventure/wine-country-trattoria; Pacific Wharf; mains lunch $15-21, dinner $17-23; ⊙lunch & dinner; ☖) If you can't quite swing the Napa Rose (p246) or Carthay Circle (p246), this sunny Cal-Italian terrace restaurant is a fine backup. Fork into Italian pastas, salads or veggie paninis, washed down with Napa Valley wines.

ℹ️ FOOD & DRINK TIPS

➜ Technically, you can't bring any food or drinks into the parks, but security-inspection staff usually look the other way at small water bottles and a few snacks.

➜ Store soft-sided coolers and other food in the all-day lockers by the not-so-appealing picnic area outside the main entrance.

➜ Within the parks, reservations are recommended at top-end restaurants. If you haven't made reservations, plan on eating at off-peak times (eg outside the noon to 3pm lunch rush, and before 6pm or after 9pm for dinner).

➜ Convenient, if overpriced, fast food and carnival-style snacks are sold everywhere in the parks.

➜ Park maps indicate restaurants and cafes where you can find healthy food options – look for the apple icon.

➜ For good-value eats and fresher menu options, exit the parks and walk to Downtown Disney (or ride the monorail).

➜ Drinking fountains are everywhere, so bring a refillable water bottle.

★ **Carthay Circle** AMERICAN $$$
(Map p240; https://disneyland.disney.go.com/dining/disney-california-adventure/carthay-circle-restaurant; Buena Vista St; mains lunch $24-34, dinner $32-45; ⊙lunch & dinner; 🖶) Decked out like a Hollywood country club, new Carthay Circle is the best dining in either park, with seasonal steaks, seafood, pasta, smart service and a good wine list. Your table needs at least one order of fried biscuits, stuffed with white cheddar, bacon and jalapeño and served with apricot honey butter.

Inquire about special packages including dinner and the World of Color (p249) show.

Downtown Disney & Disneyland Resort

Earl of Sandwich SANDWICHES $
(Map p240; 🕿714-817-7476; www.earlofsandwichusa.com; Downtown Disney; mains $4.50-7.50; ⊙8am-11pm Sun-Thu, to midnight Fri & Sat; 🖶) This counter-service chain near the Disneyland Hotel (p243) serves grilled sandwiches that are both kid- and adult-friendly. The 'original 1762' is roast beef, cheddar and horseradish, or look for chipotle chicken with avocado or holiday turkey. There are also pizza, salad and breakfast options.

Ralph Brennan's New Orleans Jazz Kitchen CAJUN $$
(Map p240; 🕿714-776-5200; http://rbjazzkitchen.com; Downtown Disney; mains lunch/dinner $14-19/$24.50-38.50; ⊙8am-10pm Sun-Thu, to 11pm Fri & Sat; 🖶) Hear live jazz combos on the weekends and piano weeknights at this resto-bar with NOLA-style Cajun and Creole dishes: gumbo, po-boy sandwiches, jambalaya, plus a (less adventurous) kids menu and specialty cocktails. There's breakfast and lunch express service if you don't have time to linger.

★ Napa Rose CALIFORNIAN $$$
(Map p240; 🕿714-300-7170; https://disneyland.disney.go.com/dining; Grand Californian Hotel & Spa; mains $38-48, 4-course prix-fixe dinner from $100; ⊙5:30-10pm; 🖶) High-back arts-and-crafts-style chairs, leaded-glass windows and towering ceilings befit Disneyland Resort's top-drawer restaurant. On the plate, seasonal 'California Wine Country' (read: NorCal) cuisine is as impeccably crafted as the Sleeping Beauty Castle. Kids menu available. Reservations essential. Enter the hotel from Disney California Adventure or Downtown Disney.

Steakhouse 55 AMERICAN $$$
(Map p240; 🕿714-781-3463; 1150 Magic Way, Disneyland Hotel; mains breakfast $14-25, dinner $31-57; ⊙7am-11pm & 5-10:30pm) Nothing at Disneyland is exactly a secret, but this clubby, grown-up hideaway comes pretty darn close. Dry-rubbed, bone-in rib eye, Australian lobster tail, heirloom potatoes and green beans with applewood-smoked bacon uphold a respectable chophouse menu. There's also a full bar, good wine list and (we hope well-behaved) kids menu.

Reservations are required at dinner.

They also do afternoon tea between noon and 3pm from Friday to Sunday (adult/child from $50/35).

Catal Restaurant MEDITERRANEAN $$$
(Map p240; 🕿714-774-4442; www.patinagroup.com/catal-restaurant; Downtown Disney; mains breakfast $9-14, lunch $16-27, dinner $26-42; ⊙hours vary, to 10pm Fri & Sat; 🖶) The chef cooks up a fusion of Californian and Mediterranean cuisines (steelhead salmon, paellas, lunchtime sandwiches, plus a kids menu) at this airy two-story restaurant decorated in a sunny Mediterranean-Provençal style with exposed beams and lemon-colored walls. Sit on the balcony: it's attached to Uva Bar (p247) and does great happy hours upstairs, from 3pm to 5pm daily.

Anaheim

Almost under the radar, Anaheim has developed some of the OC's most interesting dining, especially in the area around the Packing District (p248) and Center Street (p235), both near Anaheim City Hall.

Most restaurants on the streets surrounding Disneyland are chains, though Anaheim GardenWalk (p249) has some upscale ones. It's about a 10-minute walk from Disneyland's main gate.

More adventurous palates can head to **Little Arabia**, about 3 miles west of Disneyland, or Little Saigon (p261), about 7 miles southwest of Disneyland, in the cities of Garden Grove and Westminster.

Most restaurants on the streets surrounding Disneyland are chains, though Anaheim GardenWalk (p249) has some upscale ones. It's about a 10-minute walk from Disneyland's main gate.

★ Pour Vida MEXICAN $
(Map p254; 🕿657-208-3889; www.pourvidalatinflavor.com; 185 W Center St Promenade; tacos $2-

8; ⊙10am-7pm Mon, to 9pm Tue-Thu, to 10pm Fri, 9am-10pm Sat, 9am-7pm Sun) Chef Jimmy, who has worked in some of LA's top kitchens, returned to his Mexican roots to make some of the most gourmet tacos we've ever seen: pineapple skirt steak, tempura oyster, heirloom cauliflower...*caramba*! Even the tortillas are special, made with squid ink, spinach and a secret recipe. It's deliberately informal, all brick and concrete with chalkboard walls.

They make fresh-pressed juices like the *pasión caliente* (carrot, habanero, passion fruit, apple, peppercorns and lemon), which you can also order as margaritas.

Packing House

FOOD HALL **$**

(Map p254; 📞714-533-7225; www.anaheimpacking district.com; 440 S Anaheim St; ⊙opens 9am, closing hours vary) This 1919 former Sunkist orange packing house has a fabulous new life. Over 20 stalls and restaurants sell both sit-down and stroll-around eats and drinks: fish dinners to ramen, cocktails to shaved ice, adventurous ice cream pops to entire meals based on waffles. It's all airy and modern on the inside, with lots of spaces to hang out. Prices vary by stall, but most are pretty good value.

Healthy Junk

VEGAN **$**

(Map p254; 📞714-772-5865; www.thehealthyjunk. com; 201 Center St Promenade; mains $4-10; ⊙10am-9pm Mon-Fri, 11am-9pm Sat, 11am-5pm Sun; ✍) Vegan snacks like yam wedges with ranch dressing, veggie burgers, Tex-Mex and big salads are served in this fun counter service shop in a little food court. They even have sweets like carrot cake and triple-chocolate brownies – also vegan, naturally.

★ Olive Tree

MIDDLE EASTERN **$$**

(Map p254; 📞714-535-2878; 512 S Brookhurst St; mains $8-16; ⊙10am-9pm Mon-Sat, to 8pm Sun) In Little Arabia, this simple restaurant in a nondescript strip mall ringed with flags of Arab nations has earned accolades from local papers to *Saveur* magazine. You *could* get standards like falafel and kebabs, but daily specials are where it's at; Saturday's *kabseh* is righteous, fall-off-the-bone lamb shank over spiced rice with currants and onions.

Afterwards, stop for baklava at the bakery a few doors down.

Umami Burger

BURGERS **$$**

(Map p254; 📞714-991-8626; www.umamiburger. com; 338 S Anaheim Blvd; mains $11-15; ⊙11am-11pm Sun-Thu, to midnight Fri & Sat) The Anaheim outpost of this LA-based minichain sets the right tone for the Packing District (p248). Burgers span classic to truffled. Try the Hatch burger with roasted green chilies or the Manly with beer cheddar and bacon lardons. Get 'em with deep-fried 'smushed' potatoes with house-made ketchup, and top it off with a salted chocolate ice-cream sandwich. Full bar.

The rusted license plates on the wall were discovered during excavations of this former Packard dealership.

🍷 Drinking & Nightlife

You can't buy alcohol in Disneyland, but you can at Disney California Adventure, Downtown Disney and Disney's trio of resort hotels. Downtown Disney offers bars, live music, a 12-screen cinema and more. Some restaurants and bars stay open as late as midnight on Fridays and Saturdays.

🍸 Disneyland Resort

★ Trader Sam's Enchanted Tiki Lounge

COCKTAIL BAR

(Map p240; https://disneyland.disney.go.com/ dining/disneyland-hotel/trader-sams; 1150 Magic Way, Disneyland Hotel; ⊙11:30am-1:30am) It's tiki to the max and good, clean fun inside this faux-grass shack by the Disneyland Hotel (p243)'s pool. Look for strong, sweet cocktails like the Shrunken Zombie Head and Hippopotamai-tai served with ice cubes that light up. Order the right drink, and the walls might start moving. No, really.

Uva Bar

WINE BAR

(Map p240; 📞714-774-4442; www.patinagroup. com/uva-bar-cafe; Downtown Disney; ⊙8am-11pm Sun-Thu, to midnight Fri & Sat) *Uva* is Italian for grape, and this bar resembling a Paris Metro station is Downtown Disney's best outdoor spot to tipple wine, nibble Cal-Mediterranean tapas and people-watch from the pedestrian street's traffic circle. There are 40 wines available by the glass.

Come for happy hour at sister Catal Restaurant (p246), between 3pm and 5pm daily.

Napa Rose Lounge

LOUNGE

(Map p240; https://disneyland.disney.go.com/ dining/grand-californian-hotel/napa-rose-lounge; Grand Californian Hotel & Spa; ⊙5pm-10pm Sun-Thu, to 11pm Fri & Sat) Raise a glass to Napa as you nosh on pizzettas, artisan cheese plates and Scharffen Berger chocolate truffle cake around the fireplace in the Grand Californian (p242)'s swankiest bar.

ANAHEIM PACKING DISTRICT & CENTER STREET

The **Anaheim Packing District** (www.anaheimpackingdistrict.com; S Anaheim Bl) launched in 2013 around a long-shuttered 1925 Packard dealership and the 1919 orange-packing house a couple miles from Disneyland, near the city's actual downtown.

It relaunched in 2013–14 with chic new restaurants like **Umami Burger** (p247), the **Anaheim Brewery**, an evolving collection of shops and a park for events.

About a quarter-mile from here is **Center Street** (p235), a quietly splashy redeveloped neighborhood with an ice rink designed by Frank Gehry, and a couple of blocks packed with hipster-friendly shops selling everything from casual clothing and accessories to comic books. At **Barbeer** you can get a trim and a brewski, or check out the writerly **Ink & Bean** (p249) coffee saloon. Some of our favorite dining offerings are the fabulous **Pour Vida** (p247) taco stand and a mini food court where you might indulge in healthy junk at, um, **Healthy Junk** (p247).

ESPN Zone   SPORTS BAR
(Map p240; ☎714-300-3776; www.espnzone. com; Downtown Disney; ⊗11am-11pm Sun-Thu, to midnight Fri & Sat) Show up early and score a personal leather recliner at this sports and drinking emporium with 175 TVs – flatscreens even hang above the men's-room urinals. Ball-park food and couch-potato classics make up an all-American menu. Families gravitate toward the virtual-reality and video-game arcade upstairs.

Golden Vine Winery   BAR
(Map p240; Pacific Wharf, Disney California Adventure) This centrally located terrace is a great place for relaxing and regrouping in Disney California Adventure.

Nearby at Pacific Wharf, walk-up window **Rita's Baja Blenders** whips up frozen cocktails like marga – you know – ritas, and nonalcoholic blended strawberry and lemon drinks.

🍷 Anaheim

At last count there were about 20 craft breweries within the city of Anaheim. A couple of them, Anaheim Brewery and Unsung Brewing Company, are near each other in the Packing District. For a brew with a view, hit the rooftop lounge at the Grand Legacy at the Park Hotel (p244); time it right, and you can watch Disneyland's fireworks show.

★Blind Rabbit   COCKTAIL BAR
(Map p254; www.theblindrabbit.com; Anaheim Packing House, 440 S Anaheim Blvd; ⊗reservations 5pm-10:30pm Mon-Fri, from noon Sat & Sun) This chill, dimly lit, atmospheric speakeasy carves its own ice, makes its own juice, does regularly changing (but always creative) cocktails and has live music four nights a week.

Reserve online (until 2pm on the same day) and they'll tell you where to show up. A dress code means no flip-flops, shorts or ball caps.

Barbeer   BAR
(Map p254; ☎714-533-3737; www.facebook. com/barbeeranaheim; 165 Center St Promenade; ⊗10am-7pm Mon-Fri, to 6pm Sat, to 4pm Sun) Barber plus beer. Get it? At this hipster-cool men's styling emporium, treat yourself to a shave, a haircut and a brewski on Center Street Promenade.

Unsung Brewing Company   MICROBREWERY
(Map p254; ☎714-706-3098; www.unsungbrewing. com; 500 S Anaheim Bl; ⊗4pm-10pm Mon-Thu, 1pm-11pm Fri, 11am-11pm Sat, noon-7pm Sun) Beer with a comic-book aesthetic? Unsung calls its Buzzman light lager a mutant ale, Anthia has mango, pineapple and banana overtones and nutty Propeller-Head is brewed with coffee. Speaking of coffee, they also do cold brews. Buy a growler, and take home a comic book too.

Anaheim Brewery   BREWERY
(Map p254; www.anaheimbrew.com; 336 S Anaheim Blvd; ⊗5-9pm Tue-Thu, 5-11pm Fri, noon-11pm Sat, 1-7pm Sun) Try the surprisingly good local brew at this simple tasting room in a renovated warehouse in the Packing District (p248). Standouts include the Hefeweizen Red and Coast to Coast IPA with nice citrus notes. Four-glass tastings for $11.

Look for events like taco Tuesdays and trivia on Wednesdays.

Ink & Bean   CAFE
(Map p254; ☎714-635-2326; www.inkandbean coffee.com; 115 W Center St Promenade; ⊗7:30am-5pm Mon, to 7:30pm Tue-Fri, 8am-9pm Sat, to 5pm Sun) This cozy, literary-minded cafe serves

Stumptown coffees, sells a full complement of writing implements and gigs in live music.

House of Blues CLUB
(Map p254; ☑714-778-2583; www.houseofblues.com/anaheim; 400 W Disney Way, Anaheim Garden Walk; ⊗hours vary) Recently moved from Downtown Disney, HOB occasionally gets some heavy-hitting rock, pop, jazz and blues concerts. Call or check online for show times and tickets. Make reservations for Sunday's fun gospel brunch. Note: guests must be 21 and over to attend a show.

☆ Entertainment

☆ Disney California Adventure

★ **World of Color** LIVE PERFORMANCE
(Map p240; https://disneyland.disney.go.com/entertainment/disney-california-adventure/world-of-color; Paradise Pier) Disney California Adventure's premier show is the 22-minute *World of Color*, a dazzling nighttime display of lasers, lights and animation projected over Paradise Bay. It's so popular, you'll need a FASTPASS ticket. Otherwise, several of the restaurants around DCA offer meal-and-ticket packages. Failing that, space is available without a ticket on a first-come, first-served basis.

Hyperion Theater THEATER
(Map p240; https://disneyland.disney.go.com/entertainment/disney-california-adventure/frozen-live-at-hyperion; Hollywood Land) A live stage version of the animated movie musical *Frozen* is presented here, with actors, the hit songs and Broadway-style costumes, sets and lighting.

☆ Anaheim

Anaheim GardenWalk CINEMA, MALL
(Map p254; www.anaheimgardenwalk.com; 400 W Disney Way; ⊗11am-9pm; 🚻) This dining, shopping and entertainment complex just east of Disneyland (walk or take the ART shuttle; p252) has a family-friendly bowling alley and cineplex, all the way to the House of Blues and night club. Dining is mostly at high-end national chains.

Angel Stadium STADIUM
(Map p254; ☑888-796-4256, 714-940-2000; www.angelsbaseball.com; 2000 Gene Autry Way) The controversially (and oh-so-awkwardly) named Los Angeles Angels of Anaheim play major-league baseball here from April to early October. Single-game tickets start at $10 for nosebleed sections. Parking is $10.

City National
Grove of Anaheim CONCERT VENUE
(Map p254; ☑714-712-2700; www.citynationalgroveofanaheim.com; 2200 E Katella Ave) At this indoor 5000-seat venue, be entertained by headliners from classic rockers to modern rockers, comedy and speakers, plus 'locally grown' rock bands. Sightlines are great. Call or check online for showtimes and tickets. Parking is $12.

Honda Center STADIUM
(Map p254; ☑800-745-3000; www.hondacenter.com; 2695 E Katella Ave) The Anaheim Ducks play hockey from October to April at this indoor venue. Professional rodeo events, fight nights and megaconcerts round out the schedule. Ticket prices and parking rates vary.

🔒 Shopping

🔒 Disneyland Park & Disney California Adventure

Each 'land' has its own shopping, appropriate to its particular theme, whether the Old West, Route 66 or a seaside amusement park. There's no shortage of ways to spend on souvenirs, clothing and Disneyana and

---

DISNEYLAND FIREWORKS, PARADES & SHOWS

The fireworks spectacular above Sleeping Beauty Castle, **Remember – Dreams Come True**, happens nightly around 9:30pm in summer. (In winter, artificial snow falls on Main Street, U.S.A. after the fireworks.) In **Mickey's Soundsational Parade**, floats glide down Main Street USA with bands playing a variety of music from Latin to Bollywood, accompanying costumed characters.

At the **Princess Fantasy Faire** in **Fantasyland** (p237), your little princesses and knights can join the Royal Court and meet some Disney princesses. Storytelling and coronation ceremonies happen throughout the day in summer. Younglings can learn to harness 'The Force' at **Jedi Training Academy**, which accepts Padawans several times daily in peak season, at **Tomorrowland** (p237) Terrace.

plenty other non-Disney goods. For collectors, Disney Gallery (p250) and Off the Page (p250) sell high-end art and collectibles like original sketches and vintage reproduction prints.

You don't have to carry your purchases around all day; store them at the Newsstand (Main Street, U.S.A.; 237), Star Trader (Tomorrowland (p237)), Pioneer Mercantile (Frontierland; p238) or Engine Ear Toys (Disney California Adventure; p239). If you're staying at Disneyland, have packages sent directly to your hotel.

Bibbidi Bobbidi Boutique GIFTS & SOUVENIRS
(Map p240; ☑ reservations 714-781-7895; https://disneyland.disney.go.com/shops; Fantasyland; ⚑) Behind Sleeping Beauty Castle (p237), kids can get a full makeover as princesses, knights and more, though (fair warning) the full treatment – including hairstyle, makeup and gown – doesn't come cheap.

Disney Gallery GIFTS & SOUVENIRS
(Map p240; https://disneyland.disney.go.com; Main Street USA) Come here to view concept art and collectibles by Disney 'imagineers' and artful renderings of Disney locations from around the world.

Emporium GIFTS & SOUVENIRS
(Map p240; Main Street USA, Disneyland; ⚑) Just around the bend from the Disneyland Main Gate is this one-stop shop for a mind-boggling variety of souvenirs, clothing and Disneyana, from T-shirts to mouse ears.

Off the Page GIFTS & SOUVENIRS
(Map p240; Hollywood Land, Disney California Adventure) This shop sells animation cels, ornaments and the like, while artists at work demonstrate the creation process.

🔒 Downtown Disney

Downtown Disney is a triumph of marketing. Once in this open-air pedestrian mall, sandwiched between the two parks and the hotels, it may be hard to extract yourself. There are plenty of opportunities to drop cash in stores (not just Disney stuff either), restaurants and entertainment venues. Apart from the Disney merch, a lot of it is shops you can find elsewhere, but in the moment it's still hard to resist. Most shops here open and close with the parks.

Anna & Elsa's Boutique CLOTHING, GIFTS & SOUVENIRS
(Map p240; https://disneyland.disney.go.com/shops; Downtown Disney; ⚑) If there was ever any doubt about the popularity of *Frozen*, look no further. This giant shop sells apparel and souvenirs, sure, and by reservation the little ones can get made up as Elsa, Anna or Olaf the Snowman.

Disney Vault 28 CLOTHING, GIFTS & SOUVENIRS
(Map p240; Downtown Disney) From distressed T-shirts with edgy Cinderella prints to black tank tops patterned with white skulls, the hipster inventory is discombobulating and really intriguing, including pieces made in collaboration with familiar houses like Harajuku Lovers, Dooney & Bourke and Betsey Johnson.

D Street CLOTHING, GIFTS & SOUVENIRS
(Map p240; Downtown Disney) Fanboys and girls of all kinds – wannabe gangstas to fashionistas, skate rats, surfers and anime geeks – get their own store at Disney. If you've got tweens or teens, resistance is futile. Retro comic-book hero, Japanimation-style and Star Wars–inspired tees and toys hang on the racks next to urbanized Western wear and rockabilly dresses. It's about as counterculture as it gets in these parts.

Ridemakerz TOYS
(Map p240; Downtown Disney) Why should clothes hounds have all the fun? This shop lets you custom-build your own toy race car (*duuuuude!*). Select a chassis, body, tires (monster tires, should you want them), remote control or not, and the staff will help you put it together.

World of Disney GIFTS & SOUVENIRS
(Map p240; Downtown Disney) Pirates and princesses are hot at this minimetropolis of mouse-related merchandising. Don't miss the special room dedicated to Disney's villains – gotcha, evil Queen! Grab last-minute must-haves here.

🔒 Anaheim

Rare by Goodwill VINTAGE
(Map p254; ☑ 714-786-6642; www.ocgoodwill.org; 411 W Broadway; ☉ 10am-9pm Mon-Sat, 11am-7pm Sun) It may be a thrift store, but the vintage and gently used clothing and home goods are laid out so stylishly you'd think they cost many times more. Enter off Center St.

ℹ FASTPASS

Disneyland and Disney California Adventure's FASTPASS system can significantly cut your wait times.

➤ Walk up to a FASTPASS ticket machine – located near the entrance to select theme-park rides – and insert your park entrance ticket or annual passport. You'll receive a slip of paper showing the 'return time' for boarding (it's always at least 40 minutes later).

➤ Show up within the window of time on the ticket and join the ride's FASTPASS line. There'll still be a wait, but it's shorter (typically 15 minutes or less). Hang on to your FastPass ticket until you board the ride.

➤ If you're running late and miss the time window printed on your FASTPASS ticket, you can still try joining the FASTPASS line, although showing up before your FASTPASS time window is a no-no.

You're thinking, what's the catch, right? When you get a FASTPASS, you will have to wait at least two hours before getting another one (check the 'next available' time printed at the bottom of your ticket).

So make it count. Before getting a FASTPASS, check the display above the machine, which will tell you what the 'return time' for boarding is. If it's much later in the day, or doesn't fit your schedule, a FastPass may not be worth it. Ditto if the ride's current wait time is just 15 to 30 minutes.

Disneyland FASTPASS Attractions

Autopia (p237)

Big Thunder Mountain Railroad (p238)

Indiana Jones Adventure (p238)

Roger Rabbit's Car Toon Spin

Hyperspace Mountain (p237)

Splash Mountain (p238)

Star Tours – The Adventure Continues (p237)

DCA FASTPASS Attractions

California Screamin' (p239)

Goofy's Sky School (p242)

Grizzly River Run (p239)

Soarin' Around the World (p239)

Radiator Springs Racers (p239)

World of Color (p249)

DISNEYLAND & ORANGE COUNTY DISNEYLAND & ANAHEIM

ℹ Information

Before you arrive, consult our Disneyland Trip Planner (p48) or visit **Disneyland Resort** (☎ live assistance 714-781-7290, recorded info 714-781-4565; www.disneyland.com) for more information. You can also download the **Disneyland Explorer** app to your mobile device.

INTERNET ACCESS

There's no wi-fi internet inside the theme parks.

INTERNET RESOURCES & MOBILE APPS

Disneyland mobile app The most useful tool is Disneyland and Disney California Adventure's official smartphone app, which lets you purchase tickets, make dining reservations, view wait times and locate your favorite characters.

DisneyMaxPass Ticket add-on for $10 per day, which allows you to download, save and share all your Disney PhotoPass photos, as well as reserve digital Disney FASTPASS selections.

MousePlanet (www.mouseplanet.com) One-stop fansite for all things Disney, with news updates, podcasts, trip reports, reviews and discussion boards.

Theme Park Insider (www.themeparkinsider.com) Newsy blog, travel tips and user reviews of Disneyland rides, attractions and lodging.

Touring Plans (https://touringplans.com) The 'unofficial guide to Disneyland' since 1985. No-nonsense advice, a crowd calendar and a 'lines app.'

LOCKERS

Self-service lockers with in-and-out privileges cost $7 to $15 per day. You'll find them on **Main Street, U.S.A.** (p237) (Disneyland), in **Sunshine Plaza** (Disney California Adventure) and at the **picnic area** just outside the theme park's main entrance, near Downtown Disney.

LOST & FOUND

Lost and Found (☑714-817-2166; ⊙8am-8pm) Look for the office steps just east of Disney California Adventure's main entrance.

MEDICAL SERVICES

You'll find first-aid facilities at Disneyland (Main Street, U.S.A.), Disney California Adventure (Pacific Wharf) and Downtown Disney (next to Ralph Brennan's Jazz Kitchen).

Anaheim Urgent Care (☑714-533-2273; 831 S State College Blvd, Anaheim; ⊙8am-8pm Mon-Fri, 9am-5pm Sat & Sun) Walk-in nonemergency medical clinic.

Anaheim Global Medical Center (☑657-230-0265; www.anaheim-gmc.com; 1025 S Anaheim Blvd, Anaheim; ⊙24hr) Hospital emergency room.

MONEY

Disneyland's City Hall offers foreign-currency exchange. In Disney California Adventure, head to the guest relations lobby. Multiple ATMs are found in both theme parks and at Downtown Disney.

Travelex (☑714-687-7977; 100 West Lincoln Ave, inside US Bank, Anaheim; ⊙9am-5pm Mon-Fri, to 1pm Sat) Also exchanges foreign currency near Anaheim City Hall.

POST

There is no post office at Disneyland, but Anaheim's **Holiday Station** (www.usps.com; 1180 W Ball Rd; ⊙9am-5pm Mon-Fri) is a full-service post office.

SMOKING

Check theme-park maps for specially designated smoking areas, which are few and far between. At Downtown Disney, smoking is allowed outdoors.

TOURIST INFORMATION

For information or help inside the parks, just ask any cast member or visit Disneyland's **City Hall** (☑714-781-4565; Main Street USA) or Disney California Adventure's guest relations lobby.

Visit Anaheim (☑855-405-5020; http://visitanaheim.org; 800 W Katella Ave, Anaheim Convention Center) The city's official tourism bureau has information on lodging, dining and transportation, during events at the Convention Center.

❶ Getting There & Away

Anaheim's sparkling new transit center, **ARTIC** (Anaheim Regional Transportation Intermodal Center; 2150 E Katella Ave, Anaheim), connects trains and buses from out of town with local transport. ARTIC is about 3 miles east of the Disney Resort area.

AIR

Most international travelers arrive at Los Angeles International Airport (LAX) or San Diego (SAN), but for easy-in, easy-out domestic travel, nothing beats the easily navigated **John Wayne Airport** (p497) (SNA) in Santa Ana, served by all major US airlines and Canada's WestJet. The airport is about 14 miles south of Disneyland, near the junction of Hwy 55 and I-405 (San Diego Fwy). Ride-hailing services cost about $20 each way to the Disneyland area.

If you do arrive at LAX, it's probably not worth your time to change planes, as it's barely an hour by road. **Super Shuttle** (www.supershuttle.com; LAX/SNA to Disneyland hotels one way $17/11) operates from LAX and SNA to Disney resort hotels for $17/11 each way (more expensive to Disneyland proper).

Disneyland Resort Express (☑714-978-8855, 800-828-6699; https://dre.coachusa.com) runs buses from LAX and SNA to Disneyland-area hotels every 30 minutes to one hour from 7:30am until 10pm (adult one-way/round trip $30/48 from LAX, $20/35 from SNA; it's free for up to three children up to age 11). Reservations aren't required, except if you want to take advantage of money-saving family passes.

BUS

Anaheim Resort Transportation (ART; ☑888-364-2787; www.rideart.org; adult/child fare $3/1, day pass $5.50/2, multiple-day passes available) ART connects the Disney resorts with hotels and other locations around Anaheim and nearby. Day passes can be purchased at hotels or via the ART Ticketing app (www.rideart.org/fares-and-passes).

Greyhound (☑714-999-1256, 800-231-2222; www.greyhound.com; 2626 E Katella Ave, Anaheim, ARTIC) has several daily buses between ARTIC and Downtown LA (from $10, 40 minutes) and San Diego (from $14, 2¼ hours).

The **Orange County Transportation Authority** (OCTA; ☑714-560-6282; www.octa.net; ride/day pass $2/5) operates buses serving towns throughout the county. Both types of tickets are sold on board (cash only, exact change).

CAR & MOTORCYCLE

Disneyland Resort is just off I-5 (Santa Ana Fwy), about 30 miles southeast of Downtown LA. Take the Disneyland Dr exit if you're coming from the north, or the Katella Ave/Disney Way exit from the south.

Arriving at Disneyland Resort is like arriving at an airport. Giant, easy-to-read overhead signs indicate which ramps you need to take for the theme parks, hotels or Anaheim's streets.

All-day parking at Disneyland Resort costs $20 ($25 for oversize vehicles). Enter the 'Mickey & Friends' parking structure from southbound Disneyland Dr, off Ball Rd. Walk outside and follow the signs to board the free tram to Downtown Disney and the theme parks. The parking garage opens one hour before the parks do.

Downtown Disney parking is reserved for diners, shoppers and movie-goers. It has a different rate structure, with the first two hours free, $6 per half-hour thereafter, to a maximum of $36.

TRAIN

Amtrak (☑ 800-872-7245; www.amtrak.com; 2626 E Katella Ave, ARTIC) has almost a dozen daily trains to/from LA's Union Station ($15, 40 minutes) and San Diego ($28, 2¼ hours). Less frequent **Metrolink** (☑ 800-371-5465; www.metrolinktrains.com; 22150 E Katella Ave, Anaheim, ARTIC) commuter trains connect Anaheim to LA's Union Station ($8.75, 50 minutes), Orange ($2.50, six minutes), San Juan Capistrano ($8.50, 40 minutes) and San Clemente ($10, 50 minutes).

ⓘ Getting Around

DISNEYLAND RAILROAD

The miniature bio-diesel **Disneyland Railroad** chugs in a clockwise circle around Disneyland, stopping at Main Street, U.S.A., New Orleans Square, Mickey's Toontown and Tomorrowland, taking about 20 minutes to make a full loop. Between the Tomorrowland and Main Street USA stations, look out for **dioramas** of the Grand Canyon and a Jurassic-style 'Primeval World.' From Tomorrowland, you can catch the zero-emissions monorail directly to Downtown Disney.

MONORAIL

With an admission ticket to Disneyland, you can ride the monorail between Tomorrowland and the far end of Downtown Disney, near the Disneyland Hotel. It sure beats walking both ways along crowded Downtown Disney.

SHUTTLE

Anaheim Resort Transportation (p252) operates some 20 shuttle routes between Disneyland and area hotels, convention centers, malls, stadiums and the transit center, saving traffic jams and parking headaches. Shuttles typically start running an hour before Disneyland opens, operating from 7am to midnight daily during summer. Departures are typically two to three times per hour, depending on the route. Purchase single or multiday ART passes at kiosks near ART shuttle stops or online in advance.

Many hotels and motels offer their own free shuttles to Disneyland and other area attractions; ask when booking.

AROUND DISNEYLAND

When you've had enough of Disneyland but not amusement parks, Knott's Berry Farm, in Buena Park, was the first amusement park in the US and still pulls in crowds for its hair-raising roller coasters, Old West–style streets and adjacent Soak City (p255) water park across the street. Families will also get a kick out of the Discovery Cube (p256) science museum, while adult culture vultures should be sure to hit the Bowers Museum (p256), much respected for its top-notch exhibits of California and Pacific Island art and blockbuster special shows.

Knott's Berry Farm & Around

The biggest area attraction aside from the Disneyland Resort is this theme park teeming with charm and rides from mild to wild.

◉ Sights

★**Knott's Berry Farm**   AMUSEMENT PARK
(Map p254; ☑ 714-220-5200; www.knotts.com; 8039 Beach Blvd, Buena Park; adult/child 3-11yr $75/42; ◷ from 10am, closing hours vary 5-11pm; ℗ ♿) Old West–themed Knott's Berry Farm often teems with packs of speed-crazed adolescents testing their mettle on an intense lineup of thrill rides. Gut-wrenchers include the wooden GhostRider and the '50s-themed Xcelerator; the single-digit-aged can find tamer action at Camp Snoopy.

The park opened in 1932, when Walter Knott's boysenberries (a blackberry-raspberry hybrid) and his wife Cordelia's fried-chicken dinners attracted crowds of local farmhands. In 1941, Mr Knott built an imitation ghost town to keep them entertained, and eventually built carnival rides and charged admission. Mrs Knott kept frying the chicken, but the rides and Old West buildings became the main attraction.

Today Knott's keeps the Old West theme alive and thriving with a variety of shows and demonstrations at Ghost Town, but it's the thrill rides that draw the big crowds. **GhostRider** is the west coast's tallest, fastest and longest wooden roller coaster. The **Sierra Sidewinder** roller coaster rips through banks and turns while rotating on its axis. Nearby,

Anaheim & North Orange County

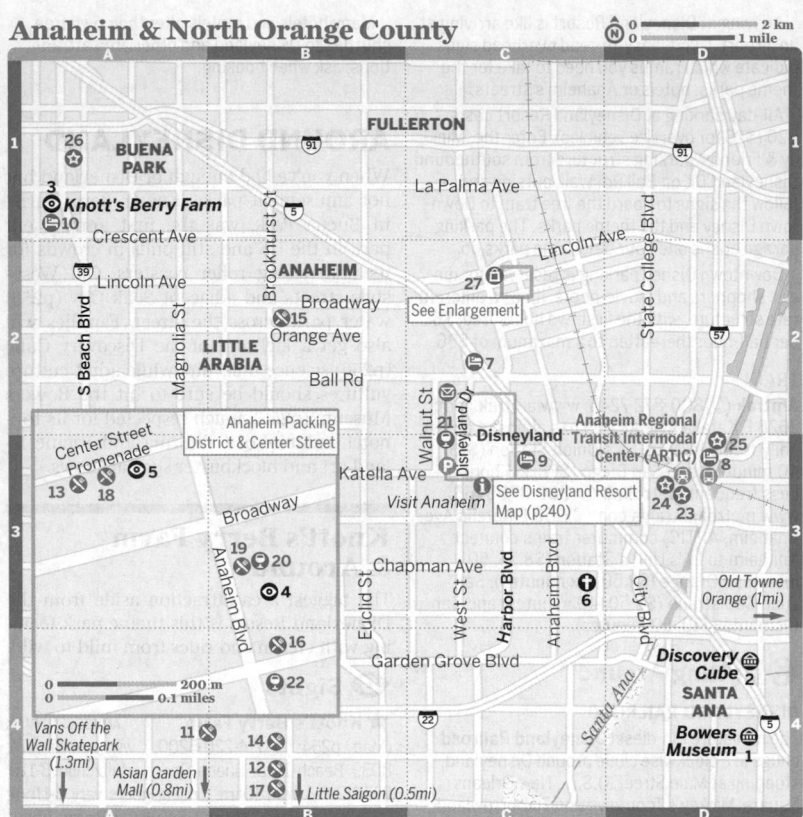

the suspended, inverted **Silver Bullet** screams through a corkscrew, a double spiral and an outside loop. From the ground, look up to see the dirty socks and bare feet of suspended riders who've removed their shoes just for fun. **Xcelerator** is a 1950s-themed roller coaster that blasts you, as if from a cannon, from zero to 82mph in under 2½ seconds; there's a hair-raising twist at the top. And one of the most popular rides, since 1969, is the giant flume, **Timber Mountain Log Rider**.

For tamer rides, **Camp Snoopy** is a kiddy wonderland populated by the *Peanuts* characters with rides like the Linus Launcher and Charlie Brown's Kite Flyer, targeted at the pre-school set. Pre-teens will probably enjoy the selection of junior coasters, flyers and scramblers nearby.

Much of the rest of the park is old-school Americana. **Main St** looks essentially the same as it did in 1941, an Old West town with blacksmith shop, thread spinner and a 'pitcher gallery' where you can dress up and,

you know, get your pitcher took. The **Calico Railroad** is an antique, narrow gauge train that routinely gets 'robbed' by bandits; you'd think management would have caught on by now. **Fiesta Village** is a colorfully painted pueblo with Mexican snack stands, game arcades and Mexican-themed rides.

Every year, Knott's Berry Farm puts on SoCal's scariest Halloween party, **Knott's Scary Farm**. On select days from late September through October 31, the park closes and reopens at night as Knott's Scary Farm. Horror-minded thrills include a dozen creepy mazes, monster-themed shows and a thousand hired hands trying to scare the bejeezus out of you in 'scare zones.' Boo!

Opening hours vary seasonally, so check online for hours as well as discounts and deals: online savings can be substantial (eg buying print-at-home tickets). Manual/motorized wheelchair rentals cost $15/45 per day. Minimum height restrictions apply for many rides

Anaheim & North Orange County

and attractions, so check the theme park's website in advance to avoid disappointment.

Knott's Berry Farm is off the I-5 Fwy or Hwy 91 (Artesia Fwy), about 6 miles north-west of Disneyland. All-day parking costs $18. There's free three-hour parking with purchase from California Marketplace.

Knott's Soak City WATER PARK
(Map p254; ☎714-220-5200; www.soakcityoc.com; 8039 Beach Blvd, Buena Park; adult/child 3-11yr $43/38; ⊙10am-5pm, 6pm or 7pm mid-May–mid-Sep; P⛑) Next door to Knott's Berry Farm (p253) is its affiliated water park, boasting a 750,000-gallon wave pool, dozens of high-speed slides, tubes and flumes (including 10 new slides for 2017), and one of the world's longest lazy river attractions. You must have a bathing suit without rivets or metal pieces to go on some slides. Bring a beach towel and a change of dry clothes.

The park is open from Memorial Day (end May) to Labor Day (start of September), plus additional May and September weekends. Look online for often-significant discounts off the full admission. Rental lockers ($10 to $22 per day) and private cabanas (from $99) are available.

🛏 Sleeping & Eating

Knott's Berry Farm Hotel HOTEL $$
(Map p254; ☎714-995-1111, 866-752-2444; www.knottshotel.com; 7675 Crescent Ave, Buena Park; r $79-169; P@🅿🛜🏊) Say 'good night,' not 'good grief,' in a Snoopy-themed room at this nine-story, 320-room hotel bordering Knott's Berry Farm (p253) and its beloved Camp Snoopy. In fact, while your kids are hugging the beagle at breakfast or dinner in the hotel's restaurant, you'll be hugging yourself for finding a low-cost room that's not too far from that *other* park.

For a little more flair, upgrade to one of the 16 Snoopy-themed rooms, in their own separate section of the hotel. These cheerful rooms, which cost more per night than stand-ards, are decorated with *Peanuts*-inspired decor. Snoopy himself wanders in for tuck-in service. A pool, spa, fitness center, and tennis and basketball courts round out the appeal. And if you need a change of pace, there's a complimentary shuttle to Disneyland.

Mrs Knott's Chicken Dinner Restaurant SOUTHERN US $$
(Map p254; ☎714-220-5055; 8039 Beach Blvd, Buena Park; chicken dinner lunch $17, dinner $22; ⊙11am-9pm Mon-Fri, 8am-10pm Sat, 7am-9pm Sun; ⛑) The restaurant that launched a

theme park. Classic, button-busting fried chicken and mashed potato dinners are served in this restaurant from 1934, newly remodeled in country style with distressed white wooden furniture.

Chicken-to-Go FAST FOOD $
(Map p254; ☑714-220-5055; www.knotts.com/ what-s-new/mrs-knott-s-chicken-dinner-restaurant; 8039 Beach Blvd, Buena Park; meals/buckets from $11/28; ☺11am-9pm Mon-Fri, 8am-10pm Sat, 8am-9pm Sun) Take-out shop for Mrs Knott's Chicken Dinner Restaurant.

Knott's Berry Farm Bakery BAKERY
(Map p254; ☑714-220-5094; Emporium Market Place, 8039 Beach Blvd, Buena Park; pie slice $4.50; ☺8:30am-9pm Sun-Thu, to 9:30pm Fri, to 10pm Sat) Knott's bakery is famous for its pies, especially boysenberry.

☆ Entertainment

Medieval Times LIVE PERFORMANCE
(Map p254; ☑866-543-9637, 714-523-1100; www. medievaltimes.com; 7662 Beach Blvd, Buena Park; adult/under 12yr $62/37; ☝) Hear ye, hear ye! All those who have sired knights-to-be and future princesses, gather ye clans and proceed forthwith for an evening-long medieval feast and performance. Yep, it's completely over-the-top but in a harmless, party-like-it's-1099 sort of way. Dinner guests root for various knights as they joust, fence and show off their horsemanship to protect the honor of the kingdom. The food is all right – roast chicken and spare ribs (vegetarian options available) – but the show's the thing.

Make reservations, show up 90 minutes early (seating is not guaranteed, even with reservations) and accept that you'll be wearing a cardboard crown for the evening. The mock castle is about a half-mile north of Knott's Berry Farm (p253). Discounted tickets online.

❶ Getting There & Away

Knott's Berry Farm is about 6 miles northwest of Disneyland, off the I-5 Fwy or Hwy 91 (Artesia Fwy). All-day parking costs $12. There's free three-hour parking for California Marketplace visitors only.

Discovery Cube

Follow the giant 10-story cube – balanced on one of its points – to the county's best educational kiddie attraction, the **Discovery Cube** (Map p254; ☑714-542-2823; www.discoverycube.org; 2500 N Main St, Santa Ana; adult/ child 3-14yr & senior $16/13, 4-D movies $2 extra;

☺10am-5pm; ℗☝). About 100 hands-on displays await, covering everything from dinosaurs to robotics, rockets to the water supply, the environment to hockey. In the Grand Hall of Science, you might learn the science of tornadoes or the physics of pulleys, while the Discovery Theater screens 4D movies.

Elsewhere, step into the eye of a hurricane or grab a seat in the Shake Shack to virtually experience a magnitude-6.4 quake. Special science-themed exhibits, like the annual Bubblefest, are fun too. 2015 saw a 44,000-sq-ft expansion of the facilities.

You'll want to allow a good four hours here (more if your kids are budding scientists). It's about 5 miles southeast of Disneyland via the I-5.

Bowers Museum & Kidseum

From its stately, Spanish Colonial–style shell, the **Bowers Museum** (Map p254; ☑714-567-3600; www.bowers.org; 2002 N Main St, Santa Ana; Tue-Fri adult/child 12-17yr & senior $13/10, Sat & Sun $15/12, special exhibit surcharge varies; ☺10am-4pm Tue-Sun; ☒53, 83) explodes onto the scene every year or so with remarkable exhibits that remind LA-centric museum-goers that the Bowers, too, is a local and national power player. Permanent exhibits are equally impressive, a rich collection of pre-Columbian, African, Chinese and Native American art, plus California art from the missions to Laguna Beach–style plein air painting. Our favorite: the Spirits and Headhunters gallery, showing jewelry, armaments, masks and religious articles of the Pacific Islands.

Docent-guided gallery tours are given every afternoon, and the airy cafe Tangata serves great lunches and California wines by the glass.

Admission to the Bowers also covers the affiliated **Kidseum**, a quick walk away; check in advance for its opening hours, which are more limited. Compared with other children's museums, this one is intimate and pretty mellow, with mostly low(ish) tech, hands-on art and cultural exhibits to keep the preschool and early elementary set entertained: drumming, dress-up, play kitchen, art projects and face-painting.

The museums are 6 miles southeast of Disneyland, off I-5 in Santa Ana. Admission is free on the first Sunday of each month. Public parking costs $6.

Christ Cathedral

About 3 miles southeast of Disneyland, this **glass monolith** (Map p254; [📞]714-971-2141; www.christcathedralcalifornia.org; 13280 Chapman Ave, Garden Grove; [🕐]tours 10am-3pm Mon-Fri, to 4pm Sat) was built in the shape of a four-pointed star and boasts 10,661 windows, seating capacity for 3000 and an organ with 16,000 pipes. Originally called 'Crystal Cathedral,' it was constructed in 1981 by architectural great Philip Johnson for the televangelist Robert Schuller. After Schuller's Crystal Cathedral Ministries went bankrupt, the Roman Catholic Diocese of Orange purchased the building. The main cathedral building is closed for renovation until late 2018, but visitors can tour the 34-acre grounds.

Old Towne Orange

The city of Orange, 7 miles southeast of Disneyland, retains its charming historical center, called Old Towne Orange. It's where locals go, and visitors will find it well worth the detour for antiques and vintage clothing shops, smart restaurants and pure SoCal nostalgia.

Orange was originally laid out by Alfred Chapman and Andrew Glassell, who in 1869 received the 1-sq-mile piece of real estate in lieu of legal fees. Orange became California's only city laid out around a central plaza, a traffic circle where present-day Glassell St and Chapman Ave meet, and it remains pleasantly walkable today.

✗ Eating

Stroll around Old Towne Orange's traffic circle, then along Glassell St to take your pick of more than a dozen atmospheric cafes, restaurants, wine bars and brewpubs, including some quietly gourmet spots.

★ Linx   HOT DOGS $
([📞]714-744-3647; www.linxdogs.com; 238 W Chapman Ave; mains $5.50-14; [🕐]11am-10pm Mon-Wed, to 11pm Thu & Fri, 10am-11pm Sat, 10am-10pm Sun) First things first: they're not hot dogs, they're 'haute' dogs, homemade and topped with your choice of combinations (the BBQ, Bacon and Blues comes with barbecue sauce, bacon marmalade and blue-cheese bacon aioli). Burgers come with fries. There's a daily-changing craft-beer selection, and bread

pudding for dessert with chocolate ganache and strawberries.

Rutabegorz   CALIFORNIAN $
([📞]714-633-3260; www.rutabegorz.com; 264 N Glassell St; mains $7-13.25; [🕐]10:30am-9pm Mon-Sat; [🚗][🍴]) Known by locals as just Ruta's, this flowering cottage north of the plaza puts a healthy spin on breakfast or lunch. Cal-Mexican, vegetarian and Middle Eastern snacks all jostle on the tables alongside comfort-food sandwiches, wraps, salads, soups and fruit smoothies. Kids menu available.

Burger Parlor   BURGERS $
([📞]714-602-8220; www.burgerparlor.com; 149 N Glassell St; mains $8-11; [🕐]11am-9pm Sun-Wed, to 11pm Thu-Sat; [🍴]) Chef Joseph Mahon has parlayed his work at a Michelin-starred restaurant into gourmet burgers that have been named the OC's best. The cheerily contemporary counter service Orange location dishes up the same award-winning Smokey and Parlor burgers, plus fries and onion rings. Bonus: you can get any burger on lettuce instead of a bun (because California).

Filling Station   DINER $
([📞]714-289-9714; www.fillingstationcafe.com; 201 N Glassell St; mains $7-16; [🕐]6:30am-9pm Sun-Thu, to 10pm Fri & Sat; [🍴]) For breakfast, not much beats this former gas station now serving *haute* pancakes, chorizo eggs, Cobb salads and patty melts instead of unleaded. Check out the vintage SoCal photographs on the walls. Sit on the dog-friendly outdoor patio, or grab a shiny counter stool or booth inside. Breakfast is served all day, lunch from 11am.

★ Watson Soda Fountain Café   DINER $$
([📞]714-202-2899; www.watsonscafe.com; 116 E Chapman Ave; mains $8-18; [🕐]7am-9pm Sun-Wed, to 10pm Thu, to midnight Fri & Sat) Established 1899, this former drugstore was recently refurbished to a period design (check out the old safe, apothecary cabinets and telephone switchboard). It offers old-fashioned soda-fountain treats such as malts, milkshakes and sundaes, as well as burgers, fries, fried pickle chips and breakfast all day.

Haven Gastropub   GASTROPUB $$
([📞]714-221-0680; www.havengastropub.com; 190 S Glassell St; items $8-27; [🕐]11am-2am Mon-Fri, from 9am Sat & Sun) Come with your sweetie or a group to share plates like beef poutine with cheese curds and sous vide egg, Brussels sprouts with flash-fried prosciutto or mac and cheese with truffle béchamel, and

the burger is so good you'll probably want to share that too. There's a great, ever-changing craft-beer list and lots of windows to watch the scene.

Felix Continental Cafe   LATIN AMERICAN $$
(☑714-633-5842; www.felixcontinentalcafe.com; 36 Plaza Sq; mains $8-17; ⊙11am-10pm Mon-Fri, 8am-10pm Sat & Sun) Longtime downtown favorite serves spiced-just-right Caribbean, Cuban and Spanish dishes, most accompanied by a hefty serving of plantains, black beans and rice. Paella is the house specialty and the roast pork is popular too. Scope out a sidewalk table if you can. Lunch served until 5pm.

Citrus City Grille   BISTRO $$$
(☑714-639-9600; www.citruscitygrille.com; 122 N Glassell St; mains lunch $9-20, dinner $12-38; ⊙11am-10pm Mon-Thu, to 2am Fri, 9:30am-2pm Sat, 9:30am-10pm Sun) Artsy and sophisticated yet casual Cal-Mediterranean bistro. It whips up creative modern classics like wild-mushroom penne, bacon-wrapped blue-cheese dates and Chilean sea bass with asparagus risotto. House-made rosemary focaccia, yum. Famous for brunch.

🛍 Shopping

Shops line up primarily north and south, and to a lesser extent east and west, of Old Towne's **plaza** (cnr Chapman Ave & Glassell St), where you can find the OC's most concentrated collection of antiques, collectibles and vintage and consignment shops. It's fun to browse and some are very well curated. That said, real bargains are rare and you'll want to make sure the pieces are authentic.

Elsewhere Vintage   VINTAGE
(☑714-771-2116; www.elsewherevintage.com; 105 W Chapman Ave; ⊙11am-7pm) A hipster's love affair, this ladies' vintage store hangs sundresses next to hats, leather handbags and fabulous costume jewelry, all with a special emphasis on the 1920s to the '60s.

Joy Ride   VINTAGE
(☑714-771-7118; www.joyridevintage.com; 109 W Chapman Ave; ⊙11am-7pm) The brother shop of Elsewhere Vintage, Joy Ride has a similar vibe, only with men's clothing: 1950s bowling shirts to immaculately maintained wool blazers, plus vintage cameras, straight-edge razors and other manly pursuits. It even has a hat-repair clinic.

Dragonfly Shops & Gardens   GIFTS & SOUVENIRS
(☑714-289-4689; www.dragonflyshopsandgardens. com; 260 N Glassell St, Orange; ⊙10am-5pm Mon-Sat, 11am-4pm Sun) Whimsical Dragonfly Shops & Gardens sells native California plants, garden-minded gifts and beaded jewelry inside a white-picketed cottage.

Matoska Trading Company   ART
(☑714-516-4940; www.matoska.com; 123 N Glassell St; ⊙11am-6pm Mon-Thu, 11am-7pm Fri & Sat, noon-6pm Sun) Everyone from Native American dancers to Hollywood costumers visits this one-of-a-kind shop selling supplies for Native American–inspired clothing, art and crafts: beads and bead looms, swatches of buffalo fur, buckskin by the pound for starters, not to mention art by Native Americans and blankets from Pendleton that pay tribute to the designs.

Orange Circle Antique Mall   ANTIQUES
(☑714-538-8160; www.orangeantiquemall.com; 118 S Glassell St; ⊙10am-4:45pm Mon, to 5:45pm Tue-Sat, 11am-5:45pm Sun) Among the many antique malls in Old Towne Orange, this one stands out for its 125 vendors over two floors, selling everything from estate jewelry and fine china to vintage clothing, pinup art, album covers and decades worth of *Life* magazine.

🛈 Getting There & Away

The drive from Anaheim takes under 20 minutes: take I-5 south to Hwy 22 east, then drive north on Grand Ave, which becomes Glassell St, for just over a mile. Both **Amtrak** (☑800-872-7245; www. amtrak.com) and **Metrolink** (☑800-371-5465; www.metrolinktrains.com) commuter trains stop at Orange's **train station** (191 N Atchison St), a few blocks west of the plaza with connections to Anaheim and LA's Union Station. **OCTA** (p252) bus line 59 also runs from Anaheim.

Richard Nixon Presidential Library & Museum

The **Nixon Library** (☑714-993-5075; www.nixon foundation.org; 18001 Yorba Linda Blvd, Yorba Linda; adult/child 5-11yr/student/senior $16/6/10/12; ⊙10am-5pm Mon-Sat, 11am-5pm Sun; ℗) offers a fascinating walk through America's modern history and that of this controversial native son of Orange County (1913–94), who served as president 1969–74. Noteworthy exhibits include a full-size replica of the White

CLUB MUD

If the road has left you feeling frazzled and achy, an hour or more at a day spa may be just what the doctor ordered. There are literally hundreds of spas throughout SoCal, from simple storefronts in strip malls to luxurious oases in rich-and-famous zip codes such as Palm Springs.

Every spa has its own 'treatment menu,' usually including a variety of massages such as Thai, shiatsu, deep-tissue, Swedish, tandem (two therapists equals four hands) and hot-stone. Beauty treatments range from classic facials and botanical wraps to exotic elixir baths and body cocktail scrubs.

For a treat, detour to Glen Ivy Hot Springs (www.glenivy.com), aka 'Club Mud,' located in inland Orange County. Famous for its red-clay mud bath, Glen Ivy also offers clear mineral-water tubs and a large swimming pool. In the mountains north of Ventura, closer to LA, **Ojai Valley Inn & Spa** (p379) is another renowned retreat. In LA Koreatown is well known for its 24-hour Eastern-style spas. One of the best is **Wi Spa** (p126).

Wherever you go, massage sessions typically cost at least $80 for 50 minutes, while a facial will set you back $60 or more. By the time you've added a 20% tip, the final tab may be high enough to warrant another stress-relieving treatment.

House East Room, recordings of conversations with Apollo 11 astronauts on the moon, access to the ex-presidential helicopter – complete with wet bar and ashtrays – and excerpts from landmark TV appearances including the Kennedy-Nixon debates and Nixon's famous self-parody on the Laugh-In comedy show.

You'll learn about Nixon's childhood in nearby Whittier, his early life and political career as senator and vice president under Dwight Eisenhower, and moments that defined his presidency: the moon landing, Vietnam War and Cold War, the Clean Air Act and the opening of the US to China.

That said, exhibits about Watergate, the infamous scandal that ultimately brought down Nixon's administration, also figure prominently. The museum's original Watergate exhibit called it a 'coup' instigated by Nixon's rivals and provided favorably edited White House tapes. That changed when the library was transferred to federal control in 2007, with oversight by the National Archives. The old exhibit was completely torn out, and now the story unfolds from many perspectives, like a spy thriller. It was a bold move, considering that 'Tricky Dick' and First Lady Pat Nixon lie buried just outside, near Nixon's birth house.

The library is in the rolling-hilled residential community of Yorba Linda in northeastern Orange County, about 10 miles northeast of Anaheim. To get here, take Hwy 57 north and exit east on Yorba Linda Blvd, then continue straight and follow the signs.

ORANGE COUNTY BEACHES

It's true you'll find gorgeous sunsets, prime surfing and just-off-the-boat seafood when traveling the OC's blissful 42 miles of surf and sand. But it's also the unexpected, serendipitous discoveries you'll remember: learning to surf the waves in Seal Beach, playing Frisbee with your pooch at Huntington Dog Beach, piloting your own boat around Newport Harbor, wandering around eclectic art displays in Laguna Beach, or spotting whales on a cruise from Dana Point.

Your mission is to find out which beach town suits you best. Seal Beach is the OC's northernmost beach town. From there, crawl along Route 1, aka Pacific Coast Hwy (PCH), south along the ocean for more than 40 miles, passing through Sunset Beach, Huntington Beach, Newport Beach, Laguna Beach, Dana Point and San Clemente. The drive takes at least an hour (much more with bumper-to-bumper beachfront traffic on summer weekends). Don't worry: it's almost always worth it.

Seal Beach

The OC's first beach town driving south from LA County, Seal is one of the last great California beach towns and a refreshing alternative to the more crowded coast further south. Its 1.5 miles of pristine beach sparkle like a crown, and that's without mentioning three-block Main St, a stoplight-free zone with mom-and-pop restaurants and indie shops that are low on 'tude and high on charm.

Although the town's east side is dominated by the sprawling retirement community Leisure World and the huge US Naval Weapons Station (look for grass-covered bunkers), all that fades away along the charming Main St and the oceanfront.

◎ Sights & Activities

Though it's unlikely you'll see any actual seals, there's plenty of beauty to be had around the town's pier.

Seal Beach Pier PIER
(Map p72) Where Main St ends, Seal Beach Pier begins, extending 1865ft over the ocean. The 1906 original fell victim to winter storms in the 1930s and has since been rebuilt three times with a wooden boardwalk. It's splintery in places, so wear shoes (no high heels!). Snap a picture of the playful bronze seal standing guard at the pier's east entrance – he may be the only one you see.

M&M Surfing School SURFING
(☎714-846-7873; www.surfingschool.com; 802 Ocean Ave; 1hr/3hr group lesson $77/85; ⊙lessons 8am-noon early Sep–mid-Jun and Sat & Sun all year, to 2pm Mon-Fri mid-Jun–early Sep; ⊕) Offers group and private lessons that include surfboard and wet-suit rental, for students age five and up. Look for its van in the parking lot just north of the pier, off Ocean Ave at 8th St.

✖ Eating

Nick's Deli DELI $
(☎562-598-5072; 223 Main St; mains $5-8.50; ⊙7am-6pm Mon-Fri, to 5pm Sat, to 4pm Sun) There's an extensive hand-scrawled menu hanging over the counter at this humble local joint where traditional deli fare is served alongside Mexican specialties. But the crowds flock here for one thing: the mad breakfast tortilla stuffed with scrambled eggs, chorizo, bacon, potatoes and cheese – basically, a heart attack on a plate. Ask for it toasted. Cash only.

Paradis ICE CREAM
(☎562-936-0196; www.paradis-icecream.com; 205 Main St; ice cream from $4-5; ⊙noon-9pm Mon-Thu, 11am-10pm Fri & Sat, 11am-9pm Sun) Paradis makes about 200 (whoa!) flavors of ice cream, of which you'll find about 16 on any given day, so there's always a reason to come back. They also do creative combos

of ice cream with coffee: latte, affogato (ice cream in espresso) and signature hot cocoa.

Crema Café BAKERY, CAFE $
(☎562-493-2501; www.cremacafe.com; 322 Main St; mains $5-13; ⊙6:30am-3pm Mon-Fri, 7am-4pm Sat & Sun; ⊕ ⊛) Service can be harried at this breezy, open-air cafe, but all is forgiven after a bite of their sweet and savory French crepes – goat cheese and turkey; chocolate; nutella – and satisfying omelets and Benedicts. In a hurry? Made-from-scratch pastries and muffins are fab, as are garden-fresh salads and toasted panini. There's a kids menu, and Crema has been voted one of the OC's most pet-friendly restaurants. Look for the daily bakery schedule online.

Beachwood BBQ BARBECUE $$
(☎562-493-4500; www.beachwoodbbq.com; 131 Main St; mains $9-20; ⊙11:30am-11pm Tue-Sun) Downtown's barbecue hut ropes in regulars with fried pickles, meats smoked using peach, maple, red oak and avocado wood, buffalo sloppy joe sandwiches, and a cool selection of microbrews (check out the website's 'Hop Cam'). For beach picnics, order takeout. Happy hours have awesome deals.

★**Walt's Wharf** SEAFOOD $$$
(☎562-598-4433; www.waltswharf.com; 201 Main St; mains lunch $13-29, dinner $17-40; ⊙11am-9pm) Everybody's favorite for fresh fish (some drive in from LA), Walt's packs them in on weekends. You can't make reservations for dinner (though they're accepted for lunch), but it's worth the wait for the oak-fire-grilled seafood and steaks in the many-windowed ground floor or upstairs in captain's chairs. Otherwise, eat at the bar.

★**Mahé** SUSHI, FUSION $$$
(☎562-431-3022; www.eatatmahe.com; 1400 Pacific Coast Hwy; mains lunch $15-20, dinner $15-39; ⊙opens 4pm Mon-Thu, 3pm Fri, 11:30am Sat, 10am Sun, closing hours vary) Raw-fish fans gather barside at this beach-chic sushi bar with live bands some nights in the back room. Baked scallop parmesan, ahi tataki wraps, and filet mignon with Gorgonzola cream all hang out on the Cal-Japanese menu. It's about five blocks from Main St but worth the walk.

◉ Drinking & Entertainment

On Main St you'll find a surprising number of Irish pubs, alongside coffee bars, though we're particularly fond of cozy Bogart's (p261), right across from the ocean.

LITTLE SAIGON

Ready for a break from big-eared mice, fried chicken and boysenberry pie? Head to Little Saigon, which straddles the cities of Westminster and Garden Grove.

About 7 miles southwest of Anaheim, Little Saigon is America's largest community of expat ethnic Vietnamese, population around 190,000, who began arriving here around the Vietnam War in the 1970s, carving out a vibrant commercial district. Even if it looks like the essence of suburban sprawl – strip malls and small homes on a grid of wide, multilane roads with no discernible center – there's a lot going on. The massive **Asian Garden Mall** (9200 Bolsa Ave; ⊗10am-7pm) is a good place to see this community in action in shops selling everything from jewelry to medicinal herbs and clothing, plus a food court.

But the best reason to visit Little Saigon is the food. Newbies might start at **Lee's Sandwiches** (☑714-636-2288; www.leessandwiches.com; 133991 Brookhurst St, Garden Grove; sandwiches from $4, breakfast from $3; ⊗24hr) serving tasty, wallet-friendly Vietnamese banh mi sandwiches on French baguette rolls, plus Vietnamese-style coffees and teas and East-meets-West pastries. Another great, inexpensive casual eatery is **Pho 79** (☑714-531-2490; www.pho79.com; 9941 Hazard Ave, Garden Grove; mains from $7-10; ⊗6am-10pm Thu-Tue, to 3pm Wed), which dishes up another Vietnamese staple, pho noodle soups, and more.

For a wider menu of rice, noodle and stir-fried dishes, visit **Brodard** (☑714-530-1744; www.brodard.net; 9892 Westminster Ave, Suite R, Garden Grove, Mall of Fortune; mains $5-14; ⊗8am-9pm Wed-Mon), known for its addictive rice-paper spring rolls, or its fancier sister, **Brodard Chateau** (☑714-899-8273; www.brodard.net; 9100 Trask Avenue, Garden Grove; mains $9-35; ⊗10:30am-9:30pm Mon-Thu, to 10pm Fri-Sun), while **Garlic & Chives** (☑714-591-5196; www.garlicandchives.com; 9892 Westminster Ave, Garden Grove, Mall of Fortune; mains $8-12, hotpots $24-32; ⊗11am-10pm Mon-Thu, from 10am Fri-Sun) is a Vietnamese fusion experience like none other. Vegetarians might opt for humble **Thien Dang** (☑714-531-1888; www.thiendangvegetarian.com; 14253 Brookhurst St, Garden Grove; mains $4-8; ⊗9am-7pm Wed-Sun).

Little Saigon lies south of Hwy 22 (Garden Grove Fwy, connecting to Orange) and east of the I-405 (San Diego Fwy).

Jazz, folk and bluegrass bands play by the pier at the foot of Main St from 6pm to 8pm every Wednesday during July and August for the annual **Summer Concerts in the Park** (http://sealbeachchamber.org; Eisenhower Park; ⊗6pm Wed Jul & Aug). The rest of the time, Main St is the kind of place where you'll find sidewalk musicians.

Bogart's Coffee House — CAFE

(☑562-431-2226; www.bogartscoffee.com; 905 Ocean Ave; ⊗6am-9pm Mon-Thu, to 10pm Fri, 7am-10pm Sat, 7am-9pm Sun; ⊛) Around the corner from Main St, sip organic espresso drinks on the leopard-print sofa and play Scrabble as you watch the surf roll in on the beach across the street. Bogart's hosts live music Friday and Saturday nights, plus a regular open mike on Tuesdays.

Shopping

Be sure to walk the full three blocks of Main St and browse the eclectic shops.

Harbour Surfboards — SPORTS & OUTDOORS

(☑562-430-5614; www.harboursurfboards.com; 329 Main St; ⊗9am-7pm, to 6pm Sun) This place has been making surfboards since 1959, but it's also about the surf-and-skate lifestyle, man. Eavesdrop on local surfers talking about their wax as you pillage the racks of hoodies, wet suits, beach T-shirts and beanie hats.

Tankfarm & Co. — FASHION & ACCESSORIES

(☑562-594-4800; www.tankfarmco.com; 212 Main St; ⊗10am-6pm Sun-Thu, to 8pm Fri & Sat) On a street dominated by women's clothing and beachwear, Seal Beach–based Tankfarm carries duds for dudes craving the outdoor lifestyle: board shorts, hoodies, flannels and blankets from brands like Herschel and Deus Ex Machina, plus its own cool tees, woven shirts and accessories from pomade to enamel mugs reading 'coffee, whiskey or beer.' Worthy goals all.

Up, Up & Away — GIFTS & SOUVENIRS

(☑562-596-7661; http://upupandawaykites.com; 139 1/2 Main St; ⊗10am-7pm Sun-Thu, to 8pm Fri & Sat) This shop specialty is kites in every color of the rainbow and tons of decorative flags: lighthouses, sailboats, sports-team logos, frogs wearing sunglasses – if you want to wave it, there's a flag for it. There are badass beach kites, nostalgic toys like Gumby and Mr Bill, and Moo Poppers that shoot balls from their mouths.

Knock Knock Toy Store TOYS
(☑562-799-8500; www.knockknocktoystore.com; 219 1/2 Main St; ⏱10am-6pm, to 5pm Sun; 👪) Thoughtfully chosen, fun and educational toys line the shelves here, from name brands to quirky one-off products like wind-up space robots.

Endless Summer CLOTHING
(☑562-430-9393; 124 Main St; ⏱11am-6pm) Teenie Wahine, Roxy and Billabong jostle for attention at this bustling store for girly tweens to college-age beach babes. It's packed to the rafters with bikinis, beach bags, shades and loads more.

Alternative Surf SURF
(www.alternativesurf.com; 330 Main St; ⏱10am-6pm) Bodyboarding central, with a full complement of boards, wet suits, apparel and other gear.

❶ Getting There & Around

Orange County Transport Authority (p252) bus 1 connects Seal Beach with the OC's other beach towns and LA's Long Beach every hour; the one-way fare is $2 (exact change). Long Beach Transit lines 131 and 171 also stop in Seal Beach.

There's two-hour free parking along Main St between downtown Seal Beach and the pier, but it's difficult to find a spot in summer. Public parking lots by the pier cost $3 per two hours, $6 all day. Free parking along residential side streets is subject to posted restrictions.

Huntington Beach

'No worries' is the phrase you'll hear over and over in Huntington Beach, the town that goes by the trademarked nickname 'Surf City USA.' In 1910 real-estate developer and railroad magnate Henry Huntington hired Hawaiian-Irish surfing star George Freeth to give demonstrations. When legendary surfer Duke Kahanamoku moved here in 1925, that solidified its status as a surf destination. Buyers for major retailers come here to see what surfers are wearing, then market the look.

Long considered a low-key, not-quite-fashionable beach community with its share of sidewalk-surfing skate rats and hollering late-night barflies, its downtown has undergone a couple of makeovers, first along **Main Street** and then at the sparkling new Pacific City (p267) shopping center.

Still, HB remains a quintessential spot to celebrate the hang-loose SoCal coastal lifestyle: consistently good waves, surf shops, a surf museum, bonfires on the sand, a canine-friendly beach, and hotels and restaurants with killer views.

◉ Sights

Huntington Beach Pier HISTORIC SITE
(cnr Main St & Pacific Coast Hwy; ⏱5am-midnight) The 1853ft Huntington Pier is one of the West Coast's longest. It has been here – in one form or another – since 1904, though the mighty Pacific has damaged giant sections or completely demolished it multiple times since then. The current concrete structure was built in 1983 to withstand 31ft waves or a 7.0-magnitude earthquake, whichever hits HB first. On the pier you can rent fishing gear from **Let's Go Fishing** (☑714-960-1392; 21 Main Street, Huntington Beach Pier; fishing sets per hour/day $6/15; ⏱hours vary) bait and tackle shop.

Huntington City Beach BEACH
(www.huntingtonbeachca.gov; ⏱5am-10pm; Ⓟ👪) One of SoCal's best beaches, the sand surrounding the pier at the foot of Main St gets packed on summer weekends with surfers, volleyball players, swimmers and families. Bathrooms and showers are located north of the pier at the back of the snack-bar complex. In the evening volleyball games give way to beach bonfires.

Bolsa Chica Conservancy Interpretive Center NATURE CENTER
(Map p72; ☑714-846-1114; www.bolsachica.org; 3842 Warner Ave, Huntington Beach; ⏱9am-4pm; Ⓟ) **FREE** Galleries in this 1400 sq ft facility feature tanks showing off local marine life and reptiles, and there's taxidermy of land and bird species. It's on the north end of the Bolsa Chica Ecological Reserve (p263). They rent out binoculars (suggested donation $3) for bird-watching in the reserve. The Bolsa Chica Conservancy leads monthly tours and cleanup days. Check website for details.

International Surfing Museum MUSEUM
(☑714-960-3483; www.surfingmuseum.org; 411 Olive Ave; adult/child $2/1; ⏱noon-5pm Tue-Sun) The world's biggest surfboard (in the *Guinness World Records*) fronts this small mu-

WETLAND WONDER: BOLSA CHICA ECOLOGICAL RESERVE

You'd be forgiven for overlooking the **Bolsa Chica Ecological Reserve** (☏714-846-1114; http://bolsachica.org; 18000 Pacific Coast Hwy; ⊙sunrise-sunset; ℙ), at least on first glance. Against a backdrop of nodding oil derricks, this flat expanse of wetlands doesn't exactly promise the unspoiled splendors of nature. However, more than 200 bird species aren't so aesthetically prejudiced, either making the wetlands their home throughout the year, or dropping by midmigration. Simply put, the restored salt marsh is an environmental success story.

This 'Little Pocket' (*bolsa chica* in Spanish) of estuarine tidal saltwater marsh – home to loons, ducks, terns, sandpipers and rare species such as the white pelican – is largely untouched, other than two circular embedded gun batteries (a legacy of WWII fears of Japanese invasion). Preservation didn't come easily, however: decades of arm-wrestling between developers and conservationists resulted, in 1997, in the state buying up some 800 acres for the reserve. Eventually, about 1450 acres were saved by a band of determined locals from numerous development projects.

The park's small **interpretive center** (p262) has lots of information about the reserve and leads occasional tours. On your own, there are multiple trails for about a 5-mile loop if you cover the whole reserve.

Sadly, Bolsa Chica is one of the last remaining coastal wetlands in SoCal – over 90% has already succumbed to development.

seum, an entertaining stop for surf-culture enthusiasts. Temporary exhibits chronicle the sport's history with photos, vintage surfboards, movie memorabilia and surf music. For the best historical tidbits, spend a minute chatting with the all-volunteer staff.

Surfers' Hall of Fame
LANDMARK
(www.hsssurf.com/shof; 300 Pacific Coast Hwy) To date, some 65 surfing legends have left their hand- and footprints in the concrete of this sidewalk, styled after Grauman's Chinese Theatre (p97) in Hollywood.

🏃 Activities

Huntington is a one-stop shop for outdoor pleasures by OC beaches. If you forgot to pack beach gear, you can rent umbrellas, beach chairs, volleyballs and other essentials from Zack's, just north of the pier. Just south of the pier on the Strand, friendly Dwight's Beach Concession, around since 1932, rents bikes, boogie boards, umbrellas and chairs. Huntington Surf & Sport (p267) also rents boards and wet suits.

Surfing

For newbie surfers, **Zack's** offers lessons. If you're an experienced surfer, keep in mind that surfing in HB is competitive. Control your longboard or draw ire from local dudes who pride themselves on being 'aggro.' Surf north of the pier.

Zack's
SURFING
(☏714-536-0215; www.zackssurfcity.com; 405 Pacific Coast Hwy; group lessons $85, surfboard rentals per hour/day $12/35, wet suits $5/15) This well-established outfit by the pier offers surfing lessons and rents all sorts of beach equipment. Lessons include equipment rental for the day.

Dwight's Beach Concession
SURFING
(☏714-536-8083; www.dwightsbeachconcession.com; 201 Pacific Coast Hwy; surfboard rentals per hour/day $10/40, bicycle rentals from $10/30; ⊙9am-5pm Mon-Fri, to 6pm Sat & Sun) Rents surfboards, bodyboards, bikes and other beach gear at competitive rates. It's HB's oldest longest running business, since 1932.

Cycling & Skating

Explore the coast while cycling or skating along the 8.5-mile **paved recreational path** running from Huntington State Beach (p266) in the south to Bolsa Chica State Beach (p266) in the north. Rent beach cruisers or tandem bikes at Zack's or Dwight's Beach Concession.

Vans Off the Wall Skatepark
OUTDOORS
(☏714-379-6666; 7471 Center Dr; helmet & pad set rentals $5; ⊙9am-8pm daily) **FREE** This custom-built facility by the OC-based sneaker and skatewear company has plenty of ramps, bowls, dips, boxes and rails for boarders to catch air. BYOB (board). Helmets and pads required for visitors under 18. The biggest

HUNTINGTON BEACH FOR CHILDREN

If you want a break from the beach scene, **Huntington Central Park** (www.huntingtonbeachca.gov; 18000 Goldenwest St; [🚻]), 3 miles north of downtown, is a green suburban retreat with a **disc golf course** (p264), down-and-dirty adventure playground featuring a rope bridge and cable slide, and two little lakes with walking paths.

For a thoughtful examination of local flora and fauna, including abundant bird life, stop by **Shipley Nature Center** (📞714-842-4772; www.shipleynature.org; 17851 Goldenwest St; ⊗9am-1pm Mon-Sat; [P][🚻]), which has kid-friendly exhibits on conservation efforts and a self-guided wetlands nature trail. Older kids may enjoy the **Bolsa Chica Ecological Reserve** (p263).

drawback is the location, about 6 miles from Huntington Beach Pier on the north side of town, so you'll need your own transport.

Frisbee

You can toss a frisbee on the beach for endless hours, or you can try the **Huntington Beach Disc Golf Course** (📞714-931-4559; www.huntingtonbeachca.gov; Huntington Central Park, 18381 Goldenwest St; admission $2-3; ⊗9am-dusk Mon-Fri, from 8am Sat & Sun), the only one in the OC.

⭐ Festivals & Events

Every Tuesday brings Surf City Nights, a street fair with a petting zoo and bounce house for the kids, crafts, sidewalk sales for the grown-ups, and live music and farmers-market goodies for everyone.

Car buffs get up early on Saturday mornings for the **Donut Derelicts Car Show** (www.donutderelicts.com; cnr Magnolia St & Adams Ave; ⊗Sat mornings), a weekly gathering of woodies, beach cruisers and pimped-out street rods at the corner of Magnolia St and Adams Ave, 2.5 miles inland from Pacific Coast Hwy.

4th of July   PARADE

(www.hb4thofjuly.org) Expect big crowds when the city closes sections of Main St and Pacific Coast Hwy for its Independence Day parade. The day-long celebration ends with evening fireworks over the pier.

Huntington Harbor
Cruise of Lights   CHRISTMAS

(www.cruiseoflights.org; 16889 Algonquin St; adult/child $19/12; ⊗mid- to late Dec) If you're here for the Christmas holidays, don't miss the evening boat tour past harborside homes twinkling with holiday lights. Run by the Philharmonic Society, cruise proceeds go to support youth music education programs.

Vans US Open of Surfing   SURFING

(www.usopenofsurfing.com; Huntington Beach Pier; ⊗late Jul & early Aug) This six-star competition lasts more than a week and draws more than 600 world-class surfers. Other festivities include beach concerts, motocross shows and skateboard jams.

Surf City Nights   FAIR

(www.surfcitynights.com; 1st 3 blocks Main St; ⊗5-9pm Tue) Every Tuesday brings Surf City Nights, a street fair with amusement for the kids, about 90 vendors doing sidewalk sales for the grown-ups, and live music and farmers-market goodies for everyone.

🛏 Sleeping

There aren't many budget options in HB, especially near the water, and *especially* especially during summer vacation season. Off-season, you may be able to score a deal. Otherwise, head inland along mind-numbing Hwy 39 toward the I-405 (San Diego Fwy) to find cheaper cookie-cutter motels and hotels.

Huntington Surf Inn   MOTEL $$

(📞714-536-2444; www.huntingtonsurfinn.com; 720 Pacific Coast Hwy; r $119-209; [P][♿][❄][🐾][📶]) You're paying for location at this two-story 1960s-era motel just north of Main St and across from the beach. Smallish rooms are individually decorated with surf and skateboard art – cool, brah – with firm mattresses and fridges, and microwaves on request. There's a small common deck area with a beach view.

⭐ Paséa   RESORT $$$

(📞888-674-3634; http://meritagecollection.com/paseahotel; 21080 Pacific Coast Hwy; r from $359; [P][♿][❄][@][📶][🏊]) This hotel is slick and serene, with tons of light and air. Floors are themed for shades of blue from denim to sky and each of its 250 shimmery, minimalist, high-ceilinged rooms has an ocean-view balcony. As if the stunning pool, gym and Balinese-inspired spa weren't enough, it also connects to Pacific City (p267).

★**Shorebreak Hotel** BOUTIQUE HOTEL **$$$**
(☑714-861-4470; www.shorebreakhotel.com; 500
Pacific Coast Hwy; r from $269; [P][⊖][❋][@][🛜][🏊]）
Stow your surfboard (lockers provided)
as you head inside HB's hippest hotel, a
stone's throw from the pier. The Shorebreak
has 'surf ambassadors,' a wet suit mural
in the lobby, pseudo-steampunk fitness
center with climbing wall, and hardwood
furniture and surfboard headboards in
geometric-patterned rooms. Minibars stock
temporary tattoos and surfboard wax, in
case you, you know, forgot yours.

Relax in the lobby over a glass of wine,
poured free for guests nightly.

**Hyatt Regency Huntington
Beach Resort & Spa** RESORT **$$$**
(☑714-698-1234, 800-492-8804; www.huntington
beach.hyatt.com; 21500 Pacific Coast Hwy; r $320-
400; [P][❋][@][🛜][🏊][🐾]）This 517-room property with conference center hulks like a
Spanish-style condo complex, but spacious,
recently renovated rooms are inviting and
have balconies for beach views and derma-
tologist-designed bath products. Look for
two outdoor saltwater swimming pools,
splash pool with slides, a 'grotto' of spa
pools, a gorgeous, 20,000 sq ft spa and direct
beach access via a pedestrian bridge.

Camp Hyatt activities are made for kids,
and in summer the hotel offers a free shuttle
to Disneyland.

Waterfront Beach Resort RESORT **$$$**
(☑714-845-8000, 800-445-8667; www.water
frontbeachresort.hilton.com; 21100 Pacific Coast
Hwy; r $279-390; [P][⊖][@][🛜][🏊]）The sprawling,
lounge-filled poolside is reminiscent of Ve-
gas, but then you see the backdrop: miles
and miles of gorgeous deep-blue sea. As you
enter, tiny surfers adorn the lobby fountain
at this 100% nonsmoking hotel, and each of
the 440 rooms in two towers has a balcony
with ocean view. Plush rooms are tempered
with earth tones.

✕ **Eating**

Huntington's dining scene has really evolved
in the last couple of years with the arrival of
Pacific City (p267). High-flying restaurants
here have unimpeded ocean views and food
to match. For something less formal and
easier on the wallet, Lot 579 is Pacific City's
gourmet food court.

For a more local, intimate experience, vis-
it the restaurants along and around Main St:
classic breakfast places, taco stands, Italian,
pubs and more.

★**Lot 579** FOOD HALL
(www.gopacificcity.com/lot-579; Pacific City, 21010
Pacific Coast Hwy; ⊙hours vary; [P][🛜][🐾]）The
food court at HB's stunning new ocean-view
mall offers some unique and fun restaurants
for pressed sandwiches (Burnt Crumbs – the
spaghetti grilled cheese is so Instagram-
mable), Aussie meat pies (Pie Not), coffee
(Portola) and ice cream (Han's). For best
views, take your takeout to the deck, or eat
at American Dream (brewpub) or Bear Flag
Fish Company.

★**Sancho's Tacos** MEXICAN **$**
(☑714-536-8226; www.sanchostacos.com; 602 Pacif-
ic Coast Hwy; mains $3-10; ⊙8am-9pm Mon-Sat, to
8pm Sun; [P]）There's no shortage of taco stands
in HB, but locals are fiercely dedicated to San-
cho's, across from the beach. This two-room
shack with patio grills flounder, shrimp and
tri-tip to order. Trippy Mexican-meets-skater
art. Eat at red leatherette booths or on the out-
door patio across from the ocean.

Sugar Shack CAFE **$**
(☑714-536-0355; www.hbsugarshack.com; 213½
Main St; mains $4.50-11; ⊙6am-2pm Mon-Tue &
Thu-Fri, to 8pm Wed, to 3pm Sat & Sun) Expect a
wait at this HB institution, or get here ear-
ly to see surfer dudes don their wet suits.
Breakfast is served all day on the bustling
Main St patio and inside, where you can
grab a spot at the counter or a two-top. Pho-
tos of surf legends plastering the walls raise
this place almost to shrine status.

**Mother's Market
& Kitchen** SUPERMARKET, VEGETARIAN **$**
(☑714-963-6667; www.mothersmarket.com/hunt
ington-beach; 19770 Beach Blvd; mains $5-10;
⊙7am-10pm; [P][🐾][🍴]）Get your organic,
health-conscious groceries here. A deli and
take-out cafe caters to all diets (eg vegetar-
ian, vegan, gluten-free, nondairy). Juice bar
open until 9:30pm daily. It's about 2 miles'
drive from central HB.

Park Bench Cafe AMERICAN **$**
(☑714-842-0775; www.parkbenchcafe.com; 17732
Goldenwest St; mains $6-15, dog menu $2.75-
4.35; ⊙7:30am-2pm Tue-Fri, to 3pm Sat & Sun;
[🍴][🐾]）Sometimes Fido likes to order too.
In a dog-friendly setting with shady out-
door picnic tables, try this casual outdoor
restaurant in Huntington Central Park.
Order an avocado-topped omelet or BLT

sandwich for yourself and a juicy 'Hound Dog Heaven' beef patty for your four-legged friend.

Cucina Alessá
ITALIAN $$

(☏714-969-2148; http://cucinaalessarestaurants.com; 520 Main St; mains lunch $9-13, dinner $12-25; ⏱11am-10pm) Every beach town needs its favorite go-to Italian kitchen. Alessa wins hearts and stomachs with classics like Neapolitan lasagna, butternut-squash ravioli and chicken masala. Lunch brings out panini, pizzas and pastas, plus breakfasts including frittata and 'famous' French toast. Get sidewalk seating, or sit behind big glass windows.

Duke's
SEAFOOD, HAWAIIAN $$

(☏714-374-6446; www.dukeshuntington.com; 317 Pacific Coast Hwy; mains lunch $14-18, dinner $14-49; ⏱3pm-9pm Mon, 11:30am-9:30pm Tue-Sat, 10am-2pm & 10am-9pm Sun) It may be touristy, but this Hawaiian-themed restaurant – named after surfing legend Duke Kahanamoku – is a kick. With unbeatable views of the beach, fresh fish and sassy cocktails, it's a primo spot to relax and show off your tan. For just drinks and appetizers, the Barefoot Bar is open between lunch and dinner.

🍷 Drinking & Nightlife

It's easy to find a bar in HB: just walk up Main St. There's everything from breweries to Irish pubs and meat markets, sometimes one and the same. And in Pacific City you'll find a few new hot spots.

★Bungalow
CLUB

(☏714-374-0399; www.thebungalow.com/hb; Pacific City, 21058 Pacific Coast Hwy, Suite 240; ⏱5pm-2am Mon-Fri, noon-2am Sat, noon-10pm Sun) This Santa Monica landmark of cool has opened a second location here in Pacific City, and with its combination of lounge spaces, outdoor patio, cozy, rustic-vintage design, specialty cocktails, DJs who know how to get the crowd going and – let's not forget – ocean views, it's already setting new standards for the OC. The food menu's pretty great too.

Saint Marc
BAR

(☏714-374-1101; www.saintmarcusa.com; Pacific City, 21058 Pacific Coast Hwy; ⏱11am-midnight Mon-Wed, to 2am Thu & Fri, 10am-2am Sat, to 10pm Sun) Indoor-outdoor Saint Marc is technically a restaurant, but it's just so darn much fun as a bar: giant beer-pong table, beer bombers, wine on draft, infused vodkas, red Solo Cup cocktails and, um, jello shots! Should you get hungry, food ranges from cheese boards to New Orleans–inflected meals, or just go for bacon by the slice from the bacon bar.

Main Street Wine Company
WINE BAR

(www.mainstreetwinecompany.com; 301 Main St, Suite 105; ⏱4pm-9pm Mon, noon-10pm Tue-Thu, noon-11pm Fri, 1pm-11pm Sat, to 9pm Sun) Boutique California-wine shop with a sleek bar, generous pours and meet-your-(wine)maker nights.

Hurricanes Bar & Grill
BAR

(☏714-374-0500; www.hurricanesbargrill.com; 2nd fl, 200 Main St; ⏱11am-1:30am) Two words:

GIMME MORE!

Want even more surf and sand? **Huntington State Beach** (☏714-536-1454; www.parks.ca.gov; ⏱6am-10pm; 🅿) extends 2 miles from Beach Blvd (Hwy 39) to the Santa Ana River and Newport Beach boundary. All-day parking costs $15. Meanwhile, dogs can romp in the surf at **Huntington Dog Beach** (www.dogbeach.org; 100 Goldenwest Street; ⏱5am-10pm; 🅿), between Goldenwest St and Seapoint Ave, north of Huntington City Beach. Nearly a mile long, it's a postcard-perfect place to play with your pooch. Parking meters cost 25¢ every 10 minutes.

Stretching alongside Pacific Coast Hwy between Huntington Dog Beach to the south and Sunset Beach to the north, **Bolsa Chica State Beach** (www.parks.ca.gov; Pacific Coast Hwy, btwn Seapoint & Warner Aves; parking $15; ⏱6am-10pm; 🅿) is a 3-mile-long strip of sand favored by surfers, volleyball players and fishers. Even though it faces a monstrous offshore oil rig, Bolsa Chica (meaning 'little pocket' in Spanish) gets mobbed on summer weekends. You'll find picnic tables, fire rings and beach showers, plus a bike path running north to Anderson Ave in Sunset Beach and south to Huntington State Beach.

meat market. But then again, any strip of beach bars worth its margarita salt needs at least one. DJs nightly, ocean view patios, a laser-light dance floor, 22 beer taps, loads of special cocktails and quite decent grub – if you're not slurping body shots by midnight, you have no one to blame but yourself.

Huntington Beach Beer Co
BAR

(☑ 714-960-5343; www.hbbeerco.com; 2nd fl, 201 Main St; ☺ from 11am, closing times vary; ☜) Cavernous brewpub with a big balcony, specializing in ales brewed in a half-dozen giant, stainless-steel kettles on site, like the HB Blonde, Brickshot Red and seasonal beers flavored with sage to cherry. Try the sampler. DJs and dancing Thursday to Saturday nights.

🛍 Shopping

You'll find lots of one-off shops in central HB and some big, mostly chain stores in the shiny new Pacific City (p267) shopping center. About halfway up Huntington Beach Pier are two tiny stores. **Surf City HB** is the only shop in town officially licensed to use the name 'Surf City' on its merchandise – pick up a beach hoodie or T-shirt. Across the way, **Kite Connection** vends single-line and deluxe spinner kites.

Pacific City
MALL

(www.gopacificcity.com; 21010 Pacific Coast Hwy; ☺ hours vary) Just south of downtown HB, this flashy, futuristic new mall sits right across Pacific Coast Hwy from the ocean. Besides large, chain retailers like H&M, Urban Outfitters and Tommy Bahama, there are interesting local merchants and about a dozen restaurants plus stands and smaller eateries in the Lot 579 (p265) food court. Nightlife venues like the **Bungalow** keep it hopping until late.

All in all, Pacific City could end up being a game changer for HB and the region, drawing shoppers, diners and party people from other parts of the city and county.

Barnabas Clothing Co.
CLOTHING

(☑ 714-374-0050; www.barnabasclothing.com; Pacific City, 21034 Pacific Coast Hwy, Suite C220; ☺ 10am-9pm, to 8pm Sun) This local maker does delicious coastal casual wear for men and women: Santa Fe–patterned fleece-lined Sherpa jackets, black corduroys, tanks, tops and graphic tees, even sweaters because hey,

it's SoCal and you never know when you're going to need one at night.

Huntington Surf & Sport
SPORTS & OUTDOORS

(www.hsssurf.com; 300 Pacific Coast Hwy; ☺ 8am-9pm Sun-Thu, to 10pm Fri & Sat) Towering behind the statue of surf hero Duke Kahanamoku at the corner of Pacific Coast Hwy and Main St, this massive store supports the Surf City vibe with vintage surf photos, the Surfers' Hall of Fame (p263) and lots of tiki-themed decor. You'll also find rows of surfboards, beachwear and surfing accessories.

HSS also rents surfboards for $10/30 per hour/day (wet suits $8/15).

American Vintage Clothing
CLOTHING

(☑ 714-969-9670; 201c Main St; ☺ 10am-8pm Mon-Fri, to 9pm Sat, to 7pm Sun) Thrift and vintage hounds check out the beautiful displays in this store: jeans to vintage Mexican surf hoodies, boots, rock T-shirts, earrings and loads of dresses arranged by decade. Enter off Walnut Ave.

ℹ Information

Visit Huntington Beach Information Kiosk (☑ 714-969-3492, 800-729-6232; www.surfcityusa.com; Pier Plaza, 325 Pacific Coast Hwy; ☺ 10:30am-7pm Mon-Fri, from 10am Sat & Sun, shorter hrs in winter) Visitor information kiosk by the pier.

ℹ Getting There & Around

Pacific Coast Hwy (PCH) runs alongside the beach. Main St intersects PCH at the pier. Heading inland, Main St ends at Hwy 39 (Beach Blvd), which connects north to I-405.

Public parking lots by the pier and beach – when you can get a spot – are 'pay and display' for $1.50 per hour, $15 daily maximum. Self-service ticket booths scattered across the parking lot take dollars or coins. More municipal lots alongside PCH and around downtown cost at least $15 per day in summer, typically with an evening flat rate of $5 after 5pm. On-street parking meters cost $1 per 40 minutes.

OCTA (p252) bus 1 connects HB with the rest of OC's beach towns every hour; one-way/day pass $2/5, payable on board (exact change). When we passed through, a free **Surf City USA Shuttle** (www.surfcityusashuttle.com; ☺ 10am-10pm Fri & Sat, 10am-8pm Sun, mid-Jun–early Sep) was making a loop around beach and inland areas.

Newport Beach

There are really three Newport Beaches: paradise for wealthy Bentley- and Porsche-driving yachtsmen and their trophy wives; perfect waves and beachside dives for surfers and stoners; and glorious sunsets and seafood for the rest of the folk, trying to live the day-to-day. Somehow, these diverse communities all seem to live – mostly – harmoniously.

For visitors, the pleasures are many: just-off-the-boat seafood, boogie-boarding the human-eating waves at the Wedge, and the ballet of yachts in the harbor. Just inland, more lifestyles of the rich and famous revolve around Fashion Island (p275), a posh outdoor mall and one of the OC's biggest shopping centers.

◉ Sights

Newport is best known for its – wait for it – beach, and the Balboa Peninsula has some of the best access to both beaches, historic architecture and retro-cool amusements.

Balboa Peninsula   AREA
Four miles long but less than a half-mile wide, the Balboa Peninsula has a white-sand beach on its ocean side and countless stylish homes, including the 1926 Lovell Beach House (p269). It's just inland from the paved beachfront recreational path, across from a small playground. Hotels, restaurants and bars cluster around the peninsula's two famous piers: Newport Pier near the western end and Balboa Pier at the eastern end. The two-mile oceanfront strip between them teems with beachgoers; people-watching is great.

Near Newport Pier, several shops rent umbrellas, beach chairs, volleyballs and other necessities. For swimming, families will find a more relaxed atmosphere and calmer waves at 10th St and 18th St. The latter beach, also known as Mothers Beach (p269), has a lifeguard, restrooms and a shower.

At the very tip of Balboa Peninsula, by the West Jetty, the Wedge is a bodysurfing, bodyboarding and knee-boarding spot for experts; newcomers should head a few blocks west. Park on Channel Rd or E Ocean Blvd and walk through tiny West Jetty View Park.

Balboa Fun Zone   AMUSEMENT PARK
(Map p270; www.thebalboafunzone.com; 600 E Bay Ave; Ferris wheel $4; ⊙ Ferris wheel 11am-6pm Sun-Thu, to 9pm Fri, to 10pm Sat; 🅟) On the harbor side of Balboa Peninsula, the Fun Zone has delighted locals and visitors since 1936. There's a small Ferris wheel (where Ryan and Marissa shared their first kiss on *The OC*), arcade games, touristy shops and restaurants, and frozen banana stands (just like the one in the TV sitcom *Arrested Development*). Nearby the landmark 1906 Balboa Pavilion (p269) is beautifully illuminated at night.

The Fun Zone is also the place to catch a harbor cruise, fishing or a whale-watching expedition, or the Balboa Island Ferry (p275) just across the channel.

★ Orange County Museum of Art   MUSEUM
(Map p270; ☑ 949-759-1122; www.ocma.net; 850 San Clemente Dr; adult/student & senior/child under 12yr $10/7.50/free; ⊙ 11am-5pm Wed-Sun, to 8pm Fri; 🅟 🛈) This engaging museum highlights California art and cutting-edge contemporary artists, with exhibitions rotating through two large spaces. Recent exhibitions have included the California-Pacific Triennial and works by Robert Rauschenberg. There's also a sculpture garden, eclectic gift shop and a theater screening classic, foreign and art-related films.

It's close to Fashion Island (p275), in case you want to get your retail fix after your culture fix.

Discovery Cube's Ocean Quest   MUSEUM
(Map p270; ☑ 949-675-8915; www.oceanquestoc. org; 600 E Bay Ave; adult/child 2 & under $5/free; ⊙ hours vary; 🅟 🛈) In the Balboa Fun Zone, this newly refurbished museum was recently taken over by Santa Ana's Discovery Cube (p256) and runs educational programs for local schools and field trips. When not hosting school groups, it opens to the public and shows traveling exhibits. Check the website for opening hours, what's on and for occasional whale-watching trips.

The Wedge   BEACH
At the end of the Balboa Peninsula, the Wedge is famous among bodyboarders and knee-boarders for its perfectly hollow waves that can swell up to 30ft high. The waves are shore-breakers that crest on the sand, not out to sea, so you can easily slam your head. There's usually a small crowd watching the action. This is not a good place for learning how to handle the currents; try a few blocks west.

Lovell Beach House   HISTORIC BUILDING
(Map p270; 1242 W Ocean Front) For a striking architectural specimen, stroll past the 1926

Lovell House, designed by seminal modernist architect Rudolf Schindler, a student of Frank Lloyd Wright's. It was built using site-cast concrete frames shaped like figures of eight. It's kind of amazing that it still exists with the encroachment all around. It's closed to the public, so you'll be looking from outside.

Balboa Pavilion HISTORIC BUILDING
(Map p270; www.balboapavilion.com; 400 Main St) Nearby the Balboa Fun Zone, the landmark 1906 Balboa Pavilion is beautifully illuminated at night. You can get boat rentals and catch ferries to Catalina Island (p228) from here.

Mothers Beach BEACH
(Map p270; Marina Park, 18th St, Balboa Peninsula;) This calm beach, known as Mothers Beach for its kid-friendly currents, has a lifeguard, restrooms and a shower.

🏃 Activities
Surfing
Surfers flock to the breaks at the small jetties surrounding the Newport Pier between 18th and 56th streets. Word of warning: locals can be territorial. For lessons, try Huntington Beach or Laguna Beach instead.

15th Street Surf & Supply SURFING
(Map p270; 949-751-7867; https://15thstsurf supply.com; 103 15th St; boogie boards per hour/ day $7/15, surfboards $15/40; 9am-7pm) Rent a full compliment of boogie boards, surfboards and accessories from wet suits to umbrellas, at this easygoing shop in business since 1961. Prices may fluctuate and shop hours are variable, so call ahead to check.

Boating
Besides the beach, the best thing about Newport Beach is its harbor. Take a boat tour, or rent your own kayak or sailboat. Even better, rent a flat-bottomed Duffy Boat, a local institution that you pilot yourself, and take a cruise with up to 12 friends.

Duffy Electric Boat Rentals BOATING
(Map p270; 949-645-6812; www.duffyofnewport beach.com; 2001 W Coast Hwy; first 2hr $199; 10am-8pm) These heated electric boats with canopies are a Newport tradition. Bring tunes, food and drinks for a fun

evening toodling around the harbor like a local. No boating experience required; maps provided.

Balboa Boat Rentals BOATING
(Map p270; 949-673-7200; http://boats4rent. com; 510 E Edgewater Pl; per hr kayaks from $18, pontoon boats $105, powerboats from $75, electric boats from $80; 10am-7pm, extended hrs in summer) By the Balboa Fun Zone (p268), this outfit rents powerboats, pontoon boats, kayaks and SUPs.

Cycling & Skating
To experience fabulous ocean views, ride a bike along the paved **recreational path** that encircles almost the entire Balboa Peninsula. Inland cyclists like the paved **scenic loop** around Upper Newport Bay Nature Preserve (p273). There are many places to rent bikes near Newport and Balboa Piers.

Diving
There's terrific diving just south of Newport Beach at the underwater park at Crystal Cove State Park (p279), where divers can check out reefs, anchors and an old military plane-crash site.

👉 Tours
Several companies offer narrated tours of glitzy Newport Harbor, departing near the Balboa Fun Zone and Balboa Pavilion. Reserve ahead for the Christmas Boat Parade.

Davey's Locker BOATING
(Map p270; 949-673-1434; www.daveyslocker. com; 400 Main St; per adult/child 3-12yr & senior 2½hr whale-watching cruise from $32/26, half-day sportfishing $41.50/34) At Balboa Pavilion; offers whale-watching and sportfishing trips.

Fun Zone Boat Co BOATING
(Map p270; 949-673-0240; www.funzoneboats. com; 700 Edgewater Pl; 45min cruise per adult/ child 5-11yr/senior from $14/7/11) Sea lion–watching and celebrity home tours depart from the Fun Zone.

Gondola Adventures BOATING
(Map p270; 888-446-6365, 949-646-2067; www.gondola.com; 3101 W Coast Hwy; 1hr cruise per couple from $135) Totally cheesy Venetian-esque gondola rides with chocolates and sparkling cider.

Newport Beach & Around

COSTA MESA

Lab (3mi); Camp (3mi);
4.4mi; Segerstrom
Center for the
Arts (5mi); South
Coast Plaza (5.5mi)

Enlargement

Superior Ave

17th St

15th St

Tustin Ave

Irvine Ave

Dover Dr

Newport Blvd

Balboa Blvd

Newport Bay

Cappy's Café (0.6mi);
Newport Channel
Inn (0.6mi);
Eat Chow (0.6mi)

W Coast Hwy

Balboa Blvd

Seashore Dr

Newport Blvd

Lido Isle

Via Lido Nord

Via Lido Soud

Bay Island

See Enlargement

Newport Bay

Bay Ave

Balboa Blvd

PACIFIC OCEAN

19th St

Newport Pier

Balboa Peninsula

✺ Festivals & Events

Christmas Boat Parade CHRISTMAS
(www.christmasboatparade.com; ☉ Dec) The
week before Christmas brings thousands
of spectators to Newport Harbor to watch a
century-old tradition. The 2½-hour parade
of up to 150 boats, including some fancy
multi-million-dollar yachts all decked out
with Christmas lights and holiday cheer, begins at 6:30pm. Watch for free from the Fun
Zone (p268) or Balboa Island (p274), or book
ahead for a harbor boat tour.

Newport Beach Film Festival FILM
(www.newportbeachfilmfest.com; ☉ mid-Apr) Roll
out the red carpet for screenings of over 350
mostly new independent and foreign films.
Some films shown here, such as *Crash*,
Waitress, *(500) Days of Summer* and *Chef*
have gone on to become classics, while earlier classics like *Sunset Boulevard* get anniversary screenings.

**Newport Beach Wine and
Food Festival** FOOD & DRINK
(www.newportwineandfood.com; ☉ late Sep)
Flashy food-and-wine fest shows off local restaurateurs, top chefs, prestigious winemakers

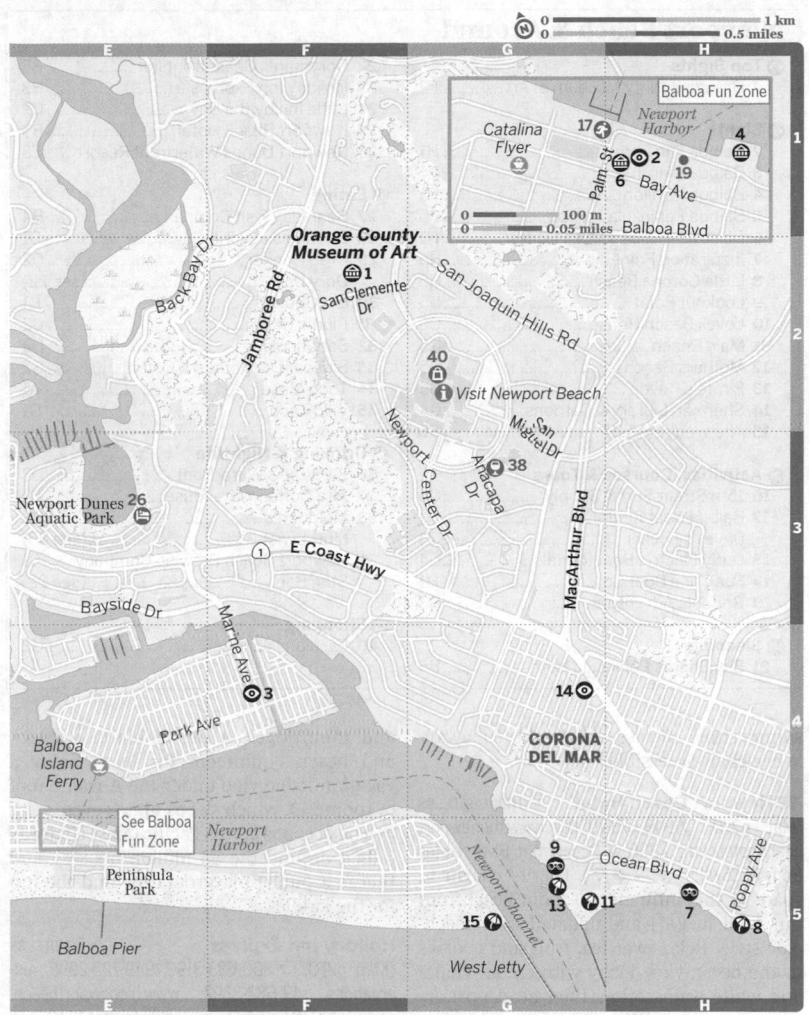

and brewmasters with live rock concerts staged near Fashion Island (p275).

🛏 Sleeping

A Newport stay ain't cheap, but outside of the peak season rates often drop 40% or more. Otherwise, to save some dough, you'll find chain hotels and motels further inland, especially around John Wayne Airport, in Costa Mesa, and around the triangle junction of Hwy 55 (Costa Mesa Fwy), toll road Hwy 73 and I-405 (San Diego Fwy).

Newport Dunes
Waterfront Resort CABIN, CAMPGROUND **$**
(Map p270; ☎ 949-729-3863; www.newport-dunes.com; 1131 Back Bay Dr; campsite from $64, cottage/1-bedroom cottage from $90/165; P@🛜🐾🏊) RVs and tents aren't required for a stay at this upscale campground: two dozen tiny, well-kept A-frames and picket-fenced one-bedroom cottages are available, all within view of Newport Bay. A fitness center and walking trails, kayak rentals, board games, family bingo, ice-cream socials, horseshoe and volleyball tournaments, an outdoor pool and playground, and

Newport Beach & Around

summertime movies on the beach await. Wheelchair-accessible.

★ **Newport Beach Hotel**   BOUTIQUE HOTEL **$$**
(Map p270; ☑ 949-673-7030; www.thenewport beachhotel.com; 2306 W Oceanfront Blvd; r/stes from $235/425; P⊖❋☎) There's charm to spare in this intimate, 20-room beachfront inn, built in 1904 and updated with beach-chic style. Relax over tea, fruit and cookies in the ocean-view lobby with rattan chairs and white wainscoting, then head upstairs where rooms of different sizes are done up with clean whites and pastel blues, some with spa tubs and ocean views.

There's a lovely wine bar at the back of the lobby.

It doesn't come cheap, but look for off-season specials. Parking is $20.

Newport Channel Inn   MOTEL **$$**
(Map p270; ☑ 949-642-3030, 800-255-8614; www. newportchannelinn.com; 6030 W Coast Hwy; r $129-199; P⊖❋☎) This 30-room, two-story 1960s-era motel is simple, homey and spotless, with genuinely friendly owners who dispense lots of local knowledge. Other perks include large rooms with microwaves

and minifridges, a big common sundeck and beach equipment for loan. Enjoy a vacation-lodge vibe under the A-frame roof of room 219, which sleeps up to seven.

The ocean is across Pacific Coast Highway (albeit around the $5 million houses), and there's a public playground behind the inn for the kiddies.

Holiday Inn Express   MOTEL **$$**
(Map p270; ☑ 800-633-3199, 949-722-2999, res-ervations 949-682-3392; www.hienewportbeach. com; 2300 W Coast Hwy; r incl breakfast $149-259; P⊖❋@☎☀) The 86 spacious rooms have up-to-date furnishings and extras like mi-crowaves, minirefrigerators and work desks. Centrally located on a busy stretch of Pacific Coast Highway, between major attractions. There's agreeable staff, a coin-op laundry, cardio equipment, hot tub and small pool heated year-round.

A lobby remodel gives more expensive properties a run for their money, and rates include a full breakfast buffet.

Little Inn by the Bay   MOTEL **$$**
(Map p270; ☑ 949-673-8800, 800-438-4466; www.littleinnbythebay.com; 2627 Newport Blvd; r

WORTH A TRIP

UPPER NEWPORT BAY ECOLOGICAL PRESERVE

The brackish water of this 752-acre **reserve** (☑ 949-640-1751; www.ocparks.com/parks/newport; 2301 University Dr; ⏱ 7am-sunset; P) ✿ **FREE**, where runoff from the San Bernardino Mountains meets the sea, supports more than 200 species of birds. This is one of the few estuaries in Southern California that has been preserved and it's an important stopover on the Pacific Flyway migration route. There are also trails for jogging and cycling. For guided tours with naturalists and weekend kayak tours of the Back Bay, contact the Newport Bay Conservancy (http://newportbay.org).

Right in the preserve, the 10,000 sq ft **Muth Interpretive Center** (☑ 949-923-2290; www.newportbay.org; 2301 University Dr, off Irvine Ave; ⏱ 10am-4pm Tue-Sun; ♿) is made from sustainable materials. Inside, you'll find displays and information about the reserve which explain how the bay is like an eggbeater and a sponge, among other scientific fun facts. There's a kid-friendly activity room with a number of small, snake-and-spider-filled terraria. Before heading out into the preserve, grab a trail map.

Built right into the hillside, the center is not visible from the parking lot. Walk past the information kiosk and down a short hill.

from $195; P ⊝ ✳ 🛜) If you're not bothered by street noise, you can walk to the beach from this 18-room mid-century motel. Recently upgraded rooms feature contemporary style, with microwave, fridge, iron and coffee maker, and some have Jacuzzis or balconies. There's beach gear and bikes to borrow.

Doryman's Oceanfront Inn   B&B $$$

(Map p270; ☑ 949-675-7300; www.dorymansinn.com; 2102 W Oceanfront; r $299-399; P ⊝ ✳ 🛜) This 2nd-floor oceanfront B&B was built in 1891 and retains that Victorian country style. Each of the 11 rooms is unique, and some boast ocean views and fireplaces. It has a great location by Newport Pier (view it from the roof deck), although it can get loud in summer with the 24-hour activities. Parking and breakfast (quiche, bagels, fruit and more) included.

Bay Shores Peninsula Hotel   HOTEL $$$

(Map p270; ☑ 800-222-6675, 949-675-3463; www.thebestinn.com; 1800 W Balboa Blvd; r incl breakfast $190-300; P ✳ @ 🛜) This three-story, reimagined motel flexes some surf-themed muscle. From *Endless Summer* posters to complimentary fresh-baked cookies and free rental movies, it's beachy, casual and customer-focused; its location at the elbow of the peninsula partially explains the steep rates. Complimentary parking, beach gear and continental breakfast buffet, best enjoyed on the 360-degree-view sun deck. Coin-op laundry available.

✕ Eating

Dozens of restaurants and pubs throughout Newport offer fish dinners (as you'd expect), plus nouveau Japanese and modern Mexican.

★ Bear Flag Fish Company   SEAFOOD $

(Map p270; ☑ 949-673-3474; www.bearflagfishco.com; 3421 Via Lido; mains $10-16; ⏱ 11am-9pm Tue-Sat, to 8pm Sun & Mon; ♿) This is *the* place for generously sized, grilled and *panko*-breaded fish tacos, ahi burritos, spankin' fresh ceviche and oysters. Pick out what you want from the ice-cold display cases, then grab a picnic-table seat. About the only way this seafood could be any fresher is if you caught and hauled it off the boat yourself! 'Guppy specials' are available for kids.

Dory Deli   DELI $

(Map p270; ☑ 949-220-7886; www.dorydeli.com; 2108 W Oceanfront; mains $7-12; ⏱ 6am-8pm Sun-Thu, to 9pm Fri & Sat) This hip new beachfront storefront does hot and cold sandwiches like the Rubinstein, Lifeguard Club and the steak-filled Rocky Balboa, plus fresh-caught fish-and-chips. For breakfast, you could be good and get the yoga pants burrito, or sin a little with chicken and waffles. Full bar too! Sure, we'll stop in after surfing...

Wild Taco   MEXICAN $

(Map p270; ☑ 949-673-9453; www.facebook.com/wildtaconewport; 407 31st St; tacos $3-4, burritos and plates $5-12; ⏱ 11am-9pm Tue-Sat, to 8pm Sun & Mon) This nifty, Baja-inspired cantina makes salsas, aguas frescas and tortillas in house and serves them with tacos of grilled

DON'T MISS

BALBOA ISLAND

In the middle of the harbor sits the **island** (http://explorebalboaisland.com; P) that time forgot. Its streets are still largely lined with tightly clustered cottages built in the 1920s and '30s when this was a summer getaway from LA. The 1.5-mile promenade that circles the island makes a terrific car-free stroll or jog. Departing from the **Balboa Fun Zone** (p268), the **ferry** (p275) lands at Agate Ave, about 0.6 miles west of Marine Ave, which is lined with swimwear boutiques, Italian trattorias and cocktail bars.

meats (*al pastor*), pork carnitas, shrimp and some delectable veggie options like grilled kale and feta. Mexican and Californian beers on tap, and margaritas are a steal. It's in a simple glass-fronted, concrete-floored room that can get loud.

Cappy's Café
DINER **$**

(Map p270; www.cappyscafe.com; 5930 W Coast Hwy; mains $6-12; ⊘ 6am-3pm Mon, Tue, Thu & Fri, to 8pm Wed, to 4pm Sat & Sun) You won't leave hungry from this bright-blue diner on the land side of Coast Hwy. It serves monster omelets, crispy bacon, country fried chicken, house-made corned beef hash, stuffed French toast and other classic blue-plate breakfasts.

Eat Chow
CALIFORNIAN **$$**

(Map p270; ☑ 949-423-7080; www.eatchownow. com; 211 62nd St; mains $9-18; ⊘ 8am-9pm Mon-Thu, to 10pm Fri, 7am-10pm Sat, 7am-9pm Sun) Hidden a block behind W Coast Hwy, Eat Chow's crowd is equal parts tatted hipsters and ladies who lunch, which makes it very Newport indeed. They all queue happily for rib-eye Thai beef salads, grilled-salmon tacos with curry slaw, and bodacious burgers like the Chow BBQ burger with homemade barbecue sauce, smoked Gouda, crispy onions and more. Groovy indie-rock soundtrack.

There's another location in **Costa Mesa** (☑ 949-650-2469; 1802 Newport Blvd; ⊘ 7am-9pm Sun-Thu, to 10pm Fri & Sat).

Crab Cooker
SEAFOOD **$$**

(Map p270; ☑ 949-673-0100; www.crabcooker. com; 2200 Newport Blvd; mains lunch/dinner $15-26/$18/26, lobster and king crab $32-43; ⊘ 11am-9pm Sun-Thu, to 10pm Fri & Sat; 🖪) Expect a

wait at this always-busy joint, a landmark since 1951. It serves great seafood and fresh crab on paper plates to an appreciative crowd wearing flip-flops and jeans. Don't miss the delish chowder – it's loaded with clams. If you're in a hurry, saunter up to the fish-market counter inside and order your seafood to go. Kids and light eaters can get fish skewers.

Sabatino's
ITALIAN **$$**

(Map p270; ☑ 949-723-0621; www.sabatinoschicagosausage.com; 251 Shipyard Way; mains lunch $13-24, dinner $15-32; ⊘ 8am-10pm) The claim to fame of this authentic Italian place on Lido Island is its handmade Chicago-style sausage, blended with Sicilian goat cheese for that cholesterol double-whammy. Family-size deli sandwiches, shrimp scampi and stuffed and baked pastas keep the locals coming back for more. It's hard to find – when you get lost, just call.

Buddha's Favorite
JAPANESE **$$**

(Map p270; ☑ 949-723-4203; www.buddhasfavorite. com; 634 Lido Park Dr; dishes $4-16; ⊘ 5:30pm-10pm Mon-Thu, to 10:30pm Fri & Sat, to 9:30pm Sun) Who are we to disagree with the Enlightened One? This dockside sushi joint's Yokohama-born chef has a hipster following for creative hot and cold appetizers like sashimi 'candy,' miso black cod, fried salmon wontons with cream cheese, and deep-fried halibut with eel sauce. Snag a table outside on the heated deck and enjoy the twinkling harbor lights.

If you're not a fan of raw fish, try tempura, soba or udon noodles, or heaping *donburi* rice bowls.

🍸 Drinking & Nightlife

The area around Newport Beach Pier is chock-a-block with drinking establishments, mostly pretty casual.

★ Alta Coffee Warehouse
COFFEE

(Map p270; www.altacoffeeshop.com; 506 31st St; ⊘ 6am-10pm Mon-Fri, from 7am Sat & Sun) Hidden on a side street, this cozy coffeehouse in a beach bungalow with a covered patio lures locals with live music and poetry readings, art on the brick walls and honest baristas who dish the lowdown on the day's soups, savories, popular comfort food and baked goods like carrot cake and cheesecake.

It's the kind of place that keeps a shelf of mugs for frequent customers, of whom there are many. The kitchen closes at 9:30pm.

★ Muldoon's
BAR

(Map p270; ☑ 949-640-4110; www.muldoonspub. com; 202 Newport Center Dr; ⊙ opens 11:30am Mon-Sat, 10am Sun, closing hours vary) At upscale, upbeat, much-admired Muldoon's, choose from indoor, outdoor (under a leafy tree) and bar seating and enjoy decent, if pricey, Irish pub grub, 10 beers on tap and live acoustic sounds Thursday through Saturday nights and many Sunday afternoons.

Our only complaint: it's a drive from the beach, in an office park by Fashion Island (p275).

3-Thirty-3 Waterfront
LOUNGE

(Map p270; ☑ 949-673-8464; www.3thirty3nb. com; 333 Bayside Dr; ⊙ 11am-2am Mon-Fri, from 9am Sat & Sun) Sip cocktails with Newport's in-crowd at this upscale restaurant lounge with killer views of the yacht-filled harbor. The crowd skews older; you might expect a 'Real Housewife' (or a Housewife hunter) to come in.

Mutt Lynch's
BAR

(Map p270; ☑ 949-675-1556; www.muttlynchs. com; 2301 W Oceanfront; ⊙ 7am-2am) By the beach, this rowdy dive (beer can chandelier, anyone?) offers schooners filled with dozens of beers on tap and cocktails made with *soju* (Korean vodka). Food from a huge menu comes in huge portions, especially at breakfast (mains $9-15). Best on 'Sunday Fundays.'

Stag Bar
BAR

(Map p270; ☑ 949-673-4470; www.stagbar.com; 121 McFadden Pl; 8am-2am) This giant space with a loooong bar reels them in for billiards, darts, creative cocktails and a chill vibe. Pub grub punches above its weight too, like skillet pancakes or breakfast pizza on weekend mornings, and daytime meatballs, salads and pizzas like the Meat Coma and Dirty Hippie.

Newport Beach Brewing Company
MICROBREWERY

(Map p270; www.newportbeachbrewingcompany. com; 2920 Newport Blvd; ⊙ 11:30am-11pm Sun-Thu, to 1am Fri & Sat; ☎) The town's only microbrewery (try their signature Newport Beach Blonde or Bisbee's ESB), 'Brewco' is a laid-back place to catch the big game or just kick it over burgers, pizzas and fried fare with your buds after a day at the beach.

🛍 Shopping

Fashion Island, inland from the beach, is Newport's biggest, most established shopping center (over 200 shops), but the new Lido Marina district is gearing up to give it a run for its money on a smaller scale: about two dozen establishments including stylish boutiques and casual indoor-outdoor dining. On Balboa Island, **Marine Avenue** is lined with darling shops in an old-fashioned village atmosphere, a good place to pick up something for the kids, unique gifts and beachy souvenirs, or jewelry, art and antiques for yourself.

Fashion Island
MALL

(Map p270; ☑ 949-721-2000, 855-658-8527; www.shopfashionisland.com; 401 Newport Center Dr; ⊙ 10am-9pm Mon-Fri, to 7pm Sat, 11am-6pm Sun) Celebrating its 50th anniversary in 2017, Fashion Island sits in the middle of a traffic loop in eastern Newport. Anchored by high-end department stores, the mall's breezy, Mediterranean-style walkways are lined with more than 200 specialty shops, upscale kiosks, 40 chain restaurants, a multiplex cinema and the occasional koi pond or burbling fountain.

ℹ Information

Visit Newport Beach (www.visitnewportbeach. com; 401 Newport Center Dr, Fashion Island, Atrium Court, 2nd fl; ⊙ 10am-9pm Mon-Fri, to 7pm Sat, to 6pm Sun) The city's official visitor center hands out free brochures and maps.

ℹ Getting There & Around

BOAT

The West Coast's largest passenger catamaran, the **Catalina Flyer** (☑ 949-673-5245; www. catalinainfo.com; 400 Main St; round-trip adult/ child 3-12yr/senior $70/53/65, per bicycle $7), makes a daily round-trip to Catalina Island, taking 75 minutes each way. It leaves Balboa Pavilion around 9am and returns before 6pm; check online for discounts.

Balboa Island Ferry (www.balboaislandferry. com; 410 S Bay Front; adult/child $1/50¢, car incl driver $2; ⊙ 6:30am-midnight Sun-Thu, to 2am Fri & Sat)

BUS

OCTA (p252) bus 1 connects Newport Beach and Fashion Island mall with the OC's other beach towns, including Corona del Mar just east, every 30 minutes to one hour. From the intersection of Newport Blvd and Pacific Coast Hwy, bus 71 heads south along the Balboa Peninsula to Main Ave every hour or so. On all routes, the one-way fare is $2 (exact change).

CAR & MOTORCYCLE

Frequently jammed from dawn till dusk, Hwy 55 (Newport Blvd) is the main access road from I-405 (San Diego Fwy); it intersects with Pacific Coast Hwy near the shore. In town, Pacific Coast Hwy is called W Coast Hwy or E Coast Hwy, both in mailing addresses and conversationally by locals.

The municipal lot beside Balboa Pier costs 50¢ per 20 minutes, or $15 per day. Street parking meters on the Balboa Peninsula cost 50¢ to $1 per hour. Free parking on residential streets, just a block or two from the sand, is time-limited and subject to other restrictions. In summer expect to circle like a hawk for a space.

Around Newport Beach

Costa Mesa

So close to Newport Beach that they're often lumped together, Costa Mesa at first glance looks like just another landlocked suburb transected by the I-405, but top venues attract some 24 million visitors each year. South Coast Plaza is SoCal's largest mall – properly termed a 'shopping resort' – while Orange County's cultural heart is steps away in the performing-arts venues Segerstrom Center for the Arts (p278) and South Coast Repertory (p278), lending the city's slogan, City of the Arts.

If that all sounds rather hoity-toity, a pair of 'anti-malls' called the Lab (p278) and the Camp (p278) bring hipster cool, while strip malls throughout town reveal cafes serving surprisingly tasty dishes, ethnic-food holes-in-the-wall, bars and clubs. A new food hall, the OC Mix (p277), is shaking it up even more. There's some distance between all of these destinations, but combined they make Costa Mesa one of the OC's most interesting enclaves.

◎ Sights

California Scenario   PUBLIC ART
(Noguchi Garden; www.segerstrommedialab.com/projects/california-scenario; 611 Anton Blvd; ◷8am-midnight) FREE The renowned sculptor Isamu Noguchi designed this 1.6 acre sculpture park, steps from the arts center near South Coast Plaza (p278) and the Segerstrom Center (p278). Noguchi's minimalist works honor the landscape of his native California, surrounding the enigmatic, reddish *Spirit of the Lima Bean* sculpture, itself cobbled together from 15 granite pieces.

🛏 Sleeping

BLVD Hotel   BOUTIQUE HOTEL $$
(☑949-631-7840; www.blvdhotels.com; 2430 Newport Bl; r $99-169; P➔❄🐾🛜) This 21st-century update of an older motel lets guests stay close to Newport Beach at less than Newport prices. The 325 sq ft rooms are smallish but well designed, with surf and city murals, wood slats and cheery colors, and renovated bathrooms have rain showers. Rates include continental breakfast and two drinks during evening happy hour.

Across from a busy highway, it's not the most glam or central of neighborhoods, but it's close to Newport Beach and shopping.

Crowne Plaza Costa Mesa   HOTEL $$
(☑714-557-3000; www.cpcostamesa.com; 3131 Bristol St; r from $129; P➔❄🛜🐾) A decently priced, central stay, with generous rooms, craftsman-style touches, friendly staff, pool and fitness room. Get a room facing the generous pool deck for more quiet. It's about halfway between South Coast Plaza and the Camp and Lab areas (about 10 minutes on foot). If walking busy Bristol St doesn't appeal, a hotel shuttle can take you.

🍴 Eating

Over the last few years, Costa Mesa has developed one of the region's most interesting dining scenes, as gourmet chefs have moved into The Lab (p278) and The Camp (p278) anti-malls, as well as the new OC Mix (p277), by the large SOCO shopping district.

★Taco Mesa   MEXICAN $
(☑949-642-0629; www.tacomesa.net; 647 W 19th St; mains $3-13; ◷7am-11pm; 🚗) 🌱 Brightly painted in Mexican Day of the Dead art, this out-of-the-way stand is a local institution for fresh, healthy, sustainably farmed tacos of steak, beer-battered fish and more, with an awesome salsa bar. We like the tacos blackened, with cheese, chipotle sauce, cabbage relish and *crema fresca*. The *niños* (kids) menu offers quesadillas and such.

Sidecar Doughnuts & Coffee   DESSERTS $
(☑949-873-5424; www.sidecardoughnuts.com; 270 E 17th St; doughnuts from $2.75; ◷6:30am-4pm Sun-Thu, to 9pm Fri & Sat; 🚗) It may be in the back corner of a nondescript strip mall, but Sidecar's a landmark nonetheless. Crowds line up out the door (especially on weekends) for what are billed the 'world's freshest doughnuts.' Changing out daily and monthly, Sidecar bakes one-of-a-kind flavors like black

velvet, Saigon cinnamon crunch, maple bacon, huckleberry, and butter and salt.

OC Mix
FOOD HALL $

(www.socoandtheocmix.com; 3303 Hyland Ave; ⏰10am-9pm, individual shop hours vary) Costa Mesa's newest food destination brings together purveyors of coffees, cheeses, oysters and more. Also here is Taco Maria, whose Michelin-starred chef started with a food truck and was recently named *Food & Wine* magazine's best new chef. It's in the middle of the SOCO outdoor mall, where foodies will also want to flock to Surfas cooking store.

Kitakata Ramen Ban Nai
RAMEN $

(☎714-557-2947; www.ramenbannai.com; 891 Baker St; ramen $8-11.50; ⏰11am-2:45pm & 5pm-9:45pm Mon & Wed-Fri, 11am-9:45pm Sat & Sun) The US location of a popular ramen chain from northeastern Japan is known for its chewy, curly, wobbly (their word) hand-crumpled noodles. The broth stews for hours yet remains light, while the *chashu* (sliced pork) is marinated in soy sauce imported from Japan. We also loved the sides of Japanese fried chicken.

It's a little place with a few dozen seats, so there's often a wait (the line moves fast).

Memphis
SOUTHERN US $$

(☎714 432 7685; www.memphiscafe.com; 2920 Bristol St; mains brunch $7-17, dinner $14-28; ⏰8am-9:30pm Sun-Wed, to 11pm Thu-Sat) Inside a vintage mid-century-modern building, this fashionable eatery is all about down-home flavor – think pulled-pork sandwiches, popcorn shrimp, gumbo and buttermilk-battered fried chicken. There's brunch daily, happy hour at the bar, and weeknight dinner specials cost a mere $10.

Plums Café
CALIFORNIAN $$

(☎949-722-7586; www.plumscafe.com; 369 E 17th St; mains $12-20; ⏰8am-3pm, dinner from 5pm) Raise your breakfast game at this gourmet caterer's bistro tucked in the corner of a cookie-cutter strip mall. With its exposed brick walls and sleek designs, Plums will have you feeling oh-so-chic as you nibble Dutch baby pancakes with Oregon pepper bacon, or alderwood smoked-salmon hash. Breakfast cocktails incorporate fun ingredients like cucumber-mint or blood orange.

Habana
LATIN AMERICAN $$

(☎714-556-0176; www.habanacostamesa.com; the Lab, 2930 Bristol St; mains lunch $13-20, dinner $20-30; ⏰11am-1am Sun-Thu, 11:30am-2am Fri & Sat)

TOP BEACHES IN ORANGE COUNTY

Seal Beach (p260)
Bolsa Chica State Beach (p266)
Huntington City Beach (p262)
Balboa Peninsula (p268)
Crystal Cove State Beach (p279)
Aliso Beach County Park (p280)
Doheny State Beach (p287)

With its flickering votive candles, ivy-covered courtyard and spicy Cuban, Mexican and Jamaican specialties, this sultry cantina whispers rendezvous. Paella, *ropa vieja* (shredded flank steak in tomato sauce) and salmon *a la parilla* (grilled) come with plantains and black beans on the side. On weekends, the bar gets jumpin' late-night.

Native Foods
VEGAN $

(www.nativefoods.com; the Camp, 2937 Bristol St; mains $8-10; ⏰11am-10pm; 🖊🦽) 🌱 Lunch in a yurt? In Orange County? Them's the digs at this vegan spot serving organic salads, veggie burgers, Native Oklahoma Classic grilled 'cheese' burger, rice bowls like the Soul Bowl (imitation chicken, beans and rice with ranch and BBQ sauce) and ooey-gooey desserts. The kids menu includes vegan mac 'n' cheese and faux chicken strips.

🍷 Drinking & Nightlife

Milk + Honey
CAFE

(☎714-708-0092; www.milkandhoneycostamesa.com; the Camp, 2981 Bristol St; ⏰7am-10pm Mon-Thu, 8am-11pm Fri & Sat, 8am-10pm Sun; 📶) This minimalist cool cafe takes fair-trade, shade-grown and organic coffee a little further, with unusual flavor combinations that (mostly) work: Spanish latte, lavender latte, plus chai tea, fruit smoothies, seasonal froyo flavors and Japanese-style shave ice with flavors like strawberry, red bean and almond. There's a small menu of sandwiches and delectable snacks like macarons and peanut butter cookie sandwiches.

Ruin
BAR

(☎714-884-3189; http://theruinbar.com; the Lab, 2930 Bristol St; ⏰4pm-1am Tue & Wed, noon-1am Thu-Sat) This intimate, eclectic bar is decorated kind of like grandma's attic...if grandma collected faux buffalo heads, piano fronts and a ski gondola, and crocheted her trees in yarn. There's a constantly changing selection of beers on tap and cocktails made from soju, the Korean distilled spirit. It's on the southern side of the Lab.

Wine Lab WINE BAR
(☑714-850-1780; www.winelabcamp.com; the Camp, 2937 Bristol St, Suite A101B; ☺noon-10pm Tue-Thu, to 11pm Fri & Sat, to 9pm Sun, 4-9pm Mon) This friendly wine and cheese bar and shop offers New World wine and craft-beer tasting flights, plus small plates of artisan cheeses and charcuterie.

☆ Entertainment

Segerstrom Center for the Arts THEATER, CONCERT HALL
(☑714-556-2787; www.scfta.org; 600 Town Center Dr) The county's main performance venue is home to the Pacific Symphony, Philharmonic Society of Orange County and Pacific Chorale. It draws international performing-arts luminaries and Broadway shows, in three main theaters. Check the website for the wide-ranging calendar.

South Coast Repertory THEATER
(☑714-708-5555; www.scr.org; 655 Town Center Dr) Next to Segerstrom Center, South Coast Rep was started by a band of plucky theater grads in the 1960s and has evolved into a multiple Tony Award–winning company. It's managed to hold true to its mission to 'explore the most urgent human and social issues of our time' with groundbreaking, original plays from fall through to spring.

🔒 Shopping

★Camp MALL
(☑714-966-6661; www.thecampsite.com; 2937 Bristol St; ☺11am-8pm Mon-Sat, to 5pm Sun, individual shop hours vary) 🌱 Vegans, treehuggers and rock climbers, lend me your ears. The Camp offers one-stop shopping for all your outdoor and natural-living needs. **Active Ride Shop** and **Seed People's Market** for outdoor gear and fair-trade home goods are among the stores clustered along a leafy outdoor walkway. Parking spaces are painted with inspirational quotes like 'Show Up for Life.'

★Lab MALL
(☑714-966-6661; www.thelab.com; 2930 Bristol St; ☺10am-9pm Sun-Thu, to 10pm Fri & Sat, individual shop hours vary; ☎) Sister property to the Camp across the street, this outdoor, ivy-covered 'anti-mall' is the original in-your-face alternative to South Coast Plaza, even if

nowadays more (cool) national chains have moved in. Sift through vintage clothing, unique sneakers and trendy duds for teens, tweens and 20-somethings. For short attention spans, contemporary art exhibitions are displayed in shipping containers at ARTery.

South Coast Plaza MALL
(☑800-782-8888; www.southcoastplaza.com; 3333 Bristol St; ☺10am-9pm Mon-Fri, to 8pm Sat, 11am-6:30pm Sun) The stats at SoCal's premier luxury shopping destination speak for themselves: About $2 billion in annual sales, over 250 boutiques, 30 restaurants, five department stores, three valet stations and 10,000 parking spaces. It's been in business for over half a century (since 1967), yet it still feels current. Grab a map from one of four concierge desks.

❶ Getting There & Away

Costa Mesa starts immediately inland from Newport Beach via Hwy 55. South Coast Plaza is off Bristol St, north of the intersection of I-405, toll road Hwy 73 and Hwy 55, about 6 miles northeast of Pacific Coast Hwy.

Several **OCTA** (p252) routes converge on South Coast Plaza, including bus 57 running along Bristol Ave south to Newport Beach's Fashion Island ($2, 20 minutes, every half-hour).

Costa Mesa is now also a stop on the **ART shuttles** (p252) serving Disneyland and Anaheim.

Corona del Mar

Just south of Balboa Peninsula is Corona del Mar, a ritzy bedroom community on the privileged eastern flanks of the Newport Channel with plenty of upscale stores and restaurants and some of SoCal's most celebrated ocean views from the bluffs, not to mention postcard-perfect beaches with rocky coves and child-friendly tide pools.

◉ Sights

Main Beach BEACH
(Corona del Mar State Beach; ☑949-644-3151; www.newportbeachca.gov; off E Shore Ave; ☺6am-10pm; 🅿⛱) This half-mile-long beach lies at the foot of rocky cliffs and offers restrooms, fire rings (arrive early to snag one) and volleyball courts.

All-day parking costs $15, but spaces fill by 9am on weekends. If you're lucky, you may find free parking atop the cliffs behind the beach along Ocean Blvd.

Lookout Point   VIEWPOINT
(3001 Ocean Blvd) Locals enjoy impromptu, though not quite legal, cocktail parties at Lookout Point, perched above the beach with views of Pirate's Cove (p279) and the Balboa Peninsula (p268). Street parking only.

Pirate's Cove   BEACH
(⛱) Take the stairs off the north end of the Main Beach (p278) parking lot down to hideaway Pirate's Cove, a waveless beach that's great for families. Scenes from the classic TV show *Gilligan's Island* were shot here.

Little Corona Beach   BEACH
(3100 Ocean Blvd; ⛱) FREE If you're seeking an escape, head down the steep hill to this secluded beach known for its tide pools. Kids love the tide pools, but be aware that the pools are being loved to death. Don't yank anything from the rocks and tread carefully: light, oxygen and heavy footsteps can kill the critters.

Because there's no parking lot here, crowds may be lighter. Look for street parking on Ocean Blvd near Poppy Ave.

Inspiration Point   VIEWPOINT
(Ocean Blvd & Orchid Ave) FREE One of the OC's most beautiful views of surf, sand, sea and sky, overlooking the curve of the bay.

Sherman Library & Gardens NOTABLE BUILDING
(☎949-673-2261; www.slgardens.org; 2647 E Pacific Coast Hwy; adult/12-18yr/child under 12yr $5/3/free; ⊙10:30am-4pm, library closed Sat & Sun; P) A variety of lush gardens awaits at Corona del Mar's prize attraction. On 2.2 acres, the profuse orchids, a rose garden, a koi pond and even a desert garden are worth a wander. The small, non-lending research library holds some 15,000 historical documents from California, Arizona, Nevada and Baja.

Admission is free on Mondays.

Crystal Cove State Park

A few miles of open beach and 2400 acres of undeveloped woodland at this **state park** (☎949-494-3539; www.parks.ca.gov; 8471 N Coast Hwy; per car $15; ⊙6am-sunset; P⛱) 🏖 let you forget you're in a crowded metropolitan area, at least once you get past the parking lots and stake out a place on the sand. Overnight guests can stay in the dozens of vintage 1930s to '50s cottages (reserve well in advance), and anyone can stop for a meal or cocktails at the landmark Beachcomber restaurant.

Crystal Cove is also an underwater park. Scuba enthusiasts can check out two historic anchors dating from the 1800s as well as the crash site of a Navy plane that went down in the 1940s. Alternatively you can just go tide pooling, fishing, kayaking and surfing along the undeveloped shoreline. On the park's inland side, miles of hiking and mountain-biking trails await.

🛏 Sleeping & Eating

★**Crystal Cove Beach Cottages** CABIN $$
(☎reservations 800-444-7275; www.crystalcovealliance.org; 35 Crystal Cove, Crystal Cove State Park Historic District; r with shared bath $35-140, cottages $171-249; ⊙check-in 4-9pm; P) Right on the beach, these two dozen preserved cottages (circa 1930s to '50s) now host guests for a one-of-a-kind stay. Each cottage is different, sleeping between two and eight people in a variety of private or dorm-style accommodations. To snag one, book on the first day of the month seven months before your intended stay – or pray for cancellations.

**Ruby's Crystal Cove
Shake Shack**   AMERICAN $
(☎949-464-0100; www.rubys.com; 7703 E Coast Hwy; items $3-11; ⊙7am-8pm, until 9 in summer; ⛱) Although this been-here-forever wooden snack stand is now owned by the Ruby's Diner chain, the shakes – and the ocean views – are as good as ever. Don't fear the date shake; it's delish. They also serve three squares a day (burgers, fries, etc) and a kids menu.

The shack is just east of the Crystal Cove/Los Trancos entrance to the state park's historic district.

Beachcomber Café   AMERICAN $$
(☎949-376-6900; www.thebeachcombercafe.com; 15 Crystal Cove; mains breakfast $9-19, lunch $14-21, dinner $20-47; ⊙7am-9:30pm) The atmospheric Beachcomber Café lets you soak up the vintage 1950s beach vibe as you tuck into macadamia-nut pancakes, roasted turkey club sandwiches or more serious surf-and-turf. Sunset is the magic hour for Polynesian tiki drinks by the sea.

Laguna Beach

It's easy to love Laguna: secluded coves, romantic cliffs, azure waves and waterfront parks imbue the city with a Riviera-like feel. But nature isn't the only draw. From public sculptures and art festivals to free summer shuttles, the city has taken thoughtful steps to promote tourism while discreetly maintaining its moneyed quality of life (MTV's reality show *Laguna Beach* being one drunken, shameless exception).

One of the earliest incorporated cities in California, Laguna has a strong tradition in the arts, starting with the plein air impressionists who lived and worked here in the early 1900s. Today it's the home of renowned arts festivals, galleries, a well-known museum and exquisitely preserved arts-and-crafts cottages and bungalows that come as a relief after seeing endless miles of suburban beige-box architecture. It's also the OC's most prominent gay enclave (even if the gay nightlife scene is a shadow of its former self).

◎ Sights

With 30 public beaches sprawling along 7 miles of coastline, Laguna Beach is perfect for do-it-yourself exploring. There's always another stunning view or hidden cove just around the bend. Although many of the coves are blocked from street view by multi-million-dollar homes, a good local map or sharp eye will take you to stairways leading from the Pacific Coast Hwy down to the beach. Just look for the 'beach access' signs, and be prepared to pass through people's backyards to reach the sand. Unlike its neighbors to the north, Laguna doesn't impose a beach curfew. You can rent beach chairs, umbrellas and boogie boards from **Main Beach Toys** (Map p282; ☑949-494-8808; 150 Laguna Ave; chairs/umbrellas/boards per day $10/10/15; ⊘9am-9pm).

Laguna Art Museum   MUSEUM
(Map p282; ☑949-494-8971; www.lagunaart museum.org; 307 Cliff Dr; adult/student & senior/ child under 13yr $7/5/free, 5-9pm 1st Thu of month free; ⊘11am-5pm Fri-Tue, to 9pm Thu) This breezy museum has changing exhibitions featuring contemporary California artists, and a permanent collection heavy on California landscapes, vintage photographs and works by early Laguna bohemians.

Free guided tours are usually given at 11am Tuesday, Thursday and Saturday, and there's a unique gift shop.

Pacific Marine Mammal Center   NATURE CENTER
(Map p282; ☑949-494-3050; www.pacificmmc. org; 20612 Laguna Canyon Rd; donations welcome; ⊘10am-4pm; 🅿️ ♿) ⚑**FREE** A nonprofit organization dedicated to rescuing and rehabilitating injured or ill marine mammals, this center northeast of town has a small staff and many volunteers who help nurse Orange County's rescued pinnipeds – mostly sea lions and seals – before releasing them back into the wild. Visitors can view outdoor pools and holding pens – but remember, this is a rescue center, not SeaWorld. Still, it's educational and heartwarming. Admission is free, but donations and gift-shop purchases (say, a stuffed animal) help.

🏃 Activities

Central Beaches

Near downtown's village, **Main Beach** has volleyball and basketball courts, a playground and restrooms. It's Laguna's best beach for swimming. Just north at **Picnic Beach**, it's too rocky to surf; tide pooling is best. Pick up a tide table at the visitors bureau.

Above Picnic Beach, the grassy, bluff-top **Heisler Park** (Map p282; 375 Cliff Dr) offers vistas of craggy coves and deep-blue sea. Bring your camera – with its palm trees and bougainvillea-dotted bluffs, the scene is definitely one for posterity. A scenic walkway also connects Heisler Park to Main Beach.

North of downtown, Crescent Bay has big hollow waves good for bodysurfing, but parking is difficult; try the bluffs atop the beach; the views here are reminiscent of the Amalfi Coast.

Southern Beaches

About 1 mile south of downtown, secluded **Victoria Beach** (Victoria Dr) has volleyball courts and La Tour, a Rapunzel's-tower-like structure from 1926. Skimboarding (at the south end) and scuba diving are popular here. Take the stairs down Victoria Dr; there's limited parking along Pacific Coast Hwy.

Further south, **Aliso Beach County Park** (☑949-923-2280; http://ocparks.com/beaches/ aliso; 31131 S Pacific Coast Hwy; parking per hr $1; ⊘6am-10pm; 🅿️ ♿) is popular with surfers, boogie boarders and skimboarders. With picnic tables, fire pits and a play area, it's also good for families. Pay-and-display parking costs $1 per hour, or drive south and park on Pacific Coast Hwy for free.

Jealously guarded by locals, **Thousand Steps Beach** (off 9th Ave) is hidden about 1 mile south of Aliso Beach. Just past Mission Hospital, park along Pacific Coast Hwy or residential side streets. At the south end of 9th St, more than 200 steps (OK, so it's not 1000) lead down to the sand. Though rocky, the beach is great for sunbathing, surfing and bodysurfing.

Diving & Snorkeling

With its coves, reefs and rocky outcroppings, Laguna is one of the best SoCal beaches for diving and snorkeling. One of the most famous spots is **Divers Cove** just below Heisler Park. It's part of the **Glenn E Vedder Ecological Reserve**, an underwater park stretching to the northern border of Main Beach. Also popular is **Shaw's Cove**. Check weather and surf conditions with the city's **marine safety forecast line** (☑949-494-6573) beforehand, as drownings have happened. The visitors bureau has tide charts.

Laguna Sea Sports   DIVING
(Map p282; ☑949-494-6965; www.beachcities scuba.com; 925 N Coast Hwy; scuba package with/ without snorkeling gear $90/65; ☺10am-6pm Mon-Thu, to 7pm Fri, 6am-7pm Sat, 6am-5pm Sun) For rentals or to rinse your gear, stop by Laguna Sea Sports near Shaw's Cove. Check out its website for more info about local dive spots and diving etiquette, as well as classes.

Surfing

Because of Laguna's coves, the surfing here isn't as stellar as it is further north. If you must, try the beaches at Thalia St, Brooks St or St Ann's Dr (but beware of rocks).

CA Surf 'n' Paddle   WATER SPORTS
(Map p282; ☑949-497-1423; www.casurfshop.com; 695 S Coast Hwy; lessons group/private $75/95; ☺8am-9pm most days) Rents surfboards ($30), wet suits ($20) and bodyboards or skimboards ($15) and offers one-hour lessons in surfing and paddleboarding.

Kayaking

Take a guided kayaking tour of the craggy coves of Laguna's coast with **La Vida Laguna** (Map p282; ☑949-275-7544; www.lavidalaguna. com; 1257 S Coast Hwy; 2hr guided tour from $85)

and you might just see a colony of sea lions. Make reservations at least a day in advance.

Hiking

Surrounded by a green belt – a rarity in SoCal – Laguna has great nature trails for hikes. If you love panoramic views, take the short, scenic drive to **Alta Laguna Park**, a locals-only park, up-canyon from town. There, the moderate **Park Avenue Nature Trail**, a 1.25-mile one-way hike, takes you through fields of spring wildflowers. Open to hikers and mountain bikers, the 2.5-mile **West Ridge Trail** follows the ridgeline of the hills above Laguna. Both trails are in-and-out trips, not loops. To reach the trailheads, take Park Ave from town to its end at Alta Laguna Blvd then turn left to the park, which has restrooms and a drinking fountain.

☞ Tours

Stop by the visitor center (p285) to pick up brochures detailing self-guided tours on foot and by public bus. The *Heritage Walking Companion* is a tour of the town's architecture with an emphasis on Laguna's many bungalows and cottages, most dating from the 1920s and '30s. Laguna also overflows with public art, from well-placed murals to freestanding sculptures in unlikely locations. The free *Public Art Brochure* has color photos of all of Laguna's public-art pieces and a map to help you navigate. Or you can just swing by Heisler Park to see almost a dozen sculptures.

🛌 Sleeping

Most lodging in Laguna is on busy Pacific Coast Hwy, so expect traffic noise; bring earplugs or ask for a room away from the road. Significant discounts may be available out of season. For cheaper motels and hotels, head about 10 miles inland to I-405 (San Diego Fwy) around Irvine.

La Casa del Camino   HISTORIC HOTEL **$$**
(Map p282; ☑949-497-6029, 855-634-5736; www. lacasadelcamino.com; 1289 S Coast Hwy; r from $159; P☀❄@🛜🐾) A bargain for downtown Laguna, this 1929 Spanish-style hotel has 36 rooms and the awesome Rooftop Lounge (p285) bar. No two rooms are the same; most have carved headboards and dark hardwood furniture. Our favorite rooms, though, are the Casa Surf Suites featuring hip design by local surf-gear companies.

Laguna Beach

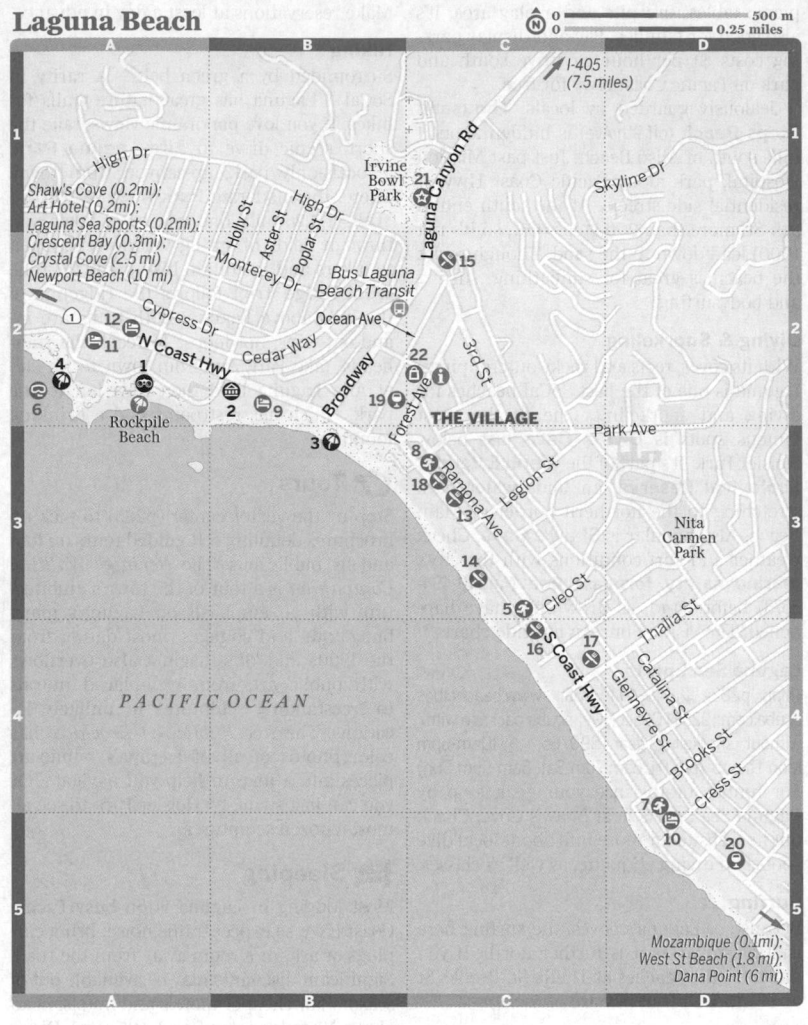

PACIFIC OCEAN

It's also got one of the best-deal resort fees in town: $16 covers parking, breakfast, wi-fi, setup of beach chairs, umbrellas and such, and access to a nearby gym.

Art Hotel
MOTEL $$

(Map p282; ☑ 949-494-6464, 877-363-7229; www.arthotellagunabeach.com; 1404 N Coast Hwy; r $184-214; P➡❋@🕸❄🐾) A mile northwest of the village, this easygoing, better-than-average shingled motel charges bargain rates, at least for Laguna. In keeping with the theme, colorful murals adorn the public

spaces – like the fantastic bas-relief of old Laguna around the pool deck – and works of a different artist hang in each of the 28 rooms. Take the shuttle downtown.

If you're sensitive to noise, you'll want to request one of the inner rooms away from busy Pacific Coast Hwy.

The Tides Inn
MOTEL $$

(Map p282; ☑ 888-777-2107, 949-494-2494; www.tideslaguna.com; 460 N Coast Hwy; r $130-200 off season, $210-400 Jul & Aug; P➡❋🕸❄🐾) A bargain for Laguna, especially considering

Laguna Beach

its convenient location just three long blocks north of the village. The feel is understated refinement: plush bedding, beachy-keen decor and inspirational quotes painted into each room. Each room is different; some have kitchenettes and many have wooden floors. Shared facilities include heated salt-water pool, barbecue grill and a fireplace for toasting marshmallows.

Thick windows help dissipate street noise.

★ Ranch at Laguna Beach
RESORT $$$

(Map p282; ☑ 949-499-2271, reservations 800-223-3309; www.theranchlb.com; 31106 S Coast Hwy; r from $399; Ⓟ☻✳☎☲) Laguna's newest resort is secluded away in Aliso Creek Canyon on the south side of town. Ninety-seven rooms, casitas and town homes are in multiple buildings spread across the 87-acre property, sporting a subtle, rustic refinement with board-and-batten construction and Mexican-tile bathrooms.

★ Montage
RESORT $$$

(Map p282; ☑ 949-715-6000; www.montagelaguna beach.com; 30801 S Coast Hwy; r from $595; Ⓟ@☎☲) You'll find nowhere more indulgent on the OC's coast than this over-the-top luxury waterside resort, especially if you hide away with your lover in a secluded bungalow. Even the most basic of its 248 rooms are plush and generous, offering California craftsman style, marble bathrooms, lemon verbena bath products and unobstructed ocean views.

★ Laguna Beach House
HOTEL $$$

(Map p282; ☑ 949-497-6645; www.thelaguna beachhouse.com; 475 N Coast Hwy; r $205-419; Ⓟ☻✳☎☲) Be it good feng shui, friendly staff or proximity to the beach, this 36-room courtyard inn feels right. From the surfboards in the lobby to colorful throw pillows and clean white walls and linens, the decor is contemporary, comfy and clean. Settle into the outdoor heated Jacuzzi with a glass of wine as the sun drops over the ocean.

Inn at Laguna Beach
HOTEL $$$

(Map p282; ☑ 949-497-9722; www.innatlagunabeach. com; 211 N Coast Hwy; r $250-500; Ⓟ✳☎☲) Pride of place goes to this three-story white, modern hotel, at the north end of Main Beach (p280). Its 70 keen rooms were recently renovated with rattan furniture, blond woods, marble, French blinds and pillow-top beds. Some have balconies overlooking the water. Extras include DVD and CD players, bathrobes, beach gear to borrow and nightly ocean-view wine reception.

You can step from the pool deck directly into Heisler Park (p280). Our favorite part is the terrace where you can bring your own lunch or dinner and enjoy 270-degree views. Staff are welcoming and professional.

A $15 resort fee covers wi-fi, those wine hours, cookies and milk, and morning coffee. Parking $30.

Eating

Laguna's dining scene will tickle foodies' fancies. Vegetarians will be happy, too, especially at the weekly **farmers market**

DON'T MISS

FIRST THURSDAYS

Once a month, downtown Laguna Beach gets festive during the **First Thursdays Gallery Art Walk** (☑949-683-6871; www.firstthursdaysartwalk.com; ⊙6-9pm 1st Thu of month). You can make the rounds of 30 local galleries and the **Laguna Art Museum** (p280) via free shuttles circling Laguna's art gallery districts.

(☑714-573-0374; www.facebook.com/lagunabeach fm; 505 Forest Ave; ⊙8am-noon Sat) in the Lumberyard parking lot, near City Hall.

Orange Inn   DINER $

(Map p282; ☑949-494-6085; www.orangeinncafe. com; 703 S Coast Hwy; mains $7-13; ⊙5:30am-5:30pm) Birthplace of the smoothie (in the *Guinness World Records*), this little shop from 1931 continues to pack in surfers fueling up before hitting the waves. It also serves date shakes, big omelets and breakfast burritos, homemade muffins and deli sandwiches on whole-wheat or sourdough bread.

Stand   VEGETARIAN, VEGAN $

(Map p282; ☑949-494-8101; www.thestandnaturalfoods.com; 238 Thalia St; mains $6-11; ⊙7am-8pm; ☑) With its friendly, indie-spirited vibe comes this tiny tribute to healthy cuisine. From hummus and guac sandwiches to sunflower sprout salads and black-beans-and-rice burritos, the menu is varied and all of it soul-satisfying. Try a smoothie or an all-natural shake. Order at the counter in the red minibarn, then cross your fingers for an outdoor patio table.

Big Fish Tavern   SEAFOOD $$

(Map p282; ☑949-715-4500; www.bigfishtavern laguna.com; 540 S Coast Hwy, Suite 200; mains $12-27; ⊙open 11:30am Mon-Sat, 11am Sun through dinner, closing hrs vary) Sustainably-raised Hawaii-style *poke* (marinated raw fish), Baja-style fish tacos, coconut shrimp and the fresh catch o' the day are about all you need. That, and views across rooftops to the ocean. And there are dozens of beers including about one-third from California. Make reservations, or wait, like, forever.

★ **Driftwood Kitchen**   AMERICAN $$$

(Map p282; ☑949-715-7700; www.driftwood-kitchen.com; 619 Sleepy Hollow Lane; mains lunch

$15-36, dinner $24-39; ⊙9-10:30am & 11am-2:30pm Mon-Fri, 5-9:30pm Sun-Thu, to 10:30pm Fri & Sat, 9am-2:30pm Sat & Sun) Ocean views and ridonkulous sunsets alone ought to be enough to bring folks in, but gourmet Driftwood steps up the food with seasonal menus centered around fresh, sustainable seafood, plus options for landlubbers. Inside it's all beachy casual, whitewashed and pale woods. And the cocktails are smart and creative.

Watermarc   AMERICAN $$$

(Map p282; ☑949-376-6272; www.watermarc restaurant.com; 448 S Coast Hwy; dinner mains $28-36; ⊙11am-10pm Sun-Thu, to 11pm Fri & Sat) At this stylish purveyor of New American cuisine, the small-plates menu ($8 to $15) ranges from filet mignon pot pie to sizzling garlic shrimp and New Zealand green lip mussels. In fact, appetizers are so good, and the cocktail list so inventive (blueberry-coconut mojito, anyone?), you might decide to skip the classic surf-and-turf dinners.

Mozambique   AFRICAN $$$

(Map p282; ☑949-715-7777; www.mozambique oc.com; 1740 S Coast Hwy; dinner mains $18-44; ⊙11am-10pm Mon-Thu, to midnight Fri & Sat, 10am-10pm Sun) Macaws and toucans welcome you to this trendy, sophisticated, three-level ode to exotically spiced dishes from southern Africa – peri-peri prawns, chicken pops, grilled pineapple to soaring steaks and seafood, in small plates to pricey surf and turf ($68). Who knows, you might see a *Real Housewives* cast member hiding out in the rooftop bar.

There's live music nightly; Sunday reggae gets jammed.

🍷 **Drinking & Nightlife**

There are almost as many watering holes in downtown's village as there are art galleries. Most cluster along S Coast Hwy and Ocean Ave, making for an easy pub crawl. If you drink, don't drive; local cops take driving under the influence (DUI) very seriously.

Although Laguna has one of SoCal's largest gay populations, the once-thriving gay nightlife has virtually vanished. The one remaining gay bar, **Main Street** (Map p282; ☑949-494-0056; www.mainstreet-bar.com; 1460 S Coast Hwy; ⊙4pm-2am Tue-Sat, to 10pm Sun; closing hours vary), is hit or miss.

FESTIVALS & THE CITY

With a dramatic canyon backdrop, Laguna's **Festival of Arts** (www.foapom.com; 650 Laguna Canyon Rd; admission $7-10; ⊙ usually 10am-11:30pm Jul & Aug; ➍) is a two-month celebration of original artwork in almost all its forms. About 140 exhibitors display artwork ranging from paintings and handcrafted furniture to scrimshaw. Begun in the 1930s by local artists looking to drum up buyers, the festival now attracts international patrons. In addition to the art show, there are kid-friendly art workshops and live music and entertainment daily. Across the road, look for the slightly more independent-minded **Sawdust Festival** (☑ 949-494-3030; www.sawdustartfestival.org; 935 Laguna Canyon Rd; adult/child 6-12yr/senior $8.50/4/7; ⊙ 10am-10pm late Jun–early Aug, to 6pm Sat & Sun late Nov–mid-Dec), which also hosts a more limited festival in late fall.

The most thrilling part of the main festival – an experience that will leave you rubbing your eyes in disbelief – is the **Pageant of the Masters** (☑ 800-487-3378; www.foapom. com; 650 Laguna Canyon Rd; tickets from $15; ⊙ 8:30pm daily mid-Jul–Aug) where human models blend seamlessly into re-creations of famous paintings. Tickets are hard to get (unless you order them months in advance) but you may be able to snag last-minute cancellations at the gate.

Laguna Beach Brewery & Grille
MICROBREWERY

(Map p282; ☑ 949-497-3381; www.lagunabeach brewery.net; 237 Ocean Ave; ⊙ 11:30am-10:30pm Tue-Thu, to 11:30pm Fri & Sat, 10am-9pm Sun) For pub grub and microbrews after a day of surfing, this place lines up copper vats behind the bar, pouring its own Miel de Laguna blond and Solar amber ales to go with regional Mexican cooking; homemade tortillas, Rosarito-style lobster tacos and ceviche. Kick back on the outdoor patio for primo people-watching. Live music Wednesdays to Saturdays.

Rooftop Lounge
BAR

(Map p282; www.rooftoplagunabeach.com; 1289 S Coast Hwy; ⊙ 11:30am-9pm Mon-Thu, to 10pm Fri & Sat, 10:30am-9pm Sun) Perched atop La Casa del Camino (p281), this bar, with 270-degree coastal views and a friendly vibe, has locals singing hallelujahs. Mango and wild berry mojitos add some spice to the cocktail menu, and you can snack on plates like meatballs in guava barbecue sauce.

Koffee Klatch
COFFEE

(Map p282; ☑ 949-376-6867; 1440 S Coast Hwy; ⊙ 7am-11pm; ☎) About a mile south of downtown, this cozy coffee shop with eclectic furniture draws an equally eclectic gay/straight/hipster crowd for coffees, breakfasts served all day, salads and ginormous cakes.

✪ Entertainment

Laguna Playhouse
THEATER

(Map p282; ☑ 949-497-2787; www.lagunaplay house.com; 606 Laguna Canyon Rd) Orange County's oldest continuously operating community theater stages lighter plays in summer, more serious works in winter.

🛍 Shopping

Downtown's village is a shopper's paradise, with hidden courtyards and eclectic little bungalows that beg further exploration. Forest Ave has the highest concentration of chic boutiques, but south of downtown, Pacific Coast Hwy has its fair share of fashionable and arty shops where you can balance your chakras or buy vintage rock albums and posters.

Hobie Surf Shop
SPORTS & OUTDOORS

(Map p282; ☑ 949-497-3304; www.hobiesurfshop. com; 294 Forest Ave; ⊙ 9am-7pm) Hobart 'Hobie' Alter started his internationally known surf line in his parents' Laguna Beach garage in 1950. Today, this is one of only a handful of logo retail shops where you can stock up on surfboards and beachwear (love those flip-flops in rainbow colors!) for both babes and dudes.

❶ Information

Visit Laguna Beach Visitors Center (☑ 949-497-9229; www.lagunabeachinfo.com; 381 Forest Ave; ⊙ 10am-5pm; ☎) Helpful staff, bus schedules, restaurant menus and free brochures on everything from hiking trails to self-guided walking tours.

❶ Getting There & Away

From I-405, take Hwy 133 (Laguna Canyon Rd) southwest. If you're coming from along the coast, Hwy 1 goes by several names in Laguna Beach: south of Broadway, downtown's main street, it's called South Coast Hwy; north of Broadway it's North Coast Hwy. Locals also call it Pacific Coast Hwy (PCH).

OCTA (p252) bus 1 heading along the coast connects Laguna Beach with Orange County's other beach towns, including Dana Point heading south, every 30 to 60 minutes. The one-way fare is $2 (exact change).

❶ Getting Around

BUS

Laguna Beach Transit (www.lagunabeachcity. net; 375 Broadway) has its central bus depot in downtown's village. Buses operate on three routes at hourly intervals (no service from 12:30pm to 1:30pm or on Sundays or public holidays). Routes are color-coded and are easy to follow. For tourists, the most important bus route is the red route that runs south of downtown along Pacific Coast Hwy. Rides cost 75¢ (exact change). All routes are free during July and August. You can pick up an information brochure and bus schedule at the **visitor center** (p285).

CAR & MOTORCYCLE

Through town, Pacific Coast Hwy moves slowly in summer, especially on weekends.

Parking lots in downtown's village charge between $10 and $20 per entry; they fill up early in the day during summer. Street parking can be hard to find near the beaches during summer, especially in the afternoons and on weekends – arrive early. Coin- and credit card–operated meters cost from $1 per hour and pay-and-display lots cost $2 per hour. Alternatively, you can park for free in residential areas, but obey time limits and posted restrictions, or you'll be towed.

FESTIVAL OF THE SWALLOWS

The famous swallows return to nest in the walls of Mission San Juan Capistrano every year around March 19, the feast of Saint Joseph, after wintering in South America. Their flight covers about 7500 miles each way. The highlight of the month-long **Festival of the Swallows** (Fiesta de las Golondrinas; ☏ 949-493-1976; www.swallowsparade. com; ☉ mid-Mar) is one of the largest nonmotorized parades in the country, which first took place in the 1930s.

If you can't find parking downtown, drive to the north or south ends of town by the beach, then ride the bus.

SHUTTLE

To alleviate summer traffic, **free trolley shuttles** travel between downtown and popular **Festival of Arts** (p285) sites in Laguna Canyon and north–south along Pacific Coast Hwy. These trolleys make continuous loops every 20 to 30 minutes between 9:30am and 11:30pm daily from late June until late August.

Around Laguna Beach

San Juan Capistrano

Famous for its swallows that fly back to town every year on March 19 (though sometimes they're just a bit early), San Juan Capistrano is home to the 'jewel of the California missions.' California missions were Roman Catholic outposts established in the late 18th and early 19th centuries. Amid that photogenic mission streetscape of adobe, tile-roofed buildings, and historic wood-built cottages, there's enough history and charm here to make almost a day of it.

'San Juan Cap' is a little town, just east of Dana Point and just over 10 miles southeast of downtown Laguna Beach.

◉ Sights

★ **Mission San Juan Capistrano** CHURCH (☏ 949-234-1300; www.missionsjc.com; 26801 Ortega Hwy; adult/child $9/6; ☉ 9am-5pm; ⊕) Plan on spending at least an hour poking around the sprawling mission's tiled roofs, covered arches, lush gardens, fountains and courtyards – including the padre's quarters, soldiers' barracks and the cemetery. Admission includes a worthwhile free audio tour with interesting stories narrated by locals. The mission is at the corner of Ortega Hwy and Camino Capistrano.

Particularly moving are the towering remains of the **Great Stone Church,** almost completely destroyed by a powerful earthquake on December 8, 1812. The **Serra Chapel** – whitewashed outside with restored frescoes inside – is believed to be the oldest existing building in California (1782). It's certainly the only one still standing in which Junípero Serra (the founder of the mission) gave Mass. Serra founded the mission on November 1, 1776, and tended it personally for many years.

There's a special audio tour for the elementary-school set, called Saved by the Mission Bell, included in children's admission.

Los Rios Historic District
HISTORIC SITE

One block southwest of the mission, next to the Capistrano train depot, this peaceful assemblage of a few dozen historic cottages and adobes now mostly houses cafes and gift shops. To see 1880s-era furnishings and decor, as well as vintage photographs, stop by the tiny **O'Neill Museum** (31831 Los Rios St; adult/child $1/50¢; ⊙9am-noon & 1-4pm Tue-Fri, noon-3pm Sat & Sun).

✖ Eating & Drinking

★El Campeon
MEXICAN $

(31921 Camino Capistrano, El Adobe Plaza; items $2-9; ⊙6:30am-9pm; ⊞) For real-deal Mexican food, in a strip mall south of the mission (p286), try this multiroom restaurant, *panadería* (bakery) and *mercado* (grocery store). Look for tacos, tostadas and burritos in freshly made tortillas, *pozole* (hominy stew) and pork *carnitas* served cafeteria-style, and *aguas frescas* (fruit drinks) in flavors like watermelon, strawberry and grapefruit.

★Ramos House Café
CALIFORNIAN $$

(✆949-443-1342; www.ramoshouse.com; 31752 Los Rios St; weekday mains $17-21, weekend brunch $44; ⊙8:30am-3pm) The best spot for breakfast or lunch in Los Rios Historic District (p287), this Old West–flavored, wood-built house from 1881 (with brick patio) docs organically raised comfort food flavored with herbs grown on-site: blueberry *pain perdu* (French toast) with lemon curd, apple-cinnamon beignets, basil-cured salmon lox or spicy crab-cake salad with smoked chili rémoulade. Breads are baked in-house daily.

El Adobe de Capistrano
MEXICAN $$

(www.eladobedecapistrano.com; 31891 Camino Capistrano; mains lunch $11-24, dinner $16-38; ⊙11am-9pm Mon-Thu, to 10pm Fri & Sat, 10am-9pm Sun) In a building that traces its origins to 1797, this sprawling, beam-ceilinged 'Mexican steakhouse' and bar does a big business in the standards (enchiladas, fajitas) through to blackened fish or lobster tacos, garlic shrimp and grilled steaks. It was a favorite of President Nixon, who lived in nearby San Clemente, which might be good or bad depending on your outlook.

Coach House
CLUB

(✆949-496-8930; www.thecoachhouse.com; 33157 Camino Capistrano; ⊙hours vary) Long-running live-music venue featuring a roster of local and national rock, indie, alternative and tribute bands; expect a cover charge of $15 to $40, depending on who's playing. Recent performers include classic rockers like Blue Öyster Cult, rockers Los Lonely Boys, plus comedy acts like Louie Anderson. Check the website for show times.

ℹ Getting There & Away

From Laguna Beach, ride **OCTA** (p252) bus 1 south to Dana Point. At the intersection of Pacific Coast Hwy and Del Obispo St, catch bus 91 northbound toward Mission Viejo, which drops you near the mission. Buses run every 30 to 60 minutes. The trips takes about an hour. You'll have to pay the one-way fare ($2, exact change) twice.

Drivers should take I-5 exit 82 (Ortega Hwy), then head west about 0.25 miles. There's free three-hour parking on streets and in municipal lots.

The **Amtrak** (✆800-872-7245; www.amtrak. com; 26701 Verdugo St) depot is one block south and west of the mission. You could arrive by train from LA ($21, 75 minutes) or San Diego ($22, 90 minutes) in time for lunch, visit the mission and be back in the city for dinner. A few daily **Metrolink** (✆800-371-5465; www.metrolink-trains.com) commuter trains link San Juan Capistrano to Orange ($8, 45 minutes), with limited connections to Anaheim.

Dana Point

Dana Point was once called 'the only romantic spot on the coast.' Too bad that quote dates from seafarer Richard Dana's voyage here in the 1830s. Its built-up, parking-lotted harbor detracts from the charm its neighbors have, but it still gets a lot of visitors to its lovely beaches and port for whale-watching, sportfishing and the like.

◎ Sights

Most attractions cluster in and around artificial Dana Point Harbor, at the foot of Golden Lantern St, just south of Pacific Coast Hwy off Dana Point Harbor Dr.

Doheny State Beach
BEACH

(✆949-496-6171; www.dohenystatebeach.org; 25300 Dana Point Harbor Dr; per car $15; ⊙park 6am-10pm, visitor center 10am-4pm Wed-Sun; 🅿⊞) Adjacent to the southern border of Dana Point Harbor, this mile-long beach is great for swimmers, surfers, surf fishers and tide poolers. You'll also find picnic tables with grills, volleyball courts and a butterfly exhibit at the 62-acre coastal park. Stop by the park's **visitor center** to check out the five aquariums, mounted birds and 500-gallon simulated tide pool. Free wi-fi at the snack bar.

Ocean Institute   MUSEUM

(☑949-496-2274; www.ocean-institute.org; 24200 Dana Pt Harbor Dr; adult/child 2-12yr $10/7.50; ☺10am-4pm Mon-Fri, 10am-3pm Sat & Sun, last entry 2:15pm; ℗☖) ✐ This child-friendly educational center encompasses four separate ocean-centric 'adventures.' It is mostly reserved for school groups on weekdays, so it's best to come on weekends to enjoy the interactive marine-focused exhibits. On Sundays, admission includes the opportunity to discover what life was like aboard an early 19th-century tall ship, the brig **Pilgrim**. Guided tours of this full-size replica of the ship sailed by Richard Dana during his journey around Cape Horn to California are offered hourly.

Salt Creek Beach   BEACH

(☑949-923-2280; www.ocparks.com/beaches/salt; 33333 S Pacific Coast Hwy, off Ritz Carlton Dr; ☺5am-midnight; ℗) Just south of the Laguna Beach boundary, this 18-acre county-run park is popular with surfers, sunbathers, bodysurfers and tide poolers. Families make the most of the park's picnic tables, grills, restrooms and showers – all sprawling beneath the elegant bluff-top Ritz-Carlton resort. Open in summer, a beach concession stand rents boogie boards, beach chairs and umbrellas. Pay-and-display parking costs $1 per hour. Call ahead to check the center's opening times, which are subject to change.

🏃 Activities

Rent bicycles at **Wheel Fun Rentals** (☑949-496-7433; www.wheelfunrentals.com; 25300 Dana Point Harbor Dr; cruiser rental per hour/day $10/28; ☺9am-sunset daily late May-early Sep, Sat & Sun early Sep-late May) at Doheny State Beach. Off Dana Point Harbor Dr, **Capo Beach Watercraft Rentals** (☑949-661-1690; www.capobeachwatercraft.com; 34512 Embarcadero Pl; jet ski before/after 11:30am per hour Mon-Fri $85/105, Sat & Sun $100/120) and **Pure Watersports Dana Point** (Dana Point Jet Ski & Kayak Center; ☑949-661-4947; www.danapointjetski.com; 34671 Puerto Pl; rentals per hr kayak and SUP from $15, jet ski from $95; ☺10am-6pm Mon-Fri, from 9am Sat & Sun) both rent kayaks for harbor paddling. For scuba rentals and dive-boat trips (from $120), try **Beach Cities Scuba** (☑949-443-3858; www.beachcitiesscuba.com; 34283 Pacific Coast Hwy; rentals without/with snorkeling gear $65/95, dive boat trips $120; ☺hours vary).

 Tours

In Mariner's Village off Dana Point Harbor Dr, Dana Wharf is the starting point for most boat tours and trips to Catalina Island. For more kid-friendly whale-watching tours and coastal cruises, book ahead with the Ocean Institute.

Capt Dave's Dolphin & Whale Safari   BOATING

(☑949-488-2828; www.dolphinsafari.com; 34451 Ensenada Pl; adult/child 3-12yr from $65/45) This popular outfit runs year-round dolphin- and whale-watching trips on a catamaran equipped with underwater viewing pods and a listening system for you to hear what's going on below the surface.

Dana Wharf Sportfishing   BOATING

(☑888-224-0603; www.danawharf.com; 34675 Golden Lantern St; sportfishing trips adult/child 3-12yr/senior from $46/29/41, whale-watching tours from $45/29/35) Half-day sportfishing trips are best for beginners. Whale-watching tours for families operate both winter and summer.

🎊 Festivals & Events

Doheny Blues Festival   MUSIC

(www.omegaevents.com/dohenyblues; Doheny State Beach; ☺mid-May) Blues, rock and soul legends perform alongside up-and-comers over a weekend of funky live-music performances and family fun at Doheny State Beach. Recent headliners have included Joe Walsh, Melissa Etheridge, Mavis Staples and Chris Isaak.

Festival of Whales   STREET CARNIVAL, CULTURAL

(www.dpfestivalofwhales.com; ☺early–mid-Mar) For two weekends, a parade, street fair, nature walks and talks, canoe races, surfing clinics, art exhibitions, live music, and surf 'woody' wagon and hot-rod show make up the merriment.

Tall Ships Festival   FAIR, SAILING

(www.tallshipsfestival.com; ☺early Sep; ☖) The Ocean Institute (p288) hosts the West Coast's largest gathering of tall ships, with living-history encampments, themed meals (mermaid breakfast, anyone?), scrimshaw carving demonstrations and lots more family-friendly marine-themed activities.

🛏 Sleeping & Eating

There are plenty of midrange chain motels near the Dana Point harbor, along Pacific Coast Hwy. At the top end of the spectrum is the oceanfront stunner, the **Ritz-Carlton Laguna Niguel** (☑949-240-2000; www.ritz carlton.com; 1 Ritz-Carlton Dr; r from $599; P ❸ ✱ @ 🀆 ✖), well-positioned for catching sunsets at Salt Creek Beach. For budget motels, head inland along I-405 (San Diego Fwy) back toward Irvine.

Jon's Fish Market   SEAFOOD $
(☑949-496-2807; 34665 Golden Lantern; mains $11-17; ☺11am-7pm Sun-Thu, to 8pm Fri & Sat, open 1hr later in summer; 🐾) Nothin' fancy about this counter-service fish market, where they do large, hearty portions of deep-fried ocean goodness: famous fish and chips, scallops, clams, shrimp and calamari, all with fries and coleslaw. Eat inside or on the dock.

Turk's   GRILL $$
(☑949-496-9028; 34683 Golden Lantern St; mains $5-16; ☺8am-2am, shorter hrs winter) At Dana Wharf, this trapped-in-amber dive bar is so dark it feels like you're drinking while jailed in the brig of a ship, but never mind. There's plenty of good pub grub (including burgers and fish-and-chips), Bloody Marys and beers, a mellow crowd and a groovy jukebox.

❶ Information

Dana Point Chamber of Commerce & Visitor Center (☑949-248-3501; www.danapoint.org; cnr Golden Lantern & Dana Point Harbor Dr; ☺9am-4pm Fri-Sun late May-early Sep) Stop at this tiny booth for tourist brochures and maps. Gung-ho volunteers sure love their city.

❶ Getting There & Away

From the harbor, **Catalina Express** (☑800-481-3470; www.catalinaexpress.com; 34675 Golden Lantern St; round-trip adult/child 2-11yr/senior $76.50/70/61) makes daily round-trips to Catalina Island, taking 90 minutes each way.

OCTA (p252) bus 1 connects Dana Point with the OC's other beach towns every 30 to 60 minutes. The one-way fare is $2 (exact change).

Four-hour public parking at the harbor is free, or pay $5 per day (overnight $10).

San Clemente

Just before reaching San Diego County, Pacific Coast Highway (PCH) slows down and rolls past the laid-back surf town of San Clemente. Home to surfing legends, top-

TRESTLES

Surfers won't want to miss world-renowned Trestles, in protected **San Onofre State Beach** (☑949-492-4872; www.parks.ca.gov; parking per day $15; P), just southeast of San Clemente. This beach is famous for its natural surf break that consistently churns out perfect waves, even in summer. There are also rugged bluff-top walking trails, swimming beaches and a developed inland **campground** (p290).

Trestles is also a great success story for environmentalists and surfers, who for over a decade fought the extension of a nearby toll road. Visit savetrestles. surfrider.org to learn more.

To reach the beach, exit I-5 at Basilone Rd, then hoof to Trestles along the nature trail.

notch surfboard companies, the Surfing Heritage & Culture Center and the dearly departed *Surfing* magazine (1964–2017), this unpretentious enclave may be one of the last spots in the OC where you can authentically live the surf lifestyle. Right on, brah.

The city center is also one of SoCal's most picturesque as the sun glimmers off the ocean. Head south off PCH and follow **Avenida del Mar** as it winds south through San Clemente's retro downtown district, where antiques and vintage shops, eclectic boutiques, cafes, restaurants and bars line the main drag. Keep curving downhill toward the ocean.

Further south along the coast, at the foot of Trafalgar Street, **T-Street** is a popular surf break, as is Trestles Beach in San Onofre State Beach (p289).

◉ Sights

San Clemente Pier   PIER
(611 Avenida Victoria; ☺4am-midnight; P) San Clemente City Beach stretches alongside this historic 1296ft-long, wood-built pier. The original 1928 pier, where Prohibition-era bootleggers once brought liquor ashore, was rebuilt most recently in 1985. Surfers go north of the pier, while swimmers and bodysurfers take the south side.

Surfing Heritage & Culture Center MUSEUM
(☑949-388-0313; www.surfingheritage.org; 110 Calle Iglesia; suggested donation $5; ☺11am-4pm

Mon-Sat; P) **FREE** This foundation gives a timeline of surfing history by exhibiting surfboards ridden by the greats from Duke Kahanamoku to Kelly Slater, and its photo archive has some 100,000 photos (a tiny fraction may be on display at any one time). Temporary exhibits (photos, skateboarding, and more) change out approximately every three months.

🛏 Sleeping

There's lovely lodging right across from the pier and worthwhile campgrounds at **San Onofre State Beach** (☎949-361-2531, reservations 800-444-7275; www.reserveamerica.com; San Mateo Campground, 830 Cristianitos Rd, San Onofre State Beach; San Mateo sites $40-65, bluff sites $40; P). There are also chain motels further inland, closer to the 5 Freeway.

★ Casa Tropicana   BOUTIQUE HOTEL $$$

(☎949-492-1234, 800-492-1245; www.casatropicana.com; 610 Avenida Victoria; r incl breakfast $250-350; P ❄ @ ☎) Right across from the pier for amazing sunsets, the breezy B&B rooms at this delightful boutique hotel all have contemporary beachy design, private Jacuzzi baths, fireplace and ocean-view decks. Rates include a nice breakfast basket and snacks and coffee in the 2nd-floor lounge.

✗ Eating

Bagel Shack   BREAKFAST $

(☎949-388-0745; www.thebagelshack.com; 777 S El Camino Real; mains $4-8; ⊙5:30am-2:30pm) Wet suit–clad crowds frequent this tiki-style breakfast and lunch place, which serves both OG breakfast sandwiches (lox and cream cheese) to new-style Cali creations like the Upper (steak, eggs, caramelized onions and pepper jack cheese). Lunch sandwiches are more predictable. They blend fruit smoothies, too. It's directly uphill from T-Street.

Pierside Kitchen & Bar   AMERICAN $$

(☎949-218-0980; www.piersidesc.com; 610 Avenida Victoria; mains $14-28; ⊙11am-11pm Mon-Thu, 11am-1am Fri, 9am-1am Sat, 9am-11pm Sun) The name really says it all at this urbane spot across from the water. Get a table by the window for the best ocean views as you chomp on a modern California menu (kale Caesar salad, bacon-wrapped dates, braised short ribs, ginger soy scallops) with some crazy-cat twists like chowder fries. Weekend brunch gets rocking with live music.

Fisherman's Restaurant & Bar   SEAFOOD $$$

(☎949-498-6390; www.thefishermansrestaurant.com; 611 Avenida Victoria; mains lunch $11-21, dinner $14-54; ⊙8am-9:30pm Sun-Thu, to 10pm Fri & Sat) Right on the pier, Fisherman's chowders, fish and chips and mesquite-grilled fresh catches come with a side of incomparable ocean views. Generous four-course Fisherman's Feasts ($29-62 per person, two or more guests) offer clams, chowder, salad and your choice of fish. Sure, you'll be with tourists (see 'right on the pier'), but hey, you're a tourist too, right? Embrace it.

🛍 Shopping

One highlight of San Clemente's shopping scene is Avenida del Mar as it slopes downhill from city hall southwest toward the beach. The tree-lined street has a low-to-the-ground feel with little boutiques selling clothing, crafts, furniture and shoes, plus cafes and specialty shops.

Rocket Fizz   FOOD & DRINKS

(☎949-492-0099; www.rocketfizz.com; 107 Avenida del Mar; ⊙11am-8:30pm Mon-Wed, 10:30am-9pm Thu & Sun, 10:30am-9:30pm Fri & Sat) This 'soda pop and candy shop' fits perfectly in picturesque San Clemente. Rocket Fizz sells old-timey American penny candy like saltwater taffy and Jolly Ranchers, plus treats from around the world (German Ritter Sport to Japanese Pocky). Then there are the unusually flavored sodas from the sublime (strawberry shortcake) to the ridiculous (peanut butter and jelly).

ℹ Getting There & Away

OCTA (p252) bus 1 heads south from Dana Point every 30 to 60 minutes. At San Clemente's **Metrolink station** (☎800-371-5465; www.metrolinktrains.com), transfer to OCTA bus 191, which runs hourly to San Clemente Pier. Unless you have a bus pass, you'll need to pay the one-way fare ($2, exact change) twice.

At least two daily **Amtrak** (☎800-872-7245; www.amtrak.com) trains between San Diego ($21, 75 minutes) and LA ($23, 90 minutes), via San Juan Capistrano and Anaheim, stop at San Clemente Pier.

San Clemente is about 6 miles southeast of Dana Point via Pacific Coast Highway. Pay-and-display parking at the pier costs $1 per hour, though good luck finding a space at peak times.

Palm Springs & the Deserts

Best Places to Eat

➜ La Copine (p310)

➜ Workshop Kitchen
+ Bar (p302)

➜ Cheeky's (p301)

➜ Red Ocotillo (p317)

➜ Inn Dining Room (p330)

Best Places to Sleep

➜ El Morocco Inn & Spa (p299)

➜ La Casa del Zorro (p316)

➜ Rimrock Ranch
Cabins (p311)

➜ L'Horizon (p298)

➜ Sacred Sands (p310)

Why Go?

There's something undeniably artistic in the way the land-scape unfolds in the California desert. Weathered volcanic peaks stand sentinel over singing sand dunes and mountains shimmering in hues from mustard yellow to vibrant pink. Hot mineral water spurts from the earth's belly to feed palm oases and soothe aching muscles in stylish spas. Tiny wildflowers push up from the hard-baked soil to celebrate springtime.

The riches of the desert soil have lured prospectors and miners, while its beauty and spirituality have tugged at the hearts of artists, visionaries and wanderers. Eccentrics, mis-fits and the military are drawn by its vastness and solitude. Hipsters and celebs come for the climate and retro flair, es-pecially in unofficial desert capital, Palm Springs. Through it all threads iconic Route 66, lined with moodily rusting roadside relics. No matter what your trail, the desert will creep into your consciousness and never fully leave.

When to Go
Palm Springs

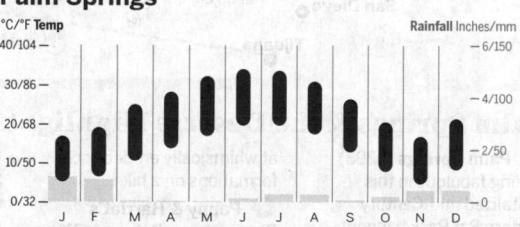

Dec–Apr Moder-ate temperatures lure in 'snowbirds' and LA week-end-trippers.

May–mid-Jun, mid-Sep–Nov Crowds thin out as temperatures arc during shoulder season.

Jun–Sep Some inns and restau-rants close in summer's heat; many of the rest offer great deals.

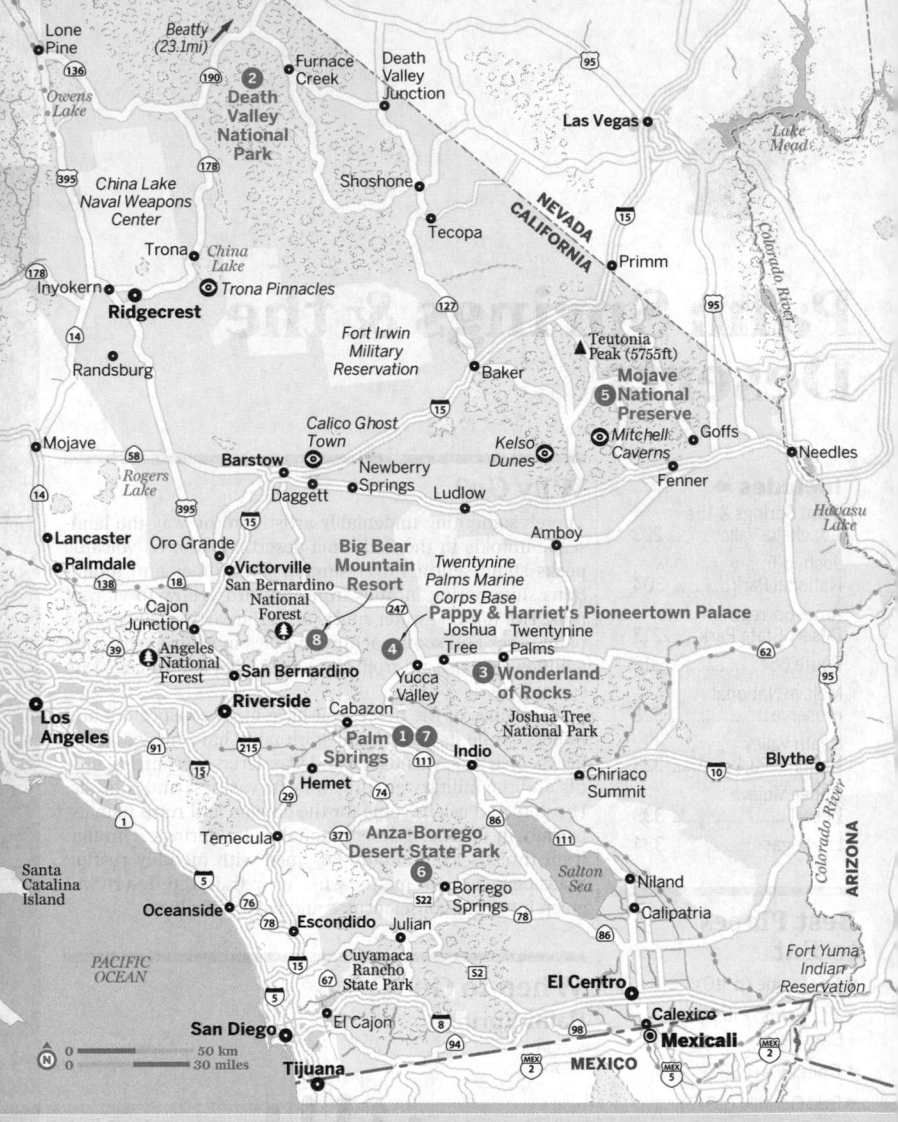

Palm Springs & the Deserts Highlights

1 **Palm Springs** (p293) Feeling fabulous in this revitalized mid-Century Modern Rat Pack hangout.

2 **Death Valley National Park** (p323) Traversing ethereal landscapes to the lowest point in the western hemisphere.

3 **Wonderland of Rocks** (p305) Marveling at whimsically eroded rock formations on a hike.

4 **Pappy & Harriet's Pioneertown Palace** (p311) Spending a rollickin' evening in a quintessential honky-tonk.

5 **Mojave National Preserve** (p322) Camping out under the stars in this starkly beautiful desert.

6 **Anza-Borrego Desert State Park** (p313) Hunting rare elephant trees and scrambling around wind caves.

7 **Palm Springs Aerial Tramway** (p295) Ascending through five zones in 10 minutes.

8 **Big Bear Mountain Resort** (p231) Schussing down the mountain in SoCal's premier ski resort.

Palm Springs & The Coachella Valley

The Rat Pack is back, baby, or at least its hangout is. In the 1950s and '60s, Palm Springs, some 100 miles east of LA, was the swinging getaway of Sinatra, Elvis and other Hollywood stars. Once the Rat Pack packed it in, though, Palm Springs surrendered to golfing retirees. However, in the mid-1990s, new generations discovered the city's retro-chic vibe and elegant mid-Century Modern structures built by famous architects. Today, retirees and snowbirds mix comfortably with hipsters, hikers and a sizeable LGBT community, on getaways from LA or from across the globe.

Palm Springs is the principal city of the Coachella Valley, a string of desert towns ranging from ho-hum Cathedral City to glamtastic Palm Desert and Coachella, home of the star-studded music festival, all linked by Hwy 111. North of Palm Springs, scruffy Desert Hot Springs draws visitors with chic boutique hotels built on top of soothing springs.

History

Cahuilla (ka-wee-ya) tribespeople have lived in the canyons on the southwest edge of the Coachella Valley for over 1000 years. Early Spanish explorers called the hot springs beneath Palm Springs *agua caliente* (hot water), which later became the name of the local Cahuilla tribe.

In 1876 the federal government carved the valley into a checkerboard of various interests. The Southern Pacific Railroad received odd-numbered sections, while the Agua Caliente were given even-numbered sections as their reservation. Casinos have made the tribes quite wealthy today.

In the town of Indio, about 20 miles southeast of Palm Springs, date palms were imported from French-held Algeria in 1890 and have become the valley's major crop, along with citrus and table grapes.

⊙ Sights

Most sights are in Palm Springs proper but there are a few blue-chip destinations such as Sunnylands (p299) or the Living Desert Zoo & Gardens (p296) worth the drive down valley.

⊙ Palm Springs

★ Palm Springs Art Museum   MUSEUM

(☑760-322-4800; www.psmuseum.org; 101 Museum Dr, Palm Springs; adult/student $12.50/free, all free 4-8pm Thu; ⊙10am-5pm Sun-Tue & Sat, noon-9pm Thu & Fri; ℗) Art fans should not miss this museum which presents changing exhibitions drawn from its stellar collection of international modern and contemporary painting, sculpture, photography and glass art. The permanent collection includes works by Henry Moore, Ed Ruscha, Mark di Suvero, Frederic Remington and many more heavy hitters. Other highlights are glass art by Dale Chihuly and William Morris and a collection of pre-Columbian figurines.

Palm Springs Art Museum, Architecture & Design Center   MUSEUM

(☑760-423-5260; www.psmuseum.org/architecture-design-center; 300 S Palm Canyon Dr, Palm Springs; ⊙10am-5pm Sat-Tue, noon-9pm Thu & Fri) **FREE** Showcasing changing exhibits drawn from the Palm Springs Art Museum's architecture and design collection, the center occupies an iconic and spiffily restored 1961 mid-Century Modern bank building by E Stewart Williams.

McCallum Adobe   NOTABLE BUILDING

(☑760-323-8297; www.pshistoricalsociety.org; 221 S Palm Canyon Dr, Palm Springs; adult/child $1/free; ⊙10am-4pm Mon & Wed-Sat, noon-3pm Sun) The town's oldest building, the 1884 McCallum Adobe, was built for John McCallum, the first permanent white settler. Today, the Palm Springs Historical Society presents changing exhibits of photos and memorabilia on the region's storied past, complemented by an engaging 24-minute video.

Agua Caliente Cultural Museum   MUSEUM

(☑760-778-1079; www.accmuseum.org; 219 S Palm Canyon Dr, Village Green Heritage Center; ⊙10am-5pm Wed-Sun Sep-May, Fri-Sun Jun-Aug) **FREE** This museum showcases the history and culture of the Agua Caliente band of Cahuilla people through permanent and changing exhibits and special events.

Ruddy's 1930s General Store Museum   MUSEUM

(☑760-327-2156; www.palmsprings.com/points/heritage/ruddy.html; 221 S Palm Canyon Dr; adult/child 95¢/free; ⊙10am-4pm Thu-Sun Oct-Jun, Sat & Sun Jul-Sep) This original 1930s general

PALM SPRINGS & THE DESERTS PALM SPRINGS & THE COACHELLA VALLEY

Palm Springs

N 0 ——— 500 m
0 ——— 0.25 miles

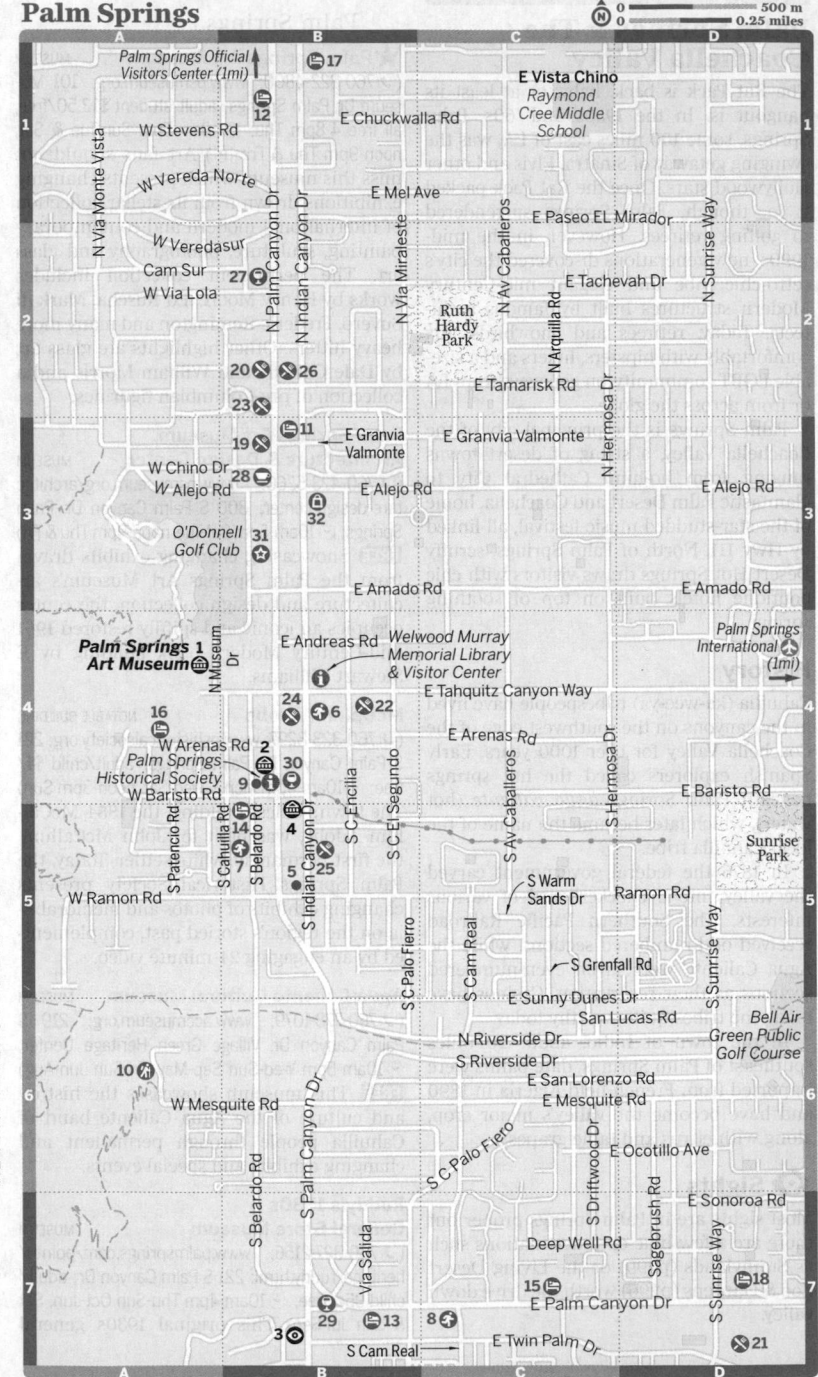

Palm Springs

store shows amazingly preserved original products from groceries to medicines, beauty aids to clothing and hardware, with period showcases and signage.

Palm Springs Air Museum MUSEUM
(☏ 760-778-6262; www.palmspringsairmuseum. org; 745 N Gene Autry Trail, Palm Springs; adult/child $16.50/9.50; ⊗ 10am-5pm; 🅿) Adjacent to the airport, this museum has an exceptional collection of WWII aircraft and flight memorabilia, a movie theater and occasional flight demonstrations. You can even climb inside functioning Boeing B17 Flying Fortress, a bomber extensively used against German industrial and military sites during WWII.

Moorten Botanical Gardens GARDENS
(☏ 760-327-6555; www.moortenbotanicalgarden. com; 1701 S Palm Canyon Dr, Palm Springs; adult/child $5/2; ⊗ 10am-4pm Thu-Tue Oct-May, Fri-Sun only Jun-Sep) Chester 'Cactus Slim' Moorten, one of the original Keystone Cops, and his wife Patricia channeled their passion for plants into this compact garden founded in 1938. Today, a stroll through this enchanting symphony of cacti, succulents and other desert flora is balm for eyes and soul.

◉ Around Palm Springs

★ **Palm Springs Aerial Tramway** CABLE CAR
(☏ 760-325-1391, 888-515-8726; www.pstramway. com; 1 Tram Way, Palm Springs; adult/child $26/17, parking $5; ⊗ 1st tram up 10am Mon-Fri, 8am Sat & Sun, last tram down 9:45pm daily, varies seasonally; 🅿 ♿) This rotating cable car climbs nearly 6000 vertical feet and covers five different vegetation zones, from the Sonoran desert floor to pine-scented Mt San Jacinto State Park, in 10 minutes during its 2.5-mile journey. From the mountain station (8561ft), which is 30°F to 40°F (up to 22°C) cooler than the desert floor, you can enjoy stupendous views, dine in two restaurants (ask about ride 'n' dine passes), explore over 50 miles of trails or visit the natural-history museum.

The valley station is about 3.5 miles off Hwy 111; the turnoff is about 3 miles north of downtown Palm Springs. Cars depart every 30 minutes and more frequently during peak times. Online tickets are available from six weeks to 24 hours in advance and highly recommended to avoid often horrendous wait times.

★ **Living Desert Zoo & Gardens**   ZOO
(☎760-346-5694; www.livingdesert.org; 47900 Portola Ave, Palm Desert; adult/child $20/10; ☺9am-5pm Oct-May, 8am-1:30pm Jun-Sep; P 🖾) 🖋 This amazing animal park showcases desert plants and animals alongside exhibits on regional geology and Native American culture. Highlights include a walk-through wildlife hospital and an African-themed village with a fair-trade market and storytelling grove. Camel rides, giraffe feeding, a spin on the endangered species carousel, and a hop-on, hop-off shuttle cost extra. It's educational, fun and worth the 15-mile drive down-valley.

Shields Date Garden   GARDENS
(☎760-347-7768; www.shieldsdategarden.com; 80-225 Hwy 111, Indio; ☺9am-5pm; P 🖾) **FREE** In business since 1924, this kooky roadside attraction is where you can watch the 15-minute documentary, *Romance and Sex Life of the Date,* try a date shake, stock up on plump blondes and brunettes (dates, that is) and, incongruously, tour a garden accented with biblical statuary.

🏃 **Activities**

★ **Indian Canyons**   HIKING
(☎760-323-6018; www.indian-canyons.com; 38520 S Palm Canyon Dr, Palm Springs; adult/child $9/5, 90min guided hike $3/2; ☺8am-5pm Oct-Jun, Fri-Sun only Jul-Sep) Streams flowing from the San Jacinto Mountains sustain rich plant varieties in oases around Palm Springs. Home to Native American communities for centuries, these canyons are a hiker's delight. Follow the Palm Canyon trail

---

WHAT THE...?

West of Palm Springs, you may do a double take when you glimpse 'Dinny the Dinosaur' and 'Mr Rex' from the I-10 at **World's Biggest Dinosaurs** (☎951-922-8700; www.cabazondinosaurs. com; 50770 Seminole Dr, Cabazon; adult/child $10/9; ☺10am-4:30pm Mon-Fri, 9am-6:30pm Sat & Sun; P 🖾). Claude K Bell, a sculptor for Knott's Berry Farm, spent over a decade crafting these concrete behemoths in the 1980s. Today you can pan for dino fossils, climb inside Rex's mouth, marvel at dozens of dinosaur models and stock up on dino souvenirs in the gift shop.

---

to the world's largest oasis of fan-palm trees, the Murray Canyon trail to a seasonal waterfall or the Andreas Canyon trail to rock formations along a year-round creek.

From downtown Palm Springs, head south on Palm Canyon Dr (continue straight when the main road turns east) for about 2 miles to the reservation entrance. From here, it's 3 miles up to the trading post and ticket booth.

Tahquitz Canyon   HIKING
(☎760-416-7044; www.tahquitzcanyon.com; 500 W Mesquite Ave, Palm Springs; adult/child $12.50/6; ☺7:30am-5pm Oct-Jun, Fri-Sun only Jul-Sep) A historic and sacred centerpiece for the Agua Caliente people, this canyon featured in the 1937 Frank Capra movie *Lost Horizon.* The visitor center has natural- and cultural-history exhibits and shows a video about the legend of Tahquitz, a shaman of the Cahuilla people. A 2-mile fairly steep and rocky trail loops around to a 60ft waterfall.

Bring a picnic, water and be sure to wear sneakers or hiking boots. Self-hiking is available until 3:30pm. Alternatively, join a 2½-hour ranger-led hike offered four times daily; reserve in advance.

In the 1960s the canyon was taken over by teenage squatters and soon became a point of contention between tribespeople, law-enforcement agencies and the squatters themselves. After the latter were booted out, it took the tribe years to haul out trash, erase graffiti and restore the site to its natural state.

Mt San Jacinto State Park   HIKING
(☎951-659-2607; www.parks.ca.gov) 🖋 **FREE** The wilderness beyond the Palm Springs Aerial Tramway mountain station is crisscrossed by 54 miles of hiking trails, including the mile-long Discovery Trail and a nontechnical but strenuous 11-mile round-trip up Mt San Jacinto (10,834ft). Free day-use wilderness permits are available at the ranger station near the tram terminal.

Applications for overnight trips cost $5 per person and can be sent in up to eight weeks in advance. See the website for the form and instructions.

Wet 'n' Wild Palm Springs   WATER PARK
(☎760-327-0499; www.wetnwildpalmsprings.com; 1500 S Gene Autry Trail, Palm Springs; adult $40, child & senior $30; ☺Apr–mid-Oct; 🖾) To keep cool on hot days, Wet 'n' Wild boasts a massive wave pool, thunderous water slides, tube rides and Flowrider surfing simulator. Some have minimum height requirements.

Call or check the website for current opening hours. Parking costs $10.

Smoke Tree Stables   HORSEBACK RIDING
(☑ 760-327-1372; www.smoketreestables.com; 2500 S Toledo Ave, Palm Springs; 1/2hr guided ride $50/120; ☺ 1hr rides hourly 8am-3pm, 2hr rides 9am, 11am & 1pm; 🐴) Near the Indian Canyons, this outfit offers public one-hour guided horse rides along the base of the mountains and two-hour tours into palm-lined Murray Canyon. Both are geared toward novice riders. Reservations are not needed but call to confirm departure times. Private tours are available by arrangement.

Stand By Golf   GOLF
(☑ 760-321-2665; www.standbygolf.com; ☺ 7am-7pm) Golf is huge here, with more than 100 public, semiprivate, private and resort golf courses scattered around the valley. This outfit books tee times for discounted same-day or next-day play at a few dozen local courses. Golf-club rentals and online bookings available.

Winter Adventure Center SKIING, SNOWSHOEING
(☑ general info 760-325-1449; www.pstramway. com/winter-adventure-center.html; snowshoe/skis rental per day $18/21; ☺ open seasonally 10am-4pm Thu-Fri & Mon, from 9am Sat & Sun, last rentals 2:30pm) Outside the Palm Springs Aerial Tramway mountain station, this outfit gets you into the snowy backcountry on snowshoes and cross-country skis, available on a first-come, first-served basis.

☞ Tours

★ Desert Tasty Tours   TOURS
(☑ 760-870-1133; www.deserttastytours.com; tours $65; ☺ 11am Mon-Sat) Get the inside scoop of Palm Springs' rejuvenated dining scene on three-hour walking tours of Palm Canyon Dr. A snack is served at each of the seven stops. Also available along El Paseo in Palm Desert.

★ Palm Springs Modern Tours   TOURS
(☑ 760-318-6118; www.palmspringsmoderntours. com; tours $85; ☺ 9:30am & 1:30pm) Three-hour minivan tour of mid-Century Modern architectural jewels by such masters as Albert Frey, Richard Neutra and John Lautner. Reservations required since the group size is restricted to a maximum of six. Private tours available.

Historical Walking Tours   TOURS
(☑ 760-323-8297; www.pshistoricalsociety.org; 221 S Palm Canyon Dr, Palm Springs; tours $20) The Palm Springs Historical Society (PSHS) runs

ELVIS HONEYMOON HIDEAWAY

Elvis and Priscilla Presley had stayed at the iconic 1960 **Alexander Estate** (☑ 760-322-1192; www.elvishoneymoon. com; 1350 Ladera Circle, Palm Springs; per person $30; ☺ tours 1pm & 3:30pm or by appointment) in 1966 and liked it so much that Elvis carried his new bride over the threshold to begin their honeymoon on May 1, 1967. Nicknamed the 'House of Tomorrow,' it consists of three floors of four concentric circles accented with glass and stone throughout. Book ahead for a chance to walk in the footsteps of the king (and even sit on his honeymoon bed!).

this bouquet of seven tours lasting between one and 2½ hours and covering history, architecture, Hollywood stars and more. Check the website for the schedule and to purchase advance tickets. Tickets are also sold at the PSHS office.

Best of the Best Tours   TOURS
(☑ 760-320-1365; www.thebestofthebesttours. com; 471 S Indian Canyon Dr, Palm Springs; tours $40-100) Established company offers tours of the Indian Canyons ($50), celebrity homes ($40), the windmills ($40) and a combination of all three ($100). Tickets must be bought in advance. Small discounts for children and seniors.

Desert Adventures   TOURS
(☑ 760-340-2345; www.red-jeep.com; tours $135-200) This outfit runs Jeep tours where you get to straddle the San Andreas Fault, explore the Indian Canyons or crisscross Joshua Tree National Park.

✪ Festivals & Events

Palm Springs and the other Coachella towns have a busy schedule of events and festivals, especially in winter. Rooms usually book out during the biggest ones such as the Coachella Music & Arts Festival and the Stagecoach Festival (p298).

★ Coachella Music & Arts Festival MUSIC
(☑ 855-771-3667; www.coachella.com; 81800 Ave 51, Indio; general/VIP $399/899; ☺ Apr) Held at Indio's Empire Polo Club over two weekends in April, this is one of the hottest indie-music festivals of its kind featuring

major headliners and the stars of tomorrow. Get tickets early or forget about it.

Desert Trip
MUSIC

(http://deserttrip.com; ⊙ mid-Oct) Debuted in 2016 and held at the same venue as Coachella (p297), albeit in autumn, this two-weekend festival has been nicknamed 'Oldchella' for the OG rockers gigged in: the Rolling Stones, Bob Dylan, Styx, Kansas and more.

Stagecoach Festival
MUSIC

(www.stagecoachfestival.com; $329) Held at Indio's Empire Polo Club, this festival celebrates new and established country-music artists.

Palm Springs
International Film Festival
FILM

(☎ 760-322-2930; www.psfilmfest.org; ⊙ early Jan) January brings a Hollywood-star-studded two-week film festival, showing more than 200 films from around the world. A short-film festival follows in June.

Modernism Week
CULTURAL

(www.modernismweek.com; ⊙ mid-Feb) Ten-day celebration of all things mid-Century Modern: architecture and home tours, films, lectures, design show and lots of parties. There are more than 250 events but tickets to some sell out quickly.

Villagefest
FOOD & DRINK

(http://villagefest.org; S Palm Canyon Dr; ⊙ 6-10pm Thu Oct-May, 7-10pm Jun-Sep) FREE Every Thursday night locals and visitors alike flock to downtown Palm Springs for this street fair with food stalls, craft vendors, music and entertainment. It runs for three blocks south of Tahquitz Canyon Way.

🛏 Sleeping

Palm Springs and the Coachella Valley offer an astonishing variety of lodging, including fine vintage-flair boutique hotels, full-on luxury resorts and chain motels. Some places don't allow children. Campers should head to Joshua Tree National Park or into the San Jacinto Mountains (via Hwy 74).

★ Arrive Hotel
BOUTIQUE HOTEL $$

(☎ 760-507-1650; www.arrivehotels.com; 1551 N Palm Canyon Dr, Palm Springs; studio from $179; P ⊛ ❀ ❄ ☷ ☎ ☷) 🐾 Ecofriendly rusted steel, wood and concrete are the main design ingredients of this new adult-only lair where the bar doubles as the reception. The 32 rooms (some with patio) tick all the requisite hipster boxes such as rain shower, Apple TV and fancy bath products. The poolside restaurant, coffee shop, ice-cream parlor and craft-beer bar score high among locals.

★ L'Horizon
BOUTIQUE HOTEL $$

(☎ 760-323-1858; http://lhorizonpalmsprings.com; 1050 E Palm Canyon Dr, Palm Springs; r $169-249; P ❀ ❄ ☎ ☷ ☷) The intimate William F Cody-designed retreat that saw Marilyn Monroe and Betty Grable lounging poolside has been rebooted as sleek and chic adult-only desert

---

TOP THREE SPAS

Get your stressed-out self to these pampering shrines to work out the kinks and turn your body into a glowing lump of tranquility. Reservations are de rigueur.

Estrella Spa at Avalon Palm Springs (☎ 760-318-3000; www.avalon-hotel.com/palm-springs/estrella-spa; 415 S Belardo Rd, Palm Springs; 1hr massage $145; ⊙ 9am-6pm Sun-Thu, to 10pm Fri & Sat) A tranquil vibe permeates this stylish retreat whose menu includes such holistic treatments as the Desert Rhythms massage or the Milk Y Way manicure/pedicure that starts with a warm fresh-milk soak.

Two Bunch Palms Spa Resort (☎ 760-676-5000; www.twobunchpalms.com/spa; 67425 Two Bunch Palms Trail, Desert Hot Springs; day-spa package from $195; ⊙ by reservation 9am-7pm Tue-Thu, 9am-8:30pm Fri, 8am-8:30pm, 8am-7pm Sun & Mon) Tim Robbins enjoyed a mud bath at this whisper-only oasis retreat in Robert Altman's film *The Player* and so can you. Nonresort guests can book (weeks in advance, please) a day-spa package that includes one healing 60-minute treatment, lunch and a soak in the hot mineral springs of the famous 'grotto.'

Feel Good Spa (☎ 760-866-6188; www.acehotel.com/palmsprings/feel-good-spa; 701 E Palm Canyon Dr, Palm Springs; 1hr massage $110-135; ⊙ by appointment 9am-6pm Sun-Thu, to 8pm Fri & Sat) At the hip Ace Hotel & Swim Club, this low-key spa offers the gamut of treatments to guests and the public, including a detoxifying hot-stone massage so you feel less guilty when bellying up to the pool bar afterwards.

DON'T MISS

SUNNY LIVING AT SUNNYLANDS

Step inside **Sunnylands Center & Gardens** (☑ 760-202-2222; www.sunnylands.org; 37977 Bob Hope Dr, Rancho Mirage; tours $20-45, center & gardens free; ☺ 9am-4pm Thu-Sun, closed early Jun–mid-Sep; ℗) the mid-century modern winter retreat of Walter and Leonore Annenberg, one of America's 'first families.' Here they entertained seven US presidents, royalty, Hollywood celebrities and heads of state. The only way to see it is on a guided 90-minute tour ($45) which must be booked far in advance via the website. No reservations are required to see the film and exhibits at the new visitor center, surrounded by magnificent desert gardens.

House-tour tickets are released at 9am on the 15th of the preceding month and usually sell out the same day. Two other types of tours are also available. The Open-Air Experience is a 45-minute first-come, first-served shuttle tour of the grounds and golf course ($20) that runs from September to April. With prior reservation, you can also join a bird tour ($35) offered Thursdays at 9:15am from November to April. Neither of these tours gives access to the house. See the website for the schedule and to buy tickets.

resort with 25 bungalows scattered across generous grounds for maximum privacy. Treat yourself to alfresco showers, a chemical-free swimming pool and private patio.

★ **El Morocco Inn & Spa** BOUTIQUE HOTEL **$$**
(☑ 888-288-9905, 760-288-2527; http://elmorocco inn.com; 66810 4th St, Desert Hot Springs; r $199-219; ℗ ☺ ✷ ☎ 🏊) Heed the call of the casbah at this drop-dead gorgeous hideaway where the scene is set for romance. Twelve exotically furnished rooms wrap around a pool deck where your enthusiastic hosts serve free 'Morocco-tinis' during happy hour. The on-site spa offers such tempting massages as 'Moroccan Rain' using an essential oil to purge the body of toxins.

Ace Hotel & Swim Club HOTEL **$$**
(☑ 760-325-9900; www.acehotel.com/palm springs; 701 E Palm Canyon Dr, Palm Springs; $180-230, ste $300-679, $31 daily resort fee; ℗ ☺ ✷ ☎ 🏊) Palm Springs goes Hollywood – with all the sass, sans the attitude – at this former Howard Johnson motel turned hipster hangout. The 176 rooms (many with patio) sport a glorified tent-cabin look and such lifestyle essentials as big flat-screen TVs and MP3 plug-in radios. Happening pool scene, low-key spa, an on-site restaurant and bar to boot.

Orbit In BOUTIQUE HOTEL **$$**
(☑ 760-323-3585, 877-966-7248; www.orbitin. com; 562 W Arenas Rd, Palm Springs; r $169-269; ℗ ☺ ✷ ☎ 🏊) Swing back to the '50s – pinkie raised and all – with free 'Orbitinis' during cocktail hour at this fabulously retro property, with high-end mid-Century Modern furniture (Eames, Noguchi et al) in only nine

rooms set around a quiet saline pool with Jacuzzi and fire pit. The long list of freebies includes bike rentals and poolside refreshments. Adults only.

Alcazar BOUTIQUE HOTEL **$$**
(☑ 760-318-9850; www.alcazarpalmsprings.com; 622 N Palm Canyon Dr; r from $119-399; ℗ ✷ @ ☎ 🏊) A fashionable (but not party) crowd makes new friends poolside before retiring to one of the 34 elegantly minimalist rooms around a pool. Some have Jacuzzi, patio, fireplace or all three. The daily $12 resort fee includes parking, bike rental, wi-fi and light breakfast. Must be 21 to check in. Two-night minimum on weekends.

Saguaro HOTEL **$$**
(☑ 760-323-1711; www.thesaguaro.com; 1800 E Palm Canyon Dr, Palm Springs; r $129-189, ste $209-279; ℗ ✷ ☎ 🏊) The hot colors of a desert blooming with wildflowers animate this updated mid-Century Modern hotel (pronounced Sah-wa-ro). Three stories of rooms look over a generous pool deck. The restaurant bar does great tacos and other south-of-the-border munchies.

Riviera Palm Springs RESORT **$$**
(☑ 760-327-8311; www.psriviera.com; 1600 Indian Canyon Dr, Palm Springs; r/ste from $119/175, resort fee $35; ℗ ✷ @ ☎ 🏊) This Rat Pack playground has been given a boho-cool makeover and sparkles brighter than ever. Expect the full range of mod-cons in nearly 400 rooms amid luscious gardens; two pools, hot tubs, restaurants and bars, a luxe spa and state-of-the-art fitness center.

The $35 resort fee includes a yoga class and bike rental, among other benefits.

Coachella Valley

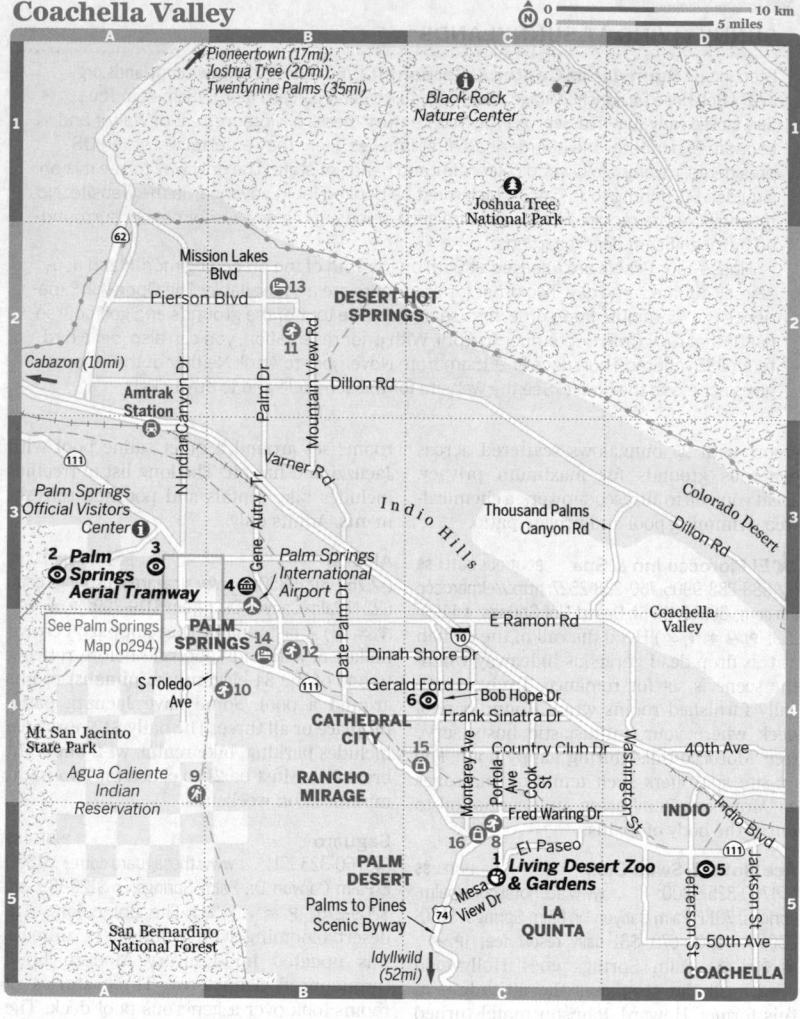

0 ————— 10 km
0 ————— 5 miles

Pioneertown (17mi);
Joshua Tree (20mi);
Twentynine Palms (35mi)

Black Rock
Nature Center

Joshua Tree
National Park

Mission Lakes Blvd
Pierson Blvd

DESERT HOT SPRINGS

Cabazon (10mi)

Amtrak Station

Dillon Rd

Indio Hills

Thousand Palms
Canyon Rd

Colorado Desert

Dillon Rd

Palm Springs
Official Visitors Center

Palm Springs Aerial Tramway

Palm Springs
International Airport

E Ramon Rd

Coachella Valley

See Palm Springs
Map (p294)

PALM SPRINGS

Dinah Shore Dr

Gerald Ford Dr

Bob Hope Dr

Frank Sinatra Dr

S Toledo Ave

CATHEDRAL CITY

RANCHO MIRAGE

Country Club Dr

40th Ave

Mt San Jacinto
State Park

Agua Caliente
Indian Reservation

Fred Waring Dr

INDIO

Indio Blvd

El Paseo

Living Desert Zoo
& Gardens

PALM DESERT

Palms to Pines
Scenic Byway

LA QUINTA

50th Ave

San Bernardino
National Forest

Idyllwild
(52mi)

COACHELLA

Coachella Valley

◉ Top Sights
1	Living Desert Zoo & Gardens	C5
2	Palm Springs Aerial Tramway	A3

◉ Sights
3	Elvis Honeymoon Hideaway	A3
4	Palm Springs Air Museum	B3
5	Shields Date Garden	D5
6	Sunnylands Center & Gardens	C4

◉ Activities, Courses & Tours
7	Covington Flats	C1
8	Funseekers	C5
9	Indian Canyons	A4

| | | |
|---|---|---|
| 10 | Smoke Tree Stables | B4 |
| 11 | Two Bunch Palms Spa Resort | B2 |
| 12 | Wet 'n' Wild Palm Springs | B4 |

◉ Sleeping
13	El Morocco Inn & Spa	B2
14	Parker Palm Springs	B4

◉ Drinking & Nightlife
	Counter Reformation	(see 14)

◉ Shopping
15	Collectors Corner	C4
16	El Paseo Shopping District	C5

Del Marcos Hotel
BOUTIQUE HOTEL **$$**

(☑ 800-676-1214, 760-325-6902; www.delmarcos hotel.com; 225 W Baristo Rd, Palm Springs; r $200-350; P ❊ 🛜 ⊠ 🐾) At this 1947 gem, designed by William F Cody, groovy lobby tunes usher you to a saltwater pool and ineffably chic mid-Century Modern rooms. The pricier ones have different bonus touches such as an Eames-style kitchen, a private redwood deck or an oversized shower.

Avalon Hotel
BOUTIQUE HOTEL **$$**

(☑ 760-320-4117; www.avalon-hotel.com/palm-springs; 415 S Belardo Rd, Palm Springs; r $159-259; P ❊ 🛜 ⊠ 🐾) Wear a Pucci dress and blend right in at this Spanish-style miniresort with 13 bungalows done up in sleek black-and-white Hollywood Regency style. After a day of lounging by the pool or getting pummeled in the spa, unwind on the patio or by the gas-burning fireplace. The on-site restaurant serves spirited California cuisine.

Caliente Tropics
MOTEL **$$**

(☑ 800-658-6034, 760-327-1391; www.caliente tropics.com; 411 E Palm Canyon Dr, Palm Springs; r $99-225; P ❊ 🛜 ⊠ 🐾) Elvis and the Rat Pack once frolicked poolside at this premier budget pick, a nicely spruced-up 1964 tiki-style motor lodge. Drift off to dreamland on quality mattresses in spacious rooms dressed in warm colors.

Parker Palm Springs
RESORT **$$$**

(☑ 760-770-5000; www.theparkerpalmsprings.com; 4200 E Palm Canyon Dr, Palm Springs; r from $295; P ❊ ☕ @ 🛜 ⊠ 🐾) This posh resort highlights whimsical decor by Jonathan Adler in public areas and rooms that include a villa once owned by Gene Autry. Stroll the lovely gardens, kick back in a hammock or try your hand at croquet and pétanque. The $30 resort charge covers parking, wi-fi and spa access.

🍴 Eating

A new line-up of zeitgeist-capturing restaurants has seriously elevated the level of dining in Palm Springs. The most exciting newcomers, including several with eye-catching design, flank N Palm Canyon Dr in the Uptown design district.

★ Cheeky's
CALIFORNIAN **$**

(☑ 760-327-7595; www.cheekysps.com; 622 N Palm Canyon Dr, Palm Springs; mains $9-14; ⊙ 8am-2pm Thu-Mon, last seating 1:30pm; ❊) Waits can be long and service only so-so at this breakfast and lunch spot, but the farm-to-table menu

dazzles with witty inventiveness. The kitchen tinkers with the menu on a weekly basis but perennial faves such as custardy scrambled eggs and grass-fed burger with pesto fries keep making appearances.

The Bloody Mary – served in a cowboy-boot-shaped glass – is an eye-opener.

Sherman's Deli & Bakery
DELI **$**

(☑ 760-325-1199; www.shermansdeli.com; 401 E Tahquitz Canyon Way, Palm Springs; sandwiches $8-18; ⊙ 7am-9pm; 🚼 ❊) Every community with a sizeable retired contingent needs a good Jewish deli. Sherman's is it. With a breezy sidewalk patio, it pulls in an all-ages crowd with its 40 sandwich varieties (great hot pastrami!), finger-lickin' rotisserie chicken, lox and bagels and to-die-for pies. Walls are festooned with head shots of celebrity regulars. Gets megabusy on weekends.

Native Foods
VEGAN **$**

(☑ 760-416-0070; www.nativefoods.com; Smoke Tree Village, 1775 E Palm Canyon Dr, Palm Springs; mains $8-11; ⊙ 11am-9pm; ❊ 🍴 ❊) From this humble mall base, Native Foods has helped pioneer America's vegan scene and now has branches all over the country. Its tempeh and seitan are made in-house and injected with complex flavors that satisfy even finicky eaters. Perennial crowd-pleasers include the 'Native nachos' with cashew cheese and the 'soul bowl' with faux chicken.

Tyler's Burgers
BURGERS **$**

(☑ 760-325-2990; www.tylersburgers.com; 149 S Indian Canyon Dr, Palm Springs; burgers & sandwiches $6.50-10; ⊙ 11am-4pm Mon-Sat; ❊) In a historic 1936 shack, owner Diana serves the same freshly ground yummy burgers on toasted buns her mom used to sell at her burger stand on the Venice Beach boardwalk. Avoid the lunchtime rush or plan on catching up on your reading at the well-stocked magazine rack. Patio seating.

Trio
CALIFORNIAN **$$**

(☑ 760-864-8746; www.triopalmsprings.com; 707 N Palm Canyon Dr, Palm Springs; mains lunch $13-16, dinner $15-30; ⊙ 11am-10pm Sun-Thu, to 11pm Fri & Sat; 🛜) The winning formula in this '60s modernist space: updated American comfort food (awesome Yankee pot roast!) amid eye-catching artwork and picture windows. The $19 prix-fixe three-course dinner (served until 6pm) is a steal, and the all-day daily happy hour lures a rocking after-work crowd with bar bites and cheap drinks.

Eight4Nine
AMERICAN $$

(☑760-325-8490; http://eight4nine.com; 849 N Palm Canyon Dr, Palm Springs; mains $18-38; ⏱11am-3pm & 5-9pm Mon-Thu, 11am-3pm & 5-11pm Fri, 9am-3pm & 5-11pm Sat, 9am-3pm & 5-9pm Sun; P❋☎) Hot pink accents the all-white high-ceilinged lounge and dining room at this popular hangout in a converted post office. Come hungry for fare that is both comforting and exciting with many dishes driven by the seasons. If you're feeling just a little peckish, sidle up to the backlit white onyx bar and order from the $9 'happy days' menu.

King's Highway
CALIFORNIAN $$

(☑760-325-9900; www.acehotel.com/palm springs/kings-highway; 701 E Palm Canyon Dr, Ace Hotel & Swim Club; mains $14-27; ⏱7am-11pm; P❋☎) A fine case of creative recycling, this former Denny's is now a diner for the 21st century where the tagliatelle is handmade, the sea bass wild-caught, the beef grass-fed, the vegetables heirloom and the cheeses artisanal. Great breakfast, too.

Wang's in the Desert
ASIAN $$

(☑760-325-9264; www.wangsinthedesert.com; 424 S Indian Canyon Dr, Palm Springs; mains $18-28; ⏱5-9pm Mon-Thu, 5-10pm Fri & Sat, 3-9pm Sun, lounge from 3pm) This mood-lit local fave with indoor koi pond delivers creatively crafted classics from around Asia – *tom ka gai* to tempura shrimp and mandarin pork – but also draws a thirsty crowd with its five-times-weekly happy hour that gets especially boisterous during Friday's 'boys night out.' On weekend nights, there's live entertainment in on-site **Venue Music Lounge**.

★ Workshop Kitchen + Bar
AMERICAN $$$

(☑760-459-3451; www.workshoppalmsprings. com; 800 N Palm Canyon Dr, Palm Springs; mains $26-45; ⏱5-10pm Mon-Sun, 10am-2pm Sun; ❋) Hidden away in the back of the ornate 1920s El Paseo building, a large patio with olive trees leads to this starkly beautiful space centered on a lofty concrete tunnel flanked by mood-lit booths. The kitchen crafts market-driven American classics reinterpreted for the 21st century and the bar is among the most happening in town.

Copley's
AMERICAN $$$

(☑760-327-9555; www.copleyspalmsprings.com; 621 N Palm Canyon Dr, Palm Springs; mains $22-40; ⏱from 5:30pm daily Oct–mid-Jun, Tue-Sun mid-Jun–Sep; P❋) After stints in the UK, Australia and Hawaii, chef Andrew Copley now concocts swoon-worthy American fare in Cary Grant's former guesthouse. Go for a classic New York steak or test the chef's imagination by ordering the Muscovy duck breast with foie-gras crème brûlée or the lavender-scented pound cake with basil ice cream.

🍷 Drinking & Nightlife

Drinking has always been in style in Palm Springs and many bars and restaurants have hugely popular happy hours that sometimes run all day. A handful of speakeasy bars have spiced up the cocktail scene and craft beer continues to be big as well. The big night out for the gay crowd is Fridays.

Palm Springs Koffi North
CAFE

(☑760-416-2244; www.kofficoffee.com; 515 N Palm Canyon Dr, Palm Springs; snacks & drinks $3-6; ⏱5:30am-7pm; ☎) Tucked among the Uptown art galleries, this is the original branch of this much-beloved local chain of hip coffeehouses. The java is organic and there are muffins, bagels and other baked goods to feed sugar cravings.

Birba
BAR

(☑760-327 5678; www.birbaps.com; 622 N Palm Canyon Dr, Palm Springs; ⏱5-11pm Sun & Wed-Thu, to midnight Fri & Sat; ☎) On a balmy night, Birba's hedge-fringed patio with twinkle lights and sunken fire pit is perfect for unwinding with a glass of wine or smooth libations like the tequila-based Heated Snake. Get a plate of *cicchetti* (Italian bar snacks) to stave off the blur or order modern pizza or pasta from the full menu.

Village Pub
PUB

(☑760-323-3265; www.palmspringsvillagepub. com; 266 S Palm Canyon Dr, Palm Springs; ⏱11am-2am Mon-Fri, 10am-2am Sat & Sun; ☎) Kick back with a cold one on the meandering patio, cheer on your favorite team on the big screen or dance til the wee hours at this all-purpose fun and charmingly divey venue in downtown Palm Springs.

★ Entertainment

Annenberg Theater
PERFORMING ARTS

(☑760-325-4490; www.psmuseum.org; 101 Museum Dr, Palm Springs) This intimate theater at the Palm Springs Art Museum (p293) has great acoustics and presents an eclectic schedule of films, lectures, theater, ballet and music performances.

Georgie's Alibi Azul
PERF

(☑760-325-5533; www.alibiazul.com; 369 N Palm Canyon Dr, Palm Canyon; ⏱11am-11pm or later;

SHHHH...TOP 3 SPEAKEASIES

It's been nearly a century since Prohibition spurred the proliferation of underground bars called speakeasies, but these days clandestine libation stations are making a big – voluntary – comeback. Palm Springs now fields its own contenders, including these prime picks.

Counter Reformation ([📞] 760-770-5000; www.theparkerpalmsprings.com/dine/counter-reformation.php; 4200 E Palm Canyon Dr, Palm Springs; ⊙ 3-10pm Mon, Thu & Fri, noon-10pm Sat & Sun) If you worship at the altar of Bacchus (the Roman god of wine), you'll be singing his praises in this dimly lit clandestine boite at the **Parker Palm Springs resort** (p301). The handpicked menu features just 17 reds, whites and champagne from small vineyards around the world.

Bootlegger Tiki ([📞] 760-318-4154; www.bootleggertiki.com; 1101 N Palm Canyon Dr, Palm Springs; ⊙ 4pm-2am) Crimson light bathes even pasty-faced hipsters into a healthy glow, as do the killer crafted cocktails at this teensy speakeasy with blowfish lamps and rattan walls. The entrance is via the Ernest coffee shop.

Seymour's ([📞] 760-892-9000; www.facebook.com/seymourspalmsprings; 233 E Palm Canyon Dr, Palm Springs; ⊙ 6pm-midnight Sun & Tue-Thu, to 2am Fri & Sat) In the back of the updated steakhouse Mr Lyons hides this furtive libation station named in honor of owner and entertainment lawyer Tara Lazar's dad. The eye-candy decor, mixing her old law books with exotic art, is easy fodder to kindle any conversation. So are the expertly shaken and stirred cocktails, including a mean martini.

[🔊] [📶] This video bar, nightclub and cafe in an old telephone exchange regales patrons with a rainbow of daily drinks specials plus events such as Sunday Disco Brunch and charity bingo. It's above the Azul tapas bar.

🔒 Shopping

Central Palm Springs has two main shopping districts along N Palm Canyon Dr, divided by Alejo Rd. North of Alejo, Uptown is more for art-and-design-inspired shops, while Downtown (south of Alejo) is ground zero for souvenirs and casual clothing. Given the city's demographic, vintage-clothing stores flourish here like few other places. West of town are two megapopular outlet malls.

Desert Hills Premium Outlets MALL
([📞] 951-849-6641; www.premiumoutlets.com/outlet/desert-hills; 48400 Seminole Dr, Cabazon; ⊙ 10am-9pm Mon-Sat, to 8pm Sun; [📶]) Bargain hunters, make a beeline for dozens of outlet stores: Gap to Gucci, Polo to Prada, Off 5th to Barneys New York. Wear comfortable shoes – this mall is huge! It's off I-10 (exit at Fields Rd), 20 minutes west of Palm Springs.

Collectors Corner VINTAGE
([📞] 760-346-1012; www.facebook.com/emccollectorscorner; 71280 Hwy 111, Rancho Mirage; ⊙ 9am-5pm Mon-Sat) It's a trek from central Palm Springs (about 12 miles), but this two-story shop is oh so worth it for its bevy of antiques, vintage clothing, jewelry and furniture. Proceeds benefit the Eisenhower Medical Center.

Angel View Resale Store THRIFT SHOP
([📞] 760-320-1733; www.angelview.org; 462 N Indian Canyon Dr, Palm Springs; ⊙ 9am-6pm Mon-Sat, 10am-5pm Sun) At this well-established thrift store, today's hipsters can shop for clothes and accessories as cool today as when they were first worn a generation or two ago.

Proceeds benefit children and adults with a disability. There are other branches throughout the Coachella Valley – see the website for locations.

Cabazon Outlets MALL
([📞] 951-922-3000; www.cabazonoutlets.com; 48750 Seminole Dr, Cabazon; ⊙ 10am-9pm) Though smaller than the adjacent Desert Hills Premium Outlets, this mall still flaunts covetable brands such as Adidas, Columbia and Guess.

El Paseo Shopping District MALL
(www.elpaseo.com; El Paseo, Palm Desert) Elegant and flower-festooned El Paseo shopping strip in Palm Desert has been dubbed the 'Rodeo Drive of the Desert.' Although it does a handful of blue-chip brands such as Escada and Gucci, most retailers are actually more in the Lululemon and Banana Republic league.

ℹ Information

Palm Springs Official Visitor Center (☏760-778-8418, 800-347-7746; www.visitpalm-springs.com; 2901 N Palm Canyon Dr, Palm Springs; ☉9am-5pm) Well-stocked and well-staffed visitor center in a 1965 Albert Frey–designed gas station at the Palm Springs Aerial Tram turnoff, 3 miles north of downtown.

Welwood Murray Memorial Library & Visitor Center (☏760-323-8296; www.visitpalm-springs.com; 100 S Palm Canyon Dr, Palm Springs; ☉9am-9pm) Small downtown branch of the regional tourist office. Also houses a historical research library and free public computers in a renovated 1941 library building.

Palm Springs Historical Society (☏760-323-8297; www.pshistoricalsociety.org; 221 S Palm Canyon Dr, Palm Springs; ☉10am-4pm Mon & Wed-Sat, noon-3pm Sun) Volunteer-staffed nonprofit organization. Maintains two museums and offers guided tours focusing on local history, architecture and celebrities.

ℹ Getting There & Away

Ask if your hotel provides free airport transfers. Otherwise, a taxi to downtown Palm Springs costs about $12 to $15, including a $2.50 airport surcharge. If you're staying in another Coachella Valley town, a ride on a shared shuttle van, such as **Sky Cap Shuttle Service** (☏760-272-5988; www.skycapshuttle.com), might work out cheaper. **SunLine** (☏800-347-8628; www.sunline.org; ticket $1, day pass $3) bus 24 stops by the airport and goes most (though, frustratingly, not all) of the way to downtown Palm Springs.

AIR

Palm Springs International Airport (p497) This regional airport is served year-round by 10 airlines, including United, American, Virgin, Delta and Alaska and has flights throughout North America.

CAR & MOTORCYCLE

Palm Springs is just over 100 miles east of Los Angeles via I-10 and 140 miles northeast of San Diego via I-15 and I-10.

ℹ Getting Around

BICYCLE

Central Palm Springs is pancake-flat, and more bike lanes are being built all the time. Many hotels have loaner bicycles.

Bike Palm Springs (☏760-832-8912; www.bikepsrentals.com; 194 S Indian Canyon Dr, Palm Springs; standard/kids/electric/tandem bikes half-day from $23/15/40/40, full-day $30/20/50/50; ☉9am-5pm)

Funseekers (☏760-340-3861; www.palmdesertbikerentals.com; 73-865 Hwy 111, Palm

Desert; bicycle 24hr from $25, 3 days from $50, week from $70, delivery & pick up $30)

BUS

SunLine Alternative-fuel-powered public buses travel around the valley, albeit slowly. Bus 111 links Palm Springs with Palm Desert (one hour) and Indio (1½ hours) via Hwy 111. Buses have air-con, wheelchair lifts and a bicycle rack. Cash only (bring exact change).

Buzz Trolley (www.new.buzzps.com; ☉11am-1am Thu-Sun) This free shuttle runs more or less every 15 minutes on a loop covering N Palm Canyon Dr from Via Escuela as far as Smoketree on E Palm Canyon and then back up Indian Canyon Dr.

CAR & MOTORCYCLE

Though you can walk to most sights in downtown Palm Springs, you'll need a car to get around the valley. Travel on Hwy 111 linking the Coachella Valley towns can be extremely slow thanks to countless of traffic lights. Depending on where you're headed, it may be quicker to take I-10.

Major rental-car companies have airport desks. Also consider two-wheelers as an alternative to getting around.

Scoot Palm Springs (☏760-413-2883; www.scootpalmsprings.com; 701 East Palm Canyon Dr, Palm Springs; half-/full-day from $80/130) From its base at the Ace Hotel & Swim Club, Scoot rents Buddy scooters made by the Genuine Scooter Company for tooling around the desert roads. Rentals include helmet, one tank of gas and unlimited mileage.

Eaglerider (☏866-464-7368, 760-718-3327; www.eaglerider.com; 74855 Country Club Dr, Palm Desert; Harley per day from $119; ☉9am-5pm) At the JW Marriot Desert Spring Hotel, the valley branch of this national chain has a big fleet of Harleys, BMW and Honda motorcycles as well as touring bikes such as the Indian Chief Vintage.

Joshua Tree National Park

Taking a page from a Dr Seuss book, the whimsical Joshua trees (actually tree-sized yuccas) welcome visitors to this 794,000-acre **park** (☏760-367-5500; www.nps.gov/jotr; 7-day entry per car $25; ☉24hr; 🅿🚻) 🦽 at the transition zone of two deserts: the low and dry Colorado and the higher, moister and slightly cooler Mojave.

Rock climbers know 'JT' as the best place to climb in California, hikers seek out hidden, shady, desert-fan-palm oases fed by natural springs and small streams, and mountain bikers are hypnotized by the desert vistas.

In springtime, the Joshua trees send up a huge single cream-colored flower. It was Mormon settlers who named the trees because the branches stretching up toward heaven reminded them of the Biblical prophet Joshua pointing the way to the promised land. The mystical quality of this stark, boulder-strewn landscape has inspired many artists, most famously the band U2, who named their 1987 album the *Joshua Tree*.

◉ Sights & Activities

Joshua Tree has three park entrances. Access the west entrance from the town of Joshua Tree, the north entrance from Twentynine Palms and the south entrance from I-10. The park's northern half harbors most of the attractions, including all the Joshua trees.

Oasis of Mara   OASIS

(☏ 760-367-5500; www.nps.gov/jotr; Utah Trail, Twentynine Palms; P) Behind the park HQ and Oasis Visitor Center, this natural oasis encompasses the original 29 palm trees that gave Twentynine Palms its name. They were planted by native Serranos who named this 'the place of little springs and much grass.' The Pinto Mountain Fault, a small branch of the San Andreas, runs through the oasis, as does a 0.5-mile, wheelchair-accessible nature trail with labeled desert plants.

★ Wonderland of Rocks   NATURAL FEATURE

(☏ 760-367-5500; www.nps.gov/jotr; P) This striking rock labyrinth extends roughly from Indian Cove in the north to Park Blvd in the south and is predictably a popular rock climbers' haunt. For a quick impression, try the 0.5-mile Indian Cove Trail or the 1-mile Barker Dam Trail. The 7-mile Willow Hole Trail and the 8-mile Boy Scout Trail present more challenging treks and should not be attempted in hot weather.

Indian Cove   LANDMARK

(☏ 760-367-5500; www.nps.gov/jotr; P) Rock hounds love the hulking caramel-colored formations in this northern corner of the park, while birders are drawn by feathered friends hiding out among the yuccas and shrubs along the half-mile Indian Cove nature trail. There's a campground for tenters and RVs with potable water.

★ Keys View   VIEWPOINT

(☏ 760-367-5500; www.nps.gov/jotr; Keys View Rd; P) From Park Blvd, it's an easy 20-minute drive up to Keys View (5185ft), where breathtaking views take in the entire Coachella Valley and extend as far as the Salton Sea. Looming in front of you are Mt San Jacinto (10,834ft) and Mt San Gorgonio (11,500ft), two of Southern California's highest peaks, while below you can spot a section of the San Andreas Fault.

Keys Ranch   HISTORIC SITE

(☏ 760-367-5500; www.nps.gov/jotr; tour adult/child $10/5; ⊘ tour schedules vary; P 🚻) Old West history buffs will delight in the 90-minute ranger-led tour of this ranch named after its builder, William Keys and his family. They built a homestead here on 160 acres in 1917 and turned it into a full working ranch, school, store and workshop. The buildings stand much as they did when Keys died in 1969. Check the website's calendar page for upcoming tour dates. Tickets must be purchased on the day at the Oasis Visitor Center (p312).

Cottonwood Spring   NATURAL FEATURE

(☏ 760-367-5500; www.nps.gov/jotr; P) Cottonwood Spring is an oasis with a natural spring that Cahuilla tribespeople depended on for centuries. Look for *morteros* – rounded depressions in the rocks used by Native Americans for grinding seeds. Miners came searching for gold here in the late 19th century.

Hiking

Leave the car behind to appreciate Joshua Tree's trippy lunar landscapes. Staff at the visitor centers can help match your time and fitness level to the perfect trail.

Boy Scout Trail   HIKING

(☏ 760-367-5500; www.nps.gov/jotr) For an immersion into the Wonderland of Rocks embark on this 8-mile one-way trail linking Indian Cove and Park Blvd (near Quail Springs picnic area). Most people prefer to start at the latter. Arrange for pick-up at the other end or plan on camping overnight. Part of the trail is unmarked and hard to follow.

Ryan Mountain Trail   HIKING

(☏ 760-367-5500; www.nps.gov/jotr) For bird's-eye park views, tackle this popular 3-mile in-and-out hike up 5458ft-high Ryan Mountain. Be sure to pack water and stamina – although not terribly long, the 1000ft elevation gain will likely make your thighs burn.

Lost Palms Oasis Trail   HIKING

(☏ 760-367-5500; www.nps.gov/jotr; Cottonwood Spring Rd) Reach this remote canyon filled with desert-fan palms on a moderately strenuous 7.5-mile hike starting from

Joshua Tree National Park

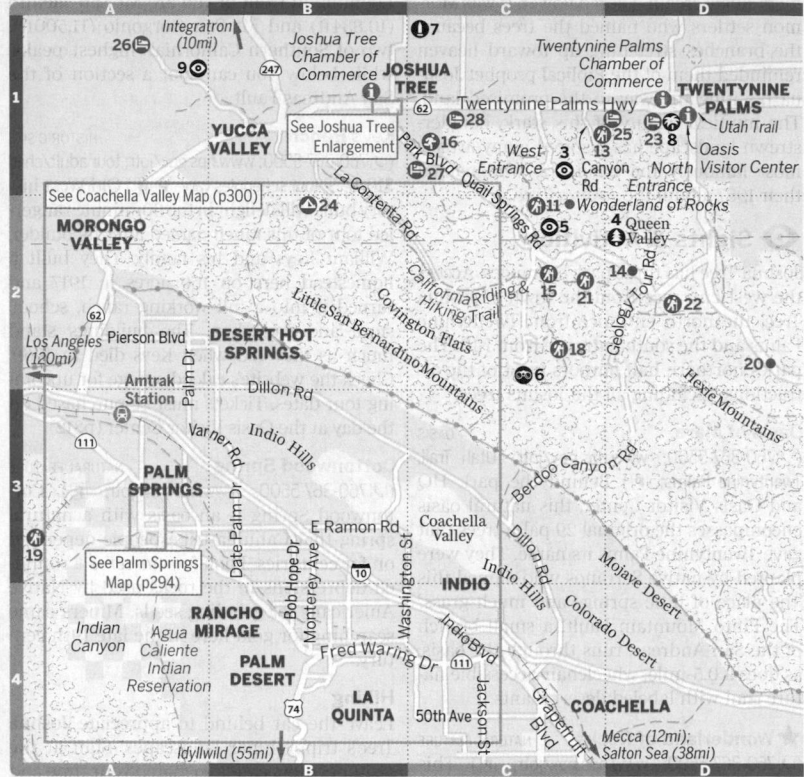

Cottonwood Spring. There's no shade, so bring lots of water and don't head out in intense summer heat.

Hidden Valley Trail
HIKING

(📞760-367-5500; www.nps.gov/jotr; Park Blvd) Some 8 miles south of the West Entrance, this whimsically dramatic cluster of rocks is a bouldering mecca, but just about anyone can enjoy a clamber on the giant rocks. An easy 1-mile trail loops around and back to the parking lot and picnic area.

Skull Rock Trail
HIKING

(📞760-367-5500; www.nps.gov/jotr; Park Blvd) Pick up this easy 1.7-mile trail around evocatively eroded rocks – one of them shaped like a skull – at **Jumbo Rocks campground** (📞760-367-5500; www.nps.gov/jotr; Park Blvd; per site $15).

Fortynine Palms Oasis Trail
HIKING

(📞760-367-5500; www.nps.gov/jotr; Canyon Rd) Escape the crowds on this moderate 3-mile, up-and-down trail to a fan-palm oasis scenically cradled by a canyon. The trailhead is at the end of Canyon Rd that veers off 29 Palms Hwy/Hwy 62, just east of the Indian Cove turnoff.

Mastodon Peak Trail
HIKING

(📞760-367-5500; www.nps.gov/jotr; Cottonwood Spring) Enjoy views of the Eagle Mountains and Salton Sea from an elevation of 3371ft on this 3-mile loop past an old gold mine from Cottonwood Spring.

Lost Horse Mine Trail
HIKING

(📞760-367-5500; www.nps.gov/jotr; Keys View Rd) A moderately strenuous in-and-out 4-mile climb that visits the remains of an authentic Old West silver and gold mine, in operation until 1931.

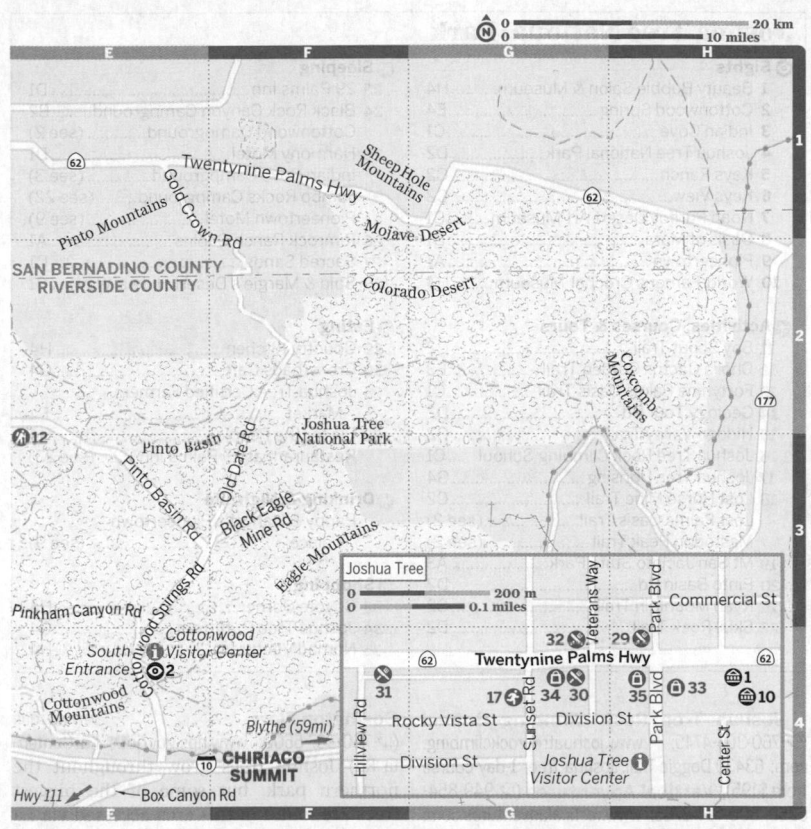

Cholla Cactus Garden Trail   HIKING

(☎760-367-5500; www.nps.gov/jotr; Pinto Basin Rd) This quarter-mile loop leads through a dense grove of 'teddy bear' cholla cactus and ocotillo plants just west of the main north-south road in the heart of the park. Wear sturdy shoes to guard against cactus spines.

Cycling

Bikes are only allowed on public paved and dirt roads that are also open to vehicles, including 29 miles of backcountry. They are not permitted on hiking trails. Popular routes include challenging **Pinkham Canyon Rd**, starting from the Cottonwood visitor center, and the long-distance **Black Eagle Mine Rd**, which starts 6.5 miles further north. **Queen Valley** has a gentler set of trails with bike racks found along the way, so people can lock up their bikes and go hiking, but it's busy with cars, as is the bumpy, sandy and steep Geology Tour Rd

(p308). There's also a wide-open network of dirt roads at Covington Flats (p308).

Rock Climbing

JT's rocks are famous for their rough, high-friction surfaces; from boulders to cracks to multipitch faces, there are more than 8000 established routes. Some of the most popular climbs are in the Hidden Valley area.

Shops catering to climbers with quality gear, advice and tours include **Joshua Tree Outfitters** (☎760-366-1848; www.joshuatreeoutfitters.com; 61707 29 Palms Hwy/Hwy 62, Joshua Tree; ⊙9am-5pm Thu-Tue), **Nomad Ventures** (☎760-366-4684; www.nomadventures.com; 61795 29 Palms Hwy/Hwy 62, Joshua Tree; ⊙8am-6pm Mon-Thu, to 8pm Fri-Sun Oct-Apr, 9am-7pm daily May-Sep) and **Coyote Corner** (☎760-366-9683; www.jtcoyotecorner.com; 6535 Park Blvd, Joshua Tree; ⊙9am-6pm).

Joshua Tree National Park

◎ Sights
1 Beauty Bubble Salon & Museum.......... H4
2 Cottonwood Spring E4
3 Indian Cove C1
4 Joshua Tree National Park D2
5 Keys Ranch C2
6 Keys View C2
7 Noah Purifoy Desert Art Museum C1
8 Oasis of Mara D1
9 Pioneertown A1
10 World-Famous Crochet Museum H4

⊙ Activities, Courses & Tours
11 Boy Scout Trail C2
12 Cholla Cactus Garden Trail E3
13 Fortynine Palms Oasis Trail C1
14 Geology Tour Rd D2
15 Hidden Valley Trail C2
16 Joshua Tree Rock Climbing School C1
17 Joshua Tree Uprising G4
18 Lost Horse Mine Trail C2
   Lost Palms Oasis Trail .... (see 2)
   Mastodon Peak Trail .... (see 2)
19 Mt San Jacinto State Park A3
20 Pinto Basin Rd D2
21 Ryan Mountain Trail C2
22 Skull Rock Trail D2

⊜ Sleeping
23 29 Palms Inn D1
24 Black Rock Canyon Campground B2
   Cottonwood Campground .... (see 2)
25 Harmony Motel D1
   Indian Cove Campground .... (see 3)
   Jumbo Rocks Campground .... (see 22)
   Pioneertown Motel .... (see 9)
26 Rimrock Ranch Cabins A1
27 Sacred Sands C1
28 Spin & Margie's Desert Hide-a-Way C1

⊗ Eating
29 Country Kitchen H4
30 Crossroads Cafe G4
31 Joshua Tree Certified Farmers
   Market F4
32 Pie for the People G4
   Restaurant at 29 Palms Inn .... (see 23)

⊙ Drinking & Nightlife
   Pappy & Harriet's Pioneertown
   Palace .... (see 9)

⊚ Shopping
33 Coyote Corner H4
34 Joshua Tree Outfitters G4
35 Nomad Ventures H4

Joshua Tree Rock Climbing School (☎760-366-4745; www.joshuatreerockclimbing. com; 63439 Doggie Trail, Joshua Tree; 1-day course from $195), **Vertical Adventures** (☎949-854-6250, 800-514-8785; www.verticaladventures.com; courses from $155; ☺Sep-May) and **Joshua Tree Uprising** (☎888-254-6266; www.josh-uatreeuprising.com; 61693 29 Palms Hwy/Hwy 62, Joshua Tree; 4/6/8hr-course from $90/100/120; ☺8am-5pm) offer guided climbs and climbing instruction starting at $120 for a one-day introduction.

⚑ Tours

Geology Tour Rd
DRIVING TOUR
(☎760-367-5500; www.nps.gov/jotr) On this 18-mile backcountry drive around Pleasant Valley, the forces of erosion, earthquakes and ancient volcanoes have played out in stunning splendor. There are 16 markers along the route – pick up a self-guided interpretive brochure and an update on road conditions at any park visitor center.

Passenger cars can usually handle the first 5 miles, but beyond Squaw Tank (marker 9) a 4WD is necessary. Pick up the road on Park Blvd about 2 miles west of Jumbo Rock campground.

Covington Flats
DRIVING TOUR
(☎760-367-5500; www.nps.gov/jotr; La Contenta Rd) Joshua trees grow throughout the northern park, but some of the biggest trees are found in this area accessed via La Contenta Rd, which runs south off Hwy 62 between Yucca Valley and Joshua Tree. For photogenic views, follow the dirt road 3.8 miles up Eureka Peak (5516ft) from the picnic area.

Pinto Basin Rd
DRIVING TOUR
(☎760-367-5500; www.nps.gov/jotr) To see the natural transition from the high Mojave Desert to the low Colorado Desert, wind down to Cottonwood Spring, a 30-mile drive from Hidden Valley passing by the Cholla Cactus Garden en route.

⊨ Sleeping

Unless you're day-tripping from Palm Springs, set up camp inside the park or base yourself in the desert communities linked by 29 Palms Hwy/Hwy 62 along the park's northern perimeter. Twentynine Palms and Yucca Valley have mostly national chain motels, while pads in Joshua Tree have plenty of charm and character.

Harmony Motel MOTEL **$**
(☑ 760-367-3351, 760-401-1309; www.harmony
motel.com; 71161 29 Palms Hwy/Hwy 62, Twentynine
Palms; r $65-85; 🅿 ⊖ ❄ 🛜 🏊) This well-kept
1950s motel, run by the charming Ash, was
where U2 stayed while working on the *Joshua Tree* album. It has a small pool and seven
large, cheerfully painted rooms (some with
kitchenette) set around a tidy desert garden
with serenely dramatic views. A light breakfast is served in the communal guest kitchen.

★ **Kate's Lazy Desert** INN **$$**
(☑ 845-688-7200; www.lazymeadow.com; 58380
Botkin Rd, Landers; Airstream $175 Mon-Thu, $200
Fri & Sat; 🅿 ⊖ ❄ 🛜 🏊) Owned by Kate Pier-
son of the B-52s, this desert camp has a coin-
sized pool (May to October) and half a dozen
Airstream trailers to sleep inside. Sporting
names such as 'Tinkerbell,' 'Planet Air' and
'Hot Lava,' each is kitted out with matching
fantasia-pop design and a double bed and
kitchenette.

Spin & Margie's Desert Hide-a-Way INN **$$**
(☑ 760-366-9124, 760-774-0850; www.deserthide
away.com; 64491 29 Palm Hwy/Hwy 62; d $145-185;
🅿 ⊖ ❄ 🛜) This handsome hacienda-style
inn is perfect for restoring calm after a long
day on the road. The five boldly colored
suites are an eccentric symphony of corru-
gated tin, old license plates and cartoon art.
Each has its own kitchen and flat-screen TV
with DVD and CD player. Knowledgeable,
gregarious owners ensure a relaxed visit.

Hicksville Trailer Palace MOTEL **$$**
(☑ 310-584-1086; www.hicksville.com; Joshua Tree;
trailer $75-225; 🅿 ❄ 🛜 🏊 🏊) Fancy sleeping
among glowing wig heads, in an Airstream
or a horse stall? Then check into one of nine
wackily decorated vintage trailers (and one
cabin) set around a saltwater pool (March
to November). All but three share facilities.
There's also a tipi with fire pit and a hot tub.
Directions provided after making reserva-
tions (to keep out looky-loos).

TOP 4 OFFBEAT ATTRACTIONS NEAR JT

The California desert is full of bizarre roadside attractions and hidden surprises, but the
area north of JT seems to harbor a disproportionate share, including these kooky gems.

Noah Purifoy Desert Art Museum (www.noahpurifoy.com; 63030 Blair Lane, Joshua Tree;
🕐 dawn-dusk; 🅿) The 'Junk Dada' sculptures and installations of African American artist
Noah Purifoy (1917–2004) are collected by the world's finest museums, but some of his
coolest works can be seen for free at his former outdoor desert studio north of Joshua
Tree. Toilets, tires, monitors, bicycles and beds are among the eclectic castoffs he turned
variously into political statements, social criticism or just plain nonsense. Pick up a pam-
phlet for a self-guided tour.

Integratron (☑ 760-364-3126; www.integratron.com; 2477 Belfield Blvd, Landers; sound baths
weekdays/weekends $30/35; 🕐 Wed-Mon; 🅿) It may look just like a white-domed structure,
but in reality it's an electrostatic generator for time travel and cell rejuvenation. Yup! At
least that's what its creator, former aerospace engineer George Van Tassel believed when
building the place in the 1950s after receiving telepathic instructions from extraterrestri-
als. Today, you can pick up on the esoteric vibes during a 60-minute 'sound bath' in the
wooden dome whose special design and location on a geomagnetic vortex generate an
extra-strong magnetic field.

Beauty Bubble Salon & Museum (☑ 760-366-9000; www.facebook.com/beautybub-
blesalonandmuseum; 61855 29 Palms Hwy/Hwy 62, Joshua Tree; museum free; 🕐 10am-6pm
Tue-Thu & Sat; 🅿) Jeff Hafler loves hair and everything to do with it, which is why his
Steel Magnolias–type home salon brims with related vintage beauty paraphernalia he's
collected for about a quarter century. Have him do your tresses up in a beehive while
surrounded by perm machines, curlers and wigs, some over 100 years old.

World-Famous Crochet Museum (www.sharielf.com/museum.html; 61855 29 Palms
Hwy/Hwy 62, Joshua Tree; 🕐 24hr) An old lime-green photo booth is the home of Bunny,
Buddy and hundreds of their crocheted friends collected by Shari Elf. The artist, singer,
fashion designer, raw-food chef and life coach has not mastered the art of crocheting
herself.

CAMPING IN JT

Of the park's eight campgrounds, only **Cottonwood** (☑760-367-5500; www.nps.gov/jotr; Pinto Basin Rd; per site \$20) and **Black Rock** (☑760-367-5500, reservations 877-444-6777; www.nps.gov/jotr; Joshua Lane; per site \$20; ℗) have potable water, flush toilets and dump stations. **Indian Cove** (☑760-367-5500, reservations 877-444-6777; www.nps.gov/jotr; Indian Cove Rd; per site \$20) and Black Rock accept reservations from October through May. The others are first-come, first-served and have pit toilets, picnic tables and fire grates. None have showers, but there are some at **Coyote Corner** (p307) in Joshua Tree. Details are available at www.nps.gov/jotr or 760-367-5500.

Between October and May, campsites fill by Thursday noon, especially during the springtime bloom. If you arrive too late, there's overflow camping on Bureau of Land Management (BLM) land north and south of the park as well as in private campgrounds. For details, download http://go.nps.gov/jtnpoverflow.

Backcountry camping is allowed 1 mile from any road or 500ft from any trailhead. There is no water in the park, so bring one to two gallons per person per day for drinking, cooking and personal hygiene. Campfires are prohibited to prevent wildfires and damage to the fragile desert floor. Free self-registration is required at a backcountry board inside the park, where you can also leave your car. For full details, download the official backcountry camping guide at http://go.nps.gov/jtnpbackcountry.

29 Palms Inn INN **$$**

(☑760-367-3505; www.29palmsinn.com; 73950 Inn Ave, Twentynine Palms; r \$170-260; ℗ ⊖ ❄@🤍❄🐾) 🥘 History oozes from every nook and cranny in this old-timey inn on the ancient Oasis of Mara (p305). Choose from air-conditioned 1934 adobe bungalows, fitted with fireplace and patio, 1950s woodframe cabins with private deck, or two-bedroom guesthouses with kitchen. Rates include breakfast and weekend walking tours around the oasis.

★ Sacred Sands B&B **$$$**

(☑760-424-6407; www.sacredsands.com; 63155 Quail Springs Rd, Joshua Tree; north/west r \$329/359, 2-night minimum; ℗⊖❄🤍) 🥘 In an isolated, pin-drop-quiet spot, these two desert-chic suites are the ultimate romantic retreat, each with a private outdoor shower, hot tub, sundeck, 2ft-thick earthen straw-bale walls and sleeping terrace under the stars. There are astounding views across the desert hills and into the National Park. Owners Scott and Steve are gracious hosts and killer breakfast cooks.

It's 4 miles south of 29 Palms Hwy (via Park Bl), 1 mile west of the park entrance.

✖ Eating

There's no food available inside the park, but the communities along Hwy 62 have big supermarkets convenient for stocking up on supplies (especially Yucca Valley). Restaurants range from mom-and-pop-run greasy spoons to organic delis, funky diners to ethnic eats. On Saturday mornings, locals gather for gossip and groceries at the **farmers market** (☑760-420-7529; www.joshuatree-farmersmarket.com; 61705 29 Palms Hwy/Hwy 62, Joshua Tree; ⊗8am-1pm Sat; ℗) in Joshua Tree.

★ La Copine AMERICAN **$**

(www.lacopinekitchen.com; 848 Old Woman Rd, Flamingo Heights; mains \$10-16; ⊗9am-3pm Thu-Sun; ℗❄) It's a long road from Philadelphia to the high desert, but that's where Nikki and Claire decided to take their farm-to-table brunch cuisine from pop-up to brick and mortar. Their roadside bistro serves zeitgeist-capturing dishes such as the signature salad with smoked salmon and poached egg, homemade crumpets and gold milk turmeric tea. Expect a wait on weekends.

Country Kitchen AMERICAN **$**

(☑760-366-8988; 61768 29 Palms Hwy/Hwy 62, Joshua Tree; mains \$4-10; ⊗6:30am-3pm Wed-Mon; ℗❄) Now run by Sarah and Dennis, this been-here-forever roadside shack gets a big thumbs up for its scrumptious home cookin'. Lines can be extra-long for breakfast on weekends, but the killer pancakes, breakfast burrito with homemade salsa and egg dishes are worth the wait. Also serves lunch.

Pie for the People PIZZA **$**

(☑760-366-0400; www.pieforthepeople.com; 61740 29 Palms Hwy/Hwy 62, Joshua Tree; pizza \$8-26; ⊗11am-9pm Sun-Thu, to 10pm Fri & Sat; ♿) This neighborhood-adored lair is in the business of thin-crust pizzas ranging from classics to creatives like the David Bowie: white pizza with mozzarella, Guinness-caramelized onions, jalapeños, pineapple, bacon and sweet plum sauce.

Crossroads Cafe AMERICAN $
(☎760-366-5414; www.crossroadscafejtree.com; 61715 29 Palms Hwy/Hwy 62, Joshua Tree; mains $6-12; ☻7am-9pm Mon-Sat, to 8pm Sun; P⬤) This JT institution is the go-to place for carb-loaded breakfast, dragged-through-the-garden salad and fresh sandwiches that make both omnivores (burgers, Reuben sandwich) and vegans ('Fake Philly' with seitan) happy.

Restaurant at 29 Palms Inn AMERICAN $$$
(☎760 367-3505; www.29spalmsinn.com; 73950 Inn Ave, Twentynine Palms; mains lunch $8-14, dinner $16-44; ☻11am-2pm Mon-Sat, 9am-2pm Sun, 5-9pm Sun-Thu, 5pm-9:30pm Fri & Sat; ⬤) This well-respected restaurant has its own organic garden and does burgers and salads at lunchtime, and grilled meats and toothsome pastas for dinner. No reservations.

 Drinking & Nightlife

Joshua Tree has a couple of artsy watering holes, often with live music featuring lo-cal and regional talent, although the most atmospheric place to steer toward after dark is Pappy & Harriet's (p311) in Pioneertown. Bars in Twentynine Palms cater mostly to marines.

 Shopping

Vintage and antiques lovers should head to the cluster of well-curated shops around the Pioneertown Rd turnoff on Hwy 62. Otherwise, Yucca Valley has mostly national chain supermarkets and big box stores along Hwy 62. Joshua Tree plays up its artistic pedigree with quirky shops and galleries in the blocks flanking Park Blvd, the main road into Joshua Tree National Park.

 Information

MEDICAL SERVICES

Hi-Desert Medical Center (☎760-366-3711; www.hdmc.org; 6601 White Feather Rd, Joshua Tree; ☻24hr) The main hospital in the Morongo Basin with 24-hour emergency care.

TELEPHONE

Cell-phone reception is extremely spotty inside the park – don't count on it! There are emergency phones at the ranger station in Indian Cove and at the Intersection Rock parking area near Hidden Valley Campground.

TURN BACK THE CLOCK AT PIONEERTOWN

Turn north off Hwy 62 onto Pioneertown Rd in Yucca Valley and drive 5 miles straight into the past. Looking like an 1870s frontier town, **Pioneertown** (www.pioneertown.com; P⬤) FREE was actually built in 1946 as a Hollywood Western movie set. Gene Autry and Roy Rogers were among the original investors and more than 50 movies and several TV shows were filmed here in the 1940s and '50s. These days, it's fun to stroll around the old buildings and drop into the local honky-tonk for refreshments. Mock gunfights take place on 'Mane St' at 2:30pm every second and fourth Saturday, April to October.

For local color, toothsome BBQ, cheap beer and kick-ass live music, drop in at **Pappy & Harriet's Pioneertown Palace** (☎760-365-5956; www.pappyandharriets.com; 53688 Pioneertown Rd, Pioneertown; mains $6-15; ☻11am-2am Thu-Sun, from 5pm Mon), a textbook honky-tonk. Monday's open-mike nights (admission free) are legendary and often bring out astounding talent. From Thursday to Saturday, local and national talent takes over the stage.

Within staggering distance is the atmospheric **Pioneertown Motel** (☎760-365-7001; www.pioneertown-motel.com; 5040 Curtis Rd, Pioneertown; r from $155; P⬤⬤⬤), where yesteryear's silver-screen stars once slept during filming and whose rooms are now filled with eccentric Western-themed memorabilia; some have kitchenettes.

Some movie stars also stayed in the knotty-pine huts reimagined as **Rimrock Ranch Cabins** (☎760-228-1297; www.rimrockranchcabins.com; 50857 Burns Canyon Rd, Pioneertown; cabins $120-220, 2-day minimum on weekends; P⬤⬤⬤), a soulful desert hideaway 4.5 miles north of Pioneertown. All have Old West decor, kitchen facilities, DVD player and private patio. For extra kookiness, book into the Airstream trailer; for stylish comfort book the Hatch House bungalow.

OFF THE BEATEN TRACK

SALTON SEA: THE DISAPPEARING LAKE

Driving along Hwy 111 southeast of Indio, you'll come across a most unexpected sight: the Salton Sea – California's largest lake in the middle of its largest desert. As you can quickly tell by the postapocalyptic mood hanging over the place, it's a troubled spot with a fascinating past, complicated present and uncertain future.

The Salton Sea is very much an 'accidental sea,' created in 1905 when high spring flooding breached irrigation canals built to bring water from the Colorado River to the farmland in the Imperial Valley. The water rushed uncontrollably into the nearest low spot – the Salton Sink – for 18 months until 1500 workers and 500,000 tons of rock managed to put a halt to the flooding. With no natural outlet, the water was here to stay: the Salton Sea – about 35 miles long and 15 miles wide – was born.

By midcentury the desert lake was stocked with fish and marketed as the 'California Riviera;' vacation homes lined its shores. The fish, in turn, attracted birds, and the sea became a prime bird-watching spot. To this day, it provides habitat for around 400 species of migratory and endangered species such as snow geese, eared grebes, ruddy ducks, white and brown pelicans, bald eagles and peregrine falcons. It is one of the most important stopovers along the Pacific Flyway.

But their survival is threatened by rising salinity from decades of phosphor and nitrogen in agricultural runoff. With hardly any rainfall and little freshwater inflow, it has increased to 56 grams per liter (versus 35 grams in the Pacific Ocean), making it impossible for most fish species to survive, tilapia being an exception. Fewer fish, in turn, make the area less attractive for birds.

Efforts to rescue the Salton Sea go back to 2003 when the California State Legislature passed the Salton Sea Restoration Act but has since failed to earmark funds for it. It did manage to talk the Imperial Irrigation District into selling some of its Colorado River water to the San Diego district in order to dilute the agricultural runoff and replenish the sea with freshwater.

Since the agreement expires in late 2017, lawmakers are scrambling to prevent an imminent ecological disaster. In March 2017, the California Natural Resources Agency unveiled a 10-year plan to restore the area and control toxic dust storms resulting from shrinking water levels by building a series of ponds and water-transfer systems. The state legislature earmarked $80.5 million for the rescue effort. It remains to be seen if it's just a drop in the bucket.

TOURIST INFORMATION

Entry permits ($25 per vehicle) are valid for seven days and come with a map and the seasonally updated *Joshua Tree Guide*.

Joshua Tree Visitor Center (www.nps.gov/jotr; 6554 Park Blvd, Joshua Tree; ◷8am-5pm; 🛜🛗) The busiest visitor center has exhibits, books and souvenirs and is just south of 29 Palms Hwy (Hwy 62) on the northern perimeter.

Oasis Visitor Center (www.nps.gov/jotr; 74485 National Park Dr, Twentynine Palms; ◷8:30am-5pm; 🛗) The easternmost visitor center is attached to the park HQ.

Black Rock Nature Center (www.nps.gov/jotr; 9800 Black Rock Canyon Rd, Yucca Valley; ◷8am-4pm Sat-Thu, to 8pm Fri Oct-May; 🛗) The westernmost visitor center is located at **Black Rock Canyon Campground** (p310).

Cottonwood Visitor Center (www.nps.gov/jotr; Cottonwood Springs; ◷8:30am-4pm; 🛗) The southern visitor center is 8 miles north of I-10.

Joshua Tree Chamber of Commerce (☏760-366-3723; www.joshuatreechamber.org; 6448 Hallee Rd, Suite 10, Joshua Tree; ◷9am-noon Wed-Sat) Info about hotels, restaurants and shops in the town of Joshua Tree, just north of Hwy 62.

Twentynine Palms Chamber of Commerce (☏760-367-6197; www.visit29.org; 73484 29 Palms Hwy/Hwy 62, Twentynine Palms; ◷10am-4pm Mon-Fri, 9am-2pm Sat & Sun; 🛜) Visitor center with gallery, gift shop, books, free wi-fi and electric-car charging station.

🛈 Getting There & Around

Joshua Tree National Park is flanked by I-10 in the south and Hwy 62 (Twentynine Palms Hwy) in the north. The park is about 140 miles east of LA via I-10 and 29 Palms Hwy (Hwy 62) and 175 miles from San Diego via I-15 and I-10. From Palm Springs it takes about an hour to reach the park's west (preferable) or south entrances.

Bus 1, operated by **Morongo Basin Transit Authority** (☑760-366-2395; www.mbtabus.com), runs hourly between 6am and 10pm along 29 Palms Hwy (Hwy 62), linking Yucca Valley and Joshua Tree with the Marine Base in Twentynine Palms. Single tickets cost $2.50, a day pass is $3.75. Cash only, exact fare required. Buses are equipped with bike racks.

Anza-Borrego Desert State Park

Shaped by an ancient sea and tectonic forces, enormous and little-developed **Anza-Borrego** (☑760-767-4205; www.parks.ca.gov; parking visitor center $5, day use in developed campgrounds $10; 🅿🚻) 🚫**FREE** covers 640,000 acres, making it the largest state park in California. Human history here goes back more than 10,000 years, as recorded by Native American pictographs and petroglyphs. The park is named for Spanish explorer Juan Bautista de Anza, who arrived in 1774, pioneering a colonial trail from Mexico and no doubt running into countless *borregos,* the wild bighorn sheep that once ranged as far south as Baja California. (Today only a few hundred of these animals survive due to drought, disease, poaching and off-highway driving.) In the 1850s Anza-Borrego became a stop along the Butterfield Stagecoach line, which delivered mail between St Louis and San Francisco.

◉ Sights & Activities

Anza-Borrego's commercial hub, Borrego Springs (population 3429), has restaurants, lodgings, stores, ATMs and gas stations. Nearby are the park visitor center and easy-to-reach sights, such as Borrego Palm Canyon and Fonts Point, that are fairly representative of the park as a whole. The Split Mountain area, east of Ocotillo Wells, is popular with off-highway vehicles (OHVs), but also contains interesting geology and spectacular wind caves. The desert's southernmost region is the least visited and, aside from Blair Valley, has few developed trails and facilities.

Many of the trailheads are accessible only by dirt roads. To find out which roads require high-clearance or 4WD vehicles, or are currently impassable, check with the park visitor center (p317).

Fonts Point   VIEWPOINT
(☑760-767-4205; www.parks.ca.gov; Anza-Borrego Desert State Park, off Rte S22) 🚫**FREE** East of Borrego Springs, a 4-mile dirt road, sometimes passable without 4WD, diverges south from County Rte S22 out to Fonts Point (1249ft). From up here a spectacular panorama unfolds over the Borrego Valley to the west and the Borrego Badlands to the south.

Vallecito County Park   HISTORIC SITE
(☑760-765-1188; www.sdparks.org; 37349 Great South Stage Rte 1849/County Rte S2, Julian; per car $3; ⊙9.30am-5pm Mon-Fri, to sunset on weekends Sep-May; 🅿) This pretty little park in a refreshing valley on the southern edge of Anza-Borrego Desert State Park centers on a replica of a historic **Butterfield Stage Station**. Its 44 primitive campsites are a handy staging ground for desert explorations.

It's 36 miles south of Borrego Springs via County Rte S2.

Agua Caliente Regional Park   SWIMMING
(☑760-765-1188; www.sdparks.org; 39555 Great Southern Overland Stage Route of 1849/County Rte

PALM SPRINGS & THE DESERTS ANZA-BORREGO DESERT STATE PARK

EASY HIKES IN ANZA-BORREGO

Kenyon Overlook (☑760-767-4205; www.parks.ca.gov; Yaqui Pass Rd/County Rte S3, Anza-Borrego Desert State Park) An easy 1-mile trail loops from the parking lot up to this viewpoint over the Vallecito Mountain and the Mescal Bajada. Views are at their golden-hued best at sunrise and sunset.

Yaqui Well Trail (☑760-767-4205; www.parks.ca.gov; Yaqui Pass Rd/County Rte S3, Anza-Borrego Desert State Park) A 1.7-mile round-trip, this easy trail passes creosote, cactus, mesquite and a natural water hole that attracts a rich variety of birds. Starts opposite Tamarisk Grove Campground.

Cactus Loop Trail (☑760-767-4205; www.parks.ca.gov; Yaqui Pass Rd/County Rte S3, Anza-Borrego Desert State Park; ⊙dawn-dusk) Short but rocky and with a steep climb built into it, this 1-mile interpretive loop takes you past a great variety of cacti while delivering sweeping views of San Felipe Wash. Wear sturdy shoes. Starts across from Tamarisk Grove Campground.

Anza-Borrego State Park

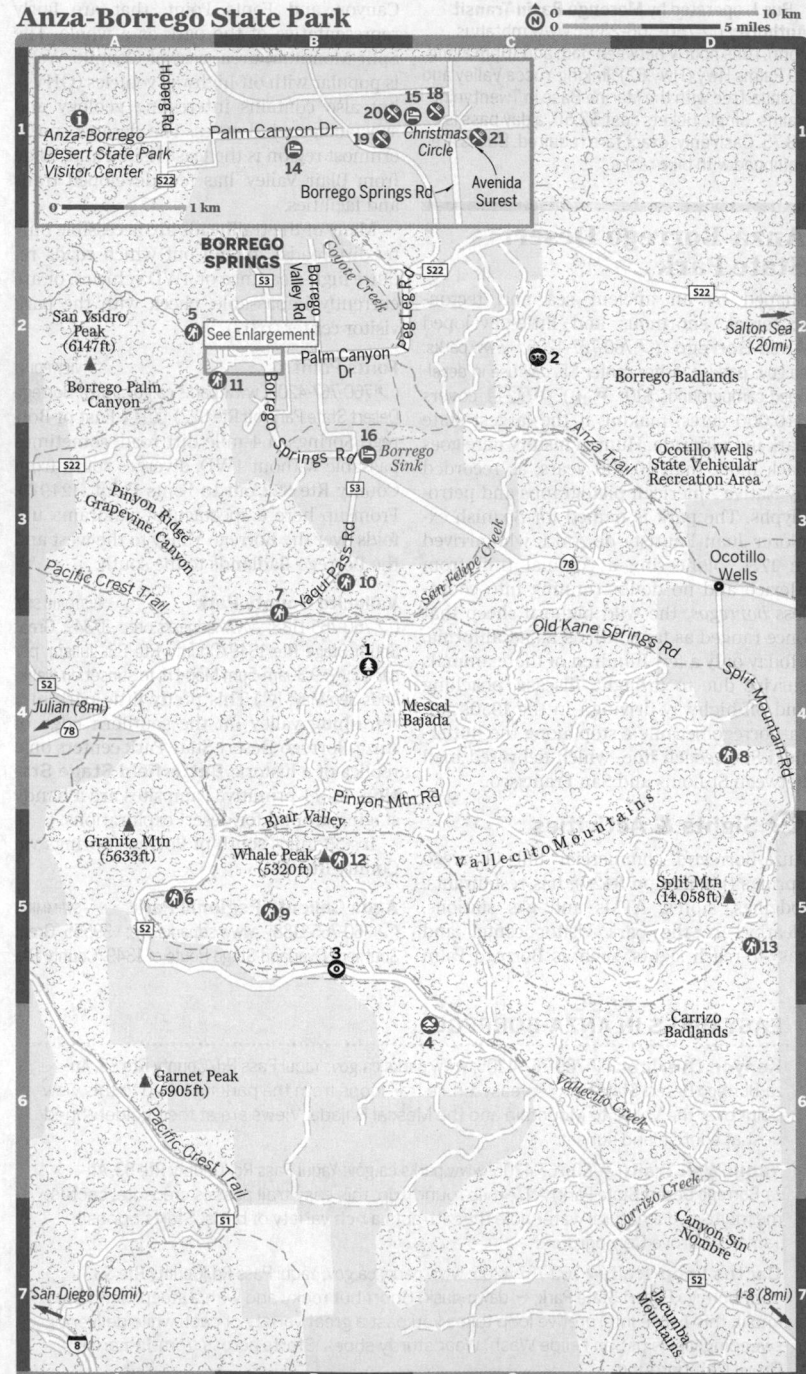

Anza-Borrego State Park

S2; per car $3; ⊙ 9:30am-5pm Mon-Fri, to sunset weekends Sep-May) In a lovely camping park on the southern edge of Anza-Borrego Desert State Park you can take a dip in two outdoor and one indoor pool fed by hot natural mineral springs. The indoor spa is heated to 102 degrees, outfitted with therapeutic Jacuzzi jets and open only to those 14 years or older.

Hiking

Borrego Palm Canyon Trail   HIKING
(☑ 760-767-4205; www.parks.ca.gov; 200 Palm Canyon Dr, Borrego Springs; day-use parking $10; ⊙ dawn-dusk) FREE This popular 3-mile loop trail starts at the top of Borrego Palm Canyon Campground, 1 mile north of the visitor center, and goes past a grove of shaggy fan palms and little waterfalls, a delightful oasis in the dry, rocky desertscape. Birds love it here and even the elusive bighorn sheep might come down for a drink.

Box Canyon   HIKING
(☑ 760-767-4205; www.parks.ca.gov; off County Rte S2) FREE A short hike takes you down into a narrow canyon where, in 1847, the Mormon Battalion (a unit of the US Army) used only hand tools to hack a wagon road through the rocks to widen the Southern Emigrant Trail, one of the most important routes for pioneer settlers to California. Past the canyon, the trail continues to a dry waterfall.

Elephant Tree Trail   HIKING
(☑ 760-767-4205; www.parks.ca.gov; Split Mountain Rd, Anza-Borrego Desert State Park) FREE The rare elephant trees get their name from their stubby trunks, thought to resemble elephant legs. Unfortunately only one living elephant tree remains along this 1-mile loop trail but it's still a nice, easy hike through a rocky wash. You'll need a high-clearance 4WD to get to the trailhead.

The turnoff is on Split Mountain Rd, about 6 miles south of Hwy 78 and Ocotillo Wells.

Pictograph/Smuggler's Canyon Trail   HIKING
(☑ 760-767-4205; www.parks.ca.gov; Blair Valley, off County Rte S2, Anza-Borrego Desert State Park) FREE In Blair Valley, this 3-mile round-trip trail skirts boulders covered in Native American pictographs and ends at a dry waterfall and a nice view of the Vallecito Valley. Take the Blair Valley turnoff on County Rte S2 and continue on the dirt road for about 3.6 miles.

Wind Caves Trail   HIKING
(☑ 760-767-4205; www.parks.ca.gov; off Split Mountain Rd, Anza-Borrego Desert State Park) FREE This steep 1-mile in-and-out trail leads up to delicate wind caves carved into sandstone outcrops. Pick it up by taking Split Mountain Rd to the dirt-road turnoff for Fish Creek and following the wash for 4 miles.

Maidenhair Falls Trail   HIKING
(☑ 760-767-4205; www.parks.ca.gov; Montezuma Valley Rd, Anza-Borrego Desert State Park) FREE This plucky 6-mile round-trip trail starts from the Hellhole Canyon Trailhead, 2 miles west of the Borrego Springs visitor center on County Rte S22 and climbs for 3 miles past several palm oases to a seasonal waterfall that supports birdlife and a variety of plants. Wear sturdy shoes as some rock scrambling is required.

OFF THE BEATEN TRACK

SALVATION MOUNTAIN

A 100ft-high hill of hand-mixed adobe and straw slathered in paint and decorated with flowers, waterfalls, birds and religious messages, **Salvation Mountain** (📞 760-624-8754; www.salvationmountaininc.org; 603 E Beal Rd, Niland; donations accepted; ⏰ dawn-dusk; 🅿) is a mighty strange sight indeed. This work of Leonard Knight (1931–2014), a passionately religious man from Vermont, was 28 years in the making. It has become one of the great works of American folk art and has even been recognized as a national treasure in the US Senate.

You'll find it in Niland, about 3 miles off Hwy 111, via Main St/Beal Rd and past train tracks and trailer parks.

Ghost Mountain Trail HIKING
(📞 760-767-4205; www.parks.ca.gov; Blair Valley, off County Rte S2, Anza-Borrego Desert State Park) **FREE** A steep 2-mile round-trip trail climbs to the sparse remains of the 1930s adobe homestead built by desert recluse Marshall South and his family. The trailhead is in the southern section of Blair Valley, at the end of a 3-mile dirt road off County Rte S2.

🛏 Sleeping

A handful of motels and hotels cluster in and around Borrego Springs, but not all are open year-round. Otherwise, camping is the only mode to spend the night in the park. Besides developed campgrounds, free backcountry camping is permitted anywhere. Note that all campfires must be in metal containers and that gathering vegetation (dead or alive) is strictly prohibited.

Vallecito County Park Campground CAMPGROUND $
(📞 reservations 858-565-3600; www.sdparks.org; 37349 Great South Stage Route 1849/County Rte S2; tent & RV sites $22; ⏰ Sep-May; 🅿) This rustic campground has 44 tent and nonhookup RV sites in a cool, green-valley refuge set around a replica of the Butterfield Stage Station. Sites come with tables, fire rings and barbecue pits. The closest supply store is at the Agua Caliente County Park, about 4 miles southeast.

Agua Caliente County Park Campground CAMPGROUND $
(📞 reservations 858-565-3600; www.sdparks.org; 39555 Great Southern Overland Stage Route of 1849/County Rte S2; tent sites $24, RV sites with partial/full hookups $29/33, cabins $70; ⏰ Sep-May; 🅿) On the southern edge of Anza-Borrego Desert State Park, this campground comes with the added bonus of natural hot-spring pools and easy access to hiking trails. It offers the gamut of camping options, including seven new glamper-friendly cabins with air-con and private bathrooms.

Borrego Palm Canyon Campground CAMPGROUND $
(📞 800-444-7275; www.reserveamerica.com; 200 Palm Canyon Dr, Borrego Springs; tent/RV sites $25/35; 🅿🐾) Near the Anza-Borrego Desert State Park visitor center (p317), this campground has award-winning toilets, campsites that are close together and an amphitheater with ranger programs.

Hacienda del Sol COTTAGES $
(📞 760-767-5442; www.haciendadelsol-borrego.com; 610 Palm Canyon Dr, Borrego Springs; r/duplex/cottages $85/145/175; 🅿🐾❄🛜🏊) Bask in the retro glow of this indie hotel where you can choose from cottages with fireplace and kitchen, spacious duplexes perfect for families or no-frills motel rooms. The pool is great for chilling or socializing.

Palms Hotel BOUTIQUE HOTEL $$
(📞 760-767-7788; www.thepalmsatindianhead.com; 2200 Hoberg Rd, Borrego Springs; r $149-249; 🅿❄🏊) This former haunt of Cary Grant, Marilyn Monroe and other old-time celebs has been reborn as a chic mid-Century Modern retreat. Connect with the era over martinis and filet mignon at the on-site steakhouse while enjoying mesmerizing desert views. Rooms are comfortable but uncluttered, with most facing the pool.

★ La Casa del Zorro RESORT $$$
(📞 760-767-0100; www.lacasadelzorro.com; 3845 Yaqui Pass Rd; r $224-350; 🅿❄🛜🏊🐾) After a top-to-bottom facelift, this venerable 1937 resort is again the region's grandest stay. The ambience exudes desert romance in 67 elegantly rustic poolside rooms and family-sized casitas sporting vaulted ceilings and marble bathtubs. A staggering 28 pools and Jacuzzi are scattered across the 42 landscaped acres, and there's a spa, five tennis courts, fun bar and gourmet restaurant.

Borrego Valley Inn INN $$$

(☏760-767-0311; www.highwaywestvacations.com; 405 Palm Canyon Dr, Borrego Springs; r $243-330; P❄✳︎⏃▨) At this rustically elegant inn, you can wrap your days tucked into rooms filled with Southwestern knickknacks and Native American weavings or into a rocking chair on your private patio. Oversized rooms orbit a courtyard filled with desert plants; some have kitchenette. Between October and May, rates include breakfast and there's a two-night minimum on weekends.

✕ Eating

Borrego Springs has a few restaurants but don't expect any culinary flights of fancy. The best supermarket is **Center Market** (☏760-767-3311; www.centermarket-borrego.com; 590 Palm Canyon Dr, Borrego Springs; ◷7am-8pm; P) in Borrego Springs. In summer many places keep shorter hours or have closing days.

Carmelita's Bar & Grill MEXICAN $

(☏760-767-5666; kfdorado@gmail.com; 575 Palm Canyon Dr, Mall; mains $5.50-18; ◷10am-9pm; P♿) This lively joint with its cheerful decor serves the best Mexican food in town, including delicious huevos rancheros. The bar staff knows how to whip up a good margarita.

★ Red Ocotillo BREAKFAST $$

(☏760-767-7400; www.facebook.com/pg/redocotillo; 721 Avenida Sureste; mains $10-20; ◷7am-8:30pm; ⏃♿▨) Empty tables are as rare as puddles in Anza-Borrego State Park at this charmer that serves quality java, all-day breakfast (try the smoked-salmon eggs Benedict) and bulging burgers and sandwiches, all at a quality standard you'd not expect out in the desert.

Carlee's AMERICAN $$

(☏760-767-3262; www.carleesplace.com; 660 Palm Canyon Dr, Borrego Springs; mains lunch $7-14, dinner $13-27; ◷11am-9pm, bar to 10pm Sun-Thu, midnight Fri & Sat; P) The menu is as long as a Tolstoy novel but the choices are good-old-fashioned Americana, hopscotching from burgers to pizza, steak to ribs, salads to pasta. It's popular with locals and visitors alike, not in the least for its full bar, pool table and live music on Saturdays.

❶ Information

Anza-Borrego Desert State Park Visitor Center (☏760-767-4205; www.parks.ca.gov; 200 Palm Canyon Dr, Borrego Springs; ◷9am-5pm daily mid-Oct–mid-May, Sat, Sun & holidays only mid-May–mid-Oct) Built partly under-ground, the stone walls of the park visitor center blend beautifully with the mountain backdrop, while inside are top-notch displays and audiovisual presentations. It's surrounded by a desert garden with a pupfish pond. The center is 1.5 miles west of central Borrego Springs.

❶ Getting There & Away

There is no public transport to Anza-Borrego Desert State Park. From Palm Springs it's 86 miles to Borrego Springs; take I-10 to Indio, then Hwy 86 south along the Salton Sea and west on to County Rte S22. From LA (150 miles) and Orange County (130 miles), take I-15 south to Hwy 79 to County Rtes S2 and S22. From San Diego (90 miles), I-8 to County Rte S2 is easiest, but if you want a more scenic ride, take twisty Hwy 79 from I-8 north through Cuyamaca Rancho State Park and into Julian, then head east on Hwy 78.

Around Anza-Borrego

Julian

The mountain hamlet of Julian, with its three-block main street, is a favorite getaway for city folk who love its quaint 1870s streetscape, gold-mining lore and famous apple pies. Prospectors, including many Confederate veterans, arrived here after the Civil War, but the population did not explode until the discovery of flecks of gold in 1869. Today, apples are the new gold with thousands of trees in the orchards flanking Hwy 178 outside town. Make sure you taste a slice of delicious apple pie, sold at bakeries all over town.

◉ Sights

Eagle Mining Co HISTORIC SITE

(☏760-765-0036; www.theeaglemining.com; 2320 C St; adult/child $10/5; ◷10am-4pm Mon-Fri, to 5pm Sat & Sun; P♿) Pan for gold and be regaled with tales of the hardscrabble life of the town's early pioneers during an hour-long underground tour through the former Eagle and High Peak gold mines.

🛏 Sleeping & Eating

Julian Gold Rush Hotel B&B $$

(☏760-765-0201; www.julianhotel.com; 2032 Main St; d $95-185; P❄✳︎⏃) At this 1897 antique-filled B&B, lace curtains, claw-foot tubs and other paraphernalia painstakingly evoke a bygone era. Rates include two-course breakfast and afternoon tea in the historic parlor, once visited by James Joyce.

Julian Pie Company

BAKERY $

(📞760-765-2449; www.julianpie.com; 2225 Main St; slices $3.50-4.50, whole pies $13-18; ⊙9am-5pm; 🖐) This famous bakery's classic apple pie is definitely crave-worthy but variations such as apple-berry crumb or the peach apple are just as tempting, especially when topped with ice cream. Buy them by the slice or take home the whole thing.

🛈 Getting There & Away

Julian sits at the junction of Hwys 78 and 79. It's about 60 miles from San Diego (via I-8 east to Hwy 79 north) and 30 miles from Borrego Springs (via Hwy 78 west).

Route 66

Completed in 1926, iconic Route 66 connected Chicago and Los Angeles across the heartland of America. During the Great Depression, thousands of migrants escaped the Dust Bowl by slogging westward in beat-up old jalopies. After WWII Americans took their newfound wealth and convertible cars on the road and headed west.

In California, Route 66 mostly follows the National Trails Hwy, prone to potholes and dangerous bumps. From the beach in Santa Monica, it rumbles through the LA basin,

---

DRIVING DIRECTIONS FOR LA TO BARSTOW

This stretch of Route 66 is about 200 miles long. From its western terminus at the Santa Monica Pier, follow Santa Monica Blvd east, turn right on Sunset Blvd and pick up the I-10 north to Pasadena. Take exit 31B and drive north, then turn right on Colorado Blvd. Continue east to Colorado Pl which turns into Huntington Dr E, which you'll follow to 2nd Ave, where you turn north, then east on Foothill Blvd through Monrovia. Jog south on S Myrtle Ave and hook a left on E Huntington Dr through Duarte. In Azusa, Huntington turns into E Foothill Blvd. Continue east through Rancho Cucamonga, Fontana and Rialto, then head north on N East St, turn left on W Highland Ave and pick up the I-215 to I-15. Drive downhill to Victorville, exiting at 7th St. Follow 7th St, then turn left at South D St and head north under I-15 where it turns into the National Trails Hwy, which runs straight into Barstow.

---

crosses over the Cajon Pass to the railway whistle-stop towns of Victorville and Barstow and runs a gauntlet of Mojave Desert ghost towns, arriving in Needles near the Nevada state line.

In larger towns, Mother Road relics may require a careful eye amid more contemporary architecture, but as you head toward Nevada, wide-open vistas and the occasional landmark remain barely changed from the days of road-trippers.

Los Angeles to Barstow

Kicking off at Route 66's western terminus in Santa Monica means first braving LA's urban and suburban sprawl. There are only a few photogenic vintage landmarks left in Pasadena, Rialto and Rancho Cucamonga, including a classic soda fountain, an orange-shaped juice stand, three retro steakhouses and a tipi hotel. Past the Cajon Pass, the route enters the vast open spaces of the Mojave. Stop to check out the sights in Victorville and Oro Grande before arriving in Barstow.

🔾 Sights

Aztec Hotel

HOTEL

(📞626-358-3231; 311 W Foothill Blvd, Monrovia) **FREE** This supposedly haunted hotel built in 1925 sports elaborate Mayan Revival-style detail and once housed a speakeasy where Hollywood celebs knocked 'em back en route to the Santa Anita racetrack.

Giant Orange

HISTORIC BUILDING

(15395 Foothill Blvd, Fontana; ⊙closed to public; 🅿) Cruising through Fontana, birthplace of the Hells Angels biker club, pause for a photo by the Giant Orange, a now-boarded-up 1930s orange-shaped juice stand of the kind that was once a fixture alongside SoCal's citrus groves. It used to offer weary Route 66 travelers 'all the juice you could drink' for a mere 10 cents.

First McDonald's Museum

MUSEUM

(📞909-885-6324; www.facebook.com/firstoriginal mcdonaldsmuseum; 1398 N E St, San Bernardino; by donation; ⊙10am-5pm; 🅿🖐) Half of the unofficial First McDonald's Museum has exhibits devoted to Route 66, with particularly interesting photographs and maps. It was first opened as a barbecue restaurant in 1940 by brothers Dick and Mac McDonald. Eventually Ray Kroc bought the rights to the name and built an empire. Today, the building is owned by Albert Okura, founder of the Juan Pollo chain of chicken shacks.

California Route 66 Museum   MUSEUM

(☑ 760-951-0436; www.califrt66museum.org; 16825 South D St, Victorville; donations welcome; ☺ 10am-4pm Thu-Sat & Mon, 11am-3pm Sun; ℙ 🏍) **FREE** Inside the old Red Rooster Cafe opposite the railroad tracks, this nostalgic collection features a kitchen sink's worth of yesteryear's treasures, including old signs and roadside memorabilia. It's worth a quick look.

Elmer's Bottle Tree Ranch   PUBLIC ART

(24266 National Trails Hwy, Oro Grande; ☺ outside 24hr; ℙ) **FREE** Colorful as a box of crayons, this roadside folk-art collection is a forest of over 200 'bottle trees' made from recycled soda and beer containers, telephone poles and weathered railroad signs.

🍴 Sleeping & Eating

Wigwam Motel   MOTEL $

(☑ 909-875-3005; www.wigwammotel.com; 2728 W Foothill Blvd, Rialto; r with bath $73-110; ℙ✳🛜🏊🐾) Get your kitsch on Route 66: stay snug in one of 19 30ft-tall concrete tipis. Built in 1949, they're equipped with nice furniture and have motel-type mod-cons. A kidney-shaped pool sits out the back.

Fair Oaks Pharmacy   DINER, ICE CREAM $

(☑ 626-799-1414; www.fairoakspharmacy.net; 1526 Mission St, South Pasadena; mains $6-11; ☺ 9am-9pm Mon-Sat, 10am-7pm Sun; 🏍) Get your kicks at this original 1915 soda fountain right on Route 66. Slurp an old-fashioned 'phosphate' (flavored syrup, soda water and 'secret potion') while waiting for a heaping sandwich or hamburger or stocking up on classic candy in the gift shops. It's touristy, sure, but fun nonetheless.

The Hat   SANDWICHES $

(☑ 626-857-0017; www.thehat.com; 611 W Alosta Ave/Rte 66, Glendora; mains $3-9; ☺ 10am-11pm Sun-Wed, to 1am Thu-Sat; 🏍) The classic sign featuring a chef's toque and the words 'World Famous Pastrami' greets hungry diners at the original Hat in Glendora where they've been piling up hot-pastrami sandwiches since 1951. Thinly sliced and generously salted, they're served on French rolls topped with au jus or gravy for dipping.

Iron Hog Restaurant & Saloon   AMERICAN $$

(☑ 760-843-0609; 20848 National Trails Hwy, Oro Grande; steaks $17-50; ☺ 8am-10pm Sun-Thu, to 2am Fri & Sat; ℙ) Roy Rodgers and Johnny Cash came by and scenes from *Easyrider* were filmed at this old-timey honky-tonk dripping with memorabilia and charac-

---

ℹ️ TIPS FOR DRIVING THE MOTHER ROAD

Sleeping

Barstow, with its chain motels, is the logical place to break the journey for a good night's sleep.

Eating

There's no shortage of eateries as you drive through the LA Basin, but as you enter the Mojave, options get thinner, with practically no pit stops between Barstow and Needles. Stock up on snacks in either town.

Navigating

For Route 66 enthusiasts who want to drive every mile of the old highway, a free turn-by-turn driving guide is available online at www.historic66.com. Also go to www.route66ca.org for more historical background, photos and info about special events.

---

ter(s). It's hugely popular with bikers and serves large portions of rib-stickers, including rattlesnake to help you connect with your inner macho. Save 2 bucks if you cook your own steak.

Magic Lamp Inn   AMERICAN $$

(☑ 909-981-8659; www.themagiclampinn.com; 8189 Foothill Blvd, Rancho Cucamonga; mains lunch $11-17, dinner $15-42; ☺ 11am-10pm Mon-Thu, 11am-2am Fri, 4:30pm-2am Sat) Easily recognized by its fabulous neon Aladdin's lamp, this 1955 Route 66 dining shrine sparkles with shiny dark woods and stained-glass windows. It serves up old-school sandwiches and steaks, including a mighty Chateaubriand carved table-side. There's music nightly and a champagne brunch on Sundays.

Sycamore Inn   STEAK $$$

(☑ 909-982-1104; www.thesycamoreinn.com; 8318 Foothill Blvd, Rancho Cucamonga; ☺ 5-9pm Mon-Thu, to 10pm Fri & Sat, 4-8:30pm Sun; ℙ✳) This storied Route 66 landmark has fed its juicy steaks to generations of meat lovers, including A-listers such as Marilyn Monroe. The menu brims with old-school faves such as oysters Rockefeller, crab cakes and shrimp cocktails to start things off before tucking into the aged and hard-carved cuts, including a 22oz porterhouse.

Barstow

At the junction of I-40 and I-15, nearly half-way between LA and Las Vegas, Barstow has been a desert travelers' crossroads for centuries. In 1776 Spanish colonial priest Francisco Garcés caravanned through, and in the mid-19th century the Old Spanish Trail passed nearby, with pioneer settlers on the Mojave River selling supplies to California immigrants. Meanwhile, mines were founded in the hills outside town. Barstow, named after a railway executive, got going as a railroad junction after 1886. After 1926 it became a major rest stop for motorists along Route 66 (Main St). Today it exists to serve nearby military bases and is still a busy pit stop for travelers.

◉ Sights

Route 66 'Mother Road' Museum MUSEUM
(☑760-255-1890; www.route66museum.org; 681 N 1st St; ☺10am-4pm Fri & Sat, 11am-4pm Sun, or by appointment; ℗♿) FREE Inside the beautifully restored **Casa del Desierto**, a 1911 Harvey House (architecturally significant railway inns named for their originator Fred Harvey), this museum documents life along the historic highway with some great old black-and-white photographs alongside eclectic relics, including a 1915 Ford Model T, a 1913 telephone switchboard and products made from locally mined minerals.

Western America Railroad Museum MUSEUM
(WARM; ☑760-256-9276; www.barstowrailmuseum.org; 685 N 1st St; ☺11am-4pm Fri-Sun; ℗) FREE Rail buffs make a beeline to the Casa del Desierto to marvel at a century's worth of railroad artifacts, including old timetables, uniforms, china and the Dog Tooth Mountain model railroad in this small museum. Outside you can see historic locomotives, bright-red cabooses and even a car used to ship racehorses.

Main Street Murals PUBLIC ART
(Main St, btwn 1st & 6th Sts; ☺24hr) FREE Barstow's Main St is well known for its history-themed murals that spruce up often empty and boarded-up buildings. Pick up a map at the Chamber of Commerce (p321).

Calico Ghost Town AMUSEMENT PARK
(☑800-862-2542; www.calicotown.com; 36600 Ghost Town Rd, Yermo; adult/child $8/5; ☺9am-5pm; ℗♿) This endearingly hokey Old West attraction consists of a cluster of pioneer-era buildings amid the ruins of a 1881 silver-mining town, reconstructed nearly a century later by Walter Knott (founder of Knott's Berry Farm). Note that optional activities such as gold panning, a mine tour and access to the 'mystery shack' are $3 extra each (or $7.50 for all). Trips on a narrow-gauge railway are $4.50. Old-timey heritage celebrations include Civil War reenactments and a bluegrass 'hootenanny.'

Take the Ghost Town Rd exit off I-15; it's about 3.5 miles uphill. There's also a **campground** (tent/RV sites with full hookup $30/40).

🍴 Sleeping & Eating

Only when the Mojave freezes over will there be no rooms left in Barstow. Just drive along E Main St and take your pick from the string of national chain motels, many with doubles from $40.

Oak Tree Inn MOTEL $
(☑888-456-8733, 760-254-1148; www.oaktreeinn.com; 35450 Yermo Rd, Yermo; r from $56; ℗ ⊜ ❋ ☎ ☷ ☒) Rooms are snug but modern and come with black-out draperies and triple-paned windows at this 65-room motel near the freeway. There's a pool and small gym for stretching after a day on the road and a 24-hour 1950s-style diner next door. It's about 10 miles east of Barstow (exit Ghost Town Rd off I-15). Kids under 12 stay free.

Peggy Sue's DINER $
(☑760-254-3370; www.peggysuesdiner.com; 35654 Yermo Rd, Yermo; mains $7.50-13; ☺6am-10pm; ℗❋♿) Built in 1954 as a simple, nine-stool, three-booth diner, Peggy Sue's has since grown into a miniempire with ice-cream shop, pizza parlor, a park out back with metal sculptures of 'diner-saurs' and kitschy-awesome gift shop. Many meals – burger to ham steak – are named after Hollywood artists. It's about 10 miles north of Barstow; take the Ghost Town Rd exit off I-15.

Lola's Kitchen MEXICAN $
(☑760-255-1007; 1244 E Main St; mains $7-9.50; ☺4am-7:30pmMon-Fri,to4:30pmSat; ℗♿) Interstate truckers, blue-collar workers and Vegas-bound hipsters all gather at this simple, colorful Mexican *cocina,* tucked away inside a strip mall and run by two sisters who make the full spectrum of honest-to-goodness Mexican faves, from quesadillas and tortas to carne asada and chile relleno. No alcohol. It's across from the Rodeway Inn.

Idle Spurs Steakhouse STEAK **$$**
(☑ 760-256-8888; www.thespurs.us; 690 Old Hwy
58; mains lunch $9-24, dinner $12-45; ⊙ 11am-9pm
Tue-Fri, from 4pm Sat & Sun; **P** **🛗**) In the saddle
since 1950, this Western-themed spot,
ringed around an atrium and a full bar, is a
fave with locals and Route 66 travelers. Sur-
render to your inner carnivore with slow-
roasted prime rib, hand-cut steaks and
succulent lobster tail. Kids menu available.

❶ Information

Barstow Area Chamber of Commerce (☑ 760-
256-8617; www.barstowroute66.com; 229 E
Main St; ⊙ 10am-4pm Mon-Thu, to 2pm Fri; 🛜)

Barstow to Needles

From Barstow, Route 66 crosses the Mojave
Desert on the National Trails Hwy that runs
mostly parallel to the I-40. Instagrammable
landmarks include the Bagdad Cafe in New-
berry Springs, Roy's Motel & Cafe in Amboy
and the schoolhouse in Goffs.

Bring a picnic since the eateries along
here, such as they are, are good for a cold
drink only.

◉ Sights

Stone Hotel HISTORIC BUILDING
(35630 Santa Fe St, Daggett; ⊙ no public entry; **P**)
Pay your respects to early desert adventurers
at the old Stone Hotel. Built in 1875 of ado-
be and stone, it once housed miners, desert
explorers and wanderers, including Sierra
Nevada naturalist John Muir and desert-
adventurer Death Valley Scotty.

The hotel is in Daggett, site of the harsh
California inspection station faced by Dust
Bowl refugees in *Grapes of Wrath*. Today,
there isn't much action, but it's a windswept
picturesque place nonetheless.

Bagdad Cafe LANDMARK
(☑ 760-257-3101; www.bagdadcafethereal.com;
46548 National Trails Hwy, Newberry Springs;
⊙ 7am-7pm) This grizzled cafe was the main
filming location of Percy Adlon's eponymous
1987 classic cult flick starring CCH Pounder
and Jack Palance. The interior is chocka-
block with posters, movie stills and mem-
orabilia while outside the old water tower
and Airstream trailer are slowly rusting
away. There's food but don't bother.

Roy's Motel & Cafe HISTORIC SITE
(www.rt66roys.com; National Old Trails Hwy, Amboy;
⊙ 7am-8pm, seasonal variations; **P**) **FREE** In the

DRIVING DIRECTIONS FOR BARSTOW TO NEEDLES

This stretch of Route 66 is about 180
miles long. Leave Barstow on I-40 east
and exit at Daggett. Drive north on A St,
cross the railroad tracks and turn right
on Santa Fe St. Continue on Santa Fe,
take your first right, then turn left to pick
up the National Trails Hwy going east. It
runs parallel to I-40, crosses it at Lavic
and continues north of I-40. This pot-
holed, crumbling backcountry stretch
crawls through ghostly desert towns. In
Ludlow turn right on Crucero Rd, cross
I-40 again and turn left. Beyond Ludlow,
the Mother Road veers away from the
freeway, leaves the National Trails Hwy
past Essex and heads north on Goffs
Rd through Fenner, where it once more
crosses I-40. Follow Goffs Rd to I-40 and
head east to Needles.

ghost town of Amboy, this beautifully kept
landmark was for decades a popular water-
ing hole for Route 66 travelers. If you believe
the lore, Roy once cooked his famous Route
66 double cheeseburger on the hood of a '63
Mercury. Although the motel is abandoned,
the gas station and store are usually open.

Amboy Crater VOLCANO
(☑ 760-326-7000; www.blm.gov/ca; ⊙ sunrise-
sunset; **P**) **FREE** Amboy Crater, off National
Trails Hwy, 2 miles west of Amboy, is a 250ft-
high, almost perfectly symmetrical volcanic
cinder cone. You can hike to the top for
great views over the lava fields where NASA
engineers field-tested the Mars Rover. The
3-mile round-trip hike doesn't have a stitch
of shade, so avoid heading out midday or in
summer.

Goffs Schoolhouse HISTORIC SITE
(☑ 760-733-4482; www.mdhca.org; 37198 Lanfair
Rd, Essex; ⊙ 9am-4pm Sat-Mon Oct-Jun, call to
confirm; **P**) **FREE** The shade of cottonwood
trees makes the 1914 Spanish Mission–style
Goffs Schoolhouse a soothing stop along this
sun-drenched stretch of highway. It stands as
part of the best-preserved pioneer settlement
in the Mojave Desert. Browsing the black-
and-white photographs of hardscrabble Dust
Bowl migrants gives an evocative glimpse
into the tough life on the edge of the Mojave.
A self-guided tour pamphlet is available.

Old Trails Bridge
BRIDGE

(⊘ no public access) East of the California–Arizona state line, south of I-40, the arched Old Trails Bridge welcomes the Mother Road to California under endless blue skies. You might recognize the bridge: the Great Depression–era Joad family used it to cross the Colorado River in the movie version of John Steinbeck's novel *Grapes of Wrath*.

Mojave National Preserve

If you're on a quest for the 'middle of nowhere,' you'll find it in the wilderness of the **Mojave National Preserve** (☎ 760-252-6100; www.nps.gov/moja; btwn I-15 & I-40; Ⓟ) 🖉 FREE, a 1.6-million-acre jumble of sand dunes, Joshua trees, volcanic cinder cones and habitats for bighorn sheep, desert tortoises, jackrabbits and coyotes. Solitude and serenity are the big draws. Daytime temperatures hover above 100°F (37°C) during summer, then plummet to around 50°F (10°C) in winter, when snowstorms are not unheard of. Strong winds will practically knock you over in spring and fall. No gas is available within the preserve.

◉ Sights & Activities

Kelso Dunes
DUNES

(off Kelbaker Rd; Ⓟ) FREE Rising to 700ft, these beautiful dunes are the country's third-tallest sand dunes. Under the right conditions they emanate low humming sounds that are caused by shifting sands. Running downhill sometimes jump-starts the effect. The trailhead to the dunes is about 3 miles on a graded dirt road west of Kelbaker Rd, 7 miles south of the Kelso Depot Visitor Center.

Cima Dome
MOUNTAIN

Visible to the south from I-15, Cima Dome is a 1500ft hunk of granite spiked with volcanic

cinder cones and crusty outcrops of basalt left by lava. Its slopes are smothered in Joshua trees that collectively make up the largest such forest in the world. For close-ups, tackle the 3-mile round-trip hike up **Teutonia Peak** (5755ft), starting on Cima Rd, 5 miles northwest of Cima.

White Horse Canyon Rd
DRIVING

This incredibly scenic 9.5-mile backcountry drive up to Mid Hills starts at Hole-in-the-Wall. Ask about current conditions at the visitor center before setting out.

Hole-in-the-Wall
HIKING, DRIVING

(Black Canyon Rd) FREE These vertical walls of rhyolite tuff (pronounced toof), which look like Swiss-cheese cliffs made of unpolished marble, are the result of a powerful prehistoric volcanic eruption that blasted rocks across the landscape. Learn how the site got its name by hiking the 0.5-mile **Rings Loop Trail** where metal rings lead down through a narrow slot-canyon once used by Native Americans to escape 19th-century ranchers.

Hole-in-the-Wall lies east of Kelso-Cima Rd via the unpaved Cedar Canyon Rd. Coming from I-40, exit at Essex Rd.

🛏 Sleeping & Eating

Camping is the only way to overnight in the preserve. Baker, on the northwestern edge along I-15, has plenty of cheap, charmless motels. Coming from the north, the casino hotels in Primm on the Nevada border offer slightly better options. If you're traveling on the I-40, Needles is the closest town to spend the night.

The only place in the park to get a bite is at the old-fashioned lunch counter in the Kelso Visitor Center. Baker is the closest town with restaurants and grocery stores.

SLOW: DESERT TORTOISE X-ING

The Mojave is the home of the desert tortoise, which can live for up to 80 years, munching on wildflowers and grasses. Its canteen-like bladder allows it to go for up to a year without drinking. Using its strong hind legs, it burrows to escape the summer heat and freezing winter temperatures and also to lay eggs. The sex of the hatchlings is determined by temperature: cooler for males, hotter for females.

Disease and shrinking habitat have decimated the desert-tortoise population. They do like to rest in the shade under parked cars (take a quick look around before just driving away) and are often hit by off-road drivers. If you see a tortoise in trouble (eg stranded in the middle of a road), call a ranger.

It's illegal to pick one up or even approach too closely and for good reason: a frightened tortoise may urinate on a perceived attacker, possibly dying of dehydration before the next rains come.

Camping

First-come, first-served sites with pit toilets and potable water are available at Hole-in-the-Wall and Mid Hills campgrounds. There's also free backcountry camping as long as you're at least 0.5 miles from developed areas and roads and 0.25 miles from any water source. Roadside camping is permitted in areas already used for the purpose. Check www.nps.gov/moja for locations or ask for details and directions at the visitor center. No permits required.

❶ Information

Hole-in-the-Wall Visitor Center (☏760-928-2572, 760-252-6104; Black Canyon Rd; ⊙9am-3pm Fri-Sun) Has seasonal ranger programs, backcountry information and road-condition updates. It's about 20 miles north of I-40 via Essex Rd.

Kelso Depot Visitor Center (☏760-252-6108; www.nps.gov/moja; Kelbaker Rd, Kelso; ⊙10am-5pm) The preserve's main visitor center is in a gracefully restored, 1920s Spanish Mission–style railway depot. The knowledgeable rangers can help you plan your day. There are also nicely presented natural- and cultural-history exhibits, a small gift store and an old-fashioned **lunch counter** (dishes $3.50 to $8.50).

❶ Getting There & Away

There is no public transport to or within Mojave National Preserve, which is hemmed in by I-15 in the north and I-40 in the south. The main entrance off I-15 is at Baker. From there it's 35 miles south to the central Kelso Depot Visitor Center via Kelbaker Rd, which links to I-40 after another 23 miles. Cima Rd and Morning Star Mine Rd near Nipton are two other northern access roads. From I-40, Essex Rd leads to the Black Canyon Rd and Hole-in-the-Wall.

Around Mojave National Preserve

Nipton

Hugging the northeastern edge of the Mojave National Preserve, this isolated Old West outpost started out in 1900 as a gold-miners' camp and soon after began seeing the railroad pass through en route from Salt Lake City to Los Angeles. Practically a ghost town today (albeit with its own solar plant!), it was sold in August 2017 for close to $5 million to American Green, an Arizona-based

marijuana-focused technology and growing company that plans to turn Nipton into a destination for pot aficionados.

Primm

Driving east on I-15 at night, the desert darkness is brightened at the Nevada state line by Primm and its three garishly blinking casino resorts. It's worth stopping if you want to fold a little gambling action into your desert getaway or need a decent and cheapish place to crash for the night. A fashion outlet mall and a nearby 18-hole golf course provide additional diversions. Coming from the east, it's a handy stopover if you're headed for Death Valley or the Mojave National Preserve.

🛏 Sleeping & Eating

Whiskey Pete's CASINO HOTEL **$**
(☏702-386-7867; www.primmvalleyresorts.com; 100 W Primm Blvd; r from $39, resort fee $15; P✸🐕📶♨) This is probably the best of the trio of badly aging casino hotels in Primm, providing you stay in one of the newly renovated rooms with pillow-top beds, big LCD TV and small fridge. The outdoor pool is only open during warmer months.

GP's STEAK **$$$**
(☏702-679-5170; www.primmvalleyresorts.com; 31900 Las Vegas Blvd; mains $23-44; ⊙5-9pm; P) The best among the largely poor or mediocre eateries in Primm, GP's trains the spotlight on quality meats and seafood, prepared in classic fashion. Kick things off with old-school continental classics such as lobster bisque or oysters Rockefeller and wrap up with the luscious cheesecake.

Death Valley National Park

The very name evokes all that is harsh, hot and hellish – a punishing, barren and lifeless place of Old Testament severity. Yet closer inspection reveals that in **Death Valley** (☏760-786-3200; www.nps.gov/deva; 7-day-pass per car $25; ⊙24hr; P🚶) 🌿 nature is putting on a truly spectacular show: singing sand dunes, water-sculpted canyons, boulders moving across the desert floor, extinct volcanic craters, palm-shaded oases, stark mountains rising to 11,000ft and plenty of endemic wildlife. This is a land of superlatives, holding the US records for hottest temperature (134°F/57°C), lowest point (Badwater, 282ft

Death Valley & Around

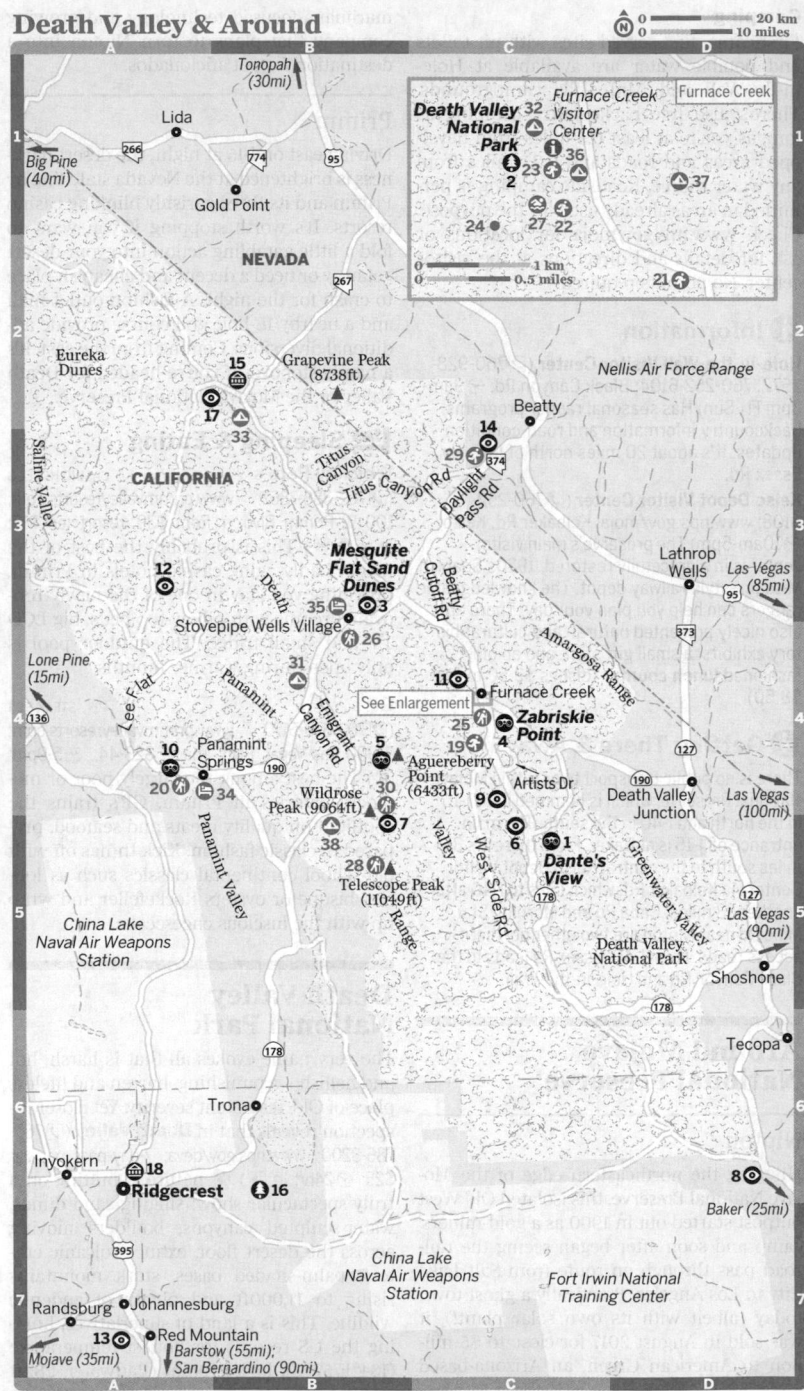

Death Valley & Around

below sea level) and largest national park outside Alaska (over 5000 sq miles).

Furnace Creek is Death Valley's commercial hub, with the park's main visitor center, a general store, gas station, post office, ATM, wi-fi, golf course, lodging and restaurants.

Park entry permits ($25 per vehicle) are valid for seven days and available from self-service pay stations at the park's access roads and at the visitor center.

◎ Sights & Activities

Families can pick up a free fun-for-all-ages *Junior Ranger Activity Booklet* at the Furnace Creek visitor center (p330), which has info-packed handouts on all kinds of activities, including hiking trails and mountain-biking routes.

◎ Furnace Creek & Around

Borax Museum MUSEUM
(☑ 760-786-2345; www.furnacecreekresort.com; Hwy 190, Ranch at Furnace Creek; ⊙ 9am-9pm Oct-May, variable summer; P 🅿) FREE On the grounds of the Ranch at Furnace Creek

(p328), this museum explains the history of borax in Death Valley, with alluring samples of local borate minerals and their uses. Out back there's a large collection of pioneer-era mining and transportation equipment.

**Ranch at Furnace Creek
Swimming Pool** SWIMMING
(☑ 760-786-2345; www.furnacecreekresort.com; Hwy 190, Ranch at Furnace Creek; nonguests $5; ⊙ 8am-11pm) This huge spring-fed pool is kept at a steady 84°F (29°C) and cleaned with a nifty flow-through system that uses minimal chlorine. It's primarily for Ranch at Furnace Creek guests, but a limited number of visitor passes are available at reception.

Furnace Creek Golf Course GOLF
(☑ 760-786-3373; www.furnacecreekresort.com/activities/golfing; Hwy 190, Furnace Creek; greens fees 9/18 holes $30/60; ⊙ year-round) For novelty's sake, play a round at the world's lowest-elevation golf course (214ft below sea level, 18 holes, par 70), redesigned by Perry Dye in 1997. It's also been certified by the Audubon Society for its environment-friendly management.

Harmony Borax Works
HISTORIC SITE

(📞760-786-3200; www.nps.gov/deva; Hwy 190) **FREE** Just north of Furnace Creek, a 0.5-mile interpretive trail follows in the footsteps of late-19th-century Chinese laborers and through the adobe ruins of Harmony Borax Works, which operated from 1883–88. Follow up with a side trip through twisting Mustard Canyon.

⊙ South of Furnace Creek

★ Zabriskie Point
VIEWPOINT

(📞760-786-3200; www.nps.gov/deva; Hwy 190; 🅿) Early morning is the best time to visit Zabriskie Point for spectacular views across golden badlands eroded into waves, pleats and gullies. It was named for a manager of the Pacific Coast Borax Company and also inspired the title of Michelangelo Antonio's 1970s movie. The cover of U2's *Joshua Tree* album was also shot here.

★ Dante's View
VIEWPOINT

(📞760-786-3200; www.nps.gov/deva; Dante's View Rd, off Hwy 190; 🅿) At 5475ft, the view of the entire southern Death Valley basin from the top of the Black Mountains is absolutely brilliant, especially at sunrise or sunset. On very clear days, you can simultaneously see the highest (Mt Whitney) and lowest (Badwater) points in the contiguous USA.

Allow about 1½ hours for the 26-mile round-trip from the turnoff at Hwy 190, east of Furnace Creek.

Golden Canyon
HIKING

(📞760-786-3200; www.nps.gov/deva; Hwy 178) Narrow canyons winding through a wonderland of golden rocks is the ammo of this trail network between Hwy 178 and Zabriskie Point. Several routes can be combined for longer treks. The most popular is a 3-mile out-and-back trek from the main trailhead off Hwy 178 to the oxidized iron cliffs of Red Cathedral. Combining it with the Gower Gulch Loop adds another mile.

★ Artists Drive
SCENIC DRIVE

(📞760-786-3200; www.nps.gov/deva; off Hwy 190) About 9 miles south of Furnace Creek, the 9-mile, one-way Artists Drive scenic loop offers 'wow' moments around every turn; it's best done in the late afternoon when exposed minerals and volcanic ash make the hills erupt in fireworks of color.

Badwater Basin
NATURAL FEATURE

(Hwy 190; 🅿) The lowest point in North America (282ft below sea level) is an eerily beautiful landscape of crinkly salt flats. Here you can walk out on to a constantly evaporating bed of salty, mineralized water that's otherworldly in its beauty. It's about 17 miles south of Furnace Creek.

Devil's Golf Course
NATURAL FEATURE

(📞760-786-3200; www.nps.gov/deva; Hwy 178; 🅿) Some 15 miles south of Furnace Creek, salt has piled up into saw-toothed miniature mountains in what was once a major lake that evaporated about 2000 years ago. You're free to explore this bizarre landscape, but don't expect to tee up.

⊙ Stovepipe Wells & Around

★ Mesquite Flat Sand Dunes
NATURAL FEATURE

(📞760-786-3200; www.nps.gov/deva; Hwy 190) The most accessible dunes in Death Valley are an undulating sea of sand rising up to 100ft high next to the highway near Stovepipe Wells Village. They're at their most photogenic at sunrise or sunset when bathed in soft light and accented by long, deep shadows. Keep an eye out for animal tracks. Full-moon nights are especially magical.

Mosaic Canyon Trail
HIKING

(📞760-786-3200; www.nps.gov/deva; Mosaic Canyon Rd, off Hwy 190, Stovepipe Wells Village) West of Stovepipe Wells Village, a 2.3-mile gravel road leads to Mosaic Canyon, where you can hike and scramble past smooth multihued rock walls. Colors are sharpest at midday.

About 1.3 miles into the hike, passage is blocked by a pile of massive boulders but it's possible to squeeze by on the left and continue the trek. Budget about 2½ hours for the 4-mile round-trip.

⊙ Northern Park

Racetrack Playa
NATURAL FEATURE

(📞760-786-3200; www.nps.gov/deva; Racetrack Rd) Past the northern end of Hwy 190, it's slow going for 27 miles on a tire-shredding dirt road (high-clearance and 4WD usually required) to the eerie Racetrack, where hundreds of sizeable rocks have etched tracks into the dry lake bed. In 2014, a group of researchers finally lifted the mystery when they actually observed the stones being moved by thin sheets of ice that were pushed by gentle winds across the desert floor. Read all about it at www.racetrackplaya.org.

Ubehebe Crater
NATURAL FEATURE

(www.nps.gov/deva; Hwy 190) Hwy 190 ends at 600ft-deep Ubehebe Crater, formed some 300 years ago by the meeting of fiery magma and cool groundwater. As the water turned into steam, it expanded until the pressure gave way to a cataclysmic explosion. The result is easily appreciated from the parking lot, but you can also walk down to the bottom or loop around the perimeter of the half-mile-wide crater.

Scotty's Castle
HISTORIC BUILDING

(📞 760-786-3200; www.nps.gov/deva; ⊘ closed) Closed due to flood damage and not likely to reopen until at least 2019, this whimsical castle was the desert home of Walter E Scott, alias 'Death Valley Scotty,' a quintessential tall-tale teller who captivated people with his stories of gold. His most lucrative friendship was with Albert Johnson, a wealthy insurance magnate from Chicago, who bankrolled this elaborate desert oasis in the 1920s.

⊙ Towards Beatty

Titus Canyon Rd
SCENIC DRIVE

(📞 760-786-3200; www.nps.gov/deva; off Hwy 374) About 2 miles outside the park boundary is the turnoff to the spectacular one-way backcountry road, Titus Canyon Rd, leading to Hwy 190 in 27 miles of rough track. The road climbs, dips and winds to a crest in the Grapevine Mountains, then slowly descends back to the desert floor past a ghost town, petroglyphs and canyon narrows.

The best light conditions are in the morning. High-clearance vehicles are highly recommended. Check road conditions at the visitor center (p330).

Goldwell Open Air Museum
MUSEUM

(📞 702-870-9946; www.goldwellmuseum.org; off Hwy 374; ⊘ park 24hr, visitor center 10am-4pm Mon-Sat, to 2pm summer; 🅿) FREE Near the ghost town of Rhyolite, just east of Death Valley National Park, this outdoor sculpture park was begun in 1984 by Belgian artist Albert Szukalski (1945–2000) with his haunting version of DaVinci's *Last Supper*. Other Belgian friends soon joined him and added other, often bizarre, sculptures. Today there are seven sculptures as well as a visitor center and small store.

Rhyolite
GHOST TOWN

(off Hwy 374; 🅿) FREE Just outside the Death Valley eastern park boundary, Rhyolite epitomizes the hurly-burly, boom-and-bust story of Western gold-rush mining towns in early 1900s. Hard to imagine today that during its peak years between 1904–16, it had 8000 residents. Highlights among the skeletal remains of houses are the Spanish Mission-style train station, a three-story bank building and a house made from 50,000 beer bottles by miner Tom Kelly.

⊙ Panamint Springs & Emigrant Canyon Rd

Father Crowley Vista
VIEWPOINT

(📞 760-786-3200; www.nps.gov/deva; off Hwy 190, Panamint Springs) This viewpoint peers deep into Rainbow Canyon, created by lava flows and scattered with multihued volcanic cinders. It's worth a quick stop on your way in or out of Death Valley. The turnoff is about 8 miles west of Panamint Springs.

Darwin Falls
HIKING

(📞 760-786-3200; www.nps.gov/deva; Hwy 190, Panamint Springs) This natural-spring-fed year-round cascade plunges into a gorge, embraced by willows that attract migratory birds. Look for the (unmarked) turnoff about 0.75 miles west of Panamint Springs, then follow the dirt road for 2.5 miles to the parking area. The 1-mile hike to the first waterfall requires some climbing over rocks and crossing small streams.

Charcoal Kilns
HISTORIC SITE

(📞 760-786-3200; www.nps.gov/deva; Emigrant Canyon Rd) Emigrant Canyon Rd climbs steeply over Emigrant Pass for the turnoff to Wildrose Canyon Rd and a lineup of 10 large beehive-shaped charcoal kilns made of stone and once used by miners to make fuel for smelting silver and lead ore. The landscape is subalpine, with forests of piñon pine and juniper; it can be covered with snow, even in spring.

Aguereberry Point
VIEWPOINT

(www.nps.gov/deva; off Emigrant Canyon Rd) Named for a lucky French miner who struck gold at the nearby Eureka Mine, Aguereberry Point sits at a lofty 6433ft above the desert floor and delivers fantastic views into the valley and out to the colorful Funeral Mountains. The best time to visit is late afternoon. The 6.5-mile road is quite rough and a high-clearance vehicle is highly recommended.

Wildrose Peak
HIKING

(☎760-786-3200; www.nps.gov/deva; Wildrose Canyon Rd) This moderate-to-strenuous trail begins near the charcoal kilns off Wildrose Canyon Rd and ascends to Wildrose Peak (9064ft). The 8.4-mile round-trip hike is best in spring or fall. The elevation gain is 2200ft, but great views start about halfway up.

Telescope Peak
HIKING

(☎760-786-3200; www.nps.gov/deva; Wildrose Canyon Rd) The park's most demanding summit is Telescope Peak (11,049ft), with views that plummet to the desert floor, which is as far below as two Grand Canyons deep! The 14-mile round-trip trail climbs 3000ft above Mahogany Flat, off upper Wildrose Canyon Rd. Summiting in winter requires ice-axe, crampons and winter-hiking experience. By June, the trail is usually free of snow. Get full details from the visitor center (p330) before setting out.

☞ Tours

Death Valley Jeep Tours
DRIVING

(www.farabeejeeps.com; Hwy 190, Furnace Creek; tours from $145, 2-person minimum; ☺Sep-May) If you want to venture into the background, but don't want to go it alone, sign up for a Jeep tour with this local company. Options include a trip down Titus Canyon ($145), out to Racetrack Playa ($280), into Echo Canyon ($150) or the more general Death Valley Experience ($195). There's a two-person minimum.

CALLING DEATH VALLEY HOME

Timbisha Shoshone tribespeople lived in the Panamint Range for centuries, visiting the valley every winter to gather acorns, hunt waterfowl, catch pupfish in marshes and cultivate small areas of corn, squash and beans. After the federal government created Death Valley National Monument in 1933, the tribe was forced to move several times and was eventually restricted to a 40-acre village site near Furnace Creek, where it still lives. In 2000 President Clinton signed an act transferring 7500 acres of land back to the Timbisha Shoshone tribe, creating the first Native American reservation inside a US national park. Learn more at www.timbisha.com.

Furnace Creek Stables
HORSEBACK RIDING

(☎760-614-1018; www.furnacecreekstables.net; Hwy 190, Furnace Creek; 1/2hr rides $55/70; ☺mid-Oct–mid-May; 🐴) Saddle up to see what Death Valley looks like from the back of a horse on guided trail rides. The one-hour ride stays on the sunbaked desert floor while the two-hour rides venture into the foothills of the Funeral Mountains for great valley views. Monthly full-moon rides are the most memorable, while 45-minute carriage rides are safe and relaxing fun for all.

★ Festivals & Events

Death Valley '49ers
CULTURAL

(www.deathvalley49ers.org; ☺early/mid-Nov) Furnace Creek hosts this weeklong historical encampment, featuring cowboy poetry, campfire sing-alongs, a gold-panning contest and a Western art show. Show up early to watch the pioneer wagons come thunderin' in.

🛏 Sleeping

Camping is plentiful but if you're looking for a place with a roof, in-park options are limited, pricey and often booked solid in springtime. Alternative bases are the gateway towns of Beatty (40 miles from Furnace Creek), Lone Pine (40 miles), Death Valley Junction (30 miles) and Tecopa (70 miles). Options a bit further afield include Ridgecrest (120 miles) and Las Vegas (140 miles).

Ranch at Furnace Creek
RESORT $$

(☎760-786-2345; www.furnacecreekresort.com; Hwy 190, Furnace Creek; cabin/r from $140/180; P☺❄🐕📶🏊) Tailor-made for families, this rambling resort with multiple, motel-style buildings has received a vigorous facelift, resulting in spiffy rooms swathed in desert colors, updated bathrooms and French doors leading to porches with comfortable patio furniture. The grounds encompass a playground, spring-fed swimming pool, tennis courts, golf course, restaurants, shops and the Borax Museum (p325).

Stovepipe Wells Village Hotel
MOTEL $$

(☎760-786-2387; www.deathvalleyhotels.com; 51880 Hwy 190, Stovepipe Wells; RV sites $33.30, r $140-210; P☺❄@📶🏊) The 83 rooms at this private resort have beds draped in quality linens and accented with cheerful Native American–patterned blankets. The small pool is cool and the on-site cowboy-style restaurant serves breakfast and dinner daily, with lunch available in the next-door saloon. Wi-fi is spotty but the new business center has two public computers and a printer.

Panamint Springs Resort   MOTEL $$
(☏ 775-482-7680; www.panamintsprings.com; Hwy 190, Panamint Springs; r $79-129, cabins $94-205; P ❄ 🐾 🎾) Elsewhere 'off-grid' is a state of mind, but it's a statement of fact at this

....

CAMPING IN DEATH VALLEY

The **national park service** (www.nps.gov/deva; campsites free-$36) operates nine campgrounds, including four tucked into the Panamint Mountains. Only Furnace Creek accepts reservations and only from mid-October to mid-April. All other campgrounds are first-come, first-served. At peak times, such as weekends during the spring wildflower bloom, campsites fill by midmorning. On those days, vast Sunset campground is your best bet for snagging a last-minute spot, plus there's always the option of free backcountry camping.

Private campgrounds catering mostly to RVers can be found in Stovepipe Wells Village (p138), Ranch at Furnace Creek (p138) and Panamint Springs Resort (p138).

Furnace Creek Ranch and Stovepipe Wells Village offer public showers ($5, including swimming-pool access). Pay at reception.

CAMPGROUND	SEASON	LOCATION	FEE	CHARACTERISTICS
Furnace Creek (Map p329; ☏ 877-444-6777; www.recreation.gov; per site without/with hookup $22/36)	year-round	valley floor	$22	pleasant grounds, some shady sites
Sunset (Map p329; ☏ 760-786-3200; www.nps.gov/deva; Hwy 190, Furnace Creek; per site $14; ⊘ mid-Oct–mid-Apr)	Oct–Apr	valley floor	$14	huge, RV-oriented
Texas Spring (Map p329; ☏ 760-786-3200; www.nps.gov/deva; off Hwy 190, Furnace Creek; per site $16; ⊘ mid-Oct–mid-May)	Oct–Apr	valley floor	$16	good for tents
Stovepipe Wells (Map p329; ☏ 760-786-3200; www.nps.gov/deva; Hwy 190, Stovepipe Wells Village; per site $14; ⊘ mid-Oct–mid-May)	Oct–Apr	valley floor	$14	parking-lot style, close to dunes
Mesquite Springs (Map p329; ☏ 760-786-3200; www.nps.gov/deva; Hwy 190; per site $14)	year-round	1800ft	$14	close to Ubehebe Crater
Emigrant (Map p329; ☏ 760-786-3200; www.nps.gov/deva; Hwy 190; ⊘ year-round) **FREE**	year-round	2100ft	free	tents only
Wildrose (Map p329; ☏ 760-786-3200; www.nps.gov/deva; Wildrose Canyon Rd, off Hwy 178) **FREE**	year-round	4100ft	free	seasonal water
Thorndike (Map p329; ☏ 760-786-3200; www.nps.gov/deva; Wildrose Canyon Rd, off Hwy 178; ⊘ Mar–Nov) **FREE**	Mar–Nov	7400ft	free	may need 4WD, no water, closed in winter
Mahogany Flat (Map p329; ☏ 760-786-3200; www.nps.gov/deva; Wildrose Canyon Rd, off Hwy 178; ⊘ Mar–Nov) **FREE**	Mar–Nov	8200ft	free	may need 4WD, no water, closed in winter

Free backcountry camping (no campfires) is allowed along dirt roads at least 1 mile away from paved roads and developed and day-use areas, and 100yd from any water source. Park your car next to the roadway and pitch your tent on a previously used campsite to minimize your impact. For a list of areas that are off-limits to backcountry camping, as well as additional regulations, check www.nps.gov/deva or stop by the visitor center (p330) where you can also pick up a free voluntary permit.

DESERT BREWS

In the middle of nowhere, **Death Valley Brewing** (☑760-852-4273; www.deathvalleybrewing.com; 102 Old Spanish Trail; ⊗noon-6pm Fri-Sun Nov-Apr) is not a mirage but the pint-sized operation of artist and brewer Jon Zellhoefer in a restored railroad tie house. He usually has nine to 12 small-batch cold ones on tap, from IPAs to Belgian ales, stouts to wheat beers, all made with water from the local mineral springs.

low-key, family-run motel with rustic cabins on the park's western border. A generator creates electricity, limited internet access comes via satellite, and phone service is dicey at best (reserve via the website).

It's part of a village that also has a restaurant-bar, a campground, a gas station and a general store.

Inn at Furnace Creek   HOTEL $$$
(☑760-786-2345; www.furnacecreekresort.com; Hwy 190; d from $450; ⊗mid-Oct–mid-May; P☕❄@🗐📶) Roll out of bed and count the colors of the desert as you pull back the curtains in your room at this 1927 Spanish Mission–style hotel. After a day of sweaty touring, enjoy languid valley views while lounging by the spring-fed swimming pool, cocktail in hand. It's the classiest place in Death Valley, but rooms would benefit from updating.

🍴 Eating & Drinking

There are restaurants and stores for stocking up on basic groceries and camping supplies in Furnace Creek, Stovepipe Wells Village and Panamint Springs. Generally speaking, restaurants are expensive and mediocre. Hours vary seasonally; some close in summer.

Toll Road Restaurant   AMERICAN $$
(☑760-786-2387; www.deathvalleyhotels.com; 51880 Hwy 190, Stovepipe Wells Village; mains $12.50-34; ⊗7-10am & 5:30-9pm; P📶) Above-par cowboy cooking happens at this ranch house, which gets Old West flair from a rustic fireplace and rickety wooden chairs and tables. Many of the mostly meaty mains are made with local ingredients, such as mesquite honey, prickly pear and piñons. Many

dishes are named after Death Valley landmarks (eg Scotty's Chicken Wings).

Panamint Springs Resort   AMERICAN $$
(☑775-482-7680; www.panamintsprings.com; Hwy 190, Panamint Springs; burgers $10-18, pizza $15-35; ⊗7am-9pm; P) It may look funky but this outback cafe serves some of the best Angus burgers, crispy salads and pizza (in three sizes) in Death Valley. Toast the panoramic views from the front porch with one of its 150 bottled beers from around the world.

Corkscrew Saloon   AMERICAN $$
(☑760-786-2345; www.furnacecreekresort.com/dining; Hwy 190, Ranch at Furnace Creek; mains $12-20; ⊗11am-11pm, seasonal variations; P📶) This gregarious joint has darts, draft beer and dynamite barbecue at dinner time, as well as pretty good, but pricey pizzas and pub grub such as onion rings and burgers. There's Badwater Ale on tap and a jukebox for entertainment. No reservations.

⭐ Inn Dining Room   INTERNATIONAL $$$
(☑760-786-2345; www.furnacecreekresort.com/dining; Inn at Furnace Creek, off Hwy 190; breakfast $10-17, mains lunch $10-14, dinner $27-58; ⊗7-10:30am & noon-2pm Mon-Sat, 7-10am & 5:30-9pm Sun mid-Oct–mid-May; P📶) This formal restaurant delivers continental cuisine with stellar views of the Panamint Mountains. For a more chilled ambience, enjoy breakfast, lunch or cocktails on the patio. Reservations are key for dinner when a 'no shorts or tank tops' policy kicks in, although you could always belly up to the bar and eat there. The Sunday brunch is a gourmet gut-buster ($35).

ℹ Information

MONEY
There are ATMs at the Ranch at Furnace Creek and in Stovepipe Wells.

TELEPHONE
Cell towers provide service at Furnace Creek and Stovepipe Wells but there's little to no coverage elsewhere in the park.

TOURIST INFORMATION
Furnace Creek Visitor Center (☑760-786-3200; www.nps.gov/deva; ⊗8am-5pm; 📶♿) The modern visitor center has engaging exhibits on the park's ecosystem and indigenous tribes as well as a gift shop, clean toilets, (slow) wi-fi and friendly rangers to answer questions and help you plan your day. First-time visitors should watch the gorgeously shot 20-minute movie *Seeing Death Valley*. Check the schedule for ranger-led activities.

ℹ️ Getting There & Away

The park's main roads (Hwys 178 and 190) are paved and in great shape, but if your travel plans include dirt roads, a high-clearance vehicle and off-road tires are highly recommended and essential on many routes. 4WD is often necessary after rains. Always check with the **visitor center** (p330) for current road conditions, especially before heading to remote areas.

Gas is available 24/7 at Furnace Creek and Stovepipe Wells Village and from 7am to 9:30pm in Panamint Springs. Prices are much higher than outside the park, especially at Panamint.

ℹ️ Getting Around

Furnace Creek Bike Rentals (☑760-786-3371; Hwy 190, Ranch at Furnace Creek; per 1/5/24hr $15/34/49; ☺Oct-Apr) The general store at the Ranch at Furnace Creek rents 24-speed mountain bikes. Cycling is allowed on designated bike trails as well as paved and dirt roads that are also open to public car travel. Bikes are not allowed on hiking trails, closed roads and service roads. Pick up route suggestions at the park's visitor center.

Farabee's Jeep Rentals (☑760-786-9872; www.deathvalleyjeeprentals.com; Hwy 190; 2-/4-door Jeep incl 200 miles $250/300; ☺Sep-May) Rent a Jeep Wrangler from this outfit to explore Death Valley's backcountry. You must be over 25 years old, have a US driver's license, credit card and proof of insurance. International visitors must purchase CDW at $60 per day. The four-door Jeeps seat up to five people. Rates include water and a GPS spot unit in case of emergency.

Around Death Valley National Park

Shoshone

Just a blip on the map, Shoshone stakes its existence on being an early-20th-century railroad stop with lodging, eating and other businesses. The railroad disappeared in 1941, but the village still caters to travelers with a gas station, store, restaurant and lodging, as well as visitor information.

◉ Sights

Shoshone Museum   MUSEUM
(Hwy 127; by donation; ☺9am-3pm Wed-Mon) A rusted Chevy parked next to antique gas pumps and other flotsam and jetsam from yesteryear are the highlights of this quirky place, so don't fret if doors are closed – unless

you want to drop by the visitor center that's also housed inside.

🛏️ Sleeping & Eating

Shoshone RV Park
& Campground   CAMPING $
(☑760-852-4569; http://shoshonevillage.com/shoshone-rv-park.html; Hwy 178; RV site with full hookup $40; ⓟ🛜🏊) This RV park on the northern end of the village has 25 full hookup sites as well as shaded tent spaces. Facilities include a pool and a laundromat.

Shoshone Inn   MOTEL $$
(☑760-852-4335; www.shoshonevillage.com; 113 Old Hwy 127; d $125-150; ☺check-in noon-10pm; ⓟ🐕❄️🛜🏊) This roadside motel has 17 contemporary rooms with dark furniture, laminate floors and comfy beds set around a shaded courtyard. Five come with kitchenette and there's also a bungalow with full kitchen. Bonus: a small, warm spring-fed pool.

Crowbar Cafe & Saloon   AMERICAN $$
(☑760-852-4224; www.shoshonevillage.com; 112 N Hwy 127; mains $10-24; ☺8am-9:30pm; ⓟ❄️🛜♿) Shoshone's only restaurant is a 1920 roadhouse next to the visitor center. Its main stocks in trade are burgers and sandwiches, but it also serves breakfast, Mexican dishes, steaks and something called 'rattlesnake' chili (sorry, there are no actual snakes in it). The attached saloon can get lively on weekend nights.

ℹ️ Information

Visitor Center (☑760-852-4524; ☺9am-3pm; 🛜) Information about Death Valley National Park and the surrounding area.

Tecopa

En route to Death Valley, the old mining town of Tecopa was named after a peacemaking Paiute chief. It is home to hot natural mineral springs, a hidden date-palm oasis and a surprisingly artistic bunch of locals.

◉ Sights & Activities

China Ranch Date Farm   FARM
(☑760-852-4415; www.chinaranch.com; China Ranch Rd; ☺9am-5pm; ⓟ♿) Fed by the mostly belowground Armagosa River and at the end of a narrow canyon, this family-run, organic date farm is a lush oasis in the middle of the blistering desert. You can go hiking or bird-watching, stock up on luscious dates or

LIFE AT DEATH VALLEY JUNCTION

An opera house in the middle of nowhere? Yes, thanks to the vision of New York dancer Marta Beckett who fell in love with the 1920s colonnaded adobe building when her car broke down nearby in 1967. For decades she entertained the curious with dance, music and mime shows at the **Amargosa Opera House** (☑ 760-852-4441; www.amargosa operahouse.com; Hwys 127, 178 & 190, Death Valley Junction; tours/shows $5/20; ☺ tours 9:30am-4pm, shows 7pm Fri & Sat, 2pm Sun; ℙ). Marta sadly passed away on January 30, 2017, but visiting performers continue to keep her legacy alive.

Tours focus on the auditorium whose walls Marta personally adorned with fanciful murals showing an audience she imagined might have attended an opera in the 16th century, including nuns, gypsies and royalty. Check at the adjacent **motel** (☑ 760-852-4441; www.amargosa-opera-house.com; Hwys 190 & 178, Death Valley Junction; r $70-80; ℙ☺@) about tours and upcoming shows.

Should you choose to spend the night, don't come looking for luxury. With no TV, no wi-fi and soft mattresses, it may lack even in basic comforts but instead delivers buckets of kookiness thanks to eccentric staff, muraled rooms and a resident ghost or two. There's a communal kitchenette. Bring supplies as there is no store and, while serving great breakfasts, healthy sandwiches and Saturday dinners, the attached farm-to-table **cafe** (☑ 760-852-4432; www.amargosacafe.org; Death Valley Junction; mains $9-19, pie per slice $5; ☺ 8am-3pm Mon, Fri, Sat & Sun, 6:30-9pm Sat; ℙ✴) ✐ does keep erratic hours. The nearest full-time restaurant is across the Nevada border about 7 miles away.

try the yummy date-nut bread. The location is well-signed from Tecopa.

Tecopa Hot Springs Campground & Pools
HOT SPRINGS

(☑ 760-852-4377; www.tecopahotspringscampground.com; 400 Tecopa Hot Springs Rd; per 24hr $7; ☺ 24hr) Men and women 'take the waters' separately in two bathhouses where nude bathing is compulsory. Private baths are available for modest types. Facilities are also used by guests of the affiliated campground (RVs and tents) across the street.

Delight's Hot Springs Resort
HOT SPRINGS

(☑ 760-852-4343; www.delightshotspringsresort.com; 368 Tecopa Hot Springs Rd; hot springs day pass 8am-5pm $15, VIP day pass 8am-10pm $20; ☺ 8am-10pm) This place has four private pools – two enclosed, two open to the sky – filled with water bubbling up from the local mineral springs at a temperature between 99°F and 104°F. There's a patio for sunning or lounging and vintage motel rooms in case you wish to spend the night.

Tecopa Hot Springs Resort
HOT SPRINGS

(☑ 760-852-4420; www.tecopahotsprings.org; 860 Tecopa Hot Springs Rd; bathing $8; ☺ 1-5pm) There are only two lockable skylit soaking tubs in this hilltop bathhouse. The water is clean but the facilities are pretty grubby. Guests at the resort campground have free 24-hour access.

🛏 Sleeping & Eating

★ Villa Anita
B&B $$

(☑ 760-852-4595; www.villaanitadv.com; 10 Sunset Rd; r from $160; ℙ✴☎) Staying at this artist-run three-room B&B feels much like bunking with good friends. Using recycled materials whenever possible, Carlo and David have fashioned one room from two boats and used bottles to build another, creating eccentric but supremely comfortable spaces to relax and reflect in. Their wacky sculptures decorate the garden where their lovely dogs like to romp.

Cynthia's
INN $$

(☑ 760-852-4580; www.discovercynthias.com; 2001 Old Spanish Trail Hwy; dm $25, r $98-138, tipi $165; ℙ☺✴☎) This congenial inn helmed by the friendly Cynthia has hostel-style bunks and eclectically decorated rooms in vintage trailers, all with private bathroom. Alternatively, you can go glamping in Native American-style tipis with thick rugs and comfy beds tucked into the nearby date-palm oasis at China Ranch. Here, bathrooms are shared. Check-in is at the inn.

McNeal's BBQ
BARBECUE $

(☑ 760-852-4343; westmcneal@gmail.com; 420 Tecopa Springs Rd; meals $7-18; ☺ 8am-7pm seasonal; ℙ) Stop by here for finger-lickin' brisket, pulled pork or ribs served with a side of toothsome coleslaw or a fresh summer salad. It's not always open, so call ahead or take your chances.

Upper Mojave Desert

The Mojave Desert is the driest desert in the US and covers a vast region, from urban areas on the northern edge of LA County to the remote unpopulated Mojave National Preserve and into southern Nevada. It's a harsh, alien landscape with sporadic mining settlements, ghost towns and vast areas set aside for weapons and aerospace testing. Historic Route 66 also traverses the Mojave whose signature plant is the endemic Joshua tree.

Mojave

Driving north on Hwy 14, Mojave is the first stop on the 'Aerospace Triangle' that also includes Boron and Ridgecrest. The modest service town is home to a huge airforce base as well as the country's first commercial space port, and has witnessed major moments in air- and space-flight history.

Being a service town, Mojave has plenty of competitively priced national motel chains along Hwys 14 and 58.

☉ Sights

Mojave Air & Space Port   NOTABLE BUILDING
(☎661-824-2433; www.mojaveairport.com; 1434 Flightline, Bldg 58; ⏰7:30am-4:30pm Mon-Fri) FREE This port made history in 2003 with the launch of SpaceShipOne, the first privately funded human space flight, thus laying the groundwork for commercial space tourism. A replica of SpaceShipOne is on display in the airport's small Legacy Park, along with a scale model of the Voyager aircraft and an original Rotary Rocket Roton, a manned spacecraft intended to deliver small satellites into space. The Voyager Cafe has some great old photographs. Enter from Airport Blvd, off Hwy 58.

Part of the airport is a huge airplane graveyard (off-limits to visitors) where retired commercial airplanes roost in the dry desert air waiting to be scavenged for spare parts.

Edwards Air Force Base   NOTABLE BUILDING
(☎661-277-3511;www.edwards.af.mil/tours;⏰tours 9:30am 1st Fri of month) FREE Storied Edwards Air Force Base is a flight-test facility for the US Air Force, NASA and civilian aircraft, and a training school for test pilots with the 'right stuff.' It was here that Chuck Yeager piloted the world's first supersonic flight, and the first space shuttles glided in after their missions. Free five-hour tours are offered on the first Friday of the month. Reservations are essential and tours fill up quickly months in advance. The website has details.

Ridgecrest & Around

Ridgecrest is a service town where you can find gas, supplies, information and cheap lodging en route to Death Valley or the Eastern Sierra Nevada. Its main raison d'être is the China Lake US Naval Air Weapons Station that sprawls for a million acres (one third the size of Delaware!) north of the town.

☉ Sights

US Naval Museum of Armament & Technology   MUSEUM
(☎760-939-3530; www.chinalakemuseum.org; 1 Pearl Harbor Way, China Lake; ⏰10am-4pm Mon-Sat) FREE Touch a Tomahawk missile or mug with a 'Fat Man' (atomic bomb, that is) at this museum on a classified US Navy base. The weapons collection will likely fascinate technology, flight, history and military buffs – and perhaps even utter pacifists. Until its relocation to a new building that's under construction at 130 E Las Flores in downtown Ridgecrest, access is restricted to US citizens; bring driver's license and proof of car insurance and prepare to spend two hours for clearance.

Trona Pinnacles   NATURE RESERVE
(Pinnacle Rd, Trona; P) FREE What do the movies *Battlestar Galactica, Star Trek V: the Final Frontier* and *Planet of the Apes* have in common? They were all filmed at Trona Pinnacles, an eerily beautiful natural landmark where some 500 calcium carbonate spires (tufa) rise up to 140ft out of an ancient lake bed in otherworldly fashion. The site sits at the end of a 5-mile dirt road off Hwy 178, about 18 miles east of Ridgecrest. Check locally for current road conditions.

Randsburg   GHOST TOWN
(P) FREE About 20 miles south of Ridgecrest, off US Hwy 395, Randsburg is a 'living ghost town,' an abandoned and now (somewhat) reinhabited gold-mining town circa 1895. You can visit a tiny historical museum, antiques shops, saloon, jailhouse and general store with soda fountain. Most places close on weekdays.

Las Vegas

It's three in the morning in a smoky casino when you spot an Elvis lookalike sauntering by arm in arm with a glittering showgirl just as a bride in a white dress shrieks 'Blackjack!'

Vegas, baby: It's the only place in the world you can see ancient hieroglyphics, the Eiffel Tower, the Brooklyn Bridge and the canals of Venice in a few short hours. Sure, they're all reproductions, but in a desert metropolis that has transformed itself into one of the most lavish getaway destinations on the planet, nothing is executed halfway – not even the illusions.

Las Vegas is the ultimate escape. Time is irrelevant here. There are no clocks, just never-ending buffets and ever-flowing drinks. This city has been constantly reinventing itself since the days of the Rat Pack. Today its pull is all-inclusive: Hollywood bigwigs gyrate at A-list ultralounges, while college kids seek cheap debauchery and grandparents whoop it up at the hot, hot penny slots. Welcome to the dream factory.

◉ Sights

Vegas' sights are primarily concentrated along the 4.2-mile stretch of Las Vegas Blvd anchored by Mandalay Bay to the south (at Russell Rd) and the **Stratosphere** (☑702-380-7777; www.stratospherehotel.com; 2000 S Las Vegas Blvd; tower entry adult/child $20/10, all-day pass incl unlimited thrill rides $40; ☺casino 24hr, tower & thrill rides 10am-1am Sun-Thu, to 2am Fri & Sat, weather permitting; P⛼) to the north (at Sahara Ave) and in the Downtown area around the intersection of Las Vegas Blvd (N Las Vegas Blvd at this point) and Fremont St. Note that while the street has the same name, there's an additional 2 miles between Downtown and the northern end of the Strip, with not much of interest in-between. It might look close if you decide to walk between the two, but you'll probably find yourself cursing in the desert heat if you do so. Ride-shares, the Monorail and Deuce bus services are by far the easiest ways to get around this spaced-out (in more ways than one) city.

◔ The Strip

★ Mandalay Bay   CASINO
(☑702-632-7700; www.mandalaybay.com; 3950 S Las Vegas Blvd; ☺24hr; P⛼) Since opening in 1999, in place of the former '50s-era Hacienda, Mandalay Bay has anchored the southern Strip. Its theme may be tropical, but it sure ain't tacky, nor is its 135,000-sq-ft casino. Well-dressed sports fans find their way to the upscale race and sports book near the high-stakes poker room. Refusing to be pigeonholed, the Bay's standout attractions are many and include the multilevel **Shark Reef Aquarium** (☑702-632-4555; www.sharkreef.com; 3950 S Las Vegas Blvd, Mandalay Bay; adult/child $25/19; ☺10am-8pm Sun-Thu, to 10pm Fri & Sat; P⛼), decadent day spas, oodles of signature dining and the unrivaled **Mandalay Bay Beach** (☑877-632-7800; www.mandalaybay.com/en/amenities/beach.html; Mandalay Bay; ☺pool 8am-5pm, Moorea Beach Club 11am-6pm; ⛼).

★ CityCenter   LANDMARK
(www.citycenter.com; 3780 S Las Vegas Blvd; P) We've seen this symbiotic relationship before (think giant hotel anchored by a mall 'concept') but the way that this futuristic-feeling complex places a small galaxy of hypermodern, chichi hotels in orbit around the glitzy **Shops at Crystals** (www.crystalsatcitycenter.com; 3720 S Las Vegas Blvd, CityCenter; ☺10am-11pm Sun-Thu, to midnight Fri & Sat) is a first. The uberupscale spread includes the subdued, stylish **Vdara** (☑702-590-2111; www.vdara.com; 2600 W Harmon Ave, CityCenter; weekday/weekend ste from $129/189; P◉❋@🔊✖🐾) 🐾, the hush-hush opulent **Mandarin Oriental** (☑702-590-8888; www.mandarinoriental.com; 3752 S Las Vegas Blvd, CityCenter; r/ste from $239/469; ❋🔊✖) and the dramatic architectural showpiece **Aria** (☑702-590-7111; www.aria.com; 3730 S Las Vegas Blvd, CityCenter; ☺24hr; P), whose sophisticated casino provides a fitting backdrop to its many drop-dead-gorgeous restaurants. CityCenter's hotels have in excess of 6700 rooms!

★ Cosmopolitan   CASINO
(☑702-698-7000; www.cosmopolitanlasvegas.com; 3708 S Las Vegas Blvd; ☺24hr; P) Hipsters who thought they were too cool for Vegas finally have a place to go where they don't need irony to endure – or enjoy – the aesthetics of the Strip. Like the new Hollywood 'It' girl, the Cosmopolitan casino looks absolutely fabulous at all times. A steady stream of ingenues and entourages parade through the lobby (with some of the coolest design elements we've seen) along with anyone else who adores contemporary art and design.

★ Bellagio   CASINO
(☑888-987-6667; www.bellagio.com; 3600 S Las Vegas Blvd; ☺24hr; P🐾) The Bellagio experience

transcends its decadent casino floor of high-limit gaming tables and in excess of 2300 slot machines; locals say odds here are less than favorable. A stop on the World Poker Tour, Bellagio's tournament-worthy poker room offers kitchen-to-gaming-table delivery around-the-clock. Most, however, come for the property's stunning architecture, interiors and amenities, including the **Conservatory & Botanical Gardens** (Bellagio; ☺24hr; P⛷) FREE, **Gallery of Fine Art** (☎702-693-7871; Bellagio; adult/child under 12yr $18/free; ☺10am-8pm, last entry 7:30pm; P⛷), unmissable **Fountains of Bellagio** (www.bellagio.com; Bellagio; ☺shows every 30min 3-8pm Mon-Fri, noon-8pm Sat, 11am-7pm Sun, every 15min 8pm-midnight Mon-Sat, from 7pm Sun; P⛷) FREE and the 2000-plus hand-blown glass flowers embellishing the hotel (p340) lobby.

★ **Paris Las Vegas**   CASINO
(☎877-603-4386; www.parislasvegas.com; 3655 S Las Vegas Blvd; ☺24hr; P) This miniversion of the French capital might lack the charm of the City of Light, but its efforts to emulate Paris' landmarks, including a 34-story Hotel de Ville and facades from the Opera House and Louvre, make it a fun stop for families and anyone yet to see the real thing. Its vaulted casino ceilings simulate sunny skies above myriad tables and slots, while its high-limit authentic French roulette wheels, sans 0 and 00, slightly improve your odds.

★ **Caesars Palace**   CASINO
(☎866-227-5938; www.caesarspalace.com; 3570 S Las Vegas Blvd; ☺24hr; P) Caesars Palace claims that its smartly renovated casino floor has more million-dollar slots than anywhere in the world, but its claims to fame are far more numerous than that. Entertainment's heavyweights Celine Dion and Elton John 'own' its custom-built **Colosseum** (☎866-227-5938; www.thecolosseum.com; Caesars Palace; tickets $55-500) theater, fashionistas saunter around the **Shops at Forum** (www.simon.com/mall/the-forum-shops-at-caesars-palace/stores; Caesars Palace; ☺10am-11pm Sun-Thu, to midnight Fri & Sat), while Caesars hotel guests quaff cocktails in the **Garden of the Gods Pool Oasis**. By night, megaclub **Omnia** (www.omniaightclub.com; Caesars Palace; cover female/male $20/40; ☺10pm-4am Tue & Thu-Sun) is the only place to get this off your face this side of Ibiza.

★ **LINQ Promenade**   STREET
(www.caesars.com/linq; ☺24hr; P⛷) You'll be delighted by the fun vibe of the Strip's newest outdoor pedestrian promenade, where you can browse the latest LA fashions, gorge yourself on cupcakes, jaburritos (where sushi rolls meet burritos!) and fish and chips, go bowling, ride the High Roller, rock out to live music, or sip pints on lazy patios beneath the desert sun.

High Roller   LANDMARK
(☎702-322-0591; www.caesars.com/linq; LINQ Promenade; adult/child from $22/9, after 5pm $32/19; ☺11:30am-2am; P⛷; Flamingo or Harrah's/Linq) The world's largest observation wheel towers 550ft above LINQ Promenade (p335). Each of the 28 air-conditioned passenger cabins is enclosed by handcrafted Italian glass. Outside, 2000 colorful LED lights glow from dusk until dawn. One revolution takes about 30 minutes and each pod can hold 40 guests. From 4pm to 7pm, select pods host the adults-only (21-plus) 'happy half hour' ($35, or $47 after 5pm) with an open bar (read all-you-can-drink) shared between your fellow riders. Things can get messy, fast.

★ **Venetian**   CASINO
(☎702-414-1000; www.venetian.com; 3355 S Las Vegas Blvd; ☺24hr; P) The Venetian's regal 120,000-sq-ft casino has marble floors, hand-painted ceiling frescoes and 120 table games, including a high-limit lounge and an elegant no-smoking poker room, where women are especially welcome (unlike at many other poker rooms in town). When combined with its younger, neighboring sibling **Palazzo** (☎702-607-7777; www.palazzo.com; 3325 S Las Vegas Blvd; ☺24hr; P), the properties claim the largest casino space in Las Vegas. Unmissable on the Strip, a highlight of this miniature replica of Venice is to take a **gondola ride** (☎702-414-4300; www.venetian.com/resort/attractions/gondola-rides.html; Venetian; shared ride per person $29, child under 3yr free, private 2-passenger ride $116; ☺indoor 10am-11pm Sun-Thu, to midnight Fri & Sat, outdoor rides 11am-10pm, weather permitting; ⛷) down its Grand Canal.

★ **Wynn & Encore Casinos**   CASINO
(☎702-770-7000; www.wynnlasvegas.com; 3131 S Las Vegas Blvd; ☺24hr; P) Steve Wynn's signature casino hotel (literally – his name is emblazoned across the top) **Wynn** (☎702-770-7000; www.wynnlasvegas.com; 3131 S Las Vegas Blvd; weekday/weekend r from $199/259; P❊@☎☎) and its younger sibling **Encore** (☎702-770-7100; www.wynnlasvegas.com; 3131 S Las Vegas

Las Vegas Strip

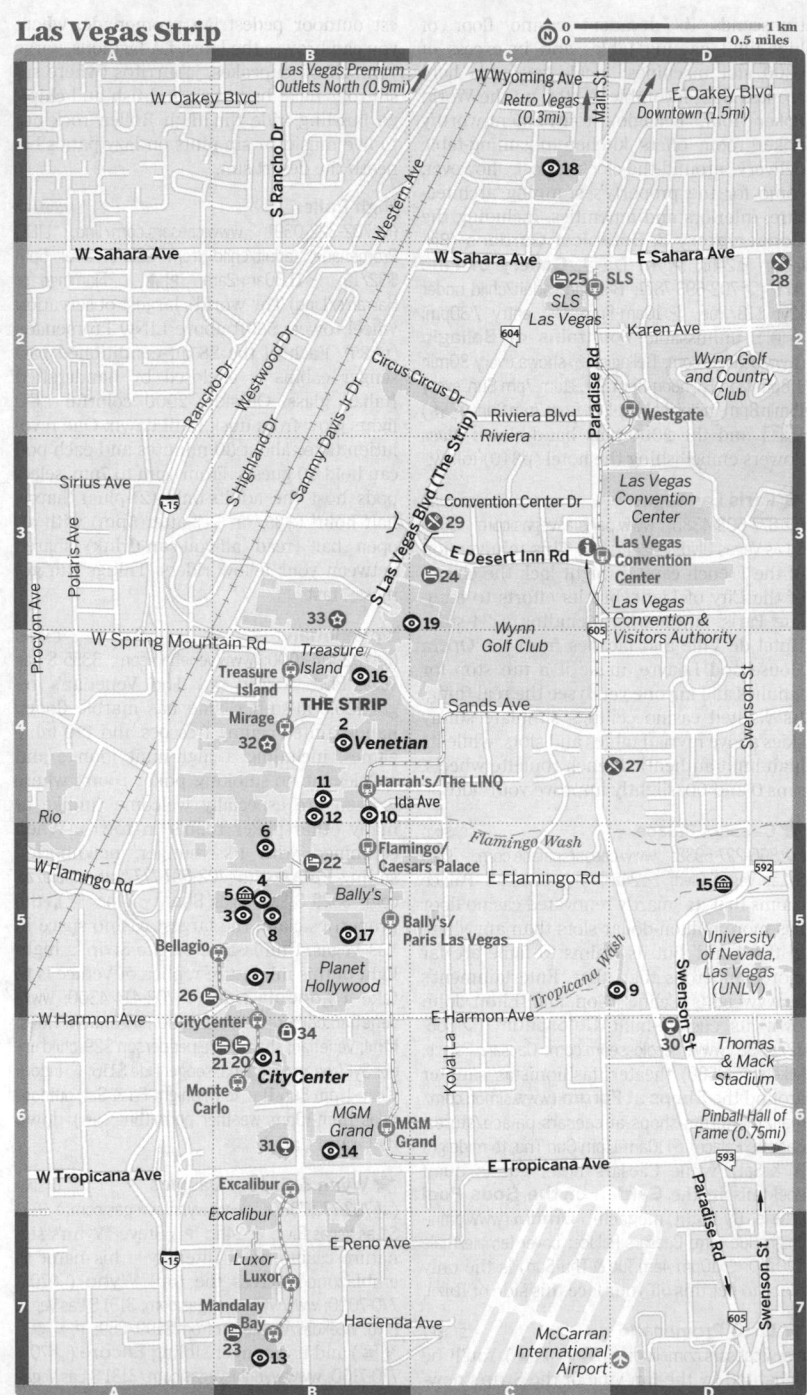

N

0 ——————— 1 km
0 ——————— 0.5 miles

W Oakey Blvd

Las Vegas Premium
Outlets North (0.9mi)

W Wyoming Ave

Retro Vegas
(0.3mi)

Main St

E Oakey Blvd
Downtown (1.5mi)

S Rancho Dr

Western Ave

⊙ 18

W Sahara Ave

W Sahara Ave

E Sahara Ave

⊗ 28

📇 25 SLS

SLS
Las Vegas

Karen Ave

Wynn Golf
and Country
Club

Paradise Rd

Circus Circus Dr

Rancho Dr

Westwood Dr

S Highland Dr

Sammy Davis Jr Dr

604

Riviera Blvd

Riviera

Westgate

Sirius Ave

I-15

Convention Center Dr

Polaris Ave

Procyon Ave

⊙ 29

E Desert Inn Rd

📇 24

Las Vegas
Convention
Center

Las Vegas
Convention
Center

605

Las Vegas
Convention &
Visitors Authority

W Spring Mountain Rd

33 ✪

⊙ 19

Wynn
Golf Club

Treasure
Island

Swenson St

Treasure
Island

⊙ 16

THE STRIP

Sands Ave

Mirage

32 ✪

2

⊙ Venetian

⊗ 27

S Las Vegas Blvd (The Strip)

Rio

11 🏠

12 ⊙

Harrah's/The LINQ

Ida Ave

⊙ 10

6 ⊙

📇 22

Flamingo/
Caesars Palace

Flamingo Wash

E Flamingo Rd

15 🏠

592

W Flamingo Rd

Bally's

4

5 🏠

3 ⊙ 8

Bally's/
Paris Las Vegas

University
of Nevada,
Las Vegas
(UNLV)

⊙ 17

Bellagio

⊙ 7

Planet
Hollywood

Tropicana Wash

⊙ 9

Swenson St

26 📇

CityCenter

W Harmon Ave

🏠 34

E Harmon Ave

⊙ 30

Thomas
& Mack
Stadium

21 20

⊙ 1

CityCenter

Koval La

Monte
Carlo

MGM
Grand

MGM
Grand

Pinball Hall of
Fame (0.75mi)

31 🏠

⊙ 14

E Tropicana Ave

593

W Tropicana Ave

Excalibur

Excalibur

E Reno Ave

Paradise Rd

I-15

Luxor

Luxor

Swenson St

Mandalay
Bay

605

23

⊙ 13

Hacienda Ave

McCarran
International
Airport

Las Vegas Strip

Blvd; r/ste from $199/259; [P][❄][@][📶][≋]) are a pair of curvaceous, copper-toned twin towers, whose entrances are obscured by high fences and lush greenery. Each hotel is unique, but their sprawling subterranean casinos converge to form the Strip's second-largest and arguably most elegant gaming floor, whose popular poker rooms lure pros around the clock and labyrinth of slot machines range from a penny to $5000 per pull!

◉ Downtown & Off-Strip

★ Mob Museum
MUSEUM

([☎] 702-229-2734; www.themobmuseum.org; 300 Stewart Ave; adult/child $24/14; ⊙ 9am-9pm; [P]; [🚌] Deuce) It's hard to say what's more impres-

sive: the museum's physical location in a historic federal courthouse where mobsters sat for federal hearings in 1950–51, the fact that the board of directors is headed up by a former FBI special agent, or the thoughtfully curated exhibits telling the story of organized crime in America. In addition to hands-on FBI equipment and mob-related artifacts, the museum boasts a series of multimedia exhibits featuring interviews with real-life Tony Sopranos.

★ Fremont Street Experience
STREET

([☎] 702-678-5600; www.vegasexperience.com; Fremont St Mall; ⊙ shows hourly dusk-midnight or 1am; [🚌] Deuce, SDX) [FREE] A five-block pedestrian mall, between Main St and N Las Vegas Blvd,

---

ℹ TOP TIPS ON DOING VEGAS RIGHT

➜ The Strip runs for miles: don't assume you can easily walk from point A to B. Consult a map first and note that pedestrian crossings are punctuated with sky bridges and escalators. Take advantage of free trams between casinos whenever possible.

➜ Meeting locals is a great way to get to know a city, but in a place of itinerants like Vegas, they're hard to find and even harder to hold. Don't be surprised if the locals are a little reserved at first: they'll be the first to tell you that nobody trusts anybody here. If that's the dominant discourse, it's a good idea to keep your own guard up a little.

➜ Areas either side of Las Vegas Blvd (especially to the east and north) can be dangerous, even during daylight hours. Exercise caution when on foot.

➜ Single women travelers should be wary of wandering too far from the Strip and avoid walking alone at night.

➜ Ride-share where possible – these services are by far the most convenient way to get around the city. Rates are great and you'll never wait long.

---

topped by an arched steel canopy and filled with computer-controlled lights, the Fremont Street Experience has brought life back Downtown. Every evening, the canopy is transformed by light-and-sound shows enhanced by 550,000 watts of wraparound sound and a larger-than-life screen lit up by 12.5-million synchronized LEDs. Soar through the air on zip lines strung underneath the canopy from **Slotzilla** (www.vegasexperience.com/slotzilla-zip-line; Fremont St Mall, Fremont Street Experience; lower line $25, upper line $45; ⊙1pm-1am Sun-Thu, to 2am Fri & Sat; 🖪; 🚌Deuce, SDX), a 12-story, slot-machine-themed platform. Gaudy, yes. Weird, yes. Busy: always.

Neon Museum – Urban Gallery　TOURS
(📞702-387-6366; www.neonmuseum.org; 450 Fremont St E, Neonopolis; ⊙24hr; 🚌Deuce, SDX) **FREE** Plaques tell the story of each restored vintage neon sign at these open-air galleries. Look for the flashy 40ft-tall cowboy on horseback, Aladdin's sparkling genie lamp, a glowing martini glass, a flaming steakhouse sign and more. The biggest assemblages are inside the Neonopolis and on the 3rd St cul-de-sac just north of the Fremont Street Experience (p337).

★ Golden Nugget　CASINO
(📞702-385-7111; www.goldennugget.com; 129 Fremont St E; ⊙24hr; 🅿🖪; 🚌Deuce, SDX) Check out the polished brass and white-leather seats in the casino: day or night, the Golden Nugget is downtown's poshest address. With classy eateries and a swimming pool famous for its shark tank, the Golden Nugget outshines its competition. This swank-carpet joint rakes in a moneyed crowd with a 38,000-sq-ft casino

populated by table games and slot machines with the same odds as at Strip megaresorts. The nonsmoking poker room hosts daily tournaments.

★ Container Park　CULTURAL CENTER
(📞702-359-9982; http://downtowncontainerpark.com; 707 Fremont St E; ⊙11am-9pm Mon-Thu, 10am-10pm Fri & Sat, to 8pm Sun) An incubator for up-and-coming fashion designers and local artisans, the edgy Container Park stacks pop-up shops on top of one another. Wander along the sidewalks and catwalks while searching out handmade jewelry, contemporary art and clothing at a dozen or so specialty boutiques, eateries and art installations. When the sun sets, the container bars come to life and host regular themed events and movie nights. It's adults only (21-plus) after 9pm.

★ National Atomic Testing Museum　MUSEUM
(📞702-794-5151; www.nationalatomictestingmuseum.org; 755 Flamingo Rd E, Desert Research Institute; adult/child $22/16; ⊙10am-5pm Mon-Sat, noon-5pm Sun; 🚌202) Fascinating multimedia exhibits focus on science, technology and the social history of the 'Atomic Age,' which lasted from WWII until atmospheric bomb testing was driven underground in 1961 and a worldwide ban on nuclear testing was declared in 1992. View footage of atomic testing and examine southern Nevada's nuclear past, present and future, from Native American ways of life to the environmental legacy of atomic testing. Don't miss the ticket booth (how could you?); it's a Nevada Test Site guard-station replica.

★**Pinball Hall of Fame** MUSEUM
(☎702-597-2627; www.pinballmuseum.org; 1610 E Tropicana Ave; per game 25¢-$1; ⊘11am-11pm Sun-Thu, to midnight Fri & Sat; ♿; ☐201) You may have more fun at this no-frills arcade than playing slot machines back on the Strip. Tim Arnold shares his collection of 200-plus vintage pinball and video games with the public. Take time to read the handwritten curatorial cards explaining the unusual history behind these restored machines.

★**Hard Rock** CASINO
(☎702-693-5000; www.hardrockhotel.com; 4455 Paradise Rd; ⊘24hr; ☐108) The world's original rock-and-roll casino houses what may be the most impressive collection of rock-star memorabilia ever assembled under one roof. Priceless items being watched over by security guards suited up like bouncers are concert attire worn by Elvis, Britney Spears and Prince; a display case filled with Beatles mementos; Jim Morrison's handwritten lyrics to one of the Doors' greatest hits; and dozens of leather jackets and guitars formerly owned by everyone from the Ramones to U2.

🛏 **Sleeping**

With over 150,000 hotel rooms and consistently high occupancy rates, prices in Vegas fluctuate constantly. Sometimes the best deals are found in advance; other times, at the last minute. As a general rule, if you find a good price on a place you love, nab it. Decent rooms Downtown start from as low as $29, while the swankiest digs on the Strip can fetch upwards of $10,000 per night!

🛏 **The Strip**

★**Aria Las Vegas Resort** CASINO HOTEL $$
(☎702-590-7111; www.arialasvegas.com; 3730 S Las Vegas Blvd, CityCenter; r weekday/weekend from $129/189; P❋@⑤⑤❄) Aria's (p334) sleek resort hotel at CityCenter (p334) has no theme, unlike the Strip's other megaproperties. Instead, its 4000-plus deluxe rooms (520 sq ft) and 560 tower suites (920-plus sq ft) are all about soothing design, spaciousness and luxury, and every room has a corner view. If you've cash to burn, **Aria Sky Suites & Villas** (☎702-590-7111; www.aria.com; Aria; ste/villa from $340/3000), a hotel-within-in-a-hotel, might be for you.

★**Cromwell Las Vegas** BOUTIQUE HOTEL $$
(☎702-777-3777; www.caesars.com/cromwell; 3595 S Las Vegas Blvd; r/ste from $199/399; P❋⑤❄❄) If you're 20- to 30-something, can hold your own with the cool kids, or you're just effortlessly stylish whatever your demographic, there are a few good reasons to choose Cromwell, the best being its location and frequently excellent rates on sassy, entry-level rooms. The others? You've got your sites set on partying at Drai's (p342) or dining downstairs at **Giada** (☎855-442-3271; www.caesars.com; Cromwell Las Vegas; mains $25-58; ⊘8am-11pm).

★**LINQ Hotel** CASINO HOTEL $$
(☎800-634-6441; www.caesars.com/linq; 3535 S Las Vegas Blvd; d/ste from $109/209; P❋❄❄) Launching onto the Las Vegas Strip in late 2014, LINQ, formerly the Quad, has cemented its position as a solid all-rounder. Its fresh, white rooms have fun splashes of color and sleek Euro-styled furniture, there's a wealth of available amenities (this being part of the Caesars group) and it has an enviable location at the center of its eponymous promenade (p335).

★**Mandalay Bay** CASINO HOTEL $$
(☎702-632-7700; www.mandalaybay.com; 3950 S Las Vegas Blvd; weekday/weekend r from $119/229; P❋@⑤❄) Anchoring the south Strip, upscale Mandalay Bay's (p334) same-named hotel (p339) has a cache of classy rooms worthy of your attention in their own right, not to mention the exclusive **Four Seasons Hotel** (☎702-632-5000; www.fourseasons.com/lasvegas; Mandalay Bay; weekday/weekend r from $229/289; P❋@⑤❄❄) and boutique **Delano** (☎877-632-7800; www.delanolasvegas.com; Mandalay Bay; r/ste from $69/129; P❋@⑤❄❄) within its bounds and a diverse range of noteworthy attractions and amenities, not least of which is Mandalay Bay Beach (p334).

★**Cosmopolitan** CASINO HOTEL $$$
(☎702-698-7575, 702-698-7000; www.cosmopolitanlasvegas.com; 3708 S Las Vegas Blvd; r/ste from $250/300; P❋@⑤❄; ☐Deuce) With at least eight distinctively different and equally stylish room types to choose from, Cosmo's digs are the hippest on the Strip. Ranging from oversized to decadent, about 2200 of its 2900 or so rooms have balconies (all but the entry-level category), many sport sunken Japanese tubs and all feature plush furnishings and design quirks you'll delight in uncovering.

If you've got cash to spare and look the part, you're going to love exploring Cosmopolitan's (p334) playground for a worldly, style-conscious and design-smart generation that's got youth on its side.

★ Bellagio
CASINO HOTEL $$$

(☑ 888-987-6667; www.bellagio.com; 3600 S Las Vegas Blvd; weekday/weekend r from $179/249; P ✳ @ 🛜 ✖ 🐕) When it opened in 1998, Bellagio was the world's most expensive hotel. Aging gracefully, it remains one of America's finest. Its sumptuous oversized guest rooms fuse classic style with modern amenities and feature palettes of platinum, indigo and muted white-gold, or rusty autumnal oranges with subtle splashes of matcha green. Cashmere throws, mood lighting and automatic drapes complete the picture.

🏨 Downtown & Off-Strip

★ El Cortez
CASINO HOTEL $

(☑ 702-385-5200; www.elcortezhotelcasino.com; 651 E Ogden Ave; weekday/weekend r from $40/80; P ✳ @ 🛜) A wide range of rooms with all kinds of vibes are available at this fun, retro property close to all the action on Fremont St. Rooms are in the 1980s tower addition to the heritage-listed 1941 El Cortez (☑ 702-385-5200; www.elcortezhotelcasino.com; 600 Fremont St E; ⊙ 24hr; 🚌 Deuce) casino and the modern, flashier El Cortez Suites, across the street. Rates offered are generally great value, though don't expect the earth.

★ Hard Rock
CASINO HOTEL $

(☑ 702-693-5000; www.hardrockhotel.com; 4455 Paradise Rd; weekday/weekend r from $45/89; P ✳ @ 🛜 ✖) Sexy, oversized rooms and HRH suites underwent a bunch of refurbishments in 2016 and 2017, making this party palace for music lovers a great alternative to staying on the Strip – there's even a free shuttle to take you there and bring you back.

★ Golden Nugget
CASINO HOTEL $

(☑ 702-385-7111; www.goldennugget.com; 129 Fremont St E; weekday/weekend r from $45/85; P ✳ @ 🛜 ✖) Pretend to relive the fabulous heyday of Vegas in the 1950s at this swank Fremont St address. Rooms in the Rush Tower are the best in the house.

🍴 Eating

The Strip has been studded with celebrity chefs for years. All-you-can-eat buffets and $10 steaks still exist, but today's high-rolling visitors demand ever more sophisticated dining experiences, with meals designed – although not personally prepared – by famous taste-makers. Flash enough cash and you can taste the same cuisine served at revered restaurants from NYC to Paris to Shanghai.

🍴 The Strip

★ Tacos El Gordo
MEXICAN $

(☑ 702-251-8226; www.tacoselgordobc.com; 3049 S Las Vegas Blvd; small plates $3-12; ⊙ 10am-2am Sun-Thu, to 4am Fri & Sat; P 🖋 🐕; 🚌 Deuce, SDX) This Tijuana-style taco shop from SoCal is just the ticket when it's way late, you've got almost no money left and you're desperately craving carne asada (beef) or *adobada* (chile-marinated pork) tacos in hot, handmade tortillas. Adventurous eaters order the authentic *sesos* (beef brains), *cabeza* (roasted cow's head) or tripe variations.

★ Umami Burger
BURGERS $

(☑ 702-761-7614; www.slslasvegas.com/dining/umami-burger; SLS, 2535 S Las Vegas Blvd; burgers $12-15; ⊙ 11am-10pm; P) SLS' (☑ 702-761-7000; www.slslasvegas.com; 2535 S Las Vegas Blvd; d from $79; P ✳ 🛜 ✖) burger offering is one of the best on the Strip, with its outdoor beer garden, extensive craft-beer selection and juicy boutique burgers made by the chain that won *GQ* magazine's prestigious 'burger of the year' crown.

★ Burger Bar
AMERICAN $$

(☑ 702-632-9364; www.burger-bar.com; Shoppes at Mandalay Place; mains $10-60; ⊙ 11am-11pm Sun-Thu, to 1am Fri & Sat; P ✳ 🐕) Since when can a hamburger be worth $60? When it's built with Kobe beef, sautéed foie gras and truffle sauce: it's the Rossini burger, the signature sandwich of chef Hubert Keller. Most menu options are more down-to-earth – diners select their own gourmet burger toppings and pair them with skinny fries and a liquor-spiked milkshake or beer float.

★ Grand Wok
CHINESE $$

(☑ 702-891-7879; www.mgmgrand.com/en/restaurants.html; MGM Grand; mains $12-28; ⊙ 11am-10pm Sun-Thu, to 11pm Fri & Sat) Come to Grand Wok, in business for over 25 years serving some of the best pan-Asian dishes you'll find this side of the Far East. Try the garlic shrimp fried rice with dried scallops. Sensational.

★**Guy Fieri's Vegas Kitchen & Bar** AMERICAN $$
(☑702-794-3139; www.caesars.com; LINQ Casino; mains $12-28; ☺9am-midnight) *Diners, Drive-ins and Dives* celebrity chef Guy Fieri has opened his first restaurant on the Strip at **LINQ Casino** (☑800-634-6441; www.caesars.com/linq; 3535 S Las Vegas Blvd; ☺24hr; P), dishing out an eclectic menu of his own design, inspired by so many years journeying America's back roads for the best and fairest down-home cooking.

★**Eiffel Tower Restaurant** FRENCH $$$
(☑702-948-6937; www.eiffeltowerrestaurant.com; Paris Las Vegas; mains lunch $14-32, dinner $32-89, tasting menu without/with wine pairings $125/205; ☺11:30am-10pm Mon-Fri, 11am-11pm Sat & Sun) At this haute eatery midway up its namesake tower, the Francophile wine list is vast, the chocolate soufflé is unforgettable, and views of the Strip and Bellagio's fountains are breathtaking. Contemporary renditions of French classics are generally well executed. Lunch is your best bet, but it's more popular to come for sunset. Reservations essential.

★**Joël Robuchon** FRENCH $$$
(☑702-891-7925; www.joel-robuchon.com/en; MGM Grand; tasting menus $120-425; ☺5-10pm) The acclaimed 'Chef of the Century' leads the pack in the French culinary invasion of the Strip. Adjacent to the **MGM Grand's** (☑877-880-0880; www.mgmgrand.com; 3799 S Las Vegas Blvd; ☺24hr; P 🅿) high-rollers' gaming area, Robuchon's plush dining rooms, done up in leather and velvet, feel like a dinner party at a 1930s Paris mansion. Complex seasonal tasting menus promise the meal of a lifetime – and they often deliver.

Reservations are essential for dinner here, as well as at the slightly less-expensive **L'Atelier de Joël Robuchon** (☑702-891-7358; www.joel-robuchon.com/en; MGM Grand; mains $41-97, tasting menu without/with wine pairings $159/265; ☺5-10:30pm; 🅿) next door, where bar seats front an exhibition kitchen.

✖ Downtown & Off-Strip

★**eat.** BREAKFAST $
(☑702-534-1515; http://eatdtlv.com; 707 Carson Ave; mains $7-14; ☺8am-3pm Mon-Fri, to 2pm Sat & Sun; 🅿) ✔ Community spirit and creative cooking provide reason enough to venture off Fremont St to find this cafe. With a concrete floor and spare decor, it can get loud as folks chow down on truffled egg sandwiches, cinnamon biscuits with strawberry compote, shrimp po'boy sandwiches and bowls of New Mexican green-chile chicken *pozole*.

Metered parking is available on the street, or take the Deuce bus to the Fremont Street Experience (p337), then walk two blocks east on Fremont and one block south on 7th, to Carson Ave.

★**Park on Fremont** GASTROPUB $
(☑702-834-3160; www.parkonfremont.com; 506 Fremont St E; light meals $9-14; ☺11am-3am) The best thing about this gorgeous little oasis away from the Fremont St frenzy are its outdoor patio and courtyard areas. OK, the burgers are great too, but not as exciting as the crispy brussels sprouts and cheesy garbage fries. It's a great place to just sit and sip a margarita and watch the crowds go by.

★**Culinary Dropout** AMERICAN $$
(☑702-522-8100; www.hardrockhotel.com; Hard Rock; mains brunch $8-14, lunch & dinner $14-32; ☺11am-11pm Mon-Thu, 11am-midnight Fri, 9am-midnight Sat, 9am-11pm Sun; 🚌108) With a pool-view patio and live bands rocking on weekends, there's no funkier gastropub around. Dip warm pretzels in provolone fondue or homemade potato chips in onion dip, then bite into fried chicken and honey biscuits. Weekend brunch (9am to 3pm on Saturday and Sunday) gives you the hair of the dog with bacon Bloody Marys. Reservations essential on weekends.

★**Firefly** TAPAS $$
(☑702-369-3971; www.fireflylv.com; 3824 Paradise Rd; shared plates $5-12, mains $15-20; ☺11:30am-1am Mon-Thu, to 2am Fri & Sat, 10am-1am Sun; 🚌108) Firefly is always packed with a fashionable local crowd, who come for well-prepared Spanish and Latin American tapas, such as *patatas bravas,* chorizo-stuffed empanadas and vegetarian bites like garbanzo beans seasoned with chili, lime and sea salt. A back-lit bar dispenses the house specialty sangria – red, white or sparkling – and fruity mojitos. Reservations strongly recommended.

Show up for happy hour from 3pm to 6pm Monday through Thursday (till 5pm on Friday).

★**Lotus of Siam** THAI $$
(☑702-735-3033; www.lotusofsiamlv.com; 953 E Sahara Ave; mains $9-30; ☺11am-2:30pm Mon-Fri, 5:30-10pm daily; 🅿; 🚌SDX) Saipin Chutima's authentic northern Thai cooking has won almost as many awards as her distinguished European and New World wine cellar. Crit-

ics have suggested this might be America's best Thai restaurant and we're sure it's up there with the best. Although the strip-mall hole-in-the-wall may not look like much, foodies flock here. Reservations essential.

★**Carson Kitchen**　　　　AMERICAN **$$**
(☏702-473-9523; www.carsonkitchen.com; 124 S 6th St; tapas & mains $8-22; ⊙11:30am-11pm Thu-Sat, to 10pm Sun-Wed; ▣ Deuce) This tiny eatery with an industrial theme of exposed beams, bare bulbs and chunky share tables hops with downtowners looking to escape the mayhem of Fremont St or the Strip's high prices. Excellent shared plates include rainbow cauliflower, watermelon and feta salad and decadent mac 'n' cheese, and there's a creative 'libations' menu.

★**Grotto**　　　　ITALIAN **$$**
(☏702-386-8341; www.goldennugget.com; 129 Fremont St E, Golden Nugget; pizza $12-15, mains $19-35; ⊙11:30am-midnight Sun-Thu, to 1am Fri & Sat; ▣ Deuce, SDX) At this Italian trattoria covered in painted murals, you'll be drawn to the sunlight-filled patio next to the Nugget's shark-tank waterslide and swimming pool. Wood-oven-fired, thin-crust pizzas, heavy pastas, and chicken, fish, veal and steak dishes are accompanied by a 200-bottle list of Italian wines. Happy hour runs 2pm to 6pm daily.

★**Andiamo Steakhouse**　　　　STEAK **$$$**
(☏702-388-2220; www.thed.com; 301 Fremont St E, The D; mains $24-79; ⊙5-11pm; ▣ Deuce, SDX) Of all the old-school steakhouses inside Downtown's carpet joints, the current front-runner is Joe Vicari's Andiamo Steakhouse. Upstairs from the casino, richly upholstered half-moon booths and impeccably polite waiters set the tone for a classic Italian steakhouse feast of surf-and-turf platters and housemade pasta, followed by a rolling dessert cart. Extensive Californian and European wine list. Reservations recommended.

🍷 Drinking & Nightlife

You don't need us to tell you that Las Vegas is party central – the Strip is ground zero for some of the country's hottest clubs and most happening bars, where you never know who you'll be rubbing shoulders with. What you might not know is that Downtown's Fremont East Entertainment District is the go-to place for Vegas' coolest nonmainstream haunts.

☕ The Strip

★**Hakkasan**　　　　CLUB
(☏702-891-3838; www.hakkasanlv.com; MGM Grand; cover $20-75; ⊙10pm-4am Wed-Sun) At this lavish Asian-inspired nightclub, international jet-set DJs like Tiësto and Steve Aoki rule the jam-packed main dance floor bordered by VIP booths and floor-to-ceiling LED screens. More offbeat sounds spin in the intimate Ling Ling Club, revealing leather sofas and backlit amber glass. Bouncers enforce the dress code: upscale nightlife attire (no athletic wear, collared shirts required for men).

★**Drai's Beachclub & Nightclub**　　　　CLUB
(☏702-777-3800; www.draislv.com; Cromwell Las Vegas; nightclub cover $20-50; ⊙nightclub 10pm-5am Thu-Sun, beach club 11am-6pm Fri-Sun) Feel ready for an after-hours party scene straight outta Hollywood? Or maybe you just wanna hang out all day poolside, then shake your booty on the petite dancefloor as DJs spin hip-hop, mash-ups and electronica? This multivenue club has you covered pretty much all day and night. Dress to kill: no sneakers, tank tops or baggy jeans.

★**Jewel**　　　　CLUB
(☏702-590-8000; www.jewelnightclub.com; Aria; cover female/male from $20/30; ⊙10:30am-4am Fri, Sat & Mon) From the creators of Hakkasan, long-awaited Jewel replaces its predecessor Haze, which failed to dazzle. Boasting five VIP suites (because it's all about being seen) and over 1400 sq ft of shimmering LED ribbon lighting, Jewel, despite accommodating up to 2000 revelers, is pitched as an 'intimate' alternative to the Strip's megaclubs. Monday nights offer locals free admission.

★**Chandelier Lounge**　　　　COCKTAIL BAR
(☏702-698-7979; www.cosmopolitanlasvegas.com/lounges-bars/chandelier; Cosmopolitan; ⊙24hr; ▣ Deuce) Towering high in the center of Cosmopolitan (p334), this ethereal cocktail bar is inventive yet beautifully simple, with three levels connected by romantic curved staircases, all draped with glowing strands of glass beads. The second level is headquarters for molecular mixology (order a martini made with liquid nitrogen), while the third specializes in floral and fruit infusions.

★**Nine Fine Irishmen**　　　　PUB
(☏702-740-6463; www.ninefineirishmen.com; New York–New York; ⊙11am-11pm, live music from 9pm;

☎) Built in Ireland and shipped piece by piece to America, this pub has cavernous interior booths and outdoor patio tables beside NYNY's Brooklyn Bridge. Genuine stouts, ales, ciders and Irish whiskeys are always stocked at the bar. Live entertainment is a mix of Celtic rock and traditional Irish country tunes, occasionally with sing-alongs and a champion Irish dancer.

★**Skyfall Lounge** BAR
(☏702-632-7575; www.delanolasvegas.com; Delano; ⊗5pm-midnight Sun-Thu, to 1:30am Fri & Sat) Enjoy unparalleled views of the southern Strip from this rooftop bar atop Mandalay Bay's Delano (p339) hotel. Sit and sip cocktails as the sun sets over the Spring Mountains to the west, then dance the night away to mellow DJ beats, spun from 9pm.

🍺 Downtown & Off-Strip

★**Beauty Bar** BAR
(☏702-598-3757; www.thebeautybar.com; 517 Fremont St E; cover free-$10; ⊗9pm-4am; 🚌Deuce) Swill a cocktail or just chill with the cool kids inside the salvaged innards of a 1950s New Jersey beauty salon. DJs and live bands rotate nightly, spinning everything from tiki lounge tunes, disco and '80s hits to punk, metal, glam and indie rock. Check the web site for special events like 'Karate Karaoke.' There's often no cover charge.

★**Commonwealth** BAR
(☏702-445-6400; www.commonwealthlv.com; 525 Fremont St E; ⊗7pm-late Tue-Sat; 🚌Deuce) It might be a little too cool for school but, whoa, that Prohibition-era interior is worth a look: plush booths, softly glowing chandeliers, Victorian-era bric-a-brac and a saloon bar. Imbibe your old-fashioned cocktails on the rooftop patio overlooking the Fremont East scene. They say there's a secret cocktail bar within the bar, but you didn't hear that from us.

★**Double Down Saloon** BAR
(☏702-791-5775; www.doubledownsaloon.com; 4640 Paradise Rd; ⊗24hr; 🚌108) This dark, psychedelic gin joint appeals to the lunatic fringe. It never closes, there's never a cover charge, the house drink is called 'ass juice' and it claims to be the birthplace of the bacon martini. When live bands aren't terrorizing the crowd, the jukebox vibrates with New Orleans jazz, British punk, Chicago blues and surf-guitar king Dick Dale.

★**Gold Spike** BAR
(☏702-476-1082; www.goldspike.com; 217 N Las Vegas Blvd; ⊗24hr) Gold Spike, with its playroom, living room and backyard, is many things: bar, nightclub, performance space, work space; sometime host of roller derbies, discos, live bands or dance parties; or just somewhere to soak up the sun with a relaxed crew and escape mainstream Vegas. Australians will think it's very Melburnian and feel right at home.

☆ Entertainment

That sensory overload of blindingly bright neon lights means you've finally landed on Las Vegas Blvd. The infamous Strip has the lion's share of gigantic casino hotels, all flashily competing to lure you (and your wallet) inside, with larger-than-life production shows, celebrity-filled nightclubs and burlesque cabarets. Head off-Strip to find jukebox dive bars, arty cocktail lounges, strip clubs and more.

★**Le Rêve the Dream** THEATER
(☏702-770-9966; http://boxoffice.wynnlasvegas.com; Wynn; tickets $105-205; ⊗shows at 7pm & 9:30pm Fri-Tue) Underwater acrobatic feats by scuba-certified performers are the centerpiece of this intimate 'aqua-in-the-round' theater, which holds a one-million-gallon swimming pool. Critics call it a less-inspiring version of Cirque's O, while devoted fans find the romantic underwater tango, thrilling high dives and visually spectacular adventures to be superior. Beware: the cheapest seats are in the 'splash zone.'

★**O** THEATER
(☏888-488-7111; www.cirquedusoleil.com; Bellagio; tickets $99-185; ⊗7pm & 9:30pm Wed-Sun) Phonetically speaking, it's the French word for water (eau). With a lithe international cast performing in, on and above water, Cirque du Soleil's O tells the tale of theater

> ### ℹ TICKET DEALS
>
> **Tix 4 Tonight** (☏877-849-4868; www.tix4tonight.com; 3200 S Las Vegas Blvd, Fashion Show Mall; ⊗10am-8pm) offers half-price tix for a limited lineup of same-day shows and small discounts on 'always sold-out' shows. It's located outside Neiman Marcus department store. Check the website for other locations around the Strip.

GETTING AROUND LAS VEGAS

Walking The Strip is 4.2 miles long – don't assume you can walk easily between casino hotels, even those that appear to be close together.

Bus Day passes on the 24-hour Deuce and faster (though not 24-hour and not servicing all casinos) SDX buses are an excellent way to get around.

Monorail Expensive, inconveniently located on the east side of the Strip and with a limited route, but great views and regular services.

Tram Operates between some casinos. Free and slow.

Taxi Expensive. Tips are expected.

Ride-share By far the best way to get around Vegas in most circumstances, and even cheaper when traveling with others.

through the ages. It's a spectacular feat of imagination and engineering, and you'll pay dearly to see it – it's one of the Strip's few shows that rarely sells discounted tickets.

Beatles LOVE THEATER
(☑702-792-7777; www.cirquedusoleil.com; Mirage; tickets $79-180; ⊙7pm & 9:30pm Thu-Mon; ☛) Another smash hit from Cirque du Soleil, *Beatles LOVE* started as the brainchild of the late George Harrison. Using *Abbey Road* master tapes, the show psychedelically fuses the musical legacy of the Beatles with Cirque's high-energy dancers and signature aerial acrobatics. Come early to photograph the trippy, rainbow-colored entryway and grab drinks at Abbey Road bar, next to Revolution Lounge.

★ **Michael Jackson ONE** THEATER
(☑702-632-7580; www.cirquedusoleil.com; Mandalay Bay; tickets from $69; ⊙7pm & 9:30pm Fri-Tue) Cirque du Soleil's musical tribute to the King of Pop blasts onto Mandalay Bay's (p334) stage with showstopping dancers and lissome acrobats and aerialists all moving to

a soundtrack of MJ's hits, moon-walking all the way back to his break-out platinum album *Thriller*. No children under five years old allowed.

🔒 Shopping

★ **Las Vegas Premium Outlets North** MALL
(☑702-474-7500; www.premiumoutlets.com/vegas north; 875 S Grand Central Pkwy; ⊙9am-9pm Mon-Sat, to 8pm Sun; ☛; ☐SDX) Vegas' biggest-ticket outlet mall features 120 mostly high-end names such as Armani, Brooks Brothers, Diane Von Furstenberg, Elle Tahari, Kate Spade, Michael Kors, Theory and Tory Burch, alongside casual brands like Banana Republic and Diesel.

Retro Vegas VINTAGE
(☑702-384-2700; www.retro-vegas.com; 1131 S Main St; ⊙11am-6pm Mon-Sat, noon-5pm Sun; ☐108, Deuce) Near Downtown's 18b Arts District, this flamingo-pink-painted antiques shop is a primo place for picking up mid-20th-century modern and swingin' 1960s and '70s gems, from artwork to home decor, as well as vintage Vegas souvenirs like casino-hotel ashtrays. Red Kat's secondhand clothing, handbags and accessories are also found here.

ℹ Information

Harmon Medical Center (☑702-796-1116; www.harmonmedicalcenter.com; 150 E Harmon Ave; ⊙8am-8pm Mon-Fri) Discounts for uninsured patients; limited translation services available.

Las Vegas Convention & Visitors Authority (LVCVA; ☑702-892-7575; www.lasvegas.com; 3150 Paradise Rd; ⊙8am-5:30pm Mon-Fri; Las Vegas Convention Center)

ℹ Getting There & Around

McCarran International Airport (LAS; ☑702-261-5211; www.mccarran.com; 5757 Wayne Newton Blvd; ☎)
The easiest and cheapest way to get to your hotel is by airport shuttle (one-way to Strip/downtown hotels from $7/9) or a shared rideshare service (from $10). As you exit baggage claim, look for shuttle-bus kiosks lining the curb; prices and destinations are clearly marked.

Santa Barbara County

Why Go?

Frankly put, this area is damn pleasant to putter around. Low-slung between lofty mountains and the shimmering Pacific, chic Santa Barbara's red-tiled roofs, white stucco buildings and Mediterranean vibe give credence to its claim of being the 'American Riviera.' It's an enticing place to loll on the beach, eat and drink extraordinarily well, shop a bit and push all your cares off to another day. The city's car-free campaign has brought electric shuttle buses, urban bike trails and earth-friendly wine tours. Mother Nature returns the love with hiking, biking, surfing, kayaking, scuba diving and camping opportunities galore, from offshore Channel Islands National Park to arty Ojai, in neighboring Ventura County. Meanwhile winemaking is booming in the bucolic Santa Ynez Mountains, west of Santa Barbara, where over a hundred wineries vie for your attention.

Best Places to Eat

➜ Santa Barbara Shellfish Company (p358)

➜ Mesa Verde (p358)

➜ Bouchon (p359)

➜ Knead (p379)

➜ Yoichi's (p358)

➜ Industrial Eats (p374)

Best Places to Sleep

➜ Belmondo El Encanto (p355)

➜ Pacific Crest Hotel (p355)

➜ Inn of the Spanish Garden (p356)

➜ Landsby (p372)

➜ Hotel Californian (p355)

When to Go
Santa Barbara

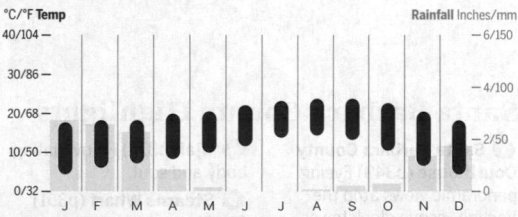

April Balmy temperatures, fewer tourists than in summer. Wildflowers bloom on Channel Islands.

June Summer vacation and beach season begin. Summer Solstice Celebration parade.

Oct Sunny blue skies and smaller crowds. Wine Country harvest festivities.

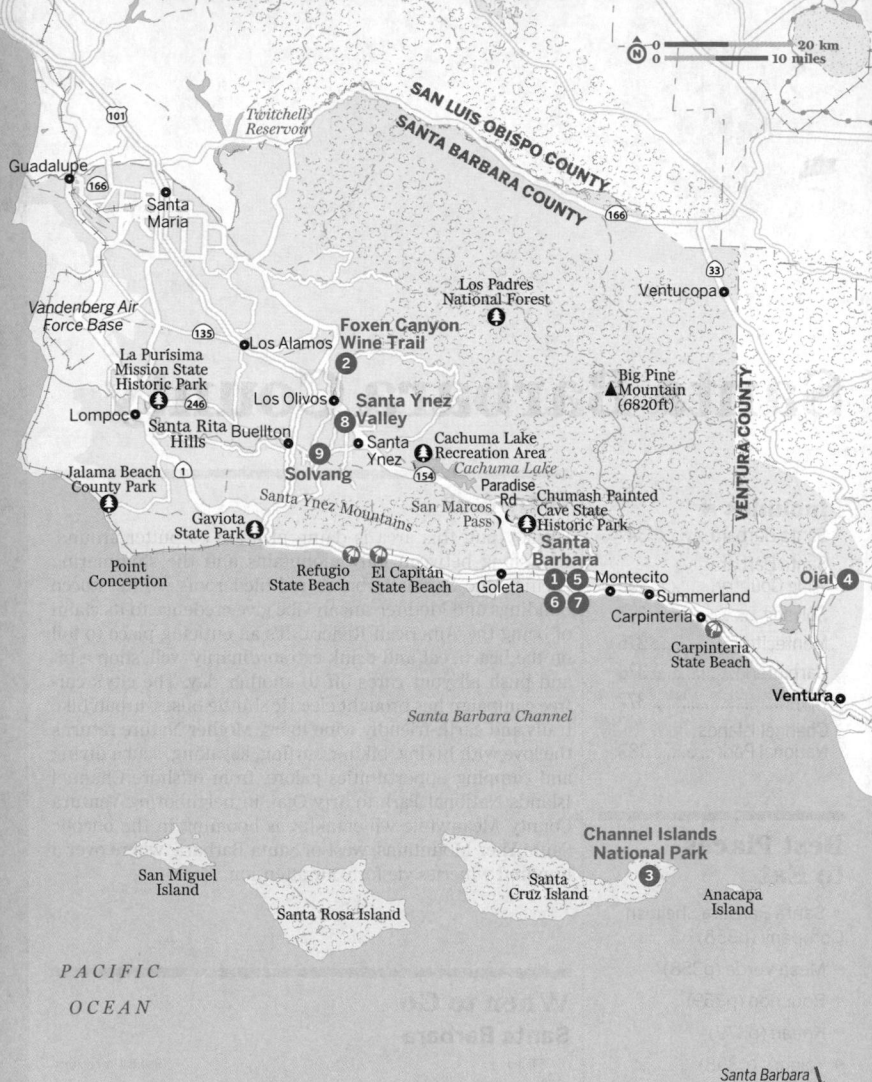

Santa Barbara
Island (30mi)

Santa Barbara County Highlights

1 **Santa Barbara County Courthouse** (p349) Eyeing panoramic views atop the *Vertigo*–esque clock tower.

2 **Foxen Canyon Wine Trail** (p366) Following this rural route to taste top Pinot Noir.

3 **Channel Islands National Park** (p383) Kayaking sea caves, hiking windswept cliffs and watching for whales.

4 **Ojai** (p377) Rejuvenating body and soul.

5 **Stearns Wharf** (p351) Strolling out to sea along California's oldest pier.

6 **Funk Zone** (p347) Ambling between wine-tasting, bars, galleries and shops in Santa Barbara's favorite neighborhood.

7 **Mission Santa Barbara** (p349) Exploring a rich vein of Spanish-colonial history.

8 **Santa Ynez Valley** (p369) Pedaling past vineyards and organic farms.

9 **Solvang** (p372) Eating *aebleskivers* (pancake popovers) by a kitschy windmill in this mock Danish village.

SANTA BARBARA

Perfect weather, beautiful buildings, excellent bars and restaurants, and activities for all tastes and budgets make Santa Barbara a great place to live (as the locals will proudly tell you) and a must-see place for visitors to Southern California. Check out the Spanish Mission church first, then just see where the day takes you.

History

For hundreds of years before the arrival of the Spanish, Chumash tribespeople thrived in this region, setting up trade routes between the mainland and the Channel Islands and constructing redwood canoes known as *tomols*. In 1542 explorer Juan Rodríguez Cabrillo sailed into the channel and claimed it for Spain – then quickly met his doom (from a gangrenous leg injury) on a nearby island.

The Chumash had little reason for concern until the permanent return of the Spanish in the late 18th century. Catholic priests established missions up and down the coast, ostensibly to convert Native Americans to Christianity. Spanish soldiers often forced the Chumash to construct the missions and presidios (military forts) and provide farm labor; they also rounded up the tribespeople on the Channel Islands and forced them to leave.

Back on the mainland, the indigenous population shrank dramatically, as many Chumash died of European diseases and ill treatment.

Mexican ranchers arrived after their country won independence in 1821. Easterners began migrating en masse after California's Gold Rush kicked off in 1849. By the late 1890s, Santa Barbara was an established vacation spot for the wealthy. After a massive earthquake in 1925, laws were passed requiring much of the city to be rebuilt in faux-but-attractive Spanish Colonial–style white-stucco buildings with red-tiled roofs.

⊙ Sights

★ MOXI   MUSEUM
(Wolf Museum of Exploration + Innovation; ☑805-770 5000; www.moxi.org; 125 State St; adult/child $14/10; ☉10am-5pm; ⊕) Part of the regeneration of this neglected strip of State St, Moxi's three floors filled with hands-on displays covering science, arts and technology themes will tempt families in, even when it's not raining outside. If all that interactivity gets too much, head to the roof terrace for views across Santa Barbara and a nerve-challenging walk across a glass ceiling.

Highlights include booths where you re-create sound effects from famous movie scenes, the 'mind ball' game where you use just your calm thoughts to move a metal ball

SANTA BARBARA COUNTY SANTA BARBARA

SANTA BARBARA COUNTY IN...

One Day

Spend the first morning exploring Santa Barbara's historic **mission** (p349) before visiting downtown's museums, landmarks and shops along **State St**, stopping at the **county courthouse** (p349) for 360-degree views from its clock tower. Grab lunch on State St and then soak up some rays at the city's **East Beach** (p352), walking out on to **Stearns Wharf** (p351) and down by the **harbor** for sunset. After dark, head to the **Funk Zone** for dinner and drinks in Santa Barbara's coolest neighborhood.

Two Days

Head up to Santa Barbara's Wine Country. Enjoy a do-it-yourself vineyards tour by car, motorcycle or bicycle along a scenic wine trail – Foxen Canyon (p366) and the Santa Rita Hills (p367) are exceptionally beautiful. Pack a picnic lunch or grab a bite in charming Los Olivos (p371) or Danish-esque Solvang (p372).

Three Days

Spend the morning cycling along the coast, surfing or sea-kayaking on the Pacific, or hiking in the Santa Ynez foothills. In the afternoon, drive to posh Montecito (p376) for shopping and people-watching, or hang loose in Carpinteria (p376), a retro beach town.

Four Days

Head east for a stop in arty Ojai (p377), up in the mountains and known for its hot springs and spas, or book a day trip from Ventura (p381) by boat to explore one of the rugged Channel Islands (p383).

Downtown Santa Barbara

SANTA BARBARA

SANTA BARBARA COUNTY SANTA BARBARA

Mission Creek

Simpson House Inn (0.3mi);
Santa Barbara
Auto Camp (0.8mi);
Agave Inn (1.4mi)

Mission Santa Barbara (0.9mi);
Santa Barbara Museum of
Natural History (1.2mi);
Belmondo El Encanto
(1.5mi); Santa Barbara
Botanic Garden (2.5mi)

W Sola St

W Anapamu St

E Anapamu St

W Figueroa St

E Figueroa St

Santa Barbara County Courthouse

W Carrillo St

E Carrillo St

MTD Transit Center

W Canon Perdido St

E De La Guerra St

W De La Guerra St

Ortega St

W Ortega St

E Ortega St

Cota St

W Cota St

E Cota St

Coronel Pl

W Haley St

E Haley St

E Gutierrez St

E Victoria St

W Mason St

W Cabrillo Blvd

Arroyo Burro Beach
County Park (2.5mi)

Leadbetter Beach (0.3mi);
Thousand Steps
Beach (1.35mi);
Shoreline Park (0.9mi);
Lazy Acres (2mi);
Mesa Verde
(2.1mi)

Shoreline Dr

Montecito St
Greyhound

Amtrak
Station

MOXI

FUNK
ZONE

Santa Barbara
Visitors Center

Natoma Ave

Cliff Dr

Outdoors Santa Barbara
Visitors Center

Lil' Toot Water Taxi

Santa
Barbara Harbor

Sand
Bar

Stearns
Wharf

De La Vina St
Chapala St
State St
San Pascual St
De La Guerra St
Castillo St
Bath St
Rancheria St
Ladera St
Anacapa St
Garden St
Santa Barbara St
Laguna St
Helena Ave
Gray Ave
Montecito St
Garden St

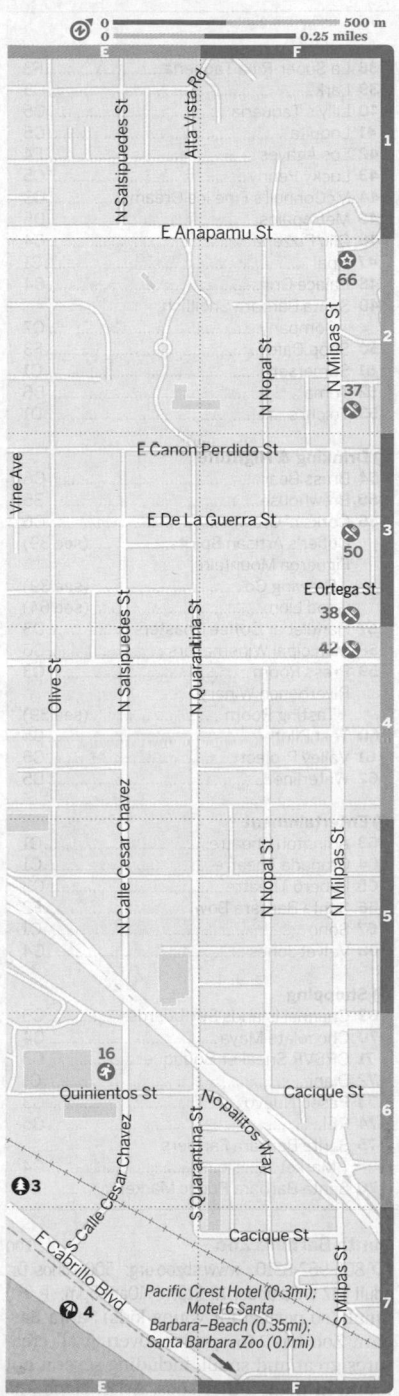

against an opponent, and workshops which feature different make-and-learn activities.

Weekends get very busy with waits for many of the exhibits, so try to come during the week when it's quieter.

★ **Santa Barbara County Courthouse**   HISTORIC BUILDING
(☎805-962-6464; http://sbcourthouse.org; 1100 Anacapa St; ⊙8am-5pm Mon-Fri, 10am-5pm Sat & Sun) FREE Built in Spanish-Moorish Revival style in 1929, the courthouse features hand-painted ceilings, wrought-iron chandeliers, and tiles from Tunisia and Spain. Step inside the hushed mural room depicting Spanish-colonial history on the 2nd floor, then head up to El Mirador, the 85ft clock tower, for arch-framed panoramas of the city, ocean and mountains.

You can explore on your own, but you'll get a lot more out of a free, one-hour docent-guided tour: 2pm daily, plus 10:30am Monday to Friday.

★ **Mission Santa Barbara**   CHURCH
(☎805-682-4713; www.santabarbaramission.org; 2201 Laguna St; adult $9, child 5-17yr $4; ⊙9am-5pm, last entry 4:15pm; P⛪) California's 'Queen of the Missions' reigns above the city on a hilltop perch over a mile north of downtown. Its imposing Ionic facade, an architectural homage to an ancient Roman chapel, is topped by an unusual twin-bell tower. Inside the mission's 1820 stone church, notice the striking Chumash artwork. In the cemetery the elaborate mausoleums of early California settlers stand out, while the graves of thousands of Chumash lie largely forgotten.

The self-guided tour starts in the pretty garden before heading to the cemetery (where Juana María, the Chumash girl made famous in *Island of the Blue Dolphins,* was buried). Next up is the church itself, followed by a series of rooms turned into a museum and exhibiting Chumash baskets, a missionary's bedroom and time-capsule black-and-white photos showing the last Chumash residents of the Mission and the damage done to the buildings after the 1925 earthquake. Docent-guided tours are usually given at 11am on Tuesday, Thursday and Friday, 10:30am on Saturday, and 12:30pm on Sunday; no reservations are taken.

The mission was established on December 4 (the feast day of St Barbara), 1786, as the 10th California mission. Of California's original 21 Spanish colonial missions, it's the only one that escaped secularization under

Downtown Santa Barbara

Mexican rule. Continuously occupied by Catholic priests since its founding, the mission is still an active parish church.

From downtown, take MTD bus 6 or 11, then walk five blocks uphill.

Santa Barbara Zoo　　　ZOO
(☏ 805-962-6310; www.sbzoo.org; 500 Ninos Dr; adult $17, child under 13 $10; ⊙ 10am-5pm; ℗ ⛟)
Small (so perfect for young kids) Santa Barbara Zoo has 146 species covering all creatures great and small, including several not found in many other zoos. Asian elephants

Little Mac and Sujatha have been together here since 1972 and are hugely popular, as are the adorable meerkats. Don't miss the chance to see endangered California condors – probably your best bet for seeing them in the whole state – and giant anteaters. The antics of the Humboldt penguins always raise a smile.

Information panels give details on the animals and their habitats, plus tips for visitors on how to help preserve the creatures' natural environments (don't buy unsustainable palm oil, for example).

Shoreline Park   PARK

(Shoreline Dr; ⏲8am-sunset; P▓) FREE For great views across the city, mountains and ocean (with the chance to spot whales in season and dolphins year-round), come to Shoreline Park, southwest of Santa Barbara. There are restrooms, picnic tables and a children's playground. Dogs are welcome.

Santa Barbara Museum
of Natural History   MUSEUM

(☎805-682-4711; www.sbnature.org; 2559 Puesta del Sol; adult $12, child 2-12yr $7, youth 13-17yr $8, incl planetarium show $16/12/12; ⏲10am-5pm; P▐) The huge whale skeleton by the entrance whets the appetite for the city's natural history museum. The usual dioramas of stuffed animals are on display in dimly lit rooms (the bird collection is especially good on local species), but the joy of this place is that once you've learned about nature inside, you can head outside to the 'Museum's Backyard', a trail through woods by a creek, and engage with the real thing.

Santa Barbara Historical Museum MUSEUM

(☎805-966-1601; www.santabarbaramuseum.com; 136 E De La Guerra St; ⏲10am-5pm Tue-Sat, from noon Sun) FREE Embracing a romantic cloistered adobe courtyard, this peaceful little museum tells the story of Santa Barbara. Its endlessly fascinating collection of local memorabilia ranges from the simply beautiful, such as Chumash woven baskets and Spanish-colonial-era textiles, to the intriguing, such as an intricately carved coffer that once belonged to Junípero Serra. Learn about the city's involvement in toppling the last Chinese monarchy, among other interesting lessons in local history.

Stearns Wharf   WATERFRONT

(www.stearnswharf.org; ⏲open daily, hours vary; P▐) FREE The southern end of State St gives way to Stearns Wharf, a rough wooden

DON'T MISS

MEETING MONARCHS
....

If you're here in late fall or winter, ask at the **Outdoors Santa Barbara Visitors Center** (p364) about the best places to see migratory monarch butterflies roosting in the trees – an extraordinary sight. See p467 for more information on roosting.

pier lined with souvenir shops, snack stands and seafood shacks. Built in 1872, it's the oldest continuously operating wharf on the West Coast, although the actual structure has been rebuilt more than once. During the 1940s it was co-owned by tough-guy actor Jimmy Cagney and his brothers. If you have kids, tow them inside the **Sea Center** (☎805-962-2526; www.sbnature.org; 211 Stearns Wharf; adult $8.50, child 2-12yr $6, youth 13-17yr $7.50; ⏲10am-5pm; P▐).

Santa Barbara Botanic Garden   GARDENS

(☎805-682-4726; www.sbbg.org; 1212 Mission Canyon Rd; adult $12, child 2-12yr $6, youth 13-17yr $8; ⏲9am-6pm Mar-Oct, to 5pm Nov-Feb; P▐▓) Take a soul-satisfying jaunt around this 40-acre botanic garden, devoted to California's native flora. Miles of partly wheelchair-accessible trails meander past cacti, redwoods and wildflowers and by the old mission dam, originally built by Chumash tribespeople to irrigate the mission's fields. Guided tours (included with admission) depart at 11am and 2pm on Saturday and Sunday, and 2pm on Monday. Leashed, well-behaved dogs are welcome.

If you're driving, head north from the mission to Foothill Blvd/Hwy 192, turn right and then left to continue on Mission Canyon Rd.

Santa Barbara Maritime Museum MUSEUM

(☎805-962-8404; www.sbmm.org; 113 Harbor Way; adult $8, child 6-17yr $5; ⏲10am-5pm Thu-Tue; P▐) On the harborfront, this jam-packed, two-story exhibition hall celebrates the town's briny history with nautical artifacts, memorabilia and hands-on exhibits, including a big-game fishing chair from which you can 'reel in' a trophy marlin. Take a virtual trip through the Santa Barbara Channel, stand on a surfboard or watch deep-sea diving documentaries in the theater. There's 90 minutes of free parking in the public lot or take the Lil' Toot water taxi (p365) from Stearns Wharf.

TOP 10 BEACHES IN SANTA BARBARA

Although Santa Barbara's beaches are beauty-pageant prize winners, don't expect sunsets over the ocean because most of this coast faces south.

East Beach (www.santabarbaraca.gov/gov/depts/parksrec; E Cabrillo Blvd; 🚾) Santa Barbara's largest and most popular beach is a long, sandy stretch sprawling east of Stearns Wharf, with volleyball nets for pick-up games, a children's play area and a snack bar. On Sunday afternoons, artists set up booths along the sidewalk, near the bike path.

Butterfly Beach (Channel Dr) No facilities but quite a high chance of celebrity spotting (the nearby Four Seasons Biltmore hotel is a popular destination for the rich and famous) at this small beach.

West Beach (W Cabrillo Blvd; 🚾) Central, palm-tree-backed stretch of sand, right next to Stearns Wharf and the harbor (swimming isn't advisable). It's also the setting for large outdoor city events such as Fourth of July celebrations.

Leadbetter Beach (📞805-564-5418; Shoreline Dr, at Loma Alta Dr; per vehicle $2; P 🚾) One of Santa Barbara's most popular beaches, always busy with surfers, wind- and kite-surfers, joggers and sunbathers. Facilities include reservable picnic areas and showers.

Goleta Beach County Park (www.countyofsb.org/parks/day-use/goleta-beach.sbc; Sandspit Rd, Goleta; ⊙8am-sunset; P) Good beach for sunbathing, swimming and picnicking (nab a prized shaded spot if you can), or strolling the 1500ft-long pier for views out to the Channel Islands.

Arroyo Burro Beach County Park (Hendry's; 📞805-568-2460; www.countyofsb.org/parks; Cliff Dr, at Las Positas Rd; ⊙8am-sunset; P 🚾🎿) Swim (lifeguards on duty), stroll or just picnic on this gem of a stretch of sand, also known as Hendry's Beach, 5 miles southwest of Santa Barbara. It's flat, wide, away from tourists and great for kids, who can go tide-pooling. It's also a popular local surf spot and the eastern section is dog-friendly (there's even a dog wash in the parking lot).

Carpinteria State Beach (p377) An idyllic, mile-long strand where kids can splash around in calm waters and go tide-pooling along the shoreline. In winter, you may spot harbor seals and sea lions hauled out on the sand, especially if you hike over a mile south along the coast to a bluff-top overlook.

El Capitán State Beach (📞805-968-1033; www.parks.ca.gov; El Capitan State Beach Rd, Goleta; $10 per vehicle; ⊙8am-sunset; P 🚾) Head down from the low cliffs to enjoy swimming (confident bathers only), surfing and fishing from this pebbly beach, overlooked by native sycamore and oak trees. The seasonal beach store opens April to mid-September and sells basic groceries and camping supplies.

Thousand Steps Beach (Shoreline Dr, southern end of Santa Cruz Blvd; ⊙sunrise-10pm) Descend the cliffs on a historic staircase (don't worry, there aren't actually a thousand steps) for some windy beachcombing and tide-pooling (only at low tide), but no swimming. The beach is also accessible from **Shoreline Park** (p351) – head west along Shoreline Dr from the park and take a left on Santa Cruz Blvd.

Santa Barbara Museum of Art MUSEUM (📞805-963-4364; www.sbmuseart.org; 1130 State St; adult $10, child 6-17yr $6, all free 5-8pm Thu; ⊙11am-5pm Tue-Wed & Fri-Sun, to 8pm Thu; 🚾) This thoughtfully curated, bite-sized art museum displays European and American masters – including Monet, Van Gogh and Degas – along with photography, classical antiquities and Asian artifacts and thought-provoking temporary exhibits. At the time of writing, some galleries were closed while the museum is retrofitted for earthquake protection.

Highlight tours of current exhibitions start at 1pm daily and are included in admission. It also has an interactive children's space, a museum shop and a cafe.

El Presidio de Santa Barbara
State Historic Park HISTORIC SITE (📞805-965-0093; www.sbthp.org; 123 E Canon Perdido St; adult $5, child under 17yr free; ⊙10:30am-4:30pm) Founded in 1782 to defend

the mission, this adobe-walled fort built by Chumash laborers was Spain's last military stronghold in Alta California. But its purpose wasn't solely to protect – the presidio also served as a social and political hub, and as a stopping point for traveling Spanish military. Today this small urban park harbors some of the city's oldest structures. On a self-guided walking tour, be sure to stop at the chapel, its interior radiant with rich hues.

🏃 Activities

Cycling

A paved **recreational path** stretches 3 miles along the waterfront in both directions from Stearns Wharf, west to Leadbetter Beach beyond the harbor and east just past East Beach. For more pedaling routes, Bike Santa Barbara (p353) offers free downloadable DIY cycling tours of the city, mountains and Wine Country, along with links to bicycle rentals and specialty shops.

Wheel Fun Rentals CYCLING
(📞805-966-2282; http://wheelfunrentalssb.com; 23 E Cabrillo Blvd; ⊙8am-8pm; 🚗) Hourly rentals of beach cruisers ($9.95), mountain bikes ($10.95) and two-/four-person surreys ($28.95/38.95), with discounted half-day and full-day rates. A second, seasonal branch is in the Fess Parker Double Tree Hotel at 633 East Cabrillo Blvd.

Santa Barbara Bikes To-Go CYCLING
(📞805-628-2444; www.sbbikestogo.com; 1 N Calle Cesar Chavez; bike rental per day $35-105; ⊙9am-5pm) Delivers top-quality road and hybrid mountain bikes to wherever you're staying in Santa Barbara. Rentals include helmets and emergency-kit saddle bags. Discounts for multiday, weekly and monthly rentals; reservations essential.

Kayaking

Paddle the calm waters of Santa Barbara's harbor or the coves of the Gaviota coast, or hitch a ride to the Channel Islands for awesome sea caves.

Santa Barbara Adventure Company KAYAKING
(📞805-884-9283; www.sbadventureco.com; 32 E Haley St; ⊙office 8am-5pm Mon-Sat; 🚗) The name says it all: if you want a company that provides a whole host of well-organized adventures then you've come to the right place. It offers everything from Channel Island kayaking ($179) to surf lessons ($89), and bike tours (from $119) to horseback riding ($150).

Paddle Sports Center KAYAKING
(📞805-617-3425; http://paddlesportsca.com; 117b Harbor Way; SUP/kayak rental from $20/12; ⊙usually 8am-6pm) Long-established, friendly outfitter offering year-round kayak and SUP rentals from Santa Barbara harbor and Goleta Beach. Walk-ins are welcome but reduced rates are available if you book online in advance.

Santa Barbara Sailing Center CRUISE, SAILING
(📞805-962-2826; www.sbsail.com; Marina 4, off Harbor Way; ⊙9am-6pm, to 5pm winter; 🚗) Climb aboard the *Double Dolphin*, a 50ft sailing catamaran, for a two-hour coastal or sunset cruise ($35). Seasonal whale-watching trips ($40) and quick half-hour spins around the harbor to view marine life ($18) are more kid-friendly. It also offers kayak and SUP rentals and tours.

Boating & Whale-Watching

Some tour companies offer year-round whale-watching boat trips, mostly to see grays in winter and spring, and humpbacks and blues in summer.

Condor Express CRUISE
(📞805-882-0088; www.condorcruises.com; 301 W Cabrillo Blvd; 2½/4½hr cruises adult from $50/99, child 5-12yr from $30/50; 🚗) Take a whale-watching excursion aboard the high-speed catamaran *Condor Express*. Whale sightings are guaranteed, so if you miss out the first time, you'll get a free voucher for another cruise.

Sunset Kidd's Sailing Cruises CRUISE
(📞805-962-8222; www.sunsetkidd.com; 125 Harbor Way; cruises $40) Take an 18-passenger sailboat on a 2½-hour whale-watching trip or a two-hour morning, afternoon, sunset-cocktail or full-moon cruise. Reservations recommended.

Surfing

Unless you're a novice, conditions are too mellow in summer – come back in winter when ocean swells kick back up. Santa Barbara's **Leadbetter Point** is best for beginners. Experts-only **Rincon Point** awaits just outside Carpinteria.

Surf-n-Wear's Beach House SURFING
(📞805-963-1281; www.surfnwear.com; 10 State St; rental per hour/day wetsuit $4/16, bodyboard $4/16, surfboard $10/35, SUP set per day $50; ⊙9am-6pm Sun-Thu, to 7pm Fri & Sat) Not far from Stearns Wharf, you can rent soft (foam) boards, bodyboards, wetsuits and SUP sets from this 1960s surf shop. It also

SANTA BARBARA ART WALKS

Prime time for downtown gallery hopping is **First Thursday** (www.santa barbaradowntown.com), from 5pm to 8pm on the first Thursday of every month, when art galleries on and off State St throw open their doors for new exhibitions, artists' receptions, wine tastings and live music, all free. Closer to the beach but similar in aim is the **Funk Zone Art Walk** (http://funkzone. net), happening on a bimonthly basis from 5pm to 8pm and featuring free events and entertainment at offbeat art galleries, bars and restaurants.

sells modern and vintage surfboards, unique T-shirts and hoodies, colorful bikinis, shades, beach bags and flip-flops.

Hiking

Gorgeous day hikes await in the foothills of the Santa Ynez Mountains and elsewhere in the Los Padres National Forest. Most trails cut through rugged chaparral and steep canyons – sweat it out and savor jaw-dropping coastal views. Spring and fall are the best seasons for hiking, when temperatures are moderate. Always carry plenty of extra water and watch out for poison oak.

To find even more local trails to explore, browse Santa Barbara Hikes online (www. sant- abarbarahikes.com) or visit the Los Padres National Forest Headquarters (p364), west of the airport.

🕝 Tours

★ Architectural Foundation of Santa Barbara 　　　　WALKING
(☏805-965-6307; www.afsb.org; adult $10, child under 12yr free; ☺10am Sat & Sun weather permitting) Take time out of your weekend for a fascinating 90-minute guided walking tour of downtown's art, history and architecture. No reservations required; call or check the website for meet-up times and places.

Santa Barbara Trolley 　　　　　　　　BUS
(☏805-965-0353; www.sbtrolley.com; adult $22, child 3-12yr $8; ☺10am-3pm; 🖪) 🖉 Biodiesel-fueled trolleys make a narrated 90-minute one-way loop stopping at 14 major tourist attractions around the city, including the Mission and the zoo. They start

from the visitor center (hourly departures 10am to 3pm) and the hop-on, hop-off tickets are valid all day (and one consecutive day) – pay the driver directly, or buy discounted tickets online in advance.

Land & Sea Tours 　　　　　　　　TOURS
(☏805-683-7600; www.out2seesb.com; 99 W Cabrillo Blvd; adult $30, child 2-9yr $15; ☺noon & 2pm, also 4pm daily May-Oct; 🖪) If you dig James Bond–style vehicles, take a narrated tour of the city on the *Land Shark,* an amphibious vehicle that drives right into the water. Trips depart from Stearns Wharf; buy tickets onboard (no reservations).

🎊 Festivals & Events

To find out what's happening now, check the events calendars at www.santabarbaraca. com and www.independent.com online.

★ Old Spanish Days Fiesta 　　　CULTURE, ART
(www.oldspanishdays-fiesta.org; ☺late Jul-early Aug) FREE The entire city fills up for this long-running – if slightly overblown – festival celebrating Santa Barbara's Spanish and Mexican colonial heritage. Festivities include outdoor bazaars and food markets, live music, flamenco dancing, horseback and rodeo events and a big ole parade.

★ Summer Solstice Celebration 　　FESTIVAL
(☏805-965-3396; www.solsticeparade.com; ☺late Jun) FREE Kicking off summer, this wildly popular and wacky float parade down State St feels like something out of Burning Man. Live music, kids' activities, food stands, a wine-and-beer garden and an arts-and-craft show happen all weekend long.

Santa Barbara County Fair 　　　　　FAIR
(☏805-925-8824; www.santamariafairpark.com; Santa Maria Fairpark, 937 S Thornburg St, Santa Maria; adult/child $10/8, child under 5yr free; ☺mid-Jul; 🖪) This old-fashioned county fair combines agriculture exhibits, carnival rides and lots of food and wine. The fairgrounds are in Santa Maria, over an hour's drive northwest of Santa Barbara via Hwy 101.

French Festival 　　　　　　　　CULTURE, ART
(☏805-963-8198; www.frenchfestival.com; Oak Park; ☺mid-Jul; 🖪; 🚪3) FREE California's biggest Francophile celebration has lots of food and wine, world music and dancing, a mock Eiffel Tower and Moulin Rouge, and even a poodle parade.

**I Madonnari Italian
Street Painting Festival** ART, FOOD
(www.imadonnarifestival.com; ☺Memorial Day weekend, generally last weekend in May; 🚗; 🚌6, 11) FREE Colorful chalk drawings adorn Mission Santa Barbara's sidewalks over Memorial Day weekend, with Italian-food vendors and arts-and-crafts booths.

**Santa Barbara
International Film Festival** FILM
(📞805-963-0023; http://sbiff.org; 1528 Chapala St, Suite 203; from $60; ☺late Jan-early Feb) Film buffs and Hollywood A-list stars show up for screenings of more than 200 independent US and foreign films.

🛏 Sleeping

Prepare for sticker shock: even basic motel rooms by the beach command over $200 in summer. Don't arrive without reservations and expect to find anything reasonably priced, especially not on weekends. A good selection of renovated motels are tucked between the harbor and the 101 freeway, just about walking distance to everything. Cheaper motels cluster along upper State St and Hwy 101 northbound to Goleta and southbound to Carpinteria, Ventura and Camarillo.

★**Santa Barbara
Auto Camp** CAMPGROUND $$
(📞888-405-7553; http://autocamp.com/sb; 2717 De La Vina St; d $175-215; 🅿❄🐾🛜🏊) 🖉 Ramp up the retro chic and bed down with vintage style in one of five shiny metal Airstream trailers parked near upper State St, north of downtown. All five architect-designed trailers have unique perks, such as a clawfoot tub or extra twin-size beds for kiddos, as well as full kitchen and complimentary cruiser bikes to borrow. Book ahead; twonight minimum may apply. Pet fee $25.

★**Hotel Californian** BOUTIQUE HOTEL $$$
(www.thehotelcalifornian.com; 36 State St; r from $400; 🅿❄🛜🏊) Hotel Californian is the new kid on the once-rundown block that is the lower end of State St. Spearheading the area's rehabilitation, it would be worth staying just for the prime location (next to the beach, Stearns Wharf and the Funk Zone) but its appeal goes way beyond geography. A winning architectural mix of Spanish Colonial and North African Moorish styles set a glamorous tone.

The hotel's original history was brief. It opened to much fanfare in 1925 and was an instant hit with both visitors and locals, until just a few short weeks later the powerful earthquake that leveled most of the city struck and forced the permanent closure of the damaged Californian. A hundred years later it's open again, and behind the original facade it's as glorious as ever.

Spread across three buildings, the spacious rooms come in four color schemes (orange, green, yellow and purple) and most have balconies along with attractive design features such as latticework and arched windows. Amenities include a spa and rooftop pool, three restaurants (open to nonguests) and boutique shopping.

★**Pacific Crest Hotel** BOUTIQUE HOTEL $$$
(📞805 966 3103; www.pacificcrestsantabarbara.com; 433 Corona del Mar Dr; r from $235; 🅿🛜🏊) 🖉 Wonderfully friendly Greg and Jennifer make sure all guests feel at home at their boutique motel, close to East Beach and the zoo. Landscaped grounds welcome you, rooms are spacious (bathrooms are small but plans are afoot to enlarge them) and come in cool, neutral tones that provide a soothing experience.

★**Belmondo El Encanto** LUXURY HOTEL $$$
(📞805-845-5800; www.elencanto.com; 800 Alvarado Pl; r from $475; 🅿❄@🛜🏊🏊) Triumphantly reborn in 2013, this 1908 icon of Santa Barbara style is a hilltop hideaway for travelers who demand the very best of everything. An infinity pool gazes out at the Pacific, while flower-filled gardens, fireplace lounges, a full-service spa and private bungalows with sun-drenched patios concoct

---

DIY WALKING TOURS

Santa Barbara's self-guided 12-block **Red Tile walking tour** is a convenient introduction to downtown's historical highlights. The tour's name comes from the half-moon-shaped red-clay tiles covering the roofs of many Spanish Revival—style buildings. You can download a free map of this walking tour, as well as other paths including along the waterfront, from Santa Barbara Car Free (www.santabarbaracarfree.org). For a lazy stroll between wine-tasting rooms, follow the city's Urban Wine Trail (p362) (www.urbanwinetrailsb.com).

the glamorous atmosphere perfectly fitted to SoCal socialites.

★ Inn of the Spanish Garden
BOUTIQUE HOTEL $$$

(☎ 805-564-4700; www.spanishgardeninn.com; 915 Garden St; r from $309; P❄✱@🛜⛱) At this Spanish Colonial–style inn, casual elegance, first-rate service and a romantic central courtyard will have you lording about like the don of your own private villa. Rooms have a balcony or patio, beds have luxurious linens and bathrooms have oversized tubs. The concierge service is top-notch. Palms surround a small outdoor pool, or unwind with a massage in your room.

Simpson House Inn
B&B $$$

(☎ 805-963-7067; www.simpsonhouseinn.com; 121 E Arrellaga St; r $325-610; P✱🛜) Whether you book an elegant room with a claw-foot bathtub or a sweet cottage with a fireplace, you'll be pampered at this Victorian-era estate ensconced by English-style gardens. From gourmet vegetarian breakfasts through evening wine, hors d'oeuvres and sweets receptions, you'll be well fed too. In-room mod cons include Netflix. Complimentary bicycles and beach gear to borrow. The hotel is perfect for a romantic break and is for adults only.

Agave Inn
MOTEL $$

(☎ 805-687-6009; www.agaveinnsb.com; 3222 State St; r from $119; P❄✱🛜) While it's still just a motel at heart, this boutique-on-a-budget property's 'Mexican pop meets modern' motif livens things up with a color palette from a Frieda Kahlo painting. Flat-screen TVs, microwaves, minifridges and air-con make it a standout option. Family-sized rooms have kitchenette and pull-out sofa beds. It's a little north of town so a car is a necessity, or good walking shoes.

Castillo Inn
MOTEL $$

(☎ 800-965-8570; www.sbcastilloinn.com; 22 Castillo St; r from $175; P@🛜) Minutes from West Beach (p352), the harbor and Stearns Wharf (p351), you can't get better priced accommodations in central Santa Barbara than at the Castillo Inn. The simply decorated rooms at this spruced-up motel are large and bright and a continental breakfast (just fruit and muffins) is included in the rate. Some rooms have terraces.

Harbor House Inn
MOTEL $$

(☎ 805-962-9745; www.harborhouseinn.com; 104 Bath St; r from $180; P❄✱🛜) Down by the harbor, this friendly, converted motel offers brightly lit studios with hardwood floors and a beachy design scheme. Most have full kitchen and one has a fireplace. Rates include a welcome basket of breakfast goodies (with a two-night minimum stay) and beach towels, chairs and umbrellas and three-speed bicycles to borrow.

SANTA BARBARA FOR CHILDREN

Santa Barbara abounds with family-friendly fun for kids of all ages, from tots to tweens.

MOXI (p347) Santa Barbara's newest hands-on, kid-friendly attraction.

Santa Barbara Museum of Natural History (p351) Giant skeletons, an insect wall and a pitch-dark planetarium captivate kids' imaginations. It's a 0.5-mile drive uphill from the mission.

Santa Barbara Maritime Museum (p351) Peer through a periscope, reel in a virtual fish, watch underwater films or check out the model ships.

Santa Barbara Sailing Center (p353) Short, one-hour sails around the harbor ($15) let young 'uns see sea lions up close.

Sea Center (p351) From touch tanks full of tide-pool critters and crawl-through aquariums to whale sing-alongs, it's interactive and educational. Hourly parking on the wharf costs $2.50.

Lil' Toot water taxi (p365) Take a joyride along the waterfront on this tiny yellow boat.

Chase Palm Park (www.santabarbaraca.gov/gov/depts/parksrec; 323 E Cabrillo Blvd; ⊗ sunrise-10pm; 🚸) FREE Antique carousel rides ($2, cash only) plus a shipwreck-themed playground decked out with seashells and a miniature lighthouse.

Arroyo Burro Beach County Park (p352) A wide, sandy beach, away from the tourists but not too far from downtown.

Hotel Indigo
BOUTIQUE HOTEL $$

(☎ 805-966-6586; www.indigosantabarbara.com; 121 State St; r from $180; ⓟ ✻ @ 🛜 🐾) 🍃 Poised between downtown and the beach, this petite Euro-chic boutique hotel has all the right touches: curated contemporary-art displays, outdoor terraces and ecofriendly green-design elements. Peruse local-interest and art-history books in the library nook, or retreat to your room and wrap yourself up in a plush bathrobe. Parking $30. Pet fee $40.

Marina Beach Motel
MOTEL $$

(☎ 805-963-9311; www.marinabeachmotel.com; 21 Bath St; r from $155; ⓟ ✻ 🛜 🐾) Family-owned since 1942, this whitewashed, one-story motor lodge that wraps around a grassy courtyard is worth a stay just for the location. Right by the beach, tidy remodeled rooms are comfy enough and some have kitchenette. Complimentary beach-cruiser bikes to borrow. Small pets OK (fee $15).

Canary Hotel
BOUTIQUE HOTEL $$$

(☎ 805-884-0300; www.canarysantabarbara.com; 31 W Carrillo St; r $325-575; ⓟ ✻ @ 🛜 🐶 🐾) 🍃 On a busy block downtown, this grand multistory hotel has a rooftop pool and sunset-watching perch for cocktails. Stylish accommodations show off four-poster beds and all mod cons. In-room spa services, Saturday yoga classes and bathroom goodies will soothe away stress, but ambient street noise may leave you sleepless (ask for an upper floor). Complimentary fitness center access and cruiser bicycles.

Hungry? Taste local farm goodness at the hotel's downstairs restaurant, **Finch & Fork**. Parking is $35; pets are welcome and stay for free.

White Jasmine Inn
B&B $$$

(☎ 805-966-0589; www.whitejasmineinnsantabarbara.com; 1327 Bath St; r $170-350; ⓟ 🛜) Tucked behind a jasmine-entwined wooden fence, this cheery inn stitches together an arts-and-crafts bungalow and two quaint cottages. Rooms all have private bath and fireplace, most are air-conditioned and come with Jacuzzi. Full breakfast basket delivered daily to your door. No children under 12 years old allowed.

Brisas del Mar
HOTEL $$$

(☎ 805-966-2219; http://brisasdelmarinn.com; 223 Castillo St; r from $210; ⓟ ✻ @ 🛜 🐶) Kudos for all the freebies (DVDs, continental breakfast, afternoon wine and cheese, evening milk and cookies), the newer Mediterranean-

---

> ## CAMPING & CABINS AROUND SANTA BARBARA
>
> You won't find a campground anywhere near downtown Santa Barbara, but less than a half-hour drive west via Hwy 101, right on the ocean, are **El Capitán & Refugio State Beaches** (☎ reservations 800-444-7275; www.reserveamerica.com; off Hwy 101; tent & RV drive-up sites $35, hike-&-bike tent sites $10; ⓟ 🐶). You'll also find family-friendly campgrounds with varying amenities in the mountainous **Los Padres National Forest** (☎ 877-444-6777; www.recreation.gov; Paradise Rd, off Hwy 154; campsites $30) and at **Cachuma Lake Recreation Area** (☎ info 805-686-5055, reservations 805-568-2460; http://reservations.sbparks.org; 2225 Hwy 154; campsites $25-45, yurts $65-90, cabins $110-140; ⓟ 🐶) off Hwy 154, closer to Santa Barbara's Wine Country.

---

style front section and the helpful staff. The outdoor pool and mountain-view sun decks are great for winding down after a day of sightseeing. It's on a noisy street three blocks north of the beach, so ask for a room in the back.

Franciscan Inn
MOTEL $$

(☎ 805-963-8845; www.franciscaninn.com; 109 Bath St; r $155-215; ⓟ ✻ 🛜 🐶) Settle into the relaxing charms of this Spanish Colonial two-story motel just over a block from the beach. Rooms differ in shape and decor, but some have kitchenette and all evince French-country charm. Embrace the friendly vibe, afternoon cookies and outdoor pool.

Motel 6 Santa Barbara-Beach
MOTEL $$

(☎ 805-564-1392; www.motel6.com; 443 Corona del Mar; r $100-210; ⓟ ✻ 🛜 🐶 🐾) The very first Motel 6 to 'leave the light on for you' has been remodeled with IKEA-esque contemporary design, flat-screen TVs and multimedia stations. It fills nightly; book ahead. Wi-fi costs $3 extra every 24 hours. Pet fee $10.

✖ Eating

Restaurants abound along downtown's State St and by the waterfront, where you'll find a few gems among the touristy claptrap. More creative kitchens are found in the Funk Zone, while east of downtown, Milpas St has great taco shops. It's wise to book well in advance (a couple of weeks) for popular places or somewhere you're particularly keen to eat.

★ Corazon Cocina
MEXICAN $

(☎ 805-845-0282; www.facebook.com/sbcorazon cocina; 38 W Victoria St; ⊗ 11am-9pm Tue-Sat, to 8pm Sun & Mon) The usual Mexican crowd-pleasers are all here (tacos *al pastor*, quesadillas, agua fresca) but made to such perfection that previous versions pale in comparison. Head into the Santa Barbara Public Market and prepare to get food drunk (and to wait a while – it's popular).

★ La Super-Rica Taqueria
MEXICAN $

(☎ 805-963-4940; 622 N Milpas St; ⊗ 11am-9pm Thu-Mon) It's small, there's usually a line and the decor is basic, but all that's forgotten once you've tried the most authentic Mexican food in Santa Barbara. The fish tacos, tamales and other Mexican staples have been drawing locals and visitors here for decades, and were loved by TV chef and author Julia Child.

★ Lucky Penny
PIZZA $

(☎ 805-284-0358; www.luckypennysb.com; 127 Anacapa St; pizzas $10-16; ⊗ 11am-9pm Sun-Thu, to 10pm Fri & Sat; ⓟ) Shiny exterior walls covered in copper pennies herald a brilliant pizza experience inside this Funk Zone favorite, right beside the Lark (p359). Always jam-packed, it's worth the wait for a crispy pizza topped with a variety of fresh ingredients, many vegetarian-friendly, or a wood-oven-fired lamb- and pork-meatball sandwich. The coffee is taken seriously too.

★ McConnell's Fine Ice Creams
DESSERTS $

(☎ 805-324-4402; www.mcconnells.com; 728 State St; pints from $10; ⊗ 11am-10pm Sun-Thu, to 11pm Fri & Sat; ⓟ) Just try walking past this place on State St if you have a sweet tooth. A Santa Barbara institution since 1949, McConnell's uses local milk and other ingredients to produce an array of flavors from the classics such as chocolate and vanilla to the adventurous like Turkish coffee and carda-mom and gingersnaps.

★ Arigato Sushi
JAPANESE $

(☎ 805-965-6074; www.arigatosb.com; 1225 State St; rolls from $7; ⊗ 5:30-10pm Sun-Thu, to 10:30pm Fri & Sat; ⓟⓟ) Phenomenally popular Arigato Sushi always has people milling around waiting for a table (no reservations taken) but it's worth the wait. Traditional and more unusual sushi, including lots of vegetarian options, plus salads and a dizzying array of hot and cold starters will make you order a sake pronto just to help you get through the menu.

It's noisy and bustling so not the place for a romantic dinner, unless you nab a table on the small patio on State St. Diners at the bar get to see the chefs in action right in front of them.

★ Mesa Verde
VEGAN $$

(☎ 805-963-4474; http://mesaverderestaurant. com; 1919 Cliff Dr; mains $15-21; ⊗ 11am-9pm; ⓟ) ⓟ Perusing the menu is usually a quick job for vegetarians – but not in Mesa Verde. There are so many delicious, innovative all-vegan dishes on offer here (the tacos with jackfruit are a highlight) that meat-avoiding procrastinators will be in torment. If in doubt, pick a selection and brace yourself for flavor-packed delights. Meat-eaters welcome (and possibly converted).

Desserts are equally inspired – don't hesitate to try the chocolate ganache if it's available.

The location is in a residential neighborhood west of the action, but it's a quick drive to get here and most definitely worth the effort.

★ Santa Barbara Shellfish Company
SEAFOOD $$

(☎ 805-966-6676; http://shellfishco.com; 230 Stearns Wharf; dishes $4-19; ⊗ 11am-9pm; ⓟⓟ) 'From sea to skillet to plate' sums up this end-of-the-wharf seafood shack that's more of a buzzing counter joint than a sit-down restaurant. Chase away the seagulls as you chow down on garlic-baked clams, crab cakes and coconut-fried shrimp at wooden picnic tables outside. Awesome lobster bisque, ocean views and the same location for almost 40 years.

★ Yoichi's
JAPANESE $$$

(☎ 805-962-6627; www.yoichis.com; 230 E Victoria St; set 7-course menu $100; ⊗ 5-10pm Tue-Sun) Headline: *kaiseki* (traditional Japanese multicourse dining) comes to Santa Barbara and wows locals. It might have limited hours, take a chunk out of your wallet and need to be booked way in advance, but none of that has stopped Yoichi's being hailed as one of Santa Barbara's best (and slightly hidden away) eating experiences.

The set menu consists of seven courses, divided into different types of dishes (soup, sashimi, grilled and so on), each of which delivers on both flavor and presentation thanks to chef Yoichi's culinary skills and the beautiful, handmade, ceramic plates on which he serves his creations. And of course there's top quality and some unusual sakes to try too.

It's tucked away on a quiet residential road a few blocks northeast of State St.

★ Lark
CALIFORNIAN $$$

(📞805-284-0370; www.thelarksb.com; 131 Anacapa St; shared plates $7-17, mains $19-48; ⊗5-10pm Tue-Sun, bar to midnight) 🍴 There's no better place in Santa Barbara County to taste the bountiful farm and fishing goodness of this stretch of SoCal coast. Named after an antique Pullman railway car, this chef-run restaurant in the Funk Zone morphs its menu with the seasons, presenting unique flavor combinations such as crispy brussels sprouts with dates or harissa and honey chicken. Make reservations. The cocktails and beer deserve serious consideration too.

★ Bouchon
CALIFORNIAN $$$

(📞805-730-1160; www.bouchonsantabarbara.com; 9 W Victoria St; mains $26-36; ⊗5-9pm Sun-Thu, to 10pm Fri & Sat) 🍴 The perfect, unhurried follow up to a day in the Wine Country is to feast on the bright, flavorful California cooking at pretty Bouchon (meaning 'wine cork'). A seasonally changing menu spotlights locally grown farm produce and ranched meats that marry beautifully with almost three dozen regional wines available by the glass. Lovebirds, book a table on the candlelit patio.

Dawn Patrol
BREAKFAST $

(📞805-962-2889; www.dawnpatrolsb.com; 324 State St; breakfast $6-13; ⊗7:30am-2pm; 🍴) Bright and colorful decor helps wake you up, and the option to build your own hash breakfast ($12.50) sets you up for exploring Santa Barbara. Bread is housemade and other ingredients are locally sourced. Add a coffee, a smoothie or a mimosa (go on, you're on vacation) and have a great start to the day.

Shop Cafe
BREAKFAST $

(📞805-845-1696; 730 N Milpas St; breakfast $6.50-15; ⊗8am-3pm; 🪑) Away from the hustle of State St, the Shop still gets crowded thanks to its top-quality breakfast offerings. The poached eggs on toast are on the healthier end of the menu spectrum. In the opposite direction are the Yolo (fried chicken, biscuit and gravy) and the Tugboat (eggs Benedict with your choice of protein).

Los Agaves
MEXICAN $

(📞805-564-2626; www.los-agaves.com; 600 N Milpas St; mains $9.25-16.95; ⊗11am-9pm Mon-Fri, 9am-9pm Sat & Sun) In the heart of east Santa Barbara's Mexican culinary scene, Los Agaves stands out for its well-cooked food and hacienda-style decor. Start with the zucchini-blossom quesadillas if they're in season and then take your pick from the mostly seafood and meat dishes. There's always a wait but that allows you time to peruse the menu carefully.

El Buen Gusto
MEXICAN $

(📞805-962-2200; 836 N Milpas St; dishes $2-8; ⊗8am-9pm; 🅿) At this red-brick strip-mall joint, order authentic south-of-the-border tacos, tortas, quesadillas and burritos with an agua fresca (fruit drink) or cold Pacifico beer. Mexican music videos and soccer games blare from the TVs. *Menudo* (tripe soup) and *birria* (spicy meat stew) are weekend specials.

Metropulos
DELI $

(📞805-899-2300; www.metrofinefoods.com; 216 E Yanonali St; dishes $2-10; ⊗8:30am-5pm Mon-Fri, 10am-5pm Sat) Before a day at the beach, pick up custom-made sandwiches and fresh salads at this gourmet deli in the Funk Zone. Artisan breads, imported cheeses, cured meats and California olives and wines will be bursting out of your picnic basket.

Lilly's Taquería
MEXICAN $

(📞805-966-9180; http://lillystacos.com; 310 Chapala St; items from $1.60; ⊗10:30am-9pm Sun, Mon, Wed & Thu, to 10pm Fri & Sat) There's almost always a line roping around this downtown taco shack at lunchtime. But it goes fast, so you'd best be snappy with your order – the *adobada* (marinated pork) and *lengua* (beef tongue) are standout choices. Second location in Goleta west of the airport, off Hwy 101.

Boathouse
CALIFORNIAN $$

(📞805-898-2628; http://boathousesb.com; 2981 Cliff Dr; mains from $14; ⊗7:30am-close; 🍴🪑) Water views and ocean air accompany your healthy dining at the Boathouse, right on Arroyo Burro Beach (p352). The outdoor patio is great for enjoying a cocktail and fancy salad with other beachgoers, while the walls inside display photos paying homage to the area's surfing and rowing heritage.

Opal
CALIFORNIAN $$

(📞805-966-9676; http://opalrestaurantandbar.com; mains $16-30; ⊗11:30am-2:30pm Mon-Sat, 5-10pm Sun-Thu, 5-11pm Fri & Sat; 🍴) Start with a cocktail (martinis are a specialty) and take your time choosing from the inventive dishes on this Californian-cuisine-meets-French-bistro-style restaurant at the top end of State

DIY DINING IN SANTA BARBARA

Stock up on fresh fruits and veggies, nuts and honey at the midweek **Santa Barbara Farmers Market** (p363), which also happens again on Saturday morning from 8:30am until 1pm at the corner of Santa Barbara and Cota Sts. Fill up a Wine Country picnic basket inside the **Santa Barbara Public Market** (p363), where gourmet food purveyors and quick-fix food stalls are open every day of the week. The best place for healthy, organic groceries is **Lazy Acres** (p361), south of Hwy 101 via W Carrillo St.

St. Strong flavors are brought together and work well in things like the homemade basil fettuccine with tiger shrimp or lemongrass salmon with Thai curry. Wine pairings are suggested for each dish.

Depending on how you're feeling, you'll either find the large open-plan dining space buzzing or noisy.

Toma
MEDITERRANEAN $$

(☎805-962-0777; www.tomarestaurant.com; 324 W Cabrillo Blvd; ⊙5pm-close) Enjoy a glass of wine or a cocktail before tucking into some tasty pasta, flatbreads or meat and seafood dishes at one of Santa Barbara's most popular restaurants. The decor's not the most exciting but the food more than compensates. Book well in advance.

Loquita
TAPAS $

(☎805-880-3380; http://loquitasb.com; 202 State St; mains from $11; ⊙5-10pm Sun-Wed, to midnight Thu-Sat, 10am-2pm Sun brunch; ✐) Spanish tapas done the Spanish way – simply and with top-quality ingredients. The wine list is a curated best-of-Spain selection too so pair your *pulpo* (octopus) with a crisp Albariño and eat with a smile on your face. Or loosen your belt for one of the best paellas this side of the Atlantic. Sunday's popular flamenco brunch is great fun.

Olio Pizzeria
ITALIAN $$

(☎805-899-2699; www.oliopizzeria.com; 11 W Victoria St; shared plates $5-24, pizzas $15-21; ⊙11:30am-10pm; ✐) Just around the corner from State St, this high-ceilinged pizzeria with a happening wine bar proffers crispy, wood-oven-baked pizzas, platters of import-ed cheeses and meats, garden-fresh *insalate* (salads), savory traditional Italian *antipasti* and sweet *dolci* (desserts). The entrance is off the parking-lot alleyway.

Somerset
CALIFORNIAN $$$

(☎805-845-7112; http://somersetsb.com; 7 E Anapamu St; mains from $28; ⊙5:30pm-close Mon-Fri, from 5pm Sat & Sun) ✐ The decor has an art-deco-meets-the-'70s wow factor and the olive-tree patio is as romantic as it gets at this relative newcomer to Santa Barbara's upscale dining scene. Chef Lauren Herman is cooking up innovative dishes similar to those that earned her James Beard awards at two LA restaurants, using only local ingredients in creative ways.

Book in advance – it's one of the hottest places in town despite some mixed reviews for the food.

Palace Grill
CAJUN, CREOLE $$

(☎805-963-5000; http://palacegrill.com; 8 E Cota St; mains lunch $10-22, dinner $17-32; ⊙11:30am-3pm daily, 5:30-10pm Sun-Thu, 5:30-11pm Fri & Sat; ☻) With all the exuberance of Mardi Gras, this N'awlins-style grill makes totally addictive baskets of housemade muffins and breads, and ginormous (if so-so) plates of jambalaya, gumbo ya-ya, blackened catfish and pecan chicken. Stiff cocktails and indulgent desserts make the grade. Act unsurprised when the staff lead the crowd in a rousing sing-along.

Brophy Brothers
SEAFOOD $$

(☎805-966-4418; www.brophybros.com; 119 Harbor Way; mains $19-26; ⊙11am-10pm; P) ✐ A long-time favorite for its fresh-off-the-dock fish and seafood, rowdy atmosphere and salty harborside setting. Slightly less claustrophobic tables on the upstairs deck are worth the long wait – they're quieter and have the best ocean views. Or skip the long lines and start knocking back oyster shooters and Bloody Marys with convivial locals at the bar.

Lazy Acres
SUPERMARKET

(☎805-564-4410; www.lazyacres.com; 302 Meigs Rd; ⊙7am-11pm Mon-Sat, to 10pm Sun; P✐) ✐ High-quality supermarket standards, plus a salad and soup bar. It's a short drive southwest of town; follow West Carrillo St which turns into Meigs St.

Drinking & Nightlife

On lower State St, most of the boisterous watering holes have happy hours, tiny dance floors and rowdy college nights. The Funk

Zone's eclectic mix of bars and wine-tasting rooms provides a trendier, more sophisticated alternative.

⭐ **Brass Bear** CRAFT BEER
(☑ 805-770-7651; www.brassbearbrewing.com; 28 Anacapa St; ⊘ noon-9pm Wed & Sun-Mon, to 10pm Thu, to 11pm Fri & Sat; 🏍🍺) Large glasses of wine and beer and a great grilled cheese make this cozy place up an alley off Anacapa (follow the murals) a worthy detour. Friendly staff add to the convivial atmosphere. Just be careful not to drink too much and end up taking some of the for-sale art on the walls home with you.

⭐ **Good Lion** COCKTAIL BAR
(☑ 805-845-8754; www.goodlioncocktails.com; 1212 State St; ⊘ 4pm-1am) Grab a cocktail at the beautiful, blue-tiled bar, then grab a book from the bookshelves and settle into a leather banquette in this petite place that has a cool Montmartre-turn-of-the-20th-century feel (candles on the tables and absinthe in many of the cocktails helps with the Parisian atmosphere).

⭐ **Municipal Winemakers** BAR
(☑ 805-931-6864; www.municipalwinemakers.com; 22 Anacapa St; tastings $12; ⊘ 11am-8pm Sun-Wed, to 11pm Thu-Sat; 🍺) Dave, the owner of Municipal Winemakers, studied the vine arts in Australia and France before applying his knowledge in this industrially decorated tasting room and bar. Pale Pink rosé is a staple and hugely popular – enjoy a bottle on the large patio. For food, you can't beat the cheese plate, or at weekends a burger van parks outside.

⭐ **Figueroa Mountain Brewing Co** BAR
(☑ 805-694-2252; www.figmtnbrew.com; 137 Anacapa St; ⊘ 11am-11pm Sun-Thu, to midnight Fri & Sat) Father and son brewers have brought their gold-medal-winning hoppy IPA, Danish red lager and double IPA from Santa Barbara's Wine Country to the Funk Zone. Knowledgeable, helpful staff will help you choose before you clink glasses on the taproom's open-air patio while acoustic acts play. Enter on Yanonali St.

Test Pilot COCKTAIL BAR
(☑ 805-845-2518; www.testpilotcocktails.com; 211 Helena Ave; ⊘ 4pm-1am Mon-Thu, 4pm-2am Fri, 2pm-2am Sat, 2pm-1am Sun) Any actual test pilot would be grounded after one of the strong but delicious cocktails at this tiki bar in the Funk Zone. The decor follows a nautical theme; the drinks keep it simple with interesting twists on traditional concoctions ($9 to $12). Expect foliage in your piña colada.

Waterline BREWERY
(☑ 805-845-1482; www.waterlinesb.com; 116-120 Santa Barbara St; ⊘ varies; 🍺) Extending the Funk Zone a little further east is no bad thing, and Waterline's combination of two taprooms (Topa Topa and Lama Dog), a restaurant (the Nook) serving elevated bar food, a wine-tasting room (Fox Wine) and a clothing, art and accessories section (Guilded Table) means you might happily spend longer here than planned.

Riverbench Winery Tasting Room WINE BAR
(☑ 805-324-4100; www.riverbench.com; 137 Anacapa St; tastings $10; ⊘ 11am-6pm) Tasting room in the Funk Zone for the Santa Maria Valley vineyard of the same name. Amiable staff can guide you through a selection of Chardonnay and Pinot Noir, or a newer sparkling wine.

Corks n' Crowns BAR
(☑ 805-845-8600; www.corksandcrowns.com; 32 Anacapa St; tastings $7-20; ⊘ 11am-7pm, last call for tastings 6pm; 🍺) Sit on the sunny porch or inside the rustic-feel hut by the fire and try out the wines and beers from Santa Barbara in general and a few international producers too. Tastings come in a flight of three for wine and four for beer – pours are generous. Board games are available – try Jenga after a tasting for added fun.

Cutler's Artisan Spirits DISTILLERY
(☑ 805-845-4040; http://cutlersartisan.com; 137 Anacapa St; tastings $10; ⊘ 1-6pm Thu-Sun) Family-run craft distillers producing whiskey, vodka, gin and apple pie (liqueur) since before (and during) Prohibition. The spirits are hard to find in stores so this is your chance to taste and then purchase up to three bottles (the maximum under local law) of their specialty liquors. The gin in particular is highly prized.

Valley Project BAR
(☑ 805-453-6768; www.thevalleyprojectwines.com; 116 E Yanonali St; tastings $12; ⊘ noon-7pm Mon-Thu, to 8pm Fri-Sun) From the sidewalk, passersby stop just to peek through the floor-to-ceiling glass windows at a wall-sized map of Santa Barbara's Wine Country, all hand-drawn in chalk. Inside, wine lovers lean on the tasting bar while sipping flights of locally grown reds and whites.

DON'T MISS

URBAN WINE TRAIL

Start Municipal Winemakers

End Waterline

Length As long you like

No wheels to head up to Santa Barbara's Wine Country? No problem. Ramble between over a dozen wine-tasting rooms (and microbreweries, too) downtown and in the Funk Zone near the beach. Pick up the Urban Wine Trail (www.urbanwinetrailsb.com) anywhere along its route. Most tasting rooms are open every afternoon or sometimes into the early evening. On weekends, join the beautiful people rubbing shoulders as they sip outstanding glasses of regional wines and listen to free live music.

For a sociable scene, start at **Municipal Winemakers** (p361) or **Corks n' Crowns** (p361), both on Anacapa St. Then head up to Yanonali St, turning left for **Riverbench Winery Tasting Room** (p361); **Cutler's Artisan Spirits** (p361) distillery, a storefront where you can sample bourbon whiskey, vodka and apple liqueur; and **Figueroa Mountain Brewing Co** (p361). Walk further west to find more wine-tippling spots.

Alternatively, turn right on Yanonali St and stop at the **Valley Project** (p362) for a liquid education about Santa Barbara's five distinct wine-growing regions. A couple of blocks east on Santa Barbara St, **Waterline** (p361) has the Fox Wine tasting room, housed in a cool, multipurpose complex that offers beer and food too.

Press Room   PUB

(☎ 805-963-8121; 15 E Ortega St; ⊙ 11am-2am) This tiny pub can barely contain the college students and European travelers who cram the place to its seams. Pop in to catch soccer games, stuff the jukebox with quarters and enjoy jovial banter with the bartender.

Hollister Brewing Company   BREWERY

(☎ 805-968-2810; www.hollisterbrewco.com; Camino Real Marketplace, 6980 Marketplace Dr, Goleta; ⊙ 11am-10pm) With over a dozen microbrews on tap, this place draws serious beer geeks out to Goleta, near the UCSB campus, off Hwy 101. IPAs are the permanent attractions, along with nitrogenated stout. Skip the food, though.

Handlebar Coffee Roasters   CAFE

(www.handlebarcoffee.com; 128 E Canon Perdido St; ⊙ 7am-5pm; 🐾) Bicycle-themed coffee shop brewing rich coffee and espresso drinks from small-batch roasted beans. Sit and sip yours on the sunny patio.

Brewhouse   BREWERY

(☎ 805-884-4664; www.sbbrewhouse.com; 229 W Montecito St; ⊙ 11am-midnight; 🛜🐾) Down by the railroad tracks, the boisterous Brewhouse crafts its own unique small-batch beer (Saint Barb's Belgian-style ales rule), serves wines by the glass, dishes up surprisingly good bar food and has cool art and rockin' live music Wednesday to Saturday nights.

☆ Entertainment

Santa Barbara's appreciation of the arts is evidenced not only by the variety of performances available on any given night, but also its gorgeous, often historic venues. For a current calendar of live music and special events, check www.independent.com online or www.newspress.com/top/section/scene.

Santa Barbara Bowl   LIVE MUSIC

(☎ 805-962-7411; http://sbbowl.com; 1122 N Milpas St; most tickets $35-125) Built by Works Progress Administration (WPA) artisans during the 1930s Great Depression, this naturally beautiful outdoor stone amphitheater has ocean views from the highest cheap seats. Kick back in the sunshine or under the stars for live rock, jazz and folk concerts in summer. Big-name acts like Brian Wilson, Radiohead and local graduate Jack Johnson have all taken the stage here.

Zodo's Bowling & Beyond   BOWLING

(☎ 805-967-0128; www.zodos.com; 5925 Calle Real, Goleta; bowling lane per hour $22-55, shoe rental $4.50; ⊙ 8:30am-1:30am Wed-Sat, to midnight Sun-Tue; 🐾) With over 40 beers on tap, pool tables and a video arcade (Skee-Ball!), this bowling alley near UCSB is good ol' family fun. Call ahead to get on the wait list and for schedules of open-play lanes and 'Glow Bowling' black-light nights with DJs. From Hwy 101 west of downtown, exit Fairview Ave north.

Arlington Theatre
THEATRE

(📞 805-963-4408; www.thearlingtontheatre.com; 1317 State St; ⊙ box office 10am-6pm Mon-Sat, to 4pm Sun) Harking back to 1931, this Mission Revival–style movie palace has a Spanish courtyard and a star-spangled ceiling. It's a drop-dead gorgeous place to attend a film-festival screening, and has a series of high-profile performers throughout the year.

Velvet Jones
MUSIC, COMEDY

(📞 805-965-8676; http://velvet-jones.com; 423 State St; most tickets $10-25) Long-running downtown punk and indie dive for rock, hip-hop, comedy and 18-plus DJ nights for the city's college crowd. Many bands stop here between gigs in LA and San Francisco.

Granada Theatre
THEATER, MUSIC

(📞 805-899-2222; www.granadasb.org; 1214 State St; ⊙ box office 10am-5:30pm Mon-Sat, noon-5pm Sun) This beautifully restored 1930s Spanish Moorish–style theater is home to the city's symphony, ballet and opera, as well as touring Broadway shows and big-name musicians.

Lobero Theatre
THEATER, MUSIC

(📞 805-963-0761; www.lobero.org; 33 E Canon Perdido St) One of California's oldest theaters (founded in 1873) presents modern dance, chamber music, jazz and world-music touring acts and stand-up comedy nights.

Soho
LIVE MUSIC

(📞 805-962-7776; www.sohosb.com; suite 205, 1221 State St; most tickets $8-50) One unpretentious brick room plus live music almost nightly equals Soho, upstairs inside a downtown office complex behind McDonald's. Lineups range from indie rock, jazz, folk and funk to world beats. Some all-ages shows.

🛍 Shopping

Downtown's **State St** is packed with shops of all kinds, and even chain stores conform to the red-roofed architectural style. The lower (beach) end has budget options, with quality and prices going up as the street does. For more local art galleries and indie shops, dive into the **Funk Zone**, east of State St, tucked in south of Hwy 101.

REI
SPORTS & OUTDOORS

(📞 805-560-1938; www.rei.com; 321 Anacapa St; ⊙ 10am-9pm Mon-Fri, to 7pm Sat, to 6pm Sun) If you forgot your tent or rock-climbing carabiners at home, the West Coast's most popular independent coop outdoor retailer is the place to pick up outdoor recreation gear, active clothing, sport shoes and topographic maps.

Santa Barbara Public Market
MARKET

(📞 805-770-7702; http://sbpublicmarket.com; 38 W Victoria St; ⊙ 7:30am-10pm Mon-Wed, 7:30am-11pm Thu & Fri, 8am-11pm Sat, 8am-10pm Sun) 🍃 Noodles, cupcakes, ice cream and Mexican magic from Corazon Cocina (p358) are just some of the tempting food options available at this central market, handy for a break from the sightseeing or for takeout picnic provisions. Stop by too for coffee and wine, and have a break in the Garden where dozens of beers come on tap.

Chocolate Maya
CHOCOLATE

(📞 805-965-5956; www.chocolatemaya.com; 15 W Gutierrez St; ⊙ 10am-6pm Mon-Fri, to 5pm Sat, to 4pm Sun) Personally sourced, fair-trade cacao from around the world means the chocolates on offer here not only taste good but make you feel good about yourself for buying them too. Truffles are a specialty and ingredients are sometimes unusual (tarragon and pineapple anyone?). Be adventurous or ask for recommendations.

Santa Barbara Farmers Market
MARKET

(📞 805-962-5354; www.sbfarmersmarket.org; 500 & 600 blocks of State St; ⊙ 4-7:30pm Tue mid-Mar–early Nov, 3-6:30pm Tue mid-Nov–mid-Mar, 8:30am-1pm Sat year-round; 🖐) 🍃 Stock up on fresh fruits and veggies, cheese, nuts and honey at the Tuesday Santa Barbara Farmers Market, which also happens again on Saturday morning at the corner of Santa Barbara and Cota Sts.

Diani
CLOTHING

(📞 805-966-7175; www.dianiboutique.com; 1324 State St, Arlington Plaza; ⊙ 10am-6pm Mon, 10am-7pm Tue-Sat, 11am-6pm Sun) Carries high-fashion, Euro-inspired designs, with a touch of funky California soul thrown in for good measure. Think Humanoid dresses, Rag & Bone skinny jeans and Stella McCartney sunglasses. A few doors down, Diani has expanded into shoes and homewares.

Channel Islands Surfboards
SPORTS & OUTDOORS

(📞 805-966-7213; www.cisurfboards.com; 36 Anacapa St; ⊙ 10am-7pm Mon-Sat, 11am-5pm Sun) Are you ready to take home a handcrafted, Southern California–born surfboard? Down in the Funk Zone, this surf shack is the place for innovative pro-worthy board designs, as well as surfer threads and beanie hats.

CRSVR Sneaker Boutique
SHOES, CLOTHING

(📞 805-962-2400; www.crsvr.com; 632 State St; ⊙ 11am-7pm) Check out this sneaker boutique run by DJs, not just for limited-editions Nikes and other athletic-shoe brands, but also T-shirts, jackets, hats and more urban styles for men.

Paseo Nuevo   MALL
(📞 805-963-7147; www.paseonuevoshopping.com; 651 Paseo Nuevo; ⏰ 10am-9pm Mon-Fri, 10am-8pm Sat, 11am-7pm Sun) This busy open-air mall is anchored by Macy's and Nordstrom department stores and offers all the usual clothing, accessories and beauty chains you could want, plus a few dining options.

🛈 Information

Santa Barbara Visitors Center (📞 805-568-1811, 805-965-3021; www.santabarbaraca.com; 1 Garden St; ⏰ 9am-5pm Mon-Sat, 10am-5pm Sun, closes 1hr earlier Nov-Jan) Pick up maps and brochures while consulting with the helpful, but busy staff. The website offers free downloadable DIY touring maps and itineraries, from famous movie locations to wine trails, art galleries and outdoors fun. Self-pay metered parking lot nearby.

Outdoors Santa Barbara Visitors Center
(📞 805-456-8752; http://outdoorsb.sbmm.org; 4th fl, 113 Harbor Way; ⏰ 11am-5pm) Inside the same building as the maritime museum, this volunteer-staffed visitor center offers info on Channel Islands National Park and a harbor-view deck.

Los Padres National Forest Headquarters
(📞 805-968-6640; www.fs.usda.gov/lpnf; 6750 Navigator Way, Goleta; ⏰ 8am-12pm & 1-4:30pm Mon-Fri) HQ for the whole Los Padres National Forest. Pick up maps, recreation passes etc.

Santa Barbara Central Library (📞 805-564-5608; www.sbplibrary.org; 40 E Anapamu St; ⏰ 10am-7pm Mon-Thu, 10am-5:30pm Fri & Sat, 1-5pm Sun; 📶) Free internet access for up to two hours (photo ID required). Reserve in advance or try a walk-in.

🛈 Getting There & Away

Small **Santa Barbara Airport** (p497), 9 miles west of downtown via Hwy 101, has scheduled flights to/from LA, San Francisco and other western US cities. A taxi to downtown or the waterfront costs about $30 to $35 plus tip. Car-rental agencies with airport lots include Alamo, Avis, Budget, Enterprise, Hertz and National; reserve in advance.

Santa Barbara Airbus (📞 805-964-7759; www.sbairbus.com) shuttles between Los Angeles International Airport (LAX) and Santa Barbara ($49/94 one-way/round-trip, 2½ hours, eight departures daily). The more people in your party, the cheaper the fare. For more discounts, prepay online.

Amtrak (📞 800-872-7245; www.amtrak.com; 209 State St) trains run south to LA ($31, 2½ hours) via Carpinteria, Ventura and Burbank's airport and north to San Luis Obispo ($22, 2¾ hours) and Oakland ($43, 8¾ hours), with stops in Paso Robles, Salinas and San Jose.

Greyhound (📞 805-965-7551; www.greyhound.com; 224 Chapala St) operates a few direct buses daily to LA ($15, three hours), Santa Cruz ($42, six hours) and San Francisco ($40, nine hours).

Vista (📞 800-438-1112; www.goventura.org) runs frequent daily 'Coastal Express' buses between Santa Barbara and Carpinteria ($3, 25 to 30 minutes) and Ventura ($3, 40 to 70 minutes); check online or call for schedules.

If you're driving on Hwy 101, take the Garden St or Carrillo St exits for downtown.

🛈 Getting Around

Local buses operated by the **Metropolitan Transit District** (MTD; 📞 805-963-3366; www.sbmtd.gov) cost $1.75 per ride (exact change, cash only). Equipped with front-loading bike racks, these buses travel all over town and to adjacent communities; ask for a free transfer upon boarding. **MTD Transit Center** (📞 805-963-3366; www.sbmtd.gov/passenger-information/transit-center.html; 1020 Chapala St; ⏰ 6am-7pm Mon-Fri, 9am-5pm Sat & Sun) has details about routes and schedules.

BUS	DESTINATION	FREQUENCY
5	Arroyo Burro Beach	hourly
11	State St, UCSB campus	every 30min
20	Montecito, Summerland, Carpinteria	hourly

MTD's electric **Downtown Shuttle** buses run along State St down to Stearns Wharf at 9am and 9:30am, and then every 15 minutes from 10am to 6pm daily. A second **Waterfront Shuttle** travels from Stearns Wharf west to the harbor and east to the zoo every 30 minutes from 10am to 6pm daily. Between Memorial Day (late May) and Labor Day (early September), both routes run every 10 to 15 minutes, including from 6pm to 9pm on Fridays and Saturdays. The fare is 50¢ per ride; transfers between routes are free.

Lil' Toot water taxi (📞 805-465-6676; www.celebrationsantabarbara.com; 113 Harbor Way; 1-way fare adult/child $5/1; ⏰ usually noon-6pm Apr-Oct, hours vary Nov-Mar; 📶) provides an ecofriendly, biodiesel-fueled ride between Stearns Wharf and the harbor, docking in front of the maritime museum. Look for ticket booths on the waterfront. Trips run every half-hour, weather permitting.

For bicycle rentals, **Wheel Fun Rentals** (p353) has two locations close to Stearns Wharf.

GO GREEN IN SANTA BARBARA

Santa Barbara's biggest eco-travel initiative is **Santa Barbara Car Free** (www.sant-abarbaracarfree.org). Browse the website for tips on seeing the city without your car, plus valuable discounts on accommodations, vacation packages, rail travel and more. Still don't believe it's possible to tour Santa Barbara without a car? Let us show you how to do it.

From LA, hop aboard the *Pacific Surfliner* or *Coast Starlight* for a memorably scenic, partly coastal ride to Santa Barbara's Amtrak station (around 2½ hours), a few blocks from the beach and downtown. Then hoof it or catch one of the electric shuttles that zips north–south along State St and east–west along the waterfront. MTD buses 6 and 11 connect with the shuttle halfway up State St and will get you within walking distance of the famous mission (get off at Los Olivos St and walk uphill). For a DIY cycling tour, **Wheel Fun Rentals** (p353) is a short walk from the train station.

Even Santa Barbara's Wine Country is getting into the sustainable swing of things. More and more vineyards are implementing biodynamic farming techniques and following organic guidelines. Many vintners and oenophiles are starting to think that the more natural the growing process, the better the wine, too. **Sustainable Vine Wine Tours** (p370) whisks you around family-owned sustainable vineyards. Minimize your carbon footprint even further by following Santa Barbara's Urban Wine Trail (www.urbanwinetrailsb.com) on foot. If you love both wine and food, *Edible Santa Barbara* magazine (http://ediblecommunities.com/santabarbara) publishes insightful articles about vineyards and restaurants that are going green. It's available free at many local markets, restaurants and wineries.

Santa Barbara County abounds with ecofriendly outdoor activities, too. Take your pick of hiking trails, cycling routes, ocean kayaking, swimming, surfing or stand up paddle boarding (SUP). If you're going whale-watching, ask around to see if there are any alternative-fueled tour boats with trained onboard naturalists.

Taxis are metered around $3 at flagfall, with an additional $3 to $4 for each mile.

Downtown street parking or parking in any of a dozen municipal lots is free for the first 75 minutes; each additional hour costs $1.50.

SANTA BARBARA WINE COUNTRY

Oak-dotted hillsides, winding country lanes, rows of grapevines stretching as far as the eye can see – it's hard not to gush about the Santa Ynez and Santa Maria Valleys and the Santa Rita Hills wine regions.

This is an area made for do-it-yourself-exploring. Locals here are friendly, from longtime landowners and farmers displaying small-town graciousness to vineyard owners who've fled big cities to follow their passion and who will happily share their knowledge and intriguing personal histories in intimate vineyard tasting rooms.

With around 100 local wineries, visiting can seem daunting, but the Santa Ynez Valley's five small towns – Los Olivos, Solvang, Buellton, Santa Ynez and Ballard – are all clustered within 10 miles of one another, so it's easy to stop, shop and eat whenever and wherever you like. Don't worry about sticking to a plan – instead, be captivated by the scenery and pull over wherever signs look welcoming.

Wineries

The big-name appellations for Santa Barbara's Wine Country are the Santa Ynez Valley, Santa Maria Valley and Santa Rita Hills, plus smaller Happy Canyon and upstart Ballard Canyon. Wine-tasting rooms abound in Los Olivos and Solvang, handy for anyone with limited time.

The Santa Ynez Valley, where you'll find most of the wineries, lies south of the Santa Maria Valley. Hwy 246 runs east–west, via Solvang, across the bottom of the Santa Ynez Valley, connecting Hwy 101 with Hwy 154. North–south secondary roads bordered by vineyards include Alamo Pintado Rd from Hwy 246 to Los Olivos, and Refugio Rd between Santa Ynez and Ballard.

If you can't stay a night or two, then a half-day trip will allow you to see one winery or tasting room, have lunch and return to Santa Barbara. Otherwise make it a full day and plan to have lunch and possibly dinner before returning to the city.

Foxen Canyon Wine Trail

The scenic Foxen Canyon Wine Trail runs north from Hwy 154, just west of Los Olivos, deep into the heart of the rural Santa Maria Valley. It's a must-see for oenophiles or anyone wanting to get off the beaten path. For the most part, it follows Foxen Canyon Rd, though a couple of top spots lie close to Santa Maria town.

★ Foxen   WINERY

(📞 805-937-4251; www.foxenvineyard.com; 7200 & 7600 Foxen Canyon Rd, Santa Maria; tastings $15-20; ⏰ 11am-4pm; 🅿) 🌿 On what was once a working cattle ranch, Foxen crafts full-fruited Pinot Noir, warm Syrah, steel-cut Chardonnay and rich Rhône-style wines, all sourced from standout vineyards. The newer tasting room (for the Rhône-style tasting) is solar-powered, while the old 'shack' – a former blacksmith's with a corrugated-metal roof, funky-cool decor and leafy patio – pours Bordeaux-style and Cal-Ital varietals.

★ Rancho Sisquoc Winery   WINERY

(📞 805-934-4332; www.ranchosisquoc.com; 6600 Foxen Canyon Rd; tastings $10; ⏰ 10am-4pm Mon-Thu, to 5pm Fri-Sun) This tranquil gem is worth the extra mileage, not just for the award-winning small-batch reds and whites, but for the delightfully rustic tasting room surrounded by pastoral views. The grounds are perfect for a picnic (fittingly, 'sisquoc' is Chumash for 'gathering place') so bring your own supplies or grab some of the on-site snacks, cheese and salami.

Turn right off Foxen Canyon Rd when you spot **San Ramon Chapel** (📞 805-937-1334; www.sanramonchapel.org; Foxen Canyon Rd; ⏰ grounds 6:30am-6:30pm; 🅿) `FREE`, look out for the 'Winery' sign and follow the narrow, partly olive-tree-lined road for a mile or two.

Demetria Estate   WINERY

(📞 805-686-2345; www.demetriaestate.com; 6701 Foxen Canyon Rd, Los Olivos; tastings $25; ⏰ by appointment; 🅿) 🌿 This hilltop retreat has the curving arches and thick wooden doors of your hospitable Greek uncle's country house, with epic views of vineyards and rolling hillsides. Tastings are by appointment only, but are worth it just to sample the biodynamically farmed Chardonnay, Syrah and Viognier, plus rave-worthy Rhône-style red blends.

Zaca Mesa Winery   WINERY

(📞 805-688-9339; www.zacamesa.com; 6905 Foxen Canyon Rd, Los Olivos; tastings $15-25, tours $30; ⏰ 10am-4pm daily year-round, to 5pm Fri & Sat late May-early Sep; 👫) Stop by this barn-style tasting room for a rustic, sipping-on-the-farm ambience. Santa Barbara's highest-elevation winery, Zaca Mesa specializes in Syrah, but is also known for its estate-grown Rhône varietals and signature Z Cuvée red blend and Z Blanc white blend. An outsized outdoor chessboard and a tree-shaded picnic area that's dog-friendly add to the laid-back atmosphere.

Firestone Vineyards   WINERY

(📞 805-688-3940; www.firestonewine.com; 5017 Zaca Station Rd; tastings $10-15, incl tour $20; ⏰ 10am-5pm; 🅿) Founded in the 1970s, Firestone is Santa Barbara's oldest estate winery. Sweeping views of the vineyard from the sleek, wood-paneled tasting room are nearly as satisfying as the value-priced Cabernet Sauvignon and Bordeaux-style blends for which it's best known. Arrive in time for a winery tour, daily at 11:15am and 1:15pm, plus 3:15pm weekends (no reservations).

Kenneth Volk Vineyards   WINERY

(📞 805-938-7896; www.volkwines.com; 5230 Tepusquet Rd, Santa Maria; tastings $10; ⏰ 10:30am-4:30pm Thu-Mon, by appointment Tue & Wed)

SANTA BARBARA WINE COUNTRY 101

Although large-scale winemaking has only been happening here since the 1980s, the climate of Santa Barbara's Wine Country has always been perfect for growing grapes. Two parallel, transverse mountain ranges – Santa Ynez and San Rafael – cradle the region and funnel coastal fog eastward off the Pacific into the valleys between. The further inland you go, the warmer it gets.

To the west, fog and low clouds may hover all day, keeping the weather crisp even in summer, while only a few miles inland, temperatures approach 100°F in July. These delicately balanced microclimates support two major types of grapes. Nearer the coast in the cooler Santa Maria Valley, Pinot Noir – a particularly fragile grape – and other Burgundian varietals such as Chardonnay thrive. Inland in the hotter Santa Ynez Valley, Rhône-style grapes do best, including Syrah and Viognier.

Only an established cult winemaker could convince oenophiles to drive so far out of their way to taste rare heritage varietals such as floral-scented Malvasia and inky Negrette, as well as standard-bearing Pinot Noir, Chardonnay, Cabernet Sauvignon and Merlot.

Riverbench Vineyard & Winery WINERY
(805-937-8340; www.riverbench.com; 6020 Foxen Canyon Rd, Santa Maria; tastings $15; 10am-4pm) Riverbench has been creating prized Pinot Noir and Chardonnay since the early 1970s and sparkling wines more recently. The rural tasting room is inside a butter-yellow arts-and-crafts farmhouse with panoramic views across the Santa Maria Valley. Out back is a picnic ground and bocce-ball court. Tours, cheese and chocolate pairings and other events available.

You can also sample their wines on Santa Barbara's Urban Wine Trail (p362).

Fess Parker Winery & Vineyard WINERY
(800-841-1104; www.fessparkerwines.com; 6200 Foxen Canyon Rd; tastings $14; 10am-5pm) Besides its on-screen appearance as Frass Canyon in the movie *Sideways,* the winery's other claim to fame is its late founder Fess Parker, best known for playing Davy Crockett on TV. Fess has now passed on, but you can still enjoy his winery's award-winning Chardonnay and Pinot Noir on the newly extended patio and buy a souvenir coonskin-cap-etched souvenir glass.

Santa Rita Hills Wine Trail

When it comes to country-road scenery, eco-conscious farming practices and top-notch Pinot Noir, the less-traveled Santa Rita Hills (www.staritahills.com) region holds its own. Almost a dozen tasting rooms line an easy driving loop west of Hwy 101 via Santa Rosa Rd and Hwy 246. Be prepared to share the roads with cyclists and an occasional John Deere tractor. More artisan winemakers hide out in the industrial warehouses of Buellton near Hwy 101 and farther afield in Lompoc, where you can combine a visit to La Purísima (p375) mission with an exploration of the town's 'Wine Ghetto,' a concentration of tasting rooms centered around Industrial Way, on the eastern edge of the town, generally open only at weekends (www.lompoctrail.com).

BEST SANTA BARBARA WINERIES FOR PICNICS

You won't have any problem finding picnic fare in Santa Barbara's Wine Country. The region is chock-full of local markets, delis and bakeries serving up portable sandwiches and salads. When picnicking at a winery, remember it's polite to buy a bottle of wine before spreading out your feast.

Beckmen Vineyards (p369)
Sunstone Vineyards & Winery (p370)
Zaca Mesa Winery (p366)
Lincourt Vineyard (p370)
Rancho Sisquoc (p366)

★**Babcock** WINERY
(805-736-1455; www.babcockwinery.com; 5175 E Hwy 246; tastings $15-18; 11am-5:30pm; P) Hillside, family-owned vineyards overflowing with different grape varietals – Chardonnay, Sauvignon Blanc, Pinot Gris, Pinot Noir, Syrah, Cabernet Sauvignon and more – that let innovative small-lot winemaker Bryan Babcock be the star: 'Slice of Heaven' and 'Ocean's Ghost' Pinot Noirs alone are worthy of a pilgrimage. The eccentrically furnished tasting room offers vintage vinyl for sale and elevated views alongside the wine.

★**Sanford Winery** WINERY
(800-426-9463; www.sanfordwinery.com; 5010 Santa Rosa Rd; tastings $20-25; 10am-4pm) Be enchanted by this romantic tasting room built of stone and handmade adobe bricks, embraced by estate vineyards on historic Rancho La Rinconada. Watch the sun sink over the vineyards from the patio with a silky Pinot Noir or citrusy Chardonnay in hand. Hour-long winery tours are given at 11am daily ($50, book at least 48 hours in advance).

Alma Rosa Winery & Vineyards WINERY
(805-688-9090; www.almarosawinery.com; 181 Industrial Way; tastings $15; noon-6:30pm Mon-Fri, from 11am Sat & Sun; P) Richard Sanford left the powerhouse winery bearing his name to start this new winery with his wife, Thekla, using sustainable, organic farming techniques. The vineyard is closed to visitors at the moment, but tastings are held in their stylish, wood-heavy tasting room

Santa Barbara Wine Country

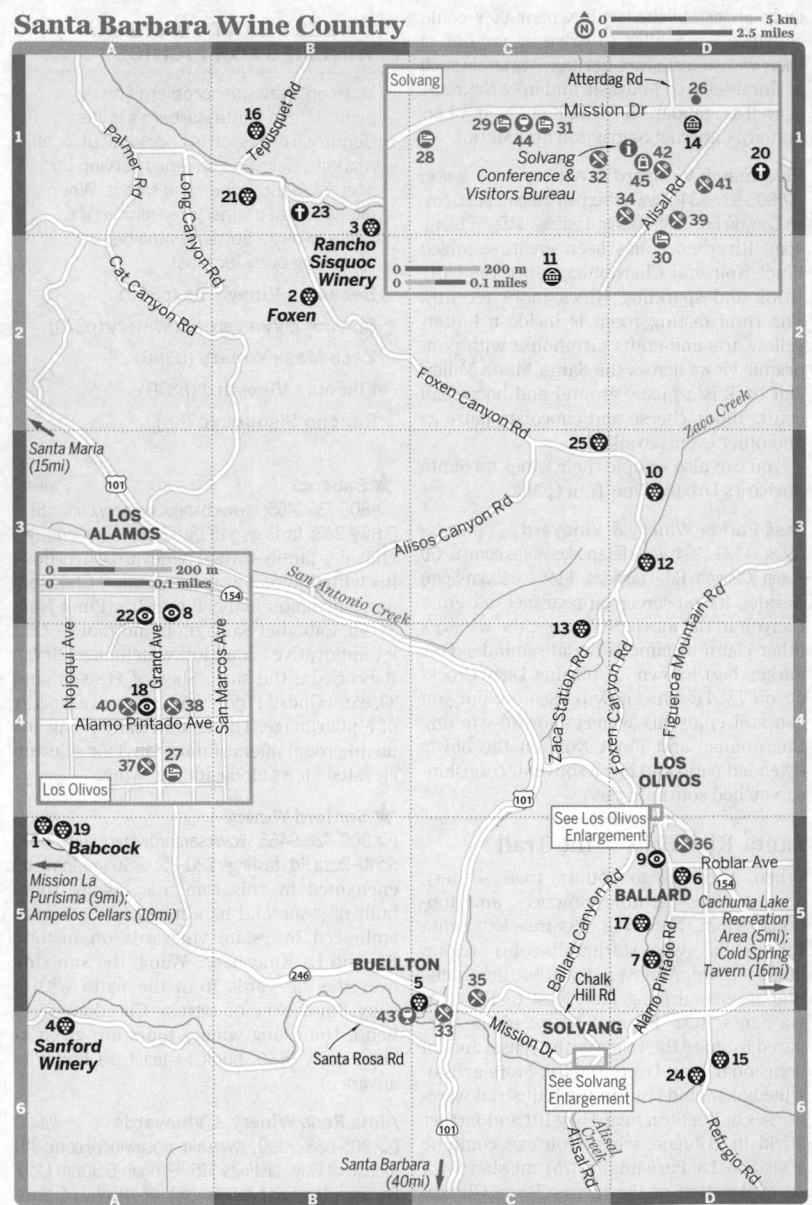

0 — 5 km
0 — 2.5 miles

Solvang

Atterdag Rd — 26

Mission Dr

29 31
44
28   Solvang
Conference &
Visitors Bureau
32   42
45
34   14
30
39
41
20
11

0 — 200 m
0 — 0.1 miles

16
Tepusquet Rd

21   23
3
**Rancho
Sisquoc
Winery**
2
Foxen

Palmer Rd
Long Canyon Rd
Cat Canyon Rd

Santa Maria
(15mi)

**LOS
ALAMOS**

101

Foxen Canyon Rd
Zaca Creek

25
10
12

Alisos Canyon Rd

San Antonio Creek
154

0 — 200 m
0 — 0.1 miles

22   8
Nojoqui Ave
Grand Ave
San Marcos Ave
40   18   38
Alamo Pintado Ave
37   27
Los Olivos

13
Zaca Station Rd
Foxen Canyon Rd
Figueroa Mountain Rd

**LOS
OLIVOS**

See Los Olivos
Enlargement

36
9   Roblar Ave
6
Ballard Canyon Rd
BALLARD
Cachuma Lake
Recreation
Area (5mi);
Cold Spring
Tavern (16mi)

17
7
Alamo Pintado Rd

1   19
Babcock

Mission La
Purísima (9mi);
Ampelos Cellars (10mi)

BUELLTON
5
35
246
43   33
Santa Rosa Rd
Mission Dr
Chalk
Hill Rd
SOLVANG

4
**Sanford
Winery**

Santa Barbara
(40mi)
101

See Solvang
Enlargement

24   15
Refugio Rd
Alisal Creek Rd
Alisal Rd

in Buellton; Pinot Noir, Chardonnay, Pinot
Blanc and Pinot Gris are what's poured.

Ampelos Cellars   TASTING ROOM
(☎ 805-736-9957; www.ampeloscellars.com; 312
N 9th Ave, Lompoc; tastings $10; ☺ 11am-5pm

Thu-Sun, to 4pm Mon) 🍃 Danish grower Peter
Work and wife Rebecca display their passion
for the vine through biodynamic farming
techniques and encyclopedic knowledge of
their lots. Their Pinot Noir, Syrah and Gre-
nache shine – you can sample them in Lom-

Santa Barbara Wine Country

poc's Wine Ghetto, an industrial area on the eastern edge of the town.

Melville WINERY
(☏805-735-7030; www.melvillewinery.com; 5185 E Hwy 246, Lompoc; tastings $10-20; ⊙11am-4pm Sun-Thu, to 5pm Fri & Sat; P) ◢ This beautiful Mediterranean hillside villa gives tastes of estate-grown, small-lot bottled Pinot Noir, Syrah and Chardonnay made by folks who believe in talking about pounds per plant, not tons per acre. Don't think there isn't variety though, with seven different clones of Pinot Noir alone grown. 'Vineyard to Bottle' tours are available noon and 2pm weekends ($25, 75 minutes).

Santa Ynez Valley

One of California's top viticulture regions, the Santa Ynez Valley is a compact area comprising a handful of small towns and dozens of vineyards. Put on the map back in 2004 by the movie *Sideways,* the area still draws the crowds and it's a hugely pleasant place to stay in upmarket lodgings, eat at high-quality restaurants and, of course, enjoy the many fine wines produced here. Los Olivos is the cutest town, Buellton the most down-to-earth, with incongruous Danish Solvang and tiny Santa Ynez and Ballard in between. Popular wineries cluster between Los Olivos and Solvang along Alamo Pintado Rd and Refugio Rd, south of Roblar Ave and west of Hwy 154.

Beckmen Vineyards WINERY
(☏805-688-8664; www.beckmenvineyards.com; 2670 Ontiveros Rd, Solvang; tastings $20; ⊙11am-5pm; P🅿🕭) ◢ Bring a picnic to one of the pond-side gazebos at this tranquil winery, where estate-grown Rhône varieties flourish on the unique terroir of Purisima Mountain. Biodynamic farming principles mean natural methods are used to prevent pests. To sample superb Syrah and a cuvée blend with Grenache, Syrah, Mourvèdre and Counoise, follow Roblar Ave west of Hwy 154 to Ontiveros Rd.

Vineyard tours are offered at 11am daily ($25 including tasting; reservations required).

WINE COUNTRY CELEBRATIONS

Santa Barbara Vintners (www.sb-countywines.com) publishes a free touring-map brochure of the county's vineyards and wine trails, which you can pick up at just about any winery or visitor center, or download the free mobile app. Special events worth planning your trip around include the **Spring Weekend** (☎805-688-0881; www.sb-vintnersweekend.com; ⊙Apr) in April and October's **Celebration of Harvest** (☎805-688-0881; www.celebrationofharvest.com; ⊙Oct).

Lincourt Vineyard

WINERY

(☎805-688-8554; www.lincourtwines.com; 1711 Alamo Pintado Rd, Solvang; tastings from $10; ⊙10am-5pm) ✷ Respected winemaker Bill Foley, who also owns Firestone Vineyard (p367) in Foxen Canyon, founded this vineyard in the 1990s on a former dairy farm. Today, the attractive, original 1926 farmhouse (built from a Sears catalog kit) is home to the tasting room: sip finely crafted Chardonnay and Pinot Noir and a dry French-style rosé, all made from locally grown grapes.

Sunstone Vineyards & Winery

WINERY

(☎805-688-9463; www.sunstonewinery.com; 125 N Refugio Rd, Santa Ynez; tastings $18; ⊙11am-5pm) ✷ Wander inside what looks like an 18th-century stone farmhouse from Provence and into a cool hillside cave housing wine barrels. Sunstone crafts Bordeaux-style wines made from 100% organically grown grapes. Bring a picnic to eat in the courtyard beneath gnarled oaks. Groups (eight or more) can order a wine-paired gourmet lunch to accompany their tasting ($30).

Kalyra Winery

WINERY

(☎805-693-8864; www.kalyrawinery.com; 343 N Refugio Rd, Santa Ynez; tastings $12-14; ⊙11am-5pm Mon-Fri, from 10am Sat & Sun; ℗) Australian Mike Brown traveled halfway around the world to combine his two loves: surfing and winemaking. Try his full-bodied red blends, unusual white varietals or sweet dessert wines (the orange muscat is a crowd-pleaser), all in bottles with Aboriginal-art-inspired labels. Kalyra also pours at Helix, a smaller venue on Buellton's Industrial Way (noon to 5pm Friday to Sunday; $15), close to several other tasting rooms.

Buttonwood Farm Winery & Vineyard

WINERY

(☎805-688-3032; www.buttonwoodwinery.com; 1500 Alamo Pintado Rd, Solvang; tastings $10-15; ⊙11am-5pm; 🚻🐾) ✷ Bordeaux and Rhône varieties do well in the sun-dappled limestone soil at this friendly winery that's perfect for wine-tasting neophytes and dog owners. The trellised back patio, bordering a fruit-tree orchard, is a pleasant spot to relax with a bottle of zingy Sauvignon Blanc.

☞ Tours

Full-day wine-tasting tours average $120 to $160 per person; most leave from Santa Barbara and some require a minimum number of participants. Wine Edventures (p371), Sustainable Vine Wine Tours (p370) and Santa Barbara Wine Country Cycling Tours (p371) are great options. The website www.sbcountywines.com has lots more.

★ Sustainable Vine Wine Tours

TOURS

(☎805-698-3911; www.sustainablevinewinetours.com; tours from $150) ✷ Biodiesel-van tours of wineries implementing organic and sustainable agricultural practices. Tours include stops at three tasting rooms, behind-the-scenes visits and organic picnic lunches. Pick-ups from any location in the Santa Barbara/Wine Country region.

Wine Edventures

TOURS

(☎805-965-9463; www.welovewines.com; tours $120) Serves up a fun-lovin' side dish of local history and behind-the-scenes wine education on its shuttle-driven tasting tours, one of which visits a microbrewery, too. Price includes a picnic lunch and a bottle of local wine. Pick-ups from just about anywhere in the local area, including many Santa Barbara and Solvang hotels, are free.

Santa Barbara Wine Country Cycling Tours

CYCLING

(☎805-686-9490; www.winecountrycycling.com; 1693 Mission Dr; tours from $170 per person; ⊙9am-6pm Mon-Fri, to 5pm Sat, to 4pm Sun) Guided and DIY bike rides start from the same building as Dr J's (p372) and come in easy to moderate versions – except the Epic Cycling Tours which cover up to 65 miles around the Santa Ynez Valley and out to **Jalama Beach** (☎recorded info 805-736-3616; www.countyofsb.org/parks/jalama; Jalama Beach Rd, Lompoc; per car $10). Multiday trips also available.

Los Olivos

The posh ranching town of Los Olivos is many visitors' first stop when exploring Santa Barbara's Wine Country. Its four-block-long main street has rustic wine-tasting rooms, bistros and boutiques seemingly airlifted straight out of Napa.

⊙ Sights

Clairmont Farms   FARM
(☑ 805-688-7505; www.clairmontfarms.com; 2480 Roblar Ave; ⊙ 11am-5pm Wed-Mon Apr-Oct, to 4pm Thu-Mon Nov-Mar; ℗ 🐾) 🐾 Natural beauty awaits just outside Los Olivos at this friendly, organic, family-owned farm, where purple lavender fields bloom like a Monet masterpiece, usually peaking mid-June to late July. Drive the olive-tree-lined drive to the tiny shop selling bath and body products, and enjoy a lavender-scented picnic outside.

🛏 Sleeping & Eating

Options are limited and choices aren't cheap round these parts, but the quality is high.

Fess Parker Wine Country
Inn & Spa   SPA HOTEL $$$
(☑ 805-688-7788; www.fessparkerinn.com; 2860 Grand Ave; r from $395; ❋ @ 🐾 🏊) Spacious rooms and suites, done out in calming, contemporary design, set the scene at this luxurious spa hotel in the center of Los Olivos. Fireplaces are standard, there's a heated pool and a decent-sized gym, and breakfast and a wine tasting are included in the price.

★ **Sides Hardware & Shoes**   AMERICAN $$$
(☑ 805-688-4820; http://sidesrestaurant.com; 2375 Alamo Pintado Ave; mains lunch $14-18, dinner $26-35; ⊙ 11am-2:30pm daily, 5-8:30pm Sun-Thu, to 9pm Fri & Sat; 🐾) Behind its historic storefront, this bistro delivers haute country cooking. For lunch you can't beat the burgers though there are lighter salads and tacos too. In the evenings (book ahead) start with the bacon steak (exactly what it says), followed by the fried chicken with garlicky kale or housemade vegetarian pasta. Sit out on the porch or in the open-plan dining room.

Los Olivos Grocery   DELI $
(☑ 805-688-5115; www.losolivosgrocery.com; 2621 W Hwy 154; ⊙ 7am-9pm; 🐾) Eat in for breakfast or lunch (grab a table on the covered porch) or get sandwiches, artisan breads, salads, specialty cheeses, pickles and everything else you'll need for a vineyard picnic to go.

Everything's produced in-house or locally. It's a couple of minutes southeast of central Los Olivos, just off Hwy 154.

Panino   SANDWICHES $
(☑ 805-688-9304; http://paninorestaurants.com; 2900 Grand Ave; sandwiches $10-12.50; ⊙ 10am-4pm; 🐾) Take your pick from a huge range of gourmet deli sandwiches and salads: curry chicken is a perennial fave, but there are robust vegetarian options too. Order at the counter, then eat outside at an umbrella-covered table. There are other branches around Santa Barbara County including in nearby Solvang and Santa Ynez.

Los Olivos Wine
Merchant & Café   CALIFORNIAN, MEDITERRANEAN $$
(☑ 805-688-7265; www.winemerchantcafe.com; 2879 Grand Ave; mains breakfast $9-12, lunch & dinner $13-29; ⊙ 11:30am-8:30pm daily, also 8-10:30am Sat & Sun) This Wine Country landmark (as seen in *Sideways*) swirls up a casual-chic SoCal ambience with its wisteria-covered trellis entrance. It stays open between lunch and dinner for antipasto platters, hearty salads and crispy pizzas and wine flights at the bar. Sit inside in the elegant dining room or outside on the covered patio.

🍷 Drinking

Bring a book and buy a bottle of wine during your day-time vineyard visits if you want something to while away your Los Olivos evenings.

Los Olivos Tasting Room   TASTING ROOM
(☑ 805-688-7406; http://site.thelosolivostasting-room.com; 2905 Grand Ave; tastings $10; ⊙ 11am-5pm) Inside a rickety 19th-century general store, this tasting room stocks rare vintages you won't find anywhere else. Well-oiled servers are by turns loquacious and gruff, but refreshingly blunt in their opinions about local wines and they pour generously.

Saarloos + Sons   TASTING ROOM
(☑ 805-688-1200; http://saarloosandsons.com; 2971 Grand Ave; tasting fee $10-15; ⊙ 11am-5pm, last pour 4:30pm) Wine snobs are given the boot at this shabby-chic tasting room pouring estate-grown, small-lot Syrah, Grenache Noir, Cabernet Sauvignon and Sauvignon Blanc. Pair your wine flight with a minicupcake and watch Los Olivos go by from the large outdoor deckchairs.

**Carhartt Vineyard
Tasting Room**   TASTING ROOM
(☎805-693-5100; www.carharttvineyard.com;
2990a Grand Ave; tasting fee $15; ⊙11am-6pm)
An unpretentious tasting room inside a
red-trimmed wooden shack that leads on
to a shady garden patio out back, where a
fun-loving younger crowd sips unfussy Zin-
fandel, Merlot and 'Not-So Petite' Syrah.

Solvang

Statues of the Little Mermaid and Hans
Christian Andersen in the middle of Wine
Country can only mean one thing: Solvang.
A Danish village founded in 1911 on what
was once a 19th-century Spanish-colonial
mission, this Santa Ynez Valley town holds
tight to its Danish heritage. With its knick-
knack stores and cutesy motels, the town is
almost as sickly sweet as the Scandinavian
pastries sold to the crowds of day-trippers.
But a few new businesses are toning down
the kitsch and upping the modern-Scandi
cool, plus the town has the best sleeping
and eating options in the valley, making it a
great base for exploration.

◎ Sights

**Hans Christian Andersen
Museum**   MUSEUM
(☎805-688-2052; www.solvangca.com/museum;
2nd fl, 1680 Mission Dr; ⊙10am-5pm; ⛹) FREE
If you remember childhood fairy tales with
fondness, stop by this tiny two-room museum. A larger-than-life bust of Denmark's
favorite storyteller welcomes you to a mix
of original letters, 1st-edition copies of his
illustrated books, and a model of Andersen's
childhood home. It's upstairs in the Book
Loft (p374) building.

Elverhøj Museum of History & Art   MUSEUM
(☎805-686-1211; www.elverhoj.org; 1624 Elver-
hoy Way; suggested donation adult $5, child under
13yr free; ⊙11am-4pm Wed-Sun; ⛹) South of
downtown, tucked away on a residential
side street, this delightful little museum has
modest but thoughtful exhibits on Solvang's
Danish heritage, as well as Danish culture,
art and history.

Old Mission Santa Ínes   CHURCH
(☎805-688-4815;   www.missionsantaines.org;
1760 Mission Dr; adult $5, child under 12yr free;
⊙9am-4:30pm; ⅋⛹) Off Hwy 246 just east
of Solvang's Alisal Rd, this historic Catholic
mission (founded in 1804) was one of the set-

tings for the Chumash revolt against Spanish-colonial cruelty in 1824. A self-guided
tour takes you through a small, dated museum, into the restored church, and through
the pretty gardens to the cemetery. It's still
an active parish today.

🏃 Activities

Solvang is best known by cyclists for the
Solvang Century races (www.bikescor.
com) in March. For self-guided cycling
tours, visit www.solvangusa.com and www.
bike-santabarbara.org online and rent a bike
from **Dr J's Bicycle Shop** (☎805-688-6263;
www.drjsbikeshop.com; 1693 Mission Dr; day rates
$45-85; ⊙9am-6pm Mon-Fri, 9am-5pm Sat, 10am-
4pm Sun).

🛌 Sleeping

Choices are the best in the region but sleeping in Solvang isn't cheap, not even at older
motels with faux-Danish exteriors. On weekends, rates skyrocket and rooms fill fast, so
book ahead.

★**Landsby**   BOUTIQUE HOTEL $$
(☎805-688-3121; www.thelandsby.com; 1576 Mis-
sion Dr; r from $149; @🅜🛜) Forget Solvang's
cheesy Danish side, the Landsby is all about
slick contemporary Scandinavian style. The
principal decorative themes in this new arriv-
al on the town's sleeping scene are white and
wood, but cool design doesn't mean there's
not a warm atmosphere. Start your day with
the complimentary breakfast and finish it
with a drink at the popular lobby bar.

The in-house **Mad & Vin restaurant**
(meaning food and wine in Danish) has sim-
ilarly chic surroundings and a good menu of
classic American dishes (mains $16 to $34).

Hamlet Inn   MOTEL $$
(☎805-688-4413; www.thehamletinn.com; 1532
Mission Dr; r $99-229; 🅟❤✳🛜) This remod-
eled motel is to Wine Country lodging what
IKEA is to interior design: a budget-friendly,
trendy alternative. Crisp, modern rooms
have bright Danish-flag bedspreads and iPod
docking stations. Free loaner bicycles and a
bocce-ball court for guests add to the appeal.

Hadsten House   BOUTIQUE HOTEL $$
(☎805-688-3210; www.hadstenhouse.com; 1450
Mission Dr; r $140-270; 🅟❤✳🛜🏊) This re-
vamped motel has luxuriously updated just
about everything, except for its routine ex-
terior. Inside, rooms are surprisingly plush,
with flat-screen TVs, comfy duvets and high-

end bath products. Spa suites come with jet tubs. There's a good in-house restaurant (Tuesday to Saturday).

Hotel Corque
BOUTIQUE HOTEL **$$$**

(☑805-688-8000; www.hotelcorque.com; 400 Alisal Rd; r $179-409; ❄@🛜🏊) This clean-lined hotel is a relief from all things Danish. Overpriced rooms may look anonymous, but they're quite spacious. Amenities include an outdoor swimming pool and hot tub, plus access to the next-door fitness center, where you can work off all those Danish butter rings.

✖️ Eating

When it comes to eating, the emphasis is most definitely on Danish dishes, with pastry-producing bakeries abounding. A couple of non-Danish standouts provide a break from the sweet stuff though, with innovative menus showing off the rich local produce.

⭐First & Oak
CALIFORNIAN **$$**

(☑805-688-1703; www.firstandoak.com; 409 First St, Mirabelle Inn; mains $12-23; ⏲5:30-8:45pm) Rich, innovative small plates in an elegant but cozy setting make First & Oak Solvang's best dining experience. The menu changes with the seasons but you can expect unusual takes on Californian cuisine such as baked beets with bee pollen and whipped goat's cheese or linguini with soft-shell crab and yuzu emulsion. Inventive desserts round off a memorable meal.

⭐Succulent Café
CALIFORNIAN **$$**

(☑805-691-9444; www.succulentcafe.com; 1555 Mission Dr; mains breakfast & lunch $5-15, dinner $16-36; ⏲10am-3pm & 5-9pm Mon & Wed-Sun, from 8:30am Sat & Sun; �foodw) 🐾 An inspired menu allows farm-fresh ingredients to speak for themselves at this family-owned gourmet cafe and market. Fuel up on breakfast biscuits with fried chicken, pulled pork and artisan grilled-cheese sandwiches for lunch, or pumpkin-seed-crusted lamb for dinner. On sunny days, eat outside on the patio, where dogs are welcome (they even have their own menu).

Paula's Pancake House
DANISH **$**

(☑805-688-2867; www.paulaspancakehouse.com; 1531 Mission Dr; pancakes from $6.50; ⏲6am-3pm; 🍴) *God Morgen!* Start the day Danish-style with a warm welcome and a hearty breakfast in which, clue in the name, pancakes feature heavily – over 30 years beating batter means Paula knows her stuff. The lunch menu ventures into burgers-and-sandwiches territory, but with breakfast served all day, there's no wrong time to put away some pancakes.

It's hugely popular and lines are long so prepare to either get here as soon as it opens or to wait a while.

Solvang Restaurant
BAKERY **$**

(☑805-688-4645; www.solvangrestaurant.com; 1672 Copenhagen Dr; items from $4; ⏲6am-3pm or 4pm Mon-Fri, to 5pm Sat & Sun; �foodw) Duck around the Danish-inscribed beams with decorative borders to order *aebleskivers* – round pancake popovers covered in powdered sugar and raspberry jam. They're so popular, there's even a special takeout window, and if you develop a fondness for them you can buy all the ingredients (and the special pan) to make your own.

Solvang Bakery
BAKERY **$**

(www.solvangbakery.com; 438 Alisal Rd; items from $3.50; ⏲7am-6:30pm Sun-Thu, to 8pm Fri & Sat; 🍴) Gingerbread is a specialty here (have a personalized holiday creation made for you) but that doesn't mean other bestsellers like the almond-butter ring and the jalapeño-cheese bread sit on the shelves for long either. The decor is exactly how you'd want this kind of place's decor to be.

Aly's
MODERN AMERICAN **$$$**

(☑805-697-7082; http://alysbyalebru.com; 451 2nd St; ⏲5-8:45pm Thu-Mon) Fine cuisine isn't usually associated with Solvang, but Aly's meat- and fish-focused dishes hit the mark. The low-lit, simply furnished dining room complements the rich, flavorful food that is sourced locally and prepared with skill. If you're struggling to choose, go with the chef's tasting menu and pair it with carefully selected wines.

Root 246
AMERICAN **$$$**

(☑805-686-8681; www.root-246.com; 420 Alisal Rd; mains $26-39, brunch buffet adult $27, child 6-12yr $11; ⏲5-9pm Tue-Thu, 5-10pm Fri & Sat, 10am-2pm & 5-9pm Sun) 🐾 Next to Hotel Corque, chef Bradley Ogden's creative farm-to-table cuisine shows an artful touch. It's hard to beat the chicken and steaks, or come for the Sunday brunch buffet. Make reservations or seat yourself in the sleek fireplace lounge to sip California wines by the glass after 4pm. Service can be hit and miss.

Drinking & Nightlife

After dinner this town is deader than an ancient Viking, with a couple of notable exceptions, Copenhagen Sausage Garden and Solvang Brewing Company.

Copenhagen Sausage Garden   BEER GARDEN
(☑805-697-7354; www.csg-solvang.com; 1660 Copenhagen Dr; ⊙10am-midnight) Another sign of Solvang's attempts to stay up late, CSG keeps the beers (and wine) flowing well into the evening on its outdoor patio. Sausages from around the world (little flags on the menu help you choose the country you want, from Spain and Italy to Denmark and the US) provide the snacks, and occasional live music provides the entertainment.

Solvang Brewing Company   BREWERY
(☑805-688-2337; http://solvangbrewing.com; 1547 Mission St; ⊙11am-midnight or later, from 4pm Wed) If you're done with wine but not with alcohol then the Brewing Company is the place to head. A decent selection of beers (including a stout and a couple of wheat ales) is complemented by filling pub grub and live music (usually Wednesday to Sunday). Plus it's one of the few places in town that stays open past sundown.

Shopping

Downtown Solvang's notoriously kitschy shops cover a half-dozen blocks south of Mission Dr/Hwy 246 between Atterdag Rd and Alisal Rd. For Danish cookbooks, handcrafted quilts and other homespun items, visit the Elverhøj Museum (p372).

★**Copenhagen House**   DESIGN
(☑805-693-5000; http://thecopenhagenhouse. com; 1660 Copenhagen Dr; ⊙10am-5.30pm Mon-Fri, to 6pm Sat & Sun) The name stays true to Solvang's Danish roots but the eclectic mix of top-quality design goods, all from the motherland, couldn't be further from the town's usual tourist tat. Keep kids happy with some Lego, treat yourself to exquisite Pandora jewelry or a Bering watch, or buy some stylish home- and kitchenware that makes you feel cooler just looking at it.

You can even educate yourself on the real Vikings with a small exhibition on Denmark's original exports.

Book Loft   BOOKS
(☑805-688-6010; www.bookloftsolvang.com; 1680 Mission Dr; ⊙9am-8pm Tue-Thu, to 9pm Fri & Sat, to 6pm Sun & Mon) Long-running, independent bookshop carrying antiquarian and Scandinavian titles and children's storybooks. The Hans Christian Andersen Museum (p372) is upstairs.

Information

Solvang Conference & Visitors Bureau
(☑805-688-6144; www.solvangusa.com; 1639 Copenhagen Dr; ⊙9am-5pm) Pick up free tourist brochures and winery maps at this kiosk in the town center, by the municipal parking lot and public restrooms.

Buellton

Tiny Buellton was once best known for Andersen's Pea Soup Restaurant, and you can still get heaping bowls of the green stuff, a tradition going back almost 100 years. If split-pea soup doesn't appeal, then the growing drinking (beer as well as wine) and eating scene on Industrial Way, just south of the 246, should do the trick instead.

Sleeping & Eating

Buellton has slightly less expensive, but more well-worn chain motels and hotels than Solvang, 3 miles further east along Hwy 246.

★**Industrial Eats**   AMERICAN $
(☑805-688-8807; http://industrialeats.com; 181 Industrial Way; mains $9-15; ⊙10am-9pm) Hugely and justifiably popular locals' hangout, housed in an eclectically decorated warehouse on Buellton's coolest street. Pizzas have traditional to what-the? toppings (eg duck and pistachio); the small plates are huge, innovative and eminently shareable; the wine and beer are top-notch. On a changing menu perennial favorites include the shrimp and pancetta on toast combo and the beef-tongue Reuben.

Ellen's Danish Pancake House   BREAKFAST $
(☑805-688-5312; www.ellensdanishpancakehouse. com; 272 Ave of Flags; mains $10-15; ⊙6am-8pm, to 2pm Mon; ℗) West of Hwy 101, just off the 246, this old-fashioned, always-busy diner is where locals congregate for friendly service and the Wine Country's best Danish pancakes and sausages. Breakfast served all day.

Hitching Post II   STEAK $$$
(☑805-688-0676; www.hitchingpost2.com; 406 E Hwy 246; mains $26-55; ⊙5-9:30pm Mon-Fri, from 4pm Sat & Sun; ♿) As seen in the movie *Sideways,* this dark-paneled chophouse offers oak-grilled steaks, pork ribs, smoked duck

MISSION LA PURÍSIMA

One of the most evocative of Southern California's missions, La Purísima was founded in 1787 and completely restored in the 1930s by the Civilian Conservation Corps (CCC). Today its a **state historic park** (☑ 805-733-3713; www.lapurisimamission.org; 2295 Purísima Rd, Lompoc; per car $6; ☉ 9am-5pm, tours at 1pm Wed-Sun & public holidays Sep-Jun, daily Jul & Aug; P) ✎ with buildings furnished just as they were during Spanish Colonial times. The mission's fields still support livestock, while outdoor gardens are planted with medicinal plants and trees once used by Chumash tribespeople.

Start in the excellent visitor center where exhibits tell the stories of the Chumash, the Spanish missionaries and the work of the CCC. Self-guided visits are the usual way to explore the buildings themselves, though guided tours, lasting 1½ to 2 hours, are available too. The mission is just outside Lompoc, about 16 miles west of Hwy 101 (take Hwy 246 west from Buellton).

breast and rack of lamb. Every old-school meal comes with a veggie tray, garlic bread, shrimp cocktail or soup, salad and potatoes. The Hitching Post makes its own Pinot Noir, and it's damn good (wine tastings at the bar start at 4pm).

🍷 Drinking & Nightlife

Bottlest Winery, Bar & Bistro   WINE BAR
(☑ 805-686-4742; http://avantwines.com; 35 Industrial Way; ☉ 11am-9pm, dinner from 5pm) Small plates and dozens of wines come together in this 'winery restaurant', formerly called Terravant. Step up to the Wine Wall to take your pick from 52 options, then add some crab cakes, pork belly or garden greens with burrata to the mix. Larger meat and fish meals are also available. Happy hour (3pm to 5pm daily) brings prices down.

Figueroa Mountain Brewing Co   BREWERY
(☑ 805-694-2252; www.figmtnbrew.com; 45 Industrial Way; ☉ 11am-9pm; ☻) Fig Mountain's original brewpub gives you a break from the wine with its award-winning, in-house-brewed beers: Hoppy Poppy, Danish Red lager and Davy Brown ale are three favorites. Soak them up with some great pub grub and enjoy the frequent live music and comedy nights. There's also a pet-friendly beer garden.

ⓘ Getting There & Around

Central Coast Shuttle (☑ 805-928-1977; www.cclax.com; 1-way/round-trip LA–Buellton $70/128; ☉ info line 8am-7:30pm Mon-Fri, 9:30am-5:30pm Sat & Sun) will bus you from LAX to Buellton for $70/128 one-way/round-trip (book in advance online to avoid a nonprepaid small additional cost). Amtrak provides a couple of daily connecting Thruway buses to and from Solvang, but only if you're catching a train (or arriving on one) in Santa Barbara.

Santa Ynez Valley Transit (☑ 805-688-5452; www.syvt.com; $1.50 each way; ☉ 7am-7pm) runs local buses equipped with bike racks on a loop around Buellton, Solvang, Santa Ynez, Ballard and Los Olivos. Buses operate roughly between 7am and 7pm Monday through Saturday; one-way rides cost $1.50 (exact change only).

AROUND SANTA BARBARA

Can't quit your day job to follow your bliss? Don't despair: a long weekend in the mountains, valleys and beaches between Santa Barbara and LA will keep you inspired until you can. In this land of daydreams, perfect waves beckon off Ventura's coast, shady trails wind skyward in the Los Padres National Forest and spiritual Zen awaits you in Ojai Valley. Surf, stroll, seek – if outdoor rejuvenation is your goal, this is the place.

And then there's Channel Islands National Park, a biodiverse chain of islands shimmering just off the coast where you can kayak majestic sea caves, scuba dive in wavy kelp forests, wander fields of wildflower blooms or simply disappear from civilization at a remote wilderness campsite.

Montecito

Well-heeled, leafy Montecito, just east of Santa Barbara in the Santa Ynez foothills, is not just home to the rich and famous but to the obscenely rich and the uber-famous.

Though many homes hide behind manicured hedges these days, a taste of the Montecito lifestyle of yesteryear can be experienced by taking a tour of **Casa del Herrero** (☑ 805-565-5653; http://casadelherrero.com; 1387 E Valley Rd; 90min tour $25; ☉ 10am & 2pm Wed & Sat,

LOTUSLAND

In 1941 the eccentric opera singer and socialite Madame Ganna Walska bought the 37 acres that make up **Lotusland** (📞 info 805-969-3767, reservations 805-969-9990; www.lotusland.org; 695 Ashley Rd, Montecito; adult $45, child 3-18yr $20; ⏱ tours by appt 10am & 1:30pm Wed-Sat mid-Feb–mid-Nov; 🅿) with her lover and yoga guru Theos Bernard. After marrying and then divorcing Bernard, she retained control of the gardens and spent the next four decades tending and expanding this incredible collection of rare and exotic plants from around the world; there are over 140 varieties of aloe alone. Come in summer when the lotuses bloom, typically during July and August.

Reservations are required for tours, but the phone is only attended from 9am to 5pm weekdays, to 1pm Saturday.

reservations 9am-5pm Mon-Sat; 🅿). The town's cafe and boutique-filled main drag is **Coast Village Rd** (exit Hwy 101 at Olive Mill Rd).

Most visitors base themselves in Santa Barbara and visit Montecito (a 15-minute drive away) as a day trip. Upmarket, beachside Four Seasons Biltmore is an option if money is no object.

From Santa Barbara, MTD (p364) buses 14 and 20 run to and from Montecito ($1.75, 20 minutes, every 40 to 60 minutes); bus 20 also connects Montecito with Summerland and Carpinteria.

Summerland

This drowsy seaside community was founded in the 1880s by HL Williams, a real-estate speculator. Williams was also a spiritualist, whose followers believed in the power of mediums to connect the living with the dead. Spiritualists were rumored to keep hidden rooms for séances – a practice that earned the town the indelicate nickname of 'Spookville.'

Today, those wanting to connect to the past wander the town's antique shops, where you won't find any bargains, but you can ooh and aah over beautiful furniture, jewelry and art from decades or even centuries gone by.

To find the beach, turn south off exit 91 instead and cross the railroad tracks to cliffside **Lookout Park** (www.countyofsb.org/parks; Lookout Park Rd; ⏱ 8am-sunset; 🚻) **FREE** with a kids' playground, picnic tables, barbecue grills and access to a wide, relatively quiet stretch of sand (leashed dogs OK).

Grab breakfast or brunch at the Victorian seaside-style **Summerland Beach Café** (📞 805-969-1019; www.summerlandbeachcafe.com; 2294 Lillie Ave; mains $7-14; ⏱ 7am-3pm Mon-Fri, to 4pm Sat & Sun; 🅿🚻👶), known for its fluffy omelets, and enjoy the ocean breezes on the patio. Or walk over to **Tinker's** (📞 805-969-1970; 2275 Ortega Hill Rd; items $5-10; ⏱ 11am-8pm; 🚻), an eat-out-of-a-basket burger shack that delivers seasoned curly fries and old-fashioned milkshakes.

From Santa Barbara, MTD bus 20 runs to Summerland ($1.75, 25 minutes, hourly) via Montecito, continuing to Carpinteria.

Carpinteria

Lying 11 miles east of Santa Barbara, the time-warped beach town of Carpinteria – so named because Chumash carpenters once built seafaring canoes here – is a laid-back place. You could easily spend an hour or two wandering in and out of antiques shops and beachy boutiques along Linden Ave, downtown's main street. To gawk at the world's largest vat of guacamole, show up for the California Avocado Festival (p377) in early October.

◉ Sights & Activities

If you're an expert surfer, **Rincon Point** has long, glassy, right point-break waves. It's about 3 miles southeast of downtown, off Hwy 101 (exit Bates Rd).

Carpinteria State Beach BEACH
(📞 805-968-1033; www.parks.ca.gov; end of Linden Ave; per car $10; ⏱ 7am-sunset; 👶) An idyllic, milelong strand where kids can splash around in calm waters and go tide-pooling along the shoreline. In winter, you may spot harbor seals and sea lions hauled out on the sand, especially if you hike over a mile south along the coast to a bluff-top overlook.

SANTA BARBARA COUNTY SUMMERLAND

✦ Festivals & Events

California Avocado Festival   FOOD & DRINK
(www.avofest.com; 800 Linden Ave; ☺early Oct)
FREE Still going strong after 30 years, the annual California Avocado Festival is one of the state's largest free events, held in downtown Carpinteria. Bands play, avocado recipes are judged and the world's largest vat of guacamole makes a guest appearance.

Surf Happens   SURFING
(☑805-966-3613; http://surfhappens.com; 13 E Haley St; 2hr private lesson from $160; ⊕) Welcoming families, beginners and 'Surf Happens Sisters,' these highly reviewed classes and camps led by expert staff incorporate the Zen of surfing. In summer, you'll begin your spiritual wave-riding journey in Carpinteria, off Hwy 101 (exit Santa Claus Lane). Make reservations in advance. The office is based in downtown Santa Barbara.

⌂ Sleeping

Carpinteria's cookie-cutter chain motels and hotels are unexciting, but usually less expensive than those in nearby Santa Barbara.

**Carpinteria State Beach
Campground**   CAMPGROUND $
(☑800-444-7275; www.reserveamerica.com; 205 Palm Ave, tent & RV drive-up sites $45-70, hike-&-bike tent sites $10) Often crowded, this oceanfront campground offers lots of family-friendly amenities including flush toilets, hot showers, picnic tables and barbecue grills. Book ahead (reservations taken up to seven months in advance).

✕ Eating & Drinking

Tacos Don Roge   MEXICAN $
(☑805-566-6546; www.facebook.com/tacosdonroge; 751 Linden Ave; items from $1.50; ☺10am-9pm) This Mexican taquería stakes its reputation on a rainbow-colored salsa bar with up to a dozen different sauces to drizzle on piquant meat-stuffed, double-rolled corn tortillas – try the jalapeño or pineapple versions. If the spiciness gets you, grab an ice cream from Rainbows next door.

Padaro Beach Grill   AMERICAN $
(☑805-566-9800; http://padarobeachgrill.com; 3765 Santa Claus Lane; mains $7-11; ☺usually 10:30am-8pm Mon-Fri, from 11am Sat & Sun; ⊕⊕) Off Hwy 101 west of downtown, this oceanfront grill makes darn good burgers (including vegan versions), grilled-fish tacos, sweet-potato fries and thick, hand-mixed

milkshakes. The palm-tree shaded garden is a relaxing place to devour them.

Corktree Cellars   CALIFORNIAN $$
(☑805-684-1400; www.corktreecellars.com; 910 Linden Ave; small plates $7.50-14; ☺usually 11:30am-9pm Tue-Thu & Sun, to 9:30pm Fri & Sat) Downtown's contemporary wine bar and bistro offers tasty California-style tapas, charcuterie and cheese plates, and a good number of wine flights ($14).

Rincon Brewery   CRAFT BEER
(☑805-684-6044; http://rinconbrewery.com; 5065 Carpinteria Ave; ☺11am-9:30pm Sun-Thu, to 11pm Fri & Sat) Swap ocean waves for 'waves of grain' (their words) and knock back Belgian-style craft beers (among others) and a long menu of standard but tasty pub grub that keeps this place busy most nights of the week.

Island Brewing Co   BREWERY
(☑805-745-8272; www.islandbrewingcompany.com; 5049 6th St, off Linden Ave; ☺noon-9pm Mon-Thu, noon-10pm Fri, 11am-10pm Sat, 11am-9pm Sun; ⊕) Wanna hang loose with friendly beach bums and drink bourbon-barrel-aged brews? Find this locals-only, industrial space with an outdoor, dog-friendly patio by the railroad tracks – look for the Island sign.

ℹ Getting There & Away

Carpinteria is 11 miles east of Santa Barbara via Hwy 101 (southbound exit Linden Ave, northbound Casitas Pass Rd). From Santa Barbara, take **MTD** (p364) bus 20 ($1.75, 40 minutes, at least hourly) via Montecito and Summerland. **Amtrak** (☑800-872-7245; www.amtrak.com; 475 Linden Ave) has an unstaffed platform downtown; buy tickets online or by phone before catching one of five daily *Pacific Surfliner* trains west to Santa Barbara ($8.50, 15 to 20 minutes) and south to Ventura ($11, 25 minutes) or LA ($29, 2½ hours).

Ojai

Hollywood director Frank Capra chose the Ojai Valley to represent a mythical Shangri-la in his 1937 movie *Lost Horizon*. Today Ojai ('OH-hi,' from the Chumash word for 'moon') attracts artists, organic farmers, spiritual seekers and anyone ready to indulge in day-spa pampering. Bring shorts and flip-flops: Shangri-la sure gets hot in summer.

⊙ Sights & Activities

Ojai Olive Oil Company FARM
(☎805-646-5964; www.ojaioliveoil.com; 1811 Ladera Rd; ⊗9am-4pm Mon-Fri, 10am-4pm Sat) FREE Outside town, family-owned Ojai Olive Oil Company has a tasting room open six days a week and offers free talks and tours on Wednesdays (1pm to 4pm) and Saturdays (10am to 4pm). They also sell at the Ojai Farmers Market (p380) on Sundays. Dip bread into the various oils (and balsamic vinegars from Modena, its home) – the milder Provençale variety is the most popular.

Meditation Mount VIEWPOINT
(☎805-646-5508; https://meditationmount.org; 10340 Reeves Rd; ⊗8:30am-sunset Wed-Sun) FREE Ojai is famous for the rosy glow that emanates from its mountains at sunset (some days), the so-called 'Pink Moment.' The ideal vantage point for catching the show is the peaceful lookout atop Meditation Mount. Head east of downtown on Ojai Ave/Hwy 150 for about 2 miles, turn left at Boccali's farm-stand restaurant and drive another 2.5 miles on Reeves Rd (there's some signage) until it heads uphill and dead-ends at a parking lot and meditation center.

As well as the view, the gardens are a scented delight and, in keeping with the name, meditation is available (8:30am guided classes, from 9am until close for private meditation).

Ojai Vineyard Tasting Room WINERY
(☎805-798-3947; www.ojaivineyard.com; 109 S Montgomery St; tastings $15; ⊗noon-6pm) Inside downtown's historic firehouse, Ojai Vineyard pours tastes of its delicate, small-batch wines. It's best known for standard-bearing Chardonnay, Pinot Noir and Syrah, but the crisp Sauvignon Blanc, dry Riesling and zippy rosé are also worth sampling.

Ojai Valley Trail HIKING
(www.traillink.com/trail/ojai-valley-trail.aspx) FREE Running beside the highway, the 9-mile Ojai Valley Trail, converted from defunct railway tracks, is popular with walkers, runners, cyclists and equestrians. Pick it up downtown two blocks south of Ojai Ave, off Bryant St, then head west through the valley.

Mob Shop CYCLING
(☎805-272-8102; www.themobshop.com; 110 W Ojai Ave; bicycle rental per hour $12, day $25-50; ⊗10am-5pm Mon & Wed-Fri, 9am-5pm Sat, 9am-4pm Sun) Bike rental (including electric and kid versions) for DIY, two-wheel exploration of Ojai, plus organized tours of the city and surrounding area. Mountain bikers can sign up for a descent of nearby Sulphur Mountain.

Spa Ojai SPA
(☎855-697-8780; www.ojairesort.com/spa-ojai; Ojai Valley Inn & Spa, 905 Country Club Rd) For the ultimate in relaxation, book a day at top-tier Spa Ojai in the Ojai Valley Inn, where nonresort guests pay an extra $20 to access swimming pools, a workout gym and mind/body fitness classes.

Day Spa of Ojai SPA
(☎805-640-1100; www.thedayspa.com; 209 N Montgomery St; treatments $21-190; ⊗10:30am-5:30pm) Soothing everyday cares away for two decades now, this family-run operation is the place to come for facials, body wraps and hot-rock treatments for men and women. It specializes in Swedish massages, starting from $88.

🛏 Sleeping

Pricey but excellent quality would best describe the local accommodations scene. Book well in advance, especially for weekends.

★Lavender Inn B&B $$
(☎805-646-6635; http://lavenderinn.com; 210 E Matilija St; r from $145; P ⊛ 🛜 🐾) For a central location in a historic 1874 schoolhouse building, you can't beat the Lavender Inn. Room decor ranges from quaint to modern; a hearty, healthy breakfast can be enjoyed on the porch overlooking the pretty garden, and the evening tapas and wine are a nice touch.

An on-site spa sees to your relaxation needs, while the in-house cookery courses can satisfy any culinary aspirations. Just remember you *are* allowed to leave to explore Ojai itself, a short walk away.

Ojai Retreat B&B $$
(☎805-646-2536; www.ojairetreat.com; 160 Besant Rd; r $90-295; ⊛ @ 🛜) On a hilltop on the outskirts of town, this peaceful place has a back-to-nature collection of 12 country arts-and-crafts-style guest rooms and cottage suites, all perfect for unplugging. Find a quiet nook for reading or writing (no TVs), ramble through the wonderful grounds, or practice your downward dog in a yoga class.

Ojai Valley Inn & Spa RESORT $$$
(☎805-646-1111, 855-697-8780; www.ojairesort.com; 905 Country Club Rd; r from $349; P ⊛ @ 🛜 🐾 🐾) At the west end of town, this pampering resort has landscaped gardens, ten-

nis courts, swimming pools, a championship golf course and a fabulous spa. Luxurious rooms are outfitted with all mod cons and some sport a fireplace and balcony. Recreational activities run the gamut from kids' camps and complimentary bikes to full-moon yoga and astrological readings. Nightly 'service' surcharge $35.

If the resort's size puts you off, don't worry – a free golf-cart shuttle will whisk you to wherever you want to be.

On-site restaurant Olivella (p380) is one of the best in town.

Emerald Iguana Inn
BOUTIQUE HOTEL $$

(📞805-646-5277; www.emeraldiguana.com; 108 Pauline St; 🕐r/ste from $179/249; 🅿❋🛜🐾) Sister property of the Blue Iguana Inn, the Emerald Iguana is oriented more toward adults looking for a getaway but within walking distance of downtown Ojai. Local art hangs on the walls, in-room spa treatments can be arranged, and packages include romantic touches (wine, roses and chocolate). Two-bed cottages, complete with full kitchen, are available alongside comfortable standard rooms.

A two-night minimum is usually required. Book well in advance for weekends.

Ojai Rancho Inn
MOTEL $$

(📞805-646-1434; http://ojairanchoinn.com; 615 W Ojai Ave; r $120-200; ❋🛜🐾🏊) At this low-slung motel next to the highway, pine-paneled rooms each have a king bed. Cottage rooms come with fireplaces, and some have whirlpool tubs and kitchenettes. Besides competitive rates, the biggest bonuses of staying here are a small pool and sauna, shuffleboard, fire pit and bicycles to borrow for the half-mile ride to downtown. Pet fee $20.

Blue Iguana Inn
INN $$

(📞805-646-5277; www.blueiguanainn.com; 11794 N Ventura Ave; r/ste from $139/169; 🛜🐾🏊) Artsy iguanas lurk everywhere at this funky architect-designed inn – on adobe walls around Mediterranean-tiled fountains and anywhere else that reptilian style could bring out a smile. Roomy bungalow and cottage suites are unique and the pool is a social scene for LA denizens. Rates include continental breakfast; two-night minimum stay on weekends. Some pets allowed with prior approval only.

For a more central location and romantic atmosphere, try the sister Emerald Iguana Inn, just north of downtown.

 Eating

You are guaranteed top-quality ingredients in Ojai. Organic, sustainable and local are part of everyday culinary life here, and in keeping with the city's bohemian, hippie vibe; vegetarians and vegans will revel in the options available. The main drag, Ojai Ave, has plenty of places serving excellent food, but equally good choices are in out-of-the-way but worth-seeking-out locations around town.

★Knead
BAKERY, CAFE $

(📞310-770-3282; http://kneadbakingcompany.com; 469 E Ojai Ave; items $3.50-16; 🕐8am-2pm Wed-Sun) Family-run artisan bakery mixing batters with the best of Ojai's fresh fruit, herbs, honey and nuts. Get a slice of sweet tart (the lemon ricotta is sensational), a savory quiche, or a made-to-order breakfast sandwich. Saturday's sticky buns fly off the shelves. Enjoy a mimosa, wine or beer too. No credit cards.

★Suzanne's Cuisine
INTERNATIONAL $$$

(📞805-640-1961; www.suzannescuisine.com; mains $18-36; 🕐11:30am-2:30pm & 5:30pm-close Mon & Wed-Sun) The eclectic menu in this Ojai locals' favorite ranges from French-inspired snails and hearty pasta dishes to healthy salads and excellent meat, fish and seafood options. It's a family-run affair with an attention to detail that reflects the dedication of the eponymous Suzanne. In summer ask for a table on the outside patio overlooking the charming garden.

Farmer & the Cook
MEXICAN, VEGETARIAN $$

(📞805-640-9608; www.farmerandcook.com; 339 W Roblar Ave; mains $8.50-14.50; 🕐8:30am-8:30pm; 🥗🪑) 🌿 Flavorful, organic, vegetarian (some vegan) homemade Mexican cooking bursts out of this roadside market, which has its own farm nearby. Come for the squash and goat's-cheese tacos or the highly rated *huarache* (tortilla, potatoes, onions, pepper, feta and more), or, at dinner Thursday to Sunday, creative pizzas and a salad bar. Smoothies are available throughout the day.

Olivella
CALIFORNIAN $$$

(📞855-697-8780; www.ojairesort.com/dining/olivella-restaurant; 905 Country Club Rd; mains $35-55; 🕐5:30-9pm Wed-Sun; 🪑) In the Ojai Valley Inn, this worth-getting-dressed-up-for (though you don't have to) restaurant is *the* place in Ojai for a special meal. Meat and pasta are the stars of the menu (the bolognese sauce is a 19th-century chef-family recipe) but salads and fish dishes are equally tasty. Or push the boat out (and loosen the belt) with the four-course experience. Service is friendly but can be disorganized.

HiHo! BURGERS $
(☑ 805-640-4446; http://hihoburger.com; 401 E Ojai Ave; burgers from $10.95; ⏰ 11:30am-8pm Wed-Sun) Sometimes even health-conscious Ojai residents just want a burger, fries and a cola. HiHo! in the heart of downtown scratches that itch. It's a simple menu: wagyu-beef patties (vegetarian burgers available) served 'classic' (lettuce, cheese, ketchup) or 'HIHO' (same but with pickles and onion jam). Sit under the umbrellas and forget kale salads exist.

Bonnie Lu's Country Cafe BREAKFAST $
(☑ 805-646-0207; www.facebook.com/bonnielus; 328 E Ojai Ave; mains from $8; ⏰ 7am-2:30pm Thu-Tue) Central, and therefore busy (expect to wait at weekends), diner where all your breakfast favorites are available including a variety of eggs Benedict, pancakes and biscuits with gravy. Not the place for a light start to the day.

Hip Vegan VEGAN $
(☑ 805-646-1750; www.hipvegancafe.com; 928 E Ojai Ave; mains $9.50-15; ⏰ 11am-5pm Mon & Thu, to 7pm Fri-Sun; ☑ 🍴) ◢ Tucked back from the street in a tiny garden (look for the arrow on the wall), this locals' kitchen stays true to Ojai's granola-crunching hippie roots with Mexican-leaning salads and sides, Asian-influenced sandwiches and classic So-Cal date shakes and teas. The interior is spartan so grab a shaded picnic table outside.

Boccali's ITALIAN $$
(☑ 805-646-6116; http://boccalis.com; 3277 Ojai-Santa Paula Rd; mains $10-19; ⏰ 4-9pm Mon & Tue, from noon Wed-Sun; ☑ 🍴) This roadside farm stand with red-and-white-checkered tablecloths does simple, big-portion Italian cooking. Much of the produce is grown behind the restaurant and the fresh tomato salad is often still warm from the garden. The real draws are the wood-oven pizzas and the seasonal strawberry shortcake. It's over 2 miles east of downtown via Ojai Ave.

🛍 Shopping

★ Bart's Books BOOKS
(☑ 805-646-3755; www.bartsbooksojai.com; 302 W Matilija St; ⏰ 9:30am-sunset) One block north of Ojai Ave, this charming, unique indoor-outdoor space sells new and well-loved tomes. It's been going for well over a half century so demands at least a half-hour browse and a purchase or two – just don't step on the lurking but surprisingly nimble cat.

Ojai Farmers Market MARKET
(☑ 805-698-5555; www.ojaicertifiedfarmersmarket. com; 300 E Matilija St; ⏰ 9am-1pm Sun) It's no surprise that in an agriculturally blessed region, Ojai's farmers market is a beauty. There are the usual high-quality fruit and vegetables on offer each Sunday, plus seafood, meat, breads, chocolate, flowers and plants.

Ojai Clothing CLOTHING
(☑ 805-640-1269; http://ojaiclothing.com; 325 E Ojai Ave; ⏰ noon-5pm Mon & Wed-Thu, noon-5:30pm Fri, 10am-5:30pm Sat, 11am-5pm Sun) Equally comfy for doing an interpretive dance or just hanging out, these earth-toned and vibrantly patterned casual pieces for women and men are made from soft cotton knits and woven fabrics.

Human Arts Gallery ARTS & CRAFTS
(☑ 805-646-1525; www.humanartsgallery.com; 246 E Ojai Ave; ⏰ 11am-5pm Mon-Sat, noon-5pm Sun) Browse the colorful handmade jewelry, sculpture, woodcarvings, glassworks, folk-art furnishings and more from over 150 American artists. A custom design service is also available if you want a unique souvenir of your Ojai visit.

❶ Information

Ojai Visitors Bureau (☑ 805-640-3606; www. ojaivisitors.com; 109 N Blanche St; ⏰ 8am-4pm Mon-Fri) Provides brochures and other material to visitors.

Ojai Ranger Station (☑ 805-646-4348; www.fs.usda.gov/detail/lpnf; 1190 E Ojai Ave; ⏰ 8am-4:30pm Mon-Fri) Camping tips and trail maps for hiking to hot springs, waterfalls and mountaintop viewpoints in the Los Padres National Forest.

Ojai Library (☑ 805-646-1639; www.vencolibrary.org/locations/ojai-library; 111 E Ojai Ave; ⏰ 10am-8pm Mon-Thu, noon-5pm Fri-Sun; 🖥) Free online computer terminals and wi-fi for public use.

❶ Getting There & Away

Ojai is around 33 miles east of Santa Barbara via scenic Hwy 150, or 15 miles inland (north) from Ventura via Hwy 33. **Gold Coast Transit** (☑ 805-487-4222; www.goldcoasttransit.org) bus 16 runs from Ventura (including a stop near the Amtrak station) to downtown Ojai ($1.50, 45 minutes, hourly).

Ventura

The primary pushing-off point for Channel Island boat trips, the beach town of San Buenaventura may not look to be the most enchanting coastal city, but it has seaside charms, especially on the historic pier and downtown along Main St, north of Hwy 101 via California St.

⊙ Sights

South of Hwy 101 via Harbor Blvd, **Ventura Harbor** is the main departure point for boats to Channel Islands National Park.

Museum of Ventura County　　MUSEUM
(☑ 805-653-0323; www.venturamuseum.org; 100 E Main St; adult $5, child 6-17yr $1; ⊙ 11am-5pm Tue-Sun; ◈) This tiny downtown museum has an excellently eclectic collection that includes exhibits on the local Chumash people and rotating exhibitions of local artists. The highlight though is the George Stuart Historical Figures gallery. An Ojai resident, Stuart made models of famous people from the past to help bring to life historical lectures he gave around the country. Look out for emperor Nero, Vlad Tepes (aka Dracula), Henry VIII (with, sadly, just two of his wives), Hitler and Putin.

San Buenaventura State Beach　　BEACH
(☑ 805-968-1033; www.parks.ca.gov; enter off San Pedro St; per car $10; ⊙ dawn-dusk; ◈) Along the waterfront off Hwy 101, this long white-sand beach is ideal for swimming, surfing or just lazing on the sand. A recreational cycling path connects to nearby **Emma Wood State Beach**, another popular spot for swimming, surfing and fishing.

Mission San Buenaventura　　CHURCH
(☑ 805-643-4318; www.sanbuenaventuramission. org; 211 E Main St; adult/child $4/2; ⊙ 10am-5pm, from 9am Sat) Ventura's Spanish-colonial roots go back to this last mission founded by Junípero Serra in California in 1782. A stroll around the mellow parish church leads you through a garden courtyard and a small museum, past statues of saints, centuries-old religious paintings and unusual, unique wooden bells.

✖ Eating

In downtown Ventura, Main St is chockablock with Mexicali taco shops, casual cafes and globally flavored kitchens.

★**Paradise Pantry**　　DELI $
(☑ 805-641-9440; www.paradisepantry.com; 222 E Main St; sandwiches $12-16; ⊙ 11am-8:30pm Tue-Thu, to 9:30pm Fri & Sat, Sun hours vary; ◢) On the cafe side of Paradise Pantry you can grab a sandwich, soup, cheese or meat plate in a quietly buzzing atmosphere. On the deli side, you can stock up on supplies for a beach or Channel Island picnic (sandwiches can be made to go) and even grab some wine or beer to wash it all down.

★**Lure Fish House**　　SEAFOOD $$$
(☑ 805-567-4400; www.lurefishhouse.com; 60 S California St; mains $17-37; ⊙ 11:30am-9pm Sun-Thu, to 10pm Fri & Sat; ◈) ◢ For seafood any fresher, you'd have to catch it yourself off Ventura pier. Go nuts ordering off a stalwart menu of sustainably caught seafood, organic regional farm produce and California wines. Make reservations or turn up at the bar during happy hour (4pm to 6pm Monday to Friday, 11:30am to 6pm Sunday) for strong cocktails, fried calamari and charbroiled oysters.

Jolly Oyster　　SEAFOOD $
(☑ 805-798-4944; www.thejollyoyster.com; 911 San Pedro St; items $5-16; ⊙ 11am-5pm Sat & Sun; ◈) ◢ At San Buenaventura State Beach, the Jolly Oyster sells its own farm-raised oysters and clams. The main option is shucking your own (seat yourself at the nearby picnic tables) though their licensed truck prepares oysters on the half shell, baked and fried oysters, clam steamers and a bay-scallop ceviche. One-hour parking free. Weekends only.

Ventura Certified Farmers Market　　MARKET $
(☑ 805-529-6266; http://vccfarmersmarkets.com; cnr Santa Clara & Palm Sts; ⊙ 8:30am-noon Sat; ◢ ◈) ◢ Over 45 farmers and food vendors show up each week, offering fresh fruits and vegetables, home-baked bread and ready-made meals – Mediterranean, Mexican and more. Another farmers market sets up at midtown's Pacific View Mall from 9am to 1pm on Wednesdays.

▼ Drinking & Nightlife

You'll find plenty of rowdy dives down by the harbor and a couple of excellent craft-beer places around town.

★**Topa Topa Brewing Company**　　CRAFT BEER
(☑ 805-628-9255; http://topatopa.beer; 104 E Thompson Blvd; ⊙ noon-9pm Mon-Thu, noon-10pm Fri & Sat, 11am-8pm Sun; ◈ ▩) Between the freeway and downtown Ventura is not

ISLAND OF THE BLUE DOPHINS

For bedtime reading aloud around the campfire, pick up Scott O'Dell's Newbery Medal–winning *Island of the Blue Dolphins*. This young adult novel was inspired by the true-life story of a girl from the Nicoleño tribe who was left behind on San Nicolas Island during the early 19th century, when her people were forced off the Channel Islands. Incredibly, the girl survived mostly alone on the island for 18 years, living in a whale-bone hut and sourcing water from a spring, before being discovered and brought to the mainland by a hunter in 1853. However, fate was not on her side: by the time she was brought to the Santa Barbara Mission she was the last surviving Nicoleña, no one could understand her native language and she died just seven weeks later. Today her body lies buried in the graveyard at Mission Santa Barbara, where a commemorative plaque is inscribed with her Christian baptismal name, Juana María.

exactly the most salubrious location, but the beer here makes up for the surroundings. Chief Peak IPA takes the medal but all the quality brewed-on-site options are worth trying. Food trucks (a different one every night; see the website for details) feed the hungry.

Surf Brewery
BREWERY

(☎ 805-644-2739; http://surfbrewery.com; suite A, 4561 Market St; ◎ 4-9pm Tue-Thu, from 1pm Fri, noon-9pm Sat, noon-7pm Sun) Operating since 2011, Surf Brewery makes big waves with its hoppy and black IPAs and rye American pale ale. Beer geeks and food trucks gather at the sociable taproom in an industrial area, about 5 miles from downtown (take Hwy 101 southbound, exit Donlon St).

Shopping

★ Copperfield's
GIFTS & SOUVENIRS

(☎ 805-667-8198; www.facebook.com/copperfieldsvta; 242 E Main St; ◎ 10am-6pm Mon-Sat, from 11am Sun) Part standard gift shop, part what can only be described as emporium of ephemera, this is the kind of place where you can buy a birthday card one day and an infra-compunctive resonance perversion ray gun the next (your guess is as good as ours). Quirky souvenirs don't come better than this.

Rocket Fizz
FOOD & DRINKS

(☎ 805-641-1222; www.rocketfizz.com; 315 E Main St; ◎ 10:30am-8pm Mon-Thu, to 9pm Fri & Sat, to 7pm Sun) Part of a national retro-style soda pop and old-fashioned candy-store chain, this is the place for stocking your cooler with all types of so-bad-but-so-good sweets and drinks before a day at the beach.

B on Main
GIFTS & SOUVENIRS

(☎ 805-643-9309; www.facebook.com/b-on-main; 446 E Main St; ◎ 10:30am-6pm Mon-Thu, 10am-7pm Fri & Sat, 11am-5pm Sun) For coastal living, B sells nifty reproductions of vintage surf posters, shabby-chic furnishings, SoCal landscape art, locally made jewelry and beachy clothing for women.

Ormachea
JEWELRY

(☎ 805-652-0484; www.ormacheajewelry.com; 451 E Main St; ◎ 11am-5:30pm Mon-Fri, to 6pm Sat, to 5pm Sun) Run by a third-generation Peruvian jewelry craftsman, Ormachea skillfully hammers out one-of-a-kind, handmade rings, pendants and bangles in a downtown studio.

ARC Foundation Thrift Store
VINTAGE

(☎ 805-650-861; www.arcvc.org; 265 E Main St; ◎ 9am-6pm Mon-Thu, 9am-7pm Fri & Sat, 10am-6pm Sun) Loads of thrift stores, antiques malls and secondhand and vintage shops cluster downtown. Most are on Main St, west of California St, where ARC is always jam-packed with bargain hunters.

ℹ Information

Ventura Visitors & Convention Bureau

(☎ 805-648-2075; www.ventura-usa.com; 101 S California St; ◎ 9am-5pm Mon-Sat, 10am-4pm Sun) Downtown visitor center handing out free maps and tourist brochures. It also contains a gift shop.

ℹ Getting There & Away

Ventura is about 30 miles southeast of Santa Barbara via Hwy 101. **Amtrak** (☎ 800-872-7245; www.amtrak.com; Harbor Blvd, at Figueroa St) operates five daily trains north to Santa Barbara ($15, 45 minutes) via Carpinteria and south to LA ($24, 2¼ hours). Amtrak's platform station is unstaffed; buy tickets in advance online or by phone. **VCTC** (Ventura County Transportation Commission; ☎ 800-438-1112; www.goventura.org) runs several daily 'Coastal Express' buses between downtown Ventura and Santa Barbara

($3, 40 to 70 minutes) via Carpinteria; check online or call for schedules.

Channel Islands National Park

Don't let this off-the-beaten-path **national park** (📞 805-658-5730; www.nps.gov/chis) 🏴 **FREE** loiter for too long on your lifetime to-do list. It's easier to access than you might think, and the payoff is immense. Imagine hiking, kayaking, scuba diving, camping and whale-watching, and doing it all amid a raw, end-of-the-world landscape. Rich in unique flora and fauna, tide pools and kelp forests, the islands are home to 145 plant and animal species found nowhere else in the world, earning them the nickname 'California's Galapagos.'

Geographically, the Channel Islands are an eight-island chain off the Southern California coast, stretching from Santa Barbara to San Diego. Five of them – San Miguel, Santa Rosa, Santa Cruz, Anacapa and tiny Santa Barbara – comprise Channel Islands National Park.

Originally the Channel Islands were inhabited by Chumash tribespeople, who were forced to move to mainland Catholic missions by Spanish military forces in the early 1800s. The islands were subsequently taken over by Mexican and American ranchers during the 19th century and the US military in the 20th, until conservation efforts began in the 1970s and '80s.

As of 2017, Santa Barbara was closed to visitors because of storm damage to its landing pier. Check the NPS website for the latest information.

◉ Sights & Activities

Anacapa and Santa Cruz, the park's most popular islands, are within an hour's boat ride of Ventura. Anacapa is a doable day trip, while Santa Cruz is better suited for overnight camping. Bring plenty of water, because none is available on either island except at Scorpion Ranch Campground on Santa Cruz.

Most visitors arrive during summer, when island conditions are hot, dusty and bone-dry. Better times to visit are during the spring wildflower bloom or in early fall, when the fog clears. Winter can be stormy, but it's also great for wildlife-watching, especially whales.

Before you shove off from the mainland, stop by Ventura Harbor's NPS Visitor Center (p385) for educational natural history exhibits, a free 25-minute nature film and, on weekends and holidays, family-friendly activities and ranger talks.

◉ Santa Cruz Island

Santa Cruz, the Channel Islands' largest at 96 sq miles, claims two mountain ranges and the park's tallest peak, Mt Diablo (2450ft). The western three-quarters is mostly wilderness, managed by the Nature Conservancy and only accessible with a permit (www.nature.org/cruzpermit). The rest, managed by the National Park Service, is ideal for an action-packed day trip or laid-back overnight stay. Boats land at either Prisoners Harbor or Scorpion Anchorage, a short walk from historic Scorpion Ranch.

You can swim, snorkel, dive and kayak here, and there are plenty of hiking options too, starting from Scorpion Anchorage. It's a 1-mile climb to captivating Cavern Point. Views don't get much better than from this windy spot. For a longer jaunt, continue 1.5 miles west, along the North Bluff Trail, to Potato Harbor. The 4.5-mile Scorpion Canyon Loop heads uphill to an old oil well and fantastic views, then drops through Scorpion

---

CALIFORNIA'S CHANNEL ISLANDS: PARADISE LOST & FOUND

Human beings have left a heavy footprint on the Channel Islands. Erosion was caused by overgrazing livestock and rabbits fed on native plants. The US military even used San Miguel as a practice bombing range. In 1969 an offshore oil spill engulfed the northern islands in an 800-sq-mile slick, killing thousands of seabirds and mammals. Meanwhile, deep-sea fishing has caused the destruction of three-quarters of the islands' kelp forests, which are key to the marine ecosystem.

Despite past abuses, the future isn't all bleak. Brown pelicans – decimated by the effects of DDT and reduced to one surviving chick in 1970 – have rebounded and are now off the endangered list, with healthy populations on West Anacapa and Santa Barbara islands. On San Miguel Island, native vegetation has returned after overgrazing sheep were removed. On Santa Cruz Island, the National Park Service and the Nature Conservancy have implemented multiyear plans to eliminate invasive plants and feral pigs.

Canyon to the campground. Alternatively, follow Smugglers Rd all the way to the pebble beach at Smugglers Cove, a strenuous 7.5-mile round-trip. From Prisoners Harbor there are several more strenuous trails including the 18-mile round-trip China Pines hike – your efforts will be rewarded by the chance to see the rare Bishop pine.

There's little shade on the island (so avoid midday summer walks), bring plenty of water (available at Scorpion Anchorage only) and make sure you're at the harbor in plenty of time to catch your return boat, otherwise you'll be stuck overnight.

Anacapa Island

Actually three separate islets totaling just over 1 sq mile, Anacapa gives a memorable introduction to the Channel Islands' ecology. It's also the best option if you're short on time. Boats dock year-round on the East Island where, after a short climb, you'll find 2 miles of trails offering fantastic views of island flora, a historic lighthouse, and rocky Middle and West Islands. You're bound to see western gulls too – the world's largest breeding colony is here.

Kayaking, diving, tide-pooling and watching seals and sea lions are popular activities, while inside the museum at the small visitor center, divers with video cameras occasionally broadcast images to a TV monitor you can watch during spring and summer.

Other Islands

The Chumash called Santa Rosa (www.nps. gov/chis/planyourvisit/santa-rosa-island.htm) 'Wima' (driftwood) because of the redwood logs that often came ashore here, with which they built plank canoes called *tomols*. This 84-sq-mile island has rare Torrey pines, sandy beaches and hundreds of plant and bird species. Beach, canyon and grasslands hiking trails abound, but high winds can make swimming, diving and kayaking tough for anyone but experts.

While 14-sq-mile San Miguel (www.nps. gov/chis/planyourvisit/san-miguel-island.htm) can guarantee solitude and a remote wilderness experience, it's often windy and shrouded in fog. Some sections are off-limits to prevent disruption of the island's fragile ecosystem, which includes a caliche forest (containing hardened calcium-carbonate castings of trees and vegetation) and seasonal colonies of seals and sea lions.

Santa Barbara (www.nps.gov/chis/planyourvisit/santa-barbara-island.htm), only 1 sq mile in size and the smallest of the islands, is a jewel box for nature lovers. Big, blooming coreopsis, cream cups and chicory are just a few of the island's memorable plant species. You'll also find the humongous northern elephant seal here as well as Scripps's murrelets, birds that nests in cliff crevices. Get more information from the island's small visitor center.

Tours

Most trips require a minimum number of participants and may be canceled due to high surf or weather conditions.

Aquasports KAYAKING
(805-968-7231; www.islandkayaking.com) Aquasports offers day and overnight kayaking trips to Santa Cruz, Anacapa and along the coast near Santa Barbara, led by professional naturalists. Prices vary from $89 to $495, depending on length of trip and whether you bring your own camping gear and arrange the ferry to the islands yourself.

Raptor Dive Charters DIVING
(805-650-7700; www.raptordive.com; 1559 Spinnaker Dr, Ventura) Certified and experienced divers can head out for some underwater

CHANNEL ISLANDS NATIONAL PARK CAMPGROUNDS

CAMPGROUND	NUMBER OF SITES	ACCESS FROM BOAT LANDING	DESCRIPTION
Anacapa	7	0.5-mile walk with over 150 stairs	High, rocky, sun-exposed and isolated
Santa Cruz (Scorpion Ranch)	31	Flat 0.5-mile walk	Popular with groups, often crowded and partly shady
Santa Barbara	10	Steep 0.25-mile walk uphill	Large, grassy and surrounded by trails
San Miguel	9	Steep 1-mile walk uphill	Windy, often foggy with volatile weather
Santa Rosa	15	Flat 1.5-mile walk	Eucalyptus grove in a windy canyon

action, including night dives, off Anacapa and Santa Cruz islands. Prices start at $120; equipment rentals are available for a surcharge; and plenty of snacks, sandwiches and drinks are available on board.

Truth Aquatics
OUTDOORS

(☎ 805-962-1127; www.truthaquatics.com; 301 W Cabrillo Blvd, Santa Barbara) Based in Santa Barbara, this long-running outfitter organizes seasonal (usually April to October) diving, kayaking and hiking day trips and three-day, all-inclusive excursions to the Channel Islands aboard specially designed dive boats.

Island Packers
CRUISE

(☎ 805-642-1393; http://islandpackers.com; 1691 Spinnaker Dr, Ventura; Channel Island day trips from $59, wildlife cruises from $68) Main provider of boats for Channel Islands visits, with day trips and overnight camping excursions available. Boats mostly set out from Ventura but a few go from nearby Oxnard. It also offers wildlife cruises year-round, including seasonal whale-watching from late December to mid-April (gray whales) and mid-May through mid-September (blue and humpback whales).

Channel Islands Kayak Center
KAYAKING

(☎ 805 984 5995; www.cikayak.com; 1691 Spinnaker Dr, Ventura; ⊙ by appointment only) Book ahead to rent kayaks and SUPs (kayak/SUP from $12.50/25) or arrange a private guided kayaking tour of Santa Cruz or Anacapa (from $180 per person, two-person minimum).

🛏 Sleeping

Each island has a primitive year-round **campground** (☎ reservations 877-444-6777; www.recreation.gov; tent sites $15) with pit toilets and picnic tables. Water is only available on Santa Rosa and Santa Cruz Islands. You must pack everything in and out, including trash. Due to fire danger, campfires aren't allowed, but enclosed, gas campstoves are OK. Advance reservations are required for all island campsites.

ℹ Information

Channel Islands National Park Visitor Center
(Robert J Lagomarsino Visitor Center; ☎ 805-658-5730; www.nps.gov/chis; 1901 Spinnaker

Dr, Ventura; ⊙ 8:30am-5pm; 🖼) Trip-planning information, books and maps are available on the mainland at the far end of Ventura Harbor. A free video, *A Treasure in the Sea*, gives background on the islands, and weekends and holidays see ranger-led free programs at 11am and 3pm.

ℹ Getting There & Away

You can access the national park by taking a boat from Ventura or Oxnard or a plane from Camarillo. Trips may be canceled anytime due to high surf or weather conditions. Reservations are essential for weekends, holidays and summer trips.

AIR

If you're prone to seasickness or just want a memorable way to get to the Channel Islands, you can take a scenic flight to Santa Rosa or San Miguel with **Channel Islands Aviation** (☎ 805-987-1301; www.flycia.com; 305 Durley Ave, Camarillo) in Camarillo. Half-day packages include hiking or a guided 4WD tour, while overnight camping excursions are more DIY.

BOAT

Island Packers offers regularly scheduled boat services to all islands, mostly from Ventura, but with a few sailings from Oxnard too. Anacapa and Santa Cruz are closer to the mainland and so less expensive to visit than other islands. Day trips are possible; overnight campers pay an additional surcharge. Be forewarned: if you do camp and seas are rough the following day, you could get stuck for an extra night or more.

San Diego & Around

Best Places to Eat

Best Places to Sleep

Why Go?

New York has its cabbie, Chicago its bluesman and Seattle its coffee-drinking boho. San Diego has its surfer dude, with his tousled hair, great tan and gentle enthusiasm; he looks like he's on a perennial vacation, and when he wishes you welcome, he really means it.

San Diego calls itself 'America's Finest City' and its breezy confidence and sunny countenance filter down to folks you encounter every day on the street. It feels like a collection of villages each with its own personality, but it's the nation's eighth-largest city and we're hard-pressed to think of a more laid-back place.

What's not to love? San Diego bursts with world-famous attractions for the entire family, including the zoo, Legoland and the museums of Balboa Park, plus a bubbling Downtown, beautiful hikes for all, more than 60 beaches and America's most perfect weather.

When to Go
San Diego

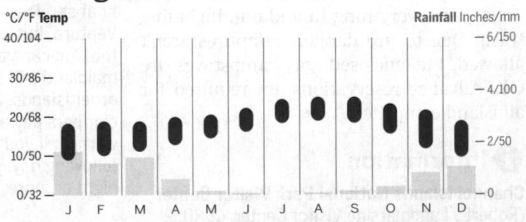

Jun–Aug High season; temperatures and hotel rates are highest. Cloudy skies in June.

Sep–Oct, Mar–May Shoulder seasons; moderate rates, warm with blue skies.

Nov–Feb Low season but far from cold, and your chance to spot whales off the coastline.

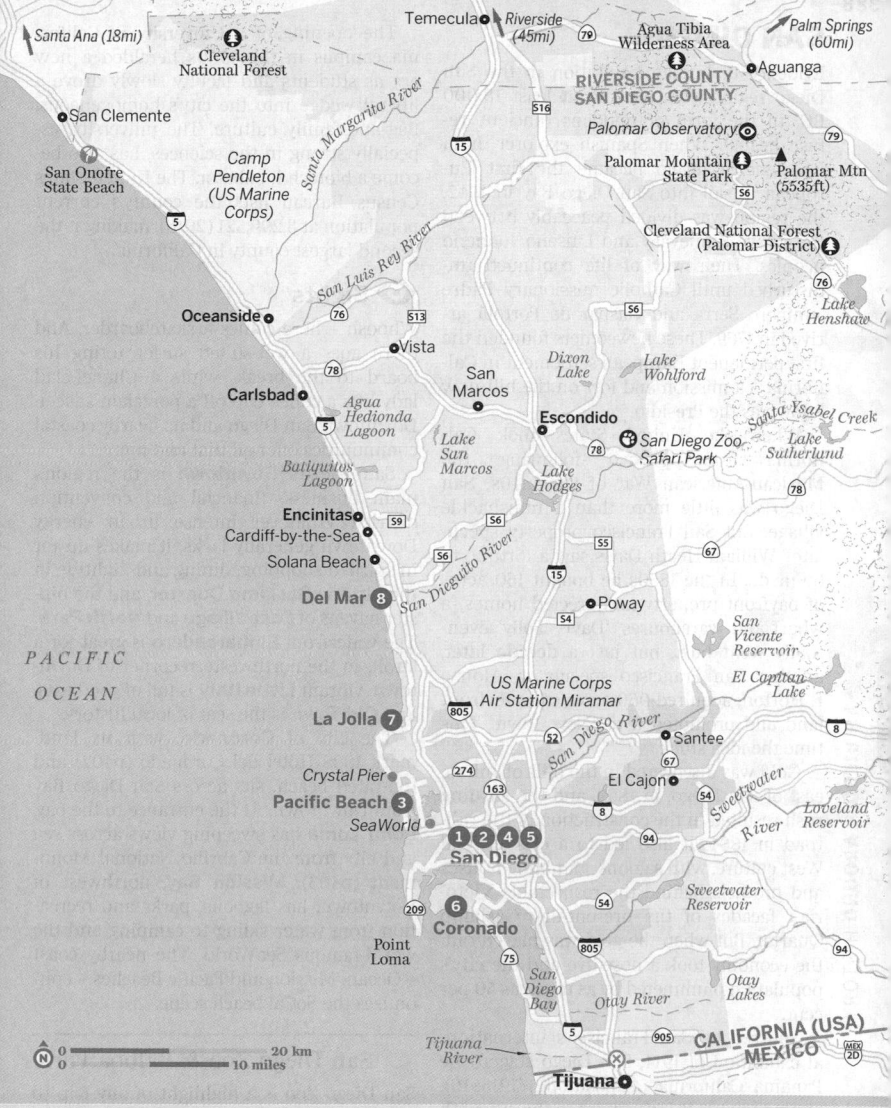

San Diego Highlights

1 San Diego Zoo (p389) Cooing at koalas and pandering to pandas.

2 Balboa Park (p388) Museum hopping, then the next great taste in Hillcrest and North Park.

3 Pacific Beach (p405) Sunning and skating on the boardwalk and catching an epic sunset on the pier.

4 Old Town Mexican Café (p418) Eating tortillas and swilling margaritas in a legendary spot.

5 Gaslamp Quarter (p421) Downtown pub-crawling and a piano show at Shout House.

6 Hotel del Coronado (p402) Marveling at the history and architecture of one of San Diego's landmarks.

7 Everyday California (p432) Kayaking at La Jolla cove and ecological reserve.

8 Del Mar Racetrack (p440) Mingling with Southern California's hoi polloi.

SAN DIEGO

Evidence of human habitation in the San Diego region goes back to at least 18,000 BC, in the form of middens (ancient refuse heaps). When Spanish explorer Juan Rodríguez Cabrillo became the first European to sail into San Diego Bay in 1542, the region was divided peacefully between the native Kumeyaay and Luiseño/Juaneño peoples. Their way of life continued undisturbed until Catholic missionary Padre Junípero Serra and Gaspar de Portolá arrived in 1769. These newcomers founded the first permanent European settlement in California – a mission and fort on the hill now known as the Presidio.

When the United States took California from Mexico following the Mexican-American War of the 1840s, San Diego was little more than a ramshackle village. But San Francisco property speculator William Heath Davis saw a fortune to be made. In the 1850s he bought 160 acres of bayfront property and erected homes, a wharf and warehouses. 'Davis' Folly' eventually went bust, but just a decade later, another San Francisco speculator, Alonzo E Horton, acquired 960 acres of waterfront land and promoted it as 'New Town.' This time the idea stuck.

Gold was discovered in the hills of Julian, east of San Diego, in 1869, and the ensuing rush resulted in the construction of the railroad in 1884. It also led to a classic Wild West culture, with saloons, gambling houses and brothels behind the respectable Victorian facades of the present-day Gaslamp Quarter. But when the gold was played out, the economy took a nosedive and the city's population plummeted by as much as 50 per cent.

Spurred by San Francisco's international exhibition of 1914, San Diego staged the Panama–California Exposition (1915–16), aiming to attract investment to the city with its deepwater port, railroad hub and perfect climate. Boosters built exhibition halls in the romantic Spanish Colonial style that still defines much of the city today.

However, it was the 1941 bombing of Pearl Harbor that permanently made San Diego. The navy's top brass quickly chose San Diego, with its excellent, protected port, as home of the US Pacific Fleet. The military literally reshaped the city, dredging the harbor, building landfill islands and constructing vast tracts of instant housing.

The opening of a University of California campus in the 1960s heralded a new era as students and faculty slowly drove a liberal wedge into the city's homogeneous, flag-and-family culture. The university, especially strong in the sciences, has also become a biotech incubator. The United States Census Bureau lists the county's current population at 3,299,521 (2016), making it the second largest county in California.

⊙ Sights

Whoosh – here comes a skateboarder. And there goes a wet-suited surfer toting his board to the break, while a Chanel-clad lady lifts a coffee cup off a porcelain saucer. Downtown San Diego and its nearby coastal communities offer all that and more.

San Diego's **Downtown** is the region's main business, financial and convention district. Whatever intense urban energy Downtown generally lacks, it makes up for in spirited shopping, dining and nightlife in the historic **Gaslamp Quarter**, and the hipster havens of **East Village** and **North Park**. The waterfront **Embarcadero** is great for a stroll; in the northwestern corner of Downtown, vibrant **Little Italy** is full of good eats, and **Old Town** is the seat of local history.

The city of **Coronado**, with its landmark 1888 Hotel del Coronado (p402) and top-rated beach, sits across San Diego Bay from Downtown. At the entrance to the bay, **Point Loma** has sweeping views across sea and city from the Cabrillo National Monument (p403). **Mission Bay**, northwest of Downtown, has lagoons, parks and recreation from water skiing to camping and the world-famous SeaWorld. The nearby coast – Ocean, Mission and Pacific Beaches – epitomizes the SoCal beach scene.

◎ San Diego Zoo & Balboa Park

San Diego Zoo is a highlight of any trip to California and should be a high priority for first-time visitors. The zoo occupies some prime real estate in Balboa Park, which itself is packed with **museums** (Map p390; 🎫 800-310-7106; www.balboapark.org/explorer; Balboa Park; multi-entry tickets from $46 adult, $27 child; 🅿 🦽) and gardens (p395). To visit all the park's sights would take days; plan your trip at the **Balboa Park Visitors Center** (Map p390; 🎫 619-239-0512; www.balboapark. org; House of Hospitality, 1549 El Prado; ⊙ 9:30am-4:30pm). Pick up a park map (suggested donation $1) and the latest opening schedule.

Discount admission coupons are widely available in local publications and at hotels and information-center kiosks. The **multi-day explorer pass** (adult/child $97/62) covers admission to Balboa Park's 17 museums and one day at the zoo; it's valid for seven days. A **one-day pass** ($46/27) excludes zoo entry, but includes five museums in one day.

The **Go San Diego** card offers up to 55 per cent off big-ticket attractions. The three-day pass (adult/child $189/169) includes San Diego Zoo, many of Balboa Park's museums, SeaWorld, Legoland, the USS *Midway* Museum and San Diego Zoo Safari Park.

Free tours depart from Balboa Park Visitors Center. To uncover the park's architectural-heritage nature and history, led by volunteers and rangers, see www.balboapark.org/explore/tours for timings.

Balboa Park is easily reached from Downtown on bus 7 along Park Blvd. By car, Park Blvd provides easy access to free parking. El Prado is a pedestrian road running through the park and between museums; visitors can access it via Laurel St, then cross Cabrillo Bridge with the Cabrillo Fwy (CA 163) 120ft below; hanging greenery here makes it look like a rainforest gorge.

The free **Balboa Park Tram** bus makes a continuous loop around the park; however, it's easiest and most enjoyable to walk.

★ **San Diego Zoo**   ZOO
(Map p390 [J]619-231-1515; http://zoo.sandiego.org; 2920 Zoo Dr; 1-day pass adult/child from $52/42; 2-visit pass to zoo &/or safari park adult/child $83.25/73.25; ⊙9am-9pm mid-Jun–early Sep, to 5pm or 6pm early Sep–mid-Jun; [P][⊞]) ◢ This justifiably famous zoo is one of SoCal's biggest attractions, showing more than 3000 animals representing more than 650 species in a beautifully landscaped setting, typically in enclosures that replicate their natural habitats. Its sister park is San Diego Zoo Safari Park (p446) in northern San Diego County.

Arrive early, as many of the animals are most active in the morning – though many perk up again in the afternoon. Pick up a map at the zoo entrance to find your favorite exhibits.

Reuben H Fleet Science Center   MUSEUM
(Map p390; [J]619-238-1233; www.rhfleet.org; 1875 El Prado; adult/child 3-12 years incl IMAX $20/17; ⊙10am-5pm Mon-Thu, to 6pm Fri-Sun; [⊞]) One of Balboa Park's most popular venues, this hands-on science museum features interactive displays and a toddler room. Look out for opportunities to build gigantic structures with Keva planks and visit the **Gallery of Illusions and Perceptions**. The biggest draw is the **Giant Dome Theater**, which screens several different films each day. The hemispherical, wraparound screen and 152-speaker state-of-the-art sound system create sensations ranging from pretty cool to mind-blowing.

SAN DIEGO IN...

One Day

Rub elbows with the locals over breakfast at **Café 222** (p415) in the **Gaslamp Quarter** then ramble around **Old Town San Diego State Historic Park** (p400) for a bit of history before lunch at **Old Town Mexican Café** (p418). Devote the afternoon to the **San Diego Zoo** (p389), which is among the world's best, and if time permits visit some of the museums or gardens in graceful **Balboa Park** (p395). For dinner and a night out, head to the hip **East Village** or back to the Gaslamp Quarter, where many restaurants have terrace seating for people-watching, and the partying ranges from posh to raucous.

Two Days

Take the ferry to Coronado for a sea-view breakfast at Marilyn Monroe's old haunt **The Del** (p402). Head to **Mission and Pacific Beaches** (p405) for a spot of California people-watching. Glam **La Jolla** beckons this afternoon: hike the trials at **Torrey Pines State Natural Reserve** (p433) or kayak ([J]858-454-6195; www.everydaycalifornia.com; 2246 Avenida de la Playa; kayak tours from $50; ⊙9am-5pm) mysterious sea caves. Try a thrilling **glider** (p436) ride for bird's-eye views of the spectacular rugged sea cliffs or browse the 1920s Spanish-revival **landmarks** (p432) and **bookstores** (p438). As the sun descends head to **Del Mar** to watch the sky turn brilliant orange and fade to black at **Pacifica Del Mar** (p439) on the roof of **Del Mar Plaza** (p440).

Balboa Park & Hillcrest

Town & Country Hotel (1mi);
Fashion Valley (1.5mi); Handlery
Hotel (1.5mi); Westfield Mission
Valley (2mi)

San Diego Chicken Pie Shop (1mi);
Adams Avenue (1.1mi)

8 Lincoln Ave

Cleveland Ave
Blaine Ave
Normal St
Centre St

Washington St

8th Ave
9th Ave

Cinema Under
the Stars (0.4mi)

40 **45** **35**

9 **38** **12**

University Ave

42

41 **44**

34

Carnitas' Snack
Shack (0.6mi)

Essex St

Vermont St

Richmond St

Herbert St

Robinson Ave

Robinson Ave

HILLCREST

6th Ave
7th Ave

10th Ave

Pennsylvania Ave

Cypress Ave

Brookes Ave

Park Blvd

3rd Ave
5th Ave

37

Brookes Ave

43

7th Ave

Myrtle Ave

Walnut Ave

15

Upas St

Upas St

1st Ave
4th Ave

Thorn St

Cabrillo Fwy

Spruce St

Richmond St

Veterans
War
Memorial

Spruce St
Footbridge
(0.1mi)

33

Zoo Dr

Zoo
Parking

17 Quince St

Balboa Dr

2
**San
Diego
Zoo**

Zoo Dr

6

31 **26**

Village Pl

Nutmeg St

**BANKERS
HILL**

Maple St

29

Plaza de
Panama

46 **5** **47**

24 **23** **30** **25**

El Prado **32** **16**

13

Laurel St

5th Ave
6th Ave

36

3

Cabrillo
Bridge

California
Triangle

1 **4**
39 **22**

21

18

Kalmia St

**Mingei
International
Museum**

11

Juniper St

Balboa
Park

27

Ivy St

10

Pan-
American
Plaza

14

Presidents Way

7

Hawthorn St

20

Park Blvd

Farenholt Ave

Wieber Ave

Grape St

19

28

Fir St

Balboa Dr

Balboa Park & Hillcrest

San Diego Natural History Museum
MUSEUM

(Map p390; ☑877-946-7797; www.sdnhm.org; 1788 El Prado; adult/youth 3-17/child under 2 $19/12/free; ☺10am-5pm; ▣) The 'Nat' houses 7.5 million specimens, including rocks, fossils and taxidermied animals, as well as an impressive dinosaur skeleton and a California fault-line exhibit, all in beautiful spaces. Kids love the movies about the natural world in the giant-screen cinema; the selections change frequently. Children's programs are held most weekends. Special exhibits (some with an extra charge) span pirates to King Tut. The museum also arranges field trips and nature walks in Balboa Park and further afield.

Spanish Village Art Center
ARTS CENTER

(Map p390; ☑619-233-9050; http://spanish villageart.com; 1770 Village Place, Balboa Park; ☺11am-4pm) **FREE** Behind the Natural History Museum is a grassy square with a magnificent Moreton Bay fig tree (sorry, climbing is prohibited). Opposite there's an enclave of small tiled cottages (billed by park authorities as 'an authentic reproduction of an ancient village in Spain') that are rented out as artists' studios, where you can watch potters, jewelry makers, glassblowers, painters and sculptors churn out their crafts.

By Spanish Village and the zoo entrance there's a 1910 **carousel** (2920 Zoo Dr; tickets $2.50; ☺11am-4:30pm Sat & Sun, to 5:30pm in summer; ▣) with most of the original hand-painted animals, and a **miniature railroad** (☑619-239-4748; 1800 Zoo Pl; $3; ☺11am-4:30pm Sat, Sun & school holidays; ▣) offering three-minute, half-mile rides.

Museum of Photographic Arts
MUSEUM

(Map p390; ☑619-238-7559; www.mopa.org; Casa de Balboa, 1649 El Prado; by donation; ☺10am-5pm Tue-Sun) Tracing the history of photography, the museum offers special exhibits from crowd-pleasing animal themes to landscapes by Ansel Adams and avant-garde cell-phone photography. The museum shop is rather good too, with photography-themed gifts, Lomography camera sets, technical reads

BALBOA PARK HISTORY

Early plans for San Diego included a 1400-acre city park at the northeastern corner of what was to become Downtown, in what was then all bare hilltops, chaparral and deep arroyos. Enter Kate O Sessions, a UC Berkeley botany graduate who in 1892 started a nursery on the site to landscape fashionable gardens for the city's emerging elite. The city granted her 30 acres of land in return for planting 100 trees a year in the park and donating 300 more for placement throughout the city. By the early 20th century, Balboa Park (named for the Spanish conquistador believed to be the first European to sight the Pacific Ocean) had become a well-loved part of San Diego.

In 1915–16, Balboa Park hosted much of the grand **Panama–California Exposition**. New Yorkers Bertram Goodhue and Carleton Winslow designed the expo's pavilions in a romantic, Spanish Colonial style with beaux-arts and baroque flourishes. The pavilions were meant to be temporary – constructed largely of stucco, chicken wire, plaster, hemp and horsehair – but they proved so popular that many were later replaced with durable concrete structures in the same style. These buildings now house the museums along **El Prado**, the main pedestrian thoroughfare in the park.

The zoo also originated with the 1915–16 exposition, which featured an assortment of animals in cages along **Park Blvd**. Local legend has it that one Dr Harry Wegeforth, hearing the roar of one of the caged lions, exclaimed, 'Wouldn't it be wonderful to have a zoo in San Diego? I believe I'll build one!' Balboa Park canyons helped to separate different species and prevent the spread of disease. By the end of WWII the **San Diego Zoo** had a strong worldwide reputation, and helped to rebuild collections of European zoos that had been devastated by the war.

Another expo, the 1935 Pacific–California Exposition, brought new buildings southwest of El Prado around the **Pan-American Plaza**. The Spanish Colonial architectural theme was expanded to include the whole New World, from indigenous styles including Pueblo and Mayan.

and books on still- and moving-picture greats like Gus Van Sant.

San Diego Model Railroad Museum   MUSEUM

(Map p390; ☎619-696-0199; www.sdmrm.org; Casa de Balboa, 1649 El Balboa; adult/child 6-14yr/child under 5 $10.75/$4/free; ☉10am-4pm Tue-Fri, 11am to 5pm Sat & Sun; 🄳) Your (inner) four-year-old child will love this railroad museum; one of the largest indoor railroad museums in the world, it has some 27,000 sq ft of amazingly landscaped working models of actual Southern California railroads and stations, both historical and contemporary.

San Diego History Center   MUSEUM

(Map p390; ☎619-232-6203; www.sandiego history.org; 1649 El Prado, Suite 3; donation recommended; ☉10am-5pm Tue-Sun) FREE The San Diego Historical Society operates this center, with permanent and temporary exhibitions on city history. Previous exhibitions have included the Place of Promise exhibition covering Kumeyaay peoples to first European contact in 1542, plus 100 years of San Diego Zoo, a celebration of San Diego children's book author Theodor Geisel (Dr Seuss, of

Cat in the Hat fame), and the evolution of the San Ysidro border crossing.

Botanical Building   GARDENS

(Map p390; www.balboapark.org/tours/bo tanical-bldg; 1549 El Prado; ☉10am-4pm) FREE The Botanical Building looks lovely from El Prado, where you can see it reflected in the large lily pond that was used for hydrotherapy in WWII when the navy took over the park. The building's central dome and two wings are covered with redwood lattice panels, which let filtered sunlight into the collection of tropical plants and ferns. The planting changes every season; in December there's a particularly beautiful poinsettia display.

Timken Museum of Art   MUSEUM

(Map p390; ☎619-239-5548; www.timken museum.org; 1500 El Prado; ☉10am-4:30pm Tue-Sat, from noon Sun) FREE Don't skip the Timken, home of the small but impressive Putnam collection, featuring works by Rembrandt, Rubens, El Greco, Cézanne and Pissarro, plus a wonderful selection of Russian icons. Built in 1965, the building stands out for *not* being in imitation-Spanish style.

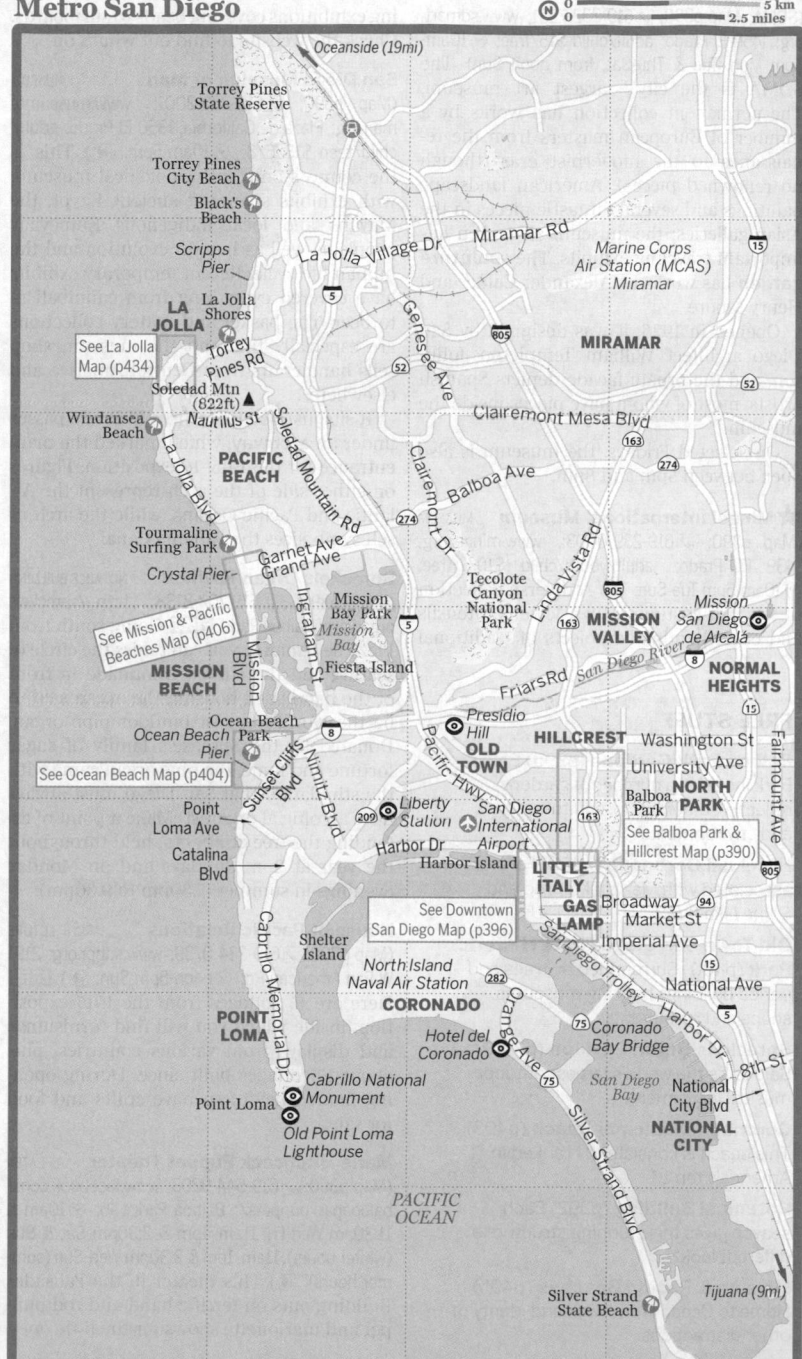

San Diego Museum of Art   MUSEUM

(SDMA; Map p390; ☑ 619-232-7931; www.sdmart. org; 1450 El Prado; adult/child $15/free; ☺ 10am-5pm Mon, Tue & Thu-Sat, from noon Sun) The SDMA is the city's largest art museum. The permanent collection has works by a number of European masters from the renaissance to the modernist eras (though no renowned pieces), American landscape paintings and several fantastic pieces in the Asian galleries; the museum also often has important traveling exhibits. The **sculpture garden** has works by Alexander Calder and Henry Moore.

Opened in 1926, it was designed by San Diego architect William Templeton Johnson, and the ornate facade depicts Spanish artists, most of whom have pieces inside the museum.

On selected Fridays, the museum is also open between 5pm and 8pm.

★ Mingei International Museum   MUSEUM

(Map p390; ☑ 619-239-0003; www.mingei.org; 1439 El Prado; adult/youth/child $10/7/free; ☺ 10am-5pm Tue-Sun; ♿) A diverse collection of folk art, costumes, toys, jewelry, utensils and other handmade objects of traditional

---

FREE STUFF

Balboa Park Gardens (p395) Balboa Park includes a number of gardens, reflecting different horticultural styles and environments.

Hotel del Coronado (p402) Forever associated with Marilyn Monroe and *Some Like It Hot.*

Old Town San Diego State Historic Park (p400) Surrounded by trees and period buildings housing museums, shops and restaurants.

Spreckels Organ Pavilion (p394) Said to be the world's largest outdoor musical instrument.

Coronado Municipal Beach (p403) This beach is consistently ranked in America's top 10.

Botanical Building (p392) Each season gives this stunning structure a different look.

Mission & Pacific Beaches (p405) Home to Ocean Front Walk and plenty of other distractions.

---

cultures from around the world, plus changing exhibitions covering beads to surfboards. Check the website to find out what's on.

San Diego Museum of Man   MUSEUM

(Map p390; ☑ 619-239-2001; www.museumofman.org; Plaza de California, 1350 El Prado; adult/child/teen $13/6/8; ☺ 10am-5pm; ♿) This is the county's only anthropological museum, with exhibits spanning ancient Egypt, the Mayans and local indigenous Kumeyaay people as well as human evolution and the human life cycle. Recent temporary exhibits have covered everything from cannibalism to beer. The basket and pottery collections are especially fine and the museum shop sells handicrafts from Central America and elsewhere.

It sits just north of where El Prado passes under an **archway**, which marked the main entrance for the 1915–16 exposition. Figures on either side of the arch represent the Atlantic and Pacific Oceans, while the arch itself symbolizes the Panama Canal.

Spreckels Organ Pavilion   NOTABLE BUILDING

(Map p390; ☑ 619-702-8138; http://spreckels organ.org; Balboa Park) **FREE** Going south from Plaza de Panama, you can't miss the circle of seating and the curved colonnade in front of the band shell housing the organ said to be the world's largest outdoor pipe organ. Donated by the Spreckels family of sugar fortune and fame, the pipe organ came with the stipulation that San Diego must always have an official organist. Make a point of attending the free **concerts**, held throughout the year at 2pm Sundays and on Monday evenings in summer (7.30pm to 9.30pm).

House of Pacific Relations   ARCHITECTURE

(Map p390; ☑ 619-234-0739; www.sdhpr.org; 2191 W Pan American Rd; ☺ noon-5pm Sun; ♿) **FREE** Here are 15 cottages from the 1915 exposition, inside which you will find furnishings and displays from various countries, plus about 15 cottages built since. During opening hours, they often have crafts and food for sale.

Marie Hitchcock Puppet Theater   THEATER

(Map p390; ☑ 619-544-9203; www.facebook.com/balboaparkpuppets/; Balboa Park; $5; ☺ 10am & 11.30am Wed-Fri, 11am, 1pm & 2:30pm Sat & Sun (winter hours), 11am, 1pm & 2.30pm Wed-Sun (summer hours); ♿) This theater in the Palisades Building puts on terrific hand and rod puppet and marionette shows for the little ones.

There have been puppet shows here since the 1940s.

San Diego Automotive Museum   MUSEUM
(Map p390; ☑ 619-231-2886; www.sdautomuseum. org; 2080 Pan American Plaza; adult/youth/child $9/4/free; ⊙10am-5pm) This museum has a permanent collection of dozens of cars and motorcycles, perfectly restored and well displayed, with classics including a 1981 De Lorean, 1990 Ferrari Testarossa, a collection of Harley Davidson and Indian motorcycles, plus a Steve McQueen exhibition. Special exhibits change quarterly.

San Diego Air & Space Museum   MUSEUM
(Map p390; ☑ 619-234-8291; www.sandiegoairand-space.org; 2001 Pan American Plaza; adult/youth/child under 2 $19.75/$10.75/free; ⊙10am-4:30pm; ⚑) The round building at the southern end of the plaza houses an excellent museum with extensive displays of aircraft throughout history – originals, replicas, models – plus memorabilia from legendary aviators, including Charles Lindbergh and astronaut John Glenn. Catch films in the 3D/4D theater.

Starlight Bowl   NOTABLE BUILDING
(Map p390; www.starlighttheatre.org; 2005 Pan American Plaza) Save Starlight (www.savestar light.org) is an initiative working to restore, revive and revitalize Starlight Bowl. The movement hopes to put on concerts, screening and hold open-air performances in this magnificent amphitheater once more.

Centro Cultural de la Raza   GALLERY
(Map p390; ☑ 619-235-6135; www.centrocultural delaraza.com; 2004 Park Blvd; suggested donation $5; ⊙noon-4pm Tue-Sun) The center hosts powerful exhibitions of Mexican and Native American art, including temporary exhibits of contemporary indigenous artwork, dance, theater and musical performances. The round, steel building, originally a water tank, is impressively painted with 240 feet of murals. It's on the edge of the main museum area of Balboa Park.

Balboa Park Gardens   GARDENS
(Map p390; ☑ 619-239-0512; www.balboapark.org/ in-the-park/Gardens; Balboa Park) Balboa Park includes a number of gardens, reflecting different horticultural styles and environments, including **Alcazar Garden**, a formal, Spanish-style garden; **Palm Canyon**, with more than 50 species of palms; **Japanese Friendship Garden** (www.niwa.org; 2215 Pan American Rd E; adult/student/child under 6yr $10/8/free; ⊙10am-7pm (last entry 6pm)); **Australian Garden**; **Rose Garden**; and **Desert Garden** (best in spring). **Florida Canyon** gives an idea of the San Diego landscape before Spanish settlement. Free tours depart the Balboa Park Visitors Center (p388) each week, covering various themes from botany to architecture. See www.balboapark.org/explore/tours for details.

Marston House   ARCHITECTURE
(Map p390; ☑ 619-297-9327; www.sohosandiego. org; 3525 7th Ave; adult/child/senior $15/7/12; ⊙10am-5pm Fri-Mon) In the far northwestern corner of Balboa Park is the former home of George Marston, philanthropist and founder of the San Diego Historical Society. Built in 1905, Marston House was designed by noted San Diego architects William Hebbard and Irving Gill, and is a fine example of the American arts-and-crafts style. Admission is by tour only.

Little Italy was settled in the mid-19th century by Italian immigrants, mostly fishermen and their families, who lived off a booming fish industry and whiskey trade.

Over the last few years, the Italian community has been joined by exciting contemporary architecture, galleries, gourmet restaurants and design and architecture businesses. Fun bars and restaurants have made this one of San Diego's hippest neighborhoods.

◎ Downtown San Diego

When Alonzo E Horton established New Town San Diego in 1867, 5th Ave was its main street, lined with saloons, gambling joints, bordellos and opium dens; it became notoriously known as the Stingaree. By the 1960s it had declined to a skid row of flophouses and bars. In the early 1980s, when developers started thinking about demolition, protests from preservationists saved the area.

Good thing. The central Downtown area, now known as the **Gaslamp Quarter**, is now prime real estate. Handsomely restored 1870s to 1920s buildings house restaurants, bars, galleries and theaters amid wrought-iron, 19th-century-style street lamps, trees and brick sidewalks. This 16-block area, south of Broadway between 4th and 6th Aves, is designated a **National Historic District**. There's still a bit of sleaze though, with a few 'adult entertainment' shops and a fair

Downtown San Diego

1st Ave
2nd Ave
3rd Ave
4th Ave

(1.5mi)

32

38

El Camino (0.15mi)

W Ivy St

Casbah (0.2mi); El Indio (1.2mi);
Shakespeare Pub & Grille (1.2mi);
Saffron (1.3mi)

LITTLE ITALY

Grape St

See Balboa Park & Hillcrest
Map (p390)

W Hawthorn St

46

Kettner Blvd

India St

Columbia St

State St

Elm St

W Grape St

San Diego Fwy

California St

W Fir St

26

30

45

W Elm St

4

20

33

W Date St

27

8

San Diego Bay

1

Maritime Museum

N Harbor Dr

County Center/
Little Italy

5

W Beech St

India St

W Cedar St

Pacific Hwy

San Diego Trolley

W Ash St

Columbia St

W A St

2nd Ave

3rd Ave

W B St

Santa Fe Depot

43

W C St

Civic Center

Cruise Ship Terminal

13

Santa Fe Depot

7

American Plaza

FINANCIAL DISTRICT

MTS Transit Store

21

22

Broadway Pier

14

Broadway

State St

Union St

Front St

1st Ave

Broadway Circle

44

51

47

Navy Pier

11

US Naval Supply Center

W E St

W F St

Kettner Blvd

W F St

24

56

Tuna La

Pantoja Park

Westfield Horton Plaza

12

W G St

DOWNTOWN

53

Tuna Harbor

Rucco Park

Seaport Village

Market St

36

54

New Children's Museum

2

28

40

42

6

W Harbor Dr

17

10

35

55

Convention Center

EMBARCADERO

San Diego Trolley

San Diego Bay

Embarcadero Marina Park

5th Ave

SAN DIEGO & AROUND SIGHTS

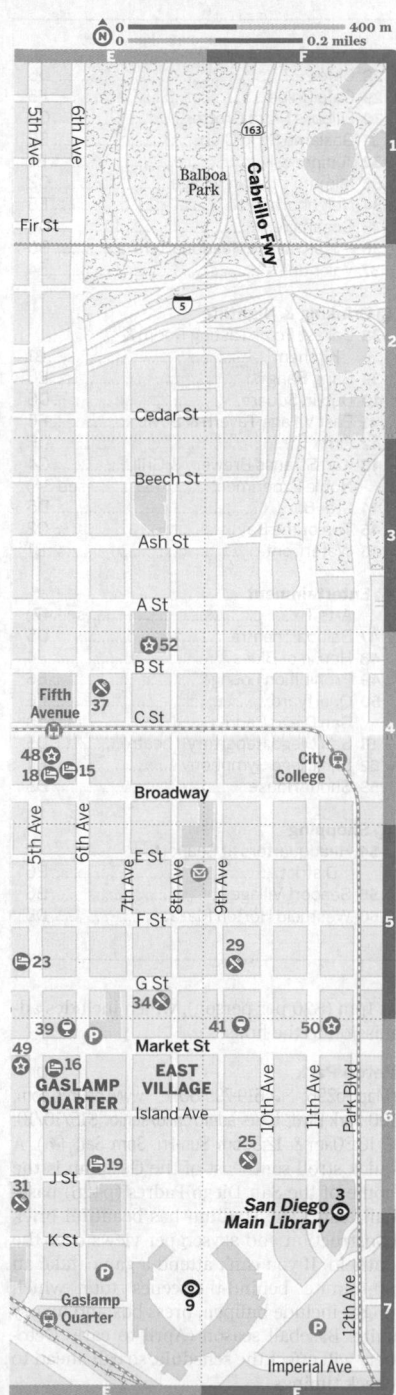

number of homeless folks, but we'll say that all lends texture.

If the Gaslamp Quarter is the center of Downtown, the **Financial District** is to the west, while east of the Gaslamp is the **East Village**, an up-and-coming enclave for local hipsters, with worldly restaurants and fun nightspots. Southwest of the Gaslamp spreads the waterfront and large hotels serving the convention center.

Museum of Contemporary Art   MUSEUM
(MCASD Downtown; Map p396; ☑ 858-454-3541; www.mcasd.org; 1001 Kettner Blvd; adult/child under 25yr/senior $10/free/$5, free 5-8pm 3rd Thu each month; ☺ 11am-5pm Thu-Tue, to 8pm 3rd Thu each month) This Financial District museum has brought an ever-changing variety of innovative artwork to San Diegans since the 1960; check the website for exhibits. Tickets are valid for seven days.

Opposite the museum, San Diego's Santa Fe Depot (aka Union Station) looks a lot like a piece from a model railway, with Spanish-style tilework and a historic Santa Fe Railway sign on top. It was built in conjunction with the 1915 exposition in the hopes that the Santa Fe Railway would make San Diego its terminus; that designation eventually went to Los Angeles.

★ **New Children's Museum**   MUSEUM
(Map p396; ☑ 619-233-8792; www.thinkplaycreate. org; 200 W Island Ave; $13; ☺ 10am-4pm Mon, Wed, Thu & Sat, 9.30am-4pm Fri, noon-4pm Sun; ⊞) This interactive children's museum offers interactive art meant for kids. Installations are designed by artists, so tykes can learn principles of movement and physics while simultaneously being exposed to art and working out the ants in their pants. Exhibits change every 18 months or so, so there's always something new.

If you need to get the kids outdoors, there's a futuristic **playground** across the street, and for a more traditional children's museum (with science exhibits and such), visit the Reuben H Fleet Science Center (p389).

San Diego Chinese Historical Museum   MUSEUM
(Map p396; ☑ 619-338-9888; www.sdchm.org; 404 3rd Ave; adult/child $5/free; ☺ 10:30am-4pm Tue-Sun) The historic heart of San Diego's Chinese community is 3rd Ave. Immigrants were once taught English and religion in the Chinese Mission Building, built in the 1920s. Displays include Chinese-American artifacts

Downtown San Diego

◉ Top Sights
1 Maritime Museum...................................A3
2 New Children's Museum.......................D6
3 San Diego Main Library.........................F6

◎ Sights
4 Amici Park...C2
5 Firehouse Museum................................C2
6 Gaslamp Museum & William
   Heath Davis House............................D6
7 Museum of Contemporary Art............B4
8 Our Lady of the Rosary Catholic
   Church..C2
9 Petco Park.. E7
10 San Diego Chinese Historical
   Museum...D6
   US Grant Hotel ....(see 22)
11 USS Midway Museum A5

☺ Activities, Courses & Tours
12 Another Side of San Diego...................D5
13 Flagship Cruises....................................A4
14 Hornblower Cruises...............................A5

☐ Sleeping
15 Courtyard by Marriott San
   Diego Downtown................................ E4
16 HI San Diego Downtown Hostel............E6
17 Horton Grand Hotel...............................D6
18 Hotel Palomar San Diego......................E4
19 Hotel Solamar...................................... E6
20 La Pensione Hotel.................................B2
21 Sofia Hotel...D4
22 US Grant Hotel......................................D4
23 USA Hostels San Diego........................ E5

⊗ Eating
24 Bandar...D5
25 Basic..F6
26 Bencotto..B2
27 Burger Lounge.......................................B2

28 Café 222..D6
29 Café Chloe..F5
30 Filippi's Pizza Grotto.............................C2
31 Gaslamp Strip Club................................E6
32 Juniper & Ivy..B1
33 Mimmo's Italian Village........................C2
34 Neighborhood..E5
35 Oceanaire...D6
36 Puesto at the Headquarters.................B6
37 Valentine's...E4

◉ Drinking & Nightlife
38 Ballast Point Tasting Room &
   Kitchen...B1
39 Bang Bang...E6
40 Dublin Square..D6
41 East Village Tavern & Bowl....................F6
42 Fluxx..D6
43 Karl Strauss Brewery & Grill.................C4
   Noble Experiment.........................(see 34)
44 Star Bar...D5
45 Top of the Bay......................................C2
46 Waterfront...B1

✪ Entertainment
   Arts Tix..(see 47)
47 Balboa Theatre......................................D5
48 House of Blues......................................E4
49 Prohibition Lounge...............................E6
50 Quartyard..F6
   San Diego Padres...........................(see 9)
51 San Diego Repertory Theatre...............D5
52 San Diego Symphony...........................E4
53 Shout House..D5

⊜ Shopping
54 Headquarters at Seaport
   District..B6
55 Seaport Village......................................B6
56 Westfield Horton Plaza.........................D5

and local art objects, and the small, white stucco structure boasts decorative red tiles, hardwood floors, and an inviting backyard.

**Gaslamp Museum & William
Heath Davis House**   MUSEUM
(Map p396; ☎619-233-4692; www.gaslampquarter.
org; 410 Island Ave; adult/senior & student $5/4,
walking tour $10/8; ☺10am-5pm Tue-Sat, noon-
4pm Sun) This house, a prefab affair brought
from Maine in 1850, contains a small museum with 19th-century furnishings, plus historic newspaper clippings in the basement.
From here, the Gaslamp Quarter Historical
Foundation leads a weekly, 90-minute **walking tour** of the neighborhood on Thursdays

at 1pm ($20 per person), which includes admission to the house.

Petco Park   STADIUM
(Map p396; ☎619-795-5011; www.padres.com;
100 Park Blvd; tours adult/child/senior $15/10/10;
☺10:30am & 12:30pm Sun-Fri, 3pm Sat; ⊞) A
quick stroll southeast of the Gaslamp is the
home of the San Diego Padres (p426) baseball team. The stadium has beautiful brick
construction and skyscraper views over the
outfield. If you can't attend a game, take an
80-minute behind-the-scenes tour which
might include bullpen, press box and luxury
suite. Baseball season (April to early October) will affect the schedule, so call ahead to
check timings.

★ **San Diego Main Library**　　LIBRARY
(Map p396; ☑ 619-236-5800; www.sandiego.gov/
public-library; 330 Park Blvd; ⊙ 9:30am-7pm Mon-
Thu, 9.30am-6pm Fri & Sat, noon-6pm Sun) FREE
A couple blocks east of Petco Park (p398),
the city's recent landmark is a beauty.
Crowned by a steel-and-mesh dome, the futuristic, nine-story library features art-filled
public spaces and plenty of learning opportunities – it has the second largest collection
of baseball memorabilia in the US. It's fully
open to the public for a wander and you can
even log on to the free wi-wi. The architect?
Rob Wellington Quigley, who also designed
the New Children's Museum (p397).

US Grant Hotel　　NOTABLE BUILDING
(Map p396; ☑ 619-232-3121; www.usgrant.net; 326
Broadway) No hotel in the region can com
pare to the Hotel del Coronado (p402) for
history, but US Grant, built in 1910, comes
close. It's on the National Register of Historic Places for its past including celebrity
guests, magnificent ballrooms, a one-time
Turkish bath and a speakeasy. Visitors can
take a tour with advance reservation by calling the concierge desk.

⊙ Uptown: Bankers Hill, Hillcrest & North Park

Uptown is roughly a triangle north of Downtown, east of Old Town and south of Mission
Valley. There aren't any big-ticket sights
here, but this string of neighborhoods is a
good place to see some Victorian and art-
deco architecture and observe day-to-day
life. Hillcrest, particularly, is one of San
Diego's most diverse and desirable neighborhoods.

In the late 19th century it was fashionable to live in the hills north of Downtown,
since only those who owned a horse-drawn
carriage could afford it. Called **Bankers Hill**
after some of the wealthy residents – or Pill
Hill because of the many doctors there – the
upscale heights had unobstructed views of
the bay and Point Loma before I-5 was built.

Among the Victorian mansions, the 1889
Long-Waterman House (Map p290; 2408 1st
Ave) is easily recognized by its towers, gables,
bay windows and verandah; it was once the
home of former California governor Robert Waterman. Also notable is the **Timken
House** (Map p390; 2508 1st Ave), one block
north. The 375ft **Spruce St Footbridge**
(btwn Front & Brant Sts) hangs over a deep canyon and the **Quince St Bridge** (Map p390;

btwn 3rd & 4th Aves) is a wood-trestle bridge
built in 1905 and refurbished in 1988 after
community activists protested its slated
demolition. In **Mission Hills**, a 1970s shingled complex at the corner of Washington
and India Sts houses mostly eateries.

The heart of Uptown is **Hillcrest**, the first
suburban real-estate development in San
Diego. Driving around, you'll see the work
of many of San Diego's best-known early-
20th-century architects, including Irving
Gill and William Templeton Johnson, alongside Mediterranean, Spanish Mission and
arts-and-crafts styles. But Hillcrest's chief
attraction is its lively street life, due largely
to its status as the center of San Diego's gay
and lesbian community.

Begin at the **Hillcrest Gateway** (Map
p390; University & 5th Ave), an illuminated electric sign that arches over University Ave at
5th Ave. East on University Ave at No 535,
look for the 1928 **Kahn Building** (Map p390;
535 University Ave), an original commercial
building with architectural elements that
border on kitsch. Hillcrest's **farmers market** (Map p390; ☑ 619-237-1632; http://hillcrest
farmersmarket.com; cnr Normal St & Lincoln Ave;
⊙ 9am-2pm Sun) 🍴 is considered one of
the best in town, and is great for people-
watching.

East of Hillcrest is the hipster neighborhood of **North Park**, centered on 30th and
University Aves. Around this area is a growing center of art in small studios and galleries around Ray St, a low-key gourmet scene,
some cool bars and an inordinate number
of hair salons.

⊙ Little Italy

Bounded by Hawthorn and Ash Sts on the
north and south, and Front St and the waterfront on the east and west, Little Italy
was settled in the mid-19th century by Italian immigrants, mostly fishermen and their
families, who created a cohesive and thriving community based on a booming fish industry and whiskey trade (which some claim
was backed by local Mafia). The community
still thrives in the many restaurants and cafes along busy India St.

Over the last few years, the Italian community has been joined by exciting contemporary architecture, and an influx of galleries,
gourmet restaurants, and design and architecture businesses have transformed Little
Italy into one of the hippest places to live,
eat and shop in downtown San Diego.

Our Lady of the Rosary
Catholic Church　　　　　　CHURCH
(Map p396; ☎619-234-4820; www.olrsd.org; cnr State & Date Sts) The rich ceiling murals here were painted by an Italian who was flown over to do the work. The church, built in 1925, is still a hub for Little Italy activity and is among San Diego's best pieces of religious art. Across the street in **Amici Park** (Union St), locals play bocce, an Italian form of outdoor bowling.

Firehouse Museum　　　　　　MUSEUM
(Map p396; ☎619-232-3473; www.sandiegofire housemuseum.com; 1572 Columbia St at Cedar St; adult/child $3/2; ☺10am-2pm Thu & Fri, to 4pm Sat & Sun; ℗) This museum preserves a historic collection of fire-fighting equipment and has exhibits depicting some of San Diego's 'hottest' moments from the late 1800s.

⊙ Old Town

Under the Mexican government, which took power in San Diego in 1821, any settlement with a population of 500 or more was entitled to become a 'pueblo,' and the area below the Presidio became the first official civilian Mexican settlement in California – the Pueblo de San Diego. A plaza was laid out around Casa de Estudillo, home of the pueblo's commandant, and within 10 years it was surrounded by about 40 huts and several houses. This square mile of land (roughly 10 times what remains in Old Town today) was also the center of American San Diego until the fire of 1872, after which the city's main body moved to what's now Downtown (then called New Town).

John Spreckels built a trolley line from New Town to Old Town in the 1920s and, to attract passengers, began restoring the old district. In 1968, the area was named Old Town State Historic Park, archaeological work began, and the few surviving original buildings were restored. Now it's a pedestrian district of shade trees, a large open plaza, and shops and restaurants.

Old Town Transit Center (www.amtrak. com; 4009 Taylor St) is an important transit hub for the *Coaster* commuter train, the **San Diego Trolley** (☎619-233-3004; www. sdmts.com) and buses. Old Town Trolley (p409) tours stop southeast of the plaza on Twiggs St. There is free parking in lots and on streets around Old Town.

★**Old Town San Diego**
State Historic Park　　　　HISTORIC SITE
(☎619-220-5422; www.parks.ca.gov; 4002 Wallace St; ☺visitor center & museums 10am-5pm daily; ℗ ♿) **FREE** This park has an excellent history museum in the **Robinson-Rose House** at the southern end of the plaza. You'll also find a diorama depicting the original pueblo at the park's **visitor center**, where you can pick up a copy of the *Old Town San Diego State Historic Park Tour Guide & Brief History* ($3), or a presentation tour (free) at 11am and 2pm daily. Personal tours cost $10 and depart at 11:30am and 1pm.

Across from the visitor center, the restored **Casa de Estudillo** is filled with authentic period furniture. Other buildings around the plaza include the first San Diego Courthouse/jail and the **Fiesta de Reyes**, just off the plaza's northwestern corner, is a colorful collection of import shops and restaurants – great for Mexican souvenirs without the trip to Tijuana. Along San Diego Ave, on the southern side of the plaza, small, historical-looking buildings (only one is authentic) house more souvenir and gift shops.

Whaley House　　　HISTORIC BUILDING
(☎619-297-7511; www.whaleyhouse.org; 2476 San Diego Ave; adult/child before 5pm $8/6, after 5pm $13/8; ☺10am-9:30pm daily summer, 10am-4:30pm Sun-Tue, to 9:30pm Thu-Sat rest of the year) Two blocks from the Old Town perimeter sits the city's oldest brick building (circa 1856), officially certified as haunted by the US Department of Commerce. Check out the collection of period furniture and clothing from when the house served as a courthouse, theater and private residence. After 5pm, admission is by tour only.

El Campo Santo　　　　　CEMETERY
(San Diego Ave, btwn Arista & Conde Sts) Continuing east, after San Diego Ave forks right at Conde St, you'll find this cemetery which dates from 1849. It is the resting place of some 20 souls, a simple dirt yard with the biographies of the deceased on signage above the graves.

Casa de Carillo　　　NOTABLE BUILDING
(cnr Juan & Wallace Sts) Just north of Old Town, this house dates from about 1820 and is said to be the oldest house in San Diego. It is now the pro shop for the public 18-hole **Presidio Hills Golf Course** (☎619-295-9476; www.pre sidiohillsgolf.com; 4136 Wallace St; greens fee $10 weekdays, $12 Fri-Sun).

Presidio Hill   HISTORIC SITE

In 1769 Padre Junípero Serra and Gaspar de Portolá established the first Spanish settlement in California overlooking the valley of the San Diego River. Walk up from Old Town along Mason St for excellent views of San Diego Bay and Mission Valley. Atop the hill, **Presidio Park** has several walking trails and shaded benches. A large cross, made with tiles from the original mission, commemorates Padre Serra.

A flagpole, a cannon, some plaques and earth walls now form the **Fort Stockton Memorial**, commemorating the fort built when American forces occupied the hill in 1846 during the Mexican-American War. The nearby **El Charro Statue**, a bicentennial gift to the city from Mexico, depicts a Mexican cowboy on horseback. Nothing remains of the original Presidio structures; the mission (p401) was later moved upriver.

Junípero Serra Museum   MUSEUM

(☑619-232-6203; www.sandiegohistory.org/serra_museum; 2727 Presidio Dr; by donation; ⊘10am-4pm Fri-Sun early Jun-early Sep, 10am-5pm Sat & Sun early Sep-early Jun; P⚫) Located at one of the most important sites in the city, the Junípero Serra Museum stands atop Presidio Hill, the place where California first began. In 1769, the first mission, known as the Mission San Diego de Alcalá, was established here before it was moved 7 miles upriver. The current Presidio building is Spanish Revival in style and houses a small but interesting collection of artifacts and pictures from San Diego's Mission and rancho periods.

It offers a good insight into the earliest days of European settlement up to 1929 when the museum was founded.

⊙ **Embarcadero & the Waterfront**

South and west of the Gaslamp Quarter, San Diego's well-manicured waterfront **promenades** stretch along Harbor Dr and are perfect for strolling or jogging. Southwest of the ship museums is Seaport Village (p427), with restaurants and gift shops, and the convention center (1989), with its sail-inspired roof that stretches for a half mile. Another gathering place is the former police headquarters (p427), now turned into a shopping center.

WORTH A TRIP

MISSION BASILICA SAN DIEGO DE ALCALA

The state's first Franciscan mission, **Mission Basilica San Diego de Alcalá** (☑619-281-8449; www.mission-sandiego.com; 10818 San Diego Mission Rd; adult/child/under 5 $5/2/free; ⊘9am-4:30pm; P⚫), is still active today. The striking painted-white structure stands proud against San Diego's blue skies. Note the five hanging bells on the church's facade – very important to daily life at any mission, they were rung to call the residents to work, mealtimes, religious services, or to signal approaching ships. A bell celebration takes place every July at the mission. The rest of the year it is open to visitors, who can learn about its history and visit the gift shop.

The mission sits north of an unlovely stretch of shopping centers and hotels along I-8 (take the Mission Gorge Rd exit); or take the **San Diego Trolley** (p400) Green Line to Mission San Diego, cutting through a scenic corridor not seen from the freeway.

★ **Maritime Museum**   MUSEUM

(Map p396; ☑619-234-9153; www.sdmaritime.org; 1492 N Harbor Dr; adult/child $16/8; ⊘9am-9pm late May-early Sep, to 8pm early Sep-late May; ⚫) This museum is easy to find: look for the 100ft-high masts of the iron-hulled square-rigger *Star of India*. Built on the Isle of Man and launched in 1863, the tall ship plied the England–India trade route, carried immigrants to New Zealand, became a trading ship based in Hawaii and, finally, ferried cargo in Alaska. It's a handsome vessel, but don't expect anything romantic or glamorous on board.

USS Midway Museum   MUSEUM

(Map p396; ☑619-544-9600; www.midway.org; 910 N Harbor Dr; adult/child $20/$10; ⊘10am-5pm, last admission 4pm; P⚫) The giant aircraft carrier USS *Midway* was one of the navy's flagships from 1945 to 1991, last playing a combat role in the First Gulf War. On the flight deck of the hulking vessel, walk right up to some 29 restored aircraft including an F-14 Tomcat and F-4 Phantom jet fighter. Admission includes an audio tour along the narrow confines of the upper decks to the bridge, admiral's war room, brig and 'pri-fly' (primary flight control; the carrier's equivalent of a control tower). Parking costs $10.

👁 Coronado

Across the bay from downtown San Diego, Coronado is a civilized escape from the jumble of the city and the chaos of the beaches. After crossing the bay by ferry or via the elegantly curved 2.12-mile-long Coronado Bay Bridge, follow the tree-lined, manicured median strip of Orange Ave a mile or so toward the commercial center, Coronado Village. Then park your car; you won't need it again until you leave.

The story of Coronado is in many ways the story of the Hotel del Coronado (p402), opened in 1888 by John D Spreckels, the millionaire who bankrolled the first rail line to San Diego, took over Coronado and turned the island into one of the West Coast's most fashionable getaways.

As an alternative to ferries, water taxis and bike rentals, bus 901 from downtown San Diego runs along Orange Ave to the Hotel del Coronado. The Old Town Trolley (p409) tour stops in front of Mc P's Irish Pub (p424).

Hotel del Coronado   HISTORIC BUILDING
(☎ 619-435-6611; www.hoteldel.com; 1500 Orange Ave, Coronado; P 🚗) Few hotels in the world are as easily recognized or as well loved as 'The Del.' The world's largest resort (p413) when it was built in 1888, the all-timber, whitewashed main building offers conical towers, cupolas, turrets, balconies, dormer windows and cavernous public spaces typical of their designers, railroad-depot architects James and Merritt Reid. Acres

---

TOP SAN DIEGO BEACHES

Choosing San Diego's best beaches is like comparing jewels at Tiffany. **Coronado Municipal Beach** (p403) has appeared on just about every top 10 list; others depend on what you're looking for.

Bodysurfing Pacific Beach (p405) and **La Jolla Shores**. Experienced bodysurfers can head to La Jolla for the big swells of Boomer Beach near La Jolla Cove, the forceful waves at **Windansea** (p435) or the beach at the end of Sea Lane.

Family friendly Shell Beach (La Jolla), 15th St Beach (Del Mar), Moonlight Beach (Encinitas).

Nude beach Black's Beach (p435).

Surf breaks With 75 miles of surfable coastline San Diego, here are some of the main spots from south to north.

➡ **Imperial Beach (via Silver Strand)** (p403) is best in winter.

➡ **Point Loma** is great for reef breaks; it's less accessible but less crowded.

➡ **Sunset Cliffs** (p405) in Ocean Beach, where some reefs are hard to access at high tide without a bit of rock climbing, is best during winter.

➡ **Pacific Beach** (p405) is the busiest beach, with a top longboarding spot to the north at Tourmaline Surfing Park.

➡ **Big Rock** (p435) is California's answer to Pipeline.

➡ **Windansea** (p435) has a hot reef break but is surfed by territorial locals.

➡ **La Jolla Shores** is good for family fun and sandbars galore.

➡ **Black's Beach** (p435) offers a fast, powerful wave.

➡ **Cardiff State Beach** (p443) has two reefs.

➡ **San Elijo State Beach** (p443) in Cardiff is known to produce barrels.

➡ **Swami's** in Encinitas has a first-class reef break.

➡ **Carlsbad State Beach** (P) has an exposed beach break with reliable conditions.

➡ **Oceanside Pier** (p449) is a popular short-boarders spot with right and left rides all year round.

Teen scene Mission Beach, Pacific Beach.

of polished wood give the interior a warm, old-fashioned feel that conjures daydreams of Panama hats and linen suits.

The hotel achieved its widest exposure when it was featured in the 1959 movie *Some Like It Hot,* which earned it a lasting association with Marilyn Monroe. Other guests have included 11 US presidents and world royalty whose pictures and mementos adorn the hotel's history gallery. There's speculation that Edward (then Prince of Wales) first met Mrs Simpson (then Mrs Spencer) when he visited in 1920, though the two did not become an item until years later.

There's an interesting resident ghost story, too, about a jilted woman who haunts the hotel; some claim she silently appears in hallways, messes with the lights and with the TV screen in the room where she had her heart broken. In case you were wondering – it's room 3327 on the 5th floor in the Victorian building.

For a taste of the Del without a stay, enjoy breakfast or lunch at the beach-view **Sheerwater** restaurant or splurge on Sunday brunch under the grand dome of the spectacular Crown Room, under chandeliers designed by L Frank Baum, who wrote *The Wonderful Wizard of Oz.*

Coronado Municipal Beach   BEACH
(www.coronado.ca.us; P) Just beyond the 'Hotel Del (p402)', this beach is consistently ranked in America's top 10. Four-and-a-half miles south of Coronado Village is the white-sand **Silver Strand State Beach** (619-435-5184; www.parks.ca.gov; 5000 Hwy 75, Coronado; per car $10, RV camping from $50; 7am-sunset; P). Both have warm, calm water, perfect for swimming and great for families.

Coronado Museum of History and Art   MUSEUM
(619-435-7242; www.coronadohistory.org; 1100 Orange Ave; 9am-5pm Mon-Fri, from 10am Sat & Sun) FREE Exhibits on local history and art and a huge archive of 20,000 photos.

Point Loma Area

On maps Point Loma looks like an elephant's trunk guarding the entrance to San Diego Bay. Highlights are the Cabrillo National Monument (p403) (at the end of the trunk), the shopping and dining of Liberty Public Market (p419) (at its base) and seafood meals around **Shelter Island**.

There's plenty of history here, too. San Diego's first fishing boats were based at Point Loma and in the 19th century whalers dragged whale carcasses here from faraway oceans to extract the precious and useful oil. Chinese fishermen settled on the harbor side of the point in the 1860s but were forced off in 1888 when the US Congress passed the Scott Act, prohibiting anyone without citizenship papers from entering the area. Portuguese fishing families arrived approximately 50 years later, around the same time that Italian immigrants settled in present-day Little Italy.

In 1927, Charles Lindbergh tested his *Spirit of St Louis* airplane on the tidal flats of **Loma Portal,** where Point Loma joins the mainland (at the elephant's neck). The following year an airport was established at his airstrip and named Lindbergh Field, now San Diego International Airport.

By WWII, the San Diego Naval Training Center by the bay had reached its peak population of around 33,000. It was decommissioned as a training center in 1997 and nowadays the attractive, 361-acre grounds and stately Spanish-style buildings, renamed Liberty Station (p427), are a mixed-use complex of restaurants, shops, food markets and galleries.

Cabrillo National Monument   MONUMENT
(619-557-5450; www.nps.gov/cabr; 1800 Cabrillo Memorial Dr; per car $10; 9am-5pm; P) Atop a steep hill at the tip of the peninsula, this is San Diego's finest locale for history, views and nature walks. It's also the best place in town to see the gray-whale migration (January to March) from land. You may forget you're in a major metropolitan area.

The **visitor center** has a comprehensive, old-school presentation on Portuguese explorer Juan Rodríguez Cabrillo's 1542 voyage up the California coast, plus exhibits on early Native Californian inhabitants and the area's natural history.

Ocean Beach

San Diego's most Bohemian seaside community is a place of seriously scruffy haircuts, facial hair and body art. You can get tattooed, shop for antiques and walk into a restaurant barefoot and shirtless without anyone batting an eyelid. **Newport Avenue,** the main drag, runs perpendicular to the beach through a compact business district of

Ocean Beach

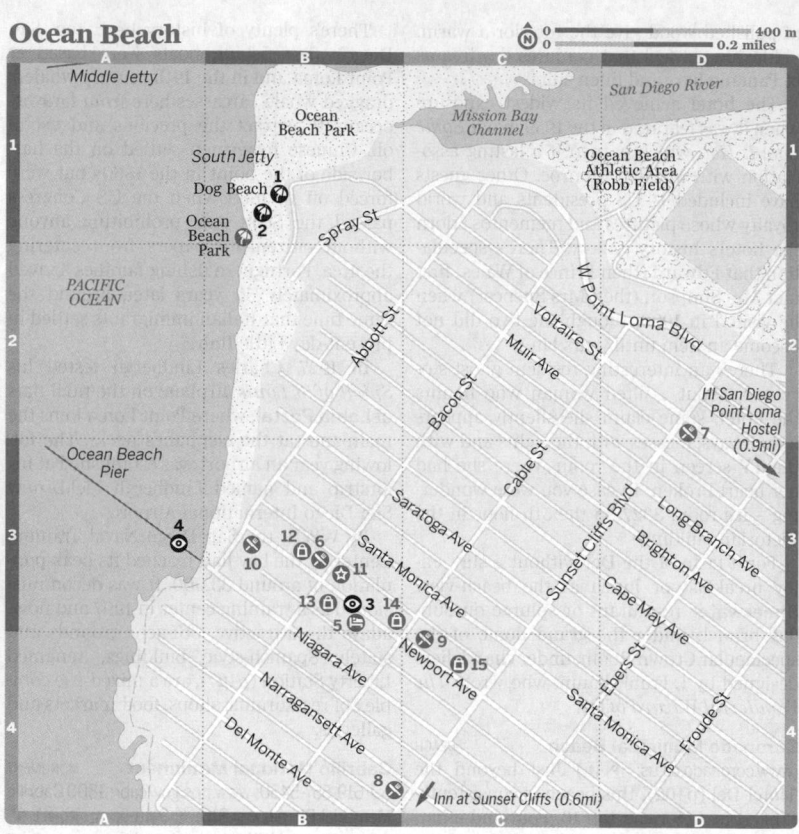

Ocean Beach

bars, surf shops, music stores, used-clothing stores and antiques consignment stores.

Ocean Beach Pier PIER
(Map p404; ☺daylight hours, times vary) This half-mile-long pier has all the architectural allure of a freeway ramp, but at its end you'll have a great perspective on the coast. There's also a **bait and tackle shop** where you can rent fishing poles ($20 per day) to fish off the pier.

Ocean Beach Coast
BEACH

(Map p404) Just north of the pier (p404), near the end of Newport Ave, is the beach scene's epicenter, with volleyball courts and sunset barbecues. Further north on **Dog Beach** (☉24hr; 🐾) pups chase birds around the marshy area where the San Diego River meets the sea. Head a few blocks south of the pier to **Sunset Cliffs Park**, where surfing and sunsets are the main attractions.

There are good surf breaks at the cliffs and, to the south, off Point Loma. Under the pier, skilful surfers slalom the pilings, but the rips and currents can be hazardous unless you know what you're doing.

Ocean Beach Farmers Market
MARKET

(Map p404; 4900 block of Newport Ave; ☉4-7pm Wed Nov-Mar, to 8pm Wed Apr-Oct) 🌿 If you're here on Wednesday afternoon, stop by the farmers market to see street performers and sample fresh food.

◉ Mission Bay, Mission Beach & Pacific Beach

The big-ticket attraction around Mission Bay is SeaWorld, while the nearby beaches are the **SoCal** of the movies: buffed surfers and bronzed bohemians pack the 3-mile-long stretch of beach. For a cruise of the area, try Bahia Belle (p409).

Mission Bay
PARK

(Map p406; www.sandiego.gov/park-and-recreation; P 🖥) Just east of Mission and Pacific Beaches (p405) is this 7-sq-mile playground, with 27 miles of shoreline and 90 acres of parks on islands, coves and peninsulas. Sailing, windsurfing and kayaking dominate northwest Mission Bay, while waterskiers zip around **Fiesta Island**. Kite flying is popular in **Mission Bay Park**, beach volleyball is big on Fiesta Island, and there's delightful cycling and inline skating on the miles of bike paths.

Although hotels, boat yards and other businesses dot about one-quarter of the land, it feels wide open. Fun fact: Spanish explorers called this expanse at the mouth of the San Diego River 'False Bay' – it formed a shallow bay when the river flowed and a marshy swamp when it didn't. After WWII, a combination of civic vision and coastal engineering turned it into a recreational area.

Mission & Pacific Beaches
BEACH

(Map p406) FREE Central San Diego's best beach scene is concentrated in a narrow strip of land between the ocean and Mission Bay. There's amazing people-watching on the **Ocean Front Walk**, the boardwalk that connects the two beaches. From South Mission Jetty to Pacific Beach Point, it's crowded with joggers, in-line skaters and cyclists any time of the year. On warm summer weekends, oiled bodies, packed like sardines, cover the beach from end to end and cheer the setting sun.

While there's lots to do here, perhaps the best use of an afternoon is to walk along the boardwalk, then spread a blanket or kick back over cocktails and take in the scenery.

A block off Mission Beach, Mission Blvd (the main north–south road), is lined with surf, smoke and swimwear shops. Cheap Rentals (p407) loans bikes, skates and surfboards.

In Pacific Beach, to the north, activity extends inland, particularly along Garnet (pronounced gar-net) Ave, lined with bars, restaurants and shops, mostly targeted at a 20-something crowd. At the ocean end of Garnet Ave, **Crystal Pier** is a mellow place to fish or gaze out to sea.

At peak times these beaches can get supercrowded: parking around noon is just not gonna happen.

Belmont Park
AMUSEMENT PARK

(☎858-228-9283; www.belmontpark.com; 3146 Mission Blvd; per ride $3-6, all-day pass adult/child $30/20; ☉from 11am daily, closing times vary; P) This old-style family-amusement park at the southern end of Mission Beach has been here since 1925. There's a large indoor pool, known as the **Plunge**, and a classic wooden roller coaster named the **Giant Dipper**, plus adventure golf, a new escape-room game, a carousel and other classics. More modern attractions include wave machines like Flowrider (p407), for simulated surfing. Even if it sits on dry land, Belmont is to San Diego what the Santa Monica Pier amusement park is to LA.

During winter months check for closures due to ride maintenance.

SeaWorld San Diego
AMUSEMENT PARK

(☎619-222-4732; www.seaworldsandiego.com; 500 SeaWorld Dr; adult/child 3-9yr $93/87, parking $17; ☉10am-7pm; P 🖥) Opened in San Diego in 1964, SeaWorld became one of California's most popular theme parks. Visitors shuttle between aquatic-themed rides, animal encounters and exhibits. However, the park's best-known attractions are also its most

Mission & Pacific Beaches

N 0 ———————— 400 m
0 ———————— 0.2 miles

Mission & Pacific Beaches

⊙ Sights
1 Mission & Pacific Beaches	A2
2 Mission Bay	B4

Activities, Courses & Tours
3 Bob's Mission Surf	A2
4 Cheap Rentals	A4
5 Mission Bay Sportcenter	B4
6 Pacific Beach Surf Shop	A2

Sleeping
7 Beach Cottages	A2
8 Catamaran Resort Hotel	B3
9 Crystal Pier Hotel & Cottages	A1
10 Tower 23	A1

⊗ Eating
JRDN	(see 10)
11 Kono's Surf Club	A1
12 World Famous	A2

Drinking & Nightlife
13 Bub's Dive	B1
14 Café 976	B1
Pacific Beach Ale House	(see 3)
15 Society Billiard Cafe	B1
16 The Grass Skirt	B2

Entertainment
17 710 Beach Club	A1

Shopping
Buffalo Exchange	(see 15)
18 Pangaea Outpost	B1
19 South Coast Wahines	A1

controversial: live shows featuring trained dolphins, sea lions and killer whales. Since the release of the 2013 documentary *Blackfish*, SeaWorld's treatment of its captive orcas has come under intense scrutiny and the company has been hit by falling visitor numbers and a catalogue of negative PR.

The film is a damning portrayal of the effects of keeping killer whales in captivity and charts the life of Tilikum, an orca at SeaWorld Orlando that was involved in the deaths of three people, including one of its trainers during a live show. Since the release of *Blackfish* many animal-welfare groups have come out in support of the film, arguing that it is harmful and stressful to keep such sensitive, complex creatures inside an enclosed tank. SeaWorld issued a statement accusing the film makers of giving false and misleading information and made plans to double the size of its orca tanks. These plans are no longer going ahead; instead the park

is in the process of investing $100 million in new attractions like Ocean Explorer, which will mix aquariums with digital technology, and promoting the park's conservation efforts. As of 2017, SeaWorld has stopped breeding the whales in captivity and has said it will phase out theatrical orca shows. Whether this effort stems the tide of public criticism is yet to be seen.

Other animal enclosures inside SeaWorld include **Penguin Encounter** where several penguin species share a habitat that simulates Antarctic living conditions. The **Wild Arctic** attraction includes polar-bear, walrus and beluga-whale enclosures, and the **Shark Encounter** offers the chance to see different species of shark as you walk through a 57ft acrylic tunnel. There are also amusement-park-style rides available like the cable-car **Bayside Skyride** and the damp **Shipwreck Rapids**.

🏃 Activities

There are plenty of hikes in San Diego, but most outdoor activities involve the ocean. These waters are a dream for surfers, paddleboarders, kayakers and boaters.

Surfing

A good number of residents moved to San Diego just for the surfing, and boy, is it good. Even beginners will understand why it's so popular.

Fall brings strong swells and offshore Santa Ana winds. In summer swells come from the south and southwest, and in winter from the west and northwest. Spring brings more frequent onshore winds, but the surfing can still be good. For the latest beach, weather and surf reports, call **San Diego County Lifeguard Services** (☑ 619-221-8824).

Beginners should head to Mission or Pacific Beach (p405) for beach breaks (soft-sand bottomed). North of Crystal Pier, **Tourmaline Surfing Park** is a crowded, but good, improvers spot for those comfortable surfing reef.

Rental rates vary depending on the quality of the equipment, but figure on soft boards from around $15/45 per hour/full-day; wetsuits cost $7/28. Packages are available.

Pacific Beach Surf Shop SURFING
(Map p406; ☑ 858-373-1138; www.pbsurfshop.com; 4150 Mission Blvd; group surfing lessons from $75; ⊘ store 9am-6pm (winter), 9am-7pm (summer)) This shop provides instruction through its Pacific Beach Surf School. It has friendly service and also rents wet suits and both soft (foam) and hard (fiberglass) boards. Call ahead for lessons, offered hourly until 3pm in winter and 5pm in summer.

Bob's Mission Surf SURFING
(Map p406; ☑ 858-483-8837; www.missionsurf.com; 4320 Mission Blvd, Pacific Beach; surfboard rentals from $10 (soft-top) $20 (hardboard); ⊘ 10am-7pm) Rent stand-up paddleboards and bikes in addition to surf equipment.

Cheap Rentals SURFING
(Map p406; ☑ 858-488-9070, 800-941-7761; 3689 Mission Blvd, Pacific Beach; foam surfboards from $7 per hour; ⊘ 10am-6pm) Rents bikes and skates ($6/15 per hour/day), plus surfboards and wet suits ($12 per day) at Pacific Beach. The store also takes reservations for rentals.

Flowrider SURFING
(Map p406; ☑ 858-228-9283; www.belmontpark.com/flow/; WaveHouse Beach Club, 3125 Ocean Front Walk; wave-riding per hour $30) FREE No surf? As of 2019, you'll be able to ride this artificial wave machine. It pumps gallons of water out creating a barreling crest; beginner waves also available. During summer months you can grab a drink and bite to eat and watch the action.

SAN DIEGO FOR KIDS

Tiny hands down, San Diego is one of America's best destinations for family travel. Here are some highlights to jump-start your vacation.

Do the **zoo** (p389); it's everything they say and more, and while you're there spend another day enjoying the rest of **Balboa Park** (p388), one of the nation's best collections of museums. The **Reuben H Fleet Science Center** (p389), **Model Railroad Museum** (p392) and **Natural History Museum** (p391) are all tailor-made for kids, and the plazas, fountains and gardens offer plenty of space for them to let off steam.

Kids elementary-school age and older will appreciate **Old Town San Diego State Historic Park** (p400) and the Mexican restaurants nearby.

Along the coast, **SeaWorld** (p405) is another national landmark (look for specials and combo tickets to keep costs down). Coronado is a calming getaway for the **Hotel del Coronado** (p402) and the kid-friendly public library. Views from **Cabrillo National Monument** (p403) inspire awe and its museum tells of the Spanish explorers, key to local history.

Teens will be in their element among the surfers, bikers and bladers in **Mission and Pacific Beaches** (p405), while up the coast in La Jolla the **Birch Aquarium** (p433) entertains as it teaches. More active kids can go snorkeling off **La Jolla Cove**.

In northern San Diego County, **Legoland** (p446) is the place for the 12-and-under set (and their parents will thrill at the workmanship of the millions of little bricks). Inland, the **San Diego Zoo Safari Park** (p446) will have the kids roaring.

Diving & Snorkeling

Off the coast of San Diego County, divers will find kelp beds, shipwrecks (including the *Yukon,* a WWII destroyer sunk off Mission Beach in 2000) and canyons deep enough to host bat ray, octopus and squid. For current conditions, call San Diego County Lifeguard Services (p407).

Fishing

The most popular public fishing piers in San Diego are Imperial Beach Pier, Embarcadero Fishing Pier, Shelter Island Fishing Pier, Ocean Beach Pier and Crystal Pier at Pacific Beach. Generally the best pier fishing is from April to October, and no license is required. For offshore fishing, catches can include barracuda, bass and yellowtail and, in summer, albacore tuna. A state fishing license is required for people over 16 for offshore fishing; visit www.wildlife.ca.gov for details or book a daily fishing trip around Coronado or Point Loma with a tour company like Point Loma Sportfishing (p408).

Point Loma Sportfishing   FISHING
([☎] 619-223-1627; www.pointlomasportfishing.com; 1403 Scott St, Point Loma; half-day trips from $45) For local half-day trips, Coronado trips and offshore tuna trips.

Seaforth Sportfishing   FISHING
([☎] 619-224-3383; www.seaforthlanding.com; 1717 Quivira Rd, Mission Bay; trips from $24-300) For fishing trips along the Baja coast and Coronado Islands. Trips include half-day, full-day, overnight and shorter whale-watching outings.

H&M Landing   FISHING
([☎] 619-222-1144; www.hmlanding.com; 2803 Emerson St, Point Loma; trips from $50) This fishing tour provider offers lobster and crab hoop-netting half-day trips, plus trips along the Mexican coast and local half-day trips (spectators welcome for $20).

Boating

San Diego offers rental of powerboats (from $130 per hour), sailboats (from $30 per hour), and kayaks (from $18 per hour) and canoes on Mission Bay from Mission Bay Sportcenter (p408). Ocean kayaking is a good way to see sea life and explore cliffs and caves inaccessible from land.

Mission Bay Sportcenter   BOATING
(Map p406; [☎] 858-488-1004; www.missionbaysportcenter.com; 1010 Santa Clara Pl; rentals $3-230) For the most fun you can have on the water, rent everything from kayaks and SUPs to a speedboat or cruising hot tub here.

Family Kayak   KAYAKING
(Map p406; [☎] 619-277-1169; www.familykayak.com; adult/child from $45/20; [⊕]) Guided sea-lion, nature and evening tours and kayak lessons. Inquire about longer tours. Locations vary.

Resort Watersports   BOATING
([☎] 858-488-2582; www.resortwatersports.com; activities $7-50) Has branches located at the Paradise Point Resort (p415), Bahia, Loews Coronado Bay Resort (p413), Catamaran (p414), Hilton San Diego and more resort hotels. Renting everything from stand up paddleboards, kayaks, sailing boats and powerboats, plus bikes and Segways.

Sailing

Experienced sailors are able to charter boats ranging from catamarans to yachts. Prices start at about $105 for four hours at Harbor Sailboats (p408) and rise steeply. Other charter operators can be found around **Shelter and Harbor Islands** (on the west side of San Diego Bay near the airport).

Harbor Sailboats   BOATING
([☎] 800-854-6625, 619-291-9568; www.harborsailboats.com; 2040 Harbor Island Dr, Suite 104; lessons for nonmembers from $350, plus port fee) Learn how to sail a basic keelboat or rent a sailboat.

Harbor Yacht Clubs   BOATING
([☎] 800-553-7245; www.harboryc.com; 1880 Harbor Island Dr; basic keelboat lesson from $350 (nonmembers)) For sailboat rentals and sailing lessons.

Whale-Watching

Gray whales pass San Diego from mid-December to late February on their way south to Baja California, and again in mid-March on their way back up to Alaskan waters. Their 12,000-mile round-trip journey is the longest migration of any mammal on earth.

Cabrillo National Monument (p403) is the best place to see the whales from land, where you'll also find exhibits, whale-related ranger programs and a shelter from which to watch the whales breach (bring binoculars).

Half-day whale-watching boat trips are offered by most of the companies that run daily fishing trips, like Seaforth Sportfishing (p408). The trips generally cost $24 per adult excursion, sometimes with a guaranteed sighting or a free ticket. Look for coupons and special offers at tourist kiosks and online.

☞ Tours

Brewery Tours of San Diego
BREWERY
(☑619-961-7999; www.brewerytoursofsandiego. com; per person $75-95) San Diego has one of America's best craft-brew scenes, with dozens of small breweries. To leave the driving to someone else, this outfit offers a variety of bus tours each week to an assortment of breweries. Price varies by amount and type of drink and food provided.

California Motorcycle Tours
MOTORCYCLE TOUR
(☑858-677-9892; www.ca-motorcycletours.com) San Diego–based outfitter offers guided trips on Harley Davidsons, including to beaches, mountains, deserts and Mexico's Baja California.

Hornblower Cruises
BOATING
(Map p396; ☑888-467-6256; www.hornblower. com; 970 N Harbor Dr; from $25 per person; 👬) In addition to sea-lion, whale, dolphin and sightseeing cruises, Hornblower specializes in sunset and catered cruises with drinks, dinner or brunch (from $37 plus tax, service and drinks).

San Diego Food Tours
FOOD & DRINK
(☑619-233-8687; http://sodiegotours.com/san-diego-food-tours/; from $50) Walking tours showcase the city's gastronomic treasures from Gaslamp, Little Italy and the Old Town, with some enthusiastic native San Diegan guides. Come hungry.

Flagship Cruises
BOATING
(Map p396; ☑619-234-4111; www.flagshipsd.com; 990 N Harbor Dr; tours adult/child from $24/12; 👬) Harbor tours and seasonal whale-watching cruises from the Embarcadero, from one to several hours long.

Old Town Trolley Tours & Seal Tours
TOURS
(☑855-396-7433; www.trolleytours.com; adult/child $40/25) Not to be confused with the municipal San Diego Trolley, this outfit operates hop-on-hop-off, open-air buses decorated like old-style streetcars, looping around the main attractions of Downtown and Coronado in about two hours, leaving every 30 minutes or so. The main trolley stand is in Old Town, but you can start or stop at any of the well-marked trolley-tour stops.

It also operates 90-minute amphibious **Seal Tours** which depart from Seaport Village (p427) and tour the bay via Shelter Island.

Another Side of San Diego
TOURS
(Map p396; ☑619-239-2111; www.anothersideof sandiegotours.com; 308 G St; tours from $75) Tour company offering Segway tours of Balboa Park, Gaslamp Quarter, La Jolla and Coronado. Plus, bike tours, brewery tours, city tours and food tours.

Bahia Belle
CRUISES
(www.sternwheelers.com; 998 W Mission Bay Dr; $10) For a lovely time without an adrenaline overload, board this floating bar disguised as a stern-wheeler paddleboat. It offers 30-minute cruises between two resort hotels, the Catamaran (p414) and the Bahia, on Friday, Saturday and Sunday March to November; and daily in July and August. Cruises start at 6:30pm; call for exact departure times.

San Diego Scenic Tours
BUS
(☑858-273-8687; www.sandiegoscenictours.com; adult/child from $38/19) Half- and full-day bus tours around San Diego and Tijuana, some of which build in time to shop and dine. Some tours combine with a harbor cruise.

Offshoot Tours
WALKING
(Map p390; ☑619-239-0512; www.balboapark. org/info/tours.php; Visitors Center, 1549 El Prado; ☉10am Sat) FREE Volunteer-led one-hour walking tours with different themes, including Balboa Park history, palm trees, desert vegetation and more.

✷ Festivals & Events

☀ March

San Diego Crew Classic
SPORTS
(www.crewclassic.org; ☉late Mar/early Apr) The national college rowing regatta takes place in Mission Bay.

☀ May

Ocean Beach Kite Festival
OUTDOORS
(www.oceanbeachkiwanis.org; ☉May; 👬) Kite making, decorating and flying, as well as competitions.

☀ June

San Diego County Fair
FAIR
(www.sdfair.com; Del Mar Fairgrounds; ☉early Jun-early Jul) More than a million people

watch headline acts, enjoy hundreds of carnival rides and shows, and pig out on 'fair fare' (plus some healthier options).

San Diego Rock 'n' Roll Marathon SPORTS
(www.runrocknroll.competitor.com; ☺ early Jun) Live bands perform at each mile mark of this 26.2-mile race, with a big concert at the finish line.

☀ July

Comic-Con International CONVENTION
(www.comic-con.org; San Diego Convention Center; ☺ late Jul) America's largest event for collectors of comic, pop-culture and movie memorabilia has gone from geek chic to trendmaker.

Opening Day at Del Mar Racetrack SPORTS
(www.dmtc.com; ☺ mid- to late Jul) Outrageous hats, cocktails and general merriment kick off the horse-racing season, 'where the turf meets the surf.' Racing through early September.

San Diego LGBT Pride LGBT
(www.sdpride.org; ☺ mid-Jul) The city's gay community celebrates in Hillcrest and Balboa Park at the month's end, with parades, parties, performances, art shows and more.

☀ September

Bayfair SPORTS
(www.sandiegobayfair.org; ☺ mid-Sep) Some of the world's fastest speedboats compete on San Diego's Mission Bay.

☀ October

Fleet Week MILITARY
(www.fleetweeksandiego.org; ☺ early Oct) The US military shows its pride in events including a sea and air parade, special tours of ships, the Miramar Air Show (the world's largest) and the Coronado Speed Festival (featuring vintage cars).

Little Italy Festa FOOD & DRINK, CULTURAL
(www.littleitalysd.com; ☺ early Oct) Come for the tastes and aromas of old Italia, and stay for Gesso Italiano, chalk art drawn directly onto the streets.

San Diego Film Festival FILM
(www.sdff.org; ☺ early Oct) The silver screen takes center stage in the Gaslamp Quarter and La Jolla, with screenings, panel discussions, parties and a chance of star sightings.

☀ November

San Diego Bay Wine & Food Festival FOOD & DRINK
(www.sandiegowineclassic.com; ☺ mid-Nov) Cooking classes, wine-tasting parties, gourmet food stands and more.

San Diego Beer Week BEER, FOOD & DRINK
(http://sdbw.org; ☺ early Nov) Celebrating all things hoppy: take part in beer-tasting breakfast, dinners with beer pairing, and roam around the giant beer garden with dozens of San Diego's best breweries and chefs.

☀ December

December Nights HOLIDAY FESTIVAL
(www.balboapark.org/decembernights; ☺ early Dec) This festival in Balboa Park includes crafts, carols and a candlelight parade.

Harbor Parade of Lights HOLIDAY FESTIVAL
(www.sdparadeoflights.org; ☺ Dec) Dozens of decorated, illuminated boats float in procession on San Diego's harbor on two Sunday evenings in December.

Las Posadas HOLIDAY FESTIVAL
(www.parks.ca.gov; ☺ Dec) This traditional Latin Christmas celebration in Old Town re-enacts Mary and Joseph seeking shelter.

🛏 Sleeping

We list high-season (summer) rates for single- or double-occupancy rooms. Prices drop significantly between September and June, but whatever time of year, ask about specials, suites and package deals. San Diego Tourism runs a **room-reservation line** (📞 800-350-6205; www.sandiego.org).

For camping try Campland on the Bay (p414) or **KOA** (📞 800-562-9877, 619-427-3601; www.sandiegokoa.com; 111 N 2nd Ave, Chula Vista; tent sites from $55, RV sites with hookups from $66, cabins from $95, deluxe cabins from $210; 🅿 @ 🛜 ⛟ 🐕), about 8 miles south, with good camping facilities for families like a pool, bike rental, Jacuzzi and off-leash dog park; deluxe cabins include linens, private bathrooms and pots and pans.

🛏 Downtown San Diego

Downtown is San Diego's most convenient place to stay, for its wealth of restaurants and hotels and its easy access to transit.

★USA Hostels San Diego   HOSTEL $

(Map p396; ☎800-438-8622, 619-232-3100; www.usahostels.com; 726 5th Ave; dm/r with shared bath from $32/80; ❄@☎) Lots of charm and color at this convivial hostel in a former Victorian-era hotel. Look for cheerful rooms, a full kitchen and a communal lounge for chilling. Rates include linens, lockers and bagels for breakfast. Surrounded by bars, it's smack-bang in the middle of Gaslamp's nightlife scene, so bring earplugs if you're a light sleeper.

HI San Diego Downtown Hostel   HOSTEL $

(Map p396; ☎619-525-1531; www.sandiegohostels.org; 521 Market St; dm with shared bath from $29, r from $85; ❄@☎) Location, location, location. This Gaslamp Quarter HI facility is steps from public transportation, restaurants and big-city fun, and it has a wide range of rooms, including some with private bathrooms. If the local nightlife doesn't suffice, there is a movie lounge and monthly art events. A continental breakfast is included and you have 24hr access.

★La Pensione Hotel   BOUTIQUE HOTEL $$

(Map p396; ☎619-236-8000, 800-232-4683; www.lapensionehotel.com; 606 W Date St; r from $145-200; P❄☎) Despite the name, Little Italy's La Pensione isn't a pension but an intimate, friendly, recently renovated hotel of 67 rooms with queen-size beds and private bathrooms. It's set around a frescoed courtyard and is just steps to the neighborhood's dining, cafes and galleries, and walking distance to most Downtown attractions. There's an attractive cafe downstairs, and a recently introduced spa. Parking is $20.

★Hotel Solamar   BOUTIQUE HOTEL $$

(Map p396; ☎619-819-9500; www.hotelsolamar.com; 435 6th Ave; r $169-299; P❄@☎⛱) A great compromise in the Gaslamp: hip style that needn't break the bank. A new pool bar is set to open in 2017, with cabanas, outdoor games (like corn hole) and skyscraper views. Rooms have sleek lines and nautical blue and neo-rococo accents for a touch of fun. There's a fitness center, in-room yoga kit, free loaner bikes and a nightly complimentary wine hour. Parking costs $47.

Hotel Palomar San Diego   CONTEMPORARY $$

(Map p396; ☎619-515-3000; www.hotelpalomar-sandiego.com; 1047 5th Ave; r from $179; P❄@☎⛱⛱) Hollywood glam in San Diego. A 9000lb bronze front door pivots to reveal Nepalese carpets and multitextured surfaces: wooden blocks to sand-dollar-shaped ceramics, stingray skin to woven leather. There's doting service, a new Mexican soul-food restaurant, lovely spa, nightly wine hour at night, and coffee and tea in the morning. Parking is $45.

Sofia Hotel   BOUTIQUE HOTEL $$

(Map p396; ☎800-826-0009, 619-234-9200; www.thesofiahotel.com; 150 W Broadway; r from $219; P⇄❄@☎⛱) Across from Westfield Horton Plaza, the historic Sofia has 211 rooms with fashionable darkwood furniture and sprightly printed fabrics. There are also in-room spa services, concierge, complimentary guided walks around the Gaslamp Quarter (Saturday and Sunday) and a fitness-and-yoga studio. The next door **Currant American brasserie** serves fresh seasonal eats in a French bistro-style setting. Valet and self-parking $36.

Courtyard by Marriott San Diego Downtown   HERITAGE HOTEL $$

(Map p396; ☎619-446-3000; www.marriott.com/sancd; 530 Broadway; r from $169; P❄@☎) Yeah, we know, Courtyard is often known for bland rooms in suburban office parks, but this Courtyard is cool because it's in a beautifully updated 1928 bank tower. Spacious rooms occupy the former offices, connected by hallways of vintage marble. Some have views to the harbor and Coronado Bay Bridge and you can play in the fitness center and billiard room.

Notable retrofits include low-wattage bulbs, digital thermostats and motion sensors. Parking is $45.

★US Grant Hotel   LUXURY HOTEL $$$

(Map p396; ☎619-232-3121, 800-237-5029; www.starwood.com; 326 Broadway; r from $211; P❄@☎) This 11-stories high 1910 hotel was built as the fancy-city counterpart to the Hotel del Coronado (p402) and has hosted everyone from Albert Einstein to Harry Truman. Today's quietly flashy lobby combines chocolate-brown and ocean-blue accents, and rooms boast original artwork on the headboards. It's owned by members of the Sycuan tribe of Native Americans. Parking costs $48.

Horton Grand Hotel   HISTORIC HOTEL $$$

(Map p396; ☎800-542-1886, 619-544-1886; www.hortongrand.com; 311 Island Ave; r from $229) At the edge of the Gaslamp, rooms in this brick hotel from 1886 are individually decorated in Victoriana and have gas fireplaces.

If you're facing the street you may get a wrought-iron balcony but also street noise from nearby theaters and clubs; rooms facing the inner courtyard are the quietest. Valet parking costs $42.

Uptown: Bankers Hills, Hillcrest & North Park

Inn at the Park HOTEL $$
(Map p390; ☑ 619-291-0999; www.shellhospitality. com/inn-at-the-park; 525 Spruce St; r from $134; P❄❋@❓) ⚡ This 80-room place, facing Balboa Park and a reasonable walk to central Hillcrest, used to be an apartment building, meaning mostly large rooms with kitchens, vast closets and Hollywood art-deco–style decor. Green initiatives include a recycling program and efficient lighting. Valet parking is $15.

Old Town

Base yourself in San Diego's Old Town and you may not need a car. Many lodgings offer free airport shuttles and there are convenient transit links on the other side of the state park.

Cosmopolitan Hotel B&B $$
(☑ 619-297-1874; http://oldtowncosmopolitan. com; 2660 Calhoun St; r $139-195; ☑ front desk 9am-9pm; P❄❓) Right in Old Town State Park, this creaky, 10-room hotel is restored to its 1870 glory and has oodles of charm, antique furnishings and is possibly haunted (!). There's a **restaurant** downstairs for lunch and dinner, with live music on Fridays and Saturday evenings. Breakfast is a simple

affair centered on coffee and scones. Free wi-fi and free parking.

Best Western Hacienda Hotel HOTEL $$
(☑ 619-298-4707, 800-888-1991; www.hacienda-hotel-oldtown.com; 4041 Harney St; r $189-340; P❋@❓❄) On four well-landscaped acres on the hillside above Old Town's restaurant row, the Hacienda has 200 rooms over eight buildings, neatly decorated in Mission style, some with pull-out sofas. Add in a workout room and Jacuzzi. Off-season rates start at around $100. Parking costs $16.

Coronado

A stay in Coronado Village – around the Hotel del Coronado (p413) – puts you close to the beach, shops and restaurants. The northern end is an easy walk to the ferry. Or get away from it all near the deserted **Silver Strand Beach**; a car is advisable here if you're looking to explore further afield.

El Cordova Hotel HISTORIC HOTEL $$
(☑ 800-229-2032, 619-435-4131; www.elcordova hotel.com; 1351 Orange Ave; r from $189; ❋@❓❄) This exceedingly cozy Spanish-style former mansion from 1902 has rooms and suites around an outdoor courtyard of shops, restaurants, pool, hot tub and barbecue grills. Rooms are charming in an antiquey sort of way, though nothing fancy; they include TVs with free HBO.

Crown City Inn MOTEL $$
(☑ 619-435-3116, 800-422-1173; www.crowncityinn. com; 520 Orange Ave; r from $140; ste from $179; P❋@❓❄) This two-story, family-owned motel is excellent value, set around a small

---

MISSION VALLEY HOTELS

Downtown rates got you down? Beach booked? A couple dozen mostly chain hotels and motels along I-8 in Mission Valley offer in quantity and price what their neighborhood lacks in charm – they're popular for conventions, family vacations and shopping excursions. Outside of the summer peak, weekday rates are occasionally as low as $100.

Handley Hotel (☑ 619-298-0511, 800-843-4343; www.handley.com; 950 Hotel Circle N; r $119-209; P❋@❓❄) The Handley has attractive furnishings (wooden armoires and writing desks) and a complimentary shuttle to area attractions. Parking costs $14.

Crowne Plaza San Diego (☑ 619-297-1101; www.cp-sandiego.com; 2270 Hotel Circle N; r from $133; P@❓❄) Leafy convention-class hotel with a Polynesian theme (koi ponds and waterfalls) and rooms with supercomfy mattresses. Parking costs $13.

Town & Country Hotel (☑ 800-772-8527, 619-291-7131; www.towncountry.com; 500 Hotel Circle N; r from $119; P@❓❄) This property is so big that golf carts are needed to shuttle between the four swimming pools, rose bushes, palms and a 10-story tower. There's a trolley stop and bridge to **Fashion Valley shopping center** (p427). Parking costs $16.

parking area with a little pool. It offers loaner bikes for easy getaways, and cookies and iced tea in the lobby. If its floral-accented rooms were beachside, they would start at $200 per night. The **bistro** on-site is a local fave.

Glorietta Bay Inn   HISTORIC HOTEL **$$**
(📞800-283-9383, 619-435-3101; www.glorietta bayinn.com; 1630 Glorietta Blvd; r from $149; 🅿✳@🛜🏊) Overshadowed by the neighboring Hotel Del, the Glorietta is built in and around the neoclassical 1908 Spreckels Mansion – 11 rooms in the mansion, 89 in boxier two-story buildings. Rooms have handsome furnishings and extras such as triple-sheeted beds and high-end bath products. Mansion rooms are more expensive and have even more luxe amenities. Rates include continental breakfast.

Stop in and see the gorgeous music room, even if you're not staying here. Parking is $15.

Coronado Inn   MOTEL **$$**
(📞800-598-6624, 619-435-4121; www.coronado-inn.com; 266 Orange Ave; r from $129, with kitchen from $159; 🅿@🛜🏊🐕) This good midrange choice near the ferry is a wood-shingled affair decked with palms, little wooden gazebos, barbecue grills and deck chairs around the pool. Continental breakfast and all-day coffee and there's free wi-fi.

★Hotel del Coronado   LUXURY HOTEL **$$$**
(📞800-468-3533, 619-435-6611; www.hoteldel. com; 1500 Orange Ave; r from $297; 🅿♿✳@🛜🏊🐕) San Diego's iconic hotel provides the essential Coronado experience: over a century of history (p402), a pool, full-service spa, shops, restaurants, manicured grounds, a white-sand beach and an ice-skating rink during Christmas season. Even the basic rooms have luxurious marbled bathrooms. Note: half the accommodations are not in the main Victorian-era hotel (368 rooms) but in an adjacent seven-story building constructed in the 1970s. For a sense of place, book a room in the original hotel. Self-parking is $39.

Loews Coronado Bay Resort   RESORT **$$$**
(📞800-235-6397, 619-424-4000; www.loews-hotels.com; 4000 Coronado Bay Rd; r $219-369; 🅿✳@🛜🏊) Way down Silver Strand (take the complimentary shuttle to Coronado Village), the 439-room Loews is reached by a causeway and has its own private marina with boat rentals. Rooms boast sea hues and rattans, the lobby is all sunny yellows and sky blues, and there are three outdoor pools, plenty of kids programs and romantic views from the chic, Mediterranean-inspired **Mistral restaurant**. Self-parking is $23.

🛏 Point Loma Area

Although it's a bit out of the way, Point Loma boasts some fun accommodations. Head to **Shelter Island** for tiki-style hotels.

HI San Diego Point Loma Hostel   HOSTEL **$**
(📞619-223-4778; www.sandiegohostels.org; 3790 Udall St; dm/r per person with shared bath from $24/45; @🛜) It's a 20-minute walk from central Ocean Beach to this little red hostel, in a largely residential area close to a market and library. Cheery private rooms are a great deal. There are often pizza nights, movie nights, karaoke and excursions around town and to Tijuana. Bus 923 runs along nearby Voltaire St. No lock-out times.

Pearl   MOTEL **$$**
(📞619-226-6100, 877-732-7573; www.thepearlsd. com; 1410 Rosecrans St; r $125-199; 🅿✳✳🛜) The mid-Century Modern Pearl feels more Palm Springs than San Diego. The 23 rooms in its 1959 shell have soothing blue hues, trippy surf motifs and fishbowls. There's a lively pool scene (including **'dive-in' movies** on Wednesday nights), or you can play Jenga or Parcheesi in the groovy, shag-carpeted lobby. Light sleepers: request a room away from busy street traffic.

Best Western Island Palms   RESORT **$$**
(📞800-922-2336, 619-222-0561; www.island palms.com; 2051 Shelter Island Dr; r from $179; 🅿✳@🛜🏊) Namesake palms adorn the lobby and grounds around this archipelago of three Polynesian-style buildings housing the resort's 227 rooms, pools and hot tubs. It has comfortable, well-maintained, upper-end-chain-motel-style rooms, plus free bike rentals. Parking is $10.

Humphrey's Half Moon Inn & Suites   RESORT **$$$**
(📞800-345-9995, 619-224-3411; www.halfmoon inn.com; 2303 Shelter Island Dr; r $170-249, ste $190-399; 🅿@🛜🏊) Fans of boating, jazz and Polynesian style will feel at home in this harborside resort. Its 182 rooms and suites are clustered amid koi ponds, paddling mallards, palms and flower beds, in wooden shingle-roofed buildings like Hawaiian lanais. Some have balconies and views of

yachts on the harbor. There's a good **jazz club** on site. Parking is $16.

🛏 Ocean Beach

Ocean Beach (OB) is a happening hippy 'hood, but it is also under the outbound flight path of San Diego airport. Light sleepers might prefer to stay elsewhere or bring earplugs.

Ocean Beach International Hostel   HOSTEL $

(Map p404; ☑ 619-223-7873, 800-339-7263; www. californiahostel.com; 4961 Newport Ave; dm $29-45, r from $110; 🛜) Central OB's cheapest option is easy to spot with its psychedelic colored exterior and peace sign on the top of the building. Only a couple of blocks from the ocean, it's a simple but friendly and fun place reserved for international travelers, with free wi-fi and breakfast. Entertainment comes in the form of music nights and board games.

Inn at Sunset Cliffs   INN $$

(☑ 619-222-7901, 866-786-2453; www.innatsunsetcliffs.com; 1370 Sunset Cliffs Blvd; r/ste from $175/289; P🐾❄@🛜🏊) At the south end of Ocean Beach, wake up to the sound of surf crashing onto the rocky shore. This low-key 1950s charmer wraps around a flower-bedecked courtyard with a small heated pool. Its 24 breezy rooms are compact, but most have attractive stone-and-tile bathrooms, and some suites have full kitchens.

🛏 Pacific Beach

Catamaran Resort Hotel   RESORT $$

(Map p406; ☑ 800-422-8386, 858-488-1081; www. catamaranresort.com; 3999 Mission Blvd; r from $139; P@🛜🏊) Tropical landscaping and tiki decor fill this resort backing onto Mission Bay (there's a luau on some summer evenings!). A plethora of activities make it a perfect place for families (sailing, kayaking, tennis, biking, skating, spa-ing, etc), or board the Bahia Belle (p409) here. Rooms are in low-rise buildings or in a 14-story tower; some have views and full kitchens.

Beach Cottages   MOTEL, COTTAGES $$

(Map p406; ☑ 858-483-7440; www.beachcottages. com; 4255 Ocean Blvd; r from $160; 🚌30, 34) Family-owned and operated, Beach Cottages has everything from plain motel rooms to cozy 1940s cottages, just across the bike path from the sand. Sure, they're nothing fancy, but there's a loveable throwback feel to the clapboard construction, ping-pong, shuffleboard and rattan furniture. Larger rooms can be a real bargain if you're traveling in a group. No air-conditioning.

Tower 23   BOUTIQUE HOTEL $$$

(Map p406; ☑ 858-270-2323, 866-869-3723; www. t23hotel.com; 723 Felspar St, Pacific Beach; r from $270; P❄@🛜🏊) If you like your oceanfront stay with contemporary cool style, this modernist place has an awesome location, minimalist decor, lots of teals and mint blues, water features and a sense of humor. There's no pool, but dude, you're right on the beach. Parking is $30.

Crystal Pier Hotel & Cottages   COTTAGE $$$

(Map p406; ☑ 800-748-5894; www.crystalpier. com; 4500 Ocean Blvd, Pacific Beach; d $185-525; P🐾❄🛜) Charming, wonderful and unlike any other place in San Diego, Crystal Pier has cottages built right on the pier above the water. Almost all 29 cottages have full ocean views and kitchens; most date from the 1930s. Newer, larger cottages sleep up to six. Book eight to 11 months in advance for summer reservations. Minimum-stay requirements vary by season. No air-conditioning. Rates include parking.

🛏 Mission Bay

Just east of Mission Beach, Mission Bay has waterfront lodging at lower prices than accommodations on the ocean.

Campland on the Bay   CAMPGROUND $

(☑ 800-422-9386, 858-581-4260; www.campland. com; 2211 Pacific Beach Dr, Mission Bay; RV & tent sites $55-432, beachfront from $225; P🛜🏊) On more than 40 acres fronting Mission Bay, amenities include a restaurant, two pools, boat rentals, full RV hookups and outdoor activities from skateboarding to sing-alongs. Price varies depending on proximity to the water; reservations are recommended. Off-season discounts.

Paradise Point Resort   RESORT $$$

(☑ 858-274-4630, 800-344-2626; www.paradise point.com; 1404 Vacation Rd; r from $149; P@🛜🏊) The grounds are so lush and dotted with so many palms that you'll feel like you're in Hawaii at this upper-end resort, whose 462 rooms are in small ground-floor bungalows. Features for kids include a putting green and summer movies in one of the five swimming pools. Full-service spa. Parking costs $38.

 Eating

San Diego has a thriving dining culture, with an emphasis on Mexican, Californian and seafood. San Diegans eat dinner early, usually around 6pm or 7pm, and most restaurants are ready to close by 10pm. Breakfast is a big affair, and there's a growing locavore and gourmet scene, especially in North Park. Less-expensive options are fun and satisfying. Reservations are recommended.

Balboa Park & Around

Big Kitchen   BREAKFAST $
(☎619-234-5789; www.bigkitchencafe.com; 3003 Grape St, South Park; mains $5-13.50; ☺7:30am-2:30pm; ⊞) Here since the '70s, this neighborhood joint is decorated with bric-a-brac, progressive bumper stickers, homages to The Beatles and pictures of Whoopi Goldberg – she once worked here as a dishwasher. The kitchen serves American classics like stacks of pancakes, 10 different types of burgers and big-bowl specialties; chili, soup and mac 'n' cheese.

★ Nomad Donuts   DESSERTS $
(☎619-431-5000;   https://nomaddonuts.com; 4504 30th St; doughnuts from $4; ☺6am-2pm Mon-Fri, 8am-2pm Sat & Sun) 🍴 If you think you know donuts, think again. This artisanal doughnut shop is headed up by pastry chef Kristianna Zabala, who hand-crafts every batch using cage-free, organic eggs and other ingredients from farmers markets. The menu changes daily, and when they're gone they're gone. Our faves include bacon flavor, charred blueberry–cream cheese, and the *ube taro* coconut doughnut.

★ Buona Forchetta   ITALIAN $$
(☎619-381-4844;   www.buonaforchettasd.com; 3001 Beech St; small plates $6-15, pizzas $8-25; ☺noon-3pm Tue-Fri, 5-10pm Mon-Thu, to 11pm Fri, noon-11pm Sat, noon-10pm Sun; ⊞) A gold-painted brick wood-fired oven imported from Italy delivers authentic Neapolitan pizzas straight to jammed-together family-sized tables at this South Park trattoria with a dog-friendly patio. No reservations can mean long waits.

★ Prado   CALIFORNIAN $$$
(Map p390; ☎619-557-9441; www.pradobalboa. com; 1549 El Prado; lunch $8-19, dinner $8-37;

☺11:30am-3pm   Mon,   11am-10pm   Tue-Thu, 11:30am-9:30pm Sat, 11am-9pm Sun; ⊞) In one of San Diego's more beautiful dining rooms, feast on Cal-eclectic cooking by one of San Diego's most renowned chefs: bakery sandwiches, lobster bucatini, and thyme-roasted Jidori half-chicken. Go for a civilized lunch on the verandah or for afternoon cocktails and appetizers in the bar.

Gaslamp Quarter

There are some 100 restaurants in the Gaslamp, many of them very good. Some have bar scenes too.

Café 222   BREAKFAST $
(☎619-236-9902; www.cafe222.com; 222 Island Ave; mains $7 11; ☺7am 1:45pm) Downtown's favorite breakfast place serves renowned peanut-butter-and-banana French toast; buttermilk, orange-pecan or granola pancakes; and eggs in scrambles or Benedicts. It also sells lunchtime sandwiches and salads, but we always go for breakfast (available until closing).

Gaslamp Strip Club   STEAK $$
(☎619-231-3140; www.gaslampsteak.com; 340 5th Ave; mains $17-27; ☺5-10pm Sun-Thu, to midnight Fri & Sat) Pull your own bottle from the wine vault, then char your own favorite cut of steak, chicken or fish on the open grills in the retro-Vegas dining room at Downtown's most novel steakhouse. No steak costs more than $27. Fab, creative martinis and pinup art by Alberto Vargas. Tons of fun. No one under 21 allowed. Happy hour 5pm–7pm Sunday–Thursday.

Oceanaire   SEAFOOD $$$
(☎619-858-2277; www.theoceanaire.com; 400 J St; mains $30-65; ☺5-10pm Sun-Thu, to 11pm Fri & Sat) The look is art-deco ocean liner, and the service is just as elegant, with an oyster bar and creations like chicken-fried lobster with truffled honey, and California sole Florentine stuffed with crab meat. If you don't feel like a total splurge, look out for happy-hour deals with bargain-priced oysters and fish tacos in the bar (times vary).

Bandar   MIDDLE EASTERN $$$
(☎619-238-0101; www.bandarrestaurant.com; 825 4th Ave; lunch $16-25, dinner $18-40; ☺11:30am-10pm Sun-Thu, to 11:30pm Fri & Sat) Exotic spices and fragrant cooking make this white-tablecloth Persian–Middle Eastern a favorite for

giant kebabs and salads that zing with flavor. Come hungry: portions are huge.

East Village

Neighborhood
PUB FOOD $$

(Map p396; 619-446-0002; www.neighbor hoodsd.com; 777 G St; mains $7-14; noon-midnight) Lit with filament bulbs and decorated with exposed beams, pipework overhead and a big mural of Downtown San Diego, this place is often used as a hangout while people are waiting to get entry to the next-door speakeasy Noble Experiment (p423), but it's a great spot in its own right, serving dozens of craft ales and hipster pub eats.

Basic
PIZZA $$

(Map p396; 619-531-8869; www.barbasic.com; 410 10th Ave; small/large pizzas from $14/32; 11:30am-2am) East Village hipsters feast on fragrant thin-crust, brick-oven-baked pizzas under Basic's high ceiling (it's in a former warehouse). Small pizzas have a large footprint but are pretty light. Toppings span the usual to the newfangled, like the mashed pie with mozzarella, mashed potatoes and bacon. Wash them down with beers (craft, naturally) or one of several cocktails.

Café Chloe
FRENCH $$$

(Map p396; 619-232-3242; www.cafechloe.com; 721 9th Ave; dinner $9-31; 8am-10pm Mon-Sat, 8:30am-9:30pm Sun) This delightful corner French bistro has a simple style and gets the standards perfect, and everything else as well. Classics include onion tart, French toast, *moules* (mussels) or steak *frites* (steak and chips) served with herb butter and salad. There's also trout salad, and wonderful egg dishes for weekend brunch.

Uptown: Bankers Hill, Hillcrest & North Park

San Diego's restaurant scene is booming here. Bankers Hill and Hillcrest are well established, and North Park is a hub of innovation.

★ Carnitas' Snack Shack
CALIFORNIAN, MEXICAN $

(619-294-7665; http://carnitassnackshack.com; 2632 University Ave; mains $8-13; 11am-midnight;) Eat honestly priced, pork-inspired slow food in a cute outdoor patio with natural wooden features. Wash dishes like the triple-threat pork sandwich (with schnitzel, bacon, pepperoncini, pickle relish, shack aioli and an Amish bun) down with local craft ales. Happy hour runs from 3pm–6pm Monday–Friday with $5 tacos, $5 drafts and $6 wines.

Bread & Cie
BAKERY, CAFE $

(Map p390; 619-683-9322; www.breadandcie. com; 350 University Ave, Hillcrest; mains $6-11; 7am-7pm Mon-Fri, to 6pm Sat, 7:30am-6pm Sun;) Aside from crafting some of San Diego's best artisan breads (including anise and fig, black olive, and walnut and raisin), this wide-open bakery-deli makes fabulous sandwiches with fillings such as curried-chicken salad and ham and Swiss cheese. Boxed lunches cost $11.50. Great pastries too.

Sipz
VEGAN $

(619-795-2889; www.sipz.com; 3914 30th St, North Park; lunch $7.75, dinner $9.25; 11am-9pm Sun-Thu, 11am-11pm Fri & Sat;) Finally, a vegan place that doesn't feel like you're slumming it. The modern decor with clean lines and bold graphics is your first clue; the menu, from cashew stir-fry to spicy basil with mock chicken or tofu, and orange mock chicken, has made believers out of North Park. Desserts span sweet rice with fresh mango to vegan cheesecake.

San Diego Chicken Pie Shop
PIES $

(619-295-0156; www.chickenpieshops.com; 2633 El Cajon Blvd, North Park; pies from $3.20, mains $5-14; 8am-8pm) It's out of the way and looks like it hasn't been redecorated since the Carter administration, but local foodies love the namesake chicken pies, with chicken, creamy gravy and vegetables. Other mains include bacon and eggs for breakfast, and fish and steaks the rest of the day.

★ Urban Solace
CALIFORNIAN $$

(619-295-6464; www.urbansolace.net; 3823 30th St, North Park; mains lunch $12-22, dinner $14-27; 11am-9pm Mon-Tue, to 9:30pm Wed-Thu, to 10:30pm Fri, 10:30am-10:30pm Sat, 9:30am-2:30pm & 4-9pm Sun) North Park's young hip gourmets revel in creative comfort food here: quinoa-veg burger; 'not your mama's' meatloaf of ground lamb, fig, pine nuts and feta; 'duckaroni' (mac 'n' cheese with duck confit); and pulled chicken and dumplings. The setting's surprisingly chill for such great eats, maybe because of the creative cocktails.

★**Hash House a Go Go** AMERICAN $$
(Map p390; 619-298-4646; www.hashhousea
gogo.com; 3628 5th Ave, Hillcrest; breakfast $10-
22, dinner mains $15-29; 7.30am-2.30pm Mon,
7:30am-2pm & 5:30-9pm Tue-Thu, to 2:30pm and
9:30pm Fri-Sun;) This buzzing bungalow
makes biscuits and gravy straight outta Indi-
ana, towering Benedicts, large-as-your-head
pancakes and – wait for it – hash seven dif-
ferent ways. Eat your whole breakfast, and
you won't need to eat the rest of the day. It's
worth coming back for the equally massive
burgers, sage-fried chicken and award-win-
ning meatloaf sandwich. No wonder it's
called 'twisted farm food.'

★**Cucina Urbana** CALIFORNIAN, ITALIAN $$$
(Map p390; 619-239-2222; www.urbankitchen
group.com/cucina-urbana-bankers-hill/; 505 Laurel
St, Bankers Hill; mains lunch $15-23, dinner $12-31;
11:30am-2pm Tue-Fri, 5-9pm Sun & Mon, 5-10pm
Tue-Thu, 5pm-midnight Fri & Sat) In this corner
place with modern rustic ambience, business gets done, celebrations get celebrated
and friends hug and kiss over refined yet affordable Cal-Ital cooking. Look for short-rib
pappardelle, pizzas like spicy coppa pork and
pineapple or pear and Gorgonzola with caramelized onion, and smart cocktails and local
'brewskies.' Reservations recommended.

Waypoint Public GASTROPUB $$
(619-255-8778; www.waypointpublic.com; 3794
30th St, North Park; mains $9-23; 4-10pm Mon-
Wed, to 11pm Thu, to 1am Fri, 8am-1am Sat, to 10pm
Sun;) Waypoint's comfort-food menu is
meant to pair craft beers with dishes: from
mussels and pork belly to a kielbasa platter
with Polish sausage, sauerkraut, apple slaw,
grained mustard and red-skin potatoes.
Walls are attractively done up in reclaimed
wood, and glass garage doors roll up to the
outside, all the better for hipster-watching
in busy North Park. Well-behaved dogs also
welcome.

Saigon on Fifth VIETNAMESE $$
(Map p390; 619-220-8828; http://saigononfifth.
menutoeat.com/; 3900 5th Ave, Hillcrest; mains
$7-16; 11am-3am;) This Vietnamese place
tries hard and succeeds, with dishes like
fresh spring rolls, fish of Hue (with garlic,
ginger and lemongrass) and rockin' 'spicy
noodles.' Staff dress nicely and the room is
elegant but not overbearing.

Baja Betty's MEXICAN $$
(Map p390; 619-269-8510; http://bajabet-
tyssd.com; 1421 University Ave, Hillcrest; mains

$8-16; 11am-1am Mon-Fri, 10am-1am Sat &
Sun) Gay-owned and straight-friendly, this
restaurant-bar is always a party with a
just-back-from-Margaritaville vibe, plus
dozens of tequilas, alongside dishes like
queso dip, fish tacos, ceviche tostadas and
spicy fajitas. There are drinks or food spe-
cials every night – like half off the menu on
Mondays and buy-one-get-one-free drinks
on Wednesdays.

Khyber Pass AFGHANI $$
(Map p390; 619-294-7579; www.khyberpass-
sandiego.com; 523 University Ave, Hillcrest; mains
$13-25; 11:30am-10pm) Afghan tapestries
and moody photos set the atmosphere in
this tall-ceilinged space, with adventure-
some Afghan cooking. If you've never had
it, it's kind of like Indian meets Lebanese:
yogurt curries, kabobs, stews and more. A
few high-end dishes (eg filet mignon or rack
of lamb kabob) are up to $25.

Little Italy

Little Italy is – surprise! – happy hunting
ground for Italian cooking and cafes on
India St and around Date St, and some
non-Italian newcomers are rounding out the
scene. Ballast Point Tasting Room & Kitchen
(p424) also does some great dishes.

Valentine's MEXICAN $
(Map p396; 619-234-8256; 1157 6th Ave; tacos
& mains $3-10; 8am-midnight Sun-Thu, to 3am
Fri & Sat) There's nothing urbane about this
home-style Mexican joint, but it's a local
institution. Apart from the usual tacos and
burritos, the carne asada fries (french fries
topped like nachos with grilled beef, sour
cream, guacamole and such) are messy,
coronary-inducing and oh so *bueno*. Late
weekend hours mean it's great after a rager.

Burger Lounge BURGERS $
(Map p396; 619-237-7878; www.burgerlounge.
com; 1608 India St; burgers $8-11; 10:30am-
10pm;) This swingin' local chain serves
chic comfort food. There's just a simple
menu, but what they do with it! Plump burgers (grass-fed beef, free-range turkey, veggie,
or Alaskan cod), crisp fries, great salads,
shakes and root-beer floats.

Mimmo's Italian Village ITALIAN $$
(Map p396; 619-239-3710; www.mimmos.biz;
1743 India St; meals $9-26; 11am-10pm Mon-Fri,
12pm-10pm Sat, 12pm-9pm Sun;) In a tall-
ceilinged space decorated like an Italian

village complete with mini Ponte Vecchio, Mimmo's deli serves salads, hot and cold sandwiches and daily lunch specials like lasagna and eggplant parmigiana.

Filippi's Pizza Grotto
PIZZA, DELI $$
(Map p396; ☎619-232-5094; www.realcheese pizza.com; 1747 India St; dishes $10-24; ⏱11am-10pm Sun & Mon, to 10:30pm Tue-Thu, to 11:30pm Fri & Sat; ⊞) There are often lines out the door for Filippi's old-school Italian cooking (pizza, spaghetti and ravioli) served on red-and-white-checked tablecloths in the dining room festooned with murals of *la bella Italia*. The front of the restaurant is an excellent Italian deli.

Bencotto
ITALIAN $$
(Map p396; ☎619-450-4786; www.lovebencotto. com; 750 W Fir St; mains $10-29; ⏱from 5pm Mon, from 11:30am Tue-Sun; ℗) Bencotto melds the old with the new of Little Italy – contemporary, angular, multistory, architect-designed, arty and green – and the food is great, too, from fresh-sliced prosciutto to pasta *a modo tuo* (your way), with more than 100 potential combos of fresh pasta and sauce.

★ Juniper & Ivy
CALIFORNIAN $$$
(Map p396; ☎619-269-9036; www.juniperandivy. com; 2228 Kettner Blvd; small plates $10-23, mains $19-45; ⏱5-10pm Sun-Thu, to 11pm Fri & Sat) The menu changes daily at chef Richard Blais' highly rated San Diego restaurant, opened in 2014. The molecular gastronomy includes dishes in the vein of lobster congee, Hawaiian snapper with Valencia Pride mango, ahi (yellowfin tuna) with creamed black trumpets, and pig-trotter *totelloni*. It's in a rockin' refurbished warehouse.

✖ Mission Hills

Mission Hills is the neighborhood north of Little Italy and west of Hillcrest. On India St, where it meets Washington St, there's a block of well-regarded eateries.

El Indio
MEXICAN $
(☎619-299-0333; www.el-indio.com; 3695 India St; dishes $3-9; ⏱8am-9pm; ℗⊞) Counter-service shop famous since 1940 for its taquitos, *mordiditas* (tiny taquitos), tamales and excellent breakfast burritos. Eat on plastic plate in a rudimentary dining room.

Saffron
THAI $$
(☎619-574-7737; www.saffronsandiego.com; 3731 India St; mains $7-15; ⏱10:30am-10pm Mon-Sat,

11am-10pm Sun) This multi-award-winning hole-in-the-wall is actually two shops – **Saffron Thai Grilled Chicken** and **Noodles & Saté**, but you can get both at either shop and enjoy it in the noodle shop. Chicken is cooked over a charcoal grill and comes with a choice of sauces, salad, jasmine rice and a menu of finger foods.

Shakespeare Pub & Grille
PUB FOOD $$
(☎619-299-0230; www.shakespearepub.com; 3701 India St; dishes $6-15; ⏱10:30am-midnight Mon-Thu, to 1am Fri, 8am-1am Sat, 8am-midnight Sun) One of San Diego's most authentic English ale houses, Shakespeare is the place for darts, soccer by satellite, beer on tap and pub grub, including fish-and-chips and bangers and mash. One thing they don't have in Britain: a great sundeck. On weekends, load up with a British breakfast: bacon, mushrooms, black and white pudding and more.

✖ Old Town

At the Mexican eateries all along San Diego Ave, hard-working cooks churn out an estimated 210,000 fresh tortillas per month, and most have great bar scenes, too. Choose your setting: party, local or sublime.

★ Old Town Mexican Café
MEXICAN $$
(☎619-297-4330; www.oldtownmexcafe.com; 2489 San Diego Ave; mains $5-17; ⏱7-11pm weekdays, to midnight weekends; ⊞) Other restaurants come and go, but this place has been in this busy adobe with hardwood booths since the 1970s. While you wait to be seated, watch the staff turn out tortillas. Then enjoy *machaca* (shredded beef with eggs, onions and peppers), carnitas and Mexican ribs. For breakfast: *chilaquiles* (tortilla chips with salsa or mole, broiled or grilled with cheese).

Fred's
MEXICAN $$
(☎619-858-8226; www.fredsmexicancafe.com; 2470 San Diego Ave; mains $9-15; ⏱11am-10pm Mon, to 11pm Sun, Wed, Thu, to 12am Fri, 10am-12am Sat) Every night, party people on a budget crowd into raucous Fred's, especially on bargain 'Taco-licious Tuesday' (with tacos from $2; 4pm–closing). The straight-down-the-middle enchiladas, burritos and tacos won't set standards, but it's hard not to love the colorful interior and rangy patio.

El Agave
MEXICAN $$$
(☎619-220-0692; www.elagave.com; 2304 San Diego Ave; mains lunch $10-20, dinner $11-33; ⏱11am-10pm; ℗) Candlelight flickers in this

romantic 2nd-floor, white-tablecloth, high-end place catering to cognoscenti. The mole is superb (there are nine types to choose from), and there are a whopping 1500 different tequilas covering just about every bit of wall space and in racks overhead, enough that it calls itself a tequila museum.

✕ Embarcadero & the Waterfront

★ Puesto at the Headquarters   MEXICAN $$
(☑ 610-233-8880; www.eatpuesto.com; 789 W Harbor Dr, The Headquarters; mains $11-19; ⊙ 11am-10pm) This eatery serves Mexican street food that knocked our *zapatos* off: innovative takes on traditional tacos like chicken (with hibiscus, chipotle, pineapple and avocado) and some out-there fillings like zucchini and cactus. Other highlights: crab guacamole, the lime-marinated shrimp ceviche and the grilled Baja striped bass.

✕ Coronado

★ Clayton's Coffee Shop   DINER $
(☑ 619-435-5425; www.facebook.com/claytons coffeeshop; 979 Orange Ave; mains $7-13; ⊙ 6am-10pm; ⊕) Some diners only look old-fashioned. This one is the real deal from the 1940s, with red leatherette swivel stools and booths with minijukeboxes. It does famous all-American breakfasts and some Mexican specialties like *machaca* with eggs and cheese, and it's not above panini and croque monsieur sandwiches. For dessert: mile-high pie from the counter.

Boney's Bayside Market   MARKET $
(☑ 619-435-0776; www.baysidemarket.com; 155 Orange Ave; sandwiches from $7; ⊙ 8am-9pm) ✐ For picnics and takeout, stop by this market near the ferry for fantastic, (mostly) healthy sandwiches and an extensive assortment of salads and organic products.

1500 Ocean   CALIFORNIAN $$$
(☑ 619-435-6611; www.hoteldel.com/1500-ocean; Hotel del Coronado, 1500 Orange Ave; mains $38-52; ⊙ 5:30-10pm Tue-Sat, plus Sun summer; ℗) It's hard to beat the romance of supping at the Hotel del Coronado (p402), especially at a table overlooking the sea from the verandah of its first-class dining room, where silver service and coastal cuisine with local ingredients set the perfect tone for popping the question or feting an important anniversary.

Primavera   ITALIAN $$$
(☑ 619-435-0454; www.primavera1st.com; 932 Orange Ave; mains $21-46; ⊙ 5-10pm) A subdued, romantic setting for Italian dining, plus a great wine list, presented by black-tied waiters. It's known for steaks, seafood dishes like shrimp in mushroom-and-white-wine sauce over pasta, and a veal chop so big two can share it. Prices are high but worth it.

✕ Point Loma Area

A hot spot for seafood restaurants, plus the recently opened Liberty Public Market with more than 30 local artisan vendors touting their flavors – you can easily spend a hour or so wandering around sampling them all.

★ Point Loma Seafoods   SEAFOOD $
(☑ 619-223-1109; www.pointlomaseafoods.com; 2805 Emerson St; mains $7-16; ⊙ 9am-7pm Mon-Sat, 10am-7pm Sun; ℗ ⊕) For off-the-boat-fresh seafood sandwiches, salads, sashimi, fried dishes and icy-cold beer, order at the counter at this fish-market-cum-deli and grab a seat at a picnic table on the upstairs harbor-view deck. It also does great sushi and takeout dishes from ceviche to clam chowder.

★ Liberty Public Market   MARKET $
(☑ 619-487-9346, http://libertypublicmarket.com; 2820 Historic Decatur Rd; ⊙ 7am-10pm) What the Ferry Building Marketplace is to San Francisco, the newly opened Liberty Public Market is to San Diego. Inside this converted old navy building are more than 30 hip artisan vendors such as Baker & Olive, Wicked Maine Lobster, Paraná Empanadas, Mastiff Sausage Company, Mama Made Thai, Le Parfait Paris, Cecilia's Taqueria and Fish-Bone Kitchen.

Stone Brewing World Bistro & Gardens   PUB FOOD $$
(☑ 619-269-2100; www.stonebrewing.com/visit/ bistros/liberty-station; Liberty Station, 2816 Historic Decatur Rd; mains lunch $15-24, dinner $16-28; ⊙ 11:30am-9pm Mon-Fri, until 10pm Sat & Sun; ℗) Local brewer Stone has transformed the former mess hall of the naval training center at Liberty Station (p427) into a temple to local craft beer. Tuck into standard-setting, spin-the-globe dishes – beer-battered fish tacos, *yakisoba* (Japanese stir-fried noodles) bowls with Jidori chicken, and spicy lamb sausage rigatoni – at long tables or comfy booths under its tall beamed ceiling, or beneath twinkling lights in its courtyard.

Corvette Diner
DINER $$

(☏619-542-1476; www.cohnrestaurants.com/corvettediner; 2965 Historic Decatur Rd; mains $11-20; ⏲11am-9pm Sun, 11:30am-9pm Mon-Thu, 11am-11pm Sat; 🖐) Your kids will be your BFFs for bringing them to this over-the-top '50s-themed diner in Liberty Station (p427). DJs spin rock-and-roll classics, waitresses wear poodle skirts and bouffant wigs, waiters dance in the aisles, kids wear drinking straws in their hair, plus there's a huge games arcade. Oh, and the food is good, too. Try the meatloaf.

Brigantine
SEAFOOD $$$

(☏619-224-2871; www.brigantine.com; 2725 Shelter Island Dr; lunch $10-19, dinner $15-32, small plates $9-15; ⏲11:30am-3pm Mon-Sat, 5-9pm daily, 10am-2pm Sun brunch) At this respected local seafood chain, lunch is heavy on sandwiches (and famous fish tacos), while dinners are fancier with dishes like marinated swordfish and wok-charred ahi. The Shelter Island Dr branch has a balcony where you can peek through palm fronds to the harbor. Awesome happy hours (4pm–7pm Tues–Sun). There are also branches in Coronado and Del Mar.

Bali Hai
POLYNESIAN $$$

(☏619-222-1181; www.balihairestaurant.com; 2230 Shelter Island Dr; dishes lunch $8-19, dinner $19-29, small plates from $10, Sun brunch adult/child $35/17; ⏲11:30am-9pm Mon-Thu, to 10pm Fri & Sat, 9:30am-9pm Sun; P) Near the tiki-themed hotels of Point Loma, this longtime, special-occasion restaurant serves Hawaiian-themed meals like tuna *poke* (cubed raw fish mixed with shōyu, sesame oil, salt, chili pepper and other condiments), *pupus* (small plates), chicken of the gods (with tangy orange-chili and a coconut–brown rice cake) and a massive Sunday champagne-brunch buffet. The best part: views clear across San Diego Bay through its circular wall of windows.

✕ Ocean Beach

★ Hodad's
BURGERS $

(Map p404; ☏619-224-4623; www.hodadies.com; 5010 Newport Ave; dishes $4-15; ⏲11am-10pm) Since the flower-power days of 1969, OB's legendary burger joint has served great shakes, massive baskets of onion rings and succulent hamburgers wrapped in paper. The walls are covered in license plates; grunge/surf-rock plays (loud!) and your bearded, tattooed server might sidle into your booth to take your order. No shirt, no shoes, no problem, dude.

Ocean Beach People's Market
VEGETARIAN $

(Map p404; ☏619-224-1387; www.obpeoplesfood.coop; 4765 Voltaire St; dishes $8, salads per pound from $7.89; ⏲8am-9pm; 🖐) 🍃 For strictly vegetarian groceries and fabulous prepared meals and salads north of central Ocean Beach, this organic cooperative does bulk foods, and excellent counter-service soups, sandwiches, salads and wraps.

Ortega's Cocina
CAFE $

(Map p404; ☏619-222-4205; http://ortegascocina.mobile-webview.com; 4888 Newport Ave; mains $4-19; ⏲8am-10pm Mon-Sat, to 9pm Sun) Tiny, family-run Ortega's is so popular that people often queue for a spot at the counter (there are indoor and sidewalk tables, too). Seafood, moles, tortas (sandwiches) and handmade tamales are the specialties, but all its dishes are soulful and classic.

Olive Tree Marketplace
MARKET $

(Map p404; ☏619-224-0443; 4805 Narragansett Ave; half sandwiches from $4.79, large sandwiches $7-8; ⏲8am-9pm) This neighborhood shop helps keep your beach picnic local, with San Diego specialties like tortilla chips from El Nopalito, baked goods from Bread & Cie (p416) and pies from Julian, plus a big menu of to-go sandwiches and local craft beers to wash them all down.

South Beach Bar & Grille
SEAFOOD, MEXICAN $

(Map p404; ☏619-226-4577; www.southbeachob.com; 5059 Newport Ave, Ocean Beach; most dishes $3-11; ⏲11am-2am) Maybe it's the lightly fried mahi and wahoo fish. Or the zippy white sauce. Or layered fresh cabbage and peppery tomato salsa. Whatever the secret, the fish tacos at this raucous beachside bar and grill are standouts. All ages welcome before 6pm.

Sundara
INDIAN $$

(Map p404; ☏619-889-0639; www.sundaracuisine.com; 1774 Sunset Cliffs Blvd; mains $11-12; ⏲5-9.30pm Sun-Thu, to 10pm Fri & Sat; 🖐) This little, modern, neat-as-a-pin place has a tiny but well-chosen menu of curries and tandoori chicken, and a much longer menu of craft and bottled beers from as far away as India. It's adorned with simple black-and-white photos of Indian street scenes.

Pacific Beach

★ Pacific Beach Fish Shop
SEAFOOD $
(☏ 858-483-1008; www.thefishshoppb.com; 1775 Garnet Ave; tacos/fish plates from $4.50/15.50; ⊙ 11am-10pm) You can't miss this fishy-themed joint with its enormous swordfish hanging outside. Inside, it's a casual, communal bench affair. Choose from more than 10 types of fresh fish at the counter, from ahi to red snapper, then pick your marinade (garlic butter to chipotle glaze), then select your style – fish plate with rice and salad, taco or sandwich perhaps?

Kono's Surf Club
CAFE $
(Map p406; ☏ 858-483-1669; www.konoscafe.com; 704 Garnet Ave, Pacific Beach; mains $5-10; ⊙ 7am-3pm Mon-Fri, to 4pm Sat & Sun; 🖼) This place makes four kinds of breakfast burritos that you eat out of a basket in view of Crystal Pier (patio seating available) alongside pancakes, eggs and Kono potatoes. It's always crowded but well worth the wait.

★ The Patio on Lamont
AMERICAN $$
(☏ 858-412-4648; www.thepatioonlamont.com; 4445 Lamont St; dishes $7-26; ⊙ 9am-midnight) Popular local hangout serving beautifully prepared New American small plates and cocktails. Try the crab and ahi tower or crispy artichoke with goat's cheese in a cozy fairy-lit patio area (with outside heaters in winter). Daily happy hours on selected beers and cocktails ($5/6) run from 3pm to 6pm and 10pm to midnight.

JRDN
CALIFORNIAN $$$
(Map p406; ☏ 858-270-5736; www.t23hotel.com/dine; Tower 23 Hotel, 723 Felspar St; breakfast & lunch dishes $11-21, dinner mains $28-49; ⊙ 9am to 4pm Mon-Fri, 5pm to 9:30pm Sun-Thu, to 10pm Fri & Sat; 🖼) 🖋 A big heaping dose of chic amid PB's congenital laid-back feel. There's both an ocean view and a futuristic interior (and most excellent bar scene). Sustainably farmed meats and seafood join local veggies to create festivals on the plate. Try dishes like farmers-market apple salad, day-boat scallops, oysters on the half shell or local yellowtail.

World Famous
SEAFOOD $$$
(Map p406; ☏ 858-272-3100; www.worldfamouspb.com; 711 Pacific Beach Dr; breakfast & lunch $9-16, dinner $15-29; ⊙ 7am-midnight) Watch the surf while enjoying 'California coastal cuisine', an ever-changing all-day menu of inventive dishes from the sea (crabcake sliders for lunch or bacon wrapped scallops for dinner), plus Mexican-style breakies, steaks, salads and lunchtime sandwiches, burgers and roasted meats. The menu changes daily and there's a great bar, too.

Drinking & Nightlife

San Diego's bar scene is diverse, ranging from live-music pubs and classic American pool bars to beach bars with tiki cocktails, gay clubs offering drag shows, and even a few hidden speakeasies. It's easy to find a local craft beer in town, or you can venture out to one of the 100 breweries or vineyards in the Temecula area.

Gaslamp Quarter

The Gaslamp has the city's highest concentration of nightlife venues. Many do double (even triple) duty as restaurants, bars and clubs.

Dublin Square
IRISH PUB
(Map p396; www.dublinsquareirishpub.com; 544 4th Ave; ⊙ 11:30am-2am weekdays, from 9am Sat & Sun) Guinness? Check. Corned beef? Check. But what sets this rambling pub apart are its long happy hours (lasting five hours early in the week) and its live music, usually in the form of a lively cover band; check the website for the schedule. Brunch is served between 9am and 2pm on weekends, and lunch and dinner from 11:30am to 10:30pm daily.

Star Bar
BAR
(Map p396; ☏ 619-234-5575; 423 E St; ⊙ 6am-2am) When you've had it with gentrified style and you're looking for a historic dive, head to this old-school bar (decorated year-round with Christmas lights) for possibly the cheapest drinks in Gaslamp. It's open 20 hours a day, 365 days a year.

★ Bang Bang
BAR
(Map p396; ☏ 619-677-2264; www.bangbangsd.com; 526 Market St; cocktails $14-26; ⊙ 5-10:30pm Wed-Thu, to 2am Fri & Sat) Beneath lantern light, the Gaslamp's hottest new spot brings in local and world-renowned DJs. Get sushi and Asian small plates like dumplings and *panko*-crusted shrimp to accompany the imaginative cocktails (some in giant goblets meant for sharing with your posse). Plus, the bathrooms are shrines to Ryan Gosling and Hello Kitty: in a word, awesome.

At the weekend and for special events, the place turns into a club: expect a cover charge later in the evening.

Fluxx
CLUB

(Map p396; www.fluxxsd.com; 500 4th Ave; ⊘9pm-2am Fri & Sat) Think Vegas in the Gaslamp. San Diego's hottest dance club has amazing design with rotating themes (jellyfish and mermaids, anyone?), DJs spinning electronic dance music and the occasional celeb sighting. Even a crowded dance floor, expensive cocktails and often steep cover charges (approx $15) can't seem to stop this place from being jam-packed.

 ### East Village

While out-of-towners frolic happily in the Gaslamp Quarter, San Diego locals and hipsters instead head east to these more insider-y bars.

Noble Experiment
BAR

(Map p396; ☎619-888-4713; http://nobleexperimentsd.com; 777 G St; ⊘7pm-2am Tue-Sun) This place is literally a find. Open a secret door and enter a contemporary speakeasy with miniature gold skulls on the walls, classical paintings on the ceilings and inventive cocktails on the list (from $12). The hard part: getting in. Text for a reservation, and they'll

---

SURF & SUDS

There are now more than 100 craft breweries operating in the San Diego area. The **San Diego Brewers Guild** (www.sandiegobrewersguild.org) counts some 40-plus member establishments. Go to the guild's website for a map or pick up one of its pamphlets around town and start planning your brewery-hopping tour. To leave the driving to someone else, **Brewery Tours of San Diego** (p409) offers bus tours to different breweries for a variety of tastes. Tour price varies by timing and whether a meal is served.

Check our recommendations to get you started and see also **Stone Brewing** (p419) and **Ballast Point Tasting Room & Kitchen** (p423).

Karl Strauss Brewery & Grill (☎619-234-2739; 1157 Columbia St; ⊘11am-10pm Sun-Thu, to 11pm Fri & Sat) Local microbrewery serving surprisingly decent pub grub (most mains $9 to $17). It's particularly proud of the mac 'n' cheese – try the Piggy Bank mac with beer-brined bacon, Black Forest ham and Andouille sausage. Every Thursday night the brewery debuts a small batch of cask brews for $5 a pint.

Stone Brewing Company (☎760-294-7866; www.stonebrew.com; 1999 Citracado Pkwy, Escondido; ⊘11am-9pm Sun-Thu, to 10pm Fri & Sat) Choose from 36 specialty beers on tap in this huge open-plan space, with natural features and a one-acre organic beer garden with water features and tropical plants. The food menu solely uses locally grown organic ingredients. A Stone Hotel, for beer enthusiasts, is expected to open on site in 2018. It will offer guests a Stone beer during check-in, and an in-room growler service.

Coronado Brewing Co (☎619-437-4452; www.coronadobrewingcompany.com; 170 Orange Ave, Coronado; ⊘from 11am) The Seacoast Pilsner, Idiot IPA and Mermaid's Red go well with the house wood-fired pizzas, or pastas, sandwiches and fries; near the ferry terminal.

Pacific Beach Ale House (☎858-581-2337; www.pbalehouse.com; 721 Grand Ave, Pacific Beach; ⊘11am-2am Mon-Fri, 9am-2am Sat & Sun) Contempo-cool setting, with an outdoor terrace overlooking Pacific Beach and a huge menu including lobster mac 'n' cheese, bison burgers and brick-oven chicken (mains $10–23).

Green Flash (☎858-622-0085; www.greenflashbrew.com; 6550 Mira Mesa Blvd; ⊘3-9pm Tue-Wed, 3-10pm Thu, 12-10pm Fri, 12-9pm Sat, 12-8pm Sun) Up to 30 beers are served in this 4,000-sq-ft tasting room and beer garden. Brewery tours run in the afternoon ($6.50 per person) and include an hour's tour of the brewery plus beer tasting.

Lost Abbey (☎800-918-6816; www.lostabbey.com; ste 104, 155 Mata Way, San Marcos; ⊘1-7pm Mon-Wed, to 8pm Thu, to 9pm Fri, 11:30am-8pm Sat, noon-6pm Sun) Using monastic and artistic Belgian brewing traditions, Lost Abbey's hoppy concept beers are freshly made on-site. There a 42-tap system in the tasting room, including seasonal and limited-edition pours. The brewer often has a food truck for the weekend; call ahead to check which will be appearing.

tell you if your requested time is available and how to find the place. It's also possible to turn up to the bar upstairs (Neighborhood; p416) and put your name on a waiting list.

East Village Tavern & Bowl   SPORTS BAR
(Map p396; ☑ 619-677-2695; www.tavernbowl.com; 930 Market St; ☺ 11am-12am Sun-Thu, to 2am Sat & Sun) This large sports bar a few blocks from baseball stadium Petco Park (p398) has six bowling lanes (thankfully, behind a wall for effective soundproofing). Pub menu (dishes $5 to $14; bacon-jam sliders, mac 'n' cheese balls) is served all day.

Uptown: Bankers Hill, Hillcrest & North Park

Nightlife in Uptown's neighborhoods reflects the varied scenes in each of them. Hillcrest has the greatest concentration of bars, particularly gay spots, while North Park has a cool, hipster vibe.

★ Polite Provisions   COCKTAIL BAR
(Map p396; ☑ 619-677-3784; www.politeprovisions. com; 4696 30th St, North Park; ☺ 3pm-2am Mon-Thu, 11:30am-2am Fri-Sun) With a French-bistro feel and plenty of old-world charm, Polite Provisions' hip clientele sip cocktails at the marble bar, under a glass ceiling, and in a beautifully designed space, complete with vintage cash register, wood-paneled walls and tiled floors. Many cocktail ingredients, syrups, sodas and infusions are homemade and displayed in apothecary-esque bottles.

The house also pours various wines and beers on tap.

★ Coin-Op Game Room   BAR, GAME ROOM
(☑ 619-255-8523; www.coinopsd.com; 3926 30th St, North Park; ☺ 4pm-1am Mon-Fri, noon-1am Sat & Sun) Dozens of classic arcade games – pinball to Mortal Kombat, Pac-Man and Big Buck Safari to Master Beer Bong – line the walls of this hipster bar in North Park. All the better to quaff craft beers and cocktails like The Dorothy Mantooth (gin, Giffard Violette, lime, cucumber, Champagne) and chow on truffle-parm tots, fried-chicken sandwiches or fried oreos.

Blind Lady Ale House   PUB
(☑ 619-225-2491; http://blindlady.blogspot.com; 3416 Adams Ave; ☺ 5pm-midnight Mon-Thu, from 11:30am Fri-Sun) A superb neighborhood pub,

with creative decor like beer cans piled floor to ceiling and longboard skateboards attached to the walls. It sells craft ales on pump and prepares fresh pizza (from $7). Vegetarians should try the meat-free Mondays offering pies with inventive flavors like the 'crows pass butternut squash' – shiitake mushrooms, sage, fontina, bechamel and lemon zest.

Nunu's Cocktail Lounge   COCKTAIL BAR
(Map p390; ☑ 619-295-2878; 3537 5th Ave, Hillcrest; bar bites from $5; ☺ 2pm-2am Mon-Thu, 12pm-2am Fri, 9am-2am Sat, 7am-2am Sun) Dark and divey, this hipster haven started pouring when JFK was president and still looks the part with its curvy booths, big bar and lovably kitsch decor. There are chicken wings, sliders, tacos and mozzarella sticks on the menu.

Little Italy

El Camino   LOUNGE
(☑ 619-685-3881; www.elcaminosd.com; 2400 India St; ☺ 5pm-late Mon-Sat, from 11am Sun) We're not sure what it means that this buzzy watering hole has a Día de los Muertos (Mexican Day of the Dead holiday) theme in the flight path of San Diego Airport – watch planes land from the outdoor patio – but whatever, dude. The clientele is cool, design mod, the cocktails strong and the Mexican victuals *fabulosos*.

Waterfront   BAR
(Map p396; ☑ 619-232-9656; www.waterfront barandgrill.com; 2044 Kettner Blvd; ☺ 6am-2am) San Diego's first liquor license was granted to this place in the 1930s (it was on the waterfront until the harbor was filled and the airport built). A room full of historic bric-a-brac, big windows looking onto the street and the spirits of those who went before make this a wonderful place to spend the afternoon or evening.

Ballast Point Tasting Room & Kitchen   PUB
(Map p396; ☑ 619-255-7213; www.ballastpoint. com; 2215 India St; ☺ 11am-11pm) This San Diego–based brewery does 4oz tasters of its beers for just $5, which could be the best deal in town. Enjoy them with a full menu including housemade pretzels, beer-steamed mussels, salads or a truffle burger.

Old Town

Old Town Saloon
BAR

(☎619-298-2209; http://oldtownsaloonsd.wixsite.com/bars; 2495 San Diego Ave; ⏰10:30am-1pm) This one's for the locals, so be cool. Swill a Bud Light, and play pool at one of four tables.

Harney Sushi
BAR

(☎619-295-3272; http://harneysushi.com; 3964 Harney St; ⏰11:30am-3pm Mon-Fri, 5:30-11pm Mon-Thu, Sun, to 12am Fri & Sat) Yes, it's a sushi bar (dishes $4 to $19), but the *bar* takes over late at night as a rotation of DJs spin music from reggae to house to techno for a hip, younger crowd.

 Coronado to Pacific Beach

Mc P's Irish Pub
PUB

(☎619-435-5280; www.mcpspub.com; 1107 Orange Ave; ⏰11am-late Mon-Sat, 10am-late Sun; 🐾) Dyed-in-the-wool Irish pub that's been here for a generation. Pints o' Guinness complement down-home Irish fare – corned beef, stew, meatloaf – as you listen to nightly live music from rock to Irish folk. Indoor and patio seating.

The Grass Skirt
COCKTAIL BAR

(Map p406; ☎858-412-5237; http://thegrassskirt.com; 910 Grand Ave; ⏰5pm-2am) Through a secret doorway, disguised as a refrigerator in the next-door **Good Time Poke** cafe, you'll step into a lost Hawaiian world with Polynesian wood carvings, thatched verandahs, fire features and tiki-girl figurines made into lamps. Sip your daiquiri or piña colada and wait for more surprises to come...listen out for immersive weather sounds and lighting effects.

Bub's Dive
BAR

(Map p406; ☎858-270-7269; http://bubspb.com; 1030 Garnet Ave, Pacific Beach; ⏰11am-2am Mon-Fri, from 10am Sat & Sun) At this rowdy spot with a frat-party atmosphere over tater tots and sliders, you might find yourself playing giant Connect Four or belting out 'Build me up, Buttercup' with a passel of new buds.

Society Billiard Cafe
BAR

(Map p406; ☎858-272-7665; 1051 Garnet Ave, Pacific Beach; ⏰noon-2pm) Why settle for a beat-up pool table in the back of a dark bar when you can visit San Diego's plushest pool hall? The billiard room has about a dozen full-sized tables, snacks and a bar.

Café 976
CAFE

(Map p406; ☎858-203-7140; www.cafe976felspar.com; 976 Felspar St, Pacific Beach; ⏰7am-5pm) Not everyone in PB spends the days surfing or the nights partying; some drink coffee and read books at this delightful side-street cafe in a converted old wooden house ensconced in rose bushes and flowering trees.

Jungle Java
CAFE

(Map p404; ☎619-224-0249; http://daniellemarie hargis.wixsite.com/jungle-java/home; 5047 Newport Ave, Ocean Beach; coffees from $2; ⏰7am-6pm Mon-Sun; 📶) Funky-dunky, canopy-covered cafe and plant shop, also crammed with crafts and art treasures. A chilled place to sip on a coffee, smoothie or chai latte, tuck into a pastry and surf the free wi-fi.

☆ Entertainment

Check out the San Diego *City Beat* or *UT San Diego* for the latest movies, theater, galleries and music gigs around town. **Arts Tix** (☎858-437-9850; www.sdartstix.com; 28 Horton Plaza (next to Balboa Theatre); ⏰10am-4pm Tue-Thu, to 6pm Fri & Sat, to 2pm Sun), in a kiosk near Westfield Horton Plaza, has half-price tickets for same-day evening or next-day matinee performances; it also offers discounted tickets to other events. **Ticketmaster** (☎800-653-8000; www.ticketmaster.com) and House of Blues (p426) sell tickets to other gigs around the city.

☆ Live Music

Prohibition Lounge
LIVE MUSIC

(Map p396; http://prohibitionsd.com; 548 5th Avenue; ⏰8:00pm-1:30am Wed-Sat) Find the unassuming doorway on 5th Ave with 'Eddie O'Hare's Law Office' on it, then flip the light switch on to alert the doorman, who'll guide you into a dimly lit basement serving craft cocktails, where patrons enjoy live jazz (music from 9:30pm). Come early as it gets busy fast; at weekends expect to put your name on a list.

Shout House
LIVE MUSIC

(Map p396; ☎619-231-6700; www.theshouthouse.com; 655 4th Ave; cover free-$10) Good, clean fun at this cavernous Gaslamp bar with dueling pianos. Talented players have an amazing repertoire, including classics, rock and more. We once heard a dirty version of 'Part of Your World' from *The Little Mermaid* (OK, maybe the fun's not so clean).

The lively crowd ranges from college age to conventioneers.

Quartyard   LIVE PERFORMANCE
(Map p396; ☑ 619-432-5303; www.quartyardsd. com; 1102 Market Street; ☺ 7am-10pm Sun-Thu, to 12am Fri & Sat) FREE Re-imagined colorful containers make up this new outdoor com-

munity space and stage in East Village, a short walk from Gas Lamp. Home to a coffee shop, beer garden, restaurant and live venue all in one, it's a great summer hangout spot when open-air performances, DJ sets and screenings take place. Note that events may be ticketed.

GAY & LESBIAN SAN DIEGO

San Diego has a sizable gay population. Historians trace the roots of San Diego's thriving gay community to WWII. Amid the enforced intimacy of military life, gay men from around the US were suddenly able to create strong, if clandestine, social networks. Postwar, many of these new friends stayed.

In the late 1960s, a newly politicized gay community made its unofficial headquarters in Hillcrest. Today, on the stretch of University Ave north of Balboa Park you'll find scattered rainbow flags and plenty of LGBTQ-friendly bars, restaurants and shops. The scene is generally more casual and friendly than in San Francisco or LA. San Diego LGBT Pride takes place in July annually with concerts, parties and a parade. For current events, visit the **San Diego Gay and Lesbian News** (www.sdgln.com).

San Diego's main LGBTQ-friendly area is Hillcrest, which has a large concentration of bars, restaurants, cafes and shops flying the rainbow flag. The scene is more casual, friendly and unpretentious than neighboring LA or San Francisco. The premier lesbian bar is **Gossip Grill**, while **Flicks**, **Rich's** and **Urban Mo's** are mixed, host various themed nights and are always lively spots to grab a drink. For current LGBTQ events and news visit the **Gay San Diego website** (http://gay-sd.com) or pick up a paper copy, distributed in newspaper racks around town.

Rich's (☑ 619-295-2195; www.richssandiego.com; 1051 University Ave; ☺ 10pm-2am Wed-Sun) In the heart of Hillcrest, DJs shower the crowd with Latin, techno, pop and house at one of San Diego's biggest gay dance clubs; Rich's also hosts the popular #LEZ ladies party on Thursdays.

Gossip Grill (☑ 619-260-8023; www.thegossipgrill.com; 1220 University Ave; ☺ noon-2am Mon-Fri, 10am-2am Sat & Sun) They pour the drinks strong at San Diego's premier lesbian bar. It has a full patio, restaurant and dance floor, decorated with plants, chandeliers and two fire pits. The menu includes wings, sliders, flatbreads, soups, salads and sandwiches (mains from $9). There are often themed events, DJs and weekly drinks offers.

Top of the Bay (☑ 619-564-3755; www.glassdoorsd.com; Porto Vista Hotel, 1835 Columbia St; ☺ 5-10pm Fri fortnightly) Start your weekend off big with after-work cocktails surrounded by fabulous people at this gay night in the bay-view penthouse restaurant of the **Porto Vista Hotel** in Little Italy.

Urban Mo's (☑ 619-491-0400; www.urbanmos.com; 308 University Ave, Hillcrest; ☺ 9am-1:30am) Urban Mo's is a Hillcrest institution and calls itself a 'hetero-friendly gay bar and restaurant.' Visit for thumping beats, casual vibes and decent bar grub. Events include everything from drag nights to line dancing and wicked happy-hour deals.

Flicks (☑ 619-297-2056; www.sdflicks.com; 1017 University Ave; ☺ 9am-late Sun, 4pm-late Mon, Wed & Thu, 2pm-late Tue & Fri, noon-late Sat) Video bar dominated by big screens, plus trivia, karaoke and more. Fun place to play pool, hang out or go for a Sunday NFL beer bust.

Fiesta Cantina (☑ 619-298-2500; www.fiestacantina.net; 142 University Ave; ☺ 12pm-2am Mon-Thu, 11.30am-2am Fri, 11am-2am Sat & Sun) A tiki-style bar with cheap multicolored cocktails as big as your head. The crowd is as diverse as the music, ranging from Latin to pop and hip-hop. There will certainly be people shaking their stuff on the small dance floor. Taco Tuesdays (all you can eat for $6) and two happy hours daily (4pm-8pm; 10:30pm-12:30am) are a big pull.

Winston's

LIVE MUSIC

(Map p404; ☑619-222-6822; www.winstonsob.com; 1921 Bacon St, Ocean Beach; ☺1pm until late) Bands play most nights, and each night has a different happening: open mike, karaoke, comedy, cover bands for the Grateful Dead and Red Hot Chili Peppers, local artists, game day etc.

House of Blues

BLUES

(Map p396; ☑619-299-2583; www.houseofblues.com/sandiego; 1055 5th Ave; ☺4-11pm) Live blues music, DJs, rock bands, karaoke, trivia nights and more. Free shows on certain nights with dinner (flatbreads, burgers, sandwiches and salads). Scheduled gigs are priced individually depending on the popularity of the artist.

710 Beach Club

LIVE MUSIC

(Map p406; ☑858-483-7844; www.710bc.com; 710 Garnet Ave, Pacific Beach; ☺11am-late) PB's main venue for live music books a solid lineup of rock, karaoke and sometimes comedy.

Casbah

LIVE MUSIC

(☑619-232-4355; www.casbahmusic.com; 2501 Kettner Blvd; $5-45) Bands from Smashing Pumpkins to Death Cab for Cutie all rocked the Casbah on their way up the charts and it's still a good place to catch tomorrow's headliners.

☆ Classical Music

San Diego Symphony

CLASSICAL MUSIC

(Map p396; ☑619-235-0800; www.sandiegosymphony.com; 750 B St, Jacobs Music Center; from $20; ☺show times vary) This accomplished orchestra presents classical and family concerts at **Jacobs Music Center**. Look for summer concerts at Embarcadero Marina Park South.

☆ Cinemas

Cinema Under the Stars

OUTDOOR CINEMA

(☑619-295-4221; www.topspresents.com; 4040 Goldfinch St; $19) This unique venue screens mostly classic American films in the open air in Mission Hills; during winter months the area is covered and the patio heated.

☆ Spectator Sports

San Diego Padres

BASEBALL

(Map p396; www.padres.com; Petco Park, 100 Park Blvd; $15-91; ☺Apr-early Oct) San Diego's Major League Baseball team team plays in the handsome Petco Park (p398) stadium in the East Village. Tickets are usually available at the gate, unless it's crucial to the standings or the LA Dodgers are in town.

☆ Theater

Theater thrives in San Diego and is one of the city's greatest cultural attractions. La Jolla Playhouse (p438) is non-profit and shows new plays and musicals. Also keep an eye out for performances at the **San Diego Junior Theatre** (Map p390; ☑619-239-1311; www.juniortheatre.com; Casa del Prado, Balboa Park; from $12; ☺show times vary) and the San Diego Repertory Theatre (p427). Book tickets at the local box offices, online or find upcoming shows via Arts Tix (p424).

Old Globe Theaters

THEATER

(Map p390; ☑619-234-5623; www.theoldglobe.org; Balboa Park) Balboa Park's Old Globe Theater dates from the 1935 Exposition, and in the 1970s the main stage was rebuilt *à la* 17th-century Globe in England, where Shakespeare's works were originally performed. This Globe puts on 15 main productions each year, plus the annual Dr. Seuss' *How the Grinch Stole Christmas!* musical, honoring the famed children's book writer who lived and died in nearby La Jolla. There are performances most days, including non-Shakespearean works.

Balboa Theatre

THEATER

(Map p396; ☑619-570-1100; http://sandiegotheatres.org; 868 4th Ave; from $35) Built in 1924, this building has a colorful past: in the '30s it screened films from Mexico City to San Diego's growing Latino audience. During World War II, it was turned into US Navy bachelor quarters. It was later closed, then (recently) underwent a $26 million refurbishment. Since 2008, this fabled stage has hosted everything from comedy to movies and operas.

San Diego Repertory Theatre

THEATER

(Map p396; ☑619-544-1000; www.sdrep.org; Lyceum Theater, 79 Horton Plaza; from $17; ☺box-office noon-6pm Tue-Sun, performance times vary) For contemporary plays and re-imagined classics and self-proclaimed 'provocative theater.'

Lamb's Players Theater

THEATER

(☑619-437-6000; www.lambsplayers.org; 1142 Orange Ave, Coronado) Well-regarded company in Coronado.

🛍 Shopping

San Diego is chock-full of shops selling everything from local-pride souvenirs to Mexican gifts, adventure goods, beachwear and interesting antiques. Keep your eyes peeled in neighborhood streets for independent shops and boutiques trading in local wares. Farmers markets are also a big hit around town. Plus, there are plenty of slightly-out-of-town malls for everyday big brands and luxury fashion items.

Adams Avenue   ANTIQUES
(www.adamsaveonline.com; Adams Ave) This is San Diego's main 'antique row,' featuring dozens of shops selling furniture, art and antiques from around the world; it cuts across some of San Diego's less-visited neighborhoods. Take a rest from all the shopping at the Blind Lady Ale House (p423), serving pizzas and craft beers.

🔒 Downtown San Diego

Headquarters at Seaport District   MALL
(Map p396; ☑ 619-235-4013; www.theheadquarters. com; 789 W Harbor Dr; ☺10am-9pm Mon-Sat, to 8pm Sun) San Diego's fairly new shopping center (opened 2013) is also one of its oldest buildings: the 1939 former police headquarters has turned into some 90 shopping, dining and entertainment options. There's a small exhibit of vintage handcuffs, helmets, badges and jail cells for you and up to 15 of your friends.

Westfield Horton Plaza   MALL
(Map p396; ☑ 619-239-8180; www.westfield.com/ hortonplaza; 342 Horton Plaza; ☺10am-8pm Mon-Sat, 11am-6pm Sun) At the edge of the Gaslamp, this five-story, seven-block shopping mall features shops big and small, including Macy's, Bebe and Forever 21. Los Angeles-based architect Jon Jerde – who also designed Universal City Walk – gave it colorful, toy-town arches and postmodernist balconies, making it feel slightly like an MC Escher drawing. Free one-hour parking, $2 per 15 minutes thereafter.

Seaport Village   SHOPPING DISTRICT
(Map p396; ☑ 619-235-4014; www.seaportvillage. com; 849 West Harbor Dr; ☺10am-10pm Jun-Aug, to 9pm Sep-May; 📶) Neither seaport nor village, this 14-acre collection of novelty shops and restaurants has a faux New England theme. It's touristy and twee but good for souvenir shopping and casual eats.

🔒 Mission Valley

Fashion Valley   MALL
(☑ 619-297-3381; www.simon.com/mall/fashion-valley; 7007 Friars Rd; ☺10am-9pm Mon-Sat, to 7pm Sun) Premier shops here include Apple, Gucci, Jimmy Choo, Louis Vuitton, Zara, H&M and Nike, plus department stores Macy's and Nordstrom.

Westfield Mission Valley   MALL
(☑ 619-296-6375; www.westfield.com/mission valley; 1640 Camino del Rio N; ☺10am-9pm Mon-Sat, 11am-6pm Sun) This mall is quite casual with shops like Target and Hot Topic.

Hazard Center   MALL
(☑ 619-543-8111; https://hazardcenter.com; 7510-7610 Hazard Center Dr; ☺hours vary per retailer) The smallest of the three Mission Valley malls, with Barnes & Noble, Joe's Crab Shack, Starbucks and Yogurtland among others.

🔒 North Park

Pigment   DESIGN
(☑ 619-501-6318; www.shoppigment.com; 3801 30th St; ☺10am-7pm Mon-Thu, to 8pm Fri & Sat, to 5pm Sun) 🖋 Organic, modern and home-grown gifts and home items, from obscure books like *How to Stay Alive in the Woods* and *Cabin Porn* to wooden water bottles, locally made candles, bags, lamps, plants and ornaments.

🔒 Point Loma Area

Liberty Station   MALL
(www.libertystation.com; 2640 Historic Decatur Rd) Between downtown and Point Loma, the former offices, barracks and mess halls of the decommissioned Naval Training Center is an up-and-coming open-air area to hang out in San Diego for shopping and dining. The new Liberty Public Market (p419) is an open-plan food hall with artisan eateries, like a smaller version of San Francisco's Ferry Building Marketplace. Meanwhile top restaurants nearby include Corvette Diner (p420) and Stone Brewing (p420).

🔒 Mission & Pacific Beaches

Pangaea Outpost   FASHION & ACCESSORIES
(Map p406; ☑ 858-224-3195; http://pangaeaout post.com; 909 Garnet Ave, Pacific Beach; ☺10am-7pm Sun-Thu, to 8pm Fri-Sat) Like a miniworld unto themselves, the 70-plus merchants

TRAVELING TO TIJUANA

Just beyond the busiest land border in the Western Hemisphere, **Tijuana, Mexico** (population around 1.7 million) was for decades a cheap, convivial escape for hard-partying San Diegans, Angelenos, sailors and college kids. A decade ago, a double-whammy of drug-related violence and global recession turned once-bustling tourist areas into ghost towns. But *tijuanenses* (as the locals call themselves) have been slowly but surely reclaiming their city. The difference from squeaky-clean San Diego is palpable from the moment you cross the border, but so are many signs of new life for those who knew TJ in the bad old days.

Avenida Revolución ('La Revo') is the main tourist drag, though its charm is marred by cheap clothing and souvenir stores, strip joints, pharmacies selling bargain-priced medications to Americans, and touts best rebuffed with a firm 'no.' It's a lot more appealing just beyond La Revo, toward and around **Avenida Constitución**, where sightseeing highlights include **Catedral de Nuestra Señora de Guadalupe** (Cathedral of our Lady of Guadalupe; cnr Av Niños Héroes & Calle 2a), Tijuana's oldest church, **Mercado El Popo** (cnr Calle 2a & Av Constitución), an atmospheric market hall selling wares from tamarind pods to religious iconography, and **Pasaje Rodríguez** (Av Revolución, btwn Calles 3a & 4a; ⏰noon-10pm), an arcade filled with hipster coffee shops, local design shops and colorful street art.

A short ride away, **Museo de las Californias** (Museum of the Californias; ☑from US 011-52-664-687-9600; www.cecut.gob.mx; Centro Cultural Tijuana, cnr Paseo de los Héroes & Av Independencia; adult/child under 12yr M$27/free; ⏰10am-6pm Tue-Sun; 🅿⏰), inside the architecturally daring **Centro Cultural Tijuana** (CECUT; ☑from US 011-52-664-687-9600; www.cecut.gob.mx; cnr Paseo de los Héroes & Av Independencia; ⏰9am-7pm Mon-Fri, 10am-7pm Sat & Sun; ⏰), aka El Cubo (the Cube), offers an excellent history of the border region from prehistory to the present; there's signage in English. If you're in town on a Friday night, check out a **lucha libre** (Mexican wrestling; ☑from US 011-52-664-250-9015; Blvd Díaz Ordaz 12421, Auditorio Municipal Fausto Gutierrez Moreno; US$8-35) match at the Auditorio Municipal Fausto Gutiérrez Moreno, where oversized men in gaudy masks do Mexican wrestling.

Tijuana's culinary claim to fame is the Caesar salad, invented at the **Hotel Caesar's** (☎664-685-16-06; www.hotelcaesars.com.mx; Av Revolución 1079; s/d M$600/750; 🅿❄🛜) and now prepared table-side with panache in the elegant dining room lined with sepia pics. Ernest Hemingway and Anthony Quinn are among the illustrious patrons to dine at **Chiki**

---

here offer a supremely eclectic selection of clothing, jewelry, wraps, handbags and semiprecious stones (just for starters!) from all around the world.

Buffalo Exchange
FASHION & ACCESSORIES

(Map p406; ☑858-273-6227; www.buffaloexchange.com/locations/san-diego/pacific-beach/; 1007 Garnet Ave, Pacific Beach; ⏰10am-8pm Mon-Sat, 11am-7pm Sun) If you need something to wear to dinner, this store carries a good selection of contemporary and vintage fashions, including designer labels.

South Coast Wahines
SURFWEAR

(Map p406; ☑858-273-7600; www.southcoast.com; 4500 Ocean Blvd, Pacific Beach; ⏰10am-6pm Mon-Sat, to 5:30pm Sun) At the foot of Garnet Ave at Crystal Pier in Pacific Beach, this store carries spiffy surf apparel for women.

🛒 Ocean Beach

Cow
MUSIC

(Map p404; ☑619-523-0236; www.facebook.com/CowRecords/; 5040 Newport Ave; ⏰10am-10pm) A music store selling new and used LPs, CDs, DVDs, cassettes, 45s, VHS, 8-tracks and stickers.

Galactic
COMICS

(Map p404; ☑619-226-6543; 4981 Newport Ave; ⏰11am-8pm) Lose time perusing the shelves of this cubbyhole comic-book store. It also rents new DVDs and has a bunch of retro arcade games to play inside.

Newport Avenue Antique Center
ANTIQUES

(Map p404; ☑619-224-1994; http://antiquesinsandiego.com; 4864 Newport Ave; ⏰11am-6pm Mon-Sat, 11am-5pm Sun) Selling one-of-a-kind, out-of-the-ordinary objects from the 1700s to the 1970s. This 7000-sq-ft space is filled with collectables from 25 dealers.

Jai (☑ from US 011-52-664-685-4955; Av Revolución 1388; mains M$100-150; ☉ 11am-10pm Mon-Sat); here since the 1940s, it still serves Spanish specialties including paella, stuffed calamari and that 'other' *tortilla* (potato-based omelet) in the simple, tiled dining room. Tijuana's also a hotbed of chef-driven contemporary Mexican cuisine. Chef Javier Plascencia has a number of spots around town including the fun storefront **Erizo** (☑ from US 011-52-686-3895; 3808 Avenida Sonora; tacos M$18-45, ceviches $62-180, ramen $90-120) for innovative takes on tacos and ceviche, worth the 10-minute taxi ride from La Revo.

Turista Libre (www.turistalibre.com) runs a variety of public and private tours in English, led by an American expat with endless enthusiasm for the city and its lesser-known nooks and crannies.

A passport is required to cross the border and to re-enter the United States. By public transport from San Diego, the **San Diego Trolley** (p400) runs from Downtown to **San Ysidro border crossing** (☑ 619-690-8900; www.cbp.gov; 720 E San Ysidro Blvd; ☉ 24hr). By car, take I-5 south and look for either signs to Mexico or for the last US exit, where you can park at one of the many lots in the area (from $10 for five hours, from $20 for 24 hours). To cross the border on foot, follow the signs to Mexico, and a turnstile, which you walk through into Mexico. Follow signs reading 'Centro Downtown.' If traveling by taxi from the Mexican side of the border, be sure to take a taxi with a meter. Uber is also available for travelers with internet service on their phones. Be aware, there can be long waits to re-enter the US by foot.

Driving into Mexico is easy for those with their own cars, but you will need to purchase extra road insurance for the time you are in Mexico, and international road-side assistance is advisable. Those with rental cars should check their provider agreements for driving in Mexico, and further insurance may be required. Phone maps/GPS is useful, as road signs can be problematic for non-Spanish speakers. Exercise caution when driving around northern Baja California. Nighttime smash-and-grab theft does happen, and there have been previous instances of carjackings in Mexico. Sensible advice is to avoid traveling at night and use toll roads where possible. Visit government travel advice websites for more information. Waits to cross back into the US via car can range from 20 minutes to three hours depending on the time of day you return. Visit https://bwt.cbp.gov for updated border wait times.

Mallory's ANTIQUES
(Map p404; ☑ 619-226-2068; 4916 Newport Ave; ☉ 10am-6pm) For furniture, gifts and jewelry.

ⓘ Information

INTERNET ACCESS

All public libraries and most coffeehouses and hotel lobbies in San Diego offer free wi-fi. Libraries also offer computer terminals for access.

San Diego Main Library (☑ 619-236-5800; www.sandiego.gov/public-library; 330 Park Blvd; ☉ 9:30am-7pm Mon-Thu, to 6pm Fri & Sat, noon-6pm Sun; ⊛) The city's new main library branch is an architectural dazzler and has all the services you could want (including wi-fi).

MEDIA

Free listings magazines *Citybeat* (http://sdcitybeat.com) and *San Diego Reader* (www.sdreader.com) cover the active music, art and theater scenes. Find them in shops and cafes.

KPBS 89.5 FM (www.kpbs.org) National public radio station.

San Diego Magazine (www.sandiegomagazine.com) Glossy monthly.

UT San Diego (www.utsandiego.com) The city's major daily.

MEDICAL SERVICES

Scripps Mercy Hospital (☑ 619-294-8111; www.scripps.org; 4077 5th Ave; ☉ 24hr) has a 24-hour emergency room. There are also 24-hour drugstores around the city, including CVS stores in Pacific Beach, Gas Lamp and Adams Ave.

MONEY

You'll find ATMs throughout San Diego.

TravelEx (☑ 858-457-2412; www.travelex.com; Westfield UTC, 4417 La Jolla Village Dr; ☉ 10am-7pm Mon-Fri, to 6pm Sat, 11am-4pm Sun) Foreign-currency exchange.

POST

For post-office locations, call 800-275-8777 or log on to www.usps.com.

Downtown Post Office (☑ 800-275-8777; www.usps.com; 815 E St; ☉ 9am-5pm Mon-Fri)

Coronado Post Office (☑619-435-1142; www.
usps.com; 1320 Ynez Pl; ☺8:30am-5pm Mon-
Fri, 9am-noon Sat)

TOURIST INFORMATION

International Visitor Information Center
(☑619-236-1242; www.sandiego.org; 1140
N Harbor Dr; ☺9am-5pm Jun-Sep, to 4pm
Oct-May) Across from the B St Cruise Ship
Terminal, helpful staff offer very detailed
neighborhood maps, sell discounted tickets to
attractions and maintain a hotel-reservation
hotline.

Coronado Visitor Center (☑866-599-7242,
619-437-8788; www.coronadovisitorcenter.
com; 1100 Orange Ave; ☺9am-5pm Mon-Fri,
10am-5pm Sat & Sun)

USEFUL WEBSITES

Lonely Planet (www.lonelyplanet.com/usa/
san-diego) Destination information, hotel
bookings, traveler forum and more.

San Diego Tourism (www.sandiego.org)
Search hotels, sights, dining, rental cars and
more, and make reservations.

ⓘ Getting There & Away

AIR

Most flights to **San Diego International Air-
port-Lindbergh Field** (p497) are domestic.
The airfield sits just 3 miles west of Downtown;
plane-spotters will thrill watching jets come
in over Balboa Park for landing. Coming from
overseas, you'll likely change flights – and clear
US customs – at one of the major US gateway
airports, such as LA, San Francisco, Chicago,
New York or Miami.

The standard one-way fare between LA and
San Diego is about $115 and takes about 35
minutes; unless you're connecting through LA,
you're usually better off driving or taking the
train.

To/from other US cities, San Diego flights
are generally up to about $140 more expensive
than to LA. All major US airlines serve San
Diego, plus Air Canada, British Airways, Mexico's
Volaris and the Canadian carrier WestJet.

BUS

Greyhound (☑619-515-1100, 800-231-2222;
www.greyhound.com; 1313 National Ave;
☺ticket office 5am-11:59pm) serves San Diego
from cities across North America from its
Downtown location. Inquire about discounts
and special fares, many available only online.

Buses depart frequently for LA; the standard
one-way/round-trip fare starts at $14 and the
trip takes 2½ to four hours. There are several
daily departures to Anaheim (singles from $12,
about 2¼ hours).

Buses to San Francisco (from $59, 12 hours,
about seven daily) require a transfer in Los
Angeles; round-trip airfares often cost about
the same. Most buses to Las Vegas (one-way
from $23, eight to nine hours, about eight daily)
require a transfer in LA or San Bernardino.

CAR & MOTORCYCLE

Allow at least two hours to reach San Diego from
LA in nonpeak traffic. With traffic, it's anybody's
guess. If there are two or more passengers in
your car you can use the high-occupancy vehicle
lanes, which will shave off a fair amount of time
in heavy traffic.

TRAIN

Amtrak (☑800-872-7245; www.amtrak.com;
1050 Kettner Blvd) runs the *Pacific Surfliner*
several times daily to Anaheim (two hours), Los
Angeles (2¾ hours) and Santa Barbara (6½
hours) from the historic **Union Station** (Santa
Fe Depot; ☑800-872-7245; 1050 Kettner Blvd;
☺3am-11:59pm). Trains run to stations in
Oceanside, Carlsbad, Encinitas, Solana Beach,
Sorrento Valley, Old Town and Downtown. Fares
start from around $30 and the coastal views
are enjoyable.

ⓘ Getting Around

BICYCLE

While in San Diego, mostly flat Pacific Beach,
Mission Beach, Mission Bay and Coronado are
all great places to ride a bike. Visit **iCommute**
(www.icommutesd.com) for maps and information about biking in the region. Public buses are
equipped with bike racks.

A few outfits rent bicycles, from mountain and
road bikes to kids bikes and cruisers. In general,
expect to pay about $8 per hour, $15–$22 per
half-day (four hours) and $25–$30 per day.

BOAT

Flagship Cruises (p409) operates the hourly
Coronado Ferry (☑800-442-7847; www.
flagshipsd.com; 990 N Harbor Dr; 1 way $4.75;
☺9am-10pm) shuttling between San Diego's
Broadway Pier (1050 N Harbor Dr) on the Embarcadero and the ferry landing at the foot of
B Ave in Coronado, two blocks south of Orange
Ave. Bikes are permitted on board at no extra
charge. Flagship also operates a water taxi,
serving mostly Downtown and Coronado.

BUS

MTS (p431) covers most of San Diego's metropolitan area, North County, La Jolla and the
beaches. It's most convenient if you're based
Downtown and not staying out late.

Useful routes to/from Downtown:

BUS ROUTE	STOPS IN SAN DIEGO
3	Balboa Park, Hillcrest, UCSD Medical Center
7	Gaslamp, Balboa Park, Zoo, Hillcrest, North Park
8/9	Old Town, Pacific Beach, SeaWorld
30	Gaslamp, Little Italy, Old Town, Pacific Beach, La Jolla, University Town Center
35	Old Town, Ocean Beach
901	Gaslamp, Coronado, Imperial Beach

CAR

All the big-name car-rental companies have desks at the **San Diego airport** (p497); lesser-known companies may be cheaper. Shop around – prices vary widely, even from day to day within the same company. The airport has free direct phones to a number of car-rental companies. Rental rates tend to be comparable to LA ($30 to $80 per day plus insurance fees). Smaller agencies include **West Coast Rent a Car** (☑ 619-544-0606; http://westcoastrentacar. net; 834 W Grape St; ☺ 9am-6pm Mon-Sat, to 5pm Sun), in Little Italy.

METROPOLITAN TRANSIT SYSTEM (MTS)

The Metropolitan Transit System runs buses and trolleys throughout central San Diego and beyond. For route and fare information, call 619-233-3004 or 800-266-6883; operators are available 5:30am to 8:30pm Monday to Friday, and 8am to 5pm Saturday and Sunday (note that the 800 number works only within San Diego). For 24-hour automated information, call 619-685-4900. Visit www.sdmts. com/schedules-real-time to plan your route online.

One paying adult may travel with up to two children aged 5 and under for free on buses with a valid MTS ticket. On Saturdays and Sundays up to two children (age 12 and under) may ride for free with one fare-paying adult (age 18 or older) on all MTS routes.

TAXI & RIDESHARE

Taxi fares vary, but plan on about $12 for a 3-mile journey. Established companies include **Orange Cab** (☑ 619-223-5555; www.orange cabsandiego.net) and **Yellow Cab** (☑ 619-444-4444; www.driveu.com). Recently app-based ride-share companies such as **Uber** (www.uber. com) and **Lyft** (www.lyft.com) have entered the market with lower fares.

TROLLEY

Municipal trolleys, not to be confused with **Old Town Trolley tourist buses** (p409), operate on three main lines in San Diego. From the transit center across from the Santa Fe Depot,

---

ℹ **BUS & TROLLEY TICKETS**

While most people get around San Diego by car, it's possible to have an entire vacation here using municipal buses and trolleys run by the **Metropolitan Transit System** (p400) and your own two feet. Most buses/trolleys cost $2.25/2.50 per ride. Transfers are not available, so purchase a day pass if you're going to be taking more than two rides in a day; a refillable **Compass Card** ($2 one-time purchase) will save hassles. The **MTS Transit Store** (☑ 619-234-1060; www. sdmts.com; 1255 Imperial Ave; ☺ 8am-5pm Mon-Fri) is one-stop shopping for route maps, tickets and one-/two-/three-/four-day passes ($5/9/12/15). Same-day passes are also available from bus drivers. At trolley stations, purchase tickets from vending machines.

Blue Line trolleys go south to San Ysidro (on the Mexico border) and north to **Old Town Transit Center** (p400). The **Green Line** runs from Gas Lamp to Old Town east through Mission Valley. The **Orange Line** connects the Convention Center and Seaport Village with Downtown, but otherwise it's less useful for visitors. Trolleys run between about 4:15am and 1am daily at 15-minute intervals during the day, and every 30 minutes in the evening. Fares are $2.50 per ride, valid for two hours from the time of purchase at vending machines on the station platforms.

LA JOLLA & NORTH COUNTY COAST

Immaculately landscaped parks, white-sand coves, upscale boutiques, top restaurants, and cliffs above deep, clear-blue waters make it easy to understand why 'La Jolla' translates from Spanish as 'The Jewel.' Pronounced la-*hoy*-yah, the name may actually date from Native Americans who inhabited the area from 10,000 years ago to the mid-19th century, and called the place 'mut la hoya, la hoya' – the place of many caves.

Northward from La Jolla, North County's coast evokes the San Diego of 40 years ago. Pretty Del Mar continues through low-key Solana Beach, Encinitas and Carlsbad (home of Legoland), before hitting Oceanside, home to Camp Pendleton Marine Base. All the beaches are terrific, and the small seaside towns are great for days of soaking up the laid-back SoCal scene and working on your tan.

All that, and only about a half-hour's drive from Downtown San Diego.

❶ Getting There & Around

North County Transit District (NCTD; ☑ 760-966-6500; www.gonctd.com) Breeze Bus 101 departs from La Jolla Village Square and follows the coastal road to Oceanside. NCTD also operates the *Coaster* train from San Diego, stopping in Solana Beach, Encinitas, Carlsbad and Oceanside. NCTD buses and trains have bike racks. A few Amtrak *Pacific Surfliner* trains stop here daily, but Greyhound buses stop only at Oceanside and San Diego's Downtown, and nowhere else in between.

La Jolla

Whether your interest is jewels or caves, you'll feel at home in this lovely enclave.

◉ Sights

◉ Historic La Jolla

For noteworthy architecture, and a little historic walking tour of La Jolla, head southwest on Prospect St to St James Episcopal Church, La Jolla Recreation Center and the Bishop's School, all built in the early 20th century. Or visit La Jolla Historical Society for regular history exhibitions.

La Jolla Historical Society   MUSEUM
(☑ 858-459-5335; www.lajollahistory.org; 780 Prospect St; ☉ 10am-4pm Mon-Fri) This place has vintage photos and beach memorabilia, plus regular exhibitions from classic cars to architecture.

La Jolla Recreation Center   NOTABLE BUILDING
(☑ 858-552-1658; www.sandiego.gov/park-and-recreation/centers/recctr/lajolla; 615 Prospect St; ☉ 10am-8pm Mon, 9am-9pm Tue & Thurs, 9am-8pm Wed, 10am-7pm Fri, 9am-3pm Sat) Commissioned by Ellen Browning Scripps and designed by famous San Diego architect Irving Gill, this notable building dates to 1915. The center has basketball courts, children's play areas, tennis courts, and picnic facilities. Check the schedule for free adult classes like Ashtanga yoga, tai chi and pilates.

St James Episcopal Church   CHURCH
(☑ 858-459-3421; 743 Prospect Street; ☉ services 7:30am, 8:45am and 10am Sun, 12pm Wed, 12pm 4th Friday of month) Classic architecture, a nice

place to stop for a photo on a historic walking tour of La Jolla.

Bishop's School   HISTORIC BUILDING
(cnr Prospect St & La Jolla Blvd) Although not open to the public, campus buildings (visible from the street) date back to 1898 and are a good example of early architecture in the area. If walking past keep a lookout for Bentham Hall, St Mary's Chapel and the Tower.

◉ La Jolla Coast

A wonderful walking path skirts the shoreline for half a mile. At the west it begins at Children's Pool, where a jetty protects the beach from big waves. Originally intended to give La Jolla's youth a safe place to frolic, this beach is now given over to sea lions, which you can view up close as they lounge on the shore.

Atop **Point La Jolla**, at the path's eastern end, **Ellen Browning Scripps Park** is a tidy expanse of green lawns and palm trees, with **La Jolla Cove** to the north. The cove's gem of a beach provides access to some of the best snorkeling there; it's also popular with rough-water swimmers.

Look for the white buoys offshore from Point La Jolla to Scripps Pier (visible to the north) that mark the San Diego-La Jolla Underwater Park Ecological Reserve (p433), a protected zone with a variety of marine life, kelp forests, reefs and canyons.

★ Children's Pool   BEACH
(La Jolla seals; 850 Coast Blvd) Built in the 1930s, La Jolla's Children's Pool was created as a family beach space, but since then it's been descended on by herds of seals and sea lions. Despite the pinnipeds' particularly pungent odor, tourists come in droves to see them larking around, swimming, fighting and mating. Visitors can get extremely close via a concrete platform surrounding the cove, and the seals don't seem to mind – but there's strictly no touching, feeding or selfies to be taken with the seals.

The future of the seals remains in debate, as divers and swimmers claim their presence increases bacteria levels in the water, yet animal-rights groups want to protect the cove and make it an official seal rookery. At the time of writing, courts ruled that the beach was to remain closed to swimmers, to protect the mums, pups and baby seals during pupping season (December 15 to May 15) when they are most vulnerable. But the future of the Children's Pool remains to be seen.

★ Cave Store   CAVE
(☑858-459-0746; www.cavestore.com; 1325 Coast Blvd; adult/child $5/3; ☺10am-4:30pm Mon-Fri, to 5pm Sat & Sun; 🖼) Waves have carved a series of caves into the sandstone cliffs east of La Jolla Cove. The largest is called **Sunny Jim Cave**, which you can access via this store. Taller visitors, watch your head as you descend the 145 steps.

San Diego-La Jolla Underwater
Park Ecological Reserve   DIVING, SNORKELING
Look for the white buoys offshore from Point La Jolla north to Scripps Pier that mark this protected zone with a variety of marine life, kelp forests, reefs and canyons. Waves have carved caves into the sandstone cliffs east of the cove.

◉ La Jolla Shores

Called simply 'the Shores,' this primarily residential area northeast of La Jolla Cove is where La Jolla's cliffs meet the wide, sandy beaches. Waves here are gentle enough for beginner surfers, and kayakers can launch from the shore without much problem. Take La Jolla Shores Dr north from Torrey Pines Rd and turn west onto Ave de la Playa.

Birch Aquarium at Scripps   AQUARIUM
(☑858-534-3474; www.aquarium.ucsd.edu; 2300 Expedition Way; adult/child $18.50/14; ☺9am-5pm; 🅿🖼) 🍴 Marine scientists were working at the Birch Aquarium at Scripps Institution of Oceanography (SIO) as early as 1910 and, helped by donations from the ever-generous Scripps family, the institute has grown to be one of the world's largest marine research institutions. It is now a part of University of California (UC) San Diego. Off N Torrey Pines Rd, the aquarium has brilliant displays. The **Hall of Fishes** has more than 60 fish tanks, simulating marine habitats from the Pacific Northwest to tropical seas.

Salk Institute   ARCHITECTURE
(☑858-453-4100; www.salk.edu; 10010 N Torrey Pines Rd; tours $15; ☺tours by reservation 11:45am Mon-Fri; 🅿) In 1960 Jonas Salk, the polio-prevention pioneer, founded the Salk Institute for biological and biomedical research. San Diego County donated 27 acres of land, the March of Dimes provided financial support

and renowned architect Louis Kahn designed the building, completed in 1965. It is regarded as a modern masterpiece, with its classically proportioned travertine-marble plaza and cubist, mirror-glass laboratory blocks framing a perfect view of the Pacific, and the fountain in the courtyard symbolizing the River of Life.

The Salk Institute attracts the best scientists to work in a research-only environment. The original buildings were expanded with new laboratories designed by Jack McAllister, a follower of Kahn's work.

Torrey Pines State
Natural Reserve   STATE PARK
(☑858-755-2063; www.torreypine.org; 12600 N Torrey Pines Rd; ☺7:15am-sunset, visitor center 10am-4pm Oct-Apr, 9am-6pm May-Sep; 🅿🖼) 🍴 FREE Between N Torrey Pines Rd and the ocean, and from the Torrey Pines Gliderport (p435) to Del Mar, this reserve preserves the last mainland stands of the Torrey pine (*Pinus torreyana*), a species adapted to sparse rainfall and sandy, stony soils. Steep sandstone gullies have eroded into wonderfully textured surfaces, and the views over the ocean and north, including whale-watching, are superb. Volunteers lead nature walks on weekends and holidays. Several trails wind through the reserve and down to the beach.

Parking is available on streets or in the park for $10 to $20.

University of California
San Diego   UNIVERSITY
(UCSD; ☑858-534-2117 (Fallen Star info); http://ucsd.edu; 9500 Gilman Dr) UCSD was established in 1960 and now has more than 30,000 students and a strong reputation, particularly for mathematics and science. It lies on rolling coastal hills in a parklike setting, surrounded by tall, fragrant eucalyptus. Its most distinctive structure is the **Geisel Library**, an upside-down pyramid named for children's author Theodor Geisel, aka Dr Seuss of *Cat in the Hat* fame; there's a collection of his drawings and books. Download a map of UCSD's excellent collection of public art at http://stuartcollection.ucsd.edu.

Fallen Star is a standout sight at UCSD – it's an angled house that juts out of the seventh floor of UCSD's Jacobs School of Engineering. Guests can step inside between 11am to 2pm on Tuesdays and Thursdays.

La Jolla

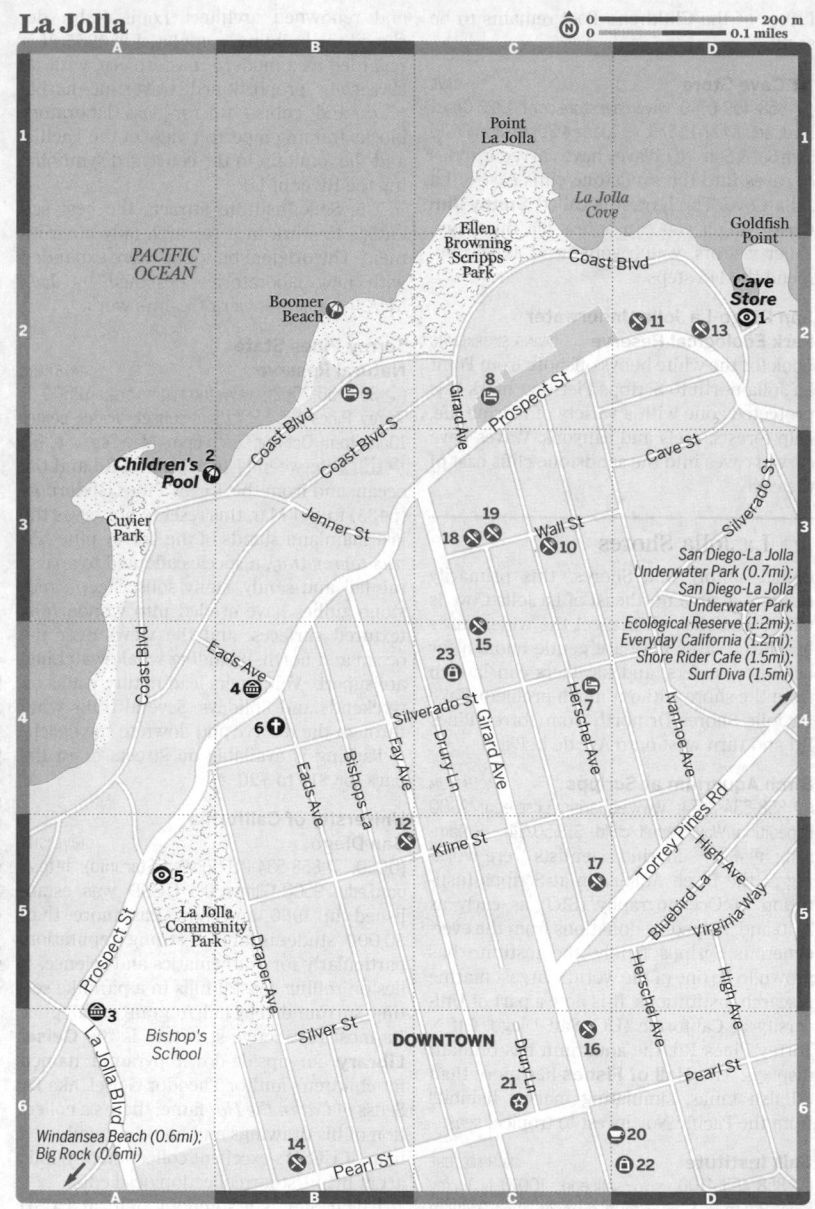

San Diego-La Jolla Underwater Park (0.7mi); San Diego-La Jolla Underwater Park Ecological Reserve (1.2mi); Everyday California (1.2mi); Shore Rider Cafe (1.5mi); Surf Diva (1.5mi)

Windansea Beach (0.6mi); Big Rock (0.6mi)

SAN DIEGO & AROUND LA JOLLA

🏃 Activities

⭐ Torrey Pines State Natural Reserve

HIKING

(📞 858-755-2063; https://torreypine.org/parks/trails.html; 12600 North Torrey Pines Rd; ⊙ 7:15am-sunset, visitor center 9am-6pm) **FREE** Walkers and hikers explore 8 miles of **trails** in 2000 acres of well-trodden coastal state park. Choose from routes of varying difficulties, including the 0.7-mile Guy Fleming Trail, with panoramic sea views and paths through wildflowers, ferns and cacti, or the 1.4-mile

La Jolla

Razor Point Trail with a good whale-spotting lookout during winter months.

La Jolla Beaches
BEACH

Some of the county's best beaches are north of the Shores in **Torrey Pines City Park**, between the Salk Institute and Torrey Pines State Natural Reserve. Hang gliders and paragliders launch into the sea breezes rising over the cliffs at Torrey Pines Gliderport, at the end of Torrey Pines Scenic Dr. It's a beautiful sight – tandem flights are available if you can't resist trying it. La Jolla Shores and Black's Beach are popular surfing spots.

San Diego-La Jolla Underwater Park
SNORKELING, DIVING

Some of California's best and most accessible diving is in this reserve, accessible from La Jolla Cove. With an average depth of 20ft, the 6000 acres of look-but-don't-touch underwater real estate are great for snorkeling too. Ever-present are the spectacular, bright-orange Garibaldi fish – California's official state fish and a protected species (there's a hefty fine for poaching one).

Windansea Beach
SURFING

Watch experienced surfers use this break, two miles south of downtown (take La Jolla Blvd south and turn west on Nautilus St); the surf's consistent peak (a powerful reef break that's not for beginners) works best at medium to low tide. However, some of the locals can be unfriendly toward outsiders.

Big Rock
SURFING

Immediately south of Windansea Beach, at the foot of Palomar Ave, is a steep, gnarly wave for expert surfers only. The name comes from the large chunk of reef protruding just offshore – it's also a great spot for tide pooling at low tide.

Surf Diva
SURFING

(☑ 858-454-8273; www.surfdiva.com; 2160 Avenida de la Playa; ⊙ store 8:30am-5pm, lesson hours vary from season to season) The wonderful women here offer surf classes from $65 and rent boards and wet suits. Men are welcome to book lessons, too.

Torrey Pines Gliderport
HANG GLIDING

(☑ 858-452-9858; www.flytorrey.com; 2800 Torrey Pines Scenic Dr; 20min paragliding $175, hang-gliding tandem flight per person $225) Conditions permitting, glider riders hang at this world-famous gliding location. It's also one of the best gliding schools in the country. Experienced pilots can join in if they have a USHGA Hang 4 (paragliders need a P3 rating) and take out an associate membership of the Torrey Pines Hang Glider Association.

🛏 Sleeping

Lodging in central La Jolla ain't cheap. We've given summer high-season (June to August) rack rates. Inquire about specials and packages, and lower rates at other times of year.

La Jolla Village Lodge
MOTEL $$

(☎877-551-2001, 858-551-2001; 1141 Silverado St; r $110-200; P☎☂☃) At the edge of downtown La Jolla, this 30-room 1950s-era motel was recently restored in period mid-century style with custom-built tables and chairs, teak headboards and new mattresses. Rooms have kitchenettes and the motel's roof deck gives long-distance views. Continental breakfast. Free parking.

★Lodge at Torrey Pines
LUXURY HOTEL $$$

(☎858-453-4420; www.lodgetorreypines.com; 11480 N Torrey Pines Rd; r from $359; P@☃) Inspired by the architecture of Greene & Greene, the turn-of-the-20th-century arts-and-crafts masters who designed the Gamble House in Pasadena, the lodge's discreetly luxurious rooms have Mission oak-and-leather furniture à la Stickley, Tiffany-style lamps, plein air paintings and basket-weave bathroom-floor tiling in marble. There's a stellar full-service spa and a croquet lawn. Parking costs $25.

La Valencia
HISTORIC HOTEL $$$

(☎858-454-0771, 800-451-0772; www.lavalencia. com; 1132 Prospect St; r from $314; P☀@ ☎☃☂) ✦ This 1926 pink-walled, Mediterranean-style landmark was designed by William Templeton Johnson. Among its 115 rooms, those in the main building are rather compact while the villas are spacious, but the property wins for its Old Hollywood romance. Even if you don't stay, consider lifting a toast – and a pinkie – to the sunset from its Spanish Revival lounge, La Sala. Parking is $30.

Estancia La Jolla Hotel & Spa
RESORT $$$

(☎877-437-8262; www.estancialajolla.com; 9700 N Torrey Pines Rd; r from $259; P☀@☎☃☂) North of the village, this rambling rancho-style resort with its pathways, patios and lush gardens is down-to-earth, romantic and cushy all at once. Unwind by the heated, saltwater pool, during an expert massage at the spa, or while sipping killer margaritas by the outdoor fireplace. Rooms feature custom furniture, luxurious linens and big bathrooms. Four restaurants.

Self-parking costs $25 per day and there's a $25 resort fee.

Pantai Inn
BOUTIQUE HOTEL $$$

(☎858-224-7600, 855-287-2682; www.pantai. com; 1003 Coast Blvd; r from $352; P☀@☎) About as close as you can stay to the beach and Scripps Park, colorful banners mark the perimeter of this Balinese-style inn. Rooms vary in size, but all have kitchens and sitting areas, and suites are filled with Balinese art and antiques. Continental breakfast is served in the Gathering Room; enjoy it on multiple ocean-view decks.

✗ Eating

Dining options are varied in La Jolla: choose from smart world-class eateries to casual street-taco joints. Look for locations of Puesto (p437) and Burger Lounge (p437) in La Jolla Village.

Harry's Coffee Shop
DINER $

(☎858-454-7381; http://harryscoffeeshop.com/; 7545 Girard Ave; dishes $5-13; ☺6am-3pm; ☂) This classic 1960 coffee shop has a posse of regulars from blue-haired socialites to sports celebs. The food is American at its best – pancakes, tuna melts, burgers (and a local concession, breakfast burritos). Wash it down with mimosas, Greyhound cocktails, Bloody Marys or beer, and soak up the special aura of the place.

★Shore Rider Cafe
CALIFORNIAN $

(☎858-412-5308; www.shoreridersd.com; 2168 Avenida de la Playa; dishes $9-15; ☺11am-10pm Mon-Thu, to 11pm Fri, 9am-11pm Sat, to 10pm Sun) For tasty eats in a surf vibe right near the beach, head to Shore Rider's new mellow open-air patio, where they play California rock and serve beer on tap and lunch plates like mahimahi and shrimp ceviche, blue cheese and bacon fries and SoCal salads. For weekend brunch (9–1pm Saturday–Sunday): shrimp ranchero, French toast or 'dinosaur eggs.'

Porkyland
MEXICAN $

(☎858-459-1708; http://goporkyland.com/locations/la-jolla/; 1030 Torrey Pines Rd; dishes $4-9; ☺9am-8pm) This tiny Mexican joint in a corner shopping center on the edge of La Jolla Village has only simple indoor-outdoor seating, but the burritos and fish tacos have a devoted following. The verde carnitas burrito ($8) will make your taste buds roar (in a good way) and still leave you money for beer.

Girard Gourmet
CAFE $

(☎858-454-3325; www.girardgourmet.com; 7837 Girard Ave; dishes $6-13; ☺8am-7pm) This Belgian-influenced deli/bakery has been serving La Jolla for 25 years. Sit in the no-frills cafe in the back of the shop and enjoy home-cooked dishes like beef Burgundy with rice, lamb stew, turkey stuffed with broccoli or a freshly made sandwich.

Burger Lounge
BURGERS $

(☑858-456-0196; www.burgerlounge.com; 1101 Wall St; burgers from $8; ⊙10:30am to 9pm Sun-Thu, to 10pm Fri-Sat) Burger chain serving cage-free chicken and grass-fed beef, local produce, plus fries and shakes.

El Pescador
SEAFOOD $$

(☑858-456-2526; www.elpescadorfishmarket.com; 634 Pearl St; mains $7-25; ⊙11am-9pm) You could pay three times as much for seafood with the tourists at fancier restaurants in town; meanwhile locals will be at this fish market and restaurant, on the edge of La Jolla Village. Order your catch from refrigerator cases and it'll be prepared into sandwich, salad or plate.

Puesto La Jolla
MEXICAN $$

(☑858-454-1260; www.eatpuesto.com; 1026 Wall St; $13-24; ⊙11am-9pm) A fabulous colorful warehouse-style restaurant dowsed in Californian spray-paint artist Chor Boogie designs. It serves Mexican street food in the form of tacos, freshly made guacamole (in six varieties) plus Baja striped bass, lime-marinated shrimp ceviche and *carnitas*. There's a decent range of tequilas, too. Sit indoors or out.

Cottage
MODERN AMERICAN $$

(☑858-454-8409; www.cottagelajolla.com; 7702 Fay Ave; breakfast $8-14, lunch $10-19; ⊙7:30am-3pm) Shhh! Don't tell anybody that the stuffed French toast, eggs La Jolla (with Canadian bacon, mushrooms, spinach and garlic, and balsamic vinegar), fish tacos and crab melt with cheddar, avocado, tomato and sourdough toast make this place a local favorite. It's crowded enough as it is, especially on weekends for brunch. Expect a wait if you arrive much after 8:30am.

Whisknladle
CALIFORNIAN $$

(☑858-551-7575; www.wnlhosp.com; 1044 Wall St; lunch $13-20, dinner $22-35; ⊙11:30am-9pm Mon-Thu, to 9.30pm Fri, 10am-9.30pm Sat, to 9pm Sun) ◢ Gourmets and gourmands alike love Whisknladle's 'slow food' preparations of local, farm-fresh ingredients, served on a breezy covered patio and meant for sharing. Every minute preparation from curing to pickling and macerating is done in-house. The menu changes often, but it's always clever. So are the cocktails (the London's Burning mixes gin and jalapeño water).

★George's at the Cove
CALIFORNIAN $$$

(☑858-454-4244; www.georgesatthecove.com; 1250 Prospect St; mains $16-46; ⊙11am-10pm Sun-Thu, to 11pm Fri & Sat) The Euro-Cal cooking is as dramatic as the oceanfront location, thanks to the bottomless imagination of chef Trey Foshee. George's has graced just about every list of top restaurants in California, and indeed the USA. Four venues allow you to enjoy it at different price points: Ocean Terrace, George's California Modern and the no-reservations Level 2 and Modern Bar.

Crab Catcher
SEAFOOD $$$

(☑858-454-9587; www.crabcatcher.com/; 1298 Prospect St; small plates from $16, mains from $26; ⊙11:30am-3pm Mon-Fri, 11am-3pm Sat, 10am-3pm Sun, 5:30pm-close) Stellar views look out to La Jolla's coastline at this fresh-fish restaurant, with clean decor, crisp white tablecloths and wrought-iron chairs on the patio. Small plates include king-crab-ceviche tacos and chilled Pacific oysters, while larger dishes like crab-stuffed fish, Maine lobster, citrus and garlic-grilled Baja tiger shrimp feature as main courses. Brunch offered on weekends.

California Modern
CALIFORNIAN $$$

(George's at the Cove; ☑858-454-4244; www.georgesatthecove.com; 1250 Prospect St; á la carte mains $28-62) The lower-floor restaurant at George's at the Cove is the place to come to splash out on a tasting menu (from $75 per person, extra for wine pairing). Menus change frequently, but expect them to be filled with creative and beautifully presented plates like coconut-and-lemon sweet potato, San Diego spiny lobster and Jidori chicken and golden raisin.

🍷 Drinking & Entertainment

While there are a few low-key bars around La Jolla, it's far from a happening nightlife scene. Most of the drinking takes place at dinner, and on restaurant patios during sunset: try **George's** (George's at the Cove; ☑858-454-4244; www.georgesatthecove.com/ocean-terrace; 1250 Prospect Street; dinner $16-40; ⊙11:30am-3pm, 4-9pm) and Crab Catcher, both overlooking the ocean.

Pannikin
CAFE

(☑858-454-5453; https://pannikincoffeeandtea.com/; 7467 Girard Ave; drinks from $2; ⊙6am-6pm; 🛜) A few blocks from the water, this clapboard shack of a cafe with a generous balcony is popular for its organic coffees,

Italian espresso and Mexican chocolate. Like all the Pannikins, it's a North County institution. Also sells sandwiches, pastries and salads.

Comedy Store COMEDY
(☑ 858-454-9176; http://lajolla.thecomedystore.com; 916 Pearl St; ☉ show times vary) One of the area's most established comedy venues, the Comedy Store also serves popcorn, drinks and barrels of laughs. Expect a cover charge (from $10 on weekdays and $20 on weekends, with a two-drink minimum) and some of tomorrow's big names. Look out for free open-mike nights.

La Jolla Playhouse THEATER
(☑ 858-550-1010; www.lajollaplayhouse.org; 2910 La Jolla Village Dr; tickets $20-75) Inside the Mandell Weiss Center for the Performing Arts, this theater has sent dozens of productions to Broadway, including *Jersey Boys*, *Peter and the Starcatcher* and 2010 Tony winner *Memphis*.

La Jolla Symphony
& Chorus CLASSICAL MUSIC
(☑ 858-534-4637; www.lajollasymphony.com; UCSD; tickets from $28) Come here for quality concerts at UCSD's Mandeville Auditorium running from October to June.

🛍 Shopping

La Jolla's skirt-and-sweater crowd pays retail for cashmere sweaters and expensive tchotchkes downtown: paintings, sculpture and decorative items. Small boutiques fill the gaps between Talbot's, Banana Republic, Ralph Lauren and Jos. A. Bank.

DG Wills and Warwick's have good book selections and host readings and author events.

Westfield UTC MALL
(UTC; ☑ 858-546-8858; www.westfield.com/utc; 4545 La Jolla Village Dr; ☉ 10am-9pm) Mall shoppers: make a beeline for this large mall out of downtown La Jolla and east of I-5; anchor stores include Nordstrom, Macy's and Sears, and for nonshoppers there are movies and an indoor ice-skating rink, **UTC Ice** (☑ 858-452-9110; https://utcice.com; 4545 La Jolla Villa Dr; $15 + $5 rental; ☉ hours vary); call for opening hours. It's also the transit hub for La Jolla.

Warwick's BOOKS
(☑ 858-454-0347; www.warwicks.com; 7812 Girard Ave; ☉ 9am-6pm Mon-Sat, 10am-5.30pm Sun)

Good range of reads, from classics to new local releases.

DG Wills BOOKS
(☑ 858-456-1800; www.dgwillsbooks.com; 7461 Girard Ave; ☉ 10am-7pm Mon-Sat, 11am-5pm Sun) A cozy cavern of books with a large collection of new and used academic works and regular book readings and talks.

ℹ Getting There & Away

Bus number 30 connects La Jolla with Bird Rock, Pacific Beach, Mission Bay Park and the **Old Town Transit Center** (p400). There's a bus stop at Silverado St and Herschel St in La Jolla. The full journey takes around 45 minutes and costs $2.25 one way.

By car, via I-5 from Downtown San Diego, take the La Jolla Pkwy exit and head west toward Torrey Pines Rd, from where it's a right turn onto Prospect St.

Del Mar

The ritziest of North County's seaside suburbs, with a Tudor aesthetic that somehow doesn't feel out of place, Del Mar boasts good (if pricey) restaurants, unique galleries, high-end boutiques and, north of town, the West Coast's most renowned horse-racing track, also the site of the annual county fair. Downtown Del Mar (sometimes called 'the village') extends for about a mile along Camino del Mar. At its hub, where 15th St crosses Camino del Mar, the tastefully designed Del Mar Plaza (p440) shopping center has restaurants, boutiques and upper-level terraces that look out to sea.

◉ Sights & Activities

California Dreamin' BALLOONING
(☑ 800-373-3359; www.californiadreamin.com; per person from $298) Brightly colored hot-air balloons are a trademark of the skies above Del Mar, on the northern fringe of the San Diego metropolitan area. For flights, contact California Dreamin', which also serves Temecula.

Seagrove Park PARK
(Coast Blvd) At the end of 15th St, this park abuts the beach and overlooks the ocean. This little stretch of well-groomed lawn is a community hub and perfect for a picnic.

🛌 Sleeping

In summer, especially around opening day at Del Mar Racetrack, rooms in Del Mar fill up and rates soar. Discounts may be available midweek. Most choices are in the town center; there are less expensive chain properties out of town, near the I-5.

Hotel Indigo San Diego Del Mar
BOUTIQUE HOTEL $$
(☑ 858-755-1501, 877-846-3446; www.hotelindigo sddelmar.com; 710 Camino Del Mar; r from $165; P❋❄@🔆≋🐾) This collection of whitewashed buildings with gray clay-tiled roofs has two outdoor heated pools, a spa, and new fitness and business centers. Rooms have hardwood floors, mosaic-tile accents and beach-inspired motifs. Some units have kitchenettes and distant ocean views. The hotel's **Ocean View Bar & Grill** serves breakfast and dinner. Free parking.

L'Auberge Del Mar Resort & Spa
RESORT $$$
(☑ 858-259-1515, 800-245-9757; www.laubergedel mar.com; 1540 Camino Del Mar; r from $299; P❋@🔆≋🐾) Rebuilt in the 1990s on the grounds of the historic Hotel del Mar, where 1920s Hollywood celebrities once frolicked, L'Auberge continues a tradition of European-style elegance with luxurious linens, a spa and lovely grounds. It feels so intimate and the service is so individual, you'd never know there are 120 rooms. Parking is $25.

Clarion Del Mar Inn
MOTEL $$$
(☑ 800-451-4515, 858-755-9765; www.delmarinn. com; 720 Camino Del Mar; r $119-449; P❄❋@🔆≋) This well-kept, 80-room upscale motel had a refurb in 2016 and tries hard to please with helpful staff, pool and large-ish rooms (many with balconies and kitchens or bathroom vanities with granite countertops). There's also an indoor-outdoor bistro.

✖ Eating

Del Mar Village has a dozen-plus restaurants from historic to chef-driven along Camino del Mar. Or head to Del Mar Plaza (p440) to check out the rooftop patio and its upscale restaurants for North County's best vantage points, especially at sunset. Try **Il Fornaio** (☑ 858-755-8876; www.ilfornaio.com/ delmar; Del Mar Plaza, 1555 Camino Del Mar; lunch $13-25, dinner $13-36; ⏱11:30am-9pm Mon-Thurs, 11:30am-10pm Fri, 11am-10pm Sat, 11am-9pm Sun) for pizzas, pastas, salads and steak; the futuristic **Pacifica Del Mar** (☑ 858-792-0476; www.pacificadelmar.com; 1555 Camino Del Mar; lunch $13-21, dinner $28-36; ⏱11:30-3pm Mon-Fri, 11am-4pm Sat-Sun, 5pm to close Mon-Sun) for

WORTH A TRIP

PRIME CANYON HIKING

A 20-minute drive inland, **Los Penasquitos Canyon Trail** (☑ county ranger 858-538-8066; www.sandiego. gov/park-and-recreation/parks/osp/ lospenasquitos; entry via Park Village Rd & Celome Way; ☺ sunrise-sunset) **FREE** consists of a series of wonderful, mostly flat, shady and sunny paths snaking through a lush valley and past a cascading waterfall surrounded by volcanic rock. The main 7-mile pathway is moderately trafficked with runners, walkers and mountain bikers. Look out for butterflies, mule deers and bobcats. Stay alert when exploring – rattlesnakes also favor these arid pathways.

fresh seafood and inventive preparations, and **Rendezvous** (☑ 858-755-2669; Del Mar Plaza, 1555 Camino Del Mar; lunch $8-12, dinner $12-17; ⏱11:30am-2:30pm Mon-Sat, 4:30pm-9pm Mon-Sat, 4:30pm-8:30pm Sun), which despite the French name serves popular Chinese and Asian fusion dishes.

Americana
MODERN AMERICAN $$
(☑ 858-794-6838; 1454 Camino del Mar; dishes breakfast & lunch $7-14, dinner $9-25; ⏱7am-late) This quietly chichi and much-loved local landmark serves a diverse lineup of regional American cuisine: cheese grits to chicken Reubens, sesame salmon on succotash to seared duck breast with Israeli couscous, plus artisan cocktails, all amid checkerboard linoleum floors, giant windows and homey wainscoting. Breakfast served until 3pm.

Zel's
CALIFORNIAN $$
(☑ 858-755-0076; www.zelsdelmar.com; 1247 Camino Del Mar; lunch $11-17, dinner $13-29; ⏱9am-10pm Sun-Thu, to midnight Fri-Sat) Zel was a longstanding local merchant, and his grandson continues the family tradition of welcoming locals and visitors, over excellent flatbread pizzas (like chicken with asparagus, truffle oil, arugula and avocado), burgers of bison, quinoa or locally raised beef, and lots of craft beers. Live music Thursday to Sunday.

En Fuego
MEXICAN $$
(☑ 858-792-6551; www.enfuegocantina.com; 1342 Camino Del Mar; mains $8-16; ⏱11:30am-11pm Sun-Thurs, to 12pm Fri-Sat) On the site of Del

Mar's first restaurant, this airy, multilevel Nuevo Mexicano spot is both restaurant and bar. Specialties on the forward-thinking menu include *borracho* shrimp (sautéed in tequila), filet mignon rancheros and honey-habanero chicken (in a sweet spicy glaze), with lots of indoor-outdoor space to enjoy them.

Brigantine SEAFOOD $$$

(858-481-1166; www.brigantine.com; 3263 Camino del Mar; lunch $9-17, dinner $16-32; 11:30am-2:30pm Mon-Sat, 5pm-8:30pm Sun-Thur, 5pm-9pm Fri-Sat) Try San Diego–style surf 'n' turf at this posh seafood joint. Menu items include wok-charred ahi, classic filet mignon, Parmesan-crusted sautéed sand dabs, and macadamia-crusted fresh mahimahi. There's an oyster bar and happy hour (all night $1 off well drinks, and $2 off bar-menu items) on Mondays and between 4pm and 6pm Tues through Sun.

Jake's Del Mar SEAFOOD $$$

(858-755-2002; www.jakesdelmar.com; 1660 Coast Blvd; lunch $13-20, dinner $15-44; 11:30am-2:30pm Tue-Sat, 5pm-9pm Mon-Thur, 5pm-9:30pm Fri, 4:30pm-9:30 pm Sat, 4:30pm-9pm Sun) Head to this beachside classic for ocean views. The atmosphere is chic and the food imaginative, like stone fruit–burrata salad with arugula, whipped avocado, honey-sherry vinaigrette and pumpkin-seed brittle, plus Dungeness crabcake and 'surfing steak' with herb-grilled jumbo shrimp, yuzu aioli and garlic potatoes.

☆ Entertainment

Del Mar Racetrack & Fairgrounds HORSE RACING

(858-792-4242; www.dmtc.com; 2260 Jimmy Durante Blvd; from $6; race season mid-Jul–early Sep) Del Mar's biggest draw during summer months was founded in 1937 by a prestigious group which included Bing Crosby. It's worth trying to brave the crowds on opening day (tickets from $10), if nothing else to see the amazing spectacle of ladies wearing over-the-top hats. The rest of the season, enjoy the visual perfection of the track's lush gardens and pink, Mediterranean-style architecture.

On opening day, the racetrack runs free double-decker shuttle buses to and from the **Solana Beach train station** (Solana Beach Transit Center; 105 N Cedros Ave).

Shopping

Del Mar Plaza MALL

(858-847-2284; http://delmarplaza.com; 1555 Camino Del Mar) Downtown Del Mar (sometimes called 'the village') extends for about a mile along Camino del Mar. This ritzy shopping mall has restaurants, shops and balconies will glorious ocean views. Underground parking is free for two hours with purchase, so ask vendors to validate your ticket.

ℹ Getting There & Away

The 101 bus runs between La Jolla and Oceanside, stopping at Camino Del Mar and15th St. Route takes approximately one hour, one-way fares $1.75.

By car, N Torrey Pines Rd from La Jolla is the most scenic approach from the south. Heading north, the road (S21) changes its name from Camino del Mar to Coast Hwy 101 to Old Hwy 101. If you're in a hurry or headed out of town, the faster I-5 parallels it to the east. Traffic can snarl everywhere during rush hour and race or fair season.

Solana Beach

Solana Beach is the next town north from Del Mar – it's not as posh, but it has good beaches and lots of contemporary style. Don't miss the Cedros Design District (p441), four blocks on Cedros Ave where interior designers from all over the region come for inspiration and merchandise from buttons to bathrooms, paint to photographs and even garden supplies. Aside from a beautiful coastline, this kind of shopping is a Solana highlight.

Belly Up (p441) is a converted warehouse and bar that consistently books good bands from jazz to funk, and big names from Jimmy Buffett and Aimee Mann to Merle Haggard and tribute bands. There's also a new microbrewery (p441) a few doors down.

◉ Sights

Cedros Design District LANDMARK

(www.shopcedros.com; Cedros Ave) A cluster of furniture, interior and design shops, plus a few restaurants, entertainment venues and galleries.

✕ Eating & Drinking

There are only a few neighborhood joints, but what Solana's unpretentious restaurant scene lacks in quantity it makes up for in quality. Choose from upscale pub food, light cafe bites and the county's best traditional Mexican restaurant.

Tony's Jacal
MEXICAN **$$**

(☑858-755-2274; www.tonysjacal.com; 621 Valley Ave; mains $6-21; ⊙lunch 11am-2pm Mon, Wed-Sat; dinner 5-9:30pm Mon, Wed, Thurs, 5-10pm Fri-Sat, 3-9:30pm Sunday) An institution in Solana Beach, the Gonzales family turned their home into a restaurant in 1946, when people would line up to sample their proper Mexican fare. And guess what? They still do. Try 50-plus traditional menu items from *camarones en mole* (shrimp in a savory sauce of Mexican chocolate) to crab-meat quesadillas with cheese and fresh corn tortillas.

Culture Brewery
BREWERY

(☑858-345-1144; https://culturebrewingco.com/; 111 S Cedros Ave, Suite 200; pints from $5; ⊙noon-9pm Mon-Sun) A rustic open-plan microbrewery, with a tasting room, on-site brewhouse, surf photography on the walls and 12 taps pouring craft beers (like tart cherry wit, milk stout or amber ale). Enjoy a pint inside at a beer-barrel table or outside on the terrace.

Belly Up
LIVE MUSIC

(☑858-481-8140; www.bellyup.com; 143 S Cedros Ave; tickets $10-45; ⊙show times vary) Live venue hosting a range of acts, local and international. Previous artists have included Ben Harper, BB King and Jimmy Cliff. Expect everything from ukulele, country, jazz and funk, and even the occasional hip-hop act.

🛍 Shopping

The Cedros Design District includes must-visit stores like **Leaping Lotus** (☑858-720-8283; www.leapinglotus.com; 240 S Cedros Ave; ⊙10am-6pm Mon-Sat, 11am-6pm Sun), in which more than 100 merchants fill the cavernous space. **Solo** (☑858-794-9016; www.solocedros.com; 309 S Cedros Ave; ⊙10am-6pm Mon-Sat, 11am-5pm Sun) sells design books, trinkets, furniture and accessories and has a design office. Other offerings include antiques shops, handcrafted-clothing boutiques, and camping and travel gear at **Adventure 16** (☑619-283-2374; www.adventure16.com; 143 S Cedros Ave, Suite M; ⊙10am-6pm Mon-Sat, 11am-5pm Sun).

❶ Getting There & Away

The 101 bus route (running from La Jolla to Oceanside roughly every hour) stops at Hwy 101 and Lomas Santa Fe Dr. The route takes around one hour and costs $1.75 per single journey.

It takes roughly 25 minutes by car to reach Solana from Downtown San Diego, heading north on the I-5.

Coaster (www.gonctd.com) commuter trains run in the morning and evening between Oceanside and downtown San Diego via Solana Beach, with fares from $8 around three daily Amtrak *Surfliner* (www.amtrak.com). Trains run through Solana Beach, with fares starting from $10. Check the websites for timetables.

Cardiff-by-the-Sea

Beachy Cardiff is good for surfing and popular with a laid-back crowd. The town center has the perfunctory supermarkets and everyday shops along San Elijo Ave, about 0.25 miles from the ocean and across the railroad tracks, but the real action is the miles of restaurants, cafes and surf shops along Hwy 101.

◉ Sights

San Elijo Lagoon
NATURE RESERVE

(☑760-623-3026; www.sanelijo.org; 2710 Manchester Ave; ⊙nature center 9am-5pm; 🅿🚶) **FREE** One of the town's main draws is this 979-acre ecological preserve popular with bird-watchers for its herons, coots, terns, ducks, egrets and more than 250 other species. A 7-mile network of trails leads through the area and the main path is pushchair-friendly.

Cardiff State Beach
BEACH

(☑760-753-5091; www.parks.ca.gov; ⊙7am-sunset; 🅿) Just south of Cardiff-by-the-Sea, the surf break on the reef here is mostly popular with longboarders, but it gets very good at low tide with a big north swell. Parking costs $10 all day or $4 for one hour.

San Elijo State Beach
BEACH

(🅿) A little north of Cardiff State Beach, San Elijo State Beach has good winter waves and $10 parking all day Monday to Thursday, $12 all day Friday through Sunday.

🍴 Eating & Drinking

Ki's Restaurant
CALIFORNIAN **$$**

(☑760-436-5236; www.kisrestaurant.com; 2591 S Coast Hwy 101; mains breakfast $6-15, lunch $9-15, dinner $6-24; ⊙8am-9pm Sun-Thu, to 8:30pm Fri & Sat; 🅿🚻) 🌿 Across from the beach, Ki's is an organic cafe-restaurant and a hub of local activity. At the juice bar on the first floor are awesome smoothies, healthy burgers,

San Diego North County Coast

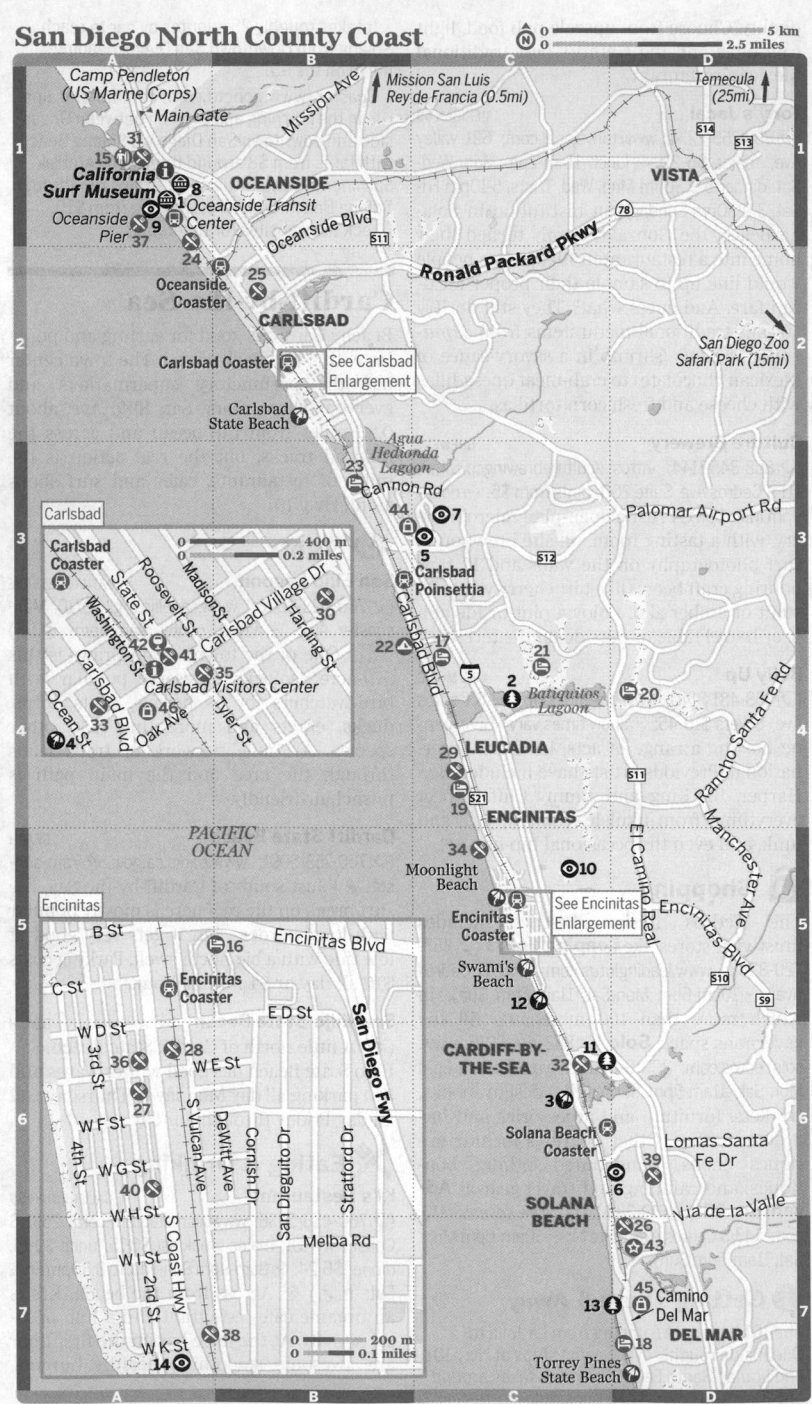

San Diego North County Coast

salads, tacos and butternut-squash-and-corn enchiladas.

★ Las Olas
MEXICAN $$

(☏760-942-1860; www.lasolasmex.com; 2655 S Coast Hwy 101; mains $9-19; ☉11am-9pm Mon-Thu, to 9:30pm Fri, 10am-9:30pm Sat, to 9pm Sun; 🖐) For fish tacos with a sea view, Las Olas is so popular it has its own traffic light, right across the street from the beach. Lobster is served in the style of the legendary Baja California lobster village, Puerto Nuevo.

House cocktails include pineapple and chili margaritas and drinks made with RIP (rum infused with pineapple). Happy hour until 6pm daily.

ⓘ Getting There & Away

The easiest way to reach Cardiff is by car, as it's a short 20- to 30-minute drive from central San Diego. However, the **North County Transit District (NCTD)** (p432) runs bus route 101, connecting UC San Diego with Torrey Pines, Del

Mar, Cardiff and Encinitas. In Cardiff, it stops near **San Elijo State Beach** (p441) and the adjacent **campground** (☑760-753-5091, reservations 800-444-7275; www.parks.ca.gov; 2050 S Coast Hwy 101; summer tent/RV sites from $35/60; P ⚡). There's another stop further south in Cardiff, outside **Ki's Restaurant** (p441) and **Cardiff State Beach** (p441). It runs roughly every hour and takes an hour from start to finish. Fares cost $1.75.

Encinitas

Peaceful Encinitas has a decidedly down-to-earth surf vibe and a laid-back, beach-town main street, perfect for a relaxing day trip or weekend escape. North of central Encinitas, yet still part of the city, is **Leucadia**, a leafy stretch of N Hwy 101 with a hippie vibe of used-clothing stores and taco shops.

◎ Sights

Self-Realization Fellowship
Retreat
RELIGIOUS SITE

(☑760-436-7220; http://encinitastemple.org; 215 K St; ☺meditation garden 9am-5pm Tue-Sat, from 11am Sun, hermitage 2-4pm Sun) **FREE** Yogi Paramahansa Yogananda founded his center here in 1937, and the town has been a magnet for holistic healers and natural-lifestyle seekers ever since. The gold lotus domes of the hermitage – conspicuous on South Coast Hwy 101 – mark the southern end of Encinitas and the turn-out for **Swami's Beach**, a powerful reef break surfed by territorial locals. The fellowship's compact but lovely **Meditation Garden** has wonderful ocean vistas, a stream and a koi pond.

San Diego Botanic Garden
GARDENS

(☑760-436-3036; www.sdbgarden.org; 230 Quail Gardens Dr; adult/child/senior $14/8/10; ☺9am-5pm; P ♿) This 37-acre garden has a large collection of California native plants as well as flora of different regions of the world, including Australia and Central America. There are special activities in the children's garden (10am Tuesday to Thursday); check the website for a schedule. Parking $2.

⛺ Sleeping

Great deals can be found in Encinitas, particularly in Leucadia along this stretch of Highway 101. The motel properties are close to shops, restaurants and the beach, but often also the highway, making them louder stays than other San Diego neighborhoods.

Leucadia Beach Inn
MOTEL $

(☑760-943-7461; www.leucadiabeachinn.org; 1322 N Coast Hwy; r $85-145; P ⚡⚡) All the sparkling-clean rooms in this charming 1920s courtyard motel have tile floors and bright paint jobs, and many have kitchenettes. The beach is a few blocks' walk. It's across Hwy 101 from the train tracks, so light sleepers should pack earplugs.

Best Western Encinitas Inn
& Suites
MOTEL $$

(☑866-236-4648, 760-942-7455; www.bwencinitas.com; 85 Encinitas Blvd; r $169-$250; P @⚡⚡⚡) Atop a hill between the freeway, shopping center and Coast Hwy is this hexagonal hotel, a few minutes on foot from the sand. Rooms, recently refurbished with new bathrooms, are well kept, with balconies: some have ocean or park views. Suites have kitchenettes and sleep sofas.

✗ Eating

Eateries in Encinitas come with plenty of charm and personality. Here you'll find cute coffee shops and cafes, country-style restaurants and even a Peruvian joint. The general menu prices are reasonable, too.

★ Fish 101
SEAFOOD $

(☑760-634-6221; www.fish101restaurant.com; 1468 N Coast Hwy 101; mains $10-14) In this casual grown-up fish shack, order at the counter, sidle up to a butcher-block table, sip craft beer or Mexican coke from a mason jar and tuck into albacore-tuna *poke*, clam chowder, shrimp po'boy or fish-and-chips. Simple grilling techniques allow the catch's natural flavors to show through, and healthy rice-bran oil is used for frying.

Swami's Café
CAFE $

(☑760-944-0612; http://swamiscafe.com; 1163 S Coast Hwy 101; mains $5-13; ☺7am-4pm Mon-Fri, 7am-5pm Sat-Sun; ✗♿) This local institution can't be beat for breakfast burritos, multigrain pancakes, stir-fries, salads, smoothies and three-egg *ohm*-lettes (sorry, we couldn't resist). Vegetarians will be satisfied, too. Most of the seating is out on an umbrella-covered patio. It's across from the Self-Realization Fellowship Retreat. There's are other locations in Carlsbad and **Oceanside** (☑760-966-1203; 202 N Coast Hwy; lunch $5-15, dinner $5-28; ☺7am-9pm Mon-Sat, to 4pm Sun).

Pannikin Coffee & Tea
CAFE $

(☑760-436-5824; https://pannikincoffeeandtea.com; 510 N Highway 101; mains $6-9; ☺6am-6pm) I n a sunny yellow, wooden building that used to be the Encinitas train station (transported from its original site), Pannikin is an adorable sprawl of nooks, crannies, balconies and lawns. The coffees, homemade muffins and pies are wonderful. They also serve a range of egg dishes, bagels and granola for breakfast and salads, melts and soups for lunch.

★ **Trattoria I Trulli**   ITALIAN $$
(☑760-943-6800; www.trattoriaitrullisd.com; 830 S Coast Hwy 101; mains lunch $9-19, dinner $9-28; ☺11am-2:30pm daily, 5-9.30pm Sun-Thu, to 10pm Fri & Sat) Country-style seating indoors and great people-watching on the sidewalk. Just one taste of the homemade ravioli or lasagna, salmon with arugula, capers and red onion, or *pollo uno zero uno* (101; chicken stuffed with cheese, spinach and artichokes in mushroom sauce) and you'll know why this mom-and-pop Italian trattoria is always packed. Reservations are recommended.

East Village Asian Diner   FUSION $$
(☑760-753-8700; www.eateastvillage.com; 628 S Coast Hwy 101; mains $9-12; ☺11:30am-2:30pm & 5-10pm Mon-Sat, to 9pm Sun; ☑) This cool diner-decorated eatery fuses mostly Korean cooking with Western and other Asian influences (witness the 'super awesome' beef-and-kimchi burrito). Try noodle dishes (Thai peanut, beef and broccoli etc), or build your own 'monk's stone pot,' a superheated rice bowl with which you can add ingredients from pulled pork to salmon. Sauces are made in-house.

Eve   VEGAN $$
(☑760-230-2560; www.eveencinitas.com; 575 S Coast Hwy 101; Buddha bowls $12; ☺8am-9pm; ☑) ❂ One part coffee shop, one part lounge and one part restaurant, this new vegan eatery serves hearty salad bowls heaped with goodness. Opt for a superfood smoothie, local kombucha or Buddha bowl. Our fave is the Legendary Hero flavor with braised kale, sprouts, beets, carrots, brown rice, hemp seed, walnuts, cranberries and tahini sauce.

Q'ero   PERUVIAN $$
(☑760-753-9050; 540 S Coast Hwy 101; meals $13-21; ☺11am-9pm Wed-Sun) The flavors of Peru tempt from this tiny, atmospheric storefront festooned with Peruvian art and iconography. Try *empanadas* (little pasties of deliciousness), *ceviche, papa rellena* (potato filled with ground beef), or pan-roasted fish simmered in fish sauce. Walk-ins only.

🍷 Drinking

There's a local beer brewery and an ale house, but the best place to drink is the saloon-style Daley Double dive bar.

Daley Double   BAR
(☑760-230-1213; 546 S Coast Hwy 101; ☺12pm-2am) Once Encinitas' most notorious dive bar, it's now Encinitas' hippest dive bar. Fantastic Old West saloon–style murals make a great backdrop for good old-fashioned sipping and flirting. Expect a line out the door on weekends.

Better Buzz Coffee   CAFE
(☑760-487-5562; www.betterbuzzcoffee.com; 578 S Coast Hwy 101; toast from $6, salads & entrees from $12; ☺5:30am-9pm) Local chain with a Scandi-design feel serving coffee, hot chocolate and smoothies, plus bites like French pastries, acai bowls, grilled sandwiches and pretentious toast (think: avocado, sesame seed, chia seed, hemp seed, lemon, crushed red pepper and microgreens).

❶ Getting There & Away

The 101 bus, costing $1.75 for a single one-zone fare, travels between La Jolla and Oceanside, stopping at **Encinitas Station** (25 E D St) roughly every 45 minutes. The entire bus route takes around one hour, depending on traffic. It takes half an hour to drive to Encinitas by car from Downtown San Diego. Roughly three Amtrak *Surfliner* trains stop at Encinitas Station per day, with fares from around $10. The NCTD *Coaster*, with single fares from $8, also goes through here, running approximately every hour during rush-hour periods.

Carlsbad

Most visitors come to Carlsbad for Legoland and head right back out, and that's too bad because they've missed the charming, intimate Carlsbad Village with shopping, dining and beaching nearby. It's bordered by I-5 and Carlsbad Blvd, which run north–south and are connected by Carlsbad Village Dr running east–west.

Carlsbad came into being with the railroad in the 1880s. John Frazier, an early homesteader, sank a well and found water that had a high mineral content, supposedly identical to that of spa water in Karlsbad, Bohemia (now in the Czech Republic). He built a grand Queen Anne–style spa hotel, which prospered until the 1930s and is now a local landmark.

SAN DIEGO ZOO SAFARI PARK

Since the early 1960s, the San Diego Zoological Society has been developing this 1800-acre, open-range zoo (☑760-747-8702; www.sdzsafaripark.org; 15500 San Pasqual Valley Rd, Escondido; 1-day adult/child $52/42, 2-visit pass to zoo and/or safari park adult/child $83.25/73.25; ⊙8am-6pm, to 7pm late Jun–mid-Aug; ℗🅗) where herds of giraffes, zebras, rhinos and other animals roam the open valley floor. For an instant safari feel, board the Africa Tram ride, which tours you around the second-largest continent in under half an hour.

Elsewhere, animals are in enclosures so naturalistic it's as if the humans are guests, and there's a petting krall and animal shows; pick up a map and schedule. Additional 'safaris,' like zip-lining, a chance to observe a cheetah whizz by while chasing a mechanical rabbit, and even sleepovers (yowza!) are available with reservations and additional payment.

The park's just north of Hwy 78, 5 miles east of I-15 from the Via Rancho Parkway exit. Plan on 45 minutes transit by car from San Diego, except in rush hour when that figure can double. For bus information contact **North County Transit District** (p432).

If you've come looking for the Carlsbad Caverns, you're outta luck. Those are in New Mexico.

⊙ Sights

Carlsbad has a number of attractions outside the village and Legoland areas. You pretty much need a car to reach them, and it's best to phone for directions since they can be hard to find.

Legoland California Resort   AMUSEMENT PARK
(☑760-918-5346; www.legoland.com/california; 1 Legoland Dr; adult/child 3-12yr from $95/89; ⊙hours vary, at least 10am-5pm year-round; ℗🅗) A fantasy environment built largely of those little colored plastic blocks from Denmark. Many rides and attractions are targeted to elementary schoolers: a junior 'driving school,' a jungle cruise lined with Lego animals, wacky 'sky cruiser' pedal cars on a track, and fairy-tale-, princess-, pirate-, adventurer- and dino-themed escapades. If you have budding scientists (age 10 and over) with you, sign them up on arrival at the park for an appointment for **Mindstorms**, where they can make computerized Lego robots. There are also lots of low-thrill activities like face-painting and princess-meeting.

Carlsbad Ranch Flower Fields   GARDENS
(☑760-431-0352; www.theflowerfields.com; 5704 Paseo del Norte; adult/child 3-10yr $14/7; ⊙usually 9am-6pm Mar–mid-May; ℗🅗) The 50-acre flower fields of Carlsbad Ranch are ablaze in a sea of the carmine, saffron and snow-white blossoms of giant tecolote ranunculus. Take the Palomar Airport Rd exit off of I-5,

head east and turn left on Paseo del Norte. It takes roughly 30 minutes from Downtown San Diego.

Batiquitos Lagoon   NATURE RESERVE
(☑760-931-0800; www.batiquitosfoundation.org; 7380 Gabbiano Ln; ⊙nature center 9am-3pm subject to volunteer availability; ℗🅗) 🎟 FREE One of the last remaining tidal wetlands in California, Batiquitos Lagoon separates Carlsbad from Encinitas. A self-guided tour lets you explore area plants, including the prickly pear cactus, coastal sage scrub and eucalyptus trees, as well as lagoon birds such as the great heron and the snowy egret. One artificial island in the lagoon is a nesting site for endangered terns and plovers. You can hike the reserve anytime, but stop by the nature center if it's open.

🏃 Activities

Chopra Center   MIND-BODY CENTER
(☑760-494-1639; www.chopra.com; 2013 Costa del Mar Rd, Omni La Costa Resort & Spa; massage treatments from $215; ⊙9am-6pm Mon-Fri, 8.30am-6pm Sat-Sun) Slow down with alternative-health guru Deepak Chopra, who leads seminars on mind-body medicine, complemented by specialized spa treatments, at this center at Omni La Costa Resort & Spa (p447).

🛏 Sleeping

If you're looking for a budget stay in Carlsbad, there's camping on the beach. Those in search of luxury have come to the right place: Carlsbad is home to fancy golf resorts and spa stays.

South Carlsbad State Park
Campground   CAMPGROUND $
(☑760-438-3143, reservations 800-444-7275; www.reserveamerica.com; 7201 Carlsbad Blvd; ocean-/streetside tent & RV sites $50/35, ocean/inland tent & RV sites with hookups $75/60; P) Three miles south of town and sandwiched between Carlsbad Blvd and the beach, this campground has more than 200 tent and RV sites; all spaces accommodate both tents and RVs.

Legoland Hotel   HOTEL $$$
(☑877-534-6526, 760-918-5346; www.legoland.com/california; 5885 The Crossings Dr; r from $328; P⊖❋@☎☀) Lego designers were let loose on this hotel, just outside Legoland's main gate, and boy is it fun. Thousands of Lego models (dragons to surfers) populate the property, and the elevator turns into a disco between floors. Each floor has its own theme (pirate, adventure, kingdom), down to the rooms' wallpaper, props (Lego cannonballs – cool!), even the shower curtains.

West Inn & Suites   HOTEL $$$
(☑866-431-9378, 760-448-4500; www.westinnandsuites.com; 4970 Avenida Encinas; r incl breakfast $179-359; P❋@☎☀☀) About halfway between Legoland and Carlsbad Village, this hyper-friendly, independently run, 86-room inn caters to both business travelers (note business and fitness centers) and vacationing families (note the sparkling pool, beach, Legoland shuttle service and nightly milk and cookies). Free wi-fi, complementary shuttles within five miles and free parking.

Omni La Costa Resort & Spa   RESORT $$$
(☑800-854-5000, 760-438-9111; www.lacosta.com; 2100 Costa Del Mar Rd; r from $322; P@☎☀☀) 🏌 Splurge-worthy La Costa offers a 400-acre, whitewashed 650-room campus overlooking Batiquitos Lagoon. It's got two PGA golf courses, excellent children's programs including pools with multiple slides, nursery and educational programming. Venues for grownups including the stunning spa and Chopra Center (p446), lovely restaurants and a touch of Hollywood history. Check for discounted packages. $20 self-parking.

Park Hyatt Aviara Resort   RESORT $$$
(☑760-603-6800; www.parkhyattaviara.com; 7100 Aviara Resort Dr; r from $349; P@☎☀☀) From the marble bathrooms in sumptuous suites to the luxurious fitness center and the Aviara Kids Academy programs, this tippy-top resort offers superb service and top-flight amenities: golf, tennis, the 15,000-sq-ft Aviara Spa and more. The **Argyle** steakhouse is worth a trip by itself. Aviara looks out over Batiquitos Lagoon (p446) and offers discounted packages. Parking costs $35.

Cape Rey Carlsbad by Hilton   RESORT $$$
(☑760-602-0800; www.carlsbadoceanfrontresortandspa.hilton.com; 1 Ponto Rd; r from $209; P⊖❋@☎☀) Most of Carlsbad's top lodgings are inland, but this swanky spot is an easy walk to the ocean across Hwy 101. Pools, spa, business and fitness centers will keep you busy on land. **Chandler's** restaurant serves three squares, including creative dinners like porcini-dusted Diver scallop and Alaskan king salmon with tomato-fennel marmalade. Parking costs $19. Resort fee $20 per night.

It's about 4 miles south of Carlsbad Village and west of Legoland, a stone's throw from the ocean.

🍴 Eating & Drinking

State St (just north of Carlsbad Village Dr) is Carlsbad's most charming stretch, with a number of restaurants worth browsing.

For a luxury experience, also check out the restaurants at Omni La Costa Resort & Spa and Park Hyatt Aviara Resort. At the other end of the scale are the brewpub Pizza Port and the local branch of Mexican Las Olas (p449).

French Bakery Cafe   BAKERY, CAFE $
(☑760-729-2241; www.carlsbadfrenchpastrycafe.com/; 1005 Carlsbad Village Dr; mains $6; ⊙7am-7pm Mon-Sat, 7.30am-5pm Sun; ☎) Its location may be in a drab-looking shopping center just off I-5, but it's the real deal for croissants and brioches (baked daily) and kick-start espresso, plus omelets, salads and sandwiches.

Pizza Port   PIZZA $$
(☑760-720-7007; www.pizzaport.com; 571 Carlsbad Village Dr; pizzas $7-24; ⊙11am-10pm Mon-Thu, to midnight Fri & Sat, 10am-11pm Sun; ◑) Rockin' and raucous local brewpub chain with surf art, rock music and 'anti-wimpy' pizzas to go with the signature Sharkbite Red Ale. Multiple locations.

Las Olas   MEXICAN
(☑760-434-5850; www.lasolasmex.com; 2939 Carlsbad Blvd; ⊙11am-9pm Mon-Thu, to 9:30pm Fri, 10am-9:30pm Sat, to 9pm Sun) A classic low-key Mexican joint serving the works: fish

tacos, ceviche, burritos, quesadillas, tostadas and more.

Vigilucci's Cucina Italiana
ITALIAN $$

(☑760-434-2500; 2943 State St; lunch $8-18, dinner $17-42; ☺11:30am-9:30pm Mon-Thurs, to 10pm Fri-Sat, to 9:30pm Sun) There's white-tablecloth service and a lovely sidewalk terrace at this State St institution. For lunch, try pastas or panini (the one with parma ham and portobello mushrooms is a fave), while dinner might be pappardelle with field mushrooms and seared diver scallops in white-truffle-and-brandy-cream sauce, or linguine alla Luciana (with baby calamari, garlic and tomato sauce).

Relm
WINE BAR

(☑760-434-9463; www.thewinerelm.com; 2917 State St; ☺from 4pm Tue-Sun) This cozy, modernist storefront pours from 50+ bottles, plus it serves cheeseboards and flatbreads to go with them. Sometimes they have live music, and the happy hour is a big pull on weekdays with red and white wines from $7, beer from $5 and 25% off food between 4pm and 6pm.

🛍 Shopping

Carlsbad Premium Outlets
OUTLET MALL

(☑760-804-9000; www.premiumoutlets.com; Paseo del Norte; ☺10am-9pm Mon-Sat, until 7pm Sun) Big-name retailers such as Calvin Klein and Coach, and purveyors of everything from cookware to jeans, have off-price boutiques among the 50 shops here. It's less than 1 mile southeast of the Cannon Rd exit off I-5.

Farenheit 451
BOOKS

(☑760-720-3373; www.farenheit451books.com; 325 Carlsbad Village Dr; ☺11am-6pm) This is an honest-to-goodness, old-style bookshop, selling mainly used books, including rare and first editions in plastic sleeves.

ℹ Information

Carlsbad Visitor Center (☑760-434-6093; www.visitcarlsbad.com; 400 Carlsbad Village Dr; ☺10am-5pm Mon-Fri, to 4pm Sat, to 3pm Sun.) Housed in the original 1887 Santa Fe train depot.

ℹ Getting There & Away

The 101 bus route runs between La Jolla's Westfield UTC shopping center and Oceanside, stopping at Carlsbad Village Station en route. Fares are $1.75 one way; the full bus journey takes roughly one hour.

Coaster and *Pacific Surfliner* trains run from Downtown's **Santa Fe Depot** (p430) along the breadth of the coastline, stopping at **Carlsbad Village Station** (☑800-872-7245; 2775 State St). *Coasters* (www.gonctd.com) run nearly every hour in the morning and evenings and start from $8 for a single one-zone journey; *Surfliner* (https://tickets.amtrak.com) trains run roughly three times a day, with fares from $10.

Oceanside

The largest North County town, Oceanside is home to many who work at giant Camp Pendleton Marine Base just to the north. The huge military presence mixes with an attractive natural setting, surf shops, head (marijuana) shops and a downtown that's slowly revitalizing.

Little remains from the 1880s streetscape, when the new Santa Fe coastal railway came through Oceanside, but a few buildings designed by Irving Gill and Julia Morgan still stand. The Welcome Center (p450) has a pamphlet describing a self-guided history walk.

👁 Sights & Activities

★ California Surf Museum
MUSEUM

(☑760-721-6876; www.surfmuseum.org; 312 Pier View Way; adult/child/student $5/free/3, first Tue of month free; ☺10am-4pm Fri-Wed, to 8pm Thu; 🅿) It's easy to spend an hour in this heartfelt museum of surf artifacts, from a timeline of surfing history to surf-themed art and a radical collection of boards, including the one chomped by a shark when it ate the arm of surfer Bethany Hamilton. Special exhibits change frequently along different themes (eg Women of Surfing and Surfers of the Vietnam War).

Mission San Luis Rey de Francia
HISTORIC SITE

(☑760-757-3651; www.sanluisrey.org; 4050 Mission Ave; adult/child 5yr & under/youth 6-18yr/senior $7/free/3/5; ☺9:30am-5pm) About 4.5 miles inland from central Oceanside, this was the largest California mission and the most successful in recruiting Native American converts. At one point some 3000 neophytes lived and worked here. After the Mexican government secularized the missions, San Luis fell into ruin; the adobe walls of the church, from 1811, are the only original parts left. Inside are displays on work and life in the mission, with some original religious art and artifacts.

Oceanside Museum of Art   MUSEUM
(www.oma-online.org; 704 Pier View Way; adult/senior/student $8/5/free; ⊙10am-4pm Tue-Sat, 1-4pm Sun) This museum underwent a recent revamp and it now stands at an impressive 16,000 sq ft in a modernist, white shell. There are about 10 rotating exhibits a year, with an emphasis on SoCal artists (especially from the San Diego region) and local cultures.

Oceanside Pier   PIER
This wooden pier extends more than 1900ft out to sea. Bait-and-tackle shops rent poles to the many anglers who line its wooden fences (per hour/day $5/15). Two major surf competitions – the West Coast Pro-Am and the National Scholastic Surf Association (NSSA) – take place near the pier each June.

Surfcamps USA   SURFING
(☑760-889-8984; www.surfcampsusa.com; 1202 N Pacific St; lessons per person from $55; 🚻) Newbies and not-so newbies can take two-hour private or group lessons from this popular operator. All equipment is included.

🛌 Sleeping & Eating

Good rates can be found on rooms in Oceanside, where accommodation mainly consists of chain hotels and motels. The Springhill Suites by Marriott is a favorite: right next to the beach, in the center of the action and with dreamy views of the Pacific Ocean.

★Springhill Suites Oceanside Downtown   HOTEL $$
(☑760-722-1003; www.shsoceanside.com; 110 N Myers St; r $149-379; P😊@🛜🏊🚻) This modern, six-story, ocean-view hotel is awash in summery yellows and sea blues in the lobby. Rooms have crisp lines and distressed-wood headboards, and ocean- and pier-view rooms have balconies or patios. Best views are from the pool and hot tub on the top floor, where there's also a fitness center. Hot breakfast buffet included.

101 Café   DINER $
(☑760-722-5220; http://101cafe.net; 631 S Coast Hwy; mains $6-10; ⊙7am-7pm Mon-Thu, to 9pm Fri-Sun; P🚻) This tiny, streamlined modern diner (1928) serves all-American classics from omelets and burgers to chicken-fried steak with country gravy, or steak and eggs and hash browns. Check out the local historic photos on the wall. If you're lucky, you'll catch the owner and can quiz him about local history.

Beach Break Café   DINER $
(☑760-439-6355; www.beachbreakcafe.net; 1802 S Coast Hwy; mains $8-11; ⊙7am-2pm; P🚻) Fuel up before surfing on omelets, scrambles and pancakes, or afterwards on sandwiches, tacos and salads at this surfers diner on the east side of the road. A second location by the harbor (280 Harbor Dr) serves the same menu in a stellar setting.

Harbor Fish & Chips   SEAFOOD $
(☑760-722-4977; 276 Harbor Dr S; mains $8-16; ⊙11am-7pm Mon-Thu, to 8pm Fri & Sat; P🚻) There's nothin' fancy about this harborside chippie from the '60s, but when the fish is fried to a deep crackle and you eat it at a picnic table on the dock while classic pop tunes play on the radio, you'll feel pretty good. There's a large local following and taxidermied catches on the walls.

That Boy Good   BARBECUE $$
(TBG; ☑760-433-4227; www.tbgbbq.com; 207 N Coast Hwy; mains $9-25; ⊙from 4pm Mon, from 11am Tue-Sun) This shrine to the Mississippi Delta serves belly-busting portions of fried chicken and waffles, dirty fries (piled with chili) and Cajun catfish. Wash it all down with a craft or canned beer or the BBQ Bloody Mary, topped with a rib.

Ruby's Diner   DINER $$
(☑760-433-7829; www.rubys.com; 1 Oceanside Pier; mains $9-14; ⊙7am-9pm Sun-Thu, to 10pm Fri & Sat; 🚻) This '50s-style diner has good burgers and milkshakes, big breakfasts and a full bar. Yes, it's a chain, but it's right at the end of the pier.

🍷 Drinking

Barrel Republic   BAR
(☑760-435-0042; http://barrelrepublic.com; 215 N Coast Highway; ⊙11:30am-12:00am Mon-Thu & Sun, 11:30am-1:00am Fri-Sat) A beer-geek's dream bar, you can pour your own beer (and a few wines) at Barrel Republic. Grab an electronic wrist band, try sips of all the beers you want, then take your bracelet to the counter and pay per ounce for what you've had. Selections of lagers, stouts, blonde ales, Pilsners and American reds rotate.

SAN DIEGO & AROUND OCEANSIDE

❶ Information

California Welcome Center (☑ 800-350-7873, 760-721-1101; www.visitoceanside.org; 928 N Coast Hwy; ⏰ 9am-5pm) Helpful, informative staff dispense coupons for local attractions, maps and information for the San Diego area, plus help book lodgings in Oceanside. It's just off the freeway exit.

❶ Getting There & Away

Local buses and trains stop at the **Oceanside Transit Center** (235 S Tremont St).

Coaster (www.gonctd.com) trains run almost an hour apart in the morning and evenings and fares start from $8 for a single one-zone journey. There are around three *Surfliner* (https://tickets.amtrak.com) trains a day, with fares from $10.

The 101 bus route (running from La Jolla to Oceanside) runs approximately every hour. It costs $1.75 per single, and takes roughly an hour from the start of the route to the end.

Traveling by car via I-5 from Downtown San Diego, take the La Jolla Pkwy exit and head west toward Torrey Pines Rd, from where it's a right turn to Oceanside's Prospect St.

TEMECULA WINE REGION

Temecula has become a popular short-break destination for its Old West Americana main street, nearly two dozen wineries and California's largest casino, Pechanga.

Temecula means 'Place of the Sun' in the language of the native Luiseño people, who were present when the first Spanish missionary, Father Fermín Lasuén, visited in 1797. In the 1820s the area became a ranching outpost for the Mission San Luis Rey, in present-day Oceanside. Later, Temecula became a stop on the Butterfield stagecoach line (1858–61) and the California Southern railroad.

But it's Temecula's late-20th-century growth that's been most astonishing, from 2700 people in 1970 – the city didn't get its first traffic light until 1984 – to some 106,700 residents today. Between Old Town and the wineries is an off-putting, 3-mile buffer zone of suburban housing developments and shopping centers. Ignore that and you'll do fine.

◉ Sights & Activities

Front St   HISTORIC SITE
Old Town Front St's turn-of-the-last-century storefronts and wooden sidewalks make for an attractive stroll – pick up the *Historic*

Old Town Temecula leaflet with building descriptions. En route, sample local agricultural bounty at shops like **Temecula Olive Oil Company** (☑ 951-693-4029; www.temeculaoliveoil.com; 28653 Old Town Front St; ⏰ 9:30am-6pm Sun-Thu, to 7pm Fri & Sat) and **Front Street Jerky** (www.frontstreetjerky.com; 28655 Old Town Front St; ⏰ 10am-6pm). Dozens of **antique dealers** populate the neighborhood, most agglomerated into large antique halls.

Temecula Valley Museum   MUSEUM
(☑ 909-694-6450; www.temeculavalleymuseum.org; 28314 Mercedes St; suggested donation $5; ⏰ 10am-4pm Tue-Sat, 1-4pm Sun; ⓟ) Just off Old Town Front St, this one-room museum tells the history of the region through artifacts from the Native American Luiseño people through to the area's Spanish period and stagecoach times, plus there's a scale model of the Mission San Luis Rey de Francia (p448), founded in 1798.

Leoness Cellars   WINERY
(☑ 951-302-7601; www.leonesscellars.com; 38311 De Portola Rd; tasting $15; ⏰ 11am-5pm Sun-Thu, 11am-6pm Fri & Sat; ⓟ) Twenty minutes' drive from Front St, this winery offers award-winning *viognier* and *melange de rêves,* plus sweeping views from its sort-of-Teutonic tower.

Longshadow Ranch   WINERY
(☑ 951-587-6221; www.longshadowranchwinery.com; 39847 Calle Contento; tasting $15; ⏰ 11am-5pm Mon-Thu, 10am-5pm Fri-Sun; ⓓ) A nice stop if you've got children in tow; the kids can look at Clydesdales at this 'Old West'-style tasting room, while mommy and daddy sip. They have bonfires on Saturday nights through spring and summer. The vineyard grows sangiovese, malbec, merlot, cabernet sauvignon and petite verdot, among other grapes.

Wilson Creek   WINERY
(www.wilsoncreekwinery.com; 35960 Rancho California Rd; tasting $20; ⏰ 10am-5pm; ⓟ) This place makes almond champagne (infused with almond oil in the fermentation process) and a chocolate-infused port.

Grapeline Temecula   TOUR
(☑ 888-894-6379; www.gogrape.com; shuttle service/tours from $69/89) To leave the driving to someone else while you're busy drinking, this outfit offers day-long wine shuttles and tours among the vineyards by minivan, with pickup at many of the area's lodgings.

PALOMAR OBSERVATORY

High on Palomar Mountain, at an elevation of 5500ft to avoid light pollution, the **Palomar Observatory** (☑760-742-2119; www.astro.caltech.edu/palomar/visitor; 35899 Canfield Rd; tour adult/child $5/3; ⊙ usually 9am-4pm, to 3pm early Nov–mid-Mar; P ♿) **FREE** is simply spectacular – as large as Rome's Pantheon, with a classic design dating from the 1930s. Run by Pasadena's prestigious California Institute of Technology, it houses five telescopes including the 200-inch Hale Telescope, once the world's largest.

On weekends between April and October, visitors can take guided tours, usually given at 11am and 1:30pm. Tickets are first-come, first-served. Bring a fleece jacket – temperatures inside the observatory hover just above freezing during cooler months.

Call ahead to check road conditions and opening hours before making the long, winding drive here.

To stretch your legs after visiting the observatory, nearby **Palomar Mountain State Park** (☑760-742-3462; www.parks.ca.gov; 19952 State Park Dr, Palomar Mountain; per car $8; ⊙ dawn-dusk; P ♿) has forested hikes along panoramic-view trails where wildflowers bloom in early summer.

California Dreamin' BALLOONING
(☑800-373-3359; www.californiadreamin.com; from $148 per person; ⊙ from 5:45am) To see the Temecula region from the air, contact this hot-air-balloon outfit, which offers hour-long rides including a post-ride breakfast. Tours meet at **Vindemia Vineyard & Winery** (33133 Vista Del Monte Rd), before balloonists are transported to the launch site.

🛏 Sleeping

Palomar Inn Hotel HISTORIC HOTEL $
(☑951-676-6503; www.palomarinntemecula.com; 28522 Old Town Front St; r weekday/weekend from $65/99; P 🎧) In the heart of Old Town, this 1927 10-room hostelry feels like a rooming house in the Old West. Eight of the rooms have shared bathrooms and the other two have private bath and kitchenette. Rooms sleep up to four and the location is primo.

Temecula Creek Inn RESORT $$
(☑888-976-3404; www.temeculacreekinn.com; 44501 Rainbow Canyon Rd; r Sun-Thu from $113, Fri & Sat from $259; P ❄🎧♨) Wake up to a view of the 27-hole golf course at this lush, green campus-style resort a few miles from Old Town. The **Corkfire Kitchen** restaurant sources from local farms, choose from dishes like lamb schnitzel, balsamic glazed short ribs and Andouille sausage breakfast. There's also an extensive whisky program, plus wines of course. Even breakfast syrup is aged in bourbon barrels. Resort fee $15 per night.

**South Coast Winery
Resort & Spa** HOTEL $$$
(☑866-994-6379, 951-587-9463; www.south coastwinery.com; 34843 Rancho California Rd; d from $199; P ❄❄🎧♨) A very Temecula way to stay – spacious villa rooms dot the edge of the vineyards, around a spa, fitness facility and recently built hotel. Your room key comes with a wine glossary, and rates include a bottle of wine, but not the nightly resort fee ($19).

🍴 Eating & Drinking

Choose an upmarket, wine-paired meal at one of Temecula's local vineyards, or casual burgers, barbecue or Mexican on Front St.

Mad Madeline's Grill BURGERS, BARBECUE $
(☑951-669-3776; www.madmadelinesgrill.com; 28495 Old Town Front St; mains $8-13; ⊙ 11am-5pm Mon-Thu, to 9pm Fri & Sat, to 7pm Sun; P ♿) Award-winning burgers (served about 20 ways) are the thing in this cheerful red-and-white wooden roadhouse in the center of Old Town, plus onion rings worth breaking your diet for. On Fridays nights, look for smoked baby-back ribs, too.

Swing Inn Cafe DINER $
(☑951-676-2321; www.swinginncafe.com; 28676 Old Town Front St; mains $7-13; ⊙ 5am-9pm; ♿) A proud local institution since 1927, with red leatherette seating and windows to watch the world go by. The Swing Inn serves three square meals, but everyone goes for breakfast – luckily it's served all day. The biscuits and gravy are renowned.

SAN DIEGO & AROUND TEMECULA WINE REGION

Bank of Mexican Food
MEXICAN $

(📞951-676-6160; 28645 Old Town Front St; mains $7-15; ⏲11am-9pm Mon-Thu, to 10pm Fri, 9am-10pm Sat, until 9am-9pm Sun; 🍴) In this handsome former bank (c 1913), try mahimahi plates, huevos rancheros or anything with the righteous Mexican rice. A patio **bar** stays open until late.

Restaurant at Ponte
CALIFORNIAN $$$

(📋951-252-1770; www.pontewinery.com; Ponte Winery, 35053 Rancho California Rd; mains $18-42; ⏲11am-4pm Mon-Thu, to 8pm Fri & Sat, to 5pm Sun) New American cuisine melds with farm-fresh flavors at this busy winery bistro, a favorite for weekend brunch on the airy patio.

Vineyard Rose
CALIFORNIAN $$$

(📋951-587-9463; 34843 Rancho California Rd; lunch mains $14-23, dinner $26-40; ⏲8am-10:45am breakfast, 11:30am-2:45pm lunch, 5:30-9pm dinner; 🅿) South Coast Winery's (p452) gracious main restaurant has an arts-and-crafts-style barn feel and vineyard views from the balcony. Salads and sandwiches are popular at lunch, or pink-pepper local sea bass and steak filet with pickled mushrooms at dinner. Plus, wine pairing recommendations, naturally. At breakfast, the bananas Foster pancake with vanilla-bean sauce may make your head spin.

Crush & Brew
BAR

(📋951-693-4567; www.crushnbrew.com; 28544 Old Town Front St, Suite 103; ⏲11:30am-10pm Sun-Thu, to midnight Fri & Sat) This attractive recent addition to Front St pays tribute to the local wine industry with wines supplied by local producers and more than 30 craft beers on tap. For food: a great selection of salads and sandwiches, plus dishes like pulled boar or pan-seared halibut.

☆ Entertainment

Many Temecula-area wineries offer entertainment, from guitar soloists to chamber concerts. Check at the visitor center or **Visit** **Temecula Valley** (www.visittemeculavalley.com) for upcoming events. If you fancy a bit of line dancing or mechanical bull-riding, try the Temecula Stampede.

Pechanga Resort & Casino
CASINO

(📋888-732-4264; www.pechanga.com; 45000 Pechanga Pkwy; ⏲24hr) This huge Native American–owned casino-hotel offers plenty of slots, blackjack and roulette. Entertainment includes stand-up acts in its comedy club, and the 1200-seat **Pechanga Theater** hosts the likes of The Pretenders and Chicago.

The Temecula Stampede
DANCE

(📋951-695-1761; www.thetemeculastampede.com; 28721 Old Town Front Street; $5-10 cover Fri & Sat; ⏲Mon, Fri & Sat 6pm-2am, Thu 8pm-2am) Large country-and-western–style dance hall offering free early-evening line-dancing lessons, plus live music, mechanical bull-riding and a touch of rock and roll.

ℹ Information

Visitor Center (📋951-491-6085, 888-363-2852; www.visittemeculavalley.com; 28690 Mercedes St; ⏲9am-5pm Mon-Sat)

ℹ Getting There & Away

Temecula is just off the I-15 freeway, which begins in San Diego. Either of the Rancho California Rd or Rte 79 exits will take you to Old Town Front St. Allow 60 minutes from San Diego, 70 from Anaheim, 80 from Palm Springs or 90 from LA.

Greyhound (📋800-231-2222, 951-676-9768; www.greyhound.com; 28464 Old Town Front St) routes head to central San Diego twice daily (from $11 one way, when purchased in advance online). Journeys take roughly one hour and thirty minutes with no traffic.

Understand Southern California

Southern California Today

Today's Southern California is the culmination of the efforts of generations of big dreamers. From Los Angeles, the fantasies spun by Hollywood have come to dominate the digital transmissions and cultural trends of the entire planet. Meanwhile, SoCal's iconic images of tanned surfers and golden sands endure, despite the all-too-real challenges that this densely populated, racially diverse and economically unequal area now faces.

Best on Film

Sunset Boulevard (1950) Madness, murder and the ultimate Hollywood drama.

Chinatown (1974) LA's twin pillars: money and water.

Boyz n the Hood (1991) Groundbreaking look at South Central's gang culture.

The Big Lebowski (1998) The Dude abides in this Coen Brothers classic.

Sideways (2004) For the love of Pinot in Santa Barbara.

(500) Days of Summer (2009) Romance and architecture in DTLA.

La La Land (2016) Old-school musical charmer for modern times.

Best in Print

The Tortilla Curtain (TC Boyle; 1995) Mexican/American culture clash and chasing the Californian dream.

My California: Journeys by Great Writers (Angel City Press; 2004) Insightful stories by different talented chroniclers.

Where I Was From (Joan Didion; 2003) California-born essayist shatters palm-fringed fantasies.

Hollywood Babylon (Kenneth Anger; 1959) 'Tell-all' book about the scandalous lives and times of Hollywood's early stars.

California Dreams vs Reality

Even if you've seen it in movies or on TV, Southern California still comes as a shock to the system. Venice skateboarders, Malibu millionaires, Deepak Chopra-quoting new-age yogis and Rodeo Drive-pillaging trophy wives aren't on different channels; they all live together here, a place where at least the pretense of tolerance for other people's beliefs, be they conservative, liberal or just plain wacky, is the essential social glue.

Current hot topics are issues of immigrants' rights, trans rights and the advent of legal recreational marijuana, alongside earnest efforts to find solutions to longstanding problems like traffic congestion and educational inequality..

Growing Pains

SoCal is not a finished work. The nightmares faced by the region in the 1990s – race riots, the Northridge earthquake – already belong to a different age. Today's issues revolve around growth: in an area that has an economy bigger than Canada's and is the headquarters for a huge range of industries, from space probes to Disneyland to the movie and TV industry and a growing tech sector, how to manage an expanding economy and population without sacrificing the environment is the biggest problem.

With burgeoning humanity comes horrific traffic and the skyrocketing costs of living and real estate. Although slowly improving, public transport is still woefully inadequate in most places, so everyone hits the tortured freeway systems, which move ever more slowly. Sheer human impact is a palpable force, especially given a recent multiyear drought and prolonged wildfire seasons that drain the state's coffers and natural resources.

There is movement, however. In 2016, Angelenos, fed up with what's typically the nation's worst traffic, voted to tax themselves to fund transit improvements. Some of that is already happening; the same year saw the debut of the Expo Line, the first rail connection between Downtown LA and the beach in Santa Monica, with more lines on the way. A major (not just transit) overhaul of the region's main airport, Los Angeles International, is also underway, due for completion by 2023.

Multicultural Mosaic

Both a success story and a victim of its very adaptability, SoCal has found that the human waves of domestic migration and international immigration continue to rise. Every New Year's Day the largest commercial for living here – Pasadena's Rose Parade – snares the imaginations of folks freezing in Wisconsin or struggling to make ends meet in the Rust Belt. Many who heed the 19th-century advice to 'Go West, young man!' wind up on SoCal's sunny shores.

Given the mix of people constantly arriving here, the good news is that it's extremely difficult to envision LA ever returning to the kind of racially charged atmosphere that sparked the 'Zoot Suit Riots' of the 1940s or the uproar that followed the 1992 'all-white jury' verdict in the beating case of Rodney King, an African American, by LA police. You may be surprised to see the amiable multiethnic mix of colleagues and friends walking along boulevards and beaches or gathering for meals at SoCal's plethora of restaurants that deliver authentic global tastes.

Work Smart, Play Hard

Some of the myths surrounding SoCal are true, it has to be admitted. You really *can* surf in the morning, spend the afternoon skiing down pine-forested slopes and end the day with cocktails at a desert hot-springs resort. Who wouldn't want to live here, even with the horrifying commute times? More to the point, who wouldn't want to visit, or even perhaps become part of, such an exciting social experiment?

Time and again, SoCal has proven itself to be resourceful, resilient and innovative. After tourism, major drivers of the economy include international trade (LA and Long Beach form the nation's largest port), technology, finance, film and TV production, health services and design. With climate change threatening, you can bet the bank that Caltech, UCLA, USC and other universities are using their big brains to solve the issues that challenge not just SoCal, but also the rest of the state, the country and the world.

POPULATION: **19.6 MILLION**

POPULATION PER SQ MI:
**SOUTHERN
CALIFORNIA: 407
LOS ANGELES: 2100
USA: 91**

AREA: **48,112 SQ MI**

if California were 100 people

40 would be Caucasian
38 would be Latino
13 would be Asian American
6 would be African American
3 would be other

belief systems
(% of population)

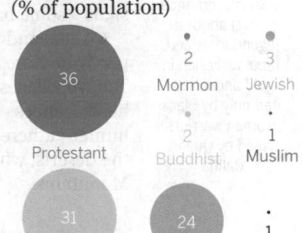

36 Protestant · 2 Mormon · 3 Jewish · 2 Buddhist · 1 Muslim · 31 Catholic · 24 other · 1 Hindu

population per sq mile

USA · California · Los Angeles

= 80 people

History

When European explorers first arrived in the 16th century, more than 100,000 Native Californians called this land home. Spanish conquistadors marched through in search of a fabled 'city of gold' before establishing Catholic missions and presidios (military forts). After winning independence from Spain, Mexico briefly ruled California, but then got trounced by the fledgling United States just before gold was discovered in 1848. Immigrant waves of star-struck California dreamers haven't stopped washing up on these Pacific shores ever since.

Native Californians

Immigration is hardly a new phenomenon here, since people have been migrating to California for millennia. Many archaeological sites have yielded evidence – from large middens of seashells along the beaches to campfire sites on the Channel Islands – of humans making their homes in Southern California as early as 13,000 years ago.

Traditional Ways of Life

The precise etymology of 'California' has never been convincingly established. Many think it derives from a 16th-century Spanish romance novel about a legendary island, fabulously rich in gold and inhabited only by black women warriors ruled by Queen Califia.

The majority of Native Californians lived in small communities and a few migrated with the seasons. Their diet was largely dependent on acorn meal, supplemented by small game such as rabbits and deer, and fish and shellfish. Native Californians were skilled craftspeople, making earthenware pots, fish nets, bows, arrows and spears with chipped stone points. Many tribes developed a knack for weaving baskets made from local grasses and plant fibers, then decorated them with geometric designs – some baskets were so tightly woven they could hold water.

Coastal and inland peoples traded but generally didn't interact much, partly because they spoke different languages. Kumeyaay, Chumash and Tongva villages dotted the coast, where people fished and paddled hand-hewn canoes, including out to the Channel Islands. Inland, nomadic hunter-gatherer bands of Cahuilla and Mojave peoples found oases in the deserts, while the Serrano camped seasonally in the San Bernardino Mountains.

TIMELINE	Around 20,000 BC	AD 1542	1602
	First people start crossing from Asia into North America via Bering Strait land bridge. The human bones found on SoCal's Santa Rosa Island date back 13,000 years.	Portuguese navigator Juan Rodríguez Cabrillo and his Spanish crew become the first Europeans to sight the mainland of New Spain's west coast, anchoring in today's San Diego Bay.	Sebastián Vizcaíno first sets foot on California soil on the feast day of San Diego de Alcalá. In honor of the saint, he names the spot San Diego.

Although there was no concept of private land ownership among Native Californians, the most common cause of conflict between indigenous peoples (that is, until Europeans arrived) was trespassing on another tribe's traditional territory. Natural resources were scarce, especially in the harsh desert, where tribes frequently skirmished.

From Conquest to Tribal Revival

Starting in the late 18th century, Spanish colonizers virtually enslaved Native Californians. Despite pockets of armed resistance and violent revolts, tribespeople were made to construct the missions and presidios (forts). Spanish soldiers, whose job was ostensibly to protect the missions and deter foreign intruders, became infamous for raping and pillaging. Meanwhile, European diseases such as smallpox and syphilis further decimated indigenous populations.

Native Californians were further dispossessed of tribal lands during the Mexican colonial and early American periods. It wasn't until the 20th century – when the US federal government began recognizing tribes as sovereign nations, including granting Native Americans citizenship and voting rights in 1924 – that California's indigenous population, once driven almost to the point of extinction, began to rebound.

Political activism, including the 'Red Power' protests of the American Indian Movement (AIM) starting in the late 1960s, led not only to a cultural renaissance, but also secured some tribes economic assistance from state and federal agencies, including California's Native American Heritage Commission established in 1978. Deprived of their traditional land base and means of livelihood centuries ago, many contemporary California tribes have turned to casino gaming to relieve unemployment and poverty on their reservations. Today tribal casinos support tens of thousands of jobs in Southern California.

A New World for Europeans

Following the conquest of Mexico in the early 16th century, Spain turned its attention toward exploring the edges of a new empire, fueled by curiosity, lust for power and, above all, greed. Tales of a golden island to the west circulated widely. In 1542 the Spanish crown sent Juan Rodríguez Cabrillo, a Portuguese explorer and retired conquistador, to find it.

The fabled land, of course, proved elusive, but Cabrillo and his crew still made it into the history books as the first Europeans to see mainland California at what is now San Diego. Cabrillo claimed the land for Spain while sitting out a storm in the harbor before sailing northward. Stopping to check out the Channel Islands, the explorer broke a leg, fell ill, died and was buried in 1543 on what is now San Miguel Island.

Native California History

Indian Canyons (p296)

Tahquitz Canyon (p296)

Autry Museum (p125)

Museum of Man (p394)

Chumash Painted Cave State Historic Park

HISTORY A NEW WORLD FOR EUROPEANS

1769	1781	1821–46	1848
Spanish captain Gaspar de Portolá leads the first European land expedition north into Alta (Upper) California, establishing colonial forts and missions with the help of priest Junípero Serra.	Spanish governor Felipe de Neve sets out from Mission San Gabriel with a tiny band of settlers, trekking west just 9 miles to establish the future Los Angeles.	During Mexico's rule over California, Spanish missions are secularized (except Santa Barbara) and their lands carved up into ranchos. Governor Pío Pico's brother-in-law snaps up San Juan Capistrano.	Signing the Treaty of Guadalupe Hidalgo on February 2, Mexico turns over one third of its territory, including California, to the US in exchange for $15 million.

SoCal's Standout Missions

San Diego (p401) (the oldest)

San Juan Capistrano (p286) (the most famous)

Santa Barbara (p349) (the only one never secularized)

La Purísima (p375) (the most complete)

The Spanish left California alone for the next half century or so, until they decided they needed to secure some ports on the Pacific coast, and sent Sebastián Vizcaíno to find them. Vizcaíno's first expedition was a disaster that didn't get past Baja (Lower) California, but in his second attempt, in 1602, he rediscovered the harbor at San Diego and became the first European to set foot in what Spaniards called Alta (Upper) California.

The Spanish Mission Period

In the 18th century, everyone wanted a toehold on the western shores of the New World. Around the 1760s, as Russian ships sailed up and down California's coast in search of otter pelts, and British trappers and explorers spread throughout the western continent, King Carlos III finally grew worried that Spain's claim to the territory might be challenged.

Conveniently, the Catholic Church was anxious to start missionary work among Native Californians, so the Church and Spanish Crown combined forces and established missions protected by presidios (forts). Native American converts were expected to live in the missions, learn trade and agricultural skills and ultimately establish pueblos, which would be like little Spanish towns. Or so the plan went.

On July 1, 1769, a sorry lot of about 100 missionaries and soldiers, led by the Franciscan priest Junípero Serra and the military commander Gaspar de Portolá, limped ashore at San Diego Bay. They had just spent several weeks at sea sailing from Baja (Lower) California; about half of their cohort had died en route and many of the survivors were sick or near death. It was an inauspicious beginning for Mission San Diego de Alcalá, the first in a chain of 21 Spanish missions in Alta (Upper) California.

The missions did achieve modest success at farming and just barely managed to become self-sufficient, an essential achievement during the 1810–21 Mexican War of Independence from Spain, when supplies from Mexico were cut off completely. As a way of colonizing California and converting the indigenous people to Christianity, however, the mission period was an abject failure. The Spanish population remained small, foreign intruders were not greatly deterred and, ultimately, more Native Californians died than were converted.

The distance between each of California's Spanish Colonial missions equaled a day's journey by horseback. Learn more about the missions' historical significance and cultural influence at www.missionscalifornia.com.

From Mexican Ranchos to Statehood

When Mexico gained its independence from Spain in 1821, many in that new nation looked to California to satisfy their thirst for private land. By the mid-1830s, almost all of the Spanish missions in Alta (Upper) California had been secularized and divvied up into land grants by Mexican governors. This gave birth to a system of Mexican ranchos, largely raising

1849	1850	1869	1874
Following the discovery of gold at Sutter's Creek in the Sierra Nevada foothills in 1848, the California Gold Rush sees the largest migration in US history.	On September 9, California becomes the 31st state of the US, entering the Union as a free (non-slave-holding) state. Its first constitution is written in Spanish and English.	Gold is discovered in Julian, near San Diego, sparking a mini mining boom. Once the gold runs out, Julian goes back to being a sleepy little town.	US Department of Agriculture ships three seedless navel orange trees to botanists in Riverside. By 1889 citrus orchards cover more than 13,000 acres of SoCal.

livestock to supply the hide and tallow trade. The new landowners, called rancheros or Californios, prospered and became the social, cultural and political fulcrums of Alta California under Mexican rule.

Meanwhile, American explorers, trappers, traders, whalers, settlers and opportunists increasingly showed interest in California. Some Americans who started businesses here converted to Catholicism, married local women and assimilated into Californio society. Impressed by California's untapped riches and imbued with Manifest Destiny (an imperialist political doctrine of extending the USA's borders from coast to coast), President Andrew Jackson sent an emissary to offer the financially strapped Mexican government $500,000 for California in 1835.

But Mexico wasn't interested in selling California, and soon a political storm was brewing. In 1836 Texas seceded from Mexico and declared itself an independent republic. When the US annexed Texas in 1845, Mexico broke off diplomatic relations and ordered all foreigners without proper papers to be deported from California. In turn, the US declared war on Mexico and began an invasion. Soon US naval units occupied every port on the California coast, but militarily speaking, California remained a sideshow while the war was mostly fought in Mexico.

The capture of Mexico City by US troops in September 1847 put an end to the fighting and led to the signing of the Treaty of Guadalupe Hidalgo on February 2, 1848, in which the Mexican government ceded much of its northern territory (including Alta California) to the USA, just in time for California's Gold Rush to begin.

Riches of Railroads, Real Estate & Oil

Many Mexican rancheros lost their land when American authorities questioned their title under the 1851 Land Act. During this period of loose government, LA was a Wild West town, filled with saloons, brothels and gambling dens. Added to the mix were thousands of Chinese immigrants who had arrived for the Gold Rush and later railroad construction work. These foreigners were viewed by many with suspicion – the state even enacted a special 'foreign miner's tax' in 1852.

The perception of LA and the rest of the region as a lawless backwater began to change with the arrival of the railroad. Completed in 1869, the transcontinental railroad shortened the trip from New York to San Francisco from two months to less than four days, elevating the latter to California's metropolitan center. SoCal's parched climate, its distance from freshwater and mining resources, and its relatively small population made it unattractive to railroad moguls. Not until the mid-1870s did wheeling and dealing result in a spur line to LA.

During the same period, agriculture diversified, with new crops – especially oranges – being grown in Southern California for markets on

Top SoCal History Books

California: A History (Kevin Starr)

City of Quartz (Mike Davis)

Journey to the Sun: Junípero Serra's Dream and the Founding of California (Gregory Orfalea)

1892	1902	1913	1915
Oil is discovered by Edward Doheny in downtown LA, near where Dodger Stadium stands today, sparking a major oil boom. Within five years, 500 wells are operational.	The first Rose Bowl football game takes place in Pasadena, with the University of Michigan defeating Stanford 49–0. The next game isn't held for another 14 years.	The Los Angeles Aqueduct, built under the direction of chief engineer William Mulholland, starts supplying water from the Owens Valley in the Eastern Sierra.	German-born Carl Laemmle builds Universal City Studios on a farm north of Hollywood, selling lunch to curious guests who come to watch the magic of moviemaking.

the East Coast and abroad. Unlike many fruits, oranges easily survived long-distance rail shipping. As oranges found their way onto New York grocery shelves, a hard-sell California advertising campaign began. Folks back East heeded the self-interested advice of crusading magazine and newspaper editor Horace Greeley to 'Go West, young man!'

Much of the land granted to the railroads in Southern California was sold in big lots to speculators who also acquired, with the help of corrupt politicians and administrators, much of the farmland that was released for new settlement. A major share of agricultural land thus became consolidated into large holdings in the hands of a few city-based landlords, establishing California's still-dominant pattern of industrial-scale 'agribusiness,' rather than small family farms. Never mind that SoCal's supply of freshwater was inadequate and that cheap agricultural labor often had to be imported.

Yet LA had other natural resources waiting to be exploited, albeit hidden underground. In 1892 a flat-broke mining prospector and real-estate speculator named Edward Doheny dug a well near downtown LA that would change SoCal forever. Inside of a year, Doheny's well was producing 40 gallons of 'black gold' (oil) per day. Flowing north from LA into Ventura and Santa Barbara Counties, SoCal's oil industry soon boomed, as fictionally depicted in the 2007 film *There Will Be Blood*.

Los Angeles' Water Wars

The growth of arid Los Angeles into a megalopolis would not have been possible without water. When the city's population surged in the early 20th century, it became clear that groundwater levels would soon be inadequate to meet its needs, let alone sustain further growth. Water had to be imported and Fred Eaton, an ex-mayor of LA, and William Mulholland, the powerful head of the LA Department of Water & Power, knew just how and where to get it: by aqueduct from the Owens Valley, which receives enormous runoff from the Sierra Nevada Mountains.

The fact that the Owens Valley was settled by farmers who needed the water for irrigation purposes bothered neither the two men nor the federal government, which actively supported LA's less-than-ethical maneuvering in acquiring land and securing water rights in the area. Voters gave Mulholland the more than $25 million needed to build the aqueduct. An amazing feat of engineering – crossing barren desert floor as well as rugged mountain terrain for 233 miles – the LA Aqueduct opened to great fanfare in 1913.

The Owens Valley, however, would never be the same. With most of its inflows diverted, Owens Lake quickly shriveled up. A bitter feud between LA and Owens Valley farmers and ranchers grew violent when some opponents to the scheme tried to sabotage the aqueduct by blowing up a

Los Angeles once had a wonderfully efficient system of streetcars, until General Motors allegedly conspired to destroy it (search online for 'GM streetcar conspiracy' and make up your own mind). It is now spending billions to reinstall train lines along those same rights of way torn up in the 1950s.

1923	1925	1927	1929
LA's famous landmark, the 45ft-tall Hollywood Sign, is erected in the Santa Monica Mountains to promote Hollywoodland subdivision. The 'land' drops off in 1949, but the sign remains.	At 6:44am on June 29, a 6.3-magnitude earthquake levels most of downtown Santa Barbara, killing 13 people. The city rebuilds in Spanish Colonial Revival style.	*The Jazz Singer* premieres at Downtown LA's Million Dollar Theater as the world's first 'talkie' movie, signaling the decline of the silent-film era. Hollywood booms.	The first Academy Awards ceremony takes place at the Hollywood Roosevelt Hotel, lasting only 15 minutes. Fewer than 300 people fork over $5 each to be part of the crowd.

section of it. All to no avail. By 1928 LA owned 90% of the water in Owens Valley and agriculture was effectively dead. These early water wars formed the basis for the 1974 noir film *Chinatown*.

These days LA still gets over half of its water supply from this aqueduct, which was extended another 105 miles to Mono Basin in 1940. The remainder of the city's water is siphoned from the Colorado and Feather Rivers; only about 15% comes from groundwater in the San Fernando Valley basin. During periods of extreme drought, water restrictions are put in place for LA residences and businesses – that's why you may have to specifically request drinking water when dining out at restaurants.

Military Might in SoCal

Along with motion pictures, aviation was another major industry to have a significant impact on Southern California, beginning in the early 20th century. During and after WWI, the Lockheed brothers and Donald Douglas established aircraft manufacturing plants in LA, while Glenn H Curtiss set up shop in San Diego and San Diego–based Ryan Airlines built the *Spirit of St Louis* for Lindbergh's celebrated transatlantic flight in 1927.

In the 1930s, the aviation industry – pumped up by billions of federal dollars for military contracts – helped lift SoCal out of the Great Depression. WWII also had a huge impact on the entire region. After the 1941 bombing of Pearl Harbor, San Diego became the headquarters of the US Pacific Fleet, changing the city forever. Farther north, Camp Pendleton, a huge Marine Corps Base, was established in 1942. Throughout WWII, local aircraft-manufacturing plants turned out planes by the thousands.

After WWII, many servicepeople settled in SoCal. The region's military-industrial complex continued to prosper during the Cold War, providing jobs in everything from avionics and missile manufacturing to helicopter and nuclear-submarine maintenance. The US Marine Corps still trains recruits and the US Navy holds advanced *Top Gun*-style training for fighter pilots here. There are submarine bases, aircraft-testing facilities, air-force bases and sprawling gunnery ranges.

Military spending peaked in the 1980s under ex-California governor and then US president Ronald Reagan, but the end of the Cold War spelled economic disaster. Budget cutbacks closed numerous military bases, forcing defense contractors to move on or diversify. Workers who had grown accustomed to regular paychecks from aerospace juggernauts like McDonnell Douglas suddenly got laid off.

Race Riots in Los Angeles

LA's long history of racial strife reached an explosive peak in the 1960s. The city was booming but not everyone was invited to the party. Many

---

SoCal's Top Military Museums & Events

USS Midway Museum (p401)

San Diego Air & Space Museum (p395)

Fleet Week & Miramar Air Show (p410)

Battleship Iowa (p199)

Fort MacArthur Military Museum (p199)

Palm Springs Air Museum (p295)

1942	**1943**	**1955**	**1965**
US Executive Order 9066 banishes 120,000 Japanese Americans to internment camps. The US federal government doesn't make monetary reparations until the 1990s.	Tension between Americans and Mexicans reaches boiling point during the Zoot Suit Riots, which pit US military servicemen against zoot-suit-clad Mexican teens while LA police look on.	Disneyland opens in Anaheim on July 18 after a quick one-year construction period. Temperatures hit 101°F, high-heeled shoes sink into the soft asphalt and drinking fountains don't work.	It takes 20,000 National Guards to quell the six-day Watts Riots in LA, which cause death, devastation and over $40 million in property damage. That same year, Rodney King is born.

CALIFORNIA IMMIGRATION: TAKE IT, THEN LEAVE IT

California has always had a love-hate relationship with its immigrants, yet owes much of its success to its cultural diversity. Newcomers are typically welcomed in periods of rapid growth, only to be rejected when times get tough.

Chinese railroad workers, for instance, were in great demand during the 1860s, but ended up being discriminated against and even violently attacked in LA over the next decade. California's Alien Land Law of 1913 even prevented resident Asians who were ineligible for US citizenship from owning agricultural land. During WWII, around 120,000 people of Japanese heritage – many of them US citizens – were forcibly placed in internment camps. African Americans came to SoCal in large numbers to take jobs during the postwar boom, but suddenly found themselves unemployed when the economy later slowed.

It is estimated that more than three million undocumented immigrants currently work in California, despite continuing efforts to seal the notoriously porous border with Mexico. Mexican and Latin American workers still do most of SoCal's farm labor and domestic work. In 1994, in the face of increasing unemployment and state budget deficits, a majority of Californians voted in favor of Proposition 187, which denied illegal immigrants access to state government services, including schools and hospitals.

Today immigration remains a volatile political topic in Southern California, especially among conservatives, some of whom employ illegal immigrants as nannies and gardeners while simultaneously calling for their expulsion. At the other end of the political spectrum, California passed a law allowing illegal immigrants to get state driver's licenses in 2013. In 2016, state lawmakers passed a bill allowing undocumented foreigners to be given access to public health care too.

In early 2017, the administration of President Donald Trump had received bids and was preparing to build the first section of its US–Mexico border wall in San Diego County.

ethnic-minority neighborhoods, predominantly African American communities with South Central foremost among them, had for decades been suffering from institutional neglect and lack of opportunity.

On a hot August day in 1965, frustration levels reached a boiling point when an African American motorist being pulled over on suspicion of drink-driving was beaten by police. Six violent days later, when the Watts Riots were over, 34 people were dead and more than 2000 were injured.

As the city licked its wounds, Governor Pat Brown appointed a commission to study the causes of the riots. They identified the problems – an unemployment rate double the LA average, overcrowded and underfunded classrooms, discriminatory housing laws etc – but lacked the vision, money and perhaps motivation to fix them. A generation later there would be a high price to pay for such indifference.

1966	1968	1969	1984
Ronald Reagan is elected Governor of California, setting a career precedent for fading film stars. He served until 1975 and in 1981 became the 40th president of the United States.	Robert Kennedy is assassinated at the Ambassador Hotel in LA by Palestinian immigrant and anti-Zionist Sirhan Sirhan, who remains in jail today in San Diego County.	UCLA professor Len Kleinrock sends data from a computer in Los Angeles to another at Stanford University, typing just two characters before the system crashes. The internet is born.	Los Angeles hosts the Summer Olympics for the second time (the first was in 1932). The USSR doesn't show up, leaving US athletes to win 83 gold medals.

Fast forward to April 29, 1992: 'Not guilty.' The words cut through the stifling air of a hushed Simi Valley courtroom. More than a year earlier – in an eerie déjà vu of 1965 – four LAPD officers had stopped Rodney King, an African American motorist, on suspicion of driving under the influence. When King initially resisted arrest, the cops allegedly started to kick, beat and shout at the man as he crouched on the sidewalk. Infamously, the whole incident was caught on videotape.

The cops' acquittal unleashed a replay of the Watts Riots on an even bigger scale, as rioting and looting spread through several neighborhoods. The National Guard patrolled the streets with machine guns, businesses and schools were ordered to close, and a dusk curfew was imposed. LA felt like a war zone. The shocking toll: 54 dead, over 2300 injured, 12,000 arrested and nearly $1 billion in property damage.

In LA, charges of police brutality and corruption splash news headlines still today, even in the wake of the Black Lives Matter movement. Given the abyss of distrust between police and some poor and minority communities, it's anybody's guess what the future holds.

Social Movers & Shakers

Unconstrained by the burden of traditions, bankrolled by elite affluence and promoted by film and TV, Southern California has long been a leader in new attitudes and social movements.

In the affluent 1950s, the emerging middle class moved to the suburbs, and no place better defined suburban life than Orange County. The Irvine Company, owner of almost 100,000 acres of private land (a legacy of 19th-century Mexican land grants), built the first 'Master Plan' communities. Strict rules governed their design – hence uniform beige-box architecture. Everybody lived on quiet streets where children could safely play, while shopping centers and strip malls were concentrated along multilane boulevards that made owning a car necessary.

When the postwar Baby Boomers hit their late teens, many rejected their parents' values and heeded LSD guru Timothy Leary's counsel to 'turn on, tune in, drop out.' Though the hippie counterculture was an international phenomenon, SoCal was at the leading edge of its music, psychedelic art and new libertarianism. Sex, drugs and rock 'n' roll ruled the day. LA's Venice Beach was a major hub and hangout for Jim Morrison, Janis Joplin and other luminaries of that era.

In the late 1960s and early '70s, New Left politics, the anti–Vietnam War movement and Black Liberation all forced their way into the political limelight, making flower power and give-peace-a-chance politics seem naive. The 1968 assassination of Robert Kennedy in LA, violent repressions of political demonstrations and the death of a spectator at a

A literally and symbolically colorful book, *A People's Guide to Los Angeles* by Laura Pulido, Laura Barraclough and Wendy Cheng, documents milestones and powerful places of struggle over race, class, gender and sexuality.

1992	1994	1994	2003
Riots explode across Los Angeles after white police officers are acquitted of the beating of motorist Rodney King.	The 6.7-magnitude Northridge earthquake strikes at 4:31am on January 17, killing 72 and causing $20 billion in property damage – one of the costliest natural disasters in US history.	Orange County, one of the wealthiest US municipalities, declares bankruptcy after the county treasurer loses $1.5 billion investing in risky derivatives and pleads guilty to six felony charges.	Arnold Schwarzenegger announces his Republican candidacy for governor on *The Tonight Show with Jay Leno*. In October's recall election, he wins by 1.3 million votes.

Rolling Stones concert at the hands of security guards (Hells Angels had been hired for the occasion) stripped the era of its innocence.

What a difference a few decades make. Since the 1980s, Southern California's new obsession has become the healthy lifestyle, with a mood-altering array of yoga and fitness classes and self-actualization workshops on offer. Leisure activities like in-line skating, skateboarding, snowboarding and mountain biking all originated in California too. Be careful what you laugh at: from pet rocks to soy burgers, kale Caesar salads to juicing, SoCal's flavor of the month is often next year's global trend.

When LA's Expo light rail line was completed in 2016, it marked the return of rail travel between Downtown LA and Santa Monica for the first time since 1953, when Red Car trolley lines were removed in favor of freeways.

Growing Pains into the 21st Century

The internet revolution, spurred by Silicon Valley up north near San Francisco, rewired California's entire economy and led to a 1990s boom in overspeculated stocks. When the bubble burst in 2000, plunging the entire state's economy into chaos, deregulation of the electricity market led to rolling blackouts and sky-high power bills. In a controversial recall election, Californians voted to give action-movie star Arnold Schwarzenegger (Republican) a shot at fixing things in 2003.

Five years later, the meltdown on Wall Street and the US recession caused another staggering financial crisis, one that took California, led by once-again Governor Jerry Brown (Democrat), several years to recover from. Meanwhile, ballistic population growth, pollution and gridlocked traffic continue to cloud SoCal's sunny skies, the need for public education and prison reform builds, and the conundrum of immigration from Mexico, which fills a critical cheap-labor shortage, remains unsolved.

2005	2007	2013	2016
Antonio Villaraigosa elected mayor of LA, the first Latino to hold that office since 1872. Born poor in East LA, he says in his victory speech, 'I will never forget where I came from.'	Wildfires sweep across drought-stricken Southern California. One million people evacuate their homes between Santa Barbara and San Diego. Extreme drought returns just three years later.	Proposition 8, a state constitutional ban on same-sex marriage that was narrowly approved by voters in 2008, is struck down after legal wrangling. Same-sex marriages resume in California.	Voters in California vote to legalize and regulate marijuana for recreational use. The new law takes effect in 2018.

The Way of Life

In the Southern California of the dream world, you wake up, have your shot of wheat-grass juice and roll down to the beach while the surf's up. Lifeguards wave as they jog by in their bathing suits. You skateboard down the boardwalk to your yoga class, where everyone admires your downward dog. A food truck pulls up with your favorite: sustainable fish tacos with organic mango chipotle salsa. But honestly, can you really make that SoCal dream come true here?

Regional Identity

Southern California is America at its extremes, with all the good and bad that this entails. Its people are among the nation's richest and poorest, most established and newest arrivals, most refined and roughest, most beautiful and most plain, most erudite and most airheaded. Success here can be spectacular, failure equally so.

What binds the residents of this region together is that they are seekers. Nearly everyone – or their forebears – arrived in Southern California by choice. Whether from across the country, across the border or across the globe, they were drawn here by a dream, be it fame on the silver screen, sand, surf and sun, making a splash in business or research, or earning cash to send home to family. It's as if America's dreamers all rushed west and stopped where the continent ran out of land. They found plenty of company on these sun-kissed shores.

The Stereotypes

Valley girls snap chewing gum in shopping malls, surfer boys shout 'Dude!' across San Diego beaches, new immigrants gather on street corners in search of day jobs, surgically enhanced babes sip mojitos poolside, rail-thin Orange County soccer moms in urban assault vehicles flip out in rush-hour traffic, and everyone works in 'the Industry' (film and TV entertainment, that is).

Southern Californians roll their eyes at these stereotypes: they didn't create NASA's Jet Propulsion Lab, SpaceX and almost half the world's movies by slacking off. According to a recent Cambridge University study, creativity, imagination and intellectualism are all defining characteristics of Californians, compared with inhabitants of other US states.

The Reality

As with everything in SoCal, if you're looking for the stereotype, that's what you'll find. But keep your eyes open and you'll find that reality is a lot more complex, and interesting.

In LA the first question you'll often hear from locals is 'What do you do for a living?' This is how people place each other and, unlike many other places in the country, nobody here is very surprised if the answer takes more than a minute. There's nothing unusual about waiting tables, for example, while working toward your dream job as an actor or screenwriter. The second question you might hear is 'Where are you from?' because most people here seem to have come from somewhere else.

SoCal inventions include the space shuttle, Mickey Mouse, whitening toothpaste, the hula hoop (or at least its trademark), Barbie, skateboard and surfboard technology, the Cobb salad and the fortune cookie.

Hollywood-esque 'happy talk' trickles down to daily interactions, sometimes to the point that people from other places can have trouble understanding what locals mean. Saying someone has 'issues' is a polite way of implying that the person has problems. 'Let's get together' is often not to be taken literally; it can actually mean 'It was great talking with you, and now I have to go.'

Then there's the car you drive. There's an underlying truth to the stereotype that owning the right car in SoCal is what the right shoes are to Italians. Fancy imports, convertibles and muscle cars still turn heads, but the status symbol *du jour* is an electric-powered Tesla Model S. That said, Angeleno hipsters, even those with means, are increasingly forgoing cars entirely and moving to neighborhoods like Downtown LA and Hollywood that can be accessed by subway, bus and bike. The high-rise condos of Downtown San Diego are another burgeoning urban scene.

In his column 'iAsk a Mexican!', *OC Weekly* editor Gustavo Arellano tackles such questions as whether sour cream on Mexican food is legit (answer: yes), alongside weighty social issues involving immigrants' rights. Read it at www.ocweekly.com.

Majorities & Minorities

Perhaps it's no coincidence that LA's current mayor, Eric Garcetti, has ancestors from Mexican, Italian, Irish and Russian Jewish backgrounds. Multiculturalism is at the city's core.

Even among the settlers who founded LA in 1781, there were different races and nationalities. Today LA is one of only two major metro areas in the nation without a majority ethnic group (the other is Honolulu). Across Southern California, immigrants from more than 140 countries have put down roots, creating the largest populations of Mexicans, Koreans, Armenians, Filipinos, Salvadorans, Guatemalans and Vietnamese outside their home countries, as well as America's largest ethnic Cambodian, Japanese and Persian communities.

All this makes LA one of the most tolerant, cosmopolitan and open-minded societies anywhere in the USA. Although there are many mono-ethnic-dominated neighborhoods, it's not uncommon to interact with people of a dozen or more ethnicities in a single day in any corner of the city. You might drop off your shirts with a Korean-run dry cleaner, have your nails done by a recent Vietnamese immigrant, pick up groceries from a Mexican grocer and a treat from the Cambodian-run doughnut shop. Dinner might just as easily be sushi, falafel, enchiladas or steak-frites.

Certainly, LA's explosive race-related incidents have received high-profile exposure, as with the riots of 1965 and again in 1992. Yet day-to-day civility between races is the norm. Animosity is hard to maintain when you encounter people of so many different ethnic backgrounds on a daily basis. Interracial couples and families – like the Garcetti – barely raise an eyebrow here.

DAMN THAT TRAFFIC JAM!

Traffic is LA's great leveler. Outsiders often marvel that it's a city without a center. That's less true than it used to be thanks to Downtown LA's redevelopment, but it's also more true in that business districts are widely dispersed. So while you could once count on traffic into Downtown in the morning and outbound in the evening, now traffic jams can happen in either direction. Or you might just as easily find the roads mysteriously clear. That same unpredictability applies to most other places in SoCal too.

Subway and light-rail lines have been extended of late, and long-range regional plans call for even more. For now, Angelenos advise to take your cell phone (with a hands-free headset – it's the law), use GPS apps such as Waze and, should you get stuck in traffic, try to be Zen about it. Those waiting for you at your destination will understand: you can blame traffic for being late every time.

Latino SoCal

One of every four US immigrants lands in California, with the largest segment coming from Mexico, followed by Central America. Almost half of LA County's residents are Latino, according to recent US Census figures, and they are soon projected to become the outright majority.

The collective influence of Latinos on SoCal life is huge. Spanish is the *lingua franca* in many restaurant kitchens, and there are hosts of Latino products on the shelves of mainstream supermarkets. Even non-Latino Angelenos can expound on different mole sauces and the advantages of corn versus flour tortillas. From Spanish-language billboards to radio and TV stations, you'll see, hear and experience Latino culture all over SoCal.

Despite their numbers, Latinos had little say in leadership until about the early 2000s; Antonio Villaraigosa made national headlines in 2005 when he became LA's first Latino mayor since 1872. Nowadays leaders throughout the city have Latino roots, as do members of LA's city council and powerful county board of supervisors, and both the California State Assembly Speaker and the leader of State Senate are Latinos from LA.

SoCal also has many representatives in the California State Assembly and US Congress. Immigration, both legal and otherwise, is always a hot-button issue, and May Day (May 1) has become the de facto time for an immigration reform rally and deportation protests in Downtown LA.

Perhaps somewhat surprisingly, San Diego is more homogeneous (read: Caucasian) than LA, despite its location closer to the border with Mexico. That said, the most recent US census showed the percentage of non-white San Diego County residents now exceeds 50%.

Other Ethnic Groups

Historically speaking, Southern California's Chinatowns, Japantowns and other ethnic neighborhoods were often the result of segregationist sentiment, not by choice. While equal opportunity may be a shared goal, in practice it's very much still a work in progress. Even racially integrated areas can still be quite segregated by ethnic group in terms of income and language.

LA's Koreatown is the largest, a vast swath between Hollywood (where you'll find the USA's first Thai Town) and Downtown LA (home of Little Tokyo, one of no fewer than three Japanese neighborhoods in LA). These days Downtown LA's Chinatown offers as much Vietnamese *pho* (noodle soup) as Chinese dim sum, while the real center of contemporary Chinese immigration to SoCal has moved east of LA to the suburban San Gabriel Valley towns of Alhambra, Monterey Park and San Gabriel, where Chinese signage is almost as prevalent as English.

Meanwhile, West LA's Venice Blvd is home to Brazilian cuisine and music, West Hollywood has a large Russian immigrant contingent, and it's not uncommon to see black-hatted Orthodox Jews walking to synagogue in the Fairfax and Pico-Robertson districts. Armenians form the largest ethnic group in Glendale, Signal Hill near Long Beach is home to a Cambodian community, Cerritos and Artesia (near the border of LA and Orange Counties) are a center for South Asian immigration, and Croatian seafarers made their home in the southern LA port town of San Pedro.

San Diego honors the heritage of its Portuguese fisherfolk in the Point Loma neighborhood. San Diego also has SoCal's only Little Italy, bursting with cafes and restaurants. Little Saigon, in the inland Orange County towns of Garden Grove and Westminster, has the largest population of ethnic Vietnamese outside Vietnam, some 190,000; many of its residents emigrated in the late 1970s, and the population tends to be vocally

Mike Davis' *City of Quartz* (1990) is an excoriating history of LA and a glimpse into its possible future; in *Ecology of Fear* (1998), he examines the decay of the natural environment in the LA Basin. Davis and collaborators also examined San Diego's underbelly in *Under the Perfect Sun: The San Diego Tourists Never See* (2003).

opposed to the current Vietnamese regime. In Anaheim's Little Arabia district, even some non-Muslim restaurants serve halal meat.

LGBT SoCal

From Palm Springs to San Diego's bohemian Hillcrest neighborhood, arty Laguna Beach and the hip neighborhoods of Silver Lake and West Hollywood (WeHo) in LA, SoCal's LGBT community is out and proud. High-profile gay men, lesbians and transgender people can be found at all levels of society, from government to business and the arts. And LA's LGBT community has dozens of ways to engage civically, from LA's LGBT film festival Outfest, SoCal's largest film festival, to fundraisers for LGBT causes, performances by LGBT choruses throughout the region, outdoors groups and many more.

That history goes back a long time. The Mattachine Society, founded in LA in 1950, has been called America's first gay rights organization. The *Advocate* magazine, PFLAG (Parents, Friends and Family of Lesbians and Gays) and America's first gay church and synagogue all started in LA. The nation's first Stonewall-style demonstration took place at the Black Cat Tavern in LA's Silver Lake neighborhood, in 1967, two years before Stonewall in New York.

In 2008 the Supreme Court of California ruled that gay and lesbian couples had the same right to marry as heterosexual couples. Over the next several months, some 18,000 same-sex couples were married in the state. The court ruling was overturned in November 2008 when, in a statewide ballot measure known as Proposition 8, the state constitution was amended to specify that marriage had to be between one man and one woman. Prop 8 eventually became the subject of multiple court challenges, whose outcomes, like so much else that originates in California, were expected to have national implications.

So what happened? In 2010 US District Court Judge Vaughn Walker struck down Prop 8 as unconstitutional. A court case challenging that decision eventually reached the US Supreme Court, which on June 26, 2013 decided by a narrow 5–4 margin not to overturn Walker's ruling. Amid celebrations by many, same-sex marriages resumed in California.

These days the energy seems to be focused on the T portion of LGBT, as issues of trans rights have taken national prominence.

Religion: Old & New

Although SoCal residents are less churchgoing than the US mainstream, and one in five professes no religion at all, this region remains one of the world's most religiously diverse. Thanks to SoCal's freewheeling reputation and attitudes, religious tolerance is (mostly) the rule here.

LA is home to the nation's largest Roman Catholic archdiocese and the second-largest Jewish community in North America, with members of almost every Protestant denomination also well represented. The world's second-largest Mormon temple is in the West LA neighborhood of Westwood, while another spectacular Mormon temple towers over the I-5 Fwy near La Jolla, in San Diego County. SoCal also has the largest community of Buddhists outside of Asia. Muslim groups estimate that some 500,000 Muslims live in Southern California.

Some mainstream faiths are also politically powerful, a few controversially so as with the Catholic church's sex-abuse scandal and Mormon support for Proposition 8, which attempted to ban same-sex marriage in California.

SoCal also has a long history of megachurches led by charismatic preachers, going back to the days of Aimee Semple McPherson, who opened the 5300-seat Angelus Temple in LA's Echo Park neighborhood back in 1923. More recently, Orange County is famously one of the USA's

Southern California has thousands of believers in Santería, a fusion of Catholicism and Yoruba beliefs first practiced by West African slaves in the Caribbean and South America. Drop by a *botànica* (herbal folk medicine shop) for charms and candles.

bastions of ultra-conservative, evangelical megachurches, with well-known televangelists Pastor Rick Warren of Saddleback Church and the Schuller family of the *Hour of Power* show broadcast from the sparkling, all-glass Crystal Cathedral until 2012 (now Christ Cathedral).

Other offshoots of mainstream religions include the yogic Self-Realization Fellowship, with large centers in Pacific Palisades and the San Diego County beach town of Encinitas. West LA's Kabbalah Centre has seen many celebrity practitioners of its version of Jewish mysticism.

Southern California has also long been a breeding ground for new religions and religious cults, which have sometimes taken over news headlines. There's a dust-up every few years or so about the Church of Scientology, which is based in Los Angeles and claims members including Hollywood celebrities. Most infamously, the UFO-millennialist cult Heaven's Gate was based in a mansion in northern San Diego County, where 38 members committed mass suicide in 1997.

Spectator Sports

LA's sports teams have long and often-winning histories, but they're also known as much for their celebrity quotient on and off the court or field as for their undeniable athletic prowess.

Case in point: the Los Angeles Lakers **basketball** team plays at Downtown LA's Staples Center, where you can watch the game alongside such famous fans as Jack Nicholson and Leonardo DiCaprio. On the court, the Lakers' roster of fabled players has included Kareem Abdul-Jabbar, Magic Johnson, Shaquille O'Neal and Kobe Bryant. LA's other NBA team, the Clippers, were former also-rans but are currently looking strong behind power players Blake Griffin, DeAndre Jordan and Chris Paul. The Clippers also play at Staples Center.

The Brooklyn Dodgers **baseball** team became the Los Angeles Dodgers in 1958, and New Yorkers have never quite forgiven LA. Ringed by hills, the classic mid-century Dodger Stadium is one of the most beautiful in baseball. San Diego's Petco Park is the gorgeous home of the San Diego Padres, in the middle of Downtown. In Orange County, you can watch the awkwardly named Los Angeles Angels of Anaheim at Angel Stadium.

SoCal's relationship with **pro football** has been, let's say, complicated. In 1994, LA's two teams, the Rams and the Raiders, both decamped, leaving no pro football in the city for more than two decades. The Rams returned in 2016, though not in their former winning ways. San Diego's NFL team, the Chargers, made the move to LA in 2017. Until a permanent football stadium opens in 2019 in Inglewood (between South LA and Los Angeles International Airport), the Rams will play at the Los Angeles Memorial Coliseum and the Chargers at StubHub center in Carson, in the South Bay.

Meanwhile **college football** is big, particularly crosstown rivals the UCLA Bruins and USC Trojans. LA's long-neglected Major League **Soccer** (MLS) team, the Galaxy, got a boost with the 2007 arrival of icon David Beckham and his $250 million price tag, but his on-and-off Galaxy career through 2012 was less than stellar.

Del Mar Racetrack in northern San Diego County is the ritziest of SoCal's **horse-racing** tracks, while LA County's historic Santa Anita Racetrack featured in the classic Marx Brothers movie *A Day at the Races* (1937) and the short-lived HBO series *Luck*. The roaring Grand Prix, a Formula 1 race, takes over the streets of Long Beach every April.

On Location: Film & TV

Imagine living in a world without Orson Welles whispering 'Rosebud,' Judy Garland clicking her sparkly red heels three times or the Terminator threatening 'I'll be back.' LA is where iconic images like these are hatched onto the big screen. But Tinseltown is about more than just movies. Every other car commercial seems to be shot in Downtown LA, and countywide locations have become backdrops for TV series. The upshot: few people come to LA without seeing something – or someone – they recognize.

The Industry in LA & Beyond

From almost the very moment that film – and later TV – became the USA's dominant entertainment medium, LA took center stage in the world of popular culture and has stood there ever since. It's also been the best (and sometimes the worst) ambassador for Southern California and the rest of the USA to the world.

You might know it as TV and movie entertainment, but to Angelenos it's simply 'the Industry.' It all began in the humble orchards of Hollywoodland, where entrepreneurial moviemakers – most of them European immigrants – established studios in the first decade of the 20th century. German-born Carl Laemmle opened Universal City Studios in 1915; Polish immigrant Samuel Goldwyn joined with Cecil B DeMille a year earlier to form Paramount Studios; and Jack Warner and his brothers arrived a few years later from Poland via Canada.

During the 1930s, '40s and '50s many famous literary figures – including F. Scott Fitzgerald, Dorothy Parker, Truman Capote and William Faulkner – did stints as Hollywood screenwriters.

SoCal's sunny weather (more than 315 days of sunshine per year) meant that most outdoor scenes could be easily shot here, and moviemaking flourished. What's more, the proximity of the Mexican border enabled filmmakers to rush their equipment to safety when challenged by the collection agents of patent holders such as Thomas Edison. Fans loved early resident LA film stars such as Charlie Chaplin and Harold Lloyd, and the first big Hollywood wedding occurred in 1920 when Douglas Fairbanks wed Mary Pickford.

Although Hollywood became the cultural and financial hub of the movie industry by the 1920s, it's a myth that production mostly took place there. Of the major studios, only Paramount Pictures is in Hollywood proper, albeit surrounded by block after block of production-related businesses such as lighting and post-production. The first big movie palaces were not located on Hollywood Blvd, but on Broadway in Downtown LA.

Most movie studios shot elsewhere around LA, in Culver City (MGM, now Sony Pictures), Studio City (Universal Studios) and Burbank (Disney and Warner Bros). Moviemaking hasn't been limited to LA either. Founded in 1910, the American Film Company (aka Flying 'A' Studios) filmed first in San Diego and then Santa Barbara, pumping out box-office hits. Balboa Studios in Long Beach was another major silent film–era dream factory.

Although LA sometimes feels like a company town, in 2014 only some 131,000 people in LA County were employed directly in film, TV and radio production, according to the California Employment Development Department. That doesn't tell the whole story, though, because the Industry indirectly supports more than half a million jobs across LA County, from high-powered attorneys to cater-waiters. The influx of new media along Silicon Beach (roughly Santa Monica to Playa del Rey), where companies from YouTube to Hulu have major facilities, is becoming another growth engine.

For stargazers or movie buffs, LA is still *the* place for a pilgrimage. You can tour major movie studios, line up alongside the red carpet for an awards ceremony, be part of a live studio audience, attend a high-wattage film festival, shop at boutiques favored by today's hottest stars and see where celebs live, eat, drink and party in real life.

SoCal on the Silver Screen

In many movies featuring the City of Angels, LA is almost a character in itself.

Classic LA Movies

Perhaps the greatest film set in LA is Roman Polanski's *Chinatown* (1974), about the city's early-20th-century water wars. *The Bad and the Beautiful* (1952) takes a hard look at the film biz, with Lana Turner recalling the exploits of an aggressive, egotistic film producer played by Kirk Douglas. In David O Selznick's *A Star Is Born* (1937), Janet Gaynor plays a woman rising to stardom as her movie-star husband declines in popularity; later remakes starred Judy Garland and Barbra Streisand.

The most memorable of James Dean's scenes in *Rebel Without a Cause* (1955) takes place above LA in Griffith Park. In *The Graduate* (1967), Dustin Hoffman and Anne Bancroft play a game of nihilism, floundering and seduction in 1960s Pasadena. Based on James Ellroy's neo-noir novel, *LA Confidential* (1997) deftly portrays the violent world of deals, sexual betrayal and double-crossing by cops during the crime-ridden 1950s.

Contemporary Films about LA

Robert Altman's *Short Cuts* (1993) weaves together several stories by Raymond Carver, showing a sadly depraved Los Angeles. Another dispiriting, multistory tale told by an award-winning ensemble is the drama *Crash* (2005). In Joel Schumacher's *Falling Down* (1993), Michael Douglas plays an unemployed defense worker for

ON LOCATION: FILM & TV SOCAL ON THE SILVER SCREEN

MILESTONES IN LA FILM HISTORY

1913

The first full-length feature Hollywood movie, a silent Western drama called *The Squaw Man*, is shot by director Cecil B DeMille.

1915

Universal City Studios (now Universal Studios Hollywood) opens, charging visitors 25¢ including lunch to watch movies being made.

1927

The first talkie, *The Jazz Singer*, ends the silent-film era. Sid Grauman opens his Chinese Theatre in Hollywood, where stars have been leaving their handprints ever since.

1928

The first Academy Awards ceremony takes place. A cartoonist named Walt Disney releases *Steamboat Willie*, the first animated short with fully synchronized sound, starring a mouse named Mickey.

1939

The Wizard of Oz is the first wide-release movie to be shown in full color. Nonetheless, it loses the Oscar for Best Picture to *Gone with the Wind*. Both were filmed in Culver City.

1950s

Communist witch hunts by the House Committee on Un-American Activities investigate and blacklist Hollywood actors, directors and screenwriters, some of whom leave for Europe.

1960

The Hollywood Walk of Fame debuts on Hollywood Blvd. Among the first celebs to be

whom a traffic jam triggers a war with the world. Quentin Tarantino, in Chandleresque fashion, creates a surreal Los Angeles from the bottom up in *Pulp Fiction* (1994).

Gritty city tales include *Stand and Deliver* (1988), based on a true story, about a take-no-prisoners LA high school teacher who successfully teaches college-level calculus to Latino gang members. John Singleton's tragic *Boyz n the Hood* (1991) stars Cuba Gooding Jr and offers a major reality check on coming-of-age as a black teenager in the inner city. In *Freedom Writers* (2007), Hilary Swank plays a Long Beach high school teacher whose students work out their feelings about race and their personal hardships through writing.

In David Lynch's surrealist *Mulholland Drive* (2001), an amnesiac woman (played by Naomi Watts) tries to put her life back together through encounters with weird and terrifying people on various edges of dark LA mindscapes. *Laurel Canyon* (2002) shows another strange view of life in LA: a young psychiatrist (Christian Bale) and his fiancée return to live with his pot-smoking mother (Frances McDormand), who's producing her latest boy toy's rock-and-roll record. Tom Ford's *A Single Man* (2009) stars Colin Firth as a gay professor in 1962 Santa Monica Canyon, who finds that love is all too fleeting.

Three of Paul Thomas Anderson's films have come to be called the 'Valley Trilogy' for their San Fernando Valley locations: *Boogie Nights* (1997)

> Easily the most famous piece of footage ever shot in Orange County is the opening of the classic *Gilligan's Island* TV series, filmed at Newport Harbor.

HOLLYWOOD ON HOLLYWOOD

Hollywood likes nothing better than to turn the camera around and make movies about itself. Self-indulgent? Maybe, but often very entertaining.

➜ *Sunset Boulevard* (1950) Gloria Swanson plays Norma Desmond, a washed-up silent-film star pining for her return, and William Holden plays the screenwriter she hires to make that happen.

➜ *Singin' in the Rain* (1952) An exuberant musical fairy tale about love in the time of talkies, starring Gene Kelly, Debbie Reynolds and Donald O'Connor.

➜ *Silent Movie* (1976) Mel Brooks' screwball comedy imagines a director trying to revive a movie studio by producing the first silent film in decades.

➜ *Postcards from the Edge* (1990) Mike Nichols directs Shirley MacLaine and Meryl Streep as a mother-daughter pair dealing with stardom's seamy underbelly.

➜ *Barton Fink* (1991) John Turturro and John Goodman engage in a battle of wits over how to write a screenplay in this dark comedy by the Coen Brothers.

➜ *The Player* (1992) In one of the most accessible films by legendary director Robert Altman, Tim Robbins plays a studio executive who takes his power too far.

➜ *Ed Wood* (1994) Tim Burton directs Johnny Depp as perhaps the worst director in Hollywood history, who was famous for wearing pink angora sweaters.

➜ *Get Shorty* (1995) Based on the Elmore Leonard novel, this comedy stars John Travolta as a mafioso who gets entangled in Hollywood and wonders which industry has fewer scruples.

➜ *Adaptation* (2002) Nicolas Cage and Meryl Streep star in this mind-bending comedy about a screenwriter's attempt to deal with writer's block and his own insecurities.

➜ *Tropic Thunder* (2008) Ben Stiller and Robert Downey Jr star in the ultimate send-up of big Hollywood action flicks. Numerous cameos include Tom Cruise as a so-bad-he's-great executive.

➜ *Hail Caesar* (2016) Coen Brothers comedy featuring Josh Brolin as a studio publicist who has to track down a movie's star, played by George Clooney, when he goes missing during production.

starred Mark Wahlberg as prodigiously endowed porn star Dirk Diggler; *Magnolia* (1999) brought together mega-stars including Tom Cruise, Julianne Moore and Philip Seymour Hoffman in a tale of interwoven family dramas; and in the darkly romantic *Punch-Drunk Love* (2002), Adam Sandler's character overcomes anger management issues.

LA Comedies

Tony Richardson's outrageously sardonic *The Loved One* (1965), based on an Evelyn Waugh novel about the funeral industry, stars Sir John Gielgud and Liberace (the latter as a huckstering mortician). Cameron Crowe wrote *Fast Times at Ridgemont High* (1982), which launched the careers of Sean Penn, Jennifer Jason Leigh, Nicolas Cage and Forest Whitaker among others, about students at a fictional San Fernando Valley high school. *Bill & Ted's Excellent Adventure* (1989) turned Keanu Reeves and Alex Winter into time-traveling San Gabriel Valley teen slackers.

The '90s produced some classic LA comedies. Steve Martin's *LA Story* (1991) hilariously parodies LA life from lattes to colonics. Julia Roberts became a screen queen for playing the definitive LA hooker with a heart of gold in Garry Marshall's romantic comedy *Pretty Woman* (1990). *Clueless* (1995) starred Alicia Silverstone as a spoiled Beverly Hills teenager in an update of the novel *Emma* by Jane Austen. *Swingers* (1996) was Vince Vaughn's breakout film as a Hollywood hipster, coining the word 'money' as a compliment and bringing 'Vegas, baby, Vegas!' into the lexicon. Jeff Bridges plays the Dude, a white-Russian-swilling bowler, slacker and stoner who finds himself in the middle of a crime in the Coen Brothers' *Big Lebowski* (1998).

More recently, LA has been the backdrop for the merry band of comedic actors led by director Judd Apatow in *The 40-Year-Old Virgin* (2005), starring Steve Carrell, and *Knocked Up* (2007) with Seth Rogen and Katherine Heigl. Some of the same actors parody themselves in the apocalyptic comedy *This is the End* (2013), as the Rapture comes to a party at James Franco's house.

Pairing Joseph Gordon-Levitt and Zooey Deschanel, *(500) Days of Summer* (2009) is not a love story but a funny story about love – and architecture – in Downtown LA. And then there's *La La Land* (2016), the musical darling starring Ryan Gosling and Emma Stone as a jazz singer and actress struggling to make a go of life and love.

SoCal Movies Beyond LA

In *Orange County* (2002), screenwriter Mike White gives a humorous snapshot of SoCal pop culture: a surfer tries to get into Stanford University and escape his oddball family, including his brother (played by Jack Black). In Nancy Meyers' comedy *It's Complicated* (2009), Meryl Streep, Alec Baldwin and Steve Martin get up to romantic shenanigans in the ritzy Santa

inaugurated with a pink star are Joanne Woodward and Burt Lancaster.

1970s
The San Fernando Valley (aka 'Silicone Valley') becomes home to the USA's adult film industry, eventually producing almost 90% of the USA's legal pornographic movies.

1975
The age of the modern blockbuster begins with the thriller *Jaws*, directed by a young filmmaker named Steven Spielberg whose string of box-office hits include *ET* and *Jurassic Park*.

1999
Independent, low-budget horror film *The Blair Witch Project* inaugurates the era of viral internet marketing, successfully racking up almost $250 million dollars in profit worldwide.

2001
In the Hollywood & Highland high-rise complex on revitalized Hollywood Blvd, the Kodak (now Dolby) Theatre becomes the permanent home of the Academy Awards ceremony.

2009
Sci-fi fantasy *Avatar* becomes the highest grossing movie of all time, encroaching on $3 billion. It beat the previous record holder, *Titanic* (1997), also directed by James Cameron.

2015
'Oscars So White' campaign challenges the lack of racial diversity in Hollywood filmmaking.

2017
As stunned audiences watched worldwide, *La La Land* was first given the Academy Award for best picture of 2016, only to have it taken away and correctly awarded to *Moonlight*.

ON LOCATION: FILM & TV SOCAL ON THE SILVER SCREEN

Barbara suburb of Montecito. Ask any oenophile about the wacky indie flick *Sideways* (2004) and you'll get an earful about Santa Barbara's Wine Country and Paul Giamatti.

The most famous film shot in San Diego was *Some Like It Hot* (1959), starring Marilyn Monroe, Jack Lemmon and Tony Curtis, in which the iconic Hotel del Coronado served as a stand-in for Florida. Giving it a close tie for most famous, Will Ferrell urges 'Stay classy, San Diego' in *Anchorman* (2004). In between are classics like Tony Scott's *Top Gun* (1986), starring a young Tom Cruise, Val Kilmer and Kelly McGillis. A spate of box-office hits in the early noughties shot in San Diego include *Almost Famous* (2000), Steven Soderbergh's *Traffic* (2000), *Bring it On* (2000) with Kirsten Dunst and *Bruce Almighty* (2003) starring Jim Carrey.

Palm Springs became a favorite getaway of Hollywood stars in the mid-20th century, partly because its distance from LA (just under 100 miles) was as far as they could travel under their restrictive studio contracts.

Shot in LA: Action Movies

Action movies shot in LA are almost too numerous to count, but here's a start. *Speed* (1994) stars Sandra Bullock and Keanu Reeves riding around LA on a bus that can't stop. In the original *Die Hard* (1988), Bruce Willis plays a cop who must rescue his wife and daughter from an attack on what's actually a 20th Century Fox Studios skyscraper. Numerous scenes from the *Iron Man* and *Fast and Furious* series were shot in locations all over LA and Orange Counties, while Downtown's Westin Bonaventure Hotel plays a starring role in Clint Eastwood's *In the Line of Fire* (1993).

Television

Ever since the first TV station began broadcasting in LA in 1931, iconic images of the city have been beamed into living rooms across America in shows such as *Dragnet* (1950s), *The Beverly Hillbillies* (1960s), *The Brady Bunch* (1970s), *LA Law* (1980s), and *Baywatch* and *Melrose Place* (1990s). The teen 'dramedy' (drama comedy) *Beverly Hills 90210* (1990s) made that LA zip code into a status symbol and *The OC* (2000s) glamorized Newport Beach.

SOCAL'S TOP FILM FESTIVALS

Besides churning out blockbuster movies, SoCal hosts dozens of high-powered film festivals every year. The following faves are worth planning your trip around (check online for schedules and ticket info).:

AFI Fest (www.afi.com/afifest; ⊘Nov) One of the most influential festivals in the country presents top-notch films by newbies and masters from around the world. *Monster* (2003), *Lincoln* (2012) and other Academy Award winners premiered here.

Los Angeles Film Festival (www.filmindependent.org/la-film-festival) This June festival corrals the best in indie movies from around the world – from shorts and music videos to full-length features and documentaries.

Outfest (www.outfest.org) The largest continuous film fest in SoCal, this 35-year-old celluloid celebration in July screens more than 200 shorts, films and videos by and about the LGBT community.

Palm Springs International Film Festival (p298) Founded in 1990 by then-mayor Sonny Bono, this balmy January festival is getting more glam every year. It's an intimate yet star-studded affair with almost 200 films from 60 countries.

Newport Beach Film Festival (p270) The buzz surrounding this competition, with 400 films over eight days in late April and early May, has been increasing steadily since Oscar-winner *Crash* premiered here in 2005.

Santa Barbara International Film Festival (p355) For almost three decades, this festival has featured independent films from around the US and abroad, with stars such as Martin Scorsese and Leonardo DiCaprio walking the red carpet.

RUNAWAY FILM & TV PRODUCTION

Entertainment is big business in LA County. According to the Los Angeles County Economic Development Corporation, in 2015 'the Industry' (film and TV production) lassoed nearly $60 billion (about 10% of the county's GDP) and employed about 250,000 people. That's before the multiplier effect of ancillary industries such as attorneys, financiers, even dry cleaners, who benefit from production work. The 2015 Otis Report on the Creative Economy of the Los Angeles Region puts that figure at $83 billion.

Beginning in about the 1990s, the high cost of filming in SoCal sent location scouts looking elsewhere, and states such as New Mexico, North Carolina, Louisiana and Georgia, and, it seems, much of Canada, temptingly offered production credits, tax incentives, state-of-the-art facilities and, in some cases, talented, non-unionized workforces. Many of these offers turned out to be so rich that studio heads and producers could not refuse.

By the early 2010s, California began to fight back with its own series of tax credits and incentives. *Variety* reported that from 2015 a tax incentive pool of $100 to $250 million would be spent annually over three years, keeping the money – and the workers and their families – in LA.

SoCal is also a versatile backdrop for edgy cable dramas, starting with HBO's *Six Feet Under,* which examined contemporary LA through the eyes of an eccentric family running a funeral home. Showtime's *Weeds* fictionalized a pot-growing SoCal widow with ties to Mexican drug cartels, while FX's *The Shield* riffed on police corruption in the City of Angels and CBS's *NCIS: Los Angeles* does the same for crime scene investigation. HBO's *Entourage* portrayed the highs, the lows and the intrigues of the Industry by following a rising young star and his posse. Showtime's *Californication* shows what happens when a successful New York novelist goes Hollywood. For more biting social satire, check out early LA-based seasons of HBO's *Curb Your Enthusiasm,* by *Seinfeld* co-creator Larry David who got Hollywood celebrities to play themselves.

If you're a fan of reality TV, you'll glimpse SoCal in an endless variety of shows from *Top Chef* to *The Real Housewives of Orange County,* as well as in MTV's drama-reality hybrid series *Laguna Beach* and *The Hills.* Next up: a reality show about the Abbey, West Hollywood's iconic gay bar.

Animation

A young cartoonist named Walt Disney arrived in LA in 1923. Five years later, he had his first breakout hit, *Steamboat Willie,* starring a mouse named Mickey. That film spawned the entire Disney empire, and dozens of other animation studios have followed with films, TV programs and special effects. Among the best known are Warner Bros (*Bugs Bunny* and friends), Hanna Barbera (*The Flintstones, The Jetsons, Yogi Bear* and *Scooby-Doo*), Dreamworks (*Shrek, Madagascar),* Film Roman *(The Simpsons, King of the Hill),* Klasky Csupo (*Rugrats*) and Nelvana (*Babar, Fairly OddParents*). Even if much of the hands-on work takes place overseas (eg South Korea), concept and supervision is done in LA.

Music & the Arts

Culture in LA? Go ahead: mock. But when Californians thank their lucky stars – or good karma, or the goddess – that they don't live in NYC, they're not only talking about beach weather. It's one of the country's most prolific – and progressive – generators of music, art and literature of all kinds. The creative spirit of SoCal's contemporary arts scene isn't afraid to be completely independent, even outlandish at times.

Music

The history of music in LA might as well be the history of American music, at least for the last 75 years. Much of the recording industry is based in LA, and the film and TV industries have proven powerful talent incubators. Today's pop-princess troublemakers and airbrushed boy bands only rose to stardom thanks to the tuneful revolutions of decades past.

Folk, Swing, Jazz, Blues & Soul

Chronologically speaking, Mexican folk music arrived first in Southern California during the rancho era. But the next big musical thing didn't come along for over a century: swing music. During the 1930s and '40s, big bands sparked a lindy-hopping craze in LA.

California's African American community grew with the 'Great Migration' during WWII's shipping and manufacturing boom, and so the West Coast blues sound was born. Texas-born bluesman T-Bone Walker worked in LA's Central Ave clubs before making hit records of his electric guitar stylings for Capitol Records.

With Beat poets riffing over improvised bass lines and audiences finger-snapping their approval, cool West Coast jazz emerged in the 1950s, including on the Sunset Strip. In the African American cultural hub along LA's Central Ave, the hard bop of Charlie Parker and Charles Mingus kept the jazz scene alive and swinging.

In the 1950s and '60s, doo-wop, rhythm and blues, and soul music were all in steady rotation at nightclubs in South Central LA, considered the 'Harlem of the West'. Soulful singer Sam Cooke ran his own hit-making record label here, attracting soul and gospel talent to LA.

The cover of Eagles' album *Hotel California* (1976) shows LA's Beverly Hills Hotel, but the group won't say which hotel actually inspired the title. The band's Don Henley has described the song as being 'about a journey from innocence to experience.'

Rock, Pop & Punk: 1950s to '80s

The first homegrown rock-and-roll talent to make it big in the 1950s was Ritchie Valens, born in the San Fernando Valley, whose 'La Bamba' was a rockified version of a Mexican folk song. Dick Dale (aka 'King of the Surf Guitar') started experimenting with reverb effects in Orange County in the 1950s, then topped the charts with his band the Del-Tones in the early '60s, influencing everyone from the Beach Boys to Jimi Hendrix. Dale's recording of 'Miserlou' featured in Tarantino's movie *Pulp Fiction*.

It's hard to say which LA band is the most emblematic of the 1960s: The Doors, the Beach Boys, the Mamas and the Papas, Joni Mitchell, the Byrds, or Crosby, Stills & Nash. The epicenter of the 1960s rock movement was LA's Laurel Canyon neighborhood, just uphill from the Sunset Strip and legendary Whisky a Go-Go nightclub, ground zero for the psychedelic rock scene.

The country-influenced pop of Eagles, Jackson Browne and Linda Ronstadt became America's soundtrack for the early 1970s, joined by the Mexican-fusion sounds of Santana and iconic funk bands War, founded in Long Beach, and Sly and the Family Stone, which got their groove on in San Francisco before moving to LA.

The 1980s saw the rise of such influential LA punk and crossover bands as X and Bad Religion (punk), Black Flag (punk/hard-core) and Suicidal Tendencies (hard-core/thrash), while more mainstream all-female bands the Bangles and the Go-Gos, new-wavers Oingo Boingo, and rockers Jane's Addiction and funky Red Hot Chili Peppers took the world by storm; the Peppers' 'Under the Bridge' (1991) is perhaps the ultimate rock anthem to LA. Bangin' out of Hollywood, Guns N' Roses was the '80s hard-rock band of choice. On avant-garde rocker Frank Zappa's 1982 single 'Valley Girl', his 14-year-old daughter Moon Unit taught the rest of America to say 'Omigo-o-od!'.

Rap, Pop, Hip-Hop & Indie: 1990s to present

Since the 1980s, LA has been a hotbed for West Coast rap and hip-hop. Eazy E, Ice Cube and Dr Dre released the seminal NWA (Niggaz With Attitude) album, *Straight Outta Compton*, in 1989, which inspired the 2015 film of the same name. Death Row Records, co-founded by Dr Dre, has launched megawatt rap talents including Long Beach bad boys Snoop Dog and Warren G. LA rapper Game's 2009 *RED Album* featured an all-star line-up of Dr Dre, Snoop Dogg and others.

In the 1990s, LA's Linkin Park combined hip-hop with metal and popularized nu metal, while alternative rock acts like Beck and Weezer gained national attention. Another key '90s band was the ska-punk-alt-rock No Doubt, of Orange County (which later launched the solo career of lead singer Gwen Stefani). From East LA, Los Lobos was the king of Chicano (Mexican-American) bands, an honor that has since passed to Ozomatli.

LA Music Radio Stations

KCRW (89.9FM) – eclectic indie music mix

KUSC (91.5FM) – classical music

KRTH (101.1FM) – all-American oldies soundtrack

KSCA (101.9FM) – popular regional Mexican tunes

KOST (103.5FM) – adult contemporary, evening love songs and dedications

KPWR (105.9FM) – hip-hop, R&B and club hits

MUSIC & THE ARTS MUSIC

SOCAL'S MUSIC FESTIVALS

All over SoCal, annual music festivals host a mix of big-name and local acts. Buy tickets early for radio station–sponsored shows. Festivals worth planning a trip around include the following:

Arroyo Seco Weekend (www.arroyosecoweekend.com; Brookside Park, Pasadena; per day from $125; ☉late Jun) Pasadena is getting into the act with this festival near the Rose Bowl, a two-day festival headlined in its debut year (2017) by Tom Petty & the Heartbreakers and Mumford & Sons.

Coachella Valley Music & Arts Festival (p297) Sweat it out in the desert in Indio, with indie bands, up-and-comers and the occasional blockbuster star over two weekends in April.

Desert Trip (p298) Coachella's autumn counterpart has been nicknamed 'Oldchella' for the OG rockers gigged in: the Rolling Stones, Bob Dylan, Styx, Kansas and more.

KCRW Summer Nights (p103) Popular, all-ages concert series popping up at different locations across LA and SoCal from June to August.

KROQ Almost Acoustic Christmas (www.kroq.cbslocal.com; ☉Dec) Winter punk and modern rock event, currently at the Forum in Inglewood.

KROQ Weenie Roast (www.kroq.cbslocal.com; ☉May or Jun) Alt-rock bands like the Fitz and the Tantrums, Garbage, Weezer and the Red Hot Chili Peppers perform at Stub Hub Center in Carson.

Stagecoach Festival (p298) All things country and western, from Shelby Lynne and Asleep at the Wheel to BBQ, on the weekend after Coachella in Indio.

SoCal pop and rock stars of the new millennium included the approachable hip-hop of LA's Black Eyed Peas, San Diego alt-rockers Stone Temple Pilots and pop-punksters Blink-182, Orange County's punk band The Offspring and, for better or for worse, LA's Robin Thicke of 'Blurred Lines' fame and LMFAO, the duo behind 'Party Rock Anthem' and 'Sexy and I Know It,' whose video was shot on Venice Beach.

Nowadays, LA-based headliners Maroon 5 with Adam Levine and Santa Barbara native Katy Perry fill stadiums, and if you're lucky enough to catch an indie performance by local bands such as Edward Sharpe and the Magnetic Zeros, Best Coast, 30 Seconds to Mars (actor Jared Leto's band) or Cherry Glazerr, you can thank us later.

Waiting for the Sun: A Rock & Roll History of Los Angeles, by Barney Hoskyns, follows the twists and turns of the SoCal music scene from the Beach Boys to Black Flag.

Film & TV Scores

John Williams, a frequent collaborator with Steven Spielberg, is perhaps the best known of legions of Hollywood film composers, having created music for *Jaws, Star Wars, Raiders of the Lost Ark, Schindler's List* and *Lincoln,* to name just a few.

The 1950s through 1980s were a golden age for film scores, including works by Elmer Bernstein (*The Magnificent Seven, Ghostbusters*), Bernard Herrmann (*Citizen Kane, Vertigo, Psycho,* the *Twilight Zone* TV series) and Ennio Morricone (*The Good, the Bad & the Ugly, A Fistful of Dollars*).

Present-day soundtrack composers include Williams, Randy Newman (*The Natural, Seabiscuit, Toy Story* movies, *Cars, Monsters U*), Oingo Boingo co-founder Danny Elfman (*Pee-wee's Big Adventure, Dick Tracy, Edward Scissorhands, Men in Black, Fifty Shades of Grey, The Simpsons* theme), Thomas Newman (*Skyfall, The Best Exotic Marigold Hotel, Finding Dory*) and Robert Lopez (*Frozen*).

You can hear historical and contemporary film music played during the Hollywood Bowl's annual movie night, when a live orchestra accompanies movie clips projected onto a giant screen.

Classical Music

First stop for fans of 'serious music' should be Downtown LA's Walt Disney Concert Hall. It's the home of one of the USA's top symphony orchestras, the LA Philharmonic, under the baton of the young Venezuelan phenom Gustavo Dudamel. The LA Phil's summer home is the Hollywood Bowl, an outdoor venue for classical, jazz and pops performances.

Not to be outdone, Orange County boasts the Segerstrom Center for the Arts in Costa Mesa, with two state-of-the-art concert halls. The San Diego Symphony performs at Copley Symphony Hall and at Embarcadero Marina Park South in summer. In Palm Springs, check the calendar for the Annenberg Theater at the Palm Springs Art Museum.

The Los Angeles Opera, under the artistic direction of Placido Domingo, plays in the Dorothy Chandler Pavilion, at the Music Center of Los

'THE DUDE' OF THE LA PHIL

In 2009 Gustavo Dudamel, not yet 30 years old, took over as conductor of the Los Angeles Philharmonic from the iconic Finnish conductor-composer Esa-Pekka Salonen, and the city took to him *con gusto*. The Venezuelan Dudamel came up musically through El Sistema, that nation's program for creating youth orchestras, culminating with his conducting the Simón Bolívar Youth Orchestra. With his shock of wild, black curls, prodigious energy on the podium and youthful enthusiasm, 'the Dude' energized LA in a way few thought possible (even if the curls have since been tamed). Just as importantly, he has brought techniques from El Sistema to this city where youth could no doubt use the outlet as much as – if not more than – those in Dudamel's homeland.

Angeles County, in Downtown LA. San Diego also has an active opera company, while the risk-taking Long Beach Opera company stages new and rare works.

Choral Music

LA is home some to some of the nation's most respected choral ensembles.

The 130-strong Los Angeles Master Chorale (http://lamasterchorale. org) has been performing historic and contemporary choral music from Beethoven to Eric Whitacre. It is now under the direction of Grant Gershon with performances at Walt Disney Concert Hall.

The 275-member Gay Men's Chorus of Los Angeles (www.gmcla.org) peforms out of the art-deco Alex Theatre in Glendale, breaking boundaries of men's choral music with consistently inventive repertoires and Broadway-style staging with professional-quality costumes, sets and dancing, and has made numerous TV performances and sung for US presidents.

One of GMCLA's newest ventures is the Trans Chorus of Los Angeles (www.transchorusla.org), America's first.

There are also Gay Men's Choruses in Orange County (Men Alive; https://menalivechorus.org) and San Diego (San Diego Gay Men's Chorus; www.sdgmc.org), and Palm Springs has two: Palm Springs Gay Men's Chorus (www.psgmc.com) and Modern Men (https://modernmen.org).

Not to be outdone, LA-based Vox Femina (www.voxfemina.org) is one of America's most acclaimed women's choruses.

Theater

In your Southern California dream you're discovered by a movie talent scout, but most actors actually get their start in theater. Home to about 25% of the nation's professional actors, LA is the second-most influential city in America for theater after NYC.

Spaces to watch around LA include the Pantages Theatre in Hollywood, the Ahmanson Theatre and Mark Taper Forum in Downtown LA and sister company Kirk Douglas Theatre in Culver City, the Geffen Playhouse close to UCLA, and the Actors' Gang Theatre, co-founded by actor Tim Robbins, in Culver City. Small theaters flourish in West Hollywood (WeHo) and North Hollywood (NoHo), the West Coast's answers to off- and off-off-Broadway. The small size of these 'equity waiver' theaters (fewer than 100 seats) allows actors to try out new material outside of the customary regulations of the Actors Equity Association union.

Influential multicultural theaters include Little Tokyo's East West Players, featuring Asian American casts, and Deaf West, which stages remarkable productions that deaf and hearing audiences can appreciate together.

Critically acclaimed outlying companies include Orange County's South Coast Repertory in Costa Mesa and La Jolla Playhouse and Shakespeare's Globe in San Diego.

Visual Arts

A 2006 exhibition at Paris' Pompidou Center called LA an 'Art Capital,' a designation that only surprised folks who haven't spent time here. NYC may be the nation's largest art market, but much of that art is made in LA. Co-founded by Walt Disney in 1961, the California Institute of Arts (CalArts), in the northern LA County suburb of Valencia, is one of the art world's premier schools. Heavy-hitting artists who have taught there include Laurie Anderson, John Baldessari, Jonathan Borofsky, Judy Chicago and Roy Lichtenstein.

SoCal's contemporary art scene brings together muralist-led social commentary, an obsessive dedication to craft and a new-media milieu

There currently seems to be an exodus of artists, galleries and those who love them, decamping from more expensive, colder places such as New York and San Francisco to DTLA's Art's District and beyond. Partly it's the weather, yes, but also the cost of living and the creative community.

LATINO MURALS IN SOCAL

Beginning in the 1930s, when the federal Works Progress Administration (WPA) sponsored schemes to uplift and beautify cities across the country, murals came to define California cityscapes. Mexican muralists Diego Rivera, David Alfaro Siqueiros and José Clemente Orozco sparked an outpouring of murals across LA that today number in the thousands. Murals gave voice to Chicano (Mexican-American) pride and protests over US Central American policies since the 1970s, notably in San Diego's Chicano Park and East LA murals by collectives such as East Los Streetscapers, still active today.

For an online directory of contemporary LA murals, including panoramic photos and directions to the sites, visit www.muralconservancy.org.

pierced by cutting-edge technology. LA's Museum of Contemporary Art (MOCA) puts on provocative and avant-garde shows, as do LA's Broad Museum, the Museum of Contemporary Art San Diego, Costa Mesa's Orange County Museum of Art and the Santa Barbara Museum of Art. More specialized art museums worth detouring for include Long Beach's Museum of Latin American Art and West LA's Hammer Museum. Leading art galleries include Hauser & Wirth in Downtown LA, Ace Gallery in Mid-City and LA Louver Gallery in Venice.

To see California-made art at its most experimental, browse the burgeoning gallery scenes in Downtown LA's Arts District and Santa Fe and Brewery arts complexes, as well as in Culver City. San Diego's Little Italy neighborhood also hosts a growing number of galleries.

In Orange County, there are vibrant art scenes in Santa Ana, home of the Bowers Museum, and in the historic artists' colony of Laguna Beach. The latter's annual Festival of Arts is capped by the Pageant of the Masters, in which actors recreate world-famous paintings on stage.

Literature

The entire state has long attracted novelists, poets and storytellers, and today SoCal's literary community is stronger than ever. You've probably already read books by Southern Californians without knowing it. Some of the best-known titles by resident writers aren't set in their home state: for example, Ray Bradbury's 1950s dystopian classic *Fahrenheit 451*.

Early-20th-Century Literature

LA sheltered many illustrious foreign writers in the first half of the 20th century, among them British immigrant Aldous Huxley and German authors Bertolt Brecht and Thomas Mann, who resided here after being exiled from their homeland during WWII. Meanwhile, much of the local writing talent always seems to be harnessed to the film industry – even literary luminaries such as F Scott Fitzgerald, William Faulkner, Dorothy Parker and Truman Capote came to LA temporarily to make a living by writing screenplays.

Starting in the 1920s, many novelists looked at LA in political terms, often viewing it unfavorably as the ultimate metaphor for capitalism. Classics in this vein include Upton Sinclair's *Oil!* (1927), a muckraking work of historical fiction with socialist overtones. Aldous Huxley's *After Many a Summer* (1939) is an ironic work based on the life of publisher William Randolph Hearst (also an inspiration for Orson Welles' film *Citizen Kane*). F Scott Fitzgerald's unfinished final novel, *The Last Tycoon* (1940), makes scathing observations about Hollywood's early years by following the life of a movie producer who is slowly working himself to death.

Few writers nail SoCal's culture as well as Joan Didion. In *Where I Was From* (2003), she contrasts California's mythology and reality. Her perceptive essays in *Slouching Toward Bethlehem* (1968) and *The White Album* (1979) narrate the social upheavals of 1960s California with an autobiographical slant.

In the 1930s, San Francisco and Los Angeles became the capitals of the pulp detective novel, examples of which were often made into noir crime films. The king of hard-boiled crime writers was Raymond Chandler, who thinly disguised his hometown Santa Monica as Bay City.

Late-20th-Century Literature & Beyond

LA fiction's banner year was 1970. Terry Southern's *Blue Movie* dived into the seamy, pornographic side of Hollywood. Joan Didion's *Play It as It Lays* depicted Angelenos with a dry, not-too-kind wit. *Post Office*, by poet-novelist Charles Bukowski, captured the down-and-out side of Downtown LA. (Bukowski himself worked at the US Postal Service's Terminal Annex.) *Chicano,* by Richard Vasquez, took a dramatic look at the Latino barrio of East LA.

The 1980s brought the startling revelations of Bret Easton Ellis' *Less than Zero,* about the cocaine-addled lives of wealthy Beverly Hills teen-agers. For a more comedic insight into LA during the go-go '80s, pick up Richard Rayner's *Los Angeles Without a Map,* which follows a British man who gets lost in his Hollywood fantasies while chasing an aspiring actress. Kate Braverman's *Palm Latitudes* traces the intersecting lives of a flamboyant prostitute, a murderous housewife and a worn-out matri-arch who maintain their strength and dignity against the backdrop of the violence and machismo of LA's Mexican barrio.

Pulp noir fiction made a comeback in LA in the 1990s. Walter Mosley's famed *Devil in a Blue Dress,* set in the Watts neighborhood of South Central LA, places its hero in impossible situations that test his desire to remain an honest man. James Ellroy's *LA Confidential,* set during the 1950s, delves into sex scandals and police corruption. Elmore Leonard's *Get Shorty* follows a Florida loan shark who moves to SoCal and gets mixed up in the movie industry. All three novels – like many of the neo-noir genre – have translated brilliantly into films.

Among contemporary LA novelists, Paul Beatty bagged both the Man Booker Prize and National Book Critics Circle Award for *The Sellout,* his 2015 satirical novel about a curmudgeon who tries to revive slavery and school segregation in a downtrodden LA suburb. Héctor Tobar, Pulitzer-winning former correspondent for the *LA Times,* wrote the *Barbarian Nurseries* (2011), in which a Mexican maid takes two children on a jour-ney across her Los Angeles when their wealthy parents disappear.

Other novelists to look for include USC English professor T Cor-aghessan Boyle, who has written prolifically about the region in novels and short stories, including *The Tortilla Curtain* and *San Miguel.* Pe-ter Lefcourt chronicles insider Hollywood in his novel *The Deal.* Lisa See's *Shanghai Girls* is set in LA's Chinatown in the 1950s, when anti-communist sentiment was prominent in US politics.

Outside LA

San Diego novelist Joseph Wambaugh draws on his own experience as a detective to craft crime-fiction novels such as *Floaters,* which centers on the 1995 America's Cup race. Abigail Padgett, also from San Diego, writes engaging mysteries that weave together themes of Native Ameri-can culture, mental illness and the SoCal desert. Sue Grafton, author of the Kinsey Millhone mystery series and the alphabet mystery series (*A is for Alibi* etc) sets her novels in Santa Barbara, though in the books it's called Santa Theresa.

To learn more about LA's literary scene, listen to the weekly *Bookworm* talk show on Santa Monica–based radio station KCRW (88.9FM). Download it as a free podcast or listen online at www.kcrw.com.

MUSIC & THE ARTS LITERATURE

Southern California Architecture

There's more to Southern California's architecture than beach houses and boardwalks. SoCal may also have a reputation for the urban sprawl by which all other sprawl is measured, but look closer and you'll discover – particularly in LA – one of the country's most architecturally dynamic regions. Freely adapting and being inspired by architectural periods and styles from around the world for centuries, SoCal architecture today reveals the element of the unexpected. It was postmodern before the word even existed.

Spanish Missions & Victorian Mansions

The first Spanish missions were built around courtyards, using materials that Native Californians and Spanish padres had at hand: adobe, limestone and grass. Many missions crumbled into disrepair as the Church's influence waned under Mexican rule, but the style remained practical for SoCal's climate. Early American settlers adapted it later into the rancho adobe style, as seen at El Pueblo de Los Angeles in Downtown LA and in San Diego's Old Town.

Once California's mid-19th-century gold rush began, nouveau-riche residents built grand mansions marked by ornamental excess in imitation of upper-class East Coast architectural fashions, in turn imported from Europe during the reign of England's Queen Victoria. One of SoCal's finest examples of Victorian whimsy is San Diego's Hotel del Coronado (1888). San Diego's Gaslamp Quarter is also filled with more modest Victorian buildings, as is the Old West mining town of Julian.

Oddball SoCal Design

Theme Building, LAX Airport

Binoculars (Google) Building, Venice

Watts Towers, South Central LA

Christ (Crystal) Cathedral, Orange County

Integratron, near Joshua Tree

Salvation Mountain, by the Salton Sea

Arts and Crafts & Art Deco

Simplicity and harmony were hallmarks of California's early-20th-century arts-and-crafts style, influenced by Japanese design principles and England's arts-and-crafts movement. The style's handmade touches marked a deliberate departure from the Industrial Revolution's mechanized design. SoCal architects Charles and Henry Greene popularized this style with their single-story bungalows in Pasadena. Overhanging eaves, airy terraces and sleeping porches formed transitions between, and extensions of, warm wooden interiors into the natural environment.

California was cosmopolitan from the start, and by the early 1920s, the emerging international art-deco style made it fashionable to copy earlier architectural periods from around the globe. No style was off-limits: neoclassical, baroque, Moorish, Mayan, Aztec or Egyptian. Downtown LA's Central Library is a prime example of this mishmash of motifs.

When it came to skyscrapers, art deco's vertical lines and symmetry created a soaring effect, often culminating in a stepped pattern toward the top, like LA's City Hall. Heavy ornamentation, especially above doors and windows, featured flowers, sunbursts and zigzags, as seen in Downtown LA's Eastern Columbia building and West Hollywood's Sunset Tower Hotel.

Streamline moderne, a derivative of art-deco, sought to incorporate the machine aesthetic, in particular the aerodynamic look of airplanes and ocean liners. Outstanding examples of this style include the Coca-Cola Building in Downtown LA, the Cross Roads of the World building in Hollywood and the Hotel Shangri-La in Santa Monica.

SoCal Modernism

Clothing-optional California has never been shy about showcasing its assets. Starting in the 1960s, California embraced the stripped-down, glass-wall aesthetics of the International style championed by Bauhaus architects Walter Gropius, Ludwig Mies van der Rohe and Le Corbusier. Its characteristics included boxlike building shapes, open floor plans, minimalist facades and abundant glass.

Austrian-born Rudolph Schindler and Richard Neutra brought modernism to LA and Palm Springs, where Swiss-born Albert Frey also worked. Their mid-century modern residential homes aimed for seamlessness between indoor and outdoor spaces with floor-to-ceiling windows perfectly suited to SoCal's see-and-be-seen culture. Neutra and Schindler were also influenced by the earlier work of Frank Lloyd Wright, who designed LA's Hollyhock House in a style he dubbed 'California Romanza.' His son, Lloyd Wright, later built the Wayfarers Chapel atop the cliffs overlooking the Pacific in Palos Verdes.

Together with Charles and Ray Eames, Neutra also contributed to the experimental Case Study Houses, several of which still jut out of the LA landscape and are often used as filming locations, as seen in *LA Confidential*. The Los Angeles Conservancy's Modern Committee aims to preserve several Case Study Houses, as well as other significant modernist structures. The Palm Springs Modern Committee celebrates that desert resort's signature architectural, design and fashion style each spring during Modernism Week (p298).

Postmodern Evolutions

Postmodernism was partly a response to the starkness of modernism's International style, and sought to re-emphasize the structural form of the building and the space around it. And true to its mythos, SoCal couldn't help wanting to embellish the facts a little anyway, veering away from strict modernism to add unlikely postmodern shapes to the local landscape, starting as early as 1965 with La Jolla's monumental Salk Institute designed by architect Louis I Kahn.

Richard Meier perfected and transcended the postmodernist vision in 1997 at the Getty Center, a cresting white wave of a building atop a sunburned West LA hilltop, which can only be approached by tram. Santa Monica resident 'starchitect' Frank Gehry is known for his deconstructivist buildings with sculptural forms and distinctive facade materials including stainless steel. Since opening in 2003, Gehry's Walt Disney Concert Hall has become an emblem of Downtown LA's re-emergence. Look closely: the ship-shaped building's exterior metal 'sails' wink cheekily at streamline moderne.

Also in Downtown LA, the Cathedral of Our Lady of the Angels, designed by Spanish architect José Rafael Moneo in 2002, echoes the grand churches of Mexico and Europe, albeit from a controversially postmodern and deconstructivist angle. Maverick architect Thom Mayne of LA's Morphosis firm has also made his mark, winning the 2005 Pritzker Prize for his futuristic, energy-efficient design of Downtown LA's Caltrans District 7 Headquarters, which is covered in a mechanical 'skin.'

Italian architect Renzo Piano's signature inside-out 'high-tech' postmodern style can be glimpsed in the sawtooth roof and red-veined exterior escalators and stairways of the Broad Contemporary Art Museum at the Los Angeles County Museum of Art. Meanwhile, Downtown LA's Grand Ave has been transformed by another postmodern museum, the Broad, designed by the NYC firm of Diller Scofidio + Renfro. Gehry's next project, a hotel, retail and residential complex opposite Walt Disney Concert Hall, is set to break ground in 2018.

Fans of the mid-century-modern tiki style will want to head to San Diego's Point Loma district, where Shelter Island feels like palmy Polynesia. Show up in August for the Tiki Oasis (www.tikioasis.com) festival of art, design, music and more.

When Downtown LA's Walt Disney Concert Hall was first built, some of its stainless-steel exterior panels reflected the sun so brightly that drivers were blinded by glare and nearby condos heated up. The offending panels had to be sanded to dull their shiny finish.

The Land & Wildlife

Much of Southern California's coast is blessed by a Mediterranean climate, with warm, dry summers and mild, wet winters. This ecological 'island' is a haven for diverse plants and animals, from SoCal hillsides covered in golden poppies to majestic migratory gray whales and monarch butterflies. Although the staggering numbers of animals that greeted the first Europeans are now a thing of the past, keep your peepers open and you'll be surprised by just how many critters still call this home.

Animals

Marine Mammals

Spend even one day along Southern California's coast and you may spot pods of bottle-nosed dolphins and porpoises swimming and doing acrobatics in the ocean. Playful sea otters and harbor seals typically stick closer to shore, especially around public piers and protected bays. To see pinnipeds, such as barking sea lions and elephant seals, in the wild rather than at SeaWorld, hop aboard a boat to Channel Islands National Park

When it comes to SoCal's superstar marine wildlife, think big. School-bus big. Gray whales make cameo appearances every year between December and April. That's when they migrate along the Pacific coast, traveling from their summertime feeding grounds in the arctic Bering Sea, down to southern breeding grounds off Baja California – and then all the way back up again. Pregnant gray whales give birth to calves weighing up to 1500lb; if lucky, those newborn whales will live up to 60 years, some growing 50ft long and weighing up to 40 tons.

You can occasionally see migrating whales spout and breach from shoreline lookouts, such as San Diego's Point Loma and Torrey Pines in La Jolla or Point Vicente on LA's Palos Verdes Peninsula. Better yet, head out to meet the cetaceans on their own own turf by going on a whale-watching tour, with departures from LA's Long Beach, San Pedro and Marina Del Rey; San Diego; Dana Point and Newport Beach in Orange County; and Ventura and Santa Barbara, northwest of LA.

Feathered Friends

Out on a boat, or just standing on a SoCal beach, you'll spot plenty of winged creatures, including hefty pelicans darting for lunch like top-gun pilots, and skinny sandpipers foraging for invertebrates in the wet sand.

SoCal is an essential stop on the migratory Pacific Flyway between Alaska and Mexico. Almost half the bird species in North America use wildlife refuges and nature preserves for rest and refueling, peaking during the wetter winter season. Grab a pair of binoculars and scan the skies over SoCal's coast and inland by the Salton Sea.

Some beaches may be closed between March and September to protect endangered western snowy plovers, who lay their eggs in exposed ground scrapes in the sand. Give these easily frightened birds plenty of space, as the presence of humans – and especially dogs – can cause them to fatally abandon their young.

SoCal's Wildlife-Watching Hot Spots

Channel Islands National Park (p383)

Death Valley National Park (p323)

Joshua Tree National Park (p304)

Mt San Jacinto Wilderness State Park (p296)

Santa Monica Mountains (p166)

The California condor is the largest flying bird in North America. In 1987 there were only two dozen or so birds left in the wild. Thanks to captive breeding and release programs, there are about 240 flying free today.

AN AUDIENCE WITH A MONARCH BUTTERFLY

Monarch butterflies are delicate-looking orange creatures that follow remarkably lengthy migration patterns to spend their winters in California and Mexico. Walt Sakai, biology professor at Santa Monica College and a recognized authority on monarch butterflies, shares with us his favorite SoCal viewing spots:

➡ SoCal's premier site is **Ellwood Main** in Goleta, west of Santa Barbara. From Hwy 101, take the Hollister Ave exit south, then turn right at the stoplight by Ellwood School. Park at the end of the road, then walk a half-mile along a signposted path. Late November and early December are the best times to see the butterflies here.

➡ In Ventura, head to **Camino Real Park** in December and January. Look for monarchs in the eucalyptus grove above the creek near the tennis courts. From Hwy 101, go north on Victoria Ave, left on Telegraph Rd, left on S Bryn Mawr St and right on Aurora Dr.

➡ In Malibu's Point Mugu State Park, **Big Sycamore Canyon** also hosts monarch butterflies, especially in sycamore trees by the hike-and-bike camping area. October is the best month to see them – they're often gone by mid-November.

Also keep an eye out for bald eagles, which soared off the endangered species list in 2007. These birds of prey have regained a foothold on the Channel Islands, and some spend their winters at Big Bear Lake near LA.

Mountain Kings

Mountain lions – also called cougars or pumas – inhabit forests and mountains throughout SoCal, especially in areas teeming with deer. Reaching up to 8ft in length and weighing as much as 175lb, this solitary animal is a formidable predator. Only a few attacks on humans have occurred, mostly where encroachment has pushed hungry lions to their limits – for example, at the borders of wilderness and rapidly developing suburbs.

Although an estimated 25,000 to 30,000 black bears roam around California, the possibilities of close encounters with bears in SoCal are extremely unlikely, and limited to the San Gabriel Mountains and the San Bernardino Mountains east of LA. The only place you'll possibly see a grizzly bear these days is on the state flag, since this species was extirpated from California during the 1920s.

Desert Critters

The desert is far from deserted, but most animals are too smart to hang out in the daytime heat, coming out only at night like bats do. Roadrunners, those black-and-white mottled ground cuckoos with long tails and punk-style mohawks, can often be spotted on roadsides. Other desert inhabitants include burrowing kit foxes, tree-climbing grey foxes, hopping jackrabbits and kangaroo rats, slow-moving desert tortoises, and a variety of snakes, lizards and spiders. Desert bighorn sheep and myriad birds flock to watering holes to SoCal's native fan-palm oases.

Plants

Native Trees & Shrubs

You've seen them on film, you've seen them on TV: swaying palm trees with trunks as slender as a giraffe's neck that are so evocative of Southern California. Well, those guys are like most locals: they're not really from here. In fact, the only native species is the fan palm, found naturally in SoCal's desert oases.

Oak trees are a different story. California has 20 native species of oak. Live, or evergreen, oaks with holly-like leaves and scaly acorns thrive

SoCal for the Birds

Ballona Wetlands (p185)

Bolsa Chica State Ecological Reserve (p263)

Malibu Lagoon State Beach (p1617)

San Elijo Lagoon (p441)

Upper Newport Bay Nature Preserve (p273)

here especially. You'll traipse past them while exploring the Santa Monica Mountains and other coastal ranges. Other common plants include the aromatic California bay laurel tree, whose long slender leaves turn purple, and manzanita shrubs with intensely red bark and small berries.

Coastal Beauties & Beyond

The Audubon Society's California chapter website (http://ca.audubon.org) offers birding checklists, photos and videos, conservation news and an interactive birding map.

The gnarled Torrey pine tree has adapted to sparse rainfall and sandy, stony soils. It grows only at Torrey Pines State Reserve near San Diego and on Santa Rosa Island in Channel Islands National Park, which is home to dozens more endemic plant species. The same is true of Catalina Island, where you'll find the Catalina ironwood and Catalina mahogany trees, flowering Santa Catalina bedstraw and succulent Catalina live-forever, all displayed at the Wrigley Memorial & Botanical Gardens.

Except in the deserts and high mountains, the hills of SoCal turn green in winter, not summer. As soon as winter rains arrive, dried-out brown grasses spring to life. As early as February, wildflowers pop up, notably the bright-orange California poppy, the state flower, which blooms into May. Resist the temptation to pick one – it's illegal ($500 fine) and besides, they wilt almost instantly when plucked from the ground.

Desert Cacti & Their Cousins

Cacti and other desert plants have adapted to the arid climate of SoCal's deserts with thin, spiny leaves that resist moisture loss (and deter grazing animals), and seed and flowering mechanisms that kick into gear during brief rains. With enough winter rainfall, wildflowers can bloom spectacularly in spring (February through April), carpeting valleys and drawing thousands of onlookers and shutterbugs.

The sheer variety of cacti found in SoCal is astonishing. Among the most common and easy to identify is cholla (*cho-ya*), which appears so furry that it's nicknamed 'teddy-bear cactus.' But it's far from cuddly and instead will bury extremely sharp, barbed spines in your skin at the slightest touch. Also watch out for catclaw acacia, nicknamed 'wait-a-minute bush' because its small, sharp, hooked thorny spikes can snatch your clothing and skin as you brush past.

A colorful photographic survey of more than 2300 of SoCal's varied wildflowers, from desert cacti to alpine blooms, awaits at www.calflora.net/bloomingplants. The Theodore Payne Foundation (http://theodore-payne.org) has tips on seeing them when in season.

Almost as widespread is prickly pear, a flat, fleshy-padded cacti that produces showy flowers in shades of red, yellow and purple, and whose juice is traditionally used as medicine by Native Americans. Then there's cactus-like creosote (actually, a small evergreen bush with a distinctive smell) and spiky ocotillo, which grows up to 20ft tall and has cane-like branches hung with blood-red flowers.

Like whimsical figments from a Dr Seuss book, Joshua trees are the largest type of yucca, and are related to agave plants. Allegedly, they were named by migrant Mormons, who thought the crooked branches resembled the outstretched arms of a biblical prophet. Joshua trees grow throughout the Mojave Desert, although their habitat and long-term survival is seriously threatened by global warming. Their heavy, creamy greenish-white flowers erupt in spring.

Survival Guide

Directory A–Z

Accommodations

Rates & Discounts

➡ Generally, midweek rates are lower except at urban hotels geared to business travelers, which lure leisure travelers with weekend deals.

➡ Discount cards (eg AAA, AARP) may get you about 10% off standard rates at participating hotels and motels.

➡ Look for motel and hotel discount coupons in freebie ad magazines at gas stations, highway rest areas, tourist information offices and online at HotelCoupons (http://hotelcoupons.com).

➡ Bargaining may be possible for walk-in guests without reservations, especially at off-peak times.

Seasons & Reservations

➡ High season is from June to August everywhere, except the deserts and mountain ski areas, where December to April are the busiest months.

➡ Demand (and prices) spike around major holidays and special events, when some properties may impose multiday minimum stays.

➡ Reservations are recommended for weekend and holiday travel year-round, and any day of the week during high season.

➡ If you walk up without reservations, always request to see a room before paying for it, especially at motels.

Smoking

➡ Some hotels are now entirely smoke-free, meaning you're not allowed to smoke anywhere on the property, or even outdoors within a certain distance of entryways.

➡ Where smoking rooms still exist at hotels, they're often left un-renovated and in less desirable locations.

➡ Expect to pay a hefty 'cleaning fee' ($100 or more) if you light up in designated nonsmoking rooms.

B&Bs

If you fancy a more idiosyncratic or perhaps more romantic alternative to impersonal motels and hotels, bed-and-breakfast inns are often a good bet. Many inhabit fine old Victorian houses or other heritage buildings, graced with antique furnishings, art and peaceful gardens. Travelers who prefer privacy, however, may find B&Bs too intimate.

Rates often include breakfast, but occasionally do not (never mind what the name 'B&B' suggests). Amenities vary widely, but rooms with TV and telephone are the exception; the cheapest units share bathrooms. Standards are high at places certified by the California Association of Boutique & Breakfast Inns (www.cabbi.com).

Most B&Bs require advance reservations; only a few will accommodate drop-in guests. Smoking is generally prohibited and children are usually not welcome. Multinight stays may be required, especially on weekends and in high season.

Camping

Camping in Southern California is a lot more than just a cheap way to spend the night. The best campsites have you waking up to ocean views, under a canopy of pine trees or next to desert

---

SLEEPING PRICE RANGES

The following price ranges refer to a private room with bathroom during high season, unless otherwise specified. Taxes and breakfast are not normally included in the price.

$ less than $100

$$ $100–250

$$$ more than $250

rock formations. Many campgrounds are open year-round, and the most popular ones (for instance, those near the beach) fill up in high season, so make reservations or arrive early.

Basic campsites with fire pits, picnic tables and access to drinking water and pit toilets are common in national forests and on Bureau of Land Management (BLM) land. Campgrounds in state and national parks usually have flush toilets and sometimes hot showers and recreational vehicle (RV) hookups. Private campgrounds are often located closer to towns and cater more to the RV crowd.

Many public and almost all private campgrounds accept both online and phone reservations for all or at least some of their campsites through one or both of the following agencies:

Recreation.gov Camping reservations in national parks, national forests (USFS) and other federal recreation lands (eg BLM).

Reserve America (☑800-444-7275; www.reserveamerica.com) For California state-park campgrounds and cabins that accept reservations.

Hostels

SoCal has five hostels affiliated with **Hostelling International USA** (☑240-650-2100; www.hiusa.org). There are two each in San Diego and LA, and one in Fullerton near Disneyland. Dorms in HI hostels are typically gender-segregated and alcohol and smoking are prohibited. HI-USA membership cards ($28 per year) get you $3 off per night and, in many cases, a third night free when you book a dorm bed for three or more consecutive nights.

Independent hostels are most common in Hollywood and Venice in LA and in San Diego. They generally have more relaxed rules, with frequent guest parties and activities. Some include a

GREEN HOTELS & MOTELS

Surprisingly, many of SoCal's hotels and motels haven't yet jumped on the environmental bandwagon. Apart from offering you the option of reusing your towels and sheets, even such simple eco-initiatives as providing recycling bins, switching to bulk soap dispensers or replacing plastic and Styrofoam cups and dropping pre-packaged items from the breakfast buffet are pretty rare. The California Green Lodging Program (www.calrecycle.ca.gov/epp/greenlodging/) is a voluntary state-run certification program – in the online directory, search for properties that have achieved the 'Environmentalist Level,' denoted by three palm trees.

light breakfast in their rates, arrange local tours or pick up guests at transportation hubs. No two hostels are alike but typical facilities include mixed dorms, semi-private rooms with shared bathrooms, communal kitchens, lockers, internet access, laundry and TV lounges.

Some hostels say they accept only international visitors (basically to keep out homeless locals), but Americans who look like travelers (eg you're in possession of a plane ticket) may be admitted, especially during slow periods.

Dorm-beds cost $25 to $60, including tax. Reservations are always a good idea, especially in high season. Most hostels take reservations online or over the phone. Booking services such as www.hostels.com, www.hostelz.com and www.hostelworld.com sometimes offer lower rates than if you contact the hostels directly.

Hotels & Motels

Hotel and motel rooms are often priced by the size and number of beds in a room, rather than the number of

occupants. A room with one double or queen-size bed usually costs the same for one or two people, while a room with a king-size bed or two double beds costs more.

There is often a small surcharge for the third and fourth person, but children under a certain age (this varies) may stay free. Cribs or rollaway cots usually incur an extra fee. Beware that suites or 'junior suites' may be simply oversized rooms; ask about the layout when booking.

Recently renovated or larger rooms, or those with a view, are likely to cost more. Descriptors like 'oceanfront' and 'ocean view' are often too liberally used, and may require a periscope to spot the surf.

Rates may include breakfast, which could be just a stale doughnut and wimpy coffee, an all-you-can-eat hot and cold buffet, or anything in between.

You can make reservations at chains by calling their central reservation lines, but to learn about specific amenities and local promotions, call the property directly.

BOOK YOUR STAY ONLINE

For more accommodations reviews by Lonely Planet authors, check out http://lonelyplanet.com/hotels/. You'll find independent reviews, as well as recommendations on the best places to stay. Best of all, you can book online.

Customs Regulations

Currently, non-US citizens and permanent residents may import up to the following limits:

➡ 1L of alcohol (if you're over 21 years old)

➡ 200 cigarettes (one carton) or 100 (non-Cuban) cigars (if you're over 18 years old)

➡ $100 worth of gifts Amounts higher than $10,000 in cash, traveler's checks, money orders and other cash equivalents must be declared. Don't even think about bringing in illegal drugs.

For more complete, up-to-date information, check with US Customs and Border Protection (www.cbp.gov).

Discount Cards

➡ **Go Los Angeles Card** (www.smartdestinations. com; 1-day pass adult/child 3-12yr $85/69, up to 5 days $315/275) Includes admission to major theme parks all over SoCal (Disney excepted); for the best deals, buy online.

➡ **Southern California CityPass** (www.citypass. com/SouthernCalifornia; adult/child from $353/324) Covers three-day admission to Disneyland and Disney California Adventure and one-day admission each to Legoland and SeaWorld, with add-ons available for the San Diego Zoo or Safari Park ($42). Passes are valid for 14 days from the first day of use. It's cheapest to buy them in advance online.

Electricity

The US electric current is 110V to 115V, 60Hz AC. Outlets are made for flat two-prong plugs (which often have a third, rounded prong for grounding). If your appliance is made for another electrical system (eg 220V),

you'll need a step-down converter, which can be bought at hardware stores and drugstores. However, most electronic devices (laptops, camera-battery chargers, etc) are built for dual-voltage use, so you will only need a plug adapter.

Type A
120V/60Hz

Type B
120V/60Hz

Embassies & Consulates

Most foreign embassies are in Washington, DC, but some countries have consular offices in Los Angeles, including the following:

Australian Consulate (☎310-229-2300; www.losangeles. consulate.gov.au; 2029 Century Park E, Suite 1350) Century City.

Canadian Consulate (☎213-346-2700; http://can-am. gc.ca/los-angeles; 550 S Hope St, 9th fl; ⊗8:30am-4:30pm Mon-Fri; MRed/Purple/Blue/Expo Lines to 7th St/Metro Center) Downtown LA.

French Consulate (☎310-235-3200; www.consulf-rance-losangeles.org; 10390 Santa Monica Blvd, Suite 410) Near Century City.

German Consulate (☎323-930-2703; www.germany. info/losangeles; 6222 Wilshire Blvd, Suite 500, Mid-City; ⊗by appointment; phone hours 8am-4pm Mon-Thu, to 1pm Fri) Mid-City.

Japanese Consulate (☎213-617-6700; www.la.us.emb-ja-pan.go.jp; 350 S Grand Ave, Suite 1700; ⊗9:30am-noon & 1-4:30pm Mon-Fri; MRed/Purple Lines to Pershing Sq) Downtown LA.

New Zealand Consulate (☎310-566-6555; www.mfat. govt.nz; 2425 Olympic Blvd, Suite 600E) Santa Monica.

UK Consulate (☎310-789-0031; www.gov.uk/government/world/organisations/brit-ish-consulate-general-los-ange-les; 2029 Century Park E, Suite 1350) Century City.

For countries not listed here, visit www.state.gov/s/cpr/rls/fco/.

Food & Drink

Check out the Eat & Drink Like a Local chapter (p52) for tasty bites of information about SoCal's culinary cornucopia.

Health

Healthcare & Insurance

For medical emergencies, call ☑911 or go to the nearest 24-hour hospital emergency room (ER). Many healthcare professionals demand payment at the time of service, especially from out-of-towners. Phone around to find a walk-in clinic or doctor who will accept your insurance.

Keep all receipts and documentation, in case your insurance provider can reimburse you. Some insurance policies require you to get pre-authorization for medical treatment before seeking help. Overseas visitors with travel health-insurance policies may need to contact a call center for an over-the-phone assessment before seeking medical treatment.

Dehydration, Heat Exhaustion & Heatstroke

➡ Take it easy as you acclimatize to SoCal's high temperatures. Always drink plenty of water. A minimum of 3L per person per day is recommended when you're active outdoors. Be sure to eat a salty snack too, as sodium is necessary for rehydration.

➡ Dehydration (lack of water) or salt deficiency can cause heat exhaustion, often characterized by heavy sweating, fatigue, lethargy, headaches, nausea, vomiting, dizziness and muscle cramps.

➡ Long, continuous exposure to high temperatures can lead to possibly fatal heatstroke, when body temperature rises to dangerous levels. Warning signs include altered mental state, hyperventilation and flushed, hot and dry skin (ie sweating stops). Immediate hospitalization is essential.

Hypothermia

➡ Skiers and hikers will find temperatures in the mountains and desert can quickly drop below freezing, especially during winter. Even a sudden spring shower or high winds can lower your body temperature rapidly.

➡ Instead of cotton, wear synthetic or wool clothing that retains warmth even when wet. Carry waterproof layers (eg Gore-Tex jacket, plastic poncho, rain pants) and high-energy, easily digestible snacks like chocolate, nuts and dried fruit.

➡ Symptoms of hypothermia include exhaustion, numbness, shivering, stumbling, slurred speech, dizzy spells, muscle cramps and irrational or even violent behavior.

➡ To treat mild hypothermia, get out of bad weather and change into dry, warm clothing. Drink hot liquids (no caffeine or alcohol) and snack on high-calorie food.

➡ For more advanced hypothermia, seek immediate medical attention.

Insurance

Getting travel insurance to cover theft, loss and medical problems is highly recommended. Some policies do not cover 'risky' activities such as scuba diving, motorcycling and skiing, so read the fine print. Make sure the policy at least covers hospital stays and an emergency flight home.

Paying for your airline ticket or rental car with a credit card may provide limited travel accident insurance. If you already have private US health insurance, or a homeowners or renters policy, find out what those policies cover and only get supplemental insurance. If you have pre-paid a large portion of your vacation, trip-cancellation insurance may be worthwhile.

Worldwide travel insurance is available at www.lonelyplanet.com/travel-insurance. You can buy, extend and claim online anytime, even if you're already on the road.

Internet Access

Cybercafes are a dying breed in LA, though free public wi-fi is proliferating, with hot spots including LAX, **Pershing Sq** (p89) and **Grand Central Market** (p90) in Downtown, **Echo Park Lake** (p120), the **Griffith Observatory** (p124), the **Hollywood & Highland mall** (p119), Venice Beach and **Santa Monica Pier** (p174). Free wi-fi is common in coffee shops and public libraries, and numerous restaurants, bars and museums also offer free wi-fi.

Although most hotels and hostels have wi-fi, some places charge for the service, or only offer it free in common areas such as the lobby.

We identify venues that provide guest internet-connected computer terminals by the internet icon; the wi-fi icon indicates that wireless access is available.

Legal Matters

Drugs & Alcohol

➡ Although California voted in 2016 to decriminalize marijuana for personal use, until the law takes effect in 2018, possession of less than 1oz of marijuana is a misdemeanor in California, and the exact details of implementation are still being determined. Possession of any other drug or more than an ounce of weed is a felony punishable by lengthy jail time. For foreigners, conviction of any drug-related offense is grounds for deportation.

➡ Police can give roadside sobriety checks to assess if you've been drinking or using drugs. If you fail, they'll require you to take a breath, urine or blood test to determine if your blood-alcohol level is over the legal limit (0.08%). Refusing to be tested is treated the same as if you had taken and failed the test.

➡ Penalties for driving under the influence (DUI) of drugs or alcohol range from license suspension and fines to jail.

➡ It's illegal to carry open containers of alcohol inside a vehicle, even if they're empty. Unless they're full and sealed, put them in the trunk.

➡ Consuming alcohol anywhere other than at a private residence or licensed premises is a no-no, which puts parks and beaches off-limits.

➡ Bars, clubs, restaurants and liquor stores often ask for photo ID to prove you are of legal drinking age (21 years old). Being 'carded' is standard practice, so don't take it personally.

Police & Security

➡ For police, fire and ambulance emergencies, dial ⏺911. For nonemergency police assistance, contact the nearest local police station (dial ⏺411 for directory assistance).

➡ If you are stopped by the police, be courteous. Don't get out of the car unless asked. Keep your hands where the officer can see them (eg on the steering wheel) at all times.

➡ There is no system of paying fines on the spot. Attempting to pay the fine to the officer may lead to a charge of attempted bribery.

➡ For traffic violations, the officer will explain your options. There is usually a 30-day period to pay a fine; most matters can be handled by mail.

➡ If you are arrested, you have the right to remain silent and are presumed innocent until proven guilty. Everyone has the right to make one phone call. If you don't have a lawyer, one will be appointed free of charge.

➡ Due to security concerns about terrorism, never leave your bags unattended, especially not at airports or bus and train stations.

LGBT Travelers

SoCal is a magnet for LGBT travelers. Hot spots include West Hollywood (WeHo), Silver Lake and Long Beach around LA, San Diego's Hillcrest neighborhood and the desert resort of Palm Springs. Some scenes are predominantly male-oriented, although women usually won't feel too left out.

Same-sex marriage is legal in California. Despite widespread tolerance, homophobic bigotry has not been completely rooted out in SoCal, especially in rural areas.

Resources

Advocate (www.advocate.com/travel) Online news, gay travel features and destination guides.

Damron (www.damron.com) Classic, advertiser-driven gay travel guides and 'Gay Scout' mobile app.

Gay & Lesbian National Hotline (888-843-4564, www.glnh.org) For counseling and referrals of any kind.

Los Angeles LGBT Center (Map p106; ⏺323-993-7400; www.lalgbtcenter.org; 1625 Schrader Blvd; ⏲9am-9pm Mon-Fri, to 1pm Sat) Offers information and health services for the LGBT community.

Mister B&B (www.misterbandb.com) Like Airbnb, but the hosts are gay.

Out Traveler (www.outtraveler.com) Free online magazine with travel tips, destination guides and hotel reviews.

Purple Roofs (www.purpleroofs.com) Online directory of LGBT accommodations.

Money

ATMs

ATMs are available 24/7 at most banks, shopping malls, airports and grocery and convenience stores. Expect a minimum surcharge of $2.50 per transaction in addition to any fees charged by your

---

SMOKING

➡ Smoking is generally prohibited inside all public buildings, including airports, shopping malls and train and bus stations, and inside all restaurants and bars.

➡ Smoking is also prohibited on many beaches and, in some cities and towns, it is illegal to smoke outdoors if you are within a certain distance of a public business.

➡ At hotels, you must specifically request a smoking room; some properties are entirely nonsmoking by law. Fines for smoking in a nonsmoking room are typically $100 to $250.

home bank. Most ATMs are connected to international networks and offer decent foreign-exchange rates.

Cash

Most people do not carry large amounts of cash for everyday use, relying instead on credit and debit cards. Some businesses refuse to accept bills larger than $20.

Credit Cards

Credit cards are almost universally accepted. In fact, it's almost impossible to rent a car, book a hotel room or buy tickets without one. Visa, MasterCard and American Express are widely accepted.

Money changers

You can exchange money at major airports, some banks and all currency-exchange offices such as American Express or Travelex. Always inquire about rates and fees. Outside big cities, exchanging money may be a problem, so make sure you have a credit card and sufficient cash.

Traveler's Checks

Traveler's checks have pretty much fallen out of use. Big-city restaurants, hotels and larger stores often will accept traveler's checks (in US dollars only), but smaller businesses and fast-food chains may refuse them.

Opening Hours

Standard opening hours are as follows. Individual opening hours vary widely.

Banks 9am–5pm Monday to Thursday, to 6pm Friday, some 9am–1:30pm Saturday

Bars 5pm–2am

Business hours (general) 9am–5pm Monday to Friday

Post offices 9am–5pm Monday to Friday, some 9am–noon Saturday

Restaurants 7:30–10:30am, 11:30am–2:30pm and 5:30–10pm

Shops 10am–6pm Monday to Saturday, noon–5pm Sunday (malls open later)

Supermarkets 8am–9pm

Post

The US Postal Service (www. usps.com) is inexpensive and reliable. For sending important documents or packages overseas, try FedEx (www. fedex.com) or UPS (www. ups.com).

Public Holidays

On the following national holidays, banks, schools and government offices (including post offices) close, and transportation, museums and other services operate on a Sunday schedule. Holidays falling on a weekend are usually observed the following Monday.

New Year's Day January 1

Martin Luther King Jr Day Third Monday in January

Presidents' Day Third Monday in February

Good Friday Friday before Easter (March/April)

Memorial Day Last Monday in May

Independence Day July 4

Labor Day First Monday in September

Columbus Day Second Monday in October

Veterans Day November 11

Thanksgiving Day Fourth Thursday in November

Christmas Day December 25

School Holidays

Colleges take a one- or two-week 'spring break' around Easter, sometime in March or April. Some hotels and resorts, especially by beaches, near theme parks and in the deserts, may raise their rates during this time. School summer vacations make July and August the busiest travel months.

Safe Travel

Don't believe everything you see in the movies. Despite its seemingly apocalyptic list of dangers – guns, violent crime, riots, earthquakes – California is a reasonably safe place to visit. The greatest danger is posed by car

TIPPING

Tipping is *not* optional. Only withhold tips in cases of outrageously bad service (in which case, a word to the manager is also warranted).

Airport skycaps and hotel bellhops $2 per bag, minimum per cart $5.

Bartenders 15% per round, minimum $1 per drink.

Concierges No tips required for simple information, up to $10 for securing last-minute restaurant reservations, sold-out show tickets etc.

Housekeeping staff $2 to $4 daily, left under the card provided; more if you're messy.

Parking valets At least $2 when handed back your car keys.

Restaurant servers and room service 18% to 20%, unless a gratuity is already charged (common for groups of six or more).

Taxi drivers 15% of metered fare, rounded up to the next dollar.

accidents. Buckle up (it's the law), no handheld phones behind the wheel and please try not to look down at your phone while walking or crossing the street. The biggest annoyances, meanwhile, are city traffic and crowds. Wildlife poses some small threats, and, of course, there is the unlikely, albeit dramatic, possibility of a natural disaster.

Earthquakes

Earthquakes happen all the time, but most are so tiny they are detectable only by sensitive seismological instruments. If you're caught in a serious shaker, heed the following advice:

➡ If indoors, get under a desk or table.

➡ Protect your head and stay clear of windows, mirrors or anything that might fall.

➡ Don't head for elevators or go running into the street.

➡ If you're in a shopping mall or large public building, expect the alarm and/or sprinkler systems to come on.

➡ If outdoors, get away from buildings, trees and power lines.

➡ If you're driving, pull over to the side of the road away from bridges, overpasses and power lines. Stay inside the car until the shaking stops.

➡ If you're on a sidewalk near buildings, duck into a doorway to protect yourself from falling bricks, glass and debris.

➡ Prepare for aftershocks.

➡ Turn on the radio and listen for bulletins.

➡ Use the telephone only if absolutely necessary.

Riptides

If you find yourself being carried offshore by a dangerous ocean current called a riptide, the important thing is to just keep afloat. Don't panic or try to swim against the current, as this will quickly exhaust you and you may drown. Instead, try to swim parallel to the shoreline and once the current stops pulling you out, swim back toward shore.

Telephone

Cell Phones

Cell-phone coverage is spotty in deserts. The only foreign phones that will work in the USA are GSM multiband models. Buy prepaid SIM cards or disposable cell phones locally.

Payphones & Phonecards

Payphones are becoming few and far between in California. Where they still exist,

they're usually coin-operated, although some accept credit cards. Local calls usually cost 50¢ minimum. For long-distance calls, you're usually better off buying a prepaid phonecard sold at supermarkets, pharmacies and electronics and convenience stores.

Phone Codes

➡ US phone numbers consist of a three-digit area code followed by a seven-digit local number.

➡ From land lines, dial ☑1 plus the area code plus the local number. If calling from a US mobile phone, the 1 is not necessary.

➡ Toll-free numbers begin with 800, 844, 855, 866, 877 or 888 and must be preceded by 1.

➡ For direct international calls, dial ☑011 plus the country code plus the area code (usually without the initial '0') plus the local phone number.

➡ The country code for the US is 1 (the same as for Canada, but beware international rates apply between the two countries).

Time

➡ Pacific Standard Time (UT minus 8 hours).

➡ During Daylight Saving Time (DST), the second Sunday in March to the first Sunday in November, clocks are set one hour ahead.

Toilets

Modern 'restrooms' are easy to find throughout SoCal. The best public facilities tend to be in hotel lobbies and upper-end restaurants, shopping malls and amusement parks. Many other shops will let you use their facilities if you ask nicely. In a pinch, gasoline stations also have toilets, but cleanliness can be an issue.

A growing number of communities, businesses and institutions now offer gen-

PRACTICALITIES

Newspapers Major dailies are the center-left *Los Angeles Times* (www.latimes.com), conservative *San Diego Union-Tribune* (www.utsandiego.com) and right-leaning *Orange County Register* (www.ocregister.com); alternative tabloids are *LA Weekly* (www.laweekly.com), *San Diego Reader* (www.sandiegoreader.com) and *OC Weekly* (www.ocweekly.com).

Radio National Public Radio (NPR), lower end of FM dial, with a variety of news and cultural programming.

TV PBS (public broadcasting), plus cable channels CNN (news), ESPN (sports), HBO (movies) and the Weather Channel.

Weights & Measures Imperial (except 1 US gallon = 0.83 imperial gallons)

der-neutral bathrooms (usually single-stall), in solidarity with the trans community.

Tourist Information

California Travel & Tourism Commission (www.visitcal-ifornia.com) is a great resource for pre-trip planning. This state-run agency also operates several California Welcome Centers (www.visitcwc.com), where staff dispense maps and brochures and may be able to help find accommodations. See regional sections for local tourism authorities.

Travelers with Disabilities

Southern California is reasonably well equipped for travelers with disabilities. Disneyland is a shining example when it comes to catering to visitors with special needs.

Download Lonely Planet's free Accessible Travel guide from http://lptravel.to/AccessibleTravel.

Communications

➜ Telephone companies provide relay operators (dial 711) for the hearing impaired.

➜ Many banks provide ATM instructions in Braille.

Mobility & Accessibility

➜ Most intersections have dropped curbs; some have audible crossing signals.

➜ The Americans with Disabilities Act (ADA) requires public buildings built after 1993 to be wheelchair-accessible, including restrooms.

➜ Motels and hotels built after 1993 must have at least one ADA-compliant accessible room; state your specific needs when making reservations.

➜ For nonpublic buildings and those built prior to 1993, including hotels, restaurants, museums and theaters,

there are no accessibility guarantees; call ahead to find out what to expect.

➜ Most national and many state parks and some other outdoor recreation areas offer paved or boardwalk-style nature trails accessible by wheelchairs.

Transportation

➜ All major airlines, Greyhound buses and Amtrak trains can accommodate people with disabilities, usually with 48 hours of advance notice required.

➜ Major car-rental agencies offer hand-controlled vehicles and vans with wheelchair lifts at no extra charge, but you must reserve these well in advance.

➜ For wheelchair-accessible van rentals, also try **Wheelchair Getaways** (☏800-642-2042; www.wheelchairgetaways.com) in LA or **Mobility Works** (☏877-275-4915; www.mobilityworks.com) with locations around LA.

➜ Local buses, trains and subway lines usually have wheelchair lifts.

➜ Seeing-eye dogs are permitted to accompany passengers traveling on public transportation.

➜ Taxi companies have at least one wheelchair-accessible van, but you'll usually need to call first.

Resources

A Wheelchair Rider's Guide to the California Coast (www.wheelingcalscoast.org) Free online directory and downloadable PDF guide for LA and Orange County coasts covers wheelchair access at beaches, parks and more.

California State Parks (http://access.parks.ca.gov) Searchable online map and database of accessible features at state parks.

Disneyland (https://disneyland.disney.go.com/guest-services/mobility-disabilities) Lists which attractions are accessible.

Visas

➜ Depending on your country of origin, the rules for entering the USA keep changing. Double-check current visa and passport requirements *before* coming to the USA.

➜ Currently, under the US Visa Waiver Program (VWP), visas are not required for citizens of 38 countries for stays up to 90 days (no extensions) as long as you have a machine-readable passport (MRP) that's valid for six months beyond your intended stay.

➜ Citizens of VWP countries must still register online with the Electronic System for Travel Authorization (https://esta.cbp.dhs.gov/) at least 72 hours before travel. Once approved, ESTA registration ($14) is valid for up to two years or until your passport expires, whichever comes first.

➜ For most Canadian citizens traveling with Canadian passports that meet current US standards, a visa for short-term visits (usually up to six months) and ESTA registration aren't required.

➜ Citizens from all other countries or whose passports don't meet current US standards need to apply for a temporary visitor visa. Best done in your home country, the process costs a nonrefundable fee (minimum $160), involves a personal interview and can take several weeks, so apply as early as possible.

➜ For up-to-date information about entry requirements and eligibility, check the visa section of the US Department of State website (http://usvisas.state.gov) or contact the nearest US embassy or consulate in your home country (for a complete list, visit www.usembassy.gov).

Transportation

GETTING THERE & AWAY

Flights, cars and tours can be booked online at lonelyplanet.com/bookings.

Entering the Region

California is an important agricultural state. To prevent the spread of pests and diseases, certain food items (including meats, fresh fruit and vegetables) may not be brought into the state. Bakery items, chocolates and hard-cured cheeses are admissible. If you drive into California across the border from Mexico or from the neighboring states of Oregon, Nevada or Arizona, you may have to stop for a quick questioning and inspection by California Department of Food and Agriculture agents.

Under the US Department of Homeland Security's Orwellian-sounding Office of Biometric Identity Management, almost all foreign visitors to the USA (excluding, for now, many Canadians, some Mexican citizens, children under age 14 and seniors over age 79) will be digitally photographed and have their electronic (inkless) fingerprints scanned upon arrival.

For more information about entering the USA, visit www.cbp.gov online.

Passports

➡ Under the Western Hemisphere Travel Initiative (WHTI), all travelers must have a valid machine-readable (MRP) passport when entering the US by air, land or sea.

➡ The only exceptions are for some US, Canadian and Mexican citizens traveling *by land* who can present another WHTI-compliant document (eg pre-approved 'trusted traveler' cards). For details, visit www.cbp.gov/travel online.

➡ All foreign passports must meet current US standards and be valid for six months longer than your intended stay in the USA.

➡ MRP passports issued or renewed after October 26, 2006 must be e-passports (ie have a digital photo and integrated chip with biometric data).

Air

Airports & Airlines

Southern California's primary international airport is Los Angeles International Airport (LAX), served by all major domestic and some 60 overseas airlines. Other airports have mostly domestic flights and are often served by low-cost carriers, such as Southwest Airlines, JetBlue, Alaska Airlines and Frontier Airlines.

Los Angeles International Airport (LAX; Map p72; www.lawa.org/welcomeLAX.aspx; 1 World Way) California's largest

---

CLIMATE CHANGE & TRAVEL

Every form of transport that relies on carbon-based fuel generates CO_2, the main cause of human-induced climate change. Modern travel is dependent on airplanes, which might use less fuel per kilometer per person than most cars but travel much greater distances. The altitude at which aircraft emit gases (including CO_2) and particles also contributes to their climate change impact. Many websites offer 'carbon calculators' that allow people to estimate the carbon emissions generated by their journey and, for those who wish to do so, to offset the impact of the greenhouse gases emitted with contributions to portfolios of climate-friendly initiatives throughout the world. Lonely Planet offsets the carbon footprint of all staff and author travel.

and busiest airport, 20 miles southwest of Downtown LA, near the beaches.

Burbank Hollywood Airport (BUR, Bob Hope Airport; Map p72; www.burbankairport.com; 2627 N Hollywood Way, Burbank) About 14 miles northwest of Downtown LA, close to Universal Studios.

John Wayne Airport (SNA; www.ocair.com; 18601 Airport Way, Santa Ana) Off the I-405 Fwy in inland Orange County.

LA/Ontario International Airport (ONT; ☑909-937-2700; www.flyontario.com; 2500 E Airport Dr; ☏) In Riverside County, east of LA, closer to some desert destinations.

Long Beach Airport (Map p72; www.lgb.org; 4100 Donald Douglas Dr, Long Beach) Easy access to LA and Orange County.

Palm Springs International Airport (PSP; Map p300; ☑760-318-3800; www.palmsprings airport.com; 3400 E Tahquitz Canyon Way, Palm Springs) In the desert, east of LA.

San Diego International Airport (SAN; ☑619-400-2404; www.san.org; 3325 N Harbor Dr; ☏) Just 4 miles from downtown San Diego.

Santa Barbara Airport (www.flysba.com; 500 Fowler Rd, Goleta; ☏) Nine miles west of downtown Santa Barbara, off Hwy 101.

Departure Tax

Departure tax is included in the price of a ticket.

Land

Border Crossings

On the US–Mexico border between San Diego and Tijuana, San Ysidro is the world's busiest border crossing. Entering Mexico is usually not a problem, but coming back into the USA almost always entails a long wait, especially if you're driving. The website http://apps.cbp.gov/bwt shows current border wait times.

US citizens do not require a visa for stays of 72 hours or less within the border zone (ie from Tijuana south to Ensenada). To get back into the USA:

➡ US citizens will need to present a valid US passport or another WHTI-compliant document (see www.cbp. gov/travel). A regular US driver's license is no longer sufficient as proof.

➡ Non-US citizens may be subject to a full immigration inspection upon returning to the US, so bring your passport and US visa if required. For current passport and visa requirements, consult http://travel.state.gov.

Bus

Greyhound (☑800-231-2222; www.greyhound.com) operates a nationwide route system serving dozens of destinations in Southern California. Some cross-border routes connect with Greyhound México (www.greyhound.com.mx) and Greyhound Canada (www.greyhound.ca). Northbound buses from Mexico can take some time to cross the US border, as US immigration authorities may insist on checking every person on board.

Car & Motorcycle

If you're driving into the USA from Canada or Mexico, bring your vehicle's registration papers, liability insurance and driver's license. Many rental agencies prohibit their vehicles from being driven across international borders.

Unless you're planning an extended stay in Mexico, driving a car from the USA across the border to Tijuana is more hassle than it's worth. Instead take the trolley from downtown San Diego, or park on the US side and walk across the border instead. If you do decide to drive, you must buy Mexican car insurance beforehand or near the border crossing.

Train

Amtrak (www.amtrak.com) operates a fairly extensive rail system throughout the USA. Trains are comfortable, if slow, and are equipped with dining cars on long-distance routes. Fares vary according to the type of seating (eg coach or business class, sleeping compartments).

Major long-distance routes to/from Southern California:

Coast Starlight Travels the West Coast daily from Seattle to LA (from $92, 35 hours) via Portland, Sacramento, Oakland, Santa Barbara and Burbank.

Southwest Chief Daily departures between Chicago and LA (from $135, 43 hours) via Kansas City, Albuquerque and Flagstaff.

Sunset Limited Thrice-weekly service between New Orleans and LA (from $130, 47 hours) via Houston, San Antonio, Tucson and northern Palm Springs.

TRAIN PASSES

Amtrak's USA Rail Pass is valid for coach-class train travel only (not Thruway buses) for 15 ($459), 30 ($689) or 45 ($899) days; children aged two to 15 pay half-price. Travel is limited to eight, 12 or 18 one-way 'segments,' respectively. A segment is not the same as a one-way trip. If reaching your destination requires riding more than one train, you'll use multiple segments. Purchase passes online, then make advance reservations for each trip segment.

Sea

The ports of LA (San Pedro), Long Beach and San Diego are important ports for pleasure cruises. Many originate here and sail up and down the coast, to Mexico or on the open ocean. Check with your cruise line about visa requirements if you will be stopping in ports outside the US.

GETTING AROUND

SoCal is famously car country, but plenty of alternatives exist. Cars are still SoCal's go-to, traffic notwithstanding, but LA has an expanding light-rail and subway network, and regional trains connect some coastal and inland destinations. In San Diego, trolleys are a popular alternative despite limited routes. Metropolitan bus travel is typically the cheapest, slowest option, but with the most extensive route network. If traveling by taxi, you must generally call for a cab, unless there is a taxi stand (don't try to hail one). Popular smartphone apps such as Uber and Lyft generally beat taxis on fares and convenience, although they are subject to 'surge pricing' at peak times.

Air

Although it is possible to fly from, say, LA to Santa Barbara, San Diego or Palm Springs, the time and cost involved don't make planes a sensible way to get around SoCal, unless you are connecting to or from another flight.

Bicycle

Although cycling is a non-polluting way to travel, SoCal distances may diminish its appeal as a primary form of transport.

That said, cities and neighborhoods throughout the region are becoming more cycle-friendly, adding bike lanes and bike-share programs. Municipal buses are equipped with bike racks, and bikes are permitted on Amtrak, light rail and subway trains.

If biking long distances, you must be able to cope with high temperatures, especially in summer and at any time of year in the deserts.

Rental & Purchase

➡ You can rent bicycles by the hour, day or week in most cities and tourist towns.

➡ Rates start at $10 per hour for beach cruisers and range up to $45 or more per day for mountain bikes; ask about multi-day and weekly discounts. A credit-card security deposit may be required.

➡ Cities and neighborhoods with short-hop bike-share programs include Downtown LA, Santa Monica, Long Beach and San Diego.

➡ Buy new models from specialty bike shops and sporting-goods stores, or used from notice boards at hostels, cafes etc.

➡ To buy or sell used bicycles, check online bulletin boards such as Craigslist (www.craigslist. org).

Road Rules

➡ Cycling is allowed on all roads and highways – even along freeways if there's no suitable alternative, such as a smaller parallel road; all mandatory exits are marked.

➡ Some cities have designated bicycle lanes, but keep your wits about you when riding in heavy traffic.

➡ Cyclists must follow the same rules of the road as vehicles. Don't expect drivers to always respect your right of way.

➡ Wearing a bicycle helmet is mandatory for riders under 18 years old.

Transporting Bicycles

➡ Municipal buses and trains are equipped with bicycle racks. Other local trains allow bicycles onboard, though possibly not during peak hours.

➡ Greyhound transports bicycles as luggage (surcharge typically $30 to $40), provided the bike is disassembled and placed in a rigid container ($10 box available at some terminals).

➡ Amtrak's *Pacific Surfliner* trains feature special bicycle racks, but be sure to reserve a spot when making your ticket reservation. On Amtrak trains without bicycle racks, bikes must be put into a box ($15 at most staffed terminals) then checked as luggage (fee $10).

Theft

➡ To prevent bicycle theft, use a heavy-duty bike lock and park in well-lit, busy areas.

➡ When parking your bike, remove accessories that can detach, such as lights and pouches.

➡ Some parking garages have special bicycle-parking areas.

➡ If possible, bring your bicycle inside your hotel room at night.

Bus

Southern California cities served by **Greyhound** (☎800-231-2222; www. greyhound.com) include LA, Anaheim, Long Beach, Santa Barbara, San Diego, Oceanside and Temecula. Frequency of service varies from 'rarely' to 'constantly,' but main routes operate every hour or so, sometimes around the clock.

Greyhound buses are usually clean, comfortable and reliable. The best seats are typically toward the front and away from the bathroom. Limited onboard amenities include wi-fi, freezing air-con (bring a sweater) and slightly reclining seats. Smoking onboard is prohibited.

Bus stations are typically dreary, often in dodgy areas; this is especially true of Downtown LA. If you arrive at night, take a taxi into town or directly to your hotel.

SAMPLE GREYHOUND FARES

ROUTE	ADULT FARE	DURATION	FREQUENCY
LA–Anaheim	$9-16	¾-1¼hr	7 per day
LA–San Diego	$13-22	2¼-3¼hr	20 per day
LA–Santa Barbara	$12-21	2¼-2¾hr	3 per day

Costs

It's easy to buy tickets online with a credit card, then pick them up (bring photo ID) at the bus terminal. You can also buy tickets over the phone or in person from a ticket agent. Ticket agents also accept debit cards, traveler's checks (in US dollars) and cash.

You may save a few dollars by purchasing tickets at least seven days in advance and by traveling between Monday and Thursday. Other promotions, including companion fares (50% off), are often available, though they may have restrictions or blackout periods. Check the website for current fare specials or ask when buying tickets.

Discounts are regularly available – on unrestricted fares only – for seniors aged over 62 (5% discount), students with a Student Advantage Card (20%) and children aged two to 11 (25%). Children under two years old ride free.

Reservations

➡ Most boarding is done on a first-come, first-served basis.

➡ Buying tickets in advance does not guarantee you a seat on any particular bus, unless you also purchase priority boarding (add $5).

➡ Arrive at least one hour prior to the scheduled departure time to secure a seat. Allow extra time on weekends and during holidays.

Car, Motorcycle & RV

The car is still king in SoCal. That said, you'll want to plan for traffic in metro areas and along coast highways, especially during weekday rush hours (7am to 10am and 3pm to 7pm) and on sunny weekends.

Parking can be costly; overnight parking can be $40 and up at downtown hotels and high-end resorts, and entertainment and spectator sports venues might charge between $10 and $35 per event. Read signage carefully before parking on city streets, as restrictions may apply.

Automobile Associations

For 24-hour emergency roadside assistance, free maps and discounts on lodging, attractions, car rentals and more:

Automobile Club of Southern California (American Automobile Association, www.calif.aaa.com)

Better World Club (www.betterworldclub.com)

Driver's Licenses

➡ Visitors may legally drive a car in California for up to 12 months with their home driver's license.

➡ If you're from overseas, an International Driving Permit (IDP) will have more credibility with traffic police and also simplify the car-rental process, especially if your license doesn't have a photo or isn't written in English.

➡ To drive a motorcycle, you'll need a valid US state motorcycle license or a specially endorsed IDP.

➡ International automobile associations can issue IDPs, valid for one year, for a fee.

Always carry your home license together with the IDP.

Insurance

California law requires liability insurance for all vehicles. When renting a car, check your auto-insurance policy from home or your travel insurance policy to see if you're already covered. If you're not, expect to pay about $20 per day.

Insurance against damage to the car itself, called Collision Damage Waiver (CDW) or Loss Damage Waiver (LDW), costs another $10 or more per day. The deductible (excess) may require you to pay the first $100 to $500 for any repairs.

Some credit cards will cover CDW/LDW, provided you charge the entire cost of the car rental to the card. If there's an accident, you may have to pay the car-rental company first, then seek reimbursement from the credit-card company.

Rental

CARS

To rent a car, you'll typically need to be at least 25 years old, hold a valid driver's license and have a major credit card (not a check or debit card). A few companies may rent to drivers aged 21 to 24, but for a hefty surcharge. If you don't have a credit card, you may occasionally be able to make a large cash deposit instead.

With advance reservations, you can often get an economy-size vehicle for about $30 per day, plus insurance, taxes and fees. Rates usually include unlimited mileage, but expect surcharges for additional drivers and one-way rentals. Airport rental locations may offer lower rates, but have higher fees; if you buy a fly-drive package, local taxes may be extra.

Child or infant safety seats are legally required; reserve them (around $10 per day) when booking your car. If you'd like to minimize

DO I NEED A CAR IN SOCAL?

Southern California is practically synonymous with car culture but, with time and patience, you can get around using public transportation. Focus your itinerary and do in-depth explorations of smaller areas rather than a big, sweeping loop. Even if you have a car, consider ditching it for at least part of the time.

Amtrak and Metrolink trains and Greyhound buses link major coastal cities, as well as some inland destinations. Many cities and towns have local bus, train and/or trolley systems, ride-hailing services are becoming ubiquitous, and beach towns are usually compact enough to explore by bicycle. Even in LA you'll be OK as long as you limit yourself to seeing just one or two neighborhoods a day.

your contribution to SoCal's polluted air, some major car-rental companies offer 'green' fleets of hybrid or bio-fueled rental cars. Expect to pay significantly more for those models and reserve them well in advance.

Check online through services like www.kayak. com or www.priceline.com to compare rental rates.

Avis (☑800-633-3469; www. avis.com)

Budget (☑800-218-7992; www. budget.com)

Enterprise (☑855-266-9289; www.enterprise.com)

Fox (☑855-571-8410; www. foxrentacar.com) Locations near LA, San Diego, Orange County, Burbank and Ontario airports.

Hertz (☑800-654-3131; www. hertz.com)

National (☑877-222-9058; www.nationalcar.com)

Rent-a-Wreck (☑877-877-0700; www.rentawreck.com) In West LA.

Simply Rent-A-Car (☑323-653-0022; www.simplyrac.com) 🖉 Rents classic and luxury cars near the Petersen Automotive Museum.

Super Cheap! Car Rental (www. supercheapcar.com) Near LAX and in Irvine, Orange County. No surcharge for drivers aged 21 to 24 years; nominal daily fee for drivers under age 21 with full-coverage insurance.

Thrifty (☑800-334-1705; www. thrifty.com)

Zipcar (☑866-494-7227; www. zipcar.com) 🖉 With locations in LA, Orange County, San Diego and Santa Barbara, this car-sharing club charges usage fees (per hour or daily) including free gas, insurance (a damage fee up to $1000 may apply) and limited mileage. Apply online (foreign drivers OK); application fee $25.

MOTORCYCLES

Motorcycle rentals and insurance are not cheap, especially if you've got your eye on a Harley. Depending on the model, it costs $100 to $250 per day plus taxes and fees, including helmets, unlimited miles and liability insurance; one-way rentals and Collision Damage Waiver cost extra. Discounts may be available for multiday and weekly rentals. Security deposits cost up to $2000 (credit card required).

Bartels' Route 66 (☑888-434-4473, 310-578-0112; www.route66riders.com; 4161 Lincoln Blvd, Marina Del Rey; ☺10am-6pm Mon-Sat) Harley-Davidson rentals in LA's Marina del Rey.

Eagle Rider (☑888-900-9901, 310-321-3180; www.eaglerider. com) SoCal rentals in LA, San Diego, Newport Beach and Palm Springs.

RECREATIONAL VEHICLES

In big cities, RVs are a nuisance since there are few places to park or plug them in. RVs are cumbersome to navigate and burn fuel at an alarming rate, but they do solve transportation, accommodations and cooking needs in one fell swoop. Outside of urban areas, it's easy to find RV campgrounds with electricity and water hookups.

Book RV rentals far in advance. Rental costs vary by size and model; expect to pay at least $100 per day, excluding mileage, vehicle prep fees and bedding and kitchen kits. If pets are allowed, a surcharge may apply.

Camper USA (☑310-929-5666; www.camperusa.com) Campervan rentals in the San Francisco Bay Area, LA and Las Vegas.

Cruise America (☑480-464-7300, 800-671-8042; www. cruiseamerica.com) RV rentals in LA, Burbank, San Diego, Oceanside and Costa Mesa.

El Monte (☑888-337-2214; www.elmonterv.com) RV rentals in LA, San Diego, Newport Beach and Van Nuys (San Fernando Valley).

Escape Campervans (☑877-270-8267, 310-672-9909; www.escapecampervans.com) Awesomely painted campervans at economical rates in LA, Las Vegas and San Francisco.

Jucy Rentals (☑800-650-4180; www.jucyrentals.com) Campervan rentals in San Francisco, LA and Las Vegas.

Vintage Surfari Wagons (☑714-585-7565; www.vwsurfari.com) VW campervan rentals in Orange County.

Road Rules

➡ Drive on the right-hand side of the road.

➡ Talking or texting on a cell phone without a hands-free device while driving is illegal.

➡ The use of seat belts is required for drivers, front-seat passengers and children under age 16.

→ Infant and child safety seats are required for children under six years old or weighing less than 60lbs.

→ All motorcyclists must wear a helmet.

→ High-occupancy (HOV) lanes marked with a diamond symbol are reserved for cars with multiple occupants, sometimes only during signposted hours.

→ Unless otherwise posted, the speed limit is 65mph on freeways, 55mph on two-lane undivided highways, 35mph on major city streets, and 25mph in business and residential districts and near schools.

→ Except where indicated, turning right at a red stoplight after coming to a full stop is permitted, although intersecting traffic still has the right of way.

→ At four-way stop signs, cars proceed in the order in which they arrived. If two cars arrive simultaneously, the one on the right has the right of way. When in doubt, wave the other driver ahead.

→ When emergency vehicles (ie police, fire or ambulance) approach from either direction, cautiously pull over to the side of the road.

→ When parking, read all posted regulations and pay close attention to any colored curbs and parking meters, or you may be ticketed and/or towed.

→ Driving under the influence of alcohol or drugs is illegal. It's also illegal to carry open

containers of alcohol, even partly full or empty ones, inside a vehicle (store them in the trunk instead).

Tours

Adventure Bus (☑888-737-5263, 909-633-7225; www.adventurebus.com) Offers camping and sleeping-bus tours of Death Valley and the Mojave Desert, departing from Las Vegas, Nevada. All ages welcome.

California Motorcycle Tours (☑858-677-9892; www.ca-motorcycletours.com) San Diego–based outfitter offers guided trips on Harley Davidsons, including to beaches, mountains, deserts and Mexico's Baja California.

Road Scholar (☑800-454-5768; www.roadscholar.org) This nonprofit organization offers educational trips – including bus and walking tours and outdoor activities such as hiking and birding – for older adults.

Train

Amtrak

Amtrak (☑800-872-7245; www.amtrak.com) runs comfortable, occasionally tardy trains throughout California. At some stations, Thruway buses provide onward connections to smaller destinations. Smoking is prohibited aboard trains and buses.

Hugging the coast for much of its route, the memorably scenic *Pacific Surfliner* is Amtrak's main rail service in SoCal. Double-decker

trains have onboard bicycle and surfboard racks and a cafe car. Business-class seats feature slightly more legroom, electrical outlets and sometimes wi-fi.

Up to 12 trains daily ply the *Surfliner* route between San Diego and LA, making stops at Oceanside (for Legoland), San Juan Capistrano and Anaheim (for Disneyland), among others. Some trains continue north to Santa Barbara via Burbank's Bob Hope Airport, Ventura and Carpinteria, and two go all the way to San Luis Obispo.

Among Amtrak's long-distance trains, which have dining and sleeping cars, the *Coast Starlight* stops in Santa Barbara, Burbank and LA, while the *Sunset Limited* travels to LA and northern Palm Springs.

COSTS

Purchase tickets at train stations, by phone, online or via Amtrak's app (in advance for the best discounts). Fares depend on the day of travel, the route, the type of seating etc. Fares may be slightly higher during peak travel times (eg summer). Round-trip tickets typically cost the same as two one-way tickets.

Usually seniors over 62 years and students with an ISIC or Student Advantage Card receive a 15% discount, while up to two children, aged two to 15 and accompanied by an adult, get 50% off. Children under two years of age ride free. AAA members save 10%. Special promotions can become available anytime,

SAMPLE AMTRAK FARES

ROUTE	COACH	BUSINESS CLASS	DURATION
LA–Anaheim	$15	$25	45min
LA–San Diego	$37	$56	2¾hr
LA–Santa Barbara	$31	$47	2¾hr
San Diego–Anaheim	$28	$42	2¼hr
San Diego–Oceanside	$18	$28	1hr
San Diego–San Juan Capistrano	$22	$33	1½hr

so check the website or ask when making reservations.

RESERVATIONS

Amtrak reservations can be made up to 11 months prior to departure. In summer and around holidays, trains sell out quickly, so book tickets as early as possible. The cheapest coach fares are usually for unreserved seats; business-class fares come with guaranteed seats.

TRAIN PASSES

Amtrak's California Rail Pass costs $159 ($80 for children aged two to 15) and is valid on all trains (except certain long-distance routes) and most connecting Thruway buses for seven days of travel within a 21-day period. Passholders must reserve each leg of travel in advance and obtain hard-copy tickets prior to boarding.

Regional Trains

Major SoCal population centers are linked to LA by a commuter-train network called **Metrolink** (☏800-371-5465; www.metrolinktrains. com). Seven lines connect Downtown LA's Union Station with the surrounding counties – Orange, Riverside, San Bernardino and Ventura – as well as northern San Diego County.

The most useful Metrolink line for visitors is the Orange County Line, stopping in Anaheim, Orange, Santa Ana, San Juan Capistrano, San Clemente and Oceanside. From Oceanside, **Coaster** (☏760-966-6500; www.gonctd. com/coaster) trains run to Downtown San Diego via Carlsbad, Encinitas, Solana Beach and Old Town.

Most trains depart during weekday morning and afternoon rush hours, with only one or two services during the day or late evening. Some lines offer limited weekend services. Tickets are available from station vending machines; fares are zone-based.

Behind the Scenes

SEND US YOUR FEEDBACK

We love to hear from travelers – your comments keep us on our toes and help make our books better. Our well-traveled team reads every word on what you loved or loathed about this book. Although we cannot reply individually to your submissions, we always guarantee that your feedback goes straight to the appropriate authors, in time for the next edition. Each person who sends us information is thanked in the next edition – the most useful submissions are rewarded with a selection of digital PDF chapters.

Visit **lonelyplanet.com/contact** to submit your updates and suggestions or to ask for help. Our award-winning website also features inspirational travel stories, news and discussions.

Note: We may edit, reproduce and incorporate your comments in Lonely Planet products such as guidebooks, websites and digital products, so let us know if you don't want your comments reproduced or your name acknowledged. For a copy of our privacy policy visit lonelyplanet.com/privacy.

WRITER THANKS

Andrea Schulte-Peevers

Big heartfelt thank yous go to the following people for their invaluable tips, insights and hospitality (in no particular order): Valerie Summers, Kristin Schmidt, Joyce Kiehl, Andrew Bender, Abigail Wines, Bruce Moore, Susan Witty, Brandy Marino and Mona Spicer.

Andrew Bender

Thanks to Denise Lengyeltoti, Christie Bacock, Melissa Perez, Jackie Alvarez, Jennifer Tong, Erin Ramsauer, Michael Ramirez, Jenny Wedge, Ashley Johnson and the many information center, hotel and restaurant staffers who gave me way more of their time than I deserved. In house, thanks especially to Clifton Wilkinson, Sarah Stocking, Anita Isalska, Judith Bamber and Kathryn Rowan.

Cristian Bonetto

A heartfelt thank you to the many Angelenos (and New Yorkers) who shared their LA secrets and insights with me, especially John-Mark Horton, Michael Amato, Andy Bender, Norge Yip, Calvin Yeung, Douglas Levine, Daphne Barahona, Nicholas Maricich, David Singleman, William J Brockschmidt, Richard Dragisic and Andy Walker. Thanks also to fellow Aussies in SoCal, Mary-ann Gardner and Natalie Yanoulis. At Lonely Planet, much gratitude to Cliff Wilkinson.

Jade Bremner

Thanks to Destination Editor Clifton Wilkinson for his support and endless knowledge about LP

guidebooks. Plus, everyone working their socks off behind the scenes – Cheree Broughton, Dianne, Jane, Neill Coen, Evan Godt and Helen Elfer. Last but not least, thanks to the friendly staff at Fig Tree Cafe for making those marvelous egg Bennies, which often set me up for the day.

Clifton Wilkinson

Thanks to the Santa Barbara County tourism people (Karna, Danielle, Chrisie) who provided excellent recommendations, including my favorite meal of the whole update. Thanks too to all the inhouse LP team, especially colleagues who listened patiently to all my pre-trip plans. And final thanks to the weather, which mostly played along with my research – except for all the mud on Santa Cruz Channel Island (if anyone finds some sunglasses, they might be the ones I lost falling over).

ACKNOWLEDGMENTS

Climate map data adapted from Peel MC, Finlayson BL & McMahon TA (2007) 'Updated World Map of the Köppen-Geiger Climate Classification', Hydrology and Earth System Sciences, 11, 163344.

Cover photograph: Hollywood Walk of Fame, Anna Loura D'Avila Wolff, istock Editorial/Getty ©

HOLLYWOOD TM & Design © 2018 Hollywood Chamber of Commerce. The Hollywood Sign (p86) and Hollywood Walk of Fame (cover, p79) are trademarks and intellectual property of the Hollywood Chamber of Commerce. All Rights Reserved.

THIS BOOK

This 5th edition of Lonely Planet's *Los Angeles, San Diego & Southern California* guidebook was written and researched by: Andrea Schulte-Peevers, Andrew Bender, Cristian Bonetto, Jade Bremner, Benedict Walker and Clifton Wilkinson. The previous edition was written by Sara Benson, Andrew Bender and Adam Skolnick.

This guidebook was produced by the following:

Destination Editors Clifton Wilkinson, Sarah Stocking
Product Editor Shona Gray
Senior Cartographer Alison Lyall
Cartographer Julie Dodkins
Book Designers Lauren Egan, Katherine Marsh, Wibowo Rusli
Assisting Editors Sarah Bailey, Andrew Bain, Judith Bamber, Melanie Dankel,

Andrea Dobbin, Carly Hall, Helen Koehne, Kellie Langdon, Jodie Martire, Kate Mathews, Katie O'Connell, Maja Vatrić
Cover Researcher Naomi Parker
Thanks to Joel Cotterell, Sasha Drew, Elizabeth Jones, Karl Kollmeier, Holly Lanza, John Malone, Susan Paterson, Patrick Wildin, Regina Wright, Tony Wheeler

Index

Map Pages **000**
Photo Pages **000**

Map Pages **000**
Photo Pages **000**

Map Legend

Sights
- Beach
- Bird Sanctuary
- Buddhist
- Castle/Palace
- Christian
- Confucian
- Hindu
- Islamic
- Jain
- Jewish
- Monument
- Museum/Gallery/Historic Building
- Ruin
- Shinto
- Sikh
- Taoist
- Winery/Vineyard
- Zoo/Wildlife Sanctuary
- Other Sight

Activities, Courses & Tours
- Bodysurfing
- Diving
- Canoeing/Kayaking
- Course/Tour
- Sento Hot Baths/Onsen
- Skiing
- Snorkeling
- Surfing
- Swimming/Pool
- Walking
- Windsurfing
- Other Activity

Sleeping
- Sleeping
- Camping
- Hut/Shelter

Eating
- Eating

Drinking & Nightlife
- Drinking & Nightlife
- Cafe

Entertainment
- Entertainment

Shopping
- Shopping

Information
- Bank
- Embassy/Consulate
- Hospital/Medical
- Internet
- Police
- Post Office
- Telephone
- Toilet
- Tourist Information
- Other Information

Geographic
- Beach
- Gate
- Hut/Shelter
- Lighthouse
- Lookout
- Mountain/Volcano
- Oasis
- Park
- Pass
- Picnic Area
- Waterfall

Population
- Capital (National)
- Capital (State/Province)
- City/Large Town
- Town/Village

Transport
- Airport
- BART station
- Border crossing
- Boston T station
- Bus
- Cable car/Funicular
- Cycling
- Ferry
- Metro/Muni station
- Monorail
- Parking
- Petrol station
- Subway/SkyTrain station
- Taxi
- Train station/Railway
- Tram
- Underground station
- Other Transport

Routes
- Tollway
- Freeway
- Primary
- Secondary
- Tertiary
- Lane
- Unsealed road
- Road under construction
- Plaza/Mall
- Steps
- Tunnel
- Pedestrian overpass
- Walking Tour
- Walking Tour detour
- Path/Walking Trail

Boundaries
- International
- State/Province
- Disputed
- Regional/Suburb
- Marine Park
- Cliff
- Wall

Hydrography
- River, Creek
- Intermittent River
- Canal
- Water
- Dry/Salt/Intermittent Lake
- Reef

Areas
- Airport/Runway
- Beach/Desert
- Cemetery (Christian)
- Cemetery (Other)
- Glacier
- Mudflat
- Park/Forest
- Sight (Building)
- Sportsground
- Swamp/Mangrove

Note: Not all symbols displayed above appear on the maps in this book

OUR STORY

A beat-up old car, a few dollars in the pocket and a sense of adventure. In 1972 that's all Tony and Maureen Wheeler needed for the trip of a lifetime – across Europe and Asia overland to Australia. It took several months, and at the end – broke but inspired – they sat at their kitchen table writing and stapling together their first travel guide, *Across Asia on the Cheap*. Within a week they'd sold 1500 copies. Lonely Planet was born.

Today, Lonely Planet has offices in Franklin, London, Melbourne, Oakland, Dublin, Beijing and Delhi, with more than 600 staff and writers. We share Tony's belief that 'a great guidebook should do three things: inform, educate and amuse'.

OUR WRITERS

Andrea Schulte-Peevers
Curator; Palm Springs & The Deserts Born and raised in Germany and educated in London and at UCLA, Andrea has earned her living as a professional travel writer for over two decades and authored or contributed to nearly 100 Lonely Planet titles, as well as to newspapers, magazines and websites around the world. She also works as a travel consultant, translator and editor.

Andrew Bender
Los Angeles; Disneyland & Orange County An award-winning travel and food writer, Andrew Bender has written three dozen Lonely Planet guidebooks, plus numerous articles for lonelyplanet.com. Outside of Lonely Planet, he writes the Seat 1A travel site for Forbes.com and is a frequent contributor to the *Los Angeles Times*, in-flight magazines and more.

Cristian Bonetto
Los Angeles Cristian has contributed to over 30 Lonely Planet guides to date, covering New York City, Italy, Venice & the Veneto, Naples & the Amalfi Coast, Denmark, Copenhagen, Sweden and Singapore. His writing has appeared in numerous publications around the world, including the *Telegraph* (UK) and *Corriere del Mezzogiorno* (Italy). He lives in Melbourne, Australia.

Jade Bremner
San Diego Jade has been a journalist for more than a decade. Wherever she goes she finds action sports to try – the weirder the better – and it's no coincidence many of her favorite places have some of the best waves in the world. Jade has edited travel magazines and sections for *Time Out* and *Radio Times* and has been a correspondent for the *Times*, CNN and the *Independent*.

Benedict Walker
Palm Springs & The Deserts Berlin-based Ben grew up in the 'burbs of Australia, spending weekends and long summers by the beach, and while he's still magnetically drawn to big mountains, beach life is in his blood. Ben thinks that the best thing about travel isn't as much about where you go as who you meet: living vicariously through the stories of strangers really adds to one's own experience.

Clifton Wilkinson
Santa Barbara County Christmases spent near Sacramento, bike rides across the Golden Gate Bridge and hiking in Yosemite National Park have all reinforced Clifton's opinion that the Golden State is the best state in the whole US, and Santa Barbara is one of its most beautiful corners. Having worked for Lonely Planet for more than 11 years, he's now based in the London office.

Published by Lonely Planet Global Limited
CRN 554153
5th edition – April 2018
ISBN 978 178 657 249 3
© Lonely Planet 2018   Photographs © as indicated 2018
10 9 8 7 6 5 4 3 2 1
Printed in Singapore